American Leaders 1789-1987

American Leaders 1789-1987

A Biographical Summary

Congressional Quarterly Inc.
1414 22nd Street N.W.
Washington, D.C. 20037

Congressional Quarterly Inc.

Congressional Quarterly Inc., an editorial research service and publishing company, serves clients in the fields of news, education, business, and government. It combines Congressional Quarterly's specific coverage of Congress, government, and politics with the more general subject range of an affiliated service, Editorial Research Reports.

Congressional Quarterly publishes the *Congressional Quarterly Weekly Report* and a variety of books, including college political science textbooks under the CQ Press imprint and public affairs paperbacks designed as timely reports to keep journalists, scholars, and the public abreast of developing issues and events. CQ also publishes information directories and reference books on the federal government, national elections, and politics, including the *Guide to Congress,* the *Guide to the U.S. Supreme Court,* the *Guide to U.S. Elections,* and *Politics in America.* The *CQ Almanac,* a compendium of legislation for one session of Congress, is published each year. *Congress and the Nation,* a record of government for a presidential term, is published every four years.

CQ publishes the *Congressional Monitor,* a daily report on current and future activities of congressional committees, and several newsletters including *Congressional Insight,* a weekly analysis of congressional action, and *Campaign Practices Reports,* a semimonthly update on campaign laws.

An electronic online information system, the Washington Alert Service, provides immediate access to CQ's databases of legislative action, votes, schedules, profiles, and analyses.

Printed in the United States of America
Second Printing

Library of Congress Cataloging-in-Publication Data

American Leaders, 1789-1987.

    1. Statesmen--United States--Biography--Dictionaries.
2. United States--Biography--Dictionaries.
I. Congressional Quarterly, Inc.
E176.A495   1987   973'.092'2 [B]   86-30937
ISBN 0-87187-413-X

Editors: Colleen McGuiness, Maria J. Sayers
Contributors: Jane S. Gilligan, Rob Gurwitt, John L. Moore, Beth Prather, David Rapp,
  Evamarie Socha, Tom Watson
Cover: Richard A. Pottern

Table of Contents

American Leaders 1789-1987

Party Abbreviations

AAD	Adams Anti Democrat		JD	Jackson Democrat
ABD	Anti Broderick Democrat		Jeff.D	Jefferson Democrat
AD	Anti Democrat		JFSt.	Jackson Free Statesman
Ad.D	Adams Democrat		KN	Know Nothing
AF	Anti Federalist		L	Liberal
AJD	Anti Jackson Democrat		Lab.	Laborite
AL	American Laborite		LD	Liberal Democrat
ALot.	Anti Lottery Democrat		L&O	Law & Order
Alliance D	Alliance Democrat		L&OW	Law & Order Whig
AM	Anti Monopolist		LR	Liberal Republican
AMas.	Anti Mason		LW	Liberation Whig
AMas. D	Anti Mason Democrat		MCD	Missouri Compromise Democrat
AMD	Anti Monopoly Democrat		N	Nullifier
AND	Anti Nebraska Democrat		NAD	Native American Democrat
ASP	American Party		Nat.	Nationalist
AR	Adams Republican		Nat.A	National American
ASW	Anti Slavery Whig		Nat.G	National Greenbacker
ATD	Anti Tammany Democrat		ND	Nullifier Democrat
AW	American Whig		New Prog.	New Progressive
C	Conservative		Nonpart.	Nonpartisan
Cal.D	Calhoun Democrat		Nonpart.R	Nonpartisan Republican
Cal.N	Calhoun Nullifier		NR	National Republican
CassD	Cass Democrat		P	Populist
CD	Clay Democrat		PD	Popular Democrat
Clinton D	Clinton Democrat		PP	People's Party
Clinton R	Clinton Republican		PR	Progressive Republican
Coal.	Coalitionist		Prog.	Progressive
Con.D	Conservative Democrat		Prohib.	Prohibitionist
Confed.D	Confederate Democrat		Protect.	Protectionist
Confed.W	Confederate Whig		Protect.TD	Protective Tariff Democrat
Const U	Constitutional Unionist		PSD	Popular Sovereignty Democrat
CR	Conservative Republican		R	Republican
CU	Conservative Unionist		Rad.	Radical
CW	Clay Whig		Read	Readjuster
D	Democrat		Ref. R	Reform Republican
DD	Douglas Democrat		RG	Republican Greenbacker
DFL	Democrat Farmer Labor		R Prog.	Republican Progressive
DR	Democratic Republican		RR	Radical Republican
E	Emancipationist		Sil.D	Silver Democrat
F	Federalist		Sil.R	Silver Republican
FA	Farmers Alliance		Soc.	Socialist
FL	Farmer Laborite		SR	State Rights Party
FS	Free-Soiler		SRD	State Rights Democrat
FSD	Free Soil Democrat		SRFT	State, Rights Free Trader
FSil.	Free Silver		SRW	State Rights Whig
FSil.R	Free Silver Republican		SRWD	State Rights War Democrat
FSW	Free Soil Whig		T	Temperance Party
Fus	Fusionist		TD	Tariff Democrat
Fus.D	Fusionist Democrat		Tyler D	Tyler Democrat
G	Greenbacker		U	Unionist
GD	Greenback Democrat		UA	Ultra Abolitionist
G-Lab.	Greenback Laborite		UC	Union Conservative
G Lab. Ref.	Greenback Labor Reformer		UD	Union Democrat
HCW	Henry Clay Whig		UL	Union Laborite
HTW	High Tariff Whig		UR	Union Republican
I	Independent		UU	Unconditional Unionist
ID	Independent Democrat		UW	Union Whig
IR	Independent Republican		UWar	Union War Party
IRad.	Independent Radical		VBD	Van Buren Democrat
IRef.	Independent Reformer		W	Whig
ISil.R	Independent Silver Republican		WD	War Democrat
IW	Independent Whig			

Presidents

The method of selecting a president was the subject of long debate at the Constitutional Convention of 1787. Several plans were proposed and rejected before the convention adopted a compromise solution, which has been modified only slightly since then.

Facing the convention when it convened May 25 was the question of whether the chief executive should be chosen by direct popular election, by Congress, by state legislatures, or by intermediate electors. Direct election was opposed because it was felt generally that the people lacked sufficient knowledge of the character and qualifications of possible candidates to make an intelligent choice. Many delegates also feared that the people of the various states would be unlikely to agree on a single person, usually casting their votes for favorite-son candidates well known to them.

The possibility of giving Congress the power to choose the president also received consideration. However, this plan was rejected, largely because of concern that it would jeopardize the principle of executive independence. Similarly, a plan favored by many delegates, to let state legislatures choose the president, was turned down because it was feared that the president might feel so indebted to the states as to allow them to encroach on federal authority.

Unable to agree on a plan, the convention on Aug. 31 appointed a "Committee of 11" to propose a solution. The committee Sept. 4 suggested a compromise under which each state would appoint presidential electors equal to the total number of its representatives and senators. The electors, chosen in a manner set forth by each state

legislature, would meet in their own states and each cast votes for two persons. The votes would be counted in Congress, with the candidate receiving a majority elected president and the second-highest candidate becoming vice president.

No distinction was made between ballots for president and vice president. Moreover, the development of national political parties and the nomination of tickets for president and vice president created further confusion. All the electors of one party tended to cast ballots for their two party nominees. But with no distinction between the presidential and vice presidential nominees, the danger arose of a tie vote between the two. That actually happened in 1800, when the Democratic Republican electors inadvertently caused a tie in the electoral college by casting equal numbers of votes for Thomas Jefferson, whom they wished to be elected president, and Aaron Burr, whom they wished to elect vice president. The election was thrown into the House of Representatives, and 36 ballots were required before Jefferson was finally elected president. The Twelfth Amendment, ratified in 1804, sought to prevent a recurrence by providing that the electors should vote separately for president and vice president.

The compromise plan constituted a great concession to the less populous states, since they were assured of three votes (two for their two senators and at least one for their representative) however small their populations might be. The plan also left important powers with the states by giving complete discretion to state legislatures to determine the method of choosing electors.

The only part of the committee's plan

Presidential Disability ...

A decade of congressional concern over the question of presidential disability was eased in 1967 by ratification of the Twenty-fifth Amendment to the Constitution. The amendment for the first time provided for continuity in carrying out the functions of the presidency in the event of presidential disability and for filling a vacancy in the vice presidency.

The ambiguity of the language of the disability clause (Article II, Section 1, Clause 5) of the Constitution had provoked occasional debate ever since the Constitutional Convention of 1787. Clause 5 provided that Congress should decide who was to succeed to the presidency if both the president and the vice president died, resigned, or became disabled. But it never had been decided how far the term "disability" extended or who would be the judge of it.

Congressional action on the problem of presidential disability was prompted by President Dwight D. Eisenhower's heart attack in 1955. Two other presidents had had serious disabilities — James A. Garfield, shot in 1881 and confined to his bed until he died two and a half months later, and Woodrow Wilson, who suffered a stroke in 1919. In each case the vice president did not assume any duties of the president for fear he would appear to be usurping the powers of the office.

As for the vice presidency, the United States has been without a vice president 18 times for a total of 40 years through 1986, after the elected vice president succeeded to the presidency, died, or resigned.

The Twenty-fifth Amendment provided that the vice president should become acting president under either one of two circumstances. If the president informed Congress that he was unable to perform his duties, the vice president would become acting president until the president could resume his responsibilities. If the vice president and a majority of the cabinet, or another body designated by Congress, found the president to be incapacitated, the vice president would become acting president until the president informed Congress that his disability had ended. Congress was given 21 days to resolve any dispute over the president's disability; a two-thirds vote of both chambers was required to overrule the president's declaration that he was no longer incapacitated.

Whenever the vacancy occurred in the office of the vice president, either by death, succession to the presidency, or resignation, the president was to nominate a vice president, and the nomination was to be confirmed by a majority vote of both houses of Congress.

The power of the president to appoint a new vice president under the terms of the Twenty-fifth Amendment was used twice since its enactment. In 1973 when Vice President Spiro T. Agnew resigned, President Richard Nixon nominated Gerald R. Ford as the new vice president. Ford was confirmed by both houses of Congress and sworn in Dec. 6, 1973. On Nixon's resignation Aug. 9, 1974, Ford succeeded to the presidency, becoming the first president in American history who was elected neither to the presidency nor to the vice presidency. Ford chose Nelson A. Rockefeller as his vice president.

Reagan Assassination Attempt

In the aftermath of the attempted assassination of President Ronald Reagan in March 1981, Vice President George Bush and members of the cabinet decided not to invoke the Twenty-fifth Amendment. However, some of the public statements made by administration officials immediately after the shooting reflected continuing confusion

... And the Line of Succession

over the issue of who is in charge when the president temporarily is unable to function. In a televised press briefing, Secretary of State Alexander M. Haig Jr. confirmed that Reagan was in surgery and under anesthesia. It was clear that Reagan was unable to make presidential decisions should the occasion require them. Attempting to reassure the country, Haig stated that he was "in control" at the White House pending the return of Bush, who was in Texas.

This assertion was followed by a question from the press about who was making administrative decisions. Haig responded, "Constitutionally, gentlemen, you have the president, the vice president, and the secretary of state in that order, and should the president decide he wants to transfer the helm to the vice president, he will do so. He has not done that."

The law applicable in the 1981 shooting was the Presidential Succession Act of 1947 (PL 80-199), as modified. Haig's response reflected the law in effect before 1947. Congress has enacted succession laws three times. The Act of March 1, 1792, provided for succession (after the vice president) of the president pro tempore of the Senate, then of the House Speaker; if those offices were vacant, states were to send electors to Washington to choose a new president. That law stood until the passage of the Presidential Succession Act of Jan. 19, 1886, which changed the line of succession to run from the vice president to the secretary of state, secretary of the Treasury, and so on through the cabinet in order of rank. As of 1979, the line of succession was the vice president, the Speaker of the House, the president pro tempore of the Senate, the secretaries of state, Treasury, defense, the attorney general, the secretaries of interior, agriculture, commerce, labor, health and human services, housing and urban development, transportation, energy, and education.

Reagan's Abdominal Surgery

The only time the Twenty-fifth Amendment was applied to a temporarily incapacitated president was on July 13, 1985, when Reagan underwent surgery to remove a cancerous polyp from his large intestine. Reagan transferred his powers to Bush just before receiving anesthesia for the surgery and signed papers reclaiming them almost as soon as he awoke, 7 hours and 54 minutes later. During that time, Bush served as acting president.

Because of the delicate wording of Reagan's official letter of notification, it remains unclear whether the Twenty-fifth Amendment was actually "invoked." Reagan stated in his letter that "I am mindful of the provisions" of the Twenty-fifth Amendment. But he added that "I do not believe that the drafters of this amendment intended its application" to situations such as his, and added that he took the action "not intending to set a precedent...."

But even though Reagan avoided designating Bush as acting president, White House officials acknowledged that Bush played that role while Reagan was in the operating room. Also, various officials contended that Reagan did, in fact, set a precedent, whether he wanted to or not. "Now it's been done," said former senator Birch Bayh, D-Ind. (1963-81), the principal author of the Twenty-fifth Amendment, in an interview on ABC News. "It seems to me they should emphasize the fact that this is a good precedent.... It's only the normal thing to do, to have an insurance policy so that somebody is always watching the store."

that aroused serious opposition was a provision giving the Senate the right to decide presidential elections in which no candidate received a majority of electoral votes. Some delegates feared that the Senate, which already had been given treaty ratification powers and the responsibility to "advise and consent" on all important executive appointments, might become too powerful. Therefore, a counterproposal was made and accepted to let the House decide in instances when the electors failed to give a majority of their votes to a single candidate. The interests of the small states were preserved by giving each state's delegation only one vote in the House on roll calls to elect a president.

The system adopted by the Constitutional Convention was a compromise born out of problems involved in diverse state voting requirements, the slavery problem, big-state vs. small-state rivalries, and the complexities of the balance of power among different branches of the government. It also apparently was as close to a direct popular election as the men who wrote the Constitution thought possible and appropriate at the time.

Only once since ratification of the Constitution has an amendment — the Twelfth Amendment — been adopted that substantially altered the method of electing the president. Other changes in the system, however, evolved over the years. The authors of the Constitution, for example, had intended that each state choose its most distinguished citizens as electors and that they would deliberate and vote as individuals in electing the president. But as strong political parties began to appear, the electors came to be chosen merely as representatives of the parties; independent voting by electors disappeared almost entirely.

Trends in Candidate Choice

As a nation the United States has never made up its mind about what background a president ought to have. Most presidents have come to the White House with long careers of public service behind them. Yet there have been notable exceptions. A look back to the eighteenth century shows just how often the fashion has changed. *(Members of Congress Who Became President, box, p. 45)*

Secretary of State

The earliest tradition developed around the secretary of state, who was considered the preeminent cabinet officer and thus the most important man in the executive branch after the president. George Washington's first secretary of state was Thomas Jefferson. Although Jefferson left the cabinet early in Washington's second term, he went on to become leader of the newly formed Democratic Republican party and its candidate for president in 1796, 1800, and 1804. Losing to John Adams in 1796, Jefferson came back to win four years later.

In turn, Jefferson's secretary of state for two terms, James Madison, won the presidency in 1808. During his first term, President Madison appointed fellow Virginian James Monroe as his secretary of state. Monroe went on to be elected to the presidency and served two terms (1817-25).

Throughout Monroe's terms, the secretary of state was John Quincy Adams, son of former president John Adams. When Monroe's second term was nearing its end, five major candidates, including Adams, entered the race to succeed him. None of the candidates managed to acquire a majority in the electoral college, and the House then chose Secretary of State Adams.

Adams was the last secretary of state to go directly from his cabinet post to the White House. After him, only two secretaries of state made it to the White House at all — Martin Van Buren and James Buchanan.

Military Background

The next cycle of American politics, from the presidency of Andrew Jackson (1829-37) to the Civil War, saw a variety of backgrounds qualify candidates for the presidency. One of the most prevalent was the military. Jackson, who ran in 1824 (unsuccessfully), 1828, and 1832, was a general in the War of 1812, gaining near-heroic stature by his defeat of the British at the Battle of New Orleans in January 1815. Like most

Nationalities of the Presidents

Listed below are the presidents and their nationalities. Seventeen presidents were of English ancestry. Eight presidents, marked in the list with an asterisk (*), were born British subjects.

President	Nationality
George Washington*	English
John Adams*	English
Thomas Jefferson*	Welsh
James Madison*	English
James Monroe*	Scotch
John Quincy Adams*	English
Andrew Jackson*	Scotch-Irish
Martin Van Buren	Dutch
William Henry Harrison*	English
John Tyler	English
James K. Polk	Scotch-Irish
Zachary Taylor	English
Millard Fillmore	English
Franklin Pierce	English
James Buchanan	Scotch-Irish
Abraham Lincoln	English
Andrew Johnson	English
Ulysses S. Grant	English-Scotch
Rutherford B. Hayes	Scotch
James A. Garfield	English
Chester A. Arthur	Scotch-Irish
Grover Cleveland	English-Irish
Benjamin Harrison	English
William McKinley	Scotch-Irish
Theodore Roosevelt	Dutch
William Howard Taft	English
Woodrow Wilson	Scotch-Irish
Warren G. Harding	English-Scotch-Irish
Calvin Coolidge	English
Herbert Hoover	Swiss-German
Franklin D. Roosevelt	Dutch
Harry S Truman	English-Scotch-Irish
Dwight D. Eisenhower	Swiss-German
John F. Kennedy	Irish
Lyndon B. Johnson	English
Richard Nixon	Scotch-Irish
Gerald R. Ford	English
Jimmy Carter	English-Scotch-Irish
Ronald Reagan	English-Scotch-Irish

SOURCE: Joseph Nathan Kane, *Facts about the Presidents: A Compilation of Biographical and Historical Information*, 4th ed. (New York: The H. W. Wilson Co., 1981). Reprinted by permission of the publisher.

military officers who have risen to the presidency, however, Jackson was only a part-time military man.

Other candidates during this era who were or had been military officers included William Henry Harrison, a Whig candidate in 1836 and 1840; Zachary Taylor, the Whig candidate in 1848; Winfield Scott, the Whig candidate in 1852; Franklin Pierce, the Democratic nominee in 1852; and John Charles Fremont, the Republican party's first presidential candidate in 1856. Thus, from 1824 through 1856, all but one presidential election featured a major candidate with a military background.

The smoldering political conflicts of the 1840s and 1850s probably contributed to the naming of military men for the presidency. Generals had usually escaped involvement in national politics and had avoided taking stands on the issues that divided the country — slavery, expansion, the currency, and the tariff.

Later on, the nature of the Civil War almost automatically led at least one of the parties to choose a military officer as presidential standard-bearer every four years. To have been on the "right" side during the war — fighting to save the Union and destroy slavery — was a major political asset in the North and Middle West, where tens of thousands of war veterans were effectively organized in the Grand Army of the Republic (GAR). The GAR became part of the backbone of the Republican party during the last third of the nineteenth century.

Consequently, it became customary for Republicans to have a Civil War officer at the head of their ticket. Except for James G. Blaine in 1884, every Republican presidential nominee from 1868 to 1900 had served as an officer in the Union Army during the Civil War. Of all the Republican nominees, however, only Ulysses S. Grant, who was elected president in 1868 and 1872, was a professional military man. The others — Rutherford B. Hayes in 1876, James A. Garfield in 1880, Benjamin Harrison in 1888 and 1892, and William McKinley in 1896 and 1900 — were civilians who volunteered for service in the Civil War.

The Democrats, who had been split over the war, had few prominent military veterans to choose from. Only twice between 1860 and 1900 did the Democrats pick a Civil War officer as their nominee, and neither was elected. In 1864, during the Civil War, the Democrats nominated Gen. George B. McClellan, the Union military commander who had fallen out with President Abraham Lincoln. And in 1880 Gen. Winfield Scott Hancock of Pennsylvania was the Democrats' choice.

The Empire State

Otherwise, Democrats tended to favor governors or former governors of New York. Their 1868 nominee was Horatio Seymour, who had been governor of New York in 1853-55 and again 1863-65. In 1876 they chose Samuel J. Tilden, New York's reform governor who was battling Tammany Hall. And in 1884 Grover Cleveland, another New York reform governor, captured the Democratic nomination. He went on to become the first Democrat to win the White House in 28 years. Cleveland also was the Democratic nominee in 1888 and 1892.

Besides being the most populous state, New York was a swing state in presidential politics. During the period from Reconstruction through the turn of the century, most Southern states voted Democratic, while the Republicans usually carried Pennsylvania, the Midwest, and New England. A New Yorker appeared as the nominee for president or vice president of at least one of the major parties in every single election from 1868 through 1892.

This general tradition was maintained through the candidacy of Thomas E. Dewey, Republican governor of New York, in 1948. Only twice between 1896 and 1948 was there no New Yorker on the national ticket of at least one of the major parties — for president or vice president. Once, in 1944, both major party presidential nominees, Democrat Franklin D. Roosevelt and Republican Dewey, were from New York.

From 1952 to 1984, however, no New Yorkers were nominated by a major party for president and only two for vice president. The latter were Rep. William E. Miller, R (1951-65), in 1964 and Rep. Geral-

Religious Affiliations of the Presidents

Listed below are the presidents and their religious affiliations. A large majority were Protestants. Of those, most (11) were Episcopalians; 7 were Presbyterians. Only 3 presidents — Thomas Jefferson, Abraham Lincoln, and Andrew Johnson — claimed no religious affiliation.

President	Religious Affiliation
George Washington	Episcopalian
John Adams	Unitarian
Thomas Jefferson	none
James Madison	Episcopalian
James Monroe	Episcopalian
John Quincy Adams	Unitarian
Andrew Jackson	Presbyterian
Martin Van Buren	Dutch Reformed
William Henry Harrison	Episcopalian
John Tyler	Episcopalian
James K. Polk	Presbyterian
Zachary Taylor	Episcopalian
Millard Fillmore	Unitarian
Franklin Pierce	Episcopalian
James Buchanan	Presbyterian
Abraham Lincoln	none
Andrew Johnson	none
Ulysses S. Grant	Methodist
Rutherford B. Hayes	Methodist
James A. Garfield	Disciples of Christ
Chester A. Arthur	Episcopalian
Grover Cleveland	Presbyterian
Benjamin Harrison	Presbyterian
William McKinley	Methodist
Theodore Roosevelt	Dutch Reformed
William Howard Taft	Unitarian
Woodrow Wilson	Presbyterian
Warren G. Harding	Baptist
Calvin Coolidge	Congregationalist
Herbert Hoover	Society of Friends (Quaker)
Franklin D. Roosevelt	Episcopalian
Harry S Truman	Baptist
Dwight D. Eisenhower	Presbyterian
John F. Kennedy	Roman Catholic
Lyndon B. Johnson	Disciples of Christ
Richard Nixon	Society of Friends (Quaker)
Gerald R. Ford	Episcopalian
Jimmy Carter	Baptist
Ronald Reagan	Episcopalian

SOURCE: Joseph Nathan Kane, *Facts about the Presidents: A Compilation of Biographical and Historical Information*, 4th ed. (New York: The H. W. Wilson Co., 1981). Reprinted by permission of publisher.

dine A. Ferraro, D (1979-85), in 1984. Dwight D. Eisenhower in 1952 and Richard Nixon in 1968 were technically residents of New York, but they were generally identified with other states. Gerald R. Ford's vice president, Nelson Rockefeller, was a former governor of New York, but he was appointed to the vice presidency. He was not asked to be on the ticket when Ford ran in 1976.

Another major swing state in the years from the Civil War through World War I was Indiana. And, in most elections, a prominent Indianan found his way onto one of the major party's national tickets. In the 13 presidential elections between 1868 and 1916, an Indianan appeared 10 times on at least one of the major parties' national tickets. However, since 1916 only one Indianan, Wendell Willkie in 1940, has been a major party's nominee.

Governors

Governors were especially favored as presidential nominees by the Democratic party from 1900 to 1956. Democratic governors who received their party's presidential nomination during this period included Woodrow Wilson in 1912, James M. Cox of Ohio in 1920, Alfred E. Smith of New York in 1928, Franklin Roosevelt in 1932, and Adlai E. Stevenson of Illinois in 1952.

During the same period, Republican presidential nominees had a wide variety of backgrounds. There were two cabinet officers, a Supreme Court justice, a U.S. senator, two governors, a private lawyer, and a general.

Vice Presidents

A sudden change took place in 1960 with the nomination of John F. Kennedy, a senator, and Nixon, a former senator and sitting vice president. It was the first time since 1860 and only the second time in the history of party nominating conventions that an incumbent vice president was chosen for the presidency. And it was only the second time in the twentieth century that an incumbent U.S. senator was nominated for the presidency. In the nineteenth century the phenomenon also was rare, with National Republican Henry Clay in 1832, Dem-

ocrat Lewis Cass in 1848, and Democrat Stephen A. Douglas in 1860 the only incumbent senators nominated for president by official party conventions. Republican James A. Garfield was a senator-elect at the time of his election in 1880. Since then, no other House member has received the presidential nomination of a major party.

The nomination of Nixon, like the nomination of Kennedy, was a sign of things to come. Beginning in 1960 the vice presidency, like the Senate, became a presidential training ground. Vice President Hubert H. Humphrey was chosen by the Democrats for president in 1968. Vice President Spiro T. Agnew was the leading contender for the 1976 Republican presidential nomination before his resignation. Former vice president Walter F. Mondale, who had served under Jimmy Carter, emerged as the Democratic choice for the presidential nomination in 1984. Even defeated vice presidential nominees have been considered for the nomination — witness Henry Cabot Lodge Jr. of Massachusetts in 1964, Edmund S. Muskie of Maine in 1972, Sargent Shriver of Maryland in 1976, and Robert Dole of Kansas in 1980.

Governors Making a Comeback?

The field of candidates for the 1980 presidential nomination continued a trend that first appeared in the 1976 campaign — the reemergence of governors as leading contenders in the nomination sweepstakes. For 16 years, beginning with Kennedy's ascension from the Senate to the White House in 1960, until 1976, senators dominated presidential campaigns. During that time every single major party nominee was a senator or former senator. This trend represented an about-face from earlier times. In the 36 years before Kennedy, the two major parties nominated only one man who ever had served in the Senate.

Yet, while there was no shortage of senators in the 1976 campaign, it was the governors who attracted the most attention. Former California governor Ronald Reagan came close to depriving incumbent Gerald Ford of the Republican presidential nomination. The Democratic nominee and eventual winner, former Georgia governor Jimmy Carter, faced a dramatic last-minute challenge from the governor of California, Jerry Brown. Reagan (successfully), Carter, and Brown were candidates again in 1980; Reagan again (successfully) in 1984.

Presidential Facts

Despite the changing political trends that shaped the selection of presidential candidates, the presidents as a group are strikingly similar. Most notably, all of the presidents have been Caucasian males. Twenty-four of the 39 men who have occupied the Oval Office were, by profession, lawyers. Twenty-five served in the military.

Eighteen presidents were governors of states or territories before assuming office. This list includes Martin Van Buren, Grover Cleveland, Theodore Roosevelt, and Franklin Roosevelt from New York; James Monroe and John Tyler from Virginia; James K. Polk and Andrew Johnson from Tennessee; Rutherford B. Hayes and William McKinley from Ohio; and Woodrow Wilson, Calvin Coolidge, Jimmy Carter, and Ronald Reagan from New Jersey, Massachusetts, Georgia, and California, respectively. In addition, William Howard Taft served as provisional governor of the Philippines; Thomas Jefferson served as the territorial governor of Virginia; Andrew Jackson held the same position in Florida, as did William Henry Harrison in Indiana.

All presidents but one, James Buchanan, were married at least once; and only one, Reagan, was divorced and remarried. Almost half of the presidents were of English ancestry; an overwhelming majority were of Protestant denominations. *(Nationalities of the Presidents, box, p. 5; Religious Affiliations of the Presidents, box, p. 7)*

The average age of the president upon taking office was 55 years. The youngest elected president was Kennedy, who was inaugurated at the age of 43. Theodore Roosevelt, however, became the youngest man ever to serve as president when, at 42, he succeeded McKinley, who was assassinated. The oldest president was Reagan. He was 69 when he took his first oath of office and, provided he serves a full second term, will be 77 when he leaves the White House in January 1989.

Franklin Roosevelt was president the longest, having served 12 years and 39 days, from March 4, 1933, until his death on April 12, 1945. Shortly thereafter the Twenty-second Amendment, ratified in 1951, limited a president to two terms. The shortest term was held by William Henry Harrison, who served 32 days from March 4, 1841, through April 4, 1841. The next shortest term was served by James Garfield, who was president for 199 days, from March 4, 1881, until he died from an assassin's wounds on Sept. 19, 1881.

Presidents: Biographies

This biographical summary lists, alphabetically, all the presidents of the United States since 1789. The material is organized as follows: name; relationship to other presidents, vice presidents, members of Congress, Supreme Court justices, or governors; party; state; date of birth; date of death (if applicable); period of service as president; congressional service, service as vice president, member of the Cabinet, governor, delegate to the Continental Congress, House or Senate majority leader, Speaker of the House, president pro tempore of the Senate, or chairman of the Democratic or Republican National Committee. *(Party abbreviations,*

box, p. x)

Under the Constitution, presidential terms from 1789 to 1933 were from March 4 to March 4; since 1934, the four-year term has been from Jan. 20 to Jan. 20. If a president began or ended his service in midterm, exact dates are shown.

The major source of information for this list was Congressional Quarterly's *Guide to U.S. Elections.* Additional data was obtained from Joseph Nathan Kane, *Facts about the Presidents: A Compilation of Biographical and Historical Information,* 4th ed. (New York: The H. W. Wilson Co., 1981).

ADAMS, John (father of John Quincy Adams, grandfather of Rep. Charles Francis Adams) (F Mass.) Oct. 30, 1735-July 4, 1826; President 1797-1801; Cont. Cong. 1774; Vice President 1789-97.

ADAMS, John Quincy (son of John Adams, father of Rep. Charles Francis Adams) (DR Mass.) July 11, 1767-Feb. 23, 1848; President 1825-29; Senate 1803-08 (Federalist); Secy. of State 1817-25; House 1831-48 (Whig).

ARTHUR, Chester Alan (R N.Y.) Oct. 5, 1830-Nov. 18, 1886; President Sept. 20, 1881-85 (succeeded James Abram Garfield, who was assassinated); Vice President March 4, 1881-Sept. 19, 1881.

BUCHANAN, James (D Pa.) April 23, 1791-June 1, 1868; President 1857-61; House 1821-31; Senate 1834-45; Secy. of State 1845-49.

CARTER, James Earl "Jimmy" Jr. (D Ga.) Oct. 1, 1924- —; President 1977-81; Gov. 1971-75.

CLEVELAND, Stephen Grover (D N.Y.) March 18, 1837-June 24, 1908; President 1885-89, 1893-97; Gov. 1883-85.

COOLIDGE, John Calvin (cousin of Gov. William Wallace Stickney of Vt.) (R Mass.) July 4, 1872-Jan. 5, 1933; President Aug. 3, 1923-29 (succeeded Warren Gamaliel Harding, who died in office); Gov. 1919-21; Vice President 1921-Aug. 3, 1923.

EISENHOWER, Dwight David (R N.Y.) Oct. 14, 1890-March 28, 1969; President 1953-61.

FILLMORE, Millard (W N.Y.) Jan. 7, 1800-March 8, 1874; President July 10, 1850-53 (succeeded Zachary Taylor, who died in office); House 1833-35, 1837-43; Vice President 1849-July 10, 1850.

FORD, Gerald Rudolph Jr. (R Mich.) July 14, 1913- —; President Aug. 9, 1974-77; House 1949-73; Vice President Dec. 6, 1973-Aug. 9, 1974.

GARFIELD, James Abram (R Ohio) Nov. 19, 1831-Sept. 19, 1881; President March 4-Sept. 19, 1881 (assassinated); House 1863-80.

GRANT, Ulysses Simpson (R Ill.) April 27, 1822-July 23, 1885; President 1869-77; Secy. of War 1867-68.

HARDING, Warren Gamaliel (R Ohio) Nov. 2, 1865-Aug. 2, 1923; President 1921-Aug. 2, 1923 (died in office); Senate 1915-21.

HARRISON, Benjamin (grandson of William Henry Harrison, son of Rep. John Scott Harrison, grandfather of Rep. William Henry Harrison) (R Ind) Aug. 20, 1833-March 13, 1901; President 1889-93; Senate 1881-87.

HARRISON, William Henry (father of Rep. John Scott Harrison, brother of Rep. Carter Basset Harrison, grandfather of Benjamin Harrison, great-great-grandfather of Rep. William Henry Harrison) (W Ohio) Feb. 9, 1773-April 4, 1841; President March 4-April 4, 1841 (died in office); House 1816-19; Senate 1825-28.

HAYES, Rutherford Birchard (R Ohio) Oct. 4, 1822-Jan. 17, 1893; President 1877-81; House 1865-67; Gov. 1868-72, 1876-77.

HOOVER, Herbert Clark (R Calif.) Aug. 10, 1874-Oct. 20, 1964; President 1929-33; Secy. of Commerce 1921-28.

JACKSON, Andrew (D Tenn.) March 15, 1767-June 8, 1845; President 1829-37; Gov. 1821 (Fla. Terr.); House 1796-97; Senate 1797-98, 1823-25.

JEFFERSON, Thomas (father-in-law of Gov. Thomas Mann Randolph of Va.) (DR Va.) April 13, 1743-July 4, 1826; President 1801-09; Cont. Cong. 1775-76, 1783-85; Gov. 1779-81 (Va. Terr.); Secy. of State 1789-93; Vice President 1797-1801.

JOHNSON, Andrew (father-in-law of Sen. David Trotter Patterson) (R Tenn.) Dec. 29, 1808-July 31, 1875; President April 15, 1865-69 (succeeded Abraham Lincoln, who was assassinated); House 1843-53 (Democrat); Gov. 1853-57 (Democrat), 1862-65 (Military); Senate 1857-62 (Democrat), 1875; Vice President March 4-April 15, 1865.

JOHNSON, Lyndon Baines (D Texas) Aug. 27, 1908-Jan. 22, 1973; President Nov. 22, 1963-69 (succeeded John Fitzgerald Kennedy, who was assassinated); House 1937-49; Senate 1949-61; Senate majority leader 1955-61; Vice President 1961-Nov. 22, 1963.

KENNEDY, John Fitzgerald (brother of Sens. Edward Moore Kennedy and Robert Francis Kennedy, grandson of Rep. John Francis Fitzgerald, uncle of Rep. Joseph Patrick Kennedy II) (D Mass.) May 29, 1917-Nov. 22, 1963; President 1961-Nov. 22, 1963 (assassinated); House 1947-53; Senate 1953-60.

LINCOLN, Abraham (R Ill.) Feb. 12, 1809-April 15, 1865; President 1861-April 15, 1865 (assassinated); House 1847-49 (Whig).

MADISON, James (DR Va.) March 16, 1751-June 28, 1836; President 1809-17; Cont. Cong. 1780-83, 1786-88; House 1789-97; Secy. of State 1801-09.

McKINLEY, William Jr. (R Ohio) Jan. 29, 1843-Sept. 14, 1901; President 1897-Sept. 14, 1901 (assassinated); House 1877-84, 1885-91; Gov. 1892-96.

MONROE, James (uncle of Rep. James Monroe) (DR Va.) April 28, 1758-July 4, 1831; President 1817-25; Cont. Cong. 1783-86; Senate 1790-94; Gov. 1799-1802, 1811; Secy. of State 1811-17.

NIXON, Richard Milhous (R Calif.) Jan. 9, 1913- —; President 1969-Aug. 9, 1974 (resigned); House 1947-50; Senate 1950-53; Vice President 1953-61.

PIERCE, Franklin (D N.H.) Nov. 23, 1804-Oct. 8, 1869; President 1853-57; House 1833-37; Senate 1837-42.

POLK, James Knox (brother of Rep. William Hawkins Polk) (D Tenn.) Nov. 2, 1795-June 15, 1849; President 1845-49; House 1825-39; Speaker 1835-39; Gov. 1839-41.

REAGAN, Ronald Wilson (R Calif.) Feb. 6, 1911- —; President 1981- —; Gov. 1967-75.

ROOSEVELT, Franklin Delano (D N.Y.) Jan. 30, 1882-April 12, 1945; President 1933-April 12, 1945 (died in office); Gov. 1929-33.

ROOSEVELT, Theodore (R N.Y.) Oct. 27, 1858-Jan. 6, 1919; President Sept. 14, 1901-09 (succeeded William McKinley Jr., who was assassinated); Gov. 1899-1901; Vice President March 4-Sept. 14, 1901.

TAFT, William Howard (brother of Rep. Charles Phelps Taft, father of Sen. Robert Alphonso Taft, grandfather of Sen. Robert Taft Jr.) (R Ohio) Sept. 15, 1857-March 8, 1930; President 1909-13; Gov. (prov.) 1901-04 (Philippines); Secy. of War 1904-08; Chief Justice United States 1921-30.

TAYLOR, Zachary (W La.) Nov. 24, 1784-July 9, 1850; President 1849-July 9, 1850 (died in office).

TRUMAN, Harry S (D Mo.) May 8, 1884-Dec. 26, 1972; President April 12, 1945-53 (succeeded Franklin Delano Roosevelt, who died in office); Senate 1935-45; Vice President Jan. 20-April 12, 1945.

TYLER, John (son of Gov. John Tyler of Va., father of Rep. David Gardiner Tyler) (W Va.) March 29, 1790-Jan. 18, 1862; President April 6, 1841-45 (succeeded William Henry Harrison, who died in office); House 1817-21 (Democratic Republican); Gov. 1825-27 (Democratic Republican); Senate 1827-36 (Democratic Republican); Pres. pro tempore 1835-36; Vice President March 4-April 6, 1841.

VAN BUREN, Martin (half brother of Rep. James Isaac Van Alen) (D N.Y.) Dec. 5, 1782-July 24, 1862; President 1837-41; Senate 1821-28; Gov. 1829; Secy. of State 1829-31; Vice President 1833-37.

WASHINGTON, George (uncle¹ of Assoc. Justice Bushrod Washington) (F Va.) Feb. 22, 1732-Dec. 14, 1799; President April 30, 1789-97; Cont. Cong. 1774-75.

WILSON, Thomas Woodrow (D N.J.) Dec. 28, 1856-Feb. 3, 1924; President 1913-21; Gov. 1911-13.

Vice Presidents

In modern times veteran political convention-watchers have come to look forward to the almost-traditional night of uncertainty as the new presidential nominee tries to come up with a running mate. But this hectic process is a recent one. During the country's first years the runner-up for the presidency automatically took the second slot.

But that system did not last long. In 1800 Thomas Jefferson and Aaron Burr found themselves in a tie for electoral votes. Neither man's supporters were willing to settle for the lesser office. The deadlock went to the House of Representatives, where Jefferson needed 36 ballots to clinch the presidency. It also led to the Twelfth Amendment, ratified in 1804, providing for electoral college balloting for presidents and vice presidents. With the emergence of political parties after 1800, candidates ran as teams. Once party conventions began in 1831, delegates, with the guidance of party bosses, began to do the choosing.

In fact, it was not until 1940 that presidential nominees began regularly handpicking their running mates. That year, after failing to persuade Secretary of State Cordell Hull to accept the vice presidency, Franklin D. Roosevelt forced Henry A. Wallace on a reluctant Democratic convention by threatening to refuse his own nomination if Wallace was rejected. The only exception to the practice Roosevelt established came in 1956, when Democrat Adlai E. Stevenson left the choice up to the convention.

Whoever is brought on board is scrutinized not so much as a policy maker, but for how well he or she balances the ticket. One of the most important factors usually is geography, but other traditional factors weighed by nominees are religion and ethnicity. In national politics of the 1980s, however, those considerations seemed to be losing their place to race and sex. While a black candidate for either spot has not been seriously considered, the Democrats chose Rep. Geraldine A. Ferraro of New York to be their vice presidential candidate in 1984, the first female to receive such an honor.

Office of the Vice President

If the selection of a running mate often has seemed like something of an afterthought, it could be because the position itself is not an especially coveted one. John Adams, the first man to hold the job, once complained, "My country has in its wisdom contrived for me the most insignificant office that ever the intention of man contrived or his imagination conceived."

More than a century later Thomas R. Marshall, Woodrow Wilson's vice president, expressed a similarly dismal view: "Once there were two brothers. One ran away to sea; the other was elected Vice President. And nothing was ever heard of either of them again."

Writing in the *Atlantic* in 1974, historian Arthur Schlesinger Jr. suggested the office be done away with. "It is a doomed office," he commented. "The Vice President has only one serious thing to do: that is, to wait around for the President to die."

Under the Constitution, the vice president does have the authority to vote in the Senate in the event of a tie. Through 1986, vice presidents had voted on 222 occasions. John Adams holds the record with 29 votes; John C. Calhoun is a close second with 28

From VP to President

Thirteen men who served as vice president (VP) have become president: John Adams, Thomas Jefferson, Martin Van Buren, John Tyler, Millard Fillmore, Andrew Johnson, Chester A. Arthur, Theodore Roosevelt, Calvin Coolidge, Harry S Truman, Richard Nixon, Lyndon B. Johnson, and Gerald R. Ford. All but Adams, Jefferson, Van Buren, and Nixon first became president on the death or resignation of their predecessor. Since 1900, eight VPs have run unsuccessfully for the presidency:

● Thomas R. Marshall, Democratic vice president under Woodrow Wilson from 1913 to 1921, failed to win the nomination in 1920.

● Charles G. Dawes, Republican vice president under Coolidge from 1925 to 1929, unsuccessfully sought the nomination in 1928 and 1932.

● John N. Garner, Democratic vice president under Franklin D. Roosevelt from 1933 to 1941, ran unsuccessfully for the nomination in 1940.

● Henry A. Wallace, Democratic vice president under Roosevelt from 1941 to 1945, was Progressive party nominee in 1948.

● Alben W. Barkley, Democratic vice president under Truman from 1949 to 1953, failed to win the 1952 nomination.

● Nixon, Republican vice president under Dwight D. Eisenhower from 1953 to 1961, was the GOP nominee in 1960.

● Hubert H. Humphrey, Democratic vice president under Lyndon Johnson from 1965 to 1969, was the Democratic nominee in 1968.

● Walter F. Mondale, Democratic vice president under Jimmy Carter from 1977 to 1981, was the Democratic nominee in 1984.

votes.

During times of a narrowly held majority in the Senate, the vice president's power could mean major victory for the administration. For example, from January 1981 to January 1987, when the Republicans were in control by just a few seats, Vice President George Bush cast the tie-breaking vote six times, on issues including the manufacture of lethal binary chemical weapons, continued production of MX intercontinental missiles, and confirmation of Daniel A. Manion as federal appeals court judge.

There is a reasonable chance that whoever becomes vice president will be able to assume the office of the presidency, either by succession or election. As of January 1987, 13 presidents had held the second-ranking post, 6 in the twentieth century. *(From VP to President, box, this page)*

Also, during the 1970s and 1980s the vice presidency evolved from the somnolent office it once was; during this period three vice presidents enjoyed responsibility their predecessors did not. Nelson A. Rockefeller, who served under Gerald R. Ford, was given considerable authority in domestic policy coordination. Vice President Walter F. Mondale was deeply involved in helping President Jimmy Carter set policy, as was Bush under President Ronald Reagan.

Vice Presidential Facts

Most of the men who became vice president came to the office with a career in public service. Thirty had served as members of Congress. Fifteen had been governors of a state or territory. Of those, six represented the state of New York — George Clinton, Daniel D. Tompkins, Martin Van Buren, Levi P. Morton, Theodore Roosevelt, and Nelson Rockefeller. Thomas Jefferson (territorial) and John Tyler represented Virginia; Elbridge Gerry and Calvin Coolidge, Massachusetts; Thomas A. Hendricks and Thomas R. Marshall, Indiana; Hannibal Hamlin, Maine; Andrew Johnson, Tennessee; and Spiro Agnew, Maryland. All except Morton served prior to their tenure as vice president. Johnson served one of his terms as military governor. *(Vice Presidents Who Served in Congress, box, p. 15)*

Vice Presidents Who Served in Congress

Listed below are the 30 vice presidents who served in Congress and the chambers in which they were members. Ten served only in the House of Representatives; 8 served only in the Senate; 12 served in both chambers. Daniel D. Tompkins, who was vice president under James Monroe, was elected to the House but resigned before the beginning of his term to accept an appointment as associate justice of the New York state supreme court.

Three other vice presidents — John Adams, Thomas Jefferson, and George Clinton — served in the Continental Congress, as did Elbridge Gerry, who is included below.

House Only

Elbridge Gerry
Millard Fillmore
Schuyler Colfax
William A. Wheeler
Levi P. Morton
Adlai E. Stevenson
James S. Sherman
John N. Garner
Gerald R. Ford
George Bush

Senate Only

Aaron Burr
Martin Van Buren
George M. Dallas
Henry Wilson
Charles W. Fairbanks
Harry S Truman
Hubert H. Humphrey
Walter F. Mondale

Both Chambers

John C. Calhoun
Richard M. Johnson
John Tyler
William R. King
John C. Breckinridge
Hannibal Hamlin

Andrew Johnson
Thomas A. Hendricks
Charles Curtis
Alben W. Barkley
Richard Nixon
Lyndon B. Johnson

SOURCE: Joseph Nathan Kane, *Facts about the Presidents: A Compilation of Biographical and Historical Information*, 4th ed. (New York: The H. W. Wilson Co., 1981). Reprinted by permission of the publisher.

The average age of the vice president upon assuming office was 53. The youngest man to become vice president was John C. Breckinridge, 36. Alben W. Barkley was the oldest vice president. He was 71 at the time of his inauguration in 1949.

Nine vice presidents succeeded to office on the death or resignation of the president under whom they were serving. Tyler, Millard Fillmore, Coolidge, and Harry S Truman assumed office after the natural death of the president; Andrew Johnson,

Chester A. Arthur, Theodore Roosevelt, and Lyndon B. Johnson after the assassination of the president; and Ford after the resignation of the president.

William R. King held the office of vice president for the shortest length of time. King, who served during the Franklin Pierce administration, was vice president from March 4, 1853, until he died on April 18 of that year. Three vice presidents — Tompkins, Marshall, and Richard Nixon — completed two full terms. Clinton and Calhoun were the only men to have served under two different presidents; Clinton under Jefferson and James Madison, Calhoun under John Quincy Adams and Andrew Jackson. Two vice presidents, Ford and Rockefeller, were appointed under the provisions of the Twenty-fifth Amendment. *(Presidential Disability and the Line of Succession, box, p. 2)*

Seven vice presidents died in office — Clinton, Gerry, Hendricks, Garret A. Hobart, King, James S. Sherman, and Henry Wilson. Two — Calhoun and Agnew — resigned.

Vice Presidents: Biographies

This biographical summary lists, alphabetically, all the vice presidents of the United States since 1789. The material is organized as follows: name; relationship to other vice presidents, presidents, members of Congress, Supreme Court justices, or governors; party, state; date of birth; date of death (if applicable); period of service as vice president; congressional service, service as president, member of the Cabinet, governor, delegate to the Continental Congress, House or Senate majority leader, Speaker of the House, president pro tempore of the Senate, or chairman of the Democratic or Republican National Committee. *(Party*

abbreviations, box, p. x)

Under the Constitution, terms of service from 1789 to 1933 were from March 4 to March 4; since 1934, service has been from Jan. 20 to Jan. 20. If a vice president began or ended his service in midterm, exact dates are shown.

The major source of information for this list was Congressional Quarterly's *Guide to U.S. Elections.* Additional data was obtained from Joseph Nathan Kane, *Facts about the Presidents: A Compilation of Biographical and Historical Information,* 4th ed. (New York: The H. W. Wilson Co., 1981).

ADAMS, John (father of Pres. John Quincy Adams, grandfather of Rep. Charles Francis Adams) (F Mass.) Oct. 30, 1735-July 4, 1826; Vice President April 21, 1789-97; Cont. Cong. 1774; President 1797-1801.

AGNEW, Spiro Theodore (R Md.) Nov. 9, 1918-—; Vice President 1969-Oct. 10, 1973 (resigned); Gov. 1967-69.

ARTHUR, Chester Alan (R N.Y.) Oct. 5, 1830-Nov. 18, 1886; Vice President March 4-Sept. 20, 1881; President Sept. 20, 1881-85 (succeeded James Abram Garfield, who was assassinated).

BARKLEY, Alben William (D Ky.) Nov. 24, 1877-April 30, 1956; Vice President 1949-53; House 1913-27; Senate 1927-49, 1955-56; Senate majority leader 1937-47.

BRECKINRIDGE, John Cabell (grandson of Sen. John Breckinridge, father of Rep. Clifton Rodes Breckinridge, cousin of Rep. Henry Donnel Foster) (D Ky.) Jan. 21, 1821-May 17, 1875; Vice President 1857-61; House 1851-55; Senate 1861.

BURR, Aaron (cousin of Rep. Theodore Dwight, father-in-law of Gov. Joseph Alston of S.C.) (DR N.Y.) Feb. 6, 1756-Sept. 14, 1836; Vice President 1801-05; Senate 1791-97.

BUSH, George Herbert Walker (son of Sen. Prescott Sheldon Bush) (R Texas) June 12, 1924-—; Vice President 1981-—; House 1967-71; Chrmn. Rep. Nat. Comm. 1973-74.

CALHOUN, John Caldwell (cousin of Sen. John Ewing Colhoun and Rep. Joseph Calhoun) (DR S.C.) March 18, 1782-March 31, 1850; Vice President 1825-Dec. 28, 1832 (resigned to become senator); House 1811-17; Secy. of War 1817-25; Senate 1832-43 (Democrat), 1845-50 (Democrat); Secy. of State 1844-45.

CLINTON, George (father of Rep. George Clinton, uncle of Rep. James Graham Clinton and Gov. De Witt Clinton of N.Y.) (DR N.Y.) July 26, 1739-April 20, 1812; Vice President 1805-April 20, 1812 (died in office); Cont. Cong. 1775-76; Gov. 1777-95, 1801-04.

COLFAX, Schuyler (R Ind.) March 23, 1823-Jan. 13, 1885; Vice President 1869-73; House 1855-69; Speaker 1863-69.

COOLIDGE, John Calvin (cousin of Gov. William Wallace Stickney of Vt.) (R Mass.) July 4, 1872-Jan. 5, 1933; Vice President 1921-Aug. 3, 1923; Gov. 1919-21; President Aug. 3, 1923-29 (succeeded Warren Gamaliel Harding, who died in office).

CURTIS, Charles (R Kan.) Jan. 25, 1860-Feb. 8, 1936; Vice President 1929-33; House 1893-1907; Senate 1907-13, 1915-29; Pres. pro tempore 1911; Senate majority leader 1924-29.

DALLAS, George Mifflin (D Pa.) July 10, 1792-Dec. 31, 1864; Vice President 1845-49; Senate 1831-33.

DAWES, Charles Gates (son of Rep. Rufus Dawes, brother of Rep. Beman Gates Dawes) (R Ill.) Aug. 27, 1865-April 23, 1951; Vice President 1925-29.

FAIRBANKS, Charles Warren (R Ind.) May 11, 1852-June 4, 1918; Vice President 1905-09; Senate 1897-1905.

FILLMORE, Millard (W N.Y.) Jan. 7, 1800-March 8, 1874; Vice President 1849-July 9, 1850; House 1833-35, 1837-43; President July 10, 1850-53 (succeeded Zachary Taylor, who died in office).

FORD, Gerald Rudolph Jr. (R Mich.) July 14, 1913- —; Vice President Dec. 6, 1973-Aug. 9, 1974; House 1949-73; President Aug. 9, 1974-77.

GARNER, John Nance (D Texas) Nov. 22, 1868-Nov. 7, 1967; Vice President 1933-Jan. 19, 1941; House 1903-33; Speaker 1931-33.

GERRY, Elbridge (great-grandfather of Sen. Peter Goelet Gerry, grandfather of Rep. Elbridge Gerry) (DR Mass.) July 17, 1744-Nov. 23, 1814; Vice President 1813-Nov. 23, 1814 (died in office); Cont. Cong. 1776-81, 1782-85; House 1789-93 (Anti Federalist); Gov. 1810-12.

HAMLIN, Hannibal (R Maine) Aug. 27, 1809-July 4, 1891; Vice President 1861-65; House 1843-47 (Democrat); Senate 1848-57 (Democrat), 1857-61, 1869-81; Gov. 1857.

HENDRICKS, Thomas Andrews (nephew of Sen. William Hendricks) (D Ind.) Sept. 7, 1819-Nov. 25, 1885; Vice President March 4-Nov. 25, 1885 (died in office); House 1851-55; Senate 1863-69; Gov. 1873-77.

HOBART, Garret Augustus (R N.J.) June 3, 1844-Nov. 21, 1899; Vice President 1897-Nov. 21, 1899 (died in office).

HUMPHREY, Hubert Horatio Jr. (husband of Sen. Muriel Buck Humphrey) (D Minn.) May 27, 1911-Jan. 13, 1978; Vice President 1965-69; Senate 1949-64, 1971-78.

JEFFERSON, Thomas (father-in-law of Gov. Thomas Mann Randolph of Va.) (DR Va.) April 13, 1743-July 4, 1826; Vice President 1797-1801; Cont. Cong. 1775-76, 1783-85; Gov. 1779-81 (Va. Terr.); Secy. of State 1789-93; President 1801-09.

JOHNSON, Andrew (father-in-law of Sen. David Trotter Patterson) (R Tenn.) Dec. 29, 1808-July 31, 1875; Vice President March 4-April 15, 1865; House 1843-53 (Democrat); Gov. 1853-57 (Democrat), 1862-65 (Military); Senate 1857-62 (Democrat), 1875; President April 15, 1865-69 (succeeded Abraham Lincoln, who was assassinated).

JOHNSON, Lyndon Baines (D Texas) Aug. 27, 1908-Jan. 22, 1973; Vice President 1961-Nov. 22, 1963; House 1937-49; Senate 1949-61; Senate majority leader 1955-61; President Nov. 22, 1963-69 (succeeded John Fitzgerald Kennedy, who was assassinated).

JOHNSON, Richard Mentor (brother of Reps. James Johnson and John Telemachus Johnson, uncle of Sen. Robert Ward Johnson) (D Ky.) Oct. 17, 1781-Nov. 19, 1850; Vice President 1837-41; House 1807-19 (Jackson Democrat), 1829-37 (Jackson Democrat); Senate 1819-29 (Jackson Democrat).

KING, William Rufus deVane (D Ala.) April 7, 1786-April 18, 1853; Vice President March 4-April 18, 1853 (died in office); House 1811-16 (N.C.); Senate 1819-44, 1848-52; Pres. pro tempore 1835-41, 1849-52.

MARSHALL, Thomas Riley (D Ind.) March 14, 1854-June 1, 1925; Vice President 1913-21; Gov. 1909-13.

MONDALE, Walter Frederick "Fritz" (D Minn.) Jan. 5, 1928- —; Vice President 1977-81; Senate 1964-76.

MORTON, Levi Parsons (R N.Y.) May 16, 1824-May 16, 1920; Vice President 1889-93; House 1879-81; Gov. 1895-97.

NIXON, Richard Milhous (R Calif.) Jan. 9, 1913- —; Vice President 1953-61; House 1947-50; Senate 1950-53; President 1969-Aug. 9, 1974.

ROCKEFELLER, Nelson Aldrich (brother of Gov. Winthrop Rockefeller of Ark., uncle of Sen. John Davison "Jay" Rockefeller IV, nephew of Rep. Richard Steere Aldrich, grandson of Sen. Nelson Wilmarth Aldrich) (R N.Y.) July 8, 1908-Jan. 26, 1979; Vice President Dec. 19, 1974-77; Gov. 1959-73.

ROOSEVELT, Theodore (R N.Y.) Oct. 27, 1858-Jan. 6, 1919; Vice President March 4-Sept. 14, 1901; Gov. 1899-1901; President Sept. 14, 1901-09 (succeeded William McKinley Jr., who was assassinated).

SHERMAN, James Schoolcraft (R N.Y.) Oct. 24, 1855-Oct. 30, 1912; Vice President 1909-Oct. 30, 1912 (died in office); House 1887-91, 1893-1909.

STEVENSON, Adlai Ewing (grandfather of Gov. Adlai Ewing Stevenson II of Ill., great-grandfather of Sen. Adlai Ewing Stevenson III) (D Ill.) Oct. 23, 1835-June 14, 1914; Vice President 1893-97; House 1875-77, 1879-81.

TOMPKINS, Daniel D. (DR N.Y.) June 21, 1774-June 11, 1825; Vice President 1817-25; Gov. 1807-17.

TRUMAN, Harry S (D Mo.) May 8, 1884-Dec. 26, 1972; Vice President Jan. 20-April 12, 1945; Senate 1935-45; President April 12, 1945-53 (succeeded Franklin Delano Roosevelt, who died in office).

TYLER, John (son of Gov. John Tyler of Va., father of Rep. David Gardiner Tyler) (W Va.) March 29, 1790-Jan. 18, 1862; Vice President March 4-April 6, 1841; Gov. 1825-27 (Democratic Republican); House 1817-21 (Democratic Republican); Senate 1827-36 (Democratic Republican); Pres. pro tempore 1835-36; President April 6, 1841-45 (succeeded William Henry Harrison, who died in office).

VAN BUREN, Martin (half brother of Rep. James Isaac Van Alen) (D N.Y.) Dec. 5, 1782-July 24, 1862; Vice President 1833-37; Senate 1821-28; Gov. 1829; Secy. of State 1829-31; President 1837-41.

WALLACE, Henry Agard (D Iowa) Oct. 7, 1888-Nov. 18, 1965; Vice President 1941-45; Secy. of Agriculture 1933-40; Secy. of Commerce 1945-46.

WHEELER, William Almon (R N.Y.) June 30, 1819-June 4, 1887; Vice President 1877-81; House 1861-63, 1869-77.

WILSON, Henry (R Mass.) Feb. 16, 1812-Nov. 22, 1875; Vice President 1873-Nov. 22, 1875 (died in office); Senate 1855-73.

Supreme Court Justices

Even though it will be 200 years old in 1989, the Supreme Court has had only 103 members, making it one of the most exclusive as well as long-lasting government entities in the world.

One hundred two justices have been men; 102 have been Caucasian. All but 12 were Protestants. The court, however, has exhibited diversity in other ways — politically, geographically, and in the age, personality, and previous service of its individual members. And there have been periodic breakthroughs when appointees with innovative ideas or controversial backgrounds first attained a seat on the court. The first Roman Catholic was appointed in 1835, the first Jew in 1916, the first black in 1967, the first woman in 1981. *(Catholic and Jewish Justices, box, p. 23)*

There are in fact no constitutional or statutory qualifications at all for serving on the Supreme Court. The Constitution simply states that "the judicial power of the United States shall be vested in one Supreme Court" as well as any lower federal courts Congress may establish (Article III, Section 1) and that the president "... by and with the Advice and Consent of the Senate, shall appoint ... Judges of the Supreme Court...." There is no age limitation, no requirement that judges be native-born citizens, nor even a requirement that appointees have a legal background.

Naturally, informal criteria for membership quickly developed. Every nominee to the court has been a lawyer. And over the years a myriad of other factors have entered into the process of presidential selection. Some of them became long-lasting traditions with virtually the force of a formal requirement. Others were as fleeting as the personal friendship between the president and the nominee.

The First Justices

George Washington, as the first president, had the responsibility of choosing the original 6 justices of the Supreme Court. The type of men he chose and the reasons he chose them foreshadowed the process of selection carried out by his successors.

In naming the first justices, Washington paid close attention to their politics, which at that time meant primarily loyalty to the new Constitution. Of the 6 original appointees, 3 had attended the Philadelphia convention that formulated the Constitution, and the other 3 had supported its adoption. John Jay, the first chief justice, was coauthor with Alexander Hamilton and James Madison of *The Federalist Papers*, a series of influential essays published in New York supporting ratification of the Constitution.

During his two terms of office (1789-97), Washington had occasion to make 5 additional Supreme Court appointments. All were staunch supporters of the Constitution and the new federal government.

Another of Washington's major considerations was geographical. The new states were a disparate group that had barely held together during the fight for independence and the confederation government of the 1780s. To help bind them more closely together, Washington consciously tried to represent each geographical area of the country in the nation's new supreme tribunal.

His first 6 appointees consisted of 3 northerners — Chief Justice John Jay from New York and Associate Justices William

Cushing of Massachusetts and James Wilson of Pennsylvania — and 3 southerners — John Blair of Virginia, James Iredell of North Carolina, and John Rutledge of South Carolina. The 5 later appointees were Oliver Ellsworth of Connecticut, Thomas Johnson and Samuel Chase of Maryland, William Paterson of New Jersey, and Rutledge, appointed a second time. Thus by the time Washington left office, 9 of the original 13 states had already achieved representation on the Supreme Court.

Appointment Opportunities

With a total of 11, Washington still holds the record for the number of Supreme Court appointments made by any president. The second highest total — 9 — belongs to President Franklin D. Roosevelt, the only president to serve more than two terms. Roosevelt also came closest since Washington to naming the entire membership of the court — only 2 justices who served prior to the Roosevelt years were still on the court at the time of his death. And 1 of them — Harlan Fiske Stone — Roosevelt elevated from associate justice to chief justice.

Presidents Andrew Jackson (1829-37) and William H. Taft (1909-13) had the next highest number of justices appointed with 6 each. Taft holds the record for a one-term president. Next in order are Abraham Lincoln (1861-65) and Dwight D. Eisenhower (1953-61) with 5 each.

Four presidents made no appointments to the Supreme Court. William Henry Harrison (1841) and Zachary Taylor (1849-50) both died in office before any vacancies occurred, and no vacancies opened up during Jimmy Carter's term (1977-81). Andrew Johnson (1865-69), who served just six weeks short of a full term, had no chance to make a court appointment because of his rancorous political battle with Congress over Reconstruction. So bitter did the struggle become that Congress in effect took away Johnson's power of appointment by passing legislation in 1866 to reduce the court to 7 members from 10 as vacancies should occur.

The legislation was occasioned by the death of Justice John Catron in 1865 and Johnson's nomination in 1866 of Henry

Stanbery to replace him. The Senate took no action on Stanbery's nomination and instead passed the bill reducing the size of the court. When Justice James Wayne died in 1867, the membership of the court automatically dropped to 8. In 1869, when the Republicans had recaptured the White House, they enacted legislation increasing the court to 9 seats, allowing President Ulysses S. Grant to make a nomination.

Nonpartisan Appointments

As political parties became an established fact of American political life, each of the major parties sought to appoint members to the Supreme Court who would espouse their view of what the federal government should and should not do.

As Washington had appointed supporters of the new Constitution, so most presidents have selected nominees with whom they were philosophically and politically in accord. Whenever a president goes to the opposite political party to find a nominee, it is the exception rather than the rule.

The first clear-cut instance of a president of one party appointing a member of the other to the Supreme Court was Republican Lincoln's selection of Democrat Stephen J. Field of California in 1863. President John Tyler, elected vice president as a Whig in 1840, appointed Democrat Samuel Nelson to the court in 1845, but by that time Tyler was no longer identified with either major political party.

After Lincoln's example, Republican presidents occasionally appointed Democrats to the court. President Benjamin Harrison selected Democrat Howell Jackson of Tennessee in 1893; Warren G. Harding appointed Democrat Pierce Butler in 1922; Herbert Hoover appointed Democrat Benjamin Cardozo in 1932; Eisenhower appointed Democrat William J. Brennan Jr. in 1956 and Richard Nixon appointed Democrat Lewis F. Powell Jr. in 1971. Republican Taft was the only president to appoint more than one member of the opposite party to the court. Three of his 6 nominees to the court were Democrats — Edward D. White, whom Taft elevated from associate justice to chief justice, and Horace Lurton and Joseph F

Catholic and Jewish Justices

The overwhelming Protestant complexion of the Supreme Court has been broken only 12 times; 91 of the 103 justices have been of Protestant background.

The first time the Protestant tradition was broken was in 1835, when President Andrew Jackson nominated Roger B. Taney, a Roman Catholic, for chief justice. Taney's religion seemed to raise no controversy at the time, however. Rather, Taney's close alliance with the controversial Jackson, whom he served as attorney general and secretary of the Treasury, was the main focus of attention.

Not until 1894 — 30 years after Taney's death — was the second Catholic, Edward D. White of Louisiana, appointed, by President Grover Cleveland. Sixteen years later, President William Howard Taft made White chief justice. As in the case of Taney, White's religion attracted no particular notice. Both Taney and White were from traditional Catholic areas of the country, and both had long been engaged in American politics without any focus on their religion. In 1897, President William McKinley chose Joseph McKenna, his attorney general and a Catholic, as an associate justice. In that appointment, however, geography was the overriding factor; McKenna came from California, as did his predecessor, Stephen J. Field.

Pierce Butler was the next Catholic appointee. President Warren G. Harding named him to the bench in 1922, largely because of Butler's political base. He was a Democrat, and Harding wanted to make a show of bipartisanship.

On Butler's death in late 1939, President Franklin D. Roosevelt picked as his successor Frank Murphy, an Irish Catholic politician who had been mayor of Detroit, governor of Michigan, and was then serving as Roosevelt's attorney general. In 1949, when Murphy died, President Harry S Truman broke the continuity of a Catholic seat on the court by naming a Protestant, Tom C. Clark. For the first time since 1894, there was no Catholic on the court.

Of all the Catholic appointments, that of William J. Brennan Jr. by President Dwight D. Eisenhower in 1956 attracted the most notice, although it too was relatively noncontroversial. But it was an election year and the Republicans were making a strong appeal to normally Democratic Catholic voters in the big cities. Some saw Brennan's appointment a part of that GOP strategy, although Eisenhower insisted it was an appointment made purely on merit.

Much more controversial than any of the Catholic nominees was Louis D. Brandeis, the first Jewish justice, named by President Woodrow Wilson in 1916. Brandeis was already a figure of great controversy because of his views on social and economic matters. Conservatives bitterly fought his nomination, and there was an element of anti-Semitism in some of the opposition. When Brandeis took his seat on the court, Justice McReynolds refused to speak to him for three years and once refused to sit next to him for a court picture-taking session.

Herbert Hoover's nomination of Benjamin Cardozo in 1932 established a so-called Jewish seat on the Supreme Court. Justice Felix Frankfurter replaced Cardozo in 1939. He in turn was replaced by Justice Arthur J. Goldberg in 1962. And when Goldberg resigned his court position to become U.S. ambassador to the United Nations, President Lyndon B. Johnson chose Abe Fortas to replace him.

But with Justice Fortas's resignation in 1969, President Richard Nixon broke the tradition of a "Jewish seat" by choosing Harry A. Blackmun of Minnesota, a Protestant.

Geographical Considerations Were Strong ...

Geography was a prime consideration in the appointment of Supreme Court justices throughout the nineteenth century. Presidents found it expedient to have each of the expanding nation's rival sections represented on the court. Whenever a justice died or resigned, his replacement usually came from the same state or a neighboring one. In addition, the justices' circuit duties, which required them to attend court sessions in their circuits periodically, made it desirable for each justice to be a native of the circuit over which he presided.

The 'New England Seat'

The most notable instance of geographical continuity was the seat traditionally held by a New Englander. William Cushing of Massachusetts was appointed an associate justice by President George Washington in 1789. From then until 1932, the seat was held by a New England appointee, usually from Massachusetts.

When Cushing died after 21 years on the court, President James Madison looked to New England for a successor. He offered the post to both former attorney general Levi Lincoln and John Quincy Adams, both from Massachusetts, but they declined. After Madison's nomination of Alexander Wolcott of Connecticut was turned down by the Senate, the president turned back to Massachusetts and selected Joseph Story, at 32 the youngest justice ever chosen. Story served 34 years, dying in 1845. President James K. Polk chose to continue the New England tradition of holding the seat by appointing Levi Woodbury of New Hampshire.

Woodbury's tenure lasted less than six years, and it fell to President Millard Fillmore to find a successor. He chose Benjamin Curtis, another Massachusetts native. Curtis resigned in 1857 after only five and a half years, largely because of his acrimonious relations with other members of the Taney court. President James Buchanan, mindful of the continued need for a New Englander on the court, chose Nathan Clifford of Maine.

Clifford served until his death in July 1881, shortly after President James A. Garfield was shot. When Garfield died in September his successor, Chester A. Arthur, chose the chief justice of the Massachusetts Supreme Court, Horace Gray, as the new justice from New England. Gray served until 1902, when he was succeeded by another Massachusetts Supreme Court chief justice, Oliver Wendell Holmes, appointed by President Theodore Roosevelt.

By the time of Holmes's appointment, however, the significance of geography had declined as a qualification for selection to the Supreme Court. President Theodore Roosevelt, in particular, was disdainful of such a prerequisite, and it was mostly accidental that Holmes came from Massachusetts. Nevertheless, his selection extended for another 30 years the tradition of the "New England seat." After Holmes's resignation in 1932, President Herbert Hoover chose as his successor Benjamin Cardozo, chief judge of New York state's highest court, thus ending the Supreme Court's longest-lasting geo

---

Lamar, southern Democrats appointed respectively in 1909 and 1910.

The only two Democrats ever to appoint Republicans to the Supreme Court were Franklin Roosevelt and Harry S Truman.

Roosevelt elevated Republican Stone from associate justice to chief justice in 1941. Truman appointed Republican senator Harold H. Burton of Ohio, an old friend and colleague from Truman's Senate days in 1945.

... In Appointment of Supreme Court Justices

graphical tradition. And while Cardozo's successor, Felix Frankfurter, was a resident of Massachusetts, that fact apparently played no role in his selection.

The 'New York Seat'

New York was another longtime holder of a specific seat on the Supreme Court. With the appointment of Justice Henry Brockholst Livingston by President Thomas Jefferson in 1806, a tradition began that continued until New Yorkers themselves ended it in 1894 by their internal quarreling.

Livingston served until his death in 1823. President James Monroe offered the post indirectly to Martin Van Buren, then a U.S. senator, but received a noncommital response. The president then chose Smith Thompson of New York, his secretary of the navy. Thompson served for 20 years. His death in 1843 came at an inopportune moment politically: President John Tyler was disliked by both Democrats and Whigs and had little political leverage. His attempts to choose a successor to Thompson met with repeated failure, the Senate defeating one nominee and forcing another to withdraw. Finally, at the last moment before leaving office in 1845, Tyler found a New Yorker acceptable to the Senate for the post. He was Justice Samuel Nelson, who continued to serve until his resignation in December 1872.

Two more New Yorkers held the seat after Nelson's retirement, Ward Hunt from 1873 to 1882 and Samuel Blatchford from 1882 to 1893. But then a bitter quarrel between New Yorkers over the seat ended the tradition. The two main New York antagonists were President Grover Cleveland and Sen. David B. Hill, old political enemies. Cleveland twice nominated a New Yorker for the post, and twice Hill used senatorial courtesy to object to the nominees. In both cases, the Senate followed its own tradition of honoring a senator's objection to a nominee of his own party from his own state and rejected Cleveland's choices. Cleveland then abandoned New York and chose U.S. Senator Edward D. White of Louisiana, who was confirmed immediately.

The 'Virginia-Maryland Seat'

Virginia and Maryland shared a seat on the Supreme Court from the first appointments in 1789 until the Civil War. John Blair of Virginia, appointed by Washington, served until 1796. Washington chose as his successor Samuel Chase of Maryland. After Chase's death in 1811, another Marylander, Gabriel Duval, was given the seat. Upon Duval's resignation in 1835, the seat went back to Virginia, with Philip Barbour holding it from 1836 to 1841 and Peter V. Daniel from 1841 to 1860. With the coming of the Civil War, there was a realignment of circuits as well as the desire of the new Republican administration to appoint more northerners and westerners to the court. The Maryland-Virginia tradition was ended when Iowan Samuel Miller was appointed as Daniel's successor by President Abraham Lincoln.

Lobbying for a Nomination

Presidential selection of justices is usually the result of a balancing of factors and a sifting of potential candidates before the president finally makes up his mind. But on a few occasions in American history a president's choice has all but been made for him by overwhelming pressure for a particular nominee.

One of the more dramatic instances of this process occurred in 1853, when President Franklin Pierce nominated John A.

Campbell of Alabama for a spot on the court. Campbell was a 41-year-old lawyer who had such a brilliant reputation that the Supreme Court justices decided they wanted him as a colleague. As a result, the entire membership of the court wrote to Pierce requesting Campbell's nomination. To emphasize their point, they sent 2 justices to the president to deliver the letters in person. Pierce complied, and Campbell was confirmed within four days.

In 1862, Lincoln was looking for a new justice from the Midwest. The Iowa congressional delegation began pressing for the appointment of Samuel Miller, a doctor and lawyer who had helped form the Iowa Republican party and had a strong reputation for moral and intellectual integrity. The movement grew rapidly until 129 of 140 House members and all but 4 senators had signed a petition for Miller's nomination. With such massive and unprecedented congressional support, Miller received Lincoln's approval despite his lack of any judicial experience. He became the first justice from west of the Mississippi River.

In 1932 a strong national movement began for the appointment of Cardozo, chief judge of the New York court of appeals, to the Supreme Court. Cardozo was a Democrat, while the president who was to make the appointment, Hoover, was a Republican. Furthermore, Cardozo was Jewish and there was already one Jew on the court, Louis D. Brandeis. Under these circumstances, it was considered unlikely Hoover would make the nomination.

But Cardozo's record was so impressive that a groundswell of support arose for him. Deans and faculty members of the nation's leading law schools, chief judges of other state courts, labor and business leaders, and powerful senators all urged Hoover to choose Cardozo. Despite his desire to appoint a western Republican, Hoover finally yielded and nominated Cardozo, who was confirmed without opposition.

Geographical Factors

George Washington's weighing of geographical factors in appointing the first justices continued as a tradition for over a century. It was reenforced by the justices's duty under the Judiciary Act of 1789 to attend circuit court sessions. Presidents strove not only for geographical balance in their appointments but considered it important that each justice be a native of the circuit over which he presided.

But the burdensome attendance requirement was curtailed by legislation during the nineteenth century until it became optional in 1891 and was abolished altogether in 1911. In the twentieth century, geography became less and less a consideration in Supreme Court nominations, although as recently as 1970 President Nixon made an issue of it in the failure of the Senate to confirm two southerners — Clement Haynsworth Jr. and G. Harrold Carswell — to the court. Nixon claimed the Senate would not confirm a conservative southerner and turned to Minnesotan Harry A. Blackmun instead.

In its heyday, the geographical factor was sometimes almost sacrosanct. The most enduring example was the so-called New England seat, which was occupied by a New Englander, usually from Massachusetts, from 1789 to 1932. There was also a seat for a New Yorker from 1806 to 1894 and a Maryland-Virginia seat from 1789 to 1860. *(Regional seats on the Supreme Court, box, p. 24)*

Geography had strong political ramifications as well. This was especially so in the case of the South. With the growth of sectional differences, particularly over the slavery issue, before the Civil War, the South felt itself to be on the defensive. One of the ways it sought to defend its interests was to gain a majority on the Supreme Court. And, indeed, 5 of the 9 justices in 1860 were from slaveholding states.

With the coming of the Civil War, the sectional balance of power shifted. Four of the 5 southern justices died between 1860 and 1867, and another — Justice John A. Campbell of Alabama — resigned to join the Confederate cause.

Not one of these justices was replaced by a southerner. Thus by 1870 every Supreme Court seat was held by a northerner or westerner. But with the gradual decline of bitterness over the war, southern members again began to appear on the court. President Rutherford B. Hayes, who sought to reconcile relations between the North and South, made the first move by appointing William B. Woods of Georgia in 1880. Woods was not a native southerner, having migrated there after the Civil War. But despite this "carpetbagger" background, he was never identified with the corruption and profligacy associated with the Reconstruction era. As a federal judge for the fifth — deep South — circuit, he gained the respect of his neighbors for his fairness and honesty.

The first native southerner appointed to the court after the Civil War was Woods's successor, Lucius Q. C. Lamar of Mississippi, appointed by President Grover Cleveland in 1888. Lamar had personally drafted Mississippi's ordinance of secession in 1861 and had served the Confederacy both as a military officer and as a diplomatic envoy to Europe. So his accession to the court was an even more significant symbol of reconciliation between the sections than Woods's appointment eight years earlier.

Thirty-one states have contributed justices to the Supreme Court. New York has by far the highest total, with 15, followed by Ohio with 9, Massachusetts with 8, and Virginia with 7. Several major states have had only 1 justice, including Texas, Indiana, and Missouri — as have such small states as Utah, Maine, and Wyoming.

Of the 19 states that have never had a native on the court, most are smaller western states. Only 6 of the 19 are east of the Mississippi River. The largest state never to have had a justice is Florida, the seventh most populous state according to the 1980 census.

The lack of representation on the court from some of the smaller states resulted in a controversy during the 1950s when North Dakota's outspoken maverick Sen. William Langer began opposing all non-North Dakotan Supreme Court nominees as a protest against big-state nominees. Langer was chairman of the Senate Judiciary Committee during the 83d Congress (1953-55). In 1954 he joined in delaying tactics against the nomination of Earl Warren as chief justice,

managing to hold off confirmation for two months. He continued his struggle for the next six years, until his death in 1959.

Only Lawyers

All of Washington's appointees were lawyers, and no president has deviated from this precedent. The legal education of the justices has changed radically over the years, however. Until the midnineteenth century, it was traditional for aspiring lawyers to study privately in a law office until they had learned the law sufficiently to pass the bar. There were no law schools as such in the early years, although some universities had courses in law. John Marshall, for example, attended a course of law lectures at William and Mary College in the 1770s. Two of the earliest justices — John Rutledge and John Blair — received their legal education in England, at the Inns of Court. A modern justice, Frank Murphy (1940-49), also studied there.

Of the 56 justices (including Rutledge and Blair) who attended law school, by far the largest number (13) attended Harvard. Yale taught 8 justices law and Columbia 5. The first justice to receive a law degree from an American university was Benjamin Curtis, who got his from Harvard in 1832.

But it was not until 1957 that the Supreme Court was composed, for the first time, entirely of law school graduates. Before that, many had attended law school but had not received degrees. The last justice never to have attended law school was James F. Byrnes, who served from 1941 to 1942. The son of poor Irish immigrants, Byrnes never even graduated from high school. He left school at age 14, worked as a law clerk and eventually became a court stenographer. Reading law in his spare time, Byrnes passed the bar at age 24.

The last justice not to have a law degree was Stanley F. Reed, who served from 1938 to 1957. He attended both the University of Virginia and Columbia law schools, but received a degree from neither.

Precourt Experience

Most justices have been active either in politics or in judicial office before coming to

Six Supreme Court Justices ...

Since the Constitution makes no stipulation that Supreme Court justices must be native-born Americans, presidents are free to name foreign-born members to the court. In all, six Supreme Court justices were born outside the United States, although one was the son of an American missionary who was temporarily living abroad. Of the remaining five, four were born in the British Isles. Only one — Felix Frankfurter — was born in a non-English-speaking country.

President George Washington appointed three of the foreign-born justices. The others were selected by Presidents Benjamin Harrison, Warren G. Harding, and Franklin D. Roosevelt. The six justices born outside the United States are:

● James Wilson, born Sept. 14, 1742, in Caskardy, Scotland. Wilson grew up in Scotland and was educated at St. Andrews University in preparation for a career in the ministry. But in 1765 he sailed for America, where he studied law and went into land speculation. A signer of the Declaration of Independence, Wilson also was a member of the 1787 Constitutional Convention and its committee of detail, which was responsible for writing the first draft of the Constitution. In 1789 Washington appointed Wilson one of the original members of the Supreme Court. In the late 1790s, Wilson's land speculations failed, and he was jailed twice for debt while riding circuit and died in a dingy inn in North Carolina.

● James Iredell, born Oct. 5, 1751, in Lewes, England. Iredell was born into an old English family allegedly descended indirectly from Oliver Cromwell's son-in-law. Through family connections, Iredell received an appointment as colonial comptroller of customs at Edenton, N.C., at the age of 17. After six years he was promoted to collector of the port of Edenton. Iredell identified with the colonial cause and resigned his job as collector in 1776. While serving in his colonial offices, Iredell had studied law and began practice in 1770. In 1788 he was a strong supporter of the new federal Constitution and worked for its ratification by North Carolina. Washington appointed him a Supreme Court justice in 1790. He served until his death in 1799 at the age of 48, the youngest justice ever to die on the court.

● William Paterson, born Dec. 24, 1745, in County Antrim, Ireland. Paterson emigrated to America with his parents when he was only two years old. He received his education at Princeton University and then read law, opening his own law practice in

the Supreme Court. In fact, only one justice — George Shiras Jr. — had never engaged in political or judicial activities before his appointment.

Judges. A total of 62 justices had some judicial experience — federal or state — before coming to the Supreme Court. Surprisingly, there have been many more who had experience on the state level (43) than on the federal level (26). (There is an overlap in the figures because 7 justices had both federal and state judicial offices.)

All except 2 of Washington's appointees had state judicial experience, the president believing that such experience was important for justices of the new federal court. But it was not until 1826 that a justice with previous federal judicial experience was appointed. He was Robert Trimble, who had served nine years as a U.S. district judge before his appointment to the Supreme Court.

Even after Trimble's appointment, judges with federal judicial experience continued to be a rarity on the Supreme Court. By 1880 only 2 other federal judges —

.. Born Outside the United States

769. Paterson was active in New Jersey affairs during the Revolutionary and Confedera-
ion periods, and served as a delegate to the Constitutional Convention in 1780-81 and
787. He was a member of the First Senate in 1789-90 and, as a member of the Judiciary
ommittee, helped write the Judiciary Act of 1789. Later, he codified the laws of the
ate of New Jersey and, in association with Alexander Hamilton, laid out plans for the
dustrial city of Paterson. He was appointed to the Supreme Court by Washington in
793 and served until his death in 1806.

• David Brewer, born Jan. 30, 1837, in Smyrna, Turkey. Brewer was a member of an
d New England family whose father was serving as a Congregational missionary in
urkey. The family returned to the United States soon after Brewer's birth. Brewer
ught his fortune in Kansas and spent most of his career in the Kansas court system and
wer federal courts. He was elevated to the Supreme Court by President Benjamin
arrison in 1890. Brewer's mother was the sister of Supreme Court Justice Stephen J.
ield (1863-97) and Cyrus W. Field, promoter of the first Atlantic cable.

• George Sutherland, born March 25, 1862, in Buckinghamshire, England.
utherland's father converted to Mormonism about the time of George's birth and
oved his family to the Utah Territory. Although the senior Sutherland soon deserted
e Mormons, the family remained in Utah, where George was educated at Brigham
oung University. When Utah entered the Union as a state in 1896, Sutherland was
ected to the state legislature. In 1900 he won a seat in the U.S. House and went on to
rve two terms in the U.S. Senate (1905-17) before being defeated for reelection. While
the Senate, he formed a close friendship to a fellow senator, Warren G. Harding of
hio. When Harding became president, he appointed Sutherland to the Supreme Court.
ater, Sutherland became one of the justices known as implacable foes of Roosevelt's
ew Deal.

• Felix Frankfurter, born Nov. 15, 1882, in Vienna, Austria. Frankfurter came to the
nited States with his parents in 1894 and grew up on the lower East Side of New York
ity. He achieved a brilliant academic record at City College and Harvard Law School,
tering practice in New York City. In 1914 he joined the Harvard Law faculty and
mained there, with time out for some governmental service during World War I, until
s appointment to the Supreme Court by Franklin Roosevelt in 1939.

hilip P. Barbour in 1836 and Peter V. Dan-
el in 1841 — had made it to the highest
ourt. After 1880, when federal circuit judge
Villiam B. Woods was appointed, the pace
icked up, and federal judicial experience
ecame an increasingly important criterion
or appointment to the Supreme Court. By
979 5 justices, a majority, had held previ-
us federal judicial office.

Politicians. Many justices have come
rom a political background, serving in Con-
ress, as governors, or as members of a cabi-
et. One president, Taft, was later ap-

pointed to the court, as chief justice, in 1921.

More than a fourth of all justices — 27
— held congressional office before their elevation to the court. An additional 6 justices
sat in the Continental Congress in the 1770s
or 1780s.

The first justice who had a congressional background was William Paterson,
who had served in the Senate from 1789 to
1790. Chief Justice John Marshall was the
first justice with cabinet experience, having
held the post of secretary of state from 1800
to 1801.

Despite the number of justices with a congressional background, few incumbent members have been nominated directly to the Supreme Court. Only one incumbent House member, James M. Wayne in 1835, has ever been named to the court, and six incumbent senators: Oliver Ellsworth in 1796, John McKinley in 1837, Levi Woodbury in 1846, Edward D. White in 1894, Hugo L. Black in 1937, and Harold H. Burton in 1945.

The Senate has traditionally confirmed its own members without much debate. But in January 1853 when lame-duck president Millard Fillmore nominated Whig senator George Badger of North Carolina to the court, the Democratic Senate postponed the nomination until the close of the congressional session in March. Then the new Democratic president, Franklin Pierce, was able to nominate his own man. The postponement of Badger's nomination was a polite way of defeating a colleague's nomination, avoiding an outright rejection.

Sen. White's nomination came about after a bitter quarrel between President Grover Cleveland and Sen. David B. Hill of New York resulted in the Senate's rejection of two Cleveland nominees from New York. Cleveland then turned to the Senate for one of its own members, White, and that body quickly accepted the choice.

Sen. Hugo Black's 1937 nomination was surrounded by controversy. Sen. Joseph T. Robinson of Arkansas, the Senate majority leader who had led the fight for President Franklin Roosevelt's so-called "court-packing" plan, was expected to get the nomination but died suddenly. So Roosevelt picked Black, one of the few southern senators other than Robinson who had championed the president in the court battle. Black's support of the controversial bill — plus what some felt was his general lack of qualifications for the Supreme Court — led to a brief but acrimonious fight over his nomination. After he was confirmed, publicity grew over his one-time membership in the Ku Klux Klan, and charges were made that he was still a member. But in a nationwide radio address, Black denied any racial or religious intolerance on his part and defused the criticism.

The last Supreme Court appointee with any previous congressional service was Sherman Minton in 1949. He had served as a U.S. senator from Indiana from 1935 to 1941, then was appointed to a circuit court of appeals judgeship. Since the retirement of Black in 1971, no Supreme Court member has had any congressional experience.

Cabinet Members. Since John Adams's secretary of state, John Marshall, was appointed to the Supreme Court, 22 other cabinet secretaries became justices, 13 of them appointed while still serving in the cabinet. Heading the list of cabinet positions that led to Supreme Court seats is that of attorney general. Nine attorneys general, including 7 incumbents, have been appointed to the court. Next came secretaries of the Treasury (4), secretaries of state (3), and secretaries of the navy (3). One postmaster general, 1 secretary of the interior, 1 secretary of war, and 1 secretary of labor were appointed to the court.

The appointment of incumbent attorneys general has been largely a twentieth-century phenomenon: 6 of the 7 appointments occurred after 1900. The other occurred just before that, when President William McKinley appointed his attorney general, Joseph McKenna. The twentieth-century incumbents named to the court were William H. Moody, appointed by Theodore Roosevelt in 1906; James C. McReynolds (Woodrow Wilson, 1914); Harlan Fiske Stone (Calvin Coolidge, 1925); Frank Murphy (Franklin Roosevelt, 1940); Robert H. Jackson (Roosevelt, 1941); and Tom C. Clark (Truman, 1949).

In the nineteenth century 2 men who had served as attorney general eventually were elevated to the Supreme Court, but in both cases appointment came after their cabinet service. They were Roger B. Taney appointed chief justice by Jackson in 1835 after serving as Jackson's attorney general from 1831 to 1833, and Nathan Clifford appointed to the court by James Buchanan in 1857 after service as James K. Polk's attorney general from 1846 to 1848.

Governors. Only six governors or former governors have ever been appointed to

Relatives on the Court

Several sets of relatives have served as Supreme Court justices. In two instances, they were on the court at the same time. There have been no father-son combinations, but one grandfather-grandson, one uncle-nephew, and one father-in-law-son-in-law tandem. At least one pair of cousins served on the court.

The two John Marshall Harlans were grandfather and grandson. The elder Harlan, a Kentucky politician, was put on the court by President Rutherford B. Hayes in 1877 and served until 1911 — one of the longest periods of service in court history. His grandson and namesake was born and grew up in Chicago, but made his career as a highly successful Wall Street lawyer. His service extended from his appointment by President Dwight D. Eisenhower in 1954 until his resignation in September 1971.

Stephen J. Field was appointed to the Supreme Court by President Abraham Lincoln in 1863. Twenty-six years later, in 1889, he was still on the court when President Benjamin Harrison named his nephew, David B. Brewer, as an associate justice. Brewer was Field's sister's son. The two served together on the court from 1889 to Field's death in 1897.

Although Justice Stanley Matthews was only four years older than Justice Horace Gray, Matthews was Gray's father-in-law. Both justices were appointed in 1881; Matthews by President James A. Garfield, and Gray later in the year by President Chester A. Arthur. They served together on the court until Matthews's death in March 1889. In June of the same year, Gray, a 61-year-old bachelor, married Matthews's daughter Jane.

The two Lamars who served on the court — Lucius Quintus Cincinnatus Lamar of Mississippi and Joseph Rucker Lamar of Georgia — were cousins. They were descendants of a Huguenot family that settled in the colonies in the 1600s. Lucius served on the court from 1888 to 1893, the first native-born southerner to be appointed after the Civil War. Joseph, appointed by President William Howard Taft, served from 1910 to 1916. Other prominent members of the same family were Mirabeau Buonaparte Lamar, second president of the Republic of Texas (1838-41), and Gazzaway Bugg Lamar, merchant, banker, and Confederate agent.

the Supreme Court. The most recent — and the most famous — was California governor Earl Warren, appointed chief justice by Eisenhower in 1953. Warren had a long political career behind him, having served as attorney general of California before winning three terms as governor of his state. In 1948 he was the Republican nominee for vice president and was briefly a candidate for the presidential nomination in 1952.

The only other incumbent governor ever appointed to the court was Charles Evans Hughes of New York, chosen by Taft in 1910. Hughes was a reform governor who had conducted investigations into fraudulent insurance practices in New York before being elected governor in 1906. He left the court in 1916 to run for president on the Republican ticket, losing narrowly to Wilson. Later he served as secretary of state under Presidents Harding and Coolidge and returned to the court in 1930 as chief justice.

The four other former governors appointed to the Supreme Court were Levi Woodbury of New Hampshire in 1846 (governor, 1823-24), Salmon P. Chase of Ohio in 1864 (governor, 1856-60), Frank Murphy of Michigan in 1940 (governor, 1937-39), and

Longest Vacancies in Court's History ...

The longest vacancy in the court's history lasted for 2 years, 3 months, and 23 days. During that period the Senate rejected four nominations by two presidents to the seat, and James Buchanan, who would serve as the 15th president of the United States, declined three invitations to fill the vacancy.

When Justice Henry Baldwin died April 21, 1844, John Tyler was president. Elected vice president on the Whig ticket in 1840, Tyler broke with the party after he had become president on William Henry Harrison's death in 1841. From then on, he was a president essentially without a party or personal popularity. At the time of Baldwin's death, one Tyler nomination to the court had already been rejected and a second was pending. Tyler first offered the Baldwin vacancy to Buchanan, who, like Baldwin, was a Pennsylvanian. When he declined, the president nominated Philadelphia attorney Judge Edward King to the seat.

Followers of Henry Clay, however, who controlled the Senate, thought Clay would win the presidency in that year's election, and they voted in June 1844 to postpone consideration of both King's nomination and Tyler's pending appointment of Reuben H. Walworth to the second vacancy. Tyler resubmitted King's name in December. Again the Senate refused to act, and Tyler was forced to withdraw the appointment.

By this time, Tyler was a lame-duck president, and Clay had lost the election to Democrat James K. Polk. Nonetheless, Tyler in February 1845 named John M. Read, a Philadelphia attorney who had support among the Democrats and the Clay Whigs in the Senate. But the Senate failed to act on the nomination before adjournment, and the vacancy was left for Polk to fill.

Polk had only slightly better luck with his appointments. After six months in office he offered the position to Buchanan, who again refused it. Another few months passed before Polk formally nominated George W. Woodward to the Baldwin vacancy in December 1845. Woodward turned out to be a hapless choice. He was opposed by one of the senators from his home state, Pennsylvania, and his extreme "American nativist" views made him unpopular with many other senators. His nomination was rejected on a 20-29 vote in January 1846.

Polk then asked Buchanan once again to take the seat. Buchanan accepted but later

William Taft in 1921 (provisional governor of the Philippines, 1901-04).

Generation Gaps

The age at which justices joined the court has varied widely. The oldest person ever initially appointed was Horace H. Lurton, who was 65 when he went on the court in 1910. Two chief justices were older than that when they achieved their office, but they had already served on the court previously: Harlan Fiske Stone was 68, in 1941; and Charles Evans Hughes 67, in 1930. Representing the younger generation,

Justices William Johnson and Joseph Story were both only 32 when they were appointed in 1804 and 1811 respectively. Story was younger than Johnson by about a month.

Only two other justices were under 40 when appointed: Bushrod Washington, nephew of the president, who was 36 when appointed in 1798, and James Iredell, who was 38 when appointed in 1790. Iredell also was the youngest justice to die on the court — 48 when he died in 1799.

The youngest justice in the twentieth century was William O. Douglas, who was 40 when appointed in 1939.

... Lasted for More Than Two Years

changed his mind and declined a third time. The president then turned to Robert C. Grier, a district court judge from Pennsylvania who proved acceptable to almost everyone. The Senate confirmed him Aug. 4, 1846, the day following his nomination.

Daniel Vacancy

The second-longest vacancy lasted almost as long as the first — 2 years, 1 month, and 16 days. It occurred when Justice Peter V. Daniel of Virginia died May 31, 1860. At this point four of the remaining justices were northerners; four were from the South. Naturally, the South wanted then-President James Buchanan to replace Daniel with another southerner; the North urged a nomination from one of its states.

Buchanan took a long time making up his mind. In February 1861, nearly eight months after the vacancy occurred, he nominated Secretary of State Jeremiah S. Black, a former chief justice of the Pennsylvania Supreme Court and U.S. attorney general. Black might have proved acceptable to southern senators, but many of them had already resigned from the Senate to join the Confederacy. Though he supported the Union, Black was not an abolitionist, and his nomination drew criticism from the northern antislavery press. Black also was opposed by Democrat Stephen A. Douglas, who had just lost the presidential election to Abraham Lincoln. Finally, Republicans in the Senate were not anxious to help fill a vacancy that they could leave open for the incoming Republican president. Had Buchanan acted earlier, it is likely that Black would have been confirmed. As it was, the Senate rejected his nomination by a one-vote margin, 25-26.

Buchanan made no further attempt to fill the Daniel vacancy. Lincoln, who soon had two more seats on the court to fill, did not name anyone to the Daniel seat until July 1862 — more than a year after his inauguration. His choice was Samuel F. Miller, a well-respected Iowa attorney. Miller's nomination had been urged by a majority of both the House and Senate and by other politicians and members of the legal profession. The Senate confirmed his nomination within half an hour of receiving it July 16, 1862.

SOURCES: Henry J. Abraham. *Justices and Presidents: A Political History of Appointments to the Supreme Court.* New York: Oxford University Press, 1974; Charles Warren. *The Supreme Court in United States History.* rev. ed. 2 vols. Boston: Little, Brown & Company, 1922, 1926.

The oldest justice ever on the court was Oliver Wendell Holmes, who retired at 90 in 1932, the court's only nonagenarian. The second-oldest member, Chief Justice Roger Taney, was 87 when he died in 1864. The following justices were in their 80s when they retired from the bench: Louis Brandeis (82), Gabriel Duval (82), Joseph McKenna (81), Stephen Field (81), and Samuel Nelson (80). As of January 1987, 80-year-old Justice William Brennan was still serving on the court. His colleague Lewis F. Powell Jr. would turn 80 in September 1987.

The youngest member ever to leave the court was Benjamin Curtis, who resigned in 1857 at 47. Others who left the court before the age of 50 were Justices Iredell, dead at 48, Alfred Moore, who retired at 48, and John Jay and John A. Campbell, who retired at 49. Jay also holds the record for number of years survived after leaving the court — 34 years. In modern times, Justice James F. Byrnes lived 29 years after resigning from the court in 1942.

Longevity

Length of service on the court has also varied greatly, from 15 months to 36 years.

Justice Byrnes served the shortest time, being confirmed by the Senate June 12, 1941, but resigning on Oct. 3, 1942, to become director of the World War II Office of Economic Stabilization.

Justice Thomas Johnson, who served from 1791 to 1793, was on the court only 16 months. Although he retired because of ill health, he lived another 26 years, dying at the age of 87.

Edwin Stanton, the controversial secretary of war during the Lincoln and Andrew Johnson administrations, was nominated for the Supreme Court by Grant. The Senate confirmed him on Dec. 20, 1869, but Stanton died of a heart attack on Dec. 24. Since he did not have a chance to begin his service on the court, he is not considered to have been a justice.

In January 1974 Justice William Douglas broke the old longevity record for service on the court, held since December 1897 by Stephen Field, who had served 34 years and 9 months when he resigned. Douglas went on to serve until November 1975, when he resigned after 36 years and 7 months on the court. Chief Justice John Marshall established the first longevity record by serving for 34 years and 5 months between 1801 and 1835. That record held until Field broke it in 1897.

Other justices who served 30 years or longer include Hugo Black (34 years, 1 month), John Marshall Harlan the first and Joseph Story (33 years each), James Wayne (32 years), John McLean (31 years), and Bushrod Washington and William Johnson (30 years each).

Black's 34 years occurred in an era of such changing membership on the court that he served at one time or another with 28 different justices, more than a quarter of the court's entire membership throughout its history.

Four or 5 years is usually the longest the court goes without a change in justices. But there was one lengthy period — 12 years — when the court maintained the same membership intact. That was from 1811, when Joseph Story was confirmed, to 1823, when Justice Henry Brockholst Livingston died.

Infirmity

Longevity of service sometimes leads to questions of disability, as justices age and are no longer capable of carrying a full load of casework. By early 1870, Justice Robert C. Grier was nearly 76. His mental and physical powers were obviously impaired, and he often seemed confused and feeble. Grier complied when a committee of his fellow justices finally approached him to urge his resignation. He died eight months later.

Among the justices urging Grier's retirement was Stephen Field. Ironically, a quarter of a century later, Field found himself in the same position as Grier. His powers had visibly declined, and he was taking less and less part in court proceedings. The other justices finally began hinting strongly that Field resign. But Field insisted on staying on the court long enough to break Chief Justice John Marshall's record for length of service.

A Disabled Court. In 1880 the court was manned by an especially infirm set of justices; 3 of the 9 were incapacitated. Justice Ward Hunt had suffered a paralytic stroke in 1879 and took no further part in court proceedings, but he refused to resign because he was not eligible for a full pension under the law then in effect. Finally, after three years, Congress passed a special law exempting Hunt from the terms of the pension law, granting him retirement at full pay if he would resign within 30 days of enactment of the exemption. Hunt resigned the same day.

Justice Nathan Clifford also had suffered a stroke that prevented him from participating in court activities. But Clifford also refused to resign, hoping to live long enough for a Democratic president to name a successor. At the time, Clifford was the only Democrat left on the court who had been named by a Democratic president. But he died while Republicans were still in power.

While Hunt and Clifford were both incapacitated, Justice Noah Swayne's mental acuity was noticeably declining. He was finally persuaded to resign by President Hayes, with the promise that Swayne's friend and fellow Ohioan Stanley Matthews would be chosen as his successor.

The most recent case of a court disability was that of Justice William Douglas, who suffered a stroke in January 1975. At first, Douglas attempted to continue his duties, but in November 1975 he resigned, citing the pain and physical disability resulting from the stroke.

Controversial Justices

The only time a justice clearly has been driven from the court by outside pressure occurred in 1969, when Justice Abe Fortas resigned. The resignation followed by less than 8 months a successful Senate filibuster against President Lyndon B. Johnson's nomination of Fortas to be chief justice. Fortas's departure from the court climaxed a furor brought on by the disclosure early in May 1969 that he had received and held for 11 months a $20,000 fee from the family foundation of a man later imprisoned for illegal stock manipulation.

A year after Fortas's resignation, an attempt was made to bring impeachment charges against Justice Douglas. General dissatisfaction with Douglas's liberal views and controversial lifestyle — combined with frustration over the Senate's rejection of 2 of President Nixon's conservative southern nominees — seemed to spark the action. House Republican leader Gerald R. Ford of Michigan, who led the attempt to impeach Douglas, charged among other things that the justice had practiced law in violation of federal law, had failed to disqualify himself in cases in which he had an interest, and violated standards of good behavior by allegedly advocating revolution. A special House Judiciary subcommittee created to investigate the charges found no grounds for impeachment.

The only Supreme Court justice ever to be impeached was Samuel Chase. A staunch Federalist who had rankled Jeffersonians with his partisan political statements and his vigorous prosecution of the Alien and Sedition Act, Chase was impeached by the House in 1804. But his critics failed to achieve the necessary two-thirds majority in the Senate for conviction.

Other, less heralded cases, have occurred from time to time that resulted in increased criticism of the justices. One early controversy surfaced in 1857, when the nation was awaiting the court's decision in the *Dred Scott* case. Justices Robert C. Grier and John Catron wrote privately to the incoming president, James Buchanan, detailing the court's discussions and foretelling the final decision. Buchanan was glad of the news and was able to say in his inaugural address that the decision was expected to come soon and that he and all Americans should acquiesce in it. But divulging the court's decision before it is publicly announced is generally considered to be unethical.

Another controversy arose 14 years later in the so-called Legal Tender Cases. The court, with 2 vacancies, had found the Civil War legal tender acts unconstitutional. But President Grant named 2 justices to fill the vacancies, and the court voted to rehear the case. With the 2 new justices — William Strong and Joseph P. Bradley — voting with the majority, the court now found the legal tender acts constitutional. It was charged that Grant had appointed the 2 knowing in advance that they would vote to reverse the court's previous decision. But historians have not turned up any evidence that there was any explicit arrangement involved.

Political activity by Supreme Court justices has usually been frowned upon — especially in the nineteenth century, when several justices manifested a hunger for their party's presidential nomination.

Justice John McLean entertained presidential ambitions throughout his long Supreme Court career (1829-61) and flirted with several political parties at various stages. In 1856 he received 190 votes on an informal first ballot at the first Republican national convention. He also sought the Republican presidential nomination in 1860.

Chief Justice Salmon Chase had aspired to the presidency before going on the bench, losing the Republican nomination to Lincoln in 1860. In 1864, while serving as Lincoln's secretary of the Treasury, he allowed himself to become the focus of an anti-Lincoln group within the Republican party. During his service on the court, in both 1868

Sixteen Chief Justices Have Served ...

John Jay
Born: Dec. 12, 1745, New York, N.Y. **Died:** May 17, 1829.
Education: King's College (now Columbia University).
Position Held at Time of Appointment: Secretary of Foreign Affairs.
Appointment: By Washington, 1789. **Resigned:** 1795.

John Rutledge
Born: September 1739, Charleston, S.C. **Died:** July 18, 1800.
Education: Inns of Court (London).
Position Held at Time of Appointment: Chief justice, South Carolina Supreme Court. (Had served as associate justice, U.S. Supreme Court, 1789-91.)
Appointment: By Washington, 1795. Recess appointment; Senate rejected confirmation in December of same year.

Oliver Ellsworth
Born: April 29, 1745, Windsor, Conn. **Died:** Nov. 26, 1807.
Education: Princeton University.
Position Held at Time of Appointment: U.S. senator.
Appointment: By Washington, 1796. **Resigned:** 1800.

John Marshall
Born: Sept. 24, 1755, Germantown, Va. **Died:** July 6, 1835.
Education: Self-taught.
Position Held at Time of Appointment: Secretary of State.
Appointment: By Adams, 1801; died in office.

Roger Brooke Taney
Born: March 17, 1777, Calvert County, Md. **Died:** Oct. 12, 1864.
Education: Dickinson College.
Position Held at Time of Appointment: Secretary of the Treasury.
Appointment: By Jackson, 1835, confirmed in 1836; died in office.

Salmon Portland Chase
Born: Jan. 13, 1808, Cornish, N.H. **Died:** May 7, 1873.
Education: Dartmouth College.
Position Held at Time of Appointment: Secretary of the Treasury.
Appointment: By Lincoln, 1864; died in office.

Morrison Remick Waite
Born: Nov. 29, 1816, Lyme, Conn. **Died:** March 23, 1888.
Education: Yale College.
Position Held at Time of Appointment: President, Ohio constitutional convention.
Appointment: By Grant, 1874; died in office.

Melville Weston Fuller
Born: Feb. 11, 1833, Augusta, Maine. **Died:** July 4, 1910.
Education: Bowdoin College, Harvard Law School.
Position Held at Time of Appointment: Attorney in Chicago.
Appointment: By Cleveland, 1888; died in office.

... In the History of the United States

Edward Douglass White

Born: Nov. 3, 1845, Lafourche Parish, La. **Died:** May 19, 1921.
Education: Mount St. Mary's College, Georgetown College.
Position Held at Time of Appointment: Associate justice, U.S. Supreme Court.
Appointment: By Taft, 1910; died in office.

William Howard Taft

Born: Sept. 15, 1857, Cincinnati, Ohio. **Died:** March 8, 1930.
Education: Yale University, Cincinnati Law School.
Previous Positions: President (1909-13); joint chairman of the National War Labor Board (1918-19).
Appointment: By Harding, 1921. **Resigned:** 1930.

Charles Evans Hughes

Born: April 11, 1862, Glens Falls, N.Y. **Died:** Aug. 27, 1948.
Education: Colgate University, Brown University, Columbia University Law School.
Position Held at Time of Appointment: Judge, Permanent Court of International Justice. (Had served as associate justice, U.S. Supreme Court, 1910-16.)
Appointment: By Hoover, 1930. **Resigned:** 1941.

Harlan Fiske Stone

Born: Oct. 11, 1872, Chesterfield, N.H. **Died:** April 22, 1946.
Education: Amherst College, Columbia University.
Position Held at Time of Appointment: Associate justice, U.S. Supreme Court.
Appointment: By Roosevelt, 1941; died in office.

Frederick Moore Vinson

Born: Jan. 22, 1890, Louisa, Ky. **Died:** Sept. 8, 1953.
Education: Centre College.
Position Held at Time of Appointment: Secretary of the Treasury.
Appointment: By Truman, 1946; died in office.

Earl Warren

Born: March 19, 1891, Los Angeles. **Died:** July 9, 1974.
Education: University of California.
Position Held at Time of Appointment: Governor of California.
Appointment: By Eisenhower, 1953, confirmed in 1954. **Resigned:** 1969.

Warren Earl Burger

Born: Sept. 17, 1907, St. Paul, Minn.
Education: University of Minnesota, St. Paul College of Law (now Mitchell College of Law).
Position Held at Time of Appointment: Judge, U.S. Court of Appeals for the District of Columbia.
Appointment: By Nixon, 1969. **Resigned:** 1986.

William Hubbs Rehnquist

Born: Oct. 1, 1924, Milwaukee, Wis.
Education: Stanford University, Harvard University, Stanford University Law School.
Position Held at Time of Appointment: Associate justice, U.S. Supreme Court.
Appointment: By Reagan, 1986.

and 1872, he made no secret of his still-burning presidential ambitions and allowed friends to maneuver politically for him.

In 1877 the Supreme Court was thrust into the election process when a dispute arose as to the outcome of the 1876 presidential election. To resolve the problem, Congress created a special electoral commission that included 5 Supreme Court justices. Each house of Congress also chose 5 members; the Democratic House choosing 5 Democrats and the Republican Senate choosing 5 Republicans.

The 5 justices were supposed to be divided evenly politically — 2 Democrats, Nathan Clifford and Stephen J. Field; 2 Republicans, Samuel Miller and William Strong; and 1 independent, David Davis.

Davis, however, withdrew from consideration because he had been elected a U.S. senator from Illinois. Justice Joseph P. Bradley, a Republican, was substituted for Davis, making the overall lineup on the commission 8 to 7 in favor of the Republicans.

The 3 Republican justices loyally supported the claims of Republican presidential aspirant Rutherford B. Hayes on all questions, and the 2 Democratic justices backed Democratic nominee Samuel J. Tilden.

The result was the election of Hayes. Justice Clifford, the chairman of the commission, was so contemptuous of the outcome that he called Hayes an illegitimate president and refused to enter the White House during his incumbency.

Supreme Court Justices: Biographies

This biographical summary lists, alphabetically, all the justices of the Supreme Court since 1789. The material is organized in the following order: name; relationship to other justices, presidents, and vice presidents; state; date of birth; date of death (if applicable); date of confirmation, date of swearing in (recess appointment noted, if applicable), date of promotion; date of confirmation, date of swearing in as chief justice (if applicable); date of resignation (in cases where the justice left the court before death); congressional service, service as president, vice president, member of the

Cabinet, governor, delegate to the Continental Congress, House or Senate majority leader, Speaker of the House, or president pro tempore of the Senate. *(Party abbreviations, box, p. x)*

The "promoted" entry is the date, according to the Supreme Court, when a sitting associate justice became the chief justice of the United States, even though he may not yet have been sworn in.

The major sources of information for this list were Congressional Quarterly's *Guide to the U.S. Supreme Court* and the United States Supreme Court.

BALDWIN, Henry (Pa.) Jan. 14, 1780-April 21, 1844; confirmed Jan. 6, 1830, sworn in Jan. 18, 1830; House 1817-22.

BARBOUR, Philip Pendleton (Va.) May 25, 1783-Feb. 25, 1841; confirmed March 15, 1836, sworn in May 12, 1836; House 1814-25, 1827-30; Speaker 1821-23.

BLACK, Hugo Lafayette (Ala.) Feb. 27, 1886-Sept. 25, 1971; confirmed Aug. 17, 1937, sworn in Aug. 19, 1937, resigned Sept. 17, 1971; Senate 1927-37.

BLACKMUN, Harry Andrew (Minn.) Nov. 12, 1908- —; confirmed May 12, 1970, sworn in June 9, 1970.

BLAIR, John Jr. (Va.) 1732-Aug. 31, 1800; confirmed Sept. 26, 1789, sworn in Feb. 2, 1790, resigned Jan. 27, 1796.

BLATCHFORD, Samuel (N.Y.) March 9, 1820-July 7, 1893; confirmed March 27, 1882, sworn in April 3, 1882.

BRADLEY, Joseph P. (N.J.) March 14, 1813-Jan. 22, 1892; confirmed March 21, 1870, sworn in March 23, 1870.

BRANDEIS, Louis Dembitz (Mass.) Nov. 13, 1856-Oct. 5, 1941; confirmed June 1, 1916, sworn in June 5, 1916, resigned Feb. 13, 1939.

BRENNAN, William Joseph Jr. (N.J.) April 25, 1906- —; confirmed March 19, 1957, sworn in Oct. 16, 1956.

BREWER, David Josiah (nephew of Stephen Johnson Field, below) (Kan.) June 20, 1837-March 28, 1910; confirmed Dec. 18, 1889, sworn in Jan. 6, 1890.

BROWN, Henry Billings (Mich.) March 2, 1836-Sept. 4, 1913; confirmed Dec. 29, 1890, sworn in Jan. 5, 1891, resigned May 28, 1906.

BURGER, Warren Earl (Minn.) Sept. 17, 1907- —; confirmed as Chief Justice June 9, 1969, sworn in June 23, 1969, resigned Sept. 26, 1986.

BURTON, Harold Hitz (Ohio) June 22, 1888-Oct. 28, 1964; confirmed Sept. 19, 1945, sworn in Oct. 1, 1945, resigned Oct. 13, 1958; Senate 1941-45.

BUTLER, Pierce (Minn.) March 17, 1866-Nov. 16, 1939; confirmed Dec. 21, 1922, sworn in Jan. 2, 1923.

BYRNES, James Francis (S.C.) May 2, 1879-April 9, 1972; confirmed June 12, 1941, sworn in July 8, 1941, resigned Oct. 3, 1942; House 1911-25; Senate 1931-41; Secy. of State 1945-47; Gov. 1951-55.

CAMPBELL, John Archibald (Ala.) June 24, 1811-March 12, 1889; confirmed March 25, 1853, sworn in April 11, 1853, resigned April 30, 1861.

CARDOZO, Benjamin Nathan (N.Y.) May 24, 1870-July 9, 1938; confirmed Feb. 24, 1932, sworn in March 14, 1932.

CATRON, John (Tenn.) 1786-May 30, 1865; confirmed March 8, 1837, sworn in May 1, 1837.

CHASE, Salmon Portland (Ohio) Jan. 13, 1808-May 7, 1873; confirmed as Chief Justice Dec. 6, 1864, sworn in Dec. 15, 1864; Senate 1849-55, 1861; Gov. 1856-60; Secy. of the Treasury 1861-64.

CHASE, Samuel (Md.) April 17, 1741-June 19, 1811; confirmed Jan. 27, 1796, sworn in Feb. 4, 1796; Cont. Cong. 1774-78, 1784-85.

CLARK, Thomas Campbell (Texas) Sept. 23, 1899-June 13, 1977; confirmed Aug. 18, 1949, sworn in Aug. 24, 1949, resigned June 12, 1967; Atty. Gen. 1945-49.

CLARKE, John Hessin (Ohio) Sept. 18, 1857-March 22, 1945; confirmed July 24, 1916, sworn in Oct. 9, 1916, resigned Sept. 18, 1922.

CLIFFORD, Nathan (Maine) Aug. 18, 1803-July 25, 1881; confirmed Jan. 12, 1858, sworn in Jan. 21, 1858; House 1839-43; Atty. Gen. 1846-48.

CURTIS, Benjamin Robbins (Mass.) Nov. 4, 1809-Sept. 15, 1874; confirmed Dec. 29, 1851, sworn in Oct. 10, 1851, resigned Sept. 30, 1857.

CUSHING, William (Mass.) March 1, 1732-Sept. 13, 1810; confirmed Sept. 26, 1789, sworn in Feb. 2, 1790.

DANIEL, Peter Vivian (Va.) April 24, 1784-May 31, 1860; confirmed March 2, 1841, sworn in Jan. 10, 1842.

DAVIS, David (Ill.) March 9, 1815-June 26, 1886; confirmed Dec. 8, 1862, sworn in Dec. 10, 1862, resigned March 4, 1877; Senate 1877-83; Pres. pro tempore 1881-83.

DAY, William Rufus (Ohio) April 17, 1849-July 9, 1923; confirmed Feb. 23, 1903, sworn in March 2, 1903, resigned Nov. 13, 1922; Secy. of State 1898.

DOUGLAS, William Orville (Conn.) Oct. 16, 1898-Jan. 19, 1980; confirmed April 4, 1939, sworn in April 17, 1939, resigned Nov. 12, 1975.

DUVALL, Gabriel (Md.) Dec. 6, 1752-March 6, 1844; confirmed Nov. 18, 1811, sworn in Nov. 23, 1811, resigned Jan. 14, 1835; House 1794-96.

ELLSWORTH, Oliver (Conn.) April 29, 1745-Nov. 26, 1807; confirmed as Chief Justice March 4, 1796, sworn in March 8, 1796; resigned Dec. 15, 1800; Cont. Cong. 1777-84; Senate 1789-96.

FIELD, Stephen Johnson (uncle of David Josiah Brewer, above) (Calif.) Nov. 4, 1816-April 9, 1899; confirmed March 10, 1863, sworn in May 20, 1863, resigned Dec. 1, 1897.

FORTAS, Abe (D.C.) June 19, 1910-April 5, 1982; confirmed Aug. 11, 1965, sworn in Oct. 4, 1965, resigned May 14, 1969.

FRANKFURTER, Felix (Mass.) Nov. 15, 1882-Feb. 22, 1965; confirmed Jan. 17, 1939, sworn in Jan. 30, 1939, resigned Aug. 28, 1962.

FULLER, Melville Weston (Ill.) Feb. 11, 1833-July 4, 1910; confirmed as Chief Justice July 20, 1888, sworn in Oct. 8, 1888.

GOLDBERG, Arthur Joseph (Ill.) Aug. 8, 1908- —; confirmed Sept. 25, 1962, sworn in Oct. 1, 1962, resigned July 25, 1965; Secy. of Labor 1961-62.

GRAY, Horace (son-in-law of Stanley Matthews, below) (Mass.) March 24, 1828-Sept. 15, 1902; confirmed Dec. 20, 1881, sworn in Jan. 9, 1882.

GRIER, Robert Cooper (Pa.) March 5, 1794-Sept. 25, 1870; confirmed Aug. 4, 1846, sworn in Aug. 10, 1846, resigned Jan. 31, 1870.

HARLAN, John Marshall (grandfather of John Marshall Harlan, below) (Ky.) June 1, 1833-Oct. 14, 1911; confirmed Nov. 29, 1877, sworn in Dec. 10, 1877.

HARLAN, John Marshall (grandson of John Marshall Harlan, above) (N.Y.) May 20, 1899-Dec. 29, 1971; confirmed March 16, 1955, sworn in March 28, 1955, resigned Sept. 23, 1971.

HOLMES, Oliver Wendell Jr. (Mass.) March 8, 1841-March 6, 1935; confirmed Dec. 4, 1902, sworn in Dec. 8, 1902, resigned Jan. 12, 1932.

HUGHES, Charles Evans (N.Y.) April 11, 1862-Aug. 27, 1948; confirmed May 2, 1910, sworn in Oct. 10, 1910, resigned June 10, 1916; confirmed as Chief Justice Feb. 13, 1930, sworn in Feb. 24, 1930, resigned June 30, 1941; Gov. 1907-10; Secy. of State 1921-25.

HUNT, Ward (N.Y.) June 14, 1810-March 24, 1886; confirmed Dec. 11, 1872, sworn in Jan. 9, 1873, resigned Jan. 27, 1882.

IREDELL, James (N.C.) Oct. 5, 1751-Oct. 20, 1799; confirmed Feb. 10, 1790, sworn in May 12, 1790.

JACKSON, Howell Edmunds (Tenn.) April 8, 1832-Aug. 8, 1895; confirmed Feb. 18, 1893, sworn in March 4, 1893; Senate 1881-86.

JACKSON, Robert Houghwout (N.Y.) Feb. 13, 1892-Oct. 9, 1954; confirmed July 7, 1941, sworn in July 11, 1941; Atty. Gen. 1940-41.

JAY, John (brother-in-law of Henry Brockholst Livingston, below) (N.Y.) Dec. 12, 1745-May 17, 1829; confirmed as Chief Justice Sept. 26, 1789, sworn in Oct 19, 1789, resigned June 29, 1795; Cont. Cong. 1774-75, 1777, 1778-79 (president); Secy. of Foreign Affairs 1784-89; Gov. 1795-1801.

JOHNSON, Thomas (Md.) Nov. 4, 1732-Oct. 26, 1819; confirmed Nov. 7, 1791, sworn in Aug. 6, 1792, resigned Feb. 1, 1793; Cont. Cong. 1774-77.

JOHNSON, William (S.C.) Dec. 27, 1771-Aug. 4, 1834; confirmed March 24, 1804, sworn in May 7, 1804.

LAMAR, Joseph Rucker (cousin of Lucius Quintus Cincinnatus Lamar, below) (Miss.) Oct. 14, 1857-Jan. 2, 1916; confirmed Dec. 15, 1910, sworn in Jan. 3, 1911.

LAMAR, Lucius Quintus Cincinnatus (cousin of Joseph Rucker Lamar, above) (Miss.) Sept. 17, 1825-Jan. 23, 1893; confirmed Jan. 16, 1888, sworn in Jan. 18, 1888; House 1857-60, 1873-77; Senate 1877-85; Secy. of the Interior 1885-88.

LIVINGSTON, Henry Brockholst (brother-in-law of John Jay, above, father-in-law of Smith Thompson, below) (N.Y.) Nov. 25, 1757-March 18, 1823; confirmed Dec. 17, 1806, sworn in Jan. 20, 1807.

LURTON, Horace Harmon (Tenn.) Feb. 26, 1844-July 12, 1914; confirmed Dec. 20, 1909, sworn in Jan. 3, 1910.

MARSHALL, John (Va.) Sept. 24, 1755-July 6, 1835; confirmed as Chief Justice Jan. 27, 1801, sworn in Feb. 4, 1801; House 1799-1800; Secy. of State, 1800-01.

MARSHALL, Thurgood (N.Y.) July 2, 1908- —; confirmed Aug. 30, 1967, sworn in Oct. 2, 1967.

MATTHEWS, Stanley (father-in-law of Horace Gray, above) (Ohio) July 21, 1824-March 22, 1889; confirmed May 12, 1881, sworn in May 17, 1881; Senate 1877-79.

McKENNA, Joseph (Calif.) Aug. 10, 1843-Nov. 21, 1926; confirmed Jan. 21, 1898, sworn in Jan. 26, 1898, resigned Jan. 5, 1925; House 1885-92; Atty. Gen. 1897-98.

McKINLEY, John (Ala.) May 1, 1780-July 19, 1852; confirmed Sept. 25, 1837, sworn in Jan. 9, 1838; Senate 1826-31, 1837; House 1833-35.

McLEAN, John (Ohio) March 11, 1785-April 4, 1861; confirmed March 7, 1829, sworn in Jan. 11, 1830; House 1813-16; Postmaster Gen. 1823-29.

McREYNOLDS, James Clark (Tenn.) Feb. 3, 1862-Aug. 24, 1946; confirmed Aug. 29, 1914, sworn in Oct. 12, 1914, resigned Jan. 31, 1941; Atty. Gen. 1913-14.

MILLER, Samuel Freeman (Iowa) April 5, 1816-Oct. 13, 1890; confirmed July 16, 1862, sworn in July 21, 1862.

MINTON, Sherman (Ind.) Oct. 20, 1890-April 9, 1965; confirmed Oct. 4, 1949, sworn in Oct. 12, 1949, resigned Oct. 15, 1956; Senate 1935-41.

MOODY, William Henry (Mass.) Dec. 23, 1853-July 2, 1917; confirmed Dec. 12, 1906, sworn in Dec. 17, 1906, resigned Nov. 20, 1910; House 1895-1902; Secy. of the Navy 1902-04; Atty. Gen. 1904-06.

MOORE, Alfred (N.C.) May 21, 1755-Oct. 15, 1810; confirmed Dec. 10, 1799, sworn in April 21, 1800, resigned Jan. 26, 1804.

MURPHY, Francis William (Mich.) April 13, 1890-July 19, 1949; confirmed Jan. 15, 1940, sworn in Feb. 5, 1940; Gov. 1937-39; Atty. Gen. 1939.

NELSON, Samuel (N.Y.) Nov. 10, 1792-Dec. 13, 1873; confirmed Feb. 14, 1845, sworn in Feb. 27, 1845, resigned Nov. 28, 1872.

O'CONNOR, Sandra Day (Ariz.) March 26, 1930- —; confirmed Sept. 21, 1981, sworn in Sept. 25, 1981.

PATERSON, William (N.J.) Dec. 24, 1745-Sept. 9, 1806; confirmed March 4, 1793, sworn in March 11, 1793; Cont. Cong. 1780-81, 1787; Senate 1789-90; Gov. 1790-93.

PECKHAM, Rufus Wheeler (N.Y.) Nov. 8, 1838-Oct. 24, 1909; confirmed Dec. 9, 1895, sworn in Jan. 6, 1896.

PITNEY, Mahlon (N.J.) Feb. 5, 1858-Dec. 9, 1924; confirmed March 13, 1912, sworn in March 18, 1912, resigned Dec. 31, 1922; House 1895-99.

POWELL, Lewis Franklin Jr. (Va.) Sept. 19, 1907- —; confirmed Dec. 6, 1971, sworn in Jan. 7, 1972.

REED, Stanley Forman (Ky.) Dec. 31, 1884-April 2, 1980; confirmed Jan. 25, 1938, sworn in Jan. 31, 1938, resigned Feb. 25, 1957.

REHNQUIST, William Hubbs (Ariz.) Oct. 1, 1924- —; confirmed Dec. 10, 1971, sworn in Jan. 7, 1972; confirmed as Chief Justice Sept. 17, 1986, sworn in Sept. 26, 1986.

ROBERTS, Owen Josephus (Pa.) May 2, 1875-May 17, 1955; confirmed May 20, 1930, sworn in June 2, 1930, resigned July 31, 1945.

RUTLEDGE, John (S.C.) Sept. 1739-July 18, 1800; confirmed Sept. 26, 1789, sworn in May 12, 1790, resigned March 5, 1791; sworn in as Chief Justice Aug. 12, 1795 (recess appointment not confirmed, service terminated Dec. 15, 1795); Cont. Cong. 1774-76, 1782-83.

RUTLEDGE, Wiley Blount (Iowa) July 29, 1894-Sept. 10, 1949; confirmed Feb. 8, 1943, sworn in Feb. 15, 1943.

SANFORD, Edward Terry (Tenn.) July 23, 1865-March 8, 1930; confirmed Jan. 29, 1923, sworn in Feb. 19, 1923.

SCALIA, Antonin (D.C.) March 11, 1936- —; confirmed Sept. 17, 1986, sworn in Sept. 26, 1986.

SHIRAS, George Jr. (Pa.) January 26, 1832-Aug. 2, 1924; confirmed July 26, 1892, sworn in Oct. 10, 1892, resigned Feb. 23, 1903.

STEVENS, John Paul (Ill.) April 20, 1920- —; confirmed Dec. 17, 1975, sworn in Dec. 19, 1975.

STEWART, Potter (Ohio) Jan. 23, 1915-Dec. 7, 1985; confirmed May 5, 1959, sworn in Oct. 14, 1958 (recess appointment), resigned July 3, 1981.

STONE, Harlan Fiske (N.Y.) Oct. 11, 1872-April 22, 1946; confirmed Feb. 5, 1925, sworn in March 2, 1925, promoted July 2, 1941; confirmed as Chief Justice June 27, 1941, sworn in July 3, 1941; Atty. Gen. 1924-25.

STORY, Joseph (Mass.) Sept. 18, 1779-Sept. 10, 1845; confirmed Nov. 18, 1811, sworn in Feb. 3, 1812; House 1808-09.

STRONG, William (Pa.) May 6, 1808-Aug. 19, 1895; confirmed Feb. 18, 1870, sworn in March 14, 1870, resigned Dec. 14, 1880; House 1847-51.

SUTHERLAND, George (Utah) March 25, 1862-July 18, 1942; confirmed Sept. 5, 1922, sworn in Oct. 2, 1922, resigned Jan. 17, 1938; House 1901-03; Senate 1905-17.

SWAYNE, Noah Haynes (Ohio) Dec. 7, 1804-June 8, 1884; confirmed Jan. 24, 1862, sworn in Jan. 27, 1862, resigned Jan. 24, 1881.

TAFT, William Howard (brother of Rep. Charles Phelps Taft, father of Sen. Robert Alphonso Taft, grandfather of Sen. Robert Taft Jr.) (Ohio) Sept. 15, 1857-March 8, 1930; confirmed as Chief Justice June 30, 1921, sworn in July 11, 1921, resigned Feb. 3, 1930; Gov. (prov.) 1901-04 (Philippines); Secy. of War 1904-08; President 1909-13.

TANEY, Roger Brooke (Md.) March 17, 1777-Oct. 12, 1864; confirmed as Chief Justice March 15, 1836, sworn in March 28, 1836; Atty. Gen. 1831-33; Acting Secy. of War 1831; Acting Secy. of the Treasury 1833-34.

THOMPSON, Smith (son-in-law of Henry Brockholst Livingston, above) (N.Y.) ca. Jan. 17, 1768-Dec. 18, 1843; confirmed Dec. 19, 1823, sworn in Sept. 1, 1823 (recess appointment); Secy. of Navy, 1819-23.

TODD, Thomas (Ky.) Jan. 23, 1765-Feb. 7, 1826; confirmed March 3, 1807, sworn in May 4, 1807.

TRIMBLE, Robert (Ky.) 1777-Aug. 25, 1828; confirmed May 9, 1826, sworn in June 16, 1826.

VAN DEVANTER, Willis (Wyo.) April 17, 1859-Feb. 8, 1941; confirmed Dec. 15, 1910, sworn in Jan. 3, 1911, resigned June 2, 1937; Atty. Gen. 1897-1903.

VINSON, Frederick Moore (Ky.) Jan. 22, 1890-Sept. 8, 1953; confirmed as Chief Justice June 20, 1946, sworn in June 24, 1946; House 1924-29, 1931-38; Secy. of the Treasury 1945-46.

WAITE, Morrison Remick (Ohio) Nov. 29, 1816-March 23, 1888; confirmed as Chief Justice Jan. 21, 1874, sworn in March 4, 1874.

WARREN, Earl (Calif.) March 19, 1891-July 9, 1974; confirmed as Chief Justice March 1, 1954, sworn in Oct. 5, 1953 (recess appointment), resigned June 23, 1969; Gov. 1943-53.

WASHINGTON, Bushrod (nephew of President George Washington) (Va.) June 5, 1762-Nov. 26, 1829; confirmed Dec. 20, 1798, sworn in Feb. 4, 1799.

WAYNE, James Moore (Ga.) 1790-July 5, 1867; confirmed Jan. 9, 1835, sworn in Jan. 14, 1835; House 1829-35.

WHITE, Byron Raymond (Colo.) June 8, 1917- —; confirmed April 11, 1962, sworn in April 16, 1962.

WHITE, Edward Douglass (La.) Nov. 3, 1845-May 19, 1921; confirmed Feb. 19, 1894, sworn in March 12, 1894, promoted Dec. 18, 1910; confirmed as Chief Justice Dec. 12, 1910, sworn in Dec. 19, 1910; Senate 1891-94.

WHITTAKER, Charles Evans (Mo.) Feb. 22, 1901-Nov. 26, 1973; confirmed March 19, 1957, sworn in March 25, 1957, resigned March 31, 1962.

WILSON, James (Pa.) Sept. 14, 1742-Aug. 21, 1798; confirmed Sept. 26, 1789, sworn in Oct. 5, 1789; Cont. Cong. 1775-77, 1783, 1785-87.

WOODBURY, Levi (N.H.) Dec. 22, 1789-Sept. 4, 1851; confirmed Jan. 3, 1846, sworn in Sept. 23, 1845; Gov. 1823-24; Senate 1825-31, 1841-45; Secy. of the Navy 1831-34; Secy. of the Treasury 1834-41.

WOODS, William Burnham (Ga.) Aug. 3, 1824-May 14, 1887; confirmed Dec. 21, 1880, sworn in Jan. 5, 1881.

Members of Congress

The American electorate makes its decision on a new Congress in November of even-numbered years. Early the following January the elected representatives and senators gather at the Capitol to begin their first session. There always are many new members along with the veterans, especially in the House. But there is a certain uniformity as well because the overall composition of Congress changes gradually. The names of persons elected to Congress change more rapidly than the characteristics of members.

American Democracy, a popular textbook of the 1960s by Robert K. Carr, Marver H. Bernstein, and Walter F. Murphy, described the "average" member of Congress: 'He is a little over 50, has served in Congress for a number of years, and has had previous political experience before coming to Congress, such as membership in his state legislature. He has a college degree, is a lawyer by profession, a war veteran, and, before coming to Congress, was a well-known and popular member of the community. He has been reasonably successful in business or the practice of law, although not so successful that he is sacrificing a huge income in giving up his private occupation for a public job. Congress is clearly not an accurate cross section of the American people but neither is it a community of intellectuals and technicians."

The description was accurate, even to the exclusive use of "he." Although the composition has changed some, most members of Congress are male Caucasian and Christian, especially Protestant. Of the 535 members in Congress at the beginning of 1987, 25 were women, 23 were black (including the nonvoting delegate from the District of Co-

lumbia), 14 were Hispanic (including the resident commissioner of Puerto Rico and the nonvoting delegates from Guam and the Virgin Islands), and a scattering were of Asian or Middle Eastern heritage.

Apart from these characteristics, it is likely that a senator served earlier in the House but rare that a representative served in the Senate. Only two former presidents served in Congress after their terms in the White House: John Quincy Adams and Andrew Johnson. *(Members of Congress Who Became President, box, p. 45)*

Although the legal profession has long been dominant among members, most other occupations — including banking, business, journalism, farming, and education — have been represented. The principal occupational groups that have been underrepresented are the clergy and workingmen. Scientists and physicians also have been underrepresented in Congress. Few blue-collar workers have served in recent decades, although a few members were from this background before coming to Congress.

Only a handful of Protestant ministers have served in Congress, and no Catholic priest had been a full-fledged member until Rep. Robert F. Drinan, D-Mass., a Jesuit, took his House seat in 1971. (Father Gabriel Richard was the nonvoting delegate of the Territory of Michigan from 1821 to 1823.) Drinan did not seek a sixth term in 1980 after Pope John Paul II that year ordered priests not to hold public office. The pope's directive also prompted Robert J. Cornell, a Catholic priest and former U.S. House member, to halt his political comeback bid in Wisconsin. Cornell, a Democrat elected in 1974, served two terms before he was de-

43

Age Structure of Congress

(Average ages at start of first session)

	House	Senate	Congress
1949	51.0	58.5	53.8
1951	52.0	56.6	53.0
1953	52.0	56.6	53.0
1955	51.4	57.2	52.2
1957	52.9	57.9	53.8
1959	51.7	57.1	52.7
1961	52.2	57.0	53.2
1963	51.7	56.8	52.7
1965	50.5	57.7	51.9
1967	50.8	57.7	52.1
1969	52.2	56.6	53.0
1971	51.9	56.4	52.7
1973	51.1	55.3	52.0
1975	49.8	55.5	50.9
1977	49.3	54.7	50.3
1979	48.8	52.7	49.5
1981	48.4	52.5	49.2
1983	45.5	53.4	47.0
1985	49.7	54.2	50.5
1987	50.7	54.4	52.5

feated in 1978. In 1987 the incoming 100th Congress contained three clergymen, including the nonvoting delegate from the District of Columbia. *(Members' Occupations, 100th Congress, box, p. 47)*

From the early days of the republic until the present, the American public often has criticized the qualifications of members of Congress. Through the years the House has received more criticism than the Senate, perhaps because senators were not elected by popular vote until 1914.

An early but still familiar critique of Congress was written in the 1830s by Alexis de Tocqueville, the French aristocrat, scholar, and astute observer of America. After he had seen both chambers in session, de Tocqueville wrote the following in *Democracy in America:*

"On entering the House of Representatives at Washington, one is struck by the vulgar demeanor of that great assembly. Often there is not a distinguished man in the whole number. Its members are almost all obscure individuals, whose names bring no associations to mind. They are mostly village lawyers, men in trade, or even persons belonging to the lower classes of society. In a country in which education is very general, it is said that the representatives of the people do not always know how to write correctly.

"At a few yards' distance is the door of the Senate, which contains within a small space a large proportion of the celebrated men of America. Scarcely an individual is to be seen in it who has not had an active and illustrious career: the Senate is composed of eloquent advocates, distinguished generals, wise magistrates, and statesmen of note, whose arguments would do honor to the most remarkable parliamentary debates of Europe."

The modern view of Congress as a whole probably is not much more charitable than de Tocqueville's opinion of the House. Many voters undoubtedly think that Mark Twain was correct when he quipped that "there is no distinctly native American criminal class except Congress." A Gallup Poll taken in August 1985 found that politicians had a poor public image. Forty-nine percent of Americans rated the honesty and ethical standards of senators and representatives as average, while 27 percent rated them as low or very low. Only 20 percent of the people interviewed gave members of Congress a high rating. (Four percent of the respondents had no opinion.)

One other major characteristic of Congress is worthy of mention: political control. The Democratic party controlled both houses for most of the five decades beginning in 1933 as the Great Depression realigned political power in the nation. Only twice — in the 80th Congress (1947-49) and the 83d Congress (1953-55) — did the Republicans have control. In 1980, however, Republicans gained 12 seats in the Senate, taking control of that chamber for the first time in a quarter century. The 1980 GOP Senate victory ended the longest one-party dominance of the Senate in American his

Members of Congress Who Became President

When Gerald R. Ford became president in 1974, he brought to 23 the number of presidents who had previous service in the House of Representatives or the Senate or both.

Following is a list of these presidents and the chambers in which they served. Three other presidents — George Washington, John Adams, and Thomas Jefferson — had served in the Continental Congress, as had two of those included below, James Madison and James Monroe.

James A. Garfield was elected to the Senate in January 1880 for a term beginning March 4, 1881, but declined to accept in December 1880 because he had been elected president. John Quincy Adams served in the House for 17 years after he had been president, and Andrew Johnson returned to the Senate five months before he died.

House Only	Senate Only
James Madison	James Monroe
James K. Polk	John Quincy Adams
Millard Fillmore	Martin Van Buren
Abraham Lincoln	Benjamin Harrison
Rutherford B. Hayes	Warren G. Harding
James A. Garfield	Harry S Truman
William McKinley	
Gerald R. Ford	

Both Chambers

Andrew Jackson	Andrew Johnson
William Henry Harrison	John F. Kennedy
John Tyler	Lyndon B. Johnson
Franklin Pierce	Richard Nixon
James Buchanan	

SOURCE: *Biographical Directory of the American Congress, 1774-1971* (Government Printing Office, 1971).

ory. Also in 1980 Republicans gained 33 seats in the House, the largest increase for the GOP since 1966. In 1982, though, the Republicans suffered the worst loss by any party at the two-year point in 60 years. The Democrats gained 26 seats, which gave them a 101-seat advantage. In the 1984 elections the GOP gained 14 House seats, leaving Democrats in the majority, but retained control of the Senate while losing 2 seats. The 1986 Senate elections gave the Democratic party its biggest gain since 1958. The

Democrats picked up 8 seats to regain the Senate majority they lost to the Republicans in 1980. In the House, the Democrats gained 5 seats giving the party an 81-seat advantage over the GOP in the 100th Congress.

Characteristics of Members

Age. The average age of members of Congress went up substantially between the Civil War period and the 1950s, but it remained fairly constant from then to the mid-1970s. In the 41st Congress (1869-71),

Congressional Service

As of 1987, the record for the longest service in Congress — 56 years — was held by Carl Hayden, D-Ariz., who retired from the Senate in 1969 at the age of 91.

Hayden gave up his job as a county sheriff to become Arizona's first representative in 1912. He was sworn in Feb. 19, 1912, five days after Arizona became a state, and served in the House for 15 years.

In 1927 he moved to the Senate where he served seven six-year terms. When Hayden retired, he was president pro tempore of the Senate and chairman of the Senate Appropriations Committee.

Runner-up to Hayden was Rep. Carl Vinson, D-Ga., who served in the House from Nov. 3, 1914, to Jan. 3, 1965. Vinson was 80 years old when he retired at the end of the 88th Congress.

the average age of members was 44.6 years; by the 85th Congress (1957-58), the average had increased by more than nine years, to 53.8. Over the next 18 years, the average fluctuated only slightly. But when the 94th Congress met in January 1975 the average dropped to 50.9 years. The difference was made in the House, where 92 freshmen members reduced the average age of representatives to 49.8 years, the first time since World War II that the average in either chamber had fallen below 50 years.

In the 96th Congress (1979-81) the representatives and senators were younger than in any Congress since 1949. The average age was 49.5 years, the first Congress since World War II in which the figure dropped below 50.

When the 97th Congress met in January 1981, the average dropped again, to 49.2 years. The average age in the Senate

dropped from 52.7 years to 52.5 years and in the House from 48.8 to 48.4 years. The House had eight members under 30, the most since World War II.

The 98th Congress (1983-85) surpassed previous records and was the youngest in at least 34 years. The average age was 47.0 years. In the House the average age dropped to 45.5 years, but the Senate grew a little older to 53.4 years.

The 99th Congress was somewhat older than its predecessor, reversing a trend that began with the 91st Congress in 1969. The average 1985 age was 50.5 years — 49.7 in the House and 54.2 in the Senate.

The 100th Congress was slightly older than its predecessor — reinforcing the reversal of a trend toward younger lawmakers. The average 1987 age was 52.5 years. The average age increased in the House to 50.7 and in the Senate to 54.4. (*Age Structure of Congress, box, p. 44*)

Occupations. From the early days of the republic, the legal profession has been the dominant occupational background of members of Congress, a development that has given that profession substantial overrepresentation. From a level of 37 percent of the House members in the First Congress, the proportion of members with a legal background rose to 70 percent in 1840, then declined slightly in subsequent years and remained at a level of 55 to 60 percent from 1950 to the mid-1970s. More than 54 percent of members of the 95th Congress (1977-79) listed law among their occupations.

The first significant decline in lawyer members began with the 96th Congress. In 1979 the 65 lawyers in the Senate represented a slight decline from 1977. But the House figures changed dramatically. For the first time in at least 30 years, lawyers made up less than a majority of the House. The loss of 17 lawyers between 1976 and 1978 marked the steepest decline among members of the legal profession since 1948.

In the 97th Congress 253 members had law degrees — 17 fewer than in the 96th Congress. The House figures were more dramatic. Only 194 representatives were lawyers, a decline of 11 from the previous Con

Members' Occupations, 100th Congress

The chart of occupations of members of the 100th Congress, which began Jan. 6, 1987, was compiled from the records of Congressional Quarterly. Some members listed more than one occupation.

Lawyers had the largest representation in Congress. One hundred eighty-four of the 435 representatives and 62 of the 100 senators cited law as a profession. The next most frequently listed professions were in business or banking followed by public service or politics.

| | House | | | Senate | | | |
Occupation	D	R	Total	D	R	Total	Congress Total
Actor/Entertainer	0	1	1	0	0	0	1
Aeronautics	0	3	3	1	1	2	5
Agriculture	10	10	20	2	3	5	25
Business or banking	66	76	142	13	15	28	170
Clergy	2	0	2	0	1	1	3
Education	24	14	38	6	6	12	50
Engineering	2	2	4	0	1	1	5
Journalism	11	9	20	6	2	8	28
Labor officials	2	0	2	0	0	0	2
Law	122	62	184	35	27	62	246
Law enforcement	6	1	7	0	0	0	7
Medicine	1	2	3	1	0	1	4
Military	0	0	0	0	1	1	1
Professional sports	3	2	5	1	0	1	6
Public service/Politics	59	35	94	13	7	20	114

gress and a drop of 28 since 1976. Lawyers in the House and Senate were no longer a majority of the members.

The trend reversed in 1983 when 261 members held law degrees — 8 more than in the previous Congress. The Senate increased from 59 to 61 lawyers, and the House grew by 6 to 200 lawyers.

Law was still the largest single profession among members of Congress in 1985, but the overall number of lawyers dropped to 251. The Senate remained at 61, but the House shrank to 190. The 100th Congress had 246 lawyers, a decrease of 5 from 1985. The House dropped to 184, but the Senate increased by 1 to 62.

The next most common profession of members has been business or banking. The 99th Congress contained 174 members previously involved in business or banking, which ranked them second to lawyers. In the 100th Congress, businessmen and bankers were still the second-largest group, although their ranks were reduced to 170. This reversed a trend that began in 1977, when businessmen and bankers gained increasingly more seats with each election. The number of members with a background in politics or public service occupations increased sharply, from 76 to 114, continuing a trend that began in 1985, when former public officials in Congress increased from 51. Other occupations that have been prominently represented in recent Congresses are education, agriculture, and journalism.

Religious Affiliations. Among reli-

Women Members of Congress ...

As of the beginning of 1987, a total of 119 women had been elected or appointed to Congress. One hundred four served in the House only, 13 in the Senate, and 2 — Margaret Chase Smith, R-Maine, and Barbara Mikulski, D-Md. — in both chambers. Following is a list of the women members, their parties and states, and the years in which they served. In addition, Mary E. Farrington, R-Hawaii (1954-57), served as a nonvoting delegate.

Senate

Rebecca L. Felton (Ind. D Ga.)*	1922
Hattie W. Caraway (D Ark.)	1931-45
Rose McConnell Long (D La.)	1936-37
Dixie Bibb Graves (D Ala.)	1937-38
Gladys Pyle (R S.D.)†	1938-39
Vera C. Bushfield (R S.D.)	1948
Margaret Chase Smith (R Maine)	1949-73
Hazel H. Abel (R Neb.)	1954
Eva K. Bowring (R Neb.)	1954
Maurine B. Neuberger (D Ore.)	1960-67
Elaine S. Edwards (D La.)	1972
Maryon Pittman Allen (D Ala.)	1978
Muriel Buck Humphrey (D Minn.)	1978
Nancy Landon Kassebaum (R Kan.)	1979-
Paula Hawkins (R Fla.)	1981-87
Barbara Mikulski (D Md.)	1987-

House

Jeannette Rankin (R Mont.)	1917-19; 1941-43
Alice M. Robertson (R Okla.)	1921-23
Winnifred S. M. Huck (R Ill.)	1922-23
Mae E. Nolan (R Calif.)	1923-25
Florence P. Kahn (R Calif.)	1925-37
Mary T. Norton (D N.J.)	1925-51
Edith N. Rogers (R Mass.)	1925-60
Katherine G. Langley (R Ky.)	1927-31
Ruth H. McCormick (R Ill.)	1929-31
Pearl P. Oldfield (D Ark.)	1929-31

Ruth B. Owen (D Fla.)	1929-33
Ruth S. B. Pratt (R N.Y.)	1929-33
Effiegene Wingo (D Ark.)	1930-33
Willa M. B. Eslick (D Tenn.)	1932-33
Marian W. Clarke (R N.Y.)	1933-35
Virginia E. Jenckes (D Ind.)	1933-39
Kathryn O'Loughlin McCarthy (D Kan.)	1933-35
Isabella S. Greenway (D Ariz.)	1934-37
Caroline L. G. O'Day (D N.Y.)	1935-43
Nan W. Honeyman (D Ore.)	1937-39
Elizabeth H. Gasque (D S.C.)†	1938-39
Clara G. McMillan (D S.C.)	1939-41
Jessie Sumner (R Ill.)	1939-47
Frances P. Bolton (R Ohio)	1940-69
Florence R. Gibbs (D Ga.)	1940-41
Margaret Chase Smith (R Maine)	1940-49
Katherine E. Byron (D Md.)	1941-43
Veronica G. Boland (D Pa.)	1942-43
Clare Boothe Luce (R Conn.)	1943-47
Winifred C. Stanley (R N.Y.)	1943-45
Willa L. Fulmer (D S.C.)	1944-45
Emily T. Douglas (D Ill.)	1945-47
Helen G. Douglas (D Calif.)	1945-51
Chase G. Woodhouse (D Conn.)	1945-47; 1949-51
Helen D. Mankin (D Ga.)	1946-47
Eliza J. Pratt (D N.C.)	1946-47
Georgia L. Lusk (D N.M.)	1947-49
Katherine P. C. St. George (R N.Y.)	1947-65
Reva Z. B. Bosone (D Utah)	1949-53

gious groups, Protestants have comprised nearly three-fourths of the membership of both houses in recent years, although Roman Catholic members have become more numerous than members belonging to any single Protestant denomination. Catholics took the lead from Methodists in 1965 and have retained it since.

At the beginning of the 100th Congress, there were 142 Catholics. More than half of the Protestant members were affiliated with four denominations: Methodists, 75; Episcopalians, 60; Presbyterians, 57; and Baptists, 52. There were 37 Jewish members.

Women in Congress

Women, who were not allowed to vote until 1920, always have been underrepre-

... More Than 100 since 1917

Cecil M. Harden (R Ind.)	1949-59	Millicent Fenwick (R N.J.)	1975-83
Edna F. Kelly (D N.Y.)	1949-69	Martha E. Keys (D Kan.)	1975-79
Vera D. Buchanan (D Pa.)	1951-55	Helen S. Meyner (D N.J.)	1975-79
Marguerite S. Church (R Ill.)	1951-63	Virginia Smith (R Neb.)	1975-
Maude E. Kee (D W.Va.)	1951-65	Gladys N. Spellman (D Md.)	1975-81
Ruth Thompson (R Mich.)	1951-57	Shirley N. Pettis (R Calif.)	1975-79
Gracie B. Pfost (D Idaho)	1953-63	Barbara A. Mikulski (D Md.)	1977-87
Leonor K. Sullivan (D Mo.)	1953-77	Mary Rose Oakar (D Ohio)	1977-
Iris F. Blitch (D Ga.)	1955-63	Beverly Barton Butcher Byron	
Edith Green (D Ore.)	1955-74	(D Md.)	1979-
Martha W. Griffiths (D Mich.)	1955-74	Geraldine Ferraro (D N.Y.)	1979-85
Coya G. Knutson (D Minn.)	1955-59	Olympia Jean Bouchles Snowe	
Kathryn E. Granahan (D Pa.)	1956-63	(R Maine)	1979-
Florence P. Dwyer (R N.J.)	1957-73	Bobbi Fiedler (R Calif.)	1981-87
Catherine D. May (R Wash.)	• 1959-71	Lynn M. Martin (R Ill.)	1981-
Edna O. Simpson (R Ill.)	1959-61	Marge Roukema (R N.J.)	1981-
Jessica McC. Weis (R N.Y.)	1959-63	Claudine Schneider (R R.I.)	1981-
Julia B. Hansen (D Wash.)	1960-74	Jean Ashbrook (R Ohio)	1982-83
Catherine D. Norrell (D Ark.)	1961-63	Barbara B. Kennelly (D Conn.)	1982-
Louise G. Reece (R Tenn.)	1961-63	Sala Burton (D Calif.)	1983-87
Corinne B. Riley (D S.C.)	1962-63	Barbara Boxer (D Calif.)	1983-
Charlotte T. Reid (R Ill.)	1963-71	Katie Hall (D Ind.)	1983-85
Irene B. Baker (R Tenn.)	1964-65	Nancy L. Johnson (R Conn.)	1983-
Patsy T. Mink (D Hawaii)	1965-77	Marcy Kaptur (D Ohio)	1983-
Lera M. Thomas (D Texas)	1966-67	Barbara Vucanovich (R Nev.)	1983-
Margaret M. Heckler (R Mass.)	1967-83	Helen Delich Bentley (R Md.)	1985-
Shirley Chisholm (D N.Y.)	1969-83	Jan Meyers (R Kan.)	1985-
Bella S. Abzug (D N.Y.)	1971-77	Cathy Long (D La.)	1985-87
Ella T. Grasso (D Conn.)	1971-75	Constance A. Morella (R Md.)	1987-
Louise Day Hicks (D Mass.)	1971-73	Elizabeth J. Patterson (D S.C.)	1987-
Elizabeth B. Andrews (D Ala.)	1972-73	Patricia Saiki (R Hawaii)	1987-
Yvonne B. Burke (D Calif.)	1973-79	Louise M. Slaughter (D N.Y.)	1987-
Marjorie S. Holt (R Md.)	1973-87		
Elizabeth Holtzman (D N.Y.)	1973-81		
Barbara C. Jordan (D Texas)	1973-79		
Patricia Schroeder (D Colo.)	1973-		
Corinne C. Boggs (D La.)	1973-		
Cardiss R. Collins (D Ill.)	1973-		
Marilyn Lloyd (D Tenn.)	1975-		

* Felton was sworn in Nov. 21, 1922, to fill the vacancy created by the death of Thomas E. Watson, D (1921-22). The next day she gave up her seat to Walter F. George, D (1922-57), the elected candidate for the vacancy.

† Never sworn in because Congress was not in session between election and expiration of term.

ented in Congress. Starting with Rep. Jeannette Rankin, R-Mont., elected in 1916, a total of 119 women had been elected or appointed to Congress by the beginning of 1987. The total included 104 in the House only, 13 in the Senate only, and 2 — Margaret Chase Smith, R-Maine, and Barbara Mikulski, D-Md. — who served in both chambers. *(Women members of Congress since 1917, box, p. 48; Number of Women Members in Congress, 1947-87, box, p. 50)*

The total of 119 is misleading, however. Two women were never sworn in because Congress was not in session between their election and the expiration of their terms. Another sat in the Senate for just one day. Several were appointed or elected to fill unexpired terms and served in Congress for

Number of Women Members in Congress 1947-87

Listed below by Congress is the number of women members of the Senate and House of Representatives from the 80th Congress through the beginning of the 100th Congress. The figures include women appointed to office as well as those chosen by voters in general elections and special elections.

Congress		Senate	House
100th	1987-89	2	23
99th	1985-87	2	23
98th	1983-85	2	22
97th	1981-83	2	21
96th	1979-81	1	16
95th	1977-79	2	18
94th	1975-77	0	19
93d	1973-75	0	16
92d	1971-73	2	13
91st	1969-71	1	10
90th	1967-69	1	11
89th	1965-67	2	10
88th	1963-65	2	11
87th	1961-63	2	17
86th	1959-61	1	16
85th	1957-59	1	15
84th	1955-57	1	16
83d	1953-55	3	12
82d	1951-53	1	10
81st	1949-51	1	9
80th	1947-49	1	7

less than a year. Only 6 women have been elected to full Senate terms.

By the beginning of 1987, 37 percent of the women members had entered Congress after their husbands. Forty-four were married to members who served before them; 41 of these (6 senators and 35 representatives) were appointed or elected to fill the unexpired terms of their late husbands. Rep.

Charlotte T. Reid, R-Ill., and Rep. Marilyn Lloyd, D-Tenn., became their parties' nominees when their husbands died between the primary and general elections. One woman, Rep. Emily Taft Douglas, D-Ill., was elected to Congress before her husband, Sen. Paul H. Douglas, D-Ill. Another woman, Rep. Martha Keys, D-Kan., married a colleague from a different state, Rep. Andrew Jacobs, D-Ind., early in 1976. The marriage, the first in congressional history, was thought to jeopardize her reelection chances, but both Keys and Jacobs returned to the 95th Congress. She, however, did lose her reelection bid in 1978.

Following the election of Rankin in 1916, the number of women in Congress increased only slightly until 1928, when 9 were elected to the House for the 71st Congress. Women's membership reached a peak of 19 (2 senators, 17 representatives) in the 87th Congress (1961-62) and did not match that until 1975, when 19 women served in the House.

The first woman named to the Senate served there only one day. On Oct. 2, 1922, Rebecca L. Felton, Independent Democrat representing Georgia, was appointed to fill the vacancy created by the death of Sen. Thomas E. Watson, D-Ga.; Senator Felton was not sworn in until Nov. 21, however, and on the next day she turned the seat over to Walter F. George, D-Ga., who had been elected to fill the vacancy. In 1931, Hattie W. Caraway, D-Ark., became the second woman to serve in Senate history when she was named to fill the vacancy created by the death of her husband, Thaddeus H. Caraway, D-Ark. In 1932 and 1938, she was elected to full six-year terms. Through the election of 1980, only 4 other women – Maurine B. Neuberger, D-Ore., Margaret Chase Smith, R-Maine, Nancy Landon Kassebaum, R-Kan., and Paula Hawkins, R-Fla. – had been elected to full Senate terms. Kassebaum, reelected in 1984, was the first woman ever elected to the Senate without being preceded in Congress by her husband. In 1986, Barbara Mikulski, Md., became the first female Democratic senator elected in her own right.

Although many women elected to Con

;ress on the basis of "widow's mandate" 1ave served only the remainder of the hus- 1and's term, others have stayed to build :trong political reputations for themselves. 3oth Senator Smith and Rep. Edith N. Rog- rs, R-Mass. — who hold the records for the ongest service by women in their respective hambers — were elected to the House to ill the unexpired terms of their late hus- 1ands. Smith served in the House until 948, when she won the first of four terms in he Senate. Rogers served in the House for ·5 years, from June 1925 until her death in ieptember 1960.

As women have become more active in 1olitics at all levels, the congressional tradi- ion of the widow's mandate has weakened. Jnly 3 of the 25 women in Congress at the 1eginning of the 100th Congress held the 3eats of their late husbands, and all had 1een elected to the positions. Corrine C. 'Lindy" (Mrs. Hale) Boggs, D-La., and 'ardiss Collins, D-Ill., had served since 973. Sala Burton, D-Calif., had served since 983.

Women have made notable gains in re- 3nt congressional elections. In 1981, for the rst time in history, there were 21 women 1embers in Congress — 19 in the House nd 2 in the Senate. (In July 1982 Rep. Jean shbrook, R-Ohio, took her husband's seat, 1ising the number to 20 in the House.) The 3nd continued in 1983 when the number)se to 21 women in the House, while the 1mber of women senators remained the 1me. By the end of the 98th Congress there 3re 22 congresswomen (Sala Burton was 3cted to fill the seat of her husband, Rep. 'hillip Burton, upon his death). Women did)t gain any seats in the 1984 elections. But . April 1985, Cathy Long, D-La., was 3cted to succeed her husband, Rep. Gillis ong, who died in January of that year.)ng's election brought the number of)men members in Congress to 25 — 23 in 1e House and 2 in the Senate.

After the 1986 elections, the number of)men remained at 25 — 23 in the House 1d 2 in the Senate. Four new House mem- 3rs offset the retirement of 4 incumbents, 1d a new female senator replaced a woman 10 lost.

Number of Black Members in Congress 1947-87

Listed below by Congress is the number of black members of the Senate and House of Representatives from the 80th Congress through the opening of the 100th Congress. The figures do not include the nonvoting delegate from the District of Columbia.

Congress		Senate	House
100th	1987-89	0	22
99th	1985-87	0	20 [1]
98th	1983-85	0	20
97th	1981-83	0	17
96th	1979-81	0	16
95th	1977-79	1	16
94th	1975-77	1	16
93d	1973-75	1	15
92d	1971-73	1	12
91st	1969-71	1	9
90th	1967-69	1	5
89th	1965-67		6
88th	1963-65		5
87th	1961-63		4
86th	1959-61		4
85th	1957-59		4
84th	1955-57		3
83d	1953-55		2
82d	1951-53		2
81st	1949-51		2
80th	1947-49		2

[1] Alton R. Waldon Jr., D-N.Y., was sworn in July 29, 1986, to fill the vacancy created by the death of Rep. Joseph P. Addabbo, D. Waldon ran for reelection but was defeated in the primary.

Hope Chamberlain wrote in *A Minority of Members: Women in the U.S. Congress:*

"Most members of this numerically select group were reared in modest economic circumstances; almost all attended college;

only a few never married. The majority have been white, Anglo-Saxon, and Protestant. Beyond hard work and the gift of intuition, however, they have had little else in common. The laws of chance, if nothing else, argue against parallels. Their geographical heritage embraces 38 of the 50 states; their precongressional careers, if any, span a broad spectrum: teaching, stenography, journalism, social work, broadcasting, the theater, law — even cowpunching."

Blacks in Congress

At the beginning of 1987, a total of 62 black Americans had served in Congress — 3 in the Senate and 59 in the House. Almost half had served in the nineteenth century after the Civil War. All but 16 of the 39 blacks elected in the twentieth century were serving in the 100th Congress when it opened. *(Black Members of Congress, box, p. 53; Number of Black Members in Congress, 1947-87, box, p. 51)*

The first black elected to Congress was John W. Menard, R-La., who won election in 1868 to an unexpired term in the 40th Congress. Menard's election was disputed, however, and the House denied him his seat. Thus the distinction of being the first black to serve in Congress went to Hiram Revels, R-Miss., who served in the Senate from February 1870 to March 1871. The first black to serve in the House was Joseph H. Rainey, R-S.C., from 1870 to 1879.

In 1874, a second black, Blanche K. Bruce, R-Miss., was elected to the Senate; Bruce was the first black member to serve a full term in the Senate and the last elected to that chamber until Edward W. Brooke, R-Mass., won in 1966. The last black elected to Congress in the nineteenth century was George Henry White, R-N.C., who won election in 1896 and 1898 but did not seek renomination in 1900.

For three decades there were no blacks in Congress. In 1928 Rep. Oscar dePriest, R-Ill., became the first black member elected in the twentieth century. Only 3 more blacks were elected during the next 25 years. But with the election of Rep. Charles C. Diggs Jr., D-Mich., in 1954, black membership began to increase. Three new black represen-

tatives were elected in the next decade. Senator Brooke won his first term in 1966. Three more blacks were elected to the House in 1968, 5 more in 1970, 3 more i 1972, 1 in a special election in 1973, and more in the 1974 general election. No addi tional blacks were elected to the 95th Con gress. Four blacks were elected to the Hous in 1978, but Senator Brooke, the only blac in the Senate, was defeated. Four mor blacks — all in the House — were elected t the 97th and 98th Congresses. No additiona black members were elected in 1984. How ever, the number of black members in th House increased by 1 on July 29, 1986, whe Alton R. Waldon Jr., D-N.Y., was sworn i to replace Rep. Joseph P. Addabbo, wh died April 10, 1986.

While black membership increased, sev eral black representatives achieved enoug seniority to be named House committe chairmen. William L. Dawson, D-Ill., serve as chairman of the Government Operation Committee from 1949 until his death i 1970. Adam Clayton Powell Jr., D-N.Y., wa chairman of the Education and Labor Com mittee from 1961 until the House strippe him of the post in 1967 because of allege misuse of committee funds. Diggs was chai man of the District of Columbia Committe from 1973 until 1979. He voluntarily reli quished his committee chairmanship aft being censured by the House on July 3 1979, for misuse of clerk-hire funds. Dig resigned from the House June 3, 1980, aft he was convicted on 29 felony counts. Ro ert N. C. Nix, D-Pa., was chairman of th Post Office and Civil Service Committe from 1977 until he was defeated in the 19 primary election. Since 1980 there ha been several more black committee chai men.

The latest member to attain the chai manship of a major committee was Willia H. Gray III, D-Pa., elected by his Dem cratic colleagues in January 1985 to cha the House Budget Committee. Rep. Char B. Rangel, D-N.Y., was one of seven depu whips in the 99th and 100th Congresse making him the highest ranking black in t House Democratic leadership.

In 1968 Rep. Shirley Chisholm, D-N.

Black Members of Congress

As of the beginning of 1987, 62 black Americans had served in Congress; 3 in the Senate and 59 in the House. Following is a list of the black members, their parties and states, and the years in which they served. In addition, John W. Menard, R-La., won a disputed election in 1868 but was not permitted to take his seat in Congress. Walter E. Fauntroy, D-D.C., began serving in 1971 as nonvoting delegate from the District of Columbia.

Senate

Hiram R. Revels (R Miss.)	1870-71
Blanche K. Bruce (R Miss.)	1875-81
Edward W. Brooke (R Mass.)	1967-79

House

Joseph H. Rainey (R S.C.)	1870-79
Jefferson F. Long (R Ga.)	1870-71
Robert B. Elliott (R S.C.)	1871-74
Robert C. DeLarge (R S.C.)	1871-73
Benjamin S. Turner (R Ala.)	1871-73
Josiah T. Walls (R Fla.)	1871-76
Richard H. Cain (R S.C.)	1873-75; 1877-79
John R. Lynch (R Miss.)	1873-77; 1882-83
James T. Rapier (R Ala.)	1873-75
Alonzo J. Ransier (R S.C.)	1873-75
Jeremiah Haralson (R Ala.)	1875-77
John A. Hyman (R N.C.)	1875-77
Charles E. Nash (R La.)	1875-77
Robert Smalls (R S.C.)	1875-79; 1882-83; 1884-87
James E. O'Hara (R N.C.)	1883-87
Henry P. Cheatham (R N.C.)	1889-93
John M. Langston (R Va.)	1890-91
Thomas E. Miller (R S.C.)	1890-91
George W. Murray (R S.C.)	1893-95; 1896-97
George H. White (R N.C.)	1897-1901
Oscar De Priest (R Ill.)	1929-35
Arthur W. Mitchell (D Ill.)	1935-43
William L. Dawson (D Ill.)	1943-70

Adam C. Powell Jr. (D N.Y.)	1945-67; 1969-71
Charles C. Diggs Jr. (D Mich.)	1955-80
Robert N. C. Nix (D Pa.)	1958-79
Augustus F. Hawkins (D Calif.)	1963-
John Conyers Jr. (D Mich.)	1965-
Louis Stokes (D Ohio)	1969-
William L. Clay (D Mo.)	1969-
Shirley Chisholm (D N.Y.)	1969-83
George W. Collins (D Ill.)	1970-72
Ronald V. Dellums (D Calif.)	1971-
Ralph H. Metcalfe (D Ill.)	1971-78
Parren J. Mitchell (D Md.)	1971-87
Charles B. Rangel (D N.Y.)	1971-
Yvonne B. Burke (D Calif.)	1973-79
Cardiss Collins (D Ill.)	1973-
Barbara C. Jordan (D Texas)	1973-79
Andrew Young (D Ga.)	1973-77
Harold E. Ford (D Tenn.)	1975-
Julian C. Dixon (D Calif.)	1979-
William H. Gray (D Pa.)	1979-
George T. Leland (D Texas)	1979-
Bennett McVey Stewart (D Ill.)	1979-81
George W. Crockett Jr. (D Mich.)	1981-
Mervin M. Dymally (D Calif.)	1981-
Gus Savage (D Ill.)	1981-
Harold Washington (D Ill.)	1981-83
Katie Hall (D Ind.)	1983-85
Charles A. Hayes (D Ill.)	1983-
Major R. Owens (D N.Y.)	1983-
Edolphus Towns (D N.Y.)	1983-
Alan Wheat (D Mo.)	1983-
Alton R. Waldon Jr. (D N.Y.)	1986-87
Mike Espy (D Miss.)	1987-
Floyd H. Flake (D N.Y.)	1987-
John Lewis (D Ga.)	1987-
Kweisi Mfume (D Md.)	1987-

SOURCES: Maurine Christopher, *America's Black Congressmen* (Thomas Y. Crowell Co., 1971), 267-269; *Biographical Directory of the American Congress, 1774-1971* (Government Printing Office, 1971).

became the first black woman to be elected to Congress. She was joined in the House by Yvonne Brathwaite Burke, D-Calif., and Barbara C. Jordan, D-Texas, who both served from 1972 until 1979. In a 1973 special election, Cardiss Collins, D-Ill., won the House seat previously held by her late husband, George W. Collins, and became the fourth black woman in Congress. The fifth black woman, Katie Hall, D-Ind., won a special election in November 1982, filling the seat vacated by the death of Adam Benjamin Jr. She lost the seat in the 1984 Indiana primary elections.

Representative Jordan and Rep. Andrew Young, D-Ga., both elected in 1972, were the first blacks in the twentieth century to represent Southern constituencies. After the 1974 election they were joined by Rep. Harold E. Ford, D-Tenn. In 1977, Young resigned to become U.S. ambassador to the United Nations. In the 1986 elections, Mike Espy, D-Miss., became the first black to win a congressional seat from that state since Reconstruction.

All 22 black members of Congress in the nineteenth century were Republicans, reflecting the political alignment of the Civil War. But in the twentieth century, through early 1987, only 2 of the 40 black members had been Republicans.

In 1971 a loose alliance of black representatives formally organized the Congressional Black Caucus, calling themselves congressmen-at-large who represented all black citizens. From 1971 through 1985, every black person elected to the House had joined the caucus. Another caucus member was Walter E. Fauntroy, D, nonvoting delegate from the District of Columbia, first elected in 1971.

Hispanics in Congress

In the early 1980s, the swelling ranks of Hispanic-Americans — 17 million people with roots to Mexico, Cuba, other Latin American nations, and Puerto Rico — sparked predictions they would emerge as a powerful voting bloc. While there has been progress, visions of a political "Hispanic Decade" appear to have been premature.

Hispanic voting levels traditionally have fallen well below the national average Aside from lack of ethnic representation Hispanic activists blame low participation on poverty, low education levels, language barriers, and alienation resulting from discrimination.

Age is another factor that diminishes Hispanic political clout. The median age of the Hispanic population is 25, 10 years younger than the national median age. Also many recently arrived Hispanic immigrant remain attached to their homeland.

In 1982, the number of Hispanics in the House jumped from 8 to 11. Much of the increase was made possible by favorable redistricting. In 1984, the number of Hispanics in the House increased again to 14. Yet Hispanics, who were 6.4 percent of the population in 1984, remained underrepresented in the House where they held only 2.8 percent of the seats.

Fourteen Hispanic representatives returned to the 100th Congress (including the resident commissioner of Puerto Rico an the nonvoting delegates from Guam and the Virgin Islands), maintaining the previous gains made by Hispanic candidates in 1984 Ten of the 11 Hispanic U.S. representative are from California, Texas, and New Mexico; 5 of these were first elected since 1982 No Hispanic candidate has been elected to the U.S. Senate since 1970, when Joseph Montoya, D-N.M., won his second and last term.

Turnover in Membership

Congress experienced high turnover rates in the nineteenth and early twentieth centuries. Throughout the nineteenth century, turnover in the House was greater than in the Senate, primarily because of the exigencies of campaign travel every two years and the tendency of state legislatures to continue reelecting the same men to the Senate. In 1869, for example, only 98 of 243 House members had served in previous Congresses. For several years after the direct election of senators was instituted by the Seventeenth Amendment in 1913, Senate turnover increased, particularly in the larger states.

In the middle of the twentieth century

Hispanic Members of Congress

As of the beginning of 1987, 20 Hispanics had served in Congress; 2 in the Senate and 18 in the House. Following is a list of the Hispanic members, their parties and states, and the years in which they served. Not included are Hispanics who served as territorial delegates (10), resident commissioners of Puerto Rico (13), or nonvoting delegates of Guam (1) or the Virgin Islands (1).

Senate

Dennis Chaves (D N.M.)	1935-62
Joseph Montoya (D N.M)	1964-77

House

Romualdo Pacheco (R Calif.)	1877-78;
	1879-83
Ladislas Lazaro (D La.)	1913-27
Benigno Cardenas Hernandez	
(R N.M.)	1915-17;
	1919-21
Nestor Montoya (R N.M.)	1921-23
Joachim Octave Fernandez (D La.)	1931-41

Antonia Manuel Fernandez (D N.M.)	1943-56
Henry B. Gonzalez (D Texas)	1961-
Edward R. Roybal (D Calif.)	1962-
E. "Kika" de la Garza (D Texas)	1965-
Manuel Lujan Jr. (R N.M.)	1969-
Herman Badillo (D N.Y.)	1971-77
Robert Garcia (D N.Y.)	1978-
Tony Coelho (D Calif)	1979-
Matthew G. Martinez (D Calif.)	1982-
Solomon P. Ortiz (D Texas)	1983-
William B. Richardson (D N.M.)	1983-
Esteban E. Torres (D Calif.)	1983-
Albert G. Bustamante (D Texas)	1985-

SOURCES: Congressional Quarterly *Weekly Report*; Congressional Hispanic Caucus.

congressional turnover held steady at a relatively low rate. In the quarter century after World War II, each Congress had an average of about 78 new members — 65 in the House and 12.7 in the Senate.

The 92d Congress opened in 1971 with 57 freshmen — 56 in the House and 11 in the Senate. The 93d Congress began in 1973 with 82 freshmen — 69 in the House and 13 in the Senate. In the next Congress the number of freshmen jumped dramatically. The 94th Congress convened early in 1975 with 102 new members — 92 representatives and 10 senators — the largest turnover in the House since 1949.

Several factors contributed to the increased turnover. The elections of 1972 and 1974 were affected by redistricting that followed the 1970 census; many House veterans had retired rather than face strong new opposition. Those two elections also were the first in which 18-year-olds were allowed to vote for members of Congress. In 1974,

probably the chief reason for change was the Watergate scandal, which put an end to the Nixon administration and badly damaged the Republican party. The Democrats gained 43 seats from the Republicans in the House, and 75 of the 92 freshman representatives at the beginning of the 94th Congress were Democrats.

Most of those Democrats managed to hold on to their seats in the 1976 elections. Of the 75 new Democrats elected in 1974 and the 4 elected since then, 78 sought reelection and 76 succeeded. The 95th Congress opened in 1977 with 85 freshmen.

In contrast to 1974, the upheaval in the 1976 elections came in the Senate. At the opening of the 95th Congress, there were 18 new members in the Senate. This marked the largest turnover in the Senate since 1958. In the 95th Congress, members elected for the first time in either 1972, 1974, or 1976 made up more than one half of the total membership of the House.

In 1978, 20 new senators were elected representing the second largest group of freshman senators since the beginning of popular Senate elections in 1914. The only larger freshman class was the one after the 1946 election — 23 senators. Three major factors accounted for the arrival of so many newcomers. Ten incumbents retired in 1978, more than in any year since World War II. Three incumbents were beaten in primaries, the most in a decade. And seven incumbents were defeated for reelection, the second highest number in 20 years.

With a record 58 open House seats in the 1978 election because of retirement, desire to seek other office, death, or primary defeat, the House gained 77 freshmen.

The 97th Congress opened in 1981 with 92 freshmen — 18 in the Senate and 74 in the House. The Republicans won Senate control for the first time since 1952, ending the longest one-party dominance of the Senate in history. They also netted the largest increase in the House since 1966.

The 1982 election broke several records. With only 5 new senators, the resulting turnover was the smallest in the 68-year history of popular Senate elections. The Senate party ratio remained the same as in the 97th Congress — 54-46 — and 95 of the 100 senators returned.

In contrast, the House had 81 new members, 57 of them Democrats. The Republicans lost 26 seats in the House, half of them were freshmen. Only three other elections in the past 30 years had brought in so many freshmen Democrats. As in the 1972 and 1974 elections, redistricting played a major part. The 1980 census shifted 17 seats from the Northeast and Midwest to the Sun Belt states of the South and West. The Democrats took 10 of these seats. The 98th Congress opened with 269 Democrats and 166 Republicans in the House.

In the 1984 elections the Republicans had a modest gain of 14 seats in the House. There were few open seats so there were only 43 new House members in the 99th Congress. The Senate had another low turnover with only 7 newcomers. On only four previous occasions since 1914 had there been fewer than 10 Senate newcomers. The

Democrats picked up 2 seats in the Senate. The 99th Congress contained 182 Republicans and 253 Democrats in the House, and 53 Republicans and 47 Democrats in the Senate.

In the 1986 Senate elections, Democrats captured a total of 9 GOP seats and lost only 1 of their own to regain Senate control back from the Republicans. The Democrats had the largest class of freshmen senators since 1958; of the 13 new senators, 11 were Democrats.

The 1986 House elections were extraordinarily good for incumbents of both parties. Only 6 House members lost in the general election, the lowest number of defeated incumbents in any post World War II election. Two representatives had lost in the primaries. The Democrats registered a net gain of 5 seats, giving the party an 81-seat edge over the GOP. The combination of open-seat outcomes and challenger victories yielded a freshman House class of 50 members, which included 23 Republicans and 27 Democrats. The 100th Congress opened Jan. 6, 1987, with 258 Democrats and 177 Republicans in the House, and 55 Democrats and 45 Republicans in the Senate.

Shifts between Chambers

From the early days of Congress there has been shifting of membership from one chamber to another. The House and the Senate are equal under the law, and representatives tend to bristle when anyone refers to their chamber as the "lower house." But that does not stop them from running for the Senate whenever they see an opening. From 1789 to 1987, a total of 544 former House members had served in the Senate while only 57 former senators had become representatives.

In recent years few former senators have gone to the House, and those who did usually had been defeated in their efforts to be reelected to the Senate. From 1962 to 1987, 117 House members tried for a place in the Senate; however, not one person left the Senate to run for the House.

Those representatives who aspire to become senators are usually taking a risk. Of the 117 representatives who ran for the Sen ate from 1962 to 1987, only 51 succeeded. Six out of 16 won in 1970, 4 out of 10 in 1972, 1 out of 6 in 1974, 5 out of 19 in 1976, 6 out of 7 in 1978, 6 out of 8 in 1980, 1 out of 2 in 1982, 4 out of 12 in 1984, and 9 out of 17 in 1986. (Two representatives were defeated in the 1986 Senate primary elections.) The risks are higher if the House members are older and have considerable seniority.

In explaining why they have left the House to try for the Senate, former representatives have cited the Senate's greater prestige and publicity, the more stable six-year term, larger staffs and more generous perquisites, increased effectiveness as legislators in a chamber of 100 members instead of 435, the Senate's greater role in foreign affairs, and the challenge of moving into a new job with a larger constituency.

Shifting of members from one chamber to the other began in the 1790s, when 19 former representatives became senators and 3 former senators moved to the House. The number of House members who became senators increased over the next several decades, reaching 55 in the years from 1800 to 1820 and 39 in the 1940s alone. The trend continued. Between 1967 and January 1987, 47 former House members assumed Senate seats. By contrast, the greatest number of former senators to become House members in any one decade was 9 in the years between 1810 and 1820. From 1900 through 1987, at least 13 former senators became members of the House. The only former senator in the House at the convening of the 100th Congress was Claude Pepper, D-Fla., who had served continuously as a representative since 1963. Pepper had been a senator from 1936 to 1951.

Perhaps the most notable shift from the Senate to the House was that of Henry Clay, Democratic Republican, Ky., who gave up his Senate seat in 1811 to assume a House seat. In his first term in the House, Clay was elected Speaker — an office he used successfully to help push the country into the War of 1812. After five terms in the House, he returned to the Senate in 1823. Another prominent House member who had once been a senator was John Quincy Adams, Whig-Mass., who also was one of only two former presidents to serve in Congress after his term in the White House. Adams, who was known as "Old Man Eloquent," was one of the most influential members of the Whig opposition to President Andrew Jackson in the 1830s.

Members of Congress: Biographies

This biographical summary lists, alphabetically, all men and women who served in Congress as senators, representatives, resident commissioners, or territorial delegates from March 4, 1789, through January 3, 1987 — the First Congress through the beginning of the 100th Congress.

The material is organized as follows: name; relationship to other members, presidents, or vice presidents; party, state (of service); date of birth; date of death (if applicable); congressional service, service as president, vice president, member of the Cabinet or Supreme Court, governor, delegate to the Continental Congress, House or Senate majority leader, Speaker of the House, president pro tempore of the Senate, or chairman of the Democratic or Republican National Committee.

If a member changed parties during his congressional service, party designation appearing after the member's name is that which applied at the end of such service and further breakdown is included after dates of congressional service. Party designation is multiple only if member was elected by two or more parties at the same time. Where service date is left open, member was serving in the 100th Congress. *(Party abbreviations, box, p. x)*

Dates of service are inclusive and may cover more than one term — six years for senators and two years for representatives. Under the Constitution, terms of service from 1789 to 1933 were from March 4 to March 4; since 1934, service has been from Jan. 3 to Jan. 3. In actual practice, members often have been sworn in on other dates at the beginning of a Congress. The exact date is shown (where available) if member began or ended his service in midterm.

The primary source of information for this list was the *Biographical Directory of the American Congress 1774-1971* compiled under the direction of the Joint Committee on Printing. Additional data were obtained from the files of the Joint Committee on Printing, the House Historian, the Senate Historian, the *Congressional Directory*, and Congressional Quarterly's *Almanac, Guide to Congress, Guide to U.S. Elections,* and *Weekly Report.*

AANDAHL, Fred George (R N.D.) April 9, 1897-April 7, 1966; House 1951-53; Gov. 1945-50.

ABBITT, Watkins Moorman (D Va.) May 21, 1908--; House Feb. 17, 1948-73.

ABBOTT, Amos (W Mass.) Sept. 10, 1786-Nov. 2, 1868; House 1843-49.

ABBOTT, Joel (D Ga.) March 17, 1776-Nov. 19, 1826; House 1817-25.

ABBOTT, Joseph (D Texas) Jan. 15, 1840-Feb. 11, 1908; House 1887-97.

ABBOTT, Joseph Carter (R N.C.) July 15, 1825-Oct. 8, 1881; Senate July 14, 1868-71.

ABBOTT, Josiah Gardner (D Mass.) Nov. 1, 1814-June 2, 1891; House July 28, 1876-77.

ABBOTT, Nehemiah (R Maine) March 29, 1804-July 26, 1877; House 1857-59.

ABDNOR, Ellis James (R S.D.) Feb. 13, 1923--; House 1973-81; Senate 1981-87.

ABEL, Hazel Hempell (R Neb.) July 10, 1888-July 30, 1966; Senate Nov. 8, 1954-Dec. 31, 1954.

ABELE, Homer E. (R Ohio) Nov. 21, 1916--; House 1963-65.

ABERCROMBIE, James (UW Ala.) 1795-July 2, 1861; House 1851-55.

ABERCROMBIE, John William (D Ala.) May 17, 1866-July 2, 1940; House 1913-17.

ABERCROMBIE, Neil (D Hawaii) June 26, 1938-- House Sept. 23, 1986-87.

ABERNETHY, Charles Laban (D N.C.) March 18, 1872-Feb. 23, 1955; House Nov. 7, 1922-35.

ABERNETHY, Thomas Gerstle (D Miss.) May 16, 1903--; House 1943-73.

ABOUREZK, James George (D S.D.) Feb. 24, 1931-- House 1971-73; Senate 1973-79.

ABZUG, Bella Savitzky (D N.Y.) July 24, 1920-- House 1971-77.

ACHESON, Ernest Francis (R Pa.) Sept. 19, 1855-May 16, 1917; House 1895-1909.

ACKER, Ephraim Leister (D Pa.) Jan. 11, 1827-May 12, 1903; House 1871-73.

ACKERMAN, Ernest Robinson (R N.J.) June 17, 1863-Oct. 18, 1931; House 1919-Oct. 18, 1931.

ACKERMAN, Gary L. (D N.Y.) Nov. 19, 1942- —; House March 2, 1983- —.

ACKLEN, Joseph Hayes (D La.) May 20, 1850-Sept. 28, 1938; House Feb. 20, 1878-81.

ADAIR, Edwin Ross (R Ind.) Dec. 14, 1907-May 7, 1983; House 1951-71.

ADAIR, Jackson Leroy (D Ill.) Feb. 23, 1887-Jan. 19, 1956; House 1933-37.

ADAIR, John (D Ky.) Jan. 9, 1757-May 19, 1840; House 1831-33; Senate Nov. 8, 1805-Nov. 18, 1806; Gov. 1820-24.

ADAIR, John Alfred McDowell (D Ind.) Dec. 22, 1864-Oct. 5, 1938; House 1907-17.

ADAMS, Alva Blanchard (D Colo.) Oct. 29, 1875-Dec. 1, 1941; Senate May 17, 1923-Nov. 30, 1924, 1933-Dec. 1, 1941.

ADAMS, Benjamin (F Mass.) Dec. 16, 1764-March 28, 1837; House Dec. 2, 1816-21.

ADAMS, Brockman "Brock" (D Wash.) Jan. 13, 1927- —; House 1965-Jan. 22, 1977; Senate 1987- —; Secy. of Transportation 1977-July 20, 1979.

ADAMS, Charles Francis (son of John Quincy Adams, grandson of President John Adams) (R Mass.) Aug. 18, 1807-Nov. 21, 1886; House 1859-May 1, 1861.

ADAMS, Charles Henry (R N.Y.) April 10, 1824-Dec. 15, 1902; House 1875-77.

ADAMS, George Everett (R Ill.) June 18, 1840-Oct. 5, 1917; House 1883-91.

ADAMS, George Madison (nephew of Green Adams) (D Ky.) Dec. 20, 1837-April 6, 1920; House 1867-75.

ADAMS, Green (uncle of George Madison Adams) (AP Ky.) Aug. 20, 1812-Jan. 18, 1884; House 1847-49 (Whig), 1859-61.

ADAMS, Henry Cullen (R Wis.) Nov. 28, 1850-July 9, 1906; House 1903-July 9, 1906.

ADAMS, John (JD N.Y.) Aug. 26, 1778-Sept. 25, 1854; House March 4-Dec. 26, 1815 (Democrat), 1833-35.

ADAMS, John Joseph (D N.Y.) Sept. 16, 1848-Feb. 16, 1919; House 1883-87.

ADAMS, John Quincy (son of President John Adams, father of Charles Francis Adams) (W Mass.) July 11, 1767-Feb. 23, 1848; Senate 1803-June 8, 1808 (Federalist); House 1831-Feb. 23, 1848; Secy. of State 1817-25; President 1825-29 (Democratic Republican).

ADAMS, Parmenio (— N.Y.) Sept. 9, 1776-Feb. 19, 1832; House Jan. 7, 1824-27.

ADAMS, Robert Jr. (R Pa.) Feb. 26, 1849-June 1, 1906; House Dec. 19, 1893-June 1, 1906.

ADAMS, Robert Huntington (JD Miss.) 1792-July 2, 1830; Senate Jan. 6, 1830-July 2, 1830.

ADAMS, Sherman (R N.H.) Jan. 8, 1899-Oct. 27, 1986; House 1945-47; Gov. 1949-53.

ADAMS, Silas (R Ky.) Feb. 9, 1839-May 5, 1896; House 1893-95.

ADAMS, Stephen (UD Miss.) Oct. 17, 1807-May 11, 1857; House 1845-47 (Democrat); Senate March 17, 1852-1857.

ADAMS, Wilbur Louis (D Del.) Oct. 23, 1884-Dec. 4, 1937; House 1933-35.

ADAMSON, William Charles (D Ga.) Aug. 13, 1854-Jan. 3, 1929; House 1897-Dec. 18, 1917.

ADDABBO, Joseph P. (D N.Y.) March 17, 1925-April 10, 1986; House 1961-April 10, 1986.

ADDAMS, William (D Pa.) April 11, 1777-May 30, 1858; House 1825-29.

ADDONIZIO, Hugh Joseph (D N.J.) Jan. 31, 1914-Feb. 2, 1981; House 1949-June 30, 1962.

ADGATE, Asa (D N.Y.) Nov. 17, 1767-Feb. 15, 1832; House June 7, 1815-17.

ADKINS, Charles (R Ill.) Feb. 7, 1863-March 31, 1941; House 1925-33.

ADRAIN, Garnett Bowditch (D N.J.) Dec. 15, 1815-Aug. 17, 1878; House 1857-61.

AHL, John Alexander (D Pa.) Aug. 16, 1813-April 25, 1882; House 1857-59.

AIKEN, David Wyatt (father of Wyatt Aiken, cousin of William Aiken) (D S.C.) March 17, 1828-April 6, 1887; House 1877-87.

AIKEN, George David (R Vt.) Aug. 20, 1892-Nov. 19, 1984; Senate Jan. 10, 1941-75; Gov. 1937-41.

AIKEN, William (cousin of David Wyatt Aiken) (D S.C.) Aug. 4, 1806-Sept. 7, 1887; House 1851-57; Gov. 1844-46.

AIKEN, Wyatt (son of David Wyatt Aiken) (D S.C.) Dec. 14, 1863-Feb. 6, 1923; House 1903-17.

AINEY, William David Blakeslee (R Pa.) April 8, 1864-Sept. 4, 1932; House Nov. 7, 1911-15.

AINSLIE, George (D Idaho) Oct. 30, 1838-May 19, 1913; House (Terr. Del.) 1879-83.

AINSWORTH, Lucien Lester (AM Iowa) June 21, 1831-April 19, 1902; House 1875-77.

AITKEN, David Demerest (R Mich.) Sept. 5, 1853-May 26, 1930; House 1893-97.

AKAKA, Daniel K. (D Hawaii) Sept. 11, 1924- —; House 1977- —.

AKERS, Thomas Peter (AP Mo.) Oct. 4, 1828-April 3, 1877; House Aug. 18, 1856-57.

AKIN, Theron (PR N.Y.) May 23, 1855-March 26, 1933; House 1911-13.

ALBAUGH, Walter Hugh (R Ohio) Jan. 2, 1890-Jan. 21, 1942; House Nov. 8, 1938-39.

ALBERT, Carl Bert (D Okla.) May 10, 1908- —; House 1947-77; House majority leader 1962-71; Speaker 1971-77.

ALBERT, William Julian (R Md.) Aug. 4, 1816-March 29, 1879; House 1873-75.

ALBERTSON, Nathaniel (D Ind.) June 10, 1800-Dec. 16, 1863; House 1849-51.

ALBOSTA, Donald Joseph (D Mich.) Dec. 5, 1925- —; House 1979-85.

ALBRIGHT, Charles (R Pa.) Dec. 13, 1830-Sept. 28, 1880; House 1873-75.

ALBRIGHT, Charles Jefferson (R Ohio) May 9, 1816-Oct. 21, 1883; House 1855-57.

ALCORN, James Lusk (R Miss.) Nov. 4, 1816-Dec. 19, 1894; Senate Dec. 1, 1871-77; Gov. 1870-71.

ALDERSON, John Duffy (D W.Va.) Nov. 29, 1854-Dec. 5, 1910; House 1889-95.

ALDRICH, Cyrus (R Minn.) June 18, 1808-Oct. 5, 1871; House 1859-63.

ALDRICH, James Franklin (son of William Aldrich) (R Ill.) April 6, 1853-March 8, 1933; House 1893-97.

ALDRICH, Nelson Wilmarth (father of Richard Steere Aldrich, cousin of William Aldrich, great-grandfather of John Davidson "Jay" Rockefeller IV, grandfather of Vice Pres. Nelson Aldrich Rockefeller and Gov. Winthrop Rockefeller of Ark.) (R R.I.) Nov. 6, 1841-April 16, 1915; House 1879-Oct. 4, 1881; Senate Oct. 5, 1881-1911.

ALDRICH, Richard Steere (son of Nelson Wilmarth Aldrich, granduncle of John Davison "Jay" Rockefeller IV, uncle of Vice Pres. Nelson Aldrich Rockefeller of Ark.) (R R.I.) Feb. 29, 1884-Dec. 25, 1941; House 1923-33.

ALDRICH, Truman Heminway (brother of William Farrington Aldrich) (R Ala.) Oct. 17, 1848-April 28, 1932; House June 9, 1896-97.

ALDRICH, William (father of James Franklin Aldrich, cousin of Nelson Wilmarth Aldrich) (R Ill.) Jan. 19, 1820-Dec. 3, 1885; House 1877-83.

ALDRICH, William Farrington (brother of Truman Heminway Aldrich) (R Ala.) March 11, 1853-Oct. 30, 1925; House March 13, 1896-97, Feb. 9, 1898-99, March 8, 1900-01.

ALESHIRE, Arthur William (D Ohio) Feb. 15, 1900-March 11, 1940; House 1937-39.

ALEXANDER, Adam Rankin (F Tenn.) ?-?; House 1823-27.

ALEXANDER, Armstead Milton (D Mo.) May 26, 1834-Nov. 7, 1892; House 1883-85.

ALEXANDER, De Alva Stanwood (R N.Y.) July 17, 1846-Jan. 30, 1925; House 1897-1911.

ALEXANDER, Evan Shelby (cousin of Nathaniel Alexander) (— N.C.) about 1767-Oct. 28, 1809; House Feb. 24, 1806-09.

ALEXANDER, Henry Porteous (W N.Y.) Sept. 13, 1801-Feb. 22, 1867; House 1849-51.

ALEXANDER, Hugh Quincy (D N.C.) Aug. 7, 1911- —; House 1953-63.

ALEXANDER, James Jr. (D Ohio) Oct. 17, 1789-Sept. 5, 1846; House 1837-39.

ALEXANDER, John (D Ohio) April 16, 1777-June 28, 1848; House 1813-17.

ALEXANDER, John Grant (R Minn.) July 16, 1893-Dec. 8, 1971; House 1939-41.

ALEXANDER, Joshua Willis (D Mo.) Jan. 22, 1852-Feb. 27, 1936; House 1907-Dec. 15, 1919; Secy. of Commerce 1919-21.

ALEXANDER, Mark (SRD Va.) Feb. 7, 1792-Oct. 7, 1883; House 1819-33.

ALEXANDER, Nathaniel (cousin of Evan Shelby Alexander) (— N.C.) March 5, 1756-March 8, 1808; House 1803-Nov. 1805; Gov. 1805-07 (Democratic Republican).

ALEXANDER, Syndenham Benoni (D N.C.) Dec. 8, 1840-June 14, 1921; House 1891-95.

ALEXANDER, William Vollie Jr. (D Ark.) Jan. 16, 1934- —; House 1969- —.

ALFORD, Julius Caesar (W Ga.) May 10, 1799-Jan. 1, 1863; House Jan. 2-March 3, 1837 (State Rights Whig), 1839-Oct. 1, 1841 (Harrison Whig).

ALFORD, Thomas Dale (D Ark.) Jan. 28, 1916- —; House 1959-63.

ALGER, Bruce Reynolds (R Texas) June 12, 1918- —; House 1955-65.

ALGER, Russell Alexander (R Mich.) Feb. 27, 1836-Jan. 24, 1907; Senate Sept. 27, 1902-Jan. 24, 1907; Gov. 1885-87; Secy. of War 1897-99.

ALLAN, Chilton (CD Ky.) April 6, 1786-Sept. 3, 1858; House 1831-37.

ALLEE, James Frank (R Del.) Dec. 2, 1857-Oct. 12, 1938; Senate March 2, 1903-07.

ALLEN, Alfred Gaither (D Ohio) July 23, 1867-Dec. 9, 1932; House 1911-17.

ALLEN, Amos Lawrence (R Maine) March 17, 1837-Feb. 20, 1911; House Nov. 6, 1899-Feb. 20, 1911.

ALLEN, Asa Leonard (D La.) Jan. 5, 1891-Jan. 5, 1969; House 1937-53.

ALLEN, Charles (FS Mass.) Aug. 9, 1797-Aug. 6, 1869; House 1849-53.

ALLEN, Charles Herbert (R Mass.) April 15, 1848-April 20, 1934; House 1885-89.

ALLEN, Clarence Emir (R Utah) Sept. 8, 1852-July 9, 1932; House Jan. 4, 1896-97.

ALLEN, Clifford Robertson (D Tenn.) Jan. 6, 1912-June 18, 1978; House Nov. 25, 1975-June 18, 1978.

ALLEN, Edward Payson (R Mich.) Oct. 28, 1839-Nov. 25, 1909; House 1887-91.

ALLEN, Elisha Hunt (son of Samuel Clesson Allen) (W Maine) Jan. 28, 1804-Jan. 1, 1883; House 1841-43.

ALLEN, Heman (W Vt.) June 14, 1777-Dec. 11, 1844; House 1831-39.

ALLEN, Heman (D Vt.) Feb. 23, 1779-April 7, 1852; House 1817-April 20, 1818.

ALLEN, Henry Crosby (R N.J.) May 13, 1872-March 7, 1942; House 1905-07.

ALLEN, Henry Dixon (D Ky.) June 24, 1854-March 9, 1924; House 1899-1903.

ALLEN, Henry Justin (R Kan.) Sept. 11, 1868-Jan. 17, 1950; Senate April 1, 1929-Nov. 30, 1930; Gov. 1919-23.

ALLEN, James Browning (D Ala.) Dec. 28, 1912-June 1, 1978; Senate 1969-June 1, 1978.

ALLEN, James Cameron (D Ill.) Jan. 29, 1822-Jan. 30, 1912; House 1853-July 18, 1856, Nov. 4, 1856-57, 1863-65.

ALLEN, John (father of John William Allen) (F Conn.) June 12, 1763-July 31, 1812; House 1797-99.

ALLEN, John Beard (R Wash.) May 18, 1845-Jan. 28, 1903; House (Terr. Del.) March 4-Nov. 11, 1889; Senate Nov. 20, 1889-93.

ALLEN, John Clayton (R Ill.) Feb. 14, 1860-Jan. 12, 1939; House 1925-33.

ALLEN, John James (brother of Robert Allen) (W Va.) Sept. 25, 1797-Sept. 18, 1871; House 1833-35.

ALLEN, John Joseph Jr. (R Calif.) Nov. 27, 1899- —; House 1947-59.

ALLEN, John Mills (D Miss.) July 8, 1846-Oct. 30, 1917; House 1885-1901.

ALLEN, John William (son of John Allen) (W Ohio) Aug. 1802-Oct. 5, 1887; House 1837-41.

ALLEN, Joseph (F Mass.) Sept. 2, 1749-Sept. 2, 1827; House Oct. 8, 1810-11.

ALLEN, Judson (D N.Y.) April 3, 1797-Aug. 6, 1880; House 1839-41.

ALLEN, Leo Elwood (R Ill.) Oct. 5, 1898-Jan. 19, 1973; House 1933-61.

ALLEN, Maryon Pittman (D Ala.) Nov. 30, 1925- —; Senate June 8, 1978-Nov. 7, 1978.

ALLEN, Nathaniel (father-in-law of Robert Lawson Rose) (— N.Y.) 1780-Dec. 22, 1832; House 1819-21.

ALLEN, Philip (TD R.I.) Sept. 1, 1785-Dec. 16, 1865; Senate July 20, 1853-59; Gov. 1851-53.

ALLEN, Robert (D Tenn.) June 19, 1778-Aug. 19, 1844; House 1819-27.

ALLEN, Robert (brother of John James Allen) (D Va.) July 30, 1794-Dec. 30, 1859; House 1827-33.

ALLEN, Robert Edward Lee (D W.Va.) Nov. 28, 1865-Jan. 28, 1951; House 1923-25.

ALLEN, Robert Gray (D Pa.) Aug. 24, 1902-Aug. 9, 1963; House 1937-41.

ALLEN, Samuel Clesson (father of Elisha Hunt Allen) (— Mass.) Jan. 5, 1772-Feb. 8, 1842; House 1817-29.

ALLEN, Thomas (D Mo.) Aug. 29, 1813-April 8, 1882; House 1881-April 8, 1882.

ALLEN, William (D Ohio) Dec. 27, 1803-July 11, 1879; House 1833-35; Senate 1837-49; Gov. 1874-76.

ALLEN, William (D Ohio) Aug. 13, 1827-July 6, 1881; House 1859-63.

ALLEN, William Franklin (D Del.) Jan. 19, 1883-June 14, 1946; House 1937-39.

ALLEN, William Joshua (son of Willis Allen) (D Ill.) June 9, 1829-Jan. 26, 1901; House June 2, 1862-65.

ALLEN, William Vincent (P Neb.) Jan. 28, 1847-Jan. 2, 1924; Senate 1893-99, Dec. 13, 1899-March 28, 1901.

ALLEN, Willis (father of William Joshua Allen) (D Ill.) Dec. 15, 1806-April 15, 1859; House 1851-55.

ALLEY, John Bassett (R Mass.) Jan. 7, 1817-Jan. 19, 1896; House 1859-67.

ALLGOOD, Miles Clayton (D Ala.) Feb. 22, 1878-March 4, 1977; House 1923-35.

ALLISON, James Jr. (father of John Allison) (W Pa.) Oct. 4, 1772-June 17, 1854; House 1823-25.

ALLISON, John (son of James Allison Jr.) (W Pa.) Aug. 5, 1812-March 23, 1878; House 1851-53, 1855-57.

ALLISON, Robert (W Pa.) March 10, 1777-Dec. 2, 1840; House 1831-33.

ALLISON, William Boyd (R Iowa) March 2, 1829-Aug. 4, 1908; House 1863-71; Senate 1873-Aug. 4, 1908.

ALLOTT, Gordon Llewellyn (R Colo.) Jan. 2, 1907- -; Senate 1955-73.

ALMON, Edward Berton (D Ala.) April 18, 1860-June 22, 1933; House 1915-June 22, 1933.

ALMOND, James Lindsay Jr. (D Va.) June 15, 1898- -; House Jan. 22, 1946-April 17, 1948; Gov. 1958-62.

ALSTON, Lemuel James (— S.C.) 1760-1836; House 1807-11.

ALSTON, William Jeffreys (W Ala.) Dec. 31, 1800-June 10, 1876; House 1849-51.

ALSTON, Willis (nephew of Nathaniel Macon) (WD N.C.) 1769-April 10, 1837; House 1799-1815, 1825-31.

ALVORD, James Church (W Mass.) April 14, 1808-Sept. 27, 1839; House 1839-Sept. 27, 1839.

AMBLER, Jacob A. (R Ohio) Feb. 18, 1829-Sept. 22, 1906; House 1869-73.

AMBRO, Jerome Anthony Jr. (D N.Y.) June 27, 1928- -; House 1975-81.

AMERMAN, Lemuel (D Pa.) Oct. 29, 1846-Oct. 7, 1897; House 1891-93.

AMES, Adelbert (father of Butler Ames, son-in-law of Benjamin Franklin Butler) (R Miss.) Oct. 31, 1835-April 12, 1933; Senate Feb. 23, 1870-Jan. 10, 1874; Gov. 1868-69 (Military), 1874-76.

AMES, Butler (son of Adelbert Ames, grandson of Benjamin Franklin Butler) (R Mass.) Aug. 22, 1871-Nov. 6, 1954; House 1903-13.

AMES, Fisher (F Mass.) April 9, 1758-July 4, 1808; House 1789-97.

AMES, Oakes (R Mass.) Jan. 10, 1804-May 8, 1873; House 1863-73.

AMLIE, Thomas Ryum (Prog. Wis.) April 17, 1897-Aug. 22, 1973; House Oct. 13, 1931-33 (Republican Progressive), 1935-39.

AMMERMAN, Joseph S. (D Pa.) July 14, 1924- -; House 1977-79.

ANCONA, Sydenham Elnathan (D Pa.) Nov. 20, 1824-June 20, 1913; House 1861-67.

ANDERSEN, Herman Carl (R Minn.) Jan. 27, 1897-July 26, 1978; House 1939-63.

ANDERSON, Albert Raney (IR Iowa) Nov. 8, 1837-Nov. 17, 1898; House 1887-89.

ANDERSON, Alexander Outlaw (son of Joseph Anderson) (D Tenn.) Nov. 10, 1794-May 23, 1869; Senate Feb. 26, 1840-41.

ANDERSON, Carl Carey (D Ohio) Dec. 2, 1877-Oct. 1, 1912; House 1909-Oct. 1, 1912.

ANDERSON, Chapman Levy (D Miss.) March 15, 1845-April 27, 1924; House 1887-91.

ANDERSON, Charles Arthur (D Mo.) Sept. 26, 1899-April 26, 1977; House 1937-41.

ANDERSON, Charles Marley (D Ohio) Jan. 5, 1845-Dec. 28, 1908; House 1885-87.

ANDERSON, Clinton Presba (D N.M.) Oct. 23, 1895-Nov. 11, 1975; House 1941-June 30, 1945; Senate 1949-73; Secy. of Agriculture 1945-48.

ANDERSON, George Alburtus (D Ill.) March 11, 1853-Jan. 31, 1896; House 1887-89.

ANDERSON, George Washington (RR Mo.) May 22, 1832-Feb. 26, 1902; House 1865-69.

ANDERSON, Glenn M. (D Calif.) Feb. 21, 1913- -; House 1969- -.

ANDERSON, Hugh Johnston (D Maine) May 10, 1801-May 31, 1881; House 1837-41; Gov. 1844-47.

ANDERSON, Isaac (Jeff.D Pa.) Nov. 23, 1760-Oct. 27, 1838; House 1803-07.

ANDERSON, James Patton (D Wash.) Feb. 16, 1822-Sept. 20, 1872; House (Terr. Del.) 1855-57.

ANDERSON, John (Jeff.D Maine) July 30, 1792-Aug. 21, 1853; House 1825-33.

ANDERSON, John Alexander (R Kan.) June 26, 1834-May 18, 1892; House 1879-91 (1887-89 Independent).

ANDERSON, John B. (R Ill.) Feb. 15, 1922- —; House 1961-81.

ANDERSON, John Zuinglius (R Calif.) March 22, 1904-Feb. 9, 1981; House 1939-53.

ANDERSON, Joseph (father of Alexander Outlaw Anderson) (— Tenn.) Nov. 5, 1757-April 17, 1837; Senate Sept. 26, 1797-1815; Pres. pro tempore Jan. 13, Feb. 28, March 2, 1805.

ANDERSON, Joseph Halstead (D N.Y.) Aug. 25, 1800-June 23, 1870; House 1843-47.

ANDERSON, Josiah McNair (W Tenn.) Nov. 29, 1807-Nov. 8, 1861; House 1849-51.

ANDERSON, LeRoy Hagen (D Mont.) Feb. 2, 1906- —; House 1957-61.

ANDERSON, Lucian (U Ky.) June 23, 1824-Oct. 18, 1898; House 1863-65.

ANDERSON, Richard Clough Jr. (— Ky.) Aug. 4, 1788-July 24, 1826; House 1817-21.

ANDERSON, Samuel (— Pa.) 1773-Jan. 17, 1850; House 1827-29.

ANDERSON, Simeon H. (father of William Clayton Anderson) (W Ky.) March 2, 1802-Aug. 11, 1840; House 1839-Aug. 11, 1840.

ANDERSON, Sydney (R Minn.) Sept. 18, 1881-Oct. 8, 1948; House 1911-25.

ANDERSON, Thomas Lilbourne (ID Mo.) Dec. 8, 1808-March 6, 1885; House 1857-61 (1857-59 American Party).

ANDERSON, Wendell Richard (D Minn.) Feb. 1, 1933- —; Senate Dec. 30, 1976-Dec. 29, 1978; Gov. 1971-76.

ANDERSON, William (Jeff.D Pa.) 1762-Dec. 16, 1829; House 1809-15, 1817-19.

ANDERSON, William Black (ID Ill.) April 2, 1830-Aug. 28, 1901; House 1875-77.

ANDERSON, William Clayton (son of Simeon H. Anderson, nephew of Albert Gallatin Talbott) (AP Ky.) Dec. 26, 1826-Dec. 23, 1861; House 1859-61.

ANDERSON, William Coleman (R Tenn.) July 10, 1853-Sept. 8, 1902; House 1895-97.

ANDERSON, William Robert (D Tenn.) June 17, 1921- —; House 1965-73.

ANDRESEN, August Herman (R Minn.) Oct. 11, 1890-Jan. 14, 1958; House 1925-33, 1935-Jan. 14, 1958.

ANDREW, Abram Piatt Jr. (R Mass.) Feb. 12, 1873-June 3, 1936; House Sept. 27, 1921-June 3, 1936.

ANDREW, John Forrester (D Mass.) Nov. 26, 1850-May 30, 1895; House 1889-93.

ANDREWS, Arthur Glenn (R Ala.) Jan. 15, 1909- —; House 1965-67.

ANDREWS, Charles (D Maine) Feb. 11, 1814-April 30, 1852; House 1851-April 30, 1852.

ANDREWS, Charles Oscar (D Fla.) March 7, 1877-Sept. 18, 1946; Senate Nov. 4, 1936-Sept. 18, 1946.

ANDREWS, Elizabeth Bullock (widow of George William Andrews) (D Ala.) Feb. 12, 1911- —; House April 4, 1972-73.

ANDREWS, George Rex (W N.Y.) Sept. 21, 1808-Dec. 5, 1873; House 1849-51.

ANDREWS, George William (husband of Elizabeth Bullock Andrews) (D Ala.) Dec. 12, 1906-Dec. 25, 1971; House March 14, 1944-Dec. 25, 1971.

ANDREWS, Ike Franklin (D N.C.) Sept. 2, 1925- —; House 1973-85.

ANDREWS, John Tuttle (D N.Y.) May 29, 1803-June 11, 1894; House 1837-39.

ANDREWS, Landaff Watson (W Ky.) Feb. 12, 1803-Dec. 23, 1887; House 1839-43.

ANDREWS, Mark (R N.D.) May 19, 1926- —; House Oct. 22, 1963-81; Senate 1981-87.

ANDREWS, Michael Allen (D Texas) Feb. 7, 1944- —; House 1983- —.

ANDREWS, Samuel George (R N.Y.) Oct. 16, 1796-June 11, 1863; House 1857-59.

ANDREWS, Sherlock James (W Ohio) Nov. 17, 1801-Feb. 11, 1880; House 1841-43.

ANDREWS, Walter Gresham (R N.Y.) July 16, 1889-March 5, 1949; House 1931-49.

ANDREWS, William Ezekiel (R Neb.) Dec. 17, 1854-Jan. 19, 1942; House 1895-97, 1919-23.

ANDREWS, William Henry (R N.M.) Jan. 14, 1846-Jan. 16, 1919; House (Terr. Del.) 1905-Jan. 7, 1912.

ANDREWS, William Noble (R Md.) Nov. 13, 1876-Dec. 27, 1937; House 1919-21.

ANDRUS, John Emory (R N.Y.) Feb. 16, 1841-Dec. 26, 1934; House 1905-13.

ANFUSO, Victor L'Episcopo (D N.Y.) March 10, 1905-Dec. 28, 1966; House 1951-53, 1955-63.

ANGEL, William G. (JD N.Y.) July 17, 1790-Aug. 13, 1858; House 1825-27, 1829-33 (1825-27 John Quincy Adams Democrat).

ANGELL, Homer Daniel (R Ore.) Jan. 12, 1875-March 31, 1968; House 1939-55.

ANKENY, Levi (R Wash.) Aug. 1, 1844-March 29, 1921; Senate 1903-09.

ANNUNZIO, Frank (D Ill.) Jan. 12, 1915- —; House 1965- —.

ANSBERRY, Timothy Thomas (D Ohio) Dec. 24, 1871-July 5, 1943; House 1907-Jan. 9, 1915.

ANSORGE, Martin Charles (R N.Y.) Jan. 1, 1882-Feb. 4, 1967; House 1921-23.

ANTHONY, Beryl Franklin Jr. (D Ark.) Feb. 21, 1938- —; House 1979- —.

ANTHONY, Daniel Read Jr. (R Kan.) Aug. 22, 1870-Aug. 4, 1931; House May 23, 1907-29.

ANTHONY, Henry Bowen (R R.I.) April 1, 1815-Sept. 2, 1884; Senate 1859-Sept. 2, 1884; Pres. pro tempore 1869-73; Gov. 1849-51 (Whig).

ANTHONY, Joseph Biles (D Pa.) June 19, 1795-Jan. 10, 1851; House 1833-37.

ANTONY, Edwin Le Roy (D Texas) Jan. 5, 1852-Jan. 16, 1913; House June 14, 1892-93.

APLIN, Henry Harrison (R Mich.) April 15, 1841-July 23, 1910; House Oct. 20, 1901-03.

APPLEBY, Stewart Hoffman (son of Theodore Frank Appleby) (R N.J.) May 17, 1890-Jan. 12, 1964; House Nov. 3, 1925-27.

APPLEBY, Theodore Frank (father of Stewart Hoffman Appleby) (R N.J.) Oct. 10, 1864-Dec. 15, 1924; House 1921-23.

APPLEGATE, Douglas (D Ohio) March 27, 1928- —; House 1977- —.

APPLETON, John (D Maine) Feb. 11, 1815-Aug. 22, 1864; House 1851-53.

APPLETON, Nathan (cousin of William Appleton) (HTW Mass.) Oct. 6, 1779-July 14, 1861; House 1831-33, June 9-Sept. 28, 1842.

APPLETON, William (cousin of Nathan Appleton) (W Mass.) Nov. 16, 1786-Feb. 15, 1862; House 1851-55 March 4-Sept. 27, 1861.

APSLEY, Lewis Dewart (R Mass.) Sept. 29, 1852-Apri 11, 1925; House 1893-97.

ARCHER, John (father of Stevenson Archer) (D Md. May 5, 1741-Sept. 28, 1810; House 1801-07.

ARCHER, Stevenson (son of John Archer, father o Stevenson Archer, below) (D Md.) Oct. 11, 1786 June 26, 1848; House Oct. 26, 1811-17, 1819-21.

ARCHER, Stevenson (son of Stevenson Archer, above grandson of John Archer) (D Md.) Feb. 28, 1827 Aug. 2, 1898; House 1867-75.

ARCHER, William Reynolds Jr. (R Texas) March 22 1928- —; House 1971- —.

ARCHER, William Segar (nephew of Joseph Egglestor (W Va.) March 5, 1789-March 28, 1855; House Jan 3, 1820-35; Senate 1841-47.

ARENDS, Leslie Cornelius (R Ill.) Sept. 27, 1895-Jul 16, 1985; House 1935-Dec. 31, 1974.

ARENS, Henry (FL Minn.) Nov. 21, 1873-Oct. 6, 196: House 1933-35.

ARENTZ, Samuel Shaw "Ulysses" (R Nev.) Jan. & 1879-June 17, 1934; House 1921-23, 1925-33.

ARMEY, Richard K. (R Texas) July 7, 1940- —; Hous 1985- —.

ARMFIELD, Robert Franklin (D N.C.) July 9, 182 Nov. 9, 1898; House 1879-83.

ARMSTRONG, David Hartley (D Mo.) Oct. 21, 181 March 18, 1893; Senate Sept. 20, 1877-Jan. 26, 187

ARMSTRONG, James (brother of John Armstrong) Pa.) Aug. 29, 1748-May 6, 1828; House 1793-95.

ARMSTRONG, John (brother of James Armstrong) (N.Y.) Nov. 25, 1758-April 1, 1843; Senate Nov. 1800-Feb. 5, 1802; Nov. 10, 1803-June 30, 1804; Sec of War 1813-14.

ARMSTRONG, Moses Kimball (D Dakota) Sept.] 1832-Jan. 11, 1906; House (Terr. Del.) 1871-75.

ARMSTRONG, Orland Kay (R Mo.) Oct. 2, 1893- House 1951-53.

ARMSTRONG, William (D Va.) Dec. 23, 1782-May] 1865; House 1825-33.

ARMSTRONG, William Hepburn (R Pa.) Sept. 7, 18: May 14, 1919; House 1869-71.

ARMSTRONG, William Lester (R Colo.) March 1937- —; House 1973-79; Senate 1979- —.

ARNELL, Samuel Mayes (R Tenn.) May 3, 1833-July 20, 1903; House July 24, 1866-71.

ARNOLD, Benedict (brother-in-law of Matthias J. Bovee) (— N.Y.) Oct. 5, 1780-March 3, 1849; House 1829-31.

ARNOLD, Isaac Newton (R Ill.) Nov. 30, 1815-April 24, 1884; House 1861-65.

ARNOLD, Laurence Fletcher (D Ill.) June 8, 1891-Dec. 6, 1966; House 1937-43.

ARNOLD, Lemuel Hastings (great-granduncle of Theodore Francis Green) (LW R.I.) Jan. 29, 1792-June 27, 1852; House 1845-47; Gov. 1831-33 (Democratic Republican).

ARNOLD, Marshall (D Mo.) Oct. 21, 1845-June 12, 1913; House 1891-95.

ARNOLD, Samuel (D Conn.) June 1, 1806-May 5, 1869; House 1857-59.

ARNOLD, Samuel Greene (granduncle of Theodore Francis Green) (R R.I.) April 12, 1821-Feb. 14, 1880; Senate Dec. 1, 1862-63.

ARNOLD, Samuel Washington (R Mo.) Sept. 21, 1879-Dec. 18, 1961; House 1943-49.

ARNOLD, Thomas Dickens (W Tenn.) May 3, 1798-May 26, 1870; House 1831-33, 1841-43.

ARNOLD, Warren Otis (R R.I.) June 3, 1839-April 1, 1910; House 1887-91, 1895-97.

ARNOLD, William Carlile (R Pa.) July 15, 1851-March 20, 1906; House 1895-99.

ARNOLD, William Wright (D Ill.) Oct. 14, 1877-Nov. 23, 1957; House 1923-Sept. 16, 1935.

ARNOT, John Jr. (D N.Y.) March 11, 1831-Nov. 20, 1886; House 1883-Nov. 20, 1886.

ARRINGTON, Archibald Hunter (uncle of Archibald Hunter Arrington Williams) (D N.C.) Nov. 13, 1809-July 20, 1872; House 1841-45.

ARTHUR, William Evans (D Ky.) March 3, 1825-May 18, 1897; House 1871-75.

ASH, Michael Woolston (— Pa.) March 5, 1789-Dec. 14, 1858; House 1835-37.

ASHBROOK, Jean S. (widow of John Milan Ashbrook, daughter-in-law of William Albert Ashbrook) (R Ohio) Sept. 21, 1934-—; House July 12, 1982-83.

ASHBROOK, John Milan (husband of Jean S. Ashbrook, son of William Albert Ashbrook) (R Ohio) Sept. 21, 1928-April 4, 1982; House 1961-April 4, 1982.

ASHBROOK, William Albert (father of John Milan Ashbrook, father-in-law of Jean S. Ashbrook) (D Ohio) July 1, 1867-Jan. 1, 1940; House 1907-21, 1935-Jan. 1, 1940.

ASHE, John Baptista (uncle of John Baptista Ashe of Tenn., Thomas Samuel Ashe and William Shepperd Ashe) (F N.C.) 1748-Nov. 27, 1802; House 1789-93; Cont. Cong. 1787.

ASHE, John Baptista (brother of William Shepperd Ashe, nephew of John Baptista Ashe of N.C. and cousin of Thomas Samuel Ashe) (W Tenn.) 1810-Dec. 29, 1857; House 1843-45.

ASHE, Thomas Samuel (nephew of John Baptista Ashe of N.C., cousin of John Baptista Ashe of Tenn. and William Shepperd Ashe) (D N.C.) July 21, 1812-Feb. 4, 1887; House 1873-77 (1873-75 Conservative).

ASHE, William Shepperd (brother of John Baptista Ashe of Tenn., nephew of John Baptista Ashe of N.C., cousin of Thomas Samuel Ashe) (D N.C.) Aug. 12, 1813-Sept. 14, 1862; House 1849-55.

ASHLEY, Chester (D Ark.) June 1, 1790-April 29, 1848; Senate Nov. 8, 1844-April 29, 1848.

ASHLEY, Delos Rodeyn (R Nev.) Feb. 19, 1828-July 18, 1873; House 1865-69.

ASHLEY, Henry (— N.Y.) Feb. 19, 1778-Jan. 14, 1829; House 1825-27.

ASHLEY, James Mitchell (great-grandfather of Thomas William Ludlow Ashley) (R Ohio) Nov. 14, 1824-Sept. 16, 1896; House 1859-69; Gov. (Mont. Terr.) 1869-70.

ASHLEY, Thomas William Ludlow (great-grandson of James Mitchell Ashley) (D Ohio) Jan. 11, 1923-—; House 1955-81.

ASHLEY, William Henry (W Mo.) 1778-March 26, 1838; House Oct. 31, 1831-37.

ASHMORE, John Durant (D S.C.) Aug. 18, 1819-Dec. 5, 1871; House 1859-Dec. 21, 1860.

ASHMORE, Robert Thomas (D S.C.) Feb. 22, 1904-—; House June 2, 1953-69.

ASHMUN, Eli Porter (father of George Ashmun) (— Mass.) June 24, 1770-May 10, 1819; Senate June 12, 1816-May 10, 1818.

ASHMUN, George (son of Eli Porter Ashmun) (W Mass.) Dec. 25, 1804-July 16, 1870; House 1845-51.

ASHURST, Henry Fountain (D Ariz.) Sept. 13, 1874-May 31, 1962; Senate March 27, 1912-41.

ASPER, Joel Funk (RR Mo.) April 20, 1822-Oct. 1, 1872; House 1869-71.

ASPIN, Les (D Wis.) July 21, 1938- —; House 1971- —.

ASPINALL, Wayne Norviel (D Colo.) April 3, 1896-Oct. 9, 1983; House 1949-73.

ASWELL, James Benjamin (D La.) Dec. 23, 1869-March 16, 1931; House 1913-March 16, 1931.

ATCHISON, David Rice (W Mo.) Aug. 11, 1807-Jan. 26, 1886; Senate Oct. 14, 1843-55; Pres. pro tempore 1846-49, 1852-54.

ATHERTON, Charles Gordon (son of Charles Humphrey Atherton) (D N.H.) July 4, 1804-Nov. 15, 1853; House 1837-43; Senate 1843-49, 1853-Nov. 15, 1853.

ATHERTON, Charles Humphrey (father of Charles Gordon Atherton) (F N.H.) Aug. 14, 1773-Jan. 8, 1853; House 1815-17.

ATHERTON, Gibson (D Ohio) Jan. 19, 1831-Nov. 10, 1887; House 1879-83.

ATKESON, William Oscar (R Mo.) Aug. 24, 1854-Oct. 16, 1931; House 1921-23.

ATKINS, Chester Greenough (D Mass.) April 14, 1948- —; House 1985- —.

ATKINS, John DeWitt Clinton (D Tenn.) June 4, 1825-June 2, 1908; House 1857-59, 1873-83.

ATKINSON, Archibald (D Va.) Sept. 15, 1792-Jan. 7, 1872; House 1843-49.

ATKINSON, Eugene Vincent (D Pa.) April 5, 1927- —; House 1979-83 (Oct. 14, 1981-83 Republican.)

ATKINSON, George Wesley (R W.Va.) June 29, 1845-April 4, 1925; House Feb. 26, 1890-91; Gov. 1897-1901.

ATKINSON, Louis Evans (R Pa.) April 16, 1841-Feb. 5, 1910; House 1883-93.

ATKINSON, Richard Merrill (D Tenn.) Feb. 6, 1894-April 29, 1947; House 1937-39.

ATWATER, John Wilbur (P N.C.) Dec. 27, 1840-July 4, 1910; House 1899-1901.

ATWOOD, David (R Wis.) Dec. 15, 1815-Dec. 11, 1889; House Feb. 23, 1870-71.

ATWOOD, Harrison Henry (R Mass.) Aug. 26, 1863-Oct. 22, 1954; House 1895-97.

AUCHINCLOSS, James Coats (R N.J.) Jan. 19, 1885-Oct. 2, 1976; House 1943-65.

AuCOIN, Les (D Ore.) Oct. 21, 1942- —; House 1975- —.

AUF DER HEIDE, Oscar Louis (D N.J.) Dec. 8, 1874-March 29, 1945; House 1925-35.

AUSTIN, Albert Elmer (stepfather of Clare Boothe Luce) (R Conn.) Nov. 15, 1877-Jan. 26, 1942; House 1939-41.

AUSTIN, Archibald (D Va.) Aug. 11, 1772-Oct. 16, 1837; House 1817-19.

AUSTIN, Richard Wilson (R Tenn.) Aug. 26, 1857-April 20, 1919; House 1909-19.

AUSTIN, Warren Robinson (R Vt.) Nov. 12, 1877-Dec. 25, 1962; Senate April 1, 1931-Aug. 2, 1946.

AVERETT, Thomas Hamlet (D Va.) July 10, 1800-June 30, 1855; House 1849-53.

AVERILL, John Thomas (R Minn.) March 1, 1825-Oct. 3, 1889; House 1871-75.

AVERY, Daniel (D N.Y.) Sept. 18, 1766-Jan. 30, 1842; House 1811-15, Sept. 30, 1816-17.

AVERY, John (R Mich.) Feb. 29, 1824-Jan. 21, 1914 House 1893-97.

AVERY, William Henry (R Kan.) Aug. 11, 1911- — House 1955-65; Gov. 1965-67.

AVERY, William Tecumsah (D Tenn.) Nov. 11, 1819 May 22, 1880; House 1857-61.

AVIS, Samuel Brashear (R W.Va.) Feb. 19, 1872-June 8 1924; House 1913-15.

AXTELL, Samuel Beach (D Calif.) Oct. 14, 1819-Aug. 6 1891; House 1867-71; Gov. (Utah Terr.) 1874-75 Gov. (N.M. Terr.) 1875 (1874-75 Republican).

AYCRIGG, John Bancker (W N.J.) July 9, 1798-Nov. 8 1856; House 1837-39, 1841-43.

AYER, Richard Small (R Va.) Oct. 9, 1829-Dec. 14, 1896 House Jan. 31, 1870-71.

AYERS, Roy Elmer (D Mont.) Nov. 9, 1882-May 23 1955; House 1933-37; Gov. 1937-41.

AYRES, Steven Beckwith (ID N.Y.) Oct. 27, 1861-Jun 1, 1929; House 1911-13.

AYRES, William Augustus (D Kan.) April 19, 1867-Feb 17, 1952; House 1915-21, 1923-Aug. 22, 1934.

AYRES, William Hanes (R Ohio) Feb. 5, 1916- —; Hous 1951-71.

BABBITT, Clinton (D Wis.) Nov. 16, 1831-March 1? 1907; House 1891-93.

BABBITT, Elijah (R Pa.) July 29, 1795-Jan. 9, 188? House 1859-63 (1859-61 Unionist).

BABCOCK, Alfred (W N.Y.) April 15, 1805-May 1? 1871; House 1841-43.

BABCOCK, Joseph Weeks (grandson of Joseph Weeks) (R Wis.) March 6, 1850-April 27, 1909; House 1893-1907.

BABCOCK, Leander (D N.Y.) March 1, 1811-Aug. 18, 1864; House 1851-53.

BABCOCK, William (− N.Y.) 1785-Oct. 20, 1838; House 1831-33.

BABKA, John Joseph (D Ohio) March 16, 1884-March 22, 1937; House 1919-21.

BACHARACH, Isaac (R N.J.) Jan. 5, 1870-Sept. 5, 1956; House 1915-37.

BACHMAN, Nathan Lynn (D Tenn.) Aug. 2, 1878-April 23, 1937; Senate Feb. 28, 1933-April 23, 1937.

BACHMAN, Reuben Knecht (D Pa.) Aug. 6, 1834-Sept. 19, 1911; House 1879-81.

BACHMANN, Carl George (R W.Va.) May 14, 1890-Jan. 22, 1980; House 1925-33.

BACON, Augustus Octavius (cousin of William Schley Howard) (D Ga.) Oct. 20, 1839-Feb. 14, 1914; Senate 1895-Feb. 14, 1914.

BACON, Ezekiel (son of John Bacon, father of William Johnson Bacon) (D Mass.) Sept. 1, 1776-Oct. 18, 1870; House Sept. 16, 1807-13.

BACON, Henry (D N.Y.) March 14, 1846-March 25, 1915; House Dec. 6, 1886-89, 1891-93.

BACON, John (father of Ezekiel Bacon, grandfather of William Johnson Bacon) (− Mass.) April 5, 1738-Oct. 25, 1820; House 1801-03.

BACON, Mark Reeves (R Mich.) Feb. 29, 1852-Aug. 20, 1941; House March 4-Dec. 13, 1917.

BACON, Robert Low (R N.Y.) July 23, 1884-Sept. 12, 1938; House 1923-Sept. 12, 1938.

BACON, William Johnson (son of Ezekiel Bacon, grandson of John Bacon) (R N.Y.) Feb. 18, 1803-July 3, 1889; House 1877-79.

BADGER, De Witt Clinton (D Ohio) Aug. 7, 1858-May 20, 1926; House 1903-05.

BADGER, George Edmund (W N.C.) April 17, 1795-May 11, 1866; Senate Nov. 25, 1846-55; Secy. of the Navy March 5-Sept. 11, 1841.

BADGER, Luther (− N.Y.) April 10, 1785-1869; House 1825-27.

BADHAM, Robert E. (R Calif.) June 9, 1929-−; House 1977-−.

BADILLO, Herman (D N.Y.) Aug. 21, 1929-−; House 1971-Dec. 31, 1977.

BAER, George Jr. (F Md.) 1763-April 3, 1834; House 1797-1801, 1815-17.

BAER, John Miller (R N.D.) March 29, 1886-Feb. 18, 1970; House July 10, 1917-21 (1917-19 Nonpartisan League).

BAFALIS, Louis Arthur (R Fla.) Sept. 28, 1929-−; House 1973-83.

BAGBY, Arthur Pendleton (D Ala.) 1794-Sept. 21, 1858; Senate Nov. 24, 1841-June 16, 1848; Gov. 1837-41.

BAGBY, John Courts (D Ill.) Jan. 24, 1819-April 4, 1896; House 1875-77.

BAGLEY, George Augustus (R N.Y.) July 22, 1826-May 12, 1915; House 1875-79.

BAGLEY, John Holroyd Jr. (D N.Y.) Nov. 26, 1832-Oct. 23, 1902; House 1875-77, 1883-85.

BAILEY, Alexander Hamilton (R N.Y.) Aug. 14, 1817-April 20, 1874; House Nov. 30, 1867-71.

BAILEY, Cleveland Monroe (D W.Va.) July 15, 1886-July 13, 1965; House 1945-47, 1949-63.

BAILEY, David Jackson (SRD Ga.) March 11, 1812-June 14, 1897; House 1851-55.

BAILEY, Donald Allen (D Pa.) July 21, 1945-−; House 1979-83.

BAILEY, Goldsmith Fox (R Mass.) July 17, 1823-May 8, 1862; House 1861-May 8, 1862.

BAILEY, James Edmund (D Tenn.) Aug. 15, 1822-Dec. 29, 1885; Senate Jan. 19, 1877-81.

BAILEY, Jeremiah (W Maine) May 1, 1773-July 6, 1853; House 1835-37.

BAILEY, John (− Mass.) 1786-June 26, 1835; House Dec. 13, 1824-31.

BAILEY, John Mosher (R N.Y.) Aug. 24, 1838-Feb. 21, 1916; House Nov. 5, 1878-81.

BAILEY, Joseph (D Pa.) March 18, 1810-Aug. 26, 1885; House 1861-65.

BAILEY, Joseph Weldon (father of Joseph Weldon Bailey Jr.) (D Texas) Oct. 6, 1862-April 13, 1929; House 1891-1901; Senate 1901-Jan. 3, 1913.

BAILEY, Joseph Weldon Jr. (son of Joseph Weldon Bailey) (D Texas) Dec. 15, 1892-July 17, 1943; House 1933-35.

BAILEY, Josiah William (D N.C.) Sept. 14, 1873-Dec. 15, 1946; Senate 1931-Dec. 15, 1946.

BAILEY, Ralph Emerson (R Mo.) July 14, 1878-April 8, 1948; House 1925-27.

BAILEY, Theodorus (D N.Y.) Oct. 12, 1758-Sept. 6, 1828; House 1793-97, 1799-1801, Oct. 6, 1801-03; Senate 1803-Jan. 16, 1804.

BAILEY, Warren Worth (D Pa.) Jan. 8, 1855-Nov. 9, 1928; House 1913-17.

BAILEY, Willis Joshua (R Kan.) Oct. 12, 1854-May 19, 1932; House 1899-1901; Gov. 1903-05.

BAILEY, Wendell (R Mo.) July 31, 1940- —; House 1981-83.

BAIRD, David (father of David Baird Jr.) (R N.J.) April 7, 1839-Feb. 25, 1927; Senate Feb. 23, 1918-19.

BAIRD, David Jr. (son of David Baird) (R N.J.) Oct. 10, 1881-Feb. 28, 1955; Senate Nov. 30, 1929-Dec. 1, 1930.

BAIRD, Joseph Edward (R Ohio) Nov. 12, 1865-June 14, 1942; House 1929-31.

BAIRD, Samuel Thomas (D La.) May 5, 1861-April 22, 1899; House 1897-April 22, 1899.

BAKER, Caleb (— N.Y.) 1762-June 26, 1849; House 1819-21.

BAKER, Charles Simeon (R N.Y.) Feb. 18, 1839-April 21, 1902; House 1885-91.

BAKER, David Jewett (D Ill.) Sept. 7, 1792-Aug. 6, 1869; Senate Nov. 12-Dec. 11, 1830.

BAKER, Edward Dickinson (R Ore.) Feb. 24, 1811-Oct. 21, 1861; House 1845-Jan. 15, 1847 (Whig Ill.), 1849-51 (Whig Ill.); Senate Oct. 2, 1860-Oct. 21, 1861.

BAKER, Ezra (— N.J.) ?-?; House 1815-17.

BAKER, Henry Moore (R N.H.) Jan. 11, 1841-May 30, 1912; House 1893-97.

BAKER, Howard Henry (husband of Irene B. Baker, father of Howard Henry Baker Jr.) (R Tenn.) Jan. 12, 1902-Jan. 7, 1964; House 1951-Jan. 7, 1964.

BAKER, Howard Henry Jr. (son of Howard Henry Baker and Irene B. Baker, son-in-law of Everett McKinley Dirksen) (R Tenn.) Nov. 15, 1925- —; Senate 1967-85; Senate majority leader 1981-85.

BAKER, Irene B. (widow of Howard Henry Baker, mother of Howard Henry Baker Jr.) (R Tenn.) Nov. 17, 1901- —; House March 10, 1964-65.

BAKER, Jacob Thompson (D N.J.) April 13, 1847-Dec. 7, 1919; House 1913-15.

BAKER, Jehu (Fus. Ill.) Nov. 4, 1822-March 1, 1903; House 1865-69, 1887-89, 1897-99 (1865-69, 1887-89 Republican).

BAKER, John (F Va.) ?-Aug. 18, 1823; House 1811-13.

BAKER, John Harris (R Ind.) Feb. 28, 1832-Oct. 21, 1915; House 1875-81.

BAKER, LaMar (R Tenn.) Dec. 19, 1915- —; House 1971-75.

BAKER, Lucien (R Kan.) June 8, 1846-June 21, 1907; Senate 1895-1901.

BAKER, Osmyn (W Mass.) May 18, 1800-Feb. 9, 1875; House Jan. 14, 1840-45.

BAKER, Richard Hugh (R La.) May 22, 1948- —; House 1987- —.

BAKER, Robert (D N.Y.) April 1862-June 15, 1943; House 1903-05.

BAKER, Stephen (R N.Y.) Aug. 12, 1819-June 9, 1875; House 1861-63.

BAKER, William (PP Kan.) April 29, 1831-Feb. 11, 1910; House 1891-97.

BAKER, William Benjamin (R Md.) July 22, 1840-May 17, 1911; House 1895-1901.

BAKER, William Henry (R N.Y.) Jan. 17, 1827-Nov. 25, 1911; House 1875-79.

BAKEWELL, Charles Montague (R Conn.) April 24, 1867-Sept. 19, 1957; House 1933-35.

BAKEWELL, Claude Ignatius (R Mo.) Aug. 9, 1912- —; House 1947-49, March 9, 1951-53.

BALDRIGE, Howard Malcolm (R Neb.) June 23, 1894-Jan. 19, 1985; House 1931-33.

BALDUS, Alvin James (D Wis.) April 27, 1926- —; House 1975-81.

BALDWIN, Abraham (F Ga.) Nov. 22, 1754-April 4, 1807; House 1789-99; Senate 1799-April 4, 1807; Pres. pro tempore 1801-02; Cont. Cong. 1785, 1787-89.

BALDWIN, Augustus Carpenter (UD Mich.) Dec. 24, 1817-Jan. 21, 1903; House 1863-65.

BALDWIN, Harry Streett (D Md.) Aug. 21, 1894-Oct. 19, 1952; House 1943-47.

BALDWIN, Henry (F Pa.) Jan. 14, 1780-April 21, 1844; House 1817-May 8, 1822; Assoc. Justice Supreme Court 1830-44.

BALDWIN, Henry Alexander (R Hawaii) Jan. 12, 1871-Oct. 8, 1946; House (Terr. Del.) March 25, 1922-23.

BALDWIN, Henry Porter (R Mich.) Feb. 22, 1814-Dec. 31, 1892; Senate Nov. 17, 1879-81; Gov. 1869-73.

BALDWIN, John (— Conn.) April 5, 1772-March 27, 1850; House 1825-29.

BALDWIN, John Denison (R Mass.) Sept. 28, 1809-July 8, 1883; House 1863-69.

BALDWIN, John Finley Jr. (R Calif.) June 28, 1915-March 9, 1966; House 1955-March 9, 1966.

BALDWIN, Joseph Clark (R N.Y.) Jan. 11, 1897-Oct. 27, 1957; House March 11, 1941-47.

BALDWIN, Melvin Riley (D Minn.) April 12, 1838-April 15, 1901; House 1893-95.

BALDWIN, Raymond Earl (R Conn.) Aug. 31, 1893-Oct. 4, 1986; Senate Dec. 27, 1946-Dec. 17, 1949; Gov. 1939-41, 1943-46.

BALDWIN, Roger Sherman (son of Simeon Baldwin) (W Conn.) Jan. 4, 1793-Feb. 19, 1863; Senate Nov. 11, 1847-51; Gov. 1844-46.

BALDWIN, Simeon (father of Roger Sherman Baldwin) (F Conn.) Dec. 14, 1761-May 26, 1851; House 1803-05.

BALL, Edward (W Ohio) Nov. 6, 1811-Nov. 22, 1872; House 1853-57.

BALL, Joseph Hurst (R Minn.) Nov. 3, 1905- —; Senate Oct. 14, 1940-Nov. 17, 1942, 1943-49.

BALL, Lewis Heisler (R Del.) Sept. 21, 1861-Oct. 18, 1932; House 1901-03; Senate March 3, 1903-05, 1919-25.

BALL, Thomas Henry (D Texas) Jan. 14, 1859-May 7, 1944; House 1897-Nov. 16, 1903.

BALL, Thomas Raymond (R Conn.) Feb. 12, 1896-June 16, 1943; House 1939-41.

BALL, William Lee (D Va.) Jan. 2, 1781-Feb. 28, 1824; House 1817-Feb. 28, 1824.

BALLENGER, T. Cass (R N.C.) Dec. 6, 1926- —; House 1987- —.

BALLENTINE, John Goff (D Tenn.) May 20, 1825-Nov. 23, 1915; House 1883-87.

BALLOU, Latimer Whipple (R R.I.) March 1, 1812-May 9, 1900; House 1875-81.

BALTZ, William Nicolas (D Ill.) Feb. 5, 1860-Aug. 22, 1943; House 1913-15.

BANDSTRA, Bert (D Iowa) Jan. 25, 1922- —; House 1965-67.

BANKHEAD, John Hollis (father of John Hollis Bankhead II and William Brockman Bankhead, grandfather of Walter Will Bankhead) (D Ala.) Sept. 13, 1842-March 1, 1920; House 1887-1907; Senate June 18, 1907-March 1, 1920.

BANKHEAD, John Hollis II (son of John Hollis Bankhead, brother of William Brockman Bankhead, father of Walter Will Bankhead) (D Ala.) July 8, 1872-June 12, 1946; Senate 1931-June 12, 1946.

BANKHEAD, Walter Will (son of John Hollis Bankhead II, grandson of John Hollis Bankhead, nephew of William Brockman Bankhead) (D Ala.) July 21, 1897- —; House Jan. 3-Feb. 1, 1941.

BANKHEAD, William Brockman (son of John Hollis Bankhead, brother of John Hollis Bankhead II, uncle of Walter Will Bankhead) (D Ala.) April 12, 1874-Sept. 15, 1940; House 1917-Sept. 15, 1940; House majority leader 1936; Speaker June 4, 1936-Sept. 15, 1940.

BANKS, John (W Pa.) Oct. 17, 1793-April 3, 1864; House 1831-36.

BANKS, Linn (D Va.) Jan. 23, 1784-Jan. 13, 1842; House April 28, 1838-Dec. 6, 1841.

BANKS, Nathaniel Prentice (R Mass.) Jan. 30, 1816-Sept. 1, 1894; House 1853-Dec. 24, 1857, Dec. 4, 1865-73, 1875-79, 1889-91 (1853-55 Coalition Democrat, 1855-57 American Party, Dec. 4, 1865-67 Union Republican, 1875-79 Liberal Republican); Speaker 1855-57; Gov. 1858-61.

BANNING, Henry Blackstone (D Ohio) Nov. 10, 1836-Dec. 10, 1881; House 1873-79.

BANNON, Henry Towne (R Ohio) June 5, 1867-Sept. 6, 1950; House 1905-09.

BANTA, Parke Monroe (R Mo.) Nov. 21, 1891-May 12, 1970; House 1947-49.

BARBER, Hiram Jr. (R Ill.) March 24, 1835-Aug. 5, 1924; House 1879-81.

BARBER, Isaac Ambrose (R Md.) Jan. 26, 1852-March 1, 1909; House 1897-99.

BARBER, Joel Allen (R Wis.) Jan. 17, 1809-June 17, 1881; House 1871-75.

BARBER, Laird Howard (D Pa.) Oct. 25, 1848-Feb. 16, 1928; House 1899-1901.

BARBER, Levi (— Ohio) Oct. 16, 1777-April 23, 1833; House 1817-19, 1821-23.

BARBER, Noyes (uncle of Edwin Barbour Morgan and Christopher Morgan) (D Conn.) April 28, 1781-Jan. 3, 1844; House 1821-35.

BARBOUR, Henry Ellsworth (R Calif.) March 8, 1877-March 21, 1945; House 1919-33.

BARBOUR, James (brother of Philip Pendleton Barbour, cousin of John Strode Barbour) (AD/SR Va.) June 10, 1775-June 7, 1842; Senate Jan. 2, 1815-March 7, 1825; Pres. pro tempore 1819; Gov. 1812-14; Secy. of War 1825-28.

BARBOUR, John Strode (father of John Strode Barbour, below, cousin of James Barbour and Philip Pendleton Barbour) (SRD Va.) Aug. 8, 1790-Jan. 12, 1855; House 1823-33.

BARBOUR, John Strode (son of John Strode Barbour, above) (D Va.) Dec. 29, 1820-May 14, 1892; House 1881-87; Senate 1889-May 14, 1892.

BARBOUR, Lucien (FS/T/KN Ind.) March 4, 1811-July 19, 1880; House 1855-57.

BARBOUR, Philip Pendleton (brother of James Barbour, cousin of John Strode Barbour) (D Va.) May 25, 1783-Feb. 25, 1841; House Sept. 19, 1814-25, 1827-Oct. 15, 1830; Speaker 1821-23; Assoc. Justice Supreme Court 1836-41.

BARBOUR, William Warren (R N.J.) July 3, 1888-Nov. 22, 1943; Senate Dec. 1, 1931-37, Nov. 9, 1938-Nov. 22, 1943.

BARCHFELD, Andrew Jackson (R Pa.) May 18, 1863-Jan. 28, 1922; House 1905-17.

BARCLAY, Charles Frederick (R Pa.) May 9, 1844-March 9, 1914; House 1907-11.

BARCLAY, David (D Pa.) 1823-Sept. 10, 1889; House 1855-57.

BARD, David (− Pa.) 1744-March 12, 1815; House 1795-99, 1803-March 12, 1815.

BARD, Thomas Robert (R Calif.) Dec. 8, 1841-March 5, 1915; Senate Feb. 7, 1900-05.

BARDEN, Graham Arthur (D N.C.) Sept. 25, 1896-Jan. 29, 1967; House 1935-61.

BARHAM, John All (R Calif.) July 17, 1843-Jan. 22, 1926; House 1895-1901.

BARING, Walter Stephan (D Nev.) Sept. 9, 1911-July 13, 1975; House 1949-53, 1957-73.

BARKER, Abraham Andrews (UR Pa.) March 30, 1816-March 18, 1898; House 1865-67.

BARKER, David Jr. (− N.H.) Jan. 8, 1797-April 1, 1834; House 1827-29.

BARKER, Joseph (D Mass.) Oct. 19, 1751-July 5, 1815; House 1805-09.

BARKLEY, Alben William (D Ky.) Nov. 24, 1877-April 30, 1956; House 1913-27; Senate 1927-Jan. 19, 1949, 1955-April 30, 1956; Senate majority leader 1937-47; Vice President 1949-53.

BARKSDALE, Ethelbert (brother of William Barksdale) (D Miss.) Jan. 4, 1824-Feb. 17, 1893; House 1883-87.

BARKSDALE, William (brother of Ethelbert Barksdale) (SRD Miss.) Aug. 21, 1821-July 2, 1863; House 1853-Jan. 12, 1861.

BARLOW, Bradley (NR Vt.) May 12, 1814-Nov. 6, 1889; House 1879-81.

BARLOW, Charles Averill (P/D Calif.) March 17, 1858-Oct. 3, 1927; House 1897-99.

BARLOW, Stephen (D Pa.) June 13, 1779-Aug. 24, 1845; House 1827-29.

BARNARD, D. Douglas Jr. (D Ga.) March 20, 1922-−; House 1977-−.

BARNARD, Daniel Dewey (W N.Y.) July 16, 1797-April 24, 1861; House 1827-29, 1839-45.

BARNARD, Isaac Dutton (F Pa.) July 18, 1791-Feb. 28, 1834; Senate 1827-Dec. 6, 1831.

BARNARD, William Oscar (R Ind.) Oct. 25, 1852-April 8, 1939; House 1909-11.

BARNES, Demas (D N.Y.) April 4, 1827-May 1, 1888; House 1867-69.

BARNES, George Thomas (D Ga.) Aug. 14, 1833-Oct. 24, 1901; House 1885-91.

BARNES, James Martin (D Ill.) Jan. 9, 1899-June 8, 1958; House 1939-43.

BARNES, Lyman Eddy (D Wis.) June 30, 1855-Jan. 16, 1904; House 1893-95.

BARNES, Michael Darr (D Md.) Sept. 3, 1943-−; House 1979-87.

BARNETT, William (SRD Ga.) March 4, 1761-April 1832; House Oct. 5, 1812-15.

BARNEY, John (F Md.) Jan. 18, 1785-Jan. 26, 1857; House 1825-29.

BARNEY, Samuel Stebbins (R Wis.) Jan. 31, 1846-Dec. 31, 1919; House 1895-1903.

BARNHART, Henry A. (D Ind.) Sept. 11, 1858-March 26, 1934; House Nov. 3, 1908-19.

BARNITZ, Charles Augustus (W Pa.) Sept. 11, 1780-Jan. 8, 1850; House 1833-35.

BARNUM, William Henry (D Conn.) Sept. 17, 1818-April 30, 1889; House 1867-May 18, 1876; Senate May 18, 1876-79; Chrmn. Dem. Nat. Comm. 1877-89.

BARNWELL, Robert (father of Robert Woodward Barnwell) (F S.C.) Dec. 21, 1761-Oct. 24, 1814; House 1791-93; Cont. Cong. 1788-89.

BARNWELL, Robert Woodward (son of Robert Barnwell) (D S.C.) Aug. 10, 1801-Nov. 24, 1882; House 1829-33; Senate June 4-Dec. 8, 1850.

BARR, Joseph Walker (D Ind.) Jan. 17, 1918- —; House 1959-61; Secy. of the Treasury 1968-69.

BARR, Samuel Fleming (R Pa.) June 15, 1829-May 29, 1919; House 1881-85.

BARR, Thomas Jefferson (D N.Y.) 1812-March 27, 1881; House Jan. 17, 1859-61.

BARRERE, Granville (nephew of Nelson Barrere) (R Ill.) July 11, 1829-Jan. 13, 1889; House 1873-75.

BARRERE, Nelson (uncle of Granville Barrere) (W Ohio) April 1, 1808-Aug. 20, 1883; House 1851-53.

BARRET, John Richard (D Mo.) Aug. 21, 1825-Nov. 2, 1903; House 1859-June 8, 1860, Dec. 3, 1860-61.

BARRETT, Frank Aloysius (R Wyo.) Nov. 10, 1892-May 30, 1962; House 1942-Dec. 31, 1950; Senate 1953-59; Gov. 1951-53.

BARRETT, William A. (D Pa.) Aug. 14, 1896-April 12, 1976; House 1945-47, 1949-April 12, 1976.

BARRETT, William Emerson (R Mass.) Dec. 29, 1858-Feb. 12, 1906; House 1895-99.

BARRINGER, Daniel Laurens (uncle of Daniel Moreau Barringer) (D N.C.) Oct. 1, 1788-Oct. 16, 1852; House Dec. 4, 1826-35.

BARRINGER, Daniel Moreau (nephew of Daniel Laurens Barringer) (W N.C.) July 30, 1806-Sept. 1, 1873; House 1843-49.

BARROW, Alexander (W La.) March 27, 1801-Dec. 19, 1846; Senate 1841-Dec. 19, 1846.

BARROW, Middleton Pope (great-grandson of Wilson Lumpkin) (D Ga.) Aug. 1, 1839-Dec. 23, 1903; Senate Nov. 15, 1882-83.

BARROW, Washington (W Tenn.) Oct. 5, 1807-Oct. 19, 1866; House 1847-49.

BARROWS, Samuel June (R Mass.) May 26, 1845-April 21, 1909; House 1897-99.

BARRY, Alexander Grant (R Ore.) Aug. 23, 1892-Dec. 28, 1952; Senate Nov. 9, 1938-39.

BARRY, Frederick George (D Miss.) Jan. 12, 1845-May 7, 1909; House 1885-89.

BARRY, Henry W. (R Miss.) April 1840-June 7, 1875; House Feb. 23, 1870-75.

BARRY, Robert Raymond (R N.Y.) May 15, 1915- —; House 1959-65.

BARRY, William Bernard (D N.Y.) July 21, 1902-Oct. 20, 1946; House Nov. 5, 1935-Oct. 20, 1946.

BARRY, William Taylor (D Ky.) Feb. 5, 1784-Aug. 30, 1835; House Aug. 8, 1810-11; Senate Dec. 16, 1814-May 1, 1816; Postmaster Gen. 1829-35.

BARRY, William Taylor Sullivan (D Miss.) Dec. 10, 1821-Jan. 29, 1868; House 1853-55.

BARSTOW, Gamaliel Henry (NR N.Y.) July 20, 1784-March 30, 1865; House 1831-33.

BARSTOW, Gideon (D Mass.) Sept. 7, 1783-March 26, 1852; House 1821-23.

BARTHOLDT, Richard (R Mo.) Nov. 2, 1855-March 19, 1932; House 1893-1915.

BARTINE, Horace Franklin (R Nev.) March 21, 1848-Aug. 27, 1918; House 1889-93.

BARTLETT, Bailey (F Mass.) Jan. 29, 1750-Sept. 9, 1830; House Nov. 27, 1797-1801.

BARTLETT, Charles Lafayette (D Ga.) Jan. 31, 1853-April 21, 1938; House 1895-1915.

BARTLETT, Dewey Follett (R Okla.) March 28, 1919-March 1, 1979; Senate 1973-79; Gov. 1967-71.

BARTLETT, Edward Lewis "Bob" (D Alaska) April 20, 1904-Dec. 11, 1968; House (Terr. Del.) 1945-59; Senate 1959-Dec. 11, 1968.

BARTLETT, Franklin (D N.Y.) Sept. 10, 1847-April 23, 1909; House 1893-97.

BARTLETT, George Arthur (D Nev.) Nov. 30, 1869-June 1, 1951; House 1907-11.

BARTLETT, Ichabod (AD N.H.) July 24, 1786-Oct. 19, 1853; House 1823-29.

BARTLETT, Josiah Jr. (— N.H.) Aug. 29, 1768-April 16, 1838; House 1811-13.

BARTLETT, Steve (R Texas) Sept. 19, 1947- —; House 1983- —.

BARTLETT, Thomas Jr. (D Vt.) June 18, 1808-Sept. 12, 1876; House 1851-53.

BARTLEY, Mordecai (— Ohio) Dec. 16, 1783-Oct. 10, 1870; House 1823-31; Gov. 1844-46 (Whig).

BARTON, Bruce (R N.Y.) Aug. 5, 1886-July 5, 1967; House Nov. 2, 1937-41.

BARTON, David (— Mo.) Dec. 14, 1783-Sept. 28, 1837; Senate Aug. 10, 1821-31.

BARTON, Joe (R Texas) Sept. 15, 1949- –; House 1985- –.

BARTON, Richard Walker (W Va.) 1800-March 15, 1859; House 1841-43.

BARTON, Samuel (JD N.Y.) July 27, 1785-Jan. 29, 1858; House 1835-37.

BARTON, Silas Reynolds (R Neb.) May 21, 1872-Nov. 7, 1916; House 1913-15.

BARTON, William Edward (cousin of Courtney Walker Hamlin) (D Mo.) April 11, 1868-July 29, 1955; House 1931-33.

BARWIG, Charles (D Wis.) March 19, 1837-Feb. 15, 1912; House 1889-95.

BASHFORD, Coles (I Ariz.) Jan. 24, 1816-April 25, 1878; House (Terr. Del.) 1867-69; Gov. 1855-58 (Republican Wis.).

BASS, Lyman Kidder (R N.Y.) Nov. 13, 1836-May 11, 1889; House 1873-77.

BASS, Perkins (R N.H.) Oct. 6, 1912- –; House 1955-63.

BASS, Ross (D Tenn.) March 17, 1918- –; House 1955-Nov. 3, 1964; Senate Nov. 4, 1964-67.

BASSETT, Burwell (D Va.) March 18, 1764-Feb. 26, 1841; House 1805-13, 1815-19, 1821-29.

BASSETT, Edward Murray (D N.Y.) Feb. 7, 1863-Oct. 27, 1948; House 1903-05.

BASSETT, Richard (grandfather of Richard Henry Bayard and James Asheton Bayard Jr., father-in-law of James Asheton Bayard Sr. and Joshua Clayton) (– Del.) April 2, 1745-Aug. 15, 1815; Senate 1789-93; Gov. 1799-1801 (Federalist).

BATE, William Brimage (D Tenn.) Oct. 7, 1826-March 9, 1905; Senate 1887-March 9, 1905; Gov. 1883-87.

BATEMAN, Ephraim (D N.J.) July 9, 1780-Jan. 28, 1829; House 1815-23; Senate Nov. 10, 1826-Jan. 12, 1829.

BATEMAN, Herbert H. (R Va.) Aug. 7, 1928- –; House 1983- –.

BATES, Arthur Laban (nephew of John Milton Thayer) (R Pa.) June 6, 1859-Aug. 26, 1934; House 1901-13.

BATES, Edward (brother of James Woodson Bates) (AAD Mo.) Sept. 4, 1793-March 25, 1869; House 1827-29; Atty. Gen. 1861-64.

BATES, George Joseph (father of William Henry Bates) (R Mass.) Feb. 25, 1891-Nov. 1, 1949; House 1937-Nov. 1, 1949.

BATES, Isaac Chapman (W Mass.) Jan. 23, 1779-March 16, 1845; House 1827-35 (Anti Jackson); Senate Jan 13, 1841-March 16, 1845.

BATES, James (D Maine) Sept. 24, 1789-Feb. 25, 1882 House 1831-33.

BATES, James Woodson (brother of Edward Bates) (– Ark.) Aug. 25, 1788-Dec. 16, 1846; House (Terr. Del.) Dec. 21, 1819-23.

BATES, Jim (D Calif.) July 21, 1941- –; House 1983- –

BATES, Joseph Bengal (D Ky.) Oct. 29, 1893-Sept. 10 1965; House June 4, 1938-53.

BATES, Martin Waltham (D Del.) Feb. 24, 1786-Jan. 1 1869; Senate Jan. 14, 1857-59.

BATES, William Henry (son of George Joseph Bates) (R Mass.) April 26, 1917-June 22, 1969; House Feb. 14 1950-June 22, 1969.

BATHRICK, Elsworth Raymond (D Ohio) Jan. 6, 1863- Dec. 23, 1917; House 1911-15, March 4-Dec. 23, 1917.

BATTIN, James F. (R Mont.) Feb. 13, 1925- –; House 1961-Feb. 27, 1969.

BATTLE, Laurie Calvin (D Ala.) May 10, 1912- – House 1947-55.

BAUCUS, Max Sieben (D Mont.) Dec. 11, 1941- – House 1975-Dec. 14, 1978; Senate Dec. 15, 1978- –.

BAUMAN, Robert Edmund (R Md.) April 4, 1937- – House Aug. 21, 1973-81.

BAUMHART, Albert David Jr. (R Ohio) June 15, 1908- –; House 1941-Sept. 2, 1942, 1955-61.

BAXTER, Portus (R Vt.) Dec. 4, 1806-March 4, 1868 House 1861-67.

BAY, William Van Ness (D Mo.) Nov. 23, 1818-Feb. 10 1894; House 1849-51.

BAYARD, James Asheton Sr. (father of Richard Henry Bayard and James Asheton Bayard Jr., grandfather of Thomas Francis Bayard Sr., great-grandfather of Thomas Francis Bayard Jr., son-in-law of Richard Bassett) (F Del.) July 28, 1767-Aug. 6, 1815; House 1797-1803; Senate Nov. 13, 1804-13.

BAYARD, James Asheton Jr. (son of James Asheton Bayard Sr., grandson of Richard Bassett, father of Thomas Francis Bayard Sr., grandfather of Thomas Francis Bayard Jr.) (D Del.) Nov. 15, 1799-June 13 1880; Senate 1851-Jan. 29, 1864, April 5, 1867-69.

BAYARD, Richard Henry (son of James Asheton Bayard Sr., grandson of Richard Bassett) (W Del.) Sept. 26, 1796-March 4, 1868; Senate June 17, 1836 Sept. 19, 1839, Jan. 12, 1841-45.

BAYARD, Thomas Francis Sr. (son of James Asheton Bayard Jr., father of Thomas Francis Bayard Jr.) (D Del.) Oct. 29, 1828-Sept. 28, 1898; Senate 1869-March 6, 1885; Pres. pro tempore 1881; Secy. of State 1885-89.

BAYARD, Thomas Francis Jr. (son of Thomas Francis Bayard Sr.) (D Del.) June 4, 1868-July 12, 1942; Senate Nov. 8, 1922-29.

BAYH, Birch Evan (D Ind.) Jan. 22, 1928- —; Senate 1963-81.

BAYLIES, Francis (brother of William Baylies) (—Mass.) Oct. 16, 1784-Oct. 28, 1852; House 1821-27.

BAYLIES, William (brother of Francis Baylies) (WD Mass.) Sept. 15, 1776-Sept. 27, 1865; House March 4-June 28, 1809, 1813-17, 1833-35.

BAYLOR, Robert Emmett Bledsoe (nephew of Jesse Bledsoe) (D Ala.) May 10, 1793-Jan. 6, 1874; House 1829-31.

BAYLY, Thomas (D Md.) Sept. 13, 1775-1829; House 1817-23.

BAYLY, Thomas Henry (son of Thomas Monteagle Bayly) (SRD Va.) Dec. 11, 1810-June 23, 1856; House May 6, 1844-June 23, 1856.

BAYLY, Thomas Monteagle (father of Thomas Henry Bayly) (D Va.) March 26, 1775-Jan. 7, 1834; House 1813-15.

BAYNE, Thomas McKee (R Pa.) June 14, 1836-June 16, 1894; House 1877-91.

BEACH, Clifton Bailey (R Ohio) Sept. 16, 1845-Nov. 15, 1902; House 1895-99.

BEACH, Lewis (D N.Y.) March 30, 1835-Aug. 10, 1886; House 1881-Aug. 10, 1886.

BEAKES, Samuel Willard (D Mich.) Jan. 11, 1861-Feb. 9, 1927; House 1913-March 3, 1917, Dec. 13, 1917-19.

BEALE, Charles Lewis (R N.Y.) March 5, 1824-Jan. 29, 1900; House 1859-61.

BEALE, James Madison Hite (D Va.) Feb. 7, 1786-Aug. 2, 1866; House 1833-37, 1849-53.

BEALE, Joseph Grant (R Pa.) March 26, 1839-May 21, 1915; House 1907-09.

BEALE, Richard Lee Tuberville (D Va.) May 22, 1819-April 21, 1893; House 1847-49, Jan. 23, 1879-81.

BEALES, Cyrus William (R Pa.) Dec. 16, 1877-Nov. 14, 1927; House 1915-17.

BEALL, James Andrew "Jack" (D Texas) Oct. 25, 1866-Feb. 12, 1929; House 1903-15.

BEALL, James Glenn (father of John Glenn Beall Jr.) (R Md.) June 5, 1894-Jan. 14, 1971; House 1943-53; Senate 1953-65.

BEALL, John Glenn Jr. (son of James Glenn Beall) (R Md.) June 19, 1927- —; House 1969-71; Senate 1971-77.

BEALL, Reasin (W Ohio) Dec. 3, 1769-Feb. 20, 1843; House April 20, 1813-June 7, 1814.

BEAM, Harry Peter (D Ill.) Nov. 23, 1892- —; House 1931-Dec. 6, 1942.

BEAMAN, Fernando Cortez (R Mich.) June 28, 1814-Sept. 27, 1882; House 1861-71.

BEAMER, John Valentine (R Ind.) Nov. 17, 1896-Sept. 8, 1964; House 1951-59.

BEAN, Benning Moulton (D N.H.) Jan. 9, 1782-Feb. 6, 1866; House 1833-37.

BEAN, Curtis Coe (R Ariz.) Jan. 4, 1828-Feb. 1, 1904; House (Terr. Del.) 1885-87.

BEARD, Edward Peter (D R.I.) Jan. 20, 1940- —; House 1975-81.

BEARD, Robin Leo Jr. (R Tenn.) Aug. 21, 1939- —; House 1973-83.

BEARDSLEY, Samuel (D N.Y.) Feb. 6, 1790-May 6, 1860; House 1831-March 29, 1836, 1843-Feb. 29, 1844.

BEATTY, John (— N.J.) Dec. 10, 1749-May 30, 1826; House 1793-95; Cont. Cong. Jan. 13-June 3, 1784, Nov. 11, 1784-Nov. 7, 1785.

BEATTY, John (R Ohio) Dec. 16, 1828-Dec. 21, 1914; House Feb. 5, 1868-73.

BEATTY, William (VBD Pa.) 1787-April 12, 1851; House 1837-41.

BEATY, Martin (W Ky.) ?-?; House 1833-35.

BEAUMONT, Andrew (D Pa.) Jan. 24, 1790-Sept. 30, 1853; House 1833-37.

BECK, Erasmus Williams (D Ga.) Oct. 21, 1833-July 22, 1898; House Dec. 2, 1872-73.

BECK, James Burnie (D Ky.) Feb. 13, 1822-May 3, 1890; House 1867-75; Senate 1877-May 3, 1890.

BECK, James Montgomery (R Pa.) July 9, 1861-April 12, 1936; House Nov. 8, 1927-Sept. 30, 1934.

BECK, Joseph David (R Wis.) March 14, 1866-Nov. 8, 1936; House 1921-29.

BECKER, Frank John (R N.Y.) Aug. 27, 1899-Sept. 4, 1981; House 1953-65.

BECKHAM, John Crepps Wickliffe (grandson of Charles Anderson Wickliffe, cousin of Robert Charles Wickliffe) (D Ky.) Aug. 5, 1869-Jan. 9, 1940; Senate 1915-21; Gov. 1900-07.

BECKNER, William Morgan (D Ky.) June 19, 1841-March 14, 1910; House Dec. 3, 1894-95.

BECKWITH, Charles Dyer (R N.J.) Oct. 22, 1838-March 27, 1921; House 1889-91.

BECKWORTH, Lindley Gary (D Texas) June 30, 1913-March 9, 1984; House 1939-53, 1957-67.

BEDE, James Adam (R Minn.) Jan. 13, 1856-April 11, 1942; House 1903-09.

BEDELL, Berkley Warren (D Iowa) March 5, 1921- —; House 1975-87.

BEDINGER, George Michael (uncle of Henry Bedinger) (— Ky.) Dec. 10, 1756-Dec. 7, 1843; House 1803-07.

BEDINGER, Henry (nephew of George Michael Bedinger) (D Va.) Feb. 3, 1812-Nov. 26, 1858; House 1845-49.

BEE, Carlos (D Texas) July 8, 1867-April 20, 1932; House 1919-21.

BEEBE, George Monroe (D N.Y.) Oct. 28, 1836-March 1, 1927; House 1875-79.

BEECHER, Philemon (F Ohio) 1775-Nov. 30, 1839; House 1817-21, 1823-29.

BEEDY, Carroll Lynwood (R Maine) Aug. 3, 1880-Aug. 30, 1947; House 1921-35.

BEEKMAN, Thomas (— N.Y.) ?-?; House 1829-31.

BEEMAN, Joseph Henry (D Miss.) Nov. 17, 1833-July 31, 1909; House 1891-93.

BEERMANN, Ralph F. (R Neb.) Aug. 13, 1912-Feb. 17, 1977; House 1961-65.

BEERS, Cyrus (D N.Y.) June 21, 1786-June 5, 1850; House Dec. 3, 1838-39.

BEERS, Edward McMath (R Pa.) May 27, 1877-April 21, 1932; House 1923-April 21, 1932.

BEESON, Henry White (D Pa.) Sept. 14, 1791-Oct. 28, 1863; House May 31, 1841-43.

BEGG, James Thomas (R Ohio) Feb. 16, 1877-March 26, 1963; House 1919-29.

BEGICH, Nicholas J. (D Alaska) April 6, 1932-?; House 1971-72. (Disappeared on an airplane flight Oct. 16, 1972, and presumed dead; congressional seat declared vacant Dec. 29, 1972.)

BEGOLE, Josiah Williams (R Mich.) Jan. 20, 1815-June 6, 1896; House 1873-75; Gov. 1883-85.

BEIDLER, Jacob Atlee (R Ohio) Nov. 2, 1852-Sept. 13, 1912; House 1901-07.

BEILENSON, Anthony Charles (D Calif.) Oct. 26, 1932- —; House 1977- —.

BEIRNE, Andrew (VBD Va.) 1771-March 16, 1845; House 1837-41.

BEITER, Alfred Florian (D N.Y.) July 7, 1894-March 11, 1974; House 1933-39, 1941-43.

BELCHER, Hiram (W Maine) Feb. 23, 1790-May 6, 1857; House 1847-49.

BELCHER, Nathan (D Conn.) June 23, 1813-June 2, 1891; House 1853-55.

BELCHER, Page Henry (R Okla.) April 21, 1899-Aug. 2, 1980; House 1951-73.

BELDEN, George Ogilvie (D N.Y.) March 28, 1797-Oct. 9, 1833; House 1827-29.

BELDEN, James Jerome (R N.Y.) Sept. 30, 1825-Jan. 1, 1904; House Nov. 8, 1887-95, 1897-99.

BELFORD, James Burns (cousin of Joseph McCrum Belford) (R Colo.) Sept. 28, 1837-Jan. 10, 1910; House Oct. 3, 1876-Dec. 13, 1877, 1879-85.

BELFORD, Joseph McCrum (cousin of James Burns Belford) (R N.Y.) Aug. 5, 1852-May 3, 1917; House 1897-99.

BELKNAP, Charles Eugene (R Mich.) Oct. 17, 1846-Jan. 16, 1929; House 1889-91, Nov. 3, 1891-93.

BELKNAP, Hugh Reid (R Ill.) Sept. 1, 1860-Nov. 12, 1901; House Dec. 27, 1895-99.

BELL, Alphonzo (R Calif.) Sept. 19, 1914- —; House 1961-77.

BELL, Charles Henry (nephew of Samuel Bell, cousin of James Bell) (R N.H.) Nov. 18, 1823-Nov. 11, 1893; Senate March 13-June 18, 1879; Gov. 1881-83.

BELL, Charles Jasper (D Mo.) Jan. 16, 1885-Jan. 21, 1978; House 1935-49.

BELL, Charles Keith (nephew of Reese Bowen Brabson (D Texas) April 18, 1853-April 21, 1913; House 1893-97.

BELL, Charles Webster (PR Calif.) June 11, 1857-April 19, 1927; House 1913-15.

BELL, Hiram (W Ohio) April 22, 1808-Dec. 21, 1855; House 1851-53.

BELL, Hiram Parks (D Ga.) Jan. 19, 1827-Aug. 17, 1907; House 1873-75, March 13, 1877-79.

BELL, James (son of Samuel Bell, uncle of Samuel Newell Bell, cousin of Charles Henry Bell) (W N.H.) Nov. 13, 1804-May 26, 1857; Senate July 30, 1855-May 26, 1857.

BELL, James Martin (D Ohio) Oct. 16, 1796-April 4, 1849; House 1833-35.

BELL, John (W Ohio) June 19, 1796-May 4, 1869; House Jan. 7-March 3, 1851.

BELL, John (W Tenn.) Feb. 15, 1797-Sept. 10, 1869; House 1827-41 (1827-29 Democrat); Speaker 1834-35; Senate Nov. 22, 1847-59; Secy. of War March 5-Sept. 12, 1841.

BELL, John Calhoun (D Colo.) Dec. 11, 1851-Aug. 12, 1933; House 1893-1903.

BELL, John Junior (D Texas) May 15, 1910-Jan. 24, 1963; House 1955-57.

BELL, Joshua Fry (W Ky.) Nov. 26, 1811-Aug. 17, 1870; House 1845-47.

BELL, Peter Hansborough (D Texas) March 11, 1810-March 8, 1898; House 1853-57; Gov. 1849-53.

BELL, Samuel (father of James Bell, grandfather of Samuel Newell Bell, uncle of Charles Henry Bell) (DR N.H.) Feb. 9, 1770-Dec. 23, 1850; Senate 1823-35; Gov. 1819-23.

BELL, Samuel Newell (grandson of Samuel Bell, nephew of James Bell) (D N.H.) March 25, 1829-Feb. 8, 1889; House 1871-73, 1875-77.

BELL, Theodore Arlington (D Calif.) July 25, 1872-Sept. 4, 1922; House 1903-05.

BELL, Thomas Montgomery (D Ga.) March 17, 1861-March 18, 1941; House 1905-31.

BELLAMY, John Dillard (D N.C.) March 24, 1854-Sept. 25, 1942; House 1899-1903.

BELLINGER, Joseph (— S.C.) 1773-Jan. 10, 1830; House 1817-19.

BELLMON, Henry Louis (R Okla.) Sept. 3, 1921-—; Senate 1969-81; Gov. 1963-67, 1987-—.

BELMONT, Oliver Hazard Perry (brother of Perry Belmont) (D N.Y.) Nov. 12, 1858-June 10, 1908; House 1901-03.

BELMONT, Perry (brother of Oliver Hazard Perry Belmont) (D N.Y.) Dec. 28, 1851-May 25, 1947; House 1881-Dec. 1, 1888.

BELSER, James Edwin (D Ala.) Dec. 22, 1805-Jan. 16, 1859; House 1843-45.

BELTZHOOVER, Frank Eckels (D Pa.) Nov. 6, 1841-June 2, 1923; House 1879-83, 1891-95.

BENDER, George Harrison (R Ohio) Sept. 29, 1896-June 18, 1961; House 1939-49, 1951-Dec. 15, 1954; Senate Dec. 16, 1954-57.

BENEDICT, Charles Brewster (D N.Y.) Feb. 7, 1828-Oct. 3, 1901; House 1877-79.

BENEDICT, Cleve (R W.Va.) March 21, 1935-—; House 1981-83.

BENEDICT, Henry Stanley (R Calif.) Feb. 20, 1878-July 10, 1930; House Nov. 7, 1916-17.

BENET, Christie (D S.C.) Dec. 26, 1879-March 30, 1951; Senate July 6-Nov. 5, 1918.

BENHAM, John Samuel (R Ind.) Oct. 24, 1863-Dec. 11, 1935; House 1919-23.

BENITEZ, Jaime (PD P.R.) Oct. 29, 1908-—; House (Res. Comm.) 1973-77.

BENJAMIN, Adam Jr. (D Ind.) Aug. 6, 1935-Sept. 7, 1982; House 1977-Sept. 7, 1982.

BENJAMIN, John Forbes (RR Mo.) Jan. 23, 1817-March 8, 1877; House 1865-71.

BENJAMIN, Judah Philip (D La.) Aug. 6, 1811-May 6, 1884; Senate 1853-Feb. 4, 1861 (1853-59 Whig).

BENNER, George Jacob (D Pa.) April 13, 1859-Dec. 30, 1930; House 1897-99.

BENNET, Augustus Witschief (son of William Stiles Bennet) (R N.Y.) Oct. 7, 1897-June 5, 1983; House 1945-47.

BENNET, Benjamin (— N.J.) Oct. 31, 1764-Oct. 8, 1840; House 1815-19.

BENNET, Hiram Pitt (CR Colo.) Sept. 2, 1826-Nov. 11, 1914; House (Terr. Del.) Aug. 19, 1861-65.

BENNET, William Stiles (father of Augustus Witschief Bennet) (R N.Y.) Nov. 9, 1870-Dec. 1, 1962; House 1905-11, Nov. 2, 1915-17.

BENNETT, Charles Edward (D Fla.) Dec. 2, 1910-—; House 1949-—.

BENNETT, Charles Goodwin (R N.Y.) Dec. 11, 1863-May 25, 1914; House 1895-99.

BENNETT, David Smith (R N.Y.) May 3, 1811-Nov. 6, 1894; House 1869-71.

BENNETT, Granville Gaylord (R Dakota) Oct. 9, 1833-June 28, 1910; House (Terr. Del.) 1879-81.

BENNETT, Hendley Stone (D Miss.) April 7, 1807-Dec. 15, 1891; House 1855-57.

BENNETT, Henry (R N.Y.) Sept. 29, 1808-May 10, 1868; House 1849-59 (1849-51 Whig).

BENNETT, John Bonifas (R Mich.) Jan. 10, 1904-Aug. 9, 1964; House 1943-45, 1947-Aug. 9, 1964.

BENNETT, Joseph Bentley (R Ky.) April 21, 1859-Nov. 7, 1923; House 1905-11.

BENNETT, Marion Tinsley (son of Philip Allen Bennett) (R Mo.) June 6, 1914- –; House Jan. 12, 1943-49.

BENNETT, Philip Allen (father of Marion Tinsley Bennett) (R Mo.) March 5, 1881-Dec. 7, 1942; House 1941-Dec. 7, 1942.

BENNETT, Risden Tyler (D N.C.) June 18, 1840-July 21, 1913; House 1883-87.

BENNETT, Thomas Warren (I Idaho) Feb. 16, 1831-Feb. 2, 1893; House (Terr. Del.) 1875-June 23, 1876; Gov. 1871-75.

BENNETT, Wallace Foster (R Utah) Nov. 13, 1898- –; Senate 1951-Dec. 20, 1974.

BENNY, Allan (D N.J.) July 12, 1867-Nov. 6, 1942; House 1903-05.

BENSON, Alfred Washburn (R Kan.) July 15, 1843-Jan. 1, 1916; Senate June 11, 1906-Jan. 23, 1907.

BENSON, Carville Dickinson (D Md.) Aug. 24, 1872-Feb. 8, 1929; House Nov. 5, 1918-21.

BENSON, Egbert (– N.Y.) June 21, 1746-Aug. 24, 1833; House 1789-93, March 4-Aug. 2, 1813; Cont. Cong. 1784-88.

BENSON, Elmer Austin (FL Minn.) Sept. 22, 1895-March 13, 1985; Senate Dec. 27, 1935-Nov. 3, 1936; Gov. 1937-39.

BENSON, Samuel Page (R Maine) Nov. 28, 1804-Aug. 12, 1876; House 1853-57 (1853-55 Whig).

BENTLEY, Alvin Morell (R Mich.) Aug. 30, 1918-April 10, 1969; House 1953-61.

BENTLEY, Helen Delich (R Md.) Nov. 28, 1923- –; House 1985- –.

BENTLEY, Henry Wilbur (D N.Y.) Sept. 30, 1838-Jan. 27, 1907; House 1891-93.

BENTON, Charles Swan (D N.Y.) July 12, 1810-May 4, 1882; House 1843-47.

BENTON, Jacob (R N.H.) Aug. 19, 1814-Sept. 29, 1892; House 1867-71.

BENTON, Lemuel (great-grandfather of George William Dargan) (D S.C.) 1754-May 18, 1818; House 1793-99.

BENTON, Maecenas Eason (D Mo.) Jan. 29, 1848-April 27, 1924; House 1897-1905.

BENTON, Thomas Hart (MCD Mo.) March 14, 1782-April 10, 1858; Senate Aug. 10, 1821-51; House 1853-55.

BENTON, William (D Conn.) April 1, 1900-March 18, 1973; Senate Dec. 17, 1949-53.

BENTSEN, Lloyd Millard Jr. (D Texas) Feb. 11, 1921- –; House Dec. 4, 1948-55; Senate 1971- –.

BEREUTER, Douglas K. (R Neb.) Oct. 6, 1939- –; House 1979- –.

BERGEN, Christopher Augustus (R N.J.) Aug. 2, 1841-Feb. 18, 1905; House 1889-93.

BERGEN, John Teunis (second cousin of Teunis Garret Bergen) (D N.Y.) 1786-March 9, 1855; House 1831-33.

BERGEN, Teunis Garret (second cousin of John Teunis Bergen) (D N.Y.) Oct. 6, 1806-April 24, 1881; House 1865-67.

BERGER, Victor Luitpold (Soc. Wis.) Feb. 28, 1860-Aug. 7, 1929; House 1911-13, 1923-29.

BERGLAND, Bob Selmer (D Minn.) July 22, 1928- –; House 1971-Jan. 22, 1977; Secy. of Agriculture 1977-81.

BERLIN, William Markle (D Pa.) March 29, 1880-Oct. 14, 1962; House 1933-37.

BERMAN, Howard L. (D Calif.) April 15, 1941- –; House 1983- –.

BERNARD, John Toussaint (FL Minn.) March 6, 1893- –; House 1937-39.

BERNHISEL, John Milton (W Utah) July 23, 1799-Sept. 28, 1881; House (Terr. Del.) 1851-59, 1861-63.

BERRIEN, John Macpherson (W Ga.) Aug. 23, 1781-Jan. 1, 1856; Senate 1825-March 9, 1829, 1841-May 1845, Nov. 14, 1845-47, Nov. 13, 1847-May 28, 1852 (1825-29 Democrat); Atty. Gen. 1829-31.

BERRY, Albert Seaton (D Ky.) May 13, 1836-Jan. 6, 1908; House 1893-1901.

BERRY, Campbell Polson (cousin of James Henderson Berry) (D Calif.) Nov. 7, 1834-Jan. 8, 1901; House 1879-83.

BERRY, Ellis Yarnal (R S.D.) Oct. 6, 1902- –; House 1951-71.

BERRY, George Leonard (D Tenn.) Sept. 12, 1882-Dec. 4, 1948; Senate May 6, 1937-Nov. 8, 1938.

BERRY, James Henderson (cousin of Campbell Polson Berry) (D Ark.) May 15, 1841-Jan. 30, 1913; Senate March 20, 1885-1907; Gov. 1883-85.

BERRY, John (D Ohio) April 26, 1833-May 18, 1879; House 1873-75.

BESHLIN, Earl Hanley (D/Prohib. Pa.) April 28, 1870-July 12, 1971; House Nov. 8, 1917-19.

BETHUNE, Edwin Ruthvin (R Ark.) Dec. 19, 1934- —; House 1979-85.

BETHUNE, Lauchlin (JD N.C.) April 15, 1785-Oct. 10, 1874; House 1831-33.

BETHUNE, Marion (R Ga.) April 8, 1816-Feb. 20, 1895; House Dec. 22, 1870-71.

BETTON, Silas (— N.H.) Aug. 26, 1768-Jan. 22, 1822; House 1803-07.

BETTS, Jackson Edward (R Ohio) May 26, 1904- —; House 1951-73.

BETTS, Samuel Rossiter (D N.Y.) June 8, 1787-Nov. 2, 1868; House 1815-17.

BETTS, Thaddeus (W Conn.) Feb. 4, 1789-April 7, 1840; Senate 1839-April 7, 1840.

BEVERIDGE, Albert Jeremiah (R Ind.) Oct. 6, 1862-April 27, 1927; Senate 1899-1911.

BEVERIDGE, John Lourie (R Ill.) July 6, 1824-May 3, 1910; House Nov. 7, 1871-Jan. 4, 1873; Gov. 1873-77.

BEVILL, Tom (D Ala.) March 27, 1921- —; House 1967- —.

BIAGGI, Mario (D N.Y.) Oct. 26, 1917- —; House 1969- —.

BIBB, George Mortimer (— Ky.) Oct. 30, 1776-April 14, 1859; Senate 1811-Aug. 23, 1814, 1829-35; Secy. of the Treasury 1844-45.

BIBB, William Wyatt (D Ga.) Oct. 2, 1780-July 10, 1820; House Jan. 26, 1807-Nov. 6, 1813; Senate Nov. 6, 1813-Nov. 9, 1816; Gov. 1819-20 (Democratic Republican Ala.)

BIBIGHAUS, Thomas Marshal (W Pa.) March 17, 1817-June 18, 1853; House 1851-53.

BIBLE, Alan Harvey (D Nev.) Nov. 20, 1909- —; Senate Dec. 2, 1954-Dec. 17, 1974.

BICKNELL, Bennet (D N.Y.) Nov. 14, 1781-Sept. 15, 1841; House 1837-39.

BICKNELL, George Augustus (D Ind.) Feb. 6, 1815-April 11, 1891; House 1877-81.

BIDDLE, Charles John (nephew of Richard Biddle) (D Pa.) April 30, 1819-Sept. 28, 1873; House July 2, 1861-63.

BIDDLE, John (W Mich.) March 2, 1792-Aug. 25, 1859; House (Terr. Del.) 1829-Feb. 21, 1831.

BIDDLE, Joseph Franklin (R Pa.) Sept. 14, 1871-Dec. 3, 1936; House Nov. 8, 1932-33.

BIDDLE, Richard (uncle of Charles John Biddle) (W Pa.) March 25, 1796-July 6, 1847; House 1837-40.

BIDEN, Joseph Robinette Jr. (D Del.) Nov. 20, 1942- —; Senate 1973- —.

BIDLACK, Benjamin Alden (D Pa.) Sept. 8, 1804-Feb. 6, 1849; House 1841-45.

BIDWELL, Barnabas (— Mass.) Aug. 23, 1763-July 27, 1833; House 1805-July 13, 1807.

BIDWELL, John (U Calif.) Aug. 5, 1819-April 4, 1900; House 1865-67.

BIEMILLER, Andrew John (D Wis.) July 23, 1906-April 3, 1982; House 1945-47, 1949-51.

BIERMANN, Frederick Elliott (D Iowa) March 20, 1884-July 1, 1968; House 1933-39.

BIERY, James Soloman (R Pa.) March 2, 1839-Dec. 3, 1904; House 1873-75.

BIESTER, Edward G. Jr. (R Pa.) Jan. 5, 1931- —; House 1967-77.

BIGBY, John Summerfield (R Ga.) Feb. 13, 1832-March 28, 1898; House 1871-73.

BIGELOW, Abijah (F Mass.) Dec. 5, 1775-April 5, 1860; House Oct. 8, 1810-March 3, 1815.

BIGELOW, Herbert Seely (D Ohio) Jan. 4, 1870-Nov. 11, 1951; House 1937-39.

BIGELOW, Lewis (— Mass.) Aug. 18, 1785-Oct. 2, 1838; House 1821-23.

BIGGS, Asa (D N.C.) Feb. 4, 1811-March 6, 1878; House 1845-47; Senate 1855-May 5, 1858.

BIGGS, Benjamin Thomas (D Del.) Oct. 1, 1821-Dec. 25, 1893; House 1869-73; Gov. 1887-91.

BIGGS, Marion (D Calif.) May 2, 1823-Aug. 2, 1910; House 1887-91.

BIGLER, William (D Pa.) Jan. 11, 1814-Aug. 9, 1880; Senate Jan. 14, 1856-61; Gov. 1852-55.

BILBO, Theodore Gilmore (D Miss.) Oct. 13, 1877-Aug. 21, 1947; Senate 1935-Aug. 21, 1947; Gov. 1916-20, 1928-32.

BILBRAY, James H. (D Nev.) May 19, 1938- —; House 1987- —.

BILIRAKIS, Michael (R Fla.) July 16, 1930- —; House 1983- —.

BILLINGHURST, Charles (R Wis.) July 27, 1818-Aug. 18, 1865; House 1855-59.

BILLMEYER, Alexander (D Pa.) Jan. 7, 1841-May 24, 1924; House Nov. 4, 1902-03.

BINDERUP, Charles Gustav (D Neb.) March 5, 1873-Aug. 19, 1950; House 1935-39.

BINES, Thomas (D N.J.) ?-April 9, 1826; House Nov. 2, 1814-15.

BINGAMAN, Jesse Francis Jr. "Jeff" (D N.M.) Oct. 3, 1943- —; Senate 1983- —.

BINGHAM, Henry Harrison (R Pa.) Dec. 4, 1841-March 22, 1912; House 1879-March 22, 1912.

BINGHAM, Hiram (father of Jonathan Brewster Bingham) (R Conn.) Nov. 19, 1875-June 6, 1956; Senate Dec. 17, 1924-33; Gov. Jan. 7-Jan. 8, 1925.

BINGHAM, John Armor (R Ohio) Jan. 21, 1815-March 19, 1900; House 1855-63, 1865-73.

BINGHAM, Jonathan Brewster (son of Hiram Bingham) (D N.Y.) April 24, 1914-July 3, 1986; House 1965-83.

BINGHAM, Kinsley Scott (R Mich.) Dec. 16, 1808-Oct. 5, 1861; House 1847-51 (Democrat); Senate 1859-Oct. 5, 1861; Gov. 1855-59.

BINGHAM, William (F Pa.) March 8, 1752-Feb. 7, 1804; Senate 1795-1801; Pres. pro tempore 1797; Cont. Cong. 1787-88.

BINNEY, Horace (W Pa.) Jan. 4, 1780-Aug. 12, 1875; House 1833-35.

BIRCH, William Fred (R N.J.) Aug. 30, 1870-Jan. 25, 1946; House Nov. 5, 1918-19.

BIRD, John (D N.Y.) Nov. 22, 1768-Feb. 2, 1806; House 1799-July 25, 1801.

BIRD, John Taylor (D N.J.) Aug. 16, 1829-May 6, 1911; House 1869-73.

BIRD, Richard Ely (R Kan.) Nov. 4, 1878-Jan. 10, 1955; House 1921-23.

BIRDSALL, Ausburn (D N.Y.) ?-July 10, 1903; House 1847-49.

BIRDSALL, Benjamin Pixley (R Iowa) Oct. 26, 1858-May 26, 1917; House 1903-09.

BIRDSALL, James (D N.Y.) 1783-July 20, 1856; House 1815-17.

BIRDSALL, Samuel (D N.Y.) May 14, 1791-Feb. 8, 1872; House 1837-39.

BIRDSEYE, Victory (W N.Y.) Dec. 25, 1782-Sept. 16, 1853; House 1815-17, 1841-43.

BISBEE, Horatio Jr. (R Fla.) May 1, 1839-March 27, 1916; House 1877-Feb. 20, 1879, Jan. 22-March 3, 1881, June 1, 1882-85.

BISHOP, Cecil William "Runt" (R Ill.) June 29, 1890-Sept. 21, 1971; House 1941-55.

BISHOP, James (W N.J.) May 11, 1816-May 10, 1895; House 1855-57.

BISHOP, Phanuel (— Mass.) Sept. 3, 1739-Jan. 6, 1812; House 1799-1807.

BISHOP, Roswell Peter (R Mich.) Jan. 6, 1843-March 4, 1920; House 1895-1907.

BISHOP, William Darius (D Conn.) Sept. 14, 1827-Feb. 4, 1904; House 1857-59.

BISSELL, William Harrison (D Ill.) April 25, 1811-March 18, 1860; House 1849-55; Gov. 1857-60 (Republican).

BIXLER, Harris Jacob (R Pa.) Sept. 16, 1870-March 29, 1941; House 1921-27.

BLACK, Edward Junius (father of George Robison Black) (D Ga.) Oct. 30, 1806-Sept. 1, 1846; House 1839-41 (State Rights Whig), Jan. 3, 1842-45.

BLACK, Eugene (D Texas) July 2, 1879-May 22, 1975; House 1915-29.

BLACK, Frank Swett (R N.Y.) March 8, 1853-March 22 1913; House 1895-Jan. 7, 1897; Gov. 1897-99.

BLACK, George Robison (son of Edward Junius Black) (D Ga.) March 24, 1835-Nov. 3, 1886; House 1881-83.

BLACK, Henry (W Pa.) Feb. 25, 1783-Nov. 28, 1841 House June 28-Nov. 28, 1841.

BLACK, Hugo Lafayette (D Ala.) Feb. 27, 1886-Sept 25, 1971; Senate 1927-Aug. 19, 1937; Assoc. Justice Supreme Court 1937-71.

BLACK, James (D Pa.) March 6, 1793-June 21, 1872 House Dec. 5, 1836-37, 1843-47.

BLACK, James Augustus (Cal.D S.C.) 1793-April 3 1848; House 1843-April 3, 1848.

BLACK, James Conquest Cross (D Ga.) May 9, 1842 Oct. 1, 1928; House 1893-March 4, 1895, Oct. 2 1895-97.

BLACK, John (— Miss.) ?-Aug. 29, 1854; Senate Nov 12, 1832-March 3, 1833, Nov. 22, 1833-Jan. 22, 1838

BLACK, John Charles (D Ill.) Jan. 27, 1839-Aug. 17, 1915; House 1893-Jan. 12, 1895.

BLACK, Loring Milton Jr. (D N.Y.) May 17, 1866-May 21, 1956; House 1923-35.

BLACKBURN, Benjamin Bentley (R Ga.) Feb. 14, 1927-—; House 1967-75.

BLACKBURN, Edmond Spencer (R N.C.) Sept. 22, 1868-March 10, 1912; House 1901-03, 1905-07.

BLACKBURN, Joseph Clay Stiles (D Ky.) Oct. 1, 1838-Sept. 12, 1918; House 1875-85; Senate 1885-97, 1901-07.

BLACKBURN, Robert E. Lee (R Ky.) April 9, 1870-Sept. 20, 1935; House 1929-31.

BLACKBURN, William Jasper (R La.) July 24, 1820-Nov. 10, 1899; House July 18, 1868-69.

BLACKLEDGE, William (father of William Salter Blackledge) (D N.C.) ?-Oct. 19, 1828; House 1803-09, 1811-13.

BLACKLEDGE, William Salter (son of William Blackledge) (D N.C.) 1793-March 21, 1857; House Feb. 7, 1821-23.

BLACKMAR, Esbon (W N.Y.) June 19, 1805-Nov. 19, 1857; House Dec. 4, 1848-49.

BLACKMON, Fred Leonard (D Ala.) Sept. 15, 1873-Feb. 8, 1921; House 1911-Feb. 8, 1921.

BLACKNEY, William Wallace (R Mich.) Aug. 28, 1876-March 14, 1963; House 1935-37, 1939-53.

BLACKWELL, Julius W. (VBD Tenn.) ?-?; House 1839-41, 1843-45.

BLAINE, James Gillespie (R Maine) Jan. 31, 1830-Jan. 27, 1893; House 1863-July 10, 1876; Speaker 1869-75; Senate July 10, 1876-March 5, 1881; Secy. of State March 5-Dec. 12, 1881, March 7, 1889-June 4, 1892.

BLAINE, John James (R Wis.) May 4, 1875-April 16, 1934; Senate 1927-33; Gov. 1921-27.

BLAIR, Austin (R Mich.) Feb. 8, 1818-Aug. 6, 1894; House 1867-73; Gov. 1861-65.

BLAIR, Bernard (W N.Y.) May 24, 1801-May 7, 1880; House 1841-43.

BLAIR, Francis Preston Jr. (D Mo.) Feb. 19, 1821-July 8, 1875; House 1857-59 (Free-Soiler), June 8-25, 1860, 1861-July 1862, 1863-June 10, 1864; Senate Jan. 20, 1871-73.

BLAIR, Henry William (R N.H.) Dec. 6, 1834-March 14, 1920; House 1875-79, 1893-95; Senate June 20, 1879-March 3, 1885, March 5, 1885-91.

BLAIR, Jacob Beeson (U W.Va.) April 11, 1821-Feb. 12, 1901; House Dec. 2, 1861-63 (Va.), Dec. 7, 1863-65.

BLAIR, James (D S.C.) 1790-April 1, 1834; House 1821-May 8, 1822, 1829-April 1, 1834 (1829-31 Union Democrat).

BLAIR, James Gorrall (LR Mo.) Jan. 1, 1825-March 1, 1904; House 1871-73.

BLAIR, John (D Tenn.) Sept. 13, 1790-July 9, 1863; House 1823-35.

BLAIR, Samuel Steel (R Pa.) Dec. 5, 1821-Dec. 8, 1890; House 1859-63.

BLAISDELL, Daniel (F N.H.) Jan. 22, 1762-Jan. 10, 1833; House 1809-11.

BLAKE, Harrison Gray Otis (R Ohio) March 17, 1818-April 16, 1876; House Oct. 11, 1859-63.

BLAKE, John Jr. (— N.Y.) Dec. 5, 1762-Jan. 13, 1826; House 1805-09.

BLAKE, John Lauris (R N.J.) March 25, 1831-Oct. 10, 1899; House 1879-81.

BLAKE, Thomas Holdsworth (AR Ind.) June 14, 1792-Nov. 28, 1849; House 1827-29.

BLAKENEY, Albert Alexander (R Md.) Sept. 28, 1850-Oct. 15, 1924; House 1901-03, 1921-23.

BLAKLEY, William Arvis (D Texas) Nov. 17, 1898-Jan. 5, 1976; Senate Jan. 15-April 28, 1957, Jan. 3-June 14, 1961.

BLANCHARD, George Washington (R Wis.) Jan. 26, 1884-Oct. 2, 1964; House 1933-35.

BLANCHARD, James Johnston (D Mich.) Aug. 8, 1942-—; House 1975-83; Gov. 1983-—.

BLANCHARD, John (W Pa.) Sept. 30, 1787-March 9, 1849; House 1845-49.

BLANCHARD, Newton Crain (D La.) Jan. 29, 1849-June 22, 1922; House 1881-March 12, 1894; Senate March 12, 1894-97; Gov. 1904-08.

BLAND, Oscar Edward (R Ind.) Nov. 21, 1877-Aug. 3, 1951; House 1917-23.

BLAND, Richard Parks (D Mo.) Aug. 19, 1835-June 15, 1899; House 1873-95, 1897-June 15, 1899.

BLAND, Schuyler Otis (D Va.) May 4, 1872-Feb. 16, 1950; House July 2, 1918-Feb. 16, 1950.

BLAND, Theodorick (— Va.) March 21, 1742-June 1, 1790; House 1789-June 1, 1790; Cont. Cong. 1780-83.

BLAND, William Thomas (grandson of John George Jackson, cousin of James Monroe Jackson) (D Mo.) Jan. 21, 1861-Jan. 15, 1928; House 1919-21.

BLANTON, Leonard Ray (D Tenn.) April 10, 1930- —; House 1967-73; Gov. 1975-79.

BLANTON, Thomas Lindsay (D Texas) Oct. 25, 1872-Aug. 11, 1957; House 1917-29, May 20, 1930-37.

BLATNIK, John Anton (D Minn.) Aug. 17, 1911- —; House 1947-Dec. 31, 1974.

BLAZ, Vincente "Ben" (R Guam) Feb. 14, 1928- —; House 1985- —.

BLEAKLEY, Orrin Dubbs (R Pa.) May 15, 1854-Dec. 3, 1927; House March 4-April 3, 1917.

BLEASE, Coleman Livingston (D S.C.) Oct. 8, 1868-Jan. 19, 1942; Senate 1925-31; Gov. 1911-15.

BLEDSOE, Jesse (uncle of Robert Emmett Bledsoe Baylor) (— Ky.) April 6, 1776-June 25, 1836; Senate 1813-Dec. 24, 1814.

BLEECKER, Harmanus (F N.Y.) Oct. 9, 1779-July 19, 1849; House 1811-13.

BLILEY, Thomas J. Jr. (R Va.) Jan. 28, 1932- —; House 1981- —.

BLISS, Aaron Thomas (R Mich.) May 22, 1837-Sept. 16, 1906; House 1889-91; Gov. 1901-05.

BLISS, Archibald Meserole (D N.Y.) Jan. 25, 1838-March 19, 1923; House 1875-83, 1885-89.

BLISS, George (D Ohio) Jan. 1, 1813-Oct. 24, 1868; House 1853-55, 1863-65.

BLISS, Philemon (R Ohio) July 28, 1813-Aug. 25, 1889; House 1855-59.

BLITCH, Iris Faircloth (D Ga.) April 25, 1912- —; House 1955-63.

BLODGETT, Rufus (D N.J.) Oct. 9, 1834-Oct. 3, 1910; Senate 1887-93.

BLOODWORTH, Timothy (— N.C.) 1736-Aug. 24, 1814; House April 6, 1790-91; Senate 1795-1801; Cont. Cong. 1786-Aug. 13, 1787.

BLOOM, Isaac (— N.Y.) 1716-April 26, 1803; House March 4-April 26, 1803.

BLOOM, Sol (D N.Y.) March 9, 1870-March 7, 1949; House 1923-March 7, 1949.

BLOOMFIELD, Joseph (DR N.J.) Oct. 5, 1753-Oct. 3, 1823; House 1817-21; Gov. 1801-12.

BLOUIN, Michael Thomas (D Iowa) Nov. 7, 1945- —; House 1975-79.

BLOUNT, James Henderson (D Ga.) Sept. 12, 1837-March 8, 1903; House 1873-93.

BLOUNT, Thomas (brother of William Blount, uncle of William Grainger Blount) (D N.C.) May 10, 1759-Feb. 7, 1812; House 1793-99, 1805-09, 1811-Feb. 7, 1812.

BLOUNT, William (father of William Grainger Blount, brother of Thomas Blount) (— Tenn.) March 26, 1749-March 21, 1800; Senate Aug. 2, 1796-July 8, 1797; Cont. Cong. 1782-83, 1786-87 (N.C.).

BLOUNT, William Grainger (son of William Blount, nephew of Thomas Blount) (D Tenn.) 1784-May 21, 1827; House Dec. 8, 1815-19.

BLOW, Henry Taylor (R Mo.) July 15, 1817-Sept. 11, 1875; House 1863-67.

BLUE, Richard Whiting (R Kan.) Sept. 8, 1841-Jan. 28, 1907; House 1895-97.

BOARDMAN, Elijah (father of William Whiting Boardman) (D Conn.) March 7, 1760-Aug. 18, 1823; Senate 1821-Aug. 18, 1823.

BOARDMAN, William Whiting (son of Elijah Boardman) (W Conn.) Oct. 10, 1794-Aug. 27, 1871; House Dec. 7, 1840-43.

BOARMAN, Alexander "Aleck" (L La.) Dec. 10, 1839-Aug. 30, 1916; House Dec. 3, 1872-73.

BOATNER, Charles Jahleal (D La.) Jan. 23, 1849-March 21, 1903; House 1889-95, June 10, 1896-97.

BOCKEE, Abraham (JD N.Y.) Feb. 3, 1784-June 1, 1865; House 1829-31, 1833-37.

BOCOCK, Thomas Stanhope (D Va.) May 18, 1815-Aug. 5, 1891; House 1847-61.

BODEN, Andrew (— Pa.) ?-Dec. 20, 1835; House 1817-21.

BODINE, Robert Nall (D Mo.) Dec. 17, 1837-March 16, 1914; House 1897-99.

BODLE, Charles (— N.Y.) 1787-Oct. 31, 1835; House 1833-35.

BOEHLERT, Sherwood L. (D N.Y.) June 28, 1936- —; House 1983- —.

BOEHNE, John William (father of John William Boehne Jr.) (D Ind.) Oct. 28, 1856-Dec. 27, 1946; House 1909-13.

BOEHNE, John William Jr. (son of John William Boehne) (D Ind.) March 2, 1895-July 5, 1973; House 1931-43.

BOEN, Haldor Erickson (PP Minn.) Jan. 2, 1851-July 23, 1912; House 1893-95.

BOGGS, Corinne Claiborne "Lindy" (widow of Thomas Hale Boggs Sr.) (D La.) March 13, 1916- —; House March 20, 1973- —.

BOGGS, James Caleb (R Del.) May 15, 1909- —; House 1947-53; Senate 1961-73; Gov. 1953-60.

BOGGS, Thomas Hale Sr. (husband of Corinne Claiborne Boggs) (D La.) Feb. 15, 1914-?; House 1941-43, 1947-73; House majority leader 1971-73. (Disappeared on an airplane flight Oct. 16, 1972, and presumed dead; congressional seat declared vacant Jan. 3, 1973.)

BOGY, Lewis Vital (D Mo.) April 9, 1813-Sept. 20, 1877; Senate 1873-Sept. 20, 1877.

BOHN, Frank Probasco (R Mich.) July 14, 1866-June 1, 1944; House 1927-33.

BOIES, William Dayton (R Iowa) Jan. 3, 1857-May 31, 1932; House 1919-29.

BOILEAU, Gerald John (Prog. Wis.) Jan. 15, 1900- —; House 1931-39 (1931-35 Republican).

BOKEE, David Alexander (W N.Y.) Oct. 6, 1805-March 15, 1860; House 1849-51.

BOLAND, Edward Patrick (D Mass.) Oct. 1, 1911- —; House 1953- —.

BOLAND, Patrick Joseph (husband of Veronica Grace Boland) (D Pa.) Jan. 6, 1880-May 18, 1942; House 1931-May 18, 1942.

BOLAND, Veronica Grace (widow of Patrick Joseph Boland) (D Pa.) March 18, 1899- —; House Nov. 19, 1942-43.

BOLES, Thomas (R Ark.) July 16, 1837-March 13, 1905; House June 22, 1868-71, Feb. 9, 1872-73.

BOLLES, Stephen (R Wis.) June 25, 1866-July 8, 1941; House 1939-July 8, 1941.

BOLLING, Richard Walker (D Mo.) May 17, 1916- —; House 1949-83.

BOLTON, Chester Castle (husband of Frances Payne Bolton, father of Oliver Payne Bolton) (R Ohio) Sept. 5, 1882-Oct. 29, 1939; House 1929-37, Jan. 3-Oct. 29, 1939.

BOLTON, Frances Payne (widow of Chester Castle Bolton, granddaughter of Henry B. Payne, mother of Oliver Payne Bolton) (R Ohio) March 29, 1885-March 9, 1977; House Feb. 27, 1940-69.

BOLTON, Oliver Payne (son of Chester Castle Bolton and Frances Payne Bolton, great-grandson of Henry B. Payne) (R Ohio) Feb. 22, 1917-Dec. 13, 1972; House 1953-57, 1963-65.

BOLTON, William P. (D Md.) July 2, 1885-Nov. 22, 1964; House 1949-51.

BOND, Charles Grosvenor (nephew of Charles Henry Grosvenor) (R N.Y.) May 29, 1877-Jan. 8, 1974; House 1921-23.

BOND, Christopher Samuel "Kit" (R Mo.) March 6, 1939- —; Senate 1987- —; Gov. 1981-85.

BOND, Shadrack (D Ill.) Nov. 24, 1773-April 12, 1832; House (Terr. Del.) Dec. 3, 1812-Aug. 2, 1813; Gov. 1818-22 (Democratic Republican).

BOND, William Key (W Ohio) Oct. 2, 1792-Feb. 17, 1864; House 1835-41.

BONE, Homer Truett (D Wash.) Jan. 25, 1883-March 11, 1970; Senate 1933-Nov. 13, 1944.

BONER, William Hill (D Tenn.) Feb. 14, 1945- —; House 1979- —.

BONHAM, Milledge Luke (SRD S.C.) Dec. 25, 1813-Aug. 27, 1890; House 1857-Dec. 21, 1860; Gov. 1862-64 (Confederate Democrat).

BONIN, Edward John (R Pa.) Dec. 23, 1904- —; House 1953-55.

BONIOR, David Edward (D Mich.) June 6, 1945- —; House 1977- —.

BONKER, Don Leroy (D Wash.) March 7, 1937- —; House 1975- —.

BONNER, Herbert Covington (D N.C.) May 16, 1891-Nov. 7, 1965; House Nov. 5, 1940-Nov. 7, 1965.

BONYNGE, Robert William (R Colo.) Sept. 8, 1863-Sept. 22, 1939; House Feb. 16, 1904-09.

BOODY, Azariah (W N.Y.) April 21, 1815-Nov. 18, 1885; House March 4-October 1853.

BOODY, David Augustus (D N.Y.) Aug. 13, 1837-Jan. 20, 1930; House March 4-Oct. 13, 1891.

BOOHER, Charles Ferris (D Mo.) Jan. 31, 1848-Jan. 21, 1921; House Feb. 19-March 3, 1889, 1907-Jan. 21, 1921.

BOOKER, George William (C Va.) Dec. 5, 1821-June 4, 1883; House Jan. 26, 1870-71.

BOON, Ratliff (JD Ind.) Jan. 18, 1781-Nov. 20, 1844; House 1825-27, 1829-39; Gov. Sept. 12-Dec. 5, 1822.

BOONE, Andrew Rechmond (D Ky.) April 4, 1831-Jan. 26, 1886; House 1875-79.

BOOTH, Newton (AM Calif.) Dec. 30, 1825-July 14, 1892; Senate 1875-81; Gov. 1871-75 (Republican).

BOOTH, Walter (FS Conn.) Dec. 8, 1791-April 30, 1870; House 1849-51.

BOOTHMAN, Melvin Morella (R Ohio) Oct. 16, 1846-March 5, 1904; House 1887-91.

BOOZE, William Samuel (R Md.) Jan. 9, 1862-Dec. 6, 1933; House 1897-99.

BORAH, William Edgar (R Idaho) June 29, 1865-Jan. 19, 1940; Senate 1907-Jan. 19, 1940.

BORCHERS, Charles Martin (D Ill.) Nov. 18, 1869-Dec. 2, 1946; House 1913-15.

BORDEN, Nathaniel Briggs (W Mass.) April 15, 1801-April 10, 1865; House 1835-39 (Van Buren Democrat), 1841-43.

BOREING, Vincent (R Ky.) Nov. 24, 1839-Sept. 16, 1903; House 1899-Sept. 16, 1903.

BOREMAN, Arthur Inghram (R W.Va.) July 24, 1823-April 19, 1896; Senate 1869-75; Gov. 1863-69.

BOREN, David Lyle (son of Lyle H. Boren) (D Okla.) April 21, 1941- −; Senate 1979- −; Gov. 1975-79.

BOREN, Lyle H. (father of David Lyle Boren) (D Okla.) May 11, 1909- −; House 1937-47.

BORLAND, Charles Jr. (− N.Y.) June 29, 1786-Feb. 23, 1852; House Nov. 8, 1821-23.

BORLAND, Solon (D Ark.) Sept. 21, 1808-Jan. 1, 1864; Senate March 30, 1848-April 3, 1853.

BORLAND, William Patterson (D Mo.) Oct. 14, 1867-Feb. 20, 1919; House 1909-Feb. 20, 1919.

BORSKI, Robert Anthony Jr. (D Pa.) Oct. 20, 1948- −; House 1983- −.

BORST, Peter I. (JD N.Y.) April 24, 1797-Nov. 14, 1848; House 1829-31.

BOSCH, Albert Henry (R N.Y.) Oct. 30, 1908- −; House 1953-Dec. 31, 1960.

BOSCHWITZ, Rudolf Eli (R Minn.) Nov. 7, 1930- −; Senate Dec. 30, 1978- −.

BOSCO, Douglas H. (D Calif.) July 28, 1946- −; House 1983- −.

BOSONE, Reva Zilpha Beck (D Utah) April 2, 1898-July 21, 1983; House 1949-53.

BOSS, John Linscom Jr. (− R.I.) Sept. 7, 1780-Aug. 1, 1819; House 1815-19.

BOSSIER, Pierre Evariste John Baptiste (Cal.D La.) March 22, 1797-April 24, 1844; House 1843-April 24, 1844.

BOTELER, Alexander Robinson (AP Va.) May 16, 1815-May 8, 1892; House 1859-61.

BOTKIN, Jeremiah Dunham (Fus. Kan.) April 24, 1849-Dec. 29, 1921; House 1897-99.

BOTTS, John Minor (HCW Va.) Sept. 16, 1802-Jan. 8, 1869; House 1839-43, 1847-49.

BOTTUM, Joseph H. (R S.D.) Aug. 7, 1903-July 4, 1984; Senate July 11, 1962-63.

BOUCHER, Frederick C. (D Va.) Aug. 1, 1946- −; House 1983- −.

BOUCK, Gabriel (nephew of Joseph Bouck) (D Wis.) Dec. 16, 1828-Feb. 21, 1904; House 1877-81.

BOUCK, Joseph (uncle of Gabriel Bouck) (D N.Y.) July 22, 1788-March 30, 1858; House 1831-33.

BOUDE, Thomas (F Pa.) May 17, 1752-Oct. 24, 1822; House 1801-03.

BOUDINOT, Elias (− N.J.) May 2, 1740-Oct. 24, 1821; House 1789-95; Cont. Cong. 1777-78, 1781-83.

BOULDIN, James Wood (brother of Thomas Tyler Bouldin) (JD Va.) 1792-March 30, 1854; House March 15, 1834-39.

BOULDIN, Thomas Tyler (brother of James Wood Bouldin) (D Va.) 1781-Feb. 11, 1834; House 1829-33, Aug. 26, 1833-Feb. 11, 1834.

BOULIGNY, Charles Dominique Joseph (uncle of John Edward Bouligny) (− La.) Aug. 22, 1773-March 1833; Senate Nov. 19, 1824-29.

BOULIGNY, John Edward (nephew of Charles Dominique Joseph Bouligny) (AP La.) Feb. 5, 1824-Feb. 20, 1864; House 1859-61.

BOULTER, Beau (R Texas) Feb. 23, 1942- −; House 1985- −.

BOUND, Franklin (R Pa.) April 9, 1829-Aug. 8, 1910; House 1885-89.

BOURN, Benjamin (F R.I.) Sept. 9, 1755-Sept. 17, 1808; House Aug. 31, 1790-96.

BOURNE, Jonathan Jr. (R Ore.) Feb. 23, 1855-Sept. 1, 1940; Senate 1907-13.

BOURNE, Shearjasub (− Mass.) June 14, 1746-March 11, 1806; House 1791-95.

BOUTELL, Henry Sherman (R Ill.) March 14, 1856-March 11, 1926; House Nov. 23, 1897-1911.

BOUTELLE, Charles Addison (R Maine) Feb. 9, 1839-May 21, 1901; House 1883-1901.

BOUTWELL, George Sewall (R Mass.) Jan. 28, 1818-Feb. 27, 1905; House 1863-March 12, 1869; Senate March 17, 1873-77; Gov. 1851-53 (Democrat); Secy. of the Treasury March 12, 1869-March 17, 1873.

BOVEE, Matthias Jacob (JD N.Y.) July 24, 1793-Sept. 12, 1872; House 1835-37.

BOW, Frank Townsend (R Ohio) Feb. 20, 1901-Nov. 13, 1972; House 1951-Nov. 13, 1972.

BOWDEN, George Edwin (nephew of Lemuel Jackson Bowden) (R Va.) July 6, 1852-Jan. 22, 1908; House 1887-91.

BOWDEN, Lemuel Jackson (uncle of George Edwin Bowden) (R Va.) Jan. 16, 1815-Jan. 2, 1864; Senate 1863-Jan. 2, 1864.

BOWDLE, Stanley Eyre (D Ohio) Sept. 4, 1868-April 6, 1919; House 1913-15.

BOWDON, Franklin Welsh (uncle of Sydney Johnston Bowie) (D Ala.) Feb. 17, 1817-June 8, 1857; House Dec. 7, 1846-51.

BOWEN, Christopher Columbus (R S.C.) Jan. 5, 1832-June 23, 1880; House July 20, 1868-71.

BOWEN, David Reece (D Miss.) Oct. 21, 1932- —; House 1973-83.

BOWEN, Henry (son of Rees Tate Bowen, nephew of John Warfield Johnston, cousin of William Bowen Campbell) (R Va.) Dec. 26, 1841-April 29, 1915; House 1883-85 (Readjuster), 1887-89.

BOWEN, John Henry (D Tenn.) Sept. 1780-Sept. 25, 1822; House 1813-15.

BOWEN, Rees Tate (father of Henry Bowen) (C Va.) Jan. 10, 1809-Aug. 29, 1879; House 1873-75.

BOWEN, Thomas Mead (R Colo.) Oct. 26, 1835-Dec. 30, 1906; Senate 1883-89; Gov. (Idaho Terr.) 1871.

BOWER, Gustavus Miller (D Va.) Dec. 12, 1790-Nov. 17, 1864; House 1843-45.

BOWER, William Horton (D N.C.) June 6, 1850-May 11, 1910; House 1893-95.

BOWERS, Eaton Jackson (D Miss.) June 17, 1865-Oct. 26, 1939; House 1903-11.

BOWERS, George Meade (R W.Va.) Sept. 13, 1863-Dec. 7, 1925; House May 9, 1916-23.

BOWERS, John Myer (— N.Y.) Sept. 25, 1772-Feb. 24, 1846; House May 26-Dec. 20, 1813.

BOWERS, William Wallace (R Calif.) Oct. 20, 1834-May 2, 1917; House 1891-97.

BOWERSOCK, Justin De Witt (R Kan.) Sept. 19, 1842-Oct. 27, 1922; House 1899-1907.

BOWIE, Richard Johns (W Md.) June 23, 1807-March 12, 1888; House 1849-53.

BOWIE, Sydney Johnston (nephew of Franklin Welsh Bowdon) (D Ala.) July 26, 1865-May 7, 1928; House 1901-07.

BOWIE, Thomas Fielder (grandnephew of Walter Bowie, brother-in-law of Reverdy Johnson) (D Md.) April 7, 1808-Oct. 30, 1869; House 1855-59.

BOWIE, Walter (granduncle of Thomas Fielder Bowie) (D Md.) 1748-Nov. 9, 1810; House March 24, 1802-05.

BOWLER, James Bernard (D Ill.) Feb. 5, 1875-July 18, 1957; House July 7, 1953-July 18, 1957.

BOWLES, Chester Bliss (D Conn.) April 5, 1901-May 25, 1986; House 1959-61; Gov. 1949-51.

BOWLES, Henry Leland (R Mass.) Jan. 6, 1866-May 17, 1932; House Sept. 29, 1925-29.

BOWLIN, James Butler (D Mo.) Jan. 16, 1804-July 19, 1874; House 1843-51.

BOWLING, William Bismarck (D Ala.) Sept. 24, 1870-Dec. 27, 1946; House Dec. 14, 1920-Aug. 16, 1928.

BOWMAN, Charles Calvin (R Pa.) Nov. 14, 1852-July 3, 1941; House 1911-Dec. 12, 1912.

BOWMAN, Frank Llewellyn (R W.Va.) Jan. 21, 1879-Sept. 15, 1936; House 1925-33.

BOWMAN, Selwyn Zadock (R Mass.) May 11, 1840-Sept. 30, 1928; House 1879-83.

BOWMAN, Thomas (D Iowa) May 25, 1848-Dec. 1, 1917; House 1891-93.

BOWNE, Obadiah (W N.Y.) May 19, 1822-April 27, 1874; House 1851-53.

BOWNE, Samuel Smith (VBD N.Y.) April 11, 1800-July 9, 1865; House 1841-43.

BOWRING, Eva Kelly (R Neb.) Jan. 9, 1892-Jan. 8, 1985; Senate April 16-Nov. 7, 1954.

BOX, John Calvin (D Texas) March 28, 1871-May 17, 1941; House 1919-31.

BOXER, Barbara (D Calif.) Nov. 11, 1940- —; House 1983- —.

BOYCE, William Henry (D Del.) Nov. 28, 1855-Feb. 6, 1942; House 1923-25.

BOYCE, William Waters (SRD S.C.) Oct. 24, 1818-Feb. 3, 1890; House 1853-Dec. 21, 1860.

BOYD, Adam (D N.J.) March 21, 1746-Aug. 15, 1835; House 1803-05, March 8, 1808-13.

BOYD, Alexander (W N.Y.) Sept. 14, 1764-April 8, 1857; House 1813-15.

BOYD, John Frank (R Neb.) Aug. 8, 1853-May 28, 1945; House 1907-09.

BOYD, John Huggins (W N.Y.) July 31, 1799-July 2, 1868; House 1851-53.

BOYD, Linn (D Ky.) Nov. 22, 1800-Dec. 17, 1859; House 1835-37, 1839-55; Speaker 1851-55.

BOYD, Sempronius Hamilton (R Mo.) May 28, 1828-June 22, 1894; House 1863-65 (Emancipationist), 1869-71.

BOYD, Thomas Alexander (R Ill.) June 25, 1830-May 28, 1897; House 1877-81.

BOYDEN, Nathaniel (R N.C.) Aug. 16, 1796-Nov. 20, 1873; House 1847-49 (Whig), July 13, 1868-69.

BOYER, Benjamin Markley (D Pa.) Jan. 22, 1823-Aug. 16, 1887; House 1865-69.

BOYER, Lewis Leonard (D Ill.) May 19, 1886-March 12, 1944; House 1937-39.

BOYKIN, Frank William (D Ala.) Feb. 21, 1885-March 12, 1969; House July 30, 1935-63.

BOYLAN, John Joseph (D N.Y.) Sept. 20, 1878-Oct. 5, 1938; House March 4, 1923-Oct. 5, 1938.

BOYLE, Charles Augustus (D Ill.) Aug. 13, 1907-Nov. 4, 1959; House 1955-Nov. 4, 1959.

BOYLE, Charles Edmund (D Pa.) Feb. 4, 1836-Dec. 15, 1888; House 1883-87.

BOYLE, John (D Ky.) Oct. 28, 1774-Feb. 28, 1834; House 1803-09.

BRABSON, Reese Bowen (uncle of Charles Keith Bell) (D Tenn.) Sept. 16, 1817-Aug. 16, 1863; House 1859-61.

BRACE, Jonathan (F Conn.) Nov. 12, 1754-Aug. 26, 1837; House Dec. 3, 1798-1800.

BRACKENRIDGE, Henry Marie (W Pa.) May 11, 1786-Jan. 18, 1871; House Oct. 13, 1840-41.

BRADBURY, George (F Mass.) Oct. 10, 1770-Nov. 7, 1823; House 1813-17.

BRADBURY, James Ware (D Maine) June 10, 1802-Jan. 6, 1901; Senate 1847-53.

BRADBURY, Theophilus (F Mass.) Nov. 13, 1739-Sept. 6, 1803; House 1795-July 24, 1797.

BRADEMAS, John (D Ind.) March 2, 1927- —; House 1959-81.

BRADFORD, Allen Alexander (R Colo.) July 23, 1815 March 12, 1888; House (Terr. Del.) 1865-67, 1869-71

BRADFORD, Taul (grandson of Micah Taul) (D Ala.) Jan. 20, 1835-Oct. 28, 1883; House 1875-77.

BRADFORD, William (— R.I.) Nov. 4, 1729-July 6 1808; Senate 1793-Oct. 1797; Pres. pro tempore 1797

BRADLEY, Edward (D Mich.) April 1808-Aug. 5, 1847 House March 4-Aug. 5, 1847.

BRADLEY, Frederick Van Ness (R Mich.) April 12 1898-May 24, 1947; House 1939-May 24, 1947.

BRADLEY, Michael Joseph (D Pa.) May 24, 1897-Nov 27, 1979; House 1937-47.

BRADLEY, Nathan Ball (R Mich.) May 28, 1831-Nov 8, 1906; House 1873-77.

BRADLEY, Stephen Row (father of William Czar Brad ley) (D Vt.) Feb. 20, 1754-Dec. 9, 1830; Senate Oc 17, 1791-95, Oct. 15, 1801-13; Pres. pro tempor 1802-03, 1808.

BRADLEY, Thomas Joseph (D N.Y.) Jan. 2, 1870-Apr 1, 1901; House 1897-1901.

BRADLEY, Thomas Wilson (R N.Y.) April 6, 1844-Ma 30, 1920; House 1903-13.

BRADLEY, William Czar (son of Stephen Row Brad ley) (D Vt.) March 23, 1782-March 3, 1867; Hous 1813-15 (War Democrat), 1823-27.

BRADLEY, William O'Connell (R Ky.) March 18, 184 May 23, 1914; Senate 1909-May 23, 1914; Gov. 189 99.

BRADLEY, William Warren "Bill" (D N.J.) July 2 1943- —; Senate 1979- —.

BRADLEY, Willis Winter (R Calif.) June 28, 1884-Au 27, 1954; House 1947-49.

BRADSHAW, Samuel Carey (W Pa.) June 10, 180 June 9, 1872; House 1855-57.

BRADY, James Dennis (R Va.) April 3, 1843-Nov. 3 1900; House 1885-87.

BRADY, James Henry (R Idaho) June 12, 1862-Jan. 1 1918; Senate Feb. 6, 1913-Jan. 13, 1918; Gov. 190 11.

BRADY, Jasper Ewing (W Pa.) March 4, 1797-Jan. 2 1871; House 1847-49.

BRADY, Nicholas Frederick (R N.J.) April 11, 1930- — Senate April 12-Dec. 20, 1982.

BRAGG, Edward Stuyvesant (D Wis.) Feb. 20, 1827-June 20, 1912; House 1877-83, 1885-87.

BRAGG, John (SRD Ala.) Jan. 14, 1806-Aug. 10, 1878; House 1851-53.

BRAGG, Thomas (D N.C.) Nov. 9, 1810-Jan. 21, 1872; Senate 1859-March 6, 1861; Gov. 1855-59.

BRAINERD, Lawrence (FS Vt.) March 16, 1794-May 9, 1870; Senate Oct. 14, 1854-55.

BRAINERD, Samuel Myron (R Pa.) Nov. 13, 1842-Nov. 21, 1898; House 1883-85.

BRAMBLETT, Ernest King (R Calif.) April 25, 1901-Dec. 27, 1966; House 1947-55.

BRANCH, John (uncle of Lawrence O'Bryan Branch, granduncle of William Augustus Blount Branch) (D N.C.) Nov. 4, 1782-Jan. 4, 1863; Senate 1823-March 9, 1829; House May 12, 1831-33; Gov. 1817-20; Secy. of the Navy 1829-31.

BRANCH, Lawrence O'Bryan (father of William Augustus Blount Branch, nephew of John Branch) (D N.C.) Nov. 28, 1820-Sept. 17, 1862; House 1855-61.

BRANCH, William Augustus Blount (son of Lawrence O'Bryan Branch, grandnephew of John Branch) (D N.C.) Feb. 26, 1847-Nov. 18, 1910; House 1891-95.

RAND, Charles (R Ohio) Nov. 1, 1871-May 23, 1966; House 1923-33.

RAND, Charles Hillyer (D Ga.) April 20, 1861-May 17, 1933; House 1917-May 17, 1933.

BRANDEGEE, Augustus (father of Frank Bosworth Brandegee) (R Conn.) July 15, 1828-Nov. 10, 1904; House 1863-67.

BRANDEGEE, Frank Bosworth (son of Augustus Brandegee) (R Conn.) July 8, 1864-Oct. 14, 1924; House Nov. 5, 1902-May 10, 1905; Senate May 10, 1905-Oct. 14, 1924.

BRANTLEY, William Gordon (D Ga.) Sept. 18, 1860-Sept. 11, 1934; House 1897-1913.

RASCO, Frank J. (D N.Y.) Oct. 15, 1932- —; House 1967-75.

RATTON, John (D S.C.) March 7, 1831-Jan. 12, 1898; House Dec. 8, 1884-85.

RATTON, Robert Franklin (D Md.) May 3, 1845-May 10, 1894; House 1893-May 10, 1894.

RATTON, Sam Gilbert (D N.M.) Aug. 19, 1888-Sept. 22, 1963; Senate 1925-June 24, 1933.

BRAWLEY, William Huggins (cousin of John James Hemphill, granduncle of Robert Witherspoon Hemphill) (D S.C.) May 13, 1841-Nov. 15, 1916; House 1891-Feb. 12, 1894.

BRAXTON, Elliott Muse (D Va.) Oct. 8, 1823-Oct. 2, 1891; House 1871-73.

BRAY, William Gilmer (R Ind.) June 17, 1903-June 4, 1979; House 1951-75.

BRAYTON, William Daniel (R R.I.) Nov. 6, 1815-June 30, 1887; House 1857-61.

BREAUX, John Berlinger (D La.) March 1, 1944- —; House Sept. 30, 1972-87; Senate 1987- —.

BREAZEALE, Phanor (D La.) Dec. 29, 1858-April 29, 1934; House 1899-1905.

BRECK, Daniel (brother of Samuel Breck) (W Ky.) Feb. 12, 1788-Feb. 4, 1871; House 1849-51.

BRECK, Samuel (brother of Daniel Breck) (F Pa.) July 17, 1771-Aug. 31, 1862; House 1823-25.

BRECKINRIDGE, Clifton Rodes (son of John Cabell Breckinridge, great-grandson of John Breckinridge) (D Ark.) Nov. 22, 1846-Dec. 3, 1932; House 1883-Sept. 5, 1890, Nov. 4, 1890-Aug. 14, 1894.

BRECKINRIDGE, James (brother of John Breckinridge) (F Va.) March 7, 1763-May 13, 1833; House 1809-17.

BRECKINRIDGE, James Douglas (— Ky.) ?-May 6, 1849; House Nov. 21, 1821-23.

BRECKINRIDGE, John (brother of James Breckinridge, grandfather of John Cabell Breckinridge, William Campbell Preston Breckinridge, great-grandfather of Clifton Rodes Breckinridge) (D Ky.) Dec. 2, 1760-Dec. 14, 1806; Senate 1801-Aug. 7, 1805; Atty. Gen. 1805-06.

BRECKINRIDGE, John Bayne (D Ky.) Nov. 29, 1913-July 29, 1979; House 1973-79.

BRECKINRIDGE, John Cabell (grandson of John Breckinridge, father of Clifton Rodes Breckinridge, cousin of Henry Donnel Foster) (D Ky.) Jan. 21, 1821-May 17, 1875; House 1851-55; Senate March 4-Dec. 4, 1861; Vice President 1857-61.

BRECKINRIDGE, William Campbell Preston (grandson of John Breckinridge, uncle of Levin Irving Handy) (D Ky.) Aug. 28, 1837-Nov. 18, 1904; House 1885-95.

BREEDING, James Floyd (D Kan.) Sept. 28, 1901-Oct. 17, 1977; House 1957-63.

BREEN, Edward G. (D Ohio) June 10, 1908- —; House 1949-Oct. 1, 1951.

BREESE, Sidney (D Ill.) July 15, 1800-June 28, 1878; Senate 1843-49.

BREHM, Walter Ellsworth (R Ohio) May 25, 1892- —; House 1943-53.

BREITUNG, Edward (R Mich.) Nov. 10, 1831-March 3, 1887; House 1883-85.

BREMNER, Robert Gunn (D N.J.) Dec. 17, 1874-Feb. 5, 1914; House 1913-Feb. 5, 1914.

BRENGLE, Francis (W Md.) Nov. 26, 1807-Dec. 10, 1846; House 1843-45.

BRENNAN, Joseph E. (D Maine) Nov. 2, 1934- —; House 1987- —; Gov. 1978-87.

BRENNAN, Martin Adlai (D Ill.) Sept. 21, 1879-July 4, 1941; House 1933-37.

BRENNAN, Vincent Morrison (R Mich.) April 22, 1890-Feb. 4, 1959; House 1921-23.

BRENNER, John Lewis (D Ohio) Feb. 2, 1832-Nov. 1, 1906; House 1897-1901.

BRENT, Richard (uncle of William Leigh Brent, nephew of Daniel Carroll) (— Va.) 1757-Dec. 30, 1814; House 1795-99, 1801-03; Senate 1809-Dec. 30, 1814.

BRENT, William Leigh (nephew of Richard Brent) (— La.) Feb. 20, 1784-July 7, 1848; House 1823-29.

BRENTANO, Lorenzo (R Ill.) Nov. 4, 1813-Sept. 18, 1891; House 1877-79.

BRENTON, Samuel (R Ind.) Nov. 22, 1810-March 29, 1857; House 1851-53 (Whig), 1855-March 29, 1857.

BRENTS, Thomas Hurley (R Wash.) Dec. 24, 1840-Oct. 23, 1916; House (Terr. Del.) 1879-85.

BRETZ, John Lewis (D Ind.) Sept. 21, 1852-Dec. 25, 1920; House 1891-95.

BREVARD, Joseph (W S.C.) July 19, 1766-Oct. 11, 1821; House 1819-21.

BREWER, Francis Beattie (R N.Y.) Oct. 8, 1820-July 29, 1892; House 1883-85.

BREWER, John Hart (R N.J.) March 29, 1844-Dec. 21, 1900; House 1881-85.

BREWER, Mark Spencer (R Mich.) Oct. 22, 1837-March 18, 1901; House 1877-81, 1887-91.

BREWER, Willis (D Ala.) March 15, 1844-Oct. 30, 1912; House 1897-1901.

BREWSTER, Daniel Baugh (D Md.) Nov. 23, 1923- —; House 1959-63; Senate 1963-69.

BREWSTER, David P. (D N.Y.) June 15, 1801-Feb. 20 1876; House 1839-43.

BREWSTER, Henry Colvin (R N.Y.) Sept. 7, 1845-Jan 29, 1928; House 1895-99.

BREWSTER, Ralph Owen (R Maine) Feb. 22, 1888 Dec. 25, 1961; House 1935-41; Senate 1941-Dec. 31 1952; Gov. 1925-29.

BRICE, Calvin Stewart (D Ohio) Sept. 17, 1845-Dec. 15 1898; Senate 1891-97; Chrmn. Dem. Nat. Comm 1889-1892.

BRICK, Abraham Lincoln (R Ind.) May 27, 1860-Apr 7, 1908; House 1899-April 7, 1908.

BRICKER, John William (R Ohio) Sept. 6, 1893-Marc 22, 1986; Senate 1947-59; Gov. 1939-45.

BRICKNER, George H. (D Wis.) Jan. 21, 1834-Aug. 1. 1904; House 1889-95.

BRIDGES, George Washington (U Tenn.) Oct. 9, 182 March 16, 1873; House Feb. 25-March 3, 1863.

BRIDGES, Henry Styles (R N.H.) Sept. 9, 1898-No 26, 1961; Senate 1937-Nov. 26, 1961; Pres. pro ten pore 1953-55; Gov. 1935-37.

BRIDGES, Samuel Augustus (D Pa.) Jan. 27, 1802-Ja 14, 1884; House March 6, 1848-49, 1853-55, 1877-7

BRIGGS, Clay Stone (D Texas) Jan. 8, 1876-April 2 1933; House 1919-April 29, 1933.

BRIGGS, Frank Obadiah (son of James Franklar Briggs) (R N.J.) Aug. 12, 1851-May 8, 1913; Sena 1907-13.

BRIGGS, Frank Parks (D Mo.) Feb. 25, 1894- —; Sena Jan. 18, 1945-47.

BRIGGS, George (AP N.Y.) May 6, 1805-June 1, 186 House 1849-53 (Whig), 1859-61.

BRIGGS, George Nixon (W Mass.) April 12, 1796-Se 11, 1861; House 1831-43; Gov. 1844-51.

BRIGGS, James Frankland (father of Frank Obadi Briggs) (R N.H.) Oct. 23, 1827-Jan. 21, 1905; Hou 1877-83.

BRIGHAM, Elbert Sidney (R Vt.) Oct. 19, 1877-July 1962; House 1925-31.

BRIGHAM, Elijah (F Mass.) July 7, 1751-Feb. 22, 18 House 1811-Feb. 22, 1816.

BRIGHAM, Lewis Alexander (R N.J.) Jan. 2, 1831-F 19, 1885; House 1879-81.

BRIGHT, Jesse David (D Ind.) Dec. 18, 1812-May 1875; Senate 1845-Feb. 5, 1862; Pres. pro temp 1854, 1856, 1860.

BRIGHT, John Morgan (D Tenn.) Jan. 20, 1817-Oct. 3, 1911; House 1871-81.

BRINKERHOFF, Henry Roelif (cousin of Jacob Brinkerhoff) (D Ohio) Sept. 23, 1787-April 30, 1844; House 1843-April 30, 1844.

BRINKERHOFF, Jacob (cousin of Henry Roelif Brinkerhoff) (D Ohio) Aug. 31, 1810-July 19, 1880; House 1843-47.

BRINKLEY, Jack Thomas (D Ga.) Dec. 22, 1930- —; House 1967-83.

BRINSON, Samuel Mitchell (D N.C.) March 20, 1870-April 13, 1922; House 1919-April 13, 1922.

BRISBIN, John (W Pa.) July 13, 1818-Feb. 3, 1880; House Jan. 13-March 3, 1851.

BRISTOW, Francis Marion (W Ky.) Aug. 11, 1804-June 10, 1864; House Dec. 4, 1854-55, 1859-61.

BRISTOW, Henry (R N.Y.) June 5, 1840-Oct. 11, 1906; House 1901-03.

BRISTOW, Joseph Little (R Kan.) July 22, 1861-July 14, 1944; Senate 1909-15.

BRITT, Charles Robin (D N.C.) June 29, 1942- —; House 1983-85.

BRITT, James Jefferson (R N.C.) March 4, 1861-Dec. 26, 1939; House 1915-17, March 1-3, 1919.

BRITTEN, Frederick Albert (R Ill.) Nov. 18, 1871-May 4, 1946; House 1913-35.

BROADHEAD, James Overton (D Mo.) May 29, 1819-Aug. 7, 1898; House 1883-85.

BROCK, Lawrence (D Neb.) Aug. 16, 1906-Aug. 28, 1968; House 1959-61.

BROCK, William Emerson (grandfather of William Emerson Brock III) (D Tenn.) March 14, 1872-Aug. 5, 1950; Senate Sept. 2, 1929-31.

BROCK, William Emerson III (grandson of William Emerson Brock) (R Tenn.) Nov. 23, 1930- —; House 1963-71; Senate 1971-77; Chrmn. Rep. Nat. Comm. 1977-81; Secy. of Labor 1985- —.

BROCKENBROUGH, William Henry (D Fla.) Feb. 23, 1812-Jan. 28, 1850; House Jan. 24, 1846-47.

BROCKSON, Franklin (D Del.) Aug. 6, 1865-March 16, 1942; House 1913-15.

BROCKWAY, John Hall (W Conn.) Jan. 31, 1801-July 29, 1870; House 1839-43.

BRODBECK, Andrew R. (D Pa.) April 11, 1860-Feb. 27, 1937; House 1913-15, 1917-19.

BRODERICK, Case (cousin of David Colbreth Broderick and Andrew Kennedy) (R Kan.) Sept. 23, 1839-April 1, 1920; House 1891-99.

BRODERICK, David Colbreth (cousin of Andrew Kennedy and Case Broderick) (D Calif.) Feb. 4, 1820-Sept. 16, 1859; Senate 1857-Sept. 16, 1859.

BRODHEAD, John (D N.H.) Oct. 5, 1770-April 7, 1838; House 1829-33.

BRODHEAD, John Curtis (D N.Y.) Oct. 27, 1780-Jan. 2, 1859; House 1831-33, 1837-39.

BRODHEAD, Joseph Davis (son of Richard Brodhead) (D Pa.) Jan. 12, 1859-April 23, 1920; House 1907-09.

BRODHEAD, Richard (father of Joseph Brodhead) (D Pa.) Jan. 5, 1811-Sept. 16, 1863; House 1843-49; Senate 1851-57.

BRODHEAD, William McNulty (D Mich.) Sept. 12, 1941- —; House 1975-83.

BROGDEN, Curtis Hooks (R N.C.) Nov. 6, 1816-Jan. 5, 1901; House 1877-79; Gov. 1874-77.

BROMBERG, Frederick George (LR/D Ala.) June 19, 1837-Sept. 4, 1930; House 1873-75.

BROMWELL, Henry Pelham Holmes (R Ill.) Aug. 26, 1823-Jan. 7, 1903; House 1865-69.

BROMWELL, Jacob Henry (R Ohio) May 11, 1848-June 4, 1924; House Dec. 3, 1894-1903.

BROMWELL, James E. (R Iowa) March 26, 1920- —; House 1961-65.

BRONSON, David (W Maine) Feb. 8, 1800-Nov. 20, 1863; House May 31, 1841-43.

BRONSON, Isaac Hopkins (D N.Y.) Oct. 16, 1802-Aug. 13, 1855; House 1837-39.

BROOCKS, Moses Lycurgus (D Texas) Nov. 1, 1864-May 27, 1908; House 1905-07.

BROOKE, Edward W. (R Mass.) Oct. 26, 1919- —; Senate 1967-79.

BROOKE, Walker (W Miss.) Dec. 25, 1813-Feb. 18, 1869; Senate Feb. 18, 1852-53.

BROOKHART, Smith Wildman (PR Iowa) Feb. 2, 1869-Nov. 15, 1944; Senate Nov. 7, 1922-April 12, 1926, 1927-33.

BROOKS, Charles Wayland (R Ill.) March 8, 1897-Jan. 14, 1957; Senate Nov. 22, 1940-49.

BROOKS, David (— N.Y.) 1756-Aug. 30, 1838; House 1797-99.

BROOKS, Edward Schroeder (R Pa.) June 14, 1867-July 12, 1957; House 1919-23.

BROOKS, Edwin Bruce (cousin of Edmund Howard Hinshaw) (R Ill.) Sept. 20, 1868-Sept. 18, 1933; House 1919-23.

BROOKS, Franklin Eli (R Colo.) Nov. 19, 1860-Feb. 7, 1916; House 1903-07.

BROOKS, George Merrick (R Mass.) July 26, 1824-Sept. 22, 1893; House Nov. 2, 1869-May 3, 1872.

BROOKS, Jack Bascom (D Texas) Dec. 18, 1922- —; House 1953- —.

BROOKS, James (D N.Y.) Nov. 10, 1810-April 30, 1873; House 1849-53 (Whig), 1863-April 7, 1866, 1867-April 30, 1873.

BROOKS, Joshua Twing (D Pa.) Feb. 27, 1884-Feb. 7, 1956; House 1933-37.

BROOKS, Micah (— N.Y.) May 14, 1775-July 7, 1857; House 1815-17.

BROOKS, Overton (nephew of John Holmes Overton) (D La.) Dec. 21, 1897-Sept. 16, 1961; House 1937-Sept. 16, 1961.

BROOKS, Preston Smith (SRD S.C.) Aug. 5, 1819-Jan. 27, 1857; House 1853-July 15, 1856, Aug. 1, 1856-Jan. 27, 1857.

BROOKSHIRE, Elijah Voorhees (D Ind.) Aug. 15, 1856-April 14, 1936; House 1889-95.

BROOM, Jacob (son of James Madison Broom) (AW Pa.) July 25, 1808-Nov. 28, 1864; House 1855-57.

BROOM, James Madison (father of Jacob Broom) (F Del.) 1776-Jan. 15, 1850; House 1805-07.

BROOMALL, John Martin (R Pa.) Jan. 19, 1816-June 3, 1894; House 1863-69.

BROOMFIELD, William S. (R Mich.) April 28, 1922- —; House 1957- —.

BROPHY, John Charles (R Wis.) Oct. 8, 1901-Dec. 26, 1976; House 1947-49.

BROSIUS, Marriott (R Pa.) March 7, 1843-March 16, 1901; House 1889-March 16, 1901.

BROTZMAN, Donald Glenn (R Colo.) June 28, 1922- —; House 1963-65, 1967-75.

BROUGHTON, Joseph Melville (D N.C.) Nov. 17, 1888-March 6, 1949; Senate Dec. 31, 1948-March 6, 1949; Gov. 1941-45.

BROUSSARD, Edwin Sidney (brother of Robert Foligny Broussard) (D La.) Dec. 4, 1874-Nov. 19, 1934; Senate 1921-33.

BROUSSARD, Robert Foligny (brother of Edwin Sidney Broussard) (D La.) Aug. 17, 1864-April 12, 1918; House 1897-1915; Senate 1915-April 12, 1918.

BROWER, John Morehead (R N.C.) July 19, 1845-Aug 5, 1913; House 1887-91.

BROWN, Aaron Venable (D Tenn.) Aug. 15, 1795-March 8, 1859; House 1839-45; Gov. 1845-47; Postmaster Gen. 1857-59.

BROWN, Albert Gallatin (D Miss.) May 31, 1813-June 12, 1880; House 1839-41, 1847-53; Senate Jan. 7, 1854-Jan. 12, 1861; Gov. 1844-48.

BROWN, Anson (W N.Y.) 1800-June 14, 1840; House 1839-June 14, 1840.

BROWN, Arthur (R Utah) March 8, 1843-Dec. 12, 1906; Senate Jan. 22, 1896-97.

BROWN, Bedford (D N.C.) June 6, 1795-Dec. 6, 1870; Senate Dec. 9, 1829-Nov. 16, 1840.

BROWN, Benjamin (nephew of John Brown) (— Mass. Sept. 23, 1756-Sept. 17, 1831; House 1815-17.

BROWN, Benjamin Gratz (grandson of John Brown of Va. and Ky.) (D Mo.) May 28, 1826-Dec. 13, 1885; Senate Nov. 13, 1863-67; Gov. 1871-73 (Liberal Republican).

BROWN, Charles (D Pa.) Sept. 23, 1797-Sept. 4, 1883; House 1841-43, 1847-49.

BROWN, Charles Elwood (R Ohio) July 4, 1834-May 22, 1904; House 1885-89.

BROWN, Charles Harrison (D Mo.) Oct. 22, 1920- —; House 1957-61.

BROWN, Clarence J. (father of Clarence J. Brown Jr. (R Ohio) July 14, 1893-Aug. 23, 1965; House 1939-Aug. 23, 1965.

BROWN, Clarence J. Jr. (son of Clarence J. Brown) (Ohio) June 18, 1927- —; House Nov. 2, 1965-83.

BROWN, Elias (W Md.) May 9, 1793-July 7, 1857; House 1829-31.

BROWN, Ernest S. (R Nev.) Sept. 25, 1903-July 23, 1965; Senate Oct. 1-Dec. 1, 1954.

BROWN, Ethan Allen (D Ohio) July 4, 1776-Feb. 24, 1852; Senate Jan. 3, 1822-25; Gov. 1818-22 (Democratic Republican).

BROWN, Foster Vincent (father of Joseph Edgar Brown) (R Tenn.) Dec. 24, 1852-March 26, 1937; House 1895-97.

BROWN, Fred Herbert (D N.H.) April 12, 1879-Feb. 3, 1955; Senate 1933-39; Gov. 1923-25.

BROWN, Garry E. (R Mich.) Aug. 12, 1923- —; House 1967-79.

BROWN, George E. Jr. (D Calif.) March 6, 1920- —; House 1963-71, 1973- —.

BROWN, George Houston (W N.J.) Feb. 12, 1810-Aug. 1, 1865; House 1851-53.

BROWN, Hank (R Colo.) Feb. 12, 1940- —; House 1981- —.

BROWN, James (brother of John Brown of Va. and Ky.) (— La.) Sept. 11, 1776-April 7, 1835; Senate Feb. 5, 1813-17, 1819-Dec. 10, 1823.

BROWN, James Sproat (D Wis.) Feb. 1, 1824-April 15, 1878; House 1863-65.

BROWN, James W. (son-in-law of Thomas Marshall Howe) (R Pa.) July 14, 1844-Oct. 23, 1909; House 1903-05.

BROWN, Jason Brevoort (D Ind.) Feb. 26, 1839-March 10, 1898; House 1889-95.

BROWN, Jeremiah (W Pa.) April 14, 1785-March 2, 1858; House 1841-45.

BROWN, John (uncle of Benjamin Brown, grandfather of John Brown Francis) (F R.I.) Jan. 27, 1736-Sept. 20, 1803; House 1799-1801.

BROWN, John (D Md.) ?-Dec. 13, 1815; House 1809-10.

BROWN, John (brother of James Brown, grandfather of Benjamin Gratz Brown) (— Va./Ky.) Sept. 12, 1757-Aug. 29, 1837; House 1789-June 1, 1792 (Ky. district of Va.); Senate June 18, 1792-1805 (Ky.); Pres. pro tempore 1803-04; Cont. Cong. (Ky. district of Va.) 1787-88.

BROWN, John (— Pa.) Aug. 12, 1772-Oct. 12, 1845; House 1821-25.

BROWN, John Brewer (D Md.) May 13, 1836-May 16, 1898; House Nov. 8, 1892-93.

BROWN, John Robert (IR Va.) Jan. 14, 1842-Aug. 4, 1927; House 1887-89.

BROWN, John W. (D N.Y.) Oct. 11, 1796-Sept. 6, 1875; House 1833-37.

BROWN, John Young (nephew of Bryan Rust Young and William Singleton Young) (D Ky.) June 28, 1835-Jan. 11, 1904; House 1859-61, 1873-77; Gov. 1891-95.

BROWN, John Young (D Ky.) Feb. 1, 1900-June 16, 1985; House 1933-35.

BROWN, Joseph Edgar (son of Foster Vincent Brown) (R Tenn.) Feb. 11, 1880-June 13, 1939; House 1921-23.

BROWN, Joseph Emerson (D Ga.) April 15, 1821-Nov. 30, 1894; Senate May 26, 1880-91; Gov. 1857-65.

BROWN, Lathrop (D N.Y.) Feb. 26, 1883-Nov. 28, 1959; House 1913-15.

BROWN, Milton (W Tenn.) Feb. 28, 1804-May 15, 1883; House 1841-47.

BROWN, Norris (R Neb.) May 2, 1863-Jan. 5, 1960; Senate 1907-13.

BROWN, Paul (D Ga.) March 31, 1880-Sept. 24, 1961; House July 5, 1933-61.

BROWN, Prentiss Marsh (D Mich.) June 18, 1889-Dec. 19, 1973; House 1933-Nov. 18, 1936; Senate Nov. 19, 1936-43.

BROWN, Robert (D Pa.) Dec. 25, 1744-Feb. 26, 1823; House Dec. 4, 1798-1815.

BROWN, Seth W. (R Ohio) Jan. 4, 1841-Feb. 24, 1923; House 1897-1901.

BROWN, Titus (— N.H.) Feb. 11, 1786-Jan. 29, 1849; House 1825-29.

BROWN, Webster Everett (R Wis.) July 16, 1851-Dec. 14, 1929; House 1901-07.

BROWN, William (— Ky.) April 19, 1779-Oct. 6, 1833; House 1819-21.

BROWN, William Gay (father of William Gay Brown Jr.) (U W.Va.) Sept. 25, 1800-April 19, 1884; House 1845-49 (Democrat Va.), 1861-63 (Va.), Dec. 7, 1863-65.

BROWN, William Gay Jr. (son of William Gay Brown) (D W.Va.) April 7, 1856-March 9, 1916; House 1911-March 9, 1916.

BROWN, William John (D Ind.) Aug. 15, 1805-March 18, 1857; House 1843-45, 1849-51.

BROWN, William Ripley (R Kan.) July 16, 1840-March 3, 1916; House 1875-77.

BROWN, William Wallace (R Pa.) April 22, 1836-Nov. 4, 1926; House 1883-87.

BROWNE, Charles (D N.J.) Sept. 28, 1875-Aug. 17, 1947; House 1923-25.

BROWNE, Edward Everts (R Wis.) Feb. 16, 1868-Nov. 23, 1945; House 1913-31.

BROWNE, George Huntington (D R.I.) Jan. 6, 1811-Sept. 26, 1885; House 1861-63.

BROWNE, Thomas Henry Bayly (R Va.) Feb. 8, 1844-Aug. 27, 1892; House 1887-91.

BROWNE, Thomas McLelland (R Ind.) April 19, 1829-July 17, 1891; House 1877-91.

BROWNING, Gordon (D Tenn.) Nov. 22, 1889-May 23, 1976; House 1923-35; Gov. 1937-39, 1949-53.

BROWNING, Orville Hickman (R Ill.) Feb. 10, 1806-Aug. 10, 1881; Senate June 26, 1861-Jan. 12, 1863; Secy. of the Interior 1866-69; Atty. Gen. ad interim 1868.

BROWNING, William John (R N.J.) April 11, 1850-March 24, 1920; House Nov. 7, 1911-March 24, 1920.

BROWNLOW, Walter Preston (nephew of William Gannaway Brownlow) (R Tenn.) March 27, 1851-July 8, 1910; House 1897-July 8, 1910.

BROWNLOW, William Gannaway (uncle of Walter Preston Brownlow) (R Tenn.) Aug. 29, 1805-April 29, 1877; Senate 1869-75; Gov. April 5, 1865-Oct. 1867.

BROWNSON, Charles Bruce (R Ind.) Feb. 5, 1914- —; House 1951-59.

BROYHILL, James T. (R N.C.) Aug. 19, 1927- —; House 1963-July 13, 1986; Senate July 14, 1986-Dec. 10, 1986.

BROYHILL, Joel Thomas (R Va.) Nov. 4, 1919- —; House 1953-Dec. 31, 1974.

BRUCE, Blanche Kelso (R Miss.) March 1, 1841-March 17, 1898; Senate 1875-81.

BRUCE, Donald Cogley (R Ind.) April 27, 1921-Aug. 31, 1969; House 1961-65.

BRUCE, Phineas (— Mass.) June 7, 1762-Oct. 4, 1809; (elected to House 1803 but did not serve).

BRUCE, Terry L. (D Ill.) March 25, 1944- —; House 1985- —.

BRUCE, William Cabell (D Md.) March 12, 1860-May 9, 1946; Senate 1923-29.

BRUCKER, Ferdinand (D Mich.) Jan. 8, 1858-March 3, 1904; House 1897-99.

BRUCKNER, Henry (D N.Y.) June 17, 1871-April 14, 1942; House 1913-Dec. 31, 1917.

BRUMBAUGH, Clement Laird (D Ohio) Feb. 28, 1863-Sept. 28, 1921; House 1913-21.

BRUMBAUGH, David Emmert (R Pa.) Oct. 8, 1894-April 22, 1977; House Nov. 2, 1943-47.

BRUMM, Charles Napoleon (father of George Franklin Brumm) (RG Pa.) June 9, 1838-Jan. 11, 1917; House 1881-89, 1895-99, Nov. 6, 1906-Jan. 4, 1909.

BRUMM, George Franklin (son of Charles Napoleon Brumm) (R Pa.) Jan. 24, 1880-May 29, 1934; House 1923-27, 1929-May 29, 1934.

BRUNDIDGE, Stephen Jr. (D Ark.) Jan. 1, 1857-Jan. 14, 1938; House 1897-1909.

BRUNNER, David B. (D Pa.) March 7, 1835-Nov. 29, 1903; House 1889-93.

BRUNNER, William Frank (D N.Y.) Sept. 15, 1887-April 23, 1965; House 1929-Sept. 27, 1935.

BRUNSDALE, Clarence Norman (R N.D.) July 9, 1891-Jan. 27, 1978; Senate Nov. 19, 1959-Aug. 7, 1960; Gov. 1951-57.

BRUSH, Henry (— Ohio) June 1778-Jan. 19, 1855; House 1819-21.

BRUYN, Andrew DeWitt (D N.Y.) Nov. 18, 1790-July 27, 1838; House 1837-July 27, 1838.

BRYAN, Guy Morrison (D Texas) Jan. 12, 1821-June 4, 1901; House 1857-59.

BRYAN, Henry H. (— Tenn.) ?-May 7, 1835; House 1819-21 (reelected 1820 but did not serve).

BRYAN, James Wesley (PR Wash.) March 11, 1874-Aug. 26, 1956; House 1913-15.

BRYAN, John Heritage (W N.C.) Nov. 4, 1798-May 19, 1870; House 1825-29.

BRYAN, Joseph (D Ga.) Aug. 18, 1773-Sept. 12, 1812; House 1803-06.

BRYAN, Joseph Hunter (— N.C.) ?-?; House 1815-19.

BRYAN, Nathan (— N.C.) 1748-June 4, 1798; House 1795-June 4, 1798.

BRYAN, Nathan Philemon (brother of William James Bryan) (D Fla.) April 23, 1872-Aug. 8, 1935; Senate 1911-17.

BRYAN, William James (brother of Nathan Philemon Bryan) (D Fla.) Oct. 10, 1876-March 22, 1908; Senate Dec. 26, 1907-March 22, 1908.

BRYAN, William Jennings (father of Ruth Bryan Owen) (D Neb.) March 19, 1860-July 26, 1925; House 1891-95; Secy. of State 1913-15.

BRYANT, John Wiley (D Texas) Feb. 22, 1947- — House 1983- —.

BRYCE, Lloyd Stephens (D N.Y.) Sept. 20, 1850-April 2, 1917; House 1887-89.

BRYSON, Joseph Raleigh (D S.C.) Jan. 18, 1893-March 10, 1953; House 1939-March 10, 1953.

BUCHANAN, Andrew (D Pa.) April 8, 1780-Dec. 2, 1848; House 1835-39.

BUCHANAN, Frank (D Ill.) June 14, 1862-April 18, 1930; House 1911-17.

BUCHANAN, Frank (husband of Vera Daerr Buchanan) (D Pa.) Dec. 1, 1902-April 27, 1951; House May 21, 1946-April 27, 1951.

BUCHANAN, Hugh (D Ga.) Sept. 15, 1823-June 11, 1890; House 1881-85.

BUCHANAN, James (D Pa.) April 23, 1791-June 1, 1868; House 1821-31; Senate Dec. 6, 1834-March 5, 1845; Secy. of State 1845-49; President 1857-61.

BUCHANAN, James (R N.J.) June 17, 1839-Oct. 30, 1900; House 1885-93.

BUCHANAN, James Paul (cousin of Edward William Pou) (D Texas) April 30, 1867-Feb. 22, 1937; House April 5, 1913-Feb. 22, 1937.

BUCHANAN, John Alexander (D Va.) Oct. 7, 1843-Sept. 2, 1921; House 1889-93.

BUCHANAN, John Hall Jr. (R Ala.) March 19, 1928--; House 1965-81.

BUCHANAN, Vera Daerr (widow of Frank Buchanan) (D Pa.) July 20, 1902-Nov. 26, 1955; House July 24, 1951-Nov. 26, 1955.

BUCHER, John Conrad (− Pa.) Dec. 28, 1792-Oct. 15, 1851; House 1831-33.

BUCK, Alfred Eliab (R Ala.) Feb. 7, 1832-Dec. 4, 1902; House 1869-71.

BUCK, Charles Francis (D La.) Nov. 5, 1841-Jan. 19, 1918; House 1895-97.

BUCK, Clayton Douglass (great-grandnephew of John Middleton Clayton) (R Del.) March 21, 1890-Jan. 27, 1965; Senate 1943-49; Gov. 1929-37.

BUCK, Daniel (father of Daniel Azro Ashley Buck) (F Vt.) Nov. 9, 1753-Aug. 16, 1816; House 1795-97.

BUCK, Daniel Azro Ashley (son of Daniel Buck) (D Vt.) April 19, 1789-Dec. 24, 1841; House 1823-25, 1827-29.

BUCK, Ellsworth Brewer (R N.Y.) July 3, 1892-Aug. 14, 1970; House June 6, 1944-49.

BUCK, Frank Henry (D Calif.) Sept. 23, 1887-Sept. 17, 1942; House 1933-Sept. 17, 1942.

BUCK, John Ransom (R Conn.) Dec. 6, 1835-Feb. 6, 1917; House 1881-83, 1885-87.

BUCKALEW, Charles Rollin (D Pa.) Dec. 28, 1821-May 19, 1899; Senate 1863-69; House 1887-91.

BUCKBEE, John Theodore (R Ill.) Aug. 1, 1871-April 23, 1936; House 1927-April 23, 1936.

BUCKINGHAM, William Alfred (R Conn.) May 28, 1804-Feb. 5, 1875; Senate 1869-Feb. 5, 1875; Gov. 1858-66.

BUCKLAND, Ralph Pomeroy (R Ohio) Jan. 20, 1812-May 27, 1892; House 1865-69.

BUCKLER, Richard Thompson (FL Minn.) Oct. 27, 1865-Jan. 23, 1950; House 1935-43.

BUCKLEY, Charles Anthony (D N.Y.) June 23, 1890-Jan. 22, 1967; House 1935-65.

BUCKLEY, Charles Waldron (R Ala.) Feb. 18, 1835-Dec. 4, 1906; House July 21, 1868-73.

BUCKLEY, James Lane (C/R N.Y.) March 9, 1923--; Senate 1971-77.

BUCKLEY, James Richard (D Ill.) Nov. 18, 1870-June 22, 1945; House 1923-25.

BUCKLEY, James Vincent (D Ill.) May 15, 1894-July 30, 1954; House 1949-51.

BUCKMAN, Clarence Bennett (R Minn.) April 1, 1851-March 1, 1917; House 1903-07.

BUCKNER, Alexander (− Mo.) 1785-June 6, 1833; Senate 1831-June 6, 1833.

BUCKNER, Aylett (son of Richard Aylett Buckner) (W Ky.) July 21, 1806-July 3, 1869; House 1847-49.

BUCKNER, Aylett Hawes (nephew of Aylett Hawes, cousin of Richard Hawes and Albert Gallatin Hawes) (D Mo.) Dec. 14, 1816-Feb. 5, 1894; House 1873-85.

BUCKNER, Richard Aylett (father of Aylett Buckner) (AD Ky.) July 16, 1763-Dec. 8, 1847; House 1823-29.

BUDD, James Herbert (D Calif.) May 18, 1851-July 30, 1908; House 1883-85; Gov. 1895-99.

BUDGE, Hamer.Harold (R Idaho) Nov. 21, 1910--; House 1951-61.

BUECHNER, Jack (R Mo.) June 6, 1940--; House 1987--.

BUEL, Alexander Woodruff (D Mich.) Dec. 13, 1813-April 19, 1868; House 1849-51.

BUELL, Alexander Hamilton (D N.Y.) July 14, 1801-Jan. 29, 1853; House 1851-Jan. 29, 1853.

BUFFETT, Howard Homan (R Neb.) Aug. 13, 1903-April 30, 1964; House 1943-49, 1951-53.

BUFFIN(G)TON, James (R Mass.) March 16, 1817-March 7, 1875; House 1855-63, 1869-March 7, 1875.

BUFFINGTON, Joseph (W Pa.) Nov. 17, 1803-Feb. 3, 1872; House 1843-47.

BUFFUM, Joseph Jr. (D N.H.) Sept. 23, 1784-Feb. 24, 1874; House 1819-21.

BUGG, Robert Malone (W Tenn.) Jan. 20, 1805-Feb. 18, 1887; House 1853-55.

BULKELEY, Morgan Gardner (cousin of Edwin Dennison Morgan) (R Conn.) Dec. 26, 1837-Nov. 6, 1922; Senate 1905-11; Gov. 1889-93.

BULKLEY, Robert Johns (D Ohio) Oct. 8, 1880-July 21, 1965; House 1911-15; Senate Dec. 1, 1930-39.

BULL, John (W Mo.) 1803-Feb. 1863; House 1833-35.

BULL, Melville (R R.I.) Sept. 29, 1854-July 5, 1909; House 1895-1903.

BULLARD, Henry Adams (W La.) Sept. 9, 1788-April 17, 1851; House 1831-Jan. 4, 1834, Dec. 5, 1850-51.

BULLOCH, William Bellinger (D Ga.) 1777-May 6, 1852; Senate April 8-Nov. 6, 1813.

BULLOCK, Robert (D Fla.) Dec. 8, 1828-July 27, 1905; House 1889-93.

BULLOCK, Stephen (F Mass.) Oct. 10, 1735-Feb. 2, 1816; House 1797-99.

BULLOCK, Wingfield (− Ky.) ?-Oct. 13, 1821; House 1821-Oct. 13, 1821.

BULOW, William John (D S.D.) Jan. 13, 1869-Feb. 26, 1960; Senate 1931-43; Gov. 1927-31.

BULWINKLE, Alfred Lee (D N.C.) April 21, 1883-Aug. 31, 1950; House 1921-29, 1931-Aug. 31, 1950.

BUMPERS, Dale (D Ark.) Aug. 12, 1925-−; Senate 1975-−; Gov. 1971-75.

BUNCH, Samuel (W Tenn.) Dec. 4, 1786-Sept. 5, 1849; House 1833-37.

BUNDY, Hezekiah Sanford (R Ohio) Aug. 15, 1817-Dec. 12, 1895; House 1865-67, 1873-75, Dec. 4, 1893-95.

BUNDY, Solomon (R N.Y.) May 22, 1823-Jan. 13, 1889; House 1877-79.

BUNKER, Berkeley Lloyd (D Nev.) Aug. 12, 1906-−; Senate Nov. 27, 1940-Dec. 6, 1942; House 1945-47.

BUNN, Benjamin Hickman (D N.C.) Oct. 19, 1844-Aug. 25, 1907; House 1889-95.

BUNNELL, Frank Charles (R Pa.) March 19, 1842-Sept. 11, 1911; House Dec. 24, 1872-73, 1885-89.

BUNNER, Rudolph (AD N.Y.) Aug. 17, 1779-July 16, 1837; House 1827-29.

BUNNING, Jim (R Ky.) Oct. 23, 1931-−; House 1987-−.

BUNTING, Thomas Lathrop (D N.Y.) April 24, 1844-Dec. 27, 1898; House 1891-93.

BURCH, John Chilton (D Calif.) Feb. 1, 1826-Aug. 31, 1885; House 1859-61.

BURCH, Thomas Granville (D Va.) July 3, 1869-March 20, 1951; House 1931-May 31, 1946; Senate May 31-Nov. 5, 1946.

BURCHARD, Horatio Chapin (R Ill.) Sept. 22, 1825-May 14, 1908; House Dec. 6, 1869-79.

BURCHARD, Samuel Dickinson (D Wis.) July 17, 1836-Sept. 1, 1901; House 1875-77.

BURCHILL, Thomas Francis (D N.Y.) Aug. 3, 1882-March 28, 1960; House 1943-45.

BURD, George (− Pa.) 1793-Jan. 13, 1844; House 1831-35.

BURDETT, Samuel Swinfin (R Mo.) Feb. 21, 1836-Sept. 24, 1914; House 1869-73.

BURDICK, Clark (R R.I.) Jan. 13, 1868-Aug. 27, 1948; House 1919-33.

BURDICK, Quentin Northrop (son of Usher Lloyd Burdick, brother-in-law of Robert Woodrow Levering) (D N.D.) June 19, 1908-−; House 1959-Aug. 8, 1960; Senate Aug. 8, 1960-−.

BURDICK, Theodore Weld (R Iowa) Oct. 7, 1836-July 16, 1898; House 1877-79.

BURDICK, Usher Lloyd (father of Quentin Northrop Burdick, father-in-law of Robert Woodrow Levering) (R N.D.) Feb. 21, 1879-Aug. 19, 1960; House 1935-45, 1949-59.

BURGENER, Clair Walter (R Calif.) Dec. 5, 1921-−; House 1973-83.

BURGES, Dempsey (− N.C.) 1751-Jan. 13, 1800; House 1795-99.

BURGES, Tristam (great-granduncle of Theodore Francis Green) (− R.I.) Feb. 26, 1770-Oct. 13, 1853; House 1825-35.

BURGESS, George Farmer (D Texas) Sept. 21, 1861-Dec. 31, 1919; House 1901-17.

BURGIN, William Olin (D N.C.) July 28, 1877-April 11, 1946; House 1939-April 11, 1946.

BURK, Henry (R Pa.) Sept. 26, 1850-Dec. 5, 1903; House 1901-Dec. 5, 1903.

BURKE, Aedanus (− S.C.) June 16, 1743-March 30, 1802; House 1789-91.

BURKE, Charles Henry (R S.D.) April 1, 1861-April 7, 1944; House 1899-1907, 1909-15.

BURKE, Edmund (D N.H.) Jan. 23, 1809-Jan. 25, 1882; House 1839-45.

BURKE, Edward Raymond (D Neb.) Nov. 28, 1880-Nov. 4, 1968; House 1933-35; Senate 1935-41.

BURKE, Frank Welsh (D Ky.) June 1, 1920- —; House 1959-63.

BURKE, J. Herbert (R Fla.) Jan. 14, 1913- —; House 1967-79.

BURKE, James Anthony (D Mass.) March 30, 1910-Oct. 13, 1983; House 1959-79.

BURKE, James Francis (R Pa.) Oct. 21, 1867-Aug. 8, 1932; House 1905-15.

BURKE, John Harley (D Calif.) June 2, 1894-May 14, 1951; House 1933-35.

BURKE, Michael Edmund (D Wis.) Oct. 15, 1863-Dec. 12, 1918; House 1911-17.

BURKE, Raymond Hugh (R Ohio) Nov. 4, 1881-Aug. 18, 1954; House 1947-49.

BURKE, Robert Emmet (D Texas) Aug. 1, 1847-June 5, 1901; House 1897-June 5, 1901.

BURKE, Thomas A. (D Ohio) Oct. 30, 1898-Dec. 5, 1971; Senate Nov. 10, 1953-Dec. 2, 1954.

BURKE, Thomas Henry (D Ohio) May 6, 1904-Sept. 12, 1959; House 1949-51.

BURKE, William Joseph (R Pa.) Sept. 25, 1862-Nov. 7, 1925; House 1919-23.

BURKE, Yvonne Brathwaite (D Calif.) Oct. 5, 1932- —; House 1973-79.

BURKETT, Elmer Jacob (R Neb.) Dec. 1, 1867-May 23, 1935; House 1899-March 4, 1905; Senate 1905-11.

BURKHALTER, Everett Glenn (D Calif.) Jan. 19, 1897-May 24, 1975; House 1963-65.

BURLEIGH, Edwin Chick (R Maine) Nov. 27, 1843-June 16, 1916; House June 21, 1897-1911; Senate 1913-June 16, 1916; Gov. 1889-93.

BURLEIGH, Henry Gordon (R N.Y.) June 2, 1832-Aug. 10, 1900; House 1883-87.

BURLEIGH, John Holmes (son of William Burleigh) (R Maine) Oct. 9, 1822-Dec. 5, 1877; House 1873-77.

BURLEIGH, Walter Atwood (R Dakota) Oct. 25, 1820-March 7, 1896; House (Terr. Del.) 1865-69.

BURLEIGH, William (father of John Holmes Burleigh) (AD Maine) Oct. 24, 1785-July 2, 1827; House 1823-July 2, 1827.

BURLESON, Albert Sidney (D Texas) June 7, 1863-Nov. 24, 1937; House 1899-March 6, 1913; Postmaster Gen. 1913-21.

BURLESON, Omar Truman (D Texas) March 19, 1906- —; House 1947-Dec. 31, 1978.

BURLINGAME, Anson (R Mass.) Nov. 14, 1820-Feb. 23, 1870; House 1855-61 (1855-59 American Party).

BURLISON, Bill Dean (D Mo.) March 15, 1933- —; House 1969-81.

BURNELL, Barker (W Mass.) Jan. 30, 1798-June 15, 1843; House 1841-June 15, 1843.

BURNES, Daniel Dee (D Mo.) Jan. 4, 1851-Nov. 2, 1899; House 1893-95.

BURNES, James Nelson (D Mo.) Aug. 22, 1827-Jan. 23, 1889; House 1883-Jan. 23, 1889.

BURNET, Jacob (F N.J.) Feb. 22, 1770-May 10, 1853; Senate Dec. 10, 1828-31.

BURNETT, Edward (D Mass.) March 16, 1849-Nov. 5, 1925; House 1887-89.

BURNETT, Henry Cornelius (D Ky.) Oct. 5, 1825-Oct. 1, 1866; House 1855-Dec. 3, 1861.

BURNETT, John Lawson (D Ala.) Jan. 20, 1854-May 13, 1919; House 1899-May 13, 1919.

BURNEY, William Evans (D Colo.) Sept. 11, 1893-Jan. 29, 1969; House Nov. 5, 1940-41.

BURNHAM, Alfred Avery (R Conn.) March 8, 1819-April 11, 1879; House 1859-63.

BURNHAM, George (R Calif.) Dec. 28, 1868-June 28, 1939; House 1933-37.

BURNHAM, Henry Eben (R N.H.) Nov. 8, 1844-Feb. 8, 1917; Senate 1901-13.

BURNS, John Anthony (D Hawaii) March 30, 1909-April 5, 1975; House (Terr. Del.) 1957-Aug. 21, 1959; Gov. 1962-74.

BURNS, Joseph (D Ohio) March 11, 1800-May 12, 1875; House 1857-59.

BURNS, Robert (D N.H.) Dec. 12, 1792-June 26, 1866; House 1833-37.

BURNSIDE, Ambrose Everett (R R.I.) May 23, 1824-Sept. 13, 1881; Senate 1875-Sept. 13, 1881; Gov. 1866-69.

BURNSIDE, Maurice Gwinn (D W.Va.) Aug. 23, 1902- —; House 1949-53, 1955-57.

BURNSIDE, Thomas (— Pa.) July 28, 1782-March 25, 1851; House Oct. 10, 1815-April 1816.

BURR, Aaron (cousin of Theodore Dwight, father-in-law of Gov. Joseph Alston of S.C.) (DR N.Y.) Feb. 6, 1756-Sept. 14, 1836; Senate 1791-97; Vice President 1801-05.

BURR, Albert George (D Ill.) Nov. 8, 1829-June 10, 1882; House 1867-71.

BURRELL, Orlando (R Ill.) July 26, 1826-June 7, 1922; House 1895-97.

BURRILL, James Jr. (great-grandfather of Theodore Francis Green) (— R.I.) April 25, 1772-Dec. 25, 1820; Senate 1817-Dec. 25, 1820.

BURROUGHS, Sherman Everett (R N.H.) Feb. 6, 1870-Jan. 27, 1923; House June 7, 1917-Jan. 27, 1923.

BURROUGHS, Silas Mainville (R N.Y.) July 16, 1810-June 3, 1860; House 1857-June 3, 1860.

BURROWS, Daniel (uncle of Lorenzo Burrows) (D Conn.) Oct. 26, 1766-Jan. 23, 1858; House 1821-23.

BURROWS, Joseph Henry (G Mo.) May 15, 1840-April 28, 1914; House 1881-83.

BURROWS, Julius Caesar (R Mich.) Jan. 9, 1837-Nov. 16, 1915; House 1873-75, 1879-83, 1885-Jan. 23, 1895; Senate Jan. 24, 1895-1911.

BURROWS, Lorenzo (nephew of Daniel Burrows) (W N.Y.) March 15, 1805-March 6, 1885; House 1849-53.

BURSUM, Holm Olaf (R N.M.) Feb. 10, 1867-Aug. 7, 1953; Senate March 11, 1921-25.

BURT, Armistead (D S.C.) Nov. 13, 1802-Oct. 30, 1883; House 1843-53.

BURTNESS, Olger Burton (R N.D.) March 14, 1884-Jan. 20, 1960; House 1921-33.

BURTON, Charles Germman (R Mo.) April 4, 1846-Feb. 25, 1926; House 1895-97.

BURTON, Clarence Godber (D Va.) Dec. 14, 1886-Jan. 18, 1982; House Nov. 2, 1948-53.

BURTON, Dan Lee (R Ind.) June 21, 1938- —; House 1983- —.

BURTON, Harold Hitz (R Ohio) June 22, 1888-Oct. 28, 1964; Senate 1941-Sept. 30, 1945; Assoc. Justice Supreme Court 1945-58.

BURTON, Hiram Rodney (R Del.) Nov. 13, 1841-June 17, 1927; House 1905-09.

BURTON, Hutchins Gordon (AD N.C.) 1774-April 21, 1836; House Dec. 6, 1819-March 23, 1824; Gov. 1824-27 (Federalist).

BURTON, John Lowell (brother of Phillip Burton, brother-in-law of Sala Burton) (D Calif.) Dec. 15, 1932- —; House June 25, 1974-83.

BURTON, Joseph Ralph (R Kan.) Nov. 16, 1850-Feb. 27, 1923; Senate 1901-June 4, 1906.

BURTON, Laurence Junior (R Utah) Oct. 30, 1926- —; House 1963-71.

BURTON, Phillip (brother of John Lowell Burton, husband of Sala Burton) (D Calif.) June 1, 1926-April 10, 1983; House Feb. 18, 1964-April 10, 1983.

BURTON, Sala (widow of Phillip Burton, sister-in-law of John Lowell Burton) (D Calif.) April 1, 1925-Feb. 1, 1987; House June 28, 1983-Feb. 1, 1987.

BURTON, Theodore Elijah (R Ohio) Dec. 20, 1851-Oct. 28, 1929; House 1889-91, 1895-1909, 1921-Dec. 15, 1928; Senate 1909-15, Dec. 15, 1928-Oct. 28, 1929.

BURWELL, William Armisted (D Va.) March 15, 1780-Feb. 16, 1821; House Dec. 1, 1806-Feb. 16, 1821.

BUSBEY, Fred Ernst (R Ill.) Feb. 8, 1895-Feb. 11, 1966; House 1943-45, 1947-49, 1951-55.

BUSBY, George Henry (D Ohio) June 10, 1794-Aug. 22, 1869; House 1851-53.

BUSBY, Thomas Jefferson (D Miss.) July 26, 1884-Oct. 18, 1964; House 1923-35.

BUSEY, Samuel Thompson (D Ill.) Nov. 16, 1835-Aug. 12, 1909; House 1891-93.

BUSH, Alvin Ray (R Pa.) June 4, 1893-Nov. 5, 1959; House 1951-Nov. 5, 1959.

BUSH, George Herbert Walker (son of Prescott Sheldon Bush) (R Texas) June 12, 1924- —; House 1967-71 Chrmn. Rep. Nat. Comm. 1973-74; Vice President 1981- —.

BUSH, Prescott Sheldon (father of George Herbert Walker Bush) (R Conn.) May 15, 1895-Oct. 8, 1972; Senate Nov. 4, 1952-63.

BUSHFIELD, Harlan John (husband of Vera Cahalan Bushfield) (R S.D.) Aug. 6, 1882-Sept. 27, 1948; Senate 1943-Sept. 27, 1948; Gov. 1939-43.

BUSHFIELD, Vera Cahalan (widow of Harlan John Bushfield) (R S.D.) Aug. 9, 1889-April 16, 1976; Senate Oct. 6-Dec. 26, 1948.

BUSHNELL, Allen Ralph (D Wis.) July 18, 1833-March 29, 1909; House 1891-93.

BUSHONG, Robert Grey (grandson of Anthony Ellmaker Roberts) (R Pa.) June 10, 1883-April 6, 1951; House 1927-29.

BUSTAMANTE, Albert G. (D Texas) April 8, 1935-−; House 1985-−.

BUTLER, Andrew Pickens (son of William Butler born in 1759, brother of William Butler born in 1790, uncle of Matthew Calbraith Butler) (SRD S.C.) Nov. 19, 1796-May 25, 1857; Senate Dec. 4, 1846-May 25, 1857.

BUTLER, Benjamin Franklin (grandfather of Butler Ames, father-in-law of Adelbert Ames) (R Mass.) Nov. 5, 1818-Jan. 11, 1893; House 1867-75, 1877-79 (Greenback); Gov. 1883-84 (Greenback/Democrat).

BUTLER, Chester Pierce (W Pa.) March 21, 1798-Oct. 5, 1850; House 1847-Oct. 5, 1850.

BUTLER, Ezra (DR Vt.) Sept. 24, 1763-July 12, 1838; House 1813-15; Gov. 1826-28.

BUTLER, Hugh Alfred (R Neb.) Feb. 28, 1878-July 1, 1954; Senate 1941-July 1, 1954.

BUTLER, James Joseph (D Mo.) Aug. 29, 1862-May 31, 1917; House 1901-June 28, 1902, Nov. 4, 1902-Feb. 26, 1903, 1903-05.

BUTLER, John Cornelius (R N.Y.) July 2, 1887-Aug. 13, 1953; House April 22, 1941-49, 1951-53.

BUTLER, John Marshall (R Md.) July 21, 1897-March 14, 1978; Senate 1951-63.

BUTLER, Josiah (D N.Y.) Dec. 4, 1779-Oct. 27, 1854; House 1817-23.

BUTLER, Manley Caldwell (R Va.) June 2, 1925-−; House Nov. 7, 1972-83.

BUTLER, Marion (P N.C.) May 20, 1863-June 3, 1938; Senate 1895-1901.

BUTLER, Matthew Calbraith (son of William Butler born in 1790, grandson of William Butler born in 1759, nephew of Andrew Pickens Butler) (D S.C.) March 8, 1836-April 14, 1909; Senate 1877-95.

BUTLER, Mounce Gore (D Tenn.) May 11, 1849-Feb. 13, 1917; House 1905-07.

BUTLER, Pierce (D S.C.) July 11, 1744-Feb. 15, 1822; Senate 1789-Oct. 25, 1796, Nov. 4, 1802-Nov. 21, 1804; Cont. Cong. 1787-88.

BUTLER, Robert Reyburn (grandson of Roderick Randum Butler) (R Ore.) Sept. 24, 1881-Jan. 7, 1933; House Nov. 6, 1928-Jan. 7, 1933.

BUTLER, Roderick Randum (grandfather of Robert Reyburn Bulter) (R Tenn.) April 9, 1827-Aug. 18, 1902; House 1867-75, 1887-89.

BUTLER, Sampson Hale (D S.C.) Jan. 3, 1803-March 16, 1848; House 1839-Sept. 27, 1842.

BUTLER, Thomas (− La.) April 14, 1785-Aug. 7, 1847; House Nov. 16, 1818-21.

BUTLER, Thomas Belden (W Conn.) Aug. 22, 1806-June 8, 1873; House 1849-51.

BUTLER, Thomas Stalker (R Pa.) Nov. 4, 1855-May 26, 1928; House 1897-May 26, 1928.

BUTLER, Walter Halben (D Iowa) Feb. 13, 1852-April 24, 1931; House 1891-93.

BUTLER, William (father of Andrew Pickens Butler and William Butler, below, grandfather of Matthew Calbraith Butler) (AF S.C.) Dec. 17, 1759-Sept. 15, 1821; House 1801-13.

BUTLER, William (son of William Butler, above, brother of Andrew Pickens Butler, father of Matthew Calbraith Butler) (W S.C.) Feb. 1, 1790-Sept. 25, 1850; House 1841-43.

BUTLER, William Morgan (R Mass.) Jan. 29, 1861-March 29, 1937; Senate Nov. 13, 1924-Dec. 6, 1926; Chrmn. Rep. Nat. Comm. 1924-28.

BUTLER, William Orlando (D Ky.) April 19, 1791-Aug. 6, 1880; House 1839-43.

BUTMAN, Samuel (− Maine) 1788-Oct. 9, 1864; House 1827-31.

BUTTERFIELD, Martin (R N.Y.) Dec. 8, 1790-Aug. 6, 1866; House 1859-61.

BUTTERWORTH, Benjamin (R Ohio) Oct. 22, 1837-Jan. 16, 1898; House 1879-83, 1885-91.

BUTTON, Daniel Evan (R N.Y.) Nov. 1, 1917-−; House 1967-71.

BUTTZ, Charles Wilson (R S.C.) Nov. 16, 1837-July 20, 1913; House Nov. 7, 1876-77.

BYNUM, Jesse Atherton (D N.C.) May 23, 1797-Sept. 23, 1868; House 1833-41.

BYNUM, William Dallas (D Ind.) June 26, 1846-Oct. 21, 1927; House 1885-95.

BYRD, Adam Monroe (D Miss.) July 6, 1859-June 21, 1912; House 1903-11.

BYRD, Harry Flood (father of Harry Flood Byrd Jr., nephew of Henry De La Warr Flood and Joel West Flood) (D Va.) June 10, 1887-Oct. 20, 1966; Senate 1933-Nov. 10, 1965; Gov. 1926-30.

BYRD, Harry Flood Jr. (son of Harry Flood Byrd) (I Va.) Dec. 20, 1914-−; Senate Nov. 12, 1965-83 (1965-71 Democrat).

BYRD, Robert Carlyle (D W.Va.) Jan. 15, 1918--; House 1953-59; Senate 1959--; Senate majority leader 1977-81, 1987--.

BYRNE, Emmet Francis (R Ill.) Dec. 6, 1896-Sept. 25, 1974; House 1957-59.

BYRNE, James Aloysius (D Pa.) June 22, 1906-Sept. 3, 1980; House 1953-73.

BYRNE, William Thomas (D N.Y.) March 6, 1876-Jan. 27, 1952; House 1937-Jan. 27, 1952.

BYRNES, James Francis (D S.C.) May 2, 1879-April 9, 1972; House 1911-25; Senate 1931-July 8, 1941; Assoc. Justice Supreme Court 1941-42; Secy. of State 1945-47; Gov. 1951-55.

BYRNES, John William (R Wis.) June 12, 1913-Jan. 12, 1985; House 1945-73.

BYRNS, Joseph Wellington (father of Joseph Wellington Byrns Jr.) (D Tenn.) July 20, 1869-June 4, 1936; House 1909-June 4, 1936; House majority leader 1933-35; Speaker 1935-June 4, 1936.

BYRNS, Joseph Wellington Jr. (son of Joseph Wellington Byrns) (D Tenn.) Aug. 15, 1903--; House 1939-41.

BYRNS, Samuel (D Mo.) March 4, 1848-July 9, 1914; House 1891-93.

BYRON, Beverly Barton Butcher (widow of Goodloe Edgar Bryon, daughter-in-law of Katharine Edgar Byron and William Devereaux) (D Md.) July 26, 1932--; House 1979--.

BYRON, Goodloe Edgar (son of Katharine Edgar Byron and William Devereux Byron, great-grandson of Louis Emory McComas, husband of Beverly Barton Butcher Byron) (D Md.) June 22, 1929-Oct. 11, 1978; House 1971-Oct. 11, 1978.

BYRON, Katharine Edgar (widow of William Devereux Byron, mother of Goodloe Edgar Byron, granddaughter of Louis Emory McComas, mother-in-law of Beverly Barton Butcher Byron) (D Md.) Oct. 25, 1903-Dec. 28, 1976; House May 27, 1941-43.

BYRON, William Devereaux (husband of Katharine Edgar Byron, father of Goodloe Edgar Byron, father-in-law of Beverly Barton Butcher Byron) (D Md.) May 15, 1895-Feb. 27, 1941; House 1939-Feb. 27, 1941.

CABANISS, Thomas Banks (cousin of Thomas Chipman McRae) (D Ga.) Aug. 31, 1835-Aug. 14, 1915; House 1893-95.

CABELL, Earle (D Texas) Oct. 27, 1906-Sept. 24, 1975; House 1965-73.

CABELL, Edward Carrington (W Fla.) Feb. 5, 1816-Feb. 28, 1896; House Oct. 6, 1845-Jan. 24, 1846, 1847-53.

CABELL, George Craighead (D Va.) Jan. 25, 1836-June 23, 1906; House 1875-87.

CABELL, Samuel Jordan (D Va.) Dec. 15, 1756-Aug. 4, 1818; House 1795-1803.

CABLE, Benjamin Taylor (D Ill.) Aug. 11, 1853-Dec. 13, 1923; House 1891-93.

CABLE, John Levi (great-grandson of Joseph Cable) (R Ohio) April 15, 1884-Sept. 15, 1971; House 1921-25, 1929-33.

CABLE, Joseph (great-grandfather of John Levi Cable) (D Ohio) April 17, 1801-May 1, 1880; House 1849-53.

CABOT, George (great-grandfather of Henry Cabot Lodge, great-great-grandfather of Henry Cabot Lodge Jr.) (F Mass.) Dec. 3, 1752-April 18, 1823; Senate 1791-June 9, 1796.

CADMUS, Cornelius Andrew (D N.J.) Oct. 7, 1844-Jan. 20, 1902; House 1891-95.

CADWALADER, John (D Pa.) April 1, 1805-Jan. 26, 1879; House 1855-57.

CADWALADER, Lambert (— N.J.) 1742-Sept. 13, 1823; House 1789-91, 1793-95; Cont. Cong. 1784-87.

CADY, Claude Ernest (D Mich.) May 28, 1878-Nov. 30, 1953; House 1933-35.

CADY, Daniel (uncle of John Watts Cady) (F N.Y. April 29, 1773-Oct. 31, 1859; House 1815-17.

CADY, John Watts (nephew of Daniel Cady) (W N.Y.) June 28, 1790-Jan. 5, 1854; House 1823-25.

CAFFERY, Donelson (grandfather of Patrick Thomson Caffery) (D La.) Sept. 10, 1835-Dec. 30, 1906; Senate Dec. 31, 1892-1901.

CAFFERY, Patrick Thomson (grandson of Donelson Caffery) (D La.) July 6, 1932--; House 1969-73.

CAGE, Harry (— Miss.) ?-1859; House 1833-35.

CAHILL, William Thomas (R N.J.) June 25, 1912--House 1959-Jan. 19, 1970; Gov. 1970-74.

CAHOON, William (AMas. Vt.) Jan. 12, 1774-May 30, 1833; House 1829-33.

CAIN, Harry Pulliam (R Wash.) Jan. 10, 1906-March 3, 1979; Senate Dec. 26, 1946-53.

CAIN, Richard Harvey (R S.C.) April 12, 1825-Jan. 18, 1887; House 1873-75, 1877-79.

CAINE, John Thomas (PP Utah) Jan. 8, 1829-Sept. 20, 1911; House (Terr. Del.) Nov. 7, 1882-93 (1882-87 Democrat).

CAKE, Henry Lutz (R Pa.) Oct. 6, 1827-Aug. 26, 1899; House 1867-71.

CALDER, William Musgrave (R N.Y.) March 3, 1869-March 3, 1945; House 1905-15; Senate 1917-23.

CALDERHEAD, William Alexander (R Kan.) Sept. 26, 1844-Dec. 18, 1928; House 1895-97, 1899-1911.

CALDWELL, Alexander (R Kan.) March 1, 1830-May 19, 1917; Senate 1871-March 24, 1873.

CALDWELL, Andrew Jackson (D Tenn.) July 22, 1837-Nov. 22, 1906; House 1883-87.

CALDWELL, Ben Franklin (D Ill.) Aug. 2, 1848-Dec. 29, 1924; House 1899-1905, 1907-09.

CALDWELL, Charles Pope (D N.Y.) June 18, 1875-July 31, 1940; House 1915-21.

CALDWELL, George Alfred (D Ky.) Oct. 18, 1814-Sept. 17, 1866; House 1843-45, 1849-51.

CALDWELL, Greene Washington (D N.C.) April 13, 1806-July 10, 1864; House 1841-43.

CALDWELL, James (D Ohio) Nov. 30, 1770-May 1838; House 1813-17.

CALDWELL, John Alexander (R Ohio) April 21, 1852-May 24, 1927; House 1889-May 4, 1894.

CALDWELL, John Henry (D Ala.) April 4, 1826-Sept. 4, 1902; House 1873-77.

CALDWELL, John William (D Ky.) Jan. 15, 1837-July 4, 1903; House 1877-83.

CALDWELL, Joseph Pearson (W N.C.) March 5, 1808-June 30, 1853; House 1849-53.

CALDWELL, Millard Fillmore (D Fla.) Feb. 6, 1897-Oct. 23, 1984; House 1933-41; Gov. 1945-49.

CALDWELL, Patrick Calhoun (SRD S.C.) March 10, 1801-Nov. 22, 1855; House 1841-43.

CALDWELL, Robert Porter (D Tenn.) Dec. 16, 1821-March 12, 1885; House 1871-73.

CALDWELL, William Parker (D Tenn.) Nov. 8, 1832-June 7, 1903; House 1875-79.

CALE, Thomas (I Alaska) Sept. 17, 1848-Feb. 3, 1941; House (Terr. Del.) 1907-09.

CALHOON, John (W Ky.) 1797-?; House 1835-39.

CALHOUN, John Caldwell (cousin of John Ewing Colhoun and Joseph Calhoun) (D S.C.) March 18, 1782-March 31, 1850; House 1811-Nov. 3, 1817; Senate Dec. 29, 1832-43, Nov. 26, 1845-March 31, 1850; Vice President 1825-Dec. 28, 1832 (Democratic Republican); Secy. of War 1817-25; Secy. of State 1844-45.

CALHOUN, Joseph (cousin of John Caldwell Calhoun and John Ewing Colhoun) (D S.C.) Oct. 22, 1750-April 14, 1817; House June 2, 1807-11.

CALHOUN, William Barron (W Mass.) Dec. 29, 1796-Nov. 8, 1865; House 1835-43.

CALKIN, Hervey Chittenden (D N.Y.) March 23, 1828-April 20, 1913; House 1869-71.

CALKINS, William Henry (R Ind.) Feb. 18, 1842-Jan. 29, 1894; House 1877-Oct. 20, 1884.

CALL, Jacob (− Ind.) ?-April 20, 1826; House Dec. 23, 1824-25.

CALL, Richard Keith (uncle of Wilkinson Call) (D Fla.) Oct. 24, 1792-Sept. 14, 1862; House (Terr. Del.) 1823-25; Gov. (Fla. Terr.) 1835-40, 1841-44.

CALL, Wilkinson (nephew of Richard Keith Call, cousin of James David Walker) (D Fla.) Jan. 9, 1834-Aug. 24, 1910; Senate 1879-97.

CALLAHAN, H. L. "Sonny" (R Ala.) Sept. 11, 1932-−; House 1985-−.

CALLAHAN, James Yancy (FSil. Okla.) Dec. 19, 1852-May 3, 1935; House (Terr. Del.) 1897-99.

CALLAN, Clair Armstrong (D Neb.) March 20, 1920-−; House 1965-67.

CALLAWAY, Howard Hollis "Bo" (R Ga.) April 2, 1927-−; House 1965-67.

CALLAWAY, Oscar (D Texas) Oct. 2, 1872-Jan. 31, 1947; House 1911-17.

CALLIS, John Benton (R Ala.) Jan. 3, 1828-Sept. 24, 1898; House July 21, 1868-69.

CALVERT, Charles Benedict (UW Md.) Aug. 24, 1808-May 12, 1864; House 1861-63.

CALVIN, Samuel (W Pa.) July 30, 1811-March 12, 1890; House 1849-51.

CAMBRELENG, Churchill Caldom (D N.Y.) Oct. 24, 1786-April 30, 1862; House 1821-39.

CAMDEN, Johnson Newlon (father of Johnson Newlon Camden Jr.) (D W.Va.) March 6, 1828-April 25, 1908; Senate 1881-87, Jan. 25, 1893-95.

CAMDEN, Johnson Newlon Jr. (son of Johnson Newlon Camden) (D Ky.) Jan. 5, 1865-Aug. 16, 1942; Senate June 16, 1914-15.

CAMERON, Angus (R Wis.) July 4, 1826-March 30, 1897; Senate 1875-81, March 14, 1881-85.

CAMERON, James Donald (son of Simon Cameron) (R Pa.) May 14, 1833-Aug. 30, 1918; Senate March 20, 1877-97; Secy. of War 1876-77; Chrmn. Rep. Nat. Comm. 1879-80.

CAMERON, Ralph Henry (R Ariz.) Oct. 21, 1863-Feb. 12, 1953; House (Terr. Del.) 1909-Feb. 18, 1912; Senate 1921-27.

CAMERON, Ronald Brooks (D Calif.) Aug. 16, 1927-—; House 1963-67.

CAMERON, Simon (father of James Donald Cameron) (R Pa.) March 8, 1799-June 26, 1889; Senate March 13, 1845-49 (Democrat), 1857-March 4, 1861, 1867-March 12, 1877; Secy. of War 1861-62.

CAMINETTI, Anthony (D Calif.) July 30, 1854-Nov. 17, 1923; House 1891-95.

CAMP, Albert Sidney (D Ga.) July 26, 1892-July 24, 1954; House Aug. 1, 1939-July 24, 1954.

CAMP, John Henry (R N.Y.) April 4, 1840-Oct. 12, 1892; House 1877-83.

CAMP, John Newbold Happy (R Okla.) May 11, 1908-—; House 1969-75.

CAMPBELL, Albert James (D Mont.) Dec. 12, 1857-Aug. 9, 1907; House 1899-1901.

CAMPBELL, Alexander (— Ohio) 1779-Nov. 5, 1857; Senate Dec. 11, 1809-13.

CAMPBELL, Alexander (I Ill.) Oct. 4, 1814-Aug. 8, 1898; House 1875-77.

CAMPBELL, Ben Nighthorse (D Colo.) April 13, 1933-—; House 1987-—.

CAMPBELL, Brookins (D Tenn.) 1808-Dec. 25, 1853; House March 4-Dec. 25, 1853.

CAMPBELL, Carroll Ashmore Jr. (R S.C.) July 24, 1940-—; House 1979-87; Gov. 1987-—.

CAMPBELL, Courtney Warren (D Fla.) April 29, 1895-Dec. 22, 1971; House 1953-55.

CAMPBELL, Ed Hoyt (R Iowa) March 6, 1882-April 26, 1969; House 1929-33.

CAMPBELL, Felix (D N.Y.) Feb. 28, 1829-Nov. 8, 1902; House 1883-91.

CAMPBELL, George Washington (D Tenn.) Feb. 9, 1769-Feb. 17, 1848; House 1803-09; Senate Oct. 8, 1811-Feb. 11, 1814, Oct. 10, 1815-April 20, 1818; Secy. of the Treasury Feb. 9-Oct. 6, 1814.

CAMPBELL, Guy Edgar (R Pa.) Oct. 9, 1871-Feb. 17, 1940; House 1917-33 (1917-23 Democrat).

CAMPBELL, Howard Edmond (R Pa.) Jan. 4, 1890-—; House 1945-47.

CAMPBELL, Jacob Miller (R Pa.) Nov. 20, 1821-Sept. 27, 1888; House 1877-79, 1881-87.

CAMPBELL, James Edwin (nephew of Lewis Davis Campbell) (D Ohio) July 7, 1843-Dec. 18, 1924; House June 20, 1884-89; Gov. 1890-92.

CAMPBELL, James Hepburn (W Pa.) Feb. 8, 1820-April 12, 1895; House 1855-57, 1859-63.

CAMPBELL, James Romulus (D Ill.) May 4, 1853-Aug. 12, 1924; House 1897-99.

CAMPBELL, John (F Md.) Sept. 11, 1765-June 23, 1828; House 1801-11.

CAMPBELL, John (brother of Robert Blair Campbell) (SRD S.C.) ?-May 19, 1845; House 1829-31 (State Rights Whig), 1837-45.

CAMPBELL, John Goulder (D Ariz.) June 25, 1827-Dec. 22, 1903; House (Terr. Del.) 1879-81.

CAMPBELL, John Hull (W Pa.) Oct. 10, 1800-Jan. 19, 1868; House 1845-47.

CAMPBELL, John Pierce Jr. (AP Ky.) Dec. 8, 1820-Oct. 29, 1888; House 1855-57.

CAMPBELL, John Wilson (D Ohio) Feb. 23, 1782-Sept. 24, 1833; House 1817-27.

CAMPBELL, Lewis Davis (uncle of James Edwin Campbell) (D Ohio) Aug. 9, 1811-Nov. 26, 1882; House 1849-May 25, 1858 (Whig), 1871-73.

CAMPBELL, Philip Pitt (R Kan.) April 25, 1862-May 26, 1941; House 1903-23.

CAMPBELL, Robert Blair (brother of John Campbell of South Carolina) (W S.C.) ?-July 12, 1862; House 1823-25 (no party designation), Feb. 27, 1834-37 (1834-35 Nullifier).

CAMPBELL, Samuel (— N.Y.) July 11, 1773-June 2, 1853; House 1821-23.

CAMPBELL, Thomas Jefferson (W Tenn.) 1786-April 13, 1850; House 1841-43.

CAMPBELL, Thompson (D Ill.) 1811-Dec. 6, 1868; House 1851-53.

CAMPBELL, Timothy John (D N.Y.) Jan. 8, 1840-April 7, 1904; House Nov. 3, 1885-89, 1891-95.

CAMPBELL, William Bowen (cousin of Henry Bowen) (D Tenn.) Feb. 1, 1807-Aug. 19, 1867; House 1837-43 (Whig), July 24, 1866-67; Gov. 1851-53.

CAMPBELL, William W. (AP N.Y.) June 10, 1806-Sept. 7, 1881; House 1845-47.

CAMPBELL, William Wildman (R Ohio) April 2, 1853-Aug. 13, 1927; House 1905-07.

CANBY, Richard Sprigg (W Ohio) Sept. 30, 1808-July 27, 1895; House 1847-49.

CANDLER, Allen Daniel (cousin of Ezekiel Samuel Candler Jr. and Milton Anthony Candler) (D Ga.) Nov. 4, 1834-Oct. 26, 1910; House 1883-91; Gov. 1898-1902.

CANDLER, Ezekiel Samuel Jr. (nephew of Milton Anthony Candler, cousin of Allen Daniel Candler) (D Miss.) Jan. 18, 1862-Dec. 18, 1944; House 1901-21.

CANDLER, John Wilson (R Mass.) Feb. 10, 1828-March 16, 1903; House 1881-83, 1889-91.

CANDLER, Milton Anthony (uncle of Ezekiel Samuel Candler Jr., cousin of Allen Daniel Candler) (D Ga.) Jan. 11, 1837-Aug. 8, 1909; House 1875-79.

CANFIELD, Gordon (R N.J.) April 15, 1898-June 20, 1972; House 1941-61.

CANFIELD, Harry Clifford (D Ind.) Nov. 22, 1875-Feb. 9, 1945; House 1923-33.

CANNON, Arthur Patrick (D Fla.) May 22, 1904-Jan. 23, 1966; House 1939-47.

CANNON, Clarence Andrew (D Mo.) April 11, 1879-May 12, 1964; House 1923-May 12, 1964.

CANNON, Frank Jenne (son of George Quayle Cannon) (R Utah) Jan. 25, 1859-July 25, 1933; House (Terr. Del.) 1895-Jan. 4, 1896; Senate Jan. 22, 1896-99.

CANNON, George Quayle (father of Frank Jenne Cannon) (R Utah) Jan. 11, 1827-April 12, 1901; House (Terr. Del.) 1873-81.

CANNON, Howard Walter (D Nev.) Jan. 26, 1912- —; Senate 1959-83.

CANNON, Joseph Gurney (R Ill.) May 7, 1836-Nov. 12, 1926; House 1873-91, 1893-1913, 1915-23; Speaker 1903-11.

CANNON, Marion (PP/D Calif.) Oct. 30, 1834-Aug. 27, 1920; House 1893-95.

CANNON, Newton (D Tenn.) May 22, 1781-Sept. 16, 1841; House Sept. 16, 1814-17, 1819-23; Gov. 1835-39 (Whig).

CANNON, Raymond Joseph (D Wis.) Aug. 26, 1894-Nov. 25, 1951; House 1933-39.

CANTOR, Jacob Aaron (D N.Y.) Dec. 6, 1854-July 2, 1921; House Nov. 4, 1913-15.

CANTRILL, James Campbell (D Ky.) July 9, 1870-Sept. 2, 1923; House 1909-Sept. 2, 1923.

CAPEHART, Homer Earl (R Ind.) June 6, 1897-Sept. 3, 1979; Senate 1945-63.

CAPEHART, James (D W.Va.) March 7, 1847-April 28, 1921; House 1891-95.

CAPERTON, Allen Taylor (son of Hugh Caperton) (D W.Va.) Nov. 21, 1810-July 26, 1876; Senate 1875-July 26, 1876.

CAPERTON, Hugh (father of Allen Taylor Caperton) (F Va.) April 17, 1781-Feb. 9, 1847; House 1813-15.

CAPOZZOLI, Louis Joseph (D N.Y.) March 6, 1901-Oct. 8, 1982; House 1941-45.

CAPPER, Arthur (R Kan.) July 14, 1865-Dec. 19, 1951; Senate 1919-49; Gov. 1915-19.

CAPRON, Adin Ballou (R R.I.) Jan. 9, 1841-March 17, 1911; House 1897-1911.

CAPSTICK, John Henry (R N.J.) Sept. 2, 1856-March 17, 1918; House 1915-March 17, 1918.

CAPUTO, Bruce F. (R N.Y.) Aug. 7, 1943- —; House 1977-79.

CARAWAY, Hattie Wyatt (widow of Thaddeus Horatius Caraway) (D Ark.) Feb. 1, 1878-Dec. 21, 1950; Senate Nov. 13, 1931-45.

CARAWAY, Thaddeus Horatius (husband of Hattie Wyatt Caraway) (D Ark.) Oct. 17, 1871-Nov. 6, 1931; House 1913-21; Senate 1921-Nov. 6, 1931.

CARDEN, Cap Robert (D Ky.) Dec. 17, 1866-June 13, 1935; House 1931-June 13, 1935.

CARDIN, Benjamin L. (D Md.) Oct. 5, 1943- —; House 1987- —.

CAREW, John Francis (nephew of Thomas Francis Magner) (D N.Y.) April 16, 1873-April 10, 1951; House 1913-Dec. 18, 1929.

CAREY, Hugh Leonard (D N.Y.) April 11, 1919- —; House 1961-Dec. 31, 1974; Gov. 1975-83.

CAREY, John (R Ohio) April 5, 1792-March 17, 1875; House 1859-61.

CAREY, Joseph Maull (father of Robert Davis Carey) (R Wyo.) Jan. 19, 1845-Feb. 5, 1924; House (Terr. Del.) 1885-July 10, 1890; Senate Nov. 15, 1890-95; Gov. 1911-15.

CAREY, Robert Davis (son of Joseph Maull Carey) (R Wyo.) Aug. 12, 1878-Jan. 17, 1937; Senate Dec. 1, 1930-37; Gov. 1919-23.

CARLETON, Ezra Child (D Mich.) Sept. 6, 1838-July 24, 1911; House 1883-87.

CARLETON, Peter (D N.H.) Sept. 19, 1755-April 29, 1828; House 1807-09.

CARLEY, Patrick J. (D N.Y.) Feb. 2, 1866-Feb. 25, 1936; House 1927-35.

CARLILE, John Snyder (U Va.) Dec. 16, 1817-Oct. 24, 1878; House 1855-57 (American Party), March 4-July 9, 1861 (American Party); Senate July 9, 1861-65.

CARLIN, Charles Creighton (D Va.) April 8, 1866-Oct. 14, 1938; House Nov. 5, 1907-19.

CARLISLE, John Griffin (D Ky.) Sept. 5, 1835-July 31, 1910; House 1877-May 26, 1890; Speaker 1883-89; Senate May 26, 1890-Feb. 4, 1893; Secy. of the Treasury 1893-97.

CARLSON, Cliffard Dale (R Ill.) Dec. 30, 1915-Aug. 28, 1977; House April 4, 1972-73.

CARLSON, Frank (R Kan.) Jan. 23, 1893- —; House 1935-47; Senate Nov. 29, 1950-69; Gov. 1947-50.

CARLTON, Henry Hull (D Ga.) May 14, 1835-Oct. 26, 1905; House 1887-91.

CARLYLE, Frank Ertel (D N.C.) April 7, 1897-Oct. 2, 1960; House 1949-57.

CARMACK, Edward Ward (D Tenn.) Nov. 5, 1858-Nov. 9, 1908; House 1897-1901; Senate 1901-07.

CARMAN, Gregory W. (R N.Y.) Jan. 31, 1937- —; House 1981-83.

CARMICHAEL, Archibald Hill (D Ala.) June 17, 1864-July 15, 1947; House Nov. 14, 1933-37.

CARMICHAEL, Richard Bennett (JD Md.) Dec. 25, 1807-Oct. 21, 1884; House 1833-35.

CARNAHAN, Albert Sidney Johnson (D Mo.) Jan. 9, 1897-March 24, 1968; House 1945-47, 1949-61.

CARNES, Thomas Petters (— Ga.) 1762-May 5, 1822; House 1793-95.

CARNEY, Charles Joseph (D Ohio) April 17, 1913- —; House Nov. 3, 1970-79.

CARNEY, William (R N.Y.) July 1, 1942- —; House 1979-87.

CARPENTER, Cyrus Clay (R Iowa) Nov. 24, 1829-May 29, 1898; House 1879-83; Gov. 1872-76.

CARPENTER, Davis (W N.Y.) Dec. 25, 1799-Oct. 22, 1878; House Nov. 8, 1853-55.

CARPENTER, Edmund Nelson (R Pa.) June 27, 1865-Nov. 4, 1952; House 1925-27.

CARPENTER, Levi D. (D N.Y.) Aug. 21, 1802-Oct. 27, 1856; House Nov. 5, 1844-45.

CARPENTER, Lewis Cass (R S.C.) Feb. 20, 1836-March 6, 1908; House Nov. 3, 1874-75.

CARPENTER, Matthew Hale (R Wis.) Dec. 22, 1824-Feb. 24, 1881; Senate 1869-75, 1879-Feb. 24, 1881; Pres. pro tempore 1873-75.

CARPENTER, Terry McGovern (D Neb.) March 28, 1900-April 27, 1978; House 1933-35.

CARPENTER, William Randolph (D Kan.) April 24, 1894-July 26, 1956; House 1933-37.

CARPER, Thomas Richard (D Del.) Jan. 23, 1947- —; House 1983- —.

CARR, Francis (father of James Carr) (D Mass.) Dec. 6, 1751-Oct. 6, 1821; House April 6, 1812-13.

CARR, James (son of Francis Carr) (— Mass.) Sept. 9, 1777-Aug. 24, 1818; House 1815-17.

CARR, John (D Ind.) April 9, 1793-Jan. 20, 1845; House 1831-37, 1839-41.

CARR, Milton Robert "Bob" (D Mich.) March 27, 1943- —; House 1975-81, 1983- —.

CARR, Nathan Tracy (D Ind.) Dec. 25, 1833-May 28, 1885; House Dec. 5, 1876-77.

CARR, Wooda Nicholas (D Pa.) Feb. 6, 1871-June 28, 1953; House 1913-15.

CARRIER, Chester Otto (R Ky.) May 5, 1897- —; House Nov. 30, 1943-45.

CARRIGG, Joseph Leonard (R Pa.) Feb. 23, 1901- —; House Nov. 6, 1951-59.

CARROLL, Charles (cousin of Daniel Carroll) (F Md.) Sept. 19, 1737-Nov. 14, 1832; Senate 1789-Nov. 30, 1792; Cont. Cong. 1776-78.

CARROLL, Charles Hobart (CW N.Y.) May 4, 1794-June 8, 1865; House 1843-47.

CARROLL, Daniel (uncle of Richard Brent, cousin of Charles Carroll) (F Md.) July 22, 1730-May 7, 1796; House 1789-91; Cont. Cong. 1780-84.

CARROLL, James (D Md.) Dec. 2, 1791-Jan. 16, 1873; House 1839-41.

CARROLL, John Albert (D Colo.) July 30, 1901-Aug. 31, 1983; House 1947-51; Senate 1957-63.

CARROLL, John Michael (D N.Y.) April 27, 1823-May 8, 1901; House 1871-73.

CARSON, Henderson Haverfield (R Ohio) Oct. 25, 1893-Oct. 5, 1971; House 1943-45, 1947-49.

CARSON, Samuel Price (D N.C.) Jan. 22, 1798-Nov. 2, 1838; House 1825-33.

CARSS, William Leighton (FL Minn.) Feb. 15, 1865-May 31, 1931; House 1919-21 (Independent), 1925-29.

CARTER, Albert Edward (R Calif.) July 5, 1881-Aug. 8, 1964; House 1925-45.

CARTER, Charles David (D Okla.) Aug. 16, 1868-April 9, 1929; House Nov. 16, 1907-27.

CARTER, John (− S.C.) Sept. 10, 1792-June 20, 1850; House Dec. 11, 1822-29.

CARTER, Luther Cullen (UR N.Y.) Feb. 25, 1805-Jan. 3, 1875; House 1859-61.

CARTER, Steven V. (D Iowa) Oct. 8, 1915-Nov. 4, 1959; House Jan. 3-Nov. 4, 1959.

CARTER, Thomas Henry (R Mont.) Oct. 30, 1854-Sept. 17, 1911; House (Terr. Del.) March 4-Nov. 7, 1889, (Rep.) Nov. 8, 1889-91; Senate 1895-1901, 1905-11; Chrmn. Rep. Nat. Comm. 1892-96.

CARTER, Tim Lee (R Ky.) Sept. 2, 1910-−; House 1965-81.

CARTER, Timothy Jarvis (D Maine) Aug. 18, 1800-March 14, 1838; House Sept. 4, 1837-March 14, 1838.

CARTER, Vincent Michael (R Wyo.) Nov. 6, 1891-Dec. 30, 1972; House 1929-35.

CARTER, William Blount (W Tenn.) Oct. 22, 1792-April 17, 1848; House 1835-41.

CARTER, William Henry (R Mass.) June 15, 1864-April 23, 1955; House 1915-19.

CARTTER, David Kellogg (D Ohio) June 22, 1812-April 16, 1887; House 1849-53.

CARTWRIGHT, Wilburn (D Okla.) Jan. 12, 1892-March 14, 1979; House 1927-43.

CARUTH, Asher Graham (D Ky.) Feb. 7, 1844-Nov. 25, 1907; House 1887-95.

CARUTHERS, Robert Looney (W Tenn.) July 31, 1800-Oct. 2, 1882; House 1841-43.

CARUTHERS, Samuel (D Mo.) Oct. 13, 1820-July 20, 1860; House 1853-59 (1853-57 Whig).

CARVILLE, Edward Peter (D Nev.) May 14, 1885-June 27, 1956; Senate July 25, 1945-47; Gov. 1939-45.

CARY, George (− Ga.) Aug. 7, 1789-Sept. 10, 1843; House 1823-27.

CARY, George Booth (D Va.) 1811-March 5, 1850; House 1841-43.

CARY, Glover H. (D Ky.) May 1, 1885-Dec. 5, 1936; House 1931-Dec. 5, 1936.

CARY, Jeremiah Eaton (D N.Y.) April 30, 1803-June 1888; House 1843-45.

CARY, Samuel Fenton (R Ohio) Feb. 18, 1814-Sept. 29, 1900; House Nov. 21, 1867-69.

CARY, Shepard (D Maine) July 3, 1805-Aug. 9, 1866; House May 10, 1844-45.

CARY, William Joseph (R Wis.) March 22, 1865-Jan. 2, 1934; House 1907-19.

CASE, Charles (D Ind.) Dec. 21, 1817-June 30, 1883; House Dec. 7, 1857-61.

CASE, Clifford Philip (R N.J.) April 16, 1904-March 5, 1982; House 1945-Aug. 16, 1953; Senate 1955-79.

CASE, Francis Higbee (R S.D.) Dec. 9, 1896-June 22, 1962; House 1937-51; Senate 1951-June 22, 1962.

CASE, Walter (− N.Y.) 1776-Oct. 7, 1859; House 1819-21.

CASEY, John Joseph (D Pa.) May 26, 1875-May 5, 1929; House 1913-17, 1919-21, 1923-25, 1927-May 5, 1929.

CASEY, Joseph (W Pa.) Dec. 17, 1814-Feb. 10, 1879; House 1849-51.

CASEY, Joseph Edward (D Mass.) Dec. 27, 1898-Sept. 1980; House 1935-43.

CASEY, Levi (− S.C.) about 1752-Feb. 3, 1807; House 1803-Feb. 3, 1807.

CASEY, Lyman Rufus (R N.D.) May 6, 1837-Jan. 26, 1914; Senate Nov. 25, 1889-93.

CASEY, Robert Randolph (D Texas) July 17, 1915-April 17, 1986; House 1959-Jan. 22, 1976.

CASEY, Samuel Lewis (R Ky.) Feb. 12, 1821-Aug. 25, 1902; House March 10, 1862-63.

CASEY, Zadoc (JD Ill.) March 7, 1796-Sept. 4, 1862; House 1833-43.

CASKIE, John Samuels (D Va.) Nov. 8, 1821-Dec. 16, 1869; House 1851-59.

CASON, Thomas Jefferson (R Ind.) Sept. 13, 1828-July 10, 1901; House 1873-77.

CASS, Lewis (D Mich.) Oct. 9, 1782-June 17, 1866; Senate 1845-May 29, 1848, 1849-57; Pres. pro tempore 1854; Gov. (Mich. Terr.) 1813-31; Secy. of War 1831-36; Secy. of State 1857-60.

CASSEDY, George (D N.J.) Sept. 16, 1783-Dec. 31, 1842; House 1821-27.

CASSEL, Henry Burd (R Pa.) Oct. 19, 1855-April 28, 1926; House Nov. 5, 1901-09.

CASSERLY, Eugene (D Calif.) Nov. 13, 1820-June 14, 1883; Senate 1869-Nov. 19, 1873.

CASSIDY, George Williams (D Nev.) April 25, 1836-June 24, 1892; House 1881-85.

CASSIDY, James Henry (R Ohio) Oct. 28, 1869-Aug. 23, 1926; House April 20, 1909-11.

CASSINGHAM, John Wilson (D Ohio) June 22, 1840-March 14, 1930; House 1901-05.

CASTELLOW, Bryant Thomas (D Ga.) July 29, 1876-July 23, 1962; House Nov. 8, 1932-37.

CASTLE, Curtis Harvey (P/D Calif.) Oct. 4, 1848-July 12, 1928; House 1897-99.

CASTLE, James Nathan (D Minn.) May 23, 1836-Jan. 2, 1903; House 1891-93.

CASTOR, George Albert (R Pa.) Aug. 6, 1855-Feb. 19, 1906; House Feb. 16, 1904-Feb. 19, 1906.

CASWELL, Lucien Bonaparte (R Wis.) Nov. 27, 1827-April 26, 1919; House 1875-83, 1885-91.

CATCHINGS, Thomas Clendinen (D Miss.) Jan. 11, 1847-Dec. 24, 1927; House 1885-1901.

CATE, George Washington (IRef. Wis.) Sept. 17, 1825-March 7, 1905; House 1875-77.

CATE, William Henderson (D Ark.) Nov. 11, 1839-Aug. 23, 1899; House 1889-March 5, 1890, 1891-93.

CATHCART, Charles William (D Ind.) July 24, 1809-Aug. 22, 1888; House 1845-49; Senate Dec. 6, 1852-53.

CATLIN, George Smith (D Conn.) Aug. 24, 1808-Dec. 26, 1851; House 1843-45.

CATLIN, Theron Ephron (R Mo.) May 16, 1878-March 19, 1960; House 1911-Aug. 12, 1912.

CATRON, Thomas Benton (R N.M.) Oct. 6, 1840-May 15, 1921; House (Terr. Del.) 1895-97; Senate March 27, 1912-17.

CATTELL, Alexander Gilmore (R N.J.) Feb. 12, 1816-April 8, 1894; Senate Sept. 19, 1866-71.

CAULFIELD, Bernard Gregory (D Ill.) Oct. 18, 1828 Dec. 19, 1887; House Feb. 1, 1875-77.

CAULFIELD, Henry Stewart (R Mo.) Dec. 9, 1873-May 11, 1966; House 1907-09; Gov. 1929-33.

CAUSEY, John Williams (D Del.) Sept. 19, 1841-Oct. 1 1908; House 1891-95.

CAUSIN, John M. S. (W Md.) 1811-Jan. 30, 1861 House 1843-45.

CAVALCANTE, Anthony (D Pa.) Feb. 6, 1897-Oct. 29 1966; House 1949-51.

CAVANAUGH, James Michael (D Mont.) July 4, 1823 Oct. 30, 1879; House May 11, 1858-59 (Minn.), 1867-71 (Terr. Del.).

CAVANAUGH, John J. III (D Neb.) Aug. 1, 1945- House 1977-81.

CAVICCHIA, Peter Angelo (R N.J.) May 22, 1879-Sept 11, 1967; House 1931-37.

CEDERBERG, Elford Alfred (R Mich.) March 6, 1918 -; House 1953-Dec. 31, 1978.

CELLER, Emanuel (D N.Y.) May 6, 1888-Jan. 15, 1981 House 1923-73.

CESSNA, John (R Pa.) June 29, 1821-Dec. 13, 1893 House 1869-71, 1873-75.

CHACE, Jonathan (R R.I.) July 22, 1829-June 30, 1917 House 1881-Jan. 26, 1885; Senate Jan. 20, 1885-April 9, 1889.

CHADWICK, E. Wallace (R Pa.) Jan. 17, 1884-Aug. 18 1969; House 1947-49.

CHAFEE, John Hubbard (R R.I.) Oct. 22, 1922- -; Senate Dec. 29, 1976- -; Gov. 1963-69.

CHAFFEE, Calvin Clifford (AP Mass.) Aug. 28, 1811 Aug. 8, 1896; House 1855-59.

CHAFFEE, Jerome Bunty (R Colo.) April 17, 1825 March 9, 1886; House (Terr. Del.) 1871-75; Senate Nov. 15, 1876-79.

CHALMERS, James Ronald (son of Joseph William Chalmers) (I Miss.) Jan. 12, 1831-April 9, 1898 House 1877-April 29, 1882 (Democrat), June 25 1884-85.

CHALMERS, Joseph Williams (father of James Ronald Chalmers) (D Miss.) Dec. 20, 1806-June 16, 1853 Senate Nov. 3, 1845-47.

CHALMERS, William Wallace (R Ohio) Nov. 1, 1861 Oct. 1, 1944; House 1921-23, 1925-31.

CHAMBERLAIN, Charles Ernest (R Mich.) July 22 1917- -; House 1957-Dec. 31, 1974.

CHAMBERLAIN, Ebenezer Mattoon (D Ind.) Aug. 20, 1805-March 14, 1861; House 1853-55.

CHAMBERLAIN, George Earle (D Ore.) Jan. 1, 1854-July 9, 1928; Senate 1909-21; Gov. 1903-09.

CHAMBERLAIN, Jacob Payson (R N.Y.) Aug. 1, 1802-Oct. 5, 1878; House 1861-63.

CHAMBERLAIN, John Curtis (F N.H.) June 5, 1772-Dec. 8, 1834; House 1809-11.

CHAMBERLAIN, William (F Vt.) April 27, 1755-Sept. 27, 1828; House 1803-05, 1809-11.

CHAMBERS, David (— Ohio) Nov. 25, 1780-Aug. 8, 1864; House Oct. 9, 1821-23.

CHAMBERS, Ezekiel Forman (W Md.) Feb. 28, 1788-Jan. 30, 1867; Senate Jan. 24, 1826-Dec. 20, 1834.

CHAMBERS, George (W Pa.) Feb. 24, 1786-March 25, 1866; House 1833-37.

CHAMBERS, Henry H. (D Ala.) Oct. 1, 1790-Jan. 24, 1826; Senate 1825-Jan. 24, 1826.

CHAMBERS, John (W Ky.) Oct. 6, 1780-Sept. 21, 1852; House Dec. 1, 1828-29, 1835-39; Gov. (Iowa Terr.) 1841-45.

CHAMPION, Edwin Van Meter (D Ill.) Sept. 18, 1890-Feb. 11, 1976; House 1937-39.

CHAMPION, Epaphroditis (F Conn.) April 6, 1756-Dec. 22, 1834; House 1807-17.

CHAMPLIN, Christopher Grant (— R.I.) April 12, 1768-March 18, 1840; House 1797-1801; Senate June 26, 1809-Oct. 2, 1811.

CHANDLER, Albert Benjamin (D Ky.) July 14, 1898-—; Senate Oct. 10, 1939-Nov. 1, 1945; Gov. 1935-39, 1955-59.

CHANDLER, John (brother of Thomas Chandler, uncle of Zachariah Chandler) (D Maine) Feb. 1, 1762-Sept. 25, 1841; House 1805-09 (Mass.); Senate June 14, 1820-29.

CHANDLER, Joseph Ripley (W Pa.) Aug. 22, 1792-July 10, 1880; House 1849-55.

CHANDLER, Rodney (R Wash.) July 13, 1942-—; House 1983-—.

CHANDLER, Thomas (brother of John Chandler, uncle of Zachariah Chandler) (D N.H.) Aug. 10, 1772-Jan. 28, 1866; House 1829-33.

CHANDLER, Thomas Alberter (R Okla.) July 26, 1871-June 22, 1953; House 1917-19, 1921-23.

CHANDLER, Walter "Clift" (D Tenn.) Oct. 5, 1887-Oct. 1, 1967; House 1935-Jan. 2, 1940.

CHANDLER, Walter Marion (R N.Y.) Dec. 8, 1867-March 16, 1935; House 1912-19 (Progressive), 1921-23.

CHANDLER, William Eaton (R N.H.) Dec. 28, 1835-Nov. 20, 1917; Senate June 14, 1887-March 3, 1889, June 18, 1889-1901; Secy. of the Navy 1882-85.

CHANDLER, Zachariah (nephew of John Chandler and Thomas Chandler, grandfather of Frederick Hale) (R Mich.) Dec. 10, 1813-Nov. 1, 1879; Senate 1857-75, Feb. 22, 1879-Nov. 1, 1879; Secy. of the Interior 1875-77; Chrmn. Rep. Nat. Comm. 1876-79.

CHANEY, John (JD Ohio) Jan. 12, 1790-April 10, 1881; House 1833-39.

CHANEY, John Crawford (R Ind.) Feb. 1, 1853-April 26, 1940; House 1905-09.

CHANLER, John Winthrop (father of William Astor Chanler) (D N.Y.) Sept. 14, 1826-Oct. 19, 1877; House 1863-69.

CHANLER, William Astor (son of John Winthrop Chanler) (D N.Y.) June 11, 1867-March 4, 1934; House 1899-1901.

CHAPIN, Alfred Clark (D N.Y.) March 8, 1848-Oct. 2, 1936; House Nov. 3, 1891-Nov. 16, 1892.

CHAPIN, Chester Williams (D Mass.) Dec. 16, 1798-June 10, 1883; House 1875-77.

CHAPIN, Graham Hurd (D N.Y.) Feb. 10, 1799-Sept. 8, 1843; House 1835-37.

CHAPMAN, Andrew Grant (son of John Grant Chapman) (D Md.) Jan. 17, 1839-Sept. 25, 1892; House 1881-83.

CHAPMAN, Augustus Alexandria (VBD Va.) March 9, 1803-June 7, 1876; House 1843-47.

CHAPMAN, Bird Beers (D Neb.) Aug. 24, 1821-Sept. 21, 1871; House (Terr. Del.) 1855-57.

CHAPMAN, Charles (W Conn.) June 21, 1799-Aug. 7, 1869; House 1851-53.

CHAPMAN, Henry (D Pa.) Feb. 4, 1804-April 11, 1891; House 1857-59.

CHAPMAN, Jim (D Texas) March 8, 1945-—; House Sept. 4, 1985-—.

CHAPMAN, John (F Pa.) Oct. 18, 1740-Jan. 27, 1800; House 1797-99.

CHAPMAN, John Grant (father of Andrew Grant Chapman) (W Md.) July 5, 1798-Dec. 10, 1856; House 1845-49.

CHAPMAN, Pleasant Thomas (R Ill.) Oct. 8, 1854-Jan. 31, 1931; House 1905-11.

CHAPMAN, Reuben (D Ala.) July 15, 1799-May 16, 1882; House 1835-47; Gov. 1847-49.

CHAPMAN, Virgil Munday (D Ky.) March 15, 1895-March 8, 1951; House 1925-29, 1931-49; Senate 1949-March 8, 1951.

CHAPMAN, William Williams (D Iowa) Aug. 11, 1808-Oct. 18, 1892; House (Terr. Del.) Sept. 10, 1838-Oct. 27, 1840.

CHAPPELL, Absalom Harris (cousin of Lucius Quintus Cincinnatus Lamar) (SRW Ga.) Dec. 18, 1801-Dec. 11, 1878; House Oct. 2, 1843-45.

CHAPPELL, John Joel (SRWD S.C.) Jan. 19, 1782-May 23, 1871; House 1813-17.

CHAPPELL, William Venroe Jr. (D Fla.) Feb. 3, 1922- —; House 1969- —.

CHAPPIE, Eugene A. (R Calif.) March 21, 1920- —; House 1981-87.

CHARLES, William Barclay (R N.Y.) April 3, 1861-Nov. 25, 1950; House 1915-17.

CHARLTON, Robert Milledge (— Ga.) Jan. 19, 1807-Jan. 18, 1854; Senate May 31, 1852-53.

CHASE, Dudley (uncle of Salmon Portland Chase and Dudley Chase Denison) (JD Vt.) Dec. 30, 1771-Feb. 23, 1846; Senate 1813-Nov. 3, 1817, 1825-31.

CHASE, George William (W N.Y.) ?-April 17, 1867; House 1853-55.

CHASE, Jackson Burton (R Neb.) Aug. 19, 1890-May 5, 1974; House 1955-57.

CHASE, James Mitchell (R Pa.) Dec. 19, 1891-Jan. 1, 1945; House 1927-33.

CHASE, Lucien Bonaparte (D Tenn.) Dec. 5, 1817-Dec. 4, 1864; House 1845-49.

CHASE, Ray P. (R Minn.) March 12, 1880-Sept. 18, 1948; House 1933-35.

CHASE, Salmon Portland (nephew of Dudley Chase, cousin of Dudley Chase Denison) (R Ohio) Jan. 13, 1808-May 7, 1873; Senate 1849-55 (Free Soil Democrat), March 4-6, 1861; Gov. 1856-60 (1856-57 Free Soil Democrat); Secy. of the Treasury 1861-July 1, 1864; Chief Justice United States 1864-73.

CHASE, Samuel (Ad.D N.Y.) ?-Aug. 3, 1838; House 1827-29.

CHASTAIN, Elijah Webb (UD Ga.) Sept. 25, 1813-April 9, 1874; House 1851-55.

CHATHAM, Richard Thurmond (D N.C.) Aug. 16, 1896-Feb. 5, 1957; House 1949-57.

CHAVES, Jose Francisco (R N.M.) June 27, 1833-Nov. 26, 1904; House (Terr. Del.) 1865-67, Feb. 20, 1869-71.

CHAVEZ, Dennis (D N.M.) April 8, 1888-Nov. 18, 1962; House 1931-35; Senate May 11, 1935-Nov. 18, 1962.

CHEADLE, Joseph Bonaparte (R Ind.) Aug. 14, 1842-May 28, 1904; House 1887-91.

CHEATHAM, Henry Plummer (R N.C.) Dec. 27, 1857-Nov. 29, 1935; House 1889-93.

CHEATHAM, Richard (W Tenn.) Feb. 20, 1799-Sept. 9, 1845; House 1837-39.

CHELF, Frank Leslie (D Ky.) Sept. 22, 1907-Sept. 1, 1982; House 1945-67.

CHENEY, Person Colby (R N.H.) Feb. 25, 1828-June 19, 1901; Senate Nov. 24, 1886-June 14, 1887; Gov. 1875-77.

CHENEY, Richard Bruce (R Wyo.) Jan. 30, 1941- —; House 1979- —.

CHENOWETH, John Edgar (R Colo.) Aug. 17, 1897-Jan. 2, 1986; House 1941-49, 1951-65.

CHESNEY, Chester Anton (D Ill.) March 9, 1916-Sept. 20, 1986; House 1949-51.

CHESNUT, James Jr. (SRD S.C.) Jan. 18, 1815-Feb. 1, 1885; Senate Dec. 3, 1858-Nov. 10, 1860.

CHETWOOD, William (JD N.J.) June 17, 1771-Dec. 17, 1857; House Dec. 5, 1836-37.

CHEVES, Langdon (D S.C.) Sept. 17, 1776-June 26, 1857; House Dec. 31, 1810-15; Speaker 1814-15.

CHICKERING, Charles Addison (R N.Y.) Nov. 26, 1843-Feb. 13, 1900; House 1893-Feb. 13, 1900.

CHILCOTT, George Miles (R Colo.) Jan. 2, 1828-March 6, 1891; House (Terr. Del.) 1867-69; Senate April 17, 1882-Jan. 27, 1883.

CHILD, Thomas Jr. (D N.Y.) March 22, 1818-March 9, 1869; House 1855-57.

CHILDS, Robert Andrew (R Ill.) March 22, 1845-Dec. 19, 1915; House 1893-95.

CHILDS, Timothy (W N.Y.) 1785-Nov. 8, 1847; House 1829-31, 1835-39, 1841-43.

CHILES, Lawton Mainor Jr. (D Fla.) April 3, 1930- —; Senate 1971- —.

CHILTON, Horace (grandson of Thomas Chilton) (D Texas) Dec. 29, 1853-June 12, 1932; Senate June 10, 1891-March 22, 1892, 1895-1901.

CHILTON, Samuel (W Va.) Sept. 7, 1804-Jan. 14, 1867; House 1843-45.

CHILTON, Thomas (grandfather of Horace Chilton) (W Ky.) July 30, 1798-Aug. 15, 1854; House Dec. 22, 1827-31, 1833-35.

CHILTON, William Edwin (D W.Va.) March 17, 1858-Nov. 7, 1939; Senate 1911-17.

CHINDBLOM, Carl Richard (R Ill.) Dec. 21, 1870-Sept. 12, 1956; House 1919-33.

CHINN, Joseph William (D Va.) Nov. 16, 1798-Dec. 5, 1840; House 1831-35.

CHINN, Thomas Withers (cousin of Robert Enoch Withers) (W La.) Nov. 22, 1791-May 22, 1852; House 1839-41.

CHIPERFIELD, Burnett Mitchell (father of Robert Bruce Chiperfield) (R Ill.) June 14, 1870-June 24, 1940; House 1915-17, 1929-33.

CHIPERFIELD, Robert Bruce (son of Burnett Mitchell Chiperfield) (R Ill.) Nov. 20, 1899-April 9, 1971; House 1939-63.

CHIPMAN, Daniel (brother of Nathaniel Chipman, granduncle of John Logan Chipman) (F Vt.) Oct. 22, 1765-April 23, 1850; House 1815-May 5, 1816.

CHIPMAN, John Logan (grandson of Nathaniel Chipman, grandnephew of Daniel Chipman) (D Mich.) June 5, 1830-Aug. 17, 1893; House 1887-Aug. 17, 1893.

CHIPMAN, John Smith (D Mich.) Aug. 10, 1800-July 27, 1869; House 1845-47.

CHIPMAN, Nathaniel (brother of Daniel Chipman, grandfather of John Logan Chipman) (− Vt.) Nov. 15, 1752-Jan. 15, 1843; Senate Oct. 17, 1797-1803.

CHIPMAN, Norton Parker (R D.C.) March 7, 1836-Feb. 1, 1924; House (Del.) April 21, 1871-75.

CHISHOLM, Shirley Anita (D N.Y.) Nov. 30, 1924- −; House 1969-83.

CHITTENDEN, Martin (− Vt.) March 12, 1769-Sept. 5, 1840; House 1803-13; Gov. 1813-15 (Federalist).

CHITTENDEN, Simeon Baldwin (R N.Y.) March 29, 1814-April 14, 1889; House Nov. 3, 1874-81.

CHITTENDEN, Thomas Cotton (W N.Y.) Aug. 30, 1788-Aug. 22, 1866; House 1839-43.

CHOATE, Rufus (W Mass.) Oct. 1, 1799-July 13, 1859; House 1831-June 30, 1834; Senate Feb. 23, 1841-45.

CHRISMAN, James Stone (D Ky.) Sept. 14, 1818-July 29, 1881; House 1853-55.

CHRISTGAU, Victor (R Minn.) Sept. 20, 1894- −; House 1929-33.

CHRISTIANCY, Isaac Peckham (R Mich.) March 12, 1812-Sept. 8, 1890; Senate 1875-Feb. 10, 1879.

CHRISTIANSON, Theodore (R Minn.) Sept. 12, 1885-Dec. 9, 1948; House 1933-37; Gov. 1925-31.

CHRISTIE, Gabriel (− Md.) 1755-April 1, 1808; House 1793-97, 1799-1801.

CHRISTOPHER, George Henry (D Mo.) Dec. 9, 1888-Jan. 23, 1959; House 1949-51, 1955-Jan. 23, 1959.

CHRISTOPHERSON, Charles Andrew (R S.D.) July 23, 1871-Nov. 2, 1951; House 1919-33.

CHUDOFF, Earl (D Pa.) Nov. 16, 1907- −; House 1949-Jan. 5, 1958.

CHURCH, Denver Samuel (D Calif.) Dec. 11, 1862-Feb. 21, 1952; House 1913-19, 1933-35.

CHURCH, Frank Forrester (D Idaho) July 25, 1924-April 7, 1984; Senate 1957-81.

CHURCH, Marguerite Stitt (widow of Ralph Edwin Church) (R Ill.) Sept. 13, 1892- −; House 1951-63.

CHURCH, Ralph Edwin (husband of Marguerite Stitt Church) (R Ill.) May 5, 1883-March 21, 1950; House 1935-41, 1943-March 21, 1950.

CHURCHILL, George Bosworth (R Mass.) Oct. 24, 1866-July 1, 1925; House March 4-July 1, 1925.

CHURCHILL, John Charles (R N.Y.) Jan. 17, 1821-June 4, 1905; House 1867-71.

CHURCHWELL, William Montgomery (D Tenn.) Feb. 20, 1826-Aug. 18, 1862; House 1851-55.

CILLEY, Bradbury (uncle of Jonathan Cilley and Joseph Cilley) (F N.H.) Feb. 1, 1760-Dec. 17, 1831; House 1813-17.

CILLEY, Jonathan (nephew of Bradbury Cilley, brother of Joseph Cilley) (JD Maine) July 2, 1802-Feb. 24, 1838; House 1837-Feb. 24, 1838.

CILLEY, Joseph (nephew of Bradbury Cilley, brother of Jonathan Cilley) (D N.H.) Jan. 4, 1791-Sept. 12, 1887; Senate June 13, 1846-47.

CITRON, William Michael (D Conn.) Aug. 29, 1896-June 7, 1976; House 1935-39.

CLAFLIN, William (R Mass.) March 6, 1818-Jan. 5, 1905; House 1877-81; Gov. 1869-72; Chrmn. Rep. Nat. Comm. 1868-72.

CLAGETT, Clifton (− N.H.) Dec. 3, 1762-Jan. 25, 1829; House 1803-05, 1817-21.

CLAGETT, William Horace (uncle of Samuel Barrett Pettengill) (R Mont.) Sept. 21, 1838-Aug. 3, 1901; House (Terr. Del.) 1871-73.

CLAGUE, Frank (R Minn.) July 13, 1865-March 25, 1952; House 1921-33.

CLAIBORNE, James Robert (D Mo.) June 22, 1882-Feb. 16, 1944; House 1933-37.

CLAIBORNE, John (son of Thomas Claiborne, brother of Thomas Claiborne Jr.) (− Va.) 1777-Oct. 9, 1808; House 1805-Oct. 9, 1808.

CLAIBORNE, John Francis Hamtramck (nephew of William Charles Cole Claiborne and Nathaniel Herbert Claiborne, great-grandfather of Herbert Claiborne Pell Jr.) (JD Miss.) April 24, 1809-May 17, 1884; House 1835-37, July 18, 1837-Feb. 5, 1838.

CLAIBORNE, Nathaniel Herbert (brother of William Charles Cole Claiborne, uncle of John Francis Hamtramck Claiborne, great-great-granduncle of Herbert Claiborne Pell Jr.) (R Va.) Nov. 14, 1777-Aug. 15, 1859; House 1825-37.

CLAIBORNE, Thomas (father of John Claiborne and Thomas Claiborne Jr.) (− Va.) Feb. 1, 1749-1812; House 1793-99, 1801-05.

CLAIBORNE, Thomas Jr. (son of Thomas Claiborne, brother of John Claiborne) (D Tenn.) May 17, 1780-Jan. 7, 1856; House 1817-19.

CLAIBORNE, William Charles Cole (brother of Nathaniel Herbert Claiborne, uncle of John Francis Hamtramck Claiborne, great-great-granduncle of Herbert Claiborne Pell Jr.) (D La.) 1775-Nov. 23, 1817; House 1797-1801 (Jefferson Democrat Tenn.); Senate March 4-Nov. 23, 1817; Gov. 1801-03 (Miss. Terr.), 1804-12 (Orleans Terr.), 1812-16 (Democratic Republican).

CLANCY, Donald D. (R Ohio) July 24, 1921-−; House 1961-77.

CLANCY, John Michael (D N.Y.) May 7, 1837-July 25, 1903; House 1889-95.

CLANCY, John Richard (D N.Y.) March 8, 1859-April 21, 1932; House 1913-15.

CLANCY, Robert Henry (R Mich.) March 14, 1882-April 23, 1962; House 1923-25 (Democrat), 1927-33.

CLAPP, Asa William Henry (D Maine) March 6, 1805-March 22, 1891; House 1847-49.

CLAPP, Moses Edwin (R Minn.) May 21, 1851-March 6, 1929; Senate Jan. 23, 1901-17.

CLARDY, John Daniel (D Ky.) Aug. 30, 1828-Aug. 20, 1918; House 1895-99.

CLARDY, Kit Francis (R Mich.) June 17, 1892-Sept. 5 1961; House 1953-55.

CLARDY, Martin Linn (D Mo.) April 26, 1844-July 5 1914; House 1879-89.

CLARK, Abraham (− N.J.) Feb. 15, 1726-Sept. 15 1794; House 1791-Sept. 15, 1794; Cont. Cong. 1776 78, 1779-83, 1787-89.

CLARK, Alvah Augustus (cousin of James Nelson Pidcock) (D N.J.) Sept. 13, 1840-Dec. 27, 1912 House 1877-81.

CLARK, Ambrose Williams (R N.Y.) Feb. 19, 1810-Oct 13, 1887; House 1861-65.

CLARK, Amos Jr. (R N.J.) Nov. 8, 1828-Oct. 31, 1912 House 1873-75.

CLARK, Charles Benjamin (R Wis.) Aug. 24, 1844-Sept 10, 1891; House 1887-91.

CLARK, Charles Nelson (R Mo.) Aug. 21, 1827-Oct. 4 1902; House 1895-97.

CLARK, Christopher Henderson (brother of James Clark, uncle of John Bullock Clark, granduncle c John Bullock Clark Jr.) (Jeff. D Va.) 1767-Nov. 21 1828; House Nov. 5, 1804-July 1, 1806.

CLARK, Clarence Don (R Wyo.) April 16, 1851-Nov. 18 1930; House Dec. 1, 1890-93; Senate Jan. 23, 1895 1917.

CLARK, Daniel (− Orleans) about 1766-Aug. 16, 1813 House (Terr. Del.) Dec. 1, 1806-09.

CLARK, Daniel (R N.H.) Oct. 24, 1809-Jan. 2, 1891 Senate June 27, 1857-July 27, 1866; Pres. pro tem pore 1864.

CLARK, David Worth (D Idaho) April 2, 1902-June 19 1955; House 1935-39; Senate 1939-45.

CLARK, Ezra Jr. (AP/R Conn.) Sept. 12, 1813-Sept. 26 1896; House 1855-59.

CLARK, Frank (D Fla.) March 28, 1860-April 14, 1936 House 1905-25.

CLARK, Frank Monroe (D Pa.) Dec. 24, 1915-−; Hous 1955-Dec. 31, 1974.

CLARK, Franklin (D Maine) Aug. 2, 1801-Aug. 24, 1874 House 1847-49.

CLARK, Henry Alden (R Pa.) Jan. 7, 1850-Feb. 1. 1944; House 1917-19.

CLARK, Henry Selby (D N.C.) Sept. 9, 1809-Jan. 1 1869; House 1845-47.

CLARK, Horace Francis (D N.Y.) Nov. 29, 1815-June 19, 1873; House 1857-61.

CLARK, James (brother of Christopher Henderson Clark, uncle of John Bullock Clark, granduncle of John Bullock Clark Jr.) (CD Ky.) Jan. 16, 1779-Aug. 27, 1839; House 1813-16, Aug. 1, 1825-31; Gov. 1836-39 (Whig).

CLARK, James Beauchamp "Champ" (father of Joel Bennett Clark) (D Mo.) March 7, 1850-March 2, 1921; House 1893-95, 1897-March 2, 1921; Speaker 1911-19.

CLARK, James West (D N.C.) Oct. 15, 1779-Dec. 20, 1843; House 1815-17.

CLARK, Jerome Bayard (D N.C.) April 5, 1882-Aug. 26, 1959; House 1929-49.

CLARK, Joel Bennett "Champ" (son of James Beauchamp Clark) (D Mo.) Jan. 8, 1890-July 13, 1954; Senate Feb. 3, 1933-45.

CLARK, John Bullock (father of John Bullock Clark Jr., nephew of Christopher Henderson Clark and James Clark) (D Mo.) April 17, 1802-Oct. 29, 1885; House Dec. 7, 1857-July 13, 1861.

CLARK, John Bullock Jr. (son of John Bullock Clark, grandnephew of Christopher Henderson Clark and James Clark) (D Mo.) Jan. 14, 1831-Sept. 7, 1903; House 1873-83.

CLARK, John Chamberlain (W N.Y.) Jan. 14, 1793-Oct. 25, 1852; House 1827-29 (Democrat), 1837-43 (1837-39 Democrat).

CLARK, Joseph Sill (D Pa.) Oct. 21, 1901- —; Senate 1957-69.

CLARK, Lincoln (D Iowa) Aug. 9, 1800-Sept. 16, 1886; House 1851-53.

CLARK, Linwood Leon (R Md.) March 21, 1876-Nov. 18, 1965; House 1929-31.

CLARK, Lot (W N.Y.) May 23, 1788-Dec. 18, 1862; House 1823-25.

CLARK, Richard Clarence "Dick" (D Iowa) Sept. 14, 1929- —; Senate 1973-79.

CLARK, Robert (D N.Y.) June 12, 1777-Oct. 1, 1837; House 1819-21.

CLARK, Rush (R Iowa) Oct. 1, 1834-April 29, 1879; House 1877-April 29, 1879.

CLARK, Samuel (D Mich.) Jan. 1800-Oct. 2, 1870; House 1833-35 (N.Y.), 1853-55.

CLARK, Samuel Mercer (R Iowa) Oct. 11, 1842-Aug. 11, 1900; House 1895-99.

CLARK, William (W Pa.) Feb. 18, 1774-March 28, 1851; House 1833-37.

CLARK, William Andrews (D Mont.) Jan. 8, 1839-March 2, 1925; Senate Dec. 4, 1899-May 15, 1900, 1901-07.

CLARK, William Thomas (R Texas) June 29, 1831-Oct. 12, 1905; House March 31, 1870-May 13, 1872.

CLARKE, Archibald Smith (brother of Staley Nichols Clarke) (— N.Y.) 1788-Dec. 4, 1821; House Dec. 2, 1816-17.

CLARKE, Bayard (AW N.Y.) March 17, 1815-June 20, 1884; House 1855-57.

CLARKE, Beverly Leonidas (D Ky.) Feb. 11, 1809-March 17, 1860; House 1847-49.

CLARKE, Charles Ezra (W N.Y.) April 8, 1790-Dec. 29, 1863; House 1849-51.

CLARKE, Frank Gay (R N.H.) Sept. 10, 1850-Jan. 9, 1901; House 1897-Jan. 9, 1901.

CLARKE, Freeman (R N.Y.) March 22, 1809-June 24, 1887; House 1863-65, 1871-75.

CLARKE, James McClure (D N.C.) June 12, 1917- —; House 1983-85, 1987- —.

CLARKE, James Paul (D Ark.) Aug. 18, 1854-Oct. 1, 1916; Senate 1903-Oct. 1, 1916; Pres. pro tempore 1913-16; Gov. 1895-97.

CLARKE, John Blades (D Ky.) April 14, 1833-May 23, 1911; House 1875-79.

CLARKE, John Davenport (husband of Marian Williams Clarke) (R N.Y.) Jan. 15, 1873-Nov. 5, 1933; House 1921-25, 1927-Nov. 5, 1933.

CLARKE, John Hopkins (W R.I.) April 1, 1789-Nov. 23, 1870; Senate 1847-53.

CLARKE, Marian Williams (widow of John Davenport Clarke) (R N.Y.) July 29, 1880-April 8, 1953; House Dec. 28, 1933-35.

CLARKE, Reader Wright (R Ohio) May 18, 1812-May 23, 1872; House 1865-69.

CLARKE, Richard Henry (D Ala.) Feb. 9, 1843-Sept. 26, 1906; House 1889-97.

CLARKE, Sidney (R Kan.) Oct. 16, 1831-June 18, 1909; House 1865-71.

CLARKE, Staley Nichols (brother of Archibald Smith Clarke) (W N.Y.) May 24, 1794-Oct. 14, 1860; House 1841-43.

CLASÓN, Charles Russell (R Mass.) Sept. 3, 1890-July 7, 1985; House 1937-49.

CLASSON, David Guy (R Wis.) Sept. 27, 1870-Sept. 6, 1930; House 1917-23.

CLAUSEN, Don Holst (R Calif.) April 27, 1923- —; House Jan. 22, 1963-83.

CLAWSON, Delwin "Del" Morgan (R Calif.) Jan. 11, 1914- —; House June 11, 1963-Dec. 31, 1978.

CLAWSON, Isaiah Dunn (W N.J.) March 30, 1822-Oct. 9, 1879; House 1855-59.

CLAY, Alexander Stephens (D Ga.) Sept. 25, 1853-Nov. 13, 1910; Senate 1897-Nov. 13, 1910.

CLAY, Brutus Junius (U Ky.) July 1, 1808-Oct. 11, 1878; House 1863-65.

CLAY, Clement Claiborne Jr. (son of Clement Comer Clay) (D Ala.) Dec. 13, 1816-Jan. 3, 1882; Senate Nov. 29, 1853-Jan. 21, 1861.

CLAY, Clement Comer (father of Clement Claiborne Clay Jr.) (D Ala.) Dec. 17, 1789-Sept. 7, 1866; House 1829-35; Senate June 19, 1837-Nov. 15, 1841; Gov. 1835-37.

CLAY, Henry (father of James Brown Clay) (— Ky.) April 12, 1777-June 29, 1852; Senate Nov. 19, 1806-07, Jan. 4, 1810-11, Nov. 10, 1831-March 31, 1842, 1849-June 29, 1852; House 1811-Jan. 19, 1814, 1815-21, 1823-March 6, 1825; Speaker Nov. 4, 1811-Jan. 19, 1814, Dec. 4, 1815-Oct. 28, 1820, Dec. 1, 1823-25; Secy. of State March 7, 1825-29.

CLAY, James Brown (son of Henry Clay) (D Ky.) Nov. 9, 1817-Jan. 26, 1864; House 1857-59.

CLAY, James Franklin (D Ky.) Oct. 29, 1840-Aug. 17, 1921; House 1883-85.

CLAY, Joseph (— Pa.) July 24, 1769-Aug. 27, 1811; House 1803-08.

CLAY, Matthew (D Va.) March 25, 1754-May 27, 1815; House 1797-1813, March 4-May 27, 1815.

CLAY, William Lacey (D Mo.) April 30, 1931- —; House 1969- —.

CLAYPOOL, Harold Kile (son of Horatio Clifford Claypool, cousin of John Barney Peterson) (D Ohio) June 2, 1886-Aug. 2, 1958; House 1937-43.

CLAYPOOL, Horatio Clifford (father of Harold Kile Claypool, cousin of John Barney Peterson) (D Ohio) Feb. 9, 1859-Jan. 19, 1921; House 1911-15, 1917-19.

CLAYTON, Augustin Smith (SRD Ga.) Nov. 27, 1783-June 21, 1839; House Jan. 21, 1832-35.

CLAYTON, Bertram Tracy (brother of Henry De Lamar Clayton) (D N.Y.) Oct. 19, 1862-May 30, 1918; House 1899-1901.

CLAYTON, Charles (R Calif.) Oct. 5, 1825-Oct. 4, 1885; House 1873-75.

CLAYTON, Henry De Lamar (brother of Bertram Tracy Clayton) (D Ala.) Feb. 10, 1857-Dec. 21, 1929 House 1897-May 25, 1914.

CLAYTON, John Middleton (nephew of Joshua Clay ton, cousin of Thomas Clayton, great-granduncle o Clayton Douglass Buck) (W Del.) July 24, 1796-Nov 9, 1856; Senate 1829-Dec. 29, 1836 (National Repub lican), 1845-Feb. 23, 1849, 1853-Nov. 9, 1856; Secy of State March 7, 1849-July 22, 1850.

CLAYTON, Joshua (father of Thomas Clayton, uncle o John Middleton Clayton, son-in-law of Richar Bassett) (— Del.) July 20, 1744-Aug. 11, 1798; Sen ate Jan. 19, 1798-Aug. 11, 1798; Gov. 1789-96 (Feder alist).

CLAYTON, Powell (R Ark.) Aug. 7, 1833-Aug. 25, 1914 Senate 1871-77; Gov. 1868-71.

CLAYTON, Thomas (son of Joshua Clayton, cousin o John Middleton Clayton) (W Del.) March 9, 1778 Aug. 21, 1854; House 1815-17 (Federalist); Senat Jan. 8, 1824-27 (Federalist), Jan. 9, 1837-47.

CLEARY, William Edward (D N.Y.) July 20, 1849-Dec 20, 1932; House March 5, 1918-21, 1923-27.

CLEMENS, Jeremiah (D Ala.) Dec. 28, 1814-May 21 1865; Senate Nov. 30, 1849-53.

CLEMENS, Sherrard (D Va.) April 28, 1820-June 30 1881; House Dec. 6, 1852-53, 1857-61.

CLEMENTE, Louis Gary (D N.Y.) June 10, 1908-Ma 13, 1968; House 1949-53.

CLEMENTS, Andrew Jackson (U Tenn.) Dec. 23, 1832 Nov. 7, 1913; House 1861-63.

CLEMENTS, Earle Chester (D Ky.) Oct. 22, 1896 March 12, 1985; House 1945-Jan. 6, 1947; Senat Nov. 27, 1950-57; Gov. 1947-50.

CLEMENTS, Isaac (R Ill.) March 31, 1837-May 31 1909; House 1873-75.

CLEMENTS, Judson Claudius (D Ga.) Feb. 12, 1846 June 18, 1917; House 1881-91.

CLEMENTS, Newton Nash (— Ala.) Dec. 23, 1837-Fe 20, 1900; House Dec. 8, 1880-81.

CLENDENIN, David (— Ohio) ? - ?; House Oct. 1 1814-17.

CLEVELAND, Chauncey Fitch (D Conn.) Feb. 16 1799-June 6, 1887; House 1849-53; Gov. 1842-44.

CLEVELAND, James Colgate (R N.H.) June 13, 1926 —; House 1963-81.

CLEVELAND, Jesse Franklin (UD Ga.) Oct. 25, 1804 June 22, 1841; House Oct. 5, 1835-39.

CLEVELAND, Orestes (D N.J.) March 2, 1829-March 30, 1896; House 1869-71.

CLEVENGER, Cliff (R Ohio) Aug. 20, 1885-Dec. 13, 1960; House 1939-59.

CLEVENGER, Raymond Francis (D Mich.) June 6, 1926- —; House 1965-67.

CLEVER, Charles P. (D N.M.) Feb. 23, 1830-July 8, 1874; House (Terr. Del.) Sept. 2, 1867-Feb. 20, 1869.

CLIFFORD, Nathan (D Maine) Aug. 18, 1803-July 25, 1881; House 1839-43; Atty. Gen. 1846-48; Assoc. Justice Supreme Court 1858-81.

CLIFT, Joseph Wales (R Ga.) Sept. 30, 1837-May 2, 1908; House July 25, 1868-69.

CLINCH, Duncan Lamont (W Ga.) April 6, 1787-Nov. 27, 1849; House Feb. 15, 1844-45.

CLINE, Cyrus (D Ind.) July 12, 1856-Oct. 5, 1923; House 1909-17.

CLINGER, William Floyd Jr. (R Pa.) April 4, 1929- —; House 1979- —.

CLINGMAN, Thomas Lanier (D N.C.) July 27, 1812-Nov. 3, 1897; House 1843-45 (Whig), 1847-May 7, 1858; Senate May 7, 1858-March 28, 1861.

CLINTON, De Witt (half brother of James Graham Clinton, cousin of George Clinton, nephew of Vice Pres. George Clinton) (DR N.Y.) March 2, 1769-Feb. 11, 1828; Senate Feb. 9, 1802-Nov. 4, 1803; Gov. 1817-23, 1825-28 (Clinton Republican).

CLINTON, George (cousin of De Witt Clinton and James Graham Clinton, son of Vice Pres. George Clinton) (D N.Y.) June 6, 1771-Sept. 16, 1809; House Feb. 14, 1805-09.

CLINTON, James Graham (half brother of De Witt Clinton, cousin of George Clinton, nephew of Vice Pres. George Clinton) (D N.Y.) Jan. 2, 1804-May 28, 1849; House 1841-45.

CLIPPINGER, Roy (R Ill.) Jan. 13, 1886-Dec. 24, 1962; House Nov. 6, 1945-49.

CLOPTON, David (SRD Ala.) Sept. 19, 1820-Feb. 5, 1892; House 1859-Jan. 21, 1861.

CLOPTON, John (D Va.) Feb. 7, 1756-Sept. 11, 1816; House 1795-99, 1801-Sept. 11, 1816.

CLOUSE, Wynne F. (R Tenn.) Aug. 29, 1883-Feb. 19, 1944; House 1921-23.

CLOVER, Benjamin Hutchinson (FA Kan.) Dec. 22, 1837-Dec. 30, 1899; House 1891-93.

CLOWNEY, William Kennedy (SRD S.C.) March 21, 1797-March 12, 1851; House 1833-35 (Nullifier), 1837-39.

CLUETT, Ernest Harold (R N.Y.) July 13, 1874-Feb. 4, 1954; House 1937-43.

CLUNIE, Thomas Jefferson (D Calif.) March 25, 1852-June 30, 1903; House 1889-91.

CLYMER, George (F Pa.) March 16, 1739-Jan. 23, 1813; House 1789-91; Cont. Cong. 1776-78, 1780-83.

CLYMER, Hiester (nephew of William Hiester, cousin of Isaac Ellmaker Hiester) (D Pa.) Nov. 3, 1827-June 12, 1884; House 1873-81.

COAD, Merwin (D Iowa) Sept. 28, 1924- —; House 1957-63.

COADY, Charles Pearce (D Md.) Feb. 22, 1868-Feb. 16, 1934; House Nov. 4, 1913-21.

COATS, Daniel R. (R Ind.) May 16, 1943- —; House 1981- —.

COBB, Amasa (R Wis.) Sept. 27, 1823-July 5, 1905; House 1863-71.

COBB, Clinton Levering (R N.C.) Aug. 25, 1842-April 30, 1879; House 1869-75.

COBB, David (F Mass.) Sept. 14, 1748-April 17, 1830; House 1793-95.

COBB, George Thomas (D N.J.) Oct. 13, 1813-Aug. 12, 1870; House 1861-63.

COBB, Howell (uncle of Howell Cobb, below) (— Ga.) Aug. 3, 1772-May 26, 1818; House 1807-12.

COBB, Howell (nephew of Howell Cobb, above) (D Ga.) Sept. 7, 1815-Oct. 9, 1868; House 1843-51, 1855-57; Speaker 1849-51; Gov. 1851-53 (Union Democrat); Secy. of the Treasury 1857-60.

COBB, James Edward (— Ala.) Oct. 5, 1835-June 2, 1903; House 1887-April 21, 1896.

COBB, Seth Wallace (D Mo.) Dec. 5, 1838-May 22, 1909; House 1891-97.

COBB, Stephen Alonzo (R Kan.) June 17, 1833-Aug. 24, 1878; House 1873-75.

COBB, Thomas Reed (D Ind.) July 2, 1828-June 23, 1892; House 1877-87.

COBB, Thomas Willis (— Ga.) 1784-Feb. 1, 1830; House 1817-21, 1823-Dec. 6, 1824; Senate Dec. 6, 1824-28.

COBB, Williamson Robert Winfield (D Ala.) June 8, 1807-Nov. 1, 1864; House 1847-Jan. 30, 1861.

COBEY, William Wilfred Jr. (R N.C.) May 13, 1939- —; House 1985-87.

COBLE, Howard (R N.C.) March 18, 1931- —; House 1985- —.

COBURN, Frank Potter (D Wis.) Dec. 6, 1858-Nov. 2, 1932; House 1891-93.

COBURN, John (R Ind.) Oct. 27, 1825-Jan. 28, 1908; House 1867-75.

COBURN, Stephen (R Maine) Nov. 11, 1817-July 4, 1882; House Jan. 2-March 3, 1861.

COCHRAN, Alexander Gilmore (D Pa.) March 20, 1846-May 1, 1928; House 1875-77.

COCHRAN, Charles Fremont (D Mo.) Sept. 27, 1846-Dec. 19, 1906; House 1897-1905.

COCHRAN, James (grandfather of James Cochrane Dobbin) (D N.C.) about 1767-April 7, 1813; House 1809-13.

COCHRAN, James (— N.Y.) Feb. 11, 1769-Nov. 7, 1848; House 1797-99.

COCHRAN, John Joseph (D Mo.) Aug. 11, 1880-March 6, 1947; House Nov. 2, 1926-47.

COCHRAN, Thomas Cunningham (R Pa.) Nov. 30, 1877-Dec. 10, 1957; House 1927-35.

COCHRAN, William Thad (R Miss.) Dec. 7, 1937- —; House 1973-Dec. 26, 1978; Senate Dec. 27, 1978- —.

COCHRANE, Aaron Van Schaick (nephew of Isaac Whitbeck Van Schaick) (R N.Y.) March 14, 1858-Sept. 7, 1943; House 1897-1901.

COCHRANE, Clark Betton (uncle of George Cochrane Hazelton and Gerry Whiting Hazelton) (R N.Y.) May 31, 1815-March 5, 1867; House 1857-61.

COCHRANE, John (SRD N.Y.) Aug. 27, 1813-Feb. 7, 1898; House 1857-61.

COCKE, John (son of William Cocke, uncle of William Michael Cocke) (— Tenn.) 1772-Feb. 16, 1854; House 1819-27.

COCKE, William (father of John Cocke, grandfather of William Michael Cocke) (— Tenn.) 1747-Aug. 22, 1828; Senate Aug. 2, 1796-March 3, 1797, April 22-Sept. 26, 1797, 1799-1805.

COCKE, William Michael (grandson of William Cocke, nephew of John Cocke) (D Tenn.) July 16, 1815-Feb. 6, 1896; House 1845-49.

COCKERILL, Joseph Randolph (D Ohio) Jan. 2, 1818-Oct. 23, 1875; House 1857-59.

COCKRAN, William Bourke (D N.Y.) Feb. 28, 1854-March 1, 1923; House 1887-89, Nov. 3, 1891-95, Feb. 23, 1904-09, 1921-March 1, 1923.

COCKRELL, Francis Marion (brother of Jeremiah Vardaman Cockrell) (D Mo.) Oct. 1, 1834-Dec. 13 1915; Senate 1875-1905.

COCKRELL, Jeremiah Vardaman (brother of Francis Marion Cockrell) (D Texas) May 7, 1832-March 18 1915; House 1893-97.

COCKS, William Willets (brother of Frederick Cocks Hicks) (R N.Y.) July 24, 1861-May 24, 1932; House 1905-11.

CODD, George Pierre (R Mich.) Dec. 7, 1869-Feb. 16 1927; House 1921-23.

CODDING, James Hodge (R Pa.) July 8, 1849-Sept. 12 1919; House Nov. 5, 1895-99.

COELHO, Anthony Lee "Tony" (D Calif.) June 15 1942- —; House 1979- —.

COFFEE, Harry Buffington (D Neb.) March 16, 1890-Oct. 3, 1972; House 1935-43.

COFFEE, John (D Ga.) Dec. 3, 1782-Sept. 25, 1836 House 1833-Sept. 25, 1836.

COFFEE, John Main (D Wash.) Jan. 23, 1897-June 1983; House 1937-47.

COFFEEN, Henry Asa (D Wyo.) Feb. 14, 1841-Dec. 1912; House 1893-95.

COFFEY, Robert Lewis Jr. (D Pa.) Oct. 21, 1918-Apr 20, 1949; House Jan. 3-April 20, 1949.

COFFIN, Charles Dustin (W Ohio) Sept. 9, 1805-Feb 28, 1880; House Dec. 20, 1837-39.

COFFIN, Charles Edward (R Md.) July 18, 1841-May 24, 1912; House Nov. 6, 1894-97.

COFFIN, Frank Morey (D Maine) July 11, 1919- — House 1957-61.

COFFIN, Howard Aldridge (R Mich.) June 11, 187 Feb. 28, 1956; House 1947-49.

COFFIN, Peleg Jr. (— Mass.) Nov. 3, 1756-March 1805; House 1793-95.

COFFIN, Thomas Chalkley (D Idaho) Oct. 25, 188 June 8, 1934; House 1933-June 8, 1934.

COFFROTH, Alexander Hamilton (D Pa.) May 1828-Sept. 2, 1906; House 1863-65, Feb. 19-July 1 1866, 1879-81.

COGHLAN, John Maxwell (R Calif.) Dec. 8, 183 March 26, 1879; House 1871-73.

COGSWELL, William (R Mass.) Aug. 23, 1838-May 22, 1895; House 1887-May 22, 1895.

COHELAN, Jeffrey (D Calif.) June 24, 1914- —; House 1959-71.

COHEN, John Sanford (D Ga.) Feb. 26, 1870-May 13, 1935; Senate April 25, 1932-Jan. 11, 1933.

COHEN, William Sebastian (R Maine) Aug. 28, 1940- —; House 1973-79; Senate 1979- —.

COHEN, William Wolfe (D N.Y.) Sept. 6, 1874-Oct. 12, 1940; House 1927-29.

COIT, Joshua (F Conn.) Oct. 7, 1758-Sept. 5, 1798; House 1793-Sept. 5, 1798.

COKE, Richard (nephew of Richard Coke Jr.) (D Texas) March 13, 1829-May 14, 1897; Senate 1877-95; Gov. Dec. 1874-76.

COKE, Richard Jr. (uncle of Richard Coke) (JD Va.) Nov. 16, 1790-March 31, 1851; House 1829-33.

COLCOCK, William Ferguson (D S.C.) Nov. 5, 1804-June 13, 1889; House 1849-53.

COLDEN, Cadwallader David (D N.Y.) April 4, 1769-Feb. 7, 1834; House Dec. 12, 1821-23.

COLDEN, Charles J. (D Calif.) Aug. 24, 1870-April 15, 1938; House 1933-April 15, 1938.

COLE, Albert McDonald (R Kan.) Oct. 13, 1901- —; House 1945-53.

COLE, Cornelius (UR Calif.) Sept. 17, 1822-Nov. 3, 1924; House 1863-65; Senate 1867-73.

COLE, Cyrenus (R Iowa) Jan. 13, 1863-Nov. 14, 1939; House July 19, 1921-33.

COLE, George Edward (D Wash.) Dec. 23, 1826-Dec. 3, 1906; House (Terr. Del.) 1863-65; Gov. (Wash. Terr.) Nov. 1866-March 4, 1867.

COLE, Nathan (R Mo.) July 26, 1825-March 4, 1904; House 1877-79.

COLE, Orsamus (W Wis.) Aug. 23, 1819-May 5, 1903; House 1849-51.

COLE, Ralph Dayton (brother of Raymond Clinton Cole) (R Ohio) Nov. 30, 1873-Oct. 15, 1932; House 1905-11.

COLE, Raymond Clinton (brother of Ralph Dayton Cole) (R Ohio) Aug. 21, 1870-Feb. 8, 1957; House 1919-25.

COLE, William Clay (R Mo.) Aug. 29, 1897-Sept. 23, 1965; House 1943-49, 1953-55.

COLE, William Hinson (D Md.) Jan. 11, 1837-July 8, 1886; House 1885-July 8, 1886.

COLE, William Purington Jr. (D Md.) May 11, 1889-Sept. 22, 1957; House 1927-29, 1931-Oct. 26, 1942.

COLE, William Sterling (R N.Y.) April 18, 1904-March 15, 1987; House 1935-Dec. 1, 1957.

COLEMAN, E. Thomas (R Mo.) May 29, 1943- —; House Nov. 2, 1976- —.

COLEMAN, Hamilton Dudley (R La.) May 12, 1845-March 16, 1926; House 1889-91.

COLEMAN, Nicholas Daniel (JD Ky.) April 22, 1800-May 11, 1874; House 1829-31.

COLEMAN, Ronald D. (D Texas) Nov. 29, 1941- —; House 1983- —.

COLEMAN, William Henry (R Pa.) Dec. 28, 1871-June 3, 1943; House 1915-17.

COLERICK, Walpole Gillespie (D Ind.) Aug. 1, 1845-Jan. 11, 1911; House 1879-83.

COLES, Isaac (father of Walter Coles) (— Va.) March 2, 1747-June 3, 1813; House 1789-91, 1793-97.

COLES, Walter (son of Isaac Coles) (D Va.) Dec. 8, 1790-Nov. 9, 1857; House 1835-45.

COLFAX, Schuyler (R Ind.) March 23, 1823-Jan. 13, 1885; House 1855-69; Speaker 1863-69; Vice President 1869-73.

COLHOUN, John Ewing (cousin of John Caldwell Calhoun and Joseph Calhoun) (D S.C.) 1750-Oct. 26, 1802; Senate 1801-Oct. 26, 1802.

COLLAMER, Jacob (R Vt.) Jan. 8, 1792-Nov. 9, 1865; House 1843-49 (Whig); Senate 1855-Nov. 9, 1865; Postmaster Gen. March 7, 1849-July 20, 1850.

COLLIER, Harold Reginald (R Ill.) Dec. 12, 1915- —; House 1957-75.

COLLIER, James William (D Miss.) Sept. 28, 1872-Sept. 28, 1933; House 1909-33.

COLLIER, John Allen (CD N.Y.) Nov. 13, 1787-March 24, 1873; House 1831-33.

COLLIN, John Francis (D N.Y.) April 30, 1802-Sept. 16, 1889; House 1845-47.

COLLINS, Cardiss (widow of George Washington Collins) (D Ill.) Sept. 24, 1931- —; House June 5, 1973- —.

COLLINS, Ela (father of William Collins) (D N.Y.) Feb. 14, 1786-Nov. 23, 1848; House 1823-25.

COLLINS, Francis Dolan (D Pa.) March 5, 1841-Nov. 21, 1891; House 1875-79.

COLLINS, George Washington (husband of Cardiss Collins) (D Ill.) March 5, 1925-Dec. 8, 1972; House Nov. 3, 1970-Dec. 8, 1972.

COLLINS, James M. (R Texas) April 29, 1916--; House Aug. 24, 1968-83.

COLLINS, Patrick Andrew (D Mass.) March 12, 1844-Sept. 13, 1905; House 1883-89.

COLLINS, Ross Alexander (D Miss.) April 25, 1880-July 14, 1968; House 1921-35, 1937-43.

COLLINS, Samuel LaFort (R Calif.) Aug. 6, 1895-June 26, 1965; House 1933-37.

COLLINS, William (son of Ela Collins) (D N.Y.) Feb. 22, 1818-June 18, 1878; House 1847-49.

COLMER, William Meyers (D Miss.) Feb. 11, 1890-Sept. 9, 1980; House 1933-73.

COLQUITT, Alfred Holt (son of Walter Terry Colquitt) (D Ga.) April 20, 1824-March 26, 1894; House 1853-55; Senate 1883-March 26, 1894; Gov. 1877-82.

COLQUITT, Walter Terry (father of Alfred Holt Colquitt) (VBD Ga.) Dec. 27, 1799-May 7, 1855; House 1839-July 21, 1840 (State Rights Whig), Jan. 3, 1842-43; Senate 1843-Feb. 1848.

COLSON, David Grant (R Ky.) April 1, 1861-Sept. 27, 1904; House 1895-99.

COLSTON, Edward (F Va.) Dec. 25, 1786-April 23, 1852; House 1817-19.

COLT, LeBaron Bradford (R R.I.) June 25, 1846-Aug. 18, 1924; Senate 1913-Aug. 18, 1924.

COLTON, Don Byron (R Utah) Sept. 15, 1876-Aug. 1, 1952; House 1921-33.

COMBEST, Larry Ed (R Texas) March 20, 1945--; House 1985--.

COMBS, George Hamilton Jr. (D Mo.) May 2, 1899-Nov. 29, 1977; House 1927-29.

COMBS, Jesse Martin (D Texas) July 7, 1889-Aug. 21, 1953; House 1945-53.

COMEGYS, Joseph Parsons (W Del.) Dec. 29, 1813-Feb. 1, 1893; Senate Nov. 19, 1856-Jan. 14, 1857.

COMER, Braxton Bragg (D Ala.) Nov. 7, 1848-Aug. 15, 1927; Senate March 5-Nov. 2, 1920; Gov. 1907-11.

COMINGO, Abram (D Mo.) Jan. 9, 1820-Nov. 10, 1889; House 1871-75.

COMINS, Linus Bacon (R Mass.) Nov. 29, 1817-Oct. 14 1892; House 1855-59 (1855-57 American Party).

COMPTON, Barnes (great-grandson of Philip Key) (D Md.) Nov. 16, 1830-Dec. 4, 1898; House 1885-March 20, 1890, 1891-May 15, 1894.

COMPTON, C. H. Ranulf (R Conn.) Sept. 16, 1878-Jan 26, 1974; House 1943-45.

COMSTOCK, Charles Carter (Fus.D Mich.) March 1818-Feb. 20, 1900; House 1885-87.

COMSTOCK, Daniel Webster (R Ind.) Dec. 16, 1840 May 19, 1917; House March 4-May 19, 1917.

COMSTOCK, Oliver Cromwell (D N.Y.) March 1, 1780 Jan. 11, 1860; House 1813-19.

COMSTOCK, Solomon Gilman (R Minn.) May 9, 1842 June 3, 1933; House 1889-91.

CONABLE, Barber B. Jr. (R N.Y.) Nov. 2, 1922-- House 1965-85.

CONARD, John (D Pa.) Nov. 1773-May 9, 1857; House 1813-15.

CONDICT, Lewis (AF N.J.) March 3, 1772-May 26 1862; House 1811-17, 1821-33.

CONDIT, John (father of Silas Condit) (D N.J.) July 1755-May 4, 1834; House 1799-1803, March 4-Nov 4, 1819; Senate Sept. 1, 1803-March 3, 1809, March 21, 1809-17.

CONDIT, Silas (son of John Condit) (CD N.J.) Aug. 1 1778-Nov. 29, 1861; House 1831-33.

CONDON, Francis Bernard (D R.I.) Nov. 11, 1891-No 23, 1965; House Nov. 4, 1930-Jan. 10, 1935.

CONDON, Robert Likens (D Calif.) Nov. 10, 1912-Jun 3, 1976; House 1953-55.

CONGER, Edwin Hurd (R Iowa) March 7, 1843-May 1 1907; House 1885-Oct. 3, 1890.

CONGER, Harmon Sweatland (W N.Y.) April 9, 181 Oct. 22, 1882; House 1847-51.

CONGER, James Lockwood (FSW Mich.) Feb. 18, 180 April 10, 1876; House 1851-53.

CONGER, Omar Dwight (R Mich.) April 1, 1818-Ju 11, 1898; House 1869-81; Senate 1881-87.

CONKLING, Alfred (father of Frederick August Conkling and Roscoe Conkling) (AJD N.Y.) Oct. 1789-Feb. 5, 1874; House 1821-23.

CONKLING, Frederick Augustus (son of Alfr Conkling, brother of Roscoe Conkling) (R N.Y.) A 22, 1816-Sept. 18, 1891; House 1861-63.

CONKLING, Roscoe (son of Alfred Conkling, brother of Frederick Augustus Conkling) (UR N.Y.) Oct. 3, 1829-April 18, 1888; House 1859-63 (Republican), 1865-March 4, 1867 (Republican); Senate 1867-May 16, 1881.

CONLAN, John Bertrand (R Ariz.) Sept. 17, 1930- —; House 1973-77.

CONN, Charles Gerard (D Ind.) Jan. 29, 1844-Jan. 5, 1931; House 1893-95.

CONNALLY, Thomas Terry (D Texas) Aug. 19, 1877-Oct. 28, 1963; House 1917-29; Senate 1929-53.

CONNELL, Charles Robert (son of William Connell) (R Pa.) Sept. 22, 1864-Sept. 26, 1922; House 1921-Sept. 26, 1922.

CONNELL, Richard Edward (D N.Y.) Nov. 6, 1857-Oct. 30, 1912; House 1911-Oct. 30, 1912.

CONNELL, William (father of Charles Robert Connell) (R Pa.) Sept. 10, 1827-March 21, 1909; House 1897-1903, Feb. 10, 1904-05.

CONNELL, William James (R Neb.) July 6, 1846-Aug. 16, 1924; House 1889-91.

CONNELLY, John Robert (D Kan.) Feb. 27, 1870-Sept. 9, 1940; House 1913-19.

CONNER, James Perry (R Iowa) Jan. 27, 1851-March 19, 1924; House Dec. 4, 1900-09.

CONNER, John Cogswell (D Texas) Oct. 14, 1842-Dec. 10, 1873; House March 31, 1870-73.

CONNER, Samuel Shepard (— Mass.) about 1783-Dec. 17, 1820; House 1815-17.

CONNERY, Lawrence Joseph (brother of William Patrick Connery Jr.) (D Mass.) Oct. 17, 1895-Oct. 19, 1941; House Sept. 28, 1937-Oct. 19, 1941.

CONNERY, William Patrick Jr. (brother of Lawrence Joseph Connery) (D Mass.) Aug. 24, 1888-June 15, 1937; House 1923-June 15, 1937.

CONNESS, John (UR Calif.) Sept. 22, 1821-Jan. 10, 1909; Senate 1863-69 (elected as a Douglas Democrat).

CONNOLLY, Daniel Ward (D Pa.) April 24, 1847-Dec. 4, 1894; House 1883-85.

CONNOLLY, James Austin (R Ill.) March 8, 1843-Dec. 15, 1914; House 1895-99.

CONNOLLY, James Joseph (R Pa.) Sept. 24, 1881-Dec. 10, 1952; House 1921-35.

CONNOLLY, Maurice (D Iowa) March 13, 1877-May 28, 1921; House 1913-15.

CONNOR, Henry William (D N.C.) Aug. 5, 1793-Jan. 6, 1866; House 1821-41.

CONOVER, Simon Barclay (R Fla.) Sept. 23, 1840-April 19, 1908; Senate 1873-79.

CONOVER, William Sheldrick II (R Pa.) Aug. 27, 1928- —; House April 25, 1972-73.

CONRAD, Charles Mynn (W La.) Dec. 24, 1804-Feb. 11, 1878; Senate April 14, 1842-43; House 1849-August 17, 1850; Secy. of War Aug. 15, 1850-March 7, 1853.

CONRAD, Frederick (F Pa.) 1759-Aug. 3, 1827; House 1803-07.

CONRAD, Gaylord Kent (D N.D.) March 12, 1948- —; Senate 1987- —.

CONRY, Joseph Aloysius (D Mass.) Sept. 12, 1868-June 22, 1943; House 1901-03.

CONRY, Michael Francis (D N.Y.) April 2, 1870-March 2, 1917; House 1909-March 2, 1917.

CONSTABLE, Albert (D Md.) June 3, 1805-Sept. 18, 1855; House 1845-47.

CONTE, Silvio Otto (R Mass.) Nov. 9, 1921- —; House 1959- —.

CONTEE, Benjamin (granduncle of Thomas Contee Worthington) (— Md.) 1755-Nov. 30, 1815; House 1789-91; Cont. Cong. 1787-88.

CONVERSE, George Leroy (D Ohio) June 4, 1827-March 30, 1897; House 1879-85.

CONWAY, Henry Wharton (cousin of Ambrose Hundley Sevier) (D Ark.) March 18, 1793-Nov. 9, 1827; House (Terr. Del.) 1823-Nov. 9, 1827.

CONWAY, Martin Franklin (R Kan.) Nov. 19, 1827-Feb. 15, 1882; House Jan. 29, 1861-63.

CONYERS, John Jr. (D Mich.) May 16, 1929- —; House 1965- —.

COOK, Burton Chauncey (R Ill.) May 11, 1819-Aug. 18, 1894; House 1865-Aug. 26, 1871.

COOK, Daniel Pope (— Ill.) 1794-Oct. 16, 1827; House 1819-27.

COOK, George Washington (R Colo.) Nov. 10, 1851-Dec. 18, 1916; House 1907-09.

COOK, Joel (R Pa.) March 20, 1842-Dec. 15, 1910; House Nov. 5, 1907-Dec. 15, 1910.

COOK, John Calhoun (ID Iowa) Dec. 26, 1846-June 7, 1920; House March 3, 1883, Oct. 9, 1883-85.

COOK, John Parsons (W Iowa) Aug. 31, 1817-April 17, 1872; House 1853-55.

COOK, Marlow Webster (R Ky.) July 27, 1926- —; Senate Dec. 17, 1968-Dec. 27, 1974.

COOK, Orchard (— Mass.) March 24, 1763-Aug. 12, 1819; House 1805-11.

COOK, Philip (D Ga.) July 30, 1817-May 24, 1894; House 1873-83.

COOK, Robert Eugene (D Ohio) May 19, 1920- —; House 1959-63.

COOK, Samuel Andrew (R Wis.) Jan. 28, 1849-April 4, 1918; House 1895-97.

COOK, Samuel Ellis (D Ind.) Sept. 30, 1860-Feb. 22, 1946; House 1923-25.

COOK, Zadock (— Ga.) Feb. 18, 1769-Aug. 3, 1863; House Dec. 2, 1816-19.

COOKE, Bates (AMas. N.Y.) Dec. 23, 1787-May 31, 1841; House 1831-33.

COOKE, Edmund Francis (R N.Y.) April 13, 1885-May 13, 1967; House 1929-33.

COOKE, Edward Dean (R Ill.) Oct. 17, 1849-June 24, 1897; House 1895-June 24, 1897.

COOKE, Eleutheros (NR Ohio) Dec. 25, 1787-Dec. 27, 1864; House 1831-33.

COOKE, Thomas Burrage (D N.Y.) Nov. 21, 1778-Nov. 20, 1853; House 1811-13.

COOLEY, Harold Dunbar (D N.C.) July 26, 1897-Jan. 15, 1974; House July 7, 1934-67.

COOLIDGE, Frederick Spaulding (father of Marcus Allen Coolidge) (D Mass.) Dec. 7, 1841-June 8, 1906; House 1891-93.

COOLIDGE, Marcus Allen (son of Frederick Spaulding Coolidge) (D Mass.) Oct. 6, 1865-Jan. 23, 1947; Senate 1931-37.

COOMBS, Frank Leslie (R Calif.) Dec. 27, 1853-Oct. 5, 1934; House 1901-03.

COOMBS, William Jerome (D N.Y.) Dec. 24, 1833-Jan. 12, 1922; House 1891-95.

COON, Samuel Harrison (R Ore.) April 15, 1903-May 8, 1981; House 1953-57.

COONEY, James (D Mo.) July 28, 1848-Nov. 16, 1904; House 1897-1903.

COOPER, Allen Foster (R Pa.) June 16, 1862-April 20, 1917; House 1903-11.

COOPER, Charles Merian (D Fla.) Jan. 16, 1856-Nov 14, 1923; House 1893-97.

COOPER, Edmund (brother of Henry Cooper) ((Tenn.) Sept. 11, 1821-July 21, 1911; House July 24 1866-67.

COOPER, Edward (R W.Va.) Feb. 26, 1873-March 1928; House 1915-19.

COOPER, George Byran (D Mich.) June 6, 1808-Aug 29, 1866; House 1859-May 15, 1860.

COOPER, George William (D Ind.) May 21, 1851-Nov 27, 1899; House 1889-95.

COOPER, Henry (brother of Edmund Cooper) (I Tenn.) Aug. 22, 1827-Feb. 4, 1884; Senate 1871-77

COOPER, Henry Allen (R Wis.) Sept. 8, 1850-March 1931; House 1893-1919, 1921-March 1, 1931.

COOPER, James (W Pa.) May 8, 1810-March 28, 186; House 1839-43; Senate 1849-55.

COOPER, James Haynes Shofner (D Tenn.) June 1 1954- —; House 1983- —.

COOPER, Jere (D Tenn.) July 20, 1893-Dec. 18, 195; House 1929-Dec. 18, 1957.

COOPER, John Gordon (R Ohio) April 27, 1872-Jan. 1955; House 1915-37.

COOPER, John Sherman (R Ky.) Aug. 23, 1901- —; Senate Nov. 6, 1946-49, Nov. 5, 1952-55, Nov. 7, 1956-7

COOPER, Mark Anthony (cousin of Eugenius Aristide Nisbet) (D Ga.) April 20, 1800-March 17, 188 House 1839-41 (State Rights Whig), Jan. 3, 184; June 26, 1843 (State Rights Whig).

COOPER, Richard Matlack (— N.J.) Feb. 29, 176 March 10, 1843; House 1829-33.

COOPER, Samuel Bronson (D Texas) May 30, 185 Aug. 21, 1918; House 1893-1905, 1907-09.

COOPER, Thomas (F Del.) 1764-1829; House 1813-1

COOPER, Thomas Buchecker (D Pa.) Dec. 29, 182 April 4, 1862; House 1861-April 4, 1862.

COOPER, William (F N.Y.) Dec. 2, 1754-Dec. 22, 18C House 1795-97, 1799-1801.

COOPER, William Craig (R Ohio) Dec. 18, 1832-Au 29, 1902; House 1885-91.

COOPER, William Raworth (D N.J.) Feb. 20, 1793-Se 22, 1856; House 1839-41.

COPELAND, Royal Samuel (D N.Y.) Nov. 7, 1868-Ju 17, 1938; Senate 1923-June 17, 1938.

COPLEY, Ira Clifton (nephew of Richard Henry Whiting) (R Prog. Ill.) Oct. 25, 1864-Nov. 1, 1947; House 1911-23.

CORBETT, Henry Winslow (UR Ore.) Feb. 18, 1827-March 31, 1903; Senate 1867-73.

CORBETT, Robert James (R Pa.) Aug. 25, 1905-April 25, 1971; House 1939-41, 1945-April 25, 1971.

CORCORAN, Thomas J. (R Ill.) May 23, 1939- —; House 1977-85.

CORDON, Guy (R Ore.) April 24, 1890-June 8, 1969; Senate March 4, 1944-55.

CORDOVA, Jorge Luis (New Prog. P.R.) April 20, 1907- —; House (Res. Comm.) 1969-73.

CORKER, Stephen Alfestus (D Ga.) May 7, 1830-Oct. 18, 1879; House Dec. 22, 1870-71.

CORLETT, William Wellington (R Wyo.) April 10, 1842-July 22, 1890; House (Terr. Del.) 1877-79.

CORLEY, Manuel Simeon (R S.C.) Feb. 10, 1823-Nov. 20, 1902; House July 25, 1868-69.

CORLISS, John Blaisdell (R Mich.) June 7, 1851-Dec. 24, 1929; House 1895-1903.

CORMAN, James C. (D Calif.) Oct. 20, 1920- —; House 1961-81.

CORNELL, Robert John (D Wis.) Dec. 16, 1919- —; House 1975-79.

CORNELL, Thomas (R N.Y.) Jan. 27, 1814-March 30, 1890; House 1867-69, 1881-83.

CORNING, Erastus (grandfather of Parker Corning) (D N.Y.) Dec. 14, 1794-April 9, 1872; House 1857-59, 1861-Oct. 5, 1863.

CORNING, Parker (grandson of Erastus Corning) (D N.Y.) Jan. 22, 1874-May 24, 1943; House 1923-37.

CORNISH, Johnston (D N.J.) June 13, 1858-June 26, 1920; House 1893-95.

CORNWELL, David Lance (D Ind.) June 14, 1945- —; House 1977-79.

CORRADA del RIO, Balthazar (New Prog. P.R.) April 10, 1935- —; House (Res. Comm.) 1977-85.

CORWIN, Franklin (nephew of Moses Bledso Corwin and Thomas Corwin) (R Ill.) Jan. 12, 1818-June 15, 1879; House 1873-75.

CORWIN, Moses Bledso (brother of Thomas Corwin, uncle of Franklin Corwin) (W Ohio) Jan. 5, 1790-April 7, 1872; House 1849-51, 1853-55.

CORWIN, Thomas (brother of Moses Bledso Corwin, uncle of Franklin Corwin) (R Ohio) July 29, 1794-Dec. 18, 1865; House 1831-May 30, 1840 (Whig), 1859-March 12, 1861; Senate 1845-July 20, 1850 (Whig); Gov. 1840-41; Secy. of the Treasury 1850-53.

COSDEN, Jeremiah (— Md.) 1768-Dec. 5, 1824; House 1821-March 19, 1822.

COSGROVE, John (D Mo.) Sept. 12, 1839-Aug. 15, 1925; House 1883-85.

COSTELLO, John Martin (D Calif.) Jan. 15, 1903-Aug. 28, 1976; House 1935-45.

COSTELLO, Peter Edward (R Pa.) June 27, 1854-Oct. 23, 1935; House 1915-21.

COSTIGAN, Edward Prentiss (D Colo.) July 1, 1874-Jan. 17, 1939; Senate 1931-37.

COTHRAN, James Sproull (D S.C.) Aug. 8, 1830-Dec. 5, 1897; House 1887-91.

COTTER, William Ross (D Conn.) July 18, 1926-Sept. 8, 1981; House 1971-Sept. 8, 1981.

COTTMAN, Joseph Stewart (IW Md.) Aug. 16, 1803-Jan. 28, 1863; House 1851-53.

COTTON, Aylett Rains (R Iowa) Nov. 29, 1826-Oct. 30, 1912; House 1871-75.

COTTON, Norris (R N.H.) May 11, 1900- —; House 1947-Nov. 7, 1954; Senate Nov. 8, 1954-Dec. 31, 1974; Aug. 8-Sept. 18, 1975.

COTTRELL, James La Fayette (D Ala.) Aug. 25, 1808-Sept. 7, 1885; House Dec. 7, 1846-47.

COUDERT, Frederick René Jr. (R N.Y.) May 7, 1898-May 21, 1972; House 1947-59.

COUDREY, Harry Marcy (R Mo.) Feb. 28, 1867-July 5, 1930; House June 23, 1906-11.

COUGHLIN, Clarence Dennis (uncle of Robert Lawrence Coughlin) (R Pa.) July 27, 1883-Dec. 15, 1946; House 1921-23.

COUGHLIN, Robert Lawrence (nephew of Clarence Dennis Coughlin) (R Pa.) April 11, 1929- —; House 1969- —.

COULTER, Richard (D Pa.) March 1788-April 21, 1852; House 1827-31 (Independent), 1831-35.

COURTER, James Andrew (R N.J.) Oct. 14, 1941- —; House 1979- —.

COURTNEY, William Wirt (D Tenn.) Sept. 7, 1889-April 6, 1961; House May 11, 1939-49.

COUSINS, Robert Gordon (R Iowa) Jan. 31, 1859-June 20, 1933; House 1893-1909.

COUZENS, James (R Mich.) Aug. 26, 1872-Oct. 22, 1936; Senate Nov. 29, 1922-Oct. 22, 1936.

COVERT, James Way (D N.Y.) Sept. 2, 1842-May 16, 1910; House 1877-81, 1889-95.

COVINGTON, George Washington (D Md.) Sept. 12, 1838-April 6, 1911; House 1881-85.

COVINGTON, James Harry (D Md.) May 3, 1870-Feb. 4, 1942; House 1909-Sept. 30, 1914.

COVINGTON, Leonard (D Md.) Oct. 30, 1768-Nov. 14, 1813; House 1805-07.

COVODE, John (R Pa.) March 18, 1808-Jan. 11, 1871; House 1855-63 (1855-57 Anti Mason Whig), 1867-69, Feb. 9, 1870-Jan. 11, 1871.

COWAN, Edgar (R Pa.) Sept. 19, 1815-Aug. 29, 1885; Senate 1861-67.

COWAN, Jacob Pitzer (D Ohio) March 20, 1823-July 9, 1895; House 1875-77.

COWEN, Benjamin Sprague (W Ohio) Sept. 27, 1793-Sept. 27, 1860; House 1841-43.

COWEN, John Kissig (D Md.) Oct. 28, 1844-April 26, 1904; House 1895-97.

COWGER, William Owen (R Ky.) Jan. 1, 1922-Oct. 2, 1971; House 1967-71.

COWGILL, Calvin (R Ind.) Jan. 7, 1819-Feb. 10, 1903; House 1879-81.

COWHERD, William Strother (D Mo.) Sept. 1, 1860-June 20, 1915; House 1897-1905.

COWLES, Charles Holden (nephew of William Henry Harrison Cowles) (R N.C.) July 16, 1875-Oct. 2, 1957; House 1909-11.

COWLES, George Washington (R N.Y.) Dec. 6, 1823-Jan. 20, 1901; House 1869-71.

COWLES, Henry Booth (− N.Y.) March 18, 1798-May 17, 1873; House 1829-31.

COWLES, William Henry Harrison (uncle of Charles Holden Cowles) (D N.C.) April 22, 1840-Dec. 30, 1901; House 1885-93.

COX, Edward Eugene (D Ga.) April 3, 1880-Dec. 24, 1952; House 1925-Dec. 24, 1952.

COX, Isaac Newton (D N.Y.) Aug. 1, 1846-Sept. 28, 1916; House 1891-93.

COX, Jacob Dolson (R Ohio) Oct. 27, 1828-Aug. 4, 1900; House 1877-79; Gov. 1866-68; Secy. of the Interior 1869-70.

COX, James (D N.J.) June 14, 1753-Sept. 12, 181⬤ House 1809-Sept. 12, 1810.

COX, James Middleton (D Ohio) March 31, 1870-Ju⬤ 15, 1957; House 1909-Jan. 12, 1913; Gov. 1913-1⬤ 1917-21.

COX, Leander Martin (AP Ky.) May 7, 1812-March 1⬤ 1865; House 1853-57 (1853-55 Whig).

COX, Nicholas Nichols (D Tenn.) Jan. 6, 1837-May 1912; House 1891-1901.

COX, Samuel Sullivan (D N.Y.) Sept. 30, 1824-Sept. 1⬤ 1889; House 1857-65 (Ohio), 1869-73, Nov. 4, 187⬤ May 20, 1885, Nov. 2, 1886-Sept. 10, 1889; Speak⬤ pro tempore 1876.

COX, William Elijah (D Ind.) Sept. 6, 1861-March 1 1942; House 1907-19.

COX, William Ruffin (D N.C.) March 11, 1831-Dec. 2⬤ 1919; House 1881-87.

COXE, William Jr. (F N.J.) May 3, 1762-Feb. 25, 183⬤ House 1813-15.

COYLE, William Radford (R Pa.) July 10, 1878-Jan. ⬤ 1962; House 1925-27, 1929-33.

COYNE, James K. (R Pa.) Nov. 17, 1946-−; Hou⬤ 1981-83.

COYNE, William J. (D Pa.) Aug. 24, 1936-−; Hou⬤ 1981-−.

CRABB, George Whitfield (W Ala.) Feb. 22, 1804-Au⬤ 15, 1846; House Sept. 4, 1838-41.

CRABB, Jeremiah (D Md.) 1760-1800; House 1795-9⬤

CRADDOCK, John Durrett (R Ky.) Oct. 26, 1881-M⬤ 20, 1942; House 1929-31.

CRADLEBAUGH, John (− Nev.) Feb. 22, 1819-F⬤ 22, 1872; House (Terr. Del.) Dec. 2, 1861-63.

CRAFTS, Samuel Chandler (W Vt.) Oct. 6, 1768-N⬤ 19, 1853; House 1817-25; Senate April 23, 1842-⬤ Gov. 1828-31 (National Republican).

CRAGIN, Aaron Harrison (AP N.H.) Feb. 3, 1821-M⬤ 10, 1898; House 1855-59 (1857-59 Republican); S⬤ ate 1865-77.

CRAGO, Thomas Spencer (R Pa.) Aug. 8, 1866-Sept. 1925; House 1911-13, 1915-21, Sept. 20, 1921-23.

CRAIG, Alexander Kerr (D Pa.) Feb. 21, 1828-July ⬤ 1892; House Feb. 26-July 29, 1892.

CRAIG, George Henry (R Ala.) Dec. 25, 1845-Jan. 1923; House Jan. 9-March 3, 1885.

CRAIG, Hector (JD N.Y.) 1775-Jan. 31, 1842; House 1823-25, 1829-July 12, 1830.

CRAIG, James (D Mo.) Feb. 28, 1818-Oct. 22, 1888; House 1857-61.

CRAIG, Larry E. (R Idaho) July 20, 1945- —; House 1981- —.

CRAIG, Robert (D Va.) 1792-Nov. 25, 1852; House 1829-33, 1835-41.

CRAIG, Samuel Alfred (R Pa.) Nov. 19, 1839-March 17, 1920; House 1889-91.

CRAIG, William Benjamin (D Ala.) Nov. 2, 1877-Nov. 27, 1925; House 1907-11.

CRAIGE, Francis Burton (D N.C.) March 13, 1811-Dec. 30, 1875; House 1853-61.

CRAIK, William (— Md.) Oct. 31, 1761-prior to 1814; House Dec. 5, 1796-1801.

CRAIL, Joe (R Calif.) Dec. 25, 1877-March 2, 1938; House 1927-33.

CRAIN, William Henry (D Texas) Nov. 25, 1848-Feb. 10, 1896; House 1885-Feb. 10, 1896.

CRALEY, Nathaniel Nieman Jr. (D Pa.) Nov. 17, 1927- —; House 1965-67.

CRAMER, John (D N.Y.) May 17, 1779-June 1, 1870; House 1833-37.

CRAMER, William Cato (R Fla.) Aug. 4, 1922- —; House 1955-71.

CRAMTON, Louis Convers (R Mich.) Dec. 2, 1875-June 23, 1966; House 1913-31.

CRANE, Daniel Bever (brother of Philip Miller Crane) (R Ill.) Jan. 10, 1936- —; House 1979-85.

CRANE, Joseph Halsey (W Ohio) Aug. 31, 1782-Nov. 13, 1851; House 1829-37.

CRANE, Philip Miller (brother of Daniel Bever Crane) (R Ill.) Nov. 3, 1930- —; House Nov. 25, 1969- —.

CRANE, Winthrop Murray (R Mass.) April 23, 1853-Oct. 2, 1920; Senate Oct. 12, 1904-13; Gov. 1900-03.

CRANFORD, John Walter (D Texas) 1862-March 3, 1899; House 1897-March 3, 1899.

CRANSTON, Alan (D Calif.) June 19, 1914- —; Senate 1969- —.

CRANSTON, Henry Young (brother of Robert Bennie Cranston) (W R.I.) Oct. 9, 1789-Feb. 12, 1864; House 1843-47.

CRANSTON, Robert Bennie (brother of Henry Young Cranston) (L&OW R.I.) Jan. 14, 1791-Jan. 27, 1873; House 1837-43 (Whig), 1847-49.

CRAPO, William Wallace (R Mass.) May 16, 1830-Feb. 28, 1926; House Nov. 2, 1875-83.

CRARY, Isaac Edwin (D Mich.) Oct. 2, 1804-May 8, 1854; House Jan. 26, 1837-41.

CRAVENS, James Addison (second cousin of James Harrison Cravens) (D Ind.) Nov. 4, 1818-June 20, 1893; House 1861-65.

CRAVENS, James Harrison (second cousin of James Addison Cravens) (W Ind.) Aug. 2, 1802-Dec. 4, 1876; House 1841-43.

CRAVENS, Jordan Edgar (cousin of William Ben Cravens) (D Ark.) Nov. 7, 1830-April 8, 1914; House 1877-83.

CRAVENS, William Ben (father of William Fadjo Cravens, cousin of Jordan Edgar Cravens) (D Ark.) Jan. 17, 1872-Jan. 13, 1939; House 1907-13, 1933-Jan. 13, 1939.

CRAVENS, William Fadjo (son of William Ben Cravens) (D Ark.) Feb. 15, 1889-April 16, 1974; House Sept. 12, 1939-49.

CRAWFORD, Coe Isaac (R S.D.) Jan. 14, 1858-April 25, 1944; Senate 1909-15; Gov. 1907-09.

CRAWFORD, Fred Lewis (R Mich.) May 5, 1888-April 13, 1957; House 1935-53.

CRAWFORD, George Walker (W Ga.) Dec. 22, 1798-July 27, 1872; House Jan. 7-March 3, 1843; Gov. 1843-47; Secy. of War 1849-50.

CRAWFORD, Joel (D Ga.) June 15, 1783-April 5, 1858; House 1817-21.

CRAWFORD, Martin Jenkins (D Ga.) March 17, 1820-July 23, 1883; House 1855-Jan. 23, 1861.

CRAWFORD, Thomas Hartley (JD Pa.) Nov. 14, 1786-Jan. 27, 1863; House 1829-33.

CRAWFORD, William (D Pa.) 1760-Oct. 23, 1823; House 1809-17.

CRAWFORD, William Harris (— Ga.) Feb. 24, 1772-Sept. 15, 1834; Senate Nov. 7, 1807-March 23, 1813; Pres. pro tempore 1812; Secy. of War 1815-16; Secy. of the Treasury 1816-25.

CRAWFORD, William Thomas (D N.C.) June 1, 1856-Nov. 16, 1913; House 1891-95, 1899-May 10, 1900, 1907-09.

CREAGER, Charles Edward (R Okla.) April 28, 1873-Jan. 11, 1964; House 1909-11.

CREAL, Edward Wester (D Ky.) Nov. 20, 1883-Oct. 13, 1943; House Nov. 5, 1935-Oct. 13, 1943.

CREAMER, Thomas James (D N.Y.) May 26, 1843-Aug. 4, 1914; House 1873-75, 1901-03.

CREBS, John Montgomery (D Ill.) April 9, 1830-June 26, 1890; House 1869-73.

CREELY, John Vaudain (R Pa.) Nov. 14, 1839-Sept. 28, 1900; House 1871-73.

CREIGHTON, William Jr. (D Ohio) Oct. 29, 1778-Oct. 8, 1851; House May 4, 1813-17, 1827-28, 1829-33.

CRESWELL, John Andrew Jackson (R Md.) Nov. 18, 1828-Dec. 23, 1891; House 1863-65; Senate March 9, 1865-67; Postmaster Gen. 1869-74.

CRETELLA, Albert William (R Conn.) April 22, 1897-May 24, 1979; House 1953-59.

CRIPPA, Edward David (R Wyo.) April 8, 1899-Oct. 20, 1960; Senate June 24-Nov. 28, 1954.

CRISFELD, John Woodland (UR Md.) Nov. 8, 1806-Jan. 12, 1897; House 1847-49 (Whig), 1861-63.

CRISP, Charles Frederick (father of Charles Robert Crisp) (D Ga.) Jan. 29, 1845-Oct. 23, 1896; House 1883-Oct. 23, 1896; Speaker 1891-95.

CRISP, Charles Robert (son of Charles Frederick Crisp) (D Ga.) Oct. 19, 1870-Feb. 7, 1937; House Dec. 19, 1896-97, 1913-Oct. 7, 1932.

CRIST, Henry (— Ky.) Oct. 20, 1764-Aug. 11, 1844; House 1809-11.

CRITCHER, John (C Va.) March 11, 1820-Sept. 27, 1901; House 1871-73.

CRITTENDEN, John Jordan (uncle of Thomas Theodore Crittenden) (U Ky.) Sept. 10, 1787-July 26, 1863; Senate 1817-19, 1835-41, March 31, 1842-June 12, 1848, 1855-61; House 1861-63; Gov. 1848-July 22, 1850 (Whig); Atty. Gen. March 5-Sept. 13, 1841, July 22, 1850-53.

CRITTENDEN, Thomas Theodore (nephew of John Jordan Crittenden) (D Mo.) Jan. 1, 1832-May 29, 1909; House 1873-75, 1877-79; Gov. 1881-85.

CROCHERON, Henry (brother of Jacob Crocheron) (D N.Y.) Dec. 26, 1772-Nov. 8, 1819; House 1815-17.

CROCHERON, Jacob (brother of Henry Crocheron) (JD N.Y.) Aug. 23, 1774-Dec. 27, 1849; House 1829-31.

CROCKER, Alva (R Mass.) Oct. 14, 1801-Dec. 26, 1874; House Jan. 2, 1872-Dec. 26, 1874.

CROCKER, Samuel Leonard (W Mass.) March 31, 1804-Feb. 10, 1883; House 1853-55.

CROCKETT, David (father of John Wesley Crockett) (W Tenn.) Aug. 17, 1786-March 6, 1836; House 1827-31 (Democrat), 1833-35.

CROCKETT, George W. Jr. (D Mich.) Aug. 10, 1909-— House Nov. 12, 1980-—.

CROCKETT, John Wesley (son of David Crockett) (W Tenn.) July 10, 1807-Nov. 24, 1852; House 1837-41

CROFT, George William (father of Theodore Gaillard Croft) (D S.C.) Dec. 20, 1846-March 10, 1904; House 1903-March 10, 1904.

CROFT, Theodore Gaillard (son of George William Croft) (D S.C.) Nov. 26, 1874-March 23, 1920; House May 17, 1904-05.

CROLL, William Martin (D Pa.) April 9, 1866-Oct. 21, 1929; House 1923-25.

CROMER, George Washington (R Ind.) May 13, 1856, Nov. 8, 1936; House 1899-1907.

CRONIN, Paul William (R Mass.) March 14, 1938-— House 1973-75.

CROOK, Thurman Charles (D Ind.) July 18, 1891-Oct. 23, 1981; House 1949-51.

CROOKE, Philip Schuyler (R N.Y.) March 2, 1810-March 17, 1881; House 1873-75.

CROSBY, Charles Noel (D Pa.) Sept. 29, 1876-Jan. 2, 1951; House 1933-39.

CROSBY, John Crawford (D Mass.) June 15, 1859-Oct. 14, 1943; House 1891-93.

CROSS, Edward (D Ark.) Nov. 11, 1798-April 6, 188; House 1839-45.

CROSS, Oliver Harian (D Texas) July 13, 1868-April 2, 1960; House 1929-37.

CROSSER, Robert (D Ohio) June 7, 1874-June 3, 195; House 1913-19, 1923-55.

CROSSLAND, Edward (D Ky.) June 30, 1827-Sept. 1, 1881; House 1871-75.

CROUCH, Edward (D Pa.) Nov. 9, 1764-Feb. 2, 182; House Oct. 12, 1813-15.

CROUNSE, Lorenzo (R Neb.) Jan. 26, 1834-May 1, 1909; House 1873-77; Gov. 1893-95.

CROUSE, George Washington (R Ohio) Nov. 23, 183, Jan. 5, 1912; House 1887-89.

CROW, Charles Augustus (R Mo.) March 31, 187, March 20, 1938; House 1909-11.

CROW, William Evans (father of William Josiah Crow) (R Pa.) March 10, 1870-Aug. 2, 1922; Senate Oct. 1, 1921-Aug. 2, 1922.

CROW, William Josiah (son of William Evans Crow) (R Pa.) Jan. 22, 1902-Oct. 13, 1974; House 1947-49.

CROWE, Eugene Burgess (D Ind.) Jan. 5, 1878-May 12, 1970; House 1931-41.

CROWELL, John (— Ala.) Sept. 18, 1780-June 25, 1846; House (Terr. Del.) Jan. 29, 1818-19, (Rep.) Dec. 14, 1819-21.

CROWELL, John (W Ohio) Sept. 15, 1801-March 8, 1883; House 1847-51.

CROWLEY, Joseph Burns (D Ohio) July 19, 1858-June 25, 1931; House 1899-1905.

CROWLEY, Miles (D Texas) Feb. 22, 1859-Sept. 22, 1921; House 1895-97.

CROWLEY, Richard (R N.Y.) Dec. 14, 1836-July 22, 1908; House 1879-83.

CROWNINSHIELD, Benjamin Williams (brother of Jacob Crowninshield) (D Mass.) Dec. 27, 1772-Feb. 3, 1851; House 1823-31; Secy. of the Navy 1814-18.

CROWNINSHIELD, Jacob (brother of Benjamin Williams Crowninshield) (D Mass.) March 31, 1770-April 15, 1808; House 1803-April 15, 1808.

CROWTHER, Frank (R N.Y.) July 10, 1870-July 20, 1955; House 1919-43.

CROWTHER, George Calhoun (R Mo.) Jan. 26, 1849-March 18, 1914; House 1895-97.

CROXTON, Thomas (D Va.) March 8, 1822-July 3, 1903; House 1885-87.

CROZIER, John Hervey (W Tenn.) Feb. 10, 1812-Oct. 25, 1889; House 1845-49.

CROZIER, Robert (R Kan.) Oct. 13, 1827-Oct. 2, 1895; Senate Nov. 24, 1873-Feb. 12, 1874.

CRUDUP, Josiah (W N.C.) Jan. 13, 1791-May 20, 1872; House 1821-23.

CRUGER, Daniel (D N.Y.) Dec. 22, 1780-July 12, 1843; House 1817-19.

CRUMP, Edward Hull (D Tenn.) Oct. 2, 1874-Oct. 16, 1954; House 1931-35.

CRUMP, George William (JD Va.) Sept. 26, 1786-Oct. 1, 1848; House Jan. 21, 1826-27.

CRUMP, Rousseau Owen (R Mich.) May 20, 1843-May 1, 1901; House 1895-May 1, 1901.

CRUMPACKER, Edgar Dean (father of Maurice Edgar Crumpacker, cousin of Shepard J. Crumpacker Jr.) (R Ind.) May 27, 1851-May 19, 1930; House 1897-1913.

CRUMPACKER, Maurice Edgar (son of Edgar Dean Crumpacker, cousin of Shepard J. Crumpacker Jr.) (R Ore.) Dec. 19, 1886-July 24, 1927; House 1925-July 24, 1927.

CRUMPACKER, Shepard J. Jr. (cousin of Edgar Dean Crumpacker and Maurice Edgar Crumpacker) (R Ind.) Feb. 13, 1917-Oct. 14, 1986; House 1951-57.

CRUTCHFIELD, William (R Tenn.) Nov. 16, 1824-Jan. 24, 1890; House 1873-75.

CULBERSON, Charles Allen (son of David Browning Culberson) (D Texas) June 10, 1855-March 19, 1925; Senate 1899-1923; Gov. 1895-99.

CULBERSON, David Browning (father of Charles Allen Culberson) (D Texas) Sept. 29, 1830-May 7, 1900; House 1875-97.

CULBERTSON, William Constantine (R Pa.) Nov. 25, 1825-May 24, 1906; House 1889-91.

CULBERTSON, William Wirt (R Ky.) Sept. 22, 1835-Oct. 31, 1911; House 1883-85.

CULBRETH, Thomas (D Md.) April 13, 1786-April 16, 1843; House 1817-21.

CULKIN, Francis Dugan (R N.Y.) Nov. 10, 1874-Aug. 4, 1943; House Nov. 6, 1928-Aug. 4, 1943.

CULLEN, Elisha Dickerson (AP Del.) April 23, 1799-Feb. 8, 1862; House 1855-57.

CULLEN, Thomas Henry (D N.Y.) March 29, 1868-March 1, 1944; House 1919-March 1, 1944.

CULLEN, William (R Ill.) March 4, 1826-Jan. 17, 1914; House 1881-85.

CULLOM, Alvan (brother of William Cullom, uncle of Shelby Moore Cullom) (W Tenn.) June 4, 1810-Dec. 6, 1896; House 1851-55.

CULLOM, Shelby Moore (nephew of Alvan Cullom and William Cullom) (R Ill.) Nov. 22, 1829-Jan. 28, 1914; House 1865-71; Senate 1883-1913; Senate majority leader 1911-13; Gov. Jan. 8, 1877-Feb. 8, 1883.

CULLOM, William (brother of Alvan Cullom, uncle of Shelby Moore Cullom) (W Tenn.) June 4, 1810-Dec. 6, 1896; House 1851-55.

CULLOP, William Allen (D Ind.) March 28, 1853-Oct. 9, 1927; House 1909-17.

CULPEPPER, John (F N.C.) 1761-Jan. 1841; House 1807-Jan. 2, 1808, Feb. 23, 1808-09, 1813-17, 1819-21, 1823-25, 1827-29.

CULVER, Charles Vernon (R Pa.) Sept. 6, 1830-Jan. 10, 1909; House 1865-67.

CULVER, Erastus Dean (W N.Y.) March 15, 1803-Oct. 13, 1889; House 1845-47.

CULVER, John Chester (D Iowa) Aug. 8, 1932- —; House 1965-75; Senate 1975-81.

CUMBACK, William (R Ind.) March 24, 1829-July 31, 1905; House 1855-57.

CUMMING, Thomas William (D N.Y.) 1814 or 1815-Oct. 13, 1855; House 1853-55.

CUMMINGS, Amos Jay (D N.Y.) May 15, 1841-May 2, 1902; House 1887-89, Nov. 5, 1889-Nov. 21, 1894, Nov. 5, 1895-May 2, 1902.

CUMMINGS, Fred Nelson (D Colo.) Sept. 18, 1864-Nov. 10, 1952; House 1933-41.

CUMMINGS, Henry Johnson Brodhead (R Iowa) May 21, 1831-April 16, 1909; House 1877-79.

CUMMINGS, Herbert Wesley (D Pa.) July 13, 1873-March 4, 1956; House 1923-25.

CUMMINS, Albert Baird (R Iowa) Feb. 15, 1850-July 30, 1926; Senate Nov. 24, 1908-July 30, 1926; Pres. pro tempore 1919-25; Gov. 1902-08.

CUMMINS, John D. (D Ohio) 1791-Sept. 11, 1849; House 1845-49.

CUNNINGHAM, Francis Alanson (D Ohio) Nov. 9, 1804-Aug. 16, 1864; House 1845-47.

CUNNINGHAM, Glenn Clarence (R Neb.) Sept. 10, 1912- —; House 1957-71.

CUNNINGHAM, John Edward III (R Wash.) March 27, 1931- —; House May 23, 1977-79.

CUNNINGHAM, Paul Harvey (R Iowa) June 15, 1890-July 16, 1961; House 1941-59.

CURLEY, Edward Walter (D N.Y.) May 23, 1873-Jan. 6, 1940; House Nov. 5, 1935-Jan. 6, 1940.

CURLEY, James Michael (D Mass.) Nov. 20, 1874-Nov. 12, 1958; House 1911-Feb. 4, 1914, 1943-47; Gov. 1935-37.

CURLIN, William Prather Jr. (D Ky.) Nov. 30, 1933- —; House Dec. 4, 1971-73.

CURRIE, Gilbert Archibald (R Mich.) Sept. 19, 1882-June 5, 1960; House 1917-21.

CURRIER, Frank Dunklee (R N.H.) Oct. 30, 1853-Nov. 25, 1921; House 1901-13.

CURRY, Charles Forrest (father of Charles Forrest Curry Jr.) (R Calif.) March 14, 1858-Oct. 10, 1930; House 1913-Oct. 10, 1930.

CURRY, Charles Forrest Jr. (son of Charles Forrest Curry) (R Calif.) Aug. 13, 1893- —; House 1931-33.

CURRY, George (R N.M.) April 3, 1863-Nov. 27, 1947; House Jan. 8, 1912-13; Gov. (N.M. Terr.) 1907-11.

CURRY, Jabez Lamar Monroe (SRD Ala.) June 5, 1825-Feb. 12, 1903; House 1857-Jan. 21, 1861.

CURTIN, Andrew Gregg (D Pa.) April 22, 1815-Oct. 7, 1894; House 1881-87; Gov. 1861-67 (Republican).

CURTIN, Willard Sevier (R Pa.) Nov. 18, 1905- —; House 1957-67.

CURTIS, Carl Thomas (R Neb.) March 15, 1905- —; House 1939-Dec. 31, 1954; Senate Jan. 1, 1955-79.

CURTIS, Carlton Brandaga (R Pa.) Dec. 17, 1811-March 17, 1883; House 1851-55 (Democrat), 1873-75.

CURTIS, Charles (R Kan.) Jan. 25, 1860-Feb. 8, 1936; House 1893-Jan. 28, 1907; Senate Jan. 29, 1907-15, 1915-29; Pres. pro tempore 1911; Senate majority leader 1924-29; Vice President 1929-33.

CURTIS, Edward (W N.Y.) Oct. 25, 1801-Aug. 2, 1856; House 1837-41.

CURTIS, George Martin (R Iowa) April 1, 1844-Feb. 1921; House 1895-99.

CURTIS, Laurence (R Mass.) Sept. 3, 1893- —; House 1953-63.

CURTIS, Newton Martin (R N.Y.) May 21, 1835-Jan. 1910; House Nov. 3, 1891-97.

CURTIS, Samuel Ryan (R Iowa) Feb. 3, 1805-Dec. 26, 1866; House 1857-Aug. 4, 1861.

CURTIS, Thomas Bradford (R Mo.) May 14, 1911- —; House 1951-69.

CUSACK, Thomas (D Ill.) Oct. 5, 1858-Nov. 19, 1926; House 1899-1901.

CUSHING, Caleb (W Mass.) Jan. 17, 1800-Jan. 2, 1879; House 1835-43; Atty. Gen. 1853-57.

CUSHMAN, Francis Wellington (R Wash.) May 1867-July 6, 1909; House 1899-July 6, 1909.

CUSHMAN, John Paine (— N.Y.) March 8, 1784-Sept. 16, 1848; House 1817-19.

CUSHMAN, Joshua (D Maine) April 11, 1761-Jan. 27, 1834; House 1819-21 (Mass.), 1821-25.

CUSHMAN, Samuel (D N.H.) June 8, 1783-May 20, 1851; House 1835-39.

CUTCHEON, Byron M. (R Mich.) May 11, 1836-April 12, 1908; House 1883-91.

CUTHBERT, Alfred (brother of John Alfred Cuthbert) (D Ga.) Dec. 23, 1785-July 9, 1856; House Dec. 13, 1813-Nov. 9, 1816, 1821-27; Senate Jan. 12, 1835-43.

CUTHBERT, John Alfred (brother of Alfred Cuthbert) (D Ga.) June 3, 1788-Sept. 22, 1881; House 1819-21.

CUTLER, Augustus William (D N.J.) Oct. 22, 1827-Jan. 1, 1897; House 1875-79.

CUTLER, Manasseh (F Mass.) May 13, 1742-July 28, 1823; House 1801-05.

CUTLER, William Parker (R Ohio) July 12, 1812-April 11, 1889; House 1861-63.

CUTTING, Bronson Murray (R N.M.) June 23, 1888-May 6, 1935; Senate Dec. 29, 1927-Dec. 6, 1928, 1929-May 6, 1935.

CUTTING, Francis Brockholst (D N.Y.) Aug. 6, 1804-June 26, 1870; House 1853-55.

CUTTING, John Tyler (R Calif.) Sept. 7, 1844-Nov. 24, 1911; House 1891-93.

CUTTS, Charles (F N.H.) Jan. 31, 1769-Jan. 25, 1846; Senate June 21, 1810-March 3, 1813, April 2-June 10, 1813.

CUTTS, Marsena Edgar (R Iowa) May 22, 1833-Sept. 1, 1883; House 1881-Sept. 1, 1883.

CUTTS, Richard (D Mass.) June 28, 1771-April 7, 1845; House 1801-13.

DADDARIO, Emilio Quincy (D Conn.) Sept. 24, 1918- —; House 1959-71.

DAGGETT, David (F Conn.) Dec. 31, 1764-April 12, 1851; Senate May 13, 1813-19.

DAGGETT, Rollin Mallory (R Nev.) Feb. 22, 1831-Nov. 12, 1901; House 1879-81.

DAGUE, Paul Bartram (R Pa.) May 19, 1898-Dec. 2, 1974; House 1947-67.

DAHLE, Herman Bjorn (R Wis.) March 30, 1855-April 25, 1920; House 1899-1903.

DAILY, Samuel Gordon (R Neb.) 1823-Aug. 15, 1866; House (Terr. Del.) May 18, 1860-65.

DALE, Harry Howard (D N.Y.) Dec. 3, 1868-Nov. 17, 1935; House 1913-Jan. 6, 1919.

DALE, Porter Hinman (R Vt.) March 1, 1867-Oct. 6, 1933; House 1915-Aug. 11, 1923; Senate Nov. 7, 1923-Oct. 6, 1933.

DALE, Thomas Henry (R Pa.) June 12, 1846-Aug. 21, 1912; House 1905-07.

D'ALESANDRO, Thomas Jr. (D Md.) Aug. 1, 1903- —; House 1939-May 16, 1947.

DALLAS, George Mifflin (D Pa.) July 10, 1792-Dec. 31, 1864; Senate Dec. 13, 1831-33; Vice President 1845-49.

DALLINGER, Frederick William (R Mass.) Oct. 2, 1871-Sept. 5, 1955; House 1915-25, Nov. 2, 1926-Oct. 1, 1932.

DALTON, Tristram (— Mass.) May 28, 1738-May 30, 1817; Senate 1789-91.

DALY, John Burrwood (D Pa.) Feb. 13, 1872-March 12, 1939; House 1935-March 12, 1939.

DALY, William Davis (D N.J.) June 4, 1851-July 31, 1900; House 1899-July 31, 1900.

DALZELL, John (R Pa.) April 19, 1845-Oct. 2, 1927; House 1887-1913.

D'AMATO, Alfonse Martello (R N.Y.) Aug. 1, 1937- —; Senate 1981- —.

D'AMOURS, Norman Edward (D N.H.) Oct. 14, 1937- —; House 1975-85.

DAMRELL, William Shapleigh (R Mass.) Nov. 29, 1809-May 17, 1860; House 1855-59 (1855-57 American Party).

DANA, Amasa (D N.Y.) Oct. 19, 1792-Dec. 24, 1867; House 1839-41, 1843-45.

DANA, Judah (D Maine) April 25, 1772-Dec. 27, 1845; Senate Dec. 7, 1836-37.

DANA, Samuel (D Mass.) June 26, 1767-Nov. 20, 1835; House Sept. 22, 1814-15.

DANA, Samuel Whittlesey (F Conn.) Feb. 13, 1760-July 21, 1830; House Jan. 3, 1797-May 10, 1810; Senate May 10, 1810-21.

DANAHER, John Anthony (R Conn.) Jan. 9, 1899- —; Senate 1939-45.

DANE, Joseph (F Maine) Oct. 25, 1778-May 1, 1858; House Nov. 6, 1820-23.

DANFORD, Lorenzo (R Ohio) Oct. 18, 1829-June 19, 1899; House 1873-79, 1895-June 19, 1899.

DANFORTH, Henry Gold (R N.Y.) June 14, 1854-April 8, 1918; House 1911-17.

DANFORTH, John Claggett (R Mo.) Sept. 5, 1936- —; Senate Dec. 27, 1976- —.

DANIEL, Charles Ezra (D S.C.) Nov. 11, 1895-Sept. 13, 1964; Senate Sept. 6-Dec. 23, 1954.

DANIEL, Henry (JD Ky.) March 15, 1786-Oct. 5, 1873; House 1827-33.

DANIEL, John Reeves Jones (D N.C.) Jan. 13, 1802-June 22, 1868; House 1841-53.

DANIEL, John Warwick (D Va.) Sept. 5, 1842-June 29, 1910; House 1885-87; Senate 1887-June 29, 1910.

DANIEL, Price Marion (D Texas) Oct. 10, 1910- -; Senate 1953-Jan. 14, 1957; Gov. Jan. 15, 1957-Jan. 15, 1963.

DANIEL, Robert Williams Jr. (R Va.) March 17, 1936- -; House 1973-83.

DANIEL, W. C. "Dan" (D Va.) May 12, 1914- -; House 1969- -.

DANIELL, Warren Fisher (D N.H.) June 26, 1826-July 30, 1913; House 1891-93.

DANIELS, Charles (R N.Y.) March 24, 1825-Dec. 20, 1897; House 1893-97.

DANIELS, Dominick V. (D N.J.) Oct. 18, 1908- -; House 1959-77.

DANIELS, Milton John (R Calif.) April 18, 1838-Dec. 1, 1914; House 1903-05.

DANIELSON, George Elmore (D Calif.) Feb. 20, 1915- -; House 1971-March 9, 1982.

DANNEMEYER, William Edward (R Calif.) Sept. 22, 1929- -; House 1979- -.

DANNER, Joel Buchanan (D Pa.) 1804-July 29, 1885; House Dec. 2, 1850-51.

DARBY, Ezra (D N.J.) June 7, 1768-Jan. 27, 1808; House 1805-Jan. 27, 1808.

DARBY, Harry (R Kan.) Jan. 23, 1895- -; Senate Dec. 2, 1949-Nov. 28, 1950.

DARBY, John Fletcher (W Mo.) Dec. 10, 1803-May 11, 1882; House 1851-53.

DARDEN, Colgate Whitehead Jr. (D Va.) Feb. 11, 1897-June 9, 1981; House 1933-37, 1939-March 1, 1941; Gov. 1942-46.

DARDEN, George "Buddy" (D Ga.) Nov. 22, 1943- -; House Nov. 10, 1983- -.

DARGAN, Edmund Strother (D Ala.) April 15, 1805-Nov. 22, 1879; House 1845-47.

DARGAN, George William (great-grandson of Lemuel Benton) (D S.C.) May 11, 1841-June 29, 1898; House 1883-91.

DARLING, Mason Cook (D Wis.) May 18, 1801-March 12, 1866; House June 9, 1848-49.

DARLING, William Augustus (R N.Y.) Dec. 27, 1817-May 26, 1895; House 1865-67.

DARLINGTON, Edward (cousin of Isaac Darlington and William Darlington, second cousin of Smedley Darlington) (AMas. Pa.) Sept. 17, 1795-Nov. 21, 1884; House 1833-39 (1833-37 Whig).

DARLINGTON, Isaac (cousin of Edward Darlington and William Darlington, second cousin of Smedley Darlington) (F Pa.) Dec. 13, 1781-April 27, 1839; House 1817-19.

DARLINGTON, Smedley (second cousin of Edward Darlington, Isaac Darlington, and William Darlington) (R Pa.) Dec. 24, 1827-June 24, 1899; House 1887-91.

DARLINGTON, William (cousin of Edward Darlington and Isaac Darlington, second cousin of Smedley Darlington) (D Pa.) April 28, 1782-April 23, 1863; House 1815-17, 1819-23.

DARRAGH, Archibald Bard (R Mich.) Dec. 23, 1840-Feb. 21, 1927; House 1901-09.

DARRAGH, Cornelius (W Pa.) 1809-Dec. 22, 1854; House March 26, 1844-47.

DARRALL, Chester Bidwell (R La.) June 24, 1842-Jan. 1, 1908; House 1869-Feb. 20, 1878, 1881-83.

DARROW, George Potter (R Pa.) Feb. 4, 1859-June 7, 1943; House 1915-37, 1939-41.

DASCHLE, Thomas Andrew (D S.D.) Dec. 9, 1947- -; House 1979-87; Senate 1987- -.

DAUB, Harold J. "Hal" Jr. (R Neb.) April 23, 1941- -; House 1981- -.

DAUGHERTY, James Alexander (D Mo.) Aug. 30, 1847-Jan. 26, 1920; House 1911-13.

DAUGHTON, Ralph Hunter (D Va.) Sept. 23, 1885-Dec. 22, 1958; House Nov. 7, 1944-47.

DAVEE, Thomas (D Maine) Dec. 9, 1797-Dec. 9, 1841; House 1837-41.

DAVENPORT, Franklin (- N.J.) Sept. 1755-July 27, 1832; Senate Dec. 5, 1798-99; House 1799-1801.

DAVENPORT, Frederick Morgan (R N.Y.) Aug. 27, 1866-Dec. 26, 1956; House 1925-33.

DAVENPORT, Harry James (D Pa.) Aug. 28, 1902-Dec. 19, 1977; House 1949-51.

DAVENPORT, Ira (R N.Y.) June 28, 1841-Oct. 6, 1904; House 1885-89.

DAVENPORT, James (brother of John Davenport of Conn.) (- Conn.) Oct. 12, 1758-Aug. 3, 1797; House Dec. 5, 1796-Aug. 3, 1797.

DAVENPORT, James Sanford (D Okla.) Sept. 21, 1864-Jan. 3, 1940; House Nov. 16, 1907-09, 1911-17.

DAVENPORT, John (brother of James Davenport) (F Conn.) Jan. 16, 1752-Nov. 28, 1830; House 1799-1817.

DAVENPORT, John (— Ohio) Jan. 9, 1788-July 18, 1855; House 1827-29.

DAVENPORT, Samuel Arza (R Pa.) Jan. 15, 1834-Aug. 1, 1911; House 1897-1901.

DAVENPORT, Stanley Woodward (D Pa.) July 21, 1861-Sept. 26, 1921; House 1899-1901.

DAVENPORT, Thomas (F Va.) ?-Nov. 18, 1838; House 1825-35.

DAVEY, Martin Luther (D Ohio) July 25, 1884-March 31, 1946; House Nov. 5, 1918-21, 1923-29; Gov. 1935-39.

DAVEY, Robert Charles (D La.) Oct. 22, 1853-Dec. 26, 1908; House 1893-95, 1897-Dec. 26, 1908.

DAVIDSON, Alexander Caldwell (D Ala.) Dec. 26, 1826-Nov. 6, 1897; House 1885-89.

DAVIDSON, Irwin Delmore (D/L N.Y.) Jan. 2, 1906-—; House 1955-Dec. 31, 1956.

DAVIDSON, James Henry (R Wis.) June 18, 1858-Aug. 6, 1918; House 1897-1913, 1917-Aug. 6, 1918.

DAVIDSON, Robert Hamilton McWhorta (D Fla.) Sept. 23, 1832-Jan. 18, 1908; House 1877-91.

DAVIDSON, Thomas Green (D La.) Aug. 3, 1805-Sept. 11, 1883; House 1855-61.

DAVIDSON, William (F N.C.) Sept. 12, 1778-Sept. 16, 1857; House Dec. 2, 1818-21.

DAVIES, Edward (W Pa.) Nov. 1779-May 18, 1853; House 1837-41.

DAVIES, John Clay (D N.Y.) May 1, 1920-—; House 1949-51.

DAVILA, Felix Cordova (U P.R.) Nov. 20, 1878-Dec. 3, 1938; House (Res. Comm.) Aug. 7, 1917-April 11, 1932.

DAVIS, Alexander Mathews (— Va.) Jan. 17, 1833-Sept. 25, 1889; House 1873-March 5, 1874.

DAVIS, Amos (brother of Garrett Davis) (W Ky.) Aug. 15, 1794-June 11, 1835; House 1833-35.

DAVIS, Charles Russell (R Minn.) Sept. 17, 1849-July 29, 1930; House 1903-25.

DAVIS, Clifford (D Tenn.) Nov. 18, 1897-June 8, 1970; House Feb. 15, 1940-65.

DAVIS, Cushman Kellogg (R Minn.) June 16, 1838-Nov. 27, 1900; Senate 1887-Nov. 27, 1900; Gov. 1874-76.

DAVIS, David (cousin of Henry Winter Davis) (I/D Ill.) March 9, 1815-June 26, 1886; Senate 1877-83; Pres. pro tempore 1881-83; Assoc. Justice Supreme Court 1862-77.

DAVIS, Ewin Lamar (D Tenn.) Feb. 5, 1876-Oct. 23, 1949; House 1919-33.

DAVIS, Garrett (brother of Amos Davis) (D Ky.) Sept. 10, 1801-Sept. 22, 1872; House 1839-47 (Henry Clay Whig); Senate Dec. 10, 1861-Sept. 22, 1872 (1861-67 Whig).

DAVIS, George Royal (R Ill.) Jan. 3, 1840-Nov. 25, 1899; House 1879-85.

DAVIS, George Thomas (W Mass.) Jan. 12, 1810-June 17, 1877; House 1851-53.

DAVIS, Glenn Robert (R Wis.) Oct. 28, 1914-—; House April 22, 1947-57, 1965-Dec. 31, 1974.

DAVIS, Henry Gassaway (brother of Thomas Beall Davis, grandfather of Davis Elkins) (D W.Va.) Nov. 16, 1823-March 11, 1916; Senate 1871-83.

DAVIS, Henry Winter (cousin of David Davis) (UU Md.) Aug. 16, 1817-Dec. 30, 1865; House 1855-61 (1855-57 American Party, 1857-61 Republican), 1863-65.

DAVIS, Horace (R Calif.) March 16, 1831-July 12, 1916; House 1877-81.

DAVIS, Jack (R Ill.) Sept. 6, 1935-—; House 1987-—.

DAVIS, Jacob Cunningham (D Ill.) Sept. 16, 1820-Dec. 25, 1883; House Nov. 4, 1856-57.

DAVIS, Jacob Erastus (D Ohio) Oct. 31, 1905-—; House 1941-43.

DAVIS, James Curran (D Ga.) May 17, 1895-Dec. 18, 1981; House 1947-63.

DAVIS, James Harvey "Cyclone" (D Texas) Dec. 24, 1853-Jan. 31, 1940; House 1915-17.

DAVIS, James John (R Pa.) Oct. 27, 1873-Nov. 22, 1947; Senate Dec. 2, 1930-45; Secy. of Labor 1921-30.

DAVIS, Jeff (D Ark.) May 6, 1862-Jan. 3, 1913; Senate 1907-Jan. 3, 1913; Gov. 1901-07.

DAVIS, Jefferson (D Miss.) June 3, 1808-Dec. 6, 1889; House 1845-June 1846; Senate Aug. 10, 1847-Sept. 23, 1851, 1857-Jan. 21, 1861; Secy. of War 1853-57.

DAVIS, John (W Mass.) Jan. 13, 1787-April 19, 1854; House 1825-Jan. 14, 1834 (National Republican); Senate Dec. 7, 1835-Dec. 1841, March 24, 1845-53; Gov. 1834-35, 1841-43.

DAVIS, John (D Pa.) Aug. 7, 1788-April 1, 1878; House 1839-41.

DAVIS, John (PP Kan.) Aug. 9, 1826-Aug. 1, 1901; House 1891-95.

DAVIS, John Givan (D Ind.) Oct. 10, 1810-Jan. 18, 1866; House 1851-55, 1857-61.

DAVIS, John James (father of John William Davis of W.Va.) (D W.Va.) May 5, 1835-March 19, 1916; House 1871-75.

DAVIS, John Wesley (D Ind.) April 16, 1799-Aug. 22, 1859; House 1835-37, 1839-41, 1843-47; Speaker 1845-47; Gov. (Oregon Terr.) 1853-54.

DAVIS, John William (son of John James Davis) (D W.Va.) April 13, 1873-March 24, 1955; House 1911-Aug. 29, 1913.

DAVIS, John William (D Ga.) Sept. 12, 1916- —; House 1961-75.

DAVIS, Joseph Jonathan (D N.C.) April 13, 1828-Aug. 7, 1892; House 1875-81.

DAVIS, Lowndes Henry (D Mo.) Dec. 13, 1836-Feb. 4, 1920; House 1879-85.

DAVIS, Mendel Jackson (D S.C.) Oct. 23, 1942- —; House April 27, 1971-81.

DAVIS, Noah (R N.Y.) Sept. 10, 1818-March 20, 1902; House 1869-July 15, 1870.

DAVIS, Reuben (D Miss.) Jan. 18, 1813-Oct. 14, 1890; House 1857-Jan. 12, 1861.

DAVIS, Richard David (D N.Y.) 1799-June 17, 1871; House 1841-45.

DAVIS, Robert Lee (R Pa.) Oct. 29, 1893- —; House Nov. 8, 1932-33.

DAVIS, Robert Thompson (R Mass.) Aug. 28, 1823-Oct. 29, 1906; House 1883-89.

DAVIS, Robert William (R Mich.) July 31, 1932- —; House 1979- —.

DAVIS, Robert Wyche (D Fla.) March 15, 1849-Sept. 15, 1929; House 1897-1905.

DAVIS, Roger (D Pa.) Oct. 2, 1762-Nov. 20, 1815; House 1811-15.

DAVIS, Samuel (F Mass.) 1774-April 20, 1831; House 1813-15.

DAVIS, Thomas (D R.I.) Dec. 18, 1806-July 26, 1895; House 1853-55.

DAVIS, Thomas Beall (brother of Henry Gassaway Davis) (D W.Va.) April 25, 1828-Nov. 26, 1911; House June 6, 1905-07.

DAVIS, Thomas Terry (— Ky.) ?-Nov. 15, 1807; House 1797-1803.

DAVIS, Thomas Treadwell (grandson of Thomas Tredwell) (U N.Y.) Aug. 22, 1810-May 2, 1872; House 1863-67.

DAVIS, Timothy (W Iowa) March 29, 1794-April 27, 1872; House 1857-59.

DAVIS, Timothy (R Mass.) April 12, 1821-Oct. 23, 1888; House 1855-59 (1855-57 American Party).

DAVIS, Warren Ransom (SRD S.C.) May 8, 1793-Jan. 29, 1835; House 1827-Jan. 29, 1835.

DAVIS, William Morris (R Pa.) Aug. 16, 1815-Aug. 5, 1891; House 1861-63.

DAVISON, George Mosby (R Ky.) March 23, 1855-Dec. 18, 1912; House 1897-99.

DAVY, John Madison (R N.Y.) June 29, 1835-April 22, 1909; House 1875-77.

DAWES, Beman Gates (son of Rufus Dawes, brother of Vice Pres. Charles Gates Dawes) (R Ohio) Jan. 14, 1870-May 15, 1953; House 1905-09.

DAWES, Henry Laurens (R Mass.) Oct. 30, 1816-Feb. 5, 1903; House 1857-75; Senate 1875-93.

DAWES, Rufus (father of Vice Pres. Charles Gates Dawes and Beman Gates Dawes) (R Ohio) July 4, 1838-Aug. 2, 1899; House 1881-83.

DAWSON, Albert Foster (R Iowa) Jan. 26, 1872-March 9, 1949; House 1905-11.

DAWSON, John (D Va.) 1762-March 31, 1814; House 1797-March 31, 1814; Cont. Cong. 1788-89.

DAWSON, John Bennett (D La.) March 17, 1798-June 26, 1845; House 1841-June 26, 1845.

DAWSON, John Littleton (D Pa.) Feb. 7, 1813-Sept. 18, 1870; House 1851-55, 1863-67.

DAWSON, William (D Mo.) March 17, 1848-Oct. 12, 1929; House 1885-87.

DAWSON, William Adams (R Utah) Nov. 5, 1903- ; House 1947-49, 1953-59.

DAWSON, William Crosby (SRW Ga.) Jan. 4, 1798-May 5, 1856; House Nov. 7, 1836-Nov. 13, 1841; Senate 1849-55.

DAWSON, William Levi (D Ill.) April 26, 1886-Nov. 9, 1970; House 1943-Nov. 9, 1970.

DAY, Rowland (D N.Y.) March 6, 1779-Dec. 23, 1853; House 1823-25, 1833-35.

DAY, Stephen Albion (R Ill.) July 13, 1882-Jan. 5, 1950; House 1941-45.

DAY, Timothy Crane (R Ohio) Jan. 8, 1819-April 15, 1869; House 1855-57.

DAYAN, Charles (D N.Y.) July 8, 1792-Dec. 25, 1877; House 1831-33.

DAYTON, Alston Gordon (R W.Va.) Oct. 18, 1857-July 30, 1920; House 1895-March 16, 1905.

DAYTON, Jonathan (F N.J.) Oct. 16, 1760-Oct. 9, 1824; House 1791-99; Speaker 1795-99; Senate 1799-1805; Cont. Cong. Nov. 6, 1787-89.

DAYTON, William Lewis (W N.J.) Feb. 17, 1807-Dec. 1, 1864; Senate July 2, 1842-51.

DEAL, Joseph Thomas (D Va.) Nov. 19, 1860-March 7, 1942; House 1921-29.

DEAN, Benjamin (D Mass.) Aug. 14, 1824-April 9, 1897; House March 28, 1878-79.

DEAN, Ezra (D Ohio) April 9, 1795-Jan. 25, 1872; House 1841-45.

DEAN, Gilbert (D N.Y.) Aug. 14, 1819-Oct. 12, 1870; House 1851-July 3, 1854.

DEAN, Josiah (D Mass.) March 6, 1748-Oct. 14, 1818; House 1807-09.

DEAN, Sidney (R Conn.) Nov. 16, 1818-Oct. 29, 1901; House 1855-59 (1855-57 American Party).

DEANE, Charles Bennett (D N.C.) Nov. 1, 1898-Nov. 24, 1969; House 1947-57.

DEAR, Cleveland (D La.) Aug. 22, 1888-Dec. 30, 1950; House 1933-37.

DEARBORN, Henry (father of Henry Alexander Scammell Dearborn) (D Mass.) Feb. 23, 1751-June 6, 1829; House 1793-97; Secy. of War 1801-09.

DEARBORN, Henry Alexander Scammell (son of Henry Dearborn) (— Mass.) March 3, 1783-July 29, 1851; House 1831-33.

DE ARMOND, David Albaugh (D Mo.) March 18, 1844-Nov. 23, 1909; House 1891-Nov. 23, 1909.

DEBERRY, Edmund (W N.C.) Aug. 14, 1787-Dec. 12, 1859; House 1829-31, 1833-45, 1849-51.

DEBOE, William Joseph (R Ky.) June 30, 1849-June 15, 1927; Senate 1897-1903.

DE BOLT, Rezin A. (D Mo.) Jan. 20, 1828-Oct. 30, 1891; House 1875-77.

DECKARD, H. Joel (R Ind.) March 7, 1942-—; House 1979-83.

DECKER, Perl D. (D Mo.) Sept. 10, 1875-Aug. 22, 1934; House 1913-19.

DeCONCINI, Dennis Webster (D Ariz.) May 8, 1937-—; Senate 1977-—.

DEEMER, Elias (R Pa.) Jan. 3, 1838-March 29, 1918; House 1901-07.

DEEN, Braswell Drue (D Ga.) June 28, 1893-Nov. 28, 1981; House 1933-39.

DEERING, Nathaniel Cobb (R Iowa) Sept. 2, 1827-Dec. 11, 1887; House 1877-83.

DeFAZIO, Peter Anthony (D Ore.) May 27, 1947-—; House 1987-—.

DE FOREST, Henry Schermerhorn (R N.Y.) Feb. 16, 1847-Feb. 13, 1917; House 1911-13.

DE FOREST, Robert Elliott (D Conn.) Feb. 20, 1845-Oct. 1, 1924; House 1891-95.

DEFREES, Joseph Hutton (R Ind.) May 13, 1812-Dec. 21, 1885; House 1865-67.

DEGENER, Edward (R Texas) Oct. 20, 1809-Sept. 11, 1890; House March 31, 1870-71.

DEGETAU, Frederico (R P.R.) Dec. 5, 1862-Jan. 20, 1914; House (Res. Comm.) 1901-05.

DE GRAFF, John Isaac (D N.Y.) Oct. 2, 1783-July 26, 1848; House 1827-29, 1837-39.

DE GRAFFENREID, Reese Calhoun (D Texas) May 7, 1859-Aug. 29, 1902; House 1897-Aug. 29, 1902.

deGRAFFENRIED, Edward (D Ala.) June 30, 1899-Nov. 5, 1974; House 1949-53.

DE HAVEN, John Jefferson (R Calif.) March 12, 1849-Jan. 26, 1913; House 1889-Oct. 1, 1890.

DEITRICK, Frederick Simpson (D Mass.) April 9, 1875-May 24, 1948; House 1913-15.

DE JARNETTE, Daniel Coleman (D Va.) Oct. 18, 1822-Aug. 20, 1881; House 1859-61.

DE LACY, Emerson Hugh (D Wash.) May 9, 1910-Aug. 19, 1986; House 1945-47.

de la GARZA, Eligio "Kika" II (D Texas) Sept. 22, 1927-—; House 1965-—.

DE LA MATYR, Gilbert (Nat./D Ind.) July 8, 1825-May 17, 1892; House 1879-81.

DE LA MONTANYA, James (D N.Y.) March 20, 1798-April 29, 1849; House 1839-41.

DELANEY, James Joseph (D N.Y.) March 19, 1901- —; House 1945-47, 1949-Dec. 31, 1978.

DELANEY, John Joseph (D N.Y.) Aug. 21, 1878-Nov. 18, 1948; House March 5, 1918-19, 1931-Nov. 18, 1948.

DELANO, Charles (R Mass.) June 24, 1820-Jan. 23, 1883; House 1859-63.

DELANO, Columbus (R Ohio) June 4, 1809-Oct. 23, 1896; House 1845-47 (Whig), 1865-67, June 3, 1868-69; Secy. of the Interior 1870-75.

DE LANO, Milton (R N.Y.) Aug. 11, 1844-Jan. 2, 1922; House 1887-91.

DELAPLAINE, Isaac Clason (Fus. N.Y.) Oct. 27, 1817-July 17, 1866; House 1861-63.

DE LARGE, Robert Carlos (R S.C.) March 15, 1842-Feb. 14, 1874; House 1871-Jan. 24, 1873.

DeLAY, Thomas Dale (R Texas) April 8, 1947- —; House 1985- —.

DELGADO, Francisco Afan (Nat. P.I.) Jan. 25, 1886-Oct. 27, 1964; House (Res. Comm.) 1935-Feb. 14, 1936.

DELLAY, Vincent John (D N.J.) June 23, 1907- —; House 1957-59 (1957 Republican).

DELLENBACK, John Richard (R Ore.) Nov. 6, 1918- —; House 1967-75.

DELLET, James (W Ala.) Feb. 18, 1788-Dec. 21, 1848; House 1839-41, 1843-45.

DELLUMS, Ronald V. (D Calif.) Nov. 24, 1935- —; House 1971- —.

de LUGO, Ron (D V.I.) Aug. 2, 1930- —; House (Terr. Del.) 1973-79, 1981- —.

DEMING, Benjamin F. (W Vt.) 1790-July 11, 1834; House 1833-July 11, 1834.

DEMING, Henry Champion (R Conn.) May 23, 1815-Oct. 8, 1872; House 1863-67.

DE MOTT, John (D N.Y.) Oct. 7, 1790-July 31, 1870; House 1845-47.

DE MOTTE, Mark Lindsey (R Ind.) Dec. 28, 1832-Sept. 23, 1908; House 1881-83.

DEMPSEY, John Joseph (D N.M.) June 22, 1879-March 11, 1958; House 1935-41, 1951-March 11, 1958; Gov. 1943-47.

DEMPSEY, Stephen Wallace (R N.Y.) May 8, 1862-March 1, 1949; House 1915-31.

DE MUTH, Peter Joseph (D Pa.) Jan. 1, 1892- —; House 1937-39.

DeNARDIS, Lawrence J. (R Conn.) March 18, 1938- —; House 1981-83.

DENBY, Edwin (grandson of Graham Newell Fitch) (R Mich.) Feb. 18, 1870-Feb. 8, 1929; House 1905-11; Secy. of the Navy 1921-24.

DENEEN, Charles Samuel (R Ill.) May 4, 1863-Feb. 5 1940; Senate Feb. 26, 1925-31; Gov. 1905-13.

DENHOLM, Frank E. (D S.D.) Nov. 29, 1923- —; House 1971-75.

DENISON, Charles (nephew of George Denison) (D Pa. Jan. 23, 1818-June 27, 1867; House 1863-June 27 1867.

DENISON, Dudley Chase (nephew of Dudley Chase cousin of Salmon Portland Chase) (R Vt.) Sept. 13 1819-Feb. 10, 1905; House 1875-79.

DENISON, Edward Everett (R Ill.) Aug. 28, 1873-June 17, 1953; House 1915-31.

DENISON, George (uncle of Charles Denison) (D Pa. Feb. 22, 1790-Aug. 20, 1831; House 1819-23.

DE NIVERNAIS, Edward James (*See* LIVERNASH Edward James).

DENNEY, Robert Vernon (R Neb.) April 11, 1916-June 26, 1981; House 1967-71.

DENNING, William (— N.Y.) April 1740-Oct. 30, 1819 House 1809-10.

DENNIS, David Worth (R Ind.) June 7, 1912- —; Hous 1969-75.

DENNIS, George Robertson (D Md.) April 8, 1822-Aug 13, 1882; Senate 1873-79.

DENNIS, John (uncle of Littleton Purnell Dennis, fa ther of John Dennis, below) (F Md.) Dec. 17, 177 Aug. 17, 1806; House 1797-1805.

DENNIS, John (son of John Dennis, above) (W Md 1807-Nov. 1, 1859; House 1837-41.

DENNIS, Littleton Purnell (nephew of John Dennis (W Md.) July 21, 1786-April 14, 1834; House 183. April 14, 1834.

DENNISON, David Short (R Ohio) July 29, 1918- — House 1957-59.

DENNY, Arthur Armstrong (R Wash.) June 20, 182 Jan. 9, 1899; House (Terr. Del.) 1865-67.

DENNY, Harmar (great-grandfather of Harmar Denn Jr.) (W Pa.) May 13, 1794-Jan. 29, 1852; House De 15, 1829-37 (1829-35 Anti Mason).

DENNY, Harmar Denny Jr. (great-grandson of Harmar Denny) (R Pa.) July 2, 1886-Jan. 6, 1966; House 1951-53.

DENNY, James William (D Md.) Nov. 20, 1838-April 12, 1923; House 1899-1901, 1903-05.

DENNY, Walter McKennon (D Miss.) Oct. 28, 1853-Nov. 5, 1926; House 1895-97.

DENOYELLES, Peter (− N.Y.) 1766-May 6, 1829; House 1813-15.

DENSON, William Henry (D Ala.) March 4, 1846-Sept. 26, 1906; House 1893-95.

DENT, George (D Md.) 1756-Dec. 2, 1813; House 1793-1801.

DENT, John Herman (D Pa.) March 10, 1908-−; House Jan. 21, 1958-79.

DENT, Stanley Hubert Jr. (D Ala.) Aug. 16, 1869-Oct. 6, 1938; House 1909-21.

DENT, William Barton Wade (D Ga.) Sept. 8, 1806-Sept. 7, 1855; House 1853-55.

DENTON, George Kirkpatrick (father of Winfield Kirkpatrick Denton) (D Ind.) Nov. 17, 1864-Jan. 4, 1926; House 1917-19.

DENTON, Jeremiah Andrew Jr. (R Ala.) July 15, 1924-−; Senate 1981-87.

DENTON, Winfield Kirkpatrick (son of George Kirkpatrick Denton) (D Ind.) Oct. 28, 1896-Nov. 2, 1971; House 1949-53, 1955-Dec. 30, 1966.

DENVER, James William (father of Matthew Rombach Denver) (ABD Calif.) Oct. 23, 1817-Aug. 9, 1892; House 1855-57; Gov. (Kansas Terr.) 1857-58.

DENVER, Matthew Rombach (son of James William Denver) (D Ohio) Dec. 21, 1870-May 13, 1954; House 1907-13.

DEPEW, Chauncey Mitchell (R N.Y.) April 23, 1834-April 5, 1928; Senate 1899-1911.

DE PRIEST, Oscar (R Ill.) March 9, 1871-May 12, 1951; House 1929-35.

DE ROUEN, Rene Louis (D La.) Jan. 7, 1874-March 27, 1942; House Aug. 23, 1927-41.

DEROUNIAN, Steven Boghos (R N.Y.) April 6, 1918-−; House 1953-65.

DERRICK, Butler Carson Jr. (D S.C.) Sept. 30, 1936-−; House 1975-−.

DERSHEM, Franklin Lewis (D Pa.) March 5, 1865-Feb. 14, 1950; House 1913-15.

DERWINSKI, Edward Joseph (R Ill.) Sept. 15, 1926-−; House 1959-83.

DE SAUSSURE, William Ford (D S.C.) Feb. 22, 1792-March 13, 1870; Senate May 10, 1852-53.

DESHA, Joseph (brother of Robert Desha) (D Ky.) Dec. 9, 1768-Oct. 12, 1842; House 1807-19; Gov. 1824-28 (Democratic Republican).

DESHA, Robert (brother of Joseph Desha) (− Tenn.) Jan. 14, 1791-Feb. 6, 1849; House 1827-31.

DESTREHAN, John Noel (− La.) 1780-1824; Senate Sept. 3-Oct. 1, 1812.

DEUSTER, Peter Victor (D Wis.) Feb. 13, 1831-Dec. 31, 1904; House 1879-85.

DEVEREUX, James Patrick Sinnott (R Md.) Feb. 20, 1903-−; House 1951-59.

DE VEYRA, Jaime Carlos (Nat. P.I.) Nov. 4, 1873-March 7, 1963; House (Res. Comm.) 1917-23.

DEVINE, Samuel Leeper (R Ohio) Dec. 21, 1915-−; House 1959-81.

DEVITT, Edward James (R Minn.) May 5, 1911-−; House 1947-49.

DE VRIES, Marion (D Calif.) Aug. 15, 1865-Sept. 11, 1939; House 1897-Aug. 20, 1900.

DEWALT, Arthur Granville (D Pa.) Oct. 11, 1864-Oct. 26, 1931; House 1915-21.

DEWART, Lewis (father of William Lewis Dewart) (JD Pa.) Nov. 14, 1780-April 26, 1852; House 1831-33.

D'EWART, Wesley Abner (R Mont.) Oct. 1, 1889-Sept. 2, 1973; House June 5, 1945-55.

DEWART, William Lewis (son of Lewis Dewart) (D Pa.) June 21, 1821-April 19, 1888; House 1857-59.

DEWEESE, John Thomas (D N.C.) June 4, 1835-July 4, 1906; House July 6, 1868-Feb. 28, 1870.

DEWEY, Charles Schuveldt (R Ill.) Nov. 10, 1880-Dec. 26, 1980; House 1941-45.

DEWEY, Daniel (W Mass.) Jan. 29, 1766-May 26, 1815; House 1813-Feb. 24, 1814.

DeWINE, Michael (R Ohio) Jan. 5, 1947-−; House 1983-−.

DE WITT, Alexander (AP Mass.) April 2, 1798-Jan. 13, 1879; House 1853-57.

DE WITT, Charles Gerrit (JD N.Y.) Nov. 7, 1789-April 12, 1839; House 1829-31.

DE WITT, David Miller (D N.Y.) Nov. 25, 1837-June 23, 1912; House 1873-75.

DE WITT, Francis Byron (R Ohio) March 11, 1849-March 21, 1929; House 1895-97.

DE WITT, Jacob Hasbrouck (Clinton D N.Y.) Oct. 2, 1784-Jan. 30, 1867; House 1819-21.

DE WOLF, James (D R.I.) March 18, 1764-Dec. 21, 1837; Senate 1821-Oct. 31, 1825.

DEXTER, Samuel (F Mass.) May 14, 1761-May 3, 1816; House 1793-95; Senate 1799-May 30, 1800; Secy. of War May 13-Dec. 31, 1800; Secy. of the Treasury Jan. 1-May 6, 1801.

DEZENDORF, John Frederick (R Va.) Aug. 10, 1834-June 22, 1894; House 1881-83.

DIAL, Nathaniel Barksdale (D S.C.) April 24, 1862-Dec. 11, 1940; Senate 1919-25.

DIBBLE, Samuel (D S.C.) Sept. 16, 1837-Sept. 16, 1913; House June 9, 1881-May 31, 1882, 1883-91.

DIBRELL, George Gibbs (D Tenn.) April 12, 1822-May 9, 1888; House 1875-85.

DICK, Charles William Frederick (R Ohio) Nov. 3, 1858-March 13, 1945; House Nov. 8, 1898-March 23, 1904; Senate March 23, 1904-11.

DICK, John (father of Samuel Bernard Dick) (R Pa.) June 17, 1794-May 29, 1872; House 1853-59 (1853-55 Whig).

DICK, Samuel Bernard (son of John Dick) (R Pa.) Oct. 26, 1836-May 10, 1907; House 1879-81.

DICKENS, Samuel (− N.C.) ?-1840; House Dec. 2, 1816-17.

DICKERMAN, Charles Heber (D Pa.) Feb. 3, 1843-Dec. 17, 1915; House 1903-05.

DICKERSON, Mahlon (brother of Philemon Dickerson) (D N.J.) April 17, 1770-Oct. 5, 1853; Senate 1817-Jan. 30, 1829; Gov. 1815-17; Secy. of the Navy 1834-38.

DICKERSON, Philemon (brother of Mahlon Dickerson) (JD N.J.) Jan. 11, 1788-Dec. 10, 1862; House 1833-Nov. 3, 1836 (Democrat), 1839-41; Gov. 1836-37 (Democrat).

DICKERSON, William Worth (D Ky.) Nov. 29, 1851-Jan. 31, 1923; House June 21, 1890-93.

DICKEY, Henry Luther (D Ohio) Oct. 29, 1832-May 23, 1910; House 1877-81.

DICKEY, Jesse Column (W Pa.) Feb. 27, 1808-Feb. 19, 1890; House 1849-51.

DICKEY, John (father of Oliver James Dickey) (W Pa. June 23, 1794-March 14, 1853; House 1843-45, 1847 49.

DICKEY, Oliver James (son of John Dickey) (R Pa. April 6, 1823-April 21, 1876; House Dec. 7, 1868-7?

DICKINSON, Clement Cabell (D Mo.) Dec. 6, 1849 Jan. 14, 1938; House Feb. 1, 1910-21, 1923-29, 1931 35.

DICKINSON, Daniel Stevens (D N.Y.) Sept. 11, 1800 April 12, 1866; Senate Nov. 30, 1844-51.

DICKINSON, David W. (nephew of William Hard Murfree) (W Tenn.) June 10, 1808-April 27, 184? House 1833-35 (Democrat), 1843-45.

DICKINSON, Edward (W Mass.) Jan. 1, 1803-June 1? 1874; House 1853-55.

DICKINSON, Edward Fenwick (D Ohio) Jan. 21, 1829 Aug. 25, 1891; House 1869-71.

DICKINSON, John Dean (W N.Y.) June 28, 1767-Ja? 28, 1841; House 1819-23 (Federalist), 1827-31.

DICKINSON, Lester Jesse (cousin of Fred Dickinso? Letts) (R Iowa) Oct. 29, 1873-June 4, 1968; Hous 1919-31; Senate 1931-37.

DICKINSON, Philemon (− N.J.) April 5, 1739-Feb. 1809; Senate Nov. 23, 1790-93; Cont. Cong. 1782-8? (Del.).

DICKINSON, Rodolphus (D Ohio) Dec. 28, 1797-Marc 20, 1849; House 1847-March 20, 1849.

DICKINSON, William Louis (R Ala.) June 5, 1925-− House 1965-−.

DICKS, Norman Devalois (D Wash.) Dec. 16, 1940-− House 1977-−.

DICKSON, David (D Miss.) ?-July 31, 1836; Hous 1835-July 31, 1836.

DICKSON, Frank Stoddard (R Ill.) Oct. 6, 1876-Feb. 2? 1953; House 1905-07.

DICKSON, John (W N.Y.) June 1, 1783-Feb. 22, 185? House 1831-35.

DICKSON, Joseph (F N.C.) April 1745-April 14, 182? House 1799-1801.

DICKSON, Samuel (W N.Y.) March 29, 1807-May ? 1858; House 1855-57.

DICKSON, William (− Tenn.) May 5, 1770-Feb. 181? House 1801-07.

DICKSON, William Alexander (D Miss.) July 20, 186? Feb. 25, 1940; House 1909-13.

DICKSTEIN, Samuel (D N.Y.) Feb. 5, 1885-April 22, 1954; House 1923-Dec. 30, 1945.

DIEKEMA, Gerrit John (R Mich.) March 27, 1859-Dec. 20, 1930; House March 17, 1908-11.

DIES, Martin (father of Martin Dies Jr.) (D Texas) March 13, 1870-July 13, 1922; House 1909-19.

DIES, Martin Jr. (son of Martin Dies) (D Texas) Nov. 5, 1900-Nov. 14, 1972; House 1931-45, 1953-59.

DIETERICH, William Henry (D Ill.) March 31, 1876-Oct. 12, 1940; House 1931-33; Senate 1933-39.

DIETRICH, Charles Elmer (D Pa.) July 30, 1889-May 20, 1942; House 1935-37.

DIETRICH, Charles Henry (R Neb.) Nov. 26, 1853-April 10, 1924; Senate March 28, 1901-05; Gov. 1901.

DIETZ, William (D N.Y.) June 28, 1778-Aug. 24, 1848; House 1825-27.

DIFFENDERFER, Robert Edward (D Pa.) June 7, 1849-April 27, 1923; House 1911-15.

DIGGS, Charles Coles Jr. (D Mich.) Dec. 2, 1922- — ; House 1955-June 3, 1980.

DILL, Clarence Cleveland (D Wash.) Sept. 21, 1884-Jan. 14, 1978; House 1915-19; Senate 1923-35.

DILLINGHAM, Paul Jr. (father of William Paul Dillingham) (D Vt.) Aug. 10, 1799-July 26, 1891; House 1843-47; Gov. 1865-67.

DILLINGHAM, William Paul (son of Paul Dillingham Jr.) (R Vt.) Dec. 12, 1843-July 12, 1923; Senate Oct. 18, 1900-July 12, 1923; Gov. 1888-90.

DILLON, Charles Hall (R S.D.) Dec. 18, 1853-Sept. 15, 1929; House 1913-19.

DILWEG, LaVern Ralph (D Wis.) Nov. 1, 1903-Jan. 2, 1968; House 1943-45.

DIMMICK, Milo Melankthon (brother of William Harrison Dimmick) (D Pa.) Oct. 30, 1811-Nov. 22, 1872; House 1849-53.

DIMMICK, William Harrison (brother of Milo Melankthon Dimmick) (D Pa.) Dec. 20, 1815-Aug. 2, 1861; House 1857-61.

DIMOCK, Davis Jr. (D Pa.) Sept. 17, 1801-Jan. 13, 1842; House 1841-Jan. 13, 1842.

DIMOND, Anthony Joseph (D Alaska) Nov. 30, 1881-May 28, 1953; House (Terr. Del.) 1933-45.

DINGELL, John David (father of John David Dingell Jr.) (D Mich.) Feb. 2, 1894-Sept. 19, 1955; House 1933-Sept. 19, 1955.

DINGELL, John David Jr. (son of John David Dingell) (D Mich.) July 8, 1926- — ; House Dec. 13, 1955- — .

DINGLEY, Nelson Jr. (R Maine) Feb. 15, 1832-Jan. 13, 1899; House Sept. 12, 1881-Jan. 13, 1899; Gov. 1874-76.

DINSMOOR, Samuel (WD N.H.) July 1, 1766-March 15, 1835; House 1811-13; Gov. 1831-34 (Jackson Democrat).

DINSMORE, Hugh Anderson (D Ark.) Dec. 24, 1850-May 2, 1930; House 1893-1905.

DioGUARDI, Joseph D. (R N.Y.) Sept. 20, 1940- — ; House 1985- — .

DIRKSEN, Everett McKinley (father-in-law of Howard H. Baker Jr.) (R Ill.) Jan. 4, 1896-Sept. 7, 1969; House 1933-49; Senate 1951-Sept. 7, 1969.

DISNEY, David Tiernan (D Ohio) Aug. 25, 1803-March 14, 1857; House 1849-55.

DISNEY, Wesley Ernest (D Okla.) Oct. 31, 1883-March 26, 1961; House 1931-45.

DITTER, John William (R Pa.) Sept. 5, 1888-Nov. 21, 1943; House 1933-Nov. 21, 1943.

DIVEN, Alexander Samuel (R N.Y.) Feb. 10, 1809-June 11, 1896; House 1861-63.

DIX, John Adams (son-in-law of John Jordan Morgan) (D N.Y.) July 24, 1798-April 21, 1879; Senate Jan. 27, 1845-49; Secy. of the Treasury Jan. 11-March 3, 1861; Gov. 1873-75 (Republican).

DIXON, Alan John (D Ill.) July 7, 1927- — ; Senate 1981- — .

DIXON, Archibald (W Ky.) April 2, 1802-April 23, 1876; Senate Sept. 1, 1852-55.

DIXON, Henry Aldous (R Utah) June 29, 1890-Jan. 22, 1967; House 1955-61.

DIXON, James (R Conn.) Aug. 5, 1814-March 27, 1873; House 1845-49 (Whig); Senate 1857-69.

DIXON, Joseph (R N.C.) April 9, 1828-March 3, 1883; House Dec. 5, 1870-71.

DIXON, Joseph Andrew (D Ohio) June 3, 1879-July 4, 1942; House 1937-39.

DIXON, Joseph Moore (R Mont.) July 31, 1867-May 22, 1934; House 1903-07; Senate 1907-13; Gov. 1921-25.

DIXON, Julian Carey (D Calif.) Aug. 8, 1934- — ; House 1979- — .

DIXON, Lincoln (D Ind.) Feb. 9, 1860-Sept. 16, 1932; House 1905-19.

DIXON, Nathan Fellows (grandfather of Nathan Fellows Dixon born in 1847, father of Nathan Fellows Dixon, below) (W R.I.) Dec. 13, 1774-Jan. 29, 1842; Senate 1839-Jan. 29, 1842.

DIXON, Nathan Fellows (son of Nathan Fellows Dixon, above, father of Nathan Fellows Dixon, below) (R R.I.) May 1, 1812-April 11, 1881; House 1849-51 (Whig), 1863-71.

DIXON, Nathan Fellows (son of Nathan Fellows Dixon, above, grandson of Nathan Fellows Dixon born in 1774) (R R.I.) Aug. 28, 1847-Nov. 8, 1897; House Feb. 12-March 3, 1885; Senate April 10, 1889-95.

DIXON, William Wirt (D Mont.) June 3, 1838-Nov. 13, 1910; House 1891-93.

DOAN, Robert Eachus (R Ohio) July 23, 1831-Feb. 24, 1919; House 1891-93.

DOAN, William (D Ohio) April 4, 1792-June 22, 1847; House 1839-43.

DOBBIN, James Cochrane (grandson of James Cochran of North Carolina) (D N.C.) Jan. 17, 1814-Aug. 4, 1857; House 1845-47; Secy. of the Navy 1853-57.

DOBBINS, Donald Claude (D Ill.) March 20, 1878-Feb. 14, 1943; House 1933-37.

DOBBINS, Samuel Atkinson (R N.J.) April 14, 1814-May 26, 1886; House 1873-77.

DOCKERY, Alexander Monroe (D Mo.) Feb. 11, 1845-Dec. 26, 1926; House 1883-99; Gov. 1901-05.

DOCKERY, Alfred (father of Oliver Hart Dockery) (W N.C.) Dec. 11, 1797-Dec. 7, 1875; House 1845-47, 1851-53.

DOCKERY, Oliver Hart (son of Alfred Dockery) (R N.C.) Aug. 12, 1830-March 21, 1906; House July 13, 1868-71.

DOCKWEILER, John Francis (D Calif.) Sept. 19, 1895-Jan. 31, 1943; House 1933-39.

DODD, Christopher John (son of Thomas Joseph Dodd) (D Conn.) May 27, 1944- —; House 1975-81; Senate 1981- —.

DODD, Edward (W N.Y.) Aug. 25, 1805-March 1, 1891; House 1855-59.

DODD, Thomas Joseph (father of Christopher John Dodd) (D Conn.) May 15, 1907-May 24, 1971; House 1953-57; Senate 1959-71.

DODDRIDGE, Philip (— Va.) May 17, 1773-Nov. 19, 1832; House 1829-Nov. 19, 1832.

DODDS, Francis Henry (R Mich.) June 9, 1858-Dec. 23, 1940; House 1909-13.

DODDS, Ozro John (D Ohio) March 22, 1840-April 18 1882; House Oct. 8, 1872-73.

DODGE, Augustus Caesar (son of Henry Dodge) (D Iowa) Jan. 2, 1812-Nov. 20, 1883; House (Terr. Del. Oct. 28, 1840-Dec. 28, 1846; Senate Dec. 7, 1848-Feb 22, 1855.

DODGE, Grenville Mellen (R Iowa) April 12, 1831-Jan 3, 1916; House 1867-69.

DODGE, Henry (father of Augustus Caesar Dodge) (— Wis.) Oct. 12, 1782-June 19, 1867; House (Terr. Del. 1841-45; Senate June 8, 1848-57; Gov. (Wis. Terr 1836-41, 1845-48.

DODGE, William Earle (R N.Y.) Sept. 4, 1805-Feb. 1883; House April 7, 1866-67.

DOE, Nicholas Bartlett (W N.Y.) June 16, 1786-Dec. 1856; House Dec. 7, 1840-41.

DOIG, Andrew Wheeler (D N.Y.) July 24, 1799-July 1 1875; House 1839-43.

DOLE, Robert J. (R Kan.) July 22, 1923- —; House 196 69; Senate 1969- —; Senate majority leader 1985-8 Chrmn. Rep. Nat. Comm. 1971-73.

DOLLINGER, Isidore (D N.Y.) Nov. 13, 1903- —; Hous 1949-Dec. 31, 1959.

DOLLIVER, James Isaac (nephew of Jonathan Prenti Dolliver) (R Iowa) Aug. 31, 1894-Dec. 10, 197 House 1945-57.

DOLLIVER, Jonathan Prentiss (uncle of James Isaa Dolliver) (R Iowa) Feb. 6, 1858-Oct. 15, 1910; Hou 1889-Aug. 22, 1900; Senate Aug. 22, 1900-Oct. 1 1910.

DOLPH, Joseph Norton (uncle of Frederick Willia Mulkey) (R Ore.) Oct. 19, 1835-March 10, 1897; Se ate 1883-95.

DOMENGEAUX, James (D La.) Jan. 6, 1907- —; Hou 1941-April 15, 1944; Nov. 7, 1944-49.

DOMENICI, Peter Vichi (R N.M.) May 7, 1932- —; Se ate 1973- —.

DOMINICK, Frederick Haskell (D S.C.) Feb. 20, 187 March 11, 1960; House 1917-33.

DOMINICK, Peter Hoyt (nephew of Howard Alexand Smith) (R Colo.) July 7, 1915-March 18, 1981; Hou 1961-63; Senate 1963-75.

DONAHEY, Alvin Victor (D Ohio) July 7, 1873-April 1946; Senate 1935-41; Gov. 1923-29.

DONDERO, George Anthony (R Mich.) Dec. 16, 188 Jan. 29, 1968; House 1933-57.

DONLEY, Joseph Benton (R Pa.) Oct. 10, 1838-Jan. 23, 1917; House 1869-71.

DONNAN, William G. (R Iowa) June 30, 1834-Dec. 4, 1908; House 1871-75.

DONNELL, Forrest C. (R Mo.) Aug. 20, 1884-March 3, 1980; Senate 1945-51; Gov. 1941-45.

DONNELL, Richard Spaight (grandson of Richard Dobbs Spaight, nephew of Richard Dobbs Spaight Jr.) (W N.C.) Sept. 20, 1820-June 3, 1867; House 1847-49.

DONNELLY, Brian Joseph (D Mass.) March 2, 1947- —; House 1979- —.

DONNELLY, Ignatius (R Minn.) Nov. 3, 1831-Jan. 1, 1901; House 1863-69

DONOHOE, Michael (D Pa.) Feb. 22, 1864-Jan. 17, 1958; House 1911-15.

DONOHUE, Harold Daniel (D Mass.) June 18, 1901-Nov. 4, 1984; House 1947-Dec. 31, 1974.

DONOVAN, Dennis D. (D Ohio) Jan. 31, 1859-April 21, 1941; House 1891-95.

DONOVAN, James George (D/R/L N.Y.) Dec. 15, 1898- —; House 1951-57.

DONOVAN, Jeremiah (D Conn.) Oct. 18, 1857-April 22, 1935; House 1913-15.

DONOVAN, Jerome Francis (D N.Y.), Feb. 1, 1872-Nov. 2, 1949; House March 5, 1918-21.

DOOLEY, Edwin Benedict (R N.Y.) April 13, 1905-Jan. 25, 1982; House 1957-63.

DOOLING, Peter Joseph (D N.Y.) Feb. 15, 1857-Oct. 18, 1931; House 1913-21.

DOOLITTLE, Dudley (D Kan.) June 21, 1881-Nov. 14, 1957; House 1913-19.

DOOLITTLE, James Rood (R Wis.) Jan. 3, 1815-July 23, 1897; Senate 1857-69.

DOOLITTLE, William Hall (R Wash.) Nov. 6, 1848-Feb. 26, 1914; House 1893-97.

DOREMUS, Frank Ellsworth (D Mich.) Aug. 31, 1865-Sept. 4, 1947; House 1911-21.

DORGAN, Byron L. (D N.D.) May 14, 1942- —; House 1981- —.

DORN, Francis Edwin (R N.Y.) April 18, 1911- —; House 1953-61.

DORN, William Jennings Bryan (D S.C.) April 14, 1916- —; House 1947-49, 1951-75.

DORNAN, Robert Kenneth (R Calif.) April 3, 1933- —; House 1977-83, 1985- —.

DORR, Charles Philips (R W.Va.) Aug. 12, 1852-Oct. 8, 1914; House 1897-99.

DORSEY, Clement (— Md.) 1778-Aug. 6, 1848; House 1825-31.

DORSEY, Frank Joseph Gerard (D Pa.) April 26, 1891-July 13, 1949; House 1935-39.

DORSEY, George Washington Emery (R Neb.) Jan. 25, 1842-June 12, 1911; House 1885-91.

DORSEY, John Lloyd Jr. (D Ky.) Aug. 10, 1891-March 22, 1960; House Nov. 4, 1930-31.

DORSEY, Stephen Wallace (R Ark.) Feb. 28, 1842-March 20, 1916; Senate 1873-79.

DORSHEIMER, William (D N.Y.) Feb. 5, 1832-March 26, 1888; House 1883-85.

DOTY, James Duane (cousin of Morgan Lewis Martin) (FS Wis.) Nov. 5, 1799-June 13, 1865; House (Terr. Del.) Jan. 14, 1839-41 (Democrat), (Rep.) 1849-53 (Democrat); Gov. (Wis. Terr.) 1841-44, (Utah Terr.) 1863-65.

DOUBLEDAY, Ulysses Freeman (JD N.Y.) Dec. 15, 1792-March 11, 1866; House 1831-33, 1835-37.

DOUGHERTY, Charles (D Fla.) Oct. 15, 1850-Oct. 11, 1915; House 1885-89.

DOUGHERTY, Charles Francis (R Pa.) June 26, 1937- —; House 1979-83.

DOUGHERTY, John (D Mo.) Feb. 25, 1857-Aug. 1, 1905; House 1899-1905.

DOUGHTON, Robert Lee (D N.C.) Nov. 7, 1863-Oct. 1, 1954; House 1911-53.

DOUGLAS, Albert (R Ohio) April 25, 1852-March 14, 1935; House 1907-11.

DOUGLAS, Beverly Browne (D Va.) Dec. 21, 1822-Dec. 22, 1878; House 1875-Dec. 22, 1878 (1875-1877 Conservative).

DOUGLAS, Emily Taft (wife of Paul Howard Douglas) (D Ill.) April 10, 1899- —; House 1945-47.

DOUGLAS, Fred James (R N.Y.) Sept. 14, 1869-Jan. 1, 1949; House 1937-45.

DOUGLAS, Helen Gahagan (D Calif.) Nov. 25, 1900-June 28, 1980; House 1945-51.

DOUGLAS, Lewis Williams (D Ariz.) July 2, 1894-March 7, 1974; House 1927-March 4, 1933.

DOUGLAS, Paul Howard (husband of Emily Taft Douglas) (D Ill.) March 26, 1892-Sept. 24, 1976; Senate 1949-67.

DOUGLAS, Stephen Arnold (PSD Ill.) April 23, 1813-June 3, 1861; House 1843-47; Senate 1847-June 3, 1861 (1847-53 Democrat).

DOUGLAS, William Harris (R N.Y.) Dec. 5, 1853-Jan. 27, 1944; House 1901-05.

DOUGLASS, John Joseph (D Mass.) Feb. 9, 1873-April 5, 1939; House 1925-35.

DOUTRICH, Isaac Hoffer (R Pa.) Dec. 19, 1871-May 28, 1941; House 1927-37.

DOVENER, Blackburn Barrett (R W.Va.) April 20, 1842-May 9, 1914; House 1895-1907.

DOW, John Goodchild (D N.Y.) May 6, 1905- —; House 1965-69, 1971-73.

DOWD, Clement (D N.C.) Aug. 27, 1832-April 15, 1898; House 1881-85.

DOWDELL, James Ferguson (SRD Ala.) Nov. 26, 1818-Sept. 6, 1871; House 1853-59.

DOWDNEY, Abraham (D N.Y.) Oct. 31, 1841-Dec. 10, 1886; House 1885-Dec. 10, 1886.

DOWDY, John Vernard (D Texas) Feb. 11, 1912- —; House Sept. 23, 1952-73.

DOWDY, Wayne (D Miss.) July 27, 1943- —; House July 9, 1981- —.

DOWELL, Cassius Clay (R Iowa) Feb. 29, 1864-Feb. 4, 1940; House 1915-35, 1937-Feb. 4, 1940.

DOWNEY, Sheridan (son of Stephen Wheeler Downey) (D Calif.) March 11, 1884-Oct. 25, 1961; Senate 1939-Nov. 30, 1950.

DOWNEY, Stephen Wheeler (father of Sheridan Downey) (R Wyo.) July 25, 1839-Aug. 3, 1902; House (Terr. Del.) 1879-81.

DOWNEY, Thomas Joseph (D N.Y.) Jan. 28, 1949- —; House 1975- —.

DOWNING, Charles (— Fla.) ?-1845; House (Terr. Del.) 1837-41.

DOWNING, Finis Ewing (D Ill.) Aug. 24, 1846-March 8, 1936; House 1895-June 5, 1896.

DOWNING, Thomas Nelms (D Va.) Feb. 1, 1919- —; House 1959-77.

DOWNS, Le Roy Donnelly (D Conn.) April 11, 1900-Jan. 18, 1970; House 1941-43.

DOWNS, Solomon Weathersbee (D La.) 1801-Aug. 14, 1854; Senate 1847-53.

DOWSE, Edward (D Mass.) Oct. 22, 1756-Sept. 3, 1828; House 1819-May 26, 1820.

DOX, Peter Myndert (grandson of John Nicholas) (D Ala.) Sept. 11, 1813-April 2, 1891; House 1869-73.

DOXEY, Charles Taylor (R Ind.) July 13, 1841-April 30, 1898; House Jan. 17-March 3, 1883.

DOXEY, Wall (D Miss.) Aug. 8, 1892-March 2, 1962; House 1929-Sept. 28, 1941; Senate Sept. 29, 1941-43.

DOYLE, Clyde Gilman (D Calif.) July 11, 1887-March 14, 1963; House 1945-47, 1949-March 14, 1963.

DOYLE, Thomas Aloysius (D Ill.) Jan. 9, 1886-Jan. 29, 1935; House Nov. 6, 1923-31.

DRAKE, Charles Daniel (R Mo.) April 11, 1811-April 1, 1892; Senate 1867-Dec. 19, 1870.

DRAKE, John Reuben (— N.Y.) Nov. 28, 1782-March 21, 1857; House 1817-19.

DRANE, Herbert Jackson (D Fla.) June 20, 1863-Aug. 11, 1947; House 1917-33.

DRAPER, Joseph (— Va.) Dec. 25, 1794-June 10, 1834; House Dec. 6, 1830-31, Dec. 6, 1832-33.

DRAPER, William Franklin (R Mass.) April 9, 1842-Jan. 28, 1910; House 1893-97.

DRAPER, William Henry (R N.Y.) June 24, 1841-Dec. 7, 1921; House 1901-13.

DRAYTON, William (UD S.C.) Dec. 30, 1776-May 24, 1846; House May 17, 1825-33.

DREIER, David T. (R Calif.) July 5, 1952- —; House 1981- —.

DRESSER, Solomon Robert (R Pa.) Feb. 1, 1842-Jan. 21, 1911; House 1903-07.

DREW, Ira Walton (D Pa.) Aug. 31, 1878-Feb. 12, 1972; House 1937-39.

DREW, Irving Webster (R N.H.) Jan. 8, 1845-April 10, 1922; Senate Sept. 2-Nov. 5, 1918.

DREWRY, Patrick Henry (D Va.) May 24, 1875-Dec. 21, 1947; House April 27, 1920-Dec. 21, 1947.

DRIGGS, Edmund Hope (D N.Y.) May 2, 1865-Sept. 27, 1946; House Dec. 6, 1897-1901.

DRIGGS, John Fletcher (R Mich.) March 8, 1813-Dec. 17, 1877; House 1863-69.

DRINAN, Robert Frederick (D Mass.) Nov. 15, 1920- —; House 1971-81.

DRISCOLL, Daniel Angelus (D N.Y.) March 6, 1875-June 5, 1955; House 1909-17.

DRISCOLL, Denis Joseph (D Pa.) March 27, 1871-Jan. 18, 1958; House 1935-37.

DRISCOLL, Michael Edward (R N.Y.) Feb. 9, 1851-Jan. 19, 1929; House 1899-1913.

DRIVER, William Joshua (D Ark.) March 2, 1873-Oct. 1, 1948; House 1921-39.

DROMGOOLE, George Coke (uncle of Alexander Dromgoole Sims) (D Va.) May 15, 1797-April 27, 1847; House 1835-41, 1843-April 27, 1847.

DRUKKER, Dow Henry (R N.J.) Feb. 7, 1872-Jan. 11, 1963; House April 7, 1914-19.

DRUM, Augustus (D Pa.) Nov. 26, 1815-Sept. 15, 1858; House 1853-55.

DRYDEN, John Fairfield (R N.J.) Aug. 7, 1839-Nov. 24, 1911; Senate Jan. 29, 1902-07.

DUBOIS, Fred Thomas (D Idaho) May 29, 1851-Feb. 14, 1930; House (Terr. Del.) 1887-July 3, 1890; Senate 1891-97, 1901-07 (1887-97 Republican, 1901 Silver Republican).

DU BOSE, Dudley McIver (D Ga.) Oct. 28, 1834-March 2, 1883; House 1871-73.

DUDLEY, Charles Edward (D N.Y.) May 23, 1780-Jan. 23, 1841; Senate Jan. 15, 1829-33.

DUDLEY, Edward Bishop (NR N.C.) Dec. 15, 1769-Oct. 30, 1855; House Nov. 10, 1829-31; Gov. 1836-41 (Whig).

DUELL, Rodolphus Holland (R N.Y.) Dec. 20, 1824-Feb. 11, 1891; House 1859-63, 1871-75.

DUER, William (W N.Y.) May 25, 1805-Aug. 25, 1879; House 1847-51.

DUFF, James Henderson (R Pa.) Jan. 21, 1883-Dec. 20, 1969; Senate Jan. 16, 1951-57; Gov. 1947-51.

DUFFEY, Warren Joseph (D Ohio) Jan. 24, 1886-July 7, 1936; House 1933-July 7, 1936.

DUFFY, Francis Ryan (D Wis.) June 23, 1888-Aug. 16, 1979; Senate 1933-39.

DUFFY, James Patrick Bernard (D N.Y.) Nov. 25, 1878-Jan. 8, 1969; House 1935-37.

DUGRO, Philip Henry (D N.Y.) Oct. 3, 1855-March 1, 1920; House 1881-83.

DUKE, Richard Thomas Walker (C Va.) June 6, 1822-July 2, 1898; House Nov. 8, 1870-73.

DULLES, John Foster (R N.Y.) Feb. 25, 1888-May 24, 1959; Senate July 7-Nov. 8, 1949; Secy. of State 1953-59.

DULSKI, Thaddeus J. (D N.Y.) Sept. 27, 1915- —; House 1959-75.

DUMONT, Ebenezer (U Ind.) Nov. 23, 1814-April 16, 1871; House 1863-67.

DUNBAR, James Whitson (R Ind.) Oct. 17, 1860-May 19, 1943; House 1919-23, 1929-31.

DUNBAR, William (D La.) 1805-March 18, 1861; House 1853-55.

DUNCAN, Alexander (W Ohio) 1788-March 23, 1853; House 1837-41, 1843-45.

DUNCAN, Daniel (W Ohio) July 22, 1806-May 18, 1849; House 1847-49.

DUNCAN, James (— Pa.) 1756-June 24, 1844; House 1821.

DUNCAN, James Henry (W Mass.) Dec. 5, 1793-Feb. 8, 1869; House 1849-53.

DUNCAN, John J. (R Tenn.) March 24, 1919- —; House 1965- —.

DUNCAN, Joseph (JD Ill.) Feb. 22, 1794-Jan. 15, 1844; House 1827-Sept. 21, 1834; Gov. 1834-38 (Whig).

DUNCAN, Richard Meloan (D Mo.) Nov. 10, 1889-Aug. 1, 1974; House 1933-43.

DUNCAN, Robert Blackford (D Ore.) Dec. 4, 1920- —; House 1963-67, 1975-81.

DUNCAN, William Addison (D Pa.) Feb. 2, 1836-Nov. 14, 1884; House 1883-Nov. 14, 1884.

DUNCAN, William Garnett (W Ky.) March 2, 1800-May 25, 1875; House 1847-49.

DUNGAN, James Irvine (D Ohio) May 29, 1844-Dec. 28, 1931; House 1891-93.

DUNHAM, Cyrus Livingston (D Ind.) Jan. 16, 1817-Nov. 21, 1877; House 1849-55.

DUNHAM, Ransom Williams (R Ill.) March 21, 1838-Aug. 19, 1896; House 1883-89.

DUNLAP, George Washington, (U Ky.) Feb. 22, 1813-June 6, 1880; House 1861-63.

DUNLAP, Robert Pickney (D Maine) Aug. 17, 1794-Oct. 20, 1859; House 1843-47; Gov. 1834-38.

DUNLAP, William Claiborne (D Tenn.) Feb. 25, 1798-Nov. 16, 1872; House 1833-37.

DUNN, Aubert Culberson (D Miss.) Nov. 20, 1896- —; House 1935-37.

DUNN, George Grundy (R Ind.) Dec. 20, 1812-Sept. 4, 1857; House 1847-49 (Whig), 1855-57.

DUNN, George Hedford (W Ind.) Nov. 15, 1794-Jan. 12, 1854; House 1837-39.

DUNN, Jim (R Mich.) July 21, 1943- —; House 1981-83.

DUNN, John Thomas (D N.J.) June 4, 1838-Feb. 22, 1907; House 1893-95.

DUNN, Matthew Anthony (D Pa.) Aug. 15, 1886-Feb. 13, 1942; House 1933-41.

DUNN, Poindexter (D Ark.) Nov. 3, 1834-Oct. 12, 1914; House 1879-89.

DUNN, Thomas Byrne (R N.Y.) March 16, 1853-July 2, 1924; House 1913-23.

DUNN, William McKee (R Ind.) Dec. 12, 1814-July 24, 1887; House 1859-63.

DUNNELL, Mark Hill (R Minn.) July 2, 1823-Aug. 9, 1904; House 1871-83, 1889-91.

DUNPHY, Edward John (D N.Y.) May 12, 1856-July 29, 1926; House 1889-95.

DUNWELL, Charles Tappan (R N.Y.) Feb. 13, 1852-June 12, 1908; House 1903-June 12, 1908.

du PONT, Henry Algernon (cousin of Thomas Coleman du Pont) (R Del.) July 30, 1838-Dec. 31, 1926; Senate June 13, 1906-17.

du PONT, Pierre Samuel "Pete" IV (R Del.) Jan. 22, 1935- —; House 1971-77; Gov. 1977-85.

du PONT, Thomas Coleman (cousin of Henry Algernon du Pont) (R Del.) Dec. 11, 1863-Nov. 11, 1930; Senate July 7, 1921-Nov. 7, 1922, 1925-Dec. 9, 1928.

DUPRE, Henry Garland (D La.) July 28, 1873-Feb. 21, 1924; House Nov. 8, 1910-Feb. 21, 1924.

DURAND, George Harman (D Mich.) Feb. 21, 1838-June 8, 1903; House 1875-77.

DURBIN, Richard Joseph (D Ill.) Nov. 21, 1944- —; House 1983- —.

DURBOROW, Alan Cathcard Jr. (D Ill.) Nov. 10, 1857-March 10, 1908; House 1891-95.

DURELL, Daniel Meserve (— N.H.) July 20, 1769-April 29, 1841; House 1807-09.

DURENBERGER, David Ferdinand (R Minn.) Aug. 19, 1934- —; Senate Nov. 8, 1978- —.

DUREY, Cyrus (R N.Y.) May 16, 1864-Jan. 4, 1933; House 1907-11.

DURFEE, Job (D R.I.) Sept. 20, 1790-July 26, 1847; House 1821-25 (1821-23 People's Party).

DURFEE, Nathaniel Briggs (R R.I.) Sept. 29, 1812-Nov. 9, 1872; House 1855-59 (1855-57 American Party).

DURGAN, George Richard (D Ind.) Jan. 20, 1872-Jan. 13, 1942; House 1933-35.

DURHAM, Carl Thomas (D N.C.) Aug. 28, 1892-April 29, 1974; House 1939-61.

DURHAM, Milton Jameson (D Ky.) May 16, 1824-Feb. 12, 1911; House 1873-79.

DURKEE, Charles (R Wis.) Dec. 10, 1805-Jan. 14, 1870; House 1849-53 (Free-Soiler); Senate 1855-61; Gov. (Utah Terr.) 1865-69.

DURKIN, John Anthony (D N.H.) March 29, 1936- —; Senate Sept. 18, 1975-Dec. 29, 1980.

DURNO, Edwin R. (R Ore.) Jan. 26, 1899-Nov. 20, 1976; House 1961-63.

DUVAL, Isaac Harding (R W.Va.) Sept. 1, 1824-July 10, 1902; House 1869-71.

DUVAL, William Pope (D Ky.) 1784-March 19, 1854; House 1813-15; Gov. (Fla. Terr.) 1822-34.

DUVALL, Gabriel (D Md.) Dec. 6, 1752-March 6, 1844; House Nov. 11, 1794-March 28, 1796; Assoc. Justice Supreme Court 1811-35.

DWIGHT, Henry Williams (— Mass.) Feb. 26, 1788-Feb. 21, 1845; House 1821-31.

DWIGHT, Jeremiah Wilbur (father of John Wilbur Dwight) (R N.Y.) April 17, 1819-Nov. 26, 1885; House 1877-83.

DWIGHT, John Wilbur (son of Jeremiah Wilbur Dwight) (R N.Y.) May 24, 1859-Jan. 19, 1928; House Nov. 2, 1902-13.

DWIGHT, Theodore (cousin of Aaron Burr) (F Conn.) Dec. 15, 1764-June 12, 1846; House Dec. 1, 1806-07.

DWIGHT, Thomas (F Mass.) Oct. 29, 1758-Jan. 2, 1819; House 1803-05.

DWINELL, Justin (— N.Y.) Oct. 28, 1785-Sept. 17, 1850; House 1823-25.

DWORSHAK, Henry Clarence (R Idaho) Aug. 29, 1894-July 23, 1962; House 1939-Nov. 5, 1946; Senate Nov. 6, 1946-49, Oct. 14, 1949-July 23, 1962.

DWYER, Bernard J. (D N.J.) Jan. 24, 1921- —; House 1981- —.

DWYER, Florence Price (R N.J.) July 4, 1902-Feb. 29, 1976; House 1959-73.

DYAL, Kenneth Warren (D Calif.) July 9, 1910-May 12, 1978; House 1965-67.

DYER, David Patterson (uncle of Leonidas Carstarphen Dyer) (R Mo.) Feb. 12, 1838-April 29, 1924; House 1869-71.

DYER, Leonidas Carstarphen (nephew of David Patterson Dyer) (R Mo.) June 11, 1871-Dec. 15, 1957; House 1911-June 19, 1914, 1915-33.

DYMALLY, Mervyn M. (D Calif.) May 12, 1926- —; House 1981- —.

DYSON, Roy (D Md.) Nov. 15, 1948- —; House 1981- —.

EAGAN, John Joseph (D N.J.) Jan. 22, 1872-June 13, 1956; House 1913-21, 1923-25.

EAGER, Samuel Watkins (R N.Y.) April 8, 1789-Dec. 23, 1860; House Nov. 2, 1830-31.

EAGLE, Joe Henry (D Texas) Jan. 23, 1870-Jan. 10, 1963; House 1913-21, Jan. 28, 1933-37.

EAGLETON, Thomas Francis (D Mo.) Sept. 4, 1929- —; Senate Dec. 28, 1968-87.

EAMES, Benjamin Tucker (R R.I.) June 4, 1818-Oct. 6, 1901; House 1871-79.

EARHART, Daniel Scofield (D Ohio) May 28, 1907-Jan. 2, 1976; House Nov. 3, 1936-37.

EARLE, Elias (uncle of Samuel Earle and John Baylis Earle, great-grandfather of John Laurens Manning Irby and Joseph Haynsworth Earle) (D S.C.) June 19, 1762-May 19, 1823; House 1805-07, 1811-15, 1817-21.

EARLE, John Baylis (nephew of Elias Earle, cousin of Samuel Earle) (— S.C.) Oct. 23, 1766-Feb. 3, 1863; House 1803-05.

EARLE, Joseph Haynsworth (great-grandson of Elias Earle, cousin of John Laurens Manning Irby, nephew of William Lowndes Yancey) (D S.C.) April 30, 1847-May 20, 1897; Senate March 4-May 20, 1897.

EARLE, Samuel (nephew of Elias Earle, cousin of John Baylis Earle) (— S.C.) Nov. 28, 1760-Nov. 24, 1833; House 1795-97.

EARLL, Jonas Jr. (cousin of Nehemiah Hezekiah Earll) (D N.Y.) 1786-Oct. 28, 1846; House 1827-31.

EARLL, Nehemiah Hezekiah (cousin of Jonas Earll Jr.) (D N.Y.) Oct. 5, 1787-Aug. 26, 1872; House 1839-41.

EARLY, Joseph Daniel (D Mass.) Jan. 31, 1933- —; House 1975- —.

EARLY, Peter (— Ga.) June 20, 1773-Aug. 15, 1817; House Jan. 10, 1803-07; Gov. 1813-15 (Democratic Republican).

EARNSHAW, Manuel (I P.I.) Nov. 19, 1862-Feb. 13, 1936; House (Res. Comm.) 1913-17.

EARTHMAN, Harold Henderson (D Tenn.) April 13, 1900- —; House 1945-47.

EAST, John Porter (R N.C.) May 5, 1931-June 29, 1986; Senate 1981-June 29, 1986.

EASTLAND, James Oliver (D Miss.) Nov. 28, 1904-Feb. 19, 1986; Senate June 30-Sept. 18, 1941, 1943-Dec. 27, 1978; Pres. pro tempore July 29, 1972-Dec. 27, 1978.

EASTMAN, Ben C. (D Wis.) Oct. 24, 1812-Feb. 2, 1856; House 1851-55.

EASTMAN, Ira Allen (nephew of Nehemiah Eastman) (D N.H.) Jan. 1, 1809-March 21, 1881; House 1839-43.

EASTMAN, Nehemiah (uncle of Ira Allen Eastman) (D N.H.) June 16, 1782-Jan. 11, 1856; House 1825-27.

EASTON, Rufus (D Mo.) May 4, 1774-July 5, 1834; House (Terr. Del.) Sept. 17, 1814-Aug. 5, 1816.

EATON, Charles Aubrey (uncle of William Robb Eaton) (R N.J.) March 29, 1868-Jan. 23, 1953; House 1925-53.

EATON, John Henry (D Tenn.) June 18, 1790-Nov. 17, 1856; Senate Sept. 5, 1818-21, Sept. 27, 1821-March 9, 1829; Secy. of War 1829-31; Gov. (Fla. Terr.) 1834-36.

EATON, Lewis (— N.Y.)?-?; House 1823-25.

EATON, Thomas Marion (R Calif.) Aug. 3, 1896-Sept. 16, 1939; House Jan. 3-Sept. 16, 1939.

EATON, William Robb (nephew of Charles Aubrey Eaton) (R Colo.) Dec. 17, 1877-Dec. 16, 1942; House 1929-33.

EATON, William Wallace (D Conn.) Oct. 11, 1816-Sept. 21, 1898; Senate Feb. 5, 1875-1881; House 1883-85.

EBERHARTER, Herman Peter (D Pa.) April 29, 1892-Sept. 9, 1958; House 1937-Sept. 9, 1958.

ECHOLS, Leonard Sidney (R W.Va.) Oct. 30, 1871-May 9, 1946; House 1919-23.

ECKART, Dennis E. (D Ohio) April 6, 1950- —; House 1981- —.

ECKERT, Charles Richard (D Pa.) Jan. 20, 1868-Oct. 26, 1959; House 1935-39.

ECKERT, Fred J. (R N.Y.) May 6, 1941- —; House 1985-87.

ECKERT, George Nicholas (W Pa.) July 4, 1802-June 28, 1865; House 1847-49.

ECKHARDT, Robert Christian (cousin of Richard Mifflin Kleberg Sr., grandnephew of Rudolph Kleberg, nephew of Harry McLeary Wurzbach) (D Texas) July 16, 1913- —; House 1967-81.

ECKLEY, Ephraim Ralph (R Ohio) Dec. 9, 1811-March 27, 1908; House 1863-69.

ECTON, Zales Nelson (R Mont.) April 1, 1898-March 3, 1961; Senate 1947-53.

EDDY, Frank Marion (R Minn.) April 1, 1856-Jan. 13, 1929; House 1895-1903.

EDDY, Norman (D Ind.) Dec. 10, 1810-Jan. 28, 1872; House 1853-55.

EDDY, Samuel (D R.I.) March 31, 1769-Feb. 3, 1839; House 1819-25.

EDELSTEIN, Morris Michael (D N.Y.) Feb. 5, 1888-June 4, 1941; House Feb. 6, 1940-June 4, 1941.

EDEN, John Rice (D Ill.) Feb. 1, 1826-June 9, 1909; House 1863-65, 1873-79, 1885-87.

EDGAR, Robert William (D Pa.) May 29, 1943- —; House 1975-87.

EDGE, Walter Evans (R N.J.) Nov. 20, 1873-Oct. 29, 1956; Senate 1919-Nov. 21, 1929; Gov. 1917-19, 1944-47.

EDGERTON, Alfred Peck (brother of Joseph Ketchum Edgerton) (D Ohio) Jan. 11, 1813-May 14, 1897; House 1851-55.

EDGERTON, Alonzo Jay (R Minn.) June 7, 1827-Aug. 9, 1896; Senate March 12-Oct. 30, 1881.

EDGERTON, Joseph Ketchum (brother of Alfred Peck Edgerton) (D Ind.) Feb. 16, 1818-Aug. 25, 1893; House 1863-65.

EDGERTON, Sidney (R Ohio) Aug. 17, 1818-July 19, 1900; House 1859-63; Gov. (Mont. Terr.) 1865-66.

EDIE, John Rufus (W Pa.) Jan. 14, 1814-Aug. 27, 1888; House 1855-59.

EDMANDS, John Wiley (W Mass.) March 1, 1809-Jan. 31, 1877; House 1853-55.

EDMISTON, Andrew (D W.Va.) Nov. 13, 1892-Aug. 28, 1966; House Nov. 28, 1933-43.

EDMOND, William (F Conn.) Sept. 28, 1755-Aug. 1, 1838; House Nov. 13, 1797-1801.

EDMONDS, George Washington (R Pa.) Feb. 22, 1864-Sept. 28, 1939; House 1913-25, 1933-35.

EDMONDSON, Edmond Augustus (brother of James Howard Edmondson) (D Okla.) April 7, 1919- —; House 1953-73.

EDMONDSON, James Howard (brother of Edmond Augustus Edmondson) (D Okla.) Sept. 27, 1925-Nov. 17, 1971; Senate Jan. 9, 1963-Nov. 3, 1964; Gov 1959-63.

EDMUNDS, George Franklin (R Vt.) Feb. 1, 1828-Feb 27, 1919; Senate April 3, 1866-Nov. 1, 1891; Pres. pro tempore 1883-85.

EDMUNDS, Paul Carrington (D Va.) Nov. 1, 1836-March 12, 1899; House 1889-95.

EDMUNDSON, Henry Alonzo (D Va.) June 14, 1814-Dec. 16, 1890; House 1849-61.

EDSALL, Joseph E. (D N.J.) 1789-1865; House 1845-49

EDWARDS, Benjamin (father of Ninian Edwards grandfather of Benjamin Edwards Grey) (— Md. Aug. 12, 1753-Nov. 13, 1829; House Jan. 2-March 3 1795.

EDWARDS, Caldwell, (D/P Mont.) Jan. 8, 1841-July 23 1922; House 1901-03.

EDWARDS, Charles Gordon (D Ga.) July 2, 1878-July 13, 1931; House 1907-17, 1925-July 13, 1931.

EDWARDS, Don (D Calif.) Jan. 6, 1915- —; House 1963 —.

EDWARDS, Don Calvin (R Ky.) July 13, 1861-Sept. 19 1938; House 1905-11.

EDWARDS, Edward Irving (D N.J.) Dec. 1, 1863-Jan 26, 1931; Senate 1923-29; Gov. 1920-23.

EDWARDS, Edwin Washington (husband of Elaine Schwartzenburg Edwards) (D La.) Aug. 7, 1927- — House Oct. 2, 1965-May 9, 1972; Gov. May 9, 1972 81, 1984- —.

EDWARDS, Elaine Schwartzenburg (wife of Edwin Washington Edwards) (D La.) March 8, 1929- — Senate Aug. 1-Nov. 13, 1972.

EDWARDS, Francis Smith (AP N.Y.) May 28, 1817 May 20, 1899; House 1855-Feb. 28, 1857.

EDWARDS, Henry Waggaman (D Conn.) Oct. 1779 July 22, 1847; House 1819-23; Senate Oct. 8, 1823-27 Gov. 1833-34, 1835-38.

EDWARDS, John (— Ky.) 1748-1837; Senate June 18 1792-95.

EDWARDS, John (D N.Y.) Aug. 6, 1781-Dec. 28, 1850 House 1837-39.

EDWARDS, John (granduncle of John Edwards Leonard) (W Pa.) 1786-June 26, 1843; House 1839-43.

EDWARDS, John (LR Ark.) Oct. 24, 1805-April 8, 1894 House 1871-Feb. 9, 1872.

DWARDS, John Cummins (D Mo.) June 24, 1804-Sept. 14, 1888; House 1841-43; Gov. 1844-48.

DWARDS, Marvin H. "Mickey" (R Okla.) July 12, 1937- —; House 1977- —.

DWARDS, Ninian (son of Benjamin Edwards) (D Ill.) March 17, 1775-July 20, 1833; Senate Dec. 3, 1818-24; Gov. 1809-18 (Ill. Terr.), 1826-30 (National Republican).

DWARDS, Samuel (F Pa.) March 12, 1785-Nov. 21, 1850; House 1819-27.

DWARDS, Thomas McKey (R N.H.) Dec. 16, 1795-May 1, 1875; House 1859-63.

DWARDS, Thomas Owen (W Ohio) March 29, 1810-Feb. 5, 1876; House 1847-49.

DWARDS, Weldon Nathaniel (D N.C.) Jan. 25, 1788-Dec. 18, 1873; House Feb. 7, 1816-27.

DWARDS, William Jackson "Jack" (R Ala.) Sept. 20, 1928- —; House 1965-85.

DWARDS, William Posey (R Ga.) Nov. 9, 1835-June 28, 1900; House July 25, 1868-69.

FNER, Valentine (D N.Y.) May 5, 1776-Nov. 20, 1865; House 1835-37.

GBERT, Albert Gallatin (D Pa.) April 13, 1828-March 28, 1896; House 1875-77.

GBERT, Joseph (D N.Y.) April 10, 1807-July 7, 1888; House 1841-43.

GE, George (— Pa.) March 9, 1748-Dec. 14, 1829; House Dec. 8, 1796-Oct. 1797.

GGLESTON, Benjamin (R Ohio) Jan. 3, 1816-Feb. 9, 1888; House 1865-69.

GGLESTON, Joseph (uncle of William Segar Archer) (D Va.) Nov. 24, 1754-Feb. 13, 1811; House Dec. 3, 1798-1801.

CHER, Edward Clayton (D Iowa) Dec. 16, 1878-Nov. 29, 1944; House 1933-Dec. 2, 1938.

CKHOFF, Anthony (D N.Y.) Sept. 11, 1827-Nov. 5, 1901; House 1877-79.

LBERG, Joshua (D Pa.) Feb. 12, 1921- —; House 1967-79.

NSTEIN, Edwin (R N.Y.) Nov. 18, 1842-Jan. 24, 1905; House 1879-81.

KWALL, William Alexander (R Ore.) June 14, 1887-Oct. 16, 1956; House 1935-37.

A, Jacob Hart (R N.H.) July 18, 1820-Aug. 21, 1884; House 1867-71.

ELAM, Joseph Barton (D La.) June 12, 1821-July 4, 1885; House 1877-81.

ELDER, James Walter (D La.) Oct. 5, 1882-Dec. 16, 1941; House 1913-15.

ELDREDGE, Charles Augustus (D Wis.) Feb. 27, 1820-Oct. 26, 1896; House 1863-75.

ELDREDGE, Nathaniel Buel (D Mich.) March 28, 1813-Nov. 27, 1893; House 1883-87.

ELIOT, Samuel Atkins (great-grandfather of Thomas Hopkinson Eliot) (W Mass.) March 5, 1798-Jan. 29, 1862; House Aug. 22, 1850-51.

ELIOT, Thomas Dawes (R Mass.) March 20, 1808-June 14, 1870; House April 17, 1854-1855 (Whig), 1859-69.

ELIOT, Thomas Hopkinson (great-grandson of Samuel Atkins Eliot) (D Mass.) June 14, 1907- —; House 1941-43.

ELIZALDE, Joaquin Miguel (— P.I.) Aug. 2, 1896-Feb. 9, 1965; House (Res. Comm.) Sept. 29, 1938-Aug. 9, 1944.

ELKINS, Davis (son of Stephen Benton Elkins, grandson of Henry Gassaway Davis) (R W.Va.) Jan. 24, 1876-Jan. 5, 1959; Senate Jan. 9-Jan. 31, 1911, 1919-25.

ELKINS, Stephen Benton (father of Davis Elkins) (R W.Va.) Sept. 26, 1841-Jan. 4, 1911; House (Terr. Del. N.M.) 1873-77; Senate 1895-Jan. 4, 1911; Secy. of War 1891-93.

ELLENBOGEN, Henry (D Pa.) April 3, 1900-July 4, 1985; House 1933-Jan. 3, 1938.

ELLENDER, Allen Joseph (D La.) Sept. 24, 1890-July 27, 1972; Senate 1937-July 27, 1972. Pres. pro tempore 1971-July 27, 1972.

ELLERBE, James Edwin (D S.C.) Jan. 12, 1867-Oct. 24, 1917; House 1905-13.

ELLERY, Christopher (D R.I.) Nov. 1, 1768-Dec. 2, 1840; Senate May 6, 1801-05.

ELLETT, Henry Thomas (D Miss.) March 8, 1812-Oct. 15, 1887; House Jan. 26-March 3, 1847.

ELLETT, Tazewell (D Va.) Jan. 1, 1856-May 19, 1914; House 1895-97.

ELLICOTT, Benjamin (D N.Y.) April 17, 1765-Dec. 10, 1827; House 1817-19.

ELLIOTT, Alfred James (D Calif.) June 1, 1895-Jan. 17, 1973; House May 4, 1937-49.

ELLIOTT, Carl Atwood (D Ala.) Dec. 20, 1913- —; House 1949-65.

ELLIOTT, Douglas Hemphill (R Pa.) June 3, 1921-June 19, 1960; House April 26-June 19, 1960.

ELLIOTT, James (F Vt.) Aug. 18, 1775-Nov. 10, 1839; House 1803-09.

ELLIOTT, James Thomas (R Ark.) April 22, 1823-July 28, 1875; House Jan. 13-March 3, 1869.

ELLIOTT, John (— Ga.) Oct. 24, 1773-Aug. 9, 1827; Senate 1819-25.

ELLIOTT, John Milton (D Ky.) May 20, 1820-March 26, 1879; House 1853-59.

ELLIOTT, Mortimer Fitzland (D Pa.) Sept. 24, 1839-Aug. 5, 1920; House 1883-85.

ELLIOTT, Richard Nash (R Ind.) April 25, 1873-March 21, 1948; House June 26, 1917-31.

ELLIOTT, Robert Brown (R S.C.) Aug. 11, 1842-Aug. 9, 1884; House 1871-Nov. 1, 1874.

ELLIOTT, William (D S.C.) Sept. 3, 1838-Dec. 7, 1907; House 1887-Sept. 23, 1890, 1891-93, 1895-June 4, 1896, 1897-1903.

ELLIS, Caleb (— N.H.) April 16, 1767-May 6, 1816; House 1805-07.

ELLIS, Chesselden (D N.Y.) 1808-May 10, 1854; House 1843-45.

ELLIS, Clyde Taylor (D Ark.) Dec. 21, 1908-Feb. 9, 1980; House 1939-43.

ELLIS, Edgar Clarence (R Mo.) Oct. 2, 1854-March 15, 1947; House 1905-09, 1921-23, 1925-27, 1929-31.

ELLIS, Ezekiel John (D La.) Oct. 15, 1840-April 25, 1889; House 1875-85.

ELLIS, Hubert Summers (R W.Va.) July 6, 1887-Dec. 3, 1959; House 1943-49.

ELLIS, Powhatan (D Miss.) Jan. 17, 1790-March 18, 1863; Senate Sept. 28, 1825-Jan. 28, 1826, 1827-July 16, 1832.

ELLIS, William Cox (F Pa.) May 5, 1787-Dec. 13, 1871; House 1821 (elected 1820 but resigned before Congress assembled), 1823-25.

ELLIS, William Russell (R Ore.) April 23, 1850-Jan. 18, 1915; House 1893-99, 1907-11.

ELLIS, William Thomas (D Ky.) July 24, 1845-Jan. 8, 1925; House 1889-95.

ELLISON, Andrew (D Ohio) 1812-about 1860; House 1853-55.

ELLISON, Daniel (R Md.) Feb. 14, 1886-Aug. 20, 1960; House 1943-45.

ELLMAKER, Amos (— Pa.) Feb. 2, 1787-Nov. 28, 185 House March 3-July 3, 1815 (elected but did n qualify, resigned before Congress assembled).

ELLSBERRY, William Wallace (D Ohio) Dec. 18, 183 Sept. 7, 1894; House 1885-87.

ELLSWORTH, Charles Clinton (R Mich.) Jan. 2 1824-June 25, 1899; House 1877-79.

ELLSWORTH, Franklin Fowler (R Minn.) July 1 1879-Dec. 23, 1942; House 1915-21.

ELLSWORTH, Matthew Harris (R Ore.) Sept. 17, 189 Feb. 7, 1986; House 1943-57.

ELLSWORTH, Oliver (father of William Wolcott Ell worth) (F Conn.) April 29, 1745-Nov. 26, 1807; Se ate 1789-March 8, 1796; Cont. Cong. 1777-84; Chi Justice United States 1796-1800.

ELLSWORTH, Robert Fred (R Kan.) June 11, 1926- House 1961-67.

ELLSWORTH, Samuel Stewart (D N.Y.) Oct. 13, 179 June 4, 1863; House 1845-47.

ELLSWORTH, William Wolcott (son of Oliver Ell worth) (W Conn.) Nov. 10, 1791-Jan. 15, 186 House 1829-July 8, 1834; Gov. 1838-42.

ELLWOOD, Reuben (R Ill.) Feb. 21, 1821-July 1, 188 House 1883-July 1, 1885.

ELLZEY, Lawrence Russell (D Miss.) March 20, 189 Dec. 7, 1977; House March 15, 1932-35.

ELMENDORF, Lucas Conrad (D N.Y.) 1758-Aug. 1843; House 1797-1803.

ELMER, Ebenezer (brother of Jonathan Elmer, fath of Lucius Quintius Cincinnatus Elmer) (D N.J.) Au 23, 1752-Oct. 18, 1843; House 1801-07. .

ELMER, Jonathan (brother of Ebenezer Elmer, uncle Lucius Quintius Cincinnatus Elmer) (F N.J.) N 29, 1745-Sept. 3, 1817; Senate 1789-91; Cont. Cor 1776-78, 1781-84, 1787-88.

ELMER, Lucius Quintius Cincinnatus (son of Ebene Elmer, nephew of Jonathan Elmer) (D N.J.) Feb. 1793-March 11, 1883; House 1843-45.

ELMER, William Price (R Mo.) March 2, 1871-May 1956; House 1943-45.

ELMORE, Franklin Harper (SRD S.C.) Oct. 15, 179 May 28, 1850; House Dec. 10, 1836-39; Senate Ap 11-May 28, 1850.

ELSAESSER, Edward Julius (R N.Y.) March 10, 190 —; House 1945-49.

ELSTON, Charles Henry (R Ohio) Aug. 1, 1891-Se 25, 1980; House 1939-53.

ELSTON, John Arthur (PR Calif.) Feb. 10, 1874-Dec. 15, 1921; House 1915-Dec. 15, 1921.

ELTSE, Ralph Roscoe (R Calif.) Sept. 13, 1885-March 18, 1971; House 1933-35.

ELVINS, Politte (R Mo.) March 16, 1878-Jan. 14, 1943; House 1909-11.

ELY, Alfred (R N.Y.) Feb. 15, 1815-May 18, 1892; House 1859-63.

ELY, Frederick David (R Mass.) Sept. 24, 1838-Aug. 6, 1921; House 1885-87.

ELY, John (D N.Y.) Oct. 8, 1774-Aug. 20, 1849; House 1839-41.

ELY, Smith Jr. (D N.Y.) April 17, 1825-July 1, 1911; House 1871-73, 1875-Dec. 11, 1876.

ELY, William (F Mass.) Aug. 14, 1765-Oct. 9, 1817; House 1805-15.

EMBREE, Elisha (W Ind.) Sept. 28, 1801-Feb. 28, 1863; House 1847-49.

EMERICH, Martin (D Ill.) April 27, 1846-Sept. 27, 1922; House 1903-05.

EMERSON, Henry Ivory (R Ohio) March 15, 1871-Oct. 28, 1953; House 1915-21.

EMERSON, Louis Woodard (R N.Y.) July 25, 1857-June 10, 1924; House 1899-1903.

EMERSON, William (R Mo.) Jan. 1, 1938-—; House 1981-—.

EMERY, David Farnham (R Maine) Sept. 1, 1948-—; House 1975-83.

EMOTT, James (F N.Y.) March 9, 1771-April 7, 1850; House 1809-13.

EMRIE, Jonas Reece (R Ohio) April 25, 1812-June 5, 1869; House 1855-57.

ENGEL, Albert Joseph (R Mich.) Jan. 1, 1888-Dec. 2, 1959; House 1935-51.

ENGLAND, Edward Theodore (R W.Va.) Sept. 29, 1869-Sept. 9, 1934; House 1927-29.

ENGLE, Clair (D Calif.) Sept. 21, 1911-July 30, 1964; House Aug. 31, 1943-59; Senate 1959-July 30, 1964.

ENGLEBRIGHT, Harry Lane (son of William Fellows Englebright) (R Calif.) Jan. 2, 1884-May 13, 1943; House Aug. 31, 1926-May 13, 1943.

ENGLEBRIGHT, William Fellows (father of Harry Lane Englebright) (R Calif.) Nov. 23, 1855-Feb. 10, 1915; House Nov. 6, 1906-11.

ENGLISH, Glenn Lee Jr. (D Okla.) Nov. 30, 1940-—; House 1975-—.

ENGLISH, James Edward (D Conn.) March 13, 1812-March 2, 1890; House 1861-65; Senate Nov. 27, 1875-May 17, 1876; Gov. 1867-69, 1870-71.

ENGLISH, Thomas Dunn (D N.J.) June 29, 1819-April 1, 1902; House 1891-95.

ENGLISH, Warren Barkley (D Calif.) May 1, 1840-Jan. 9, 1913; House April 4, 1894-95.

ENGLISH, William Eastin (son of William Hayden English) (D Ind.) Nov. 3, 1850-April 29, 1926; House May 22, 1884-85.

ENGLISH, William Hayden (father of William Eastin English) (D Ind.) Aug. 27, 1822-Feb. 7, 1896; House 1853-61.

ENLOE, Benjamin Augustine (D Tenn.) Jan. 18, 1848-July 8, 1922; House 1887-95.

ENOCHS, William Henry (R Ohio) March 29, 1842-July 13, 1893; House 1891-July 13, 1893.

EPES, James Fletcher (cousin of Sydney Parham Epes) (D Va.) May 23, 1842-Aug. 24, 1910; House 1891-95.

EPES, Sydney Parham (cousin of James Fletcher Epes) (D Va.) Aug. 20, 1865-March 3, 1900; House 1897-March 23, 1898, 1899-March 3, 1900.

EPPES, John Wayles (D Va.) April 7, 1773-Sept. 13, 1823; House 1803-11, 1813-15; Senate 1817-Dec. 4, 1819.

ERDAHL, Arlen Ingolf (R Minn.) Feb. 27, 1931-—; House 1979-83.

ERDMAN, Constantine Jacob (grandson of Jacob Erdman) (D Pa.) Sept. 4, 1846-Jan. 15, 1911; House 1893-97.

ERDMAN, Jacob (grandfather of Constantine Jacob Erdman) (D Pa.) Feb. 22, 1801-July 20, 1867; House 1845-47.

ERDREICH, Ben (D Ala.) Dec. 9, 1938-—; House 1983-—.

ERICKSON, John Edward (D Mont.) March 14, 1863-May 25, 1946; Senate March 13, 1933-Nov. 6, 1934; Gov. 1925-33.

ERK, Edmund Frederick (R Pa.) April 17, 1872-Dec. 14, 1953; House Nov. 4, 1930-33.

ERLENBORN, John Neal (R Ill.) Feb. 8, 1927-—; House 1965-85.

ERMENTROUT, Daniel (D Pa.) Jan. 24, 1837-Sept. 17, 1899; House 1881-89, 1897-Sept. 17, 1899.

ERNST, Richard Pretlow (R Ky.) Feb. 28, 1858-April 13, 1934; Senate 1921-27.

ERRETT, Russell (R Pa.) Nov. 10, 1817-April 7, 1891; House 1877-83.

ERTEL, Allen Edward (D Pa.) Nov. 7, 1936- —; House 1977-83.

ERVIN, James (Protect. S.C.) Oct. 17, 1778-July 7, 1841; House 1817-21.

ERVIN, Joseph Wilson (brother of Samuel James Ervin Jr.) (D N.C.) March 3, 1901-Dec. 25, 1945; House Jan. 3-Dec. 25, 1945.

ERVIN, Samuel James Jr. (brother of Joseph Wilson Ervin) (D N.C.) Sept. 27, 1896-April 23, 1985; House Jan. 22, 1946-47; Senate June 5, 1954-Dec. 31, 1974.

ESCH, John Jacob (R Wis.) March 20, 1861-April 27, 1941; House 1899-1921.

ESCH, Marvin L. (R Mich.) Aug. 4, 1927- —; House 1967-77.

ESHLEMAN, Edwin D. (R Pa.) Dec. 4, 1920-Jan. 10, 1985; House 1967-77.

ESLICK, Edward Everett (husband of Willa McCord Blake Eslick) (D Tenn.) April 19, 1872-June 14, 1932; House 1925-June 14, 1932.

ESLICK, Willa McCord Blake (widow of Edward Everett Eslick) (D Tenn.) Sept. 8, 1878-Feb. 18, 1961; House Aug. 4, 1932-33.

ESPY, Mike (D Miss.) Nov. 28, 1953- —; House 1987- —.

ESSEN, Frederick (R Mo.) April 22, 1863-Aug. 18, 1946; House Nov. 5, 1918-19.

ESTABROOK, Experience (— Neb.) April 30, 1813-March 26, 1894; House (Terr. Del.) 1859-May 18, 1860.

ESTEP, Harry Allison (R Pa.) Feb. 1, 1884-Feb. 28, 1968; House 1927-33.

ESTERLY, Charles Joseph (R Pa.) Feb. 8, 1888-Sept. 3, 1940; House 1925-27, 1929-31.

ESTIL, Benjamin (— Va.) March 13, 1780-July 14, 1853; House 1825-27.

ESTOPINAL, Albert (D La.) Jan. 30, 1845-April 28, 1919; House Nov. 3, 1908-April 28, 1919.

ESTY, Constantine Canaris (R Mass.) Dec. 26, 1824-Dec. 27, 1912; House Dec. 2, 1872-73.

ETHERIDGE, Emerson (W Tenn.) Sept. 28, 1819-Oct. 21, 1902; House 1853-57, 1859-61.

EUSTIS, George Jr. (brother of James Biddle Eustis) (AP La.) Sept. 28, 1828-March 15, 1872; House 1855-59.

EUSTIS, James Biddle (brother of George Eustis Jr.) (D La.) Aug. 27, 1834-Sept. 9, 1899; Senate Jan. 12, 1876-79, 1885-91.

EUSTIS, William (DR Mass.) June 10, 1753-Feb. 6, 1825; House 1801-05, Aug. 21, 1820-23; Secy. of War 1809-13; Gov. 1823-25.

EVANS, Alexander (W Md.) Sept. 13, 1818-Dec. 5, 1888; House 1847-53.

EVANS, Alvin (R Pa.) Oct. 4, 1845-June 19, 1906; House 1901-05.

EVANS, Billy Lee (D Ga.) Nov. 10, 1941- —; House 1977-83.

EVANS, Charles Robley (D Nev.) Aug. 9, 1866-Nov. 30, 1954; House 1919-21.

EVANS, Cooper (R Iowa) May 26, 1924- —; House 1981-87.

EVANS, Daniel Jackson (R Wash.) Oct. 16, 1925- — Senate Sept. 12, 1983- —; Gov. 1965-77.

EVANS, David Ellicott (D N.Y.) March 19, 1788-May 17, 1850; House March 4-May 2, 1827.

EVANS, David Reid (D S.C.) Feb. 20, 1769-March 8, 1843; House 1813-15.

EVANS, David Walter (D Ind.) Aug. 17, 1946- —; House 1975-83.

EVANS, Frank Edward (D Colo.) Sept. 6, 1923- — House 1965-79.

EVANS, George (W Maine) Jan. 12, 1797-April 6, 1867; House July 20, 1829-41; Senate 1841-47.

EVANS, Henry Clay (R Tenn.) June 18, 1843-Dec. 12, 1921; House 1889-91.

EVANS, Hiram Kinsman (R Iowa) March 17, 1863-July 9, 1941; House June 4, 1923-25.

EVANS, Isaac Newton (R Pa.) July 29, 1827-Dec. 3, 1901; House 1877-79, 1883-87.

EVANS, James La Fayette (R Ind.) March 27, 1825-May 28, 1903; House 1875-79.

EVANS, John Morgan (D Mont.) Jan. 7, 1863-March 12, 1946; House 1913-21, 1923-33.

EVANS, Joshua Jr. (D Pa.) Jan. 20, 1777-Oct. 2, 1846; House 1829-33.

EVANS, Josiah James (SRD S.C.) Nov. 27, 1786-May 6, 1858; Senate 1853-May 6, 1858.

EVANS, Lane (D Ill.) Aug. 4, 1951- —; House 1983- —.

EVANS, Lemuel Dale (AP Texas) Jan. 8, 1810-July 1, 1877; House 1855-57.

EVANS, Lynden (D Ill.) June 28, 1858-May 6, 1926; House 1911-13.

EVANS, Marcellus Hugh (D N.Y.) Sept. 22, 1884-Nov. 21, 1953; House 1935-41.

EVANS, Melvin Herbert (R V.I.) Aug. 7, 1917-Nov. 27, 1984; House (Terr. Del.) 1979-81.

EVANS, Nathan (W Ohio) June 24, 1804-Sept. 27, 1879; House 1847-51.

EVANS, Robert Emory (R Neb.) July 15, 1856-July 8, 1925; House 1919-23.

EVANS, Thomas (— Va.) ?-?; House 1797-1801.

EVANS, Thomas Beverley Jr. (R Del.) Nov. 5, 1931- —; House 1977-83; Co-Chrmn. Rep. Nat. Comm. 1971-73.

EVANS, Walter (nephew of Burwell Clark Ritter) (R Ky.) Sept. 18, 1842-Dec. 30, 1923; House 1895-99.

EVANS, William Elmer (R Calif.) Dec. 14, 1877-Nov. 12, 1959; House 1927-35.

EVARTS, William Maxwell (grandson of Roger Sherman) (R N.Y.) Feb. 6, 1818-Feb. 28, 1901; Senate 1885-91; Atty. Gen. 1868-69; Secy. of State 1877-81.

EVERETT, Edward (father of William Everett) (W Mass.) April 11, 1794-Jan. 15, 1865; House 1825-35; Senate 1853-June 1, 1854; Gov. 1836-40; Secy. of State 1852-53.

EVERETT, Horace (W Vt.) July 17, 1779-Jan. 30, 1851; House 1829-43.

EVERETT, Robert Ashton (D Tenn.) Feb. 24, 1915-Jan. 26, 1969; House Feb. 1, 1958-Jan. 26, 1969.

EVERETT, Robert William (D Ga.) March 3, 1839-Feb. 27, 1915; House 1891-93.

EVERETT, William (son of Edward Everett) (D Mass.) Oct. 10, 1839-Feb. 16, 1910; House April 25, 1893-95.

EVERHART, James Bowen (son of William Everhart) (R Pa.) July 26, 1821-Aug. 23, 1888; House 1883-87.

EVERHART, William (father of James Bowen Everhart) (W Pa.) May 17, 1785-Oct. 30, 1868; House 1853-55.

EVINS, John Hamilton (D S.C.) July 18, 1830-Oct. 20, 1884; House 1877-Oct. 20, 1884.

EVINS, Joseph Landon "Joe" (D Tenn.) Oct. 24, 1910-March 31, 1984; House 1947-77.

EWART, Hamilton Glover (R N.C.) Oct. 23, 1849-April 28, 1918; House 1889-91.

EWING, Andrew (brother of Edwin Hickman Ewing) (D Tenn.) June 17, 1813-June 16, 1864; House 1849-51.

EWING, Edwin Hickman (brother of Andrew Ewing) (W Tenn.) Dec. 2, 1809-April 24, 1902; House 1845-47.

EWING, John (W Ind.) May 19, 1789-April 6, 1858; House 1833-35, 1837-39.

EWING, John Hoge (W Pa.) Oct. 5, 1796-June 9, 1887; House 1845-47.

EWING, Presley Underwood (W Ky.) Sept. 1, 1822-Sept. 27, 1854; House 1851-Sept. 27, 1854.

EWING, Thomas (W Ohio) (father of Thomas Ewing, below) Dec. 28, 1789-Oct. 26, 1871; Senate 1831-37; July 20, 1850-51; Secy. of the Treasury 1841; Secy. of the Interior 1849-50.

EWING, Thomas (son of Thomas Ewing, above) (D Ohio) Aug. 7, 1829-Jan. 21, 1896; House 1877-81.

EWING, William Lee Davidson (JD Ill.) Aug. 31, 1795-March 25, 1846; Senate Dec. 30, 1835-37; Gov. Nov.-Dec. 1834.

EXON, John James (D Neb.) Aug. 9, 1921- —; Senate 1979- —; Gov. 1971-79.

FADDIS, Charles I. (D Pa.) June 13, 1890-April 1, 1972; House 1933-Dec. 4, 1942.

FAIR, James Graham (D Nev.) Dec. 3, 1831-Dec. 28, 1894; Senate 1881-87.

FAIRBANKS, Charles Warren (R Ind.) May 11, 1852-June 4, 1918; Senate 1897-1905; Vice President 1905-09.

FAIRCHILD, Benjamin Lewis (R N.Y.) Jan. 5, 1863-Oct. 25, 1946; House 1895-97, 1917-19, 1921-23, Nov. 6, 1923-27.

FAIRCHILD, George Winthrop (R N.Y.) May 6, 1854-Dec. 31, 1924; House 1907-19.

FAIRFIELD, John (D Maine) Jan. 30, 1797-Dec. 24, 1847; House 1835-Dec. 24, 1838; Senate 1843-Dec. 24, 1847; Gov. 1839-41, 1842-43.

FAIRFIELD, Louis William (R Ind.) Oct. 15, 1858-Feb. 20, 1930; House 1917-25.

FAISON, John Miller (D N.C.) April 17, 1862-April 21, 1915; House 1911-15.

FALCONER, Jacob Alexander (Prog. Wash.) Jan. 26, 1869-July 1, 1928; House 1913-15.

FALL, Albert Bacon (R N.M.) Nov. 26, 1861-Nov. 30, 1944; Senate March 27, 1912-March 4, 1921; Secy. of the Interior 1921-23.

FALLON, George Hyde (D Md.) July 24, 1902-March 21, 1980; House 1945-71.

FANNIN, Paul Jones (R Ariz.) Jan. 29, 1907- —; Senate 1965-77; Gov. 1959-65.

FARAN, James John (D Ohio) Dec. 29, 1808-Dec. 12, 1892; House 1845-49.

FARBSTEIN, Leonard (D N.Y.) Oct. 12, 1902- —; House 1957-71.

FARIS, George Washington (R Ind.) June 9, 1854-April 17, 1914; House 1895-1901.

FARLEE, Isaac Gray (— N.J.) May 18, 1787-Jan. 12, 1855; House 1843-45.

FARLEY, Ephraim Wilder (W Maine) Aug. 29, 1817-April 3, 1880; House 1853-55.

FARLEY, James Indus (D Ind.) Feb. 24, 1871-June 16, 1948; House 1933-39.

FARLEY, James Thompson (D Calif.) Aug. 6, 1829-Jan. 22, 1886; Senate 1879-85.

FARLEY, Michael Francis (D N.Y.) March 1, 1863-Oct. 8, 1921; House 1915-17.

FARLIN, Dudley (D N.Y.) Sept. 2, 1777-Sept. 26, 1837; House 1835-37.

FARNSLEY, Charles Rowland Peaslee (D Ky.) March 28, 1907- —; House 1965-67.

FARNSWORTH, John Franklin (R Ill.) March 27, 1820-July 14, 1897; House 1857-61, 1863-73.

FARNUM, Billie Sunday (D Mich.) April 11, 1916-Nov. 18, 1979; House 1965-67.

FARQUHAR, John Hanson (R Ind.) Dec. 20, 1818-Oct. 1, 1873; House 1865-67.

FARQUHAR, John McCreath (R N.Y.) April 17, 1832-April 24, 1918; House 1885-91.

FARR, Evarts Worcester (R N.H.) Oct. 10, 1840-Nov. 30, 1880; House 1879-Nov. 30, 1880.

FARR, John Richard (R Pa.) July 18, 1857-Dec. 11, 1933; House 1911-19, Feb. 25-March 3, 1921.

FARRELLY, John Wilson (son of Patrick Farrelly) (W Pa.) July 7, 1809-Dec. 20, 1860; House 1847-49.

FARRELLY, Patrick (father of John Wilson Farrelly) (D Pa.) 1770-Jan. 12, 1826; House 1821-Jan. 12, 1826.

FARRINGTON, James (D N.H.) Oct. 1, 1791-Oct. 29, 1859; House 1837-39.

FARRINGTON, Joseph Rider (husband of Mary Elizabeth Pruett Farrington) (R Hawaii) Oct. 15, 1897-June 19, 1954; House (Terr. Del.) 1943-June 19, 1954.

FARRINGTON, Mary Elizabeth Pruett (widow of Joseph Rider Farrington) (R Hawaii) May 30, 1898-July 21, 1984; House (Terr. Del.) July 31, 1954-57.

FARROW, Samuel (WD S.C.) 1759-Nov. 18, 1824; House 1813-15.

FARWELL, Charles Benjamin (R Ill.) July 1, 1823-Sep. 23, 1903; House 1871-May 6, 1876, 1881-83; Senate Jan. 19, 1887-91.

FARWELL, Nathan Allen (cousin of Owen Lovejoy) (R Maine) Feb. 24, 1812-Dec. 9, 1893; Senate Oct. 27, 1864-65.

FARWELL, Sewall Spaulding (R Iowa) April 26, 1834-Sept. 21, 1909; House 1881-83.

FARY, John George (D Ill.) April 11, 1911-June 7, 1984; House July 8, 1975-83.

FASCELL, Dante Bruno (D Fla.) March 9, 1917- —; House 1955- —.

FASSETT, Jacob Sloat (R N.Y.) Nov. 13, 1853-April 21, 1924; House 1905-11.

FAULKNER, Charles James (father of Charles James Faulkner, below) (D W.Va.) July 6, 1806-Nov. 1, 1884; House 1851-59 (Va.), 1875-77.

FAULKNER, Charles James (son of Charles James Faulkner, above) (D W.Va.) Sept. 21, 1847-Jan. 1, 1929; Senate 1887-99.

FAUNTROY, Walter Edward (D D.C.) Feb. 6, 1933- —; House (Delegate) March 23, 1971- —.

FAUST, Charles Lee (R Mo.) April 24, 1879-Dec. 17, 1928; House 1921-Dec. 17, 1928.

FAVROT, George Kent (D La.) Nov. 26, 1868-Dec. 26, 1934; House 1907-09, 1921-25.

FAWELL, Harris Walter (R Ill.) March 25, 1929- —; House 1985- —.

FAY, Francis Ball (W Mass.) June 12, 1793-Oct. 6, 1876; House Dec. 13, 1852-53.

FAY, James Herbert (D N.Y.) April 29, 1899-Sept. 10, 1948; House 1939-41, 1943-45.

FAY, John (D N.Y.) Feb. 10, 1773-June 21, 1855; House 1819-21.

'AZIO, Victor Herbert (D Calif.) Oct. 11, 1942- —; House 1979- —.

'EARING, Paul (F N.W. Terr.) Feb. 28, 1762-Aug. 21, 1822; House (Terr. Del.) 1801-03.

EATHERSTON, Winfield Scott (D Miss.) Aug. 8, 1820-May 28, 1891; House 1847-51.

EATHERSTONE, Lewis Porter (UL Ark.) July 28, 1851-March 14, 1922; House March 5, 1890-91.

EAZEL, William Crosson (D La.) June 10, 1895-March 16, 1965; Senate May 18-Dec. 30, 1948.

EELY, John Joseph (D Ill.) Aug. 1, 1875-Feb. 15, 1905; House 1901-03.

EIGHAN, Edward Farrell (nephew of Michael Aloysius Feighan) (D Ohio) Oct. 22, 1947- —; House 1983- —.

EIGHAN, Michael Aloysius (uncle of Edward Farrell Feighan) (D Ohio) Feb. 16, 1905- —; House 1943-71.

ELCH, Alpheus (D Mich.) Sept. 28, 1804-June 13, 1896; Senate 1847-53; Gov. 1846-47.

ELDER, John Myers (D S.C.) July 7, 1782-Sept. 1, 1851; House 1831-35.

ELLOWS, Frank (R Maine) Nov. 7, 1889-Aug. 27, 1951; House 1941-Aug. 27, 1951.

ELLOWS, John R. (D N.Y.) July 29, 1832-Dec. 7, 1896; House 1891-Dec. 31, 1893.

ELTON, Charles Norton (R Calif.) Jan. 1, 1828-Sept. 13, 1914; House 1885-89; Senate March 19, 1891-93.

ELTON, Rebecca Latimer (widow of William Harrell Felton) (D Ga.) June 10, 1835-Jan. 24, 1930; Senate Nov. 21-Nov. 22, 1922.

ELTON, William Harrell (husband of Rebecca Latimer Felton) (D Ga.) June 1, 1823-Sept. 24, 1909; House 1875-81.

ENERTY, Clare Gerald (R Pa.) July 25, 1895-July 1, 1952; House 1935-37.

ENN, Edward Hart (R Conn.) Sept. 12, 1856-Feb. 23, 1939; House 1921-31.

ENN, Stephen Southmyd (D Idaho) March 28, 1820-April 13, 1892; House (Terr. Del.) June 23, 1876-79.

ENNER, James (DR R.I.) Jan. 22, 1771-April 17, 1846; Senate 1805-Sept. 1807; Gov. 1807-11, 1824-31, 1843-45 (Law & Order).

ENTON, Ivor David (R Pa.) Aug. 3, 1889-Oct. 23, 1986; House 1939-63.

FENTON, Lucien Jerome (R Ohio) May 7, 1844-June 28, 1922; House 1895-99.

FENTON, Reuben Eaton (R N.Y.) July 4, 1819-Aug. 25, 1885; House 1853-55, 1857-Dec. 20, 1864; Senate 1869-75; Gov. 1865-69 (Union Republican).

FENWICK, Millicent Hammond (R N.J.) Feb. 25, 1910- —; House 1975-83.

FERDON, John William (R N.Y.) Dec. 13, 1826-Aug. 5, 1884; House 1879-81.

FERGUSON, Fenner (D Neb.) April 25, 1814-Oct. 11, 1859; House (Terr. Del.) 1857-59.

FERGUSON, Homer (R Mich.) Feb. 25, 1889-Dec. 17, 1982; Senate 1943-55.

FERGUSON, Phillip Colgan (D Okla.) Aug. 15, 1903-Aug. 8, 1978; House 1935-41.

FERGUSSON, Harvey Butler (D N.M.) Sept. 9, 1848-June 10, 1915; House (Terr. Del.) 1897-99, (Rep.) Jan. 8, 1912-15.

FERNALD, Bert Manfred (R Maine) April 3, 1859-Aug. 23, 1926; Senate Sept. 12, 1916-Aug. 23, 1926; Gov. 1909-11.

FERNANDEZ, Antonio Manuel (D N.M.) Jan. 17, 1902-Nov. 7, 1956; House 1943-Nov. 7, 1956.

FERNANDEZ, Joachim Octave (D La.) Aug. 14, 1896-Aug. 8, 1978; House 1931-41.

FERNOS-ISERN, Antonio (PD P.R.) May 10, 1895-Jan. 19, 1974; House (Res. Comm.) Sept. 11, 1946-65.

FERRARO, Geraldine Anne (D N.Y.) Aug. 26, 1935- —; House 1979-85.

FERRELL, Thomas Merrill (D N.J.) June 20, 1844-Oct. 20, 1916; House 1883-85.

FERRIS, Charles Goadsby (JD N.Y.) about 1796-June 4, 1848; House Dec. 1, 1834-35, 1841-43.

FERRIS, Scott (D Okla.) Nov. 3, 1877-June 8, 1945; House Nov. 16, 1907-21.

FERRIS, Woodbridge Nathan (D Mich.) Jan. 6, 1853-March 23, 1928; Senate 1923-March 23, 1928; Gov. 1913-17.

FERRISS, Orange (R N.Y.) Nov. 26, 1814-April 11, 1894; House 1867-71.

FERRY, Orris Sanford (IR/D Conn.) Aug. 15, 1823-Nov. 21, 1875; House 1859-61 (Republican); Senate 1867-Nov. 21, 1875 (1867-74 Republican).

FERRY, Thomas White (R Mich.) June 10, 1827-Oct. 13, 1896; House 1865-71; Senate 1871-83; Pres. pro tempore 1875, 1877-79.

FESS, Simeon Davison (R Ohio) Dec. 11, 1861-Dec. 23, 1936; House 1913-23; Senate 1923-35; Chrmn. Rep. Nat. Comm. 1930-32.

FESSENDEN, Samuel Clement (brother of Thomas Amory Deblois Fessenden and William Pitt Fessenden) (R Maine) March 7, 1815-April 18, 1882; House 1861-63.

FESSENDEN, Thomas Amory Deblois (brother of Samuel Clement Fessenden and William Pitt Fessenden) (R Maine) Jan. 23, 1826-Sept. 28, 1868; House Dec. 1, 1862-63.

FESSENDEN, William Pitt (brother of Samuel Clement Fessenden and Thomas Amory Deblois Fessenden) (W Maine) Oct. 16, 1806-Sept. 9, 1869; House 1841-43; Senate Feb. 10, 1854-July 1, 1864, 1865-Sept. 9, 1869; Secy. of the Treasury 1864-65.

FEW, William (D Ga.) June 8, 1748-July 16, 1828; Senate 1789-93; Cont. Cong. 1780-88.

FICKLIN, Orlando Bell (D Ill.) Dec. 16, 1808-May 5, 1886; House 1843-49, 1851-53.

FIEDLER, Bobbi (R Calif.) April 22, 1937- — ; House 1981-87.

FIEDLER, William Henry Frederick (D N.J.) Aug. 25, 1847-Jan. 1, 1919; House 1883-85.

FIELD, David Dudley (D N.Y.) Feb. 13, 1805-April 13, 1894; House Jan. 11-March 3, 1877.

FIELD, Moses Whelock (R Mich.) Feb. 10, 1828-March 14, 1889; House 1873-75.

FIELD, Richard Stockton (R N.J.) Dec. 31, 1803-May 25, 1870; Senate Nov. 21, 1862-Jan. 14, 1863.

FIELD, Scott (D Texas) Jan. 26, 1847-Dec. 20, 1931; House 1903-07.

FIELD, Walbridge Abner (R Mass.) April 26, 1833-July 15, 1899; House 1877-March 28, 1878, 1879-81.

FIELDER, George Bragg (D N.J.) July 24, 1842-Aug. 14, 1906; House 1893-95.

FIELDS, Jack (R Texas) Feb. 3, 1952- — ; House 1981- —.

FIELDS, William Craig (R N.Y.) Feb. 13, 1804-Oct. 27, 1882; House 1867-69.

FIELDS, William Jason (D Ky.) Dec. 29, 1874-Oct. 21, 1954; House 1911-Dec. 11, 1923; Gov. 1923-27.

FIESINGER, William Louis (D Ohio) Oct. 25, 1877-Sept. 11, 1953; House 1931-37.

FILLMORE, Millard (W N.Y.) Jan. 7, 1800-March 8, 1874; House 1833-35, 1837-43; Vice President 1849-July 9, 1850; President July 10, 1850-53.

FINCH, Isaac (D N.Y.) Oct. 13, 1783-June 23, 1845; House 1829-31.

FINCK, William Edward (D Ohio) Sept. 1, 1822-Jan. 25, 1901; House 1863-67, Dec. 7, 1874-75.

FINDLAY, James (brother of John Findlay and William Findlay) (JD Ohio) Oct. 12, 1770-Dec. 28, 1835; House 1825-33.

FINDLAY, John (brother of James Findlay and William Findlay) (D Pa.) March 31, 1766-Nov. 5, 1838; House Oct. 9, 1821-27.

FINDLAY, John Van Lear (D Md.) Dec. 21, 1839-April 19, 1907; House 1883-87.

FINDLAY, William (brother of James Findlay and John Findlay) (D Pa.) June 20, 1768-Nov. 12, 1846; Senate Dec. 10, 1821-27; Gov. 1817-20 (Democratic Republican).

FINDLEY, Paul (R Ill.) June 23, 1921- — ; House 1961-83.

FINDLEY, William (D Pa.) 1741 or 1742-April 4, 1821; House 1791-99, 1803-17.

FINE, John (D N.Y.) Aug. 26, 1794-Jan. 4, 1867; House 1839-41.

FINE, Sidney Asher (D N.Y.) Sept. 14, 1903-April 15, 1982; House 1951-Jan. 2, 1956.

FINERTY, John Frederick (ID Ill.) Sept. 10, 1846-June 10, 1908; House 1883-85.

FINKELNBURG, Gustavus Adolphus (LR Mo.) April 6, 1837-May 18, 1908; House 1869-71 (Republican), 1871-73.

FINLEY, Charles (son of Hugh Franklin Finley) (R Ky.) March 26, 1865-March 18, 1941; House Feb. 15, 1930-33.

FINLEY, David Edward (D S.C.) Feb. 28, 1861-Jan. 26, 1917; House 1899-Jan. 26, 1917.

FINLEY, Ebenezer Byron (nephew of Stephen Ross Harris) (D Ohio) July 31, 1833-Aug. 22, 1916; House 1877-81.

FINLEY, Hugh Franklin (father of Charles Finley) (R Ky.) Jan. 18, 1833-Oct. 16, 1909; House 1887-91.

FINLEY, Jesse Johnson (D Fla.) Nov. 18, 1812-Nov. 6, 1904; House April 19, 1876-77, Feb. 20-March 3, 1879, 1881-June 1, 1882.

FINNEGAN, Edward Rowan (D Ill.) June 5, 1905-Feb. 2, 1971; House 1961-Dec. 6, 1964.

FINNEY, Darwin Abel (R Pa.) Aug. 11, 1814-Aug. 25, 1868; House 1867-Aug. 25, 1868.

FINO, Paul Albert (R N.Y.) Dec. 15, 1913- —; House 1953-Dec. 31, 1968.

FISCHER, Israel Frederick (R N.Y.) Aug. 17, 1858- March 16, 1940; House 1895-99.

FISH, Hamilton (father of Hamilton Fish, below, grand- father of Hamilton Fish Jr. born in 1888, great- grandfather of Hamilton Fish Jr. born in 1926) (W N.Y.) Aug. 3, 1808-Sept. 7, 1893; House 1843-45; Senate 1851-57; Gov. 1849-51; Secy. of State 1869- 77.

FISH, Hamilton (son of Hamilton Fish, above, father of Hamilton Fish Jr. born in 1888, grandfather of Ham- ilton Fish Jr. born in 1926) (R N.Y.) April 17, 1849- Jan. 15, 1936; House 1909-11.

FISH, Hamilton Jr. (son of Hamilton Fish born in 1849, father of Hamilton Fish Jr., below, grandson of Hamilton Fish born in 1808) (R N.Y.) Dec. 7, 1888- —; House Nov. 2, 1920-45.

FISH, Hamilton Jr. (son of Hamilton Fish Jr., above, grandson of Hamilton Fish born in 1849, great- grandson of Hamilton Fish born in 1808) (R N.Y.) June 3, 1926- —; House 1969- —.

FISHBURNE, John Wood (cousin of Fontaine Maury Maverick) (D Va.) March 8, 1868-June 24, 1937; House 1931-33.

FISHER, Charles (D N.C.) Oct. 20, 1789-May 7, 1849; House Feb. 11, 1819-21, 1839-41.

FISHER, David (W Ohio) Dec. 3, 1794-May 7, 1886; House 1847-49.

FISHER, George (— N.Y.) March 17, 1788-March 26, 1861; House 1829-Feb. 5, 1830.

FISHER, George Purnell (UR Del.) Oct. 13, 1817-Feb. 10, 1899; House 1861-63.

FISHER, Horatio Gates (R Pa.) April 21, 1838-May 8, 1890; House 1879-83.

FISHER, Hubert Frederick (D Tenn.) Oct. 6, 1877-June 16, 1941; House 1917-31.

FISHER, John (R N.Y.) March 13, 1806-March 28, 1882; House 1869-71.

FISHER, Joseph Lyman (D Va.) Jan. 11, 1914- —; House 1975-81.

FISHER, Ovie Clark (D Texas) Nov. 22, 1903- —; House 1943-75.

FISHER, Spencer Olive (D Mich.) Feb. 3, 1843-June 1, 1919; House 1885-89.

FISK, James (D Vt.) Oct. 4, 1763-Nov. 17, 1844; House 1805-09, 1811-15; Senate Nov. 4, 1817-Jan. 8, 1818.

FISK, Jonathan (D N.Y.) Sept. 26, 1778-July 13, 1832; House 1809-11, 1813-March 1815.

FITCH, Asa (F N.Y.) Nov. 10, 1765-Aug. 24, 1843; House 1811-13.

FITCH, Ashbel Parmelee (D N.Y.) Oct. 8, 1838-May 4, 1904; House 1887-Dec. 26, 1893 (1887-89 Republi- can).

FITCH, Graham Newell (grandfather of Edwin Denby) (D Ind.) Dec. 5, 1809-Nov. 29, 1892; House 1849-53; Senate Feb. 4, 1857-61.

FITCH, Thomas (R Nev.) Jan. 27, 1838-Nov. 12, 1923; House 1869-71.

FITE, Samuel McClary (D Tenn.) June 12, 1816-Oct. 23, 1875; House March 4-Oct. 23, 1875.

FITHIAN, Floyd James (D Ind.) Nov. 3, 1928- —; House 1975-83.

FITHIAN, George Washington (D Ill.) July 4, 1854-Jan. 21, 1921; House 1889-95.

FITZGERALD, Frank Thomas (D N.Y.) May 4, 1857- Nov. 25, 1907; House March 4-Nov. 4, 1889.

FITZGERALD, John Francis (grandfather of John F. Kennedy, Robert F. Kennedy and Edward M. Ken- nedy, great-grandfather of Joseph Patrick Kennedy II) (D Mass.) Feb. 11, 1863-Oct. 2, 1950; House 1895- 1901, March 4-Oct. 23, 1919.

FITZGERALD, John Joseph (D N.Y.) March 10, 1872- May 13, 1952; House 1899-Dec. 31, 1917.

FITZGERALD, Roy Gerald (R Ohio) Aug. 25, 1875- Nov. 16, 1962; House 1921-31.

FITZGERALD, Thomas (D Mich.) April 10, 1796- March 25, 1855; Senate June 8, 1848-49.

FITZGERALD, William (JD Tenn.) Aug. 6, 1799-March 1864; House 1831-33.

FITZGERALD, William Joseph (D Conn.) March 2, 1887-May 6, 1947; House 1937-39, 1941-43.

FITZGERALD, William Thomas (R Ohio) Oct. 13, 1858-Jan. 12, 1939; House 1925-29.

FITZGIBBONS, John (D N.Y.) July 10, 1868-Aug. 4, 1941; House 1933-35.

FITZHENRY, Louis (D Ill.) June 13, 1870-Nov. 18, 1935; House 1913-15.

FITZPATRICK, Benjamin (SRD Ala.) June 30, 1802- Nov. 21, 1869; Senate Nov. 25, 1848-Nov. 30, 1849, Jan. 14, 1853-55, Nov. 26, 1855-Jan. 21, 1861; Pres. pro tempore 1857-60; Gov. 1841-45 (Democrat).

FITZPATRICK, James Martin (D N.Y.) June 27, 1869-April 10, 1949; House 1927-45.

FITZPATRICK, Morgan Cassius (D Tenn.) Oct. 29, 1868-June 25, 1908; House 1903-05.

FITZPATRICK, Thomas Young (D Ky.) Sept. 20, 1850-Jan. 21, 1906; House 1897-1901.

FITZSIMONS, Thomas (F Pa.) 1741-Aug. 26, 1811; House 1789-95; Cont. Cong. 1782-83.

FJARE, Orvin Benonie (R Mont.) April 16, 1918--; House 1955-57.

FLACK, William Henry (R N.Y.) March 22, 1861-Feb. 2, 1907; House 1903-Feb. 2, 1907.

FLAGLER, Thomas Thorn (W N.Y.) Oct. 12, 1811-Sept. 6, 1897; House 1853-57.

FLAHERTY, Lawrence James (R Calif.) July 4, 1878-June 13, 1926; House 1925-June 13, 1926.

FLAHERTY, Thomas Aloysius (D Mass.) Dec. 21, 1898-April 27, 1965; House Dec. 14, 1937-43.

FLAKE, Floyd Harold (D N.Y.) Jan. 30, 1945--; House 1987-- .

FLANAGAN, De Witt Clinton (D N.J.) Dec. 28, 1870-Jan. 15, 1946; House June 18, 1902-03.

FLANAGAN, James Winright (R Texas) Sept. 5, 1805-Sept. 28, 1887; Senate March 30, 1870-75.

FLANDERS, Alvan (R Wash.) Aug. 2, 1825-March 14, 1884; House (Terr. Del.) 1867-69; Gov. (Wash. Terr.) 1869-70.

FLANDERS, Benjamin Franklin (U La.) Jan. 26, 1816-March 13, 1896; House Dec. 3, 1862-63; Military Gov. 1867-68.

FLANDERS, Ralph Edward (R Vt.) Sept. 28, 1880-Feb. 19, 1970; Senate Nov. 1, 1946-59.

FLANNAGAN, John William Jr. (D Va.) Feb. 20, 1885-April 27, 1955; House 1931-49.

FLANNERY, John Harold (D Pa.) April 19, 1898-June 3, 1961; House 1937-42.

FLEEGER, George Washington (R Pa.) March 13, 1839-June 25, 1894; House 1885-87.

FLEETWOOD, Frederick Gleed (R Vt.) Sept. 27, 1868-Jan. 28, 1938; House 1923-25.

FLEGER, Anthony Alfred (D Ohio) Oct. 21, 1900-July 16, 1963; House 1937-39.

FLEMING, William Bennett (D Ga.) Oct. 29, 1803-Aug. 19, 1886; House Feb. 10-March 3, 1879.

FLEMING, William Henry (D Ga.) Oct. 18, 1856-June 9, 1944; House 1897-1903.

FLETCHER, Charles Kimball (R Calif.) Dec. 15, 1902-Sept. 29, 1985; House 1947-49.

FLETCHER, Duncan Upshaw (D Fla.) Jan. 6, 1859-June 17, 1936; Senate 1909-June 17, 1936.

FLETCHER, Isaac (AMas. D Vt.) Nov. 22, 1784-Oct. 19 1842; House 1837-41.

FLETCHER, Loren (R Minn.) April 10, 1833-April 15 1919; House 1893-1903, 1905-07.

FLETCHER, Richard (W Mass.) Jan. 8, 1788-June 21 1869; House 1837-39.

FLETCHER, Thomas (- Ky.) Oct. 21, 1779-?; House Dec. 2, 1816-17.

FLETCHER, Thomas Brooks (D Ohio) Oct. 10, 1879-July 1, 1945; House 1925-29, 1933-39.

FLICK, James Patton (R Iowa) Aug. 28, 1845-Feb. 25 1929; House 1889-93.

FLINT, Frank Putnam (R Calif.) July 15, 1862-Feb. 11 1929; Senate 1905-11.

FLIPPO, Ronnie G. (D Ala.) Aug. 15, 1937--; House 1977-- .

FLOOD, Daniel John (D Pa.) Nov. 26, 1903--; House 1945-47, 1949-53, 1955-Jan. 31, 1980.

FLOOD, Henry De La Warr (half brother of Joel West Flood, uncle of Harry Flood Byrd) (D Va.) Sept. 2 1865-Dec. 8, 1921; House 1901-Dec. 8, 1921.

FLOOD, Joel West (half brother of Henry De La War Flood, uncle of Harry Flood Byrd) (D Va.) Aug. 2 1894-April 27, 1964; House Nov. 8, 1932-33.

FLOOD, Thomas Schmeck (R N.Y.) April 12, 1844-Oc 28, 1908; House 1887-91.

FLORENCE, Elias (W Ohio) Feb. 15, 1797-Nov. 2 1880; House 1843-45.

FLORENCE, Thomas Birch (D Pa.) Jan. 26, 1812-Jul 3, 1875; House 1851-61.

FLORIO, James Joseph (D N.J.) Aug. 29, 1937--House 1975-- .

FLOURNOY, Thomas Stanhope (W Va.) Dec. 15, 181 March 12, 1883; House 1847-49.

FLOWER, Roswell Pettibone (D N.Y.) Aug. 7, 183 May 12, 1899; House Nov. 8, 1881-83, 1889-Sept. 1 1891; Gov. 1892-95.

FLOWERS, Walter (D Ala.) April 12, 1933-April 1 1984; House 1969-79.

OYD, Charles Albert (D N.Y.) 1791-Feb. 20, 1873; House 1841-43.

OYD, John (− Ga.) Oct. 3, 1769-June 24, 1839; House 1827-29.

OYD, John (D Va.) April 24, 1783-Aug. 17, 1837; House 1817-29; Gov. 1830-34.

OYD, John Charles (D Ark.) April 14, 1858-Nov. 4, 1930; House 1905-15.

OYD, John Gelston (D N.Y.) Feb. 5, 1806-Oct. 5, 1881; House 1839-43, 1851-53.

OYD, William (− N.Y.) Dec. 17, 1734-Aug. 4, 1821; House 1789-91; Cont. Cong. 1774-77, 1778-83.

YE, Edwin (R Maine) March 4, 1817-July 12, 1886; House Dec. 4, 1876-77.

YNN, Dennis Thomas (R Okla.) Feb. 13, 1861-June 19, 1939; House (Terr. Del.) 1893-97, 1899-1903.

YNN, Gerald Thomas (D Wis.) Oct. 7, 1910-−; House 1959-61.

YNN, Joseph Vincent (D N.Y.) Sept. 2, 1883-Feb. 6, 1940; House 1915-19.

YNT, John James Jr. (D Ga.) Nov. 8, 1914-−; House Nov. 2, 1954-79.

CHT, Benjamin Kurtz (R Pa.) March 12, 1863-March 27, 1937; House 1907-13, 1915-23, 1933-March 27, 1937.

ELKER, Otto Godfrey (R N.Y.) Dec. 29, 1875-Jan. 18, 1943; House Nov. 3, 1908-11.

ERDERER, Robert Herman (R Pa.) May 16, 1860-July 26, 1903; House 1901-July 26, 1903.

GARTY, John Edward (D R.I.) March 23, 1913-Jan. 10, 1967; House 1941-Dec. 7, 1944; 1945-Jan. 10, 1967.

GG, George Gilman (R N.H.) May 26, 1813-Oct. 5, 1881; Senate Aug. 31, 1866-67.

GLIETTA, Thomas M. (I Pa.) Dec. 3, 1928-−; House 1981-−.

LEY, James Bradford (D Ind.) Oct. 18, 1807-Dec. 5, 1886; House 1857-59.

LEY, John Robert (D Md.) Oct. 16, 1917-−; House 1959-61.

LEY, Thomas Stephen (D Wash.) March 6, 1929-−; House 1965-−.

LGER, Alonzo Dillard (brother of John Hamlin Folger) (D N.C.) July 9, 1888-April 30, 1941; House 1939-April 30, 1941.

FOLGER, John Hamlin (brother of Alonzo Dillard Folger) (D N.C.) Dec. 18, 1880-July 19, 1963; House June 14, 1941-49.

FOLGER, Walter Jr. (D Mass.) June 12, 1765-Sept. 8, 1849; House 1817-21.

FOLLETT, John Fassett (D Ohio) Feb. 18, 1831-April 15, 1902; House 1883-85.

FONG, Hiram Leong (R Hawaii) Oct. 1, 1907-−; Senate Aug. 21, 1959-77.

FOOT, Solomon (R Vt.) Nov. 19, 1802-March 28, 1866; House 1843-47 (Whig); Senate 1851-March 28, 1866 (1851-57 Whig); Pres. pro tempore 1861-64.

FOOTE, Charles Augustus (D N.Y.) April 15, 1785-Aug. 1, 1828; House 1823-25.

FOOTE, Ellsworth Bishop (R Conn.) Jan. 12, 1898-Jan. 18, 1977; House 1947-49.

FOOTE, Henry Stuart (U Miss.) Feb. 28, 1804-May 19, 1880; Senate 1847-Jan. 8, 1852; Gov. 1852-54.

FOOTE, Samuel Augustus (W Conn.) Nov. 8, 1780-Sept. 15, 1846; House 1819-21, 1823-25, 1833-May 9, 1834; Senate 1827-33; Gov. 1834-35.

FOOTE, Wallace Turner Jr. (R N.Y.) April 7, 1864-Dec. 17, 1910; House 1895-99.

FORAKER, Joseph Benson (R Ohio) July 5, 1846-May 10, 1917; Senate 1897-1909; Gov. 1886-90.

FORAN, Martin Ambrose (D Ohio) Nov. 11, 1844-June 28, 1921; House 1883-89.

FORAND, Aime Joseph (D R.I.) May 23, 1895-Jan. 18, 1972; House 1937-39, 1941-61.

FORD, Aaron Lane (D Miss.) Dec. 21, 1903-July 8, 1983; House 1935-43.

FORD, George (D Ind.) Jan. 11, 1846-Aug. 30, 1917; House 1885-87.

FORD, Gerald Rudolph Jr. (R Mich.) July 14, 1913-−; House 1949-Dec. 6, 1973; Vice President Dec. 6, 1973-Aug. 9, 1974; President Aug. 9, 1974-77.

FORD, Harold Eugene (D Tenn.) May 20, 1945-−; House 1975-−.

FORD, James (JD Pa.) May 4, 1783-Aug. 18, 1859; House 1829-33.

FORD, Leland Merritt (R Calif.) March 8, 1893-Nov. 27, 1965; House 1939-43.

FORD, Melbourne Haddock (D Mich.) June 30, 1849-April 20, 1891; House 1887-89; March 4-April 20, 1891.

'OSTER, Israel Moore (R Ohio) Jan. 12, 1873-June 10, 1950; House 1919-25.

'OSTER, John Hopkins (R Ind.) Jan. 31, 1862-Sept. 5, 1917; House May 16, 1905-09.

'OSTER, Lafayette Sabine (R Conn.) Nov. 22, 1806-Sept. 19, 1880; Senate 1855-67; Pres. pro tempore 1865-67.

'OSTER, Martin David (D Ill.) Sept. 3, 1861-Oct. 20, 1919; House 1907-19.

'OSTER, Murphy James (cousin of Jared Young Sanders) (D La.) Jan. 12, 1849-June 12, 1921; Senate 1901-13; Gov. 1892-1900 (Anti Lottery Democrat).

'OSTER, Nathaniel Greene (D Ga.) Aug. 25, 1809-Oct. 19, 1869; House 1855-57 (elected as AP candidate).

'OSTER, Stephen Clark (R Maine) Dec. 24, 1799-Oct. 5, 1872; House 1857-61.

'OSTER, Theodore (brother of Dwight Foster) (L&O R.I.) April 29, 1752-Jan. 13, 1828; Senate June 7, 1790-1803.

'OSTER, Thomas Flournoy (D Ga.) Nov. 23, 1790-Sept. 14, 1848; House 1829-35, 1841-43.

'OSTER, Wilder De Ayr (R Mich.) Jan. 8, 1819-Sept. 20, 1873; House Dec. 4, 1871-Sept. 20, 1873.

'UKE, Philip Bond (D Ill.) Jan. 23, 1818-Oct. 3, 1876; House 1859-63.

'ULKES, George Ernest (D Mich.) Dec. 25, 1878-Dec. 13, 1960; House 1933-35.

'ULKROD, William Walker (R Pa.) Nov. 22, 1846-Nov. 13, 1910; House 1907-Nov. 13, 1910.

'UNTAIN, Lawrence H. (D N.C.) April 23, 1913- —; House 1953-83.

'WLER, Charles Newell (R N.J.) Nov. 2, 1852-May 27, 1932; House 1895-1911.

'WLER, Hiram Robert (D Ill.) Feb. 7, 1851-Jan. 5, 1926; House 1911-15.

'WLER, John (— Ky.) 1755-Aug. 22, 1840; House 1797-1807.

'WLER, John Edgar (P N.C.) Sept. 8, 1866-July 4, 1930; House 1897-99.

'WLER, Joseph Smith (UR Tenn.) Aug. 31, 1820-April 1, 1902; Senate July 24, 1866-71.

'WLER, Orin (FSW Mass.) July 19, 1791-Sept. 3, 1852; House 1849-Sept. 3, 1852.

FOWLER, Samuel (grandfather of Samuel Fowler, below) (JD N.J.) Oct. 30, 1779-Feb. 20, 1844; House 1833-37.

FOWLER, Samuel (grandson of Samuel Fowler, above) (D N.J.) March 22, 1851-March 17, 1919; House 1889-93.

FOWLER, William Wyche Jr. (D Ga.) Oct. 6, 1940- —; House April 6, 1977-87; Senate 1987- —.

FOX, Andrew Fuller (D Miss.) April 26, 1849-Aug. 29, 1926; House 1897-1903.

FOX, John (D N.Y.) June 30, 1835-Jan. 17, 1914; House 1867-71.

FRANCE, Joseph Irvin (R Md.) Oct. 11, 1873-Jan. 26, 1939; Senate 1917-23.

FRANCHOT, Richard (R N.Y.) June 2, 1816-Nov. 23, 1875; House 1861-63.

FRANCIS, George Blinn (R N.Y.) Aug. 12, 1883-May 20, 1967; House 1917-19.

FRANCIS, John Brown (grandson of John Brown of R.I.) (L&O R.I.) May 31, 1791-Aug. 9, 1864; Senate Jan. 25, 1844-45; Gov. 1833-38 (Democrat).

FRANCIS, William Bates (D Ohio) Oct. 25, 1860-Dec. 5, 1954; House 1911-15.

FRANK, Augustus (nephew of William Patterson of N.Y.) (R N.Y.) July 17, 1826-April 29, 1895; House 1859-65.

FRANK, Barney (D Mass.) March 31, 1940- —; House 1981- —.

FRANK, Nathan (R/UL Mo.) Feb. 23, 1852-April 5, 1931; House 1889-91.

FRANKHAUSER, William Horace (R Mich.) March 5, 1863-May 9, 1921; House March 4-May 9, 1921.

FRANKLIN, Benjamin Joseph (D Mo.) March 1839-May 18, 1898; House 1875-79; Gov. (Ariz. Terr.) 1896-97.

FRANKLIN, Jesse (brother of Meshack Franklin) (D N.C.) March 24, 1760-Aug. 31, 1823; House 1795-97; Senate 1799-1805, 1807-13; Pres. pro tempore 1804-05; Gov. 1820-21 (Democratic Republican).

FRANKLIN, John Rankin (W Md.) May 6, 1820-Jan. 11, 1878; House 1853-55.

FRANKLIN, Meshack (brother of Jesse Franklin) (D N.C.) 1772-Dec. 18, 1839; House 1807-15.

FRANKLIN, William Webster (R Miss.) Dec. 13, 1941- —; House 1983-87.

FRASER, Donald MacKay (D Minn.) Feb. 20, 1924- — ; House 1963-79.

FRAZIER, James Beriah (father of James Beriah Frazier Jr.) (D Tenn.) Oct. 18, 1856-March 28, 1937; Senate March 21, 1905-11; Gov. 1903-05.

FRAZIER, James Beriah Jr. (son of James Beriah Frazier) (D Tenn.) June 23, 1890-Oct. 30, 1978; House 1949-63.

FRAZIER, Lynn Joseph (R N.D.) Dec. 21, 1874-Jan. 11, 1947; Senate 1923-41; Gov. 1917-21.

FREAR, James Archibald (R Wis.) Oct. 24, 1861-May 28, 1939; House 1913-35.

FREAR, Joseph Allen Jr. (D Del.) March 7, 1903- — ; Senate 1949-61.

FREDERICK, Benjamin Todd (D Iowa) Oct. 5, 1834-Nov. 3, 1903; House March 3, 1885-87.

FREDERICKS, John Donnan (R Calif.) Sept. 10, 1869-Aug. 26, 1945; House May 1, 1923-27.

FREE, Arthur Monroe (R Calif.) Jan. 15, 1879-April 1, 1953; House 1921-33.

FREEDLEY, John (W Pa.) May 22, 1793-Dec. 8, 1851; House 1847-51.

FREEMAN, Chapman (R Pa.) Oct. 8, 1832-March 22, 1904; House 1875-79.

FREEMAN, James Crawford (R Ga.) April 1, 1820-Sept. 3, 1885; House 1873-75.

FREEMAN, John D. (U Miss.) ?-Jan. 17, 1886; House 1851-53.

FREEMAN, Jonathan (uncle of Nathaniel Freeman Jr.) (F N.H.) March 21, 1745-Aug. 20, 1808; House 1797-1801.

FREEMAN, Nathaniel Jr. (nephew of Jonathan Freeman) (— Mass.) May 1, 1766-Aug. 22, 1800; House 1795-99.

FREEMAN, Richard Patrick (R Conn.) April 24, 1869-July 8, 1944; House 1915-33.

FREER, Romeo Hoyt (R W.Va.) Nov. 9, 1846-May 9, 1913; House 1899-1901.

FRELINGHUYSEN, Frederick (father of Theodore Frelinghuysen, great-great-great-grandfather of Peter Hood Ballantine Frelinghuysen Jr.) (F N.J.) April 13, 1753-April 13, 1804; Senate 1793-Nov. 12, 1796; Cont. Cong. 1778-79, 1782-83.

FRELINGHUYSEN, Frederick Theodore (nephew and adopted son of Theodore Frelinghuysen, uncle o Joseph Sherman Frelinghuysen, great-grandfathe of Peter Hood Ballantine Frelinghuysen Jr.) (R N.J. Aug. 4, 1817-May 20, 1885; Senate Nov. 12, 1866-69 1871-77; Secy. of State 1881-85.

FRELINGHUYSEN, Joseph Sherman (nephew o Frederick Theodore Frelinghuysen, cousin of Pete Hood Ballantine Frelinghuysen Jr.) (R N.J.) Marc 12, 1869-Feb. 8, 1948; Senate 1917-23.

FRELINGHUYSEN, Peter Hood Ballantine Jr. (cousi of Joseph Sherman Frelinghuysen, great-grandson Frederick Theodore Frelinghuysen, great-grea grandnephew of Theodore Frelinghuysen, grea great-great-grandson of Frederick Frelinghuysen) (N.J.) Jan. 17, 1916- — ; House 1953-75.

FRELINGHUYSEN, Theodore (son of Frederick Fr linghuysen, great-great-granduncle of Peter Hoc Ballantine Frelinghuysen Jr.) (Ad.D N.J.) March 2 1787-April 12, 1862; Senate 1829-35.

FREMONT, John Charles (FSD Calif.) Jan. 21, 181 July 13, 1890; Senate Sept. 9, 1850-51; Gov. (Ari Terr.) 1878-81.

FRENCH, Burton Lee (R Idaho) Aug. 1, 1875-Sept. 1 1954; House 1903-09, 1911-15, 1917-33.

FRENCH, Carlos (D Conn.) Aug. 6, 1835-April 14, 190 House 1887-89.

FRENCH, Ezra Bartlett (R Maine) Sept. 23, 1810-Apr 24, 1880; House 1859-61.

FRENCH, John Robert (R N.C.) May 28, 1819-Oct. 1890; House July 6, 1868-69.

FRENCH, Richard (D Ky.) June 20, 1792-May 1, 185 House 1835-37, 1843-45, 1847-49.

FRENZEL, William E. (R Minn.) July 31, 1928- — House 1971- — .

FREY, Louis Jr. (R Fla.) Jan. 11, 1934- — ; House 196 79.

FREY, Oliver Walter (D Pa.) Sept. 7, 1887-Aug. ? 1939; House Nov. 7, 1933-39.

FRICK, Henry (W Pa.) March 17, 1795-March 1, 18 House 1843-March 1, 1844.

FRIEDEL, Samuel Nathaniel (D Md.) April 18, 18 March 21, 1979; House 1953-71.

FRIES, Frank William (D Ill.) May 1, 1893- — ; Hou 1937-41.

FRIES, George (D Ohio) 1799-Nov. 13, 1866; Hou 1845-49.

FROEHLICH, Harold Vernon (R Wis.) May 12, 1932- —; House 1973-75.

FROMENTIN, Eligius (— La.) ?-Oct. 6, 1822; Senate 1813-19.

FROST, Joel (— N.Y.) ?-?; House 1823-25.

FROST, Jonas Martin III (D Texas) Jan. 1, 1942- —; House 1979- —.

FROST, Richard Graham (D Mo.) Dec. 29, 1851-Feb. 1, 1900; House 1879-March 2, 1883.

FROST, Rufus Smith (R Mass.) July 18, 1826-March 6, 1894; House 1875-July 28, 1876.

FROTHINGHAM, Louis Adams (R Mass.) July 13, 1871-Aug. 23, 1928; House 1921-Aug. 23, 1928.

FRY, Jacob Jr. (D Pa.) June 10, 1802-Nov. 28, 1866; House 1835-39.

FRY, Joseph Jr. (D Pa.) Aug. 4, 1781-Aug. 15, 1860; House 1827-31.

FRYE, William Pierce (grandfather of Wallace Humphrey White Jr.) (R Maine) Sept. 2, 1830-Aug. 8, 1911; House 1871-March 17, 1881; Senate March 18, 1881-Aug. 8, 1911; Pres. pro tempore 1896-1911.

FUGATE, Thomas Bacon (D Va.) April 10, 1899-Sept. 22, 1980; House 1949-53.

FULBRIGHT, James Franklin (D Mo.) Jan. 24, 1877-April 5, 1948; House 1923-25, 1927-29, 1931-33.

FULBRIGHT, James William (D Ark.) April 9, 1905- —; House 1943-45; Senate 1945-Dec. 31, 1974.

FULKERSON, Abram (D Va.) May 13, 1834-Dec. 17, 1902; House 1881-83 (elected as a Readjuster).

FULKERSON, Frank Ballard (R Mo.) March 5, 1866-Aug. 30, 1936; House 1905-07.

FULLER, Alvan Tufts (R Mass.) Feb. 27, 1878-April 30, 1958; House 1917-Jan. 5, 1921; Gov. 1925-29.

FULLER, Benoni Stinson (D Ind.) Nov. 13, 1825-April 14, 1903; House 1875-79.

FULLER, Charles Eugene (R Ill.) March 31, 1849-June 25, 1926; House 1903-13, 1915-June 25, 1926.

FULLER, Claude Albert (D Ark.) Jan. 20, 1876-Jan. 8, 1968; House 1929-39.

FULLER, George (D Pa.) Nov. 7, 1802-Nov. 24, 1888; House Dec. 2, 1844-45.

FULLER, Hawden Carlton (R N.Y.) Aug. 28, 1895- —; House Nov. 2, 1943-49.

FULLER, Henry Mills (W Pa.) Jan. 3, 1820-Dec. 26, 1860; House 1851-53, 1855-57.

FULLER, Philo Case (W N.Y.) Aug. 14, 1787-Aug. 16, 1855; House 1833-Sept. 2, 1836.

FULLER, Thomas James Duncan (D Maine) March 17, 1808-Feb. 13, 1876; House 1849-57.

FULLER, Timothy (D Mass.) July 11, 1778-Oct. 1, 1835; House 1817-25.

FULLER, William Elijah (R Iowa) March 30, 1846-April 23, 1918; House 1885-89.

FULLER, William Kendall (D N.Y.) Nov. 24, 1792-Nov. 11, 1883; House 1833-37.

FULLERTON, David (uncle of David Fullerton Robison) (— Pa.) Oct. 4, 1772-Feb. 1, 1843; House 1819-May 15, 1820.

FULMER, Hampton Pitts (husband of Willa Lybrand Fulmer) (D S.C.) June 23, 1875-Oct. 19, 1944; House 1921-Oct. 19, 1944.

FULMER, Willa Lybrand (widow of Hampton Pitts Fulmer) (D S.C.) Feb. 3, 1884-May 13, 1968; House Nov. 7, 1944-45.

FULTON, Andrew Steele (brother of John Hall Fulton) (W Va.) Sept. 29, 1800-Nov. 22, 1884; House 1847-49.

FULTON, Charles William (brother of Elmer Lincoln Fulton) (R Ore.) Aug. 24, 1853-Jan. 27, 1918; Senate 1903-09.

FULTON, Elmer Lincoln (brother of Charles William Fulton) (D Okla.) April 22, 1865-Oct. 4, 1939; House Nov. 16, 1907-09.

FULTON, James Grove (R Pa.) March 1, 1903-Oct. 6, 1971; House Feb. 2, 1945-Oct. 6, 1971.

FULTON, John Hall (brother of Andrew Steele Fulton) (W Va.) ?-Jan. 28, 1836; House 1833-35.

FULTON, Richard Harmon (D Tenn.) Jan. 27, 1927- —; House 1963-Aug. 14, 1975.

FULTON, William Savin (D Ark.) June 2, 1795-Aug. 15, 1844; Senate Sept. 18, 1836-Aug. 15, 1844; Gov. (Ark. Terr.) 1835-36.

FUNK, Benjamin Franklin (father of Frank Hamilton Funk) (R Ill.) Oct. 17, 1838-Feb. 14, 1909; House 1893-95.

FUNK, Frank Hamilton (son of Benjamin Franklin Funk) (R Ill.) April 5, 1869-Nov. 24, 1940; House 1921-27.

FUNSTON, Edward Hogue (R Kan.) Sept. 16, 1836-Sept. 10, 1911; House March 21, 1884-Aug. 2, 1894.

FUQUA, Don (D Fla.) Aug. 20, 1933- —; House 1963-87.

FURCOLO, Foster John (D Mass.) July 29, 1911- —; House 1949-Sept. 30, 1952; Gov. 1957-61.

FURLONG, Robert Grant (D Pa.) Jan. 4, 1886-March 19, 1973; House 1943-45.

FURLOW, Allen John (R Minn.) Nov. 9, 1890-Jan. 29, 1954; House 1925-29.

FUSTER, Jaime (PD P.R.) Jan. 12, 1941- —; House (Res. Comm.) 1985- —.

FYAN, Robert Washington (D Mo.) March 11, 1835-July 28, 1896; House 1883-85, 1891-95.

GABALDON, Isauro (Nat. P.I.) Dec. 8, 1875-Dec. 21, 1942; House (Res. Comm.) 1920-July 16, 1928.

GAGE, Joshua (D Mass.) Aug. 7, 1763-Jan. 24, 1831; House 1817-19.

GAHN, Harry Conrad (R Ohio) April 26, 1880-Nov. 2, 1962; House 1921-23.

GAILLARD, John (uncle of Theodore Gaillard Hunt) (D S.C.) Sept. 5, 1765-Feb. 26, 1826; Senate Jan. 31, 1805-Feb. 26, 1826; Pres. pro tempore 1810, 1814-18, 1820-25.

GAINES, John Pollard (W Ky.) Sept. 22, 1795-Dec. 9, 1857; House 1847-49; Gov. (Ore. Terr.) 1850-53.

GAINES, John Wesley (D Tenn.) Aug. 24, 1860-July 4, 1926; House 1897-1909.

GAINES, Joseph Holt (R W.Va.) Sept. 3, 1864-April 12, 1951; House 1901-11.

GAINES, William Embre (R Va.) Aug. 30, 1844-May 4, 1912; House 1887-89.

GAITHER, Nathan (D Ky.) Sept. 15, 1788-Aug. 12, 1862; House 1829-33.

GALBRAITH, John (D Pa.) Aug. 2, 1794-June 15, 1860; House 1833-37, 1839-41.

GALE, George (father of Levin Gale) (— Md.) June 3, 1756-Jan. 2, 1815; House 1789-91.

GALE, Levin (son of George Gale) (— Md.) April 24, 1784-Dec. 18, 1834; House 1827-29.

GALE, Richard Pillsbury (R Minn.) Oct. 30, 1900-Dec. 4, 1973; House 1941-45.

GALIFIANAKIS, Nick (D N.C.) July 22, 1928- —; House 1967-73.

GALLAGHER, Cornelius Edward (D N.J.) March 2, 1921- —; House 1959-73.

GALLAGHER, James A. (R Pa.) Jan. 16, 1869-Dec. 8 1957; House 1943-45, 1947-49.

GALLAGHER, Thomas (D Ill.) July 6, 1850-Feb. 24 1930; House 1909-21.

GALLAGHER, William James (D Minn.) May 13, 1875 Aug. 13, 1946; House 1945-Aug. 13, 1946.

GALLATIN, Albert (D Pa.) Jan. 29, 1761-Aug. 12, 1849 Senate Dec. 2, 1793-Feb. 28, 1794; House 1795-1801 Secy. of the Treasury 1801-14.

GALLEGLY, Elton William (R Calif.) March 7, 1944- — House 1987- —.

GALLEGOS, Jose Manuel (D N.M.) Oct. 30, 1815-Apri 21, 1875; House (Terr. Del.) 1853-July 23, 1856 1871-73.

GALLINGER, Jacob Harold (R N.H.) March 28, 1837 Aug. 17, 1918; House 1885-89; Senate 1891-Aug. 17 1918.

GALLIVAN, James Ambrose (D Mass.) Oct. 22, 1866 April 3, 1928; House April 7, 1914-April 3, 1928.

GALLO, Dean A. (R N.J.) Nov. 23, 1935- —; House 198! —.

GALLOWAY, Samuel (R Ohio) March 20, 1811-April 1872; House 1855-57.

GALLUP, Albert (D N.Y.) Jan. 30, 1796-Nov. 5, 185 House 1837-39.

GAMBLE, James (D Pa.) Jan. 28, 1809-Feb. 22, 188 House 1851-55.

GAMBLE, John Rankin (brother of Robert Jacksc Gamble, uncle of Ralph Abernethy Gamble) (R S.D Jan. 15, 1848-Aug. 14, 1891; House March 4-Aug. 1 1891.

GAMBLE, Ralph Abernethy (son of Robert Jacksc Gamble, nephew of John Rankin Gamble) (R N.Y May 6, 1885-March 4, 1959; House Nov. 2, 1937-5

GAMBLE, Robert Jackson (brother of John Rank Gamble, father of Ralph Abernethy Gamble) (S.D.) Feb. 7, 1851-Sept. 22, 1924; House 1895-9 1899-1901; Senate 1901-13.

GAMBLE, Roger Lawson (W Ga.) 1787-Dec. 20, 184 House 1833-35 (Democrat); 1841-43.

GAMBRELL, David Henry (D Ga.) Dec. 20, 1929- - Senate Feb. 1, 1971-Nov. 7, 1972.

GAMBRILL, Stephen Warfield (D Md.) Oct. 2, 187 Dec. 19, 1938; House Nov. 4, 1924-Dec. 19, 1938.

GAMMAGE, Robert Alton (D Texas) March 13, 193 —; House 1977-79.

GANDY, Harry Luther (D S.D.) Aug. 13, 1881-Aug. 15, 1957; House 1915-21.

GANLY, James Vincent (D N.Y.) Sept. 13. 1878-Sept. 7, 1923; House 1919-21, March 4-Sept. 7, 1923.

GANNETT, Barzillai (D Mass.) June 17, 1764-1832; House 1809-12.

GANSON, John (D N.Y.) Jan. 1, 1818-Sept. 28, 1874; House 1863-65.

GANTZ, Martin Kissinger (D Ohio) Jan. 28, 1862-Feb. 10, 1916; House 1891-93.

GARBER, Harvey Cable (D Ohio) July 6, 1866-March 23, 1938; House 1903-07.

GARBER, Jacob Aaron (R Va.) Jan. 25, 1879-Dec. 2, 1953; House 1929-31.

GARBER, Milton Cline (R Okla.) Nov. 30, 1867-Sept. 12, 1948; House 1923-33.

GARCIA, Robert (D N.Y.) Jan. 9, 1933- —; House Feb. 21, 1978- —.

GARD, Warren (D Ohio) July 2, 1873-Nov. 1, 1929; House 1913-21.

GARDENIER, Barent (F N.Y.) ?-Jan. 10, 1822; House 1807-11.

GARDNER, Augustus Peabody (uncle of Henry Cabot Lodge Jr. and John Davis Lodge) (R Mass.) Nov. 5, 1865-Jan. 14, 1918; House Nov. 3, 1902-May 15, 1917.

GARDNER, Edward Joseph (D Ohio) Aug. 7, 1898-Dec. 7, 1950; House 1945-47.

GARDNER, Francis (— N.H.) Dec. 27, 1771-June 25, 1835; House 1807-09.

GARDNER, Frank (D Ind.) May 8, 1872-Feb. 1, 1937; House 1923-29.

GARDNER, Gideon (— Mass.) May 30, 1759-March 22, 1832; House 1809-11.

GARDNER, James Carson (R N.C.) April 8, 1933- —; House 1967-69.

GARDNER, John James (R N.J.) Oct. 17, 1845-Feb. 7, 1921; House 1893-1913.

GARDNER, Mills (R Ohio) Jan. 30, 1830-Feb. 20, 1910; House 1877-79.

GARDNER, Obadiah (D Maine) Sept. 13, 1852-July 24, 1938; Senate Sept. 23, 1911-13.

GARDNER, Washington (R Mich.) Feb. 16, 1845-March 31, 1928; House 1899-1911.

GARFIELD, James Abram (R Ohio) Nov. 19, 1831-Sept. 19, 1881; House 1863-Nov. 8, 1880; President March 4-Sept. 19, 1881.

GARFIELDE, Selucius (R Wash.) Dec. 8, 1822-April 13, 1881; House (Terr. Del.) 1869-73.

GARLAND, Augustus Hill (D Ark.) June 11, 1832-Jan. 26, 1899; Senate 1877-March 6, 1885; Gov. 1874-77; Atty. General 1885-89.

GARLAND, David Shepherd (D Va.) Sept. 27, 1769-Oct. 7, 1841; House Jan. 17, 1810-11.

GARLAND, James (D Va.) June 6, 1791-Aug. 8, 1885; House 1835-41.

GARLAND, Mahlon Morris (R Pa.) May 4, 1856-Nov. 19, 1920; House 1915-Nov. 19, 1920.

GARLAND, Peter Adams (R Maine) June 16, 1923- —; House 1961-63.

GARLAND, Rice (W La.) about 1795-1861; House April 28, 1834-July 21, 1840.

GARMATZ, Edward Alexander (D Md.) Feb. 7, 1903-July 22, 1986; House July 15, 1947-73.

GARN, Edwin Jacob "Jake" (R Utah) Oct. 12, 1932- —; Senate Dec. 21, 1974- —.

GARNER, Alfred Buckwalter (R Pa.) March 4, 1873-July 30, 1930; House 1909-11.

GARNER, John Nance (D Texas) Nov. 22, 1868-Nov. 7, 1967; House 1903-33; Speaker 1931-33; Vice President 1933-41.

GARNETT, James Mercer (brother of Robert Selden Garnett, grandfather of Muscoe Russell Hunter Garnett, cousin of Charles Fenton Mercer) (D Va.) June 8, 1770-April 23, 1843; House 1805-09.

GARNETT, Muscoe Russell Hunter (grandson of James Mercer Garnett) (D Va.) July 25, 1821-Feb. 14, 1864; House Dec. 1, 1856-61.

GARNETT, Robert Selden (brother of James Mercer Garnett, cousin of Charles Fenton Mercer) (D Va.) April 26, 1789-Aug. 15, 1840; House 1817-27.

GARNSEY, Daniel Greene (JD N.Y.) June 17, 1779-May 11, 1851; House 1825-29.

GARRETT, Abraham Ellison (D Tenn.) March 6, 1830-Feb. 14, 1907; House 1871-73.

GARRETT, Clyde Leonard (D Texas) Dec. 16, 1885-Dec. 18, 1959; House 1937-41.

GARRETT, Daniel Edward (D Texas) April 28, 1869-Dec. 13, 1932; House 1913-15, 1917-19, 1921-Dec. 13, 1932.

GARRETT, Finis James (D Tenn.) Aug. 26, 1875-May 25, 1956; House 1905-29.

GARRISON, Daniel (D N.J.) April 3, 1782-Feb. 13, 1851; House 1823-27.

GARRISON, George Tankard (D Va.) Jan. 14, 1835-Nov. 14, 1889; House 1881-83; March 20, 1884-85.

GARROW, Nathaniel (D N.Y.) April 25, 1780-March 3, 1841; House 1827-29.

GARTH, William Willis (D Ala.) Oct. 28, 1828-Feb. 25, 1912; House 1877-79.

GARTNER, Fred Christian (R Pa.) March 14, 1896-Sept. 1, 1972; House 1939-41.

GARTRELL, Lucius Jeremiah (uncle of Choice Boswell Randell) (D Ga.) Jan. 7, 1821-April 7, 1891; House 1857-Jan. 23, 1861.

GARVIN, William Swan (D Pa.) July 25, 1806-Feb. 20, 1883; House 1845-47.

GARY, Frank Boyd (D S.C.) March 9, 1860-Dec. 7, 1922; Senate March 6, 1908-09.

GARY, Julian Vaughan (D Va.) Feb. 25, 1892-Sept. 6, 1973; House March 6, 1945-65.

GASQUE, Allard Henry (husband of Elizabeth "Bessie" Hawley Gasque) (D S.C.) March 8, 1873-June 17, 1938; House 1923-June 17, 1938.

GASQUE, Elizabeth "Bessie" Hawley (widow of Allard Henry Gasque — later Mrs. A. J. Van Exem) (D S.C.) ?-—; House Sept. 13, 1938-39.

GASSAWAY, Percy Lee (D Okla.) Aug. 30, 1885-May 15, 1937; House 1935-37.

GASTON, Athelston (D Pa.) April 24, 1838-Sept. 23, 1907; House 1899-1901.

GASTON, William (F N.C.) Sept. 19, 1778-Jan. 23, 1844; House 1813-17.

GATES, Seth Merrill (ASW N.Y.) Oct. 10, 1800-Aug. 24, 1877; House 1839-43.

GATHINGS, Ezekiel Candler (D Ark.) Nov. 10, 1903-May 2, 1979; House 1939-69.

GATLIN, Alfred Moore (— N.C.) April 20, 1790-?; House 1823-25.

GAUSE, Lucien Coatsworth (D Ark.) Dec. 25, 1836-Nov. 5, 1880; House 1875-79.

GAVAGAN, Joseph Andrew (D N.Y.) Aug. 20, 1892-Oct. 18, 1968; House Nov. 5, 1929-Dec. 30, 1943.

GAVIN, Leon Harry (R Pa.) Feb. 25, 1893-Sept. 15, 1963; House 1943-Sept. 15, 1963.

GAY, Edward James (grandfather of Edward James Gay, below) (D La.) Feb. 3, 1816-May 30, 1889; House 1885-May 30, 1889.

GAY, Edward James (grandson of Edward James Gay, above) (D La.) May 5, 1878-Dec. 1, 1952; Senate Nov. 6, 1918-21.

GAYDOS, Joseph M. (D Pa.) July 3, 1926-—; House Nov. 5, 1968-—.

GAYLE, John (W Ala.) Sept. 11, 1792-July 28, 1859; House 1847-49; Gov. 1831-35 (Democrat).

GAYLE, June Ward (D Ky.) Feb. 22, 1865-Aug. 5, 1942; House Jan. 15, 1900-01.

GAYLORD, James Madison (— Ohio) May 29, 1811-June 14, 1874; House 1851-53.

GAZLAY, James William (JFSt. Ohio) July 23, 1784-June 8, 1874; House 1823-25.

GEAR, John Henry (R Iowa) April 7, 1825-July 14, 1900; House 1887-91, 1893-95; Senate 1895-July 14, 1900; Gov. 1878-82.

GEARHART, Bertrand Wesley (R Calif.) May 31, 1890-Oct. 11, 1955; House 1935-49.

GEARIN, John McDermeid (D Ore.) Aug. 15, 1851-Nov. 12, 1930; Senate Dec. 13, 1905-Jan. 23, 1907.

GEARY, Thomas J. (D/AP Calif.) Jan. 18, 1854-July 6, 1929; House Dec. 9, 1890-95.

GEBHARD, John (— N.Y.) Feb. 22, 1782-Jan. 3, 1854; House 1821-23.

GEDDES, George Washington (D Ohio) July 16, 1824-Nov. 9, 1892; House 1879-87.

GEDDES, James (F N.Y.) July 22, 1763-Aug. 19, 1838; House 1813-15.

GEELAN, James Patrick (D Conn.) Aug. 11, 1901-Aug. 10, 1982; House 1945-47.

GEHRMANN, Bernard John (Prog. Wis.) Feb. 13, 1880-July 12, 1958; House 1935-43.

GEISSENHAINER, Jacob Augustus (D N.J.) Aug. 28, 1839-July 20, 1917; House 1889-95.

GEJDENSON, Samuel (D Conn.) May 20, 1948-—; House 1981-—.

GEKAS, George William (R Pa.) April 14, 1930-—; House 1983-—.

GENSMAN, Lorraine Michael (R Okla.) Aug. 26, 1878-May 27, 1954; House 1921-23.

GENTRY, Brady Preston (D Texas) March 25, 1896-Nov. 9, 1966; House 1953-57.

GENTRY, Meredith Poindexter (W Tenn.) Sept. 15, 1809-Nov. 2, 1866; House 1839-43, 1845-53.

GEORGE, Henry Jr. (D N.Y.) Nov. 3, 1862-Nov. 14, 1916; House 1911-15.

GEORGE, James Zachariah (D Miss.) Oct. 20, 1826-Aug. 14, 1897; Senate 1881-Aug. 14, 1897.

GEORGE, Melvin Clark (R Ore.) May 13, 1894-Feb. 22, 1933; House 1881-85.

GEORGE, Myron Virgil (R Kan.) Jan. 6, 1900-April 11, 1972; House Nov. 7, 1950-59.

GEORGE, Newell A. (D Kan.) Sept. 24, 1904- —; House 1959-61.

GEORGE, Walter Franklin (D Ga.) Jan. 29, 1878-Aug. 4, 1957; Senate Nov. 22, 1922-57; Pres. pro tempore 1955-57.

GEPHARDT, Richard Andrew (D Mo.) Jan. 31, 1941- —; House 1977- —.

GERAN, Elmer Hendrickson (D N.J.) Oct. 24, 1875-Jan. 12, 1954; House 1923-25.

GERLACH, Charles Lewis (R Pa.) Sept. 14, 1895-May 5, 1947; House 1939-May 5, 1947.

GERMAN, Obadiah (D N.Y.) April 22, 1766-Sept. 24, 1842; Senate 1809-15.

GERNERD, Fred Benjamin (R Pa.) Nov. 22, 1879-Aug. 7, 1948; House 1921-23.

GERRY, Elbridge (great-grandfather of Peter Goelet Gerry, grandfather of Elbridge Gerry, below) (DR Mass.) July 17, 1744-Nov. 23, 1814; House 1789-93 (Anti Federalist); Cont. Cong. 1776-81, 1782-85; Gov. 1810-12; Vice President 1813-Nov. 23, 1814.

GERRY, Elbridge (grandson of Elbridge Gerry, above) (D Maine) Dec. 6, 1813-April 10, 1886; House 1849-51.

GERRY, James (D Pa.) Aug. 14, 1796-July 19, 1873; House 1839-43.

GERRY, Peter Goelet (great-grandson of Elbridge Gerry) (D R.I.) Sept. 18, 1879-Oct. 31, 1957; House 1913-15; Senate 1917-29, 1935-47.

GEST, William Harrison (R Ill.) Jan. 7, 1838-Aug. 9, 1912; House 1887-91.

GETTYS, Thomas Smithwick (D S.C.) June 19, 1912- —; House Nov. 3, 1964-Dec. 31, 1974.

GETZ, James Lawrence (D Pa.) Sept. 14, 1821-Dec. 25, 1891; House 1867-73.

GEYER, Henry Sheffie (D Mo.) Dec. 9, 1790-March 5, 1859; Senate 1851-57.

GEYER, Lee Edward (D Calif.) Sept. 9, 1888-Oct. 11, 1941; House 1939-Oct. 11, 1941.

GHOLSON, James Herbert (D Va.) 1798-July 2, 1848; House 1833-35.

GHOLSON, Samuel Jameson (D Miss.) May 19, 1808-Oct. 16, 1883; House Dec. 1, 1836-37, July 18, 1837-Feb. 5, 1838.

GHOLSON, Thomas Jr. (D Va.) ?-July 4, 1816; House Nov. 7, 1808-July 4, 1816.

GIAIMO, Robert Nicholas (D Conn.) Oct. 15, 1919- —; House 1959-81.

GIBBONS, Sam M. (D Fla.) Jan. 20, 1920- —; House 1963- —.

GIBBS, Florence Reville (widow of Willis Benjamin Gibbs) (D Ga.) April 4, 1890-Aug. 19, 1964; House Oct. 1, 1940-41.

GIBBS, Willis Benjamin (husband of Florence Reville Gibbs) (D Ga.) April 15, 1889-Aug. 7, 1940; House 1939-Aug. 7, 1940.

GIBSON, Charles Hopper (cousin of Henry Richard Gibson) (D Md.) Jan. 19, 1842-March 31, 1900; House 1885-91; Senate Nov. 19, 1891-97.

GIBSON, Ernest Willard (father of Ernest William Gibson) (R Vt.) Dec. 29, 1872-June 20, 1940; House Nov. 6, 1923-Oct. 19, 1933; Senate Nov. 21, 1933-June 20, 1940.

GIBSON, Ernest William (son of Ernest Willard Gibson) (R Vt.) March 6, 1901-Nov. 4, 1969; Senate June 24, 1940-41; Gov. 1947-50.

GIBSON, Eustace (D W.Va.) Oct. 4, 1842-Dec. 10, 1900; House 1883-87.

GIBSON, Henry Richard (cousin of Charles Hopper Gibson) (R Tenn.) Dec. 24, 1837-May 25, 1938; House 1895-1905.

GIBSON, James King (D Va.) Feb. 18, 1812-March 30, 1879; House Jan. 28, 1870-71.

GIBSON, John Strickland (D Ga.) Jan. 3, 1893-Oct. 19, 1960; House 1941-47.

GIBSON, Paris (D Mont.) July 1, 1830-Dec. 16, 1920; Senate March 7, 1901-05.

GIBSON, Randall Lee (D La.) Sept. 10, 1832-Dec. 15, 1892; House 1875-83; Senate 1883-Dec. 15, 1892.

GIDDINGS, De Witt Clinton (D Texas) July 18, 1827-Aug. 19, 1903; House May 13, 1872-75, 1877-79.

GIDDINGS, Joshua Reed (ASW Ohio) Oct. 6, 1795-May 27, 1864; House Dec. 3, 1838-March 22, 1842; Dec. 5, 1842-59.

GIDDINGS, Napoleon Bonaparte (D Neb.) Jan. 2, 1816-Aug. 3, 1897; House (Terr. Del.) Jan. 5-March 3, 1855.

GIFFORD, Charles Laceille (R Mass.) March 15, 1871-Aug. 23, 1947; House Nov. 7, 1922-Aug. 23, 1947.

GIFFORD, Oscar Sherman (R S.D.) Oct. 20, 1842-Jan. 16, 1913; House (Terr. Del. Dakota) 1885-89, (Rep.) Nov. 2, 1889-91.

GILBERT, Abijah (R Fla.) June 18, 1806-Nov. 23, 1881; Senate 1869-75.

GILBERT, Edward (D Calif.) about 1819-Aug. 2, 1852; House Sept. 11, 1850-51.

GILBERT, Ezekiel (— N.Y.) March 25, 1756-July 17, 1841; House 1793-97.

GILBERT, George Gilmore (father of Ralph Waldo Emerson Gilbert) (D Ky.) Dec. 24, 1849-Nov. 9, 1909; House 1899-1907.

GILBERT, Jacob H. (D N.Y.) June 17, 1920-Feb. 27, 1981; House March 8, 1960-1971.

GILBERT, Newton Whiting (R Ind.) May 24, 1862-July 5, 1939; House 1905-Nov. 6, 1906.

GILBERT, Ralph Waldo Emerson (son of George Gilmore Gilbert) (D Ky.) Jan. 17, 1882-July 30, 1939; House 1921-29, 1931-33.

GILBERT, Sylvester (— Conn.) Oct. 20, 1755-Jan. 2, 1846; House Nov. 16, 1818-19.

GILBERT, William Augustus (W N.Y.) Jan. 25, 1815-May 25, 1875; House 1855-Feb. 27, 1857.

GILCHRIST, Fred Cramer (R Iowa) June 2, 1868-March 10, 1950; House 1931-45.

GILDEA, James Hilary (D Pa.) Oct. 21, 1890-—; House 1935-39.

GILES, William Branch (D Va.) Aug. 12, 1762-Dec. 4, 1830; House Dec. 7, 1790-Oct. 2, 1798 (Anti Federalist), 1801-03; Senate Aug. 11, 1804-15; Gov. 1827-30.

GILES, William Fell (D Md.) April 8, 1807-March 21, 1879; House 1845-47.

GILFILLAN, Calvin Willard (R Pa.) Feb. 20, 1832-Dec. 2, 1901; House 1869-71.

GILFILLAN, John Bachop (R Minn.) Feb. 11, 1835-Aug. 19, 1924; House 1885-87.

GILHAMS, Clarence Chauncey (R Ind.) April 11, 1860-June 5, 1912; House Nov. 6, 1906-09.

GILL, John Jr. (D Md.) June 9, 1850-Jan. 27, 1918; House 1905-11.

GILL, Joseph John (R Ohio) Sept. 21, 1846-May 22 1920; House Dec. 4, 1899-Oct. 31, 1903.

GILL, Michael Joseph (D Mo.) Dec. 5, 1864-Nov. ? 1918; House June 19, 1914-15.

GILL, Patrick Francis (D Mo.) Aug. 16, 1868-May 2? 1923; House 1909-11, Aug. 12, 1912-13.

GILL, Thomas P. (D Hawaii) April 21, 1922-—; Hous 1963-65.

GILLEN Courtland Craig (D Ind.) July 3, 1880-Sept. ? 1954; House 1931-33.

GILLESPIE, Dean Milton (R Colo.) May 3, 1884-Feb. ? 1949; House March 7, 1944-47.

GILLESPIE, Eugene Pierce (D Pa.) Sept. 24, 1852-Dec 16, 1899; House 1891-93.

GILLESPIE, James (— N.C.) ?-Jan. 11, 1805; Hous 1793-99, 1803-Jan. 11, 1805.

GILLESPIE, James Frank (D Ill.) April 18, 1869-No? 26, 1954; House 1933-35.

GILLESPIE, Oscar William (D Texas) June 20, 185? Aug. 23, 1927; House 1903-11.

GILLET, Charles William (R N.Y.) Nov. 26, 1840-De 31, 1908; House 1893-1905.

GILLET, Ransom Hooker (D N.Y.) Jan. 27, 1800-Oc 24, 1876; House 1833-37.

GILLETT, Frederick Huntington (R Mass.) Oct. 1? 1851-July 31, 1935; House 1893-1925; Speaker 191? 25; Senate 1925-31.

GILLETT, James Norris (R Calif.) Sept. 20, 1860-Ap? 20, 1937; House 1903-Nov. 4, 1906; Gov. 1907-11.

GILLETTE, Edward Hooker (son of Francis Gillette) (? Iowa) Oct. 1, 1840-Aug. 14, 1918; House 1879-81.

GILLETTE, Francis (father of Edward Hooker Gillett? (FSW Conn.) Dec. 14, 1807-Sept. 30, 1879; Sena May 24, 1854-55.

GILLETTE, Guy Mark (D Iowa) Feb. 3, 1879-March 1973; House 1933-Nov. 3, 1936; Senate Nov. 4, 193? 45, 1949-55.

GILLETTE, Wilson Darwin (R Pa.) July 1, 1880-Aug. 1951; House Nov. 4, 1941-Aug. 7, 1951.

GILLIE, George W. (R Ind.) Aug. 15, 1880-July 3, 196? House 1939-49.

GILLIGAN, John Joyce (D Ohio) March 22, 1921-—? House 1965-67; Gov. 1971-75.

GILLIS, James Lisle (D Pa.) Oct. 2, 1792-July 8, 188? House 1857-59.

GILLON, Alexander (− S.C.) 1741-Oct. 6, 1794; House 1793-Oct. 6, 1794.

GILMAN, Benjamin Arthur (R N.Y.) Dec. 6, 1922-−; House 1973-−.

GILMAN, Charles Jervis (grandnephew of Nicholas Gilman) (R Maine) Feb. 26, 1824-Feb. 5, 1901; House 1857-59.

GILMAN, Nicholas (granduncle of Charles Jervis Gilman) (D N.H.) Aug. 3, 1755-May 2, 1814; House 1789-97 (Federalist); Senate 1805-May 2, 1814.

GILMER, George Rockingham (D Ga.) April 11, 1790-Nov. 16, 1859; House 1821-23, Oct. 1, 1827-29, 1833-35; Gov. 1829-31, 1837-39 (Whig).

GILMER, John Adams (AP N.C.) Nov. 4, 1805-May 14, 1868; House 1857-61.

GILMER, Thomas Walker (D Va.) April 6, 1802-Feb. 28, 1844; House 1841-43 (Whig), 1843-Feb. 16, 1844; Gov. 1840-41 (Whig); Secy. of the Navy Feb. 15-28, 1844.

GILMER, William Franklin "Dixie" (D Okla.) June 7, 1901-June 9, 1954; House 1949-51.

GILMORE, Alfred (son of John Gilmore) (D Pa.) June 9, 1812-June 29, 1890; House 1849-53.

GILMORE, Edward (D Mass.) Jan. 4, 1867-April 10, 1924; House 1913-15.

GILMORE, John (father of Alfred Gilmore) (JD Pa.) Feb. 18, 1780-May 11, 1845; House 1829-33.

GILMORE, Samuel Louis (D La.) July 30, 1859-July 18, 1910; House March 30, 1909-July 18, 1910.

GINGERY, Don (D Pa.) Feb. 19, 1884-Oct. 15, 1961; House 1935-39.

GINGRICH, Newton Leroy (R Ga.) June 17, 1943-−; House 1979-−.

GINN, Ronald Bryan (D Ga.) May 31, 1934-−; House 1973-83.

GIST, Joseph (D S.C.) Jan. 12, 1775-March 8, 1836; House 1821-27.

GITTINS, Robert Henry (D N.Y.) Dec. 14, 1869-Dec. 25, 1957; House 1913-15.

GLASCOCK, John Raglan (D Calif.) Aug. 25, 1845-Nov. 10, 1913; House 1883-85.

GLASCOCK, Thomas (UD Ga.) Oct. 21, 1790-May 19, 1841; House Oct. 5, 1835-39.

GLASGOW, Hugh (− Pa.) Sept. 8, 1769-Jan. 31, 1818; House 1813-17.

GLASS, Carter (D Va.) Jan. 4, 1858-May 28, 1946; House Nov. 4, 1902-Dec. 16, 1918; Senate Feb. 2, 1920-May 28, 1946; Pres. pro tempore 1941-45; Secy. of the Treasury 1918-20.

GLASS, Presley Thornton (D Tenn.) Oct. 18, 1824-Oct. 9, 1902; House 1885-89.

GLATFELTER, Samuel Feiser (D Pa.) April 7, 1858-April 23, 1927; House 1923-25.

GLEN, Henry (− N.Y.) July 13, 1739-Jan. 6, 1814; House 1793-1801.

GLENN, John Herschel Jr. (D Ohio) July 18, 1921-−; Senate Dec. 24, 1974-−.

GLENN, Milton Willits (R N.J.) June 18, 1903-Dec. 14, 1967; House Nov. 5, 1957-65.

GLENN, Otis Ferguson (R Ill.) Aug. 27, 1879-March 11, 1959; Senate Dec. 3, 1928-33.

GLENN, Thomas Louis (P Idaho) Feb. 2, 1847-Nov. 18, 1918; House 1901-03.

GLICKMAN, Daniel Robert (D Kan.) Nov. 24, 1944-−; House 1977-−.

GLONINGER, John (D Pa.) Sept. 19, 1758-Jan. 22, 1836; House March 4-Aug. 2, 1813.

GLOSSBRENNER, Adam John (D Pa.) Aug. 31, 1810-March 1, 1889; House 1865-69.

GLOVER, David Delano (D Ark.) Jan. 18, 1868-April 5, 1952; House 1929-35.

GLOVER, John Milton (nephew of John Montgomery Glover) (D Mo.) June 23, 1852-Oct. 20, 1929; House 1885-89.

GLOVER, John Montgomery (uncle of John Milton Glover) (D Mo.) Sept. 4, 1822-Nov. 15, 1891; House 1873-79.

GLYNN, James Peter (R Conn.) Nov. 12, 1867-March 6, 1930; House 1915-23, 1925-March 6, 1930.

GLYNN, Martin Henry (D N.Y.) Sept. 27, 1871-Dec. 14, 1924; House 1899-1901; Gov. 1913-15.

GODDARD, Calvin (F Conn.) July 17, 1768-May 2, 1842; House May 14, 1801-05.

GODSHALK, William (R Pa.) Oct. 25, 1817-Feb. 6, 1891; House 1879-83.

GODWIN, Hannibal Lafayette (D N.C.) Nov. 3, 1873-June 9, 1929; House 1907-21.

GOEBEL, Herman Philip (R Ohio) April 5, 1853-May 4, 1930; House 1903-11.

GOEKE, John Henry (D Ohio) Oct. 28, 1869-March 25, 1930; House 1911-15.

GOFF, Abe McGregor (R Idaho) Dec. 21, 1899-Nov. 23, 1984; House 1947-49.

GOFF, Guy Despard (son of Nathan Goff, father of Louise Goff Reece, father-in-law of Brazilla Carroll Reece) (R W.Va.) Sept. 13, 1866-Jan. 7, 1933; Senate 1925-31.

GOFF, Nathan (father of Guy Despard Goff, grandfather of Louise Goff Reece) (R W.Va.) Feb. 9, 1843-April 24, 1920; House 1883-89; Senate April 1, 1913-19; Secy. of the Navy Jan. 6-March 5, 1881.

GOGGIN, William Leftwich (W Va.) May 31, 1807-Jan. 3, 1870; House 1839-43, April 25, 1844-45, 1847-49.

GOLD, Thomas Ruggles (F N.Y.) Nov. 4, 1764-Oct. 24, 1827; House 1809-13, 1815-17.

GOLDEN, James Stephen (R Ky.) Sept. 10, 1891-Sept. 6, 1971; House 1949-55.

GOLDER, Benjamin Martin (R Pa.) Dec. 23, 1891-Dec. 30, 1946; House 1925-33.

GOLDFOGLE, Henry Mayer (D N.Y.), May 23, 1856-June 1, 1929; House 1901-15, 1919-21.

GOLDSBOROUGH, Charles (great-grandfather of Thomas Alan Goldsborough and Winder Laird Henry) (F Md.) July 15, 1765-Dec. 13, 1834; House 1805-17; Gov. 1819.

GOLDSBOROUGH, Phillips Lee (R Md.) Aug. 6, 1865-Oct. 22, 1946; Senate 1929-35; Gov. 1912-16.

GOLDSBOROUGH, Robert Henry (great-grandfather of Winder Laird Henry) (W Md.) Jan. 4, 1779-Oct. 5, 1836; Senate May 21, 1813-19 (Federalist); Jan. 13, 1835-Oct. 5, 1836.

GOLDSBOROUGH, Thomas Alan (great-grandson of Charles Goldsborough) (D Md.) Sept. 16, 1877-June 16, 1951; House 1921-April 5, 1939.

GOLDTHWAITE, George Thomas (D Ala.) Dec. 10, 1809-March 16, 1879; Senate 1871-77.

GOLDWATER, Barry Morris (father of Barry Morris Goldwater Jr.) (R Ariz.) Jan. 1, 1909- —; Senate 1953-65, 1969-87.

GOLDWATER, Barry Morris Jr. (son of Barry Morris Goldwater) (R Calif.) July 15, 1938- —; House April 29, 1969-83.

GOLDZIER, Julius (D Ill.) Jan. 20, 1854-Jan. 20, 1925; House 1893-95.

GOLLADAY, Edward Isaac (brother of Jacob Shall Golladay) (D Tenn.) Sept. 9, 1830-July 11, 1897; House 1871-73.

GOLLADAY, Jacob Shall (brother of Edward Isaac Golladay) (D Ky.) Jan. 19, 1819-May 20, 188?; House Dec. 5, 1867-Feb. 28, 1870.

GONZALEZ, Henry B. (D Texas) May 3, 1916- — House Nov. 4, 1961- —.

GOOCH, Daniel Linn (D Ky.) Oct. 28, 1853-April 1? 1913; House 1901-05.

GOOCH, Daniel Wheelwright (R Mass.) Jan. 8, 182? Nov. 11, 1891; House Jan. 31, 1858-Sept. 1, 186? 1873-75.

GOOD, James William (R Iowa) Sept. 24, 1866-Nov. 1? 1929; House 1909-June 15, 1921; Secy. of War Marc 5-Nov. 18, 1929.

GOODALL, Louis Bertrand (R Maine) Sept. 23, 185? June 26, 1935; House 1917-21.

GOODE, John Jr. (D Va.) May 27, 1829-July 14, 190? House 1875-81.

GOODE, Patrick Gaines (W Ohio) May 10, 1798-Oct. 1 1862; House 1837-43.

GOODE, Samuel (— Va.) March 21, 1756-Nov. 14, 182? House 1799-1801.

GOODE, William Osborne (D Va.) Sept. 16, 1798-July 1859; House 1841-43, 1853-July 3, 1859.

GOODELL, Charles Ellsworth (R N.Y.) March 16, 192? Jan. 21, 1987; House May 26, 1959-Sept. 10, 196? Senate Sept. 10, 1968-71.

GOODENOW, John Milton (JD Ohio) 1782-July 2? 1838; House 1829-April 9, 1830.

GOODENOW, Robert (brother of Rufus Kir Goodenow) (W Maine) April 19, 1800-May 15, 187? House 1851-53.

GOODENOW, Rufus King (brother of Robe? Goodenow) (W Maine) April 24, 1790-March 2? 1863; House 1849-51.

GOODHUE, Benjamin (F Mass.) Sept. 20, 1748-July 2? 1814; House 1789-June 1796; Senate June 11, 179? Nov. 8, 1800.

GOODIN, John Randolph (D Kan.) Dec. 14, 1836-De? 18, 1885; House 1875-77.

GOODING, Frank Robert (R Idaho) Sept. 16, 1859-Ju? 24, 1928; Senate Jan. 15, 1921-June 24, 1928; Go? 1905-08.

GOODLING, George Atlee (father of William Frankl? Goodling) (R Pa.) Sept. 26, 1896-Oct. 17, 198? House 1961-65, 1967-75.

GOODLING, William Franklin (son of George Atl? Goodling) (R Pa.) Dec. 5, 1927- —; House 1975- —

GOODNIGHT, Isaac Herschel (D Ky.) Jan. 31, 1849-July 24, 1901; House 1889-95.

GOODRICH, Chauncey (brother of Elizur Goodrich) (F Conn.) Oct. 20, 1759-Aug. 18, 1815; House 1795-1801; Senate Oct. 25, 1807-May 1813.

GOODRICH, Elizur (brother of Chauncey Goodrich) (F Conn.) March 24, 1761-Nov. 1, 1849; House 1799-1801.

GOODRICH, John Zacheus (W Mass.) Sept. 27, 1804-April 19, 1885; House 1851-55.

GOODRICH, Milo (R N.Y.) Jan. 3, 1814-April 15, 1881; House 1871-73.

GOODWIN, Angier Louis (R Mass.) Jan. 30, 1881-June 20, 1975; House 1943-55.

GOODWIN, Forrest (R Maine) June 14, 1862-May 28, 1913; House March 4-May 28, 1913.

GOODWIN, Godfrey Gummer (R Minn.) Jan. 11, 1873-Feb. 16, 1933; House 1925-Feb. 16, 1933.

GOODWIN, Henry Charles (R N.Y.) June 25, 1824-Nov. 12, 1860; House Nov. 7, 1854-55, 1857-59.

GOODWIN, John Noble (R Ariz.) Oct. 18, 1824-April 29, 1887; House (Rep. Maine) 1861-63, (Terr. Del.) 1865-67; Gov. (Ariz. Terr.) 1863-65.

GOODWIN, Philip Arnold (R N.Y.) Jan. 20, 1882-June 6, 1937; House 1933-June 6, 1937.

GOODWIN, Robert Kingman (R Iowa) May 23, 1905-Feb. 21, 1983; House March 5, 1940-41.

GOODWIN, William Shields (D Ark.) May 2, 1866-Aug. 9, 1937; House 1911-21.

GOODWYN, Albert Taylor (D Ala.) Dec. 17, 1842-July 2, 1931; House April 22, 1896-97.

GOODWYN, Peterson (D Va.) 1745-Feb. 21, 1818; House 1803-Feb. 21, 1818.

GOODYEAR, Charles (D N.Y.) April 26, 1804-April 9, 1876; House 1845-47, 1865-67.

GOODYKOONTZ, Wells (R W.Va.) June 3, 1872-March 2, 1944; House 1919-23.

GORDON, Bart (D Tenn.) Jan. 24, 1949- — ; House 1985- —.

GORDON, George Washington (D Tenn.) Oct. 5, 1836-Aug. 9, 1911; House 1907-Aug. 9, 1911.

GORDON, James (F N.Y.) Oct. 31, 1739-Jan. 17, 1810; House 1791-95.

GORDON, James (— Miss.) Dec. 6, 1833-Nov. 28, 1912; Senate Dec. 27, 1909-Feb. 22, 1910.

GORDON, John Brown (D Ga.) Feb. 6, 1832-Jan. 9, 1904; Senate 1873-May 26, 1880, 1891-97; Gov. 1886-90.

GORDON, Robert Bryarly (D Ohio) Aug. 6, 1855-Jan. 3, 1923; House 1899-1903.

GORDON, Samuel (D N.Y.) April 28, 1802-Oct. 28, 1873; House 1841-43, 1845-47.

GORDON, Thomas Sylvy (D Ill.) Dec. 17, 1893-Jan. 22, 1959; House 1943-59.

GORDON, William (— N.H.) April 12, 1763-May 8, 1802; House 1797-June 12, 1800.

GORDON, William (D Ohio) Dec. 15, 1862-Jan. 16, 1942; House 1913-19.

GORDON, William Fitzhugh (D Va.) Jan. 13, 1787-Aug. 28, 1858; House Jan. 25, 1830-35.

GORE, Albert Arnold (father of Albert Arnold Gore Jr.) (D Tenn.) Dec. 26, 1907- — ; House 1939-Dec. 4, 1944, 1945-53; Senate 1953-71.

GORE, Albert Arnold Jr. (son of Albert Arnold Gore) (D Tenn.) March 31, 1948- — ; House 1977-85; Senate 1985- —.

GORE, Christopher (— Mass.) Sept. 21, 1758-March 1, 1827; Senate May 5, 1813-May 30, 1816; Gov. 1809-10 (Federalist).

GORE, Thomas Pryor (D Okla.) Dec. 10, 1870-March 16, 1949; Senate Dec. 11, 1907-21, 1931-37.

GORHAM, Benjamin (— Mass.) Feb. 13, 1775-Sept. 27, 1855; House Nov. 6, 1820-23, July 23, 1827-31, 1833-35.

GORMAN, Arthur Pue (D Md.) March 11, 1839-June 4, 1906; Senate 1881-99, 1903-June 4, 1906.

GORMAN, George Edmund (D Ill.) April 13, 1873-Jan. 13, 1935; House 1913-15.

GORMAN, James Sedgwick (D Mich.) Dec. 28, 1850-May 27, 1923; House 1891-95.

GORMAN, John Jerome (R Ill.) June 2, 1883-Feb. 24, 1949; House 1921-23, 1925-27.

GORMAN, Willis Arnold (D Ind.) Jan. 12, 1816-May 20, 1876; House 1849-53; Gov. (Minn. Terr.) 1853-57.

GORSKI, Chester Charles (D N.Y.) June 22, 1906-April 25, 1975; House 1949-51.

GORSKI, Martin (D Ill.) Oct. 30, 1886-Dec. 4, 1949; House 1943-Dec. 4, 1949.

GORTON, Thomas Slade III (R Wash.) Jan. 8, 1928- — ; Senate 1981-87.

GOSS, Edward Wheeler (R Conn.) April 27, 1893- —; House Nov. 4, 1930-35.

GOSS, James Hamilton (R S.C.) Aug. 9, 1820-Oct. 31, 1886; House July 18, 1868-69.

GOSSETT, Charles Clinton (D Idaho) Sept. 2, 1888-Sept. 20, 1974; Senate Nov. 17, 1945-47; Gov. Jan.-Nov. 16, 1945.

GOSSETT, Ed Lee (D Texas) Jan. 27, 1902- —; House 1939-July 31, 1951.

GOTT, Daniel (W N.Y.) July 10, 1794-July 6, 1864; House 1847-51.

GOULD, Arthur Robinson (R Maine) March 16, 1857-July 24, 1946; Senate Nov. 30, 1926-31.

GOULD, Herman Day (W N.Y.) Jan. 16, 1799-Jan. 26, 1852; House 1849-51.

GOULD, Norman Judd (grandson of Norman Buel Judd) (R N.Y.) March 15, 1877-Aug. 20, 1964; House Nov. 2, 1915-23.

GOULD, Samuel Wadsworth (D Maine) Jan. 1, 1852-Dec. 19, 1935; House 1911-13.

GOULDEN, Joseph Aloysius (D N.Y.) Aug. 1, 1844-May 3, 1915; House 1903-11, 1913-May 3, 1915.

GOURDIN, Theodore (D S.C.) March 20, 1764-Jan. 17, 1826; House 1813-15.

GOVAN, Andrew Robison (— S.C.) Jan. 13, 1794-June 27, 1841; House Dec. 4, 1822-27.

GOVE, Samuel Francis (R Ga.) March 9, 1822-Dec. 3, 1900; House June 25, 1868-69.

GRABOWSKI, Bernard F. (D Conn.) June 11, 1923- —; House 1963-67.

GRADISON, Willis David Jr. (R Ohio) Dec. 28, 1928- —; House 1975- —.

GRADY, Benjamin Franklin (D N.C.) Oct. 10, 1831-March 6, 1914; House 1891-95.

GRAFF, Joseph Verdi (R Ill.) July 1, 1854-Nov. 10, 1921; House 1895-1911.

GRAHAM, Daniel Robert "Bob" (D Fla.) Nov. 9, 1936- —; Senate 1987- —; Gov. 1978-87.

GRAHAM, Frank Porter (D N.C.) Oct. 14, 1886-Feb. 16, 1972: Senate March 29, 1949-Nov. 26, 1950.

GRAHAM, George Scott (R Pa.) Sept. 13, 1850-July 4, 1931; House 1913-July 4, 1931.

GRAHAM, James (brother of William Alexander Graham) (W N.C.) Jan. 7, 1793-Sept. 25, 1851; House 1833-March 29, 1836, Dec. 5, 1836-1843, 1845-47.

GRAHAM, James Harper (R N.Y.) Sept. 18, 1812-Jun 23, 1881; House 1859-61.

GRAHAM, James McMahon (D Ill.) April 14, 1852-Oc 23, 1945; House 1909-15.

GRAHAM, John Hugh (D N.Y.) April 1, 1835-July 1, 1895; House 1893-95.

GRAHAM, Louis Edward (R Pa.) Aug. 4, 1880-Nov. 1965; House 1939-55.

GRAHAM, William (W Ind.) March 16, 1782-Aug. 1 1858; House 1837-39.

GRAHAM, William Alexander (brother of James Graham) (W N.C.) Sept. 5, 1804-Aug. 11, 1875; Senat Nov. 25, 1840-43; Gov. 1845-49; Secy. of the Nav 1850-52.

GRAHAM, William Harrison (R Pa.) Aug. 3, 184 March 2, 1923; House Nov. 29, 1898-1903, 1905-1

GRAHAM, William Johnson (R Ill.) Feb. 7, 1872-No 10, 1937; House 1917-June 7, 1924.

GRAMM, William Philip "Phil" (R Texas) July 8, 194 —; House 1979-January 5, 1983 (Democrat), Feb. 2 1983-85; Senate 1985- —.

GRAMMER, Elijah Sherman (R Wash.) April 3, 186 Nov. 19, 1936; Senate Nov. 22, 1932-33.

GRANAHAN, Kathryn Elizabeth (widow of Willia Thomas Granahan) (D Pa.) Dec. 7, 1906-July 1 1979; House Nov. 6, 1956-63.

GRANAHAN, William Thomas (husband of Kathry Elizabeth Granahan) (D Pa.) July 26, 1895-May 2 1956; House 1945-47, 1949-May 25, 1956.

GRANATA, Peter Charles (R Ill.) Oct. 28, 1898-- House 1931-April 5, 1932.

GRANDY, Frederick Lawrence (R Iowa) June 29, 194 —; House 1987- —.

GRANFIELD, William Joseph (D Mass.) Dec. 18, 188 May 28, 1959; House Feb. 11, 1930-37.

GRANGER, Amos Phelps (cousin of Francis Grange (W N.Y.) June 3, 1789-Aug. 20, 1866; House 1855-5

GRANGER, Bradley Francis (D Mich.) March 12, 182 Nov. 4, 1882; House 1861-63.

GRANGER, Daniel Larned Davis (D R.I.) May 30, 185 Feb. 14, 1909; House 1903-Feb. 14, 1909.

GRANGER, Francis (cousin of Amos Phelps Grange (W N.Y.) Dec. 1, 1792-Aug. 31, 1868; House 1835-: 1839-March 5, 1841, Nov. 27, 1841-43; Postmas Gen. March 6-Sept. 18, 1841.

GRANGER, Miles Tobey (D Conn.) Aug. 12, 1817-Oct. 21, 1895; House 1887-89.

GRANGER, Walter Keil (D Utah) Oct. 11, 1888-April 21, 1978; House 1941-53.

GRANT, Abraham Phineas (D N.Y.) April 5, 1804-Dec. 11, 1871; House 1837-39.

GRANT, George McInvale (D Ala.) July 11, 1897-Nov. 3, 1982; House June 14, 1938-65.

GRANT, John Gaston (R N.C.) Jan. 1, 1858-June 21, 1923; House 1909-11.

GRANT, Robert Allen (R Ind.) July 31, 1905- — ; House 1939-49.

GRANT, William (D Fla.) Feb. 21, 1943- — ; House 1987- —.

GRANTLAND, Seaton (U Ga.) June 8, 1782-Oct. 18, 1864; House 1835-39.

GRASSLEY, Charles Ernest (R Iowa) Sept. 17, 1933- — ; House 1975-81; Senate 1981- —.

GRASSO, Ella Tambussi (D Conn.) May 10, 1919-Feb. 5, 1981; House 1971-75; Gov. 1975-Dec. 31, 1980.

GRAVEL, Maurice Robert "Mike" (D Alaska) May 13, 1930- — ; Senate 1969-81.

GRAVELY, Joseph Jackson (R Mo.) Sept. 25, 1828-April 28, 1872; House 1867-69.

GRAVES, Alexander (D Mo.) Aug. 25, 1844-Dec. 23, 1916; House 1883-85.

GRAVES, Dixie Bibb (D Ala.) July 26, 1882-Jan. 21, 1965; Senate Aug. 20, 1937-Jan. 10, 1938.

GRAVES, William Jordan (W Ky.) 1805-Sept. 27, 1848; House 1835-41.

GRAY, Edward Winthrop (R N.J.) Aug. 18, 1870-June 10, 1942; House 1915-19.

GRAY, Edwin (— Va.) July 18, 1743-?; House 1799-1813.

GRAY, Finly Hutchinson (D Ind.) July 21, 1863-May 8, 1947; House 1911-17, 1933-39.

GRAY, George (D Del.) May 4, 1840-Aug. 7, 1925; Senate March 18, 1885-99.

GRAY, Hiram (D N.Y.) July 10, 1801-May 6, 1890; House 1837-39.

GRAY, John Cowper (— Va.) 1783-May 18, 1823; House Aug. 28, 1820-21.

GRAY, Joseph Anthony (D Pa.) Feb. 25, 1884-May 8, 1966; House 1935-39.

GRAY, Kenneth James (D Ill.) Nov. 14, 1924- — ; House 1955-Dec. 31, 1974, 1985- —.

GRAY, Oscar Lee (D Ala.) July 2, 1865-Jan. 2, 1936; House 1915-19.

GRAY, William H. III (D Pa.) Aug. 20, 1941- — ; House 1979- —.

GRAYSON, William (father of William John Grayson, uncle of Alexander Dalrymple Orr) (AF Va.) 1740-March 12, 1790; Senate 1789-March 12, 1790; Cont. Cong. 1785-87.

GRAYSON, William John (son of William Grayson, cousin of Alexander Dalrymple Orr) (W S.C.) Nov. 2, 1788-Oct. 4, 1863; House 1833-37.

GREELEY, Horace (W N.Y.) Feb. 3, 1811-Nov. 29, 1872; House Dec. 4, 1848-49.

GREEN, Bryam (— N.Y.) April 15, 1786-Oct. 18, 1865; House 1843-45.

GREEN, Edith (D Ore.) Jan. 17, 1910- — ; House 1955-Dec. 31, 1974.

GREEN, Frederick William (D Ohio) Feb. 18, 1816-June 18, 1879; House 1851-55.

GREEN, Henry Dickinson (D Pa.) May 3, 1857-Dec. 29, 1929; House Nov. 7, 1899-1903.

GREEN, Innis (D Pa.) Feb. 26, 1776-Aug. 4, 1839; House 1827-31.

GREEN, Isaiah Lewis (— Mass.) Dec. 28, 1761-Dec. 5, 1841; House 1805-09, 1811-13.

GREEN, James Stephen (D Mo.) Feb. 28, 1817-Jan. 19, 1870; House 1847-51; Senate Jan. 12, 1857-61.

GREEN, Robert Alexis (D Fla.) Feb. 10, 1892-Feb. 9, 1973; House 1925-Nov. 25, 1944.

GREEN, Robert Stockton (D N.J.) March 25, 1831-May 7, 1895; House 1885-Jan. 17, 1887; Gov. 1887-90.

GREEN, Sedgwick William "Bill" (R N.Y.) Oct. 16, 1929- — ; House Feb. 21, 1978- —.

GREEN, Theodore Francis (grandnephew of Samuel Greene Arnold, great-grandnephew of Tristam Burges, great-grandson of James Burrill Jr., great-grandnephew of Lemuel Hastings Arnold) (D R.I.) Oct. 2, 1867-May 19, 1966; Senate 1937-61; Gov. 1933-37.

GREEN, Wharton Jackson (grandson of Jesse Wharton, cousin of Matt Whitaker Ransom) (D N.C.) Feb. 28, 1831-Aug. 6, 1910; House 1883-87.

GREEN, William Joseph Jr. (father of William Joseph Green III) (D Pa.) March 5, 1910-Dec. 21, 1963; House 1945-47, 1949-Dec. 21, 1963.

GREEN, William Joseph III (son of William Joseph Green Jr.) (D Pa.) June 24, 1938- —; House April 28, 1964-77.

GREEN, William Raymond (R Iowa) Nov. 7, 1856-June 11, 1947; House June 5, 1911-March 31, 1928.

GREEN, Willis (W Ky.) ?-?; House 1839-45.

GREENE, Albert Collins (W R.I.) April 15, 1792-Jan. 8, 1863; Senate 1845-51.

GREENE, Frank Lester (R Vt.) Feb. 10, 1870-Dec. 17, 1930; House July 30, 1912-1923; Senate 1923-Dec. 17, 1930.

GREENE George Woodward (D N.Y.) July 4, 1831-July 21, 1895; House 1869-Feb. 17, 1870.

GREENE, Ray (— R.I.) Feb. 2, 1765-Jan 11, 1849; Senate Nov. 13, 1797-March 5, 1801.

GREENE, Thomas Marston (— Miss.) Feb. 26, 1758-Feb. 7, 1813; House (Terr. Del.) Dec. 6, 1802-03.

GREENE, William Laury (P Neb.) Oct. 3, 1849-March 11, 1899; House 1897-March 11, 1899.

GREENE, William Stedman (R Mass.) April 28, 1841-Sept. 22, 1924; House May 31, 1898-Sept. 22, 1924.

GREENHALGE, Frederic Thomas (R Mass.) July 19, 1842-March 5, 1896; House 1889-91; Gov. 1894-96.

GREENLEAF, Halbert Stevens (D N.Y.) April 12, 1827-Aug. 25, 1906; House 1883-85, 1891-93.

GREENMAN, Edward Whitford (D N.Y.) Jan. 26, 1840-Aug. 3, 1908; House 1887-89.

GREENUP, Christopher (— Ky.) 1750-April 27, 1818; House Nov. 9, 1792-1797; Gov. 1804-08.

GREENWAY, Isabella Selmes (later Mrs. Harry Orland King) (D Ariz.) March 22, 1886-Dec. 18, 1953; House Oct. 3, 1933-37.

GREENWOOD, Alfred Burton (D Ark.) July 11, 1811-Oct. 4, 1889; House 1853-59.

GREENWOOD, Arthur Herbert (D Ind.) Jan. 31, 1880-April 26, 1963; House 1923-39.

GREENWOOD, Ernest (D N.Y.) Nov. 25, 1884-June 15, 1955; House 1951-53.

GREEVER, Paul Ranous (D Wyo.) Sept. 28, 1891-Feb. 16, 1943; House 1935-39.

GREGG, Alexander White (D Texas) Jan. 31, 1855-April 30, 1919; House 1903-19.

GREGG, Andrew (grandfather of James Xavier McLanahan) (— Pa.) June 10, 1755-May 20, 1835 House 1791-1807; Senate 1807-13; Pres. pro tempore 1809.

GREGG, Curtis Hussey (D Pa.) Aug. 9, 1865-Jan. 18 1933; House 1911-13.

GREGG, James Madison (D Ind.) June 26, 1806-June 16, 1869; House 1857-59.

GREGG, Judd (R N.H.) Feb. 14, 1947- —; House 1981 —.

GREGORY, Dudley Sanford (W N.J.) Feb. 5, 1800-Dec 8, 1874; House 1847-49.

GREGORY, Noble Jones (brother of William Voris Gregory) (D Ky.) Aug. 30, 1897-Sept. 26, 1971 House 1937-59.

GREGORY, William Voris (brother of Noble Jones Gregory) (D Ky.) Oct. 21, 1877-Oct. 10, 1936; House 1927-Oct. 10, 1936.

GREIG, John (W N.Y.) Aug. 6, 1779-April 9, 1858 House May 21-Sept. 25, 1841.

GREIGG, Stanley Lloyd (D Iowa) May 7, 1931- — House 1965-67.

GRENNELL, George Jr. (— Mass.) Dec. 25, 1786-Nov 19, 1877; House 1829-39.

GRESHAM, Walter (D Texas) July 22, 1841-Nov. 6 1920; House 1893-95.

GREY, Benjamin Edwards (grandson of Benjamin Edwards) (W Ky.) ?-?; House 1851-55.

GRIDER, George William (D Tenn.) Oct. 1, 1912- — House 1965-67.

GRIDER, Henry (W Ky.) July 16, 1796-Sept. 7, 1866 House 1843-47, 1861-Sept. 7, 1866.

GRIEST, William Walton (R Pa.) Sept. 22, 1858-Dec. 1929; House 1909-Dec. 5, 1929.

GRIFFIN, Anthony Jerome (D N.Y.) April 1, 1866-Jan 13, 1935; House March 5, 1918-Jan. 13, 1935.

GRIFFIN, Charles Hudson (great-great-grandson of Isaac Griffin) (D Miss.) May 9, 1926- —; House March 12, 1968-1973.

GRIFFIN, Daniel Joseph (D N.Y.) March 26, 1880-Dec 11, 1926; House 1913-Dec. 31, 1917.

GRIFFIN, Isaac (great-grandfather of Eugene McLanahan Wilson, great-great-grandfather of Charles Hudson Griffin) (D Pa.) Feb. 27, 1756-Oct. 12, 1827; House Feb. 16, 1813-17.

GRIFFIN, John King (SRW S.C.) Aug. 13, 1789-Aug. 1, 1841; House 1831-41.

GRIFFIN, Levi Thomas (D Mich.) May 23, 1837-March 17, 1906; House Dec. 4, 1893-95.

GRIFFIN, Michael (R Wis.) Sept. 9, 1842-Dec. 29, 1899; House Nov. 5, 1894-99.

GRIFFIN, Robert Paul (R Mich.) Nov. 6, 1923- —; House 1957-May 10, 1966; Senate May 11, 1966-79.

GRIFFIN, Samuel (— Va.) ?-Nov. 3, 1810; House 1789-95.

GRIFFIN, Thomas (— Va.) 1773-Oct. 7, 1837; House 1803-05.

GRIFFITH, Francis Marion (D Ind.) Aug. 21, 1849-Feb. 8, 1927; House Dec. 6, 1897-1905.

GRIFFITH, John Keller (D La.) Oct. 16, 1882-Sept. 25, 1942; House 1937-41.

GRIFFITH, Samuel (D Pa.) Feb. 14, 1816-Oct. 1, 1893; House 1871-73.

GRIFFITHS, Martha Wright (D Mich.) Jan. 29, 1912- —; House 1955-Dec. 31, 1974.

GRIFFITHS, Percy Wilfred (R Ohio) March 30, 1893-June 12, 1984; House 1943-49.

GRIGGS, James Mathews (D Ga.) March 29, 1861-Jan. 5, 1910; House 1897-Jan. 5, 1910.

GRIGSBY, George Barnes (D Alaska) Dec. 2, 1874-May 9, 1962; House (Terr. Del.) June 3, 1920-March 1, 1921.

GRIMES, James Wilson (R Iowa) Oct. 20, 1816-Feb. 7, 1872; Senate 1859-Dec. 6, 1869; Gov. 1854-58 (Whig).

GRIMES, Thomas Wingfield (D Ga.) Dec. 18, 1844-Oct. 28, 1905; House 1887-91.

GRINNELL, Joseph (brother of Moses Hicks Grinnell) (W Mass.) Nov. 17, 1788-Feb. 7, 1885; House Dec. 7, 1843-51.

GRINNELL, Josiah Bushnell (R Iowa) Dec. 22, 1821-March 31, 1891; House 1863-67.

GRINNELL, Moses Hicks (brother of Joseph Grinnell) (W N.Y.) March 3, 1803-Nov. 24, 1877; House 1839-41.

GRISHAM, Wayne Richard (R Calif.) Jan. 10, 1923- —; House 1979-83.

GRISWOLD, Dwight Palmer (R Neb.) Nov. 27, 1893-April 12, 1954; Senate Nov. 5, 1952-April 12, 1954; Gov. 1941-47.

GRISWOLD, Gaylord (F N.Y.) Dec. 18, 1767-March 1, 1809; House 1803-05.

GRISWOLD, Glenn Hasenfratz (D Ind.) Jan. 20, 1890-Dec. 5, 1940; House 1931-39.

GRISWOLD, Harry Wilbur (R Wis.) May 19, 1886-July 4, 1939; House Jan. 3-July 4, 1939.

GRISWOLD, John Ashley (D N.Y.) Nov. 18, 1822-Feb. 22, 1902; House 1869-71.

GRISWOLD, John Augustus (R N.Y.) Nov. 11, 1822-Oct. 31, 1872; House 1863-69 (1863-65 Democrat).

GRISWOLD, Matthew (grandson of Roger Griswold) (R Pa.) June 6, 1833-May 19, 1919; House 1891-93, 1895-97.

GRISWOLD, Roger (grandfather of Matthew Griswold) (F Conn.) May 21, 1762-Oct. 25, 1812; House 1795-1805; Gov. 1811-12.

GRISWOLD, Stanley (— Ohio) Nov. 14, 1763-Aug. 21, 1815; Senate May 18-Dec. 11, 1809.

GROESBECK, William Slocum (D Ohio) July 24, 1815-July 7, 1897; House 1857-59.

GRONNA, Asle Jorgenson (R N.D.) Dec. 10, 1858-May 4, 1922; House 1905-Feb. 2, 1911; Senate Feb. 2, 1911-21.

GROOME, James Black (D Md.) April 4, 1838-Oct. 5, 1893; Senate 1879-85; Gov. 1874-76.

GROSS, Chester Heilman (R Pa.) Oct. 13, 1888-Jan. 9, 1973; House 1939-41, 1943-49.

GROSS, Ezra Carter (D N.Y.) July 11, 1787-April 9, 1829; House 1819-21.

GROSS, Harold Royce (R Iowa) June 30, 1899- —; House 1949-1975.

GROSS, Samuel (D Pa.) Nov. 10, 1774-March 19, 1844; House 1819-23.

GROSVENOR, Charles Henry (uncle of Charles Grosvenor Bond) (R Ohio) Sept. 20, 1833-Oct. 30, 1917; House 1885-91, 1893-1907.

GROSVENOR, Thomas Peabody (F N.Y.) Dec. 20, 1778-April 24, 1817; House Jan. 29, 1813-17.

GROTBERG, John E. (R Ill.) March 21, 1925-Nov. 15, 1986; House 1985-Nov. 15, 1986.

GROUT, Jonathan (D Mass.) July 23, 1737-Sept. 8, 1807; House 1789-91.

GROUT, William Wallace (R Vt.) May 24, 1836-Oct. 7, 1902; House 1881-83; 1885-1901.

GROVE, William Barry (F N.C.) Jan. 15, 1764-March 30, 1818; House 1791-1803.

GROVER, Asa Porter (D Ky.) Feb. 18, 1819-July 20, 1887; House 1867-69.

GROVER, James R. Jr. (R N.Y.) March 5, 1919-–; House 1963-75.

GROVER, La Fayette (D Ore.) Nov. 29, 1823-May 10, 1911; House Feb. 15-March 3, 1859; Senate 1877-83; Gov. 1870-77.

GROVER, Martin (NAD N.Y.) Oct. 20, 1811-Aug. 23, 1875; House 1845-47.

GROW, Galusha Aaron (R Pa.) Aug. 31, 1823-March 31, 1907; House 1851-63 (1851-57 Free Soil Democrat), Feb. 26, 1894-1903; Speaker 1861-63.

GRUENING, Ernest (D Alaska) Feb. 6, 1887-June 26, 1974; Senate 1959-69; Gov. (Alaska Terr.) 1939-53.

GRUNDY, Felix (WD Tenn.) Sept. 11, 1777-Dec. 19, 1840; House 1811-14; Senate Oct. 19, 1829-July 4, 1838, Nov. 19, 1839-Dec. 19, 1840; Atty. Gen. 1838-39.

GRUNDY, Joseph Ridgway (R Pa.) Jan. 13, 1863-March 3, 1961; Senate Dec. 11, 1929-Dec. 1, 1930.

GUARINI, Frank Joseph (D N.J.) Aug. 20, 1924-–; House 1979-–.

GUBSER, Charles Samuel (R Calif.) Feb. 1, 1916-–; House 1953-Dec. 31, 1974.

GUDE, Gilbert (R Md.) March 9, 1923-–; House 1967-77.

GUDGER, James Madison Jr. (father of Katherine Gudger Langley, father-in-law of John Wesley Langley) (D N.C.) Oct. 22, 1855-Feb. 29, 1920; House 1903-07, 1911-15.

GUDGER, Lamar (D N.C.) April 30, 1919-–; House 1977-81.

GUENTHER, Richard William (R Wis.) Nov. 30, 1845-April 5, 1913; House 1881-89.

GUERNSEY, Frank Edward (R Maine) Oct. 15, 1866-Jan. 1, 1927; House Nov. 3, 1908-17.

GUEVARA, Pedro (Nat. P.I.) Feb. 23, 1879-Jan. 19, 1937; House (Res. Comm.) 1923-Feb. 14, 1936.

GUFFEY, Joseph F. (D Pa.) Dec. 29, 1870-March 6, 1959; Senate 1935-47.

GUGGENHEIM, Simon (R Colo.) Dec. 30, 1867-Nov. 2, 1941; Senate 1907-13.

GUILL, Ben Hugh (R Texas) Sept. 8, 1909-–; House May 6, 1950-51.

GUION, Walter (D La.) April 3, 1849-Feb. 7, 1927; Senate April 22-Nov. 5, 1918.

GUNCKEL, Lewis B. (R Ohio) Oct. 15, 1826-Oct. 3, 1903; House 1873-75.

GUNDERSON, Steven (R Wis.) May 10, 1951-–; House 1981-–.

GUNN, James (– Ga.) March 13, 1753-July 30, 1801; Senate 1789-1801; Cont. Cong. 1788-89.

GUNN, James (P Idaho) March 6, 1843-Nov. 5, 1911; House 1897-99.

GUNTER, Thomas Montague (D Ark.) Sept. 18, 1826-Jan. 12, 1904; House June 16, 1874-83.

GUNTER, William Dawson Jr. (D Fla.) July 16, 1934-–; House 1973-75.

GURLEY, Henry Hosford (W La.) May 20, 1788-March 16, 1833; House 1823-31.

GURLEY, John Addison (R Ohio) Dec. 9, 1813-Aug. 19, 1863; House 1859-63.

GURNEY, Edward John (R Fla.) Jan. 12, 1914-–; House 1963-69; Senate 1969-Dec. 31, 1974.

GURNEY, John Chandler "Chan" (R S.D.) May 21, 1896-March 9, 1985; Senate 1939-51.

GUSTINE, Amos (D Pa.) 1789-March 3, 1844; House May 4, 1841-43.

GUTHRIE, James (D Ky.) Dec. 5, 1792-March 13, 1869; Senate 1865-Feb. 7, 1868; Secy. of the Treasury 1853-57.

GUYER, Tennyson (R Ohio) Nov. 29, 1913-April 12, 1981; House 1973-April 12, 1981.

GUYER, Ulysses Samuel (R Kan.) Dec. 13, 1868-June 5, 1943; House Nov. 4, 1924-25, 1927-June 5, 1943.

GUYON, James Jr. (F N.Y.) Dec. 24, 1778-March 9, 1846; House Jan. 14, 1820-21.

GWIN, William McKendree (D Calif.) Oct. 9, 1805-Sept. 3, 1885; House 1841-43 (Miss.); Senate Sept. 9, 1850-55, Jan. 13, 1857-61.

GWINN, Ralph Waldo (R N.Y.) March 29, 1884-Feb. 27, 1962; House 1945-59.

GWYNNE, John William (R Iowa) Oct. 20, 1889-–; House 1935-49.

HABERSHAM, Richard Wylly (SRD Ga.) Dec. 1786-Dec. 2, 1842; House 1839-Dec. 2, 1842.

HACKETT, Richard Nathaniel (D N.C.) Dec. 4, 1866-Nov. 22, 1923; House 1907-09.

HACKETT, Thomas C. (D Ga.) ?-Oct. 8, 1851; House 1849-51.

HACKLEY, Aaron Jr. (−N.Y.) May 6, 1783-Dec. 28, 1868; House 1819-21.

HACKNEY, Thomas (D Mo.) Dec. 11, 1861-Dec. 24, 1946; House 1907-09.

HADLEY, Lindley Hoag (R Wash.) June 19, 1861-Nov. 1, 1948; House 1915-33.

HADLEY, William Flavius Lester (R Ill.) June 15, 1847-April 25, 1901; House Dec. 2, 1895-97.

HAGAN, G. Elliott (D Ga.) May 24, 1916--; House 1961-73.

HAGANS, John Marshall (R W.Va.) Aug. 13, 1838-June 17, 1900; House 1873-75.

HAGEDORN, Thomas Michael (R Minn.) Nov. 27, 1943--; House 1975-83.

HAGEN, Harlan Francis (D Calif.) Oct. 8, 1914--; House 1953-67.

HAGEN, Harold Christian (R Minn.) Nov. 10, 1901-March 19, 1957; House 1943-55 (1943-45 Farmer Laborite).

HAGER, Alva Lysander (R Iowa) Oct. 29, 1850-Jan. 29, 1923; House 1893-99.

HAGER, John Sharpenstein (AMD Calif.) March 12, 1818-March 19, 1890; Senate Dec. 23, 1873-75.

HAGGOTT, Warren Armstrong (R Colo.) May 18, 1864-April 29, 1958; House 1907-09.

HAHN, John (D Pa.) Oct. 30, 1776-Dec. 26, 1823; House 1815-17.

HAHN, Michael (R La.) Nov. 24, 1830-March 15, 1886; House Dec. 3, 1862-63 (Unionist), 1885-March 15, 1886; Gov. 1864-65 (State Rights Free Trader).

HAIGHT, Charles (D N.J.) Jan. 4, 1838-Aug. 1, 1891; House 1867-71.

HAIGHT, Edward (D N.Y.) March 26, 1817-Sept. 15, 1885; House 1861-63.

HAILE, William (− Miss.) 1797-March 7, 1837; House July 10, 1826-Sept. 12, 1828.

HAILEY, John (D Idaho) Aug. 29, 1835-April 10, 1921; House (Terr. Del.) 1873-75, 1885-87.

HAINER, Eugene Jerome (R Neb.) Aug. 16, 1851-March 17, 1929; House 1893-97.

HAINES, Charles Delemere (D N.Y.) June 9, 1856-April 11, 1929; House 1893-95.

HAINES, Harry Luther (D Pa.) Feb. 1, 1880-March 29, 1947; House 1931-39, 1941-43.

HALDEMAN, Richard Jacobs (D Pa.) May 19, 1831-Oct. 1, 1886; House 1869-73.

HALE, Artemas (W Mass.) Oct. 20, 1783-Aug. 3, 1882; House 1845-49.

HALE, Eugene (father of Frederick Hale) (R Maine) June 9, 1836-Oct. 7, 1918; House 1869-79; Senate 1881-1911.

HALE, Fletcher (R N.H.) Jan. 22, 1883-Oct. 22, 1931; House 1925-Oct. 22, 1931.

HALE, Frederick (son of Eugene Hale, grandson of Zachariah Chandler, cousin of Robert Hale) (R Maine) Oct. 7, 1874-Sept. 28, 1963; Senate 1917-41.

HALE, James Tracy (R Pa.) Oct. 14, 1810-April 6, 1865; House 1859-65.

HALE, John Blackwell (D Mo.) Feb. 27, 1831-Feb. 1, 1905; House 1885-87.

HALE, John Parker (FS N.H.) March 31, 1806-Nov. 19, 1873; House 1843-45 (Democrat); Senate 1847-53, July 30, 1855-65.

HALE, Nathan Wesley (R Tenn.) Feb. 11, 1860-Sept. 16, 1941; House 1905-09.

HALE, Robert (cousin of Frederick Hale) (R Maine) Nov. 29, 1889-Nov. 30, 1976; House 1943-59.

HALE, Robert Safford (R N.Y.) Sept. 24, 1822-Dec. 14, 1881; House Dec. 3, 1866-67, 1873-75.

HALE, Salma (D N.H.) March 7, 1787-Nov. 19, 1866; House 1817-19.

HALE, William (F N.H.) Aug. 6, 1765-Nov. 8, 1848; House 1809-11, 1813-17.

HALEY, Elisha (D Conn.) Jan. 21, 1776-Jan. 22, 1860; House 1835-39.

HALEY, James Andrew (D Fla.) Jan. 4, 1899-Aug. 6, 1981; House 1953-77.

HALL, Albert Richardson (R Ind.) Aug. 27, 1884-Nov. 29, 1969; House 1925-31.

HALL, Augustus (D Iowa) April 29, 1814-Feb. 1, 1861; House 1855-57.

HALL, Benton Jay (D Iowa) Jan. 13, 1835-Jan. 5, 1894; House 1885-87.

HALL, Bolling (WD Ga.) Dec. 25, 1767-Feb. 25, 1836; House 1811-17.

HALL, Chapin (R Pa.) July 12, 1816-Sept. 12, 1879; House 1859-61.

HALL, Darwin Scott (R Minn.) Jan. 23, 1844-Feb. 23, 1919; House 1889-91.

HALL, David McKee (D N.C.) May 16, 1918-Jan. 29, 1960; House 1959-Jan. 29, 1960.

HALL, Durward Gorham (R Mo.) Sept. 14, 1910- —; House 1961-73.

HALL, Edwin Arthur (R N.Y.) Feb. 11, 1909- —; House Nov. 7, 1939-53.

HALL, George (D N.Y.) May 12, 1770-March 20, 1840; House 1819-21.

HALL, Hiland (W Vt.) July 20, 1795-Dec. 18, 1885; House Jan. 1, 1833-43; Gov. 1858-60 (Republican).

HALL, Homer William (R Ill.) July 22, 1870-Sept. 22, 1954; House 1927-33.

HALL, James Knox Polk (D Pa.) Sept. 30, 1844-Jan. 5, 1915; House 1899-Nov. 29, 1902.

HALL, Joseph (D Maine) June 26, 1793-Dec. 31, 1859; House 1833-37.

HALL, Joshua Gilman (R N.H.) Nov. 5, 1828-Oct. 31, 1898; House 1879-83.

HALL, Katie Beatrice Green (D Ind.) April 3, 1938- —; House Nov. 29, 1982-85.

HALL, Lawrence Washington (D Ohio) 1819-Jan. 18, 1863; House 1857-59.

HALL, Leonard Wood (R N.Y.) Oct. 2, 1900-June 2, 1979; House 1939-Dec. 31, 1952; Chrmn. Rep. Nat. Comm. 1953-57.

HALL, Nathan Kelsey (W N.Y.) March 28, 1810-March 2, 1874; House 1847-49; Postmaster Gen. 1850-52.

HALL, Norman (D Pa.) Nov. 17, 1829-Sept. 29, 1917; House 1887-89.

HALL, Obed (D N.H.) Dec. 23, 1757-April 1, 1828; House 1811-13.

HALL, Osee Matson (D Minn.) Sept. 10, 1847-Nov. 26, 1914; House 1891-95.

HALL, Philo (R S.D.) Dec. 31, 1865-Oct. 7, 1938; House 1907-09.

HALL, Ralph M. (D Texas) May 3, 1923- —; House 1981- —.

HALL, Robert Bernard (R Mass.) Jan. 28, 1812-April 15, 1868; House 1855-59 (1855-57 American Party).

HALL, Robert Samuel (D Miss.) March 10, 1879-June 10, 1941; House 1929-33.

HALL, Sam Blakeley Jr. (D Texas) Jan. 11, 1924- —; House June 19, 1976-May 27, 1985.

HALL, Thomas (R N.D.) June 6, 1869-Dec. 4, 1958; House Nov. 4, 1924-33.

HALL, Thomas H. (D N.C.) June 1773-June 30, 1853; House 1817-25, 1827-35.

HALL, Tim Lee (D Ill.) June 11, 1925- —; House 1975-77.

HALL, Tony Patrick (D Ohio) Jan. 16, 1942- —; House 1979- —.

HALL, Uriel Sebree (son of William Augustus Hall, nephew of Willard Preble Hall) (D Mo.) April 12, 1852-Dec. 30, 1932; House 1893-97.

HALL, Willard (D Del.) Dec. 24, 1780-May 10, 1875; House 1817-Jan. 22, 1821.

HALL, Willard Preble (brother of William Augustus Hall, uncle of Uriel Sebree Hall) (D Mo.) May 9, 1820-Nov. 2, 1882; House 1847-53; Gov. 1864-65.

HALL, William (D Tenn.) Feb. 11, 1775-Oct. 7, 1856; House 1831-33; Gov. 1829 (Democratic Republican).

HALL, William Augustus (father of Uriel Sebree Hall, brother of Willard Preble Hall) (D Mo.) Oct. 15, 1815-Dec. 15, 1888; House Jan. 20, 1862-65.

HALL, Wilton Earle (D S.C.) March 11, 1901-Feb. 25, 1980; Senate Nov. 20, 1944-45.

HALLECK, Charles Abraham (R Ind.) Aug. 22, 1900-March 3, 1986; House Jan. 29, 1935-69; House majority leader 1947-49, 1953-55.

HALLOCK, John Jr. (D N.Y.) July 1783-Dec. 6, 1840; House 1825-29.

HALLOWAY, Ransom (W N.Y.) about 1793-April 6, 1851; House 1849-51.

HALLOWELL, Edwin (D Pa.) April 2, 1844-Sept. 13, 1916; House 1891-93.

HALPERN, Seymour (R N.Y.) Nov. 19, 1913- —; House 1959-73.

HALSELL, John Edward (D Ky.) Sept. 11, 1826-Dec. 26, 1899; House 1883-87.

HALSEY, George Armstrong (R N.J.) Dec. 7, 1827-April 1, 1894; House 1867-69, 1871-73.

HALSEY, Jehiel Howell (son of Silas Halsey, brother of Nicoll Halsey) (JD N.Y.) Oct. 7, 1788-Dec. 5, 1867; House 1829-31.

HALSEY, Nicoll (son of Silas Halsey, brother of Jehiel Howell Halsey) (D N.Y.) March 8, 1782-March 3, 1865; House 1833-35.

HALSEY, Silas (father of Jehiel Howell Halsey and Nicoll Halsey) (D N.Y.) Oct. 6, 1743-Nov. 19, 1832; House 1805-07.

HALSEY, Thomas Jefferson (R Mo.) May 4, 1863-March 17, 1951; House 1929-31.

HALSTEAD, William (W N.J.) June 4, 1794-March 4, 1878; House 1837-39, 1841-43.

HALTERMAN, Frederick (R Pa.) Oct. 22, 1831-March 22, 1907; House 1895-97.

HALVORSON, Kittel (FA/Prohib. Minn.) Dec. 15, 1846-July 12, 1936; House 1891-93.

HAMBLETON, Samuel (D Md.) Jan. 8, 1812-Dec. 9, 1886; House 1869-73.

HAMER, Thomas Lyon (uncle of Thomas Ray Hamer) (D Ohio) July 1800-Dec. 2, 1846; House 1833-39.

HAMER, Thomas Ray (nephew of Thomas Lyon Hamer) (R Idaho) May 4, 1864-Dec. 22, 1950; House 1909-11.

HAMILL, James Alphonsus (D N.J.) March 30, 1877-Dec. 15, 1941; House 1907-21.

HAMILL, Patrick (D Md.) April 28, 1817-Jan. 15, 1895; House 1869-71.

HAMILTON, Andrew Holman (D Ind.) June 7, 1834-May 9, 1895; House 1875-79.

HAMILTON, Andrew Jackson (brother of Morgan Calvin Hamilton) (ID Texas) Jan. 28, 1815-April 11, 1875; House 1859-61; Military Gov. 1862-65; Provisional Gov. 1865-66.

HAMILTON, Charles Mann (R N.Y.) Jan. 23, 1874-Jan. 3, 1942; House 1913-19.

HAMILTON, Charles Memorial (R Fla.) Nov. 1, 1840-Oct. 22, 1875; House July 1, 1868-71.

HAMILTON, Cornelius Springer (R Ohio) Jan. 2, 1821-Dec. 22, 1867; House March 4-Dec. 22, 1867.

HAMILTON, Daniel Webster (D Iowa) Dec. 20, 1861-Aug. 21, 1936; House 1907-09.

HAMILTON, Edward La Rue (R Mich.) Dec. 9, 1857-Nov. 2, 1923; House 1897-1921.

HAMILTON, Finley (D Ky.) June 19, 1886-Jan. 10, 1940; House 1933-35.

HAMILTON, James Jr. (SRFT S.C.) May 8, 1786-Nov. 15, 1857; House Dec. 13, 1822-29; Gov. 1830-32 (State Rights Democrat).

HAMILTON, John (D Pa.) Nov. 25, 1754-Aug. 22, 1837; House 1805-07.

HAMILTON, John M. (D W.Va.) March 16, 1855-Dec. 27, 1916; House 1911-13.

HAMILTON, John Taylor (D Iowa) Oct. 16, 1843-Jan. 25, 1925; House 1891-93.

HAMILTON, Lee Herbert (D Ind.) April 20, 1931-—; House 1965-—.

HAMILTON, Morgan Calvin (brother of Andrew Jackson Hamilton) (R Texas) Feb. 25, 1809-Nov. 21, 1893; Senate March 31, 1870-77.

HAMILTON, Norman Rond (D Va.) Nov. 13, 1877-March 26, 1964; House 1937-39.

HAMILTON, Robert (D N.J.) Dec. 9, 1809-March 14, 1878; House 1873-77.

HAMILTON, William Thomas (D Md.) Sept. 8, 1820-Oct. 26, 1888; House 1849-55; Senate 1869-75; Gov. 1880-84.

HAMLIN, Courtney Walker (cousin of William Edward Barton) (D Mo.) Oct. 27, 1858-Feb. 16, 1950; House 1903-05, 1907-19.

HAMLIN, Edward Stowe (W Ohio) July 6, 1808-Nov. 23, 1894; House Oct. 8, 1844-45.

HAMLIN, Hannibal (R Maine) Aug. 27, 1809-July 4, 1891; House 1843-47 (Democrat); Senate June 8, 1848-Jan. 7, 1857 (Democrat), 1857-Jan. 17, 1861, 1869-81; Gov. Jan. 8-Feb. 25, 1857; Vice President 1861-65.

HAMLIN, Simon Moulton (D Maine) Aug. 10, 1866-July 27, 1939; House 1935-37.

HAMMER, William Cicero (D N.C.) March 24, 1865-Sept. 26, 1930; House 1921-Sept. 26, 1930.

HAMMERSCHMIDT, John Paul (R Ark.) May 4, 1922-—; House 1967-—.

HAMMETT, William H. (D Miss.) ?-?; House 1843-45.

HAMMOND, Edward (D Md.) March 17, 1812-Oct. 19, 1882; House 1849-53.

HAMMOND, Jabez Delno (D N.Y.) Aug. 2, 1778-Aug. 18, 1855; House 1815-17.

HAMMOND, James Henry (SRD S.C.) Nov. 15, 1807-Nov. 13, 1864; House 1835-Feb. 26, 1836 (State Rights Free Trader); Senate Dec. 7, 1857-Nov. 11, 1860; Gov. 1842-44 (Democrat).

HAMMOND, John (R N.Y.) Aug. 17, 1827-May 28, 1889; House 1879-83.

HAMMOND, Nathaniel Job (D Ga.) Dec. 26, 1833-April 20, 1899; House 1879-87.

HAMMOND, Peter Francis (D Ohio) June 30, 1887-April 2, 1971; House Nov. 30, 1936-37.

HAMMOND, Robert Hanna (VBD Pa.) April 28, 1791-June 2, 1847; House 1837-41.

HAMMOND, Samuel (D Ga.) Sept. 21, 1757-Sept. 11, 1842; House 1803-Feb. 2, 1805; Gov. (Upper Louisiana Terr.) 1805-24.

HAMMOND, Thomas (D Ind.) Feb. 27, 1843-Sept. 21, 1909; House 1893-95.

HAMMOND, Winfield Scott (D Minn.) Nov. 17, 1863-Dec. 30, 1915; House 1907-Jan. 6, 1915; Gov. 1915.

HAMMONS, David (D Maine) May 12, 1808-Nov. 7, 1888; House 1847-49.

HAMMONS, Joseph (JD N.H.) March 3, 1787-March 29, 1836; House 1829-33.

HAMPTON, James Giles (W N.J.) June 13, 1814-Sept. 22, 1861; House 1845-49.

HAMPTON, Moses (W Pa.) Oct. 28, 1803-June 27, 1878; House 1847-51.

HAMPTON, Wade (grandfather of Wade Hampton, below) (D S.C.) 1752-Feb. 4, 1835; House 1795-97, 1803-05.

HAMPTON, Wade (grandson of Wade Hampton, above, son-in-law of George McDuffie) (D S.C.) March 28, 1818-April 11, 1902; Senate 1879-91; Gov. 1876-79.

HANBACK, Lewis (R Kan.) March 27, 1839-Sept. 7, 1897; House 1883-87.

HANBURY, Harry Alfred (R N.Y.) Jan. 1, 1863-Aug. 22, 1940; House 1901-03.

HANCE, Kent Ronald (D Texas) Nov. 14, 1942- –; House 1979-85.

HANCHETT, Luther (R Wis.) Oct. 25, 1825-Nov. 24, 1862; House 1861-Nov. 24, 1862.

HANCOCK, Clarence Eugene (R N.Y.) Feb. 13, 1885-Jan. 3, 1948; House Nov. 8, 1927-47.

HANCOCK, Franklin Wills Jr. (D N.C.) Nov. 1, 1894-Jan. 23, 1969; House Nov. 4, 1930-39.

HANCOCK, George (D Va.) June 13, 1754-July 18, 1820; House 1793-97.

HANCOCK, John (D Texas) Oct. 24, 1824-July 19, 1893; House 1871-77, 1883-85.

HAND, Augustus Cincinnatus (D N.Y.) Sept. 4, 1803-March 8, 1878; House 1839-41.

HAND, Thomas Millet (R N.J.) July 7, 1902-Dec. 26 1956; House 1945-Dec. 26, 1956.

HANDLEY, William Anderson (D Ala.) Dec. 15, 1834 June 23, 1909; House 1871-73.

HANDY, Levin Irving (nephew of William Campbel Preston Breckenridge) (D Del.) Dec. 24, 1861-Feb. ? 1922; House 1897-99.

HANKS, James Millander (D Ark.) Feb. 12, 1833-Ma 24, 1909; House 1871-73.

HANLEY, James M. (D N.Y.) July 19, 1920- –; Hous 1965-81.

HANLY, James Franklin (R Ind.) April 4, 1863-Aug. 1 1920; House 1895-97; Gov. 1905-09.

HANNA, John (R Ind.) Sept. 3, 1827-Oct. 24, 188? House 1877-79.

HANNA, John Andre (grandfather of Archibal McAllister) (AF Pa.) 1762-July 23, 1805; Hous 1797-July 23, 1805.

HANNA, Louis Benjamin (R N.D.) Aug. 9, 1861-Apr 23, 1948; House 1909-Jan. 7, 1913; Gov. 1913-17.

HANNA, Marcus Alonzo (father of Ruth Hanna McCor mick) (R Ohio) Sept. 24, 1837-Feb. 15, 1904; Senat March 5, 1897-Feb. 15, 1904; Chrmn. Rep. Na Comm. 1896-1904.

HANNA, Richard Thomas (D Calif.) June 9, 1914- – House 1963-Dec. 31, 1974.

HANNA, Robert (W Ind.) April 6, 1786-Nov. 16, 185? Senate Aug. 19, 1831-Jan. 3, 1832.

HANNAFORD, Mark Warren (D Calif.) Feb. 7, 192? June 2, 1985; House 1975-79.

HANNEGAN, Edward Allen (D Ind.) June 25, 180? Feb. 25, 1859; House 1833-37; Senate 1843-49.

HANRAHAN, Robert Paul (R Ill.) Feb. 25, 1934- – House 1973-75.

HANSBROUGH, Henry Clay (R N.D.) Jan. 30, 184? Nov. 16, 1933; House Nov. 2, 1889-91; Senate 189? 1909.

HANSEN, Clifford Peter (R Wyo.) Oct. 16, 1912- – Senate 1967-Dec. 31, 1978; Gov. 1963-67.

HANSEN, George Vernon (R Idaho) Sept. 14, 1930- – House 1965-69, 1975-85.

HANSEN, James V. (R Utah) Aug. 14, 1932- –; Hous 1981- –.

HANSEN, John Robert (D Iowa) Aug. 24, 1901-Sept. 2: 1974; House 1965-67.

ANSEN, Julia Butler (D Wash.) June 14, 1907- —; House Nov. 8, 1960-Dec. 31, 1974.

ANSEN, Orval Howard (R Idaho) Aug. 3, 1926- —; House 1969-75.

ANSON, Alexander Contee (F Md.) Feb. 27, 1786-April 23, 1819; House 1813-16; Senate Dec. 20, 1816-April 23, 1819.

ARALSON, Hugh Anderson (D Ga.) Nov. 13, 1805-Sept. 25, 1854; House 1843-51.

ARALSON, Jeremiah (R Ala.) April 1, 1846-about 1916; House 1875-77.

ARD, Gideon (W N.Y.) April 29, 1797-April 27, 1885; House 1833-37.

ARDEMAN, Thomas Jr. (D Ga.) Jan. 12, 1825-March 6, 1891; House 1859-Jan. 23, 1861, 1883-85.

ARDEN, Cecil Murray (R Ind.) Nov. 21, 1894-Dec. 5, 1984; House 1949-59.

ARDENBERGH, Augustus Albert (D N.J.) May 18, 1830-Oct. 5, 1889; House 1875-79, 1881-83.

ARDIN, Benjamin (cousin of Martin Davis Hardin) (W Ky.) Feb. 29, 1784-Sept. 24, 1852; House 1815-17, 1819-23, 1833-37.

ARDIN, John J. (son of Martin Davis Hardin) (W Ill.) Jan. 6, 1810-Feb. 23, 1847; House 1843-45.

ARDIN, Martin Davis (cousin of Benjamin Hardin, father of John J. Hardin) (D Ky.) June 21, 1780-Oct. 8, 1823; Senate Nov. 13, 1816-17.

ARDING, Aaron (UD Ky.) Feb. 20, 1805-Dec. 24, 1875; House 1861-67.

ARDING, Abner Clark (R Ill.) Feb. 10, 1807-July 19, 1874; House 1865-69.

ARDING, Benjamin Franklin (R Ore.) Jan. 4, 1823-June 16, 1899; Senate Sept. 12, 1862-65.

ARDING, John Eugene (R Ohio) June 27, 1877-July 26, 1959; House 1907-09.

ARDING, Ralph R. (D Idaho) Sept. 9, 1929- —; House 1961-65.

ARDING, Warren Gamaliel (R Ohio) Nov. 2, 1865-Aug. 2, 1923; Senate 1915-Jan. 13, 1921; President 1921-Aug. 2, 1923.

ARDWICK, Thomas William (D Ga.) Dec. 9, 1872-Jan. 31, 1944; House 1903-Nov. 2, 1914; Senate Nov. 4, 1914-19; Gov. 1921-23.

ARDY, Alexander Merrill (R Ind.) Dec. 16, 1847-Aug. 31, 1927; House 1895-97.

HARDY, Guy Urban (R Colo.) April 4, 1872-Jan. 26, 1947; House 1919-33.

HARDY, John (D N.Y.) Sept. 19, 1835-Dec. 9, 1913; House Dec. 5, 1881-85.

HARDY, Porter Jr. (D Va.) June 1, 1903- —; House 1947-69.

HARDY, Rufus (D Texas) Dec. 16, 1855-March 13, 1943; House 1907-23.

HARE, Butler Black (father of James Butler Hare) (D S.C.) Nov. 25, 1875-Dec. 30, 1967; House 1925-33, 1939-47.

HARE, Darius Dodge (D Ohio) Jan. 9, 1843-Feb. 10, 1897; House 1891-95.

HARE, James Butler (son of Butler Black Hare) (D S.C.) Sept. 4, 1918-July 16, 1966; House 1949-51.

HARE, Silas (D Texas) Nov. 13, 1827-Nov. 26, 1907; House 1887-91.

HARGIS, Denver David (D Kan.) July 22, 1921- —; House 1959-61.

HARKIN, Thomas Richard (D Iowa) Nov. 19, 1939- —; House 1975-85; Senate 1985- —.

HARLAN, Aaron (cousin of Andrew Jackson Harlan) (W Ohio) Sept. 8, 1802-Jan. 8, 1868; House 1853-59.

HARLAN, Andrew Jackson (cousin of Aaron Harlan) (D Ind.) March 29, 1815-May 19, 1907; House 1849-51, 1853-55.

HARLAN, Byron Berry (D Ohio) Oct. 22, 1886-Nov. 11, 1949; House 1931-39.

HARLAN, James (W Ky.) June 22, 1800-Feb. 18, 1863; House 1835-39.

HARLAN, James (R Iowa) Aug. 26, 1820-Oct. 5, 1899; Senate Dec. 31, 1855-Jan. 12, 1857 (Whig), Jan. 29, 1857-May 15, 1865, 1867-73; Secy. of the Interior May 15, 1865-July 27, 1866.

HARLESS, Richard Fielding (D Ariz.) Aug. 6, 1905-Nov. 24, 1970; House 1943-49.

HARMANSON, John Henry (D La.) Jan. 15, 1803-Oct. 24, 1850; House 1845-Oct. 24, 1850.

HARMER, Alfred Crout (R Pa.) Aug. 8, 1825-March 6, 1900; House 1871-75, 1877-March 6, 1900.

HARMON, Randall S. (D Ind.) July 19, 1903-Aug. 18, 1982; House 1959-61.

HARNESS, Forest Arthur (R Ind.) June 24, 1895-July 29, 1974; House 1939-49.

HARPER, Alexander (W Ohio) Feb. 5, 1786-Dec. 1, 1860; House 1837-39, 1843-47, 1851-53.

HARPER, Francis Jacob (D Pa.) March 5, 1800-March 18, 1837; House March 4-18, 1837.

HARPER, James (W Pa.) March 28, 1780-March 31, 1873; House 1833-37 (1833-35 Clay Democrat).

HARPER, James Clarence (C N.C.) Dec. 6, 1819-Jan. 8, 1890; House 1871-73.

HARPER, John Adams (WD N.H.) Nov. 2, 1779-June 18, 1816; House 1811-13.

HARPER, Joseph Morrill (D N.H.) June 21, 1787-Jan. 15, 1865; House 1831-35; Gov. 1831.

HARPER, Robert Goodloe (F Md.) Jan. 1765-Jan. 14, 1825; House Feb. 5, 1795-1801 (S.C.); Senate Jan. 29-Dec. 6, 1816.

HARPER, William (SRD S.C.) Jan. 17, 1790-Oct. 10, 1847; Senate March 8-Nov. 29, 1826.

HARRELD, John William (R Okla.) Jan. 24, 1872-Dec. 26, 1950; House Nov. 8, 1919-21; Senate 1921-27.

HARRIES, William Henry (D Minn.) Jan. 15, 1843-July 23, 1921; House 1891-93.

HARRINGTON, Henry William (D Ind.) Sept. 12, 1825-March 20, 1882; House 1863-65.

HARRINGTON, Michael Joseph (D Mass.) Sept. 2, 1936- —; House Sept. 30, 1969-79.

HARRINGTON, Vincent Francis (D Iowa) May 16, 1903-Nov. 29, 1943; House 1937-Sept. 5, 1942.

HARRIS, Benjamin Gwinn (D Md.) Dec. 13, 1805-April 4, 1895; House 1863-67.

HARRIS, Benjamin Winslow (father of Robert Orr Harris) (R Mass.) Nov. 10, 1823-Feb. 7, 1907; House 1873-83.

HARRIS, Charles Murray (D Ill.) April 10, 1821-Sept. 20, 1896; House 1863-65.

HARRIS, Christopher Columbus (D Ala.) Jan. 28, 1842-Dec. 28, 1935; House May 11, 1914-15.

HARRIS, Claude Jr. (D Ala.) June 29, 1940- —; House 1987- —.

HARRIS, Fred Roy (D Okla.) Nov. 13, 1930- —; Senate Nov. 4, 1964-73; Chrmn. Dem. Nat. Comm. 1969-70.

HARRIS, George Emrick (R Miss.) Jan. 6, 1827-March 19, 1911; House Feb. 23, 1870-73.

HARRIS, Henry Richard (D Ga.) Feb. 2, 1828-Oct. 15, 1909; House 1873-79, 1885-87.

HARRIS, Henry Schenck (D N.J.) Dec. 27, 1850-May 1902; House 1881-83.

HARRIS, Herbert Eugene II (D Va.) April 14, 1926- -- House 1975-81.

HARRIS, Ira (grandfather of Henry Riggs Rathbone) (N.Y.) May 31, 1802-Dec. 2, 1875; Senate 1861-67.

HARRIS, Isham Green (D Tenn.) Feb. 10, 1818-July 1897; House 1849-53; Senate 1877-July 8, 1897; Pre pro tempore 1893-95; Gov. 1857-62.

HARRIS, James Morrison (AP Md.) Nov. 20, 1817-Ju 16, 1898; House 1855-61.

HARRIS, John (cousin of Robert Harris) (− N.Y.) Sep 26, 1760-Nov. 1824; House 1807-09.

HARRIS, John Spafford (R La.) Dec. 18, 1825-Jan. 2 1906; Senate July 8, 1868-71.

HARRIS, John Thomas (cousin of John Hill of Virgini (D Va.) May 8, 1823-Oct. 14, 1899; House 1859-6 1871-81.

HARRIS, Mark (− Maine) Jan. 27, 1779-March 2, 184 House Dec. 2, 1822-23.

HARRIS, Oren (D Ark.) Dec. 20, 1903- —; House 194 Feb. 2, 1966.

HARRIS, Robert (cousin of John Harris) (− Pa.) Se 5, 1768-Sept. 3, 1851; House 1823-27.

HARRIS, Robert Orr (son of Benjamin Winslow Harr (R Mass.) Nov. 8, 1854-June 13, 1926; House 191 13.

HARRIS, Sampson Willis (D Ala.) Feb. 23, 1809-April 1857; House 1847-57.

HARRIS, Stephen Ross (uncle of Ebenezer Byr Finley) (R Ohio) May 22, 1824-Jan. 15, 1905; Hou 1895-97.

HARRIS, Thomas K. (D Tenn.) ?-March 18, 18 House 1813-15.

HARRIS, Thomas Langrell (D Ill.) Oct. 29, 1816-N 24, 1858; House 1849-51, 1855-Nov. 24, 1858.

HARRIS, Wiley Pope (D Miss.) Nov. 9, 1818-Dec. 1891; House 1853-55.

HARRIS, William Alexander (father of William Alexa der Harris, below) (D Va.) Aug. 24, 1805-March 1864; House 1841-43.

HARRIS, William Alexander (son of William Alexand Harris, above) (D Kan.) Oct. 29, 1841-Dec. 20, 19 House 1893-95 (Populist); Senate 1897-1903.

HARRIS, William Julius (great-grandson of Charles Hooks) (D Ga.) Feb. 3, 1868-April 18, 1932; Senate 1919-April 18, 1932.

HARRIS, Winder Russell (D Va.) Dec. 3, 1888-Feb. 24, 1973; House April 8, 1941-Sept. 15, 1944.

HARRISON, Albert Galliton (VBD Mo.) June 26, 1800-Sept. 7, 1839; House 1835-39.

HARRISON, Benjamin (grandson of William Henry Harrison, son of John Scott Harrison, grandfather of William Henry Harrison of Wyoming) (R Ind.) Aug. 20, 1833-March 13, 1901; Senate 1881-87; President 1889-93.

HARRISON, Burr Powell (son of Thomas Walter Harrison) (D Va.) July 2, 1904-Dec. 29, 1973; House Nov. 6, 1946-63.

HARRISON, Byron Patton "Pat" (D Miss.) Aug. 29, 1881-June 22, 1941; House 1911-19; Senate 1919-June 22, 1941; Pres. pro tempore 1941.

HARRISON, Carter Bassett (brother of William Henry Harrison born in 1773) (— Va.) ?-April 18, 1808; House 1793-99.

HARRISON, Carter Henry (D Ill.) Feb. 15, 1825-Oct. 28, 1893; House 1875-79.

HARRISON, Francis Burton (D N.Y.) Dec. 18, 1873-Nov. 21, 1957; House 1903-05, 1907-Sept. 1, 1913.

HARRISON, Frank (D Pa.) Feb. 2, 1940-—; House 1983-85.

HARRISON, George Paul (D Ala.) March 19, 1841-July 17, 1922; House Nov. 6, 1894-97.

HARRISON, Horace Harrison (R Tenn.) Aug. 7, 1829-Dec. 20, 1885; House 1873-75.

HARRISON, John Scott (son of William Henry Harrison born in 1773, father of Benjamin Harrison) (W Ohio) Oct. 4, 1804-May 25, 1878; House 1853-57.

HARRISON, Richard Almgill (UD Ohio) April 8, 1824-July 30, 1904; House July 4, 1861-63.

HARRISON, Robert Dinsmore (R Neb.) Jan. 26, 1897-June 11, 1977; House Dec. 4, 1951-59.

HARRISON, Samuel Smith (D Pa.) 1780-April 1853; House 1833-37.

HARRISON, Thomas Walter (father of Burr Powell Harrison) (D Va.) Aug. 5, 1856-May 9, 1935; House Nov. 7, 1916-Dec. 15, 1922, 1923-29.

HARRISON, William Henry (father of John Scott Harrison, brother of Carter Basset Harrison, grandfather of Benjamin Harrison, great-great-grandfather of William Henry Harrison of Wyoming) (W Ohio) Feb. 9, 1773-April 4, 1841; House (Terr. Del.) 1799-May 14, 1800; (Rep.) Oct. 8, 1816-19; Senate 1825-May 20, 1828; Gov. (Indiana Terr.) 1801-13; President March 4-April 4, 1841.

HARRISON, William Henry (great-great-grandson of William Henry Harrison, grandson of Benjamin Harrison and Alvin Saunders) (R Wyo.) Aug. 10, 1896-—; House 1951-55, 1961-65, 1967-69.

HARSHA, William Howard (R Ohio) Jan. 1, 1921-—; House 1961-81.

HART, Alphonso (R Ohio) July 4, 1830-Dec. 23, 1910; House 1883-85.

HART, Archibald Chapman (D N.J.) Feb. 27, 1873-July 24, 1935; House Nov. 5, 1912-March 3, 1913, July 22, 1913-17.

HART, Edward Joseph (D N.J.) March 25, 1893-April 20, 1961; House 1935-55.

HART, Elizur Kirke (D N.Y.) April 8, 1841-Feb. 18, 1893; House 1877-79.

HART, Emanuel Bernard (D N.Y.) Oct. 27, 1809-Aug. 29, 1897; House 1851-53.

HART, Gary Warren (D Colo.) Nov. 28, 1937-—; Senate 1975-87.

HART, Joseph Johnson (D Pa.) April 18, 1859-July 13, 1926; House 1895-97.

HART, Michael James (D Mich.) July 16, 1877-Feb. 14, 1951; House Nov. 3, 1931-35.

HART, Philip Aloysius (D Mich.) Dec. 10, 1912-Dec. 26, 1976; Senate 1959-Dec. 26, 1976.

HART, Roswell (R N.Y.) Aug. 4, 1824-April 20, 1883; House 1865-67.

HART, Thomas Charles (R Conn.) June 12, 1877-July 4, 1971; Senate Feb. 15, 1945-Nov. 5, 1946.

HARTER, Dow Watters (D Ohio) Jan. 2, 1885-Sept. 4, 1971; House 1933-43.

HARTER, John Francis (R N.Y.) Sept. 1, 1897-Dec. 20, 1947; House 1939-41.

HARTER, Michael Daniel (grandson of Robert Moore) (D Ohio) April 6, 1846-Feb. 22, 1896; House 1891-95.

HARTKE, Rupert Vance (D Ind.) May 31, 1919-—; Senate 1959-77.

HARTLEY, Fred Allan Jr. (R N.J.) Feb. 22, 1902-May 11, 1969; House 1929-49.

HARTLEY, Thomas (− Pa.) Sept. 7, 1748-Dec. 21, 1800; House 1789-Dec. 21, 1800.

HARTMAN, Charles Sampson (Sil.R Mont.) March 1, 1861-Aug. 3, 1929; House 1893-99 (1893-97 Republican).

HARTMAN, Jesse Lee (R Pa.) June 18, 1853-Feb. 17, 1930; House 1911-13.

HARTNETT, Thomas F. (R S.C.) Aug. 7, 1941- −; House 1981-87.

HARTRIDGE, Julian (D Ga.) Sept. 9, 1829-Jan. 8, 1879; House 1875-Jan. 8, 1879.

HARTZELL, William (D Ill.) Feb. 20, 1837-Aug. 14, 1903; House 1875-79.

HARVEY, David Archibald (R Okla.) March 20, 1845-May 24, 1916; House (Terr. Del.) Nov. 4, 1890-93.

HARVEY, James (R Mich.) July 4, 1922- −; House 1961-Jan. 31, 1974.

HARVEY, James Madison (R Kan.) Sept. 21, 1833-April 15, 1894; Senate Feb. 2, 1874-77; Gov. 1869-73.

HARVEY, Jonathan (brother of Matthew Harvey) (− N.H.) Feb. 25, 1780-Aug. 23, 1859; House 1825-31.

HARVEY, Matthew (brother of Jonathan Harvey) (D N.H.) June 21, 1781-April 7, 1866; House 1821-25; Gov. 1830-31 (Jackson Democrat).

HARVEY, Ralph (R Ind.) Aug. 9, 1901- −; House Nov. 4, 1947-59, 1961-Dec. 30, 1966.

HASBROUCK, Abraham Bruyn (cousin of Abraham Joseph Hasbrouck) (NR N.Y.) Nov. 29, 1791-Feb. 24, 1879; House 1825-27.

HASBROUCK, Abraham Joseph (cousin of Abraham Bruyn Hasbrouck) (Clinton D N.Y.) Oct. 16, 1773-Jan. 12, 1845; House 1813-15.

HASBROUCK, Josiah (− N.Y.) March 5, 1755-March 19, 1821; House April 28, 1803-05, 1817-19.

HASCALL, Augustus Porter (W N.Y.) June 24, 1800-June 27, 1872; House 1851-53.

HASKELL, Dudley Chase (grandfather of Otis Halbert Holmes) (R Kan.) March 23, 1842-Dec. 16, 1883; House 1877-Dec. 16, 1883.

HASKELL, Floyd Kirk (D Colo.) Feb. 7, 1916- −; Senate 1973-79.

HASKELL, Harry Garner Jr. (R Del.) May 27, 1921- −; House 1957-59.

HASKELL, Reuben Locke (R N.Y.) Oct. 5, 1878-Oct. 2, 1971; House 1915-Dec. 31, 1919.

HASKELL, William T. (nephew of Charles Ready) (W Tenn.) July 21, 1818-March 12, 1859; House 1847-49.

HASKIN, John Bussing (D N.Y.) Aug. 27, 1821-Sept. 18, 1895; House 1857-61.

HASKINS, Kittredge (R Vt.) April 8, 1836-Aug. 7, 1916; House 1901-09.

HASTERT, J. Dennis (R Ill.) Jan. 2, 1942- −; House 1987- −.

HASTINGS, Daniel Oren (R Del.) March 5, 1874-May 9, 1966; Senate Dec. 10, 1928-37.

HASTINGS, George (D N.Y.) March 13, 1807-Aug. 29, 1866; House 1853-55.

HASTINGS, James Fred (R N.Y.) April 10, 1926- − House 1969-Jan. 20, 1976.

HASTINGS, John (JD Ohio) 1778-Dec. 8, 1854; House 1839-43.

HASTINGS, Serranus Clinton (D Iowa) Nov. 14, 1813-Feb. 18, 1893; House Dec. 28, 1846-47.

HASTINGS, Seth (father of William Soden Hastings) (F Mass.) April 8, 1762-Nov. 19, 1831; House Aug. 24, 1801-07.

HASTINGS, William Soden (son of Seth Hastings) (W Mass.) June 3, 1798-June 17, 1842; House 1837-June 17, 1842.

HASTINGS, William Wirt (D Okla.) Dec. 31, 1866-April 8, 1938; House 1915-21, 1923-35.

HATCH, Carl Atwood (D N.M.) Nov. 27, 1889-Sept. 15, 1963; Senate Oct. 10, 1933-49.

HATCH, Herschel Harrison (R Mich.) Feb. 17, 1837-Nov. 30, 1920; House 1883-85.

HATCH, Israel Thompson (D N.Y.) June 30, 1808-Sept. 24, 1875; House 1857-59.

HATCH, Jethro Ayers (R Ind.) June 18, 1837-Aug. 1912; House 1895-97.

HATCH, Orrin Grant (R Utah) March 22, 1934- −; Senate 1977- −.

HATCH, William Henry (D Mo.) Sept. 11, 1833-Dec. 1896; House 1879-95.

HATCHER, Charles F. (D Ga.) July 1, 1939- −; House 1981- −.

HATCHER, Robert Anthony (D Mo.) Feb. 24, 1819-Dec. 4, 1886; House 1873-79.

HATFIELD, Henry Drury (R W.Va.) Sept. 15, 1875-Oct. 23, 1962; Senate 1929-35; Gov. 1913-17.

HATFIELD, Mark Odom (R Ore.) July 12, 1922-–;
Senate Jan. 10, 1967-–; Gov. 1959-67.

HATFIELD, Paul Gerhart (D Mont.) April 29, 1928-–;
Senate Jan. 22-Dec. 14, 1978.

HATHAWAY, Samuel Gilbert (D N.Y.) July 18, 1780-
May 2, 1867; House 1833-35.

HATHAWAY, William Dodd (D Maine) Feb. 21, 1924-
–; House 1965-73; Senate 1973-79.

HATHORN, Henry Harrison (R N.Y.) Nov. 28, 1813-
Feb. 20, 1887; House 1873-77.

HATHORN, John (F N.Y.) Jan. 9, 1749-Feb. 19, 1825;
House 1789-91, 1795-97; Cont. Cong. 1788.

HATTON, Robert Hopkins (AP Tenn.) Nov. 2, 1826-
May 31, 1862; House 1859-61.

HAUGEN, Gilbert Nelson (R Iowa) April 21, 1859-July
18, 1933; House 1899-1933.

HAUGEN, Nils Pederson (R Wis.) March 9, 1849-April
23, 1931; House 1887-95.

HAUGHEY, Thomas (R Ala.) 1826-Aug. 1869; House
July 21, 1868-69.

HAUN, Henry Peter (D Calif.) Jan. 18, 1815-June 6,
1860; Senate Nov. 3, 1859-March 4, 1860.

HAVEN, Nathaniel Appleton (F N.H.) July 19, 1762-
March 13, 1831; House 1809-11.

HAVEN, Solomon George (W N.Y.) Nov. 27, 1810-Dec.
24, 1861; House 1851-57.

HAVENNER, Franck Roberts (D Calif.) Sept. 20, 1882-
July 24, 1967; House 1937-41 (1937-39 Progressive),
1945-53.

HAVENS, Harrison Eugene (R Mo.) Dec. 15, 1837-Aug.
16, 1916; House 1871-75.

HAVENS, James Smith (D N.Y.) May 28, 1859-Feb. 27,
1927; House April 19, 1910-11.

HAVENS, Jonathan Nicoll (D N.Y.) June 18, 1757-Oct.
25, 1799; House 1795-Oct. 25, 1799.

HAWES, Albert Gallatin (brother of Richard Hawes,
nephew of Aylett Hawes, granduncle of Harry
Bartow Hawes, cousin of Aylett Hawes Buckner)
(JD Ky.) April 1, 1804-March 14, 1849; House 1831-
37.

HAWES, Aylett (uncle of Richard Hawes, Albert Gallatin Hawes and Aylett Hawes Buckner) (D Va.) April
21, 1768-Aug. 31, 1833; House 1811-17.

HAWES, Harry Bartow (grandnephew of Albert Gallatin Hawes) (D Mo.) Nov. 15, 1869-July 31, 1947;
House 1921-Oct. 15, 1926; Senate Dec. 6, 1926-Feb.
3, 1933.

HAWES, Richard (brother of Albert Gallatin Hawes,
nephew of Aylett Hawes, cousin of Aylett Hawes
Buckner) (W Ky.) Feb. 6, 1797-May 25, 1877; House
1837-41.

HAWK, Robert Moffett Allison (R Ill.) April 23, 1839-
June 29, 1882; House 1879-June 29, 1882.

HAWKES, Albert Wahl (R N.J.) Nov. 20, 1878-May 9,
1971; Senate 1943-49.

HAWKES, James (– N.Y.) Dec. 13, 1776-Oct. 2, 1865;
House 1821-23.

HAWKINS, Augustus F. (D Calif.) Aug. 31, 1907-–;
House 1963-–.

HAWKINS, Benjamin (uncle of Micajah Thomas Hawkins) (F N.C.) Aug. 15, 1754-June 6, 1816; Senate
Nov. 27, 1789-95; Cont. Cong. 1781-84, 1786-87.

HAWKINS, George Sydney (D Fla.) 1808-March 15,
1878; House 1857-Jan. 21, 1861.

HAWKINS, Isaac Roberts (R Tenn.) May 16, 1818-Aug.
12, 1880; House July 24, 1866-71.

HAWKINS, Joseph (Ad.D N.Y.) Nov. 14, 1781-April 20,
1832; House 1829-31.

HAWKINS, Joseph H. (F Ky.) ?-1823; House March 29,
1814-15.

HAWKINS, Micajah Thomas (nephew of Benjamin
Hawkins and Nathaniel Macon) (D N.C.) May 20,
1790-Dec. 22, 1858; House Dec. 15, 1831-41.

HAWKINS, Paula (R Fla.) Jan. 24, 1927-–; Senate
1981-87.

HAWKS, Charles Jr. (R Wis.) July 7, 1899-Jan. 6, 1960;
House 1939-41.

HAWLEY, John Baldwin (R Ill.) Feb. 9, 1831-May 24,
1895; House 1869-75.

HAWLEY, Joseph Roswell (R Conn.) Oct. 31, 1826-
March 17, 1905; House Dec. 2, 1872-75, 1879-81;
Senate 1881-1905; Gov. 1866-67.

HAWLEY, Robert Bradley (R Texas) Oct. 25, 1849-Nov.
28, 1921; House 1897-1901.

HAWLEY, Willis Chatman (R Ore.) May 5, 1864-July
24, 1941; House 1907-33.

HAWS, John Henry Hobart (W N.Y.) 1809-Jan. 27,
1858; House 1851-53.

HAY, Andrew Kessler (W N.J.) Jan. 19, 1809-Feb. 7, 1881; House 1849-51.

HAY, James (D Va.) Jan. 9, 1856-June 12, 1931; House 1897-Oct. 1, 1916.

HAY, John Breese (R Ill.) Jan. 8, 1834-June 16, 1916; House 1869-73.

HAYAKAWA, Samuel Ichiye (R Calif.) July 18, 1906- —; Senate Jan. 2, 1977-83.

HAYDEN, Carl Trumbull (D Ariz.) Oct. 2, 1877-Jan. 25, 1972; House Feb. 19, 1912-27; Senate 1927-69; Pres. pro tempore 1957-69.

HAYDEN, Edward Daniel (R Mass.) Dec. 27, 1833-Nov. 15, 1908; House 1885-89.

HAYDEN, Moses (— N.Y.) 1786-Feb. 13, 1830; House 1823-27.

HAYES, Charles Arthur (D Ill.) Feb. 17, 1918- —; House Sept. 12, 1983- —.

HAYES, Everis Anson (R Calif.) March 10, 1855-June 3, 1942; House 1905-19.

HAYES, James Alison "Jimmy" (D La.) Dec. 21, 1946- —; House 1987- —.

HAYES, Philip Cornelius (R Ill.) Feb. 3, 1833-July 13, 1916; House 1877-81.

HAYES, Philip Harold (D Ind.) Sept. 1, 1940- —; House 1975-77.

HAYES, Rutherford Birchard (R Ohio) Oct. 4, 1822-Jan. 17, 1893; House 1865-July 20, 1867; President 1877-81; Gov. 1868-72, 1876-77.

HAYES, Walter Ingalls (D Iowa) Dec. 9, 1841-March 14, 1901; House 1887-95.

HAYMOND, Thomas Sherwood (W Va.) Jan. 15, 1794-April 5, 1869; House Nov. 8, 1849-51.

HAYMOND, William Summerville (D/L Ind.) Feb. 20, 1823-Dec. 24, 1885; House 1875-77.

HAYNE, Arthur Peronneau (brother of Robert Young Hayne) (D S.C.) March 12, 1790-Jan. 7, 1867; Senate May 11-Dec. 2, 1858.

HAYNE, Robert Young (brother of Arthur Peronneau Hayne, son-in-law of Charles Pinckney) (TD S.C.) Nov. 10, 1791-Sept. 24, 1839; Senate 1823-Dec. 13, 1832; Gov. 1832-34 (State Rights Democrat).

HAYNES, Charles Eaton (U Ga.) April 15, 1784-Aug. 29, 1841; House 1825-31 (Democrat).

HAYNES, Martin Alonzo (R N.H.) July 30, 1842-Nov. 28, 1919; House 1883-87.

HAYNES, William Elisha (cousin of George William Palmer) (D Ohio) Oct. 19, 1829-Dec. 5, 1914; House 1889-93.

HAYS, Charles (R Ala.) Feb. 2, 1834-June 24, 1879; House 1869-77.

HAYS, Edward Dixon (R Mo.) April 28, 1872-July 25, 1941; House 1919-23.

HAYS, Edward Retilla (R Iowa) May 26, 1847-Feb. 28 1896; House Nov. 4, 1890-91.

HAYS, Lawrence Brooks (D Ark.) Aug. 9, 1898-Oct. 12 1981; House 1943-59.

HAYS, Samuel (D Pa.) Sept. 10, 1783-July 1, 1868 House 1843-45.

HAYS, Samuel Lewis (D Va.) Oct. 20, 1794-March 17 1871; House 1841-43.

HAYS, Wayne Levere (D Ohio) May 13, 1911- —; House 1949-Sept. 1, 1976.

HAYWARD, Monroe Leland (R Neb.) Dec. 22, 1840 Dec. 5, 1899; Senate March 8-Dec. 5, 1899.

HAYWARD, William Jr. (D Md.) 1787-Oct. 19, 1836 House 1823-25.

HAYWOOD, William Henry Jr. (D N.C.) Oct. 23, 1801 Oct. 7, 1852; Senate 1843-July 25, 1846.

HAYWORTH, Donald (D Mich.) Jan. 13, 1898-Feb. 25 1982; House 1955-57.

HAZARD, Nathaniel (D R.I.) 1776-Dec. 17, 1820; House 1819-Dec. 17, 1820.

HAZELTINE, Abner (W N.Y.) June 10, 1793-Dec. 20 1879; House 1833-37.

HAZELTINE, Ira Sherwin (RG Mo.) July 13, 1821-Jan 13, 1899; House 1881-83.

HAZELTON, George Cochrane (brother of Gerry Whiting Hazelton, nephew of Clark Betton Cochrane) (R Wis.) Jan. 3, 1832-Sept. 4, 1922; House 1877-83.

HAZELTON, Gerry Whiting (brother of George Cochrane Hazelton, nephew of Clark Betton Cochrane) (R Wis.) Feb. 24, 1829-Sept. 19, 1920 House 1871-75.

HAZELTON, John Wright (R N.J.) Dec. 10, 1814-Dec 20, 1878; House 1871-75.

HAZLETT, James Miller (R Pa.) Oct. 14, 1864-Nov. 1940; House March 4-Oct. 20, 1927.

HEALD, William Henry (R Del.) Aug. 27, 1864-June 1939; House 1909-13.

HEALEY, Arthur Daniel (D Mass.) Dec. 29, 1889-Sept. 16, 1948; House 1933-Aug. 3, 1942.

HEALEY, James Christopher (D N.Y.) Dec. 24, 1909-Dec. 16, 1981; House Feb. 7, 1956-65.

HEALY, Joseph (D N.H.) Aug. 21, 1776-Oct. 10, 1861; House 1825-29.

HEALY, Ned R. (D Calif.) Aug. 9, 1905-Sept. 10, 1977; House 1945-47.

HEARD, John Thaddeus (D Mo.) Oct. 29, 1840-Jan. 27, 1927; House 1885-95.

HEARST, George (father of William Randolph Hearst) (D Calif.) Sept. 3, 1820-Feb. 28, 1891; Senate March 23-Aug. 4, 1886, 1887-Feb. 28, 1891.

HEARST, William Randolph (son of George Hearst) (D N.Y.) April 29, 1863-Aug. 14, 1951; House 1903-07.

HEATH, James P. (D Md.) Dec. 21, 1777-June 12, 1854; House 1833-35.

HEATH, John (R Va.) May 8, 1758-Oct. 13, 1810; House 1793-97.

HEATON, David (R N.C.) March 10, 1823-June 25, 1870; House July 15, 1868-June 25, 1870.

HEATON, Robert Douglas (R Pa.) July 1, 1873-June 11, 1933; House 1915-19.

HEATWOLE, Joel Prescott (R Minn.) Aug. 22, 1856-April 4, 1910; House 1895-1903.

HEBARD, William (W Vt.) Nov. 29, 1800-Oct. 20, 1875; House 1849-53.

HEBERT, Felix (R R.I.) Dec. 11, 1874-Dec. 14, 1969; Senate 1929-35.

HEBERT, Felix Edward (D La.) Oct. 12, 1901-Dec. 29, 1979; House 1941-77.

HECHLER, Ken (D W.Va.) Sept. 20, 1914- —; House 1959-77.

HECHT, Jacob "Chic" (R Nev.) Nov. 30, 1928- —; Senate 1983- —.

HECKLER, Margaret M. (R Mass.) June 21, 1931- —; House 1967-83; Secy. Health and Human Services 1983-85.

HEDGE, Thomas (R Iowa) June 24, 1844-Nov. 28, 1920; 1899-1907.

HEDRICK, Erland Harold (D W.Va.) Aug. 9, 1894-Sept. 20, 1954; House 1945-53.

HEFFERNAN, James Joseph (D N.Y.) Nov. 8, 1888-Jan. 27, 1967; House 1941-53.

HEFLIN, Howell Thomas (nephew of James Thomas Heflin) (D Ala.) June 19, 1921- —; Senate 1979- —.

HEFLIN, James Thomas (uncle of Howell Thomas Heflin, nephew of Robert Stell Heflin) (D Ala.) April 9, 1869-April 22, 1951; House May 10, 1904-Nov. 1, 1920; Senate Nov. 3, 1920-31.

HEFLIN, Robert Stell (uncle of James Thomas Heflin) (R Ala.) April 15, 1815-Jan. 24, 1901; House 1869-71.

HEFLY, Joel M. (R Colo.) April 18, 1935- —; House 1987- —.

HEFNER, Willie Gathrel (D N.C.) April 11, 1930- —; House 1975- —.

HEFTEL, Cecil (D Hawaii) Sept. 30, 1924- —; House 1977-July 11, 1986.

HEIDINGER, James Vandaveer (R Ill.) July 17, 1882-March 22, 1945; House 1941-March 22, 1945.

HEILMAN, William (great-grandfather of Charles Marion La Follette) (R Ind.) Oct. 1, 1824-Sept. 22, 1890; House 1879-83.

HEINER, Daniel Brodhead (R Pa.) Dec. 30, 1854-Feb. 14, 1944; House 1893-97.

HEINKE, George Henry (R Neb.) July 22, 1882-Jan. 2, 1940; House 1939-Jan. 2, 1940.

HEINTZ, Victor (R Ohio) Nov. 20, 1876-Dec. 27, 1968; House 1917-19.

HEINZ, Henry John III (R Pa.) Oct. 23, 1938- —; House Nov. 2, 1971-77; Senate 1977- —.

HEISKELL, John Netherland (D Ark.) Nov. 2, 1872-Dec. 28, 1972; Senate Jan. 6-Jan. 29, 1913.

HEITFELD, Henry (P Idaho) Jan. 12, 1859-Oct. 21, 1938; Senate 1897-1903.

HELGESEN, Henry Thomas (R N.D.) June 26, 1857-April 10, 1917; House 1911-April 10, 1917.

HELLER, Louis Benjamin (D N.Y.) Feb. 10, 1905- —; House Feb. 15, 1949-July 21, 1954.

HELM, Harvey (D Ky.) Dec. 2, 1865-March 3, 1919; House 1907-March 3, 1919.

HELMICK, William (R Ohio) Sept. 6, 1817-March 31, 1888; House 1859-61.

HELMS, Jesse Alexander (R N.C.) Oct. 18, 1921- —; Senate 1973- —.

HELMS, William (D N.J.) ?-1813; House 1801-11.

HELSTOSKI, Henry (D N.J.) March 21, 1925- —; House 1965-77.

HELVERING, Guy Tresillian (D Kan.) Jan. 10, 1878-July 4, 1946; House 1913-19.

HEMENWAY, James Alexander (R Ind.) March 8, 1860-Feb. 10, 1923; House 1895-1905; Senate 1905-09.

HEMPHILL, John (uncle of John James Hemphill, great-granduncle of Robert Witherspoon Hemphill) (SRD Texas) Dec. 18, 1803-Jan. 4, 1862; Senate 1859-July 11, 1861.

HEMPHILL, John James (cousin of William Huggins Brawley, nephew of John Hemphill, granduncle of Robert Witherspoon Hemphill) (D S.C.) Aug. 25, 1849-May 11, 1912; House 1883-93.

HEMPHILL, Joseph (JD Pa.) Jan. 7, 1770-May 29, 1842; House 1801-03 (Federalist), 1819-26 (Federalist), 1829-31.

HEMPHILL, Robert Witherspoon (great-grandnephew of John Hemphill, grandnephew of John James Hemphill and William Huggins Brawley, great-great-grandson of Robert Witherspoon) (D S.C.) May 10, 1915-Dec. 25, 1983; House 1957-May 1, 1964.

HEMPSTEAD, Edward (− Mo.) June 3, 1780-Aug. 10, 1817; House (Terr. Del.) Nov. 9, 1812-Sept. 17, 1814.

HENDEE, George Whitman (R Vt.) Nov. 30, 1832-Dec. 6, 1906; House 1873-79.

HENDERSON, Archibald (F N.C.) Aug. 7, 1768-Oct. 21, 1822; House 1799-1803.

HENDERSON, Bennett H. (− Tenn.) Sept. 5, 1784-?; House 1815-17.

HENDERSON, Charles Belknap (D Nev.) June 8, 1873-Nov. 8, 1954; Senate Jan. 12, 1918-21.

HENDERSON, David Bremner (R Iowa) March 14, 1840-Feb. 25, 1906; House 1883-1903; Speaker 1899-1903.

HENDERSON, David Newton (D N.C.) April 16, 1921-−; House 1961-77.

HENDERSON, James Henry Dickey (UR Ore.) July 23, 1810-Dec. 13, 1885; House 1865-67.

HENDERSON, James Pinckney (SRD Texas) March 31, 1808-June 4, 1858; Senate Nov. 9, 1857-June 4, 1858; Gov. 1846-47.

HENDERSON, John (W Miss.) Feb. 28, 1797-Sept. 15, 1857; Senate 1839-45.

HENDERSON, John Brooks (D Mo.) Nov. 16, 1826-April 12, 1913; Senate Jan. 17, 1862-69.

HENDERSON, John Earl (R Ohio) Jan. 4, 1917-−; House 1955-61.

HENDERSON, John Steele (D N.C.) Jan. 6, 1846-Oct 9, 1916; House 1885-95.

HENDERSON, Joseph (− Pa.) Aug. 2, 1791-Dec. 25 1863; House 1833-37.

HENDERSON, Samuel (R Pa.) Nov. 27, 1764-Nov. 17 1841; House Oct. 11, 1814-15.

HENDERSON, Thomas (F N.J.) Aug. 15, 1743-Dec. 15 1824; House 1795-97; Gov. 1793.

HENDERSON, Thomas Jefferson (R Ill.) Nov. 29 1824-Feb. 6, 1911; House 1875-95.

HENDON, William A. (R N.C.) Nov. 9, 1944-−; Hous 1981-83, 1985-87.

HENDRICK, John Kerr (D Ky.) Oct. 10, 1849-June 20 1921; House 1895-97.

HENDRICKS, Joseph Edward (D Fla.) Sept. 24, 1903 −; House 1937-49.

HENDRICKS, Thomas Andrews (nephew of Willian Hendricks) (D Ind.) Sept. 7, 1819-Nov. 25, 1885 House 1851-55; Senate 1863-69; Gov. 1873-77; Vic President 1885.

HENDRICKS, William (uncle of Thomas Andrew Hendricks) (D Ind.) Nov. 12, 1782-May 16, 1850 House Dec. 11, 1816-July 25, 1822; Senate 1825-37 Gov. 1822-25 (Democratic Republican).

HENDRICKSON, Robert Clymer (R N.J.) Aug. 1 1898-Dec. 7, 1964; Senate 1949-55.

HENDRIX, Joseph Clifford (D N.Y.) May 25, 1853-No 9, 1904; House 1893-95.

HENKLE, Eli Jones (D Md.) Nov. 24, 1828-Nov. 1893; House 1875-81.

HENLEY, Barclay (son of Thomas Jefferson Henley) (Calif.) March 17, 1843-Feb. 15, 1914; House 1883-8

HENLEY, Thomas Jefferson (father of Barclay Henle (D Ind.) April 2, 1810-Jan. 2, 1865; House 1843-4

HENN, Bernhart (D Iowa) 1817-Aug. 30, 1865; Hous 1851-55.

HENNEY, Charles William Francis (D Wis.) Feb. 1884-Nov. 16, 1969; House 1933-35.

HENNINGS, Thomas Carey Jr. (D Mo.) June 25, 190 Sept. 13, 1960; House 1935-Dec. 31, 1940; Sena 1951-Sept. 13, 1960.

HENRY, Charles Lewis (R Ind.) July 1, 1849-May 1927; House 1895-99.

HENRY, Daniel Maynadier (D Md.) Feb. 19, 1823-Au 31, 1899; House 1877-81.

IENRY, Edward Stevens (R Conn.) Feb. 10, 1836-Oct. 10, 1921; House 1895-1913.

IENRY, John (D Md.) Nov. 1750-Dec. 16, 1798; Senate 1789-Dec. 10, 1797; Gov. 1797-98; Cont. Cong. 1778-81, 1784-87.

IENRY, John (W Ill.) Nov. 1, 1800-April 28, 1882; House Feb. 5-March 3, 1847.

IENRY, John Flournoy (− Ky.) Jan. 17, 1793-Nov. 12, 1873; House Dec. 11, 1826-27.

IENRY, Lewis (R N.Y.) June 8, 1885-July 23, 1941; House April 11, 1922-23.

IENRY, Patrick (uncle of Patrick Henry, below) (D Miss.) Feb. 12, 1843-May 18, 1930; House 1897-1901.

IENRY, Patrick (nephew of Patrick Henry, above) (D Miss.) Feb. 15, 1861-Dec. 28, 1933; House 1901-03.

IENRY, Paul B. (R Mich.) July 9, 1942-−; House 1985-−.

IENRY, Robert Kirkland (R Wis.) Feb. 9, 1890-Nov. 20, 1946; House 1945-Nov. 20, 1946.

ENRY, Robert Lee (D Texas) May 12, 1864-July 9, 1931; House 1897-1917.

ENRY, Robert Pryor (CD Ky.) Nov. 24, 1788-Aug. 25, 1826; House 1823-Aug. 25, 1826.

ENRY, Thomas (W Pa.) 1779-July 20, 1849; House 1837-43.

ENRY, William (W Vt.) March 22, 1788-April 16, 1861; House 1847-51.

ENRY, Winder Laird (great-grandson of Charles Goldsborough and Robert Henry Goldsborough) (D Md.) Dec. 20, 1864-July 5, 1940; House Nov. 6, 1894-95.

ENSLEY, Walter Lewis (D Mo.) Sept. 3, 1871-July 18, 1946; House 1911-19.

EPBURN, William Peters (great-grandson of Matthew Lyon) (R Iowa) Nov. 4, 1833-Feb. 7, 1916; House 1881-87, 1893-1909.

ERBERT, Hilary Abner (D Ala.) March 12, 1834-March 5, 1919; House 1877-93; Secy. of the Navy 1893-97.

ERBERT, John Carlyle (F Md.) Aug. 16, 1775-Sept. 1, 1846; House 1815-19.

ERBERT, Philemon Thomas (D Calif.) Nov. 1, 1825-July 23, 1864; House 1855-57.

EREFORD, Frank (D W.Va.) July 4, 1825-Dec. 21, 1891; House 1871-Jan. 31, 1877; Senate Jan. 31, 1877-81.

HERGER, Walter William "Wally" II (R Calif.) May 20, 1945-−; House 1987-−.

HERKIMER, John (D N.Y.) 1773-June 8, 1848; House 1817-19, 1823-25.

HERLONG, Albert Sydney Jr. (D Fla.) Feb. 14, 1909-−; House 1949-69.

HERMANN, Binger (R Ore.) Feb. 19, 1843-April 15, 1926; House 1885-97, June 1, 1903-07.

HERNANDEZ, Benigno Cardenas (R N.M.) Feb. 13, 1862-Oct. 18, 1954; House 1915-17, 1919-21.

HERNANDEZ, Joseph Marion (W Fla.) Aug. 4, 1793-June 8, 1857; House (Terr. Del.) Sept. 30, 1822-23.

HERNDON, Thomas Hord (D Ala.) July 1, 1828-March 28, 1883; House 1879-March 28, 1883.

HERNDON, William Smith (D Texas) Nov. 27, 1835-Oct. 11, 1903; House 1871-75.

HEROD, William (W Ind.) March 31, 1801-Oct. 20, 1871; House Jan. 25, 1837-39.

HERRICK, Anson (son of Ebenezer Herrick) (D N.Y.) Jan. 21, 1812-Feb. 6, 1868; House 1863-65.

HERRICK, Ebenezer (father of Anson Herrick) (− Maine) Oct. 21, 1785-May 7, 1839; House 1821-27.

HERRICK, Joshua (D Maine) March 18, 1793-Aug. 30, 1874; House 1843-45.

HERRICK, Manuel (R Okla.) Sept. 20, 1876-Feb. 29, 1952; House 1921-23.

HERRICK, Richard Platt (W N.Y.) March 23, 1791-June 20, 1846; House 1845-June 20, 1846.

HERRICK, Samuel (D Ohio) April 14, 1779-June 4, 1852; House 1817-21.

HERRING, Clyde LaVerne (D Iowa) May 3, 1879-Sept. 15, 1945; Senate Jan. 15, 1937-43; Gov. 1933-37.

HERSEY, Ira Greenlief (R Maine) March 31, 1858-May 6, 1943; House 1917-29.

HERSEY, Samuel Freeman (R Maine) April 12, 1812-Feb. 3, 1875; House 1873-Feb. 3, 1875.

HERSMAN, Hugh Steel (D Calif.) July 8, 1872-March 7, 1954; House 1919-21.

HERTEL, Dennis M. (D Mich.) Dec. 7, 1938-−; House 1981-−.

HERTER, Christian Archibald (R Mass.) March 28, 1895-Dec. 30, 1966; House 1943-53; Gov. 1953-57; Secy. of State 1959-61.

HESELTON, John Walter (R Mass.) March 17, 1900-Aug. 19, 1962; House 1945-59.

HESS, William Emil (R Ohio) Feb. 13, 1898- —; House 1929-37, 1939-49, 1951-61.

HEWITT, Abram Stevens (D N.Y.) July 31, 1822-Jan. 18, 1903; House 1875-79, 1881-Dec. 30, 1886; Chrmn. Dem. Nat. Comm. 1876-77.

HEWITT, Goldsmith Whitehouse (D Ala.) Feb. 14, 1834-May 27, 1895; House 1875-79, 1881-85.

HEYBURN, Weldon Brinton (R Idaho) May 23, 1852-Oct. 17, 1912; Senate 1903-Oct. 17, 1912.

HIBBARD, Ellery Albee (cousin of Harry Hibbard) (D N.H.) July 31, 1826-July 24, 1903; House 1871-73.

HIBBARD, Harry (cousin of Ellery Albee Hibbard) (D N.H.) June 1, 1816-July 28, 1872; House 1849-55.

HIBSHMAN, Jacob (R Pa.) Jan. 31, 1772-May 19, 1852; House 1819-21.

HICKENLOOPER, Bourke Blakemore (R Iowa) July 21, 1896-Sept. 4, 1971; Senate 1945-69; Gov. 1943-45.

HICKEY, Andrew James (R Ind.) Aug. 27, 1872-Aug. 20, 1942; House 1919-31.

HICKEY, John Joseph (D Wyo.) Aug. 22, 1911-Sept. 22, 1970; Senate 1961-Nov. 6, 1962; Gov. 1959-61.

HICKMAN, John (R Pa.) Sept. 11, 1810-March 23, 1875; House 1855-63 (1855-59 Democrat, 1859-61 Douglas Democrat).

HICKS, Floyd Verne (D Wash.) May 29, 1915- —; House 1965-77.

HICKS, Frederick Cocks (original name: Frederick Hicks Cocks, brother of William Willets Cocks) (R N.Y.) March 6, 1872-Dec. 14, 1925; House 1915-23.

HICKS, Josiah Duane (R Pa.) Aug. 1, 1844-May 9, 1923; House 1893-99.

HICKS, Louise Day (D Mass.) Oct. 16, 1923- —; House 1971-73.

HICKS, Thomas Holliday (UR Md.) Sept. 2, 1798-Feb. 14, 1865; Senate Dec. 29, 1862-Feb. 14, 1865; Gov. 1858-62 (American Party).

HIESTAND, Edgar Willard (R Calif.) Dec. 3, 1888-Aug. 19, 1970; House 1953-63.

HIESTAND, John Andrew (R Pa.) Oct. 2, 1824-Dec. 13, 1890; House 1885-89.

HIESTER, Daniel (brother of John Hiester, cousin o Joseph Hiester, uncle of William Hiester and Danie Hiester, below) (— Md.) June 25, 1747-March 7 1804; House 1789-July 1, 1796 (Pa.), 1801-March 7 1804.

HIESTER, Daniel (son of John Hiester, nephew of Dan iel Hiester, above) (— Pa.) 1774-March 8, 1834 House 1809-11.

HIESTER, Isaac Ellmaker (son of William Hieste cousin of Hiester Clymer) (W Pa.) May 29, 1824 Feb. 6, 1871; House 1853-55.

HIESTER, John (brother of Daniel Hiester born i 1747, cousin of Joseph Hiester, uncle of Willian Hiester) (— Pa.) April 9, 1745-Oct. 15, 1821; Hous 1807-09.

HIESTER, Joseph (cousin of John Hiester and Danie Hiester born in 1747, grandfather of Henry Augustu Muhlenberg) (F Pa.) Nov. 18, 1752-June 10, 183; House Dec. 1, 1799-1805, 1815-Dec. 1820; Gov. 182C 23 (Democratic Republican).

HIESTER, William (father of Isaac Ellmaker Hieste uncle of Hiester Clymer, nephew of John Hieste and Daniel Hiester born in 1747) (W Pa.) Oct. 1 1790-Oct. 13, 1853; House 1831-37.

HIGBY, William (R Calif.) Aug. 18, 1813-Nov. 27, 188 House 1863-69.

HIGGINS, Anthony (R Del.) Oct. 1, 1840-June 26, 191 Senate 1889-95.

HIGGINS, Edwin Werter (R Conn.) July 2, 1874-Sep 24, 1954; House Oct. 2, 1905-13.

HIGGINS, John Patrick (D Mass.) Feb. 19, 1893-Aug. 1955; House 1935-Sept. 30, 1937.

HIGGINS, William Lincoln (R Conn.) March 8, 186 Nov. 19, 1951; House 1933-37.

HIGHTOWER, Jack English (D Texas) Sept. 6, 1926- - House 1975-85.

HILBORN, Samuel Greeley (R Calif.) Dec. 9, 1834-Ap 19, 1899; House Dec. 5, 1892-April 4, 1894, 1895-9

HILDEBRANDT, Fred Herman (D S.D.) Aug. 2, 187 Jan. 26, 1956; House 1933-39.

HILDEBRANT, Charles Quinn (R Ohio) Oct. 17, 186 March 31, 1953; House 1901-05.

HILER, John P. (R Ind.) April 24, 1953- —; House 198 —.

HILL, Benjamin Harvey (cousin of Hugh Lawson Wh Hill) (D Ga.) Sept. 14, 1823-Aug. 16, 1882; Hou May 5, 1875-77; Senate 1877-Aug. 16, 1882.

ILL, Charles Augustus (R Ill.) Aug. 23, 1833-May 29, 1902; House 1889-91.

ILL, Clement Sidney (ID Ky.) Feb. 13, 1813-Jan. 5, 1892; House 1853-55.

ILL, David Bennett (D N.Y.) Aug. 29, 1843-Oct. 20, 1910; Senate Jan. 7, 1892-97; Gov. 1885-92.

ILL, Ebenezer J. (R Conn.) Aug. 4, 1845-Sept. 27, 1917; House 1895-1913, 1915-Sept. 27, 1917.

ILL, Hugh Lawson White (cousin of Benjamin Harvey Hill) (D Tenn.) March 1, 1810-Jan. 18, 1892; House 1847-49.

ILL, Isaac (D N.H.) April 6, 1788-March 22, 1851; Senate 1831-May 30, 1836; Gov. 1836-39.

ILL, John (D N.C.) April 9, 1797-April 24, 1861; House 1839-41.

ILL, John (cousin of John Thomas Harris) (W Va.) July 18, 1800-April 19, 1880; House 1839-41.

LL, John (R N.J.) June 10, 1821-July 24, 1884; House 1867-73, 1881-83.

LL, John Boynton Philip Clayton (R Md.) May 2, 1879-May 23, 1941; House 1921-27.

LL, Joseph Lister (D Ala.) Dec. 29, 1894-Dec. 21, 1984; House Aug. 14, 1923-Jan. 11, 1938; Senate Jan. 11, 1938-69.

LL, Joshua (UR Ga.) Jan. 10, 1812-March 6, 1891; House 1857-Jan. 23, 1861 (American Party); Senate Feb. 1, 1871-73.

LL, Knute (D Wash.) July 31, 1876-Dec. 3, 1963; House 1933-43.

LL, Mark Langdon (— Maine) June 30, 1772-Nov. 26, 1842; House 1819-21 (Mass.), 1821-23.

LL, Nathaniel Peter (R Colo.) Feb. 18, 1832-May 22, 1900; Senate 1879-85.

LL, Ralph (R Ind.) Oct. 12, 1827-Aug. 20, 1899; House 1865-67.

LL, Robert Potter (D Okla.) April 18, 1874-Oct. 29, 1937; House 1913-15 (Ill.), Jan. 3-Oct. 29, 1937.

LL, Samuel Billingsley (D Wash.) April 2, 1875-March 16, 1958; House Sept. 25, 1923-June 25, 1936.

LL, William David (D Ohio) Oct. 1, 1833-Dec. 26, 1906; House 1879-81, 1883-87.

LL, William Henry (F N.C.) May 1, 1767-1809; House 1799-1803.

LL, William Henry (R N.Y.) March 23, 1877-July 24, 1972; House 1919-21.

HILL, William Luther (D Fla.) Oct. 17, 1873-Jan. 5, 1951; Senate July 1-Nov. 3, 1936.

HILL, William Silas (R Colo.) Jan. 20, 1886-Aug. 28, 1972; House 1941-59.

HILL, Wilson Shedric (D Miss.) Jan. 19, 1863-Feb. 14, 1921; House 1903-09.

HILLELSON, Jeffrey Paul (R Mo.) March 9, 1919- —; House 1953-55.

HILLEN, Solomon Jr. (D Md.) July 10, 1810-June 26, 1873; House 1839-41.

HILLHOUSE, James (F Conn.) Oct. 20, 1754-Dec. 29, 1832; House 1791-96; Senate Dec. 6, 1796-June 10, 1810; Pres. pro tempore 1801.

HILLIARD, Benjamin Clark (D Colo.) Jan. 9, 1868-Aug. 7, 1951; House 1915-19.

HILLIARD, Henry Washington (W Ala.) Aug. 4, 1808-Dec. 17, 1892; House 1845-51.

HILLINGS, Patrick Jerome (R Calif.) Feb. 19, 1923- —; House 1951-59.

HILLIS, Elwood Haynes (R Ind.) March 6, 1926- —; House 1971-87.

HILLYER, Junius (D Ga.) April 23, 1807-June 21, 1886; House 1851-55.

HIMES, Joseph Hendrix (R Ohio) Aug. 15, 1885-Sept. 9, 1960; House 1921-23.

HINDMAN, Thomas Carmichael (D Ark.) Jan. 28, 1828-Sept. 27, 1868; House 1859-61.

HINDMAN, William (— Md.) April 1, 1743-Jan. 19, 1822; House Jan. 30, 1793-99; Senate Dec. 12, 1800-Nov. 19, 1801; Cont. Cong. 1784-88.

HINDS, Asher Crosby (R Maine) Feb. 6, 1863-May 1, 1919; House 1911-17.

HINDS, James (R Ark.) Dec. 5, 1833-Oct. 22, 1868; House June 22-Oct. 22, 1868.

HINDS, Thomas (D Miss.) Jan. 9, 1780-Aug. 23, 1840; House Oct. 21, 1828-31.

HINEBAUGH, William Henry (Prog. Ill.) Dec. 16, 1867-Sept. 22, 1943; House 1913-15.

HINES, Richard (D N.C.) ?-Nov. 20, 1851; House 1825-27.

HINES, William Henry (D Pa.) March 15, 1856-Jan. 17, 1914; House 1893-95.

HINRICHSEN, William Henry (D Ill.) May 27, 1850-Dec. 18, 1907; House 1897-99.

HINSHAW, Andrew Jackson (R Calif.) Aug. 4, 1923- —; House 1973-77.

HINSHAW, Edmund Howard (cousin of Edwin Bruce Brooks) (R Neb.) Dec. 8, 1860-June 15, 1932; House 1903-11.

HINSHAW, John Carl Williams (R Calif.) July 28, 1894-Aug. 5, 1956; House 1939-Aug. 5, 1956.

HINSON, Jon C. (R Miss.) March 16, 1942- —; House 1979-April 13, 1981.

HIRES, George (R N.J.) Jan. 26, 1835-Feb. 16, 1911; House 1885-89.

HISCOCK, Frank (R N.Y.) Sept. 6, 1834-June 18, 1914; House 1877-87; Senate 1887-93.

HISE, Elijah (D Ky.) July 4, 1802-May 8, 1867; House Dec. 3, 1866-May 8, 1867.

HITCHCOCK, Gilbert Monell (son of Phineas Warrener Hitchcock) (D Neb.) Sept. 18, 1859-Feb. 3, 1934; House 1903-05, 1907-11; Senate 1911-23.

HITCHCOCK, Herbert Emery (D S.D.) Aug. 22, 1867-Feb. 17, 1958; Senate Dec. 29, 1936-Nov. 8, 1938.

HITCHCOCK, Peter (— Ohio) Oct. 19, 1781-March 4, 1854; House 1817-19.

HITCHCOCK, Phineas Warrener (father of Gilbert Monell Hitchcock) (R Neb.) Nov. 30, 1831-July 10, 1881; House (Terr. Del.) 1865-March 1, 1867; Senate 1871-77.

HITT, Robert Roberts (R Ill.) Jan. 16, 1834-Sept. 19, 1906; House Nov. 7, 1882-Sept. 19, 1906.

HOAG, Truman Harrison (D Ohio) April 9, 1816-Feb. 5, 1870; House 1869-Feb. 5, 1870.

HOAGLAND, Moses (D Ohio) June 19, 1812-April 16, 1865; House 1849-51.

HOAR, Ebenezer Rockwood (son of Samuel Hoar, brother of George Frisbie Hoar, father of Sherman Hoar, uncle of Rockwood Hoar) (R Mass.) Feb. 21, 1816-Jan. 31, 1895; House 1873-75; Atty. Gen. 1869-70.

HOAR, George Frisbie (son of Samuel Hoar, brother of Ebenezer Rockwood Hoar, father of Rockwood Hoar, uncle of Sherman Hoar) (R Mass.) Aug. 29, 1826-Sept. 30, 1904; House 1869-77; Senate 1877-Sept. 30, 1904.

HOAR, Rockwood (son of George Frisbie Hoar, nephew of Ebenezer Rockwood Hoar, cousin of Sherman Hoar, grandson of Samuel Hoar) (R Mass.) Aug. 24, 1855-Nov. 1, 1906; House 1905-Nov. 1, 1906.

HOAR, Samuel (father of Ebenezer Rockwood Hoar ar George Frisbie Hoar, grandfather of Sherman Ho and Rockwood Hoar) (W Mass.) May 18, 1778-No 2, 1856; House 1835-37.

HOAR, Sherman (son of Ebenezer Rockwood Hoa nephew of George Frisbee Hoar, cousin of Rockwo Hoar, grandson of Samuel Hoar) (D Mass.) July 3 1860-Oct. 7, 1898; House 1891-93.

HOARD, Charles Brooks (R N.Y.) June 5, 1805-Nov. 2 1886; House 1857-61.

HOBART, Aaron (D Mass.) June 26, 1787-Sept. 1858; House Nov. 24, 1820-27.

HOBART, John Sloss (— N.Y.) May 6, 1738-Feb. 1805; Senate Jan. 11-April 16, 1798.

HOBBIE, Selah Reeve (JD N.Y.) March 10, 1797-Mar 23, 1854; House 1827-29.

HOBBS, Samuel Francis (D Ala.) Oct. 5, 1887-May 1952; House 1935-51.

HOBLITZELL, Fetter Schrier (D Md.) Oct. 7, 18 May 2, 1900; House 1881-85.

HOBLITZELL, John Dempsey Jr. (R W.Va.) Dec. 1912-Jan. 6, 1962; Senate Jan. 25-Nov. 4, 1958.

HOBSON, Richmond Pearson (D Ala.) Aug. 17, 18 March 16, 1937; House 1907-15.

HOCH, Daniel Knabb (D Pa.) Jan. 31, 1866-Oct. 1960; House 1943-47.

HOCH, Homer (R Kan.) July 4, 1879-Jan. 30, 19 House 1919-33.

HOCHBRUECKNER, George Joseph (D N.Y.) Se 20, 1938- —; House 1987- —.

HODGES, Asa (R Ark.) Jan. 22, 1822-June 6, 19 House 1873-75.

HODGES, Charles Drury (D Ill.) Feb. 4, 1810-Apri 1884; House Jan. 4-March 3, 1859.

HODGES, George Tisdale (R Vt.) July 4, 1789-Aug 1860; House Dec. 1, 1856-57.

HODGES, James Leonard (— Mass.) April 24, 17 March 8, 1846; House 1827-33.

HODGES, Kaneaster Jr. (D Ark.) Aug. 20, 1938- —; S ate Dec. 10, 1977-79.

HOEPPEL, John Henry (D Calif.) Feb. 10, 1881-Se 21, 1976; House 1933-37.

HOEVEN, Charles Bernard (R Iowa) March 30, 18 Nov. 9, 1980; House 1943-65.

OEY, Clyde Roark (D N.C.) Dec. 11, 1877-May 12, 1954; House Dec. 16, 1919-21; Senate 1945-May 12, 1954; Gov. 1937-41.

OFFECKER, John Henry (father of Walter Oakley Hoffecker) (R Del.) Sept. 12, 1827-June 16, 1900; House 1899-June 16, 1900.

OFFECKER, Walter Oakley (son of John Henry Hoffecker) (R Del.) Sept. 20, 1854-Jan. 23, 1934; House Nov. 6, 1900-01.

OFFMAN, Carl Henry (R Pa.) Aug. 12, 1896- —; House May 21, 1946-47.

OFFMAN, Clare Eugene (R Mich.) Sept. 10, 1875-Nov. 3, 1967; House 1935-63.

OFFMAN, Elmer Joseph (R Ill.) July 7, 1899-June 25, 1976; House 1959-65.

OFFMAN, Harold Giles (R N.J.) Feb. 7, 1896-June 4, 1954; House 1927-31; Gov. 1935-38.

OFFMAN, Henry William (AP Md.) Nov. 10, 1825-July 28, 1895; House 1855-57.

OFFMAN, Josiah Ogden (W N.Y.) May 3, 1793-May 1, 1856; House 1837-41.

OFFMAN, Michael (D N.Y.) Oct. 11, 1787-Sept. 27, 1848; House 1825-33.

OFFMAN, Richard William (R Ill.) Dec. 23, 1893-July 6, 1975; House 1949-57.

OGAN, Earl Lee (D Ind.) March 13, 1920- —; House 1959-61.

OGAN, John (D Mo.) Jan. 2, 1805-Feb. 5, 1892; House 1865-67.

OGAN, Lawrence Joseph (R Md.) Sept. 30, 1928- —; House 1969-75.

OGAN, Michael Joseph (R N.Y.) April 22, 1871-May 7, 1940; House 1921-23.

OGAN, William (JD N.Y.) July 17, 1792-Nov. 25, 1874; House 1831-33.

OGE, John (brother of William Hoge) (D Pa.) Sept. 10, 1760-Aug. 4, 1824; House Nov. 2, 1804-05.

OGE, John Blair (D W.Va.) Feb. 2, 1825-March 1, 1896; House 1881-83.

OGE, Joseph Pendleton (D Ill.) Dec. 15, 1810-Aug. 14, 1891; House 1843-47.

OGE, Solomon Lafayette (R S.C.) July 11, 1836-Feb. 23, 1909; House April 8, 1869-71, 1875-77.

OGE, William (brother of John Hoge) (F Pa.) 1762-Sept. 25, 1814; House 1801-Oct. 15, 1804, 1807-09.

HOGEBOOM, James Lawrence (W N.Y.) Aug. 25, 1766-Dec. 23, 1839; House 1823-25.

HOGG, Charles Edgar (father of Robert Lynn Hogg) (D W.Va.) Dec. 21, 1852-June 14, 1935; House 1887-89.

HOGG, David (R Ind.) Aug. 21, 1886-Oct. 23, 1973; House 1925-33.

HOGG, Herschel Millard (R Colo.) Nov. 21, 1853-Aug. 27, 1934; House 1903-07.

HOGG, Robert Lynn (son of Charles Edgar Hogg) (R W.Va.) Dec. 30, 1893-July 21, 1973; House Nov. 4, 1930-33.

HOGG, Samuel (D Tenn.) April 18, 1783-May 28, 1842; House 1817-19.

HOIDALE, Einar (D Minn.) Aug. 17, 1870-Dec. 5, 1952; House 1933-35.

HOLADAY, William Perry (R Ill.) Dec. 14, 1882-Jan. 29, 1946; House 1923-33.

HOLBROCK, Greg John (D Ohio) June 21, 1906- —; House 1941-43.

HOLBROOK, Edward Dexter (D Idaho) May 6, 1836-June 18, 1870; House (Terr. Del.) 1865-69.

HOLCOMBE, George (D N.J.) March 1786-Jan. 14, 1828; House 1821-Jan. 14, 1828.

HOLIFIELD, Chester Earl (D Calif.) Dec. 3, 1903- —; House 1943-Dec. 31, 1974.

HOLLADAY, Alexander Richmond (D Va.) Sept. 18, 1811-Jan. 29, 1877; House 1849-53.

HOLLAND, Cornelius (D Maine) July 9, 1783-June 2, 1870; House Dec. 6, 1830-33.

HOLLAND, Edward Everett (D Va.) Feb. 26, 1861-Oct. 23, 1941; House 1911-21.

HOLLAND, Elmer Joseph (D Pa.) Jan. 8, 1894-Aug. 9, 1968; House May 19, 1942-43; Jan. 24, 1956-Aug. 9, 1968.

HOLLAND, James (AF N.C.) 1754-May 19, 1823; House 1795-97, 1801-11.

HOLLAND, Kenneth Lamar (D S.C.) Nov. 24, 1934- —; House 1975-83.

HOLLAND, Spessard Lindsey (D Fla.) July 10, 1892-Nov. 6, 1971; Senate Sept. 25, 1946-71; Gov. 1941-45.

HOLLEMAN, Joel (VBD Va.) Oct. 1, 1799-Aug. 5, 1844; House 1839-40.

HOLLENBECK, Harold Capistran (R N.J.) Dec. 29, 1938- —; House 1977-83.

HOLLEY, John Milton (W N.Y.) Nov. 10, 1802-March 8, 1848; House 1847-March 8, 1848.

HOLLIDAY, Elias Selah (R Ind.) March 5, 1842-March 13, 1936; House 1901-09.

HOLLINGS, Ernest Frederick "Fritz" (D S.C.) Jan. 1, 1922- —; Senate Nov. 9, 1966- —; Gov. 1959-63.

HOLLINGSWORTH, David Adams (R Ohio) Nov. 21, 1844-Dec. 3, 1929; House 1909-11, 1915-19.

HOLLIS, Henry French (D N.H.) Aug. 30, 1869-July 7, 1949; Senate March 13, 1913-19.

HOLLISTER, John Baker (R Ohio) Nov. 7, 1890-Jan. 4, 1979; House Nov. 3, 1931-37.

HOLLOWAY, Clyde (R La.) Nov. 28, 1943- —; House 1987- —.

HOLLOWAY, David Pierson (PP Ind.) Dec. 7, 1809-Sept. 9, 1883; House 1855-57.

HOLMAN, Rufus Cecil (R Ore.) Oct. 14, 1877-Nov. 27, 1959; Senate 1939-45.

HOLMAN, William Steele (D Ind.) Sept. 6, 1822-April 22, 1897; House 1859-65, 1867-77, 1881-95, March 4-April 22, 1897.

HOLMES, Adoniram Judson (R Iowa) March 2, 1842-Jan. 21, 1902; House 1883-89.

HOLMES, Charles Horace (R N.Y.) Oct. 24, 1827-Oct. 2, 1874; House Dec. 6, 1870-71.

HOLMES, David (DR Miss.) March 10, 1769-Aug. 20, 1832; House 1797-1809 (Va.); Senate Aug. 30, 1820-Sept. 25, 1825; Gov. 1809-17 (Miss. Terr.), 1817-20.

HOLMES, Elias Bellows (W N.Y.) May 22, 1807-July 31, 1866; House 1845-49.

HOLMES, Gabriel (— N.C.) 1769-Sept. 26, 1829; House 1825-Sept. 26, 1829; Gov. 1821-24 (Democratic Republican).

HOLMES, Isaac Edward (D S.C.) April 6, 1796-Feb. 24, 1867; House 1839-51.

HOLMES, John (D Maine) March 14, 1773-July 7, 1843; House 1817-March 15, 1820 (Mass.); Senate June 13, 1820-27, Jan. 15, 1829-33.

HOLMES, Otis Halbert "Hal" (grandson of Dudley Chase Haskell) (R Wash.) Feb. 22, 1902-July 27, 1977; House 1943-59.

HOLMES, Pehr Gustaf (R Mass.) April 9, 1881-Dec. 19, 1952; House 1931-47.

HOLMES, Sidney Tracy (R N.Y.) Aug. 14, 1815-Jan. 16, 1890; House 1865-67.

HOLMES, Uriel (F Conn.) Aug. 26, 1764-May 18, 182 House 1817-18.

HOLSEY, Hopkins (UD Ga.) Aug. 25, 1779-March 3 1859; House Oct. 5, 1835-39.

HOLT, Hines (W Ga.) April 27, 1805-Nov. 4, 186 House Feb. 1-March 3, 1841.

HOLT, Joseph Franklin 3d (R Calif.) July 6, 1924- House 1953-61.

HOLT, Marjorie Sewell (R Md.) Sept. 17, 1920- House 1973-87.

HOLT, Orrin (D Conn.) March 13, 1792-June 20, 185 House Dec. 5, 1836-39.

HOLT, Rush Dew (D W.Va.) June 19, 1905-Feb. 8, 195 Senate June 21, 1935-41.

HOLTEN, Samuel (— Mass.) June 9, 1738-Jan. 2, 181 House 1793-95; Cont. Cong. 1778-80, 1782-87.

HOLTON, Hart Benton (R Md.) Oct. 13, 1835-Jan. 1907; House 1883-85.

HOLTZMAN, Elizabeth (D N.Y.) Aug. 11, 1941- House 1973-81.

HOLTZMAN, Lester (D N.Y.) June 1, 1913- —; Hou 1953-Dec. 31, 1961.

HONEYMAN, Nan Wood (D Ore.) July 15, 1881-D 10, 1970; House 1937-39.

HOOD, George Ezekial (D N.C.) Jan. 25, 1875-March 1960; House 1915-19.

HOOK, Enos (D Pa.) Dec. 3, 1804-July 15, 1841; Hou 1839-April 18, 1941.

HOOK, Frank Eugene (D Mich.) May 26, 1893-June 1982; House 1935-43, 1945-47.

HOOKER, Charles Edward (D Miss.) 1825-Jan. 8, 19 House 1875-83, 1887-95, 1901-03.

HOOKER, James Murray (D Va.) Oct. 29, 1873-Aug 1940; House Nov. 8, 1921-25.

HOOKER, Warren Brewster (R N.Y.) Nov. 24, 18 March 5, 1920; House 1891-Nov. 10, 1898.

HOOKS, Charles (great-grandfather of William Ju Harris) (D N.C.) Feb. 20, 1768-Oct. 18, 1843; Ho Dec. 2, 1816-17, 1819-25.

HOOPER, Benjamin Stephen (Read. Va.) March 1835-Jan. 17, 1898; House 1883-85.

HOOPER, Joseph Lawrence (R Mich.) Dec. 22, 18 Feb. 22, 1934; House Aug. 18, 1925-Feb. 22, 193

OOPER, Samuel (R Mass.) Feb. 3, 1808-Feb. 14, 1875; House Dec. 2, 1861-Feb. 14, 1875.

OOPER, William Henry (D Utah) Dec. 25, 1813-Dec. 30, 1882; House (Terr. Del.) 1859-61, 1865-73.

OPE, Clifford Ragsdale (R Kan.) June 9, 1893-May 16, 1970; House 1927-57.

OPKINS, Albert Cole (R Pa.) Sept. 15, 1837-June 9, 1911; House 1891-95.

OPKINS, Albert Jarvis (R Ill.) Aug. 15, 1846-Aug. 23, 1922; House Dec. 7, 1885-1903; Senate 1903-09.

OPKINS, Benjamin Franklin (R Wis.) April 22, 1829-Jan. 1, 1870; House 1867-Jan. 1, 1870.

OPKINS, David William (R Mo.) Oct. 31, 1897-Oct. 14, 1968; House Feb. 5, 1929-33.

OPKINS, Francis Alexander "Frank" (D Ky.) May 27, 1853-June 5, 1918; House 1903-07.

OPKINS, George Washington (D Va.) Feb. 22, 1804-March 1, 1861; House 1835-47, 1857-59.

OPKINS, James Herron (D Pa.) Nov. 3, 1832-June 17, 1904; House 1875-77, 1883-85.

OPKINS, Larry Jones (R Ky.) Oct. 25, 1933- —; House 1979- —.

OPKINS, Nathan Thomas (R Ky.) Oct. 27, 1852-Feb. 11, 1927; House Feb. 18-March 3, 1897.

OPKINS, Samuel (D Ky.) April 9, 1753-Sept. 16, 1819; House 1813-15.

OPKINS, Samuel Isaac (D Va.) Dec. 12, 1843-Jan. 15, 1914; House 1887-89.

OPKINS, Samuel Miles (— N.Y.) May 9, 1772-March 9, 1837; House 1813-15.

OPKINS, Stephen Tyng (R N.Y.) March 25, 1849-March 3, 1892; House 1887-89.

OPKINSON, Joseph (F Pa.) Nov. 12, 1770-Jan. 15, 1842; House 1815-19.

OPWOOD, Robert Freeman (R Pa.) July 24, 1856-March 1, 1940; House 1915-17.

ORAN, Walter Franklin (R Wash.) Oct. 15, 1898-Dec. 19, 1966; House 1943-65.

ORN, Henry (JD Pa.) 1786-Jan. 12, 1862; House 1831-33.

ORNBECK, John Westbrook (W Pa.) Jan. 24, 1804-Jan. 16, 1848; House 1847-Jan. 16, 1848.

ORNOR, Lynn Sedwick (D W.Va.) Nov. 3, 1874-Sept. 23, 1933; House 1931-Sept. 23, 1933.

HORR, Ralph Ashley (R Wash.) Aug. 12, 1884-Jan. 26, 1960; House 1931-33.

HORR, Roswell Gilbert (R Mich.) Nov. 26, 1830-Dec. 19, 1896; House 1879-85.

HORSEY, Outerbridge (F Del.) March 5, 1777-June 9, 1842; Senate Jan. 12, 1810-21.

HORSFORD, Jerediah (W N.Y.) March 8, 1791-Jan. 14, 1875; House 1851-53.

HORTON, Frank Jefferson (R N.Y.) Dec. 12, 1919- —; House 1963- —.

HORTON, Frank Ogilvie (R Wyo.) Oct. 18, 1882-Aug. 17, 1948; House 1939-41.

HORTON, Thomas Raymond (R N.Y.) April 1822-July 26, 1894; House 1855-57.

HORTON, Valentine Baxter (W Ohio) Jan. 29, 1802-Jan. 14, 1888; House 1855-59, 1861-63.

HOSKINS, George Gilbert (R N.Y.) Dec. 24, 1824-June 12, 1893; House 1873-77.

HOSMER, Craig (R Calif.) May 6, 1915-Oct. 11, 1982; House 1953-Dec. 31, 1974.

HOSMER, Hezekiah Lord (— N.Y.) June 7, 1765-June 9, 1814; House 1797-99.

HOSTETLER, Abraham Jonathan (D Ind.) Nov. 22, 1818-Nov. 24, 1899; House 1879-81.

HOSTETTER, Jacob (D Pa.) May 9, 1754-June 29, 1831; House Nov. 16, 1818-21.

HOTCHKISS, Giles Waldo (R N.Y.) Oct. 25, 1815-July 5, 1878; House 1863-67, 1869-71.

HOTCHKISS, Julius (R Conn.) July 11, 1810-Dec. 23, 1878; House 1867-69.

HOUCK, Jacob Jr. (D N.Y.) Jan. 14, 1801-Oct. 2, 1857; House 1841-43.

HOUGH, David (— N.H.) March 13, 1753-April 18, 1831; House 1803-07.

HOUGH, William Jervis (D N.Y.) March 20, 1795-Oct. 4, 1869; House 1845-47.

HOUGHTON, Alanson Bigelow (grandfather of Amory Houghton Jr.) (R N.Y.) Oct. 10, 1863-Sept. 15, 1941; House 1919-Feb. 28, 1922.

HOUGHTON, Amory Jr. (grandson of Alanson Bigelow Houghton) (R N.Y.) Aug. 7, 1926- —; House 1987- —.

HOUGHTON, Sherman Otis (R Calif.) April 10, 1828-Aug. 31, 1914; House 1871-75.

HOUK, George Washington (D Ohio) Sept. 25, 1825-Feb. 9, 1894; House 1891-Feb. 9, 1894.

HOUK, John Chiles (son of Leonidas Campbell Houk) (R Tenn.) Feb. 26, 1860-June 3, 1923; House Dec. 7, 1891-95.

HOUK, Leonidas Campbell (father of John Chiles Houk) (R Tenn.) June 8, 1836-May 25, 1891; House 1879-May 25, 1891.

HOUSE, John Ford (D Tenn.) Jan. 9, 1827-June 28, 1904; House 1875-83.

HOUSEMAN, Julius (D Mich.) Dec. 8, 1832-Feb. 8, 1891; House 1883-85.

HOUSTON, Andrew Jackson (son of Samuel Houston) (D Texas) June 21, 1854-June 26, 1941; Senate April 21-June 26, 1941.

HOUSTON, George Smith (D Ala.) Jan. 17, 1809-Dec. 31, 1879; House 1841-49, 1851-Jan. 21, 1861; Senate March 4-Dec. 31, 1879; Gov. 1874-78 (Union Democrat).

HOUSTON, Henry Aydelotte (D Del.) July 10, 1847-April 5, 1925; House 1903-05.

HOUSTON, John Mills (D Kan.) Sept. 15, 1890-April 29, 1975; House 1935-43.

HOUSTON, John Wallace (uncle of Robert Griffith Houston) (W Del.) May 4, 1814-April 26, 1896; House 1845-51.

HOUSTON, Robert Griffith (nephew of John Wallace Houston) (R Del.) Oct. 13, 1867-Jan. 29, 1946; House 1925-33.

HOUSTON, Samuel (father of Andrew Jackson Houston, cousin of David Hubbard) (D Texas) March 2, 1793-July 26, 1863; House 1823-27 (Tenn.); Senate Feb. 21, 1846-59; Gov. 1827-April 16, 1829, 1859-61.

HOUSTON, Victor Stewart Kaleoaloha (R Hawaii) July 22, 1876-July 31, 1959; House (Terr. Del.) 1927-33.

HOUSTON, William Cannon (D Tenn.) March 17, 1852-Aug. 30, 1931; House 1905-19.

HOVEY, Alvin Peterson (R Ind.) Sept. 6, 1821-Nov. 23, 1891; House 1887-Jan. 17, 1889; Gov. 1889-91.

HOWARD, Benjamin (– Ky.) 1760-Sept. 18, 1814; House 1807-April 10, 1810; Gov. (La. Terr.) 1810-12.

HOWARD, Benjamin Chew (son of John Eager Howard) (D Md.) Nov. 5, 1791-March 6, 1872; House 1829-33, 1835-39.

HOWARD, Edgar (D Neb.) Sept. 16, 1858-July 19, 1951; House 1923-35.

HOWARD, Everette Burgess (D Okla.) Sept. 19, 1873-April 3, 1950; House 1919-21, 1923-25, 1927-29.

HOWARD, Guy Victor (R Minn.) Nov. 28, 1879-Aug. 20 1954; Senate Nov. 4, 1936-37.

HOWARD, Jacob Merritt (R Mich.) July 10, 1805-April 2, 1871; House 1841-43; Senate Jan. 17, 1862-7 (1841-43 Whig, 1862-71 Republican).

HOWARD, James John (D N.J.) July 24, 1927-–; House 1965-–.

HOWARD, John Eager (father of Benjamin Chew Howard) (F Md.) June 4, 1752-Oct. 12, 1827; Senate Nov 30, 1796-1803; Pres. pro tempore 1801; Gov. 1788-91 Cont. Cong. 1784-88.

HOWARD, Jonas George (D Ind.) May 22, 1825-Oct. 1911; House 1885-89.

HOWARD, Milford Wriarson (P Ala.) Dec. 18, 1862 Dec. 28, 1937; House 1895-99.

HOWARD, Tilghman Ashurst (D Ind.) Nov. 14, 1797 Aug. 16, 1844; House Aug. 5, 1839-July 1, 1840.

HOWARD, Volney Erskine (D Texas) Oct. 22, 1809 May 14, 1889; House 1849-53.

HOWARD, William (D Ohio) Dec. 31, 1817-June 1891; House 1859-61.

HOWARD, William Alanson (R Mich.) April 8, 181 April 10, 1880; House 1855-59, May 15, 1860-6 Gov. (Dakota Terr.) 1878-80.

HOWARD, William Marcellus (D Ga.) Dec. 6, 1857-Ju 5, 1932; House 1897-1911.

HOWARD, William Schley (cousin of Augustus Oct vius Bacon) (D Ga.) June 29, 1875-Aug. 1, 195 House 1911-19.

HOWE, Albert Richards (R Miss.) Jan. 1, 1840-June 1884; House 1873-75.

HOWE, Allan Turner (D Utah) Sept. 6, 1927-–; Hou 1975-77.

HOWE, James Robinson (R N.Y.) Jan. 27, 1839-Sept. 2 1914; House 1895-99.

HOWE, John W. (FSW Pa.) 1801-Dec. 1, 1873; Hou 1849-53.

HOWE, Thomas Marshall (father-in-law of James Brown) (W Pa.) April 20, 1808-July 20, 1877; Hou 1851-55.

HOWE, Thomas Y. Jr. (D N.Y.) 1801-July 15, 186 House 1851-53.

HOWE, Timothy Otis (UR Wis.) Feb. 24, 1816-Mar 25, 1883; Senate 1861-79; Postmaster Gen. 1882-8

HOWELL, Benjamin Franklin (R N.J.) Jan. 27, 184 Feb. 1, 1933; House 1895-1911.

HOWELL, Charles Robert (D N.J.) April 23, 1904-July 5, 1973; House 1949-55.

HOWELL, Edward (D N.Y.) Oct. 16, 1792-Jan. 30, 1871; House 1833-35.

HOWELL, Elias (father of James Bruen Howell) (W Ohio) 1792-May 1844; House 1835-37.

HOWELL, George (R Pa.) June 28, 1859-Nov. 19, 1913; House 1903-Feb. 10, 1904.

HOWELL, George Evan (R Ill.) Sept. 21, 1905-Jan. 18, 1980; House 1941-Oct. 5, 1947.

HOWELL, James Bruen (son of Elias Howell) (R Iowa) July 4, 1816-June 17, 1880; Senate Jan. 18, 1870-71.

HOWELL, Jeremiah Brown (F R.I.) Aug. 28, 1771-Feb. 5, 1822; Senate 1811-17.

HOWELL, Joseph (R Utah) Feb. 17, 1857-July 18, 1918; House 1903-17.

HOWELL, Nathaniel Woodhull (− N.Y.) Jan. 1, 1770-Oct. 15, 1851; House 1813-15.

HOWELL, Robert Beecher (R Neb.) Jan. 21, 1864-March 11, 1933; Senate 1923-March 11, 1933.

HOWEY, Benjamin Franklin (nephew of Charles Creighton Stratton) (R N.J.) March 17, 1828-Feb. 6, 1895; House 1883-85.

HOWLAND, Benjamin (D R.I.) July 27, 1755-May 1, 1821; Senate Oct. 29, 1804-09.

HOWLAND, Leonard Paul (R Ohio) Dec. 5, 1865-Dec. 23, 1942; House 1907-13.

HOXWORTH, Stephen Arnold (D Ill.) May 1, 1860-Jan. 25, 1930; House 1913-15.

HOYER, Steny (D Md.) June 14, 1939- −; House June 3, 1981- −.

HRUSKA, Roman Lee (R Neb.) Aug. 16, 1904- −; House 1953-Nov. 8, 1954; Senate Nov. 8, 1954-Dec. 27, 1976.

HUBARD, Edmund Wilcox (D Va.) Feb. 20, 1806-Dec. 9, 1878; House 1841-47.

HUBBARD, Asahel Wheeler (father of Elbert Hamilton Hubbard) (R Iowa) Jan. 19, 1819-Sept. 22, 1879; House 1863-69.

HUBBARD, Carroll Jr. (D Ky.) July 7, 1937- −; House 1975- −.

HUBBARD, Chester Dorman (father of William Pallister Hubbard) (R W.Va.) Nov. 25, 1814-Aug. 23, 1891; House 1865-69.

HUBBARD, David (cousin of Samuel Houston) (SRD Ala.) 1792-Jan. 20, 1874; House 1839-41, 1849-51.

HUBBARD, Demas Jr. (R N.Y.) Jan. 17, 1806-Sept. 2, 1873; House 1865-67.

HUBBARD, Elbert Hamilton (son of Asahel Wheeler Hubbard) (R Iowa) Aug. 19, 1849-June 4, 1912; House 1905-June 4, 1912.

HUBBARD, Henry (D N.H.) May 3, 1784-June 5, 1857; House 1829-35; Senate 1835-41; Gov. 1842-44.

HUBBARD, Joel Douglas (R Mo.) Nov. 6, 1860-May 26, 1919; House 1895-97.

HUBBARD, John Henry (R Conn.) March 24, 1804-July 30, 1872; House 1863-67.

HUBBARD, Jonathan Hatch (F Vt.) May 7, 1768-Sept. 20, 1849; House 1809-11.

HUBBARD, Levi (D Mass.) Dec. 19, 1762-Feb. 18, 1836; House 1813-15.

HUBBARD, Richard Dudley (D Conn.) Sept. 7, 1818-Feb. 28, 1884; House 1867-69; Gov. 1877-79.

HUBBARD, Samuel Dickinson (W Conn.) Aug. 10, 1799-Oct. 8, 1855; House 1845-49; Postmaster Gen. 1852-53.

HUBBARD, Thomas Hill (D N.Y.) Dec. 5, 1781-May 21, 1857; House 1817-19, 1821-23.

HUBBARD, William Pallister (son of Chester Dorman Hubbard) (R W.Va.) Dec. 24, 1843-Dec. 5, 1921; House 1907-11.

HUBBELL, Edwin Nelson (D N.Y.) Aug. 13, 1815-?; House 1865-67.

HUBBELL, James Randolph (R Ohio) July 13, 1824-Nov. 26, 1890; House 1865-67.

HUBBELL, Jay Abel (R Mich.) Sept. 15, 1829-Oct. 13, 1900; House 1873-83.

HUBBELL, William Spring (D N.Y.) Jan. 17, 1801-Nov. 16, 1873; House 1843-45.

HUBBS, Orlando (R N.C.) Feb. 18, 1840-Dec. 5, 1930; House 1881-83.

HUBER, Robert James (R Mich.) Aug. 29, 1922- −; House 1973-75.

HUBER, Walter B. (D Ohio) June 29, 1903-Aug. 8, 1982; House 1945-51.

HUBLEY, Edward Burd (JD Pa.) 1792-Feb. 23, 1856; House 1835-39.

HUCK, Winnifred Sprague Mason (daughter of William Ernest Mason) (R Ill.) Sept. 14, 1882-Aug. 24, 1936; House Nov. 7, 1922-23.

HUCKABY, Thomas Jerry (D La.) July 19, 1941--; House 1977--.

HUDD, Thomas Richard (D Wis.) Oct. 2, 1835-June 22, 1896; House March 8, 1886-89.

HUDDLESTON, George (father of George Huddleston Jr.) (D Ala.) Nov. 11, 1869-Feb. 29, 1960; House 1915-37.

HUDDLESTON, George Jr. (son of George Huddleston) (D Ala.) March 19, 1920-Sept. 14, 1971; House 1955-65.

HUDDLESTON, Walter Darlington (D Ky.) April 15, 1926--; Senate 1973-85.

HUDNUT, William Herbert III (R Ind.) Oct. 17, 1932---; House 1973-75.

HUDSON, Charles (W Mass.) Nov. 14, 1795-May 4, 1881; House May 3, 1841-49.

HUDSON, Grant Martin (R Mich.) July 23, 1868-Oct. 26, 1955; House 1923-31.

HUDSON, Thomas Jefferson (P Kan.) Oct. 30, 1839-Jan. 4, 1923; House 1893-95.

HUDSPETH, Claude Benton (D Texas) May 12, 1877-March 19, 1941; House 1919-31.

HUFF, George Franklin (R Pa.) July 16, 1842-April 18, 1912; House 1891-93, 1895-97, 1903-11.

HUFFMAN, James Wylie (D Ohio) Sept. 13, 1894--; Senate Oct. 8, 1945-Nov. 5, 1946.

HUFTY, Jacob (D N.J.) ?-May 20, 1814; House 1808-May 20, 1814.

HUGER, Benjamin (- S.C.) 1768-July 7, 1823; House 1799-1805, 1815-17.

HUGER, Daniel (father of Daniel Elliott Huger) (- S.C.) Feb. 20, 1742-July 6, 1799; House 1789-93; Cont. Cong. 1786-88.

HUGER, Daniel Elliott (son of Daniel Huger) (SRD S.C.) June 28, 1779-Aug. 21, 1854; Senate 1843-45.

HUGHES, Charles (D N.Y.) Feb. 27, 1822-Aug. 10, 1887; House 1853-55.

HUGHES, Charles James Jr. (D Colo.) Feb. 16, 1853-Jan. 11, 1911; Senate 1909-Jan. 11, 1911.

HUGHES, Dudley Mays (D Ga.) Oct. 10, 1848-Jan. 20, 1927; House 1909-17.

HUGHES, George Wurtz (D Md.) Sept. 30, 1806-Sept. 3█ 1870; House 1859-61.

HUGHES, Harold Everett (D Iowa) Feb. 10, 1922--; Senate 1969-75; Gov. 1963-69.

HUGHES, James (D Ind.) Nov. 24, 1823-Oct. 24, 187█ House 1857-59.

HUGHES, James Anthony (R W.Va.) Feb. 27, 1861█ March 2, 1930; House 1901-15, 1927-March 2, 193█

HUGHES, James Frederic (D Wis.) Aug. 7, 1883-Aug. █ 1940; House 1933-35.

HUGHES, James Hurd (D Del.) Jan. 14, 1867-Aug. 2█ 1953; Senate 1937-43.

HUGHES, James Madison (D Mo.) April 7, 1809-Feb█ 26, 1861; House 1843-45.

HUGHES, Thomas Hurst (W N.J.) Jan. 10, 1769-Nov█ 10, 1839; House 1829-33.

HUGHES, William (D N.J.) April 3, 1872-Jan. 30, 191█ House 1903-05, 1907-Sept. 27, 1912; Senate 191█ Jan. 30, 1918.

HUGHES, William John (D N.J.) Oct. 17, 1932--; House 1975--.

HUGHSTON, Jonas Abbott (W N.Y.) 1808-Nov. 1█ 1862; House 1855-57.

HUGUNIN, Daniel Jr. (- N.Y.) Feb. 6, 1790-June 2█ 1850; House Dec. 15, 1825-27.

HUKRIEDE, Theodore Waldemar (R Mo.) Nov. █ 1878-April 14, 1945; House 1921-23.

HULBERT, George Murray (D N.Y.) May 14, 188█ April 26, 1950; House 1915-Jan. 1, 1918.

HULBERT, John Whitefield (F Mass.) June 1, 177█ Oct. 19, 1831; House Sept. 26, 1814-17.

HULBURD, Calvin Tilden (R N.Y.) June 5, 1809-O█ 25, 1897; House 1863-69.

HULICK, George Washington (R Ohio) June 29, 183█ Aug. 13, 1907; House 1893-97.

HULING, James Hall (R W.Va.) March 24, 1844-Ap█ 23, 1918; House 1895-97.

HULINGS, Willis James (R Pa.) July 1, 1850-Aug. █ 1924; House 1913-15 (Progressive), 1919-21.

HULL, Cordell (D Tenn.) Oct. 2, 1871-July 23, 195█ House 1907-21, 1923-31; Senate 1931-March 3, 193█ Chrmn. Dem. Nat. Comm. 1921-24; Secy. of Sta█ 1933-44.

HULL, Harry Edward (R Iowa) March 12, 1864-Jan. █ 1938; House 1915-25.

HULL, John Albert Tiffin (R Iowa) May 1, 1841-Sept. 26, 1928; House 1891-1911.

HULL, Merlin (R Wis.) Dec. 18, 1870-May 17, 1953; House 1929-31, 1935-May 17, 1953 (1935-47 Progressive).

HULL, Morton Denison (R Ill.) Jan. 13, 1867-Aug. 20, 1937; House April 3, 1923-33.

HULL, Noble Andrew (D Fla.) March 11, 1827-Jan. 28, 1907; House 1879-Jan. 22, 1881.

HULL, William Edgar (R Ill.) Jan. 13, 1866-May 30, 1942; House 1923-33.

HULL, William Raleigh Jr. (D Mo.) April 17, 1906-Aug. 15, 1977; House 1955-73.

HUMPHREY, Augustin Reed (R Neb.) Feb. 18, 1859-Dec. 10, 1937; House Nov. 7, 1922-23.

HUMPHREY, Charles (D N.Y.) Feb. 14, 1792-April 17, 1850; House 1825-27.

HUMPHREY, Gordon John (R N.H.) Oct. 7, 1940- —; Senate 1979- —.

HUMPHREY, Herman Leon (R Wis.) March 14, 1830-June 10, 1902; House 1877-83.

HUMPHREY, Hubert Horatio Jr. (husband of Muriel Buck Humphrey) (D Minn.) May 27, 1911-Jan. 13, 1978; Senate 1949-Dec. 29, 1964, 1971-Jan. 13, 1978; Vice President 1965-69.

HUMPHREY, James (R N.Y.) Oct. 9, 1811-June 16, 1866; House 1859-61, 1865-June 16, 1866.

HUMPHREY, James Morgan (D N.Y.) Sept. 21, 1819-Feb. 9, 1899; House 1865-69.

HUMPHREY, Muriel Buck (widow of Hubert Horatio Humphrey Jr.) (D Minn.) Feb. 20, 1912- —; Senate Jan. 25, 1978-Nov. 7, 1978.

HUMPHREY, Reuben (— N.Y.) Sept. 2, 1757-Aug. 12, 1831; House 1807-09.

HUMPHREY, William Ewart (R Wash.) March 31, 1862-Feb. 14, 1934; House 1903-17.

HUMPHREYS, Andrew (D Ind.) March 30, 1821-June 14, 1904; House Dec. 5, 1876-77.

UMPHREYS, Benjamin Grubb (father of William Yerger Humphreys) (D Miss.) Aug. 17, 1865-Oct. 16, 1923; House 1903-Oct. 16, 1923.

UMPHREYS, Parry Wayne (D Tenn.) 1778-Feb. 12, 1839; House 1813-15.

UMPHREYS, Robert (D Ky.) Aug. 20, 1893-Dec. 31, 1977; Senate June 21-Nov. 6, 1956.

HUMPHREYS, William Yerger (son of Benjamin Grubb Humphreys) (D Miss.) Sept. 9, 1890-Feb. 26, 1933; House Nov. 27, 1923-25.

HUNGATE, William Leonard (D Mo.) Dec. 24, 1922- —; House Nov. 3, 1964-77.

HUNGERFORD, John Newton (R N.Y.) Dec. 31, 1825-April 2, 1883; House 1877-79.

HUNGERFORD, John Pratt (D Va.) Jan. 2, 1761-Dec. 21, 1833; House March 4-Nov. 29, 1811, 1813-17.

HUNGERFORD, Orville (D N.Y.) Oct. 29, 1790-April 6, 1851; House 1843-47.

HUNT, Carleton (nephew of Theodore Gaillard Hunt) (D La.) Jan. 1, 1836-Aug. 14, 1921; House 1883-85.

HUNT, Hiram Paine (W N.Y.) May 23, 1796-Aug. 14, 1865; House 1835-37, 1839-43.

HUNT, James Bennett (D Mich.) Aug. 13, 1799-Aug. 15, 1857; House 1843-47.

HUNT, John Edmund (R N.J.) Nov. 25, 1908- —; House 1967-75.

HUNT, John Thomas (D Mo.) Feb. 2, 1860-Nov. 30, 1916; House 1903-07.

HUNT, Jonathan (NR Vt.) Aug. 12, 1787-May 15, 1832; House 1827-May 15, 1832.

HUNT, Lester Callaway (D Wyo.) July 8, 1892-June 19, 1954; Senate 1949-June 19, 1954; Gov. 1943-49.

HUNT, Samuel (— N.H.) July 8, 1765-July 7, 1807; House Dec. 6, 1802-05.

HUNT, Theodore Gaillard (nephew of John Gaillard, uncle of Carleton Hunt) (W La.) Oct. 23, 1805-Nov. 15, 1893; House 1853-55.

HUNT, Washington (W N.Y.) Aug. 5, 1811-Feb. 2, 1867; House 1843-49; Gov. 1851-53.

HUNTER, Allan Oakley (R Calif.) June 15, 1916- —; House 1951-55.

HUNTER, Andrew Jackson (D Ill.) Dec. 17, 1831-Jan. 12, 1913; House 1893-95, 1897-99.

HUNTER, Duncan L. (R Calif.) May 31, 1948- —; House 1981- —.

HUNTER, John (F S.C.) 1732-1802; House 1793-95; Senate Dec. 8, 1796-Nov. 26, 1798.

HUNTER, John Feeney (D Ohio) Oct. 19, 1896-Dec. 19, 1957; House 1937-43.

HUNTER, John Ward (— N.Y.) Oct. 15, 1807-April 16, 1900; House Dec. 4, 1866-67.

HUNTER, Morton Craig (R Ind.) Feb. 5, 1825-Oct. 25, 1896; House 1867-69, 1873-79.

HUNTER, Narsworthy (− Miss.) ?-March 11, 1802; House (Terr. Del.) 1801-March 11, 1802.

HUNTER, Richard Charles (D Neb.) Dec. 3, 1884-Jan. 23, 1941; Senate Nov. 7, 1934-35.

HUNTER, Robert Mercer Taliaferro (D Va.) April 21, 1809-July 18, 1887; House 1837-43 (State Rights Whig), 1845-47; Senate 1847-March 28, 1861; Speaker 1839-41.

HUNTER, Whiteside Godfrey (R Ky.) Dec. 25, 1841-Nov. 2, 1917; House 1887-89, 1895-97, Nov. 10, 1903-05.

HUNTER, William (R Vt.) Jan. 3, 1754-Nov. 30, 1827; House 1817-19.

HUNTER, William (F R.I.) Nov. 26, 1774-Dec. 3, 1849; Senate Oct. 28, 1811-21.

HUNTER, William Forrest (W Ohio) Dec. 10, 1808-March 30, 1874; House 1849-53.

HUNTER, William H. (D Ohio) ?-1842; House 1837-39.

HUNTINGTON, Abel (D N.Y.) Feb. 21, 1777-May 18, 1858; House 1833-37.

HUNTINGTON, Benjamin (− Conn.) April 19, 1736-Oct. 16, 1800; House 1789-91; Cont. Cong. 1780-84, 1787-88.

HUNTINGTON, Ebenezer (W Conn.) Dec. 26, 1754-June 17, 1834; House Oct. 11, 1810-11, 1817-19.

HUNTINGTON, Jabez Williams (W Conn.) Nov. 8, 1788-Nov. 1, 1847; House 1829-Aug. 16, 1834; Senate May 4, 1840-Nov. 1, 1847.

HUNTON, Eppa (D Va.) Sept. 22, 1822-Oct. 11, 1908; House 1873-81; Senate May 28, 1892-95.

HUNTSMAN, Adam (JD Tenn.) ?-?; House 1835-37.

HUOT, Joseph Oliva (D N.H.) Aug. 11, 1917-Aug. 5, 1983; House 1965-67.

HURD, Frank Hunt (D Ohio) Dec. 25, 1840-July 10, 1896; House 1875-77, 1879-81, 1883-85.

HURLBUT, Stephen Augustus (R Ill.) Nov. 29, 1815-March 27, 1882; House 1873-77.

HURLEY, Denis Michael (R N.Y.) March 14, 1843-Feb. 26, 1899; House 1895-Feb. 26, 1899.

HUSTED, James William (R N.Y.) March 16, 1870-Jan. 2, 1925; House 1915-23.

HUSTING, Paul Oscar (D Wis.) April 25, 1866-Oct. 21, 1917; Senate 1915-Oct. 21, 1917.

HUTCHESON, Joseph Chappell (D Texas) May 18 1842-May 25, 1924; House 1893-97.

HUTCHINS, John (cousin of Wells Andrews Hutchins (R Ohio) July 25, 1812-Nov. 20, 1891; House 1859 63.

HUTCHINS, Waldo (D N.Y.) Sept. 30, 1822-Feb. 8 1891; House Nov. 4, 1879-85.

HUTCHINS, Wells Andrews (cousin of John Hutchins (D Ohio) Oct. 8, 1818-Jan. 25, 1895; House 1863-65

HUTCHINSON, Edward (R Mich.) Oct. 13, 1914-Jul 22, 1985; House 1963-77.

HUTCHINSON, Elijah Cubberley (R N.J.) Aug. 1855-June 25, 1932; House 1915-23.

HUTCHINSON, John G. (D W.Va.) Feb. 4, 1935- House June 10, 1980-81.

HUTTO, Earl Dewitt (D Fla.) May 12, 1926-−; Hous 1979-−.

HUTTON, John Edward (D Mo.) March 28, 1828-De 28, 1893; House 1885-89.

HUYLER, John (D N.J.) April 9, 1808-Jan. 9, 187 House 1857-59.

HYDE, DeWitt Stephen (R Md.) March 21, 1909- House 1953-59.

HYDE, Henry John (R Ill.) April 18, 1924-−; Hous 1975-−.

HYDE, Ira Barnes (R Mo.) Jan. 18, 1838-Dec. 6, 192 House 1873-75.

HYDE, Samuel Clarence (R Wash.) April 22, 184 March 7, 1922; House 1895-97.

HYMAN, John Adams (R N.C.) July 23, 1840-Sept. 1 1891; House 1875-77.

HYNEMAN, John M. (D Pa.) April 25, 1771-April 1 1816; House 1811-Aug. 2, 1813.

HYNES, William Joseph (Ref. R Ark.) March 31, 184 April 2, 1915; House 1873-75.

ICHORD, Richard H. (D Mo.) June 27, 1926-−; Hou 1961-81.

IGLESIAS, Santiago (formerly Santiago Iglesi Pantin) (Coal. P.R.) Feb. 22, 1872-Dec. 5, 193 House (Res. Comm.) 1933-Dec. 5, 1939.

IGOE, James Thomas (D Ill.) Oct. 23, 1883-Dec. 2, 197 House 1927-33.

IGOE, Michael Lambert (D Ill.) April 16, 1885-Aug. 2 1967; House Jan. 3-June 2, 1935.

GOE, William Leo (D Mo.) Oct. 19, 1879-April 20, 1953; House 1913-21.

HRIE, Peter Jr. (JD Pa.) Feb. 3, 1796-March 29, 1871; House Oct. 13, 1829-33.

KARD, Frank Neville (D Texas) Jan. 30, 1914- —; House Sept. 8, 1951-Dec. 15, 1961.

KIRT, George Pierce (D Ohio) Nov. 3, 1852-Feb. 12, 1927; House 1893-95.

LSLEY, Daniel (D Mass.) May 30, 1740-May 10, 1813; House 1807-09.

MHOFF, Lawrence E. (D Ohio) Dec. 28, 1895- —; House 1933-39, 1941-43.

MLAY, James Henderson (— N.J.) Nov. 26, 1764-March 6, 1823; House 1797-1801.

NGALLS, John James (R Kan.) Dec. 29, 1833-Aug. 16, 1900; Senate 1873-91; Pres. pro tempore 1887-91.

IGE, Samuel Williams (nephew of William Marshall Inge) (D Ala.) Feb. 22, 1817-June 10, 1868; House 1847-51.

IGE, William Marshall (uncle of Samuel Williams Inge) (D Tenn.) 1802-46; House 1833-35.

IGERSOLL, Charles Jared (brother of Joseph Reed Ingersoll) (D Pa.) Oct. 3, 1782-May 14, 1862; House 1813-15, 1841-49.

IGERSOLL, Colin Macrae (son of Ralph Isaacs Ingersoll) (D Conn.) March 11, 1819-Se, t. 13, 1903; House 1851-55.

IGERSOLL, Ebon Clark (R Ill.) Dec. 12, 1831-May 31, 1879; House May 20, 1864-71.

IGERSOLL, Joseph Reed (brother of Charles Jared Ingersoll) (W Pa.) June 14, 1786-Feb. 20, 1868; House 1835-37, Oct. 12, 1841-49.

IGERSOLL, Ralph Isaacs (father of Colin Macrae Ingersoll) (D Conn.) Feb. 8, 1789-Aug. 26, 1872; House 1825-33.

IGHAM, Samuel (D Conn.) Sept. 5, 1793-Nov. 10, 1881; House 1835-39.

IGHAM, Samuel Delucenna (Jeff. D Pa.) Sept. 16, 1779-June 5, 1860; House 1813-July 6, 1818, Oct. 8, 1822-29; Secy. of the Treasury 1829-31.

IHOFE, James Mountain (R Okla.) Nov. 17, 1934- —; House 1987- —.

IOUYE, Daniel Ken (D Hawaii) Sept. 7, 1924- —; House Aug. 21, 1959-63; Senate 1963- —.

IRBY, John Laurens Manning (great-grandson of Elias Earle) (D S.C.) Sept. 10, 1854-Dec. 9, 1900; Senate 1891-97.

IREDELL, James (DR N.C.) Nov. 2, 1788-April 13, 1853; Senate Dec. 15, 1828-31; Gov. 1827-28.

IRELAND, Andrew P. (R Fla.) Aug. 23, 1930- —; House 1977- — (1977-July 5, 1984, Democrat).

IRELAND, Clifford Cady (R Ill.) Feb. 14, 1878-May 24, 1930; House 1917-23.

IRION, Alfred Briggs (D La.) Feb. 18, 1833-May 21, 1903; House 1885-87.

IRVIN, Alexander (W Pa.) Jan. 18, 1800-March 20, 1874; House 1847-49.

IRVIN, James (W Pa.) Feb. 18, 1800-Nov. 28, 1862; House 1841-45.

IRVIN, William W. (D Ohio) 1778-March 28, 1842; House 1829-33.

IRVINE, William (— Pa.) Nov. 3, 1741-July 29, 1804; House 1793-95; Cont. Cong. 1786-88.

IRVINE, William (R N.Y.) Feb. 14, 1820-Nov. 12, 1882; House 1859-61.

IRVING, Theodore Leonard (D Mo.) March 24, 1898-March 8, 1962; House 1949-53.

IRVING, William (D N.Y.) Aug. 15, 1766-Nov. 9, 1821; House Jan. 22, 1814-19.

IRWIN, Donald J. (D Conn.) Sept. 7, 1926- —; House 1959-61, 1965-69.

IRWIN, Edward Michael (R Ill.) April 14, 1869-Jan. 30, 1933; House 1925-31.

IRWIN, Harvey Samuel (R Ky.) Dec. 10, 1844-Sept. 3, 1916; House 1901-03.

IRWIN, Jared (D Pa.) Jan. 19, 1768-?; House 1813-17.

IRWIN, Thomas (D Pa.) Feb. 22, 1785-May 14, 1870; House 1829-31.

IRWIN, William Wallace (W Pa.) 1803-Sept. 15, 1856; House 1841-43.

ISACKS, Jacob C. (— Tenn.) ?-?; House 1823-33.

ISACSON, Leo (AL N.Y.) April 20, 1910- —; House Feb. 17, 1948-49.

ITTNER, Anthony Friday (R Mo.) Oct. 8, 1837-Feb. 22, 1931; House 1877-79.

IVERSON, Alfred Sr. (D Ga.) Dec. 3, 1798-March 5, 1873; House 1847-49; Senate 1855-Jan. 28, 1861.

IVES, Irving McNeil (R N.Y.) Jan. 24, 1896-Feb. 24, 1962; Senate 1947-59.

IVES, Willard (D N.Y.) July 7, 1806-April 19, 1896; House 1851-53.

IZAC, Edouard Victor Michel (D Calif.) Dec. 18, 1891- —; House 1937-47.

IZARD, Ralph (— S.C.) Jan. 23, 1742-May 30, 1804; Senate 1789-95; Pres. pro tempore 1794-95; Cont. Cong. 1782-83.

IZLAR, James Ferdinand (D S.C.) Nov. 25, 1832-May 26, 1912; House April 12, 1894-95.

JACK, Summers Melville (R Pa.) July 18, 1852-Sept. 16, 1945; House 1899-1903.

JACK, William (D Pa.) July 19, 1788-Feb. 28, 1852; House 1841-43.

JACKSON, Alfred Metcalf (D Kan.) July 14, 1860-June 11, 1924; House 1901-03.

JACKSON, Amos Henry (R Ohio) May 10, 1846-Aug. 30, 1924; House 1903-05.

JACKSON, Andrew (D Tenn.) March 15, 1767-June 8, 1845; House Dec. 5, 1796-Sept. 26, 1797; Senate Sept. 26, 1797-April 1798, 1823-Oct. 14, 1825; Gov. (Florida Terr.) March 10-July 18, 1821; President 1829-37.

JACKSON, David Sherwood (D N.Y.) 1813-Jan. 20, 1872; House 1847-April 19, 1848.

JACKSON, Donald L. (R Calif.) Jan. 23, 1910-May 27, 1981; House 1947-61.

JACKSON, Ebenezer Jr. (W Conn.) Jan. 31, 1796-Aug. 17, 1874; House Dec. 1, 1834-35.

JACKSON, Edward Brake (son of George Jackson, brother of John George Jackson) (D Va.) Jan. 25, 1793-Sept. 8, 1826; House Oct. 23, 1820-23.

JACKSON, Fred Schuyler (R Kan.) April 19, 1868-Nov. 21, 1931; House 1911-13.

JACKSON, George (father of John George Jackson and Edward Brake Jackson) (— Va.) Jan. 9, 1757-May 17, 1831; House 1795-97, 1799-1803.

JACKSON, Henry Martin (D Wash.) May 31, 1912-Sept. 1, 1983; House 1941-53; Senate 1953-Sept. 1, 1983; Chrmn. Dem. Nat. Comm. 1960-61.

JACKSON, Howell Edmunds (D Tenn.) April 8, 1832-Aug. 8, 1895; Senate 1881-April 14, 1886; Assoc. Justice Supreme Court 1893-95.

JACKSON, Jabez Young (son of Sen. James Jackson, uncle of Rep. James Jackson) (UD Ga.) July 1790-? House Oct. 5, 1835-39.

JACKSON, James (father of Jabez Young Jackson, grandfather of James Jackson, below) (— Ga.) Sep 21, 1757-March 19, 1806; House 1789-91; Senate 1793-95, 1801-March 19, 1806; Gov. 1798-180 (Democratic Republican).

JACKSON, James (grandson of James Jackson, above, nephew of Jabez Young Jackson) (D Ga.) Oct. 1 1819-Jan. 13, 1887; House 1857-Jan. 23, 1861.

JACKSON, James Monroe (cousin of William Thom Bland) (D W.Va.) Dec. 3, 1825-Feb. 14, 1901; Hous 1889-Feb. 3, 1890.

JACKSON, James Streshley (U Ky.) Sept. 27, 1823-Oc 8, 1862; House March 4-Dec. 13, 1861.

JACKSON, John George (son of George Jackson, brother of Edward Brake Jackson, grandfather William Thomas Bland) (D Va.) Sept. 22, 177 March 28, 1825; House 1803-Sept. 28, 1810, 1813-1

JACKSON, Joseph Webber (D Ga.) Dec. 6, 1796-Sep 29, 1854; House March 4, 1850-53.

JACKSON, Oscar Lawrence (R Pa.) Sept. 2, 1840-Fe 16, 1920; House 1885-89.

JACKSON, Richard Jr. (F R.I.) July 3, 1764-April 1 1838; House Nov. 11, 1808-15.

JACKSON, Samuel Dillon (D Ind.) May 28, 1895-Mar 8, 1951; Senate Jan. 28-Nov. 13, 1944.

JACKSON, Thomas Birdsall (D N.Y.) March 24, 179 April 23, 1881; House 1837-41.

JACKSON, William (W Mass.) Sept. 2, 1783-Feb. 2 1855; House 1833-37.

JACKSON, William Humphreys (father of Willia Purnell Jackson) (R Md.) Oct. 15, 1839-April 1915; House 1901-05, 1907-09.

JACKSON, William Purnell (son of William Hu phreys Jackson) (R Md.) Jan. 11, 1868-March 1939; Senate Nov. 29, 1912-Jan. 28, 1914.

JACKSON, William Terry (W N.Y.) Dec. 29, 1794-Se 15, 1882; House 1849-51.

JACOBS, Andrew Sr. (father of Andrew Jacobs Jr., ther-in-law of Martha Elizabeth Keys) (D Ind.) F 22, 1906-—; House 1949-51.

JACOBS, Andrew Jr. (son of Andrew Jacobs Sr., hu band of Martha Elizabeth Keys) (D Ind.) Feb. 1932-—; House 1965-73, 1975-—.

ACOBS, Ferris Jr. (R N.Y.) March 20, 1836-Aug. 30, 1886; House 1881-83.

ACOBS, Israel (− Pa.) June 9, 1726-about Dec. 10, 1796; House 1791-93.

ACOBS, Orange (R Wash.) May 2, 1827-May 21, 1914; House (Terr. Del.) 1875-79.

ACOBSEN, Bernhard Martin (father of William Sebastian Jacobsen) (D Iowa) March 26, 1862-June 30, 1936; House 1931-June 30, 1936.

ACOBSEN, William Sebastian (son of Bernhard Martin Jacobsen) (D Iowa) Jan. 15, 1887-April 10, 1955; House 1937-43.

ACOBSTEIN, Meyer (D N.Y.) Jan. 25, 1880-April 18, 1963; House 1923-29.

ACOWAY, Henderson Madison (D Ark.) Nov. 7, 1870-Aug. 4, 1947; House 1911-23.

ADWIN, Cornelius Comegys (R Pa.) March 27, 1835-Aug. 17, 1913; House 1881-83.

AMES, Addison Davis (grandfather of John Albert Whitaker) (R Ky.) Feb. 27, 1850-June 10, 1947; House 1907-09.

AMES, Amaziah Bailey (R N.Y.) July 1, 1812-July 6, 1883; House 1877-81.

AMES, Benjamin Franklin (R Pa.) Aug. 1, 1885-Jan. 26, 1961; House 1949-59.

AMES, Charles Tillinghast (Protect.TD R.I.) Sept. 15, 1805-Oct. 17, 1862; Senate 1851-57.

AMES, Darwin Rush (R N.Y.) May 14, 1834-Nov. 19, 1908; House 1883-87.

AMES, Francis (W Pa.) April 4, 1799-Jan. 4, 1886; House 1839-41.

AMES, Hinton (D N.C.) April 24, 1884-Nov. 3, 1948; House Nov. 4, 1930-31.

AMES, Ollie Murray (D Ky.) July 27, 1871-Aug. 28, 1918; House 1903-13; Senate 1913-Aug. 28, 1918.

AMES, Rorer Abraham (D Va.) March 1, 1859-Aug. 6, 1921; House June 15, 1920-Aug. 6, 1921.

AMES, William Francis "Frank" (R Mich.) May 23, 1873-Nov. 17, 1945; House 1915-35.

AMESON, John (D Mo.) March 6, 1802-Jan. 24, 1857; House Dec. 12, 1839-41, 1843-45, 1847-49.

AMIESON, William Darius (D Iowa) Nov. 9, 1873-Nov. 18, 1949; House 1909-11.

ANES, Henry Fisk (W/AM Vt.) Oct. 10, 1792-June 6, 1879; House Dec. 2, 1834-37.

JARMAN, John (R Okla.) July 17, 1915-Jan. 15, 1982; House 1951-77 (1951-Jan. 24, 1975, Democrat).

JARMAN, Pete (D Ala.) Oct. 31, 1892-Feb. 17, 1955; House 1937-49.

JARNAGIN, Spencer (W Tenn.) 1792-June 25, 1853; Senate Oct. 17, 1843-47.

JARRETT, Benjamin (R Pa.) July 18, 1881-July 20, 1944; House 1937-43.

JARRETT, William Paul (D Hawaii) Aug. 22, 1877-Nov. 10, 1929; House (Terr. Del.) 1923-27.

JARVIS, Leonard (D Maine) Oct. 19, 1781-Oct. 18, 1854; House 1829-37.

JARVIS, Thomas Jordan (D N.C.) Jan. 18, 1836-June 17, 1915; Senate April 19, 1894-Jan. 23, 1895; Gov. 1879-85.

JAVITS, Jacob Koppel (R N.Y.) May 18, 1904-March 7, 1986; House 1947-Dec. 31, 1954; Senate Jan. 9, 1957-81.

JAYNE, William (− Dakota) Oct. 8, 1826-March 20, 1916; House (Terr. Del.) 1863-June 17, 1864; Gov. 1861-63.

JEFFERIS, Albert Webb (R Neb.) Dec. 7, 1868-Sept. 14, 1942; House 1919-23.

JEFFERS, Lamar (D Ala.) April 16, 1888-June 1, 1983; House June 7, 1921-35.

JEFFORDS, Elza (R Miss.) May 23, 1826-March 19, 1885; House 1883-85.

JEFFORDS, James Merrill (R Vt.) May 11, 1934-−; House 1975-−.

JEFFREY, Harry Palmer (R Ohio) Dec. 26, 1901-−; House 1943-45.

JEFFRIES, James Edmund (R Kan.) June 1, 1925-−; House 1979-83.

JEFFRIES, Walter Sooy (R N.J.) Oct. 16, 1893-Oct. 11, 1954; House 1939-41.

JENCKES, Thomas Allen (R R.I.) Nov. 2, 1818-Nov. 4, 1875; House 1863-71.

JENCKES, Virginia Ellis (D Ind.) Nov. 6, 1877-Jan. 9, 1975; House 1933-39.

JENIFER, Daniel (NR Md.) April 15, 1791-Dec. 18, 1855; House 1831-33, 1835-41.

JENISON, Edward Halsey (R Ill.) July 27, 1907-−; House 1947-53.

JENKINS, Albert Gallatin (D Va.) Nov. 10, 1830-May 21, 1864; House 1857-61.

JENKINS, Edgar Lanier (D Ga.) Jan. 4, 1933- —; House 1977- —.

JENKINS, John James (R Wis.) Aug. 24, 1843-June 8, 1911; House 1895-1909.

JENKINS, Lemuel (D N.Y.) Oct. 20, 1789-Aug. 18, 1862; House 1823-25.

JENKINS, Mitchell (R Pa.) Jan. 24, 1896-Sept. 15, 1977; House 1947-49.

JENKINS, Robert (— Pa.) July 10, 1769-April 18, 1848; House 1807-11.

JENKINS, Thomas Albert (R Ohio) Oct. 28, 1880-Dec. 21, 1959; House 1925-59.

JENKINS, Timothy (D N.Y.) Jan. 29, 1799-Dec. 24, 1859; House 1845-49, 1851-53.

JENKS, Arthur Byron (R N.H.) Oct. 15, 1866-Dec. 14, 1947; House 1937-June 9, 1938, 1939-43.

JENKS, George Augustus (D Pa.) March 26, 1836-Feb. 10, 1908; House 1875-77.

JENKS, Michael Hutchinson (W Pa.) May 21, 1795-Oct. 16, 1867; House 1843-45.

JENNER, William Ezra (R Ind.) July 21, 1908-March 9, 1985; Senate Nov. 14, 1944-45, 1947-59.

JENNESS, Benning Wentworth (D N.H.) July 14, 1806-Nov. 16, 1879; Senate Dec. 1, 1845-June 13, 1846.

JENNINGS, David (— Ohio) 1787-1834; House 1825-May 25, 1826.

JENNINGS, John Jr. (R Tenn.) June 6, 1880-Feb. 27, 1956; House Dec. 30, 1939-51.

JENNINGS, Jonathan (D Ind.) 1784-July 26, 1834; House Dec. 2, 1822-31; Gov. 1816-22 (Democratic Republican).

JENNINGS, William Pat (D Va.) Aug. 20, 1919- —; House 1955-67.

JENRETTE, John Wilson Jr. (D S.C.) May 19, 1936- —; House 1975-Dec. 10, 1980.

JENSEN, Benton Franklin "Ben" (R Iowa) Dec. 16, 1892-Feb. 5, 1970; House 1939-65.

JEPSEN, Roger William (R Iowa) Dec. 23, 1928- —; Senate 1979-85.

JETT, Thomas Marion (D Ill.) May 1, 1862-Jan. 10, 1939; House 1897-1903.

JEWETT, Daniel Tarbox (R Mo.) Sept. 14, 1807-Oct. 7, 1906; Senate Dec. 19, 1870-Jan. 20, 1871.

JEWETT, Freeborn Garrettson (JD N.Y.) Aug. 4, 179? Jan. 27, 1858; House 1831-33.

JEWETT, Hugh Judge (brother of Joshua Husban Jewett) (D Ohio) July 1, 1817-March 6, 1898; Hous 1873-June 23, 1874.

JEWETT, Joshua Husband (brother of Hugh Judg Jewett) (D Ky.) Sept. 30, 1815-July 14, 1861; Hous 1855-59.

JEWETT, Luther (F Vt.) Dec. 24, 1772-March 8, 186 House 1815-17.

JOELSON, Charles S. (D N.J.) Jan. 27, 1916- —; Hous 1961-Sept. 4, 1969.

JOHANSEN, August Edgar (R Mich.) July 21, 1905- — House 1955-65.

JOHNS, Joshua Leroy (R Wis.) Feb. 27, 1881-March 1 1947; House 1939-43.

JOHNS, Kensey Jr. (F Del.) Dec. 10, 1791-March ? 1857; House Oct. 2, 1827-31.

JOHNSON, Adna Romulus (R Ohio) Dec. 14, 1860-Ju 11, 1938; House 1909-11.

JOHNSON, Albert (R Wash.) March 5, 1869-Jan. 1 1957; House 1913-33.

JOHNSON, Albert Walter (R Pa.) April 17, 1906- House Nov. 5, 1963-77.

JOHNSON, Andrew (father-in-law of David Trot Patterson) (R Tenn.) Dec. 29, 1808-July 31, 18` House 1843-53 (Democrat); Senate Oct. 8, 1857- (Democrat), March 4-July 31, 1875; Gov. 1853- (Democrat), 1862-65 (Military); Vice Preside March 4-April 15, 1865; President April 15, 1865- ●

JOHNSON, Anton Joseph (R Ill.) Oct. 20, 1878-Ap 16, 1958; House 1939-49.

JOHNSON, Ben (D Ky.) May 20, 1858-June 4, 19 House 1907-27.

JOHNSON, Byron Lindberg (D Colo.) Oct. 12, 1917- House 1959-61.

JOHNSON, Calvin Dean (R Ill.) Nov. 22, 1898- House 1943-45.

JOHNSON, Cave (D Tenn.) Jan. 11, 1793-Nov. 23, 18 House 1829-37, 1839-45; Postmaster Gen. 1845-4

JOHNSON, Charles (— N.Y.) ?-July 23, 1802; Ho 1801-July 23, 1802.

JOHNSON, Charles Fletcher (D Maine) Feb. 14, 18 Feb. 15, 1930; Senate 1911-17.

JOHNSON, Dewey William (FL Minn.) March 14, 18 Sept. 18, 1941; House 1937-39.

HNSON, Edwin Carl (D Colo.) Jan. 1, 1884-May 30, 1970; Senate 1937-55; Gov. 1933-37, 1955-57.

HNSON, Edwin Stockton (D S.D.) Feb. 26, 1857-July 19, 1933; Senate 1915-21.

HNSON, Francis (Ad.D Ky.) June 19, 1776-May 16, 1842; House Nov. 13, 1820-27.

HNSON, Frederick Avery (− N.Y.) Jan. 2, 1833-July 17, 1893; House 1883-87.

HNSON, Fred Gustus (R Neb.) Oct. 16, 1876-April 30, 1951; House 1929-31.

HNSON, George William (D W.Va.) Nov. 10, 1869-Feb. 24, 1944; House 1923-25, 1933-43.

HNSON, Glen Dale (D Okla.) Sept. 11, 1911-Feb. 10, 1983; House 1947-49.

HNSON, Grove Lawrence (father of Hiram Warren Johnson) (R Calif.) March 27, 1841-Feb. 1, 1926; House 1895-97.

HNSON, Harold Terry (D Calif.) Dec. 2, 1907-−; House 1959-81.

HNSON, Harvey Hull (D Ohio) Sept. 7, 1808-Feb. 4, 1896; House 1853-55.

HNSON, Henry S. (W La.) Sept. 14, 1783-Sept. 4, 1864; Senate Jan. 12, 1818-May 27, 1824, Feb. 12, 1844-49; House Sept. 25, 1834-39; Gov. 1824-28 (Democratic-Republican).

HNSON, Henry Underwood (R Ind.) Oct. 28, 1850-June 4, 1939; House 1891-99.

HNSON, Herschel Vespasian (D Ga.) Sept. 18, 1812-Aug. 16, 1880; Senate Feb. 4, 1848-49; Gov. 1853-57.

HNSON, Hiram Warren (son of Grove Lawrence Johnson) (R Calif.) Sept. 2, 1866-Aug. 6, 1945; Senate March 16, 1917-Aug. 6, 1945; Gov. 1911-17.

HNSON, Jacob (R Utah) Nov. 1, 1847-Aug. 15, 1925; House 1913-15.

HNSON, James (D Va.) ?-Dec. 7, 1825; House 1813-Feb. 1, 1820.

HNSON, James (brother of Richard Mentor Johnson and John Telemachus Johnson, uncle of Robert Ward Johnson) (D Ky.) Jan. 1, 1774-Aug. 14, 1826; House 1825-Aug. 14, 1826.

HNSON, James (U Ga.) Feb. 12, 1811-Nov. 20, 1891; House 1851-53; Provisional Gov. 1865.

HNSON, James Augustus (D Calif.) May 16, 1829-May 11, 1896; House 1867-71.

HNSON, James Hutchins (− N.H.) June 3, 1802-Sept. 2, 1887; House 1845-49.

JOHNSON, James Leeper (W Ky.) Oct. 30, 1818-Feb. 12, 1877; House 1849-51.

JOHNSON, James Paul (R Colo.) June 2, 1930-−; House 1973-81.

JOHNSON, Jed Joseph (father of Jed Johnson Jr.) (D Okla.) July 31, 1888-May 8, 1963; House 1927-47.

JOHNSON, Jed Jr. (son of Jed Joseph Johnson) (D Okla.) Dec. 17, 1939-−; House 1965-67.

JOHNSON, Jeromus (D N.Y.) Nov. 2, 1775-Sept. 7, 1846; House 1825-29.

JOHNSON, John (I Ohio) 1805-Feb. 5, 1867; House 1851-53.

JOHNSON, John Telemachus (brother of James Johnson of Ky. and Richard Mentor Johnson, uncle of Robert Ward Johnson) (JD Ky.) Oct. 5, 1788-Dec. 17, 1856; House 1821-25.

JOHNSON, Joseph (uncle of Waldo Porter Johnson) (D Va.) Dec. 19, 1785-Feb. 27, 1877; House 1823-27, Jan. 21-March 3, 1833, 1835-41, 1845-47; Gov. 1852-56.

JOHNSON, Joseph Travis (D S.C.) Feb. 28, 1858-May 8, 1919; House 1901-April 19, 1915.

JOHNSON, Justin Leroy (R Calif.) April 8, 1888-March 26, 1961; House 1943-57.

JOHNSON, Lester Roland (D Wis.) June 16, 1901-July 24, 1975; House Oct. 13, 1953-65.

JOHNSON, Luther Alexander (D Texas) Oct. 29, 1875-June 6, 1965; House 1923-July 17, 1946.

JOHNSON, Lyndon Baines (D Texas) Aug. 27, 1908-Jan. 22, 1973; House April 10, 1937-49; Senate 1949-61; Senate majority leader 1955-61; Vice President 1961-Nov. 22, 1963; President Nov. 22, 1963-69.

JOHNSON, Magnus (FL Minn.) Sept. 19, 1871-Sept. 13, 1936; Senate July 16, 1923-25; House 1933-35.

JOHNSON, Martin Nelson (R N.D.) March 3, 1850-Oct. 21, 1909; House 1891-99; Senate March 4-Oct. 21, 1909.

JOHNSON, Nancy Lee (R Conn.) Jan. 5, 1935-−; House 1983-−.

JOHNSON, Noadiah (D N.Y.) 1795-April 4, 1839; House 1833-35.

JOHNSON, Noble Jacob (R Ind.) Aug. 23, 1887-March 17, 1968; House 1925-31, 1939-July 1, 1948.

JOHNSON, Paul Burney (D Miss.) March 23, 1880-Dec. 26, 1943; House 1919-23; Gov. 1940-43.

JOHNSON, Perley Brown (W Ohio) Sept. 8, 1798-Feb. 9, 1870; House 1843-45.

JOHNSON, Philip (R Pa.) Jan. 17, 1818-Jan. 29, 1867; House 1861-Jan. 29, 1867.

JOHNSON, Reverdy (brother-in-law of Thomas Fielder Bowie) (D Md.) May 21, 1796-Feb. 10, 1876; Senate 1845-March 7, 1849 (Whig), 1863-July 10, 1868; Atty Gen. 1849-50.

JOHNSON, Richard Mentor (brother of James Johnson of Ky. and John Telemachus Johnson, uncle of Robert Ward Johnson) (D Ky.) Oct. 17, 1781-Nov. 19, 1850; House 1807-19, 1829-37 (Jackson Democrat); Senate Dec. 10, 1819-29 (Jackson Democrat); Vice President 1837-41.

JOHNSON, Robert Davis (D Mo.) Aug. 12, 1883-Oct. 23, 1961; House Sept. 29, 1931-33.

JOHNSON, Robert Ward (nephew of James Johnson of Ky., John Telemachus Johnson and Richard Mentor Johnson) (D Ark.) July 22, 1814-July 26, 1879; House 1847-53; Senate July 6, 1853-61.

JOHNSON, Royal Cleaves (R S.D.) Oct. 3, 1882-Aug. 2, 1939; House 1915-33.

JOHNSON, Thomas F. (D Md.) June 26, 1909--; House 1959-63.

JOHNSON, Tim (D S.D.) Dec. 28, 1946--; House 1987--.

JOHNSON, Tom Loftin (D Ohio) July 18, 1854-April 10, 1911; House 1891-95.

JOHNSON, Waldo Porter (nephew of Joseph Johnson) (D Mo.) Sept. 16, 1817-Aug. 14, 1885; Senate March 17, 1861-Jan. 10, 1862.

JOHNSON, William Cost (W Md.) Jan. 14, 1806-April 14, 1860; House 1833-35, 1837-43.

JOHNSON, William Richard (R Ill.) May 15, 1875-Jan. 2, 1938; House 1925-33.

JOHNSON, William Samuel (− Conn.) Oct. 7, 1727-Nov. 14, 1819; Senate 1789-March 4, 1791; Cont. Cong. 1784-87.

JOHNSON, William Ward (R Calif.) March 9, 1892-June 8, 1963; House 1941-45.

JOHNSTON, Charles (W N.Y.) Feb. 14, 1793-Sept. 1, 1845; House 1839-41.

JOHNSTON, Charles Clement (brother of Joseph Eggleston Johnston, uncle of John Warfield Johnston) (SRD Va.) April 30, 1795-June 17, 1832; House 1831-June 17, 1832.

JOHNSTON, David Emmons (D W.Va.) April 10, 1845-July 7, 1917; House 1899-1901.

JOHNSTON, James Thomas (R Ind.) Jan. 19, 1839-Ju 19, 1904; House 1885-89.

JOHNSTON, John Bennett Jr. (D La.) June 10, 193 −; Senate Nov. 14, 1972-−.

JOHNSTON, John Brown (D N.Y.) July 10, 1882-Ja 11, 1960; House 1919-21.

JOHNSTON, John Warfield (uncle of Henry Bowe nephew of Charles Clement Johnston and Josep Eggleston Johnston) (C Va.) Sept. 9, 1818-Feb. 2 1889; Senate Jan. 26, 1870-March 3, 1871, March 1 1871-83.

JOHNSTON, Joseph Eggleston (brother of Charl Clement Johnston, uncle of John Warfield Joh ston) (D Va.) Feb. 3, 1807-March 21, 1891; Hou 1879-81.

JOHNSTON, Joseph Forney (D Ala.) March 23, 184 Aug. 8, 1913; Senate Aug. 6 1907-Aug. 8, 1913; Go 1896-1900.

JOHNSTON, Josiah Stoddard (D La.) Nov. 24, 178 May 19, 1833; House 1821-23; Senate Jan. 15, 182 May 19, 1833.

JOHNSTON, Olin DeWitt Talmadge (father of Eliz beth Johnston Patterson) (D S.C.) Nov. 18, 189 April 18, 1965; Senate 1945-April 18, 1965; G 1935-39, 1943-45.

JOHNSTON, Rienzi Melville (cousin of Benjamin E ward Russell) (D Texas) Sept. 9, 1849-Feb. 28, 19 Senate Jan. 4-29, 1913.

JOHNSTON, Rowland Louis (R Mo.) April 23, 187 Sept. 22, 1939; House 1929-31.

JOHNSTON, Samuel (F N.C.) Dec. 15, 1733-Aug. 1 1816; Senate Nov. 27, 1789-93; Cont. Cong. 1780-8 Gov. 1789.

JOHNSTON, Thomas Dillard (D N.C.) April 1, 184 June 22, 1902; House 1885-89.

JOHNSTON, W. Eugene (R N.C.) March 3, 1936-- House 1981-83.

JOHNSTON, William (D Ohio) 1819-May 1, 186 House 1863-65.

JOHNSTONE, George (D S.C.) April 18, 1846-March 1921; House 1891-93.

JOLLEY, John Lawlor (R S.D.) July 14, 1840-Dec. 1 1926; House Dec. 7, 1891-93.

JONAS, Benjamin Franklin (D La.) July 19, 1834-De 21, 1911; Senate 1879-85.

JONAS, Charles Andrew (father of Charles Raper J nas) (R N.C.) Aug. 14, 1876-May 25, 1955; Hou 1929-31.

JONAS, Charles Raper (son of Charles Andrew Jonas) (R N.C.) Dec. 9, 1904- — ; House 1953-73.

JONAS, Edgar Allan (R Ill.) Oct. 14, 1885-Nov. 14, 1965; House 1949-55.

JONES, Alexander Hamilton (R N.C.) July 21, 1822-Jan. 29, 1901; House July 6, 1868-71.

JONES, Andrieus Aristieus (D N.M.) May 16, 1862-Dec. 20, 1927; Senate 1917-Dec. 20, 1927.

JONES, Benjamin (D Ohio) April 13, 1787-April 24, 1861; House 1833-37.

JONES, Burr W. (D Wis.) March 9, 1846-Jan. 7, 1935; House 1883-85.

JONES, Charles William (D Fla.) Dec. 24, 1834-Oct. 11, 1897; Senate 1875-87.

JONES, Daniel Terryll (D N.Y.) Aug. 17, 1800-March 29, 1861; House 1851-55.

JONES, Ed (D Tenn.) April 20, 1912- — ; House March 25, 1969- —.

JONES, Evan John (R Pa.) Oct. 23, 1872-Jan. 9, 1952; House 1919-23.

JONES, Francis (— Tenn.) ?-?; House 1817-23.

JONES, Frank (D N.H.) Sept. 15, 1832-Oct. 2, 1902; House 1875-79.

JONES, George (— Ga.) Feb. 25, 1766-Nov. 13, 1838; Senate Aug. 27-Nov. 7, 1807.

JONES, George Wallace (— Iowa) April 12, 1804-July 22, 1896; House (Terr. Del.) 1835-April 1836 (Mich.), April 1836-Jan. 14, 1839 (Wis.); Senate Dec. 7, 1848-59.

JONES, George Washington (D Tenn.) March 15, 1806-Nov. 14, 1884; House 1843-59.

JONES, George Washington (G Texas) Sept. 5, 1828-July 11, 1903; House 1879-83.

JONES, Hamilton Chamberlain (D N.C.) Sept. 26, 1884-Aug. 10, 1957; House 1947-53.

JONES, Homer Raymond (R Wash.) Sept. 3, 1893-Nov. 26, 1970; House 1947-49.

JONES, Isaac Dashiell (W Md.) Nov. 1, 1806-July 5, 1893; House 1841-43.

JONES, James (R Ga.) ?-Jan. 11, 1801; House 1799-Jan. 11, 1801.

JONES, James (D Va.) Dec. 11, 1772-April 25, 1848; House 1819-23.

JONES, James Chamberlain (W Tenn.) June 7, 1809-Oct. 29, 1859; Senate 1851-57; Gov. 1841-45.

JONES, James Henry (D Texas) Sept. 13, 1830-March 22, 1904; House 1883-87.

JONES, James Kimbrough (D Ark.) Sept. 29, 1839-June 1, 1908; House 1881-Feb. 19, 1885; Senate March 4, 1885-1903; Chrmn. Dem. Nat. Comm. 1896-1904.

JONES, James Robert (D Okla.) May 5, 1939- — ; House 1973-87.

JONES, James Taylor (D Ala.) July 20, 1832-Feb. 15, 1895; House 1877-79, Dec. 3, 1883-89.

JONES, Jehu Glancy (D Pa.) Oct. 7, 1811-March 24, 1878; House 1851-53, Feb. 4, 1854-Oct. 30, 1858.

JONES, John James (D Ga.) Nov. 13, 1824-Oct. 19, 1898; House 1859-Jan. 23, 1861.

JONES, John Marvin (D Texas) Feb. 26, 1886-March 4, 1976; House 1917-Nov. 20, 1940.

JONES, John Percival (R Nev.) Jan. 27, 1829-Nov. 27, 1912; Senate 1873-1903.

JONES, John Sills (R Ohio) Feb. 12, 1836-April 11, 1903; House 1877-79.

JONES, John William (W Ga.) April 14, 1806-April 27, 1871; House 1847-49.

JONES, John Winston (D Va.) Nov. 22, 1791-Jan. 29, 1848; House 1835-45; Speaker 1843-45.

JONES, Morgan (D N.Y.) Feb. 26, 1830-July 13, 1894; House 1865-67.

JONES, Nathaniel (D N.Y.) Feb. 17, 1788-July 20, 1866; House 1837-41.

JONES, Owen (D Pa.) Dec. 29, 1819-Dec. 25, 1878; House 1857-59.

JONES, Paul Caruthers (D Mo.) March 12, 1901-Feb. 10, 1981; House Nov. 2, 1948-69.

JONES, Phineas (R N.J.) April 18, 1819-April 19, 1884; House 1881-83.

JONES, Robert Emmett Jr. (D Ala.) June 12, 1912- — ; House Jan. 28, 1947-77.

JONES, Robert Franklin (F Ohio) June 25, 1907-June 22, 1968; House 1939-Sept. 2, 1947.

JONES, Roland (D La.) Nov. 18, 1813-Feb. 5, 1869; House 1853-55.

JONES, Seaborn (D Ga.) Feb. 1, 1788-March 18, 1864; House 1833-35, 1845-47.

JONES, Thomas Laurens (D Ky.) Jan. 22, 1819-June 20, .1887; House 1867-71, 1875-77.

JONES, Walter (D Va.) Dec. 18, 1745-Dec. 31, 1815; House 1797-99, 1803-11.

JONES, Walter B. (D N.C.) Aug. 19, 1913--; House Feb. 5, 1966- -.

JONES, Wesley Livsey (R Wash.) Oct. 9, 1863-Nov. 19, 1932; House 1899-1909; Senate 1909-Nov. 19, 1932.

JONES, William (D Pa.) 1760-Sept. 6, 1831; House 1801-03; Secy. of the Navy 1813-14.

JONES, William Atkinson (D Va.) March 21, 1849-April 17, 1918; House 1891-April 17, 1918.

JONES, William Carey (FSil. R Wash.) April 5, 1855-June 14, 1927; House 1897-99.

JONES, William Theopilus (R Wyo.) Feb. 20, 1842-Oct. 9, 1882; House (Terr. Del.) 1871-73.

JONES, Woodrow Wilson (D N.C.) Jan. 26, 1914--; House Nov. 7, 1950-57.

JONKMAN, Bartel John (R Mich.) April 28, 1884-June 13, 1955; House Feb. 19, 1940-49.

JONTZ, Jim (D Ind.) Dec. 18, 1951- -; House 1987- -.

JORDAN, Barbara Charline (D Texas) Feb. 21, 1936- -; House 1973-79.

JORDAN, Benjamin Everett (D N.C.) Sept. 8, 1896-March 15, 1974; Senate April 19, 1958-73.

JORDAN, Isaac M. (D Ohio) May 5, 1835-Dec. 3, 1890; House 1883-85.

JORDAN, Leonard Beck (R Idaho) May 15, 1899-June 30, 1983; Senate Aug. 6, 1962-73; Gov. 1951-55.

JORDEN, Edwin James (R Pa.) Aug. 30, 1863-Sept. 7, 1903; House Feb. 23-March 4, 1895.

JORGENSEN, Joseph (R Va.) Feb. 11, 1844-Jan. 21, 1888; House 1877-83.

JOSEPH, Antonio (D N.M.) Aug. 25, 1846-April 19, 1910; House (Terr. Del.) 1885-95.

JOST, Henry Lee (D Mo.) Dec. 6, 1873-July 13, 1950; House 1923-25.

JOY, Charles Frederick (R Mo.) Dec. 11, 1849-April 13, 1921; House 1893-April 3, 1894, 1895-1903.

JOYCE, Charles Herbert (R Vt.) Jan. 30, 1830-Nov. 22, 1916; House 1875-83.

JOYCE, James (R Ohio) July 2, 1870-March 25, 1931; House 1909-11.

JUDD, Norman Buel (grandfather of Norman Judd Gould) (R Ill.) Jan. 10, 1815-Nov. 10, 1878; House 1867-71.

JUDD, Walter Henry (R Minn.) Sept. 25, 1898- - House 1943-63.

JUDSON, Andrew Thompson (D Conn.) Nov. 29, 1784 March 17, 1853; House 1835-July 4, 1836.

JULIAN, George Washington (R Ind.) May 5, 1817-July 7, 1899; House 1849-51 (Free-Soiler), 1861-71.

JUNKIN, Benjamin Franklin (R Pa.) Nov. 12, 1822-Oct. 9, 1908; House 1859-61.

JUUL, Niels (R Ill.) April 27, 1859-Dec. 4, 1929; House 1917-21.

KADING, Charles August (R Wis.) Jan. 14, 1874-June 19, 1956; House 1927-33.

KAHN, Florence Prag (widow of Julius Kahn) (R Calif.) Nov. 9, 1868-Nov. 16, 1948; House 1925-37.

KAHN, Julius (husband of Florence Prag Kahn) (R Calif.) Feb. 28, 1861-Dec. 18, 1924; House 1899-1903 1905-Dec. 18, 1924.

KALANIANAOLE, Jonah Kuhio (R Hawaii) March 26 1871-Jan. 7, 1922; House (Terr. Del.) 1903-Jan. 7 1922.

KALBFLEISCH, Martin (D N.Y.) Feb. 8, 1804-Feb. 12 1873; House 1863-65.

KANE, Elias Kent (D Ill.) June 7, 1794-Dec. 12, 1835 Senate 1825-Dec. 12, 1835.

KANE, Nicholas Thomas (D N.Y.) Sept. 12, 1846-Sept 14, 1887; House March 4-Sept. 14, 1887.

KANJORSKI, Paul E. (D Pa.) April 2, 1937- -; Hous 1985- -.

KAPTUR, Marcia Carolyn (D Ohio) June 17, 1946- - House 1983- -.

KARCH, Charles Adam (D Ill.) March 17, 1875-Nov. 6 1932; House 1931-Nov. 6, 1932.

KARNES, David (R Neb.) Dec 12, 1948- -; Senat March 13, 1987- -.

KARST, Raymond Willard (D Mo.) Dec. 31, 1902- - House 1949-51.

KARSTEN, Frank Melvin (D Mo.) Jan. 7, 1913- - House 1947-69.

KARTH, Joseph Edward (D Minn.) Aug. 26, 1922- - House 1959-77.

KASEM, George Albert (D Calif.) April 6, 1919- - House 1959-61.

KASICH, John R. (R Ohio) May 13, 1952- —; House 1983- —.

KASSEBAUM, Nancy Landon (R Kan.) July 29, 1932- —; Senate Dec. 23, 1978- —.

KASSON, John Adam (R Iowa) Jan. 11, 1822-May 19, 1910; House 1863-67, 1873-77, 1881-July 13, 1884.

KASTEN, Robert Walter Jr. (R Wis.) June 19, 1942- —; House 1975-79; Senate 1981- —.

KASTENMEIER, Robert William (D Wis.) Jan. 24, 1924- —; House 1959- —.

KAUFMAN, David Spangler (D Texas) Dec. 18, 1813-Jan. 31, 1851; House March 30, 1846-Jan. 31, 1851.

KAVANAGH, Edward (D Maine) April 27, 1795-Jan. 20, 1844; House 1831-35; Gov. 1843-44.

KAVANAUGH, William Marmaduke (D Ark.) March 3, 1866-Feb. 21, 1915; Senate Jan. 29-March 3, 1913.

KAYNOR, William Kirk (R Mass.) Nov. 29, 1884-Dec. 20, 1929; House March 4-Dec. 20, 1929.

KAZEN, Abraham Jr. (D Texas) Jan. 17, 1919- —; House 1967-85.

KEAN, Hamilton Fish (father of Robert Winthrop Kean, brother of John Kean) (R N.J.) Feb. 27, 1862-Dec. 27, 1941; Senate 1929-35.

KEAN, John (brother of Hamilton Fish Kean, uncle of Robert Winthrop Kean) (R N.J.) Dec. 4, 1852-Nov. 4, 1914; House 1883-85, 1887-89; Senate 1899-1911.

KEAN, Robert Winthrop (son of Hamilton Fish Kean, nephew of John Kean) (R N.J.) Sept. 28, 1893-Sept. 22, 1980; House 1939-59.

KEARNEY, Bernard William (R N.Y.) May 23, 1889-June 3, 1976; House 1943-59.

KEARNS, Carroll Dudley (R Pa.) May 7, 1900-June 11, 1976; House 1947-63.

KEARNS, Charles Cyrus (R Ohio) Feb. 11, 1869-Dec. 17, 1931; House 1915-31.

KEARNS, Thomas (R Utah) April 11, 1862-Oct. 18, 1918; Senate Jan. 23, 1901-05.

KEATING, Edward (D Colo.) July 9, 1875-March 18, 1965; House 1913-19.

KEATING, Kenneth Barnard (R N.Y.) May 18, 1900-May 5, 1975; House 1947-59; Senate 1959-65.

KEATING, William John (R Ohio) March 30, 1927- —; House 1971-Jan. 3, 1974.

KEE, James (son of John and Maude Elizabeth Kee) (D W.Va.) April 15, 1917- —; House 1965-73.

KEE, John (husband of Maude Elizabeth Kee, father of James Kee) (D W.Va.) Aug. 22, 1874-May 8, 1951; House 1933-May 8, 1951.

KEE, Maude Elizabeth (widow of John Kee, mother of James Kee) (D W.Va.) ?-Feb. 16, 1975; House July 17, 1951-65.

KEEFE, Frank Bateman (R Wis.) Sept. 23, 1887-Feb. 5, 1952; House 1939-51.

KEENEY, Russell Watson (R Ill.) Dec. 29, 1897-Jan. 11, 1958; House 1957-Jan. 11, 1958.

KEESE, Richard (D N.Y.) Nov. 23, 1794-Feb. 7, 1883; House 1827-29.

KEFAUVER, Carey Estes (D Tenn.) July 26, 1903-Aug. 10, 1963; House Sept. 13, 1939-49; Senate 1949-Aug. 10, 1963.

KEHOE, James Nicholas (D Ky.) July 15, 1862-June 16, 1945; House 1901-05.

KEHOE, James Walter (D Fla.) April 25, 1870-Aug. 20, 1938; House 1917-19.

KEHR, Edward Charles (D Mo.) Nov. 5, 1837-April 20, 1918; House 1875-77.

KEIFER, Joseph Warren (R Ohio) Jan. 30, 1836-April 22, 1932; House 1877-85, 1905-11; Speaker 1881-83.

KEIGHTLEY, Edwin William (R Mich.) Aug. 7, 1843-May 4, 1926; House 1877-79.

KEIM, George May (uncle of William High Keim) (D Pa.) March 23, 1805-June 10, 1861; House March 17, 1838-43.

KEIM, William High (nephew of George May Keim) (D Pa.) June 13, 1813-May 18, 1862; House Dec. 7, 1858-59.

KEISTER, Abraham Lincoln (R Pa.) Sept. 10, 1852-May 26, 1917; House 1913-17.

KEITH, Hastings (R Mass.) Nov. 22, 1915- —; House 1959-73.

KEITT, Laurence Massillon (D S.C.) Oct. 4, 1824-June 4, 1864; House 1853-July 16, 1856, Aug. 6, 1856-Dec. 1860.

KELIHER, John Austin (D Mass.) Nov. 6, 1866-Sept. 20, 1938; House 1903-11.

KELLER, Kent Ellsworth (D Ill.) June 4, 1867-Sept. 3, 1954; House 1931-41.

KELLER, Oscar Edward (IR Minn.) July 30, 1878-Nov. 21, 1927; House July 1, 1919-27.

KELLEY, Augustine Bernard (D Pa.) July 9, 1883-Nov. 20, 1957; House 1941-Nov. 20, 1957.

KELLEY, Harrison (R Kan.) May 12, 1836-July 24, 1897; House Dec. 2, 1889-91.

KELLEY, John Edward (D/PP S.D.) March 27, 1853-Aug. 5, 1941; House 1897-99.

KELLEY, Patrick Henry (R Mich.) Oct. 7, 1867-Sept. 11, 1925; House 1913-23.

KELLEY, William Darrah (R Pa.) April 12, 1814-Jan. 9, 1890; House 1861-Jan. 9, 1890.

KELLOGG, Charles (− N.Y.) Oct. 3, 1773-May 11, 1842; House 1825-27.

KELLOGG, Francis William (R Ala.) May 30, 1810-Jan. 13, 1879; House 1859-65 (Mich.); July 22, 1868-69.

KELLOGG, Frank Billings (R Minn.) Dec. 22, 1856-Dec. 21, 1937; Senate 1917-23; Secy. of State 1925-29.

KELLOGG, Orlando (W N.Y.) June 18, 1809-Aug. 24, 1865; House 1847-49, 1863-Aug. 24, 1865.

KELLOGG, Stephen Wright (R Conn.) April 5, 1822-Jan. 27, 1904; House 1869-73.

KELLOGG, William (R Ill.) July 8, 1814-Dec. 20, 1872; House 1857-63.

KELLOGG, William Pitt (R La.) Dec. 8, 1830-Aug. 10, 1918; Senate July 9, 1868-Nov. 1, 1872, 1877-83; House 1883-85; Gov. 1873-77.

KELLY, Edna Flannery (D N.Y.) Aug. 20, 1906-−; House Nov. 8, 1949-69.

KELLY, Edward Austin (D Ill.) April 3, 1892-Aug. 30, 1969; House 1931-43, 1945-47.

KELLY, George Bradshaw (D N.Y.) Dec. 12, 1900-June 26, 1971; House 1937-39.

KELLY, James (− Pa.) July 17, 1760-Feb. 4, 1819; House 1805-09.

KELLY, James Kerr (D Ore.) Feb. 16, 1819-Sept. 15, 1903; Senate 1871-77.

KELLY, John (D N.Y.) April 21, 1821-June 1, 1886; House 1855-Dec. 25, 1858.

KELLY, Melville Clyde (R Pa.) Aug. 4, 1883-April 29, 1935; House 1913-15, 1917-35.

KELLY, Richard (R Fla.) July 31, 1924-−; House 1975-81.

KELLY, William (− Ala.) Sept. 22, 1786-Aug. 24, 1834; Senate Dec. 12, 1822-25.

KELSEY, William Henry (R N.Y.) Oct. 2, 1812-April 20, 1879; House 1855-59 (Whig), 1867-71.

KELSO, John Russell (IRad. Mo.) March 23, 1831-Jan 26, 1891; House 1865-67.

KEM, James Preston (R Mo.) April 2, 1890-Feb. 24 1965; Senate 1947-53.

KEM, Omar Madison (P Neb.) Nov. 13, 1855-Feb. 13 1942; House 1891-97.

KEMBLE, Gouverneur (D N.Y.) Jan. 25, 1786-Sept. 16 1875; House 1837-41.

KEMP, Bolivar Edwards (D La.) Dec. 28, 1871-June 19 1933; House 1925-June 19, 1933.

KEMP, Jack French (R N.Y.) July 13, 1935-−; House 1971-−.

KEMPSHALL, Thomas (W N.Y.) about 1796-Jan. 14 1865; House 1839-41.

KENAN, Thomas (D N.C.) Feb. 26, 1771-Oct. 22, 1843 House 1805-11.

KENDALL, Charles West (D Nev.) April 22, 1828-June 25, 1914; House 1871-75.

KENDALL, Elva Roscoe (R Ky.) Feb. 14, 1893-Jan. 29 1968; House 1929-31.

KENDALL, John Wilkerson (father of Joseph Morgan Kendall) (D Ky.) June 26, 1834-March 7, 1892 House 1891-March 7, 1892.

KENDALL, Jonas (father of Joseph Gowing Kendall) (F Mass.) Oct. 27, 1757-Oct. 22, 1844; House 1819 21.

KENDALL, Joseph Gowing (son of Jonas Kendall) (− Mass.) Oct. 27, 1788-Oct. 2, 1847; House 1829-33.

KENDALL, Joseph Morgan (son of John Wilkerson Kendall) (D Ky.) May 12, 1863-Nov. 5, 1933; House April 21, 1892-93, 1895-Feb. 18, 1897.

KENDALL, Nathan Edward (R Iowa) March 17, 1868 Nov. 5, 1936; House 1909-13; Gov. 1921-25.

KENDALL, Samuel Austin (R Pa.) Nov. 1, 1859-Jan. 8 1933; House 1919-Jan. 8, 1933.

KENDRICK, John Benjamin (D Wyo.) Sept. 6, 1857 Nov. 3, 1933; Senate 1917-Nov. 3, 1933; Gov. 1915 17.

KENNA, John Edward (D W.Va.) April 10, 1848-Jan 11, 1893; House 1877-83; Senate 1883-Jan. 11, 1893

KENNEDY, Ambrose (R R.I.) Dec. 1, 1875-March 10 1967; House 1913-23.

KENNEDY, Ambrose Jerome (D Md.) Jan. 6, 1893-Aug 29, 1950; House Nov. 8, 1932-41.

KENNEDY, Andrew (cousin of Case Broderick) (D Ind.) July 24, 1810-Dec. 31, 1847; House 1841-47.

KENNEDY, Anthony (brother of John Pendleton Kennedy) (U Md.) Dec. 21, 1810-July 31, 1892; Senate 1857-63.

KENNEDY, Charles Augustus (R Iowa) March 24, 1869-Jan. 10, 1951; House 1907-21.

KENNEDY, Edward Moore (brother of John Fitzgerald Kennedy and Robert Francis Kennedy, grandson of John Francis Fitzgerald, uncle of Joseph Patrick Kennedy II) (D Mass.) Feb. 22, 1932- —; Senate Nov. 7, 1962- —.

KENNEDY, James (R Ohio) Sept. 3, 1853-Nov. 9, 1928; House 1903-11.

KENNEDY, John Fitzgerald (brother of Edward Moore Kennedy and Robert Francis Kennedy, grandson of John Francis Fitzgerald, uncle of Joseph Patrick Kennedy II) (D Mass.) May 29, 1917-Nov. 22, 1963; House 1947-53; Senate 1953-Dec. 22, 1960; President 1961-Nov. 22, 1963.

KENNEDY, John Lauderdale (R Neb.) Oct. 27, 1854-Aug. 30, 1946; House 1905-07.

KENNEDY, John Pendleton (brother of Anthony Kennedy) (W Md.) Oct. 25, 1795-Aug. 18, 1870; House April 25, 1838-39, 1841-45; Secy. of the Navy 1852-53.

KENNEDY, Joseph Patrick II (son of Robert Francis Kennedy, nephew of Edward Moore Kennedy and John Fitzgerald Kennedy, great-grandson of John Francis Fitzgerald) (D Mass.) Sept. 24, 1952- —; House 1987- —.

KENNEDY, Martin John (D N.Y.) Aug. 29, 1892-Oct. 27, 1955; House March 11, 1930-45.

KENNEDY, Michael Joseph (D N.Y.) Oct. 25, 1897-Nov. 1, 1949; House 1939-43.

KENNEDY, Robert Francis (brother of Edward Moore Kennedy and John Fitzgerald Kennedy, grandson of John Francis Fitzgerald, father of Joseph Patrick Kennedy II) (D N.Y.) Nov. 20, 1925-June 6, 1968; Senate 1965-June 6, 1968; Atty. Gen. 1961-64.

KENNEDY, Robert Patterson (R Ohio) Jan. 23, 1840-May 6, 1918; House 1887-91.

KENNEDY, William (F N.C.) July 31, 1768-Oct. 11, 1834; House 1803-05, 1809-11, Jan. 30, 1813-15.

KENNEDY, William (D Conn.) Dec. 19, 1854-June 19, 1918; House 1913-15.

KENNELLY, Barbara Bailey (D Conn.) July 10, 1936- —; House Jan. 25, 1982- —.

KENNETT, Luther Martin (AP Mo.) March 15, 1807-April 12, 1873; House 1855-57.

KENNEY, Edward Aloysius (D N.J.) Aug. 11, 1884-Jan. 27, 1938; House 1933-Jan. 27, 1938.

KENNEY, Richard Rolland (D Del.) Sept. 9, 1856-Aug. 14, 1931; Senate 1897-1901.

KENNON, William Sr. (cousin of William Kennon Jr.) (D Ohio) May 14, 1793-Nov. 2, 1881; House 1829-33, 1835-37.

KENNON, William Jr. (cousin of William Kennon Sr.) (D Ohio) June 12, 1802-Oct. 19, 1867; House 1847-49.

KENT, Everett (D Pa.) Nov. 15, 1888-Oct. 13, 1963; House 1923-25, 1927-29.

KENT, Joseph (NR Md.) Jan. 14, 1779-Nov. 24, 1837; House 1811-15 (Federalist), 1819-Jan. 6, 1826 (Republican); Senate 1833-Nov. 24, 1837; Gov. 1826-29 (Democratic Republican).

KENT, Moss (F N.Y.) April 3, 1766-May 30, 1838; House 1813-17.

KENT, William (I Calif.) March 29, 1864-March 13, 1928; House 1911-17 (1911-13 Progressive Republican).

KENYON, William Scheuneman (R N.Y.) Dec. 13, 1820-Feb. 10, 1896; House 1859-61.

KENYON, William Squire (R Iowa) June 10, 1869-Sept. 9, 1933; Senate April 12, 1911-Feb. 24, 1922.

KEOGH, Eugene James (D N.Y.) Aug. 30, 1907- —; House 1937-67.

KERN, Frederick John (D Ill.) Sept. 6, 1864-Nov. 9, 1931; House 1901-03.

KERN, John Worth (D Ind.) Dec. 20, 1849-Aug. 17, 1917; Senate 1911-17; Senate majority leader 1913-17.

KERNAN, Francis (D N.Y.) Jan. 14, 1816-Sept. 7, 1892; House 1863-65; Senate 1875-81.

KERR, Daniel (R Iowa) June 18, 1836-Oct. 8, 1916; House 1887-91.

KERR, James (D Pa.) Oct. 2, 1851-Oct. 31, 1908; House 1889-91.

KERR, John (father of John Kerr Jr., cousin of Bartlett Yancey, granduncle of John Hosea Kerr) (D Va.) Aug. 4, 1782-Sept. 29, 1842; House 1813-15, Oct. 30, 1815-17.

KERR, John Jr. (son of John Kerr) (W N.C.) Feb. 10, 1811-Sept. 5, 1879; House 1853-55.

KERR, John Bozman (son of John Leeds Kerr) (W Md.) March 5, 1809-Jan. 27, 1878; House 1849-51.

KERR, John Hosea (grandnephew of John Kerr) (D N.C.) Dec. 31, 1873-June 21, 1958; House Nov. 6, 1923-53.

KERR, John Leeds (father of John Bozman Kerr) (W Md.) Jan. 15, 1780-Feb. 21, 1844; House 1825-29, 1831-33; Senate Jan. 5, 1841-43.

KERR, Joseph (D Ohio) 1765-Aug. 22, 1837; Senate Dec. 10, 1814-15.

KERR, Josiah Leeds (R Md.) Jan. 10, 1861-Sept. 27, 1920; House Nov. 6, 1900-01.

KERR, Michael Crawford (D Ind.) March 15, 1827-Aug. 19, 1876; House 1865-73, 1875-Aug. 19, 1876; Speaker 1875-76.

KERR, Robert Samuel (D Okla.) Sept. 11, 1896-Jan. 1, 1963; Senate 1949-Jan. 1, 1963; Gov. 1943-47.

KERR, Winfield Scott (R Ohio) June 23, 1852-Sept. 11, 1917; House 1895-1901.

KERRIGAN, James (D N.Y.) Dec. 25, 1828-Nov. 1, 1899; House 1861-63.

KERRY, John Forbes (D Mass.) Dec. 22, 1943- —; Senate 1985- —.

KERSHAW, John (D S.C.) Sept. 12, 1765-Aug. 4, 1829; House 1813-15.

KERSTEN, Charles Joseph (R Wis.) May 26, 1902-Oct. 31, 1972; House 1947-49, 1951-55.

KETCHAM, John Clark (R Mich.) Jan. 1, 1873-Dec. 4, 1941; House 1921-33.

KETCHAM, John Henry (R N.Y.) Dec. 21, 1832-Nov. 4, 1906; House 1865-73, 1877-93, 1897-Nov. 4, 1906.

KETCHUM, William Matthew (R Calif.) Sept. 2, 1921-June 24, 1978; House 1973-June 24, 1978.

KETCHUM, Winthrop Welles (R Pa.) June 29, 1820-Dec. 6, 1879; House 1875-July 19, 1876.

KETTNER, William (D Calif.) Nov. 20, 1864-Nov. 11, 1930; House 1913-21.

KEY, David McKendree (D Tenn.) Jan. 27, 1824-Feb. 3, 1900; Senate Aug. 18, 1875-Jan. 19, 1877; Postmaster Gen. 1877-80.

KEY, John Alexander (D Ohio) Dec. 30, 1871-March 4, 1954; House 1913-19.

KEY, Philip (cousin of Philip Barton Key, great-grand-father of Barnes Compton) (— Md.) 1750-Jan. 4, 1820; House 1791-93.

KEY, Philip Barton (cousin of Philip Key) (F Md.) April 12, 1757-July 28, 1815; House 1807-13.

KEYES, Elias (R Vt.) April 14, 1758-July 9, 1844; House 1821-23.

KEYES, Henry Wilder (R N.H.) May 23, 1863-June 19 1938; Senate 1919-37; Gov. 1917-19.

KEYS, Martha Elizabeth (wife of Andrew Jacobs Jr., daughter-in-law of Andrew Jacobs Sr.) (D Kan. Aug. 10, 1930- —; House 1975-79.

KIDDER, David (W Maine) Dec. 8, 1787-Nov. 1, 1860 House 1823-27.

KIDDER, Jefferson Parish (R Dakota) June 4, 1815 Oct. 2, 1883; House (Terr. Del.) 1875-79.

KIDWELL, Zedekiah (D Va.) Jan. 4, 1814-April 27 1872; House 1853-57.

KIEFER, Andrew Robert (R Minn.) May 25, 1832-Ma 1, 1904; House 1893-97.

KIEFNER, Charles Edward (R Mo.) Nov. 25, 1869-Dec 13, 1942; House 1925-27, 1929-31.

KIESS, Edgar Raymond (R Pa.) Aug. 26, 1875-July 20 1930; House 1913-July 20, 1930.

KILBOURNE, James (D Ohio) Oct. 19, 1770-April 9 1850; House 1813-17.

KILBURN, Clarence Evans (R N.Y.) April 13, 1893 May 20, 1975; House Feb. 13, 1940-65.

KILDAY, Paul Joseph (D Texas) March 29, 1900-Oct 12, 1968; House 1939-Sept. 24, 1961.

KILDEE, Dale Edward (D Mich.) Sept. 16, 1929- — House 1977- —.

KILGORE, Constantine Buckley (D Texas) Feb. 20 1835-Sept. 23, 1897; House 1887-95.

KILGORE, Daniel (D Ohio) 1793-Dec. 12, 1851; House Dec. 1, 1834-July 4, 1838.

KILGORE, David (R Ind.) April 3, 1804-Jan. 22, 1879 House 1857-61.

KILGORE, Harley Martin (D W.Va.) Jan. 11, 1893-Feb 28, 1956; Senate 1941-Feb. 28, 1956.

KILGORE, Joe Madison (D Texas) Dec. 10, 1918- — House 1955-65.

KILLE, Joseph (D N.J.) April 12, 1790-March 1, 1865 House 1839-41.

KILLINGER, John Weinland (R Pa.) Sept. 18, 1824 June 30, 1896; House 1859-63, 1871-75, 1877-81.

KIMBALL, Alanson Mellen (R Wis.) March 12, 1827-May 26, 1913; House 1875-77.

KIMBALL, Henry Mahlon (R Mich.) Aug. 27, 1878-Oct. 19, 1935; House Jan. 3-Oct. 19, 1935.

KIMBALL, William Preston (D Ky.) Nov. 4, 1857-Feb. 24, 1926; House 1907-09.

KIMMEL, William (D Md.) Aug. 15, 1812-Dec. 28, 1886; House 1877-81.

KINCAID, John (D Ky.) Feb. 15, 1791-Feb. 7, 1873; House 1829-31.

KINCHELOE, David Hayes (D Ky.) April 9, 1877-April 16, 1950; House 1915-Oct. 5, 1930.

KINDEL, George John (D Colo.) March 2, 1855-Feb. 28, 1930; House 1913-15.

KINDNESS, Thomas Norman (R Ohio) Aug. 26, 1929- −; House 1975-87.

KINDRED, John Joseph (D N.Y.) July 15, 1864-Oct. 23, 1937; House 1911-13, 1921-29.

KING, Adam (D Pa.) 1790-May 6, 1835; House 1827-33.

KING, Andrew (D Mo.) March 20, 1812-Nov. 18, 1895; House 1871-73.

KING, Austin Augustus (UD Mo.) Sept. 21, 1802-April 22, 1870; House 1863-65; Gov. 1848-53 (Democrat).

KING, Carleton James (R N.Y.) June 15, 1904-Nov. 19, 1977; House 1961-Dec. 31, 1974.

KING, Cecil Rhodes (D Calif.) Jan. 13, 1898-March 17, 1974; House Aug. 25, 1942-69.

KING, Cyrus (half brother of Rufus King) (F Mass.) Sept. 6, 1772-April 25, 1817; House 1813-17.

KING, Daniel Putnam (W Mass.) Jan. 8, 1801-July 25, 1850; House 1843-July 25, 1850.

KING, David Sjodahl (son of William Henry King) (D Utah) June 20, 1917-−; House 1959-63, 1965-67.

KING, Edward John (R Ill.) July 1, 1867-Feb. 17, 1929; House 1915-Feb. 17, 1929.

KING, George Gordon (W R.I.) June 9, 1807-July 17, 1870; House 1849-53.

KING, Henry (brother of Thomas Butler King, uncle of John Floyd King) (D Pa.) July 6, 1790-July 13, 1861; House 1831-35.

KING, James Gore (son of Rufus King, brother of John Alsop King) (W N.J.) May 8, 1791-Oct. 3, 1853; House 1849-51.

KING, John (D N.Y.) 1775-Sept. 1, 1836; House 1831-33.

KING, John Alsop (son of Rufus King, brother of James Gore King) (W N.Y.) Jan. 3, 1788-July 7, 1867; House 1849-51; Gov. 1857-59 (Republican).

KING, John Floyd (son of Thomas Butler King, nephew of Henry King) (D La.) April 20, 1842-May 8, 1915; House 1879-87.

KING, John Pendleton (D Ga.) April 3, 1799-March 19, 1888; Senate Nov. 21, 1833-Nov. 1, 1837.

KING, Karl Clarence (R Pa.) Jan. 26, 1897-April 16, 1974; House Nov. 6, 1951-57.

KING, Perkins (D N.Y.) Jan. 12, 1784-Nov. 29, 1875; House 1829-31.

KING, Preston (R N.Y.) Oct. 14, 1806-Nov. 12, 1865; House 1843-47 (Democrat), 1849-53 (Democrat); Senate 1857-63.

KING, Rufus (half brother of Cyrus King, father of John Alsop King and James Gore King) (F N.Y.) March 24, 1755-April 29, 1827; Senate July 16, 1789-May 20, 1796, 1813-25; Cont. Cong. 1784-87 (Mass.).

KING, Rufus H. (W N.Y.) Jan. 20, 1820-Sept. 13, 1890; House 1855-57.

KING, Samuel Wilder (R Hawaii) Dec. 17, 1886-March 24, 1959; House (Terr. Del.) 1935-43; Gov. (Hawaii Terr.) 1953-57.

KING, Thomas Butler (brother of Henry King, father of John Floyd King) (W Ga.) Aug. 27, 1800-May 10, 1864; House 1839-43, 1845-50.

KING, William Henry (father of David Sjodahl King) (D Utah) June 3, 1863-Nov. 27, 1949; House 1897-99, April 2, 1900-01; Senate 1917-41; Pres. pro tempore 1941.

KING, William Rufus deVane (D Ala.) April 7, 1786-April 18, 1853; House 1811-Nov. 4, 1816 (N.C.); Senate Dec. 14, 1819-April 15, 1844, July 1, 1848-Dec. 20, 1852; Pres. pro tempore 1835-41, 1849-52; Vice President March 4-April 18, 1853.

KING, William Smith (R Minn.) Dec. 16, 1828-Feb. 24, 1900; House 1875-77.

KINGSBURY, William Wallace (D Minn.) June 4, 1828-April 17, 1892; House (Terr. Del.) 1857-May 11, 1858.

KINKAID, Moses Pierce (R Neb.) Jan. 24, 1856-July 6, 1922; House 1903-July 6, 1922.

KINKEAD, Eugene Francis (D N.J.) March 27, 1876-Sept. 6, 1960; House 1909-Feb. 4, 1915.

KINNARD, George L. (D Ind.) 1803-Nov. 26, 1836; House 1833-Nov. 26, 1836.

KINNEY, John Fitch (D Utah) April 2, 1816-Aug. 16, 1902; House (Terr. Del.) 1863-65.

KINSELLA, Thomas (D N.Y.) Dec. 31, 1832-Feb. 11, 1884; House 1871-73.

KINSEY, Charles (− N.J.) 1773-June 25, 1849; House 1817-19, Feb. 2, 1820-21.

KINSEY, William Medcalf (R Mo.) Oct. 28, 1846-June 20, 1931; House 1889-91.

KINSLEY, Martin (− Mass.) June 2, 1754-June 20, 1835; House 1819-21.

KINZER, John Roland (R Pa.) March 28, 1874-July 25, 1955; House Jan. 28, 1930-47.

KIPP, George Washington (D Pa.) March 28, 1847-July 24, 1911; House 1907-09, March 4-July 24, 1911.

KIRBY, William Fosgate (D Ark.) Nov. 16, 1867-July 26, 1934; Senate Nov. 8, 1916-21.

KIRK, Andrew Jackson (R Ky.) March 19, 1866-May 25, 1933; House Feb. 13, 1926-27.

KIRKLAND, Joseph (− N.Y.) Jan. 18, 1770-Jan. 26, 1844; House 1821-23.

KIRKPATRICK, Littleton (D N.J.) Oct. 19, 1797-Aug. 15, 1859; House 1843-45.

KIRKPATRICK, Sanford (D Iowa) Feb. 11, 1842-Feb. 13, 1932; House 1913-15.

KIRKPATRICK, Snyder Solomon (R Kan.) Feb. 21, 1848-April 5, 1909; House 1895-97.

KIRKPATRICK, William (D N.Y.) Nov. 7, 1769-Sept. 2, 1832; House 1807-09.

KIRKPATRICK, William Huntington (son of William Sebring Kirkpatrick) (R Pa.) Oct. 2, 1885-Nov. 28, 1970; House 1921-23.

KIRKPATRICK, William Sebring (father of William Huntington Kirkpatrick) (R Pa.) April 21, 1844-Nov. 3, 1932; House 1897-99.

KIRKWOOD, Samuel Jordan (R Iowa) Dec. 20, 1813-Sept. 1, 1894; Senate Jan. 13, 1866-67, 1877-March 7, 1881; Gov. 1860-64, 1876-77; Secy. of the Interior 1881-82.

KIRTLAND, Dorrance (− N.Y.) July 28, 1770-May 23, 1840; House 1817-19.

KIRWAN, Michael Joseph (D Ohio) Dec. 2, 1886-July 27, 1970; House 1937-July 27, 1970.

KISSEL, John (R N.Y.) July 31, 1864-Oct. 3, 1938; House 1921-23.

KITCHELL, Aaron (D N.J.) July 10, 1744-June 25, 1820; House 1791-93, Jan. 29, 1795-97, 1799-1801, Senate 1805-March 12, 1809.

KITCHEN, Bethuel Middleton (R W.Va.) March 21, 1812-Dec. 15, 1895; House 1867-69.

KITCHENS, Wade Hampton (D Ark.) Dec. 26, 1878-Aug. 22, 1966; House 1937-41.

KITCHIN, Alvin Paul (nephew of Claude Kitchin and William Walton Kitchin, grandson of William Hodges Kitchin) (D N.C.) Sept. 13, 1908-Oct. 22, 1983; House 1957-63.

KITCHIN, Claude (son of William Hodges Kitchin, brother of William Walton Kitchin, uncle of Alvin Paul Kitchin) (D N.C.) March 24, 1869-May 31, 1923; House 1901-May 31, 1923; House majority leader 1915-19.

KITCHIN, William Hodges (father of Claude Kitchin and William Walton Kitchin, grandfather of Alvin Paul Kitchin) (D N.C.) Dec. 22, 1837-Feb. 2, 1901; House 1879-81.

KITCHIN, William Walton (son of William Hodges Kitchin, brother of Claude Kitchin, uncle of Alvin Paul Kitchin) (D N.C.) Oct. 9, 1866-Nov. 9, 1924; House 1897-Jan. 11, 1909; Gov. 1909-13.

KITTERA, John Wilkes (father of Thomas Kittera) (− Pa.) Nov. 1752-June 6, 1801; House 1791-1801.

KITTERA, Thomas (son of John Wilkes Kittera) (− Pa.) March 21, 1789-June 16, 1839; House Oct. 16, 1826-27.

KITTREDGE, Alfred Beard (R S.D.) March 28, 1861-May 4, 1911; Senate July 11, 1901-09.

KITTREDGE, George Washington (AND N.H.) Jan. 31, 1805-March 6, 1881; House 1853-55.

KLEBERG, Richard Mifflin Sr. (nephew of Rudolph Kleberg, cousin of Robert Christian Eckhardt) (D Texas) Nov. 18, 1887-May 8, 1955; House Nov. 24, 1931-45.

KLEBERG, Rudolph (granduncle of Robert Christian Eckhardt, uncle of Richard Mifflin Kleberg Sr.) (D Texas) June 26, 1847-Dec. 28, 1924; House April 1896-1903.

KLECZKA, John Casimir (R Wis.) May 6, 1885-April 21, 1959; House 1919-23.

KLECZKA, Gerald (D Wis.) Nov. 26, 1943- −; House Apr. 10, 1984- −.

KLEIN, Arthur George (D N.Y.) Aug. 8, 1904-Feb. 20, 1968; House July 29, 1941-45, Feb. 19, 1946-Dec. 31, 1956.

KLEINER, John Jay (D Ind.) Feb. 8, 1845-April 8, 1911; House 1883-87.

KLEPPE, Thomas S. (R N.D.) July 1, 1919- —; House 1967-71; Secy. of the Interior July 17, 1975-77.

KLEPPER, Frank B. (R Mo.) June 22, 1864-Aug. 4, 1933; House 1905-07.

KLINE, Ardolph Loges (R N.Y.) Feb. 21, 1858-Oct. 13, 1930; House 1921-23.

KLINE, Isaac Clinton (R Pa.) Aug. 18, 1858-Dec. 2, 1947; House 1921-23.

KLINE, Marcus Charles Lawrence (D Pa.) March 26, 1855-March 10, 1911; House 1903-07.

LINGENSMITH, John Jr. (D Pa.) 1785-?; House 1835-39.

KLOEB, Frank Le Blond (grandson of Francis Celeste Le Blond) (D Ohio) June 16, 1890-March 11, 1976; House 1933-Aug. 19, 1937.

KLOTZ, Robert (D Pa.) Oct. 27, 1819-May 1, 1895; House 1879-83.

KLUCZYNSKI, John Carl (D Ill.) Feb. 15, 1896-Jan. 26, 1975; House 1951-Jan. 26, 1975.

KLUTTZ, Theodore Franklin (D N.C.) Oct. 4, 1848-Nov. 18, 1918; House 1899-1905.

NAPP, Anthony Lausett (brother of Robert McCarty Knapp) (D Ill.) June 14, 1828-May 24, 1881; House Dec. 12, 1861-65.

NAPP, Charles (father of Charles Junius Knapp) (R N.Y.) Oct. 8, 1797-May 14, 1880; House 1869-71.

NAPP, Charles Junius (son of Charles Knapp) (R N.Y.) June 30, 1845-June 1, 1916; House 1889-91.

NAPP, Charles Luman (R N.Y.) July 4, 1847-Jan. 3, 1929; House Nov. 5, 1901-11.

NAPP, Chauncey Langdon (R Mass.) Feb. 26, 1809-May 31, 1898; House 1855-59 (1855-57 American Party).

NAPP, Robert McCarty (brother of Anthony Lausett Knapp) (D Ill.) April 21, 1831-June 24, 1889; House 1873-75, 1877-79.

NICKERBOCKER, Herman (F N.Y.) July 27, 1779-Jan. 30, 1855; House 1809-11.

NIFFIN, Frank Charles (D Ohio) April 26, 1894-April 30, 1968; House 1931-39.

NIGHT, Charles Landon (R Ohio) June 18, 1867-Sept. 26, 1933; House 1921-23.

KNIGHT, Jonathan (W Pa.) Nov. 22, 1787-Nov. 22, 1858; House 1855-57.

KNIGHT, Nehemiah (father of Nehemiah Rice Knight) (AF R.I.) March 23, 1746-June 13, 1808; House 1803-June 13, 1808.

KNIGHT, Nehemiah Rice (son of Nehemiah Knight) (D R.I.) Dec. 31, 1780-April 18, 1854; Senate Jan. 9, 1821-41 (1821-35 Anti Federalist); Gov. 1817-21 (Democratic Republican).

KNOPF, Philip (R Ill.) Nov. 18, 1847-Aug. 14, 1920; House 1903-09.

KNOTT, James Proctor (D Ky.) Aug. 29, 1830-June 18, 1911; House 1867-71, 1875-83; Gov. 1883-87.

KNOWLAND, Joseph Russell (father of William Fife Knowland) (R Calif.) Aug. 5, 1873-Feb. 1, 1966; House Nov. 8, 1904-15.

KNOWLAND, William Fife (son of Joseph Russell Knowland) (R Calif.) June 26, 1908-Feb. 23, 1974; Senate Aug. 26, 1945-59; Senate majority leader 1953-55.

KNOWLES, Freeman Tulley (P S.D.) Oct. 10, 1846-June 1, 1910; House 1897-99.

KNOWLTON, Ebenezer (R Maine) Dec. 6, 1815-Sept. 10, 1874; House 1855-57.

KNOX, James (W Ill.) July 4, 1807-Oct. 8, 1876; House 1853-57.

KNOX, Philander Chase (R Pa.) May 6, 1853-Oct. 12, 1921; Senate June 10, 1904-March 4, 1909, 1917-Oct. 12, 1921; Atty. Gen. 1901-04; Secy. of State 1909-13.

KNOX, Samuel (R Mo.) March 21, 1815-March 7, 1905; House June 10, 1864-65.

KNOX, Victor Alfred (R Mich.) Jan. 13, 1899-Dec. 13, 1976; House 1953-65.

KNOX, William Shadrach (R Mass.) Sept. 10, 1843-Sept. 21, 1914; House 1895-1903.

KNUTSON, Coya Gjesdal (DFL Minn.) Aug. 22, 1912- —; House 1955-59.

KNUTSON, Harold (R Minn.) Oct. 20, 1880-Aug. 21, 1953; House 1917-49.

KOCH, Edward Irving (D/L N.Y.) Dec. 12, 1924- —; House 1969-Dec. 31, 1977.

KOCIALKOWSKI, Leo Paul (D Ill.) Aug. 16, 1882-Sept. 27, 1958; House 1933-43.

KOGOVSEK, Raymond Peter (D Colo.) Aug. 19, 1941- —; House 1979-85.

KOLBE, James Thomas (R Ariz.) June 28, 1942- —; House 1985- —.

KOLTER, Joseph Paul (D Pa.) Sept. 3, 1926- —; House 1983- —.

KONIG, George (D Md.) Jan. 26, 1865-May 31, 1913; House 1911-May 31, 1913.

KONNYU, Ernest Leslie (R Calif.) May 17, 1937- —; House 1987- —.

KONOP, Thomas Frank (D Wis.) Aug. 17, 1879-Oct. 17, 1964; House 1911-17.

KOONTZ, William Henry (R Pa.) July 15, 1830-July 4, 1911; House July 18, 1866-69.

KOPP, Arthur William (R Wis.) Feb. 28, 1874-June 2, 1967; House 1909-13.

KOPP, William Frederick (R Iowa) June 20, 1869-Aug. 24, 1938; House 1921-33.

KOPPLEMANN, Herman Paul (D Conn.) May 1, 1880-Aug. 11, 1957; House 1933-39, 1941-43, 1945-47.

KORBLY, Charles Alexander (D Ind.) March 24, 1871-July 26, 1937; House 1909-15.

KORELL, Franklin Frederick (R Ore.) July 23, 1889-June 7, 1965; House Oct. 18, 1927-31.

KORNEGAY, Horace Robinson (D N.C.) March 12, 1924- —; House 1961-69.

KOSTMAYER, Peter Houston (D Pa.) Sept. 27, 1946- —; House 1977-81, 1983- —.

KOWALSKI, Frank (D Conn.) Oct. 18, 1907-Oct. 11, 1974; House 1959-63.

KRAMER, Charles (D Calif.) April 18, 1879-Jan. 20, 1943; House 1933-43.

KRAMER, Kenneth Bentley (R Colo.) Feb. 19, 1942- —; House 1979-87.

KRAUS, Milton (R Ind.) June 26, 1866-Nov. 18, 1942; House 1917-23.

KREBS, Jacob (D Pa.) March 13, 1782-Sept. 26, 1847; House Dec. 4, 1826-March 3, 1827.

KREBS, John Hans (D Calif.) Dec. 17, 1926- —; House 1975-79.

KREBS, Paul J. (D N.J.) May 26, 1912- —; House 1965-67.

KREIDER, Aaron Shenk (R Pa.) June 26, 1863-May 19, 1929; House 1913-23.

KREMER, George (— Pa.) Nov. 21, 1775-Sept. 11, 1854; House 1823-29.

KRIBBS, George Frederic (D Pa.) Nov. 8, 1846-Sept. 8 1938; House 1891-95.

KRONMILLER, John (R Md.) Dec. 6, 1858-June 19 1928; House 1909-11.

KRUEGER, Otto (R N.D.) Sept. 7, 1890-June 6, 196? House 1953-59.

KRUEGER, Robert Charles (D Texas) Sept. 19, 1935 —; House 1975-79.

KRUSE, Edward H. Jr. (D Ind.) Oct. 22, 1918- —; Hous 1949-51.

KUCHEL, Thomas Henry (R Calif.) Aug. 15, 1910- — Senate Jan. 2, 1953-69.

KUHNS, Joseph Henry (W Pa.) Sept. 1800-Nov. 16 1883; House 1851-53.

KULP, Monroe Henry (R Pa.) Oct. 23, 1858-Oct. 19 1911; House 1895-99.

KUNKEL, Jacob Michael (D Md.) July 13, 1822-April 1870; House 1857-61.

KUNKEL, John Christian (grandfather of John Cra Kunkel) (W Pa.) Sept. 18, 1816-Oct. 14, 1870; Hou 1855-59.

KUNKEL, John Crain (grandson of John Christi Kunkel, great-grandson of John Sergeant, grea great-grandson of Robert Whitehill) (R Pa.) July 2 1898-July 27, 1970; House 1939-51, May 16, 196 Dec. 30, 1966.

KUNZ, Stanley Henry (D Ill.) Sept. 26, 1864-April 2 1946; House 1921-31, April 5, 1932-33.

KUPFERMAN, Theodore R. (R N.Y.) May 12, 1920- House Feb. 8, 1966-69.

KURTZ, Jacob Banks (R Pa.) Oct. 31, 1867-Sept. 16 1960; House 1923-35.

KURTZ, William Henry (D Pa.) Jan. 31, 1804-June 24 1868; House 1851-55.

KUSTERMANN, Gustav (R Wis.) May 24, 1850-De 25, 1919; House 1907-11.

KUYKENDALL, Andrew Jackson (R Ill.) March 1815-May 11, 1891; House 1865-67.

KUYKENDALL, Dan H. (R Tenn.) July 9, 1924- — House 1967-75.

KVALE, Ole Juulson (father of Paul John Kvale) (F Minn.) Feb. 6, 1869-Sept. 11, 1929; House 1923-Sep 11, 1929 (1923-25 Independent Republican).

KVALE, Paul John (son of Ole Juulson Kvale) (F Minn.) March 27, 1896-June 14, 1960; House Oct. 1 1929-39.

KYL, John Henry (father of Jon Kyl) (R Iowa) May 9, 1919--; House Dec. 15, 1959-65, 1967-73.

KYL, Jon (son of John Henry Kyl) (R Ariz.) April 25, 1942--; House 1987--.

KYLE, James Henderson (I S.D.) Feb. 24, 1854-July 1, 1901; Senate 1891-July 1, 1901.

KYLE, John Curtis (D Miss.) July 17, 1851-July 6, 1913; House 1891-97.

KYLE, Thomas Barton (R Ohio) March 10, 1856-Aug. 13, 1915; House 1901-05.

KYROS, Peter N. (D Maine) July 11, 1925--; House 1967-75.

LA BRANCHE, Alcee Louis (D La.) 1806-Aug. 17, 1861; House 1843-45.

LACEY, Edward Samuel (R Mich.) Nov. 26, 1835-Oct. 2, 1916; House 1881-85.

LACEY, John Fletcher (R Iowa) May 30, 1841-Sept. 29, 1913; House 1889-91, 1893-1907.

LACOCK, Abner (D Pa.) July 9, 1770-April 12, 1837; House 1811-13; Senate 1813-19.

LADD, Edwin Freemont (Nonpart.R N.D.) Dec. 13, 1859-June 22, 1925; Senate 1921-June 22, 1925.

LADD, George Washington (D/G Maine) Sept. 28, 1818-Jan. 30, 1892; House 1879-83.

LA DOW, George Augustus (D Ore.) March 18, 1826-May 1, 1875; House March 4-May 1, 1875.

LaFALCE, John Joseph (D N.Y.) Oct. 6, 1939--; House 1975--.

LAFEAN, Daniel Franklin (R Pa.) Feb. 7, 1861-April 18, 1922; House 1903-13, 1915-17.

LAFFERTY, Abraham Walter (PR Ore.) June 10, 1875-Jan. 15, 1964; House 1911-15.

LAFFOON, Polk (D Ky.) Oct. 24, 1844-Oct. 22, 1906; House 1885-89.

LAFLIN, Addison Henry (R N.Y.) Oct. 24, 1823-Sept. 24, 1878; House 1865-71.

LA FOLLETTE, Charles Marion (great-grandson of William Heilman) (R Ind.) Feb. 27, 1898--; House 1943-47.

LA FOLLETTE, Robert Marion (father of Robert Marion La Follette Jr.) (R Wis.) June 14, 1855-June 18, 1925; House 1885-91; Senate Jan. 2, 1906-June 18, 1925; Gov. 1901-06.

LA FOLLETTE, Robert Marion Jr. (son of Robert Marion La Follette) (Prog. Wis.) Feb. 6, 1895-Feb. 24, 1953; Senate Sept. 30, 1925-47 (Sept. 30, 1925-35 Republican Progressive).

LA FOLLETTE, William Leroy (R Wash.) Nov. 30, 1860-Dec. 20, 1934; House 1911-19.

LAFORE, John Armand Jr. (R Pa.) May 25, 1905--; House Nov. 5, 1957-61.

LAGAN, Matthew Diamond (D La.) June 20, 1829-April 8, 1901; House 1887-89, 1891-93.

LAGOMARSINO, Robert John (R Calif.) Sept. 4, 1926--; House March 5, 1974--.

LA GUARDIA, Fiorello Henry (R Prog. N.Y.) Dec. 11, 1882-Sept. 20, 1947; House 1917-19 (Republican), 1923-33 (1923-25 Republican, 1925-27 Socialist).

LAHM, Samuel (D Ohio) April 22, 1812-June 16, 1876; House 1847-49.

LAIDLAW, William Grant (R N.Y.) Jan. 1, 1840-Aug. 19, 1908; House 1887-91.

LAIRD, James (R Neb.) June 20, 1849-Aug. 17, 1889; House 1883-Aug. 17, 1889.

LAIRD, Melvin Robert (R Wis.) Sept. 1, 1922--; House 1953-Jan. 21, 1969; Secy. of Defense 1969-73.

LAIRD, William Ramsey III (D W.Va.) June 2, 1916-Jan. 7, 1974; Senate March 13-Nov. 6, 1956.

LAKE, William Augustus (W Miss.) Jan. 6, 1808-Oct. 15, 1861; House 1855-57.

LAMAR, Henry Graybill (D Ga.) July 10, 1798-Sept. 10, 1861; House Dec. 7, 1829-33.

LAMAR, James Robert (D Mo.) March 28, 1866-Aug. 11, 1923; House 1903-05, 1907-09.

LAMAR, John Basil (D Ga.) Nov. 5, 1812-Sept. 15, 1862; House March 4-July 29, 1843.

LAMAR, Lucius Quintus Cincinnatus (uncle of William Bailey Lamar, cousin of Absalom Harris Chappell) (D Miss.) Sept. 17, 1825-Jan. 23, 1893; House 1857-December 1860, 1873-77; Senate 1877-March 6, 1885; Secy. of the Interior 1885-88; Assoc. Justice Supreme Court 1888-93.

LAMAR, William Bailey (nephew of Lucius Quintus Cincinnatus Lamar) (D Fla.) June 12, 1853-Sept. 26, 1928; House 1903-09.

LAMB, Alfred William (D Mo.) March 18, 1824-April 29, 1888; House 1853-55.

LAMB, John (D Va.) June 12, 1840-Nov. 21, 1924; House 1897-1913.

LAMB, John Edward (D Ind.) Dec. 26, 1852-Aug. 23, 1914; House 1883-85.

LAMBERT, John (DR N.J.) Feb. 24, 1746-Feb. 4, 1823; House 1805-09; Senate 1809-15; Gov. 1802-03.

LAMBERTSON, William Purnell (R Kan.) March 23, 1880-Oct. 26, 1957; House 1929-45.

LAMBETH, John Walter (D N.C.) Jan. 10, 1896-Jan. 12, 1961; House 1931-39.

LAMISON, Charles Nelson (D Ohio) 1826-April 24, 1896; House 1871-75.

LAMNECK, Arthur Philip (D Ohio) March 12, 1880-April 23, 1944; House 1931-39.

LAMPERT, Florian (R Wis.) July 8, 1863-July 18, 1930; House Nov. 5, 1918-July 18, 1930.

LAMPORT, William Henry (R N.Y.) May 27, 1811-July 21, 1891; House 1871-75.

LANCASTER, Columbia (D Wash.) Aug. 26, 1803-Sept. 15, 1893; House (Terr. Del.) April 12, 1854-55.

LANCASTER, Harold Martin (D N.C.) March 24, 1943- —; House 1987- —.

LANDERS, Franklin (D Ind.) March 22, 1825-Sept. 10, 1901; House 1875-77.

LANDERS, George Marcellus (D Conn.) Feb. 22, 1813-March 27, 1895; House 1875-79.

LANDES, Silas Zephaniah (D Ill.) May 15, 1842-May 23, 1910; House 1885-89.

LANDGREBE, Earl F. (R Ind.) Jan. 21, 1916-June 29, 1986; House 1969-75.

LANDIS, Charles Beary (brother of Frederick Landis) (R Ind.) July 9, 1858-April 24, 1922; House 1897-1909.

LANDIS, Frederick (brother of Charles Beary Landis) (R Ind.) Aug. 18, 1872-Nov. 15, 1934; House 1903-07.

LANDIS, Gerald Wayne (R Ind.) Feb. 23, 1895-Sept. 6, 1971; House 1939-49.

LANDRUM, John Morgan (D La.) July 3, 1815-Oct. 18, 1861; House 1859-61.

LANDRUM, Phillip Mitchell (D Ga.) Sept. 10, 1909- —; House 1953-77.

LANDRY, Joseph Aristide (W La.) July 10, 1817-March 9, 1881; House 1851-53.

LANDY, James (D Pa.) Oct. 13, 1813-July 25, 1875; House 1857-59.

LANE, Amos (father of James Henry Lane) (D Ind.) March 1, 1778-Sept. 2, 1849; House 1833-37.

LANE, Edward (D Ill.) March 27, 1842-Oct. 30, 1912; House 1887-95.

LANE, Harry (grandson of Joseph Lane, nephew of La-Fayette Lane) (D Ore.) Aug. 28, 1855-May 23, 1917, Senate 1913-May 23, 1917.

LANE, Henry Smith (R Ind.) Feb. 24, 1811-June 18, 1881; House Aug. 3, 1840-43 (Whig); Senate 1861-67; Gov. Jan. 14-16, 1861.

LANE, James Henry (son of Amos Lane) (R Kan.) June 22, 1814-July 11, 1866; House 1853-55 (Democrat Ind.); Senate April 4, 1861-July 11, 1866.

LANE, Joseph (father of LaFayette Lane, grandfather of Harry Lane) (D Ore.) Dec. 14, 1801-April 19, 1881 House (Terr. Del.) June 2, 1851-Feb. 14, 1859; Senate Feb. 14, 1859-61; Gov. (Ore. Terr.) 1849-50, May 16-19, 1853.

LANE, Joseph Reed (R Iowa) May 6, 1858-May 1, 1931 House 1899-1901.

LANE, LaFayette (son of Joseph Lane, uncle of Harry Lane) (D Ore.) Nov. 12, 1842-Nov. 23, 1896; House Oct. 25, 1875-77.

LANE, Thomas Joseph (D Mass.) July 6, 1898- —; House Dec. 30, 1941-63.

LANGDON, Chauncey (F Vt.) Nov. 8, 1763-July 23 1830; House 1815-17.

LANGDON, John (D N.H.) June 26, 1741-Sept. 18 1819; Senate 1789-1801; Pres. pro tempore 1789 1792-94; Cont. Cong. 1775-76, 1783; Gov. 1788, 1805- 09, 1810-12.

LANGEN, Odin Elsford Stanley (R Minn.) Jan. 5, 1913 July 6, 1976; House 1959-71.

LANGER, William (R N.D.) Sept. 30, 1886-Nov. 8, 195 Senate 1941-Nov. 8, 1959; Gov. 1932-34, 1937-39 (Independent).

LANGHAM, Jonathan Nicholas (R Pa.) Aug. 4, 1861 May 21, 1945; House 1909-15.

LANGLEY, John Wesley (husband of Katherine Gudger Langley, son-in-law of James Madison Gudger Jr.) (R Ky.) Jan. 14, 1868-Jan. 17, 1932; House 1907 Jan. 11, 1926.

LANGLEY, Katherine Gudger (wife of John Wesley Langley, daughter of James Madison Gudger Jr.) (Ky.) Feb. 14, 1888-Aug. 15, 1948; House 1927-31.

LANGSTON, John Mercer (R Va.) Dec. 14, 1829-No 15, 1897; House Sept. 23, 1890-91.

LANHAM, Fritz Garland (son of Samuel Willis Tucker Lanham) (D Texas) Jan. 3, 1880-July 31, 1965; House April 19, 1919-47.

LANHAM, Henderson Lovelace (D Ga.) Sept. 14, 1888-Nov. 10, 1957; House 1947-Nov. 10, 1957.

LANHAM, Samuel Willis Tucker (father of Fritz Garland Lanham) (D Texas) July 4, 1846-July 29, 1908; House 1883-93, 1897-Jan. 15, 1903; Gov. 1903-07.

LANING, Jay Ford (R Ohio) May 15, 1853-Sept. 1, 1941; House 1907-09.

LANKFORD, Menalcus (R Va.) March 14, 1883-Dec. 27, 1937; House 1929-33.

LANKFORD, Richard Estep (D Md.) July 22, 1914- —; House 1955-65.

LANKFORD, William Chester (D Ga.) Dec. 7, 1877-Dec. 10, 1964; House 1919-33.

LANMAN, James (D Conn.) June 14, 1767-Aug. 7, 1841; Senate 1819-25.

LANNING, William Mershon (R N.J.) Jan. 1, 1849-Feb. 16, 1912; House 1903-June 6, 1904.

LANSING, Frederick (R N.Y.) Feb. 16, 1838-Jan. 31, 1894; House 1889-91.

LANSING, Gerrit Yates (JD N.Y.) Aug. 4, 1783-Jan. 3, 1862; House 1831-37.

LANSING, William Esselstyne (R N.Y.) Dec. 29, 1821-July 29, 1883; House 1861-63, 1871-75.

LANTAFF, William Courtland (D Fla.) July 31, 1913-Jan. 28, 1970; House 1951-55.

LANTOS, Tom (D Calif.) Feb. 1, 1928- —; House 1981- —.

LANZETTA, James Joseph (D N.Y.) Dec. 21, 1894-Oct. 27, 1956; House 1933-35, 1937-39.

LAPHAM, Elbridge Gerry (R N.Y.) Oct. 18, 1814-Jan. 8, 1890; House 1875-July 29, 1881; Senate Aug. 2, 1881-85.

LAPHAM, Oscar (D R.I.) June 29, 1837-March 29, 1926; House 1891-95.

LAPORTE, John (— Pa.) Nov. 4, 1798-Aug. 22, 1862; House 1833-37.

LARCADE, Henry Dominique Jr. (D La.) July 12, 1890-March 15, 1966; House 1943-53.

LARNED, Simon (— Mass.) Aug. 3, 1753-Nov. 16, 1817; House Nov. 5, 1804-05.

LARRABEE, Charles Hathaway (D Wis.) Nov. 9, 1820-Jan. 20, 1883; House 1859-61.

LARRABEE, William Henry (D Ind.) Feb. 21, 1870-Nov. 16, 1960; House 1931-43.

LARRAZOLO, Octaviano Ambrosio (R N.M.) Dec. 7, 1859-April 7, 1930; Senate Dec. 7, 1928-29; Gov. 1919-21.

LARRINAGA, Tulio (U P.R.) Jan. 15, 1847-April 28, 1917; House (Res. Comm.) 1905-11.

LARSEN, William Washington (D Ga.) Aug. 12, 1871-Jan. 5, 1938; House 1917-33.

LARSON, Oscar John (R Minn.) May 20, 1871-Aug. 1, 1957; House 1921-25.

LA SERE, Emile (D La.) 1802-Aug. 14, 1882; House Jan. 29, 1846-51.

LASH, Israel George (R N.C.) Aug. 18, 1810-April 1, 1878; House July 20, 1868-71.

LASSITER, Francis Rives (grandnephew of Francis Everod Rives) (D Va.) Feb. 18, 1866-Oct. 31, 1909; House April 19, 1900-03, 1907-Oct. 31, 1909.

LATHAM, George Robert (R W.Va.) March 9, 1832-Dec. 16, 1917; House 1865-67.

LATHAM, Henry Jepson (R N.Y.) Dec. 10, 1908- —; House 1945-Dec. 31, 1958.

LATHAM, Louis Charles (D N.C.) Sept. 11, 1840-Oct. 16, 1895; House 1881-83, 1887-89.

LATHAM, Milton Slocum (D Calif.) May 23, 1827-March 4, 1882; House 1853-55; Senate March 5, 1860-63; Gov. Jan. 9-14, 1860.

LATHROP, Samuel (R Mass.) May 1, 1772-July 11, 1846; House 1819-27.

LATHROP, William (R Ill.) April 17, 1825-Nov. 19, 1907; House 1877-79.

LATIMER, Asbury Churchwell (D S.C.) July 31, 1851-Feb. 20, 1908; House 1893-1903; Senate 1903-Feb. 20, 1908.

LATIMER, Henry (— Del.) April 24, 1752-Dec. 19, 1819; House Feb. 14, 1794-Feb. 7, 1795; Senate Feb. 7, 1795-Feb. 28, 1801.

LATTA, Delbert Leroy (R Ohio) March 5, 1920- —; House 1959- —.

LATTA, James Polk (D Neb.) Oct. 31, 1844-Sept. 11, 1911; House 1909-Sept. 11, 1911.

LATTIMORE, William (— Miss.) Feb. 9, 1774-April 3, 1843; House (Terr. Del.) 1803-07, 1813-17.

LAURANCE, John (— N.Y.) 1750-Nov. 11, 1810; House 1789-93; Senate Nov. 9, 1796-Aug. 1800; Pres. pro tempore 1798-99; Cont. Cong. 1785-87.

LAUSCHE, Frank John (D Ohio) Nov. 14, 1895--; Senate 1957-69; Gov. 1945-47, 1949-57.

LAUTENBERG, Frank Raleigh (D N.J.) Jan. 23, 1924- --; Senate Dec. 27, 1982--.

LAW, Charles Blakeslee (R N.Y.) Feb. 5, 1872-Sept. 15, 1929; House 1905-11.

LAW, John (son of Lyman Law, grandson of Amasa Learned) (D Ind.) Oct. 28, 1796-Oct. 7, 1873; House 1861-65.

LAW, Lyman (father of John Law) (F Conn.) Aug. 19, 1770-Feb. 3, 1842; House 1811-17.

LAWLER, Frank (D Ill.) June 25, 1842-Jan. 17, 1896; House 1885-91.

LAWLER, Joab (W Ala.) June 12, 1796-May 8, 1838; House 1835-May 8, 1838.

LAWRENCE, Abbott (W Mass.) Dec. 16, 1792-Aug. 18, 1855; House 1835-37, 1839-Sept. 18, 1840.

LAWRENCE, Cornelius Van Wyck (cousin of Effingham Lawrence) (JD N.Y.) Feb. 28, 1791-Feb. 20, 1861; House 1833-May 14, 1834.

LAWRENCE, Effingham (cousin of Cornelius Van Wyck Lawrence) (D La.) March 2, 1820-Dec. 9, 1878; House March 3, 1875.

LAWRENCE, George Pelton (R Mass.) May 19, 1859-Nov. 21, 1917; House Nov. 2, 1897-1913.

LAWRENCE, George Van Eman (son of Joseph Lawrence) (R Pa.) Nov. 13, 1881-Oct. 2, 1904; House 1865-69 (Whig), 1883-85.

LAWRENCE, Henry Franklin (R Mo.) Jan. 31, 1868-Jan. 12, 1950; House 1921-23.

LAWRENCE, John Watson (D N.Y.) Aug. 1800-Dec. 20, 1888; House 1845-47.

LAWRENCE, Joseph (father of George Van Eman Lawrence) (W Pa.) 1786-April 17, 1842; House 1825-29, 1841-April 17, 1842.

LAWRENCE, Samuel (brother of William Thomas Lawrence) (-- N.Y.) May 23, 1773-Oct. 20, 1837; House 1823-25.

LAWRENCE, Sidney (D N.Y.) Dec. 31, 1801-May 9, 1892; House 1847-49.

LAWRENCE, William (D Ohio) Sept. 2, 1814-Sept. 8, 1895; House 1857-59.

LAWRENCE, William (R Ohio) June 26, 1819-May 8, 1899; House 1865-71, 1873-77.

LAWRENCE, William Thomas (brother of Samuel Lawrence) (-- N.Y.) May 7, 1788-Oct. 25, 1859; House 1847-49.

LAWS, Gilbert Lafayette (R Neb.) March 11, 1838-April 25, 1907; House Dec. 2, 1889-91.

LAWSON, John Daniel (R N.Y.) Feb. 18, 1816-Jan. 24, 1896; House 1873-75.

LAWSON, John William (D Va.) Sept. 13, 1837-Feb. 21, 1905; House 1891-93.

LAWSON, Thomas Graves (D Ga.) May 2, 1835-April 16, 1912; House 1891-97.

LAWYER, Thomas (-- N.Y.) Oct. 14, 1785-May 21, 1868; House 1817-19.

LAXALT, Paul Dominique (R Nev.) Aug. 2, 1922-- Senate Dec. 18, 1974-87; Gov. 1967-71.

LAY, Alfred Morrison (D Mo.) May 20, 1836-Dec. 8, 1879; House March 4-Dec. 8, 1879.

LAY, George Washington (W N.Y.) July 26, 1798-Oct. 21, 1860; House 1833-37.

LAYTON, Caleb Rodney (R Del.) Sept. 8, 1851-Nov. 11, 1930; House 1919-23.

LAYTON, Fernando Coello (D Ohio) April 11, 1847-June 22, 1926; House 1891-97.

LAZARO, Ladislas (D La.) June 5, 1872-March 30, 1927; House 1913-March 30, 1927.

LAZEAR, Jesse (D Pa.) Dec. 12, 1804-Sept. 2, 1877; House 1861-65.

LEA, Clarence Frederick (D Calif.) July 11, 1874-June 20, 1964; House 1917-49.

LEA, Luke (brother of Pryor Lea, great-grandfather of Luke Lea, below) (UD Tenn.) Jan. 21, 1783-June 17, 1851; House 1833-37.

LEA, Luke (great-grandson of Luke Lea, above) (D Tenn.) April 12, 1879-Nov. 18, 1945; Senate 1911-17.

LEA, Pryor (brother of Luke Lea) (JD Tenn.) Aug. 31, 1794-Sept. 14, 1879; House 1827-31.

LEACH, Anthony Claude "Buddy" Jr. (D La.) March 30, 1934--; House 1979-81.

LEACH, DeWitt Clinton (R Mich.) Nov. 23, 1822-Dec. 21, 1909; House 1857-61.

LEACH, James A. S. (R Iowa) Oct. 15, 1942--; House 1977--.

LEACH, James Madison (C N.C.) Jan. 17, 1815-June 1891; House 1859-61 (Whig), 1871-75.

LEACH, Robert Milton (R Mass.) April 2, 1879-Feb. 18, 1952; House Nov. 4, 1924-25.

LEADBETTER, Daniel Parkhurst (JD Ohio) Sept. 10, 1797-Feb. 26, 1870; House 1837-41.

LEAHY, Edward Laurence (D R.I.) Feb. 9, 1886-July 22, 1953; Senate Aug. 24, 1949-Dec. 18, 1950.

LEAHY, Patrick Joseph (D Vt.) March 31, 1940- —; Senate 1975- —.

LEAKE, Eugene Walter (D N.J.) July 13, 1877-Aug. 23, 1959; House 1907-09.

LEAKE, Shelton Farrar (D Va.) Nov. 30, 1812-March 4, 1884; House 1845-47, 1859-61.

LEAKE, Walter (DR Miss.) May 25, 1762-Nov. 17, 1825; Senate Dec. 10, 1817-May 15, 1820; Gov. 1822-25.

LEARNED, Amasa (grandfather of John Law) (— Conn.) Nov. 15, 1750-May 4, 1825; House 1791-95.

LEARY, Cornelius Lawrence Ludlow (U Md.) Oct. 22, 1813-March 21, 1893; House 1861-63.

LEATH, James Marvin (D Texas) May 6, 1931- —; House 1979- —.

LEATHERWOOD, Elmer O. (R Utah) Sept. 4, 1872-Dec. 24, 1929; House 1921-Dec. 24, 1929.

LEAVENWORTH, Elias Warner (R N.Y.) Dec. 20, 1803-Nov. 25, 1887; House 1875-77.

LEAVITT, Humphrey Howe (JD Ohio) June 18, 1796-March 15, 1873; House Dec. 6, 1830-July 10, 1834.

LEAVITT, Scott (R Mont.) June 16, 1879-Oct. 19, 1966; House 1923-33.

LEAVY, Charles Henry (D Wash.) Feb. 16, 1884-Sept. 25, 1952; House 1937-Aug. 1, 1942.

LE BLOND, Francis Celeste (grandfather of Frank Le Blond Kloeb) (D Ohio) Feb. 14, 1821-Nov. 9, 1902; House 1863-67.

LeBOUTILLIER, John (R N.Y.) May 26, 1953- —; House 1981-83.

LECOMPTE, Joseph (D Ky.) Dec. 15, 1797-April 25, 1851; House 1825-33.

LE COMPTE, Karl Miles (R Iowa) May 25, 1887-Sept. 30, 1972; House 1939-59.

LEDERER, Raymond Francis (D Pa.) May 19, 1938- —; House 1977-May 5, 1981.

LEE, Blair (great-grandson of Richard Henry Lee) (D Md.) Aug. 9, 1857-Dec. 25, 1944; Senate Jan. 28, 1914-17.

LEE, Frank Hood (D Mo.) March 29, 1873-Nov. 20, 1952; House 1933-35.

LEE, Gary A. (R N.Y.) Aug. 18, 1933- —; House 1979-83.

LEE, Gideon (JD N.Y.) April 27, 1778-Aug. 21, 1841; House Nov. 4, 1835-37.

LEE, Gordon (D Ga.) May 29, 1859-Nov. 7, 1927; House 1905-27.

LEE, Henry (brother of Richard Bland Lee, grandfather of William Henry Fitzhugh Lee) (F Va.) Jan. 29, 1756-March 25, 1818; House 1799-1801; Cont. Cong. 1785-88; Gov. 1791-94.

LEE, John (D Md.) Jan. 30, 1788-May 17, 1871; House 1823-25.

LEE, Joshua (D N.Y.) 1783-Dec. 19, 1842; House 1835-37.

LEE, Joshua Bryan (D Okla.) Jan. 23, 1892-Aug. 10, 1967; House 1935-37; Senate 1937-43.

LEE, Moses Lindley (R N.Y.) May 29, 1805-May 19, 1876; House 1859-61.

LEE, Richard Bland (brother of Henry Lee) (— Va.) Jan. 20, 1761-March 12, 1827; House 1789-95.

LEE, Richard Henry (great-grandfather of Blair Lee) (— Va.) Jan. 20, 1732-June 19, 1794; Senate 1789-Oct. 8, 1792; Pres. pro tempore 1791-92; Cont. Cong. 1774-80, 1784-87.

LEE, Robert Emmett (D Pa.) Oct. 12, 1868-Nov. 19, 1916; House 1911-15.

LEE, Robert Quincy (D Texas) Jan. 12, 1869-April 18, 1930; House 1929-April 18, 1930.

LEE, Silas (F Mass.) July 3, 1760-March 1, 1814; House 1799-Aug. 20, 1801.

LEE, Thomas (D N.J.) Nov. 28, 1780-Nov. 2, 1856; House 1833-37.

LEE, Warren Isbell (R N.Y.) Feb. 5, 1876-Dec. 25, 1955; House 1921-23.

LEE, William Henry Fitzhugh (grandson of Henry Lee) (D Va.) May 31, 1837-Oct. 15, 1891; House 1887-Oct. 15, 1891.

LEECH, James Russell (R Pa.) Nov. 19, 1888-Feb. 5, 1952; House 1927-Jan. 29, 1932.

LEEDOM, John Peter (D Ohio) Dec. 20, 1847-March 18, 1895; House 1881-83.

LEET, Isaac (D Pa.) 1801-June 10, 1844; House 1839-41.

LeFANTE, Joseph Anthony (D N.J.) Sept. 8, 1928- —; House 1977-Dec. 23, 1978.

LE FEVER, Jacob (father of Frank Jacob LeFevre) (R N.Y.) April 20, 1830-Feb. 4, 1905; House 1893-97.

LE FEVER, Joseph (D Pa.) April 3, 1760-Oct. 17, 1826; House 1811-13.

LE FEVRE, Benjamin (D Ohio) Oct. 8, 1838-March 7, 1922; House 1879-87.

LE FEVRE, Frank Jacob (son of Jacob Le Fever) (R N.Y.) Nov. 30, 1874-April 29, 1941; House 1905-07.

LE FEVRE, Jay (R N.Y.) Sept. 6, 1893-April 26, 1970; House 1943-51.

LEFFERTS, John (D N.Y.) Dec. 17, 1785-Sept. 18, 1829; House 1813-15.

LEFFLER, Isaac (brother of Shepherd Leffler) (− Va.) Nov. 7, 1788-March 8, 1866; House 1827-29.

LEFFLER, Shepherd (brother of Isaac Leffler) (D Iowa) April 24, 1811-Sept. 7, 1879; House Dec. 28, 1846-51.

LEFTWICH, Jabez (− Va.) Sept. 22, 1765-June 22, 1855; House 1821-25.

LEFTWICH, John William (D Tenn.) Sept. 7, 1826-March 6, 1870; House July 24, 1866-67.

LEGARDA Y TUASON, Benito (− P.I.) Sept. 27, 1853-Aug. 27, 1915; House (Res. Comm.) Nov. 22, 1907-13.

LEGARE, George Swinton (D S.C.) Nov. 11, 1869-Jan. 31, 1913; House 1903-Jan. 31, 1913.

LEGARE, Hugh Swinton (UD S.C.) Jan. 2, 1797-June 20, 1843; House 1837-39; Atty. Gen. 1841-43; Secy. of State 1843.

LEGGETT, Robert L. (D Calif.) July 26, 1926-−; House 1963-79.

LEHLBACH, Frederick Reimold (nephew of Herman Lehlbach) (R N.J.) Jan. 31, 1876-Aug. 4, 1937; House 1915-37.

LEHLBACH, Herman (uncle of Frederick Reimold Lehlbach) (R N.J.) July 3, 1845-Jan. 11, 1904; House 1885-91.

LEHMAN, Herbert Henry (D N.Y.) March 28, 1878-Dec. 5, 1963; Senate Nov. 9, 1949-57; Gov. 1933-42.

LEHMAN, Richard Henry (D Calif.) July 20, 1948-−; House 1983-−.

LEHMAN, William (D Fla.) Oct. 4, 1913-−; House 1973-−.

LEHMAN, William Eckart (D Pa.) Aug. 21, 1821-July 19, 1895; House 1861-63.

LEHR, John Camillus (D Mich.) Nov. 18, 1878-Feb. 1 1958; House 1933-35.

LEIB, Michael (D Pa.) Jan. 8, 1760-Dec. 8, 1822; Hous 1799-Feb. 14, 1806; Senate Jan. 9, 1809-Feb. 1 1814.

LEIB, Owen D. (D Pa.) ?-June 17, 1848; House 1845-4

LEIDY, Paul (D Pa.) Nov. 13, 1813-Sept. 11, 187 House Dec. 7, 1857-59.

LEIGH, Benjamin Watkins (W Va.) June 18, 1781-Fe 2, 1849; Senate Feb. 26, 1834-July 4, 1836.

LEIGHTY, Jacob D. (R Ind.) Nov. 15, 1839-Oct. 1 1912; House 1895-97.

LEIPER, George Gray (D Pa.) Feb. 3, 1786-Nov. 1 1868; House 1829-31.

LEISENRING, John (R Pa.) June 3, 1853-Jan. 19, 190 House 1895-97.

LEITER, Benjamin Franklin (R Ohio) Oct. 13, 181 June 17, 1866; House 1855-59.

LELAND, George Thomas "Mickey" (D Texas) Nov. 2 1944-−; House 1979-−.

LEMKE, William (R N.D.) Aug. 13, 1878-May 30, 19£ House 1933-41 (Nonpartisan Republican), 1943-M 30, 1950.

LE MOYNE, John Valcoulon (D Ill.) Nov. 17, 1828-Ju 27, 1918; House May 6, 1876-77.

LENAHAN, John Thomas (D Pa.) Nov. 15, 1852-Ap 28, 1920; House 1907-09.

L'ENGLE, Claude (D Fla.) Oct. 19, 1868-Nov. 6, 19 House 1913-15.

LENNON, Alton Asa (D N.C.) Aug. 17, 1906-Dec. 1986; Senate July 10, 1953-Nov. 28, 1954; Hou 1957-73.

LENROOT, Irvine Luther (R Wis.) Jan. 31, 1869-Ja 26, 1949; House 1909-April 17, 1918; Senate April 1918-27.

LENT, James (JD N.Y.) 1782-Feb. 22, 1833; Hou 1829-Feb. 22, 1833.

LENT, Norman Frederick (R N.Y.) March 23, 1931-House 1971-−.

LENTZ, John Jacob (D Ohio) Jan. 27, 1856-July 1931; House 1897-1901.

LEONARD, Fred Churchill (R Pa.) Feb. 16, 1856-D 5, 1921; House 1895-97.

LEONARD, George (− Mass.) July 4, 1729-July 1819; House 1789-91, 1795-97.

LEONARD, John Edwards (grandnephew of John Edwards of Pa.) (R La.) Sept. 22, 1845-March 15, 1878; House 1877-March 15, 1878.

LEONARD, Moses Gage (D N.Y.) July 10, 1809-March 20, 1899; House 1843-45.

LEONARD, Stephen Banks (D N.Y.) April 15, 1793-May 8, 1876; House 1835-37, 1839-41.

LESHER, John Vandling (D Pa.) July 27, 1866-May 3, 1932; House 1913-21.

LESINSKI, John (father of John Lesinski Jr.) (D Mich.) Jan. 3, 1885-May 27, 1950; House 1933-May 27, 1950.

LESINSKI, John Jr. (son of John Lesinski) (D Mich.) Dec. 28, 1914- —; House 1951-65.

LESSLER, Montague (R N.Y.) Jan. 1, 1869-Feb. 17, 1938; House Jan. 7, 1902-03.

LESTER, Posey Green (D Va.) March 12, 1850-Feb. 9, 1929; House 1889-93.

LESTER, Rufus Ezekiel (D Ga.) Dec. 12, 1837-June 16, 1906; House 1889-June 16, 1906.

LETCHER, John (D Va.) March 29, 1813-Jan. 26, 1884; House 1851-59; Gov. 1860-63.

LETCHER, Robert Perkins (W Ky.) Feb. 10, 1788-Jan. 24, 1861; House 1823-33 (1823-27 Clay Democrat), Aug. 6, 1834-35; Gov. 1840-44.

LETTS, Fred Dickinson (cousin of Lester Jesse Dickinson) (R Iowa) April 26, 1875-Jan. 19, 1965; House 1925-31.

LEVER, Asbury Francis (D S.C.) Jan. 5, 1875-April 28, 1940; House Nov. 5, 1901-Aug. 1, 1919.

LEVERING, Robert Woodrow (son-in-law of Usher L. Burdick, brother-in-law of Quentin N. Burdick) (D Ohio) Oct. 3, 1914- —; House 1959-61.

LEVIN, Carl Milton (brother of Sander Martin Levin) (D Mich.) June 28, 1934- —; Senate 1979- —.

LEVIN, Lewis Charles (AP Pa.) Nov. 10, 1808-March 14, 1860; House 1845-51.

LEVIN, Sander Martin (brother of Carl Milton Levin) (D Mich.) Sept. 6, 1931- —; House 1983- —.

LEVINE, Mel (D Calif.) June 7, 1943- —; House 1983- —.

LEVITAS, Elliott Harris (D Ga.) Dec. 26, 1930- —; House 1975-85.

LEVY, David (R Fla.) (*See* YULEE, David Levy.)

LEVY, Jefferson Monroe (D N.Y.) April 16, 1852-March 6, 1924; House 1899-1901, 1911-15.

LEVY, William Mallory (D La.) Oct. 31, 1827-Aug. 14, 1882; House 1875-77.

LEWIS, Abner (W N.Y.) ?-?; House 1845-47.

LEWIS, Barbour (R Tenn.) Jan. 5, 1818-July 15, 1893; House 1873-75.

LEWIS, Burwell Boykin (D Ala.) July 7, 1838-Oct. 11, 1885; House 1875-77, 1879-Oct. 1, 1880.

LEWIS, Charles Swearinger (D Va.) Feb. 26, 1821-Jan. 22, 1878; House Dec. 4, 1854-55.

LEWIS, Clarke (D Miss.) Nov. 8, 1840-March 13, 1896; House 1889-93.

LEWIS, David John (D Md.) May 1, 1869-Aug. 12, 1952; House 1911-17, 1931-39.

LEWIS, Dixon Hall (D Ala.) Aug. 10, 1802-Oct. 25, 1848; House 1829-April 22, 1844 (State Rights Democrat); Senate April 22, 1844-Oct. 25, 1848.

LEWIS, Earl Ramage (R Ohio) Feb. 22, 1887-Feb. 1, 1956; House 1939-41, 1943-49.

LEWIS, Edward Taylor (D La.) Oct. 26, 1834-April 26, 1927; House 1883-85.

LEWIS, Elijah Banks (D Ga.) March 27, 1854-Dec. 10, 1920; House 1897-1909.

LEWIS, Fred Ewing (R Pa.) Feb. 8, 1865-June 27, 1949; House 1913-15.

LEWIS, James Hamilton (D Ill.) May 18, 1863-April 9, 1939; House 1897-99 (Wash.); Senate March 26, 1913-19, 1931-April 9, 1939.

LEWIS, Jerry (R Calif.) Oct. 21, 1934- —; House 1979- —.

LEWIS, John (D Ga.) Feb. 19, 1940- —; House 1987- —.

LEWIS, John Francis (R Va.) March 1, 1818-Sept. 2, 1895; Senate Jan. 26, 1870-75.

LEWIS, John Henry (R Ill.) July 21, 1830-Jan. 6, 1929; House 1881-83.

LEWIS, John William (R Ky.) Oct. 14, 1841-Dec. 20, 1913; House 1895-97.

LEWIS, Joseph Horace (D Ky.) Oct. 29, 1824-July 6, 1904; House May 10, 1870-73.

LEWIS, Joseph Jr. (F Va.) 1772-March 30, 1834; House 1803-17.

LEWIS, Lawrence (D Colo.) June 22, 1879-Dec. 9, 1943; House 1933-Dec. 9, 1943.

LEWIS, Robert Jacob (R Pa.) Dec. 30, 1864-July 24, 1933; House 1901-03.

LEWIS, Thomas (− Va.) ?-?; House 1803-March 5, 1804.

LEWIS, Thomas F. (R Fla.) Oct. 26, 1924-−; House 1983-−.

LEWIS, William (R Ky.) Sept. 22, 1868-Aug. 8, 1959; House April 24, 1948-49.

LEWIS, William J. (D Va.) July 4, 1766-Nov. 1, 1828; House 1817-19.

LIBBEY, Harry (R Va.) Nov. 22, 1843-Sept. 30, 1913; House 1883-87.

LIBONATI, Roland Victor (D Ill.) Dec. 29, 1900-−; House Dec. 31, 1957-65.

LICHTENWALNER, Norton Lewis (D Pa.) June 1, 1889-May 3, 1960; House 1931-33.

LICHTENWALTER, Franklin Herbert (R Pa.) March 28, 1910-March 4, 1973; House Sept. 9, 1947-51.

LIEB, Charles (D Ind.) May 20, 1852-Sept. 1, 1928; House 1913-17.

LIEBEL, Michael Jr. (D Pa.) Dec. 12, 1870-Aug. 8, 1927; House 1915-17.

LIGHTFOOT, Jim Ross (R Iowa) Sept. 27, 1939-−; House 1985-−.

LIGON, Robert Fulwood (D Ala.) Dec. 16, 1823-Oct. 11, 1901; House 1877-79.

LIGON, Thomas Watkins (D Md.) May 10, 1810-Jan. 12, 1881; House 1845-49; Gov. 1854-58.

LILLEY, George Leavens (R Conn.) Aug. 3, 1859-April 21, 1909; House 1903-Jan. 5, 1909; Gov. Jan. 5-April 21, 1909.

LILLEY, Mial Eben (R Pa.) May 30, 1850-Feb. 28, 1915; House 1905-07.

LILLY, Samuel (D N.J.) Oct. 28, 1815-April 3, 1880; House 1853-55.

LILLY, Thomas Jefferson (D W.Va.) June 3, 1878-April 2, 1956; House 1923-25.

LILLY, William (R Pa.) June 3, 1821-Dec. 1, 1893; House March 4-Dec. 1, 1893.

LINCOLN, Abraham (R Ill.) Feb. 12, 1809-April 15, 1865; House 1847-49 (Whig); President 1861-April 15, 1865.

LINCOLN, Enoch (son of Levi Lincoln, brother of Levi Lincoln Jr.) (DR Maine) Dec. 28, 1788-Oct. 8, 1829; House Nov. 4, 1818-21 (Mass.), 1821-26; Gov. 1827-29.

LINCOLN, Levi (father of Enoch Lincoln and Levi Lin coln Jr.) (D Mass.) May 15, 1749-April 14, 182 House Dec. 15, 1800-March 5, 1801; Atty. Gen. 180 05; Gov. 1808-09.

LINCOLN, Levi Jr. (son of Levi Lincoln, brother Enoch Lincoln) (W Mass.) Oct. 25, 1782-May 2 1868; House Feb. 17, 1834-March 16, 1841; Go 1825-34 (Anti Democrat/National Republican).

LINCOLN, William Slosson (R N.Y.) Aug. 13, 181 April 21, 1893; House 1867-69.

LIND, James Francis (D Pa.) Oct. 17, 1900-−; Hou 1949-53.

LIND, John (D Minn.) March 25, 1854-Sept. 18, 193 House 1887-93 (Republican), 1903-05; Gov. 189 1901.

LINDBERG, Charles Augustus (R Minn.) Jan. 20, 185 May 24, 1924; House 1907-17.

LINDLEY, James Johnson (W Mo.) Jan. 1, 1822-Ap 18, 1891; House 1853-57.

LINDQUIST, Francis Oscar (R Mich.) Sept. 27, 186 Sept. 25, 1924; House 1913-15.

LINDSAY, George Henry (father of George Washingt Lindsay) (D N.Y.) Jan. 7, 1837-May 25, 1916; Hou 1901-13.

LINDSAY, George Washington (son of George Her Lindsay) (D N.Y.) March 28, 1865-March 15, 19 House 1923-35.

LINDSAY, John Vliet (R N.Y.) Nov. 24, 1921-−; Hou 1959-Dec. 31, 1965.

LINDSAY, William (D Ky.) Sept. 4, 1835-Oct. 15, 19 Senate Feb. 15, 1893-1901.

LINDSEY, Stephen Decatur (R Maine) March 3, 18 April 26, 1884; House 1877-83.

LINDSLEY, James Girard (R N.Y.) March 19, 18 Dec. 4, 1898; House 1885-87.

LINDSLEY, William Dell (D Ohio) Dec. 25, 18 March 11, 1890; House 1853-55.

LINEBERGER, Walter Franklin (R Calif.) July 1883-Oct. 9, 1943; House 1921-27.

LINEHAN, Neil Joseph (D Ill.) Sept. 23, 1895-Aug. 1967; House 1949-51.

LINK, Arthur Albert (D N.D.) May 24, 1914-−; Ho 1971-73; Gov. 1973-81.

LINK, William Walter (D Ill.) Feb. 12, 1884-Sept. 1950; House 1945-47.

INN, Archibald Ladley (W N.Y.) Oct. 15, 1802-Oct. 10, 1857; House 1841-43.

INN, James (D N.J.) 1749-Jan. 5, 1821; House 1799-1801.

INN, John (− N.J.) Dec. 3, 1763-Jan. 5, 1821; House 1817-Jan. 5, 1821.

INN, Lewis Fields (D Mo.) Nov. 5, 1796-Oct. 3, 1843; Senate Oct. 25, 1833-Oct. 3, 1843.

INNEY, Romulus Zachariah (R N.C.) Dec. 26, 1841-April 15, 1910; House 1895-1901.

INTHICUM, John Charles (D Md.) Nov. 26, 1867-Oct. 5, 1932; House 1911-Oct. 5, 1932.

INTON, William Seelye (R Mich.) Feb. 4, 1856-Nov. 22, 1927; House 1893-97.

PINSKI, William Oliver (D Ill.) Dec. 22, 1937-−; House 1983-−.

PPITT, Henry Frederick (R R.I.) Oct. 12, 1856-Dec. 28, 1933; Senate 1911-17.

PSCOMB, Glenard Paul (R Calif.) Aug. 19, 1915-Feb. 1, 1970; House Nov. 10, 1953-Feb. 1, 1970.

SLE, Marcus Claiborne (D Ky.) Sept. 23, 1862-July 7, 1894; House 1893-July 7, 1894.

TCHFIELD, Elisha (D N.Y.) July 12, 1785-Aug. 4, 1859; House 1821-25.

TTAUER, Lucius Nathan (R N.Y.) Jan. 20, 1859-March 2, 1944; House 1897-1907.

TTLE, Chauncey Bundy (D Kan.) Feb. 10, 1877-Sept. 29, 1952; House 1925-27.

TTLE, Edward Campbell (R Kan.) Dec. 14, 1858-June 27, 1924; House 1917-June 27, 1924.

TTLE, Edward Preble (D Mass.) Nov. 7, 1791-Feb. 6, 1875; House Dec. 13, 1852-53.

TTLE, John (R Ohio) April 25, 1837-Oct. 18, 1900; House 1885-87.

TTLE, John Sebastian (D Ark.) March 15, 1851-Oct. 29, 1916; House Dec. 3, 1894-Jan. 14, 1907; Gov. Jan. 8-Feb. 11, 1907.

TTLE, Joseph James (D N.Y.) June 5, 1841-Feb. 11, 1913; House Nov. 3, 1891-93.

TTLE, Peter (D Md.) Dec. 11, 1775-Feb. 5, 1830; House 1811-13, Sept. 2, 1816-29.

TTLEFIELD, Charles Edgar (R Maine) June 21, 1851-May 2, 1915; House June 19, 1899-Sept. 30, 1908.

LITTLEFIELD, Nathaniel Swett (CassD Maine) Sept. 20, 1804-Aug. 15, 1882; House 1841-43 (Democrat), 1849-51.

LITTLEJOHN, DeWitt Clinton (R N.Y.) Feb. 7, 1818-Oct. 27, 1892; House 1863-65.

LITTLEPAGE, Adam Brown (D W.Va.) April 14, 1859-June 29, 1921; House 1911-13, 1915-19.

LITTLETON, Martin Wiley (D N.Y.) Jan. 12, 1872-Dec. 19, 1934; House 1911-13.

LITTON, Jerry Lon (D Mo.) May 12, 1937-Aug. 3, 1976; House 1973-Aug. 3, 1976.

LIVELY, Robert Maclin (D Texas) Jan. 6, 1855-Jan. 15, 1929; House July 23, 1910-11.

LIVERMORE, Arthur (son of Samuel Livermore, brother of Edward St. Loe Livermore) (D N.H.) July 29, 1766-July 1, 1853; House 1817-21, 1823-25.

LIVERMORE, Edward St. Loe (son of Samuel Livermore, brother of Arthur Livermore) (F Mass.) April 5, 1762-Sept. 15, 1832; House 1807-11.

LIVERMORE, Samuel (father of Arthur Livermore and Edward St. Loe Livermore) (− N.H.) May 14, 1732-May 18, 1803; House 1789-93; Senate 1793-June 12, 1801; Pres. pro tempore 1796, 1800; Cont. Cong. 1780-82, 1785.

LIVERNASH, Edward James (subsequently Edward James de Nivernais) (UL/D Calif.) Feb. 14, 1866-June 1, 1938; House 1903-05.

LIVINGSTON, Edward (D La.) May 28, 1764-May 23, 1836; House 1795-1801 (N.Y.), 1823-29; Senate 1829-May 24, 1831; Secy. of State 1831-33.

LIVINGSTON, Henry Walter (− N.Y.) 1768-Dec. 22, 1810; House 1803-07.

LIVINGSTON, Leonidas Felix (D Ga.) April 3, 1832-Feb. 11, 1912; House 1891-1911.

LIVINGSTON, Robert LeRoy (F N.Y.) ?-?; House 1809-May 6, 1812.

LIVINGSTON, Robert Linligthgow Jr. (R La.) April 30, 1943-−; House Sept. 7, 1977-−.

LLOYD, Edward (granduncle of Lloyd Lowndes Jr.) (D Md.) July 22, 1779-June 2, 1834; House Dec. 3, 1806-09; Senate 1819-Jan. 14, 1826; Gov. 1809-11 (Democratic Republican).

LLOYD, James (D Md.) 1745-1820; Senate Dec. 11, 1797-Dec. 1, 1800.

LLOYD, James (F Mass.) Dec. 1769-April 5, 1831; Senate June 9, 1808-May 1, 1813, June 5, 1822-May 23, 1826.

LLOYD, James Frederick (D Calif.) Sept. 27, 1922-—; House 1975-81.

LLOYD, James Tilghman (D Mo.) Aug. 28, 1857-April 3, 1944; House June 1, 1897-1917.

LLOYD, Marilyn Laird (D Tenn.) Jan. 3, 1929-—; House 1975-—.

LLOYD, Sherman Parkinson (R Utah) Jan. 11, 1914-Dec. 15, 1979; House 1963-65, 1967-73.

LLOYD, Wesley (D Wash.) July 24, 1883-Jan. 10, 1936; House 1933-Jan. 10, 1936.

LOAN, Benjamin Franklin (Rad. Mo.) Oct. 4, 1819-March 30, 1881; House 1863-69 (1863-67 Emancipationist).

LOBECK, Charles Otto (D Neb.) April 6, 1852-Jan. 30, 1920; House 1911-19.

LOCHER, Cyrus (D Ohio) March 8, 1878-Aug. 17, 1929; Senate April 5-Dec. 14, 1928.

LOCKE, Francis (nephew of Matthew Locke) (D N.C.) Oct. 31, 1776-Jan. 8, 1823; Senate 1814-Dec. 5, 1815.

LOCKE, John (— Mass.) Feb. 14, 1764-March 29, 1855; House 1823-29.

LOCKE, Matthew (uncle of Francis Locke, great-great-great-grandfather of Effiegene Locke Wingo) (D N.C.) 1730-Sept. 7, 1801; House 1793-99.

LOCKHART, James (D Ind.) Feb. 13, 1806-Sept. 7, 1857; House 1851-53, March 4-Sept. 7, 1857.

LOCKHART, James Alexander (D N.C.) June 2, 1850-Dec. 24, 1905; House 1895-June 5, 1896.

LOCKWOOD, Daniel Newton (D N.Y.) June 1, 1844-June 1, 1906; House 1877-79, 1891-95.

LODGE, Henry Cabot (grandfather of Henry Cabot Lodge Jr. and John Davis Lodge, great-grandson of George Cabot) (R Mass.) May 12, 1850-Nov. 9, 1924; House 1887-93; Senate 1893-Nov. 9, 1924; Senate majority leader 1919-24.

LODGE, Henry Cabot Jr. (grandson of Henry Cabot Lodge, brother of John Davis Lodge, nephew of Augustus Peabody Gardner, great-great grandson of George Cabot) (R Mass.) July 5, 1902-Feb. 27, 1986; Senate 1937-Feb. 3, 1944, 1947-53.

LODGE, John Davis (grandson of Henry Cabot Lodge, brother of Henry Cabot Lodge Jr., nephew of Augustus Peabody Gardner, great-great grandson of George Cabot) (R Conn.) Oct. 20, 1903-Oct. 29, 1985; House 1947-51; Gov. 1951-55.

LOEFFLER, Thomas Gilbert (R Texas) Aug. 1, 1946-—; House 1979-87.

LOFLAND, James Ruch (R Del.) Nov. 2, 1823-Feb. 1(1894; House 1873-75.

LOFT, George William (D N.Y.) Feb. 6, 1865-Nov. 1943; House Nov. 4, 1913-17.

LOFTIN, Scott Marion (D Fla.) Sept. 14, 1878-Sept. 2 1953; Senate May 26-Nov. 3, 1936.

LOGAN, George (D Pa.) Sept. 9, 1753-April 9, 182 Senate July 13, 1801-07.

LOGAN, Henry (D Pa.) April 14, 1784-Dec. 26, 186 House 1835-39.

LOGAN, John Alexander (R Ill.) Feb. 9, 1826-Dec. 2 1886; House 1859-April 2, 1862 (Democrat), 1867-7 Senate 1871-77, 1879-Dec. 26, 1886.

LOGAN, Marvel Mills (D Ky.) Jan. 7, 1874-Oct. 3, 193 Senate 1931-Oct. 3, 1939.

LOGAN, William (D Ky.) Dec. 8, 1776-Aug. 8, 18: Senate 1819-May 28, 1820.

LOGAN, William Turner (D S.C.) June 21, 1874-Se 15, 1941; House 1921-25.

LOGUE, James Washington (D Pa.) Feb. 22, 1863-A 27, 1925; House 1913-15.

LONDON, Meyer (Soc. N.Y.) Dec. 29, 1871-June 1926; House 1915-19, 1921-23.

LONERGAN, Augustine (D Conn.) May 20, 1874-O 18, 1947; House 1913-15, 1917-21, 1931-33; Sena 1933-39.

LONG, Alexander (D Ohio) Dec. 24, 1816-Nov. 28, 18 House 1863-65.

LONG, Cathy (widow of Gillis William Long) (D L Feb. 7, 1924-—; House April 4, 1985-87.

LONG, Chester Isaiah (R Kan.) Oct. 12, 1860-July 1934; House 1895-97, 1899-March 4, 1903; Sen 1903-09.

LONG, Clarence Dickinson (D Md.) Dec. 11, 1908- House 1963-85.

LONG, Edward Henry Carroll (W Md.) Sept. 28, 18 Oct. 16, 1865; House 1845-47.

LONG, Edward Vaughn (D Mo.) July 18, 1908-Nov 1972; Senate Sept. 23, 1960-Dec. 27, 1968.

LONG, George Shannon (brother of Huey Pierce " Kingfish" Long, brother-in-law of Rose McCon Long, uncle of Russell Billiu Long, cousin of G William Long) (D La.) Sept. 11, 1883-March 1958; House 1953-March 22, 1958.

ONG, Gillis William (husband of Cathy Long, cousin of Huey Pierce "the Kingfish" Long, Rose McConnell Long, Russell Billiu Long and George Shannon Long) (D La.) May 4, 1923-Jan. 20, 1985; House 1963-65, 1973-Jan. 20, 1985.

ONG, Huey Pierce "the Kingfish" (husband of Rose McConnell Long, father of Russell Billiu Long, brother of George Shannon Long, cousin of Gillis William Long) (D La.) Aug. 30, 1893-Sept. 10, 1935; Senate Jan. 25, 1932-Sept. 10, 1935; Gov. 1928-32.

ONG, Jefferson Franklin (R Ga.) March 3, 1836-Feb. 5, 1900; House Dec. 22, 1870-71.

ONG, John (W N.C.) Feb. 26, 1785-Aug. 11, 1857; House 1821-29.

ONG, John Benjamin (D Texas) Sept. 8, 1843-April 27, 1924; House 1891-93.

ONG, John Davis (R Mass.) Oct. 27, 1838-Aug. 28, 1915; House 1883-89; Gov. 1880-83; Secy. of the Navy 1897-1902.

ONG, Lewis Marshall (D Ill.) June 22, 1883-Sept. 9, 1957; House 1937-39.

ONG, Oren Ethelbirt (D Hawaii) March 4, 1889-May 6, 1965; Senate Aug. 21, 1959-63; Gov. (Hawaii Terr.) 1951-53.

ONG, Rose McConnell (widow of Huey Pierce "the Kingfish" Long, mother of Russell Billiu Long, sister-in-law of George Shannon Long) (D La.) April 8, 1892-May 27, 1970; Senate Jan. 31, 1936-37.

ONG, Russell Billiu (son of Huey Pierce "the Kingfish" Long and Rose McConnell Long, nephew of George Shannon Long) (D La.) Nov. 3, 1918- —; Senate Dec. 31, 1948-87.

ONG, Speedy Oteria (D La.) June 16, 1928- —; House 1965-73.

ONGFELLOW, Stephen (F Maine) June 23, 1775-Aug. 2, 1849; House 1823-25.

ONGNECKER, Henry Clay (R Pa.) April 17, 1820-Sept. 16, 1871; House 1859-61.

ONGWORTH, Nicholas (nephew of Bellamy Storer) (R Ohio) Nov. 5, 1869-April 9, 1931; House 1903-13, 1915-April 9, 1931; House majority leader 1923-25; Speaker 1925-31.

ONGYEAR, John Wesley (R Mich.) Oct. 22, 1820-March 11, 1875; House 1863-67.

OOFBOUROW, Frederick Charles (R Utah) Feb. 8, 1874-July 8, 1949; House Nov. 4, 1930-33.

OOMIS, Andrew Williams (W Ohio) June 27, 1797-Aug. 24, 1873; House March 4-Oct. 20, 1837.

LOOMIS, Arphaxed (D N.Y.) April 9, 1798-Sept. 15, 1885; House 1837-39.

LOOMIS, Dwight (R Conn.) July 27, 1821-Sept. 17, 1903; House 1859-63.

LORD, Bert (R N.Y.) Dec. 4, 1869-May 24, 1939; House 1935-May 24, 1939.

LORD, Frederick William (W N.Y.) Dec. 11, 1800-May 24, 1860; House 1847-49.

LORD, Henry William (R Mich.) March 8, 1821-Jan. 25, 1891; House 1881-83.

LORD, Scott (D N.Y.) Dec. 11, 1820-Sept. 10, 1885; House 1875-77.

LORE, Charles Brown (D Del.) March 16, 1831-March 6, 1911; House 1883-87.

LORIMER, William (R Ill.) April 27, 1861-Sept. 13, 1934; House 1895-1901, 1903-June 17, 1909; Senate June 18, 1909-July 13, 1912.

LORING, George Bailey (R Mass.) Nov. 8, 1817-Sept. 13, 1891; House 1877-81.

LOSER, Joseph Carlton (D Tenn.) Oct. 1, 1892-July 31, 1984; House 1957-63.

LOTT, Chester Trent (R Miss.) Oct. 9, 1941- —; House 1973- —.

LOUD, Eugene Francis (R Calif.) March 12, 1847-Dec. 19, 1908; House 1891-1903.

LOUD, George Alvin (R Mich.) June 18, 1852-Nov. 13, 1925; House 1903-13, 1915-17.

LOUDENSLAGER, Henry Clay (R N.J.) May 22, 1852-Aug. 12, 1911; House 1893-Aug. 12, 1911.

LOUGHRIDGE, William (R Iowa) July 11, 1827-Sept. 26, 1889; House 1867-71, 1873-75.

LOUNSBERY, William (D N.Y.) Dec. 25, 1831-Nov. 8, 1905; House 1879-81.

LOUTTIT, James Alexander (R Calif.) Oct. 16, 1848-July 26, 1906; House 1885-87.

LOVE, Francis Johnson (R W.Va.) Jan. 23, 1901- —; House 1947-49.

LOVE, James (— Ky.) May 12, 1795-June 12, 1874; House 1833-35.

LOVE, John (D Va.) ?-Aug. 17, 1822; House 1807-11.

LOVE, Peter Early (D Ga.) July 7, 1818-Nov. 8, 1866; House 1859-Jan. 23, 1861.

LOVE, Rodney Marvin (D Ohio) July 18, 1908- —; House 1965-67.

LOVE, Thomas Cutting (W N.Y.) Nov. 30, 1789-Sept. 17, 1853; House 1835-37.

LOVE, William Carter (D N.C.) 1784-1835; House 1815-17.

LOVE, William Franklin (D Miss.) March 29, 1850-Oct. 16, 1898; House 1897-Oct. 16, 1898.

LOVEJOY, Owen (cousin of Nathan Allen Farwell) (R Ill.) Jan. 6, 1811-March 25, 1864; House 1857-March 25, 1864.

LOVERING, Henry Bacon (D Mass.) April 8, 1841-April 5, 1911; House 1883-87.

LOVERING, William Croad (R Mass.) Feb. 25, 1835-Feb. 4, 1910; House 1897-Feb. 4, 1910.

LOVETT, John (F N.Y.) Feb. 20, 1761-Aug. 12, 1818; House 1813-17.

LOVETTE, Oscar Byrd (R Tenn.) Dec. 20, 1871-July 6, 1934; House 1931-33.

LOVRE, Harold Orrin (R S.D.) Jan. 30, 1904-Jan. 17, 1972; House 1949-57.

LOW, Frederick Ferdinand (R Calif.) June 30, 1828-July 21, 1894; House June 3, 1862-63; Gov. 1863-67 (Unionist).

LOW, Philip Burrill (R N.Y.) May 6, 1836-Aug. 23, 1912; House 1895-99.

LOWDEN, Frank Orren (R Ill.) Jan. 26, 1861-March 20, 1943; House Nov. 6, 1906-11; Gov. 1917-21.

LOWE, David Perley (R Kan.) Aug. 22, 1823-April 10, 1882; House 1871-75.

LOWE, William Manning (GD Ala.) June 12, 1842-Oct. 12, 1882; House 1879-81, June 3-Oct. 12, 1882.

LOWELL, Joshua Adams (D Maine) March 20, 1801-March 13, 1874; House 1839-43.

LOWENSTEIN, Allard K. (D-L N.Y.) Jan. 16, 1929-March 14, 1980; House 1969-71.

LOWER, Christian (D Pa.) Jan. 7, 1740-Dec. 19, 1806; House 1805-Dec. 19, 1806.

LOWERY, Bill (R Calif.) May 2, 1947-—; House 1981-—.

LOWNDES, Lloyd Jr. (grandnephew of Edward Lloyd) (R Md.) Feb. 21, 1845-Jan. 8, 1905; House 1873-75; Gov. 1896-1900.

LOWNDES, Thomas (brother of William Lowndes) (F S.C.) Jan. 22, 1766-July 8, 1843; House 1801-05.

LOWNDES, William (brother of Thomas Lowndes) (D S.C.) Feb. 11, 1782-Oct. 27, 1822; House 1811-May 1822.

LOWREY, Bill Green (D Miss.) May 25, 1862-Sept. 1947; House 1921-29.

LOWRIE, Walter (D Pa.) Dec. 10, 1784-Dec. 14, 186 Senate 1819-25.

LOWRY, Michael E. (D Wash.) March 8, 1939-—; Hous 1979-—.

LOWRY, Robert (D Ind.) April 2, 1824-Jan. 27, 190 House 1883-87.

LOYALL, George (D Va.) May 29, 1789-Feb. 24, 186 House March 9, 1830-31, 1833-37.

LOZIER, Ralph Fulton (D Mo.) Jan. 28, 1866-May 2 1945; House 1923-35.

LUCAS, Edward (brother of William Lucas) (D Va Oct. 20, 1780-March 4, 1858; House 1833-37.

LUCAS, John Baptiste Charles (D Pa.) Aug. 14, 175 Aug. 17, 1842; House 1803-05.

LUCAS, Scott Wike (D Ill.) Feb. 19, 1892-Feb. 22, 196 House 1935-39; Senate 1939-51; Senate majori leader 1949-51.

LUCAS, William (brother of Edward Lucas) (D Va Nov. 30, 1800-Aug. 29, 1877; House 1839-41, 1843-4

LUCAS, William Vincent (R S.D.) July 3, 1835-Nov. 1 1921; House 1893-95.

LUCAS, Wingate Hezekiah (D Texas) May 1, 1908- House 1947-55.

LUCE, Clare Boothe (stepdaughter of Albert Elmer A tin) (R Conn.) April 10, 1903-—; House 1943-47.

LUCE, Robert (R Mass.) Dec. 2, 1862-April 17, 19 House 1919-35, 1937-41.

LUCKEY, Henry Carl (D Neb.) Nov. 22, 1868-Dec. 1956; House 1935-39.

LUCKING, Alfred (D Mich.) Dec. 18, 1856-Dec. 1, 19 House 1903-05.

LUDLOW, Louis Leon (D Ind.) June 24, 1873-Nov. 1950; House 1929-49.

LUECKE, John Frederick (D Mich.) July 4, 1889-Ma 21, 1952; House 1937-39.

LUFKIN, Willfred Weymouth (R Mass.) March 1879-March 28, 1934; House Nov. 6, 1917-June 1921.

LUGAR, Richard Green (R Ind.) April 4, 1932-—; S ate 1977-—.

UHRING, Oscar Raymond (R Ind.) Feb. 11, 1879-Aug. 20, 1944; House 1919-23.

UJAN, Manuel Jr. (R N.M.) May 12, 1928- —; House 1969- —.

UKEN, Thomas Andrew (D Ohio) July 9, 1925- —; House March 5, 1974-75, 1977- —.

UKENS, Donald Earl "Buz" (R Ohio) Feb. 11, 1931- —; House 1967-71, 1987- —.

UMPKIN, Alva Moore (D S.C.) Nov. 13, 1886-Aug. 1, 1941; Senate July 22-Aug. 1, 1941.

UMPKIN, John Henry (nephew of Wilson Lumpkin) (D Ga.) June 13, 1812-July 10, 1860; House 1843-49, 1855-57.

UMPKIN, Wilson (uncle of John Henry Lumpkin, grandfather of Middleton Pope Barrow) (D Ga.) Jan. 14, 1783-Dec. 28, 1870; House 1815-17, 1827-31; Senate Nov. 22, 1837-41; Gov. 1831-35 (Union Democrat).

UNA, Tranquillino (R N.M.) Feb. 25, 1849-Nov. 20, 1892; House (Terr. Del.) 1881-March 5, 1884.

UNDEEN, Ernest (FL Minn.) Aug. 4, 1878-Aug. 31, 1940; House 1917-19 (Republican), 1933-37; Senate 1937-Aug. 31, 1940.

UNDIN, Frederick (R Ill.) May 18, 1868-Aug. 20, 1947; House 1909-11.

UNDINE, Stanley N. (D N.Y.) Feb. 4, 1939- —; House March 8, 1976-87.

UNGREN, Daniel Edward (R Calif.) Sept. 22, 1946- —; House 1979- —.

UNN, George Richard (D N.Y.) June 23, 1873-Nov. 27, 1948; House 1917-19.

USK, Georgia L. (D N.M.) May 12, 1893-Jan. 5, 1971; House 1947-49.

USK, Hall Stoner (D Ore.) Sept. 21, 1883-May 15, 1983; Senate March 16-Nov. 8, 1960.

UTTRELL, John King (D Calif.) June 27, 1831-Oct. 4, 1893; House 1873-79.

YBRAND, Archibald (R Ohio) May 23, 1840-Feb. 7, 1910; House 1897-1901.

YLE, Aaron (D Pa.) Nov. 17, 1759-Sept. 24, 1825; House 1809-17.

YLE, John Emmett Jr. (D Texas) Sept. 4, 1910- —; House 1945-55.

YMAN, Joseph (R Iowa) Sept. 13, 1840-July 9, 1890; House 1885-89.

LYMAN, Joseph Stebbins (— N.Y.) Feb. 14, 1785-March 21, 1821; House 1819-21.

LYMAN, Samuel (— Mass.) Jan. 25, 1749-June 5, 1802; House 1795-Nov. 6, 1800.

LYMAN, Theodore (I Mass.) Aug. 23, 1833-Sept. 9, 1897; House 1883-85.

LYMAN, William (D Mass.) Dec. 7, 1755-Sept. 2, 1811; House 1793-97.

LYNCH, John (R Maine) Feb. 18, 1825-July 21, 1892; House 1865-73.

LYNCH, John (D Pa.) Nov. 1, 1843-Aug. 17, 1910; House 1887-89.

LYNCH, John Roy (R Miss.) Sept. 10, 1847-Nov. 2, 1939; House 1873-77, April 29, 1882-83.

LYNCH, Thomas (D Wis.) Nov. 21, 1844-May 4, 1898; House 1891-95.

LYNCH, Walter Aloysius (D N.Y.) July 7, 1894-Sept. 10, 1957; House Feb. 20, 1940-51.

LYNDE, William Pitt (D Wis.) Dec. 16, 1817-Dec. 18, 1885; House June 5, 1848-49, 1875-79.

LYON, Asa (F Vt.) Dec. 31, 1763-April 4, 1841; House 1815-17.

LYON, Caleb (I N.Y.) Dec. 7, 1822-Sept. 8, 1875; House 1853-55; Gov. (Idaho Terr.) 1864-66.

LYON, Chittenden (son of Matthew Lyon) (D Ky.) Feb. 22, 1787-Nov. 23, 1842; House 1827-35.

LYON, Francis Strother (W Ala.) Feb. 25, 1800-Dec. 31, 1882; House 1835-39.

LYON, Homer Le Grand (D N.C.) March 1, 1879-May 31, 1956; House 1921-29.

LYON, Lucius (D Mich.) Feb. 26, 1800-Sept. 24, 1851; House (Terr. Del.) 1833-35, (Rep.) 1843-45; Senate Jan. 26, 1837-39.

LYON, Matthew (father of Chittenden Lyon, great-grandfather of William Peters Hepburn) (— Ky.) July 14, 1746-Aug. 1, 1822; House 1797-1801 (Vt.), 1803-11.

LYTLE, Robert Todd (nephew of John Rowan) (JD Ohio) May 19, 1804-Dec. 22, 1839; House 1833-March 10, 1834, Dec. 27, 1834-35.

MAAS, Melvin Joseph (R Minn.) May 14, 1898-April 13, 1964; House 1927-33, 1935-45.

MacCRATE, John (R N.Y.) March 29, 1885-June 9, 1976; House 1919-Dec. 30, 1920.

MacDONALD, John Lewis (D Minn.) Feb. 22, 1838-July 13, 1903; House 1887-89.

MACDONALD, Moses (D Maine) April 8, 1815-Oct. 18, 1869; House 1851-55.

MACDONALD, Torbert Hart (D Mass.) June 6, 1917-May 21, 1976; House 1955-May 21, 1976.

MacDONALD, William Josiah (Prog. Mich.) Nov. 17, 1873-March 29, 1946; House Aug. 26, 1913-15.

MacDOUGALL, Clinton Dugald (R N.Y.) June 14, 1839-May 24, 1914; House 1873-77.

MACE, Daniel (R Ind.) Sept. 5, 1811-July 26, 1867; House 1851-57 (1851-55 Democrat).

MacGREGOR, Clarence (R N.Y.) Sept. 16, 1872-Feb. 18, 1952; House 1919-Dec. 31, 1928.

MacGREGOR, Clark (R Minn.) July 12, 1922- -; House 1961-71.

MACHEN, Hervey Gilbert (D Md.) Oct. 14, 1916- -; House 1965-69.

MACHEN, Willis Benson (D Ky.) April 10, 1810-Sept. 29, 1893; Senate Sept. 27, 1872-73.

MACHIR, James (- Va.) ?-June 25, 1827; House 1797-99.

MACHROWICZ, Thaddeus Michael (D Mich.) Aug. 21, 1899-Feb. 17, 1970; House 1951-Sept. 18, 1961.

MACIEJEWSKI, Anton Frank (D Ill.) Jan. 3, 1893-Sept. 25, 1949; House 1939-Dec. 8, 1942.

MacINTYRE, Archibald Thompson (D Ga.) Oct. 27, 1822-Jan. 1, 1900; House 1871-73.

MACIORA, Lucien John (D Conn.) Aug. 17, 1902- -; House 1941-43.

MACK, Connie III (R Fla.) Oct. 29, 1940- -; House 1983- -.

MACK, Peter Francis Jr. (D Ill.) Nov. 1, 1916-July 4, 1986; House 1949-63.

MACK, Russell Vernon (R Wash.) June 13, 1891-March 28, 1960; House June 7, 1947-March 28, 1960.

MACKAY, James Armstrong (D Ga.) June 25, 1919- -; House 1965-67.

MacKAY, Kenneth Hood "Buddy" (D Fla.) March 22, 1933- -; House 1983- -.

MACKEY, Edmund William McGregor (R S.C.) March 8, 1846-Jan. 27, 1884; House 1875-July 19, 1876 (Independent Republican), May 31, 1882-Jan. 27, 1884.

MACKEY, Levi Augustus (D Pa.) Nov. 25, 1819-Feb. 8 1889; House 1875-79.

MACKIE, John C. (D Mich.) June 1, 1920- -; Hous 1965-67.

MacKINNON, George Edward (R Minn.) April 2: 1906- -; House 1947-49.

MacLAFFERTY, James Henry (R Calif.) Feb. 27, 1871 June 9, 1937; House Nov. 7, 1922-25.

MACLAY, Samuel (brother of William Maclay, fathe of William Plunkett Maclay) (- Pa.) June 17, 174 Oct. 5, 1811; House 1795-97; Senate 1803-Jan. 1809.

MACLAY, William (brother of Samuel Maclay, uncle c William Plunkett Maclay) (D Pa.) July 20, 173˙ April 16, 1804; Senate 1789-91.

MACLAY, William (- Pa.) March 22, 1765-Jan. 1825; House 1815-19.

MACLAY, William Brown (D N.Y.) March 20, 181: Feb. 19, 1882; House 1843-49, 1857-61.

MACLAY, William Plunkett (son of Samuel Macla nephew of William Maclay) (D Pa.) Aug. 23, 177 Sept. 2, 1842; House Oct. 8, 1816-21.

MACON, Nathaniel (uncle of Willis Alston and Micaja Thomas Hawkins, great-grandfather of Charl Henry Martin of North Carolina) (D N.C.) Dec. 1 1757-June 29, 1837; House 1791-Dec. 13, 1815; Se ate Dec. 13, 1815-Nov. 14, 1828; Speaker 1801-0 Pres. pro tempore 1826-27.

MACON, Robert Bruce (D Ark.) July 6, 1859-Oct. 1925; House 1903-13.

MACY, John B. (D Wis.) March 26, 1799-Sept. 24, 185 House 1853-55.

MACY, William Kingsland (R N.Y.) Nov. 21, 1889-Ju 15, 1961; House 1947-51.

MADDEN, Martin Barnaby (R Ill.) March 20, 185 April 27, 1928; House 1905-April 27, 1928.

MADDEN, Ray John (D Ind.) Feb. 25, 1892- -; Hou 1943-77.

MADDOX, John W. (D Ga.) June 3, 1848-Sept. 27, 192 House 1893-1905.

MADIGAN, Edward Rell (R Ill.) Jan. 13, 1936- - House 1973- -.

MADISON, Edmond Haggard (R Kan.) Dec. 18, 186 Sept. 18, 1911; House 1907-Sept. 18, 1911.

MADISON, James (DR Va.) March 16, 1751-June 2 1836; House 1789-97; Cont. Cong. 1780-83, 1786-8 Secy. of State 1801-09; President 1809-17.

MAFFETT, James Thompson (R Pa.) Feb. 2, 1837-Dec. 19, 1912; House 1887-89.

MAGEE, Clare (D Mo.) March 31, 1899-Aug. 7, 1969; House 1949-53.

MAGEE, James McDevitt (R Pa.) April 5, 1877-April 16, 1949; House 1923-27.

MAGEE, John (D N.Y.) Sept. 3, 1794-April 5, 1868; House 1827-31.

MAGEE, John Alexander (D Pa.) Oct. 14, 1827-Nov. 18, 1903; House 1873-75.

MAGEE, Walter Warren (R N.Y.) May 23, 1861-May 25, 1927; House 1915-May 25, 1927.

MAGINNIS, Martin (D Mont.) Oct. 27, 1841-March 27, 1919; House (Terr. Del.) 1873-85.

MAGNER, Thomas Francis (uncle of John Francis Carew) (D N.Y.) March 8, 1860-Dec. 22, 1945; House 1889-95.

MAGNUSON, Donald Hammer (D Wash.) March 7, 1911-Oct. 5, 1979; House 1953-63.

MAGNUSON, Warren Grant (D Wash.) April 12, 1905- —; House 1937-Dec. 13, 1944; Senate Dec. 14, 1944-81; Pres. pro tempore Jan. 15, 1979-81.

MAGOON, Henry Sterling (R Wis.) Jan. 31, 1832-March 3, 1889; House 1875-77.

MAGRADY, Frederick William (R Pa.) Nov. 24, 1863-Aug. 27, 1954; House 1925-33.

MAGRUDER, Allan Bowie (D La.) 1775-April 15, 1822; Senate Sept. 3, 1812-13.

MAGRUDER, Patrick (— Md.) 1768-Dec. 24, 1819; House 1805-07.

MAGUIRE, Gene Andrew (D N.J.) March 11, 1939- —; House 1975-81.

MAGUIRE, James George (D Calif.) Feb. 22, 1853-June 20, 1920; House 1893-99.

MAGUIRE, John Arthur (D Neb.) Nov. 29, 1870-July 1, 1939; House 1909-15.

MAHAN, Bryan Francis (D Conn.) May 1, 1856-Nov. 16, 1923; House 1913-15.

MAHANY, Rowland Blennerhassett (R N.Y.) Sept. 28, 1864-May 2, 1937; House 1895-99.

MAHER, James Paul (D N.Y.) Nov. 3, 1865-July 31, 1946; House 1911-21.

MAHON, Gabriel Heyward Jr. (D S.C.) Nov. 11, 1889-June 11, 1962; House Nov. 3, 1936-39.

MAHON, George Herman (D Texas) Sept. 22, 1900-Nov. 19, 1985; House 1935-79.

MAHON, Thaddeus Maclay (R Pa.) May 21, 1840-May 31, 1916; House 1893-1907.

MAHONE, William (Read. Va.) Dec. 1, 1826-Oct. 8, 1895; Senate 1881-87.

MAHONEY, Peter Paul (D N.Y.) June 25, 1848-March 27, 1889; House 1885-89.

MAHONEY, William Frank (D Ill.) Feb. 22, 1856-Dec. 27, 1904; House 1901-Dec. 27, 1904.

MAILLIARD, William Somers (R Calif.) June 10, 1917- —; House 1953-March 5, 1974.

MAIN, Verner Wright (R Mich.) Dec. 16, 1885-July 6, 1965; House Dec. 17, 1935-37.

MAISH, Levi (D Pa.) Nov. 22, 1837-Feb. 26, 1899; House 1875-79, 1887-91.

MAJOR, James Earl (D Ill.) Jan. 5, 1887-Jan. 4, 1972; House 1923-25, 1927-29, 1931-Oct. 6, 1933.

MAJOR, Samuel Collier (D Mo.) July 2, 1869-July 28, 1931; House 1919-21, 1923-29, March 4-July 28, 1931.

MAJORS, Thomas Jefferson (R Neb.) June 25, 1841-July 11, 1932; House Nov. 5, 1878-79.

MALBONE, Francis (F R.I.) March 20, 1759-June 4, 1809; House 1793-97; Senate March 4-June 4, 1809.

MALBY, George Roland (R N.Y.) Sept. 16, 1857-July 5, 1912; House 1907-July 5, 1912.

MALLARY, Richard Walker (R Vt.) Feb. 21, 1929- —; House Jan. 7, 1972-75.

MALLARY, Rollin Carolas (— Vt.) May 27, 1784-April 16, 1831; House Jan. 13, 1820-April 16, 1831.

MALLORY, Francis (W Va.) Dec. 12, 1807-March 26, 1860; House 1837-39, Dec. 28, 1840-43.

MALLORY, Meredith (D N.Y.) ?-?; House 1839-41.

MALLORY, Robert (UD Ky.) Nov. 15, 1815-Aug. 11, 1885; House 1859-65.

MALLORY, Rufus (UR Ore.) Jan. 10, 1831-April 30, 1914; House 1867-69.

MALLORY, Stephen Russell (father of Stephen Russell Mallory, below) (D Fla.) 1812-Nov. 9, 1873; Senate 1851-Jan. 21, 1861.

MALLORY, Stephen Russell (son of Stephen Russell Mallory, above) (D Fla.) Nov. 2, 1848-Dec. 23, 1907; House 1891-95; Senate May 15, 1897-Dec. 23, 1907.

MALONE, George Wilson (R Nev.) Aug. 7, 1890-May 19, 1961; Senate 1947-59.

MALONEY, Francis Thomas (D Conn.) March 31, 1894-Jan. 16, 1945; House 1933-35; Senate 1935-Jan. 16, 1945.

MALONEY, Franklin John (R Pa.) March 29, 1899-Sept. 15, 1958; House 1947-49.

MALONEY, Paul Herbert (D La.) Feb. 14, 1876-March 26, 1967; House 1931-Dec. 15, 1940, 1943-47.

MALONEY, Robert Sarsfield (R Mass.) Feb. 3, 1881-Nov. 8, 1934; House 1921-23.

MANAHAN, James (R Minn.) March 12, 1866-Jan. 8, 1932; House 1913-15.

MANASCO, Carter (D Ala.) Jan. 3, 1902-—; House June 24, 1941-49.

MANDERSON, Charles Frederick (R Neb.) Feb. 9, 1837-Sept. 28, 1911; Senate 1883-95; Pres. pro tempore 1891-93.

MANGUM, Willie Person (W N.C.) May 10, 1792-Sept. 7, 1861; House 1823-March 18, 1826; Senate 1831-Nov. 26, 1836, Nov. 25, 1840-53; Pres. pro tempore 1842-45.

MANKIN, Helen Douglas (D Ga.) Sept. 11, 1896-July 25, 1956; House Feb. 12, 1946-47.

MANLOVE, Joe Jonathan (R Mo.) Oct. 1, 1876-Jan. 31, 1956; House 1923-33.

MANN, Abijah Jr. (D N.Y.) Sept. 24, 1793-Sept. 6, 1868; House 1833-37.

MANN, Edward Coke (D S.C.) Nov. 21, 1880-Nov. 11, 1931; House Oct. 7, 1919-21.

MANN, Horace (FS Mass.) May 4, 1796-Aug. 2, 1859; House April 3, 1848-53 (1848-51 Whig).

MANN, James (D La.) June 22, 1822-Aug. 26, 1868; House July 18-Aug. 26, 1868.

MANN, James Robert (R Ill.) Oct. 20, 1856-Nov. 30, 1922; House 1897-Nov. 30, 1922.

MANN, James Robert (D S.C.) April 27, 1920-—; House 1969-79.

MANN, Job (D Pa.) March 31, 1795-Oct. 8, 1873; House 1835-37, 1847-51.

MANN, Joel Keith (D Pa.) Aug. 1, 1780-Aug. 28, 1857; House 1831-35.

MANNING, John Jr. (D N.C.) July 30, 1830-Feb. 12, 1899; House Dec. 7, 1870-71.

MANNING, Richard Irvine I (cousin of John Peter Richardson II) (D S.C.) May 1, 1789-May 1, 1836; House Dec. 8, 1834-May 1, 1836; Gov. 1824-26 (Democratic Republican).

MANNING, Vannoy Hartrog (D Miss.) July 26, 1839-Nov. 3, 1892; House 1877-83.

MANSFIELD, Joseph Jefferson (D Texas) Feb. 9, 1861-July 12, 1947; House 1917-July 12, 1947.

MANSFIELD, Michael Joseph (D Mont.) March 16, 1903-—; House 1943-53; Senate 1953-77; Senate majority leader 1961-77.

MANSON, Mahlon Dickerson (D Ind.) Feb. 20, 1820-Feb. 4, 1895; House 1871-73.

MANSUR, Charles Harley (D Mo.) March 6, 1835-April 16, 1895; House 1887-93.

MANTLE, Lee (R Mont.) Dec. 13, 1851-Nov. 18, 1934; Senate Jan. 16, 1895-99.

MANTON, Thomas J. (D N.Y.) Nov. 3, 1932-—; House 1985-—.

MANZANARES, Francisco Antonio (D N.M.) Jan. 25, 1843-Sept. 17, 1904; House (Terr. Del.) March 5, 1884-85.

MAPES, Carl Edgar (R Mich.) Dec. 26, 1874-Dec. 12, 1939; House 1913-Dec. 12, 1939.

MARABLE, John Hartwell (NR Tenn.) Nov. 18, 1786-April 11, 1844; House 1825-29.

MARAZITI, Joseph James (R N.J.) June 15, 1912-—; House 1973-75.

MARCANTONIO, Vito (AL N.Y.) Dec. 10, 1902-Aug. 9, 1954; House 1935-37 (Republican), 1939-51.

MARCHAND, Albert Gallatin (son of David Marchand) (D Pa.) Feb. 27, 1811-Feb. 5, 1848; House 1839-43.

MARCHAND, David (father of Albert Gallatin Marchand) (— Pa.) Dec. 10, 1776-March 11, 1832; House 1817-21.

MARCY, Daniel (D N.H.) Nov. 7, 1809-Nov. 3, 1893; House 1863-65.

MARCY, William Learned (JD N.Y.) Dec. 12, 1786-July 4, 1857; Senate 1831-Jan. 1, 1833; Gov. 1833-39; Secy. of War 1845-49; Secy. of State 1853-57.

MARDIS, Samuel Wright (D Ala.) June 12, 1800-Nov. 14, 1836; House 1831-35.

MARION, Robert (— S.C.) ?-?; House 1805-Dec. 4, 1810.

MARKELL, Henry (son of Jacob Markell) (D N.Y.) Feb. 7, 1792-Aug. 30, 1831; House 1825-29.

MARKELL, Jacob (father of Henry Markell) (F N.Y.) May 8, 1770-Nov. 26, 1852; House 1813-15.

MARKEY, Edward John (D Mass.) July 11, 1946--; House Nov. 2, 1976--.

MARKHAM, Henry Harrison (R Calif.) Nov. 16, 1840-Oct. 9, 1923; House 1885-87; Gov. 1891-95.

MARKLEY, Philip Swenk (D Pa.) July 2, 1789-Sept. 12, 1834; House 1823-27.

MARKS, Marc Lincoln (R Pa.) Feb. 12, 1927--; House 1977-83.

MARKS, William (D Pa.) Oct. 13, 1778-April 10, 1858; Senate 1825-31.

MARLAND, Ernest Whitworth (D Okla.) May 8, 1874-Oct. 3, 1941; House 1933-35; Gov. 1935-39.

MARLENEE, Ronald Charles (R Mont.) Aug. 8, 1935- --; House 1977--.

MARQUETTE, Turner Mastin (R Neb.) July 19, 1831-Dec. 22, 1894; House March 2-3, 1867.

MARR, Alem (D Pa.) June 18, 1787-March 29, 1843; House 1829-31.

MARR, George Washington Lent (-- Tenn.) May 25, 1779-Sept. 5, 1856; House 1817-19.

MARRIOTT, David Daniel (R Utah) Nov. 2, 1939--; House 1977-85.

MARSALIS, John Henry (D Colo.) May 9, 1904--; House 1949-51.

MARSH, Benjamin Franklin (R Ill.) 1839-June 2, 1905; House 1877-83, 1893-1901, 1903-June 2, 1905.

MARSH, Charles (father of George Perkins Marsh) (F Vt.) July 10, 1765-Jan. 11, 1849; House 1815-17.

MARSH, George Perkins (son of Charles Marsh) (W Vt.) March 15, 1801-July 24, 1882; House 1843-May 1849.

MARSH, John O. Jr. (D Va.) Aug. 7, 1926--; House 1963-71.

MARSHALL, Alexander Keith (AP Ky.) Feb. 11, 1808-April 28, 1884; House 1855-57.

MARSHALL, Alfred (D Maine) about 1797-Oct. 2, 1868; House 1841-43.

MARSHALL, Edward Chauncey (D Calif.) June 29, 1821-July 9, 1893; House 1851-53.

MARSHALL, Fred (D Minn.) March 13, 1906-June 5, 1985; House 1949-63.

MARSHALL, George Alexander (D Ohio) Sept. 14, 1851-April 21, 1899; House 1897-99.

MARSHALL, Humphrey (grandfather of Humphrey Marshall, below, father of Thomas Alexander Marshall, cousin of John Marshall) (F Ky.) 1760-July 1, 1841; Senate 1795-1801.

MARSHALL, Humphrey (grandson of Humphrey Marshall, above) (AP Ky.) Jan. 13, 1812-March 28, 1872; House 1849-Aug. 4, 1852 (Whig), 1855-59.

MARSHALL, James William (D Va.) March 31, 1844-Nov. 27, 1911; House 1893-95.

MARSHALL, John (uncle of Thomas Francis Marshall, cousin of Humphrey Marshall) (-- Va.) Sept. 24, 1755-July 6, 1835; House 1799-June 7, 1800; Secy. of State June 6, 1800-March 4, 1801; Chief Justice United States 1801-35.

MARSHALL, Leroy Tate (R Ohio) Nov. 8, 1883-Nov. 22, 1950; House 1933-37.

MARSHALL, Lycurgus Luther (R Ohio) July 9, 1888-Jan. 12, 1958; House 1939-41.

MARSHALL, Samuel Scott (D Ill.) March 12, 1821-July 26, 1890; House 1855-59, 1865-75.

MARSHALL, Thomas Alexander (son of Humphrey Marshall) (W Ky.) Jan. 15, 1794-April 17, 1871; House 1831-35.

MARSHALL, Thomas Francis (nephew of John Marshall) (-- Ky.) June 7, 1801-Sept. 22, 1864; House 1841-43.

MARSHALL, Thomas Frank (R N.D.) March 7, 1854-Aug. 20, 1921; House 1901-09.

MARSTON, Gilman (R N.H.) Aug. 20, 1811-July 3, 1890; House 1859-63, 1865-67; Senate March 4-June 18, 1889.

MARTIN, Alexander (-- N.C.) 1740-Nov. 10, 1807; Senate 1793-99; Gov. 1789-92.

MARTIN, Augustus Newton (D Ind.) March 23, 1847-July 11, 1901; House 1889-95.

MARTIN, Barclay (uncle of Lewis Tillman) (D Tenn.) Dec. 17, 1802-Nov. 8, 1890; House 1845-47.

MARTIN, Benjamin Franklin (D W.Va.) Oct. 2, 1828-Jan. 20, 1895; House 1877-81.

MARTIN, Charles (D Ill.) May 20, 1856-Oct. 28, 1917; House March 4-Oct. 28, 1917.

MARTIN, Charles Drake (D Ohio) Aug. 5, 1829-Aug. 27, 1911; House 1859-61.

MARTIN, Charles Henry (great-grandson of Nathaniel Macon) (P N.C.) Aug. 28, 1848-April 19, 1931; House June 5, 1896-99.

MARTIN, Charles Henry (D Ore.) Oct. 1, 1863-Sept. 22, 1946; House 1931-35; Gov. 1935-39.

MARTIN, David O'Brien (R N.Y.) April 26, 1944- —; House 1981- —.

MARTIN, David Thomas (R Neb.) July 9, 1907- —; House 1961-Dec. 31, 1974.

MARTIN, Eben Wever (R S.D.) April 12, 1855-May 22, 1932; House 1901-07, Nov. 3, 1908-15.

MARTIN, Edward (R Pa.) Sept. 18, 1879-March 19, 1967; Senate 1947-59; Gov. 1943-47.

MARTIN, Edward Livingston (D Del.) March 29, 1837-Jan. 22, 1897; House 1879-83.

MARTIN, Elbert Sevier (brother of John Preston Martin) (AP Va.) about 1829-Sept. 3, 1876; House 1859-61.

MARTIN, Frederick Stanley (W N.Y.) April 25, 1794-June 28, 1865; House 1851-53.

MARTIN, George Brown (grandson of John Preston Martin) (D Ky.) Aug. 18, 1876-Nov. 12, 1945; Senate Sept. 7, 1918-19.

MARTIN, James D. (R Ala.) Sept. 1, 1918- —; House 1965-67.

MARTIN, James Grubbs (R N.C.) Dec. 11, 1935- —; House 1973-85; Gov. 1985- —.

MARTIN, John (D Kan.) Nov. 12, 1833-Sept. 3, 1913; Senate 1893-95.

MARTIN, John Andrew (D Colo.) April 10, 1868-Dec. 23, 1939; House 1909-13, 1933-Dec. 23, 1939.

MARTIN, John Cunningham (D Ill.) April 29, 1880-Jan. 27, 1952; House 1939-41.

MARTIN, John Mason (son of Joshua Lanier Martin) (D Ala.) Jan. 20, 1837-June 16, 1898; House 1885-87.

MARTIN, John Preston (brother of Elbert Sevier Martin, grandfather of George Brown Martin) (D Ky.) Oct. 11, 1811-Dec. 23, 1862; House 1845-47.

MARTIN, Joseph John (R N.C.) Nov. 21, 1833-Dec. 18, 1900; House 1879-Jan. 29, 1881.

MARTIN, Joseph William Jr. (R Mass.) Nov. 3, 1884-March 6, 1968; House 1925-67; Speaker 1947-49, 1953-55; Chrmn. Rep. Nat. Comm. 1940-42.

MARTIN, Joshua Lanier (father of John Mason Martin) (D Ala.) Dec. 5, 1799-Nov. 2, 1856; House 1835-39; Gov. 1845-47.

MARTIN, Lewis J. (D N.J.) Feb. 22, 1844-May 5, 1913; House March 4-May 5, 1913.

MARTIN, Lynn Morley (R Ill.) Dec. 26, 1939- —; House 1981- —.

MARTIN, Morgan Lewis (cousin of James Duane Doty) (D Wis.) March 31, 1805-Dec. 10, 1887; House (Terr Del.) 1845-47.

MARTIN, Patrick Minor (R Calif.) Nov. 25, 1924-July 18, 1968; House 1963-65.

MARTIN, Robert Nicols (D Md.) Jan. 14, 1798-July 20 1870; House 1825-27.

MARTIN, Thomas Ellsworth (R Iowa) Jan. 18, 1893 June 27, 1971; House 1939-55; Senate 1955-61.

MARTIN, Thomas Staples (D Va.) July 29, 1847-Nov 12, 1919; Senate 1895-Nov. 12, 1919; Senate majority leader 1917-19.

MARTIN, Whitmell Pugh (D La.) Aug. 12, 1867-April 6 1929; House 1915-April 6, 1929 (1915-19 Progres sive).

MARTIN, William Dickinson (D S.C.) Oct. 20, 1789 Nov. 17, 1833; House 1827-31.

MARTIN, William Harrison (D Texas) May 23, 1823 Feb. 3, 1898; House Nov. 4, 1887-91.

MARTINDALE, Henry Clinton (W N.Y.) May 6, 1780 April 22, 1860; House 1823-31, 1833-35.

MARTINE, James Edgar (D N.J.) Aug. 25, 1850-Feb 26, 1925; Senate 1911-17.

MARTINEZ, Matthew G. (D. Calif.) Feb. 14, 1929- — House July 15, 1982- —.

MARVIN, Dudley (W N.Y.) May 9, 1786-June 25, 1856 House 1823-29 (Adams Democrat), 1847-49.

MARVIN, Francis (R N.Y.) March 8, 1828-Aug. 14 1905; House 1893-95.

MARVIN, James Madison (U N.Y.) Feb. 27, 1809-Apri 25, 1901; House 1863-69.

MARVIN, Richard Pratt (W N.Y.) Dec. 23, 1803-Jan 11, 1892; House 1837-41.

MASON, Armistead Thomson (son of Stevens Thomso Mason) (D Va.) Aug. 4, 1787-Feb. 6, 1819; Senat Jan. 3, 1816-17.

MASON, Harry Howland (D Ill.) Dec. 16, 1873-Marc 10, 1946; House 1935-37.

MASON, James Brown (F R.I.) Jan. 1775-Aug. 31, 181 House 1815-19.

MASON, James Murray (JD Va.) Nov. 3, 1798-April 28, 1871; House 1837-39; Senate Jan. 21, 1847-March 28, 1861; Pres. pro tempore 1857.

MASON, Jeremiah (F N.H.) April 27, 1768-Oct. 14, 1848; Senate June 10, 1813-June 16, 1817.

MASON, John Calvin (JD Ky.) Aug. 4, 1802-Aug. 1865; House 1849-53, 1857-59.

MASON, John Thomson (D Md.) May 9, 1815-March 28, 1873; House 1841-43.

MASON, John Young (D Va.) April 18, 1799-Oct. 3, 1859; House 1831-Jan. 11, 1837; Secy. of the Navy 1844-45, 1846-49; Atty. Gen. 1845-46.

MASON, Jonathan (F Mass.) Aug. 30, 1752-Nov. 1, 1831; Senate Nov. 14, 1800-03; House 1817-May 15, 1820.

MASON, Joseph (R N.Y.) March 30, 1828-May 31, 1914; House 1879-83.

MASON, Moses Jr. (D Maine) June 2, 1789-June 25, 1866; House 1833-37.

MASON, Noah Morgan (R Ill.) July 19, 1882-March 29, 1965; House 1937-63.

MASON, Samson (W Ohio) July 24, 1793-Feb. 1, 1869; House 1835-43.

MASON, Stevens Thomson (father of Armistead Thomson Mason) (D Va.) Dec. 29, 1760-May 10, 1803; Senate Nov. 18, 1794-May 10, 1803.

MASON, William (D N.Y.) Sept. 10, 1786-Jan. 13, 1860; House 1835-37.

MASON, William Ernest (father of Winnifred Sprague Mason Huck) (R Ill.) July 7, 1850-June 16, 1921; House 1887-91, 1917-June 16, 1921; Senate 1897-1903.

MASSEY, William Alexander (R Nev.) Oct. 7, 1856-March 5, 1914; Senate July 1, 1912-Jan. 29, 1913.

MASSEY, Zachary David (R Tenn.) Nov. 14, 1864-July 13, 1923; House Nov. 8, 1910-11.

MASSINGALE, Samuel Chapman (D Okla.) Aug. 2, 1870-Jan. 17, 1941; House 1935-Jan. 17, 1941.

MASTERS, Josiah (D N.Y.) Nov. 22, 1763-June 30, 1822; House 1805-09.

MATHEWS, Frank Asbury Jr. (R N.J.) Aug. 3, 1890-Feb. 5, 1964; House Nov. 6, 1945-49.

MATHEWS, George (− Ga.) Aug. 30, 1739-Aug. 30, 1812; House 1789-91; Gov. 1793-96 (Democratic Republican).

MATHEWS, George Arthur (R Dakota) June 4, 1852-April 19, 1941; House (Terr. Del.) March 4-Nov. 2, 1889.

MATHEWS, James (D Ohio) June 4, 1805-March 30, 1887; House 1841-45.

MATHEWS, Vincent (F N.Y.) June 29, 1766-Aug. 23, 1846; House 1809-11.

MATHEWSON, Elisha (D R.I.) April 18, 1767-Oct. 14, 1853; Senate Oct. 26, 1807-11.

MATHIAS, Charles McCurdy Jr. (R Md.) July 24, 1922-−; House 1961-69; Senate 1969-87.

MATHIAS, Robert B. (R Calif.) Nov. 17, 1930-−; House 1967-75.

MATHIOT, Joshua (W Ohio) April 4, 1800-July 30, 1849; House 1841-43.

MATHIS, Marvin Dawson (D Ga.) Nov. 30, 1940-−; House 1971-81.

MATLACK, James (− N.J.) Jan. 11, 1775-Jan. 16, 1840; House 1821-25.

MATSON, Aaron (− N.H.) 1770-July 18, 1855; House 1821-25.

MATSON, Courtland Cushing (D Ind.) April 25, 1841-Sept. 4, 1915; House 1881-89.

MATSUI, Robert Takeo (D Calif.) Sept. 17, 1941-−; House 1979-−.

MATSUNAGA, Spark Masayuki (D Hawaii) Oct. 8, 1916-−; House 1963-77; Senate 1977-−.

MATTESON, Orsamus Benajah (W N.Y.) Aug. 28, 1805-Dec. 22, 1889; House 1849-51, 1853-Feb. 27, 1857, March 4, 1857-59.

MATTHEWS, Charles (R Pa.) Oct. 15, 1856-Dec. 12, 1932; House 1911-13.

MATTHEWS, Donald Ray "Billy" (D Fla.) Oct. 3, 1907-−; House 1953-67.

MATTHEWS, Nelson Edwin (R Ohio) April 14, 1852-Oct. 13, 1917; House 1915-17.

MATTHEWS, Stanley (uncle of Henry Watterson) (R Ohio) July 21, 1824-March 22, 1889; Senate March 21, 1877-79; Assoc. Justice Supreme Court 1881-89.

MATTHEWS, William (− Md.) April 26, 1755-?; House 1797-99.

MATTINGLY, Mack (R Ga.) Jan. 7, 1931-−; Senate 1981-87.

MATTOCKS, John (W Vt.) March 4, 1777-Aug. 14, 1847; House 1821-23, 1825-27, 1841-43; Gov. 1843-44.

MATTOON, Ebenezer (F Mass.) Aug. 19, 1755-Sept. 11, 1843; House Feb. 2, 1801-03.

MATTOX, James Albon (D Texas) Aug. 29, 1943- — ; House 1977-83.

MAURICE, James (D N.Y.) Nov. 7, 1814-Aug. 4, 1884; House 1853-55.

MAURY, Abram Poindexter (cousin of Fontaine Maury Maverick) (W Tenn.) Dec. 26, 1801-July 22, 1848; House 1835-39.

MAVERICK, Fontaine Maury (cousin of Abram Poindexter Maury, nephew of James Luther Slayden, cousin of John Wood Fishburne) (D Texas) Oct. 23, 1895-June 7, 1954; House 1935-39.

MAVROULES, Nicholas (D Mass.) Nov. 1, 1929- — ; House 1979- —.

MAXEY, Samuel Bell (D Texas) March 30, 1825-Aug. 16, 1895; Senate 1875-87.

MAXWELL, Augustus Emmett (grandfather of Emmett Wilson) (D Fla.) Sept. 21, 1820-May 5, 1903; House 1853-57.

MAXWELL, George Clifford (father of John Patterson Bryan Maxwell, uncle of George Maxwell Robeson) (— N.J.) May 31, 1771-March 16, 1816; House 1811-13.

MAXWELL, John Patterson Bryan (son of George Clifford Maxwell, uncle of George Maxwell Robeson) (W N.J.) Sept. 3, 1804-Nov. 14, 1845; House 1837-39, 1841-43.

MAXWELL, Lewis (NR Va.) April 17, 1790-Feb. 13, 1862; House 1827-33.

MAXWELL, Samuel (Fus. Neb.) May 20, 1825-Feb. 11, 1901; House 1897-99.

MAXWELL, Thomas (D N.Y.) Feb. 16, 1792-Nov. 4, 1864; House 1829-31.

MAY, Andrew Jackson (D Ky.) June 24, 1875-Sept. 6, 1959; House 1931-47.

MAY, Catherine Dean Barnes (R Wash.) May 18, 1914- — ; House 1959-71.

MAY, Edwin Hyland Jr. (R Conn.) May 28, 1924- — ; House 1957-59.

MAY, Henry (D Md.) Feb. 13, 1816-Sept. 25, 1866; House 1853-55, 1861-63.

MAY, Mitchell (D N.Y.) July 10, 1870-March 24, 1961; House 1899-1901.

MAY, William L. (D Ill.) about 1793-Sept. 29, 1849; House Dec. 1, 1834-39.

MAYALL, Samuel (D Maine) June 21, 1816-Sept. 17, 1892; House 1853-55.

MAYBANK, Burnet Rhett (D S.C.) March 7, 1899-Sept. 1, 1954; Senate Nov. 5, 1941-Sept. 1, 1954; Gov. 1939-41.

MAYBURY, William Cotter (D Mich.) Nov. 20, 1848-May 6, 1909; House 1883-87.

MAYFIELD, Earle Bradford (D Texas) April 12, 1881-June 23, 1964; Senate 1923-29.

MAYHAM, Stephen Lorenzo (D N.Y.) Oct. 8, 1826-March 3, 1908; House 1869-71, 1877-79.

MAYNARD, Harry Lee (D Va.) June 8, 1861-Oct. 23, 1922; House 1901-11.

MAYNARD, Horace (R Tenn.) Aug. 30, 1814-May 3, 1882; House 1857-63 (American Party), July 24, 1866-75; Postmaster Gen. 1880-81.

MAYNARD, John (W N.Y.) ?-March 24, 1850; House 1827-29, 1841-43.

MAYNE, Wiley (R Iowa) Jan. 19, 1917- — ; House 1967-75.

MAYO, Robert Murphy (Read. Va.) April 28, 1836-March 29, 1896; House 1883-March 20, 1884.

MAYRANT, William (— S.C.) ?-?; House 1815-Oct. 21, 1816.

MAYS, Dannite Hill (D Fla.) April 28, 1852-May 9, 1930; House 1909-13.

MAYS, James Henry (D Utah) June 29, 1868-April 19, 1926; House 1915-21.

MAZZOLI, Romano Louis (D Ky.) Nov. 2, 1932- — ; House 1971- —.

McADOO, William (D N.J.) Oct. 25, 1853-June 7, 1930; House 1883-91.

McADOO, William Gibbs (D Calif.) Oct. 31, 1863-Feb. 1, 1941; Senate 1933-Nov. 8, 1938; Secy. of the Treasury 1913-18.

McALEER, William (D Pa.) Jan. 6, 1838-April 19, 1912; House 1891-95, 1897-1901.

McALLISTER, Archibald (grandson of John Andre Hanna) (D Pa.) Oct. 12, 1813-July 18, 1883; House 1863-65.

McANDREWS, James (D Ill.) Oct. 22, 1862-Aug. 3, 1942; House 1901-05, 1913-21, 1935-41.

McARDLE, Joseph A. (D Pa.) June 29, 1903-Dec. 27, 1967; House 1939-Jan. 5, 1942.

McARTHUR, Clifton Nesmith (grandson of James Willis Nesmith) (R Ore.) June 10, 1879-Dec. 9, 1923; House 1915-23.

McARTHUR, Duncan (D Ohio) Jan. 14, 1772-April 29, 1839; House March 4-April 5, 1813, 1823-25; Gov. 1830-32 (National Republican).

McBRIDE, George Wycliffe (brother of John Rogers McBride) (R Ore.) March 13, 1854-June 18, 1911; Senate 1895-1901.

McBRIDE, John Rogers (brother of George Wycliffe McBride) (R Ore.) Aug. 22, 1832-July 20, 1904; House 1863-65.

McBRYDE, Archibald (D N.C.) Sept. 28, 1766-Feb. 15, 1816; House 1809-13.

McCAIN, John Sidney II (R Ariz.) Aug. 29, 1936- —; House 1983-87; Senate 1987- —.

McCALL, John Ethridge (R Tenn.) Aug. 14, 1859-Aug. 8, 1920; House 1895-97.

McCALL, Samuel Walker (R Mass.) Feb. 28, 1851-Nov. 4, 1923; House 1893-1913; Gov. 1916-19.

McCANDLESS, Alfred A. (R Calif.) July 23, 1927- —; House 1983- —.

McCANDLESS, Lincoln Loy (D Hawaii) Sept. 18, 1859-Oct. 5, 1940; House (Terr. Del.) 1933-35.

McCARRAN, Patrick Anthony (D Nev.) Aug. 8, 1876-Sept. 28, 1954; Senate 1933-Sept. 28, 1954.

McCARTHY, Dennis (R N.Y.) March 19, 1814-Feb. 14, 1886; House 1867-71.

McCARTHY, Eugene Joseph (D Minn.) March 29, 1916- —; House 1949-59; Senate 1959-71.

McCARTHY, John Henry (D N.Y.) Nov. 16, 1850-Feb. 5, 1908; House 1889-Jan. 14, 1891.

McCARTHY, John Jay (R Neb.) July 19, 1857-March 30, 1943; House 1903-07.

McCARTHY, Joseph Raymond (R Wis.) Nov. 14, 1908-May 2, 1957; Senate 1947-May 2, 1957.

McCARTHY, Kathryn O'Loughlin (*See* O'LOUGHLIN, Kathryn Ellen).

McCARTHY, Richard Dean (D N.Y.) Sept. 24, 1927- —; House 1965-71.

McCARTY, Andrew Zimmerman (W N.Y.) July 14, 1808-April 23, 1879; House 1855-57.

McCARTY, Johnathan (W Ind.) Aug. 3, 1795-March 30, 1852; House 1831-37.

McCARTY, Richard (D N.Y.) Feb. 19, 1780-May 18, 1844; House 1821-23.

McCARTY, William Mason (W Va.) about 1789-Dec. 20, 1863; House Jan. 25, 1840-41; Gov. (Fla. Terr.) 1827.

McCAUSLEN, William Cochran (D Ohio) 1796-March 13, 1863; House 1843-45.

McCLAMMY, Charles Washington (D N.C.) May 29, 1839-Feb. 26, 1896; House 1887-91.

McCLEAN, Moses (D Pa.) June 17, 1804-Sept. 30, 1870; House 1845-47.

McCLEARY, James Thompson (R Minn.) Feb. 5, 1853-Dec. 17, 1924; House 1893-1907.

McCLEERY, James (R La.) Dec. 2, 1837-Nov. 5, 1871; House March 4-Nov. 5, 1871.

McCLELLAN, Abraham (D Tenn.) Oct. 4, 1789-May 3, 1866; House 1837-43.

McCLELLAN, Charles A. O. (D Ind.) May 25, 1835-Jan. 31, 1898; House 1889-93.

McCLELLAN, George (D N.Y.) Oct. 10, 1856-Feb. 20, 1927; House 1913-15.

McCLELLAN, George Brinton (D N.Y.) Nov. 23, 1865-Nov. 30, 1940; House 1895-Dec. 21, 1903.

McCLELLAN, John Little (D Ark.) Feb. 25, 1896-Nov. 28, 1977; House 1935-39; Senate 1943-Nov. 28, 1977.

McCLELLAN, Robert (D N.Y.) Oct. 2, 1806-June 28, 1860; House 1837-39, 1841-43.

McCLELLAND, Robert (D Mich.) Aug. 1, 1807-Aug. 30, 1880; House 1843-49; Gov. 1851-53; Secy. of the Interior 1853-57.

McCLELLAND, William (D Pa.) March 2, 1842-Feb. 7, 1892; House 1871-73.

McCLENACHAN, Blair (— Pa.) ?-May 8, 1812; House 1797-99.

McCLERNAND, John Alexander (D Ill.) May 30, 1812-Sept. 20, 1900; House 1843-51, Nov. 8, 1859-Oct. 28, 1861.

McCLINTIC, James Vernon (D Okla.) Sept. 8, 1878-April 22, 1948; House 1915-35.

McCLINTOCK, Charles Blaine (R Ohio) May 25, 1886-Feb. 1, 1965; House 1929-33.

McCLORY, Robert (R Ill.) Jan. 31, 1908- —; House 1963-83.

McCLOSKEY, Augustus (D Texas) Sept. 23, 1878-July 21, 1950; House 1929-Feb. 10, 1930.

McCLOSKEY, Francis X. (D Ind.) June 12, 1939- —; House 1983-85, May 1, 1985- —.

McCLOSKEY, Paul N. "Pete" Jr. (R Calif.) Sept. 29, 1927- —; House Dec. 12, 1967-83.

McCLURE, Addison S. (R Ohio) Oct. 10, 1839-April 17, 1903; House 1881-83, 1895-97.

McCLURE, Charles (D Pa.) 1804-Jan. 10, 1846; House 1837-39, Dec. 7, 1840-41.

McCLURE, James A. (R Idaho) Dec. 27, 1924- —; House 1967-73; Senate 1973- —.

McCLURG, Joseph Washington (Rad. Mo.) Feb. 22, 1818-Dec. 2, 1900; House 1863-68 (1863-65 Emancipationist); Gov. 1869-71 (Republican).

McCOID, Moses Ayres (R Iowa) Nov. 5, 1840-May 19, 1904; House 1879-85.

McCOLLISTER, John Yetter (R Neb.) June 10, 1921- —; House 1971-77.

McCOLLUM, Bill (R Fla.) July 12, 1944- —; House 1981- —.

McCOMAS, Louis Emory (grandfather of Katherine Edgar Byron, great-grandfather of Goodloe Edgar Byron) (R Md.) Oct. 28, 1846-Nov. 10, 1907; House 1883-91; Senate 1899-1905.

McCOMAS, William (W Va.) 1795-June 3, 1865; House 1833-37.

McCONNELL, Addison Mitchell Jr. (R Ky.) Feb. 20, 1942- —; Senate 1985- —.

McCONNELL, Felix Grundy (D Ala.) April 1, 1809-Sept. 10, 1846; House 1843-Sept. 10, 1846.

McCONNELL, Samuel Kerns Jr. (R Pa.) April 6, 1901- —; House Jan. 18, 1944-Sept. 1, 1957.

McCONNELL, William John (R Idaho) Sept. 18, 1839-March 30, 1925; Senate Dec. 18, 1890-91; Gov. 1893-97.

McCOOK, Anson George (R N.Y.) Oct. 10, 1835-Dec. 30, 1917; House 1877-83.

McCORD, Andrew (— N.Y.) about 1754-1808; House 1803-05.

McCORD, James Nance (D Tenn.) March 17, 1879-Sept. 2, 1968; House 1943-45; Gov. 1945-49.

McCORD, Myron Hawley (R Wis.) Nov. 26, 1840-April 27, 1908; House 1889-91; Gov. (Ariz. Terr.) 1897-98.

McCORKLE, Joseph Walker (D Calif.) June 24, 1819-March 18, 1884; House 1851-53.

McCORKLE, Paul Grier (D S.C.) Dec. 19, 1863-June 2, 1934; House Feb. 24-March 3, 1917.

McCORMACK, John William (D Mass.) Dec. 21, 1891-Nov. 22, 1980; House Nov. 6, 1928-71; House majority leader 1940-47, 1949-53, 1955-62; Speaker 1962-71.

McCORMACK, Mike (D Wash.) Dec. 14, 1921- —; House 1971-81.

McCORMICK, Henry Clay (R Pa.) June 30, 1844-May 26, 1902; House 1887-91.

McCORMICK, James Robinson (D Mo.) Aug. 1, 1824-May 19, 1897; House Dec. 17, 1867-73.

McCORMICK, John Watts (R Ohio) Dec. 20, 1831-June 25, 1917; House 1883-85.

McCORMICK, Joseph Medill (husband of Ruth Hanna McCormick) (R Ill.) May 16, 1877-Feb. 25, 1925; House 1917-19; Senate 1919-Feb. 25, 1925.

McCORMICK, Nelson B. (P Kan.) Nov. 20, 1847-April 10, 1914; House 1897-99.

McCORMICK, Richard Cunningham (R N.Y.) May 23, 1832-June 2, 1901; House (Unionist Terr. Del. Ariz.) 1869-75, (Rep.) 1895-97; Gov. (Unionist Ariz. Terr.) 1866.

McCORMICK, Ruth Hanna (daughter of Marcus Alonzo Hanna, widow of Joseph Medill McCormick and of Albert Gallatin Simms) (R Ill.) March 27, 1880-Dec. 31, 1944; House 1929-31.

McCORMICK, Washington Jay (R Mont.) Jan. 4, 1884-March 7, 1949; House 1921-23.

McCOWEN, Edward Oscar (R Ohio) June 29, 1877-Nov. 4, 1953; House 1943-49.

McCOY, Robert (— Pa.) ?-June 7, 1849; House Nov. 22, 1831-33.

McCOY, Walter Irving (D N.J.) Dec. 8, 1859-July 17, 1933; House 1911-Oct. 3, 1914.

McCOY, William (D Va.) ?-1864; House 1811-33.

McCRACKEN, Robert McDowell (R Idaho) March 1, 1874-May 16, 1934; House 1915-17.

McCRARY, George Washington (R Iowa) Aug. 29, 1835-June 23, 1890; House 1869-77; Secy. of War 1877-79.

McCRATE, John Dennis (D Maine) Oct. 1, 1802-Sept. 11, 1879; House 1845-47.

McCREARY, George Deardorff (R Pa.) Sept. 28, 1846-July 26, 1915; House 1903-13.

McCREARY, James Bennett (D Ky.) July 8, 1838-Oct. 8, 1918; House 1885-97; Senate 1903-09; Gov. 1875-79, 1911-15.

McCREARY, John (– S.C.) 1761-Nov. 4, 1833; House 1819-21.

McCREDIE, William Wallace (R Wash.) April 27, 1862-May 10, 1935; House Nov. 2, 1909-11.

McCREERY, Thomas Clay (D Ky.) Dec. 12, 1816-July 10, 1890; Senate Feb. 19, 1868-71, 1873-79.

McCREERY, William (– Md.) 1750-March 8, 1814; House 1803-09.

McCREERY, William (D Pa.) May 17, 1786-Sept. 27, 1841; House 1829-31.

McCULLOCH, George (D Pa.) Feb. 22, 1792-April 6, 1861; House Nov. 20, 1839-41.

McCULLOCH, John (W Pa.) Nov. 15, 1806-May 15, 1879; House 1853-55.

McCULLOCH, Philip Doddridge Jr. (D Ark.) June 23, 1851-Nov. 26, 1928; House 1893-1903.

McCULLOCH, Roscoe Conkling (R Ohio) Nov. 27, 1880-March 17, 1958; House 1915-21; Senate Nov. 5, 1929-Nov. 30, 1930.

McCULLOCH, William Moore (R Ohio) Nov. 24, 1901-Feb. 22, 1980; House Nov. 4, 1947-73.

McCULLOGH, Welty (R Pa.) Oct. 10, 1847-Aug. 31, 1889; House 1887-89.

McCULLOUGH, Hiram (D Md.) Sept. 26, 1813-March 4, 1885; House 1865-69.

McCULLOUGH, Thomas Grubb (– Pa.) April 20, 1785-Sept. 10, 1848; House Oct. 17, 1820-21.

McCUMBER, Porter James (R N.D.) Feb. 3, 1858-May 18, 1933; Senate 1899-1923.

McCURDY, David K. (D Okla.) March 30, 1950-–; House 1981-–.

McDADE, Joseph Michael (R Pa.) Sept. 29, 1931-–; House 1963-–.

McDANIEL, William (D Mo.) ?-about 1854; House Dec. 7, 1846-47.

McDANNOLD, John James (D Ill.) Aug. 29, 1851-Feb. 3, 1904; House 1893-95.

McDEARMON, James Calvin (D Tenn.) June 13, 1844-July 19, 1902; House 1893-97.

McDERMOTT, Allan Langdon (D N.J.) March 30, 1854-Oct. 26, 1908; House Dec. 3, 1900-07.

McDERMOTT, James Thomas (D Ill.) Feb. 13, 1872-Feb. 7, 1938; House 1907-July 21, 1914, 1915-17.

McDILL, Alexander Stuart (R Wis.) March 18, 1822-Nov. 12, 1875; House 1873-75.

McDILL, James Wilson (R Iowa) March 4, 1834-Feb. 28, 1894; House 1873-77; Senate March 8, 1881-83.

McDONALD, Alexander (R Ark.) April 10, 1832-Dec. 13, 1903; Senate June 22, 1868-71.

McDONALD, Edward Francis (D N.J.) Sept. 21, 1844-Nov. 5, 1892; House 1891-Nov. 5, 1892.

McDONALD, Jack H. (R Mich.) June 28, 1932-–; House 1967-73.

McDONALD, John (R Md.) May 24, 1837-Jan. 30, 1917; House 1897-99.

McDONALD, Joseph Ewing (D Ind.) Aug. 29, 1819-June 21, 1891; House 1849-51; Senate 1875-81.

McDONALD, Lawrence Patton (D Ga.) April 1, 1935-Sept. 1, 1983; House 1975-Sept. 1, 1983.

McDONOUGH, Gordon Leo (R Calif.) Jan. 2, 1895-June 25, 1968; House 1945-63.

McDOUGALL, James Alexander (D Calif.) Nov. 19, 1817-Sept. 3, 1867; House 1853-55; Senate 1861-67.

McDOWELL, Alexander (R Pa.) March 4, 1845-Sept. 30, 1913; House 1893-95.

McDOWELL, Harris Brown Jr. (D Del.) Feb. 10, 1906-–; House 1955-57, 1959-67.

McDOWELL, James (D Va.) Oct. 13, 1796-Aug. 24, 1851; House March 6, 1846-51; Gov. 1843-46.

McDOWELL, James Foster (D Ind.) Dec. 3, 1825-April 18, 1887; House 1863-65.

McDOWELL, John Anderson (D Ohio) Sept. 25, 1853-Oct. 2, 1927; House 1897-1901.

McDOWELL, John Ralph (R Pa.) Nov. 6, 1902-Dec. 11, 1957; House 1939-41, 1947-49.

McDOWELL, Joseph (father of Joseph Jefferson McDowell, cousin of Joseph McDowell, below) (– N.C.) Feb. 15, 1756-Feb. 5, 1801; House 1797-99.

McDOWELL, Joseph (P G) (cousin of Joseph McDowell, above) (– N.C.) Feb. 25, 1758-March 7, 1799; House 1793-95.

McDOWELL, Joseph Jefferson (son of Joseph McDowell) (D Ohio) Nov. 13, 1800-Jan. 17, 1877; House 1843-47.

McDUFFIE, George (father-in-law of Wade Hampton) (D S.C.) Aug. 10, 1790-March 11, 1851; House 1821-34; Senate Dec. 23, 1842-Aug. 17, 1846; Gov. 1834-36 (State Rights Democrat).

McDUFFIE, John (D Ala.) Sept. 25, 1883-Nov. 1, 1950; House 1919-March 2, 1935.

McDUFFIE, John Van (R Ala.) May 16, 1841-Nov. 18, 1896; House June 4, 1890-91.

McENERY, Samuel Douglas (D La.) May 28, 1837-June 28, 1910; Senate 1897-June 28, 1910; Gov. 1881-88.

McETTRICK, Michael Joseph (D Mass.) June 22, 1848-Dec. 31, 1921; House 1893-95.

McEWAN, Thomas Jr. (R N.J.) Feb. 26, 1854-Sept. 11, 1926; House 1895-99.

McEWEN, Robert Cameron (R N.Y.) Jan. 5, 1920- —; House 1965-81.

McEWEN, Robert D. (R Ohio) Jan. 12, 1950- —; House 1981- —.

McFADDEN, Louis Thomas (R Pa.) July 25, 1876-Oct. 1, 1936; House 1915-35.

McFADDEN, Obadiah Benton (D Wash.) Nov. 18, 1815-June 25, 1875; House (Terr. Del.) 1873-75.

McFALL, John Joseph (D Calif.) Feb. 20, 1918- —; House 1957-Dec. 31, 1978.

McFARLAN, Duncan (— N.C.) ?-Sept. 7, 1816; House 1805-07.

McFARLAND, Ernest William (D Ariz.) Oct. 9, 1894-June 8, 1984; Senate 1941-53; Senate majority leader 1951-53; Gov. 1955-59.

McFARLAND, William (D Tenn.) Sept. 15, 1821-April 12, 1900; House 1875-77.

McFARLANE, William Doddridge (D Texas) July 17, 1894-Feb. 18, 1980; House 1933-39.

McGANN, Lawrence Edward (D Ill.) Feb. 2, 1852-July 22, 1928; House 1891-Dec. 2, 1895.

McGARVEY, Robert Neill (R Pa.) Aug. 14, 1888-June 28, 1952; House 1947-49.

McGAUGHEY, Edward Wilson (W Ind.) Jan. 16, 1817-Aug. 6, 1852; House 1845-47, 1849-51.

McGAVIN, Charles (R Ill.) Jan. 10, 1874-Dec. 17, 1940; House 1905-09.

McGEE, Gale William (D Wyo.) March 17, 1915- —; Senate 1959-77.

McGEHEE, Daniel Rayford (D Miss.) Sept. 10, 1883-Feb. 9, 1962; House 1935-47.

McGILL, George (D Kan.) Feb. 12, 1879-May 14, 1963; Senate Dec. 1, 1930-39.

McGILLICUDDY, Daniel John (D Maine) Aug. 27 1859-July 30, 1936; House 1911-17.

McGINLEY, Donald Francis (D Neb.) June 30, 1920- — House 1959-61.

McGLENNON, Cornelius Augustine (D N.J.) Dec. 10 1878-June 13, 1931; House 1919-21.

McGLINCHEY, Herbert Joseph (D Pa.) Nov. 7, 1904 —; House 1945-47.

McGOVERN, George Stanley (D S.D.) July 19, 1922- — House 1957-61; Senate 1963-81.

McGOWAN, Jonas Hartzell (R Mich.) April 2, 1837 July 5, 1909; House 1877-81.

McGRANERY, James Patrick (D Pa.) July 8, 1895-Dec 23, 1962; House 1937-Nov. 17, 1943; Atty. Gen. 1952 53.

McGRATH, Christopher Columbus (D N.Y.) May 15 1902-July 7, 1986; House 1949-53.

McGRATH, James Howard (D R.I.) Nov. 28, 1903-Sept 2, 1966; Senate 1947-Aug. 23, 1949; Gov. 1941-45 Chrmn. Dem. Nat. Comm. 1947-49; Atty. Gen. 1949 52.

McGRATH, John Joseph (D Calif.) July 23, 1872-Aug 25, 1951; House 1933-39.

McGRATH, Raymond J. (R N.Y.) March 27, 1941- — House 1981- —.

McGRATH, Thomas C. Jr. (D N.J.) April 22, 1927- — House 1965-67.

McGREGOR, J. Harry (R Ohio) Sept. 30, 1896-Oct. 1 1958; House Feb. 27, 1940-Oct. 7, 1958.

McGREW, James Clark (R W.Va.) Sept. 14, 1813-Sept 18, 1910; House 1869-73.

McGROARTY, John Steven (D Calif.) Aug. 20, 1862 Aug. 7, 1944; House 1935-39.

McGUGIN, Harold Clement (R Kan.) Nov. 22, 1893 March 7, 1946; House 1931-35.

McGUIRE, Bird Segle (cousin of William Neville) (I Okla.) Oct. 13, 1865-Nov. 9, 1930; House (Terr. Del 1903-07, (Rep.) Nov. 16, 1907-15.

McGUIRE, John Andrew (D Conn.) Feb. 28, 1906-Ma 28, 1976; House 1949-53.

McHATTON, Robert Lytle (JD Ky.) Nov. 17, 1788-Ma 20, 1835; House Dec. 7, 1826-29.

McHENRY, Henry Davis (son of John Hardin McHenry) (D Ky.) Feb. 27, 1826-Dec. 17, 1890; House 1871-73.

McHENRY, John Geiser (D Pa.) April 26, 1868-Dec. 27, 1912; House 1907-Dec. 27, 1912.

McHENRY, John Hardin (father of Henry Davis McHenry) (W Ky.) Oct. 13, 1797-Nov. 1, 1871; House 1845-47.

McHUGH, Matthew Francis (D N.Y.) Dec. 6, 1938--; House 1975--.

McILVAINE, Abraham Robinson (W Pa.) Aug. 14, 1804-Aug. 22, 1863; House 1843-49.

McILVAINE, Joseph (D N.J.) Oct. 2, 1769-Aug. 19, 1826; Senate Nov. 12, 1823-Aug. 19, 1826.

McINDOE, Walter Duncan (R Wis.) March 30, 1819-Aug. 22, 1872; House Jan. 26, 1863-67.

McINTIRE, Clifford Guy (R Maine) May 4, 1908-Oct. 1, 1974; House Oct. 22, 1951-65.

McINTIRE, Rufus (JD Maine) Dec. 19, 1784-April 28, 1866; House Sept. 10, 1827-35.

McINTIRE, William Watson (R Md.) June 30, 1850-March 30, 1912; House 1897-99.

McINTOSH, Robert John (R Mich.) Sept. 16, 1922--; House 1957-59.

McINTYRE, John Joseph (D Wyo.) Dec. 17, 1904-Nov. 30, 1974; House 1941-43.

McINTYRE, Thomas James (D N.H.) Feb. 20, 1915--; Senate Nov. 7, 1962-79.

McJUNKIN, Ebenezer (R Pa.) March 28, 1819-Nov. 10, 1907; House 1871-Jan. 1, 1875.

McKAIG, William McMahone (D Md.) July 29, 1845-June 6, 1907; House 1891-95.

McKAY, James Iver (D N.C.) 1793-Sept. 4, 1853; House 1831-49.

McKAY, Koln Gunn (D Utah) Feb. 23, 1925--; House 1971-81.

McKEAN, James Bedell (nephew of Samuel McKean) (R N.Y.) Aug. 5, 1821-Jan. 5, 1879; House 1859-63.

McKEAN, Samuel (uncle of James Bedell McKean) (D Pa.) April 7, 1787-Dec. 14, 1841; House 1823-29; Senate 1833-39.

McKEE, George Colin (R Miss.) Oct. 2, 1837-Nov. 17, 1890; House 1869-75.

McKEE, John (- Ala.) 1771-Aug. 12, 1832; House 1823-29.

McKEE, Samuel (D Ky.) Oct. 13, 1774-Oct. 16, 1826; House 1809-17.

McKEE, Samuel (R Ky.) Nov. 5, 1833-Dec. 11, 1898; House 1865-67, June 22, 1868-69.

McKEIGHAN, William Arthur (I Neb.) Jan. 19, 1842-Dec. 15, 1895; House 1891-95 (1891-93 Democrat).

McKELLAR, Kenneth Douglas (D Tenn.) Jan. 29, 1869-Oct. 25, 1957; House Nov. 9, 1911-17; Senate 1917-53; Pres. pro tempore 1945-47, 1949-53.

McKENNA, Joseph (R Calif.) Aug. 10, 1843-Nov. 21, 1926; House 1885-92; Atty. Gen. 1897-98; Assoc. Justice Supreme Court 1898-1925.

McKENNAN, Thomas McKean Thompson (W Pa.) March 31, 1794-July 9, 1852; House 1831-39, May 30, 1842-43; Secy. of the Interior Aug. 15-Sept. 12, 1850.

McKENNEY, William Robertson (D Va.) Dec. 2, 1851-Jan. 3, 1916; House 1895-May 2, 1896.

McKENTY, Jacob Kerlin (D Pa.) Jan. 19, 1827-Jan. 3, 1866; House Dec. 3, 1860-61.

McKENZIE, Charles Edgar (D La.) Oct. 3, 1896-June 7, 1956; House 1943-47.

McKENZIE, James Andrew (uncle of John McKenzie Moss) (D Ky.) Aug. 1, 1840-June 25, 1904; House 1877-83.

McKENZIE, John Charles (R Ill.) Feb. 18, 1860-Sept. 17, 1941; House 1911-25.

McKENZIE, Lewis (UC Va.) Oct. 7, 1810-June 28, 1895; House Feb. 16-March 3, 1863 (Unionist), Jan. 31, 1870-71.

McKEON, John (D N.Y.) March 29, 1808-Nov. 22, 1883; House 1835-37, 1841-43.

McKEOUGH, Raymond Stephen (D Ill.) April 29, 1888-Dec. 16, 1979; House 1935-43.

McKEOWN, Thomas Deitz (D Okla.) June 4, 1878-Oct. 22, 1951; House 1917-21, 1923-35.

McKERNAN, John R. Jr. (R Maine) May 20, 1948--; House 1983-87; Gov. 1987--.

McKEVITT, James Douglas "Mike" (R Colo.) Oct. 26, 1928--; House 1971-73.

McKIBBIN, Joseph Chambers (D Calif.) May 14, 1824-July 1, 1896; House 1857-59.

McKIM, Alexander (uncle of Isaac McKim) (D Md.) Jan. 10, 1748-Jan. 18, 1832; House 1809-15.

McKIM, Isaac (nephew of Alexander McKim) (D Md.) July 21, 1775-April 1, 1838; House Jan. 4, 1823-25, 1833-April 1, 1838.

McKINIRY, Richard Francis (D N.Y.) March 23, 1878-May 30, 1950; House 1919-21.

McKINLAY, Duncan E. (R Calif.) Oct. 6, 1862-Dec. 30, 1914; House 1905-11.

McKINLEY, John (JD Ala.) May 1, 1780-July 19, 1852; Senate Nov. 27, 1826-31, March 4-April 22, 1837; House 1833-35; Assoc. Justice Supreme Court 1838-52.

McKINLEY, William (D Va.) ?-?; House Dec. 21, 1810-11.

McKINLEY, William Brown (R Ill.) Sept. 5, 1856-Dec. 7, 1926; House 1905-13, 1915-21; Senate 1921-Dec. 7, 1926.

McKINLEY, William Jr. (R Ohio) Jan. 29, 1843-Sept. 14, 1901; House 1877-May 27, 1884, 1885-91; Gov. 1892-96; President 1897-Sept. 14, 1901.

McKINNEY, James (R Ill.) April 14, 1852-Sept. 29, 1934; House Nov. 7, 1905-13.

McKINNEY, John Franklin (D Ohio) April 12, 1827-June 13, 1903; House 1863-65, 1871-73.

McKINNEY, Luther Franklin (D N.H.) April 25, 1841-July 30, 1922; House 1887-89, 1891-93.

McKINNEY, Stewart Brett (R Conn.) Jan. 30, 1931- —; House 1971- —.

McKINNON, Clinton Dotson (D Calif.) Feb. 5, 1906- —; House 1949-53.

McKISSOCK, Thomas (W N.Y.) April 17, 1790-June 26, 1866; House 1849-51.

McKNEALLY, Martin B. (R N.Y.) Dec. 31, 1914- —; House 1969-71.

McKNIGHT, Robert (R Pa.) Jan. 20, 1820-Oct. 25, 1885; House 1859-63.

McLACHLAN, James (R Calif.) Aug. 1, 1852-Nov. 21, 1940; House 1895-97, 1901-11.

McLAIN, Frank Alexander (D Miss.) Jan. 29, 1852-Oct. 10, 1920; House Dec. 12, 1898-1909.

McLANAHAN, James Xavier (grandson of Andrew Gregg) (D Pa.) 1809-Dec. 16, 1861; House 1849-53.

McLANE, Louis (father of Robert Milligan McLane) (F Del.) May 28, 1786-Oct. 7, 1857; House 1817-27; Senate 1827-April 16, 1829; Secy. of the Treasury 1831-33; Secy. of State 1833-34.

McLANE, Patrick (D Pa.) March 14, 1875-Nov. 13 1946; House 1919-Feb. 25, 1921.

McLANE, Robert Milligan (son of Louis McLane) (D Md.) June 23, 1815-April 16, 1898; House 1847-51 1879-83; Gov. 1884-85.

McLAUGHLIN, Charles Francis (D Neb.) June 19 1887-Feb. 5, 1976; House 1935-43.

McLAUGHLIN, James Campbell (R Mich.) Jan. 26 1858-Nov. 29, 1932; House 1907-Nov. 29, 1932.

McLAUGHLIN, Joseph (R Pa.) June 9, 1867-Nov. 21 1926; House 1917-19, 1921-23.

McLAUGHLIN, Melvin Orlando (R Neb.) Aug. 8, 1876 June 18, 1928; House 1919-27.

McLAURIN, Anselm Joseph (D Miss.) March 26, 1848 Dec. 22, 1909; Senate Feb. 7, 1894-95, 1901-Dec. 22 1909; Gov. 1896-1900.

McLAURIN, John Lowndes (D S.C.) May 9, 1860-Jul 29, 1934; House Dec. 5, 1892-May 31, 1897; Senate June 1, 1897-1903.

McLEAN, Alney (— Ky.) June 10, 1779-Dec. 30, 1841 House 1815-17, 1819-21.

McLEAN, Donald Holman (R N.J.) March 18, 1884 Aug. 19, 1975; House 1933-45.

McLEAN, Finis Ewing (brother of John McLean of Ill uncle of James David Walker) (W Ky.) Feb. 19 1806-April 12, 1881; House 1849-51.

McLEAN, George Payne (R Conn.) Oct. 7, 1857-June 6 1932; Senate 1911-29; Gov. 1901-03.

McLEAN, James Henry (R Mo.) Aug. 13, 1829-Aug. 12 1886; House Dec. 15, 1882-83.

McLEAN, John (brother of William McLean) (W Ohio) March 11, 1785-April 4, 1861; House 1813-16 Postmaster Gen. 1823-29; Assoc. Justice Supreme Court 1830-61.

McLEAN, John (brother of Finis Ewing McLean, uncl of James David Walker) (D Ill.) Feb. 4, 1791-Oct. 14 1830; House Dec. 3, 1818-19; Senate Nov. 23, 1824 25, 1829-Oct. 14, 1830.

McLEAN, Samuel (D Mont.) Aug. 7, 1826-July 16, 1877 House (Terr. Del.) Jan. 6, 1865-67.

McLEAN, William (brother of John McLean of Ohio (— Ohio) Aug. 10, 1794-Oct. 12, 1839; House 1823 29.

McLEAN, William Pinkney (D Texas) Aug. 9, 1836 March 13, 1925; House 1873-75.

McLEMORE, Atkins Jefferson "Jeff" (D Texas) March 13, 1857-March 4, 1929; House 1915-19.

McLENE, Jeremiah (D Ohio) 1767-March 19, 1837; House 1833-37.

McLEOD, Clarence John (R Mich.) July 3, 1895-May 15, 1959; House Nov. 2, 1920-21, 1923-37, 1939-41.

McLOSKEY, Robert Thaddeus (R Ill.) June 26, 1907- −; House 1963-65.

McMAHON, Gregory (R N.Y.) March 19, 1915-−; House 1947-49.

McMAHON, James O'Brien (D Conn.) Oct. 6, 1903-July 28, 1952; Senate 1945-July 28, 1952.

McMAHON, John A. (nephew of Clement Laird Vallandigham) (D Ohio) Feb. 19, 1833-March 8, 1923; House 1875-81.

McMANUS, William (− N.Y.) 1780-Jan. 18, 1835; House 1825-27.

McMASTER, William Henry (R S.D.) May 10, 1877-Sept. 14, 1968; Senate 1925-31; Gov. 1921-25.

McMILLAN, Alexander (− N.C.) ?-1817; House 1817.

McMILLAN, Clara Gooding (widow of Thomas Sanders McMillan) (D S.C.) Aug. 17, 1894-Nov. 8, 1976; House Nov. 7, 1939-41.

McMILLAN, J. Alex (R N.C.) May 9, 1932-−; House 1985-−.

McMILLAN, James (R Mich.) May 12, 1838-Aug. 10, 1902; Senate 1889-Aug. 10, 1902.

McMILLAN, John Lanneau (D S.C.) ?-Sept. 3, 1977; House 1939-73.

McMILLAN, Samuel (R N.Y.) Aug. 6, 1850-May 6, 1924; House 1907-09.

McMILLAN, Samuel James Renwick (R Minn.) Feb. 22, 1826-Oct. 3, 1897; Senate 1875-87.

McMILLAN, Thomas Sanders (husband of Clara Gooding McMillan) (D S.C.) Nov. 27, 1888-Sept. 29, 1939; House 1925-Sept. 29, 1939.

McMILLAN, William (− N.W. Terr.) March 2, 1764-May 1804; House (Terr. Del.) Nov. 24, 1800-01.

McMILLEN, Rolla Coral (R Ill.) Oct. 5, 1880-May 6, 1961; House June 13, 1944-51.

McMILLEN, Thomas (D Md.) May 26, 1952-−; House 1987-−.

McMILLIN, Benton (D Tenn.) Sept. 11, 1845-Jan. 8, 1933; House 1879-Jan. 6, 1899; Gov. 1899-1903.

McMORRAN, Henry Gordon (R Mich.) June 11, 1844-July 19, 1929; House 1903-13.

McMULLEN, Chester Bartow (D Fla.) Dec. 6, 1902-Nov. 3, 1953; House 1951-53.

McMULLEN, Fayette (D Va.) May 18, 1805-Nov. 8, 1880; House 1849-57; Gov. (Wash. Terr.) 1857-61.

McMURRAY, Howard Johnstone (D Wis.) March 3, 1901-Aug. 14, 1961; House 1943-45.

McNAGNY, William Forgy (D Ind.) April 19, 1850-Aug. 24, 1923; House 1893-95.

McNAIR, John (D Pa.) June 8, 1800-Aug. 12, 1861; House 1851-55.

McNAMARA, Patrick Vincent (D Mich.) Oct. 4, 1894-April 30, 1966; Senate 1955-April 30, 1966.

McNARY, Charles Linza (R Ore.) June 12, 1874-Feb. 25, 1944; Senate May 29, 1917-Nov. 5, 1918, Dec. 18, 1918-Feb. 25, 1944.

McNARY, William Sarsfield (D Mass.) March 29, 1863-June 26, 1930; House 1903-07.

McNEELY, Thompson Ware (D Ill.) Oct. 5, 1835-July 23, 1921; House 1869-73.

McNEILL, Archibald (− N.C.) ?-1849; House 1821-23, 1825-27.

McNULTA, John (R Ill.) Nov. 9, 1837-Feb. 22, 1900; House 1873-75.

McNULTY, Frank Joseph (D N.J.) Aug. 10, 1872-May 26, 1926; House 1923-25.

McNULTY, James Francis Jr. (D Ariz.) Oct. 18, 1925-−; House 1983-85.

McPHERSON, Edward (R Pa.) July 31, 1830-Dec. 14, 1895; House 1859-63.

McPHERSON, Isaac Vanbert (R Mo.) March 8, 1868-Oct. 31, 1931; House 1919-23.

McPHERSON, John Rhoderic (D N.J.) May 9, 1833-Oct. 8, 1897; Senate 1877-95.

McPHERSON, Smith (R Iowa) Feb. 14, 1848-Jan. 17, 1915; House 1899-June 6, 1900.

McQUEEN, John (D S.C.) Feb. 9, 1804-Aug. 30, 1867; House Feb. 12, 1849-Dec. 21, 1860.

McRAE, John Jones (SRD Miss.) Jan. 10, 1815-May 30, 1868; Senate Dec. 1, 1851-March 17, 1852 (Democrat); House Dec. 7, 1858-Jan. 12, 1861; Gov. 1854-58 (Democrat).

McRAE, Thomas Chipman (cousin of Thomas Banks Cabaniss) (D Ark.) Dec. 21, 1851-June 2, 1929; House Dec. 7, 1885-1903; Gov. 1921-25.

McREYNOLDS, Samuel Davis (D Tenn.) April 16, 1872-July 11, 1939; House 1923-July 11, 1939.

McROBERTS, Samuel (D Ill.) April 12, 1799-March 27, 1843; Senate 1841-March 27, 1843.

McRUER, Donald Campbell (R Calif.) March 10, 1826-Jan. 29, 1898; House 1865-67.

McSHANE, John Albert (D Neb.) Aug. 25, 1850-Nov. 10, 1923; House 1887-89.

McSHERRY, James (− Pa.) July 29, 1776-Feb. 3, 1849; House 1821-23.

McSPADDEN, Clem Rogers (D Okla.) Nov. 9, 1925- −; House 1973-75.

McSWAIN, John Jackson (D S.C.) May 1, 1875-Aug. 6, 1936; House 1921-Aug. 6, 1936.

McSWEEN, Harold Barnett (D La.) July 19, 1926- −; House 1959-63.

McSWEENEY, John (D Ohio) Dec. 19, 1890-Dec. 13, 1969; House 1923-29, 1937-39, 1949-51.

McVEAN, Charles (D N.Y.) 1802-Dec. 22, 1848; House 1833-35.

McVEY, Walter Lewis (R Kan.) Feb. 19, 1922- −; House 1961-63.

McVEY, William Estus (R Ill.) Dec. 13, 1885-Aug. 10, 1958; House 1951-Aug. 10, 1958.

McVICKER, Roy Harrison (D Colo.) Feb. 20, 1924-Sept. 15, 1973; House 1965-67.

McWILLIAMS, John Dacher (R Conn.) July 23, 1891-March 30, 1975; House 1943-45.

McWILLIE, William (D Miss.) Nov. 17, 1795-March 3, 1869; House 1849-51; Gov. 1857-59.

MEACHAM, James (W Vt.) Aug. 16, 1810-Aug. 23, 1856; House Dec. 3, 1849-Aug. 23, 1856.

MEAD, Cowles (− Ga.) Oct. 18, 1776-May 17, 1844; House March 4-Dec. 24, 1805.

MEAD, James Michael (D N.Y.) Dec. 27, 1885-March 15, 1964; House 1919-Dec. 2, 1938; Senate Dec. 3, 1938-47.

MEADE, Edwin Ruthven (D N.Y.) July 6, 1836-Nov. 28, 1889; House 1875-77.

MEADE, Hugh Allen (D Md.) April 4, 1907-July 8, 1949; House 1947-49.

MEADE, Richard Kidder (D Va.) July 29, 1803-April 20, 1862; House Aug. 5, 1847-53.

MEADE, Wendell Howes (R Ky.) Jan. 18, 1912- −; House 1947-49.

MEADER, George (R Mich.) Sept. 13, 1907- −; House 1951-65.

MEANS, Rice William (R Colo.) Nov. 16, 1877-Jan. 30, 1949; Senate Dec. 1, 1924-27.

MEBANE, Alexander (− N.C.) Nov. 26, 1744-July 5, 1795; House 1793-95.

MECHEM, Edwin Leard (R N.M.) July 2, 1912- −; Senate Nov. 30, 1962-Nov. 3, 1964; Gov. 1951-55, 1957-59, 1961-62.

MEDILL, William (D Ohio) Feb. 1802-Sept. 2, 1865; House 1839-43; Gov. 1853-56.

MEECH, Ezra (D Vt.) July 26, 1773-Sept. 23, 1856; House 1819-21, 1825-27.

MEEDS, Lloyd (D Wash.) Dec. 11, 1927- −; House 1965-79.

MEEKER, Jacob Edwin (R Mo.) Oct. 7, 1878-Oct. 16, 1918; House 1915-Oct. 16, 1918.

MEEKISON, David (D Ohio) Nov. 14, 1849-Feb. 12, 1915; House 1897-1901.

MEEKS, James Andrew (D Ill.) March 7, 1864-Nov. 10, 1946; House 1933-39.

MEIGS, Henry (D N.Y.) Oct. 28, 1782-May 20, 1861; House 1819-21.

MEIGS, Return Jonathan Jr. (D Ohio) Nov. 17, 1765-March 29, 1825; Senate Dec. 12, 1808-May 1, 1810; Gov. 1810-14 (Democratic Republican); Postmaster Gen. 1814-23.

MEIKLEJOHN, George de Rue (R Neb.) Aug. 26, 1857-April 19, 1929; House 1893-97.

MELCHER, John (D Mont.) Sept. 6, 1924- −; House June 24, 1969-77; Senate 1977- −.

MELLEN, Prentiss (− Mass.) Oct. 11, 1764-Dec. 31, 1840; Senate June 5, 1818-May 15, 1820.

MELLISH, David Batcheller (R N.Y.) Jan. 2, 1831-May 23, 1874; House 1873-May 23, 1874.

MENEFEE, Richard Hickman (W Ky.) Dec. 4, 1809-Feb. 21, 1841; House 1837-39.

MENGES, Franklin (R Pa.) Oct. 26, 1858-May 12, 1956; House 1925-31.

MENZIES, John William (U Ky.) April 12, 1819-Oct. 3, 1897; House 1861-63.

MERCER, Charles Fenton (cousin of Robert Selden Garnett) (D Va.) June 16, 1778-May 4, 1858; House 1817-Dec. 26, 1839.

MERCER, David Henry (R Neb.) July 9, 1857-Jan. 10, 1919; House 1893-1903.

MERCER, John Francis (D Md.) May 17, 1759-Aug. 30, 1821; House Feb. 5, 1792-April 13, 1794; Cont. Cong. 1782-85 (Va.); Gov. 1801-03 (Democratic Republican).

MERCUR, Ulysses (R Pa.) Aug. 12, 1818-June 6, 1887; House 1865-Dec. 2, 1872.

MEREDITH, Elisha Edward (D Va.) Dec. 26, 1848-July 29, 1900; House Dec. 9, 1891-97.

MERIWETHER, David (father of James Meriwether, grandfather of James A. Meriwether) (D Ga.) April 10, 1755-Nov. 16, 1822; House Dec. 6, 1802-07.

MERIWETHER, David (D Ky.) Oct. 30, 1800-April 4, 1893; Senate July 6-Aug. 31, 1852; Gov. (N.M. Terr.) 1853-55.

MERIWETHER, James (son of David Meriwether of Ga., uncle of James A. Meriwether) (— Ga.) 1789-1854; House 1825-27.

MERIWETHER, James A. (nephew of James Meriwether, grandson of David Meriwether of Ga.) (W Ga.) Sept. 20, 1806-April 18, 1852; House 1841-43.

MERRIAM, Clinton Levi (R N.Y.) March 25, 1824-Feb. 18, 1900; House 1871-75.

MERRICK, William Duhurst (father of William Matthew Merrick) (W Md.) Oct. 25, 1793-Feb. 5, 1857; Senate Jan. 4, 1838-45.

MERRICK, William Matthew (son of William Duhurst Merrick) (D Md.) Sept. 1, 1818-Feb. 4, 1889; House 1871-73.

MERRILL, D. Bailey (R Ind.) Nov. 22, 1912- —; House 1953-55.

MERRILL, Orsamus Cook (D Vt.) June 18, 1775-April 12, 1865; House 1817-Jan. 12, 1820.

MERRIMAN, Truman Adams (D N.Y.) Sept. 5, 1839-April 16, 1892; House 1885-89.

MERRIMON, Augustus Summerfield (D N.C.) Sept. 15, 1830-Nov. 14, 1892; Senate 1873-79.

MERRITT, Edwin Albert (R N.Y.) July 25, 1860-Dec. 4, 1914; House Nov. 5, 1912-Dec. 4, 1914.

MERRITT, Matthew Joseph (D N.Y.) April 2, 1895-Sept. 29, 1946; House 1935-45.

MERRITT, Samuel Augustus (D Idaho) Aug. 15, 1827-Sept. 8, 1910; House (Terr. Del.) 1871-73.

MERRITT, Schuyler (R Conn.) Dec. 16, 1853-April 1, 1953; House Nov. 6, 1917-31, 1933-37.

MERROW, Chester Earl (R N.H.) Nov. 15, 1906-Feb. 10, 1974; House 1943-63.

MERWIN, Orange (— Conn.) April 7, 1777-Sept. 4, 1853; House 1825-29.

MESICK, William Smith (R Mich.) Aug. 26, 1856-Dec. 1, 1942; House 1897-1901.

MESKILL, Thomas Joseph (R Conn.) Jan. 30, 1928- —; House 1967-71; Gov. 1971-75.

METCALF, Arunah (D N.Y.) Aug. 15, 1771-Aug. 15, 1848; House 1811-13.

METCALF, Jesse Houghton (R R.I.) Nov. 16, 1860-Oct. 9, 1942; Senate Nov. 5, 1924-37.

METCALF, Lee Warren (D Mont.) Jan. 28, 1911-Jan. 12, 1978; House 1953-61; Senate 1961-Jan. 12, 1978.

METCALF, Victor Howard (R Calif.) Oct. 10, 1853-Feb. 20, 1936; House 1899-July 1, 1904; Secy. of Commerce and Labor 1904-06; Secy of the Navy 1906-08.

METCALFE, Henry Bleecker (D N.Y.) Jan. 20, 1805-Feb. 7, 1881; House 1875-77.

METCALFE, Lyne Shackelford (R Mo.) April 21, 1822-Jan. 31, 1906; House 1877-79.

METCALFE, Ralph Harold (D Ill.) May 29, 1910-Oct. 10, 1978; House 1971-Oct. 10, 1978.

METCALFE, Thomas (D Ky.) March 20, 1780-Aug. 18, 1855; House 1819-June 1, 1828; Senate June 23, 1848-49; Gov. 1828-32 (National Republican).

METZ, Herman August (D N.Y.) Oct. 19, 1867-May 17, 1934; House 1913-15.

METZENBAUM, Howard Morton (D Ohio) June 4, 1917- —; Senate Jan. 4-Dec. 23, 1974, Dec. 29, 1976- —.

MEYER, Adolph (D La.) Oct. 19, 1842-March 8, 1908; House 1891-March 8, 1908.

MEYER, Herbert Alton (R Kan.) Aug. 30, 1886-Oct. 2, 1950; House 1947-Oct. 2, 1950.

MEYER, John Ambrose (D Md.) May 15, 1899-Oct. 2, 1969; House 1941-43.

MEYER, William Henry (D Vt.) Dec. 29, 1914-Dec. 16, 1983; House 1959-61.

MEYERS, Benjamin Franklin (D Pa.) July 6, 1833-Aug. 11, 1918; House 1871-73.

MEYERS, Jan (R Kan.) July 20, 1928- —; House 1985- —.

MEYNER, Helen Stevenson (D N.J.) March 5, 1929- —; House 1975-79.

MEZVINSKY, Edward Maurice (D Iowa) Jan. 17, 1937- —; House 1973-77.

MFUME, Kweisi (D Md.) Oct. 24, 1948- —; House 1987- —.

MICA, Daniel Andrew (D Fla.) Feb. 4, 1944- —; House 1979- —.

MICHAELSON, Magne Alfred (R Ill.) Sept. 7, 1878-Oct. 26, 1949; House 1921-31.

MICHALEK, Anthony (R Ill.) Jan. 16, 1878-Dec. 21, 1916; House 1905-07.

MICHEL, Robert Henry (R Ill.) March 2, 1923- —; House 1957- —.

MICHENER, Earl Cory (R Mich.) Nov. 30, 1876-July 4, 1957; House 1919-33, 1935-51.

MICKEY, J. Ross (D Ill.) Jan. 5, 1856-March 20, 1928; House 1901-03.

MIDDLESWARTH, Ner (W Pa.) Dec. 12, 1783-June 2, 1865; House 1853-55.

MIDDLETON, George (D N.J.) Oct. 14, 1800-Dec. 31, 1888; House 1863-65.

MIDDLETON, Henry (D S.C.) Sept. 28, 1770-June 14, 1846; House 1815-19; Gov. 1810-12 (Democratic Republican).

MIERS, Robert Walter (D Ind.) Jan. 27, 1848-Feb. 20, 1930; House 1897-1905.

MIKULSKI, Barbara Ann (D Md.) July 20, 1936- —; House 1977-87; Senate 1987- —.

MIKVA, Abner J. (D Ill.) Jan. 21, 1926- —; House 1969-73, 1975-Sept. 26, 1979.

MILES, Frederick (R Conn.) Dec. 19, 1815-Nov. 20, 1896; House 1879-83, 1889-91.

MILES, John Esten (D N.M.) July 28, 1884-Oct. 7, 1971; House 1949-51; Gov. 1939-43.

MILES, Joshua Weldon (D Md.) Dec. 9, 1858-March 4, 1929; House 1895-97.

MILES, William Porcher (D S.C.) July 4, 1822-May 11, 1899; House 1857-Dec. 1860.

MILFORD, Dale (D Texas) Feb. 18, 1926- —; House 1973-79.

MILLARD, Charles Dunsmore (R N.Y.) Dec. 1, 1873-Dec. 11, 1944; House 1931-Sept. 29, 1937.

MILLARD, Joseph Hopkins (R Neb.) April 20, 1836-Jan. 13, 1922; Senate March 28, 1901-07.

MILLARD, Stephen Columbus (R N.Y.) Jan. 14, 1841-June 21, 1914; House 1883-87.

MILLEDGE, John (— Ga.) 1757-Feb. 9, 1818; House Nov. 22, 1792-93, 1795-99, 1801-May 1802; Senate June 19, 1806-Nov. 14, 1809; Pres. pro tempore 1809; Gov. 1802-06 (Democratic Republican).

MILLEN, John (D Ga.) 1804-Oct. 15, 1843; House March 4-Oct. 15, 1843.

MILLER, Arthur Lewis (R Neb.) May 24, 1892-March 16, 1967; House 1943-59.

MILLER, Bert Henry (D Idaho) Dec. 15, 1879-Oct. 8, 1949; Senate Jan. 3-Oct. 8, 1949.

MILLER, Clarence Benjamin (R Minn.) March 13, 1872-Jan. 10, 1922; House 1909-19.

MILLER, Clarence E. (R Ohio) Nov. 1, 1917- —; House 1967- —.

MILLER, Clement Woodnutt (nephew of Thomas Woodnutt Miller) (D Calif.) Oct. 28, 1916-Oct. 7, 1962; House 1959-Oct. 7, 1962.

MILLER, Daniel Fry (W Iowa) Oct. 4, 1814-Dec. 9, 1895; House Dec. 20, 1850-51.

MILLER, Daniel H. (JD Pa.) ?-1846; House 1823-31.

MILLER, Edward Edwin (R Ill.) July 22, 1880-Aug. 1, 1946; House 1923-25.

MILLER, Edward Tylor (R Md.) Feb. 1, 1895-Jan. 20, 1968; House 1947-59.

MILLER, George (D Calif.) May 17, 1945- —; House 1975- —.

MILLER, George Funston (R Pa.) Sept. 5, 1809-Oct. 21, 1885; House 1865-69.

MILLER, George Paul (D Calif.) Jan. 15, 1891-Dec. 2, 1982; House 1945-73.

MILLER, Homer Virgil Milton (D Ga.) April 29, 1814-May 31, 1896; Senate Feb. 24-March 3, 1871.

MILLER, Howard Shultz (D Kan.) Feb. 27, 1879-Jan. 7, 1970; House 1953-55.

MILLER, Jack Richard (R Iowa) June 6, 1916- —; Senate 1961-73.

MILLER, Jacob Welsh (W N.J.) Aug. 29, 1800-Sept. 30, 1862; Senate 1841-53.

MILLER, James Francis (D Texas) Aug. 1, 1830-July 3, 1902; House 1883-87.

MILLER, James Monroe (R Kan.) May 6, 1852-Jan. 20, 1926; House 1899-1911.

MILLER, Jesse (father of William Henry Miller) (D Pa.) 1800-Aug. 20, 1850; House 1833-Oct. 30, 1836.

MILLER, John (− N.Y.) Nov. 10, 1774-March 31, 1862; House 1825-27.

MILLER, John (VBD Mo.) Nov. 25, 1781-March 18, 1846; House 1837-43; Gov. 1826-32 (Jackson Democrat).

MILLER, John Elvis (D Ark.) May 15, 1888-Jan. 30, 1981; House 1931-Nov. 14, 1937; Senate Nov. 15, 1937-March 31, 1941.

MILLER, John Franklin (uncle of John Franklin Miller, below) (R Calif.) Nov. 21, 1831-March 8, 1886; Senate 1881-March 8, 1886.

MILLER, John Franklin (nephew of John Franklin Miller, above) (R Wash.) June 9, 1862-May 28, 1936; House 1917-31.

MILLER, John Gaines (W Mo.) Nov. 29, 1812-May 11, 1856; House 1851-May 11, 1856.

MILLER, John Krepps (D Ohio) May 25, 1819-Aug. 11, 1863; House 1847-51.

MILLER, John R. (R Wash.) May 23, 1938- −; House 1985- −.

MILLER, Joseph (D Ohio) Sept. 9, 1819-May 27, 1862; House 1857-59.

MILLER, Killian (W N.Y.) July 30, 1785-Jan. 9, 1859; House 1855-57.

MILLER, Louis Ebenezer (R Mo.) April 30, 1899-Nov. 1, 1952; House 1943-45.

MILLER, Lucas Miltiades (D Wis.) Sept. 15, 1824-Dec. 4, 1902; House 1891-93.

MILLER, Morris Smith (father of Rutger Bleecker Miller) (F N.Y.) July 31, 1779-Nov. 16, 1824; House 1813-15.

MILLER, Orrin Larrabee (R Kan.) Jan. 11, 1856-Sept. 11, 1926; House 1895-97.

MILLER, Pleasant Moorman (− Tenn.) ?-1849; House 1809-11.

MILLER, Rutger Bleecker (son of Morris Smith Miller) (D N.Y.) July 28, 1805-Nov. 12, 1877; House Nov. 9, 1836-37.

MILLER, Samuel Franklin (R N.Y.) May 27, 1827-March 16, 1892; House 1863-65, 1875-77.

MILLER, Samuel Henry (R Pa.) April 19, 1840-Sept. 4, 1918; House 1881-85, 1915-17.

MILLER, Smith (D Ind.) May 30, 1804-March 21, 1872; House 1853-57.

MILLER, Stephen Decatur (N S.C.) May 8, 1787-March 8, 1838; House Jan. 2, 1817-19 (Democrat); Senate 1831-March 2, 1833; Gov. 1828-30 (Democrat).

MILLER, Thomas Byron (R Pa.) Aug. 11, 1896-March 20, 1976; House May 9, 1942-45.

MILLER, Thomas Ezekiel (R S.C.) June 17, 1849-April 8, 1938; House Sept. 24, 1890-91.

MILLER, Thomas Woodnutt (uncle of Clement Woodnutt Miller) (R Del.) June 26, 1886-May 5, 1973; House 1915-17.

MILLER, Ward MacLaughlin (R Ohio) Nov. 29, 1902- −; House Nov. 8, 1960-61.

MILLER, Warner (R N.Y.) Aug. 12, 1838-March 21, 1918; House 1879-July 26, 1881; Senate July 27, 1881-87.

MILLER, Warren (R W.Va.) April 2, 1847-Dec. 29, 1920; House 1895-99.

MILLER, William Edward (R N.Y.) March 22, 1914-June 24, 1983; House 1951-65; Chrmn. Rep. Nat. Comm. 1961-64.

MILLER, William Henry (son of Jesse Miller) (D Pa.) Feb. 28, 1829-Sept. 12, 1870; House 1863-65.

MILLER, William Jennings (R Conn.) March 12, 1899-Nov. 22, 1950; House 1939-41, 1943-45, 1947-49.

MILLER, William Starr (− N.Y.) Aug. 22, 1793-Nov. 9, 1854; House 1845-47.

MILLIGAN, Jacob Le Roy (D Mo.) March 9, 1889-March 9, 1951; House Feb. 14, 1920-21, 1923-35.

MILLIGAN, John Jones (W Del.) Dec. 10, 1795-April 20, 1875; House 1831-39.

MILLIKEN, Charles William (D Ky.) Aug. 15, 1827-Oct. 16, 1915; House 1873-77.

MILLIKEN, Seth Llewellyn (R Maine) Dec. 12, 1831-April 18, 1897; House 1883-April 18, 1897.

MILLIKEN, William H. Jr. (R Pa.) Aug. 19, 1897-July 4, 1969; House 1959-65.

MILLIKIN, Eugene Donald (R Colo.) Feb. 12, 1891-July 26, 1958; Senate Dec. 20, 1941-57.

MILLINGTON, Charles Stephen (R N.Y.) March 13, 1855-Oct. 25, 1913; House 1909-11.

MILLS, Daniel Webster (R Ill.) Feb. 25, 1838-Dec. 16, 1904; House 1897-99.

MILLS, Elijah Hunt (F Mass.) Dec. 1, 1776-May 5, 1829; House 1815-19; Senate June 12, 1820-27.

MILLS, Newt Virgus (D La.) Sept. 27, 1899- —; House 1937-43.

MILLS, Ogden Livingston (R N.Y.) Aug. 23, 1884-Oct. 11, 1937; House 1921-27; Secy. of the Treasury 1932-33.

MILLS, Roger Quarles (D Texas) March 30, 1832-Sept. 2, 1911; House 1873-March 28, 1892; Senate March 29, 1892-99.

MILLS, Wilbur Daigh (D Ark.) May 24, 1909- —; House 1939-77.

MILLS, William Oswald (R Md.) Aug. 12, 1924-May 24, 1973; House May 27, 1971-May 24, 1973.

MILLSON, John Singleton (D Va.) Oct. 1, 1808-March 1, 1874; House 1849-61.

MILLSPAUGH, Frank Crenshaw (R Mo.) Jan. 14, 1872-July 8, 1947; House 1921-Dec. 5, 1922.

MILLWARD, William (W Pa.) June 30, 1822-Nov. 28, 1871; House 1855-57, 1859-61.

MILNES, Alfred (R Mich.) May 28, 1844-Jan. 15, 1916; House Dec. 2, 1895-97.

MILNES, William Jr. (C Va.) Dec. 8, 1827-Aug. 14, 1889; House Jan. 27, 1870-71.

MILNOR, James (F Pa.) June 20, 1773-April 8, 1844; House 1811-13.

MILNOR, William (F Pa.) June 26, 1769-Dec. 13, 1848; House 1807-11, 1815-17, 1821-May 8, 1822.

MILTON, John Gerald (D N.J.) Jan. 21, 1881-April 14, 1977; Senate Jan. 18-Nov. 8, 1938.

MILTON, William Hall (D Fla.) March 2, 1864-Jan. 4, 1942; Senate March 27, 1908-09.

MINAHAN, Daniel Francis (D N.J.) Aug. 8, 1877-April 29, 1947; House 1919-21, 1923-25.

MINER, Ahiman Louis (W Vt.) Sept. 23, 1804-July 19, 1886; House 1851-53.

MINER, Charles (F Pa.) Feb. 1, 1780-Oct. 26, 1865; House 1825-29.

MINER, Henry Clay (D N.Y.) March 23, 1842-Feb. 22, 1900; House 1895-97.

MINER, Phineas (W Conn.) Nov. 27, 1777-Sept. 15, 1839; House Dec. 1, 1834-35.

MINETA, Norman Yoshio (D Calif.) Nov. 12, 1931- —; House 1975- —.

MINISH, Joseph George (D N.J.) Sept. 1, 1916- —; House 1963-85.

MINK, Patsy Takemoto (D Hawaii) Dec. 6, 1927- —; House 1965-77.

MINOR, Edward Sloman (R Wis.) Dec. 13, 1840-July 26, 1924; House 1895-1907.

MINSHALL, William Edwin Jr. (R Ohio) Oct. 24, 1911- —; House 1955-75.

MINTON, Sherman (D Ind.) Oct. 20, 1890-April 9, 1965; Senate 1935-41; Assoc. Justice Supreme Court 1949-56.

MITCHEL, Charles Burton (D Ark.) Sept. 19, 1815-Sept. 20, 1864; Senate March 4-July 11, 1861.

MITCHELL, Alexander (father of John Lendrum Mitchell) (D Wis.) Oct. 18, 1817-April 19, 1887; House 1871-75.

MITCHELL, Alexander Clark (R Kan.) Oct. 11, 1860-July 7, 1911; House March 4-July 7, 1911.

MITCHELL, Anderson (W N.C.) June 13, 1800-Dec. 24, 1876; House April 27, 1842-43.

MITCHELL, Arthur Wergs (D Ill.) Dec. 22, 1883-May 9, 1968; House 1935-43.

MITCHELL, Charles F. (W N.Y.) about 1808-?; House 1837-41.

MITCHELL, Charles Le Moyne (D Conn.) Aug. 6, 1844-March 1, 1890; House 1883-87.

MITCHELL, Donald Jerome (R N.Y.) May 8, 1923- —; House 1973-83.

MITCHELL, Edward Archibald (R Ind.) Dec. 2, 1910-Dec. 11, 1979; House 1947-49.

MITCHELL, George' Edward (D Md.) March 3, 1781-June 28, 1832; House 1823-27, Dec. 7, 1829-June 28, 1832.

MITCHELL, George John (D Maine) Aug. 20, 1933- ; Senate May 19, 1980- —.

MITCHELL, Harlan Erwin (D Ga.) Aug. 17, 1924- ; House Jan. 8, 1958-61.

MITCHELL, Henry (JD N.Y.) 1784-Jan. 12, 1856; House 1833-35.

MITCHELL, Hugh Burnton (D Wash.) March 22, 1907- —; Senate Jan. 10, 1945-Dec. 25, 1946; House 1949-53.

MITCHELL, James Coffield (— Tenn.) March 1786-Aug. 7, 1843; House 1825-29.

MITCHELL, James S. (D Pa.) 1784-1844; House 1821-27.

MITCHELL, John (D Pa.) March 8, 1781-Aug. 3, 1849; House 1825-29.

MITCHELL, John Hipple (R Ore.) June 22, 1835-Dec. 8, 1905; Senate 1873-79, Nov. 18, 1885-97, 1901-Dec. 8, 1905.

MITCHELL, John Inscho (R Pa.) July 28, 1838-Aug. 20, 1907; House 1877-81; Senate 1881-87.

MITCHELL, John Joseph (D Mass.) May 9, 1873-Sept. 13, 1925; House Nov. 8, 1910-11, April 15, 1913-15.

MITCHELL, John Lendrum (son of Alexander Mitchell) (D Wis.) Oct. 19, 1842-June 29, 1904; House 1891-93; Senate 1893-99.

MITCHELL, John Murray (R N.Y.) March 18, 1858-May 31, 1905; House June 2, 1896-99.

MITCHELL, John Ridley (D Tenn.) Sept. 26, 1877-Feb. 26, 1962; House 1931-39.

MITCHELL, Nahum (F Mass.) Feb. 12, 1769-Aug. 1, 1853; House 1803-05.

MITCHELL, Parren James (D Md.) April 29, 1922-—; House 1971-87.

MITCHELL, Robert (D Ohio) 1778-Nov. 13, 1848; House 1833-35.

MITCHELL, Stephen Mix (F Conn.) Dec. 9, 1743-Sept. 30, 1835; Senate Dec. 2, 1793-95; Cont. Cong. 1783-88.

MITCHELL, Thomas Rothmaler (— S.C.) May 1783-Nov. 2, 1837; House 1821-23, 1825-29, 1831-33.

MITCHELL, William (R Ind.) Jan. 19, 1807-Sept. 11, 1865; House 1861-63.

MITCHILL, Samuel Latham (D N.Y.) Aug. 20, 1764-Sept. 7, 1831; House 1801-Nov. 22, 1804, Dec. 4, 1810-13; Senate Nov. 23, 1804-09.

MIZE, Chester L. (R Kan.) Dec. 25, 1917-—; House 1965-71.

MIZELL, Wilmer David (R N.C.) Aug. 13, 1930-—; House 1969-75.

MOAKLEY, John Joseph (D Mass.) April 27, 1927-—; House 1973-— (1973-75 Independent Democrat).

MOBLEY, William Carlton (D Ga.) Dec. 7, 1906-—; House March 2, 1932-33.

MOELLER, Walter Henry (D Ohio) March 15, 1910-—; House 1959-63, 1965-67.

MOFFATT, Seth Crittenden (R Mich.) Aug. 10, 1841-Dec. 22, 1887; House 1885-Dec. 22, 1887.

MOFFET, John (D Pa.) April 5, 1831-June 19, 1884; House March 4-April 9, 1869.

MOFFETT, Anthony Joseph (D Conn.) Aug. 18, 1944-—; House 1975-83.

MOFFITT, Hosea (F N.Y.) Nov. 17, 1757-Aug. 31, 1825; House 1813-17.

MOFFITT, John Henry (R N.Y.) Jan. 8, 1843-Aug. 14, 1926; House 1887-91.

MOLINARI, Guy V. (R N.Y.) Nov. 23, 1928-—; House 1981-—.

MOLLOHAN, Alan B. (son of Robert Homer Mollohan) (D W.Va.) May 14, 1943-—; House 1983-—.

MOLLOHAN, Robert Homer (father of Alan B. Mollohan) (D W.Va.) Sept. 18, 1909-—; House 1953-57, 1969-83.

MOLONY, Richard Sheppard (D Ill.) June 28, 1811-Dec. 14, 1891; House 1851-53.

MONAGAN, John Stephen (D Conn.) Dec. 23, 1911-—; House 1959-73.

MONAGHAN, Joseph Patrick (D Mont.) March 26, 1906-—; House 1933-37.

MONAHAN, James Gideon (R Wis.) Jan. 12, 1855-Dec. 5, 1923; House 1919-21.

MONAST, Louis (R R.I.) July 1, 1863-April 16, 1936; House 1927-29.

MONDALE, Walter Frederick "Fritz" (D Minn.) Jan. 5, 1928-—; Senate Dec. 30, 1964-Dec. 29, 1976; Vice-President 1977-81.

MONDELL, Franklin Wheeler (R Wyo.) Nov. 6, 1860-Aug. 6, 1939; House 1895-97, 1899-1923; House majority leader 1919-23.

MONELL, Robert (— N.Y.) 1786-Nov. 29, 1860; House 1819-21, 1829-Feb. 21, 1831.

MONEY, Hernando De Soto (D Miss.) Aug. 26, 1839-Sept. 18, 1912; House 1875-85, 1893-97; Senate Oct. 8, 1897-1911.

MONKIEWICZ, Boleslaus Joseph (R Conn.) Aug. 8, 1898-July 2, 1971; House 1939-41, 1943-45.

MONROE, James (uncle of James Monroe, below) (DR Va.) April 28, 1758-July 4, 1831; Senate Nov. 9, 1790-May 27, 1794; Cont. Cong. 1783-86; Gov. 1799-1802, 1811; Secy. of State 1811-17; President 1817-25.

MONROE, James (nephew of James Monroe, above) (W N.Y.) Sept. 10, 1799-Sept. 7, 1870; House 1839-41.

MONROE, James (R Ohio) July 18, 1821-July 6, 1898; House 1871-81.

MONRONEY, Almer Stillwell Mike (D Okla.) March 2, 1902-Feb. 13, 1980; House 1939-51; Senate 1951-69.

MONSON, David Smith (R Utah) June 20, 1935-—; House 1985-87.

MONTAGUE, Andrew Jackson (D Va.) Oct. 3, 1862-Jan. 24, 1937; House 1913-Jan. 24, 1937; Gov. 1902-06.

MONTET, Numa Francois (D La.) Sept. 17, 1892-Oct. 12, 1985; House Aug. 6, 1929-37.

MONTGOMERY, Alexander Brooks (D Ky.) Dec. 11, 1837-Dec. 27, 1910; House 1887-95.

MONTGOMERY, Daniel Jr. (D Pa.) Oct. 30, 1765-Dec. 30, 1831; House 1807-09.

MONTGOMERY, Gillespie V. "Sonny" (D Miss.) Aug. 5, 1920-—; House 1967-—.

MONTGOMERY, John (D Md.) 1764-July 17, 1828; House 1807-April 29, 1811.

MONTGOMERY, John Gallagher (D Pa.) June 27, 1805-April 24, 1857; House March 4-April 24, 1857.

MONTGOMERY, Samuel James (R Okla.) Dec. 1, 1896-June 4, 1957; House 1925-27.

MONTGOMERY, Thomas (D Ky.) 1779-April 2, 1828; House 1813-15, Aug. 1, 1820-23.

MONTGOMERY, William (— Pa.) Aug. 3, 1736-May 1, 1816; House 1793-95; Cont. Cong. 1784-85.

MONTGOMERY, William (D N.C.) Dec. 29, 1789-Nov. 27, 1844; House 1835-41.

MONTGOMERY, William (D Pa.) April 11, 1818-April 28, 1870; House 1857-61.

MONTOYA, Joseph Manuel (D N.M.) Sept. 24, 1915-June 5, 1978; House April 9, 1957-Nov. 3, 1964; Senate Nov. 4, 1964-77.

MONTOYA, Nestor (R N.M.) April 14, 1862-Jan. 13, 1923; House 1921-Jan. 13, 1923.

MOODY, Arthur Edson Blair (D Mich.) Feb. 13, 1902-July 20, 1954; Senate April 23, 1951-Nov. 4, 1952.

MOODY, Gideon Curtis (R S.D.) Oct. 16, 1832-March 17, 1904; Senate Nov. 2, 1889-91.

MOODY, James Montraville (R N.C.) Feb. 12, 1858-Feb. 5, 1903; House 1901-Feb. 5, 1903.

MOODY, Jim (D Wis.) Sept. 2, 1935-—; House 1983-—

MOODY, Malcolm Adelbert (R Ore.) Nov. 30, 1854-March 19, 1925; House 1899-1903.

MOODY, William Henry (R Mass.) Dec. 23, 1853-July 2, 1917; House Nov. 5, 1895-May 1, 1902; Secy. of the Navy 1902-04; Atty. Gen. 1904-06; Assoc. Justice Supreme Court 1906-10.

MOON, John Austin (D Tenn.) April 22, 1855-June 26, 1921; House 1897-1921.

MOON, John Wesley (R Mich.) Jan. 18, 1836-April 5, 1898; House 1893-95.

MOON, Reuben Osborne (R Pa.) July 22, 1847-Oct. 25, 1919; House Nov. 2, 1903-13.

MOONEY, Charles Anthony (D Ohio) Jan. 5, 1879-May 29, 1931; House 1919-21, 1923-May 29, 1931.

MOONEY, William Crittenden (R Ohio) June 15, 1855-July 24, 1918; House 1915-17.

MOOR, Wyman Bradbury Seavy (D Maine) Nov. 1811-March 10, 1869; Senate Jan. 5-June 7, 1848.

MOORE, Allen Francis (R Ill.) Sept. 30, 1869-Aug. 1945; House 1921-25.

MOORE, Andrew (father of Samuel McDowell Moore) (— Va.) 1752-April 14, 1821; House 1789-97, March 5-Aug. 11, 1804; Senate Aug. 11, 1804-09.

MOORE, Arch Alfred Jr. (R W.Va.) April 16, 1923-; House 1957-69; Gov. 1969-77, 1985-—.

MOORE, Arthur Harry (D N.J.) July 3, 1879-Nov. 1952; Senate 1935-Jan. 17, 1938; Gov. 1926-29, 1932-35, 1938-41.

MOORE, Charles Ellis (R Ohio) Jan. 3, 1884-April 1941; House 1919-33.

MOORE, Edward Hall (R Okla.) Nov. 19, 1871-Sept. 1950; Senate 1943-49.

MOORE, Eliakim Hastings (R Ohio) June 19, 1812-April 4, 1900; House 1869-71.

MOORE, Ely (D N.Y.) July 4, 1798-Jan. 27, 1861; House 1835-39.

MOORE, Gabriel (— Ala.) 1785-June 9, 1845; House 1821-29; Senate 1831-37; Gov. 1829-31.

MOORE, Heman Allen (D Ohio) Aug. 27, 1809-April 1844; House 1843-April 3, 1844.

MOORE, Henry Dunning (W Pa.) April 13, 1817-Aug. 11, 1887; House 1849-53.

MOORE, Horace Ladd (D Kan.) Feb. 25, 1837-May 1, 1914; House Aug. 2, 1894-95.

MOORE, Jesse Hale (R Ill.) April 22, 1817-July 11, 1883; House 1869-73.

MOORE, John (W La.) 1788-June 17, 1867; House Dec. 17, 1840-43, 1851-53.

MOORE, John Matthew (D Texas) Nov. 18, 1862-Feb. 3, 1940; House June 6, 1905-13.

MOORE, John William (D Ky.) June 9, 1877-Dec. 11, 1941; House Nov. 3, 1925-29, June 1, 1929-33.

MOORE, Joseph Hampton (R Pa.) March 8, 1864-May 2, 1950; House Nov. 6, 1906-Jan. 4, 1920.

MOORE, Laban Theodore (Nat.A. Ky.) Jan. 13, 1829-Nov. 9, 1892; House 1859-61.

MOORE, Littleton Wilde (D Texas) March 25, 1835-Oct. 29, 1911; House 1887-93.

MOORE, Nicholas Ruxton (D Md.) July 21, 1756-Oct. 7, 1816; House 1803-11, 1813-15.

MOORE, Orren Cheney (R N.H.) Aug. 10, 1839-May 12, 1893; House 1889-91.

MOORE, Oscar Fitzallen (R Ohio) Jan. 27, 1817-June 24, 1885; House 1855-57.

MOORE, Paul John (D N.J.) Aug. 5, 1868-Jan. 10, 1938; House 1927-29.

MOORE, Robert (grandfather of Michael Daniel Harter) (— Pa.) March 30, 1778-Jan. 14, 1831; House 1817-21.

MOORE, Robert Lee (D Ga.) Nov. 27, 1867-Jan. 14, 1940; House 1923-25.

MOORE, Robert Walton (D Va.) Feb. 6, 1859-Feb. 8, 1941; House May 27, 1919-31.

MOORE, Samuel (D Pa.) Feb. 8, 1774-Feb. 18, 1861; House Oct. 13, 1818-May 20, 1822.

MOORE, Samuel McDowell (son of Andrew Moore) (W Va.) Feb. 9, 1796-Sept. 17, 1875; House 1833-35.

MOORE, Sydenham (D Ala.) May 25, 1817-May 31, 1862; House 1857-Jan. 21, 1861.

MOORE, Thomas (— S.C.) 1759-July 11, 1822; House 1801-13, 1815-17.

MOORE, Thomas Love (— Va.) ?-1862; House Nov. 13, 1820-23.

MOORE, Thomas Patrick (D Ky.) 1797-July 21, 1853; House 1823-29.

MOORE, William (R N.J.) Dec. 25, 1810-April 26, 1878; House 1867-71.

MOORE, William Henson (R La.) Oct. 4, 1939-—; House Jan. 7, 1975-87.

MOORE, William Robert (R Tenn.) March 28, 1830-June 12, 1909; House 1881-83.

MOORE, William Sutton (R Pa.) Nov. 18, 1822-Dec. 30, 1877; House 1873-75.

MOOREHEAD, Tom Van Horn (R Ohio) April 12, 1898-—; House 1961-63.

MOORES, Merrill (R Ind.) April 21, 1856-Oct. 21, 1929; House 1915-25.

MOORHEAD, Carlos John (R Calif.) May 6, 1922-—; House 1973-—.

MOORHEAD, James Kennedy (R Pa.) Sept. 7, 1806-March 6, 1884; House 1859-69.

MOORHEAD, William Singer (D Pa.) April 8, 1923-—; House 1959-81.

MOORMAN, Henry DeHaven (D Ky.) June 9, 1880-Feb. 3, 1939; House 1927-29.

MORAN, Edward Carleton Jr. (D Maine) Dec. 29, 1894-July 12, 1967; House 1933-37.

MORANO, Albert Paul (R Conn.) Jan. 18, 1908-—; House 1951-59.

MOREHEAD, Charles Slaughter (W Ky.) July 7, 1802-Dec. 21, 1868; House 1847-51; Gov. 1855-59 (American Party).

MOREHEAD, James Turner (W Ky.) May 24, 1797-Dec. 28, 1854; Senate 1841-47; Gov. 1834-36 (Democrat).

MOREHEAD, James Turner (W N.C.) Jan. 11, 1799-May 5, 1875; House 1851-53.

MOREHEAD, John Henry (D Neb.) Dec. 3, 1861-May 30, 1942; House 1923-35; Gov. 1913-17.

MOREHEAD, John Motley (R N.C.) July 20, 1866-Dec. 13, 1923; House 1909-11.

MORELLA, Constance Albanese (R Md.) Feb. 12, 1931-—; House 1987-—.

MOREY, Frank (R La.) July 11, 1840-Sept. 22, 1889; House 1869-June 8, 1876.

MOREY, Henry Lee (R Ohio) April 8, 1841-Dec. 29, 1902; House 1881-June 20, 1884, 1889-91.

MORGAN, Charles Henry (R Mo.) July 5, 1842-Jan. 4, 1912; House 1875-79, 1883-85, 1893-95, 1909-11 (1875-95 Democrat).

MORGAN, Christopher (brother of Edwin Barbour Morgan, nephew of Noyes Barber) (W N.Y.) June 4, 1808-April 3, 1877; House 1839-43.

MORGAN, Daniel (F Va.) 1736-July 6, 1802; House 1797-99.

MORGAN, Dick Thompson (R Okla.) Dec. 6, 1853-July 4, 1920; House 1909-July 4, 1920.

MORGAN, Edwin Barbour (brother of Christopher Morgan, nephew of Noyes Barber) (R N.Y.) May 2, 1806-Oct. 13, 1881; House 1853-59.

MORGAN, Edwin Dennison (cousin of Morgan Gardner Bulkeley) (UR N.Y.) Feb. 8, 1811-Feb. 14, 1883; Senate 1863-69; Chrmn. Rep. Nat. Comm. 1856-64, 1872-76; Gov. 1859-63 (Republican).

MORGAN, George Washington (D Ohio) Sept. 20, 1820-July 26, 1893; House 1867-June 3, 1868, 1869-73.

MORGAN, James (F N.J.) Dec. 29, 1756-Nov. 11, 1822; House 1811-13.

MORGAN, James Bright (D Miss.) March 14, 1833-June 18, 1892; House 1885-91.

MORGAN, John Jordan (father-in-law of John Adams Dix) (D N.Y.) 1770-July 29, 1849; House 1821-25, Dec. 1, 1834-35.

MORGAN, John Tyler (D Ala.) June 20, 1824-June 11, 1907; Senate 1877-June 11, 1907.

MORGAN, Lewis Lovering (D La.) March 2, 1876-June 10, 1950; House Nov. 5, 1912-17.

MORGAN, Robert Burren (D N.C.) Oct. 5, 1925- —; Senate 1975-81.

MORGAN, Stephen (R Ohio) Jan. 25, 1854-Feb. 9, 1928; House 1899-1905.

MORGAN, Thomas Ellsworth (D Pa.) Oct. 13, 1906- —; House 1945-77.

MORGAN, William Mitchell (R Ohio) Aug. 1, 1870-Sept. 17, 1935; House 1921-31.

MORGAN, William Stephen (D Va.) Sept. 7, 1801-Sept. 3, 1878; House 1835-39.

MORIN, John Mary (R Pa.) April 18, 1868-March 3, 1942; House 1913-29.

MORITZ, Theodore Leo (D Pa.) Feb. 10, 1892- —; House 1935-37.

MORPHIS, Joseph Lewis (R Miss.) April 17, 1831-July 29, 1913; House Feb. 23, 1870-73.

MORRELL, Daniel Johnson (R Pa.) Aug. 8, 1821-Au 20, 1885; House 1867-71.

MORRELL, Edward de Veaux (R Pa.) Aug. 7, 186 Sept. 1, 1917; House Nov. 6, 1900-07.

MORRIL, David Lawrence (DR N.H.) June 10, 177: Jan. 28, 1849; Senate 1817-23; Gov. 1824-27.

MORRILL, Anson Peaslee (brother of Lot Myric Morrill) (R Maine) June 10, 1803-July 4, 188 House 1861-63; Gov. 1855-56.

MORRILL, Edmund Needham (R Kan.) Feb. 12, 183 March 14, 1909; House 1883-91; Gov. 1895-97.

MORRILL, Justin Smith (UR Vt.) April 14, 1810-De 28, 1898; House 1855-67 (Whig); Senate 1867-De 28, 1898.

MORRILL, Lot Myrick (brother of Anson Peasle Morrill) (R Maine) May 3, 1813-Jan. 10, 1883; Se ate Jan. 17, 1861-69, Oct. 30, 1869-July 7, 1876; Go 1858-61; Secy. of the Treasury 1876-77.

MORRILL, Samuel Plummer (R Maine) Feb. 11, 181 Aug. 4, 1892; House 1869-71.

MORRIS, Calvary (W Ohio) Jan. 15, 1798-Oct. 13, 187 House 1837-43.

MORRIS, Daniel (R N.Y.) Jan. 4, 1812-April 22, 188 House 1863-67.

MORRIS, Edward Joy (W Pa.) July 16, 1815-Dec. 3 1881; House 1843-45, 1857-June 8, 1861.

MORRIS, Gouverneur (uncle of Lewis Robert Morr (F N.Y.) Jan. 31, 1752-Nov. 6, 1816; Senate April 1800-03; Cont. Cong. 1777-78.

MORRIS, Isaac Newton (son of Thomas Morris of Oh brother of Jonathan David Morris) (D Ill.) Jan. 2 1812-Oct. 29, 1879; House 1857-61.

MORRIS, James Remley (son of Joseph Morris) Ohio) Jan. 10, 1819-Dec. 24, 1899; House 1861-6:

MORRIS, Jonathan David (son of Thomas Morris Ohio, brother of Isaac Newton Morris) (D Ohio) O 8, 1804-May 16, 1875; House 1847-51.

MORRIS, Joseph (father of James Remley Morris) Ohio) Oct. 16, 1795-Oct. 23, 1854; House 1843-47

MORRIS, Joseph Watkins (D Ky.) Feb. 26, 1879-D 21, 1937; House Nov. 30, 1923-25.

MORRIS, Lewis Robert (nephew of Gouverneur Morr (F Vt.) Nov. 2, 1760-Dec. 29, 1825; House 1797-18

MORRIS, Mathias (W Pa.) Sept. 12, 1787-Nov. 9, 18: House 1835-39.

ORRIS, Robert (father of Thomas Morris of N.Y.) (−
Pa.) Jan. 20, 1734-May 8, 1806; Senate 1789-95;
Cont. Cong. 1776-78.

ORRIS, Robert Page Walter (R Minn.) June 30, 1853-
Dec. 16, 1924; House 1897-1903.

ORRIS, Samuel Wells (D Pa.) Sept. 1, 1786-May 25,
1847; House 1837-41.

ORRIS, Thomas (son of Robert Morris) (− N.Y.)
Feb. 26, 1771-March 12, 1849; House 1801-03.

ORRIS, Thomas (father of Isaac Newton Morris and
Jonathan David Morris) (D Ohio) Jan. 3, 1776-Dec.
7, 1844; Senate 1833-39.

ORRIS, Thomas Gayle (D N.M.) Aug. 20, 1919-−;
House 1959-69.

ORRIS, Toby (D Okla.) Feb. 28, 1899-Sept. 1, 1973;
House 1947-53, 1957-61.

ORRISON, Bruce A. (D Conn.) Oct. 8, 1944-−; House
1983-−.

ORRISON, Cameron A. (D N.C.) Oct. 5, 1869-Aug. 20,
1953; Senate Dec. 13, 1930-Dec. 4, 1932; House 1943-
45; Gov. 1921-25.

ORRISON, George Washington (D N.H.) Oct. 16,
1809-Dec. 21, 1888; House Oct. 8, 1850-51, 1853-55.

ORRISON, James Hobson (D La.) Dec. 8, 1908-−;
House 1943-67.

ORRISON, James Lowery Donaldson (D Ill.) April 12,
1816-Aug. 14, 1888; House Nov. 4, 1856-57.

ORRISON, John Alexander (D Pa.) Jan. 31, 1814-
July 25, 1904; House 1851-53.

ORRISON, Martin Andrew (D Ind.) April 15, 1862-
July 9, 1944; House 1909-17.

ORRISON, Sid (R Wash.) May 13, 1933-−; House
1981-−.

ORRISON, William Ralls (D Ill.) Sept. 14, 1825-Sept.
29, 1909; House 1863-65, 1873-87.

ORRISSEY, John (D N.Y.) Feb. 12, 1831-May 1,
1878; House 1867-71.

ORROW, Dwight Whitney (R N.J.) Jan. 11, 1873-Oct.
5, 1931; Senate Dec. 3, 1930-Oct. 5, 1931.

ORROW, Jeremiah (W Ohio) Oct. 6, 1771-March 22,
1852; House Oct. 17, 1803-13 (Democrat), Oct. 13,
1840-43; Senate 1813-19 (Democrat); Gov. 1822-26
(Jackson Democrat).

ORROW, John (− Va.) ?-?; House 1805-09.

MORROW, John (D N.M.) April 19, 1865-Feb. 25, 1935;
House 1923-29.

MORROW, William W. (R Calif.) July 15, 1843-July 24,
1929; House 1885-91.

MORSE, Elijah Adams (R Mass.) May 25, 1841-June 5,
1898; House 1889-97.

MORSE, Elmer Addison (R Wis.) May 11, 1870-Oct. 4,
1945; House 1907-13.

MORSE, F. Bradford (R Mass.) Aug. 7, 1921-−; House
1961-May 1, 1972.

MORSE, Freeman Harlow (R Maine) Feb. 19, 1807-Feb.
5, 1891; House 1843-45 (Whig), 1857-61.

MORSE, Isaac Edward (D La.) May 22, 1809-Feb. 11,
1866; House Dec. 2, 1844-51.

MORSE, Leopold (D Mass.) Aug. 15, 1831-Dec. 15, 1892;
House 1877-85, 1887-89.

MORSE, Oliver Andrew (R N.Y.) March 26, 1815-April
20, 1870; House 1857-59.

MORSE, Wayne Lyman (D Ore.) Oct. 20, 1900-July 22,
1974; Senate 1945-69 (1945-Oct. 24, 1952, Republican, Oct. 24, 1952-Feb. 17, 1955, Independent).

MORTON, Jackson (brother of Jeremiah Morton) (W
Fla.) Aug. 10, 1794-Nov. 20, 1874; Senate 1849-55.

MORTON, Jeremiah (brother of Jackson Morton) (W
Va.) Sept. 3, 1799-Nov. 28, 1878; House 1849-51.

MORTON, Levi Parsons (R N.Y.) May 16, 1824-May 16,
1920; House 1879-March 21, 1881; Vice President
1889-93; Gov. 1895-97.

MORTON, Marcus (D Mass.) Dec. 19, 1784-Feb. 6, 1864;
House 1817-21; Gov. 1825 (Democratic Republican),
1840-41, 1843-44.

MORTON, Oliver Hazard Perry Throck (UR Ind.) Aug.
4, 1823-Nov. 1, 1877; Senate 1867-Nov. 1, 1877; Gov.
1861-67 (Republican).

MORTON, Rogers Clark Ballard (brother of Thruston
Ballard Morton) (R Md.) Sept. 19, 1914-April 19,
1979; House 1963-Jan. 29, 1971; Chrmn. Rep. Nat.
Comm. 1969-71; Secy. of the Interior 1971-75; Secy.
of Commerce 1975-76.

MORTON, Thruston Ballard (brother of Rogers Clark
Ballard Morton) (R Ky.) Aug. 19, 1907-August 14,
1982; House 1947-53; Senate 1957-Dec. 16, 1968;
Chrmn. Rep. Nat. Comm. 1959-61.

MOSELEY, Jonathan Ogden (R Conn.) April 9, 1762-
Sept. 9, 1838; House 1805-21.

MOSELEY, William Abbott (W N.Y.) Oct. 20, 1798-
Nov. 19, 1873; House 1843-47.

MOSER, Guy Louis (D Pa.) Jan. 23, 1866-May 9, 1961; House 1937-43.

MOSES, Charles Leavell (D Ga.) May 2, 1856-Oct. 10, 1910; House 1891-97.

MOSES, George Higgins (R N.H.) Feb. 9, 1869-Dec. 20, 1944; Senate Nov. 6, 1918-33; Pres. pro tempore 1925-33.

MOSES, John (D N.D.) June 12, 1885-March 3, 1945; Senate Jan. 3-March 3, 1945; Gov. 1939-45.

MOSGROVE, James (D/G Pa.) June 14, 1821-Nov. 27, 1900; House 1881-83.

MOSHER, Charles Adams (R Ohio) May 7, 1906-Nov. 16, 1984; House 1961-77.

MOSIER, Harold Gerard (D Ohio) July 24, 1889-Aug. 7, 1971; House 1937-39.

MOSS, Frank Edward (D Utah) Sept. 23, 1911- —; Senate 1959-77.

MOSS, Hunter Holmes Jr. (R W.Va.) May 26, 1874-July 15, 1916; House 1913-July 15, 1916.

MOSS, John Emerson Jr. (D Calif.) April 13, 1913- —; House 1953-Dec. 31, 1978.

MOSS, John McKenzie (nephew of James Andrew McKenzie) (R Ky.) Jan. 3, 1868-June 11, 1929; House March 25, 1902-03.

MOSS, Ralph Wilbur (D Ind.) April 21, 1862-April 26, 1919; House 1909-17.

MOTT, Gordon Newell (R Nev.) Oct. 21, 1812-April 27, 1887; House (Terr. Del.) 1863-Oct. 31, 1864.

MOTT, James (D N.J.) Jan. 18, 1739-Oct. 18, 1823; House 1801-05.

MOTT, James Wheaton (R Ore.) Nov. 12, 1883-Nov. 12, 1945; House 1933-Nov. 12, 1945.

MOTT, Luther Wright (R N.Y.) Nov. 30, 1874-July 10, 1923; House 1911-July 10, 1923.

MOTT, Richard (R Ohio) July 21, 1804-Jan. 22, 1888; House 1855-59.

MOTTL, Ronald Milton (D Ohio) Feb. 6, 1934- —; House 1975-83.

MOULDER, Morgan Moore (D Mo.) Aug. 31, 1904-Nov. 12, 1976; House 1949-63.

MOULTON, Mace (D N.H.) May 2, 1796-May 5, 1867; House 1845-47.

MOULTON, Samuel Wheeler (D Ill.) Jan. 20, 1821-June 3, 1905; House 1865-67, 1881-85.

MOUSER, Grant Earl (father of Grant Earl Mouser Jr. (R Ohio) Sept. 11, 1868-May 6, 1949; House 1905-0

MOUSER, Grant Earl Jr. (son of Grant Earl Mouser) (Ohio) Feb. 20, 1895-Dec. 21, 1943; House 1929-33

MOUTON, Alexandre (D La.) Nov. 19, 1804-Feb. 1 1885; Senate Jan. 12, 1837-March 1, 1842; Gov. 184 46.

MOUTON, Robert Louis (D La.) Oct. 20, 1892-Nov. 2 1956; House 1937-41.

MOXLEY, William James (R Ill.) May 22, 1851-Aug. 1938; House Nov. 23, 1909-11.

MOYNIHAN, Daniel Patrick (D N.Y.) March 16, 192 —; Senate 1977- —.

MOYNIHAN, Patrick Henry (R Ill.) Sept. 25, 1869-M 20, 1946; House 1933-35.

MOZLEY, Norman Adolphus (R Mo.) Dec. 11, 186 May 9, 1922; House 1895-97.

MRAZEK, Robert J. (D N.Y.) Nov. 5, 1945- —; Hou 1983- —.

MRUK, Joseph (R N.Y.) Nov. 6, 1903- —; House 194 45.

MUDD, Sydney Emanuel (father of Sydney Eman Mudd, below) (R Md.) Feb. 12, 1858-Oct. 21, 19 House March 20, 1890-91, 1897-1911.

MUDD, Sydney Emanuel (son of Sydney Eman Mudd, above) (R Md.) June 20, 1885-Oct. 11, 19 House 1915-Oct. 11, 1924.

MUHLENBERG, Francis Swaine (son of John Pe Gabriel Muhlenberg, nephew of Frederick August Conrad Muhlenberg) (NR Ohio) April 22, 1795-D 17, 1831; House Dec. 19, 1828-29.

MUHLENBERG, Frederick Augustus (great-gre grandson of Frederick Augustus Conrad Muhl berg, great-great-grandnephew of John Peter (briel Muhlenberg) (R Pa.) Sept. 25, 1887-Jan 1980; House 1947-49.

MUHLENBERG, Frederick Augustus Conrad (brot of John Peter Gabriel Muhlenberg, uncle of Fran Swaine Muhlenberg and Henry Augustus Phi Muhlenberg, great-great-grandfather of Freder Augustus Muhlenberg) (— Pa.) Jan. 1, 1750-June 1801; House 1789-97; Speaker 1789-91, 1793- Cont. Cong. 1779-80.

MUHLENBERG, Henry Augustus (son of Henry A gustus Philip Muhlenberg, grandson of Jose Hiester) (D Pa.) July 21, 1823-Jan. 9, 1854; Ho 1853-Jan. 9, 1854.

MUHLENBERG, Henry Augustus Philip (father of Henry Augustus Muhlenberg, nephew of John Peter Gabriel Muhlenberg and Frederick Augustus Conrad Muhlenberg) (JD Pa.) May 13, 1782-Aug. 11, 1844; House 1829-Feb. 9, 1838.

MUHLENBERG, John Peter Gabriel (father of Francis Swaine Muhlenberg, brother of Frederick Augustus Conrad Muhlenberg, uncle of Henry Augustus Philip Muhlenberg, great-great-granduncle of Frederick Augustus Muhlenberg) (D Pa.) Oct. 1, 1746-Oct. 1, 1807; House 1789-91, 1793-95, 1799-1801; Senate March 4-June 30, 1801.

MULDOWNEY, Michael Joseph (R Pa.) Aug. 10, 1889-March 30, 1947; House 1933-35.

MULDROW, Henry Lowndes (D Miss.) Feb. 8, 1837-March 1, 1905; House 1877-85.

MULKEY, Frederick William (nephew of Joseph Norton Dolph) (R Ore.) Jan. 6, 1874-May 5, 1924; Senate Jan. 23-March 3, 1907, Nov. 6-Dec. 17, 1918.

MULKEY, William Oscar (D Ala.) July 27, 1871-June 30, 1943; House June 29, 1914-15.

MULLER, Nicholas (D N.Y.) Nov. 15, 1836-Dec. 12, 1917; House 1877-81, 1883-87, 1899-Dec. 1, 1902.

MULLIN, Joseph (R N.Y.) Aug. 6, 1811-May 17, 1882; House 1847-49.

MULLINS, James (R Tenn.) Sept. 15, 1807-June 26, 1873; House 1867-69.

MULTER, Abraham Jacob (D N.Y.) Dec. 24, 1900- —; House Nov. 4, 1947-Dec. 31, 1967.

MUMFORD, George (D N.C.) ?-Dec. 31, 1818; House 1817-Dec. 31, 1818.

MUMFORD, Gurdon Saltonstall (F N.Y.) Jan. 29, 1764-April 30, 1831; House 1805-11.

MUMMA, Walter Mann (R Pa.) Nov. 20, 1890-Feb. 25, 1961; House 1951-Feb. 25, 1961.

MUNDT, Karl Earl (R S.D.) June 3, 1900-Aug. 16, 1974; House 1939-Dec. 30, 1948; Senate Dec. 31, 1948-73.

MUNGEN, William (D Ohio) May 12, 1821-Sept. 9, 1887; House 1867-71.

MURCH, Thompson Henry (G Lab. Ref. Maine) March 29, 1838-Dec. 15, 1886; House 1879-83.

MURDOCK, John Robert (D Ariz.) April 20, 1885-Feb. 14, 1972; House 1937-53.

MURDOCK, Orrice Abram Jr. "Abe" (D Utah) July 18, 1893-Sept. 15, 1979; House 1933-41; Senate 1941-47.

MURDOCK, Victor (R Kan.) March 18, 1871-July 8, 1945; House May 26, 1903-15; Chrmn. Prog. Party Nat. Comm. 1915-16.

MURFREE, William Hardy (uncle of David W. Dickinson) (D N.C.) Oct. 2, 1781-Jan. 19, 1827; House 1813-17.

MURKOWSKI, Frank H. (R Alaska) March 28, 1933- —; Senate 1981- —.

MURPHEY, Charles (D Ga.) May 9, 1799-Jan. 16, 1861; House 1851-53.

MURPHY, Arthur Phillips (R Mo.) Dec. 10, 1870-Feb. 1, 1914; House 1905-07, 1909-11.

MURPHY, Austin J. (D Pa.) June 17, 1927- —; House 1977- —.

MURPHY, Benjamin Franklin (R Ohio) Dec. 24, 1867-March 6, 1938; House 1919-33.

MURPHY, Edward Jr. (D N.Y.) Dec. 15, 1836-Aug. 3, 1911; Senate 1893-99.

MURPHY, Everett Jerome (R Ill.) July 24, 1852-April 10, 1922; House 1895-97.

MURPHY, George Lloyd (R Calif.) July 4, 1902- —; Senate Jan. 1, 1965-Jan. 2, 1971.

MURPHY, Henry Cruse (D N.Y.) July 5, 1810-Dec. 1, 1882; House 1843-45, 1847-49.

MURPHY, James Joseph (D N.Y.) Nov. 3, 1898-Oct. 19, 1962; House 1949-53.

MURPHY, James William (D Wis.) April 17, 1858-July 11, 1927; House 1907-09.

MURPHY, Jeremiah Henry (D Iowa) Feb. 19, 1835-Dec. 11, 1893; House 1883-87.

MURPHY, John (D Ala.) 1785-Sept. 21, 1841; House 1833-35; Gov. 1825-29 (Jackson Democrat).

MURPHY, John Michael (D N.Y.) Aug. 3, 1926- —; House 1963-81.

MURPHY, John William (D Pa.) April 26, 1902-March 28, 1962; House 1943-July 17, 1946.

MURPHY, Maurice J. Jr. (R N.H.) Oct. 3, 1927- —; Senate Dec. 7, 1961-Nov. 6, 1962.

MURPHY, Morgan Francis (D Ill.) April 16, 1933- —; House 1971-81.

MURPHY, Nathan Oakes (R Ariz.) Oct. 14, 1849-Aug. 22, 1908; House (Terr. Del.) 1895-97; Gov. (Ariz. Terr.) 1892-94, 1898-1902.

MURPHY, Richard Louis (D Iowa) Nov. 6, 1875-July 16, 1936; Senate 1933-July 16, 1936.

MURPHY, William Thomas (D Ill.) Aug. 7, 1899-Jan. 29, 1978; House 1959-71.

MURRAY, Ambrose Spencer (brother of William Murray) (R N.Y.) Nov. 27, 1807-Nov. 8, 1885; House 1855-59.

MURRAY, George Washington (R S.C.) Sept. 22, 1853-April 21, 1926; House 1893-95, June 4, 1896-97.

MURRAY, James Cunningham (D Ill.) May 16, 1917- —; House 1955-57.

MURRAY, James Edward (D Mont.) May 3, 1876-March 23, 1961; Senate Nov. 7, 1934-61.

MURRAY, John (cousin of Thomas Murray Jr.) (— Pa.) 1768-March 7, 1834; House Oct. 14, 1817-21.

MURRAY, John L. (D Ky.) Jan. 25, 1806-Jan. 31, 1842; House 1837-39.

MURRAY, Reid Fred (R Wis.) Oct. 16, 1887-April 29, 1952; House 1939-April 29, 1952.

MURRAY, Robert Maynard (D Ohio) Nov. 28, 1841-Aug. 2, 1913; House 1883-85.

MURRAY, Thomas Jefferson (D Tenn.) Aug. 1, 1894-Nov. 28, 1971; House 1943-67.

MURRAY, Thomas Jr. (cousin of John Murray) (D Pa.) 1770-Aug. 26, 1823; House Oct. 9, 1821-23.

MURRAY, William (brother of Ambrose Spencer Murray) (D N.Y.) Oct. 1, 1803-Aug. 25, 1875; House 1851-55.

MURRAY, William Francis (D Mass.) Sept. 7, 1881-Sept. 21, 1918; House 1911-Sept. 28, 1914.

MURRAY, William Henry (D Okla.) Nov. 21, 1869-Oct. 15, 1956; House 1913-17; Gov. 1931-35.

MURRAY, William Vans (F Md.) Feb. 9, 1760-Dec. 11, 1803; House 1791-97.

MURTHA, John Patrick Jr. (D Pa.) Jan. 17, 1932- —; House Feb. 5, 1974- —.

MUSKIE, Edmund Sixtus (D Maine) March 28, 1914- —; Senate 1959-May 7, 1980; Gov. 1955-59; Secy. of State May 8, 1980-81.

MUSSELWHITE, Harry Webster (D Mich.) May 23, 1868-Dec. 14, 1955; House 1933-35.

MUSTO, Raphael (D Pa.) March 30, 1929- —; House April 15, 1980-81.

MUTCHLER, Howard (son of William Mutchler) (D Pa.) Feb. 12, 1859-Jan. 4, 1916; House Aug. 7, 1893-95, 1901-03.

MUTCHLER, William (father of Howard Mutchler) (D Pa.) Dec. 21, 1831-June 23, 1893; House 1875-77, 1881-85, 1889-June 23, 1893.

MYERS, Amos (R Pa.) April 23, 1824-Oct. 18, 1893; House 1863-65.

MYERS, Francis John (D Pa.) Dec. 18, 1901-July 5, 1956; House 1939-45; Senate 1945-51.

MYERS, Gary Arthur (R Pa.) Aug. 16, 1937- —; House 1975-79.

MYERS, Henry Lee (D Mont.) Oct. 9, 1862-Nov. 11, 1943; Senate 1911-23.

MYERS, John Thomas (R Ind.) Feb. 8, 1927- —; House 1967- —.

MYERS, Leonard (R Pa.) Nov. 13, 1827-Feb. 11, 1904; House 1863-69, April 9, 1869-75.

MYERS, Michael J. "Ozzie" (D Pa.) May 4, 1943- —; House Nov. 2, 1976-Oct. 2, 1980.

MYERS, William Ralph (D Ind.) June 12, 1836-April 18, 1907; House 1879-81.

NABERS, Benjamin Duke (U Miss.) Nov. 7, 1812-Sept. 6, 1878; House 1851-53.

NAGLE, Dave R. (D Iowa) April 15, 1943- —; House 1987- —.

NAPHEN, Henry Francis (D Mass.) Aug. 14, 1852-June 8, 1905; House 1899-1903.

NAPIER, John L. (R S.C.) May 16, 1947- —; House 1981-83.

NAREY, Harry Elsworth (R Iowa) May 15, 1885-Aug. 18, 1962; House Nov. 3, 1942-43.

NASH, Charles Edmund (R La.) May 23, 1844-June 21, 1913; House 1875-77.

NATCHER, William Huston (D Ky.) Sept. 11, 1909- —; House Aug. 1, 1953- —.

NAUDAIN, Arnold (NR Del.) Jan. 6, 1790-Jan. 4, 1872; Senate Jan. 13, 1830-June 16, 1836.

NAYLOR, Charles (W Pa.) Oct. 6, 1806-Dec. 24, 1872; House June 29, 1837-41.

NEAL, Henry Safford (R Ohio) Aug. 25, 1828-July 13, 1906; House 1877-83.

NEAL, John Randolph (D Tenn.) Nov. 26, 1836-March 26, 1889; House 1885-89.

NEAL, Lawrence Talbot (D Ohio) Sept. 22, 1844-Nov. 3, 1905; House 1873-77.

NEAL, Stephen Lybrook (D N.C.) Nov. 7, 1934- —; House 1975- —.

NEAL, William Elmer (R W.Va.) Oct. 14, 1875-Nov. 12, 1959; House 1953-55, 1957-59.

NEALE, Raphael (— Md.) ?-Oct. 19, 1833; House 1819-25.

NEDZI, Lucien Norbert (D Mich.) May 28, 1925- —; House Nov. 7, 1961-81.

NEECE, William Henry (D Ill.) Feb. 26, 1831-Jan. 3, 1909; House 1883-87.

NEEDHAM, James Carson (R Calif.) Sept. 17, 1864-July 11, 1942; House 1899-1913.

NEELEY, George Arthur (D Kan.) Aug. 1, 1879-Jan. 1, 1919; House Nov. 11, 1912-15.

NEELY, Matthew Mansfield (D W.Va.) Nov. 9, 1874-Jan. 18, 1958; House Oct. 14, 1913-21, 1945-47; Senate 1923-29, 1931-Jan. 12, 1941, 1949-Jan. 18, 1958; Gov. 1941-45.

NEGLEY, James Scott (R Pa.) Dec. 22, 1826-Aug. 7, 1901; House 1869-75, 1885-87.

NEILL, Robert (D Ark.) Nov. 12, 1838-Feb. 16, 1907; House 1893-97.

NELLIGAN, James L. (R Pa.) Feb. 14, 1929- —; House 1981-83.

NELSEN, Ancher (R Minn.) Oct. 11, 1904- —; House 1959-75.

NELSON, Adolphus Peter (R Wis.) March 28, 1872-Aug. 21, 1927; House Nov. 5, 1918-23.

NELSON, Arthur Emanuel (R Minn.) May 10, 1892-April 11, 1955; Senate Nov. 18, 1942-43.

NELSON, Charles Pembroke (son of John Edward Nelson) (R Maine) July 2, 1907-June 8, 1962; House 1949-57.

NELSON, Clarence William "Bill" (D Fla.) Sept. 29, 1942- —; House 1979- —.

NELSON, Gaylord Anton (D Wis.) June 4, 1916- —; Senate 1963-81; Gov. 1959-63.

NELSON, Homer Augustus (D N.Y.) Aug. 31, 1829-April 25, 1891; House 1863-65.

NELSON, Hugh (D Va.) Sept. 30, 1768-March 18, 1836; House 1811-Jan. 14, 1823.

NELSON, Jeremiah (F Mass.) Sept. 14, 1769-Oct. 2, 1838; House 1805-07, 1815-25, 1831-33.

NELSON, John (son of Roger Nelson) (D Md.) June 1, 1794-Jan. 18, 1860; House 1821-23; Atty. Gen. 1843-45.

NELSON, John Edward (father of Charles Pembroke Nelson) (R Maine) July 12, 1874-April 11, 1955; House March 27, 1922-33.

NELSON, John Mandt (R Wis.) Oct. 10, 1870-Jan. 29, 1955; House Sept. 4, 1906-19, 1921-33.

NELSON, Knute (R Minn.) Feb. 2, 1843-April 28, 1923; House 1883-89; Senate 1895-April 28, 1923; Gov. 1893-95.

NELSON, Roger (father of John Nelson) (D Md.) 1759-June 7, 1815; House Nov. 6, 1804-May 14, 1810.

NELSON, Thomas Amos Rogers (U Tenn.) March 19, 1812-Aug. 24, 1873; House 1859-61.

NELSON, Thomas Maduit (D Va.) Sept. 27, 1782-Nov. 10, 1853; House Dec. 4, 1816-19.

NELSON, William (W N.Y.) June 29, 1784-Oct. 3, 1869; House 1847-51.

NELSON, William Lester (D Mo.) Aug. 4, 1875-Dec. 31, 1946; House 1919-21, 1925-33, 1935-43.

NES, Henry (I Pa.) May 20, 1799-Sept. 10, 1850; House 1843-45, 1847-Sept. 10, 1850.

NESBIT, Walter (D Ill.) May 1, 1878-Dec. 6, 1938; House 1933-35.

NESBITT, Wilson (D S.C.) ?-May 13, 1861; House 1817-19.

NESMITH, James Willis (cousin of Joseph Gardner Wilson, grandfather of Clifton Nesmith McArthur) (D Ore.) July 23, 1820-June 17, 1885; Senate 1861-67; House Dec. 1, 1873-75.

NEUBERGER, Maurine Brown (widow of Richard Lewis Neuberger) (D Ore.) Jan. 9, 1907- —; Senate Nov. 9, 1960-67.

NEUBERGER, Richard Lewis (husband of Maurine Brown Neuberger) (D Ore.) Dec. 26, 1912-March 9, 1960; Senate 1955-March 9, 1960.

NEVILLE, Joseph (— Va.) 1730-March 4, 1819; House 1793-95.

NEVILLE, William (cousin of Bird Segle McGuire) (P Neb.) Dec. 29, 1843-April 5, 1909; House Dec. 4, 1899-1903.

NEVIN, Robert Murphy (R Ohio) May 5, 1850-Dec. 17, 1912; House 1901-07.

NEW, Anthony (D Ky.) 1747-March 2, 1833; House 1793-1805 (Va.), 1811-13, 1817-19, 1821-23.

NEW, Harry Stewart (R Ind.) Dec. 31, 1858-May 9, 1937; Senate 1917-23; Chrmn. Rep. Nat. Comm. 1907-08; Postmaster Gen. 1923-29.

NEW, Jeptha Dudley (D Ind.) Nov. 28, 1830-July 9, 1892; House 1875-77, 1879-81.

NEWBERRY, John Stoughton (father of Truman Handy Newberry) (R Mich.) Nov. 18, 1826-Jan. 2, 1887; House 1879-81.

NEWBERRY, Truman Handy (son of John Stoughton Newberry) (R Mich.) Nov. 5, 1864-Oct. 3, 1945; Senate 1919-Nov. 18, 1922; Secy. of the Navy 1908-09.

NEWBERRY, Walter Cass (D Ill.) Dec. 23, 1835-July 20, 1912; House 1891-93.

NEWBOLD, Thomas (D N.J.) Aug. 2, 1760-Dec. 18, 1823; House 1807-13.

NEWCOMB, Carman Adam (R Mo.) July 1, 1830-April 6, 1902; House 1867-69.

NEWELL, William Augustus (R N.J.) Sept. 5, 1817-Aug. 8, 1901; House 1845-51 (Whig), 1865-67; Gov. 1857-60, (Wash. Terr.) 1880-84.

NEWHALL, Judson Lincoln (R Ky.) March 26, 1870-July 23, 1952; House 1929-31.

NEWHARD, Peter (D Pa.) July 26, 1783-Feb. 19, 1860; House 1839-43.

NEWLANDS, Francis Griffith (D Nev.) Aug. 28, 1848-Dec. 24, 1917; House 1893-1903; Senate 1903-Dec. 24, 1917.

NEWMAN, Alexander (D Va.) Oct. 5, 1804-Sept. 8, 1849; House March 4-Sept. 8, 1849.

NEWNAN, Daniel (SRD Ga.) about 1780-Jan. 16, 1851; House 1831-33.

NEWSHAM, Joseph Parkinson (R La.) May 24, 1837-Oct. 22, 1919; House July 18, 1868-69, May 23, 1870-71.

NEWSOME, John Parks (D Ala.) Feb. 13, 1893-Nov. 10, 1961; House 1943-45.

NEWTON, Cherubusco (D La.) May 15, 1848-May 26, 1910; House 1887-89.

NEWTON, Cleveland Alexander (R Mo.) Sept. 3, 1873-Sept. 17, 1945; House 1919-27.

NEWTON, Eben (W Ohio) Oct. 16, 1795-Nov. 6, 1885; House 1851-53.

NEWTON, Thomas Jr. (D Va.) Nov. 21, 1768-Aug. 5, 1847; House 1801-29, March 4, 1829-March 9, 1830, 1831-33.

NEWTON, Thomas Willoughby (W Ark.) Jan. 18, 1804 Sept. 22, 1853; House Feb. 6-March 3, 1847.

NEWTON, Walter Hughes (R Minn.) Oct. 10, 1880-Aug 10, 1941; House 1919-June 30, 1929.

NEWTON, Willoughby (W Va.) Dec. 2, 1802-May 23 1874; House 1843-45.

NIBLACK, Silas Leslie (cousin of William Ellis Niblack) (D Fla.) March 17, 1825-Feb. 13, 1883 House Jan. 29-March 3, 1873.

NIBLACK, William Ellis (cousin of Silas Leslie Niblack) (D Ind.) May 19, 1822-May 7, 1893; Hous Dec. 7, 1857-61, 1865-75.

NICHOLAS, John (brother of Wilson Cary Nicholas uncle of Robert Carter Nicholas) (DR Va.) about 1757-Dec. 31, 1819; House 1793-1801.

NICHOLAS, Robert Carter (nephew of John Nicholas and Wilson Cary Nicholas) (D La.) 1793-Dec. 24 1857; Senate Jan. 13, 1836-41.

NICHOLAS, Wilson Cary (brother of John Nicholas uncle of Robert Carter Nicholas) (DR Va.) Jan. 31 1761-Oct. 10, 1820; Senate Dec. 5, 1799-May 22 1804; House 1807-Nov. 27, 1809; Gov. 1814-16.

NICHOLLS, John Calhoun (D Ga.) April 25, 1834-Dec 25, 1893; House 1879-81, 1883-85.

NICHOLLS, Samuel Jones (D S.C.) May 7, 1885-Nov 23, 1937; House Sept. 14, 1915-21.

NICHOLLS, Thomas David (D Pa.) Sept. 16, 1870-Jan 19, 1931; House 1907-11.

NICHOLS, Charles Archibald (R Mich.) Aug. 25, 1876 April 25, 1920; House 1915-April 25, 1920.

NICHOLS, John (I N.C.) Nov. 14, 1834-Sept. 22, 1917 House 1887-89.

NICHOLS, John Conover "Jack" (D Okla.) Aug. 31 1896-Nov. 7, 1945; House 1935-July 3, 1943.

NICHOLS, Matthias H. (R Ohio) Oct. 3, 1824-Sept. 1 1862; House 1853-59 (1853-55 Whig).

NICHOLS, William (D Ala.) Oct. 16, 1918- ; Hou 1967- .

NICHOLSON, Alfred Osborn Pope (D Tenn.) Aug. 31 1808-March 23, 1876; Senate Dec. 25, 1840-Feb. 1842, 1859-61.

NICHOLSON, Donald William (R Mass.) Aug. 11, 1888 Feb. 16, 1968; House Nov. 18, 1947-59.

NICHOLSON, John (D N.Y.) 1765-Jan. 20, 1820; Hou 1809-11.

NICHOLSON, John Anthony (D Del.) Nov. 17, 1827-Nov. 4, 1906; House 1865-69.

NICHOLSON, Joseph Hopper (D Md.) May 15, 1770-March 4, 1817; House 1799-March 1, 1806.

NICHOLSON, Samuel Danford (R Colo.) Feb. 22, 1859-March 24, 1923; Senate 1921-March 24, 1923.

NICKLES, Donald L. (R Okla.) Dec. 6, 1948- –; Senate 1981- –.

NICOLL, Henry (D N.Y.) Oct. 23, 1812-Nov. 28, 1879; House 1847-49.

NIEDRINGHAUS, Frederick Gottlieb (uncle of Henry Frederick Niedringhaus) (R Mo.) Oct. 21, 1837-Nov. 25, 1922; House 1889-91.

NIEDRINGHAUS, Henry Frederick (nephew of Frederick Gottlieb Niedringhaus) (R Mo.) Dec. 15, 1864-Aug. 3, 1941; House 1927-33.

NIELSON, Howard Curtis (R Utah) Sept. 12, 1924- –; House 1983- –.

NILES, Jason (R Miss.) Dec. 19, 1814-July 7, 1894; House 1873-75.

NILES, John Milton (D Conn.) Aug. 20, 1787-May 31, 1856; Senate Dec. 21, 1835-39, 1843-49; Postmaster Gen. 1840-41.

NILES, Nathaniel (– Vt.) April 3, 1741-Oct. 31, 1828; House Oct. 17, 1791-95.

NIMTZ, F. Jay (R Ind.) Dec. 1, 1915- –; House 1957-59.

NISBET, Eugenius Aristides (cousin of Mark Anthony Cooper) (W Ga.) Dec. 7, 1803-March 18, 1871; House 1839-Oct. 12, 1841.

NIVEN, Archibald Campbell (D N.Y.) Dec. 8, 1803-Feb. 21, 1882; House 1845-47.

NIX, Robert Nelson Cornelius Sr. (D Pa.) Aug. 9, 1905- –; House May 20, 1958-79.

NIXON, George Stuart (R Nev.) April 2, 1860-June 5, 1912; Senate 1905-June 5, 1912.

NIXON, John Thompson (R N.J.) Aug. 31, 1820-Sept. 28, 1889; House 1859-63.

NIXON, Richard Milhous (R Calif.) Jan. 9, 1913- –; House 1947-Nov. 30, 1950; Senate Dec. 1, 1950-Jan. 1, 1953; Vice President 1953-61; President 1969-Aug. 9, 1974.

NOBLE, David Addison (D Mich.) Nov. 9, 1802-Oct. 13, 1876; House 1853-55.

NOBLE, James (DR Ind.) Dec. 16, 1785-Feb. 26, 1831; Senate Dec. 11, 1816-Feb. 26, 1831.

NOBLE, Warren Perry (D Ohio) June 14, 1820-July 9, 1903; House 1861-65.

NOBLE, William Henry (D N.Y.) Sept. 22, 1788-Feb. 5, 1850; House 1837-39.

NODAR, Robert Joseph Jr. (R N.Y.) March 23, 1916- –; House 1947-49.

NOELL, John William (father of Thomas Estes Noell) (D Mo.) Feb. 22, 1816-March 14, 1863; House 1859-March 14, 1863.

NOELL, Thomas Estes (son of John William Noell) (Rad. Mo.) April 3, 1839-Oct. 3, 1867; House 1865-Oct. 3, 1867.

NOLAN, John Ignatius (husband of Mae Ella Nolan) (R Calif.) Jan. 14, 1874-Nov. 18, 1922; House 1913-Nov. 18, 1922.

NOLAN, Mae Ella (widow of John Ignatius Nolan) (R Calif.) Sept. 20, 1886-July 9, 1973; House Jan. 23, 1923-25.

NOLAN, Michael Nicholas (D N.Y.) May 4, 1833-May 31, 1905; House 1881-83.

NOLAN, Richard Michael (D Minn.) Dec. 17, 1943- –; House 1975-81.

NOLAN, William Ignatius (R Minn.) May 14, 1874-Aug. 3, 1943; House June 17, 1929-33.

NOLAND, James E. (D Ind.) April 22, 1920- –; House 1949-51.

NOONAN, Edward Thomas (D Ill.) Oct. 23, 1861-Dec. 19, 1923; House 1899-1901.

NOONAN, George Henry (R Texas) Aug. 20, 1828-Aug. 17, 1907; House 1895-97.

NORBECK, Peter (R S.D.) Aug. 27, 1870-Dec. 20, 1936; Senate 1921-Dec. 20, 1936; Gov. 1917-21.

NORBLAD, Albin Walter Jr. (R Ore.) Sept. 12, 1908-Sept. 20, 1964; House Jan. 11, 1946-Sept. 20, 1964.

NORCROSS, Amasa (R Mass.) Jan. 26, 1824-April 2, 1898; House 1877-83.

NORMAN, Fred Barthold (R Wash.) March 21, 1882-April 18, 1947; House 1943-45, Jan. 3-April 18, 1947.

NORRELL, Catherine Dorris (widow of William Frank Norrell) (D Ark.) March 30, 1901-Aug. 26, 1981; House April 18, 1961-63.

NORRELL, William Frank (husband of Catherine Dorris Norrell) (D Ark.) Aug. 29, 1896-Feb. 15, 1961; House 1939-Feb. 15, 1961.

NORRIS, Benjamin White (R Ala.) Jan. 22, 1819-Jan. 26, 1873; House July 21, 1868-69.

NORRIS, George William (IR Neb.) July 11, 1861-Sept. 2, 1944; House 1903-13; Senate 1913-43 (1913-37 Republican).

NORRIS, Moses Jr. (D N.H.) Nov. 8, 1799-Jan. 11, 1855; House 1843-47; Senate 1849-Jan. 11, 1855.

NORTH, Solomon Taylor (R Pa.) May 24, 1853-Oct. 19, 1917; House 1915-17.

NORTH, William (F N.Y.) 1755-Jan. 3, 1836; Senate May 5-Aug. 17, 1798.

NORTHWAY, Stephen Asa (R Ohio) June 19, 1833-Sept. 8, 1898; House 1893-Sept. 8, 1898.

NORTON, Daniel Sheldon (UC Minn.) April 12, 1829-July 13, 1870; Senate 1865-July 13, 1870.

NORTON, Ebenezer Foote (D N.Y.) Nov. 7, 1774-May 11, 1851; House 1829-31.

NORTON, Elijah Hise (D Mo.) Nov. 24, 1821-Aug. 5, 1914; House 1861-63.

NORTON, James (D S.C.) Oct. 8, 1843-Oct. 14, 1920; House Dec. 6, 1897-1901.

NORTON, James Albert (D Ohio) Nov. 11, 1843-July 24, 1912; House 1897-1903.

NORTON, Jesse Olds (R Ill.) Dec. 25, 1812-Aug. 3, 1875; House 1853-57, 1863-65.

NORTON, John Nathaniel (D Neb.) May 12, 1878-Oct. 5, 1960; House 1927-29, 1931-33.

NORTON, Mary Teresa (D N.J.) March 7, 1875-Aug. 2, 1959; House 1925-51.

NORTON, Miner Gibbs (R Ohio) May 11, 1857-Sept. 7, 1926; House 1921-23.

NORTON, Nelson Ira (R N.Y.) March 30, 1820-Oct. 28, 1887; House Dec. 6, 1875-77.

NORTON, Patrick Daniel (R N.D.) May 17, 1876-Oct. 14, 1953; House 1913-19.

NORTON, Richard Henry (D Mo.) Nov. 6, 1849-March 15, 1918; House 1889-93.

NORVELL, John (D Mich.) Dec. 21, 1789-April 24, 1850; Senate Jan. 26, 1837-41.

NORWOOD, Thomas Manson (D Ga.) April 26, 1830-June 19, 1913; Senate Nov. 14, 1871-77; House 1885-89.

NOTT, Abraham (F S.C.) Feb. 5, 1768-June 19, 1830; House 1799-1801.

NOURSE, Amos (– Maine) Dec. 17, 1794-April 7, 1877; Senate Jan. 16-March 3, 1857.

NOWAK, Henry James (D N.Y.) Feb. 21, 1935-–; House 1975-–.

NOYES, John (F Vt.) April 2, 1764-Oct. 26, 1841; Hous 1815-17.

NOYES, Joseph Cobham (W Maine) Sept. 22, 1798-Jul 28, 1868; House 1837-39.

NUCKOLLS, Stephen Friel (D Wyo.) Aug. 16, 1825 Feb. 14, 1879; House (Terr. Del.) Dec. 6, 1869-71.

NUCKOLLS, William Thompson (– S.C.) Feb. 23 1801-Sept. 27, 1855; House 1827-33.

NUGEN, Robert Hunter (D Ohio) July 16, 1809-Feb. 28 1872; House 1861-63.

NUGENT, John Frost (D Idaho) June 28, 1868-Sept. 18 1931; Senate Jan. 22, 1918-Jan. 14, 1921.

NUNN, David Alexander (R Tenn.) July 26, 1833-Sep 11, 1918; House 1867-69, 1873-75.

NUNN, Samuel Augustus (D Ga.) Sept. 8, 1938-–; Sei ate Nov. 8, 1972-–.

NUTE, Alonzo (R N.H.) Feb. 12, 1826-Dec. 24, 189 House 1889-91.

NUTTING, Newton Wright (R N.Y.) Oct. 22, 1840-Oc 15, 1889; House 1883-85, 1887-Oct. 15, 1889.

NYE, Frank Mellen (R Minn.) March 7, 1852-Nov. 2 1935; House 1907-13.

NYE, Gerald Prentice (R N.D.) Dec. 19, 1892-July 1 1971; Senate Nov. 14, 1925-45.

NYE, James Warren (R Nev.) June 10, 1815-Dec. 2 1876; Senate Dec. 16, 1864-73; Gov. (Nev. Terr 1861-64.

NYGAARD, Hjalmar (R N.D.) March 24, 1906-July 1 1963; House 1961-July 18, 1963.

OAKAR, Mary Rose (D Ohio) March 5, 1940-–; Hou 1977-–.

OAKEY, Peter Davis (R Conn.) Feb. 25, 1861-Nov. 1 1920; House 1915-17.

OAKLEY, Thomas Jackson (Clinton D. N.Y.) Nov. 1 1783-May 11, 1857; House 1813-15 (Federalis 1827-May 9, 1828.

OAKMAN, Charles Gibb (R Mich.) Sept. 4, 1903-O 28,.1973; House 1953-55.

OATES, William Calvin (D Ala.) Dec. 1, 1835-Sept. 1910; House 1881-Nov. 5, 1894; Gov. 1894-96.

OBERSTAR, James Louis (D Minn.) Sept. 10, 1934-–; House 1975-–.

OBEY, David Ross (D Wis.) Oct. 3, 1938- —; House April 1, 1969- —.

O'BRIEN, Charles Francis Xavier (D N.J.) March 7, 1879-Nov. 14, 1940; House 1921-25.

O'BRIEN, George Donoghue (D Mich.) Jan. 1, 1900-Oct. 25, 1957; House 1937-39, 1941-47, 1949-55.

O'BRIEN, George Miller (R Ill.) June 17, 1917-July 17, · 1986; House 1973-July 17, 1986.

O'BRIEN, James (ATD N.Y.) March 13, 1841-March 5, 1907; House 1879-81.

O'BRIEN, James Henry (D N.Y.) July 15, 1860-Sept. 2, 1924; House 1913-15.

O'BRIEN, Jeremiah (D Maine) Jan. 21, 1778-May 30, 1858; House 1823-29.

O'BRIEN, Joseph John (R N.Y.) Oct. 9, 1897-Jan. 23, 1953; House 1939-45.

O'BRIEN, Leo William (D N.Y.) Sept. 21, 1900-May 4, 1982; House April 1, 1952-67.

O'BRIEN, Thomas Joseph (D Ill.) April 30, 1878-April 14, 1964; House 1933-39, 1943-April 14, 1964.

O'BRIEN, William James (D Md.) May 28, 1836-Nov. 13, 1905; House 1873-77.

O'BRIEN, William Smith (D W.Va.) Jan. 8, 1862-Aug. 10, 1948; House 1927-29.

OCAMPO, Pablo (— P.I.) Jan. 25, 1853-Feb. 5, 1925; House (Res. Comm.) Nov. 22, 1907-Nov. 22, 1909.

OCHILTREE, Thomas Peck (I Texas) Oct. 26, 1837-Nov. 25, 1902; House 1883-85.

O'CONNELL, David Joseph (D N.Y.) Dec. 25, 1868-Dec. 29, 1930; House 1919-21, 1923-Dec. 29, 1930.

O'CONNELL, Jeremiah Edward (D R.I.) July 8, 1883-Sept. 18, 1964; House 1923-27, 1929-May 9, 1930.

O'CONNELL, Jerry Joseph (D Mont.) June 14, 1909-Jan. 16, 1956; House 1937-39.

O'CONNELL, John Matthew (D R.I.) Aug. 10, 1872-Dec. 6, 1941; House 1933-39.

O'CONNELL, Joseph Francis (D Mass.) Dec. 7, 1872-Dec. 10, 1942; House 1907-11.

O'CONNOR, Charles (R Okla.) Oct. 26, 1878-Nov. 15, 1940; House 1929-31.

O'CONNOR, James (D La.) April 4, 1870-Jan. 7, 1941; House June 5, 1919-31.

O'CONNOR, James Francis (D Mont.) May 7, 1878-Jan. 15, 1945; House 1937-Jan. 15, 1945.

O'CONNOR, John Joseph (D N.Y.) Nov. 23, 1885-Jan. 26, 1960; House Nov. 6, 1923-39.

O'CONNOR, Michael Patrick (D S.C.) Sept. 29, 1831-April 26, 1881; House 1879-April 26, 1881.

O'CONOR, Herbert Romulus (D Md.) Nov. 17, 1896-March 4, 1960; Senate 1947-53; Gov. 1939-47.

O'DANIEL, Wilbert Lee "Pappy" (D Texas) March 11, 1890-May 11, 1969; Senate Aug. 4, 1941-49; Gov. 1939-41.

O'DAY, Caroline Love Goodwin (D N.Y.) June 22, 1875-Jan. 4, 1943; House 1935-43.

ODDIE, Tasker Lowndes (R Nev.) Oct. 24, 1870-Feb. 18, 1950; Senate 1921-33; Gov. 1911-15.

ODELL, Benjamin Baker Jr. (R N.Y.) Jan. 14, 1854-May 9, 1926; House 1895-99; Gov. 1901-05.

ODELL, Moses Fowler (D N.Y.) Feb. 24, 1818-June 13, 1866; House 1861-65.

ODELL, Nathaniel (D N.Y.) Oct. 10, 1828-Oct. 30, 1904; House 1875-77.

O'DONNELL, James (R Mich.) March 25, 1840-March 17, 1915; House 1885-93.

O'FERRALL, Charles Triplett (D Va.) Oct. 21, 1840-Sept. 22, 1905; House May 5, 1884-Dec. 28, 1893; Gov. 1894-98.

OGDEN, Aaron (F N.J.) Dec. 3, 1756-April 19, 1839; Senate Feb. 28, 1801-03; Gov. 1812-13.

OGDEN, Charles Franklin (R Ky.) ?-April 10, 1933; House 1919-23.

OGDEN, David A. (F N.Y.) Jan. 10, 1770-June 9, 1829; House 1817-19.

OGDEN, Henry Warren (D La.) Oct. 21, 1842-July 23, 1905; House May 12, 1894-99.

OGLE, Alexander (father of Charles Ogle, grandfather of Andrew Jackson Ogle) (D Pa.) Aug. 10, 1766-Oct. 14, 1832; House 1817-19.

OGLE, Andrew Jackson (grandson of Alexander Ogle) (W Pa.) March 25, 1822-Oct. 14, 1852; House 1849-51.

OGLE, Charles (son of Alexander Ogle) (W Pa.) 1798-May 10, 1841; House 1837-May 10, 1841.

OGLESBY, Richard James (cousin of Woodson Ratcliffe Oglesby) (R Ill.) July 25, 1824-April 24, 1899; Senate 1873-79; Gov. 1865-69, Jan. 13-23, 1873, 1885-89.

OGLESBY, Woodson Ratcliffe (cousin of Richard James Oglesby) (D N.Y.) Feb. 9, 1867-April 30, 1955; House 1913-17.

O'GORMAN, James Aloysius (D N.Y.) May 5, 1860-May 17, 1943; Senate 1911-17.

O'GRADY, James Mary Early (R N.Y.) March 31, 1863-Nov. 3, 1928; House 1899-1901.

O'HAIR, Frank Trimble (D Ill.) March 12, 1870-Aug. 3, 1932; House 1913-15.

O'HARA, Barratt (D Ill.) April 28, 1882-Aug. 11, 1969; House 1949-51, 1953-69.

O'HARA, James Edward (R N.C.) Feb. 26, 1844-Sept. 15, 1905; House 1883-87.

O'HARA, James Grant (D Mich.) Nov. 8, 1925- —; House 1959-77.

O'HARA, Joseph Patrick (R Minn.) Jan. 23, 1895-March 4, 1975; House 1941-59.

OHLIGER, Lewis Phillip (D Ohio) Jan. 3, 1843-Jan. 9, 1923; House Dec. 5, 1892-93.

O'KONSKI, Alvin Edward (R Wis.) May 26, 1904- —; House 1943-73.

OLCOTT, Jacob Van Vechten (R N.Y.) May 17, 1856-June 1, 1940; House 1905-11.

OLCOTT, Simeon (F N.H.) Oct. 1, 1735-Feb. 22, 1815; Senate June 17, 1801-05.

OLDFIELD, Pearl Peden (widow of William Allan Oldfield) (D Ark.) Dec. 2, 1876-April 12, 1962; House Jan. 9, 1929-31.

OLDFIELD, William Allan (husband of Pearl Peden Oldfield) (D Ark.) Feb. 4, 1874-Nov. 19, 1928; House 1909-Nov. 19, 1928.

OLDS, Edson Baldwin (D Ohio) June 3, 1802-Jan. 24, 1869; House 1849-55.

O'LEARY, Denis (D N.Y.) Jan. 22, 1863-Sept. 27, 1943; House 1913-Dec. 31, 1914.

O'LEARY, James Aloysius (D N.Y.) April 23, 1889-March 16, 1944; House 1935-March 16, 1944.

OLIN, Abram Baldwin (son of Gideon Olin, cousin of Henry Olin) (R N.Y.) Sept. 21, 1808-July 7, 1879; House 1857-63.

OLIN, Gideon (father of Abram Baldwin Olin, uncle of Henry Olin) (D Vt.) Nov. 2, 1743-Jan. 21, 1823; House 1803-07.

OLIN, Henry (nephew of Gideon Olin, cousin of Abram Baldwin Olin) (Jeff.D Vt.) May 7, 1768-Aug. 16, 1837; House Dec. 13, 1824-25.

OLIN, James R. (D Va.) Feb. 28, 1920- —; House 198? —.

OLIVER, Andrew (D N.Y.) Jan. 16, 1815-March 6, 188? House 1853-57.

OLIVER, Daniel Charles (D N.Y.) Oct. 6, 1865-Marc 26, 1924; House 1917-19.

OLIVER, Frank (D N.Y.) Oct. 2, 1883-Jan. 1, 196? House 1923-June 18, 1934.

OLIVER, George Tener (R Pa.) Jan. 26, 1848-Jan. 2, 1919; Senate March 17, 1909-17.

OLIVER, James Churchill (D Maine) Aug. 6, 1895-De 25, 1986; House 1937-43 (Republican); 1959-61.

OLIVER, Mordecai (W Mo.) Oct. 22, 1819-April 2 1898; House 1853-57.

OLIVER, Samuel Addison (R Iowa) July 21, 1833-Ju? 7, 1912; House 1875-79.

OLIVER, William Bacon (cousin of Sydney Parha? Epes) (D Ala.) May 23, 1867-May 27, 1948; Hou? 1915-37.

OLIVER, William Morrison (D N.Y.) Oct. 15, 1792-Ju 21, 1863; House 1841-43.

OLMSTED, Marlin Edgar (R Pa.) May 21, 1847-July ? 1913; House 1897-1913.

OLNEY, Richard (D Mass.) Jan. 5, 1871-Jan. 15, 193? House 1915-21.

O'LOUGHLIN, Kathryn Ellen (later married a? served as Kathryn O'Loughlin McCarthy) (D Kar? April 24, 1894-Jan. 16, 1952; House 1933-35.

OLPP, Archibald Ernest (R N.J.) May 12, 1882-July ? 1949; House 1921-23.

OLSEN, Arnold (D Mont.) Dec. 17, 1916- —; Hou? 1961-71.

OLSON, Alec G. (D Minn.) Sept. 11, 1930- —; Hou? 1963-67.

O'MAHONEY, Joseph Christopher (D Wyo.) Nov. 1884-Dec. 1, 1962; Senate Jan. 1, 1934-53; Nov. ? 1954-61.

O'MALLEY, Matthew Vincent (D N.Y.) June 26, 187? May 26, 1931; House March 4-May 26, 1931.

O'MALLEY, Thomas David Patrick (D Wis.) March ? 1903- —; House 1933-39.

O'NEAL, Emmet (D Ky.) April 14, 1887-July 18, 196? House 1935-47.

O'NEAL, Maston Emmett Jr. (D Ga.) July 19, 1907- House 1965-71.

O'NEALL, John Henry (D Ind.) Oct. 30, 1838-July 15, 1907; House 1887-91.

O'NEIL, Joseph Henry (D Mass.) March 23, 1853-Feb. 19, 1935; House 1889-95.

O'NEILL, Charles (R Pa.) March 21, 1821-Nov. 25, 1893; House 1863-71, 1873-Nov. 25, 1893.

O'NEILL, Edward Leo (D N.J.) July 10, 1903-Dec. 12, 1948; House 1937-39.

O'NEILL, Harry Patrick (D Pa.) Feb. 10, 1889-June 24, 1953; House 1949-53.

O'NEILL, John (D Ohio) Dec. 17, 1822-May 25, 1905; House 1863-65.

O'NEILL, John Joseph (D Mo.) June 25, 1846-Feb. 19, 1898; House 1883-89, 1891-93, April 3, 1894-95.

O'NEILL, Thomas Phillip "Tip" Jr. (D Mass.) Dec. 9, 1912- —; House 1953-87; House majority leader 1973-77; Speaker 1977-87.

O'REILLY, Daniel (D N.Y.) June 3, 1838-Sept. 23, 1911; House 1879-81.

ORMSBY, Stephen (D Ky.) 1759-1844; House 1811-13, April 20, 1813-17.

ORR, Alexander Dalrymple (nephew of William Grayson, cousin of William John Grayson (— Ky.) Nov. 6, 1761-June 21, 1835; House Nov. 8, 1792-97.

ORR, Benjamin (F Mass.) Dec. 1, 1772-Sept. 3, 1828; House 1817-19.

ORR, Jackson (R Iowa) Sept. 21, 1832-March 15, 1926; House 1871-75.

ORR, James Lawrence (D S.C.) May 12, 1822-May 5, 1873; House 1849-59; Speaker 1857-59; Gov. 1865-68 (Republican).

ORR, Robert Jr. (D Pa.) March 5, 1786-May 22, 1876; House Oct. 11, 1825-29.

ORTH, Godlove Stein (R Ind.) April 22, 1817-Dec. 16, 1882; House 1863-71, 1873-75, 1879-Dec. 16, 1882.

ORTIZ, Solomon Porfirio (D Texas) June 3, 1937- —; House 1983- —.

OSBORN, Thomas Ward (R Fla.) March 9, 1836-Dec. 18, 1898; Senate June 25, 1868-73.

OSBORNE, Edwin Sylvanus (R Pa.) Aug. 7, 1839-Jan. 1, 1900; House 1885-91.

OSBORNE, Henry Zenas (R Calif.) Oct. 4, 1848-Feb. 8, 1923; House 1917-Feb. 8, 1923.

OSBORNE, John Eugene (D Wyo.) June 19, 1858-April 24, 1953; House 1897-99; Gov. 1893-95.

OSBORNE, Thomas Burr (W Conn.) July 8, 1798-Sept. 2, 1869; House 1839-43.

OSGOOD, Gayton Pickman (D Mass.) July 4, 1797-June 26, 1861; House 1833-35.

O'SHAUNESSY, George Francis (D R.I.) May 1, 1868-Nov. 28, 1934; House 1911-19.

OSIAS, Camilo (Nat. P.I.) March 23, 1889- —; House (Res. Comm.) 1929-35.

OSMER, James H. (R Pa.) Jan. 23, 1832-Oct. 3, 1912; House 1879-81.

OSMERS, Frank Charles Jr. (R N.J.) Dec. 30, 1907-May 21, 1977; House 1939-43, Nov. 6, 1951-65.

OSTERTAG, Harold Charles (R N.Y.) June 22, 1896-May 2, 1985; House 1951-65.

O'SULLIVAN, Eugene Daniel (D Neb.) May 31, 1883-Feb. 7, 1968; House 1949-51.

O'SULLIVAN, Patrick Brett (D Conn.) Aug. 11, 1887-Nov. 10, 1978; House 1923-25.

OTERO, Mariano Sabino (nephew of Miguel Antonio Otero) (R N.M.) Aug. 29, 1844-Feb. 1, 1904; House (Terr. Del.) 1879-81.

OTERO, Miguel Antonio (uncle of Mariano Sabino Otero) (D N.M.) June 21, 1829-May 30, 1882; House (Terr. Del.) July 23, 1856-61.

OTEY, Peter Johnston (D Va.) Dec. 22, 1840-May 4, 1902; House 1895-May 4, 1902.

OTIS, Harrison Gray (F Mass.) Oct. 8, 1765-Oct. 28, 1848; House 1797-1801; Senate 1817-May 30, 1822.

OTIS, John (W Maine) Aug. 3, 1801-Oct. 17, 1856; House 1849-51.

OTIS, John Grant (PP Kan.) Feb. 10, 1838-Feb. 22, 1916; House 1891-93.

OTIS, Norton Prentiss (R N.Y.) March 18, 1840-Feb. 20, 1905; House 1903-Feb. 20, 1905.

OTJEN, Theobald (R Wis.) Oct. 27, 1851-April 11, 1924; House 1895-1907.

O'TOOLE, Donald Lawrence (D N.Y.) Aug. 1, 1902-Sept. 12, 1964; House 1937-53.

OTTINGER, Richard Lawrence (D N.Y.) Jan. 27, 1929- —; House 1965-71, 1975-85.

OURY, Granville Henderson (D Ariz.) March 12, 1825-Jan. 11, 1891; House (Terr. Del.) 1881-85.

OUTHWAITE, Joseph Hodson (D Ohio) Dec. 5, 1841-Dec. 9, 1907; House 1885-95.

OUTLAND, George Elmer (D Calif.) Oct. 8, 1906- —; House 1943-47.

OUTLAW, David (cousin of George Outlaw) (W N.C.) Sept. 14, 1806-Oct. 22, 1868; House 1847-53.

OUTLAW, George (cousin of David Outlaw) (JD N.C.) ?-Aug. 15, 1825; House Jan. 19-March 3, 1825.

OVERMAN, Lee Slater (D N.C.) Jan. 3, 1854-Dec. 12, 1930; Senate 1903-Dec. 12, 1930.

OVERMYER, Arthur Warren (D Ohio) May 31, 1879-March 8, 1952; House 1915-19.

OVERSTREET, James (— S.C.) Feb. 11, 1773-May 24, 1822; House 1819-May 24, 1822.

OVERSTREET, James Whetstone (D Ga.) Aug. 28, 1866-Dec. 4, 1938; House Oct. 3, 1906-07, 1917-23.

OVERSTREET, Jesse (R Ind.) Dec. 14, 1859-May 27, 1910; House 1895-1909.

OVERTON, Edward Jr. (R Pa.) Feb. 4, 1836-Sept. 18, 1903; House 1877-81.

OVERTON, John Holmes (uncle of Overton Brooks) (D La.) Sept. 17, 1875-May 14, 1948; House May 12, 1931-33; Senate 1933-May 14, 1948.

OVERTON, Walter Hampden (D La.) 1788-Dec. 24, 1845; House 1829-31.

OWEN, Allen Ferdinand (W Ga.) Oct. 9, 1816-April 7, 1865; House 1849-51.

OWEN, Emmett Marshall (D Ga.) Oct. 19, 1877-June 21, 1939; House 1933-June 21, 1939.

OWEN, George Washington (— Ala.) Oct. 20, 1796-Aug. 18, 1837; House 1823-29.

OWEN, James (D N.C.) Dec. 7, 1784-Sept. 4, 1865; House 1817-19.

OWEN, Robert Dale (D Ind.) Nov. 9, 1800-June 24, 1877; House 1843-47.

OWEN, Robert Latham (D Okla.) Feb. 3, 1856-July 19, 1947; Senate Dec. 11, 1907-25.

OWEN, Ruth Bryan (later Mrs. Borge Rohde, daughter of William Jennings Bryan) (D Fla.) Oct. 2, 1885-July 26, 1954; House 1929-33.

OWEN, William Dale (R Ind.) Sept. 6, 1846-1906; House 1885-91.

OWENS, Douglas Wayne (D Utah) May 2, 1937- —; House 1973-75, 1987- —.

OWENS, George Welshman (U Ga.) Aug. 29, 1786-March 2, 1856; House 1835-39.

OWENS, James W. (D Ohio) Oct. 24, 1837-March 30, 1900; House 1889-93.

OWENS, Major Robert Odell (D N.Y.) June 28, 1936- — House 1983- —.

OWENS, Thomas Leonard (R Ill.) Dec. 21, 1897-June 7, 1948; House 1947-June 7, 1948.

OWENS, William Claiborne (D Ky.) Oct. 17, 1849-Nov 18, 1925; House 1895-97.

OWSLEY, Bryan Young (W Ky.) Aug. 19, 1798-Oct. 27, 1849; House 1841-43.

OXLEY, Michael Garver (R Ohio) Feb. 11, 1944- — House July 21, 1981- —.

PACE, Stephen (D Ga.) March 9, 1891-April 5, 1970; House 1937-51.

PACHECO, Romualdo (R Calif.) Oct. 31, 1831-Jan. 23, 1899; House 1877-Feb. 7, 1878, 1879-83; Gov. Feb. 27-Dec. 9, 1875.

PACKARD, Jasper (R Ind.) Feb. 1, 1832-Dec. 13, 1899; House 1869-75.

PACKARD, Ron (R Calif.) Jan. 19, 1931- —; House 1983- —.

PACKER, Asa (D Pa.) Dec. 29, 1805-May 17, 1879; House 1853-57.

PACKER, Horace Billings (R Pa.) Oct. 11, 1851-April 13, 1940; House 1897-1901.

PACKER, John Black (R Pa.) March 21, 1824-July 7, 1891; House 1869-77.

PACKWOOD, Robert William (R Ore.) Sept. 11, 1932- —; Senate 1969- —.

PADDOCK, Algernon Sidney (R Neb.) Nov. 9, 1830-Oct. 17, 1897; Senate 1875-81, 1887-93.

PADDOCK, George Arthur (R Ill.) March 24, 1885-Dec. 29, 1964; House 1941-43.

PADGETT, Lemuel Phillips (D Tenn.) Nov. 28, 1855-Aug. 2, 1922; House 1901-Aug. 2, 1922.

PAGAN, Bolivar (Coal. P.R.) May 16, 1897-Feb. 9, 1961; House (Res. Comm.) Dec. 26, 1939-45.

PAGE, Carroll Smalley (R Vt.) Jan. 10, 1843-Dec. 3, 1925; Senate Oct. 21, 1908-23; Gov. 1890-92.

PAGE, Charles Harrison (D R.I.) July 19, 1843-July 21, 1912; House Feb. 21-March 3, 1887, 1891-93, April 5, 1893-95.

PAGE, Henry (D Md.) June 28, 1841-Jan. 7, 1913; House 1891-Sept. 3, 1892.

AGE, Horace Francis (R Calif.) Oct. 20, 1833-Aug. 23, 1890; House 1873-83.

AGE, John (D Va.) April 17, 1744-Oct. 11, 1808; House 1789-97; Gov. 1802-05.

AGE, John (D N.H.) May 21, 1787-Sept. 8, 1865; Senate June 8, 1836-37; Gov. 1839-42.

AGE, Robert (F Va.) Feb. 4, 1765-Dec. 8, 1840; House 1799-1801.

AGE, Robert Newton (D N.C.) Oct. 26, 1859-Oct. 3, 1933; House 1903-17.

AGE, Sherman (JD N.Y.) May 9, 1779-Sept. 27, 1853; House 1833-37.

AIGE, Calvin DeWitt (R Mass.) May 20, 1848-April 24, 1930; House Nov. 26, 1913-25.

AIGE, David Raymond (D Ohio) April 8, 1844-June 30, 1901; House 1883-85.

AINE, Elijah (F Vt.) Jan. 21, 1757-April 28, 1842; Senate 1795-Sept. 1, 1801.

AINE, Halbert Eleazer (R Wis.) Feb. 4, 1826-April 14, 1905; House 1865-71.

AINE, Robert Treat (AP N.C.) Feb. 18, 1812-Feb. 8, 1872; House 1855-57.

AINE, William Wiseham (D Ga.) Oct. 10, 1817-Aug. 5, 1882; House Dec. 22, 1870-71.

ALEN, Rufus (W N.Y.) Feb. 25, 1807-April 26, 1844; House 1839-41.

ALFREY, John Gorham (W Mass.) May 2, 1796-April 26, 1881; House 1847-49.

ALMER, Alexander Mitchell (D Pa.) May 4, 1872-May 11, 1936; House 1909-15; Atty. Gen. 1919-21.

ALMER, Beriah (− N.Y.) 1740-May 20, 1812; House 1803-05.

ALMER, Cyrus Maffet (R Pa.) Feb. 12, 1887-Aug. 16, 1959; House 1927-29.

ALMER, Francis Wayland "Frank" (R Iowa) Oct. 11, 1827-Dec. 3, 1907; House 1869-73.

ALMER, George William (nephew of John Palmer, cousin of William Elisha Haynes) (R N.Y.) Jan. 13, 1818-March 2, 1916; House 1857-61.

ALMER, Henry Wilber (R Pa.) July 10, 1839-Feb. 15, 1913; House 1901-07, 1909-11.

ALMER, John (uncle of George William Palmer) (D N.Y.) Jan. 29, 1785-Dec. 8, 1840; House 1817-19, 1837-39.

PALMER, John McAuley (D Ill.) Sept. 13, 1817-Sept. 25, 1900; Senate 1891-97; Gov. 1869-73 (Republican).

PALMER, John William (R Mo.) Aug. 20, 1866-Nov. 3, 1958; House 1929-31.

PALMER, Thomas Witherell (R Mich.) Jan. 25, 1830-June 1, 1913; Senate 1883-89.

PALMER, William Adams (D Vt.) Sept. 12, 1781-Dec. 3, 1860; Senate Oct. 20, 1818-25; Gov. 1831-35.

PALMISANO, Vincent Luke (D Md.) Aug. 5, 1882-Jan. 12, 1953; House 1927-39.

PANETTA, Leon Edward (D Calif.) June 28, 1938-−; House 1977-−.

PANTIN, Santiago Iglesias (*See* IGLESIAS, Santiago).

PAREDES, Quintin (Nat. P.I.) Sept. 9, 1884-−; House (Res. Comm.) Feb. 14, 1936-Sept. 29, 1938.

PARK, Frank (D Ga.) March 3, 1864-Nov. 20, 1925; House Nov. 5, 1913-25.

PARKE, Benjamin (D Ind.) Sept. 22, 1777-July 12, 1835; House (Terr. Del.) Dec. 12, 1805-March 1, 1808.

PARKER, Abraham X. (R N.Y.) Nov. 14, 1831-Aug. 9, 1909; House 1881-89.

PARKER, Amasa Junius (D N.Y.) June 2, 1807-May 13, 1890; House 1837-39.

PARKER, Andrew (D Pa.) May 21, 1805-Jan. 15, 1864; House 1851-53.

PARKER, Homer Cling (D Ga.) Sept. 25, 1885-June 22, 1946; House Sept. 10, 1931-35.

PARKER, Hosea Washington (D N.H.) May 30, 1833-Aug. 21, 1922; House 1871-75.

PARKER, Isaac (− Mass.) June 17, 1768-July 26, 1830; House 1797-99.

PARKER, Isaac Charles (R Mo.) Oct. 15, 1838-Nov. 17, 1896; House 1871-75.

PARKER, James (D Mass.) 1768-Nov. 9, 1837; House 1813-15, 1819-21.

PARKER, James (grandfather of Richard Wayne Parker) (D N.J.) March 3, 1776-April 1, 1868; House 1833-37.

PARKER, James Southworth (R N.Y.) June 3, 1867-Dec. 19, 1933; House 1913-Dec. 19, 1933.

PARKER, John Mason (W N.Y.) June 14, 1805-Dec. 16, 1873; House 1855-59.

PARKER, Josiah (− Va.) May 11, 1751-March 18, 1810; House 1789-1801.

PARKER, Nahum (− N.H.) March 4, 1760-Nov. 12, 1839; Senate 1807-June 1, 1810.

PARKER, Richard (D Va.) Dec. 22, 1810-Nov. 10, 1893; House 1849-51.

PARKER, Richard Elliott (D Va.) Dec. 27, 1783-Sept. 6, 1840; Senate Dec. 12, 1836-March 13, 1837.

PARKER, Richard Wayne (grandson of James Parker) (R N.J.) Aug. 6, 1848-Nov. 28, 1923; House 1895-1911, Dec. 1, 1914-19, 1921-23.

PARKER, Samuel Wilson (W Ind.) Sept. 9, 1805-Feb. 1, 1859; House 1851-55.

PARKER, Severn Eyre (− Va.) July 19, 1787-Oct. 21, 1836; House 1819-21.

PARKER, William Henry (− S.D.) May 5, 1847-June 26, 1908; House 1907-June 26, 1908.

PARKS, Gorham (D Maine) May 27, 1794-Nov. 23, 1877; House 1833-37.

PARKS, Tilman Bacon (D Ark.) May 14, 1872-Feb. 12, 1950; House 1921-37.

PARMENTER, William (D Mass.) March 30, 1789-Feb. 25, 1866; House 1837-45.

PARRAN, Thomas (R Md.) Feb. 12, 1860-March 29, 1955; House 1911-13.

PARRETT, William Fletcher (D Ind.) Aug. 10, 1825-June 30, 1895; House 1889-93.

PARRIS, Albion Keith (cousin of Virgil Delphini Parris) (DR Maine) Jan. 19, 1788-Feb. 22, 1857; House 1815-Feb. 3, 1818 (Mass.); Senate 1827-Aug. 26, 1828; Gov. 1822-27.

PARRIS, Stanford E. (R Va.) Sept. 9, 1929-−; House 1973-75, 1981-−.

PARRIS, Virgil Delphini (cousin of Albion Keith Parris) (SRD Maine) Feb. 18, 1807-June 13, 1874; House May 29, 1838-41.

PARRISH, Isaac (D Ohio) March 1804-Aug. 9, 1860; House 1839-41, 1845-47.

PARRISH, Lucian Walton (D Texas) Jan. 10, 1878-March 27, 1922; House 1919-March 27, 1922.

PARROTT, John Fabyan (D N.H.) Aug. 8, 1767-July 9, 1836; House 1817-19; Senate 1819-25.

PARROTT, Marcus Junius (R Kan.) Oct. 27, 1828-Oct. 4, 1879; House (Terr. Del.) 1857-Jan. 29, 1861.

PARSONS, Claude VanCleve (D Ill.) Oct. 7, 1895-May 23, 1941; House Nov. 4, 1930-41.

PARSONS, Edward Young (D Ky.) Dec. 12, 1841-Jul 8, 1876; House 1875-July 8, 1876.

PARSONS, Herbert (R N.Y.) Oct. 28, 1869-Sept. 1 1925; House 1905-11.

PARSONS, Richard Chappel (R Ohio) Oct. 10, 182€ Jan. 9, 1899; House 1873-75.

PARTRIDGE, Donald Barrows (R Maine) June 7, 189 June 5, 1946; House 1931-33.

PARTRIDGE, Frank Charles (R Vt.) May 7, 186 March 2, 1943; Senate Dec. 23, 1930-March 31, 193

PARTRIDGE, George (− Mass.) Feb. 8, 1740-July 1828; House 1789-Aug. 14, 1790; Cont. Cong. 177 82, 1783-85.

PARTRIDGE, Samuel (D N.Y.) Nov. 29, 1790-Marc 30, 1883; House 1841-43.

PASCHAL, Thomas Moore (D Texas) Dec. 15, 184 Jan. 28, 1919; House 1893-95.

PASCO, Samuel (D Fla.) June 28, 1834-March 13, 191 Senate May 19, 1887-April 19, 1899.

PASHAYAN, Charles Sahag "Chip" Jr. (R Calif March 27, 1941-−; House 1979-−.

PASSMAN, Otto Ernest (D La.) June 27, 1900-- House 1947-77.

PASTORE, John Orlando (D R.I.) March 17, 1907-- Senate Dec. 19, 1950-Dec. 28, 1976; Gov. 1945-50.

PATERSON, John (− N.Y.) 1744-July 19, 1808; Hous 1803-05.

PATERSON, William (F N.J.) Dec. 24, 1745-Sept. 1806; Senate 1789-Nov. 13, 1790; Cont. Cong. 178(81, 1787; Gov. 1790-93; Assoc. Justice Suprem Court 1793-1806.

PATMAN, William N. (son of Wright Patman) (Texas) March 26, 1927-−; House 1981-85.

PATMAN, Wright (father of William N. Patman) (Texas) Aug. 6, 1893-March 7, 1976; House 192 March 7, 1976.

PATRICK, Luther (D Ala.) Jan. 23, 1894-May 26, 195 House 1937-43, 1945-47.

PATTEN, Edward James (D N.J.) Aug. 22, 1905-- House 1963-81.

PATTEN, Harold Ambrose (D Ariz.) Oct. 6, 1907-Sep 6, 1969; House 1949-55.

PATTEN, John (− Del.) April 26, 1746-Dec. 26, 180 House 1793-Feb. 14, 1794, 1795-97; Cont. Con 1785-86.

ATTEN, Thomas Gedney (D N.Y.) Sept. 12, 1861-Feb. 23, 1939; House 1911-17.

ATTERSON, David Trotter (son-in-law of Andrew Johnson) (D Tenn.) Feb. 28, 1818-Nov. 3, 1891; Senate July 24, 1866-69.

ATTERSON, Edward White (D Kan.) Oct. 4, 1895-March 6, 1940; House 1935-39.

ATTERSON, Elizabeth Johnston (daughter of Olin DeWitt Talmadge Johnston) (D S.C.) Nov. 18, 1939- —; House 1987- —.

ATTERSON, Ellis Ellwood (D Calif.) Nov. 28, 1897- —; House 1945-47.

ATTERSON, Francis Ford Jr. (R N.J.) July 30, 1867-Nov. 30, 1935; House Nov. 2, 1920-27.

ATTERSON, George Robert (R Pa.) Nov. 9, 1863-March 21, 1906; House 1901-March 21, 1906.

ATTERSON, George Washington (brother of William Patterson) (R N.Y.) Nov. 11, 1799-Oct. 15, 1879; House 1877-79.

ATTERSON, Gilbert Brown (D N.C.) May 29, 1863-Jan. 26, 1922; House 1903-07.

ATTERSON, James O'Hanlon (D S.C.) June 25, 1857-Oct. 25, 1911; House 1905-11.

ATTERSON, James Thomas (R Conn.) Oct. 20, 1908- —; House 1947-59.

ATTERSON, James Willis (R N.H.) July 2, 1823-May 4, 1893; House 1863-67; Senate 1867-73.

ATTERSON, Jerry Mumford (D Calif.) Oct. 25, 1934- —; House 1975-85.

ATTERSON, John (half brother of Thomas Patterson) (D Ohio) Feb. 10, 1771-Feb. 7, 1848; House 1823-25.

ATTERSON, John James (R S.C.) Aug. 8, 1830-Sept. 28, 1912; Senate 1873-79.

ATTERSON, Josiah (father of Malcolm Rice Patterson) (D Tenn.) April 14, 1837-Feb. 10, 1904; House 1891-97.

ATTERSON, Lafayette Lee (D Ala.) Aug. 23, 1888- —; House Nov. 6, 1928-33.

ATTERSON, Malcolm Rice (son of Josiah Patterson) (D Tenn.) June 7, 1861-March 8, 1935; House 1901-Nov. 5, 1906; Gov. 1907-11.

ATTERSON, Roscoe Conkling (R Mo.) Sept. 15, 1876-Oct. 22, 1954; House 1921-23; Senate 1929-35.

ATTERSON, Thomas (half brother of John Patterson) (D Pa.) Oct. 1, 1764-Nov. 16, 1841; House 1817-25.

PATTERSON, Thomas J. (W N.Y.) about 1808-?; House 1843-45.

PATTERSON, Thomas MacDonald (D Colo.) Nov. 4, 1839-July 23, 1916; House (Terr. Del.) 1875-Aug. 1, 1876; (Rep.) Dec. 13, 1877-79; Senate 1901-07.

PATTERSON, Walter (— N.Y.) ?-?; House 1821-23.

PATTERSON, William (brother of George Washington Patterson, uncle of Augustus Frank) (W N.Y.) June 4, 1789-Aug. 14, 1838; House 1837-Aug. 14, 1838.

PATTERSON, William (D Ohio) 1790-Aug. 17, 1868; House 1833-37.

PATTISON, Edward Worthington (D N.Y.) April 29, 1932- —; House 1975-79.

PATTISON, John M. (D Ohio) June 13, 1847-June 18, 1906; House 1891-93; Gov. Jan. 8-June 18, 1906.

PATTON, Charles Emory (son of John Patton, brother of John Patton Jr., cousin of William Irvin Swoope) (— Pa.) July 5, 1859-Dec. 15, 1937; House 1911-15.

PATTON, David Henry (D Ind.) Nov. 26, 1837-Jan. 17, 1914; House 1891-93.

PATTON, John (father of Charles Emory Patton and John Patton Jr., uncle of William Irvin Swoope) (R Pa.) Jan. 6, 1823-Dec. 23, 1897; House 1861-63, 1887-89.

PATTON, John Jr. (son of John Patton, brother of Charles Emory Patton, cousin of William Irvin Swoope) (R Mich.) Oct. 30, 1850-May 24, 1907; Senate May 5, 1894-Jan. 14, 1895.

PATTON, John Denniston (D Pa.) Nov. 28, 1829-Feb. 22, 1904; House 1883-85.

PATTON, John Mercer (D Va.) Aug. 10, 1797-Oct. 29, 1858; House Nov. 25, 1830-April 7, 1838; Gov. 1841 (State Rights Whig).

PATTON, Nat (D Texas) Feb. 26, 1884-July 27, 1957; House 1935-45.

PAUL, John (father of John Paul, below) (Read. Va.) June 30, 1839-Nov. 1, 1901; House 1881-Sept. 5, 1883.

PAUL, John (son of John Paul, above) (R Va.) Dec. 9, 1883-Feb. 13, 1964; House Dec. 15, 1922-23.

PAUL, Ronald Ernest (R Texas) Aug. 20, 1935- —; House April 3, 1976-77, 1979-85.

PAULDING, William Jr. (D N.Y.) March 7, 1770-Feb. 11, 1854; House 1811-13.

PAWLING, Levi (D Pa.) July 25, 1773-Sept. 7, 1845; House 1817-19.

PAYNE, Frederick George (R Maine) July 24, 1904-June 15, 1978; Senate 1953-59; Gov. 1949-52.

PAYNE, Henry B. (grandfather of Frances Payne Bolton) (D Ohio) Nov. 30, 1810-Sept. 9, 1896; House 1875-77; Senate 1885-91.

PAYNE, Sereno Elisha (R N.Y.) June 26, 1843-Dec. 10, 1914; House 1883-87, 1889-Dec. 10, 1914; House majority leader 1899-1911.

PAYNE, William Winter (D Ala.) Jan. 2, 1807-Sept. 2, 1874; House 1841-47.

PAYNTER, Lemuel (D Pa.) 1788-Aug. 1, 1863; House 1837-41.

PAYNTER, Thomas Hanson (D Ky.) Dec. 9, 1851-March 8, 1921; House 1889-Jan. 5, 1895; Senate 1907-13.

PAYSON, Lewis Edwin (R Ill.) Sept. 17, 1840-Oct. 4, 1909; House 1881-91.

PEACE, Roger Craft (D S.C.) May 19, 1899-Aug. 20, 1968; Senate Aug. 5-Nov. 4, 1941.

PEARCE, Charles Edward (R Mo.) May 29, 1842-Jan. 30, 1902; House 1897-1901.

PEARCE, Dutee Jerauld (D R.I.) April 3, 1789-May 9, 1849; House 1825-37.

PEARCE, James Alfred (D Md.) Dec. 8, 1804-Dec. 20, 1862; House 1835-39 (Whig), 1841-43 (Whig); Senate 1843-Dec. 20, 1862 (1843-61 Whig).

PEARCE, John Jamison (W Pa.) Feb. 28, 1826-May 26, 1912; House 1855-57.

PEARRE, George Alexander (R Md.) July 16, 1860-Sept. 19, 1923; House 1899-1911.

PEARSON, Albert Jackson (D Ohio) May 20, 1846-May 15, 1905; House 1891-95.

PEARSON, Herron Carney (D Tenn.) July 31, 1890-April 24, 1953; House 1935-43.

PEARSON, James Blackwood (R Kan.) May 7, 1920- —; Senate Jan. 31, 1962-Dec. 23, 1978.

PEARSON, John James (W Pa.) Oct. 25, 1800-May 30, 1888; House Dec. 5, 1836-37.

PEARSON, Joseph (F N.C.) 1776-Oct. 27, 1834; House 1809-15.

PEARSON, Richmond (R N.C.) Jan. 26, 1852-Sept. 12, 1923; House 1895-99, May 10, 1900-01.

PEASE, Donald James (D Ohio) Sept. 26, 1931- —; House 1977- —.

PEASE, Henry Roberts (R Miss.) Feb. 19, 1835-Jan. 2 1907; Senate Feb. 3, 1874-75.

PEASLEE, Charles Hazen (D N.H.) Feb. 6, 1804-Sep 18, 1866; House 1847-53.

PEAVEY, Hubert Haskell (R Wis.) Jan. 12, 1881-Nov 21, 1937; House 1923-35.

PECK, Erasmus Darwin (R Ohio) Sept. 16, 1808-Dec. 25 1876; House April 23, 1870-73.

PECK, George Washington (D Mich.) June 4, 1818-Jun 30, 1905; House 1855-57.

PECK, Jared Valentine (D N.Y.) Sept. 21, 1816-Dec. 2 1891; House 1853-55.

PECK, Lucius Benedict (D Vt.) Nov. 17, 1802-Dec. 28 1866; House 1847-51.

PECK, Luther Christopher (W N.Y.) Jan. 1800-Feb. 4 1876; House 1837-41.

PECKHAM, Rufus Wheeler (D N.Y.) Dec. 20, 1809 Nov. 22, 1873; House 1853-55.

PEDDIE, Thomas Baldwin (R N.J.) Feb. 11, 1808-Fe 16, 1889; House 1877-79.

PEDEN, Preston Elmer (D Okla.) June 28, 1914- - House 1947-49.

PEEK, Harmanus (— N.Y.) June 24, 1782-Sept. 2 1838; House 1819-21.

PEEL, Samuel West (D Ark.) Sept. 13, 1831-Dec. 1 1924; House 1883-93.

PEELLE, Stanton Judkins (R Ind.) Feb. 11, 1843-Sep 4, 1928; House 1881-May 22, 1884.

PEERY, George Campbell (D Va.) Oct. 28, 1873-Oct. 1 1952; House 1923-29; Gov. 1934-38.

PEFFER, William Alfred (P Kan.) Sept. 10, 1831-Oct. 1912; Senate 1891-97.

PEGRAM, John (— Va.) Nov. 16, 1773-April 8, 183 House April 21, 1818-19.

PEIRCE, Joseph (— N.H.) June 25, 1748-Sept. 12, 181 House 1801-02.

PEIRCE, Robert Bruce Fraser (R Ind.) Feb. 17, 184 Dec. 5, 1898; House 1881-83.

PELHAM, Charles (R Ala.) March 12, 1835-Jan. 1908; House 1873-75.

PELL, Claiborne de Borda (son of Herbert Claibor Pell Jr., great-great grandson of John Francis Ha tramck Claiborne) (D R.I.) Nov. 22, 1918- —; Sena 1961- —.

PELL, Herbert Claiborne Jr. (great-grandson of John Francis Hamtramck Claiborne, great-great-grand-nephew of William Charles Cole Claiborne and Nathaniel Herbert Claiborne, father of Claiborne de Borda Pell) (D N.Y.) Feb. 16, 1884-July 17, 1961; House 1919-21.

PELLY, Thomas Minor (R Wash.) Aug. 22, 1902-Nov. 21, 1973; House 1953-73.

PELTON, Guy Ray (W N.Y.) Aug. 3, 1824-July 24, 1890; House 1855-57.

PENCE, Lafayette (P/Sil.D Colo.) Dec. 23, 1857-Oct. 22, 1923; House 1893-95.

PENDLETON, Edmund Henry (W N.Y.) 1788-Feb. 25, 1862; House 1831-33.

PENDLETON, George Cassety (D Texas) April 23, 1845-Jan. 19, 1913; House 1893-97.

PENDLETON, George Hunt (son of Nathanael Greene Pendleton) (D Ohio) July 19, 1825-Nov. 24, 1889; House 1857-65; Senate 1879-85.

PENDLETON, James Monroe (R R.I.) Jan. 10, 1822-Feb. 16, 1889; House 1871-75.

PENDLETON, John Overton (D W.Va.) July 4, 1851-Dec. 24, 1916; House 1889-Feb. 26, 1890, 1891-95.

PENDLETON, John Strother (W Va.) March 1, 1802-Nov. 19, 1868; House 1845-49.

PENDLETON, Nathanael Green (father of George Hunt Pendleton) (W Ohio) Aug. 25, 1793-June 16, 1861; House 1841-43.

PENINGTON, John Brown (D Del.) Dec. 20, 1825-June 1, 1902; House 1887-91.

PENN, Alexander Gordon (D La.) May 10, 1799-May 7, 1866; House Dec. 30, 1850-53.

PENNIMAN, Ebenezer Jenckes (W/FS Mich.) Jan. 11, 1804-April 12, 1890; House 1851-53.

PENNINGTON, Alexander Cumming McWhorter (cousin of William Pennington) (W N.J.) July 2, 1810-Jan. 25, 1867; House 1853-57.

PENNINGTON, William (cousin of Alexander Cumming McWhorter Pennington) (R N.J.) May 4, 1796-Feb. 16, 1862; House 1859-61; Speaker 1859-61; Gov. 1837-43 (Democratic Republican).

PENNY, Timothy J. (D Minn.) Nov. 19, 1951- —; House 1983- —.

PENNYBACKER, Isaac Samuels (cousin of Green Berry Samuels) (D Va.) Sept. 3, 1805-Jan. 12, 1847; House 1837-39; Senate Dec. 3, 1845-Jan. 12, 1847.

PENROSE, Boies (R Pa.) Nov. 1, 1860-Dec. 31, 1921; Senate 1897-Dec. 31, 1921.

PEPPER, Claude Denson (D Fla.) Sept. 8, 1900- —; Senate Nov. 4, 1936-51; House 1963- —.

PEPPER, George Wharton (R Pa.) March 16, 1867-May 24, 1961; Senate Jan. 9, 1922-27.

PEPPER, Irvin St. Clair (D Iowa) June 10, 1876-Dec. 22, 1913; House 1911-Dec. 22, 1913.

PERCE, Legrand Winfield (R Miss.) June 19, 1836-March 16, 1911; House Feb. 23, 1870-73.

PERCY, Charles Harting (father-in-law of John Davison "Jay" Rockefeller IV) (R Ill.) Sept. 27, 1919- —; Senate 1967-85.

PERCY, Le Roy (D Miss.) Nov. 9, 1860-Dec. 24, 1929; Senate Feb. 23, 1910-13.

PEREA, Francisco (cousin of Pedro Perea) (R N.M.) Jan. 9, 1830-May 21, 1913; House (Terr. Del.) 1863-65.

PEREA, Pedro (cousin of Francisco Perea) (R N.M.) April 22, 1852-Jan. 11, 1906; House (Terr. Del.) 1899-1901.

PERHAM, Sidney (R Maine) March 27, 1819-April 10, 1907; House 1863-69; Gov. 1871-74.

PERKINS, Bishop (D N.Y.) Sept. 5, 1787-Nov. 20, 1866; House 1853-55.

PERKINS, Bishop Walden (R Kan.) Oct. 18, 1841-June 20, 1894; House 1883-91; Senate Jan. 1, 1892-93.

PERKINS, Carl C. "Chris" (son of Carl Dewey Perkins) (D Ky.) Aug. 6, 1954- —; House 1985- —.

PERKINS, Carl Dewey (father of Carl C. "Chris" Perkins) (D Ky.) Oct. 15, 1912-Aug. 3, 1984; House 1949-Aug. 3, 1984.

PERKINS, Elias (F Conn.) April 5, 1767-Sept. 27, 1845; House 1801-03.

PERKINS, George Clement (R Calif.) Aug. 23, 1839-Feb. 26, 1923; Senate July 26, 1893-1915; Gov. 1880-83.

PERKINS, George Douglas (R Iowa) Feb. 29, 1840-Feb. 3, 1914; House 1891-99.

PERKINS, James Breck (R N.Y.) Nov. 4, 1847-March 11, 1910; House 1901-March 11, 1910.

PERKINS, Jared (W N.H.) Jan. 5, 1793-Oct. 15, 1854; House 1851-53.

PERKINS, John Jr. (D La.) July 1, 1819-Nov. 28, 1885; House 1853-55.

PERKINS, Randolph (R N.J.) Nov. 30, 1871-May 25, 1936; House 1921-May 25, 1936.

PERKY, Kirtland Irving (D Idaho) Feb. 8, 1867-Jan. 9, 1939; Senate Nov. 18, 1912-Feb. 5, 1913.

PERLMAN, Nathan David (R N.Y.) Aug. 2, 1887-June 29, 1952; House Nov. 2, 1920-27.

PERRILL, Augustus Leonard (D Ohio) Jan. 20, 1807-June 2, 1882; House 1845-47.

PERRY, Aaron Fyfe (R Ohio) Jan. 1, 1815-March 11, 1893; House 1871-72.

PERRY, Eli (D N.Y.) Dec. 25, 1799-May 17, 1881; House 1871-75.

PERRY, John Jasiel (R Maine) Aug. 2, 1811-May 2, 1897; House 1855-57, 1859-61.

PERRY, Nehemiah (Const.U N.J.) March 30, 1816-Nov. 1, 1881; House 1861-65.

PERRY, Thomas Johns (D Md.) Feb. 17, 1807-June 27, 1871; House 1845-47.

PERRY, William Hayne (D S.C.) June 9, 1839-July 7, 1902; House 1885-91.

PERSON, Seymour Howe (R Mich.) Feb. 2, 1879-April 7, 1957; House 1931-33.

PERSONS, Henry (D Ga.) Jan. 30, 1834-June 17, 1910; House 1879-81.

PESQUERA, Jose Lorenzo (Nonpart. P.R.) Aug. 10, 1882-July 25, 1950; House (Res. Comm.) April 15, 1932-33.

PETER, George (D Md.) Sept. 28, 1779-June 22, 1861; House Oct. 7, 1816-19, 1825-27.

PETERS, Andrew James (D Mass.) April 3, 1872-June 26, 1938; House 1907-Aug. 15, 1914.

PETERS, John Andrew (uncle of John Andrew Peters, below) (R Maine) Oct. 9, 1822-April 2, 1904; House 1867-73.

PETERS, John Andrew (nephew of John Andrew Peters, above) (R Maine) Aug. 13, 1864-Aug. 22, 1953; House Sept. 8, 1913-Jan. 2, 1922.

PETERS, Mason Summers (D/P Kan.) Sept. 3, 1844-Feb. 14, 1914; House 1897-99.

PETERS, Samuel Ritter (R Kan.) Aug. 16, 1842-April 21, 1910; House 1883-91.

PETERSEN, Andrew Nicholas (R N.Y.) March 10, 1870-Sept. 28, 1952; House 1921-23.

PETERSON, Hugh (D Ga.) Aug. 21, 1898-Oct. 3, 1961; House 1935-47.

PETERSON, James Hardin (D Fla.) Feb. 11, 1894-March 28, 1978; House 1933-51.

PETERSON, John Barney (cousin of Horatio Clifford Claypool and Harold Kile Claypool) (D Ind.) July 4, 1850-July 16, 1944; House 1913-15.

PETERSON, Morris Blaine (D Utah) March 26, 1906-July 15, 1985; House 1961-63.

PETRI, Thomas E. (R Wis.) May 28, 1940- — ; House April 9, 1979- —.

PETRIE, George (R N.Y.) Sept. 8, 1793-May 8, 1879; House 1847-49.

PETRIKIN, David (D Pa.) Dec. 1, 1788-March 1, 1847; House 1837-41.

PETTENGILL, Samuel Barrett (nephew of William Horace Clagett) (D Ind.) Jan. 19, 1886-March 20, 1974; House 1931-39.

PETTIBONE, Augustus Herman (R Tenn.) Jan. 21, 1835-Nov. 26, 1918; House 1881-87.

PETTIGREW, Ebenezer (W N.C.) March 10, 1783-July 8, 1848; House 1835-37.

PETTIGREW, Richard Franklin (R S.D.) July 23, 1848-Oct. 5, 1926; House (Terr. Del.) 1881-83; Senate Nov. 2, 1889-1901.

PETTIS, Jerry Lyle (husband of Shirley Neal Pettis) (R Calif.) July 18, 1916-Feb. 14, 1975; House 1967-Feb. 14, 1975.

PETTIS, Shirley Neal (widow of Jerry Lyle Pettis) (R Calif.) July 12, 1924- — ; House April 29, 1975-79.

PETTIS, Solomon Newton (R Pa.) Oct. 10, 1827-Sept. 18, 1900; House Dec. 7, 1868-69.

PETTIS, Spencer Darwin (D Mo.) 1802-Aug. 28, 1831; House 1829-Aug. 28, 1831.

PETTIT, John (D Ind.) June 24, 1807-Jan. 17, 1877; House 1843-49; Senate Jan. 11, 1853-55.

PETTIT, John Upfold (R Ind.) Sept. 11, 1820-March 21, 1881; House 1855-61.

PETTUS, Edmund Winston (D Ala.) July 6, 1821-July 27, 1907; Senate 1897-July 27, 1907.

PEYSER, Peter A. (D N.Y.) Sept. 7, 1921- — ; House 1971-77 (Republican), 1979-83.

PEYSER, Theodore Albert (D N.Y.) Feb. 18, 1873-Aug. 8, 1937; House 1933-Aug. 8, 1937.

PEYTON, Balie (brother of Joseph Hopkins Peyton) (W Tenn.) Nov. 26, 1803-Aug. 18, 1878; House 1833-37,

PEYTON, Joseph Hopkins (brother of Balie Peyton) (W Tenn.) May 20, 1808-Nov. 11, 1845; House 1843-Nov. 11, 1845.

PEYTON, Samuel Oldham (D Ky.) Jan. 8, 1804-Jan. 4, 1870; House 1847-49, 1857-61.

PFEIFER, Joseph Lawrence (D N.Y.) Feb. 6, 1892-April 19, 1974; House 1935-51.

PFEIFFER, William Louis (R N.Y.) May 29, 1907- —; House 1949-51.

PFOST, Gracie Bowers (D Idaho) March 12, 1906-Aug. 11, 1965; House 1953-63.

PHEIFFER, William Townsend (R N.Y.) July 15, 1898- —; House 1941-43.

PHELAN, James (D Tenn.) Dec. 7, 1856-Jan. 30, 1891; House 1887-Jan. 30, 1891.

PHELAN, James Duval (D Calif.) April 20, 1861-Aug. 7, 1930; Senate 1915-21.

PHELAN, Michael Francis (D Mass.) Oct. 22, 1875-Oct. 12, 1941; House 1913-21.

PHELPS, Charles Edward (UC Md.) May 1, 1833-Dec. 27, 1908; House 1865-69 (1865-67 Union War Party).

PHELPS, Darwin (R Pa.) April 17, 1807-Dec. 14, 1879; House 1869-71.

PHELPS, Elisha (father of John Smith Phelps) (D Conn.) Nov. 16, 1779-April 6, 1847; House 1819-21, 1825-29.

PHELPS, James (son of Lancelot Phelps) (D Conn.) Jan. 12, 1822-Jan. 15, 1900; House 1875-83.

PHELPS, John Smith (son of Elisha Phelps) (D Mo.) Dec. 22, 1814-Nov. 20, 1886; House 1845-63; Gov. 1877-81.

PHELPS, Lancelot (father of James Phelps) (D Conn.) Nov. 9, 1784-Sept. 1, 1866; House 1835-39.

PHELPS, Oliver (D N.Y.) Oct. 21, 1749-Feb. 21, 1809; House 1803-05.

PHELPS, Samuel Shethar (W Vt.) May 13, 1793-March 25, 1855; Senate 1839-51; Jan. 17, 1853-March 16, 1854.

PHELPS, Timothy Guy (R Calif.) Dec. 20, 1824-June 11, 1899; House 1861-63.

PHELPS, William Wallace (D Minn.) June 1, 1826-Aug. 3, 1873; House May 11, 1858-59.

PHELPS, William Walter (R N.J.) Aug. 24, 1839-June 17, 1894; House 1873-75, 1883-89.

PHILBIN, Philip Joseph (D Mass.) May 29, 1898-June 14, 1972; House 1943-71.

PHILIPS, John Finis (D Mo.) Dec. 31, 1834-March 13, 1919; House 1875-77, Jan. 10, 1880-81.

PHILLIPS, Alfred Noroton (D Conn.) April 23, 1894-Jan. 18, 1970; House 1937-39.

PHILLIPS, Dayton Edward (R Tenn.) March 29, 1910-Oct. 23, 1980; House 1947-51.

PHILLIPS, Fremont Orestes (R Ohio) March 16, 1856-Feb. 21, 1936; House 1899-1901.

PHILLIPS, Henry Myer (D Pa.) June 30, 1811-Aug. 28, 1884; House 1857-59.

PHILLIPS, John (F Pa.) ?-?; House 1821-23.

PHILLIPS, John (R Calif.) Sept. 11, 1887-Dec. 18, 1983; House 1943-57.

PHILLIPS, Philip (D Ala.) Dec. 13, 1807-Jan. 14, 1884; House 1853-55.

PHILLIPS, Stephen Clarendon (W Mass.) Nov. 4, 1801-June 26, 1857; House Dec. 1, 1834-Sept. 28, 1838.

PHILLIPS, Thomas Wharton (father of Thomas Wharton Phillips Jr.) (R Pa.) Feb. 23, 1835-July 21, 1912; House 1893-97.

PHILLIPS, Thomas Wharton Jr. (son of Thomas Wharton Phillips) (R Pa.) Nov. 21, 1874-Jan. 2, 1956; House 1923-27.

PHILLIPS, William Addison (R Kan.) Jan. 14, 1824-Nov. 30, 1893; House 1873-79.

PHILSON, Robert (— Pa.) 1759-July 25, 1831; House 1819-21.

PHIPPS, Lawrence Cowle (R Colo.) Aug. 30, 1862-March 1, 1958; Senate 1919-31.

PHISTER, Elijah Conner (D Ky.) Oct. 8, 1822-May 16, 1887; House 1879-83.

PHOENIX, Jonas Phillips (W N.Y.) Jan. 14, 1788-May 4, 1859; House 1843-45, 1849-51.

PICKENS, Andrew (grandfather of Francis Wilkinson Pickens) (D S.C.) Sept. 13, 1739-Aug. 11, 1817; House 1793-95.

PICKENS, Francis Wilkinson (grandson of Andrew Pickens) (ND S.C.) April 7, 1805-Jan. 25, 1869; House Dec. 8, 1834-43; Gov. 1860-62 (State Rights Democrat).

PICKENS, Israel (D Ala.) Jan. 30, 1780-April 24, 1827; House 1811-17 (N.C.); Senate Feb. 17-Nov. 27, 1826; Gov. 1821-25 (Democratic Republican).

PICKERING, Timothy (F Mass.) July 17, 1745-Jan. 29, 1829; Senate 1803-11; House 1813-17; Postmaster Gen. 1791-95; Secy. of War 1795; Secy. of State 1795-1800.

PICKETT, Charles Edgar (R Iowa) Jan. 14, 1866-July 20, 1930; House 1909-13.

PICKETT, Owen B. (D Va.) Aug. 31, 1930- —; House 1987- —.

PICKETT, Thomas Augustus (Tom) (D Texas) Aug. 14, 1906-June 7, 1980; House 1945-June 30, 1952.

PICKLE, J. J. "Jake" (D Texas) Oct. 11, 1913- —; House Dec. 21, 1963- —.

PICKLER, John Alfred (R S.D.) Jan. 24, 1844-June 13, 1910; House Nov. 2, 1889-97.

PICKMAN, Benjamin Jr. (— Mass.) Sept. 30, 1763-Aug. 16, 1843; House 1809-11.

PIDCOCK, James Nelson (cousin of Alvah Augustus Clark) (D N.J.) Feb. 8, 1836-Dec. 17, 1899; House 1885-89.

PIERCE, Charles Wilson (D Ala.) Oct. 7, 1823-Feb. 18, 1907; House July 21, 1868-69.

PIERCE, Franklin (D N.H.) Nov. 23, 1804-Oct. 8, 1869; House 1833-37; Senate 1837-Feb. 28, 1842; President 1853-57.

PIERCE, Gilbert Ashville (R N.D.) Jan. 11, 1839-Feb. 15, 1901; Senate Nov. 21, 1889-91; Gov. (N.D. Terr.) 1884-86.

PIERCE, Henry Lillie (R Mass.) Aug. 23, 1825-Dec. 17, 1896; House Dec. 1, 1873-77.

PIERCE, Ray Vaughn (R N.Y.) Aug. 6, 1840-Feb. 4, 1914; House 1879-Sept. 18, 1880.

PIERCE, Rice Alexander (D Tenn.) July 3, 1848-July 12, 1936; House 1883-85, 1889-93, 1897-1905.

PIERCE, Wallace Edgar (R N.Y.) Dec. 9, 1881-Jan. 3, 1940; House 1939-Jan. 3, 1940.

PIERCE, Walter Marcus (D Ore.) May 30, 1861-March 27, 1954; House 1933-43; Gov. 1923-27.

PIERSON, Isaac (W N.J.) Aug. 15, 1770-Sept. 22, 1833; House 1827-31.

PIERSON, Jeremiah Halsey (F N.Y.) Sept. 13, 1766-Dec. 12, 1855; House 1821-23.

PIERSON, Job (D N.Y.) Sept. 23, 1791-April 9, 1860; House 1831-35.

PIGOTT, James Protus (D Conn.) Sept. 11, 1852-July 1, 1919; House 1893-95.

PIKE, Austin Franklin (R N.H.) Oct. 16, 1819-Oct. 8 1886; House 1873-75; Senate 1883-Oct. 8, 1886.

PIKE, Frederick Augustus (R Maine) Dec. 9, 1816-Dec 2, 1886; House 1861-69.

PIKE, James (AP N.H.) Nov. 10, 1818-July 26, 1895 House 1855-59.

PIKE, Otis G. (D N.Y.) Aug. 31, 1921- —; House 1961-79

PILCHER, John Leonard (D Ga.) Aug. 27, 1898-Aug. 20 1981; House Feb. 4, 1953-65.

PILE, William Anderson (R Mo.) Feb. 11, 1829-July 7 1889; House 1867-69; Gov. 1869-70 (N.M.).

PILES, Samuel Henry (R Wash.) Dec. 28, 1858-March 11, 1940; Senate 1905-11.

PILLION, John Raymond (R N.Y.) Aug. 10, 1904-Dec 31, 1978; House 1953-65.

PILSBURY, Timothy (Cal.D Texas) April 12, 1789-Nov. 23, 1858; House March 30, 1846-49.

PINCKNEY, Charles (father of Henry Laurens Pinckney, father-in-law of Robert Young Hayne) (D S.C.) Oct. 26, 1757-Oct. 29, 1824; Senate Dec. 1798-1801; House 1819-21; Cont. Cong. 1784-87 Gov. 1789-92, 1796-98, 1806-08.

PINCKNEY, Henry Laurens (son of Charles Pinckney (D S.C.) Sept. 24, 1794-Feb. 3, 1863; House 1833-37

PINCKNEY, John McPherson (D Texas) May 4, 1845-April 24, 1905; House Nov. 17, 1903-April 24, 1905

PINCKNEY, Thomas (F S.C.) Oct. 23, 1750-Nov. 2 1828; House Nov. 23, 1797-1801; Gov. 1787-89.

PINDALL, James (F Va.) about 1783-Nov. 22, 1825 House 1817-July 26, 1820.

PINDAR, John Sigsbee (D N.Y.) Nov. 18, 1835-June 30 1907; House 1885-87; Nov. 4, 1890-91.

PINE, William Bliss (R Okla.) Dec. 30, 1877-Aug. 25 1942; Senate 1925-31.

PINERO, Jesus T. (PD P.R.) April 16, 1897-Nov. 19 1952; House (Res. Comm.) 1945-Sept. 2, 1946; Gov. 1946-48.

PINKNEY, William (— Md.) March 17, 1764-Feb. 25 1822; House March 4-Nov. 1791, 1815-April 18, 1816 Senate Dec. 21, 1819-Feb. 25, 1822; Atty. Gen. 1811-14.

PIPER, William (— Pa.) Jan. 1, 1774-1852; House 1811-17.

PIPER, William Adam (D Calif.) May 21, 1826-Aug. 5 1899; House 1875-77.

PIRCE, William Almy (R R.I.) Feb. 29, 1824-March 5, 1891; House 1885-Jan. 25, 1887.

PIRNIE, Alexander (R N.Y.) April 16, 1903-June 12, 1982; House 1959-73.

PITCHER, Nathaniel (D N.Y.) Nov. 30, 1777-May 25, 1836; House 1819-23, 1831-33; Gov. 1828 (Democratic Republican).

PITKIN, Timothy (F Conn.) Jan. 21, 1766-Dec. 18, 1847; House Sept. 16, 1805-19.

PITMAN, Charles Wesley (W Pa.) ?-June 8, 1871; House 1849-51.

PITNEY, Mahlon (R N.J.) Feb. 5, 1858-Dec. 9, 1924; House 1895-Jan. 10, 1899; Assoc. Justice Supreme Court 1912-22.

PITTENGER, William Alvin (R Minn.) Dec. 29, 1885-Nov. 26, 1951; House 1929-33, 1935-37, 1939-47.

PITTMAN, Key (D Nev.) Sept. 19, 1872-Nov. 10, 1940; Senate Jan. 29, 1913-Nov. 10, 1940; Pres. pro tempore March 9, 1933-Nov. 10, 1940.

PLAISTED, Harris Merrill (R Maine) Nov. 2, 1828-Jan. 31, 1898; House Sept. 13, 1875-77; Gov. 1881-83 (Democrat).

PLANT, David (NR Conn.) March 29, 1783-Oct. 18, 1851; House 1827-29.

PLANTS, Tobias Avery (R Ohio) March 17, 1811-June 19, 1887; House 1865-69.

PLATER, Thomas (— Md.) May 9, 1769-May 1, 1830; House 1801-05.

PLATT, Edmund (R N.Y.) Feb. 2, 1865-Aug. 7, 1939; House 1913-June 7, 1920.

PLATT, James Henry Jr. (R Va.) July 13, 1837-Aug. 13, 1894; House Jan. 26, 1870-75.

PLATT, Jonas (F N.Y.) June 30, 1769-Feb. 22, 1834; House 1799-1801.

PLATT, Orville Hitchcock (R Conn.) July 19, 1827-April 21, 1905; Senate 1879-April 21, 1905.

PLATT, Thomas Collier (R N.Y.) July 15, 1833-March 6, 1910; House 1873-77; Senate March 4-May 16, 1881, 1897-1909.

PLAUCHE, Vance Gabriel (D La.) Aug. 25, 1897-April 2, 1976; House 1941-43.

PLEASANTS, James Jr. (DR Va.) Oct. 24, 1769-Nov. 9, 1836; House 1811-Dec. 14, 1819; Senate Dec. 14, 1819-Dec. 15, 1822; Gov. 1822-25.

PLOESER, Walter Christian (R Mo.) Jan. 7, 1907-—; House 1941-49.

PLOWMAN, Thomas Scales (D Ala.) June 8, 1843-July 26, 1919: House 1897-Feb. 9, 1898.

PLUMB, Preston B. (R Kan.) Oct. 12, 1837-Dec. 20, 1891; Senate 1877-Dec. 20, 1891.

PLUMB, Ralph (R Ill.) March 29, 1816-April 8, 1903; House 1885-89.

PLUMER, Arnold (D Pa.) June 6, 1801-April 28, 1869; House 1837-39, 1841-43.

PLUMER, George (D Pa.) Dec. 5, 1762-June 8, 1843; House 1821-27.

PLUMER, William (father of William Plumer Jr.) (F N.H.) June 25, 1759-Dec. 22, 1850; Senate June 17, 1802-07; Gov. 1812-13, 1816-19 (1812-19 Democratic Republican).

PLUMER, William Jr. (son of William Plumer) (D N.H.) Feb. 9, 1789-Sept. 18, 1854; House 1819-25.

PLUMLEY, Charles Albert (son of Frank Plumley) (R Vt.) April 14, 1875-Oct. 31, 1964; House Jan. 16, 1934-51.

PLUMLEY, Frank (father of Charles Albert Plumley) (R Vt.) Dec. 17, 1844-April 30, 1924; House 1909-15.

PLUMMER, Franklin E. (— Miss.) ?-Sept. 24, 1847; House 1831-35.

POAGE, William Robert (D Texas) Dec. 28, 1899-Jan. 3, 1987; House 1937-Dec. 31, 1978.

PODELL, Bertram L. (D N.Y.) Dec. 27, 1925-—; House Feb. 20, 1968-75.

POEHLER, Henry (D Minn.) Aug. 22, 1833-July 18, 1912; House 1879-81.

POFF, Richard Harding (R Va.) Oct. 19, 1923-—; House 1953-Aug. 29, 1972.

POINDEXTER, George (D Miss.) 1779-Sept. 5, 1855; House (Terr. Del.) 1807-13; (Rep.) Dec. 10, 1817-19; Senate Oct. 15, 1830-35; Pres. pro tempore 1834; Gov. 1820-22 (Democratic Republican).

POINDEXTER, Miles (R Wash.) April 22, 1868-Sept. 21, 1946; House 1909-11; Senate 1911-23.

POINSETT, Joel Roberts (D S.C.) March 2, 1779-Dec. 12, 1851; House 1821-March 7, 1825; Secy. of War 1837-41.

POLANCO-ABREU, Santiago (PD P.R.) Oct. 30, 1920-—; House 1965-69.

POLAND, Luke Potter (R Vt.) Nov. 1, 1815-July 2, 1887; Senate Nov. 21, 1865-67; House 1867-75, 1883-85.

POLK, Albert Fawcett (D Del.) Oct. 11, 1869-Feb. 14, 1955; House 1917-19.

POLK, James Gould (D Ohio) Oct. 6, 1896-April 28, 1959; House 1931-41, 1949-April 28, 1959.

POLK, James Knox (brother of William Hawkins Polk) (D Tenn.) Nov. 2, 1795-June 15, 1849; House 1825-39; Speaker 1835-39; Gov. 1839-41; President 1845-49.

POLK, Rufus King (D Pa.) Aug. 23, 1866-March 5, 1902; House 1899-March 5, 1902.

POLK, Trusten (D Mo.) May 29, 1811-April 16, 1876; Senate 1857-Jan. 10, 1862; Gov. 1857.

POLK, William Hawkins (brother of James Knox Polk) (D Tenn.) May 24, 1815-Dec. 16, 1862; House 1851-53.

POLLARD, Ernest Mark (R Neb.) April 15, 1869-Sept. 24, 1939; House July 18, 1905-09.

POLLARD, Henry Moses (R Mo.) June 14, 1836-Feb. 23, 1904; House 1877-79.

POLLOCK, Howard W. (R Alaska) April 11, 1920- -; House 1967-71.

POLLOCK, James (W Pa.) Sept. 11, 1810-April 19, 1890; House April 5, 1844-49; Gov. 1855-58.

POLLOCK, William Pegues (D S.C.) Dec. 9, 1870-June 2, 1922; Senate Nov. 6, 1918-19.

POLSLEY, Daniel Haymond (R W.Va.) Nov. 28, 1803-Oct. 14, 1877; House 1867-69.

POMERENE, Atlee (D Ohio) Dec. 6, 1863-Nov. 12, 1937; Senate 1911-23.

POMEROY, Charles (R Iowa) Sept. 3, 1825-Feb. 11, 1891; House 1869-71.

POMEROY, Samuel Clarks (R Kan.) Jan. 3, 1816-Aug. 27, 1891; Senate April 4, 1861-73.

POMEROY, Theodore Medad (R N.Y.) Dec. 31, 1824-March 23, 1905; House 1861-69; Speaker Dec. 7, 1868-March 3, 1869.

POND, Benjamin (D N.Y.) 1768-Oct. 6, 1814; House 1811-13.

POOL, Joe Richard (D Texas) Feb. 18, 1911-July 14, 1968; House 1963-July 14, 1968.

POOL, John (uncle of Walter Freshwater Pool) (W N.C.) June 16, 1826-Aug. 16, 1884; Senate July 4, 1868-73.

POOL, Walter Freshwater (nephew of John Pool) (R N.C.) Oct. 10, 1850-Aug. 25, 1883; House March 4-Aug. 25, 1883.

POOLE, Theodore Lewis (R N.Y.) April 10, 1840-Dec 23, 1900; House 1895-97.

POPE, James Pinckney (D Idaho) March 31, 1884-Jan 23, 1966; Senate 1933-39.

POPE, John (D Ky.) 1770-July 12, 1845; Senate 1807-13 House 1837-43; Pres. pro tempore 1811; Gov. (Ark Terr.) 1829-35.

POPE, Nathaniel (− Ill.) Jan. 5, 1784-Jan. 22, 1850 House (Terr. Del.) Sept. 5, 1816-Sept. 5, 1818.

POPE, Patrick Hamilton (D Ky.) March 17, 1806-May 4 1841; House 1833-35.

POPPLETON, Earley Franklin (D Ohio) Sept. 29, 1834 May 6, 1899; House 1875-77.

PORTER, Albert Gallatin (R Ind.) April 20, 1824-May 3, 1897; House 1859-63; Gov. 1881-85.

PORTER, Alexander (W La.) 1786-Jan. 13, 1844; Senate Dec. 19, 1833-Jan. 5, 1837.

PORTER, Augustus Seymour (nephew of Peter Buel Porter) (W Mich.) Jan. 18, 1798-Sept. 18, 1872; Senate Jan. 20, 1840-45.

PORTER, Charles Howell (R Va.) June 21, 1833-July 9 1897; House Jan. 26, 1870-73.

PORTER, Charles Orlando (D Ore.) April 4, 1919- − House 1957-61.

PORTER, Gilchrist (W Mo.) Nov. 1, 1817-Nov. 1, 1894 House 1851-53, 1855-57.

PORTER, Henry Kirke (− Pa.) Nov. 24, 1840-April 10 1921; House 1903-05.

PORTER, James (D N.Y.) April 18, 1787-Feb. 7, 1839 House 1817-19.

PORTER, John (− Pa.) ?-?; House Dec. 8, 1806-11.

PORTER, John Edward (R Ill.) June 1, 1935- -; House Jan. 24, 1980- -.

PORTER, Peter Augustus (grandson of Peter Buell Porter) (IR/D N.Y.) Oct. 10, 1853-Dec. 15, 1925; House 1907-09.

PORTER, Peter Buell (grandfather of Peter Augustus Porter, uncle of Augustus Seymour Porter) (D N.Y. Aug. 4, 1773-March 20, 1844; House 1809-13, 1815 Jan. 23, 1816; Secy. of War 1828-29.

PORTER, Stephen Geyer (R Pa.) May 18, 1869-June 27 1930; House 1911-June 27, 1930.

PORTER, Timothy H. (− N.Y.) ?-about 1840; House 1825-27.

OSEY, Francis Blackburn (R Ind.) April 28, 1848-Oct. 31, 1915; House Jan. 29-March 3, 1889.

OSEY, Thomas (— La.) July 9, 1750-March 19, 1818; Senate Oct. 8, 1812-Feb. 4, 1813; Gov. (Ind. Terr.) 1813-16.

OST, George Adams (D Pa.) Sept. 1, 1854-Oct. 31, 1925; House 1883-85.

OST, James Douglas (D Ohio) Nov. 25, 1863-April 1, 1921; House 1911-15.

OST, Jotham Jr. (F N.Y.) April 4, 1771-May 15, 1817; House 1813-15.

OST, Morton Everel (D Wyo.) Dec. 25, 1840-March 19, 1933; House (Terr. Del.) 1881-85.

OST, Philip Sidney (R Ill.) March 19, 1833-Jan. 6, 1895; House 1887-Jan. 6, 1895.

OSTON, Charles Debrille (R Ariz.) April 20, 1825-June 24, 1902; House (Terr. Del.) Dec. 5, 1864-65.

OTTER, Allen (I Mich.) Oct. 2, 1818-May 8, 1885; House 1875-77.

OTTER, Charles Edward (R Mich.) Oct. 30, 1916-Nov. 23, 1979; House Aug. 26, 1947-Nov. 4, 1952; Senate Nov. 5, 1952-59.

OTTER, Clarkson Nott (D N.Y.) April 25, 1825-Jan. 23, 1882; House 1869-75, 1877-79.

OTTER, Elisha Reynolds (father of Elisha Reynolds Potter, below) (F R.I.) Nov. 5, 1764-Sept. 26, 1835; House Nov. 15, 1796-97, 1809-15.

OTTER, Elisha Reynolds (son of Elisha Reynolds Potter, above) (W R.I.) June 20, 1811-April 10, 1882; House 1843-45.

OTTER, Emery Davis (D Ohio) Oct. 7, 1804-Feb. 12, 1896; House 1843-45, 1849-51.

OTTER, John Fox (R Wis.) May 11, 1817-May 18, 1899; House 1857-63.

OTTER, Orlando Brunson (UD N.Y.) March 10, 1823-Jan. 2, 1894; House 1883-85.

OTTER, Robert (JD N.C.) about 1800-March 2, 1841; House 1829-Nov. 1831.

OTTER, Samuel John (— R.I.) June 29, 1753-Oct. 14, 1804; Senate 1803-Oct. 14, 1804.

OTTER, William Wilson (D Pa.) Dec. 18, 1792-Oct. 28, 1839; House 1837-Oct. 28, 1839.

OTTLE, Emory Bemsley (R N.Y.) July 4, 1815-April 18, 1891; House 1857-61.

POTTS, David Jr. (W Pa.) Nov. 27, 1794-June 1, 1863; House 1831-39.

POTTS, David Matthew (R N.Y.) March 12, 1906-Sept. 11, 1976; House 1947-49.

POTTS, Richard (F Md.) July 19, 1753-Nov. 26, 1808; Senate Jan. 10, 1793-Oct. 24, 1796; Cont. Cong. 1781-82.

POU, Edward William (cousin of James Paul Buchanan) (D N.C.) Sept. 9, 1863-April 1, 1934; House 1901-April 1, 1934.

POULSON, C. Norris (R Calif.) July 23, 1895-Sept. 25, 1982; House 1943-45, 1947-June 11, 1953.

POUND, Thaddeus Coleman (R Wis.) Dec. 6, 1833-Nov. 21, 1914; House 1877-83.

POWELL, Adam Clayton Jr. (D N.Y.) Nov. 29, 1908-April 4, 1972; House 1945-67, 1969-71.

POWELL, Alfred H. (— Va.) March 6, 1781-1831; House 1825-27.

POWELL, Cuthbert (son of Levin Powell) (W Va.) March 4, 1775-May 8, 1849; House 1841-43.

POWELL, Joseph (D Pa.) June 23, 1828-April 24, 1904; House 1875-77.

POWELL, Lazarus Whitehead (D Ky.) Oct. 6, 1812-July 3, 1867; Senate 1859-65; Gov. 1851-55.

POWELL, Levin (father of Cuthbert Powell) (F Va.) 1737-Aug. 23, 1810; House 1799-1801.

POWELL, Paulus (D Va.) 1809-June 10, 1874; House 1849-59.

POWELL, Samuel (— Tenn.) July 10, 1776-Aug. 2, 1841; House 1815-17.

POWELL, Walter E. (R Ohio) April 25, 1931- — ; House 1971-75.

POWER, Thomas Charles (R Mont.) May 22, 1839-Feb. 16, 1923; Senate Jan. 2, 1890-95.

POWERS, Caleb (R Ky.) Feb. 1, 1869-July 25, 1932; House 1911-19.

POWERS, David Lane (R N.J.) July 29, 1896-March 28, 1968; House 1933-Aug. 30, 1945.

POWERS, Gershom (JD N.Y.) July 11, 1789-June 25, 1831; House 1829-31.

POWERS, Horace Henry (R Vt.) May 29, 1835-Dec. 8, 1913; House 1891-1901.

POWERS, Llewellyn (R Maine) Oct. 14, 1836-July 28, 1908; House 1877-79, April 8, 1901-July 28, 1908; Gov. 1897-1901.

POWERS, Samuel Leland (R Mass.) Oct. 26, 1848-Nov. 30, 1929; House 1901-05.

POYDRAS, Julien de Lallande (— Orleans) April 3, 1740-June 14, 1824; House (Terr. Del.) 1809-11.

PRACHT, Charles Frederick (R Pa.) Oct. 20, 1880-Dec. 22, 1950; House 1943-45.

PRALL, Anning Smith (D N.Y.) Sept. 17, 1870-July 23, 1937; House Nov. 6, 1923-35.

PRATT, Charles Clarence (R Pa.) April 23, 1854-Jan. 27, 1916; House 1909-11.

PRATT, Daniel Darwin (R Ind.) Oct. 26, 1813-June 17, 1877; Senate 1869-75.

PRATT, Eliza Jane (D N.C.) March 5, 1902-May 13, 1981; House May 25, 1946-47.

PRATT, Harcourt Joseph (R N.Y.) Oct. 23, 1866-May 21, 1934; House 1925-33.

PRATT, Harry Hayt (R N.Y.) Nov. 11, 1864-Nov. 13, 1932; House 1915-19.

PRATT, Henry Otis (R Iowa) Feb. 11, 1838-May 22, 1931; House 1873-77.

PRATT, James Timothy (D Conn.) Dec. 14, 1802-April 11, 1887; House 1853-55.

PRATT, Joseph Marmaduke (R Pa.) Sept. 4, 1891-July 19, 1946; House Jan. 18, 1944-45.

PRATT, Le Gage (D N.J.) Dec. 14, 1852-March 9, 1911; House 1907-09.

PRATT, Ruth Sears Baker (R N.Y.) Aug. 24, 1877-Aug. 23, 1965; House 1929-33.

PRATT, Thomas George (W Md.) Feb. 18, 1804-Nov. 9, 1869; Senate Jan. 12, 1850-57 (1856-57 Conservative Democrat); Gov. 1845-48.

PRATT, Zadock (D N.Y.) Oct. 30, 1790-April 6, 1871; House 1837-39, 1843-45.

PRAY, Charles Nelson (R Mont.) April 6, 1868-Sept. 12, 1963; House 1907-13.

PRENTISS, John Holmes (brother of Samuel Prentiss) (D N.Y.) April 17, 1784-June 26, 1861; House 1837-41.

PRENTISS, Samuel (brother of John Holmes Prentiss) (W Vt.) March 31, 1782-Jan. 15, 1857; Senate 1831-April 11, 1842.

PRENTISS, Sergeant Smith (— Miss.) Sept. 30, 1808-July 1, 1850; House May 30, 1838-39.

PRESCOTT, Cyrus Dan (R N.Y.) Aug. 15, 1836-Oct. 23, 1902; House 1879-83.

PRESSLER, Larry Lee (R S.D.) March 29, 1942-—; House 1975-79; Senate 1979-—.

PRESTON, Francis (father of William Campbell Preston, uncle of William Ballard Preston and William Preston) (— Va.) Aug. 2, 1765-May 26, 1836; House 1793-97.

PRESTON, Jacob Alexander (W Md.) March 12, 1796-Aug. 2, 1868; House 1843-45.

PRESTON, Prince Hulon Jr. (D Ga.) July 5, 1908-Feb. 8, 1961; House 1947-61.

PRESTON, William (nephew of Francis Preston, cousin of William Ballard Preston and William Campbell Preston) (W Ky.) Oct. 16, 1816-Sept. 21, 1887; House Dec. 6, 1852-55.

PRESTON, William Ballard (nephew of Francis Preston, cousin of William Preston and William Campbell Preston) (W Va.) Nov. 25, 1805-Nov. 16, 1862; House 1847-49; Secy. of the Navy 1849-50.

PRESTON, William Campbell (son of Francis Preston, cousin of William Preston and William Ballard Preston) (Cal.N S.C.) Dec. 27, 1794-May 22, 1860; Senate Nov. 26, 1833-Nov. 29, 1842.

PREYER, Lunsford Richardson (D N.C.) Jan. 11, 1919-—; House 1969-81.

PRICE, Andrew (D La.) April 2, 1854-Feb. 5, 1909; House Dec. 2, 1889-97.

PRICE, Charles Melvin (D Ill.) Jan. 1, 1905-—; House 1945-—.

PRICE, David Eugene (D N.C.) Aug. 17, 1940-—; House 1987-—.

PRICE, Emory Hilliard (D Fla.) Dec. 3, 1899-Feb. 11, 1976; House 1943-49.

PRICE, Hiram (R Iowa) Jan. 10, 1814-May 30, 1901; House 1863-69, 1877-81.

PRICE, Hugh Hiram (son of William Thompson Price) (R Wis.) Dec. 2, 1859-Dec. 25, 1904; House Jan. 18-March 3, 1887.

PRICE, Jesse Dashiell (D Md.) Aug. 15, 1863-May 14, 1939; House Nov. 3, 1914-19.

PRICE, Robert Dale (R Texas) Sept. 7, 1927-—; House 1967-75.

PRICE, Rodman McCamley (D N.J.) May 5, 1816-June 7, 1894; House 1851-53; Gov. 1854-57.

PRICE, Samuel (— W.Va.) July 28, 1805-Feb. 25, 1884; Senate Aug. 26, 1876-Jan. 26, 1877.

PRICE, Sterling (D Mo.) Sept. 20, 1809-Sept. 29, 1867; House 1845-Aug. 12, 1846; Gov. 1853-57.

PRICE, Thomas Lawson (D Mo.) Jan. 19, 1809-July 15, 1870; House Jan. 21, 1862-63.

PRICE, William Pierce (D Ga.) Jan. 29, 1835-Nov. 4, 1908; House Dec. 22, 1870-73.

PRICE, William Thompson (father of Hugh Hiram Price) (R Wis.) June 17, 1824-Dec. 6, 1886; House 1883-Dec. 6, 1886.

PRIDEMORE, Auburn Lorenzo (D Va.) June 27, 1837-May 17, 1900; House 1877-79.

PRIEST, James Percy (D Tenn.) April 1, 1900-Oct. 12, 1956; House 1941-Oct. 12, 1956.

PRINCE, Charles Henry (R Ga.) May 9, 1837-April 3, 1912; House July 25, 1868-69.

PRINCE, George Washington (R Ill.) March 4, 1854-Sept. 26, 1939; House Dec. 2, 1895-1913.

PRINCE, Oliver Hillhouse (- Ga.) 1787-Oct. 9, 1837; Senate Nov. 7, 1828-29.

PRINCE, William (- Ind.) 1772-Sept. 8, 1824; House 1823-Sept. 8, 1824.

PRINDLE, Elizur H. (R N.Y.) May 6, 1829-Oct. 7, 1890; House 1871-73.

PRINGEY, Joseph Colburn (R Okla.) May 22, 1858-Feb. 11, 1935; House 1921-23.

PRINGLE, Benjamin (W N.Y.) Nov. 9, 1807-June 7, 1887; House 1853-57.

PRITCHARD, George Moore (son of Jeter Connelly Pritchard) (R N.C.) Jan. 4, 1886-April 24, 1955; House 1929-31.

PRITCHARD, Jeter Connelly (father of George Moore Pritchard) (R N.C.) July 12, 1857-April 10, 1921; Senate Jan. 23, 1895-1903.

PRITCHARD, Joel McFee (R Wash.) May 5, 1925- —; House 1973-85.

PROCTOR, Redfield (R Vt.) June 1, 1831-March 4, 1908; Senate Nov. 2, 1891-March 4, 1908; Gov. 1878-80; Secy. of War 1889-91.

PROFFIT, George H. (W Ind.) Sept. 7, 1807-Sept. 7, 1847; House 1839-43.

PROKOP, Stanley A. (D Pa.) ?-Nov. 11, 1977; House 1959-61.

PROSSER, William Farrand (R Tenn.) March 16, 1834-Sept. 23, 1911; House 1869-71.

PROUTY, Solomon Francis (R Iowa) Jan. 17, 1854-July 16, 1927; House 1911-15.

PROUTY, Winston Lewis (R Vt.) Sept. 1, 1906-Sept. 10, 1971; House 1951-59; Senate 1959-Sept. 10, 1971.

PROXMIRE, William (D Wis.) Nov. 11, 1915- —; Senate Aug. 28, 1957- —.

PRUYN, John Van Schaick Lansing (D N.Y.) June 22, 1811-Nov. 21, 1877; House Dec. 7, 1863-65, 1867-69.

PRYOR, David Hampton (D Ark.) Aug. 29, 1934- —; House Nov. 8, 1966-73; Senate 1979- —; Gov. 1975-79.

PRYOR, Luke (D Ala.) July 5, 1820-Aug. 5, 1900; Senate Jan. 7-Nov. 23, 1880; House 1883-85.

PRYOR, Roger Atkinson (D Va.) July 19, 1828-March 14, 1919; House Dec. 7, 1859-61.

PUCINSKI, Roman Conrad (D Ill.) May 13, 1919- —; House 1959-73.

PUGH, George Ellis (D Ohio) Nov. 28, 1822-July 19, 1876; Senate 1855-61.

PUGH, James Lawrence (D Ala.) Dec. 12, 1820-March 9, 1907; House 1859-Jan. 21, 1861; Senate Nov. 24, 1880-97.

PUGH, John (D Pa.) June 2, 1761-July 13, 1842; House 1805-09.

PUGH, John Howard (R N.J.) June 23, 1827-April 30, 1905; House 1877-79.

PUGH, Samuel Johnson (R Ky.) Jan. 28, 1850-April 17, 1922; House 1895-1901.

PUGSLEY, Cornelius Amory (D N.Y.) July 17, 1850-Sept. 10, 1936; House 1901-03.

PUGSLEY, Jacob Joseph (R Ohio) Jan. 25, 1838-Feb. 5, 1920; House 1887-91.

PUJO, Arsène Paulin (D La.) Dec. 16, 1861-Dec. 31, 1939; House 1903-13.

PULITZER, Joseph (D N.Y.) April 10, 1847-Oct. 29, 1911; House 1885-April 10, 1886.

PURCELL, Graham Boynton Jr. (D Texas) May 5, 1919- —; House Jan. 27, 1962-73.

PURCELL, William Edward (D N.D.) Aug. 3, 1856-Nov. 23, 1928; Senate Feb. 1, 1910-Feb. 1, 1911.

PURDY, Smith Meade (D N.Y.) July 31, 1796-March 30, 1870; House 1843-45.

PURMAN, William James (R Fla.) April 11, 1840-Aug. 14, 1928; House 1873-Jan. 25, 1875, March 4, 1875-77.

PURNELL, Fred Sampson (R Ind.) Oct. 25, 1882-Oct. 21, 1939; House 1917-33.

PURSELL, Carl Duane (R Mich.) Dec. 19, 1932- —; House 1977- —.

PURTELL, William Arthur (R Conn.) May 6, 1897-May 31, 1978; Senate Aug. 29-Nov. 4, 1952, 1953-59.

PURVIANCE, Samuel Anderson (W Pa.) Jan. 10, 1809-Feb. 14, 1882; House 1855-59.

PURVIANCE, Samuel Dinsmore (F N.C.) Jan. 7, 1774-about 1806; House 1803-05.

PURYEAR, Richard Clauselle (W N.C.) Feb. 9, 1801-July 30, 1867; House 1853-57.

PUSEY, William Henry Mills (D Iowa) July 29, 1826-Nov. 15, 1900; House 1883-85.

PUTNAM, Harvey (W N.Y.) Jan. 5, 1793-Sept. 20, 1855; House Nov. 7, 1838-39, 1847-51.

PYLE, Gladys (R S.D.) Oct. 4, 1890- —; Senate Nov. 9, 1938-39.

QUACKENBUSH, John Adam (R N.Y.) Oct. 15, 1828-May 11, 1908; House 1889-93.

QUARLES, James Minor (W Tenn.) Feb. 8, 1823-March 3, 1901; House 1859-61.

QUARLES, Joseph Very (R Wis.) Dec. 16, 1843-Oct. 7, 1911; Senate 1899-1905.

QUARLES, Julian Minor (D Va.) Sept. 25, 1848-Nov. 18, 1929; House 1899-1901.

QUARLES, Tunstall (D Ky.) about 1770-Jan. 7, 1855; House 1817-June 15, 1820.

QUAY, Matthew Stanley (R Pa.) Sept. 30, 1833-May 28, 1904; Senate 1887-99, Jan. 16, 1901-May 28, 1904; Chrmn. Rep. Nat. Comm. 1888-91.

QUAYLE, James Danforth (R Ind.) Feb. 4, 1947- —; House 1977-81; Senate 1981- —.

QUAYLE, John Francis (D N.Y.) Dec. 1, 1868-Nov. 27, 1930; House 1923-Nov. 27, 1930.

QUEZON, Manuel Luis (Nat. P.I.) Aug. 19, 1878-Aug. 1, 1944; House (Res. Comm.) Nov. 23, 1909-Oct. 15, 1916; Pres. (P.I.) 1935-44.

QUIE, Albert Harold (R Minn.) Sept. 18, 1923- —; House Feb. 18, 1958-79; Gov. 1979-83.

QUIGG, Lemuel Ely (R N.Y.) Feb. 12, 1863-July 1, 1919; House Jan. 30, 1894-99.

QUIGLEY, James Michael (D Pa.) March 30, 1918- —; House 1955-57, 1959-61.

QUILLEN, James H. "Jimmy" (R Tenn.) Jan. 11, 1916- —; House 1963- —.

QUIN, Percy Edwards (D Miss.) Oct. 30, 1872-Feb. 4 1932; House 1913-Feb. 4, 1932.

QUINCY, Josiah (F Mass.) Feb. 4, 1772-July 1, 1864 House 1805-13.

QUINN, James Leland (D Pa.) Sept. 8, 1875-Nov. 12 1960; House 1935-39.

QUINN, John (D N.Y.) Aug. 9, 1839-Feb. 23, 1903 House 1889-91.

QUINN, Peter Anthony (D N.Y.) May 10, 1904-Dec. 23 1974; House 1945-47.

QUINN, Terence John (D N.Y.) Oct. 16, 1836-June 18 1878; House 1877-June 18, 1878.

QUINN, Thomas Vincent (D N.Y.) March 16, 1903- — House 1949-Dec. 30, 1951.

QUITMAN, John Anthony (D Miss.) Sept. 1, 1799-July 17, 1858; House 1855-July 17, 1858; Gov. 1835-36 1850-51.

RABAUT, Louis Charles (D Mich.) Dec. 5, 1886-Nov 12, 1961; House 1935-47, 1949-Nov. 12, 1961.

RABIN, Benjamin J. (D N.Y.) June 3, 1896-Feb. 22 1969; House 1945-Dec. 31, 1947.

RACE, John Abner (D Wis.) May 12, 1914-Nov. 10 1983; House 1965-67.

RADCLIFFE, Amos Henry (R N.J.) Jan. 16, 1870-Dec 29, 1950; House 1919-23.

RADCLIFFE, George Lovick (D Md.) Aug. 22, 1877 July 29, 1974; Senate 1935-47.

RADFORD, William (D N.Y.) June 24, 1814-Jan. 18 1870; House 1863-67.

RADWAN, Edmund Patrick (R N.Y.) Sept. 22, 1911 Sept. 7, 1959; House 1951-59.

RAGON, Heartsill (D Ark.) March 20, 1885-Sept. 15 1940; House 1923-June 16, 1933.

RAGSDALE, James Willard (D S.C.) Dec. 14, 1872-Jul 23, 1919; House 1913-July 23, 1919.

RAHALL, Nick Joe II (D W.Va.) May 20, 1949- — House 1977- —.

RAILSBACK, Thomas F. (R Ill.) Jan. 22, 1932- — House 1967-83.

RAINES, John (R N.Y.) May 6, 1840-Dec. 16, 1909 House 1889-93.

RAINEY, Henry Thomas (D Ill.) Aug. 20, 1860-Aug. 19 1934; House 1903-21, 1923-Aug. 19, 1934; House majority leader 1931-33; Speaker 1933-34.

AINEY, John William (D Ill.) Dec. 21, 1880-May 4, 1923; House April 2, 1918-May 4, 1923.

AINEY, Joseph Hayne (R S.C.) June 21, 1832-Aug. 2, 1887; House Dec. 12, 1870-79.

AINEY, Lilius Bratton (D Ala.) July 27, 1876-Sept. 27, 1959; House Sept. 30, 1919-23.

AINS, Albert M. (D Ala.) March 11, 1902- —; House 1945-65.

AKER, John Edward (D Calif.) Feb. 22, 1863-Jan. 22, 1926; House 1911-Jan. 22, 1926.

ALSTON, Samuel Moffett (D Ind.) Dec. 1, 1857-Oct. 14, 1925; Senate 1923-Oct. 14, 1925; Gov. 1913-17.

AMEY, Frank Marion (R Ill.) Sept. 23, 1881-March 27, 1942; House 1929-31.

AMEY, Homer Alonzo (R Ohio) March 2, 1891-April 13, 1960; House 1943-49.

AMSAY, Robert Lincoln (D W.Va.) March 24, 1877-Nov. 14, 1956; House 1933-39, 1941-43, 1949-53.

AMSEY, Alexander (R Minn.) Sept. 8, 1815-April 22, 1903; House 1843-47 (Whig Pa.); Senate 1863-75; Gov. 1849-53 (Minn. Terr.), 1860-63; Secy. of War 1879-81.

AMSEY, John Rathbone (R N.J.) April 25, 1862-April 10, 1933; House 1917-21.

AMSEY, Robert (W Pa.) Feb. 15, 1780-Dec. 12, 1849; House 1833-35, 1841-43.

AMSEY, William (D Pa.) Sept. 7, 1779-Sept. 29, 1831; House 1827-Sept. 29, 1831.

AMSEY, William Sterrett (D Pa.) June 12, 1810-Oct. 17, 1840; House 1839-Oct. 17, 1840.

AMSEYER, Christian William (R Iowa) March 13, 1875-Nov. 1, 1943; House 1915-33.

AMSPECK, Robert C. Word (D Ga.) Sept. 5, 1890-Sept. 10, 1972; House Oct. 2, 1929-Dec. 31, 1945.

ANDALL, Alexander (W Md.) Jan. 3, 1803-Nov. 21, 1881; House 1841-43.

ANDALL, Benjamin (W Maine) Nov. 14, 1789-Oct. 11, 1859; House 1839-43.

ANDALL, Charles Hiram (Prohib./D/R/Prog. Calif.) July 23, 1865-Feb. 18, 1951; House 1915-21.

ANDALL, Charles Sturtevant (R Mass.) Feb. 20, 1824-Aug. 17, 1904; House 1889-95.

ANDALL, Clifford Ellsworth (R Wis.) Dec. 25, 1876-Oct. 16, 1934; House 1919-21.

RANDALL, Samuel Jackson (D Pa.) Oct. 10, 1828-April 13, 1890; House 1863-April 13, 1890; Speaker 1876-81.

RANDALL, William Harrison (R Ky.) July 15, 1812-Aug. 1, 1881; House 1863-67.

RANDALL, William Joseph (D Mo.) July 16, 1909- —; House March 3, 1959-77.

RANDELL, Choice Boswell (nephew of Lucius Jeremiah Gartrell) (D Texas) Jan. 1, 1857-Oct. 19, 1945; House 1901-13.

RANDOLPH, James Fitz (father of Theodore Fitz Randolph) (— N.J.) June 26, 1791-Jan. 25, 1872; House Dec. 1, 1827-33.

RANDOLPH, James Henry (R Tenn.) Oct. 18, 1825-Aug. 22, 1900; House 1877-79.

RANDOLPH, Jennings (D W.Va.) March 8, 1902- —; House 1933-47; Senate Nov. 5, 1958-85.

RANDOLPH, John (SRD Va.) June 2, 1773-May 24, 1833; House 1799-1813, 1815-17, 1819-Dec. 26, 1825, 1827-29, March 4-May 24, 1833; Senate Dec. 26, 1825-27.

RANDOLPH, Joseph Fitz (W N.J.) March 14, 1803-March 20, 1873; House 1837-43.

RANDOLPH, Theodore Fitz (son of James Fitz Randolph) (D N.J.) June 24, 1826-Nov. 7, 1883; Senate 1875-81; Gov. 1869-72.

RANDOLPH, Thomas Mann (son-in-law of Pres. Thomas Jefferson) (DR Va.) Oct. 1, 1768-June 20, 1828; House 1803-07; Gov. 1819-22.

RANEY, John Henry (R Mo.) Sept. 28, 1849-Jan. 23, 1928; House 1895-97.

RANGEL, Charles Bernard (D N.Y.) June 1, 1930- —; House 1971- —.

RANKIN, Christopher (D Miss.) 1788-March 14, 1826; House 1819-March 14, 1826.

RANKIN, Jeannette (R Mont.) June 11, 1880-May 18, 1973; House 1917-19, 1941-43.

RANKIN, John Elliott (D Miss.) March 29, 1882-Nov. 26, 1960; House 1921-53.

RANKIN, Joseph (D Wis.) Sept. 25, 1833-Jan. 24, 1886; House 1883-Jan. 24, 1886.

RANNEY, Ambrose Arnold (R Mass.) April 17, 1821-March 5, 1899; House 1881-87.

RANSDELL, Joseph Eugene (D La.) Oct. 7, 1858-July 27, 1954; House Aug. 29, 1899-1913; Senate 1913-31.

RANSIER, Alonzo Jacob (R S.C.) Jan. 3, 1834-Aug. 17, 1882; House 1873-75.

RANSLEY, Harry Clay (R Pa.) Feb. 5, 1863-Nov. 7, 1941; House Nov. 2, 1920-37.

RANSOM, Matt Whitaker (cousin of Wharton Jackson Green) (D N.C.) Oct. 8, 1826-Oct. 8, 1904; Senate Jan. 30, 1872-95; Pres. pro tempore 1895.

RANTOUL, Robert Jr. (D Mass.) Aug. 13, 1805-Aug. 7, 1852; Senate Feb. 1-March 3, 1851; House March 4, 1851-Aug. 7, 1852.

RAPIER, James Thomas (R Ala.) Nov. 13, 1837-May 31, 1883; House 1873-75.

RARICK, John Richard (D La.) Jan. 29, 1924- —; House 1967-75.

RARIDEN, James (W Ind.) Feb. 14, 1795-Oct. 20, 1856; House 1837-41.

RATCHFORD, William Richard (D Conn.) May 24, 1934- —; House 1979-85.

RATHBONE, Henry Riggs (grandson of Ira Harris) (R Ill.) Feb. 12, 1870-July 15, 1928; House 1923-July 15, 1928.

RATHBUN, George Oscar (D N.Y.) 1803-Jan. 5, 1870; House 1843-47.

RAUCH, George Washington (D Ind.) Feb. 22, 1876-Nov. 4, 1940; House 1907-17.

RAUM, Green Berry (R Ill.) Dec. 3, 1829-Dec. 18, 1909; House 1867-69.

RAVENEL, Arthur Jr. (R S.C.) March 29, 1927- —; House 1987- —.

RAWLINS, Joseph Lafayette (D Utah) March 28, 1850-May 24, 1926; House (Terr. Del.) 1893-95; Senate 1897-1903.

RAWLS, Morgan (D Ga.) June 29, 1829-Oct. 18, 1906; House 1873-March 24, 1874.

RAWSON, Charles Augustus (R Iowa) May 29, 1867-Sept. 2, 1936; Senate Feb. 24-Dec. 1, 1922.

RAY, George Washington (R N.Y.) Feb. 3, 1844-Jan. 10, 1925; House 1883-85, 1891-Sept. 11, 1902.

RAY, John Henry (R N.Y.) Sept. 27, 1886-May 21, 1975; House 1953-63.

RAY, Joseph Warren (R Pa.) May 25, 1849-Sept. 15, 1928; House 1889-91.

RAY, Ossian (R N.H.) Dec. 13, 1835-Jan. 28, 1892; House Jan. 8, 1881-85.

RAY, Richard Belmont (D Ga.) Feb. 2, 1927- —; Hous 1983- —.

RAY, William Henry (R Ill.) Dec. 14, 1812-Jan. 25, 188 House 1873-75.

RAYBURN, Sam (D Texas) Jan. 6 1882-Nov. 16, 196 House 1913-Nov. 16, 1961; House majority lead 1937-40; Speaker 1940-47, 1949-53, 1955-61.

RAYFIEL, Leo Frederick (D N.Y.) March 22, 1888-No 18, 1978; House 1945-Sept. 13, 1947.

RAYMOND, Henry Jarvis (R N.Y.) Jan. 24, 1820-Ju 18, 1869; House 1865-67; Chrmn. Rep. Nat. Com 1864-66.

RAYMOND, John Baldwin (R Dakota) Dec. 5, 184 Jan. 3, 1886; House (Terr. Del.) 1883-85.

RAYNER, Isidor (D Md.) April 11, 1850-Nov. 25, 191 House 1887-89, 1891-95; Senate 1905-Nov. 25, 191

RAYNER, Kenneth (W N.C.) June 20, 1808-March 1884; House 1839-45.

REA, David (D Mo.) Jan. 19, 1831-June 13, 1901; Hou 1875-79.

REA, John (D Pa.) Jan. 27, 1755-Feb. 26, 1829; Hou 1803-11, May 11, 1813-15.

READ, Almon Heath (D Pa.) June 12, 1790-June 1844; House March 18, 1842-June 3, 1844.

READ, George (— Del.) Sept. 18, 1733-Sept. 21, 179 Senate 1789-Sept. 18, 1793; Cont. Cong. 1774-77.

READ, Jacob (F S.C.) 1751-July 17, 1816; Senate 179 1801; Pres. pro tempore 1798; Cont. Cong. 1783-8

READ, Nathan (F Mass.) July 2, 1759-Jan. 20, 184 House Nov. 25, 1800-03.

READ, William Brown (D Ky.) Dec. 14, 1817-Aug. 1880; House 1871-75.

READE, Edwin Godwin (AP N.C.) Nov. 13, 1812-O 18, 1894; House 1855-57.

READING, John Roberts (D Pa.) Nov. 1, 1826-Feb. 1886; House 1869-April 13, 1870.

READY, Charles (uncle of William T. Haskell) (Tenn.) Dec. 22, 1802-June 4, 1878; House 1853-5

REAGAN, John Henninger (D Texas) Oct. 8, 18 March 6, 1905; House 1857-61, 1875-March 4, 18 Senate March 4, 1887-June 10, 1891.

REAMES, Alfred Evan (D Ore.) Feb. 5, 1870-March 1943; Senate Feb. 1-Nov. 8, 1938.

REAMS, Henry Frazier (I Ohio) Jan. 15, 1897-Sept. 1971; House 1951-55.

REAVIS, Charles Frank (R Neb.) Sept. 5, 1870-May 26, 1932; House 1915-June 3, 1922.

REBER, John (R Pa.) Feb. 1, 1858-Sept. 26, 1931; House 1919-23.

REDDEN, Monroe Minor (D N.C.) Sept. 24, 1901- —; House 1947-53.

REDFIELD, William Cox (D N.Y.) June 18, 1858-June 13, 1932; House 1911-13; Secy. of Commerce 1913-19.

REDING, John Randall (D N.H.) Oct. 18, 1805-Oct. 8, 1892; House 1841-45.

REDLIN, Rolland W. (D N.D.) Feb. 29, 1920- —; House 1965-67.

REECE, Brazilla Carroll (husband of Louise Goff Reece, son-in-law of Guy Despard Goff) (R Tenn.) Dec. 22, 1889-March 19, 1961; House 1921-31, 1933-47, 1951-March 19, 1961; Chrmn. Rep. Nat. Comm. 1946-48.

REECE, Louise Goff (widow of Brazilla Carroll Reece, daughter of Guy Despard Goff, granddaughter of Nathan Goff) (R Tenn.) Nov. 6, 1898-May 14, 1970; House May 16, 1961-63.

REED, Charles Manning (W Pa.) April 3, 1803-Dec. 16, 1871; House 1843-45.

REED, Chauncey William (R Ill.) June 2, 1890-Feb. 9, 1956; House 1935-Feb. 9, 1956.

REED, Clyde Martin (R Kan.) Oct. 19, 1871-Nov. 8, 1949; Senate 1939-Nov. 8, 1949; Gov. 1929-31.

REED, Daniel Alden (R N.Y.) Sept. 15, 1875-Feb. 19, 1959; House 1919-Feb. 19, 1959.

REED, David Aiken (R Pa.) Dec. 21, 1880-Feb. 10, 1953; Senate Aug. 8, 1922-35.

REED, Edward Cambridge (D N.Y.) March 8, 1793-May 1, 1883; House 1831-33.

REED, Eugene Elliott (D N.H.) April 23, 1866-Dec. 15, 1940; House 1913-15.

REED, Isaac (W Maine) Aug. 22, 1809-Sept. 19, 1887; House June 25, 1852-53.

REED, James Alexander (D Mo.) Nov. 9, 1861-Sept. 8, 1944; Senate 1911-29.

REED, James Byron (D Ark.) Jan. 2, 1881-April 27, 1935; House Oct. 20, 1923-29.

REED, John (father of John Reed, below) (F Mass.) Nov. 11, 1751-Feb. 17, 1831; House 1795-1801.

REED, John (son of John Reed, above) (W Mass.) Sept. 2, 1781-Nov. 25, 1860; House 1813-17 (Federalist), 1821-41.

REED, Joseph Rea (R Iowa) March 12, 1835-April 2, 1925; House 1889-91.

REED, Philip (— Md.) 1760-Nov. 2, 1829; Senate Nov. 25, 1806-13; House 1817-19, March 19, 1822-23.

REED, Robert Rentoul (W Pa.) March 12, 1807-Dec. 14, 1864; House 1849-51.

REED, Stuart Felix (R W.Va.) Jan. 8, 1866-July 4, 1935; House 1917-25.

REED, Thomas Brackett (R Maine) Oct. 18, 1839-Dec. 7, 1902; House 1877-Sept. 4, 1899; Speaker 1889-91, 1895-99.

REED, Thomas Buck (D Miss.) May 7, 1787-Nov. 26, 1829; Senate Jan. 28, 1826-27, March 4-Nov. 26, 1829.

REED, William (F Mass.) June 6, 1776-Feb. 18, 1837; House 1811-15.

REEDER, William Augustus (R Kan.) Aug. 28, 1849-Nov. 7, 1929; House 1899-1911.

REES, Edward Herbert (R Kan.) June 3, 1886-Oct. 25, 1969; House 1937-61.

REES, Rollin Raymond (R Kan.) Jan. 10, 1865-May 30, 1935; House 1911-13.

REES, Thomas M. (D Calif.) March 26, 1925- —; House Dec. 15, 1965-77.

REESE, David Addison (W Ga.) March 3, 1794-Dec. 16, 1871; House 1853-55.

REESE, Seaborn (D Ga.) Nov. 28, 1846-March 1, 1907; House Dec. 4, 1882-87.

REEVES, Albert Lee Jr. (R Mo.) May 31, 1906- —; House 1947-49.

REEVES, Henry Augustus (D N.Y.) Dec. 7, 1832-March 4, 1916; House 1869-71.

REEVES, Walter (R Ill.) Sept. 25, 1848-April 9, 1909; House 1895-1903.

REGAN, Kenneth Mills (D Texas) March 6, 1893-Aug. 15, 1959; House Aug. 23, 1947-55.

REGULA, Ralph Strauss (R Ohio) Dec. 3, 1924- —; House 1973- —.

REID, Charles Chester (D Ark.) June 15, 1868-May 20, 1922; House 1901-11.

REID, Charlotte Thompson (R Ill.) Sept. 27, 1913- —; House 1963-Oct. 7, 1971.

REID, David Settle (nephew of Thomas Settle) (D N.C.) April 19, 1813-June 19, 1891; House 1843-47; Senate Dec. 6, 1854-59; Gov. 1851-54.

REID, Frank R. (R Ill.) April 18, 1879-Jan. 25, 1945; House 1923-35.

REID, Harry (D Nev.) Dec. 2, 1939- —; House 1983-87; Senate 1987- —.

REID, James Wesley (D N.C.) June 11, 1849-Jan. 1, 1902; House Jan. 28, 1885-Dec. 31, 1886.

REID, John William (D Mo.) June 14, 1821-Nov. 22, 1881; House March 4-Aug. 3, 1861.

REID, Ogden Rogers (D N.Y.) June 24, 1925- —; House 1963-75 (1963-March 22, 1972 Republican).

REID, Robert Raymond (D Ga.) Sept. 8, 1789-July 1, 1841; House Feb. 18, 1819-23; Gov. (Fla. Terr.) 1839-41.

REIFEL, Benjamin (R S.D.) Sept. 19, 1906- —; House 1961-71.

REILLY, James Bernard (D Pa.) Aug. 12, 1845-May 14, 1924; House 1875-79, 1889-95.

REILLY, John (D Pa.) Feb. 22, 1836-April 19, 1904; House 1875-77.

REILLY, Michael Kieran (D Wis.) July 15, 1869-Oct. 14, 1944; House 1913-17, Nov. 4, 1930-39.

REILLY, Thomas Lawrence (D Conn.) Sept. 20, 1859-July 6, 1924; House 1911-15.

REILLY, Wilson (D Pa.) Aug. 8, 1811-Aug. 26, 1885; House 1857-59.

REILY, Luther (D Pa.) Oct. 17, 1794-Feb. 20, 1854; House 1837-39.

REINECKE, Edwin (R Calif.) Jan. 7, 1924- —; House 1965-Jan. 21, 1969.

RELFE, James Hugh (D Mo.) Oct. 17, 1791-Sept. 14, 1863; House 1843-47.

REMANN, Frederick (R Ill.) May 10, 1847-July 14, 1895; House March 4-July 14, 1895.

RENCHER, Abraham (D N.C.) Aug. 12, 1798-July 6, 1883; House 1829-39, 1841-43; Gov. (N.M.) 1857-61.

RESA, Alexander John (D Ill.) Aug. 4, 1887-July 4, 1964; House 1945-47.

RESNICK, Joseph Yale (D N.Y.) July 13, 1924-Oct. 6, 1969; House 1965-69.

REUSS, Henry Schoellkopf (D Wis.) Feb. 22, 1912- —; House 1955-83.

REVELS, Hiram Rhodes (R Miss.) Sept. 27, 1827-Jan. 16, 1901; Senate Feb. 23, 1870-71.

REVERCOMB, William Chapman (R W.Va.) July 20, 1895-Oct. 6, 1979; Senate 1943-49, Nov. 7, 1956-59.

REYBURN, John Edgar (father of William Stuart Reyburn) (R Pa.) Feb. 7, 1845-Jan. 4, 1914; House Feb. 18, 1890-97, Nov. 6, 1906-March 31, 1907.

REYBURN, William Stuart (son of John Edgar Reyburn) (R Pa.) Dec. 17, 1882-July 25, 1946; House May 23, 1911-13.

REYNOLDS, Edwin Ruthvin (R N.Y.) Feb. 16, 1816-July 4, 1908; House Dec. 5, 1860-61.

REYNOLDS, Gideon (W N.Y.) Aug. 9, 1813-July 13, 1896; House 1847-51.

REYNOLDS, John (D Ill.) Feb. 26, 1789-May 8, 1865; House Dec. 1, 1834-37, 1839-43; Gov. 1830-34 (National Republican).

REYNOLDS, John Hazard (R N.Y.) June 21, 1819-Sept. 24, 1875; House 1859-61.

REYNOLDS, John Merriman (R Pa.) March 5, 1848-Sept. 14, 1933; House 1905-Jan. 17, 1911.

REYNOLDS, Joseph (D N.Y.) Sept. 14, 1785-Sept. 24, 1864; House 1835-37.

REYNOLDS, Robert Rice (D N.C.) June 18, 1884-Feb. 13, 1963; Senate Dec. 5, 1932-45.

REYNOLDS, Samuel Williams (R Neb.) Aug. 11, 1890- —; Senate July 3-Nov. 7, 1954.

RHEA, John (D Tenn.) 1753-May 27, 1832; House 1803-15, 1817-23.

RHEA, John Stockdale (D/P Ky.) March 9, 1855-July 29, 1924; House 1897-March 25, 1902, 1903-05.

RHEA, William Francis (D Va.) April 20, 1858-March 23, 1931; House 1899-1903.

RHETT, Robert Barnwell (formerly Robert Barnwell Smith) (D S.C.) Dec. 24, 1800-Sept. 14, 1876; House 1837-49; Senate Dec. 18, 1850-May 7, 1852.

RHINOCK, Joseph Lafayette (D Ky.) Jan. 4, 1863-Sept. 20, 1926; House 1905-11.

RHODES, George Milton (D Pa.) Feb. 24, 1898-Oct. 24, 1978; House 1949-69.

RHODES, John J. III (son of John Jacob Rhodes) (R Ariz.) Sept. 8, 1943- —; House 1987- —.

RHODES, John Jacob (father of John J. Rhodes III) (R Ariz.) Sept. 18, 1916- —; House 1953-83.

RHODES, Marion Edwards (R Mo.) Jan. 4, 1868-Dec. 25, 1928; House 1905-07, 1919-23.

RIBICOFF, Abraham Alexander (D Conn.) April 9, 1910- —; House 1949-53; Senate 1963-81; Gov. 1955-61; Secy. of Health, Education and Welfare 1961-62.

RICAUD, James Barroll (AP Md.) Feb. 11, 1808-Jan. 24, 1866; House 1855-59.

RICE, Alexander Hamilton (R Mass.) Aug. 30, 1818-July 22, 1895; House 1859-67; Gov. 1876-79.

RICE, Americus Vespucius (D Ohio) Nov. 18, 1835-April 4, 1904; House 1875-79.

RICE, Benjamin Franklin (R Ark.) May 26, 1828-Jan. 19, 1905; Senate June 23, 1868-73.

RICE, Edmund (brother of Henry Mower Rice) (D Minn.) Feb. 14, 1819-July 11, 1889; House 1887-89.

RICE, Edward Young (D Ill.) Feb. 8, 1820-April 16, 1883; House 1871-73.

RICE, Henry Mower (brother of Edmund Rice) (D Minn.) Nov. 29, 1817-Jan. 15, 1894; House (Terr. Del.) 1853-57; Senate May 11, 1858-63.

RICE, John Birchard (R Ohio) June 23, 1832-Jan. 14, 1893; House 1881-83.

RICE, John Blake (R Ill.) May 28, 1809-Dec. 17, 1874; House 1873-Dec. 17, 1874.

RICE, John Hovey (R Maine) Feb. 5, 1816-March 14, 1911; House 1861-67.

RICE, John McConnell (D Ky.) Feb. 19, 1831-Sept. 18, 1895; House 1869-73.

RICE, Theron Moses (Nat.G Mo.) Sept. 21, 1829-Nov. 7, 1895; House 1881-83.

RICE, Thomas (— Mass.) March 30, 1768-Aug. 25, 1854; House 1815-19.

RICE, William Whitney (R Mass.) March 7, 1826-March 1, 1896; House 1877-87.

RICH, Carl West (R Ohio) Sept. 12, 1898-June 26, 1972; House 1963-65.

RICH, Charles (D Vt.) Sept. 13, 1771-Oct. 15, 1824; House 1813-15.

RICH, John Tyler (R Mich.) April 23, 1841-March 28, 1926; House April 5, 1881-83; Gov. 1893-97.

RICH, Robert Fleming (R Pa.) June 23, 1883-April 28, 1968; House Nov. 4, 1930-43, 1945-51.

RICHARD, Gabriel (— Mich.) Oct. 15, 1767-Sept. 13, 1832; House (Terr. Del.) 1823-25.

RICHARDS, Charles Lenmore (D Nev.) Oct. 3, 1877-Dec. 22, 1953; House 1923-25.

RICHARDS, Jacob (D Pa.) 1773-July 20, 1816; House 1803-09.

RICHARDS, James Alexander Dudley (D Ohio) March 22, 1845-Dec. 4, 1911; House 1893-95.

RICHARDS, James Prioleau (D S.C.) Aug. 31, 1894-Feb. 21, 1979; House 1933-57.

RICHARDS, John (brother of Matthias Richards) (— Pa.) April 18, 1753-Nov. 13, 1822; House 1795-97.

RICHARDS, John (— N.Y.) April 13, 1765-April 18, 1850; House 1823-25.

RICHARDS, Mark (D Vt.) July 15, 1760-Aug. 10, 1844; House 1817-21.

RICHARDS, Matthias (brother of John Richards) (— Pa.) Feb. 26, 1758-Aug. 4, 1830; House 1807-11.

RICHARDSON, David Plunket (R N.Y.) May 28, 1833-June 21, 1904; House 1879-83.

RICHARDSON, George Frederick (D Mich.) July 1, 1850-March 1, 1923; House 1893-95.

RICHARDSON, Harry Alden (R Del.) Jan. 1, 1853-June 16, 1928; Senate 1907-13.

RICHARDSON, James Daniel (D Tenn.) March 10, 1843-July 24, 1914; House 1885-1905.

RICHARDSON, James Montgomery (D Ky.) July 1, 1858-Feb. 9, 1925; House 1905-07.

RICHARDSON, John Peter II (cousin of Richard Irvine Manning I) (SRD S.C.) April 14, 1801-Jan. 24, 1864; House Dec. 19, 1836-39; Gov. 1840-42.

RICHARDSON, John Smythe (D S.C.) Feb. 29, 1828-Feb. 24, 1894; House 1879-83.

RICHARDSON, Joseph (— Mass.) Feb. 1, 1778-Sept. 25, 1871; House 1827-31.

RICHARDSON, William (D Ala.) May 8, 1839-March 31, 1914; House Aug. 6, 1900-March 31, 1914.

RICHARDSON, William Alexander (D Ill.) Jan. 16, 1811-Dec. 27, 1875; House Dec. 6, 1847-Aug. 25, 1856, 1861-Jan. 29, 1863; Senate Jan. 30, 1863-65.

RICHARDSON, William Blaine (D N.M.) Nov. 15, 1947- —; House 1983- —.

RICHARDSON, William Emanuel (D Pa.) Sept. 3, 1886-Nov. 3, 1948; House 1933-37.

RICHARDSON, William Merchant (F Mass.) Jan. 4, 1774-March 15, 1838; House Nov. 4, 1811-April 18, 1814.

RICHMOND, Frederick William (D N.Y.) Nov. 15, 1923- —; House 1975-August 25, 1982.

RICHMOND, Hiram Lawton (R Pa.) May 17, 1810-Feb. 19, 1885; House 1873-75.

RICHMOND, James Buchanan (D Va.) Feb. 27, 1842-April 30, 1910; House 1879-81.

RICHMOND, Jonathan (− N.Y.) July 31, 1774-July 28, 1853; House 1819-21.

RICKETTS, Edwin Darlington (R Ohio) Aug. 3, 1867-July 3, 1937; House 1915-17, 1919-23.

RIDDICK, Carl Wood (R Mont.) Feb. 25, 1872-July 9, 1960; House 1919-23.

RIDDLE, Albert Gallatin (R Ohio) May 28, 1816-May 16, 1902; House 1861-63.

RIDDLE, George Read (D Del.) 1817-March 29, 1867; House 1851-55; Senate Feb. 2, 1864-March 29, 1867.

RIDDLE, Haywood Yancey (D Tenn.) June 20, 1834-March 28, 1879; House Dec. 14, 1875-79.

RIDDLEBERGER, Harrison Holt (Read. Va.) Oct. 4, 1844-Jan. 24, 1890; Senate 1883-89.

RIDER, Ira Edgar (D N.Y.) Nov. 17, 1868-May 29, 1906; House 1903-05.

RIDGE, Thomas Joseph (R Pa.) Aug. 26, 1945- −; House 1983- −.

RIDGELY, Edwin Reed (PP/D Kan.) May 9, 1844-April 23, 1927; House 1897-1901.

RIDGELY, Henry Moore (F Del.) Aug. 6, 1779-Aug. 6, 1847; House 1811-15; Senate Jan. 12, 1827-29.

RIDGWAY, Joseph (W Ohio) May 6, 1783-Feb. 1, 1861; House 1837-43.

RIDGWAY, Robert (C Va.) April 21, 1823-Oct. 16, 1870; House Jan. 27-Oct. 16, 1870.

RIEGLE, Donald Wayne Jr. (D Mich.) Feb. 4, 1938- −; House 1967-Dec. 30, 1976 (1967-Feb. 27, 1973, Republican); Senate Dec. 30, 1976- −.

RIEHLMAN, Roy Walter (R N.Y.) Aug. 26, 1899-July 16, 1978; House 1947-65.

RIFE, John Winebrenner (R Pa.) Aug. 14, 1846-April 17, 1908; House 1889-93.

RIGGS, James Milton (D Ill.) April 17, 1839-Nov. 18, 1933; House 1883-87.

RIGGS, Jetur Rose (D N.J.) June 20, 1809-Nov. 5, 1869; House 1859-61.

RIGGS, Lewis (D N.Y.) Jan. 16, 1789-Nov. 6, 1870; House 1841-43.

RIGNEY, Hugh McPheeters (D Ill.) July 31, 1873-Oct 12, 1950; House 1937-39.

RIKER, Samuel (− N.Y.) April 8, 1743-May 19, 1823 House Nov. 5, 1804-05, 1807-09.

RILEY, Corinne Boyd (widow of John Jacob Riley) (I S.C.) July 4, 1893-April 12, 1979; House April 10 1962-63.

RILEY, John Jacob (husband of Corinne Boyd Riley) (I S.C.) Feb. 1, 1895-Jan. 1, 1962; House 1945-49, 1951 Jan. 1, 1962.

RINAKER, John Irving (R Ill.) Nov. 1, 1830-Jan. 15 1915; House June 5, 1896-97.

RINALDO, Matthew John (R N.J.) Sept. 1, 1931- − House 1973- −.

RINGGOLD, Samuel (D Md.) Jan. 15, 1770-Oct. 18 1829; House Oct. 15, 1810-15, 1817-21.

RIORDAN, Daniel Joseph (D N.Y.) July 7, 1870-Apri 28, 1923; House 1899-1901, Nov. 6, 1906-April 28 1923.

RIPLEY, Eleazar Wheelock (brother of James Wheelock Ripley) (D La.) April 15, 1782-March 2, 1839 House 1835-March 2, 1839.

RIPLEY, James Wheelock (brother of Eleazar Wheelock Ripley) (D Maine) March 12, 1786-June 1 1835; House Sept. 11, 1826-March 12, 1830.

RIPLEY, Thomas C. (− N.Y.) ?-?; House Dec. 7, 1846 47.

RISENHOOVER, Theodore Marshall (D Okla.) Nov. 1934- −; House 1975-79.

RISK, Charles Francis (R R.I.) Aug. 19, 1897-Dec. 2 1943; House Aug. 6, 1935-37, 1939-41.

RISLEY, Elijah (W N.Y.) May 7, 1787-Jan. 9, 187 House 1849-51.

RITCHEY, Thomas (D Ohio) Jan. 19, 1801-March 1863; House 1847-49, 1853-55.

RITCHIE, Byron Foster (son of James Monroe Ritchi (D Ohio) Jan. 29, 1853-Aug. 22, 1928; House 1893-9

RITCHIE, David (R Pa.) Aug. 19, 1812-Jan. 24, 186 House 1853-59.

RITCHIE, James Monroe (father of Byron Fost Ritchie) (R Ohio) July 28, 1829-Aug. 17, 1918; Hou 1881-83.

RITCHIE, John (D Md.) Aug. 12, 1831-Oct. 27, 188 House 1871-73.

RITTER, Burwell Clark (uncle of Walter Evans) (C Ky Jan. 6, 1810-Oct. 1, 1880; House 1865-67.

ITTER, Donald Lawrence (R Pa.) Oct. 21, 1940- -; House 1979- -.

ITTER, John (D Pa.) Feb. 6, 1779-Nov. 24, 1851; House 1843-47.

IVERA, Luis Munoz (U P.R.) July 17, 1859-Nov. 15, 1916; House (Res. Comm.) 1911-Nov. 15, 1916.

IVERS, Lucius Mendel (D S.C.) Sept. 28, 1905-Dec. 28, 1970; House 1941-Dec. 28, 1970.

IVERS, Ralph Julian (D Alaska) May 23, 1903-Aug. 14, 1976; House 1959-67.

IVERS, Thomas (AP Tenn.) Sept. 18, 1819-March 18, 1863; House 1855-57.

IVES, Francis Everod (granduncle of Francis Rives Lassiter) (D Va.) Jan. 14, 1792-Dec. 26, 1861; House 1837-41.

IVES, William Cabell (W Va.) May 4, 1792-April 25, 1868; House 1823-29 (Democrat); Senate Dec. 10, 1832-Feb. 22, 1834 (Democrat), 1836-39 (Democrat), Jan. 18, 1841-45.

IVES, Zeno John (R Ill.) Feb. 22, 1874-Sept. 2, 1939; House 1905-07.

IXEY, John Franklin (D Va.) Aug. 1, 1854-Feb. 8, 1907; House 1897-Feb. 8, 1907.

IZLEY, Ross (R Okla.) July 5, 1892-March 4, 1969; House 1941-49.

OACH, Sidney Crain (R Mo.) July 25, 1876-June 29, 1934; House 1921-25.

OACH, William Nathaniel (D N.D.) Sept. 25, 1840-Sept. 7, 1902; Senate 1893-99.

OANE, John (father of John Jones Roane) (D Va.) Feb. 9, 1766-Nov. 15, 1838; House 1809-15, 1827-31, 1835-37.

OANE, John Jones (son of John Roane) (D Va.) Oct. 31, 1794-Dec. 18, 1869; House 1831-33.

OANE, William Henry (D Va.) Sept. 17, 1787-May 11, 1845; House 1815-17; Senate March 14, 1837-41.

OARK, Charles Wickliffe (R Ky.) Jan. 22, 1887-April 5, 1929; House March 4-April 5, 1929.

OBB, Edward (D Mo.) March 19, 1857-March 13, 1934; House 1897-1905.

OBBINS, Asher (W R.I.) Oct. 26, 1757-Feb. 25, 1845; Senate Oct. 31, 1825-39.

OBBINS, Edward Everett (R Pa.) Sept. 27, 1860-Jan. 25, 1919; House 1897-99, 1917-Jan. 25, 1919.

ROBBINS, Gaston Ahi (D Ala.) Sept. 26, 1858-Feb. 22, 1902; House 1893-March 13, 1896, 1899-March 8, 1900.

ROBBINS, George Robbins (W N.J.) Sept. 24, 1808-Feb. 22, 1875; House 1855-59.

ROBBINS, John (D Pa.) 1808-April 27, 1880; House 1849-55, 1875-77.

ROBBINS, William McKendree (D N.C.) Oct. 26, 1828-May 5, 1905; House 1873-79.

ROBERTS, Anthony Ellmaker (grandfather of Robert Grey Bushong) (W Pa.) Oct. 29, 1803-Jan. 25, 1885; House 1855-59.

ROBERTS, Brigham Henry (D Utah) March 13, 1857-Sept. 27, 1933; House 1899-Jan. 25, 1900.

ROBERTS, Charles Boyle (D Md.) April 19, 1842-Sept. 10, 1899; House 1875-79.

ROBERTS, Clint (R S.D.) Jan. 30, 1935- -; House 1981-83.

ROBERTS, Edwin Ewing (R Nev.) Dec. 12, 1870-Dec. 11, 1933; House 1911-19.

ROBERTS, Ellis Henry (R N.Y.) Sept. 30, 1827-Jan. 8, 1918; House 1871-75.

ROBERTS, Ernest William (R Mass.) Nov. 22, 1858-Feb. 27, 1924; House 1899-1917.

ROBERTS, Herbert Ray (D Texas) March 28, 1913- -; House Jan. 30, 1962-81.

ROBERTS, Jonathan (DR Pa.) Aug. 16, 1771-July 24, 1854; House 1811-Feb. 24, 1814; Senate Feb. 24, 1814-21.

ROBERTS, Kenneth Allison (D Ala.) Nov. 1, 1912- -; House 1951-65.

ROBERTS, Pat (R Kan.) April 20, 1936- -; House 1981- -.

ROBERTS, Robert Whyte (D Miss.) Nov. 28, 1784-Jan. 4, 1865; House 1843-47.

ROBERTS, William Randall (D N.Y.) Feb. 6, 1830-Aug. 9, 1897; House 1871-75.

ROBERTSON, Alice Mary (R Okla.) Jan. 2, 1854-July 1, 1931; House 1921-23.

ROBERTSON, A. Willis (D Va.) May 27, 1887-Nov. 1, 1971; House 1933-Nov. 5, 1946; Senate Nov. 6, 1946-67.

ROBERTSON, Charles Raymond (R N.D.) Sept. 5, 1889-Feb. 18, 1951; House 1941-43, 1945-49.

ROBERTSON, Edward Vivian (R Wyo.) May 27, 1881-April 15, 1963; Senate 1943-49.

ROBERTSON, Edward White (father of Samuel Matthews Robertson) (D La.) June 13, 1823-Aug. 2, 1887; House 1877-83, March 4-Aug. 2, 1887.

ROBERTSON, George (− Ky.) Nov. 18, 1790-May 16, 1874; House 1817-21.

ROBERTSON, John (brother of Thomas Bolling Robertson) (W Va.) April 13, 1787-July 5, 1873; House Dec. 8, 1834-39.

ROBERTSON, Samuel Matthews (son of Edward White Robertson) (D La.) Jan. 1, 1852-Dec. 24, 1911; House Dec. 5, 1887-1907.

ROBERTSON, Thomas Austin (D Ky.) Sept. 9, 1848-July 18, 1892; House 1883-87.

ROBERTSON, Thomas Bolling (brother of John Robertson) (D La.) Feb. 27, 1779-Oct. 5, 1828; House April 30, 1812-April 20, 1818; Gov. 1820-24 (Democratic Republican).

ROBERTSON, Thomas James (R S.C.) Aug. 3, 1823-Oct. 13, 1897; Senate July 15, 1868-77.

ROBERTSON, William Henry (R N.Y.) Oct. 10, 1823-Dec. 7, 1898; House 1867-69.

ROBESON, Edward John Jr. (D Va.) Aug. 9, 1890-March 10, 1966; House May 2, 1950-59.

ROBESON, George Maxwell (nephew of George Clifford Maxwell) (R N.J.) March 16, 1829-Sept. 27, 1897; House 1879-83; Secy. of the Navy 1869-77.

ROBIE, Reuben (D N.Y.) July 15, 1799-Jan. 21, 1872; House 1851-53.

ROBINSON, Arthur Raymond (R Ind.) March 12, 1881-March 17, 1961; Senate Oct. 20, 1925-35.

ROBINSON, Christopher (AP R.I.) May 15, 1806-Oct. 3, 1889; House 1859-61.

ROBINSON, Edward (W Maine) Nov. 25, 1796-Feb. 19, 1857; House April 28, 1838-39.

ROBINSON, George Dexter (R Mass.) Jan. 20, 1834-Feb. 22, 1896; House 1877-Jan. 7, 1884; Gov. 1884-87.

ROBINSON, James Carroll (D Ill.) Aug. 19, 1823-Nov. 3, 1886; House 1859-65, 1871-75.

ROBINSON, James Kenneth (R Va.) May 14, 1916-−; House 1971-85.

ROBINSON, James McClellan (D Ind.) May 31, 1861-Jan. 16, 1942; House 1897-1905.

ROBINSON, James Sidney (R Ohio) Oct. 14, 1827-Ja 14, 1892; House 1881-Jan. 12, 1885.

ROBINSON, James Wallace (R Ohio) Nov. 26, 182 June 28, 1898; House 1873-75.

ROBINSON, James William (D Utah) Jan. 19, 187 Dec. 2, 1964; House 1933-47.

ROBINSON, John Buchanan (R Pa.) May 23, 1846-Ja 28, 1933; House 1891-97.

ROBINSON, John Larne (D Ind.) May 3, 1813-Mar 21, 1860; House 1847-53.

ROBINSON, John McCracken (D Ill.) April 10, 179 April 25, 1843; Senate Dec. 11, 1830-41.

ROBINSON, John Seaton (D Neb.) May 4, 1856-M 25, 1903; House 1899-1903.

ROBINSON, Jonathan (brother of Moses Robinson) (Vt.) Aug. 11, 1756-Nov. 3, 1819; Senate Oct. 1807-15.

ROBINSON, Joseph Taylor (D Ark.) Aug. 26, 1872-J 14, 1937; House 1903-Jan. 14, 1913; Senate 1913-J 14, 1937; Senate majority leader 1933-37; Gov. J 16-March 8, 1913.

ROBINSON, Leonidas Dunlap (D N.C.) April 22, 18 Nov. 7, 1941; House 1917-21.

ROBINSON, Milton Stapp (R Ind.) April 20, 1832-J 28, 1892; House 1875-79.

ROBINSON, Moses (brother of Jonathan Robinson) Vt.) March 20, 1741-May 26, 1813; Senate Oct. 1791-Oct. 15, 1796; Gov. 1789-90.

ROBINSON, Orville (D N.Y.) Oct. 28, 1801-Dec. 1882; House 1843-45.

ROBINSON, Thomas John Bright (R Iowa) Aug. 1868-Jan. 27, 1958; House 1923-33.

ROBINSON, Thomas Jr. (D Del.) 1800-Oct. 28, 18 House 1839-41.

ROBINSON, Tommy (D Ark.) March 7, 1942-−; Ho 1985-−.

ROBINSON, William Erigena (D N.Y.) May 6, 18 Jan. 23, 1892; House 1867-69, 1881-85.

ROBISON, David Fullerton (nephew of David Full ton) (W Pa.) May 28, 1816-June 24, 1859; Hou 1855-57.

ROBISON, Howard Winfield (R N.Y.) Oct. 30, 1915-House Jan. 14, 1958-75.

ROBSION, John Marshall (father of John Marshall Robsion Jr.) (R Ky.) Jan. 2, 1873-Feb. 17, 1948; House 1919-Jan. 10, 1930, 1935-Feb. 17, 1948; Senate Jan. 11-Nov. 30, 1930.

ROBSION, John Marshall Jr. (son of John Marshall Robsion) (R Ky.) Aug. 28, 1904- —; House 1953-59.

ROCHESTER, William Beatty (D N.Y.) Jan. 29, 1789-June 14, 1838; House 1821-April 1823.

ROCKEFELLER, John Davison "Jay" IV (great-grandson of Nelson Wilmarth Aldrich, grandnephew of Richard Steere Aldrich, nephew of Vice Pres. Nelson Aldrich Rockefeller and Gov. Winthrop Rockefeller of Ark., son-in-law of Charles Harting Percy) (D W.Va.) June 18, 1937- —; Senate Jan. 15, 1985- —; Gov. 1977-85.

ROCKEFELLER, Lewis Kirby (R N.Y.) Nov. 25, 1875-Sept. 18, 1948; House Nov. 2, 1937-43.

ROCKHILL, William (D Ind.) Feb. 10, 1793-Jan. 15, 1865; House 1847-49.

ROCKWELL, Francis Williams (son of Julius Rockwell) (R Mass.) May 26, 1844-June 26, 1929; House Jan. 17, 1884-91.

ROCKWELL, Hosea Hunt (D N.Y.) May 31, 1840-Dec. 18, 1918; House 1891-93.

ROCKWELL, John Arnold (W Conn.) Aug. 27, 1803-Feb. 10, 1861; House 1845-49.

ROCKWELL, Julius (father of Francis Williams Rockwell) (W Mass.) April 26, 1805-May 19, 1888; House 1843-51; Senate June 3, 1854-Jan. 31, 1855.

ROCKWELL, Robert Fay (R Colo.) Feb. 11, 1886-Sept. 29, 1950; House Dec. 9, 1941-49.

RODDENBERY, Seaborn Anderson (D Ga.) Jan. 12, 1870-Sept. 25, 1913; House Feb. 16, 1910-Sept. 25, 1913.

RODENBERG, William August (R Ill.) Oct. 30, 1865-Sept. 10, 1937; House 1899-1901, 1903-13, 1915-23.

RODEY, Bernard Shandon (R N.M.) March 1, 1856-March 10, 1927; House (Terr. Del.) 1901-05.

RODGERS, Robert Lewis (R Pa.) June 2, 1875-May 9, 1960; House 1939-47.

RODINO, Peter Wallace Jr. (D N.J.) June 7, 1909- —; House 1949- —.

RODMAN, William (D Pa.) Oct. 7, 1757-July 27, 1824; House 1811-13.

RODNEY, Caesar Augustus (cousin of George Brydges Rodney) (D Del.) Jan. 4, 1772-June 10, 1824; House 1803-05, 1821-Jan. 24, 1822; Senate Jan. 24, 1822-Jan. 29, 1823; Atty. Gen. 1807-11.

RODNEY, Daniel (F Del.) Sept. 10, 1764-Sept. 2, 1846; House Oct. 1, 1822-23; Senate Nov. 8, 1826-Jan. 12, 1827; Gov. 1814-17.

RODNEY, George Brydges (cousin of Caesar Augustus Rodney) (W Del.) April 2, 1803-June 18, 1883; House 1841-45.

ROE, Dudley George (D Md.) March 23, 1881-Jan. 4, 1970; House 1945-47.

ROE, James A. (D N.Y.) July 9, 1896-April 22, 1967; House 1945-47.

ROE, Robert A. (D N.J.) Feb. 28, 1924- —; House Nov. 4, 1969- —.

ROEMER, Buddy (D La.) Oct. 4, 1943- —; House 1981- —.

ROGERS, Andrew Jackson (D N.J.) July 1, 1828-May 22, 1900; House 1863-67.

ROGERS, Anthony Astley Cooper (D Ark.) Feb. 14, 1821-July 27, 1899; House 1869-71.

ROGERS, Byron Giles (D Colo.) Aug. 1, 1900-Dec. 31, 1983; House 1951-71.

ROGERS, Charles (W N.Y.) April 30, 1800-Jan. 13, 1874; House 1843-45.

ROGERS, Dwight Laing (father of Paul Grant Rogers) (D Fla.) Aug. 17, 1886-Dec. 1, 1954; House 1945-Dec. 1, 1954.

ROGERS, Edith Nourse (widow of John Jacob Rogers) (R Mass.) 1881-Sept. 10, 1960; House June 30, 1925-Sept. 10, 1960.

ROGERS, Edward (D N.Y.) May 30, 1787-May 29, 1857; House 1839-41.

ROGERS, George Frederick (D N.Y.) March 19, 1887-Nov. 20, 1948; House 1945-47.

ROGERS, Harold (R Ky.) Dec. 31, 1937- —; House 1981- —.

ROGERS, James (D S.C.) Oct. 24, 1795-Dec. 21, 1873; House 1835-37, 1839-43.

ROGERS, John (D N.Y.) May 9, 1813-May 11, 1879; House 1871-73.

ROGERS, John Henry (D Ark.) Oct. 9, 1845-April 16, 1911; House 1883-91.

ROGERS, John Jacob (husband of Edith Nourse Rogers) (R Mass.) Aug. 18, 1881-March 28, 1925; House 1913-March 28, 1925.

ROGERS, Paul Grant (son of Dwight Laing Rogers) (D Fla.) June 4, 1921- —; House Jan. 11, 1955-79.

ROGERS, Sion Hart (D N.C.) Sept. 30, 1825-Aug. 14, 1874; House 1853-55 (Whig), 1871-73.

ROGERS, Thomas Jones (father of William Findlay Rogers) (D Pa.) 1781-Dec. 7, 1832; House March 3, 1818-April 20, 1824.

ROGERS, Walter Edward (D Texas) July 19, 1908- —; House 1951-67.

ROGERS, Will (D Okla.) Dec. 12, 1898-Aug. 3, 1983; House 1933-43.

ROGERS, Will Jr. (D Calif.) Oct. 20, 1911- —; House 1943-May 23, 1944.

ROGERS, William Findlay (son of Thomas Jones Rogers) (D N.Y.) March 1, 1820-Dec. 16, 1899; House 1883-85.

ROGERS, William Nathaniel (D N.H.) Jan. 10, 1892-Sept. 25, 1945; House 1923-25, Jan. 5, 1932-37.

ROHRBOUGH, Edward Gay (R W.Va.) 1874-Dec. 12, 1956; House 1943-45, 1947-49.

ROLLINS, Edward Henry (R N.H.) Oct. 3, 1824-July 31, 1889; House 1861-67; Senate 1877-83.

ROLLINS, James Sidney (C Mo.) April 19, 1812-Jan. 9, 1888; House 1861-65.

ROLPH, Thomas (R Calif.) Jan. 17, 1885-May 10, 1956; House 1941-45.

ROMAN, James Dixon (W Md.) Aug. 11, 1809-Jan. 19, 1867; House 1847-49.

ROMEIS, Jacob (R Ohio) Dec. 1, 1835-March 8, 1904; House 1885-89.

ROMERO, Trinidad (R N.M.) June 15, 1835-Aug. 28, 1918; House (Terr. Del.) 1877-79.

ROMJUE, Milton Andrew (D Mo.) Dec. 5, 1874-Jan. 23, 1968; House 1917-21, 1923-43.

ROMULO, Carlos Pena (— P.I.) Jan. 14, 1901- —; House (Res. Comm.) Aug. 10, 1944-July 4, 1946.

RONAN, Daniel J. (D Ill.) July 13, 1914-Aug. 13, 1969; House 1965-Aug. 13, 1969.

RONCALIO, Teno (D Wyo.) March 23, 1916- —; House 1965-67, 1971-Dec. 30, 1978.

RONCALLO, Angelo Dominick (R N.Y.) May 28, 1927- —; House 1973-75.

ROONEY, Fred B. (D Pa.) Nov. 6, 1925- —; House Jul 30, 1963-79.

ROONEY, John James (D N.Y.) Nov. 29, 1903-Oct. 2ϵ 1975; House June 6, 1944-Dec. 31, 1974.

ROOSEVELT, Franklin Delano Jr. (son of Pres. Frank lin Delano Roosevelt, brother of James Roosevel (D N.Y.) Aug. 17, 1914- —; House May 17, 1949-5 (1949-51 Liberal/Four Freedoms).

ROOSEVELT, James (son of Pres. Franklin Delan Roosevelt, brother of Franklin Delano Roosevelt Jr (D Calif.) Dec. 23, 1907- —; House 1955-Sept. 3ϵ 1965.

ROOSEVELT, James I. (uncle of Robert Barnwell Ro sevelt) (D N.Y.) Dec. 14, 1795-April 5, 1875; Hous 1841-43.

ROOSEVELT, Robert Barnwell (nephew of James Roosevelt, uncle of Theodore Roosevelt) (D N.Y Aug. 7, 1829-June 14, 1906; House 1871-73.

ROOT, Elihu (R N.Y.) Feb. 15, 1845-Feb. 7, 1937; Sena 1909-15; Secy. of War 1899-1904; Secy. of Sta 1905-09.

ROOT, Erastus (D N.Y.) March 16, 1773-Dec. 24, 184 House 1803-05, 1809-11, Dec. 26, 1815-17, 1831-3ϵ

ROOT, Joseph Mosley (W Ohio) Oct. 7, 1807-April 1879; House 1845-51.

ROOTS, Logan Holt (R Ark.) March 26, 1841-May ϵ 1893; House June 22, 1868-71.

ROSE, Charles Gradison III (D N.C.) Aug. 10, 1939- House 1973- —.

ROSE, John Marshall (R Pa.) May 18, 1856-April ϵ 1923; House 1917-23.

ROSE, Robert Lawson (son of Robert Selden Rose, sc in-law of Nathaniel Allen) (W N.Y.) Oct. 12, 18C March 14, 1877; House 1847-51.

ROSE, Robert Selden (father of Robert Lawson Ro (— N.Y.) Feb. 24, 1774-Nov. 24, 1835; House 18 27, 1829-31.

ROSECRANS, William Starke (D Calif.) Sept. 6, 18ϵ March 11, 1898; House 1881-85.

ROSENBLOOM, Benjamin Louis (R W.Va.) June 1880-March 22, 1965; House 1921-25.

ROSENTHAL, Benjamin S. (D/L N.Y.) June 8, 19ϵ Jan. 4, 1983; House Feb. 20, 1962-Jan. 4, 1983.

ROSIER, Joseph (D W.Va.) Jan. 24, 1870-Oct. 7, 19 Senate Jan. 13, 1941-Nov. 17, 1942.

ROSS, Edmund Gibson (R Kan.) Dec. 7, 1826-May 8, 1907; Senate July 19, 1866-71; Gov. (N.M. Terr.) 1885-89 (Democrat).

ROSS, Henry Howard (W N.Y.) May 9, 1790-Sept. 14, 1862; House 1825-27.

ROSS, James (F Pa.) July 12, 1762-Nov. 27, 1847; Senate April 24, 1794-1803; Pres. pro tempore 1798-99.

ROSS, John (father of Thomas Ross) (— Pa.) Feb. 24, 1770-Jan. 31, 1834; House 1809-11, 1815-Feb. 24, 1818.

ROSS, Jonathan (R Vt.) April 30, 1826-Feb. 23, 1905; Senate Jan. 11, 1899-Oct. 18, 1900.

ROSS, Lewis Winans (D Ill.) Dec. 8, 1812-Oct. 20, 1895; House 1863-69.

ROSS, Miles (D N.J.) April 30, 1827-Feb. 22, 1903; House 1875-83.

ROSS, Robert Tripp (R N.Y.) June 4, 1903-October 1, 1981; House 1947-49, Feb. 19, 1952-53.

ROSS, Sobieski (R Pa.) May 16, 1828-Oct. 24, 1877; House 1873-77.

ROSS, Thomas (son of John Ross) (D Pa.) Dec. 1, 1806-July 7, 1865; House 1849-53.

ROSS, Thomas Randolph (D Ohio) Oct. 26, 1788-June 28, 1869; House 1819-25.

ROSSDALE, Albert Berger (R N.Y.) Oct. 23, 1878-April 17, 1968; House 1921-23.

ROSTENKOWSKI, Daniel David "Dan" (D Ill.) Jan. 2, 1928- —; House 1959- —.

ROTH, Tobias A. (R Wis.) Oct. 10, 1938- —; House 1979- —.

ROTH, William V. Jr. (R Del.) July 22, 1921- —; House 1967-Dec. 31, 1970; Senate Jan. 1, 1971- —.

ROTHERMEL, John Hoover (D Pa.) March 7, 1856-Aug. 1922; House 1907-15.

ROTHWELL, Gideon Frank (D Mo.) April 24, 1836-Jan. 18, 1894; House 1879-81.

ROUDEBUSH, Richard Lowell (R Ind.) Jan. 18, 1918- —; House 1961-71.

ROUKEMA, Marge (R N.J.) Sept. 19, 1929- —; House 1981- —.

ROUSE, Arthur Blythe (D Ky.) June 20, 1874-Jan. 25, 1956; House 1911-27.

ROUSH, John Edward (D Ind.) Sept. 12, 1920- —; House 1959-69, 1971-77.

ROUSSEAU, Lovell Harrison (R Ky.) Aug. 4, 1818-Jan. 7, 1869; House 1865-July 21, 1866, Dec. 3, 1866-67.

ROUSSELOT, John Harbin (R Calif.) Nov. 1, 1927- —; House 1961-63, June 30, 1970-83.

ROUTZOHN, Harry Nelson (R Ohio) Nov. 4, 1881-April 14, 1953; House 1939-41.

ROWAN, John (uncle of Robert Todd Lytle) (D Ky.) July 12, 1773-July 13, 1843; House 1807-09; Senate 1825-31.

ROWAN, Joseph (D N.Y.) Sept. 8, 1870-Aug. 3, 1930; House 1919-21.

ROWAN, William A. (D Ill.) Nov. 24, 1882-May 31, 1961; House 1943-47.

ROWBOTTOM, Harry Emerson (R Ind.) Nov. 3, 1884-March 22, 1934; House 1925-31.

ROWE, Edmund (R Ohio) Dec. 21, 1892- —; House 1943-45.

ROWE, Frederick William (R N.Y.) March 19, 1863-June 20, 1946; House 1915-21.

ROWE, Peter (D N.Y.) March 10, 1807-April 17, 1876; House 1853-55.

ROWELL, Jonathan Harvey (R Ill.) Feb. 10, 1833-May 15, 1908; House 1883-91.

ROWLAND, Alfred (D N.C.) Feb. 9, 1844-Aug. 2, 1898; House 1887-91.

ROWLAND, Charles Hedding (R Pa.) Dec. 20, 1860-Nov. 24, 1921; House 1915-19.

ROWLAND, James Roy Jr. (D Ga.) Feb. 3, 1926- —; House 1983- —.

ROWLAND, John G. (R Conn.) May 24, 1957- —; House 1985- —.

ROY, Alphonse (D N.H.) Oct. 26, 1897-Oct. 5, 1967; House June 9, 1938-39.

ROY, William Robert (D Kan.) Feb. 23, 1926- —; House 1971-75.

ROYBAL, Edward R. (D Calif.) Feb. 10, 1916- —; House 1963- —.

ROYCE, Homer Elihu (R Vt.) June 14, 1819-April 24, 1891; House 1857-61.

ROYER, William H. (R Calif.) April 11, 1920- —; House April 9, 1979-81.

ROYSE, Lemuel Willard (R Ind.) Jan. 19, 1847-Dec. 18, 1946; House 1895-99.

RUBEY, Thomas Lewis (D Mo.) Sept. 27, 1862-Nov. 2, 1928; House 1911-21, 1923-Nov. 2, 1928.

RUCKER, Atterson Walden (D Colo.) April 3, 1847-July 19, 1924; House 1909-13.

RUCKER, Tinsley White (D Ga.) March 24, 1848-Nov. 18, 1926; House Jan. 11-March 3, 1917.

RUCKER, William Waller (D Mo.) Feb. 1, 1855-May 30, 1936; House 1899-1923.

RUDD, Eldon Dean (R Ariz.) July 15, 1920- —; House 1977-87.

RUDD, Stephen Andrew (D N.Y.) Dec. 11, 1874-March 31, 1936; House 1931-March 31, 1936.

RUDMAN, Warren (R N.H.) May 13, 1930- —; Senate Dec. 29, 1980- —.

RUFFIN, James Edward (D Mo.) July 24, 1893-April 9, 1977; House 1933-35.

RUFFIN, Thomas (D N.C.) Sept. 9, 1820-Oct. 13, 1863; House 1853-61.

RUGGLES, Benjamin (D Ohio) Feb. 21, 1783-Sept. 2, 1857; Senate 1815-33.

RUGGLES, Charles Herman (— N.Y.) Feb. 10, 1789-June 16, 1865; House 1821-23.

RUGGLES, John (D Maine) Oct. 8, 1789-June 20, 1874; Senate Jan. 20, 1835-41.

RUGGLES, Nathaniel (F Mass.) Nov. 11, 1761-Dec. 19, 1819; House 1813-19.

RUMPLE, John Nicholas William (R Iowa) March 4, 1841-Jan. 31, 1903; House 1901-Jan. 31, 1903.

RUMSEY, David (W N.Y.) Dec. 25, 1810-March 12, 1883; House 1847-51.

RUMSEY, Edward (W Ky.) Nov. 5, 1796-April 6, 1868; House 1837-39.

RUMSFELD, Donald (R Ill.) July 9, 1932- —; House 1963-May 25, 1969; Secy. of Defense 1975-77.

RUNK, John (W N.J.) July 3, 1791-Sept. 22, 1872; House 1845-47.

RUNNELS, Harold Lowell (D N.M.) March 17, 1924-Aug. 5, 1980; House 1971-Aug. 5, 1980.

RUPLEY, Arthur Ringwalt (PR Pa.) Nov. 13, 1868-Nov. 11, 1920; House 1913-15.

RUPPE, Philip E. (R Mich.) Sept. 29, 1926- —; House 1967-79.

RUPPERT, Jacob Jr. (D N.Y.) Aug. 5, 1867-Jan. 13, 1939; House 1899-1907.

RUSK, Harry Welles (D Md.) Oct. 17, 1852-Jan. 2? 1926; House Nov. 2, 1886-97.

RUSK, Jeremiah McLain (R Wis.) June 17, 1830-No' 21, 1893; House 1871-77; Gov. 1882-89; Secy. of Agr¹ culture 1889-93.

RUSK, Thomas Jefferson (D Texas) Dec. 5, 1803-Ju¹ 29, 1857; Senate Feb. 21, 1846-July 29, 1857; Pre' pro tempore 1857.

RUSS, John (D Conn.) Oct. 29, 1767-June 22, 183' House 1819-23.

RUSSELL, Benjamin Edward (cousin of Rienzi Melvi¹ Johnston) (D Ga.) Oct. 5, 1845-Dec. 4, 1909; Hou' 1893-97.

RUSSELL, Charles Addison (R Conn.) March 2, 185' Oct. 23, 1902; House 1887-Oct. 23, 1902.

RUSSELL, Charles Hinton (R Nev.) Dec. 27, 1903-- House 1947-49; Gov. 1951-59.

RUSSELL, Daniel Lindsay (R N.C.) Aug. 7, 1845-M' 14, 1908; House 1879-81; Gov. 1897-1901.

RUSSELL, David Abel (W N.Y.) 1780-Nov. 24, 186' House 1835-41.

RUSSELL, Donald Stuart (D S.C.) Feb. 22, 1906- Senate April 22, 1965-67; Gov. 1963-65.

RUSSELL, Gordon James (D Texas) Dec. 22, 185' Sept. 14, 1919; House Nov. 4, 1902-June 14, 191'

RUSSELL, James McPherson (father of Samuel Ly' Russell) (W Pa.) Nov. 10, 1786-Nov. 14, 1870; Hou' Dec. 21, 1841-43.

RUSSELL, Jeremiah (D N.Y.) Jan. 26, 1786-Sept. ¹ 1867; House 1843-45.

RUSSELL, John (— N.Y.) Sept. 7, 1772-Aug. 2, 18' House 1805-09.

RUSSELL, John Edwards (D Mass.) Jan. 20, 1834-C 28, 1903; House 1887-89.

RUSSELL, Jonathan (D Mass.) Feb. 27, 1771-Feb. 1832; House 1821-23.

RUSSELL, Joseph (D N.Y.) ?-?; House 1845-47, 18' 53.

RUSSELL, Joseph James (D Mo.) Aug. 23, 1854-C 22, 1922; House 1907-09, 1911-19.

RUSSELL, Joshua Edward (R Ohio) Aug. 9, 1867-J' 21, 1953; House 1915-17.

RUSSELL, Leslie W. (— N.Y.) April 15, 1840-Feb 1903; House March 4-Sept. 11, 1891.

RUSSELL, Richard Brevard (D Ga.) Nov. 2, 1897-Jan. 21, 1971; Senate Jan. 12, 1933-Jan. 21, 1971; Pres. pro tempore 1969-71; Gov. 1931-33.

RUSSELL, Richard Manning (D Mass.) March 3, 1891-Feb. 27, 1977; House 1935-37.

RUSSELL, Sam Morris (D Texas) Aug. 9, 1889-Oct. 19, 1971; House 1941-47.

RUSSELL, Samuel Lyon (son of James McPherson Russell) (W Pa.) July 30, 1816-Sept. 27, 1891; House 1853-55.

RUSSELL, William (W Ohio) 1782-Sept. 28, 1845; House 1827-33 (Jackson Democrat), 1841-43.

RUSSELL, William Augustus (R Mass.) April 22, 1831-Jan. 10, 1899; House 1879-85.

RUSSELL, William Fiero (D N.Y.) Jan. 14, 1812-April 29, 1896; House 1857-59.

RUSSO, Martin Anthony (D Ill.) Jan. 23, 1944- —; House 1975- —.

RUST, Albert (D Ark.) ?-April 3, 1870; House 1855-57, 1859-61.

RUTH, Earl B. (R N.C.) Feb. 7, 1916- —; House 1969-75.

RUTHERFORD, Albert Greig (R Pa.) Jan. 3, 1879-Aug. 10, 1941; House 1937-Aug. 10, 1941.

RUTHERFORD, J. T. (D Texas) May 30, 1921- —; House 1955-63.

RUTHERFORD, Robert (— Va.) Oct. 20, 1728-Oct. 1803; House 1793-97.

RUTHERFORD, Samuel (D Ga.) March 15, 1870-Feb. 4, 1932; House 1925-Feb. 4, 1932.

RUTHERFURD, John (F N.J.) Sept. 20, 1760-Feb. 23, 1840; Senate 1791-Dec. 5, 1799.

RUTLEDGE, John Jr. (F S.C.) 1766-Sept. 1, 1819; House 1797-1803.

RYALL, Daniel Bailey (D N.J.) Jan. 30, 1798-Dec. 17, 1864; House 1839-41.

RYAN, Elmer James (D Minn.) May 26, 1907-Feb. 1, 1958; House 1935-41.

RYAN, Harold M. (D Mich.) Feb. 6, 1911- —; House Feb. 13, 1962-65.

RYAN, James Wilfrid (D Pa.) Oct. 16, 1858-Feb. 26, 1907; House 1899-1901.

RYAN, Leo Joseph (D Calif.) May 5, 1925-Nov. 18, 1978; House 1973-Nov. 18, 1978.

RYAN, Thomas (R Kan.) Nov. 25, 1837-April 5, 1914; House 1877-April 4, 1889.

RYAN, Thomas Jefferson (R N.Y.) June 17, 1890-Nov. 10, 1968; House 1921-23.

RYAN, William (D N.Y.) March 8, 1840-Feb. 18, 1925; House 1893-95.

RYAN, William Fitts (D/L N.Y.) June 28, 1922-Sept. 17, 1972; House 1961-Sept. 17, 1972.

RYAN, William Henry (D N.Y.) May 10, 1860-Nov. 18, 1939; House 1899-1909.

RYON, John Walker (D Pa.) March 4, 1825-March 12, 1901; House 1879-81.

RYTER, John Francis (D Conn.) Feb. 4, 1914-Feb. 5, 1978; House 1945-47.

SABATH, Adolph Joachim (D Ill.) April 4, 1866-Nov. 6, 1952; House 1907-Nov. 6, 1952.

SABIN, Alvah (W Vt.) Oct. 23, 1793-Jan. 22, 1885; House 1853-57.

SABIN, Dwight May (R Minn.) April 25, 1843-Dec. 22, 1902; Senate 1883-89; Chrmn. Rep. Nat. Comm. 1883-84.

SABINE, Lorenzo (W Mass.) Feb. 28, 1803-April 14, 1877; House Dec. 13, 1852-53.

SABO, Martin Olav (D Minn.) Feb. 28, 1938- —; House 1979- —.

SACKETT, Frederick Mosley (R Ky.) Dec. 17, 1868-May 18, 1941; Senate 1925-Jan. 9, 1930.

SACKETT, William Augustus (W N.Y.) Nov. 18, 1811-Sept. 6, 1895; House 1849-53.

SACKS, Leon (D Pa.) Oct. 7, 1902-March 11, 1972; House 1937-43.

SADLAK, Antoni Nicholas (R Conn.) June 13, 1908-Oct. 18, 1969; House 1947-59.

SADLER, Thomas William (D Ala.) April 17, 1831-Oct. 29, 1896; House 1885-87.

SADOWSKI, George Gregory (D Mich.) March 12, 1903-Oct. 9, 1961; House 1933-39, 1943-51.

SAGE, Ebenezer (D N.Y.) Aug. 16, 1755-Jan. 20, 1834; House 1809-15.

SAGE, Russell (W N.Y.) Aug. 4, 1816-July 22, 1906; House 1853-57.

SAIKI, Patricia (R Hawaii) May 28, 1930- —; House 1987- —.

SAILLY, Peter (D N.Y.) April 20, 1754-March 16, 1826; House 1805-07.

ST. GEORGE, Katharine Price Collier (R N.Y.) July 12, 1896-May 2, 1983; House 1947-65.

ST GERMAIN, Fernand Joseph (D R.I.) Jan. 9, 1928--; House 1961--.

ST. JOHN, Charles (R N.Y.) Oct. 8, 1818-July 6, 1891; House 1871-75.

ST. JOHN, Daniel Bennett (W N.Y.) Oct. 8, 1808-Feb. 18, 1890; House 1847-49.

ST. JOHN, Henry (D Ohio) July 16, 1783-May 1869; House 1843-47.

ST. MARTIN, Louis (D La.) May 17, 1820-Feb. 9, 1893; House 1851-53, 1885-87.

ST. ONGE, William Leon (D Conn.) Oct. 9, 1914-May 1, 1970; House 1963-May 1, 1970.

SALINGER, Pierre Emil George (D Calif.) June 14, 1925--; Senate Aug. 4-Dec. 31, 1964.

SALMON, Joshua S. (D N.J.) Feb. 2, 1846-May 6, 1902; House 1899-May 6, 1902.

SALMON, William Charles (D Tenn.) April 3, 1868-May 13, 1925; House 1923-25.

SALTONSTALL, Leverett (great-grandfather of Leverett Saltonstall, below) (W Mass.) June 13, 1783-May 8, 1845; House Dec. 5, 1838-43.

SALTONSTALL, Leverett (great-grandson of Leverett Saltonstall, above) (R Mass.) Sept. 1, 1892-June 17, 1979; Senate Jan. 4, 1945-67; Gov. 1939-45.

SAMFORD, William James (D Ala.) Sept. 16, 1844-June 11, 1901; House 1879-81; Gov. 1900-01.

SAMMONS, Thomas (grandfather of John Henry Starin) (D N.Y.) Oct. 1, 1762-Nov. 20, 1838; House 1803-07, 1809-13.

SAMPLE, Samuel Caldwell (D Ind.) Aug. 15, 1796-Dec. 2, 1855; House 1843-45.

SAMPSON, Ezekiel Silas (R Iowa) Dec. 6, 1831-Oct. 7, 1892; House 1875-79.

SAMPSON, Zabdiel (D Mass.) Aug. 22, 1781-July 19, 1828; House 1817-July 26, 1820.

SAMUEL, Edmund William (R Pa.) Nov. 27, 1857-March 7, 1930; House 1905-07.

SAMUELS, Green Berry (cousin of Isaac Samuels Pennybacker) (D Va.) Feb. 1, 1806-Jan. 5, 1859; House 1839-41.

SANBORN, John Carfield (R Idaho) Sept. 28, 188? May 16, 1968; House 1947-51.

SANDAGER, Harry (R R.I.) April 12, 1887-Dec. 2 1955; House 1939-41.

SANDERS, Archie Dovell (R N.Y.) June 17, 1857-Ju? 15, 1941; House 1917-33.

SANDERS, Everett (R Ind.) March 8, 1882-May 1 1950; House 1917-25; Chrmn. Rep. Nat. Comr 1932-34.

SANDERS, Jared Young (father of Jared Young San? ers Jr., cousin of Murphy James Foster) (D La.) Ja? 29, 1867-March 23, 1944; House 1917-21; Gov. 190? 12.

SANDERS, Jared Young Jr. (son of Jared Young San? ers) (D La.) April 20, 1892-Nov. 29, 1960; House M? 1, 1934-37, 1941-43.

SANDERS, Morgan Gurley (D Texas) July 14, 187? Jan. 7, 1956; House 1921-39.

SANDERS, Newell (R Tenn.) July 12, 1850-Jan. 2? 1939; Senate April 11, 1912-Jan. 24, 1913.

SANDERS, Wilbur Fiske (R Mont.) May 2, 1834-July 1905; Senate Jan. 1, 1890-93.

SANDFORD, James T. (-- Tenn.) ?-?; House 1823-2?

SANDFORD, Thomas (D Ky.) 1762-Dec. 10, 18?? House 1803-07.

SANDIDGE, John Milton (D La.) Jan. 7, 1817-Mar? 30, 1890; House 1855-59.

SANDLIN, John Nicholas (D La.) Feb. 24, 1872-D? 25, 1957; House 1921-37.

SANDMAN, Charles William Jr. (R N.J.) Oct. 23, 192? Aug. 26, 1985; House 1967-75.

SANDS, Joshua (-- N.Y.) Oct. 12, 1757-Sept. 13, 18?? House 1803-05, 1825-27.

SANFORD, John (father of Stephen Sanford, grand? ther of John Sanford, below) (D N.Y.) June 3, 180? Oct. 4, 1857; House 1841-43.

SANFORD, John (son of Stephen Sanford, grandson John Sanford, above) (R N.Y.) Jan. 18, 1851-Se? 26, 1939; House 1889-93.

SANFORD, John W. A. (UD Ga.) Aug. 28, 1798-Se? 12, 1870; House March 4-July 25, 1835.

SANFORD, Jonah (great-grandfather of Rollin Bre? ster Sanford) (JD N.Y.) Nov. 30, 1790-Dec. 25, 18?? House Nov. 3, 1830-31.

SANFORD, Nathan (D N.Y.) Nov. 4, 1777-Oct. ? 1838; Senate 1815-21, Jan. 14, 1826-31.

SANFORD, Rollin Brewster (great-grandson of Jonah Sanford) (R N.Y.) May 18, 1874-May 16, 1957; House 1915-21.

SANFORD, Stephen (son of John Sanford born in 1803, father of John Sanford born in 1851) (R N.Y.) May 26, 1826-Feb. 13, 1913; House 1869-71.

SANFORD, Terry (D N.C.) Aug. 20, 1917- —; Senate Dec. 10, 1986- —; Gov. 1961-65.

SANTANGELO, Alfred Edward (D N.Y.) June 4, 1912-March 30, 1978; House 1957-63.

SANTINI, James David (D Nev.) Aug. 13, 1937- —; House 1975-83.

SAPP, William Fletcher (nephew of William Robinson Sapp) (R Iowa) Nov. 20, 1824-Nov. 22, 1890; House 1877-81.

SAPP, William Robinson (uncle of William Fletcher Sapp) (W Ohio) March 4, 1804-Jan. 3, 1875; House 1853-57.

SARASIN, Ronald Arthur (R Conn.) Dec. 31, 1934- —; House 1973-79.

SARBACHER, George William Jr. (R Pa.) Sept. 30, 1919-March 4, 1973; House 1947-49.

SARBANES, Paul Spyros (D Md.) Feb. 3, 1933- —; House 1971-77; Senate 1977- —.

SARGENT, Aaron Augustus (R Calif.) Sept. 28, 1827-Aug. 14, 1887; House 1861-63, 1869-73; Senate 1873-79.

SASSCER, Lansdale Ghiselin (D Md.) Sept. 30, 1893-Nov. 5, 1964; House Feb. 3, 1939-53.

SASSER, James Ralph (D Tenn.) Sept. 30, 1931- —; Senate 1977- —.

SATTERFIELD, Dave Edward Jr. (father of David Edward Satterfield III) (D Va.) Sept. 11, 1894-Dec. 27, 1946; House Nov. 2, 1937-Feb. 15, 1945.

SATTERFIELD, Dave Edward III (son of Dave Edward Satterfield Jr.) (D Va.) Dec. 2, 1920- —; House 1965-81.

SAUERHERING, Edward (R Wis.) June 24, 1864-March 1, 1924; House 1895-99.

SAULSBURY, Eli (brother of Willard Saulsbury born in 1820, uncle of Willard Saulsbury born in 1861) (D Del.) Dec. 29, 1817-March 22, 1893; Senate 1871-89.

SAULSBURY, Willard (brother of Eli Saulsbury, father of Willard Saulsbury, below) (D Del.) June 2, 1820-April 6, 1892; Senate 1859-71.

SAULSBURY, Willard (son of Willard Saulsbury, above, nephew of Eli Saulsbury) (D Del.) April 17, 1861-Feb. 20, 1927; Senate 1913-19; Pres. pro tempore 1916-19.

SAUND, Daliph Singh (D Calif.) Sept. 20, 1899-April 22, 1973; House 1957-63.

SAUNDERS, Alvin (grandfather of William Henry Harrison of Wyoming) (R Neb.) July 12, 1817-Nov. 1, 1899; Senate March 5, 1877-83; Gov. (Neb. Terr.) 1861-67.

SAUNDERS, Edward Watts (D Va.) Oct. 20, 1860-Dec. 16, 1921; House Nov. 6, 1906-Feb. 29, 1920.

SAUNDERS, Romulus Mitchell (D N.C.) March 3, 1791-April 21, 1867; House 1821-27, 1841-45.

SAUTHOFF, Harry (Prog. Wis.) June 3, 1879-June 16, 1966; House 1935-39, 1941-45.

SAVAGE, Charles Raymon (D Wash.) April 12, 1906-Jan. 14, 1976; House 1945-47.

SAVAGE, Gus (D Ill.) Oct. 30, 1925- —; House 1981- —.

SAVAGE, John (D N.Y.) Feb. 22, 1779-Oct. 19, 1863; House 1815-19.

SAVAGE, John Houston (— Tenn.) Oct. 9, 1815-April 5, 1904; House 1849-53, 1855-59.

SAVAGE, John Simpson (D Ohio) Oct. 30, 1841-Nov. 24, 1884; House 1875-77.

SAWTELLE, Cullen (D Maine) Sept. 25, 1805-Nov. 10, 1887; House 1845-47, 1849-51.

SAWYER, Frederick Adolphus (R S.C.) Dec. 12, 1822-July 31, 1891; Senate July 16, 1868-73.

SAWYER, Harold S. (R Mich.) March 21, 1920- —; House 1977-85.

SAWYER, John Gilbert (R N.Y.) June 5, 1825-Sept. 5, 1898; House 1885-91.

SAWYER, Lemuel (D N.C.) 1777-Jan. 9, 1852; House 1807-13, 1817-23, 1825-29.

SAWYER, Lewis Ernest (D Ark.) June 24, 1867-May 5, 1923; House March 4-May 5, 1923.

SAWYER, Philetus (R Wis.) Sept. 22, 1816-March 29, 1900; House 1865-75; Senate 1881-93.

SAWYER, Samuel Locke (D Mo.) Nov. 27, 1813-March 29, 1890; House 1879-81.

SAWYER, Samuel Tredwell (D N.C.) 1800-Nov. 29, 1865; House 1837-39.

SAWYER, Tom (D Ohio) Aug. 15, 1945- —; House 1987- —.

SAWYER, William (D Ohio) Aug. 5, 1803-Sept. 18, 1877; House 1845-49.

SAXBE, William B. (R Ohio) June 24, 1916- —; Senate 1969-Jan. 3, 1974; Atty. Gen. 1974-75.

SAXTON, H. James (R N.J.) Jan. 22, 1943- —; House 1985- —.

SAY, Benjamin (— Pa.) 1756-April 23, 1813; House Nov. 16, 1808-June 1809.

SAYERS, Joseph Draper (D Texas) Sept. 23, 1841-May 15, 1929; House 1885-Jan. 16, 1899; Gov. 1899-1903.

SAYLER, Henry Benton (cousin of Milton Sayler) (R Ind.) March 31, 1836-June 18, 1900; House 1873-75.

SAYLER, Milton (cousin of Henry Benton Sayler) (D Ohio) Nov. 4, 1831-Nov. 17, 1892; House 1873-79; Speaker pro tempore 1876.

SAYLOR, John Phillips (R Pa.) July 23, 1908-Oct. 28, 1973; House Sept. 13, 1949-Oct. 28, 1973.

SCALES, Alfred Moore (D N.C.) Nov. 26, 1827-Feb. 9, 1892; House 1857-59, 1875-Dec. 30, 1884; Gov. 1885-89.

SCAMMAN, John Fairfield (D Maine) Oct. 24, 1786-May 22, 1858; House 1845-47.

SCANLON, Thomas Edward (D Pa.) Sept. 18, 1896-Aug. 9, 1955; House 1941-45.

SCARBOROUGH, Robert Bethea (D S.C.) Oct. 29, 1861-Nov. 23, 1927; House 1901-05.

SCHADEBERG, Henry Carl (R Wis.) Oct. 12, 1913-Dec. 11, 1985; House 1961-65, 1967-71.

SCHAEFER, Daniel L. (R Colo.) Jan. 25, 1936- —; House April 7, 1983- —.

SCHAEFER, Edwin Martin (D Ill.) May 14, 1887-Nov. 8, 1950; House 1933-43.

SCHAFER, John Charles (R Wis.) May 7, 1893-June 9, 1962; House 1923-33, 1939-41.

SCHALL, Thomas David (R Minn.) June 4, 1878-Dec. 22, 1935; House 1915-25; Senate 1925-Dec. 22, 1935.

SCHELL, Richard (D N.Y.) May 15, 1810-Nov. 10, 1879; House Dec. 7, 1874-75.

SCHENCK, Abraham Henry (uncle of Isaac Teller) (D N.Y.) Jan. 22, 1775-June 1, 1831; House 1815-17.

SCHENCK, Ferdinand Schureman (JD N.J.) Feb. 11, 1790-May 16, 1860; House 1833-37.

SCHENCK, Paul Fornshell (R Ohio) April 19, 1899-Nov. 30, 1968; House Nov. 6, 1951-65.

SCHENCK, Robert Cumming (R Ohio) Oct. 4, 1809 March 23, 1890; House 1843-51 (Whig), 1863-Jan. 5 1871.

SCHERER, Gordon Harry (R Ohio) Dec. 26, 1906- — House 1953-63.

SCHERLE, William Joseph (R Iowa) March 14, 1923- — House 1967-75.

SCHERMERHORN, Abraham Maus (W N.Y.) Dec. 1 1791-Aug. 22, 1855; House 1849-53.

SCHERMERHORN, Simon Jacob (D N.Y.) Sept. 25 1827-July 21, 1901; House 1893-95.

SCHEUER, James Haas (D N.Y.) Feb. 6, 1920- — House 1965-73, 1975- —.

SCHIFFLER, Andrew Charles (R W.Va.) Aug. 10, 1889 March 27, 1970; House 1939-41, 1943-45.

SCHIRM, Charles Reginald (R Md.) Aug. 12, 1864-Nov 2, 1918; House 1901-03.

SCHISLER, Darwin Gale (D Ill.) March 2, 1933- — House 1965-67.

SCHLEICHER, Gustave (D Texas) Nov. 19, 1823-Jar 10, 1879; House 1875-Jan. 10, 1879.

SCHLEY, William (D Ga.) Dec. 10, 1786-Nov. 20, 1858 House 1833-July 1, 1835; Gov. 1835-37 (Union Democrat).

SCHMIDHAUSER, John Richard (D Iowa) Jan. 1922- —; House 1965-67.

SCHMITT, Harrison Hagan (R N.M.) July 3, 1935- — Senate 1977-83.

SCHMITZ, John George (R Calif.) Aug. 12, 1930- — House June 30, 1970-73.

SCHNEEBELI, Gustav Adolphus (R Pa.) May 23, 185? Feb. 6, 1923; House 1905-07.

SCHNEEBELI, Herman T. (R Pa.) July 7, 1907-May 1982; House April 26, 1960-77.

SCHNEIDER, Claudine (R R.I.) March 25, 1947- — House 1981- —.

SCHNEIDER, George John (Prog. Wis.) Oct. 30, 187? March 12, 1939; House 1923-33 (Republican), 193? 39.

SCHOEPPEL, Andrew Frank (R Kan.) Nov. 23, 189? Jan. 21, 1962; Senate 1949-Jan. 21, 1962; Gov. 194? 47.

SCHOOLCRAFT, John Lawrence (W N.Y.) 1804-Ju 7, 1860; House 1849-53.

SCHOONMAKER, Cornelius Corneliusen (grandfather of Marius Schoonmaker) (− N.Y.) June 1745-96; House 1791-93.

SCHOONMAKER, Marius (grandson of Cornelius Corneliusen Schoonmaker) (W N.Y.) April 24, 1811-Jan. 5, 1894; House 1851-53.

SCHROEDER, Patricia Scott (D Colo.) July 30, 1940-−; House 1973-−.

SCHUETTE, William Duncan (R Mich.) Oct. 13, 1953-−; House 1985-−.

SCHUETZ, Leonard William (D Ill.) Nov. 16, 1887-Feb. 13, 1944; House 1931-Feb. 13, 1944.

SCHULTE, William Theodore (D Ind.) Aug. 19, 1890-Dec. 7, 1966; House 1933-43.

SCHULZE, Richard Taylor (R Pa.) Aug. 7, 1929-−; House 1975-−.

SCHUMAKER, John Godfrey (D N.Y.) June 27, 1826-Nov. 23, 1905; House 1869-71, 1873-77.

SCHUMER, Charles E. (D N.Y.) Nov. 23, 1951-−; House 1981-−.

SCHUNEMAN, Martin Gerretsen (D N.Y.) Feb. 10, 1764-Feb. 21, 1827; House 1805-07.

SCHUREMAN, James (F N.J.) Feb. 12, 1756-Jan. 22, 1824; House 1789-91, 1797-99, 1813-15; Senate 1799-Feb. 16, 1801; Cont. Cong. 1786-87.

SCHURZ, Carl (R Mo.) March 2, 1829-May 14, 1906; Senate 1869-75; Secy. of the Interior 1877-81.

SCHUYLER, Karl Cortlandt (R Colo.) April 3, 1877-July 31, 1933; Senate Dec. 7, 1932-33.

SCHUYLER, Philip Jeremiah (son of Philip John Schuyler) (− N.Y.) Jan. 21, 1768-Feb. 21, 1835; House 1817-19.

SCHUYLER, Philip John (father of Philip Jeremiah Schuyler) (F N.Y.) Nov. 20, 1733-Nov. 18, 1804; Senate 1789-91, 1797-Jan. 3, 1798; Cont. Cong. 1775-81.

SCHWABE, George Blaine (brother of Max Schwabe) (R Okla.) July 26, 1886-April 2, 1952; House 1945-49, 1951-April 2, 1952.

SCHWABE, Max (brother of George Blaine Schwabe) (R Mo.) Dec. 6, 1905-−; House 1943-49.

SCHWARTZ, Henry Herman "Harry" (D Wyo.) May 18, 1869-April 24, 1955; Senate 1937-43.

SCHWARTZ, John (D Pa.) Oct. 27, 1793-June 20, 1860; House 1859-June 20, 1860.

SCHWEIKER, Richard Schultz (R Pa.) June 1, 1926-−; House 1961-69; Senate 1969-81. Secy. of Health and Human Services 1981-83.

SCHWELLENBACH, Lewis Baxter (D Wash.) Sept. 20, 1894-June 10, 1948; Senate 1935-Dec. 16, 1940; Secy. of Labor 1945-48.

SCHWENGEL, Frederick Delbert (R Iowa) May 28, 1907-−; House 1955-65, 1967-73.

SCHWERT, Pius Louis (D N.Y.) Nov. 22, 1892-March 11, 1941; House 1939-March 11, 1941.

SCOBLICK, James Paul (R Pa.) May 10, 1909-−; House Nov. 5, 1946-49.

SCOFIELD, Glenni William (R Pa.) March 11, 1817-Aug. 30, 1891; House 1863-75.

SCOTT, Byron Nicholson (D Calif.) March 21, 1903-−; House 1935-39.

SCOTT, Charles Frederick (R Kan.) Sept. 7, 1860-Sept. 18, 1938; House 1901-11.

SCOTT, Charles Lewis (D Calif.) Jan. 23, 1827-April 30, 1899; House 1857-61.

SCOTT, David (− Pa.) ?-?; House 1817 (elected 1816 but resigned before Congress assembled).

SCOTT, Frank Douglas (R Mich.) Aug. 25, 1878-Feb. 12, 1951; House 1915-27.

SCOTT, George Cromwell (R Iowa) Aug. 8, 1864-Oct. 6, 1948; House Nov. 5, 1912-15, 1917-19.

SCOTT, Hardie (son of John Roger Kirkpatrick Scott) (R Pa.) June 7, 1907-−; House 1947-53.

SCOTT, Harvey David (R Ind.) Oct. 18, 1818-July 11, 1891; House 1855-57.

SCOTT, Hugh Doggett Jr. (R Pa.) Nov. 11, 1900-−; House 1941-45, 1947-59; Senate 1959-77; Chrmn. Rep. Nat. Comm'. 1948-49.

SCOTT, John (− Mo.) May 18, 1785-Oct. 1, 1861; House (Terr. Del.) Aug. 6, 1816-Jan. 13, 1817, Aug. 5, 1817-March 3, 1821, (Rep.) Aug. 10, 1821-27.

SCOTT, John (father of John Scott, below) (− Pa.) Dec. 25, 1784-Sept. 22, 1850; House 1829-31.

SCOTT, John (son of John Scott, above) (R Pa.) July 24, 1824-Nov. 29, 1896; Senate 1869-75.

SCOTT, John Guier (D Mo.) Dec. 26, 1819-May 16, 1892; House Dec. 7, 1863-65.

SCOTT, John Roger Kirkpatrick (father of Hardie Scott) (R Pa.) July 6, 1873-Dec. 9, 1945; House 1915-Jan. 5, 1919.

SCOTT, Lon Allen (R Tenn.) Sept. 25, 1888-Feb. 11, 1931; House 1921-23.

SCOTT, Nathan Bay (R W.Va.) Dec. 18, 1842-Jan. 2, 1924; Senate 1899-1911.

SCOTT, Owen (D Ill.) July 6, 1848-Dec. 21, 1928; House 1891-93.

SCOTT, Ralph James (D N.C.) Oct. 15, 1905-Aug. 5, 1983; House 1957-67.

SCOTT, Thomas (— Pa.) 1739-March 2, 1796; House 1789-91, 1793-95.

SCOTT, William Kerr (D N.C.) April 17, 1896-April 16, 1958; Senate Nov. 29, 1954-April 16, 1958; Gov. 1949-53.

SCOTT, William Lawrence (D Pa.) July 2, 1828-Sept. 19, 1891; House 1885-89.

SCOTT, William Lloyd (R Va.) July 1, 1915-—; House 1967-73; Senate 1973-Jan. 1, 1979.

SCOVILLE, Jonathan (D N.Y.) July 14, 1830-March 4, 1891; House Nov. 12, 1880-83.

SCRANTON, George Whitfield (second cousin of Joseph Augustine Scranton) (R Pa.) May 11, 1811-March 24, 1861; House 1859-March 24, 1861.

SCRANTON, Joseph Augustine (great-grandfather of William Warren Scranton, second cousin of George Whitfield Scranton) (R Pa.) July 26, 1838-Oct. 12, 1908; House 1881-83, 1885-87, 1889-91, 1893-97.

SCRANTON, William Warren (great-grandson of Joseph Augustine Scranton) (R Pa.) July 19, 1917-—; House 1961-63; Gov. 1963-67.

SCRIVNER, Errett Power (R Kan.) March 20, 1898-May 5, 1978; House Sept. 14, 1943-59.

SCROGGY, Thomas Edmund (R Ohio) March 18, 1843-March 6, 1915; House 1905-07.

SCRUGHAM, James Graves (D Nev.) Jan. 19, 1880-June 2, 1945; House 1933-Dec. 7, 1942; Senate Dec. 7, 1942-June 23, 1945; Gov. 1923-27.

SCUDDER, Henry Joel (uncle of Townsend Scudder) (R N.Y.) Sept. 18, 1825-Feb. 10, 1886; House 1873-75.

SCUDDER, Hubert Baxter (R Calif.) Nov. 5, 1888-July 4, 1968; House 1949-59.

SCUDDER, Isaac Williamson (R N.J.) 1816-Sept. 10, 1881; House 1873-75.

SCUDDER, John Anderson (D N.J.) March 22, 1759-Nov. 6, 1836; House Oct. 31, 1810-11.

SCUDDER, Townsend (nephew of Henry Joel Scudder (D N.Y.) July 26, 1865-Feb. 22, 1960; House 1899-1901, 1903-05.

SCUDDER, Tredwell (— N.Y.) Jan. 1, 1778-Oct. 31, 1834; House 1817-19.

SCUDDER, Zeno (W Mass.) Aug. 18, 1807-June 26, 1857; House 1851-March 4, 1854.

SCULL, Edward (R Pa.) Feb. 5, 1818-July 10, 1900, House 1887-93.

SCULLY, Thomas Joseph (D N.J.) Sept. 19, 1868-Dec. 14, 1921; House 1911-21.

SCURRY, Richardson (D Texas) Nov. 11, 1811-April 9, 1862; House 1851-53.

SEAMAN, Henry John (AP N.Y.) April 16, 1805-May 3, 1861; House 1845-47.

SEARING, John Alexander (D N.Y.) May 14, 1805-May 6, 1876; House 1857-59.

SEARS, William Joseph (D Fla.) Dec. 4, 1874-March 30, 1944; House 1915-29, 1933-37.

SEARS, Willis Gratz (R Neb.) Aug. 16, 1860-June 1, 1949; House 1923-31.

SEATON, Frederick Andrew (R Neb.) Dec. 11, 1909-Jan. 16, 1974; Senate Dec. 10, 1951-Nov. 4, 1952; Secy. of the Interior 1956-61.

SEAVER, Ebenezer (D Mass.) July 5, 1763-March 1, 1844; House 1803-13.

SEBASTIAN, William King (D Ark.) 1812-May 20, 1865; Senate May 12, 1848-July 11, 1861.

SEBELIUS, Keith George (R Kan.) Sept. 10, 1916-Aug. 5, 1982; House 1969-81.

SECCOMBE, James (R Ohio) Feb. 12, 1893-Aug. 23, 1970; House 1939-41.

SECREST, Robert Thompson (D Ohio) Jan. 22, 1904-—; House 1933-Aug. 3, 1942, 1949-Sept. 26, 1954, 1963-67.

SEDDON, James Alexander (D Va.) July 13, 1815-Aug. 19, 1880; House 1845-47, 1849-51.

SEDGWICK, Charles Baldwin (R N.Y.) March 15, 1815-Feb. 3, 1883; House 1859-63.

SEDGWICK, Theodore (F Mass.) May 9, 1746-Jan. 24, 1813; House 1789-June 1796, 1799-1801; Speaker 1799-1801; Senate June 11, 1796-99; Pres. pro tempore 1798; Cont. Cong. 1785-88.

SEELEY, John Edward (R N.Y.) Aug. 1, 1810-March 30, 1875; House 1871-73.

EELY-BROWN, Horace Jr. (R Conn.) May 12, 1908-April 9, 1982; House 1947-49, 1951-59, 1961-63.

EELYE, Julius Hawley (I Mass.) Sept. 14, 1824-May 12, 1895; House 1875-77.

EERLEY, John Joseph (D Iowa) March 13, 1852-Feb. 23, 1931; House 1891-93.

EGAR, Joseph Eggleston (U Va.) June 1, 1804-April 30, 1880; House March 15, 1862-63.

EGER, George Nicholas (R N.J.) Jan. 4, 1866-Aug. 26, 1940; House 1923-Aug. 26, 1940.

EIBERLING, Francis (R Ohio) Sept. 20, 1870-Feb. 1, 1945; House 1929-33.

EIBERLING, John Frederick (D Ohio) Sept. 8, 1918--; House 1971-87.

ELBY, Thomas Jefferson (D Ill.) Dec. 4, 1840-March 10, 1917; House 1901-03.

ELDEN, Armistead Inge Jr. (D Ala.) Feb. 20, 1921-Nov. 14, 1985; House 1953-69.

ELDEN, Dudley (D N.Y.) ?-Nov. 7, 1855; House 1833-July 1, 1834.

ELDOMRIDGE, Harry Hunter (D Colo.) Oct. 1, 1864-Nov. 2, 1927; House 1913-15.

ELLS, Sam Riley (R Tenn.) Aug. 2, 1871-Nov. 2, 1935; House 1911-21.

ELVIG, Conrad George (R Minn.) Oct. 11, 1877-Aug. 2, 1953; House 1927-33.

ELYE, Lewis (I N.Y.) July 11, 1803-Jan. 27, 1883; House 1867-69.

EMMES, Benedict Joseph (D Md.)-Nov. 1, 1789-Feb. 10, 1863; House 1829-33.

EMPLE, James (D Ill.) Jan. 5, 1798-Dec. 20, 1866; Senate Dec. 4, 1843-47.

ENER, James Beverley (R Va.) May 18, 1837-Nov. 18, 1903; House 1873-75.

ENEY, George Ebbert (D Ohio) May 29, 1832-June 11, 1905; House 1883-91.

ENEY, Joshua (- Md.) March 4, 1756-Oct. 20, 1798; House 1789-May 1, 1792; Cont. Cong. 1787-88.

ENNER, George Frederick Jr. (D Ariz.) Nov. 24, 1921--; House 1963-67.

ENSENBRENNER, Frank James Jr. (R Wis.) June 14, 1943--; House 1979--.

ENTER, William Tandy (W Tenn.) May 12, 1801-Aug. 28, 1848; House 1843-45.

SERGEANT, John (grandfather of John Sergeant Wise and Richard Alsop Wise, great-grandfather of John Crain Kunkel, father-in-law of Henry Alexander Wise) (F Pa.) Dec. 5, 1779-Nov. 23, 1852; House Oct. 10, 1815-23, 1827-29, 1837-Sept. 15, 1841.

SESSINGHAUS, Gustavus (R Mo.) Nov. 8, 1838-Nov. 16, 1887; House March 2-3, 1883.

SESSIONS, Walter Loomis (R N.Y.) Oct. 4, 1820-May 27, 1896; House 1871-75, 1885-87.

SETTLE, Evan Evans (D Ky.) Dec. 1, 1848-Nov. 16, 1899; House 1897-Nov. 16, 1899.

SETTLE, Thomas (uncle of David Settle Reid, grandfather of Thomas Settle, below) (D N.C.) March 9, 1789-Aug. 5, 1857; House 1817-21.

SETTLE, Thomas (grandson of Thomas Settle, above) (R N.C.) March 10, 1865-Jan. 20, 1919; House 1893-97.

SEVERANCE, Luther (W Maine) Oct. 26, 1797-Jan. 25, 1855; House 1843-47.

SEVIER, Ambrose Hundley (cousin of Henry Wharton Conway) (D Ark.) Nov. 10, 1801-Dec. 31, 1848; House (Terr. Del.) Feb. 13, 1828-June 15, 1836 (Whig); Senate Sept. 18, 1836-March 15, 1848.

SEVIER, John (D Tenn.) Sept. 23, 1745-Sept. 24, 1815; House 1789-91 (N.C.), 1811-Sept. 24, 1815; Gov. 1796-1801 (Democratic Republican), 1803-09 (Democratic Republican).

SEWALL, Charles S. (- Md.) 1779-Nov. 3, 1848; House Oct. 1, 1832-33, Jan. 2-March 3, 1843.

SEWALL, Samuel (- Mass.) Dec. 11, 1757-June 8, 1814; House Dec. 7, 1796-Jan. 10, 1800.

SEWARD, James Lindsay (D Ga.) Oct. 30, 1813-Nov. 21, 1886; House 1853-59.

SEWARD, William Henry (R N.Y.) May 16, 1801-Oct. 10, 1872; Senate 1849-61 (1849-55 Whig); Secy. of State 1861-69; Gov. 1839-43 (Whig).

SEWELL, William Joyce (R N.J.) Dec. 6, 1835-Dec. 27, 1901; Senate 1881-87, 1895-Dec. 27, 1901.

SEXTON, Leonidas (R Ind.) May 19, 1827-July 4, 1880; House 1877-79.

SEYBERT, Adam (D Pa.) May 16, 1773-May 2, 1825; House Oct. 10, 1809-15, 1817-19.

SEYMOUR, David Lowrey (D N.Y.) Dec. 2, 1803-Oct. 11, 1867; House 1843-45, 1851-53.

SEYMOUR, Edward Woodruff (son of Origen Storrs Seymour) (D Conn.) Aug. 30, 1832-Oct. 16, 1892; House 1883-87.

SEYMOUR, Henry William (R Mich.) July 21, 1834-April 7, 1906; House Feb. 14, 1888-89.

SEYMOUR, Horatio (uncle of Origen Storrs Seymour) (CD Vt.) May 31, 1778-Nov. 21, 1857; Senate 1821-33.

SEYMOUR, Origen Storrs (father of Edward Woodruff Seymour, nephew of Horatio Seymour) (D Conn.) Feb. 9, 1804-Aug. 12, 1881; House 1851-55.

SEYMOUR, Thomas Hart (D Conn.) Sept. 29, 1807-Sept. 3, 1868; House 1843-45; Gov. 1850-53.

SEYMOUR, William (D N.Y.) about 1780-Dec. 28, 1848; House 1835-37.

SHACKELFORD, John Williams (D N.C.) Nov. 16, 1844-Jan. 18, 1883; House 1881-Jan. 18, 1883.

SHACKLEFORD, Dorsey William (D Mo.) Aug. 27, 1853-July 15, 1936; House Aug. 29, 1899-1919.

SHAFER, Jacob K. (D Idaho) Dec. 26, 1823-Nov. 22, 1876; House (Terr. Del.) 1869-71.

SHAFER, Paul Werntz (R Mich.) April 27, 1893-Aug. 17, 1954; House 1937-Aug. 17, 1954.

SHAFFER, Joseph Crockett (R Va.) Jan. 19, 1880-Oct. 19, 1958; House 1929-31.

SHAFROTH, John Franklin (D Colo.) June 9, 1854-Feb. 20, 1922; House 1895-Feb. 15, 1904 (1895-97 Republican, 1897-1903 Silver Republican/Democrat); Senate 1913-19; Gov. 1909-13.

SHALLENBERGER, Ashton Cokayne (D Neb.) Dec. 23, 1862-Feb. 22, 1938; House 1901-03, 1915-19, 1923-29, 1931-35; Gov. 1909-11.

SHALLENBERGER, William Shadrack (R Pa.) Nov. 24, 1839-April 15, 1914; House 1877-83.

SHAMANSKY, Robert N. (D Ohio) April 18, 1927- —; House 1981-83.

SHANKLIN, George Sea (D Ky.) Dec. 23, 1807-April 1, 1883; House 1865-67.

SHANKS, John Peter Cleaver (R Ind.) June 17, 1826-Jan. 23, 1901; House 1861-63, 1867-75.

SHANLEY, James Andrew (D Conn.) April 1, 1896-April 5, 1965; House 1935-43.

SHANNON, James Michael (D Mass.) April 4, 1952- —; House 1979-85.

SHANNON, Joseph Bernard (D Mo.) March 17, 1867-March 28, 1943; House 1931-43.

SHANNON, Richard Cutts (R N.Y.) Feb. 12, 1839-Oct. 5, 1920; House 1895-99.

SHANNON, Thomas (brother of Wilson Shannon) Ohio) Nov. 15, 1786-March 16, 1843; House Dec. 1826-27.

SHANNON, Thomas Bowles (R Calif.) Sept. 21, 182 Feb. 21, 1897; House 1863-65.

SHANNON, Wilson (brother of Thomas Shannon) Ohio) Feb. 24, 1802-Aug. 30, 1877; House 1853-! Gov. 1838-40, 1842-44, 1855-56 (Kansas Terr.).

SHARON, William (R Neb.) Jan. 9, 1821-Nov. 13, 18! Senate 1875-81.

SHARP, Edgar Allan (R N.Y.) June 3, 1876-Nov. 1948; House 1945-47.

SHARP, Philip Riley (D Ind.) July 15, 1942- —; Ho 1975- —.

SHARP, Solomon P. (D Ky.) 1780-Nov. 7, 1825; Ho 1813-17.

SHARP, William Graves (D Ohio) March 14, 1859-N 17, 1922; House 1909-July 23, 1914.

SHARPE, Peter (— N.Y.) ?-?; House 1823-25.

SHARTEL, Cassius McLean (R Mo.) April 27, 18! Sept. 27, 1943; House 1905-07.

SHATTUC, William Bunn (R Ohio) June 11, 1841-J 13, 1911; House 1897-1903.

SHAW, Aaron (D Ill.) Dec. 19, 1811-Jan. 7, 1887; Ho 1857-59, 1883-85.

SHAW, Albert Duane (R N.Y.) Dec. 21, 1841-Feb. 1901; House Nov. 6, 1900-Feb. 10, 1901.

SHAW, E. Clay (R Fla.) April 19, 1939- —; House 19! —.

SHAW, Frank Thomas (D Md.) Oct. 7, 1841-Feb. 1923; House 1885-89.

SHAW, George Bullen (R Wis.) March 12, 1854-Aug. 1894; House 1893-Aug. 27, 1894.

SHAW, Guy Loren (R Ill.) May 16, 1881-May 19, 19 House 1921-23.

SHAW, Henry (son of Samuel Shaw) (F Mass.) 17! Oct. 17, 1857; House 1817-21.

SHAW, Henry Marchmore (D N.C.) Nov. 20, 1819-N 1, 1864; House 1853-55, 1857-59.

SHAW, John Gilbert (D N.C.) Jan. 16, 1859-July 1932; House 1895-97.

SHAW, Samuel (father of Henry Shaw) (D Vt.) D 1768-Oct. 23, 1827; House Sept. 6, 1808-13.

HAW, Tristram (− N.H.) May 23, 1786-March 14, 1843; House 1839-43.

HEAFE, James (F N.H.) Nov. 16, 1755-Dec. 5, 1829; House 1799-1801; Senate 1801-June 14, 1802.

HEAKLEY, James (D Pa.) April 24, 1829-Dec. 10, 1917; House 1875-77; Gov. (Alaska Terr.) 1893-97.

HEATS, Charles Christopher (R Ala.) April 10, 1839-May 27, 1904; House 1873-75.

HEEHAN, Timothy Patrick (R Ill.) Feb. 21, 1909- −; House 1951-59.

HEFFER, Daniel (D Pa.) May 24, 1783-Feb. 16, 1880; House 1837-39.

HEFFEY, Daniel (F Va.) 1770-Dec. 3, 1830; House 1809-17.

HEFFIELD, William Paine (father of William Paine Sheffield, below) (R R.I.) Aug. 30, 1820-June 2, 1907; House 1861-63; Senate Nov. 19, 1884-Jan. 20, 1885.

HEFFIELD, William Paine (son of William Paine Sheffield, above) (R R.I.) June 1, 1857-Oct. 19, 1919; House 1909-11.

HELBY, Richard Craig (D Ala.) May 6, 1934- −; House 1979-87; Senate 1987- −.

HELDEN, Carlos Douglas (R Mich.) June 10, 1840-June 24, 1904; House 1897-1903.

HELDON, Lionel Allen (R La.) Aug. 30, 1828-Jan. 17, 1917; House 1869-75; Gov. (N.M. Terr.) 1881-85.

HELDON, Porter (R N.Y.) Sept. 29, 1831-Aug. 15, 1908; House 1869-71.

HELL, George Washington (D S.C.) Nov. 13, 1831-Dec. 15, 1899; House 1891-95.

HELLABARGER, Samuel (R Ohio) Dec. 10, 1817-Aug. 7, 1896; House 1861-63, 1865-69, 1871-73.

HELLEY, Charles Miller (D Ala.) Dec. 28, 1833-Jan. 20, 1907; House 1877-81, Nov. 7, 1882-Jan. 9, 1885.

HELLEY, John Francis (D Calif.) Sept. 3, 1905-Sept. 1, 1974; House Nov. 8, 1949-Jan. 7, 1964.

HELTON, Samuel Azariah (R Mo.) Sept. 3, 1858-Sept. 13, 1948; House 1921-23.

HEPARD, Charles Biddle (D N.C.) Dec. 5, 1807-Oct. 31, 1843; House 1837-41.

HEPARD, William (− Mass.) Dec. 1, 1737-Nov. 16, 1817; House 1797-1803.

HEPARD, William Biddle (NR N.C.) May 14, 1799-June 20, 1852; House 1829-37.

SHEPLER, Matthias (D Ohio) Nov. 11, 1790-April 7, 1863; House 1837-39.

SHEPLEY, Ether (D Maine) Nov. 2, 1789-Jan. 15, 1877; Senate 1833-March 3, 1836.

SHEPPARD, Harry Richard (D Calif.) Jan. 10, 1885-April 28, 1969; House 1937-65.

SHEPPARD, John Levi (father of Morris Sheppard) (D Texas) April 13, 1852-Oct. 11, 1902; House 1899-Oct. 11, 1902.

SHEPPARD, Morris (son of John Levi Sheppard) (D Texas) May 28, 1875-April 9, 1941; House Nov. 15, 1902-Feb. 3, 1913; Senate Feb. 3, 1913-April 9, 1941.

SHEPPERD, Augustine Henry (W N.C.) Feb. 24, 1792-July 11, 1864; House 1827-39, 1841-43, 1847-51.

SHERBURNE, John Samuel (− N.H.) 1757-Aug. 2, 1830; House 1793-97.

SHEREDINE, Upton (D Md.) 1740-Jan. 14, 1800; House 1791-93.

SHERIDAN, George Augustus (L La.) Feb. 22, 1840-Oct. 7, 1896; House 1873-75.

SHERIDAN, John Edward (D Pa.) Sept. 15, 1902- −; House Nov. 7, 1939-47.

SHERLEY, Joseph Swagar (D Ky.) Nov. 28, 1871-Feb. 13, 1941; House 1903-19.

SHERMAN, James Schoolcraft (R N.Y.) Oct. 24, 1855-Oct. 30, 1912; House 1887-91, 1893-1909; Vice President 1909-Oct. 30, 1912.

SHERMAN, John (R Ohio) May 10, 1823-Oct. 22, 1900; House 1855-March 21, 1861; Senate March 21, 1861-March 8, 1877, 1881-March 4, 1897; Pres. pro tempore 1886; Secy. of the Treasury 1877-81; Secy. of State 1897-98.

SHERMAN, Judson W. (R N.Y.) 1808-Nov. 12, 1881; House 1857-59.

SHERMAN, Lawrence Yates (R Ill.) Nov. 8, 1858-Sept. 15, 1939; Senate March 26, 1913-21.

SHERMAN, Roger (grandfather of William Maxwell Evarts) (− Conn.) April 19, 1721-July 23, 1793; House 1789-91; Senate June 13, 1791-July 23, 1793; Cont. Cong. 1774-81, 1783-84.

SHERMAN, Socrates Norton (R N.Y.) July 22, 1801-Feb. 1, 1873; House 1861-63.

SHERRILL, Eliakim (W N.Y.) Feb. 16, 1813-July 4, 1863; House 1847-49.

SHERROD, William Crawford (D Ala.) Aug. 17, 1835-March 24, 1919; House 1869-71.

SHERWIN, John Crocker (R Ill.) Feb. 8, 1838-Jan. 1, 1904; House 1879-83.

SHERWOOD, Henry (D Pa.) Oct. 9, 1813-Nov. 10, 1896; House 1871-73.

SHERWOOD, Isaac R. (D Ohio) Aug. 13, 1835-Oct. 15, 1925; House 1873-75 (Republican), 1907-21, 1923-25.

SHERWOOD, Samuel (F N.Y.) April 24, 1779-Oct. 31, 1862; House 1813-15.

SHERWOOD, Samuel Burr (F Conn.) Nov. 26, 1767-April 27, 1833; House 1817-19.

SHIEL, George Knox (D Ore.) 1825-Dec. 12, 1893; House July 30, 1861-63.

SHIELDS, Benjamin Glover (W Ala.) 1808-?; House 1841-43.

SHIELDS, Ebenezer J. (W Tenn.) Dec. 22, 1778-April 21, 1846; House 1835-39.

SHIELDS, James (uncle of James Shields, below) (JD Ohio) April 13, 1762-Aug. 13, 1831; House 1829-31.

SHIELDS, James (nephew of James Shields, above) (D Mo.) May 10, 1810-June 1, 1879; Senate March 6-15, 1849 (Ill.), Oct. 27, 1849-55 (Ill.), May 11, 1858-59 (Minn.), Jan. 27-March 3, 1879.

SHIELDS, John Knight (D Tenn.) Aug. 15, 1858-Sept. 30, 1934; Senate 1913-25.

SHINN, William Norton (JD N.J.) Oct. 24, 1782-Aug. 18, 1871; House 1833-37.

SHIPHERD, Zebulon Rudd (F N.Y.) Nov. 15, 1768-Nov. 1, 1841; House 1813-15.

SHIPLEY, George Edward (D Ill.) April 21, 1927-–; House 1959-79.

SHIPSTEAD, Henrik (R Minn.) Jan. 8, 1881-June 26, 1960; Senate 1923-47 (1923-41 Farmer Laborite).

SHIRAS, George III (IR Pa.) Jan. 1, 1859-March 24, 1942; House 1903-05.

SHIVELY, Benjamin Franklin (D Ind.) March 20, 1857-March 14, 1916; House Dec. 1, 1884-85 (National Anti Monopolist), 1887-93; Senate 1909-March 14, 1916.

SHOBER, Francis Edwin (father of Francis Emanuel Shober) (D N.C.) March 12, 1831-May 29, 1896; House 1869-73.

SHOBER, Francis Emanuel (son of Francis Edwin Shober) (D N.Y.) Oct. 24, 1860-Oct. 7, 1919; House 1903-05.

SHOEMAKER, Francis Henry (FL Minn.) April 25, 1889-July 24, 1958; House 1933-35.

SHOEMAKER, Lazarus Denison (R Pa.) Nov. 5, 18?? Sept. 9, 1893; House 1871-75.

SHONK, George Washington (R Pa.) April 26, 185? Aug. 14, 1900; House 1891-93.

SHORT, Dewey Jackson (R Mo.) April 7, 1898-Nov. ? 1979; House 1929-31, 1935-57.

SHORT, Don Levingston (R N.D.) June 22, 1903-M? 10, 1982; House 1959-65.

SHORTER, Eli Sims (D Ala.) March 15, 1823-April ? 1879; House 1855-59.

SHORTRIDGE, Samuel Morgan (R Calif.) Aug. 1861-Jan. 15, 1952; Senate 1921-33.

SHOTT, Hugh Ike (R W Va.) Sept. 3, 1866-Oct. 12, 19? House 1929-33; Senate Nov. 18, 1942-43.

SHOUP, George Laird (grandfather of Richard Gar? Shoup) (R Idaho) June 15, 1836-Dec. 21, 1904; S? ate Dec. 18, 1890-1901; Gov. 1889-90 (Idaho Ter? Oct. 1-Dec. 1890.

SHOUP, Richard Garner (grandson of George La? Shoup) (R Mont.) Nov. 29, 1923-–; House 1971-?

SHOUSE, Jouett (D Kan.) Dec. 10, 1879-June 2, 19? House 1915-19.

SHOWALTER, Joseph Baltzell (R Pa.) Feb. 11, 18? Dec. 3, 1932; House April 20, 1897-1903.

SHOWER, Jacob (I Md.) Feb. 22, 1803-May 25, 18? House 1853-55.

SHREVE, Milton William (R Pa.) May 3, 1858-Dec. 1939; House 1913-15, 1919-33.

SHRIVER, Garner E. (R Kan.) July 6, 1912-–; Ho? 1961-77.

SHUFORD, Alonzo Craig (P N.C.) March 1, 1858-F? 8, 1933; House 1895-99.

SHUFORD, George Adams (D N.C.) Sept. 5, 1895-D? 8, 1962; House 1953-59.

SHULL, Joseph Horace (D Pa.) Aug. 17, 1848-Aug? 1944; House 1903-05.

SHULTZ, Emanuel (R Ohio) July 25, 1819-Nov. 5, 19? House 1881-83.

SHUMWAY, Norman David (R Calif.) July 28, 1934-House 1979-–.

SHUSTER, E. G. "Bud" (R Pa.) Jan. 23, 1932-–; Ho? 1973-–.

SIBAL, Abner Woodruff (R Conn.) April 11, 1921-House 1961-65.

SIBLEY, Henry Hastings (son of Solomon Sibley) (− Minn.) Feb. 20, 1811-Feb. 18, 1891; House (Terr. Del.) Oct. 30, 1848-49 (Wis.), July 7, 1849-53; Gov. 1858-60.

SIBLEY, Jonas (D Mass.) March 7, 1762-Feb. 5, 1834; House 1823-25.

SIBLEY, Joseph Crocker (R Pa.) Feb. 18, 1850-May 19, 1926; House 1893-95 (Democrat/People's Party/ Prohibitionist), 1899-1907 (1899-1901 Democrat).

SIBLEY, Mark Hopkins (W N.Y.) 1796-Sept. 8, 1852; House 1837-39.

SIBLEY, Solomon (father of Henry Hastings Sibley) (− Mich.) Oct. 7, 1769-April 4, 1846; House (Terr. Del.) Nov. 20, 1820-23.

SICKLES, Carlton R. (D Md.) June 15, 1921-−; House 1963-67.

SICKLES, Daniel Edgar (D N.Y.) Oct. 10, 1825-May 3, 1914; House 1857-61, 1893-95.

SICKLES, Nicholas (D N.Y.) Sept. 11, 1801-May 13, 1845; House 1835-37.

SIEGEL, Isaac (R N.Y.) April 12, 1880-June 29, 1947; House 1915-23.

SIEMINSKI, Alfred Dennis (D N.J.) Aug. 23, 1911-−; House 1951-59.

SIKES, Robert Louis Fulton (D Fla.) June 3, 1906-−; House 1941-Oct. 19, 1944, 1945-79.

SIKORSKI, Gerry (D Minn.) April 26, 1948-−; House 1983-−.

SILER, Eugene (R Ky.) June 26, 1900-−; House 1955-65.

SILJANDER, Mark Deli (R Mich.) June 11, 1951-−; House April 28, 1981-87.

SILL, Thomas Hale (NR Pa.) Oct. 11, 1783-Feb. 7, 1856; House March 14, 1826-27, 1829-31.

SILSBEE, Nathaniel (D Mass.) Jan. 14, 1773-July 14, 1850; House 1817-21; Senate May 31, 1826-35.

SILVESTER, Peter (grandfather of Peter Henry Silvester) (− N.Y.) 1734-Oct. 15, 1808; House 1789-93.

SILVESTER, Peter Henry (grandson of Peter Silvester) (W N.Y.) Feb. 17, 1807-Nov. 29, 1882; House 1847-51.

SIMKINS, Eldred (D S.C.) Aug. 30, 1779-Nov. 17, 1831; House Jan. 24, 1818-21.

SIMMONS, Furnifold McLendel (D N.C.) Jan. 20, 1854-April 30, 1940; House 1887-89; Senate 1901-31.

SIMMONS, George Abel (R N.Y.) Sept. 8, 1791-Oct. 27, 1857; House 1853-57.

SIMMONS, James Fowler (W R.I.) Sept. 10, 1795-July 10, 1864; Senate 1841-47, 1857-Aug. 15, 1862.

SIMMONS, James Samuel (nephew of Milton George Urner) (R N.Y.) Nov. 25, 1861-Nov. 28, 1935; House 1909-13.

SIMMONS, Robert Glenmore (R Neb.) Dec. 25, 1891-Dec. 27, 1969; House 1923-33.

SIMMS, Albert Gallatin (husband of Ruth Hanna Mc-Cormick) (R N.M.) Oct. 8, 1882-Dec. 29, 1964; House 1929-31.

SIMMS, William Emmett (D Ky.) Jan. 2, 1822-June 25, 1898; House 1859-61.

SIMON, Joseph (R Ore.) Feb. 7, 1851-Feb. 14, 1935; Senate Oct. 8, 1898-1903.

SIMON, Paul Martin (D Ill.) Nov. 29, 1928-−; House 1975-85; Senate 1985-−.

SIMONDS, William Edgar (R Conn.) Nov. 24, 1842-March 14, 1903; House 1889-91.

SIMONS, Samuel (D Conn.) 1792-Jan. 13, 1847; House 1843-45.

SIMONTON, Charles Bryson (D Tenn.) Sept. 8, 1838-June 10, 1911; House 1879-83.

SIMONTON, William (W Pa.) Feb. 12, 1788-May 17, 1846; House 1839-43.

SIMPKINS, John (R Mass.) June 27, 1862-March 27, 1898; House 1895-March 27, 1898.

SIMPSON, Alan Kooi (son of Milward Lee Simpson) (R Wyo.) Sept. 2, 1931-−; Senate Jan. 1, 1979-−.

SIMPSON, Edna Oakes (widow of Sidney Elmer "Sid" Simpson) (R Ill.) Oct. 28, 1891-−; House 1959-61.

SIMPSON, James Jr. (R Ill.) Jan. 7, 1905-Feb. 29, 1960; House 1933-35.

SIMPSON, Jeremiah "Jerry" (P Kan.) March 31, 1842-Oct. 23, 1905; House 1891-95, 1897-99.

SIMPSON, Kenneth Farrand (R N.Y.) May 4, 1895-Jan. 25, 1941; House Jan. 3-Jan. 25, 1941.

SIMPSON, Milward Lee (father of Alan Kooi Simpson) (R Wyo.) Nov. 12, 1897-−; Senate Nov. 7, 1962-67; Gov. 1955-59.

SIMPSON, Richard Franklin (D S.C.) March 24, 1798-Oct. 28, 1882; House 1843-49.

SIMPSON, Richard Murray (R Pa.) Aug. 30, 1900-Jan. 7, 1960; House May 11, 1937-Jan. 7, 1960.

SIMPSON, Sidney Elmer "Sid" (husband of Edna Oakes Simpson) (R Ill.) Sept. 20, 1894-Oct. 26, 1958; House 1943-Oct. 26, 1958.

SIMS, Alexander Dromgoole (nephew of George Coke Dromgoole) (D S.C.) June 12, 1803-Nov. 22, 1848; House 1845-Nov. 22, 1848.

SIMS, Hugo Sheridan Jr. (D S.C.) Oct. 14, 1921- —; House 1949-51.

SIMS, Leonard Henly (D Mo.) Feb. 6, 1807-Feb. 28, 1886; House 1845-47.

SIMS, Thetus Willrette (D Tenn.) April 25, 1852-Dec. 17, 1939; House 1897-1921.

SINCLAIR, James Herbert (R N.D.) Oct. 9, 1871-Sept. 5, 1943; House 1919-35.

SINGISER, Theodore Frelinghuysen (R Idaho) March 15, 1845-Jan. 23, 1907; House (Terr. Del.) 1883-85.

SINGLETON, James Washington (D Ill.) Nov. 23, 1811-April 4, 1892; House 1879-83.

SINGLETON, Otho Robards (D Miss.) Oct. 14, 1814-Jan. 11, 1889; House 1853-55, 1857-Jan. 12, 1861, 1875-87.

SINGLETON, Thomas Day (N S.C.) ?-Nov. 25, 1833; House March 3-Nov. 25, 1833.

SINNICKSON, Clement Hall (grandnephew of Thomas Sinnickson) (R N.J.) Sept. 16, 1834-July 24, 1919; House 1875-79.

SINNICKSON, Thomas (granduncle of Clement Hall Sinnickson, uncle of Thomas Sinnickson, below) (— N.J.) Dec. 21, 1744-May 15, 1817; House 1789-91, 1797-99.

SINNICKSON, Thomas (nephew of Thomas Sinnickson, above) (— N.J.) Dec. 13, 1786-Feb. 17, 1873; House Dec. 1, 1828-29.

SINNOTT, Nicholas John (R Ore.) Dec. 6, 1870-July 20, 1929; House 1913-May 31, 1928.

SIPE, William Allen (D Pa.) July 1, 1844-Sept. 10, 1935; House Dec. 5, 1892-95.

SIROVICH, William Irving (D N.Y.) March 18, 1882-Dec. 17, 1939; House 1927-Dec. 17, 1939.

SISISKY, Norman (D Va.) June 9, 1927- —; House 1983- —.

SISK, Bernice Frederic (D Calif.) Dec. 14, 1910- —; House 1955-79.

SISSON, Frederick James (D N.Y.) March 31, 1879-Oct. 20, 1949; House 1933-37.

SISSON, Thomas Upton (D Miss.) Sept. 22, 1869-Sept. 26, 1923; House 1909-23.

SITES, Frank Crawford (D Pa.) Dec. 24, 1864-May 23 1935; House 1923-25.

SITGREAVES, Charles (D N.J.) April 22, 1803-March 17, 1878; House 1865-69.

SITGREAVES, Samuel (F Pa.) March 16, 1764-April 4 1827; House 1795-98.

SITTLER, Edward Lewis Jr. (R Pa.) April 21, 1908-Dec 26, 1978; House 1951-53.

SKAGGS, David E. (D Colo.) Feb. 22, 1943- —; House 1987- —.

SKEEN, Joseph R. (R N.M.) June 30, 1927- —; House 1981- —.

SKELTON, Charles (D N.J.) April 19, 1806-May 20 1879; House 1851-55.

SKELTON, Ike N. (D Mo.) Dec. 20, 1931- —; House 1977- —.

SKILES, William Woodburn (R Ohio) Dec. 11, 1849 Jan. 9, 1904; House 1901-Jan. 9, 1904.

SKINNER, Charles Rufus (R N.Y.) Aug. 4, 1844-June 30, 1928; House Nov. 8, 1881-85.

SKINNER, Harry (brother of Thomas Gregory Skinner) (P N.C.) May 25, 1855-May 19, 1929; House 1895-99

SKINNER, Richard (D Vt.) May 30, 1778-May 23, 1833 House 1813-15; Gov. 1820-23.

SKINNER, Thomas Gregory (brother of Harry Skinner (D N.C.) Jan. 22, 1842-Dec. 22, 1907; House Nov. 20 1883-87, 1889-91.,

SKINNER, Thomas Joseph (D Mass.) May 24, 1752 Jan. 20, 1809; House Jan. 27, 1797-99, 1803-Aug. 10 1804.

SKUBITZ, Joe (R Kan.) May 6, 1906- —; House 1963 Dec. 31, 1978.

SLACK, John Mark Jr. (D W.Va.) March 18, 1915 March 17, 1980; House 1959-March 17, 1980.

SLADE, Charles (D Ill.) ?-July 26, 1834; House 1833 July 26, 1834.

SLADE, William (W Vt.) May 9, 1786-Jan. 18, 1859 House Nov. 1, 1831-43; Gov. 1844-46.

SLATER, James Harvey (D Ore.) Dec. 28, 1826-Jan. 28 1899; House 1871-73; Senate 1879-85.

SLATTERY, James Charles (D Kan.) Aug. 4, 1948- —; House 1983- —.

SLATTERY, James Michael (D Ill.) July 29, 1878-Aug. 28, 1948; Senate April 14, 1939-Nov. 21, 1940.

SLAUGHTER, Daniel French Jr. (R Va.) May 20, 1925- —; House 1985- —.

SLAUGHTER, Louise M. (D N.Y.) Aug. 14, 1929- —; House 1987- —.

SLAUGHTER, Roger Caldwell (D Mo.) July 17, 1905-June 2, 1974; House 1943-47.

SLAYDEN, James Luther (uncle of Fontaine Maury Maverick) (D Texas) June 1, 1853-Feb. 24, 1924; House 1897-1919.

SLAYMAKER, Amos (— Pa.) March 11, 1755-June 12, 1837; House Oct. 11, 1814-15.

SLEMONS, William Ferguson (D Ark.) March 15, 1830-Dec. 10, 1918; House 1875-81.

SLEMP, Campbell (father of Campbell Bascom Slemp) (R Va.) Dec. 2, 1839-Oct. 13, 1907; House 1903-Oct. 13, 1907.

SLEMP, Campbell Bascom (son of Campbell Slemp) (R Va.) Sept. 4, 1870-Aug. 7, 1943; House Dec. 17, 1907-23.

SLIDELL, John (SRD La.) 1793-July 26, 1871; House 1843-Nov. 10, 1845; Senate Dec. 5, 1853-Feb. 4, 1861.

SLINGERLAND, John I. (R N.Y.) March 1, 1804-Oct. 26, 1861; House 1847-49.

SLOAN, Andrew (R Ga.) June 10, 1845-Sept. 22, 1883; House March 24, 1874-75.

SLOAN, Andrew Scott (brother of Ithamar Conkey Sloan) (R Wis.) June 12, 1820-April 8, 1895; House 1861-63.

SLOAN, Charles Henry (R Neb.) May 2, 1863-June 2, 1946; House 1911-19, 1929-31.

SLOAN, Ithamar Conkey (brother of Andrew Scott Sloan) (R Wis.) May 9, 1822-Dec. 24, 1898; House 1863-67.

SLOAN, James (— N.J.) ?-Nov. 1811; House 1803-09.

SLOANE, John (W Ohio) 1779-May 15, 1856; House 1819-29.

SLOANE, Jonathan (W Ohio) Nov. 1785-April 25, 1854; House 1833-37.

SLOCUM, Henry Warner (D N.Y.) Sept. 24, 1827-April 14, 1894; House 1869-73, 1883-85.

SLOCUMB, Jesse (F N.C.) 1780-Dec. 20, 1820; House 1817-Dec. 20, 1820.

SLOSS, Joseph Humphrey (Con.D Ala.) Oct. 12, 1826-Jan. 27, 1911; House 1871-75.

SMALL, Frank Jr. (R Md.) July 15, 1896-Oct. 24, 1973; House 1953-55.

SMALL, John Humphrey (D N.C.) Aug. 29, 1858-July 13, 1946; House 1899-1921.

SMALL, William Bradbury (R N.H.) May 17, 1817-April 7, 1878; House 1873-75.

SMALLS, Robert (R S.C.) April 5, 1839-Feb. 22, 1915; House 1875-79, July 19, 1882-83, March 18, 1884-87.

SMART, Ephraim Knight (D Maine) Sept. 3, 1813-Sept. 29, 1872; House 1847-49, 1851-53.

SMART, James Stevenson (R N.Y.) June 14, 1842-Sept. 17, 1903; House 1873-75.

SMATHERS, George Armistead (nephew of William Howell Smathers) (D Fla.) Nov. 14, 1913- —; House 1947-51; Senate 1951-69.

SMATHERS, William Howell (uncle of George Armistead Smathers) (D N.J.) Jan. 7, 1891-Sept. 24, 1955; Senate April 15, 1937-43.

SMELT, Dennis (— Ga.) about 1750-?; House Sept. 1, 1806-11.

SMILIE, John (D Pa.) 1741-Dec. 30, 1812; House 1793-95, 1799-Dec. 30, 1812.

SMITH, Abraham Herr (R Pa.) March 7, 1815-Feb. 16, 1894; House 1873-85.

SMITH, Addison Taylor (R Idaho) Sept. 5, 1862-July 5, 1956; House 1913-33.

SMITH, Albert (D Maine) Jan. 3, 1793-May 29, 1867; House 1839-41.

SMITH, Albert (R N.Y.) June 22, 1805-Aug. 27, 1870; House 1843-47.

SMITH, Albert Lee (R Ala.) Aug. 31, 1931- —; House 1981-83.

SMITH, Arthur (— Va.) Nov. 15, 1785-March 30, 1853; House 1821-25.

SMITH, Ballard (— Va.) ?-?; House 1815-21.

SMITH, Benjamin A. II (D Mass.) March 26, 1916- —; Senate Dec. 27, 1960-Nov. 7, 1962.

SMITH, Bernard (— N.Y.) July 5, 1776-July 16, 1835; House 1819-21.

SMITH, Caleb Blood (W Ind.) April 16, 1808-Jan. 7, 1864; House 1843-49; Secy. of the Interior 1861-63.

SMITH, Charles Bennett (D N.Y.) Sept. 14, 1870-May 21, 1939; House 1911-19.

SMITH, Charles Brooks (R W.Va.) Feb. 24, 1844-Dec. 7, 1899; House Feb. 3, 1890-91.

SMITH, Christopher H. (R N.J.) March 4, 1953-—; House 1981-—.

SMITH, Clyde Harold (husband of Margaret Chase Smith) (R Maine) June 9, 1876-April 8, 1940; House 1937-April 8, 1940.

SMITH, Daniel (— Tenn.) Oct. 28, 1748-June 6, 1818; Senate Oct. 6, 1798-99, 1805-March 31, 1809.

SMITH, David Highbaugh (D Ky.) Dec. 19, 1854-Dec. 17, 1928; House 1897-1907.

SMITH, Delazon (D Ore.) Oct. 5, 1816-Nov. 19, 1860; Senate Feb. 14-March 3, 1859.

SMITH, Denny (R Ore.) Jan. 19, 1938-—; House 1981-—.

SMITH, Dietrich Conrad (R Ill.) April 4, 1840-April 18, 1914; House 1881-83.

SMITH, Edward Henry (D N.Y.) May 5, 1809-Aug. 7, 1885; House 1861-63.

SMITH, Ellison DuRant (D S.C.) Aug. 1, 1866-Nov. 17, 1944; Senate 1909-Nov. 17, 1944.

SMITH, Frances Ormand Jonathan (D Maine) Nov. 23, 1806-Oct. 14, 1876; House 1833-39.

SMITH, Francis Raphael (D Pa.) Sept. 25, 1911-—; House 1941-43.

SMITH, Frank Ellis (D Miss.) Feb. 21, 1918-—; House 1951-Nov. 14, 1962.

SMITH, Frank Leslie (R Ill.) Nov. 24, 1867-Aug. 30, 1950; House 1919-21; Senate (elected 1926 but never served).

SMITH, Frank Owens (D Md.) Aug. 27, 1859-Jan. 29, 1924; House 1913-15.

SMITH, Frederick Cleveland (R Ohio) July 29, 1884-July 16, 1956; House 1939-51.

SMITH, George (— Pa.) ?-?; House 1809-13.

SMITH, George Joseph (R N.Y.) Nov. 7, 1859-Dec. 24, 1913; House 1903-05.

SMITH, George Luke (R La.) Dec. 11, 1837-July 9, 1884; House Nov. 24, 1873-75.

SMITH, George Ross (R Minn.) May 28, 1864-Nov. 7, 1952; House 1913-17.

SMITH, George Washington (R Ill.) Aug. 18, 1846-Nov. 30, 1907; House 1889-Nov. 30, 1907.

SMITH, Gerrit (UA N.Y.) March 6, 1797-Dec. 28, 1874; House 1853-Aug. 7, 1854.

SMITH, Gomer Griffith (D Okla.) July 11, 1896-May 26, 1953; House Dec. 10, 1937-39.

SMITH, Green Clay (son of John Speed Smith) (U Ky.) July 4, 1826-June 29, 1895; House 1863-July 13, 1866; Gov. (Mont. Terr.) 1866-69.

SMITH, H. Allen (R Calif.) Oct. 8, 1909-—; House 1957-73.

SMITH, Henry (PP Wis.) July 22, 1838-Sept. 16, 1916; House 1887-89.

SMITH, Henry Cassorte (R Mich.) June 2, 1856-Dec. 7, 1911; House 1899-1903.

SMITH, Henry P. III (R N.Y.) Sept. 29, 1911-—; House 1965-75.

SMITH, Hezekiah Bradley (D/G N.J.) July 24, 1816-Nov. 3, 1887; House 1879-81.

SMITH, Hiram Ypsilanti (R Iowa) March 22, 1843-Nov. 4, 1894; House Dec. 2, 1884-85.

SMITH, Hoke (D Ga.) Sept. 2, 1855-Nov. 27, 1931; Senate Nov. 16, 1911-21; Secy. of the Interior 1893-96; Gov. 1907-09, 1911.

SMITH, Horace Boardman (R N.Y.) Aug. 18, 1826-Dec. 26, 1888; House 1871-75.

SMITH, Howard Alexander (uncle of Peter H. Dominick) (R N.J.) Jan. 30, 1880-Oct. 27, 1966; Senate Dec. 7, 1944-59.

SMITH, Howard Worth (D Va.) Feb. 2, 1883-Oct. 3, 1976; House 1931-67.

SMITH, Isaac (F N.J.) 1740-Aug. 29, 1807; House 1795-97.

SMITH, Isaac (D Pa.) Jan. 4, 1761-April 4, 1834; House 1813-15.

SMITH, Israel (D Vt.) April 4, 1759-Dec. 2, 1810; House Oct. 17, 1791-97, 1801-03; Senate 1803-Oct. 1, 1807; Gov. 1807-08.

SMITH, James Jr. (D N.J.) June 12, 1851-April 1, 1927; Senate 1893-99.

SMITH, James Strudwick (D N.C.) Oct. 15, 1790-Aug. 1859; House 1817-21.

SMITH, James Vernon (R Okla.) July 23, 1926-June 23, 1973; House 1967-69.

SMITH, Jedediah Kilburn (− N.H.) Nov. 7, 1770-Dec. 17, 1828; House 1807-09.

SMITH, Jeremiah (brother of Samuel Smith of N.H., uncle of Robert Smith) (F N.H.) Nov. 29, 1759-Sept. 21, 1842; House 1791-July 26, 1797; Gov. 1809-10.

SMITH, John (D Ohio) 1735-June 10, 1816; Senate April 1, 1803-April 25, 1808.

SMITH, John (D Va.) May 7, 1750-March 5, 1836; House 1801-15.

SMITH, John (D N.Y.) Feb. 12, 1752-Aug. 12, 1816; House Feb. 6, 1800-Feb. 23, 1804; Senate Feb. 23, 1804-13.

SMITH, John (father of Worthington Curtis Smith) (D Vt.) Aug. 12, 1789-Nov. 26, 1858; House 1839-41.

SMITH, John Ambler (R Va.) Sept. 23, 1847-Jan. 6, 1892; House 1873-75.

SMITH, John Armstrong (R Ohio) Sept. 23, 1814-March 7, 1892; House 1869-73.

SMITH, John Cotton (F Conn.) Feb. 12, 1765-Dec. 7, 1845; House Nov. 17, 1800-Aug. 1806; Gov. 1812-17.

SMITH, John Hyatt (IR/D N.Y.) April 10, 1824-Dec. 7, 1886; House 1881-83.

SMITH, John Joseph (D Conn.) Jan. 25, 1904-Feb. 16, 1980; House 1935-Nov. 4, 1941.

SMITH, John M. C. (R Mich.) Feb. 6, 1853-March 30, 1923; House 1911-21, June 28, 1921-March 30, 1923.

SMITH, John Quincy (R Ohio) Nov. 5, 1824-Dec. 30, 1901; House 1873-75.

SMITH, John Speed (father of Green Clay Smith) (D Ky.) July 1, 1792-June 6, 1854; House Aug. 6, 1821-23.

SMITH, John T. (D Pa.) ?-?; House 1843-45.

SMITH, John Walter (D Md.) Feb. 5, 1845-April 19, 1925; House 1899-Jan. 12, 1900; Senate March 25, 1908-21; Gov. 1900-04.

SMITH, Joseph F. (D Pa.) Jan. 24, 1920-−; House July 28, 1981-83.

SMITH, Joseph Luther (D W.Va.) May 22, 1880-Aug. 23, 1962; House 1929-45.

SMITH, Joseph Showalter (D Ore.) June 20, 1824-July 13, 1884; House 1869-71.

SMITH, Josiah (− Mass.) Feb. 26, 1738-April 4, 1803; House 1801-03.

SMITH, Lamar Seeligson (R Texas) Nov. 19, 1947-−; House 1987-−.

SMITH, Lawrence Henry (R Wis.) Sept. 15, 1892-Jan. 22, 1958; House Aug. 29, 1941-Jan. 22, 1958.

SMITH, Lawrence Jack "Larry" (D Fla.) April 25, 1941-−; House 1983-−.

SMITH, Madison Roswell (D Mo.) July 9, 1850-June 18, 1919; House 1907-09.

SMITH, Marcus Aurelius (D Ariz.) Jan. 24, 1851-April 7, 1924; House (Terr. Del.) 1887-95, 1897-99, 1901-03, 1905-09; Senate March 27, 1912-21.

SMITH, Margaret Chase (widow of Clyde Harold Smith) (R Maine) Dec. 14, 1897-−; House June 3, 1940-49; Senate 1949-73.

SMITH, Martin Fernand (D Wash.) May 28, 1891-Oct. 25, 1954; House 1933-43.

SMITH, Nathan (brother of Nathaniel Smith, uncle of Truman Smith) (W Conn.) Jan. 8, 1770-Dec. 6, 1835; Senate 1833-Dec. 6, 1835.

SMITH, Nathaniel (brother of Nathan Smith, uncle of Truman Smith) (F Conn.) Jan. 6, 1762-March 9, 1822; House 1795-99.

SMITH, Neal Edward (D Iowa) March 23, 1920-−; House 1959-−.

SMITH, O'Brien (− S.C.) about 1756-April 27, 1811; House 1805-07.

SMITH, Oliver Hampton (W Ind.) Oct. 23, 1794-March 19, 1859; House 1827-29 (Jackson Democrat); Senate 1837-43.

SMITH, Perry (D Conn.) May 12, 1783-June 8, 1852; Senate 1837-43.

SMITH, Ralph Tyler (R Ill.) Oct. 6, 1915-Aug. 13, 1972; Senate Sept. 17, 1969-Nov. 3, 1970.

SMITH, Robert (nephew of Jeremiah Smith and Samuel Smith of N.H.) (D Ill.) June 12, 1802-Dec. 21, 1867; House 1843-49, 1857-59.

SMITH, Robert Barnwell (*See* RHETT, Robert Barnwell).

SMITH, Robert Clinton (R N.H.) March 30, 1941-−; House 1985-−.

SMITH, Robert Freeman (R Ore.) June 16, 1931-−; House 1983-−.

SMITH, Samuel (D Md.) July 27, 1752-April 22, 1839; House 1793-1803, Jan. 31, 1816-Dec. 17, 1822; Senate 1803-15, Dec. 17, 1822-23; Pres. pro tempore 1805-08.

SMITH, Samuel (− Pa.) ?-?; House Nov. 7, 1805-11.

SMITH, Samuel (brother of Jeremiah Smith, uncle of Robert Smith) (F N.H.) Nov. 11, 1765-April 25, 1842; House 1813-15.

SMITH, Samuel A. (ID Pa.) 1795-May 15, 1861; House Oct. 13, 1829-33.

SMITH, Samuel Axley (D Tenn.) June 26, 1822-Nov. 25, 1863; House 1853-59.

SMITH, Samuel William (R Mich.) Aug. 23, 1852-June 19, 1931; House 1897-1915.

SMITH, Sylvester Clark (R Calif.) Aug. 26, 1858-Jan. 26, 1913; House 1905-Jan. 26, 1913.

SMITH, Thomas (F Pa.) ?-Jan. 29, 1846; House 1815-17.

SMITH, Thomas (D Ind.) May 1, 1799-April 12, 1876; House 1839-41, 1843-47.

SMITH, Thomas Alexander (D Md.) Sept. 3, 1850-May 1, 1932; House 1905-07.

SMITH, Thomas Francis (D N.Y.) July 24, 1865-April 11, 1923; House April 12, 1917-21.

SMITH, Thomas Vernor (D Ill.) April 26, 1890-May 24, 1964; House 1939-41.

SMITH, Truman (nephew of Nathan Smith and Nathaniel Smith) (W Conn.) Nov. 27, 1791-May 3, 1884; House 1839-43, 1845-49; Senate 1849-May 24, 1854.

SMITH, Virginia Dodd (R Neb.) June 30, 1911-−; House 1975-−.

SMITH, Walter Inglewood (R Iowa) July 10, 1862-Jan. 27, 1922; House Dec. 3, 1900-March 15, 1911.

SMITH, William (F Md.) April 12, 1728-March 27, 1814; House 1789-91; Cont. Cong. 1777-78.

SMITH, William (D S.C.) 1762-June 26, 1840; Senate Dec. 4, 1816-23, Nov. 29, 1826-31.

SMITH, William (− S.C.) Sept. 20, 1751-June 22, 1837; House 1797-99.

SMITH, William (− Va.) ?-?; House 1821-27.

SMITH, William (D Va.) Sept. 6, 1797-May 18, 1887; House 1841-43, 1853-61; Gov. 1846-49, 1864-65 (Confederate Democrat).

SMITH, William Alden (R Mich.) May 12, 1859-Oct. 11, 1932; House 1895-Feb. 9, 1907; Senate Feb. 9, 1907-19.

SMITH, William Alexander (R N.C.) Jan. 9, 1828-May 16, 1888; House 1873-75.

SMITH, William Ephraim (D Ga.) March 14, 1829-March 11, 1890; House 1875-81.

SMITH, William Jay (R Tenn.) Sept. 24, 1823-Nov. 29, 1913; House 1869-71.

SMITH, William Loughton (F S.C.) 1758-Dec. 19, 1812; House 1789-July 10, 1797.

SMITH, William Nathan Harrell (D N.C.) Sept. 24, 1812-Nov. 14, 1889; House 1859-61.

SMITH, William Orlando (R Pa.) June 13, 1859-May 12, 1932; House 1903-07.

SMITH, William Robert (D Texas) Aug. 18, 1863-Aug. 16, 1924; House 1903-17.

SMITH, William Russell (AP Ala.) March 27, 1815-Feb. 26, 1896; House 1851-57 (1851-55 Union Whig).

SMITH, William Stephens (F N.Y.) Nov. 8, 1755-June 10, 1816; House 1813-15.

SMITH, Willis (D N.C.) Dec. 19, 1887-June 26, 1953; Senate Nov. 27, 1950-June 26, 1953.

SMITH, Wint (R Kan.) Oct. 7, 1892-April 27, 1976; House 1947-61.

SMITH, Worthington Curtis (son of John Smith of Vt.) (R Vt.) April 23, 1823-Jan. 2, 1894; House 1867-73.

SMITHERS, Nathaniel Barratt (R Del.) Oct. 8, 1818-Jan. 16, 1896; House Dec. 7, 1863-65.

SMITHWICK, John Harris (D Fla.) July 17, 1872-Dec. 2, 1948; House 1919-27.

SMOOT, Reed (R Utah) Jan. 10, 1862-Feb. 9, 1941; Senate 1903-33.

SMYSER, Martin Luther (R Ohio) April 3, 1851-May 6, 1908; House 1889-91, 1905-07.

SMYTH, Alexander (− Va.) 1765-April 17, 1830; House 1817-25, 1827-April 17, 1830.

SMYTH, George Washington (D Texas) May 16, 1803-Feb. 21, 1866; House 1853-55.

SMYTH, William (R Iowa) Jan. 3, 1824-Sept. 30, 1870; House 1869-Sept. 30, 1870.

SNAPP, Henry (father of Howard Malcolm Snapp) (R Ill.) June 30, 1822-Nov. 26, 1895; House Dec. 4, 1871-73.

SNAPP, Howard Malcolm (son of Henry Snapp) (R Ill.) Sept. 27, 1855-Aug. 14, 1938; House 1903-11.

SNEED, William Henry (AP Tenn.) Aug. 27, 1812-Sept. 18, 1869; House 1855-57.

NELL, Bertrand Hollis (R N.Y.) Dec. 9, 1870-Feb. 2, 1958; House Nov. 2, 1915-39.

NIDER, Samuel Prather (R Minn.) Oct. 9, 1845-Sept. 24, 1928; House 1889-91.

NODGRASS, Charles Edward (nephew of Henry Clay Snodgrass) (D Tenn.) Dec. 28, 1866-Aug. 3, 1936; House 1899-1903.

NODGRASS, Henry Clay (uncle of Charles Edward Snodgrass) (D Tenn.) March 29, 1848-April 22, 1931; House 1891-95.

NODGRASS, John Fryall (D Va.) March 2, 1804-June 5, 1854; House 1853-June 5, 1854.

NOOK, John Stout (D Ohio) Dec. 18, 1862-Sept. 19, 1952; House 1901-05, 1917-19.

NOVER, Horace Greeley (R Mich.) Sept. 21, 1847-July 21, 1924; House 1895-99.

NOW, Donald Francis (R Maine) Sept. 6, 1877-Feb. 12, 1958; House 1929-33.

NOW, Herman Wilber (D Ill.) July 3, 1836-Aug. 25, 1914; House 1891-93.

NOW, William W. (D N.Y.) April 27, 1812-Sept. 3, 1886; House 1851-53.

NOWE, Olympia Jean Bouchles (R Maine) Feb. 21, 1947- —; House 1979- —.

NYDER, Adam Wilson (VBD Ill.) Oct. 6, 1799-May 14, 1842; House 1837-39.

NYDER, Charles Philip (D W.Va.) June 9, 1847-Aug. 21, 1915; House May 15, 1883-89.

NYDER, Homer Peter (R N.Y.) Dec. 6, 1863-Dec. 30, 1937; House 1915-25.

NYDER, John (— Pa.) Jan. 29, 1793-Aug. 15, 1850; House 1841-43.

NYDER, John Buell (D Pa.) July 30, 1877-Feb. 24, 1946; House 1933-Feb. 24, 1946.

NYDER, Marion Gene (R Ky.) Jan. 26, 1928- —; House 1963-65, 1967-87.

NYDER, Melvin Claude (R W.Va.) Oct. 29, 1898- —; House 1947-49.

NYDER, Oliver P. (R Ark.) Nov. 13, 1833-Nov. 22, 1882; House 1871-75.

OLARZ, Stephen Joshua (D N.Y.) Sept. 12, 1940- —; House 1975- —.

OLLERS, Augustus Rhodes (W Md.) May 1, 1814-Nov. 26, 1862; House 1841-43, 1853-55.

SOLOMON, Gerald B. (R N.Y.) Aug. 14, 1930- —; House 1979- —.

SOMERS, Andrew Lawrence (D N.Y.) March 21, 1895-April 6, 1949; House 1925-April 6, 1949.

SOMERS, Peter J. (D Wis.) April 12, 1850-Feb. 15, 1924; House Aug. 27, 1893-95.

SOMES, Daniel Eton (R Maine) May 20, 1815-Feb. 13, 1888; House 1859-61.

SORG, Paul John (D Ohio) Sept. 23, 1840-May 28, 1902; House May 21, 1894-97.

SOSNOWSKI, John Bartholomew (R Mich.) Dec. 8, 1883-July 16, 1968; House 1925-27.

SOULE, Nathan (— N.Y.) ?-?; House 1831-33.

SOULE, Pierre (SRD La.) Aug. 28, 1801-March 26, 1870; Senate Jan. 21-March 3, 1847, 1849-April 11, 1853.

SOUTH, Charles Lacy (D Texas) July 22, 1892-Dec. 20, 1965; House 1935-43.

SOUTHALL, Robert Goode (D Va.) Dec. 26, 1852-May 25, 1924; House 1903-07.

SOUTHARD, Henry (father of Isaac Southard and Samuel Lewis Southard) (D N.J.) Oct. 7, 1747-May 22, 1842; House 1801-11, 1815-21.

SOUTHARD, Isaac (son of Henry Southard, brother of Samuel Lewis Southard) (CD N.J.) Aug. 30, 1783-Sept. 18, 1850; House 1831-33.

SOUTHARD, James Harding (R Ohio) Jan. 20, 1851-Feb. 20, 1919; House 1895-1907.

SOUTHARD, Milton Isaiah (D Ohio) Oct. 20, 1836-May 4, 1905; House 1873-79.

SOUTHARD, Samuel Lewis (son of Henry Southard, brother of Isaac Southard) (W N.J.) June 9, 1787-June 26, 1842; Senate Jan. 26, 1821-23 (Democrat), 1833-June 26, 1842; Pres. pro tempore 1841-42; Secy. of the Navy 1823-29; Gov. 1832-33.

SOUTHGATE, William Wright (W Ky.) Nov. 27, 1800-Dec. 26, 1849; House 1837-39.

SOUTHWICK, George Newell (R N.Y.) March 7, 1863-Oct. 17, 1912; House 1895-99, 1901-11.

SOWDEN, William Henry (D Pa.) June 6, 1840-March 3, 1907; House 1885-89.

SPAIGHT, Richard Dobbs (grandfather of Richard Spaight Donnell, father of Richard Dobbs Spaight Jr.) (D N.C.) March 25, 1758-Sept. 6, 1802; House Dec. 10, 1798-1801; Cont. Cong. 1782-85; Gov. 1792-95.

SPAIGHT, Richard Dobbs Jr. (son of Richard Dobbs Spaight, uncle of Richard Spaight Donnell) (D N.C.) 1796-May 2, 1850; House 1823-25; Gov. 1835-36.

SPALDING, Burleigh Folsom (R N.D.) Dec. 3, 1853-March 17, 1934; House 1899-1901, 1903-05.

SPALDING, George (R Mich.) Nov. 12, 1836-Sept. 13, 1915; House 1895-99.

SPALDING, Rufus Paine (WD Ohio) May 3, 1798-Aug. 29, 1886; House 1863-69.

SPALDING, Thomas (− Ga.) March 26, 1774-Jan. 5, 1851; House Dec. 24, 1805-06.

SPANGLER, David (W Ohio) Dec. 2, 1796-Oct. 18, 1856; House 1833-37.

SPANGLER, Jacob (F Pa.) Nov. 28, 1767-June 17, 1843; House 1817-April 20, 1818.

SPARKMAN, John Jackson (D Ala.) Dec. 20, 1899-Nov. 16, 1985; House 1937-Nov. 5, 1946; Senate Nov. 6, 1946-79.

SPARKMAN, Stephen Milancthon (D Fla.) July 29, 1849-Sept. 26, 1929; House 1895-1917.

SPARKS, Charles Isaac (R Kan.) Dec. 20, 1872-April 30, 1937; House 1929-33.

SPARKS, William Andrew Jackson (D Ill.) Nov. 19, 1828-May 7, 1904; House 1875-83.

SPAULDING, Elbridge Gerry (U N.Y.) Feb. 24, 1809-May 5, 1897; House 1849-51 (Whig), 1859-63.

SPAULDING, Oliver Lyman (R Mich.) Aug. 2, 1833-July 30, 1922; House 1881-83.

SPEAKS, John Charles (R Ohio) Feb. 11, 1859-Nov. 6, 1945; House 1921-31.

SPEARING, James Zacharie (D La.) April 23, 1864-Nov. 2, 1942; House April 22, 1924-31.

SPECTER, Arlen (R Pa.) Feb. 12, 1930-−; Senate 1981-−.

SPEED, Thomas (− Ky.) Oct. 25, 1768-Feb. 20, 1842; House 1817-19.

SPEER, Emory (I Ga.) Sept. 3, 1848-Dec. 13, 1918; House 1879-83 (1879-81 Democrat).

SPEER, Peter Moore (R Pa.) Dec. 29, 1862-Aug. 3, 1933; House 1911-13.

SPEER, Robert Milton (D Pa.) Sept. 8, 1838-Jan. 17, 1890; House 1871-75.

SPEER, Thomas Jefferson (R Ga.) Aug. 31, 1837-Aug. 18, 1872; House 1871-Aug. 18, 1872.

SPEIGHT, Jesse (D Miss.) Sept. 22, 1795-May 1, 1847 House 1829-37 (N.C.); Senate 1845-May 1, 1847.

SPELLMAN, Gladys Noon (D Md.) March 1, 1918-− House 1975-Feb. 24, 1981.

SPENCE, Brent (D Ky.) Dec. 24, 1874-Sept. 18, 1967 House 1931-63.

SPENCE, Floyd Davidson (R S.C.) April 9, 1928-− House 1971-−.

SPENCE, John Selby (uncle of Thomas Ara Spence) (I Md.) Feb. 29, 1788-Oct. 24, 1840; House 1823-25 1831-33; Senate Dec. 31, 1836-Oct. 24, 1840.

SPENCE, Thomas Ara (nephew of John Selby Spence (W Md.) Feb. 20, 1810-Nov. 10, 1877; House 1843-45.

SPENCER, Ambrose (father of John Canfield Spencer (D N.Y.) Dec. 13, 1765-March 13, 1848; House 1829-31.

SPENCER, Elijah (D N.Y.) 1775-Dec. 15, 1852; Hous 1821-23.

SPENCER, George Eliphaz (R Ala.) Nov. 1, 1836-Feb. 19, 1893; Senate July 13, 1868-79.

SPENCER, George Lloyd (D Ark.) March 27, 1893-Jan. 14, 1981; Senate April 1, 1941-43.

SPENCER, James Bradley (D N.Y.) April 26, 1781 March 26, 1848; House 1837-39.

SPENCER, James Grafton (D Miss.) Sept. 13, 1844-Feb. 22, 1926; House 1895-97.

SPENCER, John Canfield (son of Ambrose Spencer) (I N.Y.) Jan. 8, 1788-May 18, 1855; House 1817-19 Secy. of War 1841-43; Secy. of the Treasury 1843-44.

SPENCER, Richard (D Md.) Oct. 29, 1796-Sept. 3, 1868 House 1829-31.

SPENCER, Selden Palmer (R Mo.) Sept. 16, 1862-May 16, 1925; Senate Nov. 6, 1918-May 16, 1925.

SPENCER, William Brainerd (D La.) Feb. 5, 1835-Feb. 12, 1882; House June 8, 1876-Jan. 8, 1877.

SPERRY, Lewis (D Conn.) Jan. 23, 1848-June 22, 1922 House 1891-95.

SPERRY, Nehemiah Day (R Conn.) July 10, 1827-Nov. 13, 1911; House 1895-1911.

SPIGHT, Thomas (D Miss.) Oct. 25, 1841-Jan. 5, 1924 House July 5, 1898-1911.

SPINK, Cyrus (R Ohio) March 24, 1793-May 31, 1859 House March 4-May 31, 1859.

PINK, Solomon Lewis (R Dakota) March 20, 1831-Sept. 22, 1881; House (Terr. Del.) 1869-71.

PINNER, Francis Elias (D N.Y.) Jan. 21, 1802-Dec. 31, 1890; House 1855-61.

PINOLA, Francis Barretto (D N.Y.) March 19, 1821-April 14, 1891; House 1887-April 14, 1891.

PONG, William Belser Jr. (D Va.) Sept. 29, 1920- —; Senate Dec. 31, 1966-73.

POONER, Henry Joshua (R R.I.) Aug. 6, 1839-Feb. 9, 1918; House Dec. 5, 1881-91.

POONER, John Coit (R Wis.) Jan. 6, 1843-June 11, 1919; Senate 1885-91, 1897-April 30, 1907.

PRAGUE, Charles Franklin (grandson of Peleg Sprague of Maine) (R Mass.) June 10, 1857-Jan. 30, 1902; House 1897-1901.

PRAGUE, Peleg (— N.H.) Dec. 10, 1756-April 20, 1800; House Dec. 15, 1797-99.

PRAGUE, Peleg (grandfather of Charles Franklin Sprague) (NR Maine) April 27, 1793-Oct. 13, 1880; House 1825-29; Senate 1829-Jan. 1, 1835.

PRAGUE, William (W Mich.) Feb. 23, 1809-Sept. 19, 1868; House 1849-51.

PRAGUE, William (uncle of William Sprague, below) (W R.I.) Nov. 3, 1799-Oct. 19, 1856; House 1835-37; Senate Feb. 18, 1842-Jan. 17, 1844; Gov. 1838-39.

PRAGUE, William (nephew of William Sprague, above) (R R.I.) Sept. 12, 1830-Sept. 11, 1915; Senate 1863-75; Gov. 1860-63 (Unionist).

PRAGUE, William Peter (R Ohio) May 21, 1827-March 3, 1899; House 1871-75.

PRATT, John M. Jr. (D S.C.) Nov. 1, 1942- —; House 1983- —.

PRIGG, James Cresap (brother of Michael Cresap Sprigg) (— Ky.) 1802-Oct. 3, 1852; House 1841-43.

PRIGG, Michael Cresap (brother of James Cresap Sprigg) (D Md.) July 1, 1791-Dec. 18, 1845; House 1827-31.

PRIGG, Richard Jr. (nephew of Thomas Sprigg) (— Md.) ?-?; House May 5, 1796-99, 1801-Feb. 11, 1802.

PRIGG, Thomas (uncle of Richard Sprigg Jr.) (— Md.) 1747-Dec. 13, 1809; House 1793-97.

PRIGGS, John Thomas (D N.Y.) April 5, 1825-Dec. 23, 1888; House 1883-87.

PRINGER, Raymond Smiley (R Ind.) April 26, 1882-Aug. 28, 1947; House 1939-Aug. 28, 1947.

SPRINGER, William Lee (R Ill.) April 12, 1909- —; House 1951-73.

SPRINGER, William McKendree (D Ill.) May 30, 1836-Dec. 4, 1903; House 1875-95.

SPROUL, Elliott Wilford (R Ill.) Dec. 28, 1856-June 22, 1935; House 1921-31.

SPROUL, William Henry (R Kan.) Oct. 14, 1867-Dec. 27, 1932; House 1923-31.

SPRUANCE, Presley (W Del.) Sept. 11, 1785-Feb. 13, 1863; Senate 1847-53.

SQUIRE, Watson Carvosso (R Wash.) May 18, 1838-June 7, 1926; Senate Nov. 20, 1889-97; Gov. (Wash. Terr.) 1884-87.

STACK, Edmund John (D Ill.) Jan. 31, 1874-April 12, 1957; House 1911-13.

STACK, Edward John (D Fla.) April 29, 1910- —; House 1979-81.

STACK, Michael Joseph (D Pa.) Sept. 29, 1888-Dec. 14, 1960; House 1935-39.

STACKHOUSE, Eli Thomas (D S.C.) March 27, 1824-June 14, 1892; House 1891-June 14, 1892.

STAEBLER, Neil (D Mich.) July 11, 1905- —; House 1963-65.

STAFFORD, Robert Theodore (R Vt.) Aug. 8, 1913- —; House 1961-Sept. 16, 1971; Senate Sept. 16, 1971- —; Gov. 1959-61.

STAFFORD, William Henry (R Wis.) Oct. 12, 1869-April 22, 1957; House 1903-11, 1913-19, 1921-23, 1929-33.

STAGGERS, Harley Orrin (father of Harley Orrin Staggers Jr.) (D W.Va.) Aug. 3, 1907- —; House 1949-81.

STAGGERS, Harley Orrin Jr. (son of Harley Orrin Staggers) (D W.Va.) Feb. 22, 1951- —; House 1983- —.

STAHLE, James Alonzo (R Pa.) Jan. 11, 1829-Dec. 21, 1912; House 1895-97.

STAHLNECKER, William Griggs (D N.Y.) June 20, 1849-March 26, 1902; House 1885-93.

STALBAUM, Lynn Ellsworth (D Wis.) May 15, 1920- —; House 1965-67.

STALKER, Gale Hamilton (R N.Y.) Nov. 7, 1889-Nov. 4, 1985; House 1923-35.

STALLINGS, Jesse Francis (D Ala.) April 4, 1856-March 18, 1928; House 1893-1901.

STALLINGS, Richard H. (D Idaho) Oct. 10, 1940- —; House 1985- —.

STALLWORTH, James Adams (D Ala.) April 7, 1822-Aug. 31, 1861; House 1857-Jan. 21, 1861.

STANARD, Edwin Obed (R Mo.) Jan. 5, 1832-March 12, 1914; House 1873-75.

STANBERY, William (JD Ohio) Aug. 10, 1788-Jan. 23, 1873; House Oct. 9, 1827-33.

STANDIFER, James (W Tenn.) ?-Aug. 20, 1837; House 1823-25, 1829-Aug. 20, 1837.

STANDIFORD, Elisha David (D Ky.) Dec. 28, 1831-July 26, 1887; House 1873-75.

STANFIELD, Robert Nelson (R Ore.) July 9, 1877-April 13 1945; Senate 1921-27.

STANFIL, William Abner (R Ky.) Jan. 16, 1892-June 12, 1971; Senate Nov. 19, 1945-Nov. 5, 1946.

STANFORD, Amasa Leland (R Calif.) March 9, 1824-June 21, 1893; Senate 1885-June 21, 1893; Gov. 1862-63.

STANFORD, Richard (grandfather of William Robert Webb) (D N.C.) March 2, 1767-April 9, 1816; House 1797-April 9, 1816.

STANGELAND, Arlan Ingehart (R Minn.) Feb. 8, 1930- —; House March 1, 1977- —.

STANLEY, Augustus Owsley (D Ky.) May 21, 1867-Aug. 13, 1958; House 1903-15; Senate May 19, 1919-25; Gov. 1915-19.

STANLEY, Thomas Bahnson (D Va.) July 16, 1890-July 10, 1970; House Nov. 5, 1946-Feb. 3, 1953; Gov. 1954-58.

STANLEY, Winifred Claire (R N.Y.) Aug. 14, 1909- —; House 1943-45.

STANLY, Edward (son of John Stanly) (W N.C.) July 13, 1810-July 12, 1872; House 1837-43, 1849-53.

STANLY, John (father of Edward Stanly) (— N.C.) April 9, 1774-Aug. 2, 1834; House 1801-03, 1809-11.

STANTON, Benjamin (W Ohio) June 4, 1809-June 2, 1872; House 1851-53, 1855-61.

STANTON, Frederick Perry (D Tenn.) Dec. 22, 1814-June 4, 1894; House 1845-55; Gov. (Kan. Terr.) 1858-61.

STANTON, James Vincent (D Ohio) Feb. 27, 1932- —; House 1971-77.

STANTON, John William (R Ohio) Feb. 20, 1924- —; House 1965-83.

STANTON, Joseph Jr. (D R.I.) July 19, 1739-1807; Senate June 7, 1790-93; House 1801-07.

STANTON, Richard Henry (D Ky.) Sept. 9, 1812-March 20, 1891; House 1849-55.

STANTON, William Henry (D Pa.) July 28, 1843-March 28, 1900; House Nov. 7, 1876-77.

STARIN, John Henry (grandson of Thomas Sammons) (R N.Y.) Aug. 27, 1825-March 21, 1909; House 1877-81.

STARK, Benjamin (D Ore.) June 26, 1820-Oct. 10, 1898; Senate Oct. 29, 1861-Sept. 12, 1862.

STARK, Fortney Hillman "Pete" (D Calif.) Nov. 11, 1931- —; House 1973- —.

STARK, William Ledyard (D Neb.) July 29, 1853-Nov. 11, 1922; House 1897-1903.

STARKEY, Frank Thomas (D Minn.) Feb. 18, 1892-May 14, 1968; House 1945-47.

STARKWEATHER, David Austin (D Ohio) Jan. 21, 1802-July 12, 1876; House 1839-41, 1845-47.

STARKWEATHER, George Anson (D N.Y.) May 19, 1794-Oct. 15, 1879; House 1847-49.

STARKWEATHER, Henry Howard (R Conn.) April 29, 1826-Jan. 28, 1876; House 1867-Jan. 28, 1876.

STARNES, Joe (D Ala.) March 31, 1895-Jan. 9, 1962; House 1935-45.

STARR, John Farson (R N.J.) March 25, 1818-Aug. 1904; House 1863-67.

STATON, David Mick (R W.Va.) Feb. 11, 1940- —; House 1981-83.

STAUFFER, Simon Walter (R Pa.) Aug. 13, 1888-Sept. 26, 1975; House 1953-55, 1957-59.

STEAGALL, Henry Bascom (D Ala.) May 19, 1873-Nov. 22, 1943; House 1915-Nov. 22, 1943.

STEARNS, Asahel (F Mass.) June 17, 1774-Feb. 5, 1839; House 1815-17.

STEARNS, Foster Waterman (R N.H.) July 29, 1881-June 4, 1956; House 1939-45.

STEARNS, Ozora Pierson (R Minn.) Jan. 15, 1831-June 2, 1896; Senate Jan. 23-March 3, 1871.

STEBBINS, Henry George (WD N.Y.) Sept. 15, 1811-Dec. 9, 1881; House 1863-Oct. 24, 1864.

STECK, Daniel Frederick (D Iowa) Dec. 16, 1881-Dec. 31, 1950; Senate April 12, 1926-31.

TEDMAN, Charles Manly (D N.C.) Jan. 29, 1841-Sept. 23, 1930; House 1911-Sept. 23, 1930.

TEDMAN, William (F Mass.) Jan. 21, 1765-Aug. 31, 1831; House 1803-July 16, 1810.

TEED, Thomas Jefferson (D Okla.) March 2, 1904-June 7, 1983; House 1949-81.

TEELE, George Washington (R Ind.) Dec. 13, 1839-July 12, 1922; House 1881-89, 1895-1903; Gov. (Okla. Terr.) 1890-91.

TEELE, Henry Joseph (D Pa.) May 10, 1860-March 19, 1933; House 1915-21.

TEELE, John (F N.C.) Nov. 1, 1764-Aug. 14, 1815; House 1789-93.

TEELE, John Benedict (D N.Y.) March 28, 1814-Sept. 24, 1866; House 1861-65.

TEELE, John Nevett (W Md.) Feb. 22, 1796-Aug. 13, 1853; House May 29, 1834-37.

TEELE, Leslie Jasper (D Ga.) Nov. 21, 1868-July 24, 1929; House 1927-July 24, 1929.

TEELE, Robert Hampton (R Conn.) Nov. 3, 1938- —; House Nov. 3, 1970-75.

TEELE, Thomas Jefferson (D Iowa) March 19, 1853-March 20, 1920; House 1915-17.

TEELE, Walter Leak (D N.C.) April 18, 1823-Oct. 16, 1891; House 1877-81.

TEELE, William Gaston (D N.J.) Dec. 17, 1820-April 22, 1892; House 1861-65.

TEELE, William Randolph (D Wyo) July 24, 1842-Nov. 30, 1901; House (Terr. Del.) 1873-77.

TEELMAN, Alan Watson (R Texas) March 15, 1942- —; House 1973-77.

TEENERSON, Halvor (R Minn.) June 30, 1852-Nov. 22, 1926; House 1903-23.

TEENROD, Lewis (D Va.) May 27, 1810-Oct. 3, 1862; House 1839-45.

TEERS, Newton Ivan Jr. (R Md.) Jan 13, 1917- —; House 1977-79.

TEFAN, Karl (R Neb.) March 1, 1884-Oct. 2, 1951; House 1935-Oct. 2, 1951.

TEIGER, Sam (R Ariz.) March 10, 1929- —; House 1967-77.

TEIGER, William Albert (R Wis.) May 15, 1938-Dec. 4, 1978; House 1967-Dec. 4, 1978.

STEIWER, Frederick (R Ore.) Oct. 13, 1883-Feb. 3, 1939; Senate 1927-Jan. 31, 1938.

STENGER, William Shearer (D Pa.) Feb. 13, 1840-March 29, 1918; House 1875-79.

STENGLE, Charles Irwin (D N.Y.) Dec. 5, 1869-Nov. 23, 1953; House 1923-25.

STENHOLM, Charles Walter (D Texas) Oct. 26, 1938- —; House 1979- —.

STENNIS, John Cornelius (D Miss.) Aug. 3, 1901- —; Senate Nov. 5, 1947- —; Pres. pro tempore 1987- —.

STEPHENS, Abraham P. (D N.Y.) Feb. 18, 1796-Nov. 25, 1859; House 1851-53.

STEPHENS, Alexander Hamilton (great-granduncle of Robert Grier Stephens Jr.) (D Ga.) Feb. 11, 1812-March 4, 1883; House Oct. 2, 1843-59, Dec. 1, 1873-Nov. 4, 1882; Gov. 1882-83.

STEPHENS, Ambrose Everett Burnside (R Ohio) June 3, 1862-Feb. 12, 1927; House 1919-Feb. 12, 1927.

STEPHENS, Dan Voorhees (D Neb.) Nov. 4, 1868-Jan. 13, 1939; House Nov. 7, 1911-19.

STEPHENS, Hubert Durrett (D Miss.) July 2, 1875-March 14, 1946; House 1911-21; Senate 1923-35.

STEPHENS, John Hall (D Texas) Nov. 22, 1847-Nov. 18, 1924; House 1897-1917.

STEPHENS, Philander (JD Pa.) 1788-July 8, 1842; House 1829-33.

STEPHENS, Robert Grier Jr. (great-grandnephew of Alexander Hamilton Stephens) (D Ga.) Aug. 14, 1913- —; House 1961-77.

STEPHENS, William Dennison (R Calif.) Dec. 26, 1859-April 25, 1944; House 1911-July 22, 1916; Gov. 1917-23.

STEPHENSON, Benjamin (D Ill.) ?-Oct. 10, 1822; House (Terr. Del.) Sept. 3, 1814-16.

STEPHENSON, Isaac (brother of Samuel Merritt Stephenson) (R Wis.) June 18, 1829-March 15, 1918; House 1883-89; Senate May 17, 1907-15.

STEPHENSON, James (F Va.) March 20, 1764-Aug. 7, 1833; House 1803-05, 1809-11, Oct. 28, 1822-25.

STEPHENSON, Samuel Merritt (brother of Isaac Stephenson) (R Mich.) Dec. 23, 1831-July 31, 1907; House 1889-97.

STERETT, Samuel (AF Md.) 1758-July 12, 1833; House 1791-93.

STERIGERE, John Benton (D Pa.) July 31, 1793-Oct. 13, 1852; House 1827-31.

STERLING, Ansel (brother of Micah Sterling) (— Conn.) Feb. 3, 1782-Nov. 6, 1853; House 1821-25.

STERLING, Bruce Foster (D Pa.) Sept. 28, 1870-April 26, 1945; House 1917-19.

STERLING, John Allen (brother of Thomas Sterling) (R Ill.) Feb. 1, 1857-Oct. 17, 1918; House 1903-13, 1915-Oct. 17, 1918.

STERLING, Micah (brother of Ansel Sterling) (F N.Y.) Nov. 5, 1784-April 11, 1844; House 1821-23.

STERLING, Thomas (brother of John Allen Sterling) (R S.D.) Feb. 21, 1851-Aug. 26, 1930; Senate 1913-25.

STETSON, Charles (D Maine) Nov. 2, 1801-March 27, 1863; House 1849-51.

STETSON, Lemuel (D N.Y.) March 13, 1804-May 17, 1868; House 1843-45.

STEVENS, Aaron Fletcher (R N.H.) Aug. 9, 1819-May 10, 1887; House 1867-71.

STEVENS, Bradford Newcomb (D Ill.) Jan. 3, 1813-Nov. 10, 1885; House 1871-73.

STEVENS, Charles Abbot (brother of Moses Tyler Stevens, cousin of Isaac Ingalls Stevens) (R Mass.) Aug. 9, 1816-April 7, 1892; House Jan. 27-March 3, 1875.

STEVENS, Frederick Clement (R Minn.) Jan. 1, 1861-July 1, 1923; House 1897-1915.

STEVENS, Hestor Lockhart (D Mich.) Oct. 1, 1803-May 7, 1864; House 1853-55.

STEVENS, Hiram Sanford (D Ariz.) March 20, 1832-March 22, 1893; House (Terr. Del.) 1875-79.

STEVENS, Isaac Ingalls (cousin of Charles Abbot Stevens and Moses Tyler Stevens) (D Wash.) March 25, 1818-Sept. 1, 1862; House (Terr. Del.) 1857-61; Gov. (Wash. Terr.) 1853-57.

STEVENS, James (D Conn.) July 4, 1768-April 4, 1835; House 1819-21.

STEVENS, Moses Tyler (brother of Charles Abbot Stevens, cousin of Isaac Ingalls Stevens) (D Mass.) Oct. 10, 1825-March 25, 1907; House 1891-95.

STEVENS, Raymond Bartlett (D N.H.) June 18, 1874-May 18, 1942; House 1913-15.

STEVENS, Robert Smith (D N.Y.) March 27, 1824-Feb. 23, 1893; House 1883-85.

STEVENS, Thaddeus (R Pa.) April 4, 1792-Aug. 11, 1868; House 1849-53 (Whig), 1859-Aug. 11, 1868.

STEVENS, Theodore F. "Ted" (R Alaska) Nov. 18, 1923- —; Senate Dec. 24, 1968- —.

STEVENSON, Adlai Ewing (great-grandfather of Adla Ewing Stevenson III, grandfather of Gov. Adlai Ew ing Stevenson II of Ill.) (D Ill.) Oct. 23, 1835-Jun 14, 1914; House 1875-77, 1879-81; Vice Presiden 1893-97.

STEVENSON, Adlai Ewing III (great-grandson of Adl Ewing Stevenson, son of Adlai Ewing Stevenson II o Ill.) (D Ill.) Oct. 10, 1930- —; Senate Nov. 17, 197 81.

STEVENSON, Andrew (father of John White Steve son) (D Va.) Jan. 21, 1784-Jan. 25, 1857; House 182 June 2, 1834; Speaker 1827-34.

STEVENSON, James S. (— Pa.) 1780-Oct. 16, 183 House 1825-29.

STEVENSON, Job Evans (R Ohio) Feb. 10, 1832-Ju 24, 1922; House 1869-73.

STEVENSON, John White (son of Andrew Stevenso (D Ky.) May 4, 1812-Aug. 10, 1886; House 1857-6 Senate 1871-77; Gov. 1867-71.

STEVENSON, William Francis (D S.C.) Nov. 23, 186 Feb. 12, 1942; House 1917-33.

STEVENSON, William Henry (R Wis.) Sept. 23, 189 March 19, 1978; House 1941-49.

STEWARD, Lewis (D Ill.) Nov. 21, 1824-Aug. 27, 189 House 1891-93.

STEWART, Alexander (R Wis.) Sept. 12, 1829-May 2 1912; House 1895-1901.

STEWART, Andrew (father of Andrew Stewart, belov (W Pa.) June 11, 1791-July 16, 1872; House 1821-2 (Democrat), 1831-35 (Democrat), 1843-49.

STEWART, Andrew (son of Andrew Stewart, above) (Pa.) April 6, 1836-Nov. 9, 1903; House 1891-Feb. 2 1892.

STEWART, Arthur Thomas "Tom" (D Tenn.) Jan. 1 1892-Oct. 10, 1972; Senate Jan. 16, 1939-49.

STEWART, Bennett McVey (D Ill.) Aug. 6, 1915- - House 1979-81.

STEWART, Charles (D Texas) May 30, 1836-Sept. 2 1895; House 1883-93.

STEWART, David (W Md.) Sept. 13, 1800-Jan. 5, 185 Senate Dec. 6, 1849-Jan. 12, 1850.

STEWART, David Wallace (R Iowa) Jan. 22, 1887-Fe 10, 1974; Senate Aug. 7, 1926-27.

STEWART, Donald Wilbur (D Ala.) Feb. 8, 1940- - Senate Nov. 8, 1978-81.

STEWART, Jacob Henry (R Minn.) Jan. 15, 1829-Au 25, 1884; House 1877-79.

STEWART, James (− N.C.) Nov. 11, 1775-Dec. 29, 1821; House Jan. 5, 1818-19.

STEWART, James Augustus (D Md.) Nov. 24, 1808-April 3, 1879; House 1855-61.

STEWART, James Fleming (R N.J.) June 15, 1851-Jan. 21, 1904; House 1895-1903.

STEWART, John (D Pa.) ?-1820; House Jan. 15, 1801-05.

STEWART, John (D Conn.) Feb. 10, 1795-Sept. 16, 1860; House 1843-45.

STEWART, John David (D Ga.) Aug. 2, 1833-Jan. 28, 1894; House 1887-91.

STEWART, John George (R Del.) June 2, 1890-May 24, 1970; House 1935-37.

STEWART, John Knox (R N.Y.) Oct. 20, 1853-June 27, 1919; House 1899-1903.

STEWART, John Wolcott (R Vt.) Nov. 24, 1825-Oct. 29, 1915; House 1883-91; Senate March 24-Oct. 21, 1908; Gov. 1870-72.

STEWART, Paul (D Okla.) Feb. 27, 1892-Nov. 13, 1950; House 1943-47.

STEWART, Percy Hamilton (D N.J.) Jan. 10, 1867-June 30, 1951; House Dec. 1, 1931-33.

STEWART, Thomas Elliott (CR N.Y.) Sept. 22, 1824-Jan. 9, 1904; House 1867-69.

STEWART, William (R Pa.) Sept. 10, 1810-Oct. 17, 1876; House 1857-61.

STEWART, William Morris (R Nev.) Aug. 9, 1827-April 23, 1909; Senate Dec. 15, 1864-75, 1887-1905.

STIGLER, William Grady (D Okla.) July 7, 1891-Aug. 21, 1952; House March 28, 1944-Aug. 21, 1952.

STILES, John Dodson (D Pa.) Jan. 15, 1822-Oct. 29, 1896; House June 3, 1862-65, 1869-71.

STILES, William Henry (D Ga.) Jan. 1, 1808-Dec. 20, 1865; House 1843-45.

STILLWELL, Thomas Neel (R Ind.) Aug. 29, 1830-Jan. 14, 1874; House 1865-67.

STINESS, Walter Russell (R R.I.) March 13, 1854-March 17, 1924; House 1915-23.

STINSON, K. William "Bill" (R Wash.) April 20, 1930--; House 1963-65.

STIVERS, Moses Dunning (R N.Y.) Dec. 30, 1828-Feb. 2, 1895; House 1889-91.

STOBBS, George Russell (R Mass.) Feb. 7, 1877-Dec. 23, 1966; House 1925-31.

STOCKBRIDGE, Francis Brown (R Mich.) April 9, 1826-April 30, 1894; Senate 1887-April 30, 1894.

STOCKBRIDGE, Henry Jr. (R Md.) Sept. 18, 1856-March 22, 1924; House 1889-91.

STOCKDALE, Thomas Ringland (D Miss.) March 28, 1828-Jan. 8, 1899; House 1887-95.

STOCKMAN, David Alan (R Mich.) Nov. 10, 1946--; House 1977-Jan. 27, 1981; Director, Office of Management and Budget 1981-85.

STOCKMAN, Lowell (R Ore.) April 12, 1901-Aug. 10, 1962; House 1943-53.

STOCKSLAGER, Strother Madison (D Ind.) May 7, 1842-June 1, 1930; House 1881-85.

STOCKTON, John Potter (son of Robert Field Stockton, grandson of Richard Stockton) (D N.J.) Aug. 2, 1826-Jan. 22, 1900; Senate March 15, 1865-March 27, 1866, 1869-75.

STOCKTON, Richard (father of Robert Field Stockton, grandfather of John Potter Stockton) (F N.J.) April 17, 1764-March 7, 1828; Senate Nov. 12, 1796-99; House 1813-15.

STOCKTON, Robert Field (son of Richard Stockton, father of John Potter Stockton) (D N.J.) Aug. 20, 1795-Oct. 7, 1866; Senate 1851-Jan. 10, 1853.

STODDARD, Ebenezer (− Conn.) May 6, 1785-Aug. 19, 1847; House 1821-25.

STODDERT, John Truman (JD Md.) Oct. 1, 1790-July 19, 1870; House 1833-35.

STOKELY, Samuel (W Ohio) Jan. 25, 1796-May 23, 1861; House 1841-43.

STOKES, Edward Lowber (R Pa.) Sept. 29, 1880-Nov. 8, 1964; House Nov. 3, 1931-35.

STOKES, James William (D S.C.) Dec. 12, 1853-July 6, 1901; House 1895-June 1, 1896; Nov. 3, 1896-July 6, 1901.

STOKES, Louis (D Ohio) Feb. 23, 1925--; House 1969--.

STOKES, Montfort (D N.C.) March 12, 1762-Nov. 4, 1842; Senate Dec. 4, 1816-23; Gov. 1830-32.

STOKES, William Brickly (R Tenn.) Sept. 9, 1814-March 14, 1897; House 1859-61 (Whig), July 24, 1866-71.

STOLL, Philip Henry (D S.C.) Nov. 5, 1874-Oct. 29, 1958; House Oct. 7, 1919-23.

STONE, Alfred Parish (D Ohio) June 28, 1813-Aug. 2, 1865; House Oct. 8, 1844-45.

STONE, Charles Warren (R Pa.) June 29, 1843-Aug. 15, 1912; House Nov. 4, 1890-99.

STONE, Claudius Ulysses (D Ill.) May 11, 1879-Nov. 13, 1957; House 1911-17.

STONE, David (D N.C.) Feb. 17, 1770-Oct. 7, 1818; House 1799-1801; Senate 1801-Feb. 17, 1807, 1813-Dec. 24, 1814; Gov. 1808-10 (Democratic Republican).

STONE, Eben Francis (R Mass.) Aug. 3, 1822-Jan. 22, 1895; House 1881-87.

STONE, Frederick (grandson of Michael Jenifer Stone) (D Md.) Feb. 7, 1820-Oct. 17, 1899; House 1867-71.

STONE, James W. (D Ky.) 1813-Oct. 13, 1854; House 1843-45, 1851-53.

STONE, John Wesley (R Mich.) July 18, 1838-March 24, 1922; House 1877-81.

STONE, Joseph Champlin (R Iowa) July 30, 1829-Dec. 3, 1902; House 1877-79.

STONE, Michael Jenifer (grandfather of Frederick Stone) (— Md.) 1747-1812; House 1789-91.

STONE, Richard Bernard (D Fla.) Sept. 22, 1928-—; Senate Jan. 1, 1975-Dec. 31, 1980.

STONE, Ulysses Stevens (R Okla.) Dec. 17, 1878-Dec. 8, 1962; House 1929-31.

STONE, William (W Tenn.) Jan. 26, 1791-Feb. 18, 1853; House Sept. 14, 1837-39.

STONE, William Alexis (R Pa.) April 18, 1846-March 1, 1920; House 1891-Nov. 9, 1898; Gov. 1899-1903.

STONE, William Henry (D Mo.) Nov. 7, 1828-July 9, 1901; House 1873-77.

STONE, William Joel (D Mo.) May 7, 1848-April 14, 1918; House 1885-91; Senate 1903-April 14, 1918; Gov. 1893-97.

STONE, William Johnson (D Ky.) June 26, 1841-March 12, 1923; House 1885-95.

STORER, Bellamy (father of Bellamy Storer, below) (W Ohio) March 26, 1796-June 1, 1875; House 1835-37.

STORER, Bellamy (son of Bellamy Storer, above, uncle of Nicholas Longworth) (R Ohio) Aug. 28, 1847-Nov. 12, 1922; House 1891-95.

STORER, Clement (— N.H.) Sept. 20, 1760-Nov. 21, 1830; House 1807-09; Senate June 27, 1817-19.

STORKE, Thomas More (D Calif.) Nov. 23, 1876-Oct. 12, 1971; Senate Nov. 9, 1938-39.

STORM, Frederic (R N.Y.) July 2, 1844-June 9, 1935; House 1901-03.

STORM, John Brutzman (D Pa.) Sept. 19, 1838-Aug. 13, 1901; House 1871-75, 1883-87.

STORRS, Henry Randolph (brother of William Lucius Storrs) (F N.Y.) Sept. 3, 1787-July 29, 1837; House 1817-21, 1823-31.

STORRS, William Lucius (brother of Henry Randolph Storrs) (W Conn.) March 25, 1795-June 25, 1861; House 1829-33, 1839-June 1840.

STORY, Joseph (D Mass.) Sept. 18, 1779-Sept. 10, 1845; House May 23, 1808-09; Assoc. Justice Supreme Court 1812-45.

STOUGHTON, William Lewis (R Mich.) March 20, 1827-June 6, 1888; House 1869-73.

STOUT, Byron Gray (D Mich.) Jan. 12, 1829-June 19, 1896; House 1891-93.

STOUT, Lansing (D Ore.) March 27, 1828-March 4, 1871; House 1859-61.

STOUT, Tom (D Mont.) May 20, 1879-Dec. 26, 1965; House 1913-17.

STOVER, John Hubler (R Mo.) April 24, 1833-Oct. 27, 1889; House Dec. 7, 1868-69.

STOW, Silas (F N.Y.) Dec. 21, 1773-Jan. 19, 1827; House 1811-13.

STOWELL, William Henry Harrison (R Va.) July 26, 1840-April 27, 1922; House 1871-77.

STOWER, John G. (JD N.Y.) ?-?; House 1827-29.

STRADER, Peter Wilson (D Ohio) Nov. 6, 1818-Feb. 25, 1881; House 1869-71.

STRAIT, Horace Burton (R Minn.) Jan. 26, 1835-Feb. 25, 1894; House 1873-79, 1881-87.

STRAIT, Thomas Jefferson (Alliance D S.C.) Dec. 25, 1846-April 18, 1924; House 1893-99.

STRANAHAN, James Samuel Thomas (W N.Y.) April 25, 1808-Sept. 3, 1898; House 1855-57.

STRANG, Michael Lathrop (R Col.) June 17, 1929-— House 1985-87.

STRANGE, Robert (D N.C.) Sept. 20, 1796-Feb. 19 1854; Senate Dec. 5, 1836-Nov. 16, 1840.

STRATTON, Charles Creighton (uncle of Benjamin Franklin Howey) (W N.J.) March 6, 1796-March 30 1859; House 1837-39, 1841-43; Gov. 1845-48.

STRATTON, John (− Va.) Aug. 19, 1769-May 10, 1804; House 1801-03.

STRATTON, John Leake Newbold (R N.J.) Nov. 27, 1817-May 17, 1899; House 1859-63.

STRATTON, Nathan Taylor (D N.J.) March 17, 1813-March 9, 1887; House 1851-55.

STRATTON, Samuel Studdiford (D N.Y.) Sept. 27, 1916-−; House 1959-−.

STRATTON, William Grant (R Ill.) Feb. 26, 1914-−; House 1941-43, 1947-49; Gov. 1953-61.

STRAUB, Christian Markle (D Pa.) 1804-?; House 1853-55.

STRAUS, Isidor (D N.Y.) Feb. 6, 1845-April 15, 1912; House Jan. 30, 1894-95.

STRAWBRIDGE, James Dale (R Pa.) April 7, 1824-July 19, 1890; House 1873-75.

STREET, Randall S. (D N.Y.) 1780-Nov. 21, 1841; House 1819-21.

STRICKLAND, Randolph (R Mich.) Feb. 4, 1823-May 5, 1880; House 1869-71.

STRINGER, Lawrence Beaumont (D Ill.) Feb. 24, 1866-Dec. 5, 1942; House 1913-15.

STRINGFELLOW, Douglas (R Utah) Sept. 24, 1922-Oct. 19, 1966; House 1953-55.

STRODE, Jesse Burr (R Neb.) Feb. 18, 1845-Nov. 10, 1924; House 1895-99.

STROHM, John (W Pa.) Oct. 16, 1793-Sept. 12, 1884; House 1845-49.

STRONG, Caleb (F Mass.) Jan. 9, 1745-Nov. 7, 1819; Senate 1789-June 1, 1796; Gov. 1800-07, 1812-16.

STRONG, James (F N.Y.) 1783-Aug. 8, 1847; House 1819-21, 1823-31.

STRONG, James George (R Kan.) April 23, 1870-Jan. 11, 1938; House 1919-33.

STRONG, Julius Levi (R Conn.) Nov. 8, 1828-Sept. 7, 1872; House 1869-Sept. 7, 1872.

STRONG, Luther Martin (R Ohio) June 23, 1838-April 26, 1903; House 1893-97.

STRONG, Nathan Leroy (R Pa.) Nov. 12, 1859-Dec. 14, 1939; House 1917-35.

STRONG, Selah Brewster (D N.Y.) May 1, 1792-Nov. 29, 1872; House 1843-45.

STRONG, Solomon (F Mass.) March 2, 1780-Sept. 16, 1850; House 1815-19.

STRONG, Stephen (D N.Y.) Oct. 11, 1791-April 15, 1866; House 1845-47.

STRONG, Sterling Price (D Texas) Aug. 17, 1852-March 28, 1936; House 1933-35.

STRONG, Theron Rudd (cousin of William Strong of Pa.) (D N.Y.) Nov. 7, 1802-May 14, 1873; House 1839-41.

STRONG, William (D Vt.) 1763-Jan. 28, 1840; House 1811-15, 1819-21.

STRONG, William (cousin of Theron Rudd Strong) (D Pa.) May 6, 1808-Aug. 19, 1895; House 1847-51; Assoc. Justice Supreme Court 1870-80.

STROTHER, George French (father of James French Strother of Va., great-grandfather of James French Strother of W.Va.) (D Va.) 1783-Nov. 28, 1840; House 1817-Feb. 10, 1820.

STROTHER, James French (son of George French Strother, grandfather of James French Strother, below) (W Va.) Sept. 4, 1811-Sept. 20, 1860; House 1851-53.

STROTHER, James French (grandson of James French Strother, above, great-grandson of George French Strother) (R W.Va.) June 29, 1868-April 10, 1930; House 1925-29.

STROUSE, Myer (D Pa.) Dec. 16, 1825-Feb. 11, 1878; House 1863-67.

STROWD, William Franklin (P N.C.) Dec. 7, 1832-Dec. 12, 1911; House 1895-99.

STRUBLE, Isaac S. (R Iowa) Nov. 3, 1843-Feb. 17, 1913; House 1883-91.

STRUDWICK, William Francis (F N.C.) ?-1812; House Nov. 28, 1796-97.

STUART, Alexander Hugh Holmes (cousin of Archibald Stuart) (W Va.) April 2, 1807-Feb. 13, 1891; House 1841-43; Secy. of the Interior 1850-53.

STUART, Andrew (D Ohio) Aug. 3, 1823-April 30, 1872; House 1853-55.

STUART, Archibald (cousin of Alexander Hugh Holmes Stuart) (W Va.) Dec. 2, 1795-Sept. 20, 1855; House 1837-39.

STUART, Charles Edward (D Mich.) Nov. 25, 1810-May 19, 1887; House Dec. 6, 1847-49, 1851-53; Senate 1853-59.

STUART, David (D Mich.) March 12, 1816-Sept. 12, 1868; House 1853-55.

STUART, John Todd (D Ill.) Nov. 10, 1807-Nov. 23, 1885; House 1839-43 (Whig), 1863-65.

STUART, Philip (F Md.) 1760-Aug. 14, 1830; House 1811-19.

STUBBLEFIELD, Frank Albert (D Ky.) April 5, 1907-Oct. 14, 1977; House 1959-Dec. 31, 1974.

STUBBS, Henry Elbert (D Calif.) March 4, 1881-Feb. 28, 1937; House 1933-Feb. 28, 1937.

STUCKEY, Williamson Sylvester Jr. (D Ga.) May 25, 1935--; House 1967-77.

STUDDS, Gerry Eastman (D Mass.) May 12, 1937--; House 1973--.

STUDLEY, Elmer Ebenezer (R N.Y.) Sept. 24, 1869-Sept. 6, 1942; House 1933-35.

STULL, Howard William (R Pa.) April 11, 1876-April 22, 1949; House April 26, 1932-33.

STUMP, Herman (D Md.) Aug. 8, 1837-Jan. 9, 1917; House 1889-93.

STUMP, Robert (R Ariz.) April 4, 1927--; House 1977-- (1977-83 Democrat).

STURGEON, Daniel (D Pa.) Oct. 27, 1789-July 3, 1878; Senate Jan. 14, 1840-51.

STURGES, Jonathan (father of Lewis Burr Sturges) (-- Conn.) Aug. 23, 1740-Oct. 4, 1819; House 1789-93; Cont. Cong. 1774-87.

STURGES, Lewis Burr (son of Jonathan Sturges) (F Conn.) March 15, 1763-March 30, 1844; House Sept. 16, 1805-17.

STURGISS, George Cookman (R W.Va.) Aug. 16, 1842-Feb. 26, 1925; House 1907-11.

STURTEVANT, John Cirby (R Pa.) Feb. 20, 1835-Dec. 20, 1912; House 1897-99.

SULLIVAN, Christopher Daniel (D N.Y.) July 14, 1870-Aug. 3, 1942; House 1917-41.

SULLIVAN, George (-- N.H.) Aug. 29, 1771-April 14, 1838; House 1811-13.

SULLIVAN, John Andrew (D Mass.) May 10, 1868-May 31, 1927; House 1903-07.

SULLIVAN, John Berchmans (husband of Leonor Kretzer Sullivan) (D Mo.) Oct. 10, 1897-Jan. 29, 1951; House 1941-43, 1945-47, 1949-Jan. 29, 1951.

SULLIVAN, Leonor Kretzer (widow of John Berchmans Sullivan) (D Mo.) Aug. 21, 1903--; House 1953-77.

SULLIVAN, Maurice Joseph (D Nev.) Dec. 7, 1884-Aug. 9, 1953; House 1943-45.

SULLIVAN, Patrick Joseph (R Wyo.) March 17, 1865-April 8, 1935; Senate Dec. 5, 1929-Nov. 20, 1930.

SULLIVAN, Patrick Joseph (R Pa.) Oct. 12, 1877-Dec. 31, 1946; House 1929-33.

SULLIVAN, Timothy Daniel (D N.Y.) July 23, 1862-Aug. 31, 1913; House 1903-July 27, 1906, March 4-Aug. 31, 1913.

SULLIVAN, William Van Amberg (D Miss.) Dec. 18, 1857-March 21, 1918; House 1897-May 31, 1898; Senate May 31, 1898-1901.

SULLOWAY, Cyrus Adams (R N.H.) June 8, 1839-March 11, 1917; House 1895-1913, 1915-March 11, 1917.

SULZER, Charles August (brother of William Sulzer) (D Alaska) Feb. 24, 1879-April 28, 1919; House (Ter Del.) 1917-Jan. 7, 1919, March 4-April 28, 1919.

SULZER, William (brother of Charles August Sulzer) (D N.Y.) March 18, 1863-Nov. 6, 1941; House 1895 Dec. 31, 1912; Gov. 1913.

SUMMERS, George William (W Va.) March 4, 1804 Sept. 19, 1868; House 1841-45.

SUMMERS, John William (R Wash.) April 29, 1870 Sept. 25, 1937; House 1919-33.

SUMNER, Charles (R Mass.) Jan. 6, 1811-March 11 1874; Senate April 24, 1851-March 11, 1874 (1851-5' Democrat/Free-Soiler).

SUMNER, Charles Allen (D Calif.) Aug. 2, 1835-Jan. 31 1903; House 1883-85.

SUMNER, Daniel Hadley (D Wis.) Sept. 15, 1837-May 29, 1903; House 1883-85.

SUMNER, Jessie (R Ill.) July 17, 1898--; House 1939 47.

SUMNERS, Hatton William (D Texas) May 30, 1875 April 19, 1962; House 1913-47.

SUMTER, Thomas (grandfather of Thomas De Lag Sumter) (D S.C.) Aug. 14, 1734-June 1, 1832; House 1789-93, 1797-Dec. 15, 1801; Senate Dec. 15, 1801 Dec. 16, 1810.

SUMTER, Thomas De Lage (grandson of Thomas Sum ter) (D S.C.) Nov. 14, 1809-July 2, 1874; House 1839 43.

SUNDQUIST, Donald Kenneth (R Tenn.) March 15 1936--; House 1983--.

SUNDSTROM, Frank Leander (R N.J.) Jan. 5, 1901 May 23, 1980; House 1943-49.

SUNIA, Fofo I. F. (D American Samoa) March 13, 1937 --; House 1981--.

UTHERLAND, Daniel Alexander (R Alaska) April 17, 1869-March 24, 1955; House (Terr. Del.) 1921-31.

UTHERLAND, George (R Utah) March 25, 1862-July 18, 1942; House 1901-03; Senate 1905-17; Assoc. Justice Supreme Court 1922-38.

UTHERLAND, Howard (R W.Va.) Sept. 8, 1865-March 12, 1950; House 1913-17; Senate 1917-23.

UTHERLAND, Jabez Gridley (D Mich.) Oct. 6, 1825-Nov. 20, 1902; House 1871-73.

UTHERLAND, Joel Barlow (JD Pa.) Feb. 26, 1792-Nov. 15, 1861; House 1827-37.

UTHERLAND, Josiah (D N.Y.) June 12, 1804-May 25, 1887; House 1851-53.

UTHERLAND, Roderick Dhu (P Neb.) April 27, 1862-Oct. 18, 1915; House 1897-1901.

UTPHIN, William Halstead (D N.J.) Aug. 30, 1887-Oct. 14, 1972; House 1931-43.

UTTON, James Patrick "Pat" (D Tenn.) Oct. 31, 1915- —; House 1949-55.

VAN, Samuel (— N.J.) 1771-Aug. 24, 1844; House 1821-31.

VANK, Fletcher B. (D Okla.) April 24, 1875-March 16, 1950; House 1921-29, 1931-35.

VANN, Edward (D N.Y.) March 10, 1862-Sept. 19, 1945; House Nov. 4, 1902-03.

VANN, Thomas (D Md.) Feb. 3, 1809-July 24, 1883; House 1869-79; Gov. 1866-69 (Union Democrat).

VANSON, Charles Edward (R Iowa) Jan. 3, 1879-Aug. 22, 1970; House 1929-33.

VANSON, Claude Augustus (D Va.) March 31, 1862-July 7, 1939; House 1893-Jan. 30, 1906; Senate Aug. 1, 1910-33; Gov. 1906-10; Secy. of the Navy 1933-39.

VANWICK, John (D Pa.) 1740-Aug. 1, 1798; House 1795-Aug. 1, 1798.

VART, Peter (— N.Y.) July 5, 1752-Nov. 3, 1829; House 1807-09.

VARTZ, Joshua William (R Pa.) June 9, 1867-May 27, 1959; House 1925-27.

VASEY, John Philip (R Maine) Sept. 4, 1839-May 27, 1928; House Nov. 3, 1908-11.

VEARINGEN, Henry (D Ohio) about 1792-?; House Dec. 3, 1838-41.

VEAT, Lorenzo De Medici (D Maine) May 26, 1818-July 26, 1898; House 1863-65.

SWEENEY, Mac (R Texas) Sept. 15, 1955- —; House 1985- —.

SWEENEY, Martin Leonard (father of Robert E. Sweeney) (D Ohio) April 15, 1885-May 1, 1960; House Nov. 3, 1931-43.

SWEENEY, Robert E. (son of Martin Leonard Sweeney) (D Ohio) Nov. 4, 1924- —; House 1965-67.

SWEENEY, William Northcut (D Ky.) May 5, 1832-April 21, 1895; House 1869-71.

SWEENY, George (— Ohio) Feb. 22, 1796-Oct. 10, 1877; House 1839-43.

SWEET, Burton Erwin (R Iowa) Dec. 10, 1867-Jan. 3, 1957; House 1915-23.

SWEET, Edwin Forrest (D Mich.) Nov. 21, 1847-April 2, 1935; House 1911-13.

SWEET, John Hyde (R Neb.) Sept. 1, 1880-April 4, 1964; House April 9, 1940-41.

SWEET, Thaddeus C. (R N.Y.) Nov. 16, 1872-May 1, 1928; House Nov. 6, 1923-May 1, 1928.

SWEET, Willis (R Idaho) Jan. 1, 1856-July 9, 1925; House Oct. 1, 1890-95.

SWEETSER, Charles (D Ohio) Jan. 22, 1808-April 14, 1864; House 1849-53.

SWENEY, Joseph Henry (R Iowa) Oct. 2, 1845-Nov. 11, 1918; House 1889-91.

SWICK, Jesse Howard (R Pa.) Aug. 6, 1879-Nov. 17, 1952; House 1927-35.

SWIFT, Allen (D Wash.) Sept. 12, 1935- —; House 1979- —.

SWIFT, Benjamin (F Vt.) April 3, 1781-Nov. 11, 1847; House 1827-31; Senate 1833-39.

SWIFT, George Robinson (D Ala.) Dec. 19, 1887-Sept. 10, 1972; Senate June 15-Nov. 5, 1946.

SWIFT, Oscar William (R N.Y.) April 11, 1869-June 30, 1940; House 1915-19.

SWIFT, Zephaniah (F Conn.) Feb. 27, 1759-Sept. 27, 1823; House 1793-97.

SWIGERT, John Leonard (R Colo.) Aug. 30, 1931-Dec. 27, 1982; (elected to House 1982 but did not serve).

SWINBURNE, John (R N.Y.) May 30, 1820-March 28, 1889; House 1885-87.

SWINDALL, Charles (R Okla.) Feb. 13, 1876-June 19, 1939; House Nov. 2, 1920-21.

SWINDALL, Patrick Lynn (R Ga.) Oct. 18, 1950- —; House 1985- —.

SWING, Philip David (R Calif.) Nov. 30, 1884-Aug. 8, 1963; House 1921-33.

SWITZER, Robert Mauck (R Ohio) March 6, 1863-Oct. 28, 1952; House 1911-19.

SWOOPE, Jacob (F Va.) ?-1832; House 1809-11.

SWOOPE, William Irvin (nephew of John Patton) (R Pa.) Oct. 3, 1862-Oct. 9, 1930; House 1923-27.

SWOPE, Guy Jacob (D Pa.) Dec. 26, 1892-July 25, 1969; House 1937-39; Gov. (P.R.) 1941.

SWOPE, John Augustus (D Pa.) Dec. 25, 1827-Dec. 6, 1910; House Dec. 23, 1884-March 3, 1885, Nov. 3, 1885-87.

SWOPE, King (R Ky.) Aug. 10, 1893-April 23, 1961; House Aug. 2, 1919-21.

SWOPE, Samuel Franklin (R Ky.) March 1, 1809-April 19, 1865; House 1855-57 (1855-56 American Party).

SYKES, George (D N.J.) Sept. 20, 1802-Feb. 25, 1880; House 1843-45, Nov. 4, 1845-47.

SYMES, George Gifford (R Colo.) April 28, 1840-Nov. 3, 1893; House 1885-89.

SYMINGTON, James Wadsworth (son of William Stuart Symington, grandson of James Wolcott Wadsworth Jr., great-grandson of James Wolcott Wadsworth) (D Mo.) Sept. 28, 1927- —; House 1969-77.

SYMINGTON, William Stuart (father of James Wadsworth Symington, son-in-law of James Wolcott Wadsworth Jr.) (D Mo.) June 26, 1901- —; Senate 1953-Dec. 27, 1976.

SYMMS, Steven Douglas (R Idaho) April 23, 1938- —; House 1973-81; Senate 1981- —.

SYNAR, Michael Lynn (D Okla.) Oct. 17, 1950- —; House 1979- —.

SYPHER, Jacob Hale (R La.) June 22, 1837-May 9, 1905; House July 18, 1868-69, Nov. 7, 1870-75.

TABER, John (R N.Y.) May 5, 1880-Nov. 22, 1965; House 1923-63.

TABER, Stephen (son of Thomas Taber II) (D N.Y.) March 7, 1821-April 23, 1886; House 1865-69.

TABER, Thomas II (father of Stephen Taber) (D N.Y.) May 19, 1785-March 21, 1862; House Nov. 5, 1828-29.

TABOR, Horace Austin Warner (R Colo.) Nov. 26, 183▪ April 10, 1899; Senate Jan. 27-March 3, 1883.

TACKETT, Boyd (D Ark.) May 9, 1911- —; House 194▪ 53.

TAFFE, John (R Neb.) Jan. 30, 1827-March 14, 188▪ House 1867-73.

TAFT, Charles Phelps (brother of Pres. William Howa▪ Taft, uncle of Robert Alphonso Taft) (R Ohio) De▪ 21, 1843-Dec. 31, 1929; House 1895-97.

TAFT, Kingsley Arter (R Ohio) July 19, 1903-March 2▪ 1970; Senate Nov. 5, 1946-47.

TAFT, Robert Alphonso (son of Pres. William Howa▪ Taft, father of Robert Taft Jr., nephew of Charl▪ Phelps Taft) (R Ohio) Sept. 8, 1889-July 31, 195▪ Senate 1939-July 31, 1953; Senate majority lead▪ 1953.

TAFT, Robert Jr. (son of Robert Alphonso Taft, gran▪ son of Pres. William Howard Taft, grandnephew ▪ Charles Phelps Taft) (R Ohio) Feb. 26, 1917- ▪ House 1963-65, 1967-71; Senate 1971-Dec. 28, 197▪

TAGGART, Joseph (D Kan.) June 15, 1867-Dec. 3, 19▪ House Nov. 7, 1911-17.

TAGGART, Samuel (F Mass.) March 24, 1754-April ▪ 1825; House 1803-17.

TAGGART, Thomas (D Ind.) Nov. 17, 1856-March ▪ 1929; Senate March 20-Nov. 7, 1916; Chrmn. De▪ Nat. Comm. 1904-08.

TAGUE, Peter Francis (D Mass.) June 4, 1871-Sept. ▪ 1941; House 1915-19, Oct. 23, 1919-25.

TAIT, Charles (D Ga.) Feb. 1, 1768-Oct. 7, 1835; Sen▪ Nov. 27, 1809-19.

TALBERT, William Jasper (D S.C.) Oct. 6, 1846-Feb.▪ 1931; House 1893-1903.

TALBOT, Isham (— Ky.) 1773-Sept. 25, 1837; Sen▪ Jan. 3, 1815-19, Oct. 19, 1820-25.

TALBOT, Joseph Edward (R Conn.) March 18, 19▪ April 30, 1966; House Jan. 20, 1942-47.

TALBOT, Silas (F N.Y.) Jan. 11, 1751-June 30, 18▪ House 1793-95.

TALBOTT, Albert Gallatin (uncle of William Clayt▪ Anderson) (D Ky.) April 4, 1808-Sept. 9, 18▪ House 1855-59.

TALBOTT, Joshua Frederick Cockey (D Md.) July ▪ 1843-Oct. 5, 1918; House 1879-85, 1893-95, 1903-C▪ 5, 1918.

TALCOTT, Burt L. (R Calif.) Feb. 22, 1920- —; Ho▪ 1963-77.

ALCOTT, Charles Andrew (D N.Y.) June 10, 1857-Feb. 27, 1920; House 1911-15.

ALIAFERRO, Benjamin (− Ga.) 1750-Sept. 3, 1821; House 1799-1802.

ALIAFERRO, James Piper (D Fla.) Sept. 30, 1847-Oct. 6, 1934; Senate April 20, 1899-1911.

ALIAFERRO, John (W Va.) 1768-Aug. 12, 1852; House 1801-03 (Democrat), Nov. 29, 1811-13 (Democrat), March 24, 1824-31 (Democrat), 1835-43.

ALLE, Henry Oscar (R Iowa) Jan. 12, 1892-March 14, 1969; House 1939-59.

ALLMADGE, Benjamin (father of Frederick Augustus Tallmadge) (F Conn.) Feb. 25, 1754-March 7, 1835; House 1801-17.

ALLMADGE, Frederick Augustus (son of Benjamin Tallmadge) (W N.Y.) Aug. 29, 1792-Sept. 17, 1869; House 1847-49.

ALLMADGE, James Jr. (D N.Y.) Jan. 20, 1778-Sept. 29, 1853; House June 6, 1817-19.

ALLMADGE, Nathaniel Pitcher (D N.Y.) Feb. 8, 1795-Nov. 2, 1864; Senate 1833-June 17, 1844; Gov. (Wis. Terr.) 1844-45.

ALLMAN, Peleg (D Mass.) July 24, 1764-March 12, 1840; House 1811-13.

ALLON, Robert M. (D S.C.) Aug. 8, 1946-−; House 1983-−.

ALMADGE, Herman Eugene (D Ga.) Aug. 9, 1913-−; Senate 1957-81; Gov. 1947, 1948-55.

ANNEHILL, Adamson (D Pa.) May 23, 1750-Dec. 23, 1820; House 1813-15.

ANNER, Adolphus Hitchcock (R N.Y.) May 23, 1833-Jan. 14, 1882; House 1869-71.

APPAN, Benjamin (D Ohio) May 25, 1773-April 12, 1857; Senate 1839-45.

APPAN, Mason Weare (R N.H.) Oct. 20, 1817-Oct. 25, 1886; House 1855-61.

ARBOX, John Kemble (D Mass.) May 6, 1838-May 28, 1887; House 1875-77.

ARR, Christian (− Pa.) May 25, 1765-Feb. 24, 1833; House 1817-21.

ARSNEY, John Charles (D Mo.) Nov. 7, 1845-Sept. 4, 1920; House 1889-Feb. 17, 1896.

ARSNEY, Timothy Edward (D Mich.) Feb. 4, 1849-June 8, 1909; House 1885-89.

TARVER, Malcolm Connor (D Ga.) Sept. 25, 1885-March 5, 1960; House 1927-47.

TATE, Farish Carter (D Ga.) Nov. 20, 1856-Feb. 7, 1922; House 1893-1905.

TATE, Magnus (F Va.) 1760-March 30, 1823; House 1815-17.

TATGENHORST, Charles Jr. (R Ohio) Aug. 19, 1883-Jan. 13, 1961; House Nov. 8, 1927-29.

TATOM, Absalom (R N.C.) 1742-Dec. 20, 1802; House 1795-June 1, 1796.

TATNALL, Josiah (− Ga.) 1764-June 6, 1803; Senate Feb. 20, 1796-99; Gov. 1801-02 (Democratic Republican).

TATTNALL, Edward Fenwick (− Ga.) 1788-Nov. 21, 1832; House 1821-27.

TAUKE, Thomas Joseph (R Iowa) Oct. 11, 1950-−; House 1979-−.

TAUL, Micah (grandfather of Taul Bradford) (D Ky.) May 14, 1785-May 27, 1850; House 1815-17.

TAULBEE, William Preston (D Ky.) Oct. 22, 1851-March 11, 1890; House 1885-89.

TAURIELLO, Anthony Francis (D N.Y.) Aug. 14, 1899-Dec. 21, 1983; House 1949-51.

TAUZIN, W. J. "Billy" (D La.) June 14, 1943-−; House May 22, 1980-−.

TAVENNER, Clyde Howard (D Ill.) Feb. 4, 1882-Feb. 6, 1942; House 1913-17.

TAWNEY, James Albertus (R Minn.) Jan. 3, 1855-June 12, 1919; House 1893-1911.

TAYLER, Robert Walker (R Ohio) Nov. 26, 1852-Nov. 25, 1910; House 1895-1903.

TAYLOR, Abner (R Ill.) 1829-April 13, 1903; House 1889-93.

TAYLOR, Alexander Wilson (R Pa.) March 22, 1815-May 7, 1893; House 1873-75.

TAYLOR, Alfred Alexander (son of Nathaniel Green Taylor, brother of Robert Love Taylor) (R Tenn.) Aug. 6, 1848-Nov. 25, 1931; House 1889-95; Gov. 1921-23.

TAYLOR, Arthur Herbert (D Ind.) Feb. 29, 1852-Feb. 20, 1922; House 1893-95.

TAYLOR, Benjamin Irving (D N.Y.) Dec. 21, 1877-Sept. 5, 1946; House 1913-15.

TAYLOR, Caleb Newbold (R Pa.) July 27, 1813-Nov. 15, 1887; House 1867-69, April 13, 1870-71.

TAYLOR, Chester William (son of Samuel Mitchell Taylor) (D Ark.) July 16, 1883-July 17, 1931; House Oct. 31, 1921-23.

TAYLOR, Dean Park (R N.Y.) Jan. 1, 1902-Oct. 16, 1977; House 1943-61.

TAYLOR, Edward Livingston Jr. (R Ohio) Aug. 10, 1869-March 10, 1938; House 1905-13.

TAYLOR, Edward Thomas (D Colo.) June 19, 1858-Sept. 3, 1941; House 1909-Sept. 3, 1941.

TAYLOR, Ezra Booth (R Ohio) July 9, 1823-Jan. 29, 1912; House Dec. 13, 1880-93.

TAYLOR, Gene (R Mo.) Feb. 10, 1928- —; House 1973- —.

TAYLOR, George (D N.Y.) Oct. 19, 1820-Jan. 18, 1894; House 1857-59.

TAYLOR, George Washington (D Ala.) Jan. 16, 1849-Dec. 21, 1932; House 1897-1915.

TAYLOR, Glen Hearst (D Idaho) April 12, 1904-April 28, 1984; Senate 1945-51.

TAYLOR, Herbert Worthington (R N.J.) Feb. 19, 1869-Oct. 15, 1931; House 1921-23, 1925-27.

TAYLOR, Isaac Hamilton (R Ohio) April 18, 1840-Dec. 18, 1936; House 1885-87.

TAYLOR, James Alfred (D W.Va.) Sept. 25, 1878-June 9, 1956; House 1923-27.

TAYLOR, James Willis (R Tenn.) Aug. 28, 1880-Nov. 14, 1939; House 1919-Nov. 14, 1939.

TAYLOR, John (D Va.) May 17, 1754-Aug. 20, 1824; Senate Oct. 18, 1792-May 11, 1794, June 4-Dec. 7, 1803, Dec. 18, 1822-Aug. 20, 1824.

TAYLOR, John (D S.C.) May 4, 1770-April 16, 1832; House 1807-Dec. 30, 1810; Senate Dec. 31, 1810-Nov. 1816; Gov. 1826-28.

TAYLOR, John (— S.C.) ?-?; House 1815-17.

TAYLOR, John Clarence (D S.C.) March 2, 1890-March 25, 1983; House 1933-39.

TAYLOR, John James (D N.Y.) April 27, 1808-July 1, 1892; House 1853-55.

TAYLOR, John Lampkin (W Ohio) March 7, 1805-Sept. 6, 1870; House 1847-55.

TAYLOR, John May (D Tenn.) May 18, 1838-Feb. 17, 1911; House 1883-87.

TAYLOR, John W. (D N.Y.) March 26, 1784-Sept. 8, 1854; House 1813-33; Speaker 1820-21, 1825-27.

TAYLOR, Jonathan (D Ohio) 1796-April 1848; Hou 1839-41.

TAYLOR, Joseph Danner (R Ohio) Nov. 7, 1830-Sep 19, 1899; House Jan. 2, 1883-85, 1887-93.

TAYLOR, Miles (D La.) July 16, 1805-Sept. 23, 187 House 1855-Feb. 5, 1861.

TAYLOR, Nathaniel Green (father of Alfred Alexand Taylor and Robert Love Taylor) (W Tenn.) Dec. 2 1819-April 1, 1887; House March 30, 1854-55, Ju 24, 1866-67.

TAYLOR, Nelson (D N.Y.) June 8, 1821-Jan. 16, 189 House 1865-67.

TAYLOR, Robert (— Va.) April 29, 1763-July 3, 184 House 1825-27.

TAYLOR, Robert Love (son of Nathaniel Green Tayl brother of Alfred Alexander Taylor) (D Tenn.) Ju 31, 1850-March 31, 1912; House 1879-81; Sena 1907-March 31, 1912; Gov. 1887-91, 1897-99.

TAYLOR, Roy Arthur (D N.C.) Jan. 31, 1910- —; Hou June 25, 1960-77.

TAYLOR, Samuel Mitchell (father of Chester Willi Taylor) (D Ark.) May 25, 1852-Sept. 13, 1921; Hou Jan. 15, 1913-Sept. 13, 1921.

TAYLOR, Vincent Albert (R Ohio) Dec. 6, 1845-Dec. 1922; House 1891-93.

TAYLOR, Waller (D Ind.) before 1786-Aug. 26, 18 Senate Dec. 11, 1816-25.

TAYLOR, William (D N.Y.) Oct. 12, 1791-Sept. 1865; House 1833-39.

TAYLOR, William (D Va.) April 5, 1788-Jan. 17, 18 House 1843-Jan. 17, 1846.

TAYLOR, William Penn (W Va.) ?-?; House 1833-3

TAYLOR, Zachary (R Tenn.) May 9, 1849-Feb. 19, 19 House 1885-87.

TAZEWELL, Henry (father of Littleton Wa Tazewell) (— Va.) Nov. 15, 1753-Jan. 24, 1799; S ate Dec. 29, 1794-Jan. 24, 1799; Pres. pro temp 1794-96.

TAZEWELL, Littleton Waller (son of Henry Tazew (D Va.) Dec. 17, 1774-May 6, 1860; House Nov. 1800-01; Senate Dec. 7, 1824-July 16, 1832; Pres. tempore 1832; Gov. 1834-36.

TEAGUE, Charles McKevett (R Calif.) Sept. 18, 19 Jan. 1, 1974; House 1955-Jan. 1, 1974.

TEAGUE, Olin Earl (D Texas) April 6, 1910-Jan. 1981; House Aug. 24, 1946-Dec. 31, 1978.

EESE, Frederick Halstead (D N.J.) Oct. 21, 1823-Jan. 7, 1894; House 1875-77.

EIGAN, Henry George (FL Minn.) Aug. 7, 1881-March 12, 1941; House 1937-39.

ELFAIR, Thomas (D Ga.) March 2, 1780-Feb. 18, 1818; House 1813-17.

ELLER, Henry Moore (D Colo.) May 23, 1830-Feb. 23, 1914; Senate Nov. 15, 1876-April 17, 1882 (Republican), 1885-1909 (1885-97 Republican, 1897-1903 Independent-Silver Republican); Secy. of the Interior 1882-85.

ELLER, Isaac (nephew of Abraham Henry Schenck) (D N.Y.) Feb. 7, 1799-April 30, 1868; House Nov. 7, 1854-55.

ELLER, Ludwig (D N.Y.) June 22, 1911-Oct. 4, 1965; House 1957-61.

EMPLE, Henry Wilson (R Pa.) March 31, 1864-Jan. 11, 1955; House 1913-15 (Progressive Republican), Nov. 2, 1915-33.

EMPLE, William (D Del.) Feb. 28, 1814-May 28, 1863; House March 4-May 28, 1863.

EMPLETON, Thomas Weir (R Pa.) Nov. 8, 1867-Sept. 5, 1935; House 1917-19.

ENER, John Kinley (R Pa.) July 25, 1863-May 19, 1946; House 1909-Jan. 16, 1911; Gov. 1911-15.

ENEROWICZ, Rudolph Gabriel (D Mich.) June 14, 1890-Aug. 31, 1963; House 1939-43.

EN EYCK, Egbert (— N.Y.) April 18, 1779-April 11, 1844; House 1823-Dec. 15, 1825.

EN EYCK, John Conover (R N.J.) March 12, 1814-Aug. 24, 1879; Senate 1859-65.

EN EYCK, Peter Gansevoort (D N.Y.) Nov. 7, 1873-Sept. 2, 1944; House 1913-15, 1921-23.

ENNEY, Samuel (— N.H.) Nov. 27, 1748-Feb. 6, 1816; House Dec. 8, 1800-07.

ENZER, Herbert (D N.Y.) Nov. 1, 1905-—; House 1965-69.

CRRELL, George Butler (D Texas) Dec. 5, 1862-April 18, 1947; House 1933-35.

CRRELL, James C. (UD Ga.) Nov. 7, 1806-Dec. 1, 1835; House March 4-July 8, 1835.

CRRELL, Joseph Meriwether (D Ga.) June 6, 1861-Nov. 17, 1912; Senate Nov. 17, 1910-July 14, 1911; Gov. 1902-07.

CRRELL, William (D Ga.) 1778-July 4, 1855; House 1817-21.

TERRY, David Dickson (son of William Leake Terry) (D Ark.) Jan. 31, 1881-Oct. 7, 1963; House Dec. 19, 1933-43.

TERRY, John H. (R N.Y.) Nov. 14, 1924-—; House 1971-73.

TERRY, Nathaniel (— Conn.) Jan. 30, 1768-June 14, 1844; House 1817-19.

TERRY, William (C Va.) Aug. 14, 1824-Sept. 5, 1888; House 1871-73, 1875-77.

TERRY, William Leake (father of David Dickson Terry) (D Ark.) Sept. 27, 1850-Nov. 4, 1917; House 1891-1901.

TEST, John (W Ind.) Nov. 12, 1771-Oct. 9, 1849; House 1823-27 (Clay Democrat), 1829-31.

TEWES, Donald Edgar (R Wis.) Aug. 4, 1916-—; House 1957-59.

THACHER, George (F Mass.) April 12, 1754-April 6, 1824; House 1789-1801; Cont. Cong. 1787.

THACHER, Thomas Chandler (D Mass.) July 20, 1858-April 11, 1945; House 1913-15.

THATCHER, Maurice Hudson (R Ky.) Aug. 15, 1870-Jan. 6, 1973; House 1923-33.

THATCHER, Samuel (D Mass.) July 1, 1776-July 18, 1872; House Dec. 6, 1802-05.

THAYER, Andrew Jackson (D Ore.) Nov. 27, 1818-April 28, 1873; House March 4-July 30, 1861.

THAYER, Eli (father of John Alden Thayer) (R Mass.) June 11, 1819-April 15, 1899; House 1857-61.

THAYER, Harry Irving (R Mass.) Sept. 10, 1869-March 10, 1926; House 1925-March 10, 1926.

THAYER, John Alden (son of Eli Thayer) (D Mass.) Dec. 22, 1857-July 31, 1917; House 1911-13.

THAYER, John Milton (uncle of Arthur Laban Bates) (R Neb.) Jan. 24, 1820-March 19, 1906; Senate March 1, 1867-71; Gov. 1875-79 (Wyo. Terr.), 1887-91, 1891-92.

THAYER, John Randolph (D Mass.) March 9, 1845-Dec. 19, 1916; House 1899-1905.

THAYER, Martin Russell (R Pa.) Jan. 27, 1819-Oct. 14, 1906; House 1863-67.

THEAKER, Thomas Clarke (R Ohio) Feb. 1, 1812-July 16, 1883; House 1859-61.

THIBODEAUX, Bannon Goforth (— La.) Dec. 22, 1812-March 5, 1866; House 1845-49.

THILL, Lewis Dominic (R Wis.) Oct. 18, 1903- —; House 1939-43.

THISTLEWOOD, Napoleon Bonaparte (R Ill.) March 30, 1837-Sept. 15, 1915; House Feb. 15, 1908-13.

THOM, William Richard (D Ohio) July 7, 1885-Aug. 28, 1960; House 1933-39, 1941-43, 1945-47.

THOMAS, Albert (husband of Lera M. Thomas) (D Texas) April 12, 1898-Feb. 15, 1966; House 1937-Feb. 15, 1966.

THOMAS, Benjamin Franklin (CU Mass.) Feb. 12, 1813-Sept. 27, 1878; House June 11, 1861-63.

THOMAS, Charles Randolph (father of Charles Randolph Thomas, below) (R N.C.) Feb. 7, 1827-Feb. 18, 1891; House 1871-75.

THOMAS, Charles Randolph (son of Charles Randolph Thomas, above) (D N.C.) Aug. 21, 1861-March 8, 1931; House 1899-1911.

THOMAS, Charles Spalding (D Colo.) Dec. 6, 1849-June 24, 1934; Senate Jan. 15, 1913-21; Gov. 1899-1901.

THOMAS, Christopher Yancy (R Va.) March 24, 1818-Feb. 11, 1879; House March 5, 1874-75.

THOMAS, David (D N.Y.) June 11, 1762-Nov. 11, 1831; House 1801-May 1, 1808.

THOMAS, Elbert Duncan (D Utah) June 17, 1883-Feb. 11, 1953; Senate 1933-51.

THOMAS, Francis (UR Md.) Feb. 3, 1799-Jan. 22, 1876; House 1831-41 (Jackson Democrat), 1861-69; Gov. 1842-45 (Democrat).

THOMAS, George Morgan (R Ky.) Nov. 23, 1828-Jan. 7, 1914; House 1887-89.

THOMAS, Henry Franklin (R Mich.) Dec. 17, 1843-April 16, 1912; House 1893-97.

THOMAS, Isaac (D Tenn.) Nov. 4, 1784-Feb. 2, 1859; House 1815-17.

THOMAS, James Houston (D Tenn.) Sept. 22, 1808-Aug. 4, 1876; House 1847-51, 1859-61.

THOMAS, Jesse Burgess (W Ill.) 1777-May 4, 1853; House (Terr. Del.) Oct. 22, 1808-09 (Ind.); Senate Dec. 3, 1818-29.

THOMAS, John (R Idaho) Jan. 4, 1874-Nov. 10, 1945; Senate June 30, 1928-33, Jan. 27, 1940-Nov. 10, 1945.

THOMAS, John Chew (F Md.) Oct. 15, 1764-May 10, 1836; House 1799-1801.

THOMAS, John Lewis Jr. (R Md.) May 20, 1835-Oct. 15, 1893; House Dec. 4, 1865-67.

THOMAS, John Parnell (R N.J.) Jan. 16, 1895-Nov. 1 1970; House 1937-Jan. 2, 1950.

THOMAS, John Robert (R Ill.) Oct. 11, 1846-Jan. 1 1914; House 1879-89.

THOMAS, John William Elmer (D Okla.) Sept. 8, 187 Sept. 19, 1965; House 1923-27; Senate 1927-51.

THOMAS, Lera M. (widow of Albert Thomas) (Texas) Aug. 3, 1900- —; House March 30, 1966-6'

THOMAS, Lot (R Iowa) Oct. 17, 1843-March 17, 19C House 1899-1905.

THOMAS, Ormsby Brunson (R Wis.) Aug. 21, 1832-O(24, 1904; House 1885-91.

THOMAS, Philemon (D La.) Feb. 9, 1763-Nov. 18, 18◆ House 1831-35.

THOMAS, Phillip Francis (D Md.) Sept. 12, 1810-O◆ 2, 1890; House 1839-41, 1875-77; Gov. 1848-51; Se◆ of the Treasury 1860-61.

THOMAS, Richard (F Pa.) Dec. 30, 1744-Jan. 19, 18◆ House 1795-1801.

THOMAS, Robert Lindsay (D Ga.) Nov. 20, 1943- - House 1983- —.

THOMAS, Robert Young Jr. (D Ky.) July 13, 1855-Se◆ 3, 1925; House 1909-Sept. 3, 1925.

THOMAS, William Aubrey (R Ohio) June 7, 1866-Se◆ 8, 1951; House Nov. 8, 1904-11.

THOMAS, William David (R N.Y.) March 22, 1880-M◆ 17, 1936; House Jan. 30, 1934-May 17, 1936.

THOMAS, William Marshall (R Calif.) Dec. 6, 1941-House 1979- —.

THOMASON, Robert Ewing (D Texas) May 30, 18◆ Nov. 8, 1973; House 1931-July 31, 1947.

THOMASSON, William Poindexter (W Ky.) Oct. 1797-Dec. 29, 1882; House 1843-47.

THOMPSON, Albert Clifton (R Ohio) Jan. 23, 18 Jan. 26, 1910; House 1885-91.

THOMPSON, Benjamin (W Mass.) Aug. 5, 1798-Se◆ 24, 1852; House 1845-47, 1851-Sept. 24, 1852.

THOMPSON, Charles James (R Ohio) Jan. 24, 18◆ March 27, 1932; House 1919-31.

THOMPSON, Charles Perkins (D Mass.) July 30, 18◆ Jan. 19, 1894; House 1875-77.

THOMPSON, Charles Winston (D Ala.) Dec. 30, 18◆ March 20, 1904; House 1901-March 20, 1904.

THOMPSON, Chester Charles (D Ill.) Sept. 19, 1893-Jan. 30, 1971; House 1933-39.

THOMPSON, Clark Wallace (D Texas) Aug. 6, 1896-Dec. 16, 1981; House June 24, 1933-35, Aug. 23, 1947-Dec. 30, 1966.

THOMPSON, Fountain Land (D N.D.) Nov. 18, 1854-Feb. 4, 1942; Senate Nov. 10, 1909-Jan. 31, 1910.

THOMPSON, Frank Jr. (D N.J.) July 26, 1918- –; House 1955-81.

THOMPSON, George Western (D Va.) May 14, 1806-Feb. 24, 1888; House 1851-July 30, 1852.

THOMPSON, Hedge (– N.J.) Jan. 28, 1780-July 23, 1828; House 1827-July 23, 1828.

THOMPSON, Jacob (D Miss.) May 15, 1810-March 24, 1885; House 1839-51; Secy. of the Interior 1857-61.

THOMPSON, James (D Pa.) Oct. 1, 1806-Jan. 28, 1874; House 1845-51.

THOMPSON, Joel (F N.Y.) Oct. 3, 1760-Feb. 8, 1843; House 1813-15.

THOMPSON, John (D N.Y.) March 20, 1749-1823; House 1799-1801, 1807-11.

THOMPSON, John (R N.Y.) July 4, 1809-June 1, 1890; House 1857-59.

THOMPSON, John Burton (W Ky.) Dec. 14, 1810-Jan. 7, 1874; House Dec. 7, 1840-43, 1847-51; Senate 1853-59.

THOMPSON, John McCandless (brother of William George Thompson) (R Pa.) Jan. 4, 1829-Sept. 3, 1903; House Dec. 22, 1874-75, 1877-79.

THOMPSON, Joseph Bryan (D Okla.) April 29, 1871-Sept. 18, 1919; House 1913-Sept. 18, 1919.

THOMPSON, Philip (– Ky.) Aug. 20, 1789-Nov. 25, 1836; House 1823-25.

THOMPSON, Philip Burton Jr. (D Ky.) Oct. 15, 1845-Dec. 15, 1909; House 1879-85.

THOMPSON, Philip Rootes (D Va.) March 26, 1766-July 27, 1837; House 1801-07.

THOMPSON, Richard Wigginton (W Ind.) June 9, 1809-Feb. 9, 1900; House 1841-43, 1847-49; Secy. of the Navy 1877-80.

THOMPSON, Robert Augustine (father of Thomas Larkin Thompson) (D Va.) Feb. 14, 1805-Aug. 31, 1876; House 1847-49.

THOMPSON, Ruth (R Mich.) Sept. 15, 1887-April 5, 1970; House 1951-57.

THOMPSON, Standish Fletcher (R Ga.) Feb. 5, 1925- –; House 1967-73.

THOMPSON, Theo Ashton (D La.) March 31, 1916-July 1, 1965; House 1953-July 1, 1965.

THOMPSON, Thomas Larkin (son of Robert Augustine Thompson) (D Calif.) May 31, 1838-Feb. 1, 1898; House 1887-89.

THOMPSON, Thomas Weston (– N.H.) March 15, 1766-Oct. 1, 1821; House 1805-07; Senate June 24, 1814-17.

THOMPSON, Waddy Jr. (W S.C.) Jan. 8, 1798-Nov. 23, 1868; House Sept. 10, 1835-41.

THOMPSON, Wiley (D Ga.) Sept. 23, 1781-Dec. 28, 1835; House 1821-33.

THOMPSON, William (D Iowa) Nov. 10, 1813-Oct. 6, 1897; House 1847-June 29, 1850.

THOMPSON, William George (brother of John McCandless Thompson) (R Iowa) Jan. 17, 1830-April 2, 1911; House Oct. 14, 1879-83.

THOMPSON, William Henry (D Neb.) Dec. 14, 1853-June 6, 1937; Senate May 24, 1933-Nov. 6, 1934.

THOMPSON, William Howard (D Kan.) Oct. 14, 1871-Feb. 9, 1928; Senate 1913-19.

THOMSON, Alexander (– Pa.) Jan. 12, 1788-Aug. 2, 1848; House Dec. 6, 1824-May 1, 1826.

THOMSON, Charles Marsh (PR Ill.) Feb. 13, 1877-Dec. 30, 1943; House 1913-15.

THOMSON, Edwin Keith (R Wyo) Feb. 8, 1919-Dec. 9, 1960; House 1955-Dec. 9, 1960; (elected to Senate 1960 but did not serve).

THOMSON, John (D Ohio) Nov. 20, 1780-Dec. 2, 1852; House 1825-27, 1829-37.

THOMSON, John Renshaw (D N.J.) Sept. 25, 1800-Sept. 12, 1862; Senate 1853-Sept. 12, 1862.

THOMSON, Mark (F N.J.) 1739-Dec. 14, 1803; House 1795-99.

THOMSON, Vernon Wallace (R Wis.) Nov. 5, 1905- –; House 1961-Dec. 31, 1974; Gov. 1957-59.

THONE, Charles (R Neb.) Jan. 4, 1924- –; House 1971-79; Gov. 1979-83.

THORINGTON, James (W Iowa) May 7, 1816-June 13, 1887; House 1855-57.

THORKELSON, Jacob (R Mont.) Sept. 24, 1876-Nov. 20, 1945; House 1939-41.

THORNBERRY, William Homer (D Texas) Jan. 9, 1909- –; House 1949-Dec. 20, 1963.

THORNBURGH, Jacob Montgomery (R Tenn.) July 3, 1837-Sept. 19, 1890; House 1873-79.

THORNTON, Anthony (D Ill.) Nov. 9, 1814-Sept. 10, 1904; House 1865-67.

THORNTON, John Randolph (D La.) Aug. 25, 1846-Dec. 28, 1917; Senate Dec. 7, 1910-15.

THORNTON, Raymond Hoyt Jr. (D Ark.) July 16, 1928- —; House 1973-79.

THORP, Robert Taylor (R Va.) March 12, 1850-Nov. 26, 1938; House May 2, 1896-97, March 23, 1898-99.

THORPE, Roy Henry (R Neb.) Dec. 13, 1874-Sept. 19, 1951; House Nov. 7, 1922-23.

THROCKMORTON, James Webb (D Texas) Feb. 1, 1825-April 21, 1894; House 1875-79, 1883-87; Gov. 1866-67.

THROOP, Enos Thompson (D N.Y.) Aug. 21, 1784-Nov. 1, 1874; House 1815-June 4, 1816; Gov. 1829-33 (Jackson Democrat).

THROPP, Joseph Earlston (R Pa.) Oct. 4, 1847-July 27, 1927; House 1899-1901.

THRUSTON, Bruckner (D Ky.) Feb. 8, 1764-Aug. 30, 1845; Senate 1805-Dec. 18, 1809.

THURMAN, Allen Granberry (D Ohio) Nov. 13, 1813-Dec. 12, 1895; House 1845-47; Senate 1869-81; Pres. pro tempore 1879-81.

THURMAN, John Richardson (W N.Y.) Oct. 6, 1814-July 24, 1854; House 1849-51.

THURMOND, James Strom (R S.C.) Dec. 5, 1902- —; Senate Dec. 24, 1954-April 4, 1956 (Democrat), Nov. 7, 1956- — (1956-Sept. 16, 1964, Democrat); Pres. pro tempore 1981-87; Gov. 1947-51 (Democrat).

THURSTON, Benjamin Babcock (D R.I.) June 29, 1804-May 17, 1886; House 1847-49, 1851-57.

THURSTON, John Mellen (R Neb.) Aug. 21, 1847-Aug. 9, 1916; Senate 1895-1901.

THURSTON, Lloyd (R Iowa) March 27, 1880-May 7, 1970; House 1925-39.

THURSTON, Samuel Royal (D Ore.) April 15, 1816-April 9, 1851; House (Terr. Del.) 1849-51.

THYE, Edward John (R Minn.) April 26, 1896-Aug. 28, 1969; Senate 1947-59; Gov. 1943-47.

TIBBATTS, John Wooleston (D Ky.) June 12, 1802-July 5, 1852; House 1843-47.

TIBBITS, George (F N.Y.) Jan. 14, 1763-July 19, 1849; House 1803-05.

TIBBOTT, Harve (R Pa.) May 27, 1885-Dec. 31, 1969 House 1939-49.

TICHENOR, Isaac (F Vt.) Feb. 8, 1754-Dec. 11, 1838 Senate Oct. 18, 1796-Oct. 17, 1797, 1815-21; Gov 1797-1807, 1808-09.

TIERNAN, Robert Owens (D R.I.) Feb. 24, 1929- — House March 28, 1967-75.

TIERNEY, William Laurence (D Conn.) Aug. 6, 1876 April 13, 1958; House 1931-33.

TIFFIN, Edward (D Ohio) June 19, 1766-Aug. 9, 1829 Senate 1807-09; Gov. 1803-07 (Democratic Republi can).

TIFT, Nelson (D Ga.) July 23, 1810-Nov. 21, 1891; Hous July 25, 1868-69.

TILDEN, Daniel Rose (W Ohio) Nov. 5, 1804-March 1890; House 1843-47.

TILLINGHAST, Joseph Leonard (cousin of Thoma Tillinghast) (W R.I.) 1791-Dec. 30, 1844; Hous 1837-43.

TILLINGHAST, Thomas (cousin of Joseph Leonar Tillinghast) (— R.I.) Aug. 21, 1742-Aug. 26, 182 House Nov. 13, 1797-99, 1801-03.

TILLMAN, Benjamin Ryan (brother of George Dic nysius Tillman) (D S.C.) Aug. 11, 1847-July 3, 1918 Senate 1895-July 3, 1918; Gov. 1890-94.

TILLMAN, George Dionysius (brother of Benjami Ryan Tillman) (D S.C.) Aug. 21, 1826-Feb. 2, 190 House 1879-June 19, 1882, 1883-93.

TILLMAN, John Newton (D Ark.) Dec. 13, 1859-Marc 9, 1929; House 1915-29.

TILLMAN, Lewis (nephew of Barclay Martin) (' Tenn.) Aug. 18, 1816-May 3, 1886; House 1869-71

TILLOTSON, Thomas (— N.Y.) 1750-May 5, 183 House March 4-Aug. 10, 1801.

TILSON, John Quillin (R Conn.) April 5, 1866-Aug. 1 1958; House 1909-13, 1915-Dec. 3, 1932; House ma jority leader 1925-31.

TIMBERLAKE, Charles Bateman (R Colo.) Sept. 2 1854-May 31, 1941; House 1915-33.

TINCHER, Jasper Napoleon (R Kan.) Nov. 2, 187 Nov. 6, 1951; House 1919-27.

TINKHAM, George Holden (R Mass.) Oct. 29, 187 Aug. 28, 1956; House 1915-43.

TIPTON, John (D Ind.) Aug. 14, 1786-April 5, 183 Senate Jan. 3, 1832-39.

TIPTON, Thomas Foster (R Ill.) Aug. 29, 1833-Feb. 7, 1904; House 1877-79.

TIPTON, Thomas Weston (R Neb.) Aug. 5, 1817-Nov. 26, 1899; Senate March 1, 1867-75.

TIRRELL, Charles Quincy (R Mass.) Dec. 10, 1844-July 31, 1910; House 1901-July 31, 1910.

TITUS, Obadiah (D N.Y.) Jan. 20, 1789-Sept. 2, 1854; House 1837-39.

TOBEY, Charles William (R N.H.) July 22, 1880-July 24, 1953; House 1933-39; Senate 1939-July 24, 1953; Gov. 1929-31.

TOD, John (D Pa.) 1779-March 1830; House 1821-24.

TODD, Albert May (Fus. Mich.) June 3, 1850-Oct. 6, 1931; House 1897-99.

TODD, John Blair Smith (D Dakota) April 4, 1814-Jan. 5, 1872; House (Terr. Del.) Dec. 9, 1861-63, June 17, 1864-65.

TODD, Lemuel (R Pa.) July 29, 1817-May 12, 1891; House 1855-57, 1873-75.

TODD, Paul Harold Jr. (D Mich.) Sept. 22, 1921- —; House 1965-67.

TOLAN, John Harvey (D Calif.) Jan. 15, 1877-June 30, 1947; House 1937-47.

TOLAND, George Washington (W Pa.) Feb. 8, 1796-Jan. 30, 1869; House 1837-43.

TOLL, Herman (D Pa.) March 15, 1907-July 26, 1967; House 1959-67.

TOLLEFSON, Thor Carl (R Wash.) May 2, 1901-Dec. 30, 1982; House 1947-65.

TOLLEY, Harold Sumner (R N.Y.) Jan. 16, 1894-May 20, 1956; House 1925-27.

TOMLINSON, Gideon (D Conn.) Dec. 31, 1780-Oct. 8, 1854; House 1819-27; Senate 1831-37; Gov. 1827-31 (Democratic Republican).

TOMLINSON, Thomas Ash (W N.Y.) March 1802-June 18, 1872; House 1841-43.

TOMPKINS, Arthur Sidney (R N.Y.) Aug. 26, 1865-Jan. 20, 1938; House 1899-1903.

TOMPKINS, Caleb (— N.Y.) Dec. 22, 1759-Jan. 1, 1846; House 1817-21.

TOMPKINS, Christopher (— Ky.) March 24, 1780-Aug. 9, 1858; House 1831-35.

TOMPKINS, Cydnor Bailey (father of Emmett Tompkins) (R Ohio) Nov. 8, 1810-July 23, 1862; House 1857-61.

TOMPKINS, Emmett (son of Cydnor Bailey Tompkins) (R Ohio) Sept. 1, 1853-Dec. 18, 1917; House 1901-03.

TOMPKINS, Patrick Watson (W Miss.) 1804-May 8, 1953; House 1847-49.

TONGUE, Thomas H. (R Ore.) June 23, 1844-Jan. 11, 1903; House 1897-Jan. 11, 1903.

TONRY, Richard Alvin (D La.) June 25, 1935- —; House Jan. 3-May 4, 1977.

TONRY, Richard Joseph (D N.Y.) Sept. 30, 1893-Jan. 17, 1971; House 1935-37.

TOOLE, Joseph Kemp (D Mont.) May 12, 1851-March 11, 1929; House (Terr. Del.) 1885-89; Gov. 1889-93, 1901-08.

TOOMBS, Robert (SRD Ga.) July 2, 1810-Dec. 15, 1885; House 1845-53; Senate 1853-Feb. 4, 1861.

TORRENS, James H. (D N.Y.) Sept. 12, 1874-April 5, 1952; House Feb. 29, 1944-47.

TORRES, Estaban Edward (D Calif.) Jan. 27, 1930- —; House 1983- —.

TORRICELLI, Robert G. (D N.J.) Aug. 26, 1951- —; House 1983- —.

TOUCEY, Isaac (D Conn.) Nov. 5, 1796-July 30, 1869; House 1835-39; Senate May 12, 1852-57; Gov. 1846-47; Atty. Gen. 1848-49; Secy. of the Navy 1857-61.

TOU VELLE, William Ellsworth (D Ohio) Nov. 23, 1862-Aug. 14, 1951; House 1907-11.

TOWE, Harry Lancaster (R N.J.) Nov. 3, 1898- —; House 1943-Sept. 7, 1951.

TOWELL, David Gilmer (R Nev.) June 9, 1937- —; House 1973-75.

TOWER, John Goodwin (R Texas) Sept. 29, 1925- —; Senate June 15, 1961-85.

TOWEY, Frank William Jr. (D N.J.) Nov. 5, 1895-Sept. 4, 1979; House 1937-39.

TOWNE, Charles Arnette (D N.Y.) Nov. 21, 1858-Oct. 22, 1928; House 1895-97 (Republican Minn.), 1905-07; Senate Dec. 5, 1900-Jan. 28, 1901 (Minn.).

TOWNER, Horace Mann (R Iowa) Oct. 23, 1855-Nov. 23, 1937; House 1911-April 1, 1923; Gov. (P.R.) 1923-29.

TOWNS, Edolphus (D N.Y.) July 21, 1934- —; House 1983- —.

TOWNS, George Washington Bonaparte (D Ga.) May 4, 1801-July 15, 1854; House 1835-Sept. 1, 1836 (Union Democrat), 1837-39 (Union Democrat), Jan. 5, 1846-47; Gov. 1847-51.

TOWNSEND, Amos (R Ohio) 1821-March 17, 1895; House 1877-83.

TOWNSEND, Charles Champlain (R Pa.) Nov. 24, 1841-July 10, 1910; House 1889-91.

TOWNSEND, Charles Elroy (R Mich.) Aug. 15, 1856-Aug. 3, 1924; House 1903-11; Senate 1911-23.

TOWNSEND, Dwight (D N.Y.) Sept. 26, 1826-Oct. 29, 1899; House Dec. 5, 1864-65, 1871-73.

TOWNSEND, Edward Waterman (D N.J.) Feb. 10, 1855-March 15, 1942; House 1911-15.

TOWNSEND, George (D N.Y.) 1769-Aug. 17, 1844; House 1815-19.

TOWNSEND, Hosea (R Colo.) June 16, 1840-March 4, 1909; House 1889-93.

TOWNSEND, John Gillis Jr. (R Del.) May 31, 1871-April 10, 1964; Senate 1929-41; Gov. 1917-21.

TOWNSEND, Martin Ingham (R N.Y.) Feb. 6, 1810-March 8, 1903; House 1875-79.

TOWNSEND, Washington (R Pa.) Jan. 20, 1813-March 18, 1894; House 1869-77.

TOWNSHEND, Norton Strange (D Ohio) Dec. 25, 1815-July 13, 1895; House 1851-53.

TOWNSHEND, Richard Wellington (D Ill.) April 30, 1840-March 9, 1889; House 1877-March 9, 1889.

TRACEWELL, Robert John (R Ind.) May 7, 1852-July 28, 1922; House 1895-97.

TRACEY, Charles (D N.Y.) May 27, 1847-March 24, 1905; House Nov. 8, 1887-95.

TRACEY, John Plank (R Mo.) Sept. 18, 1836-July 24, 1910; House 1895-97.

TRACY, Albert Haller (brother of Phineas Lyman Tracy) (D N.Y.) June 17, 1793-Sept. 19, 1859; House 1819-25.

TRACY, Andrew (W Vt.) Dec. 15, 1797-Oct. 28, 1868; House 1853-55.

TRACY, Henry Wells (IR Pa.) Sept. 24, 1807-April 11, 1886; House 1863-65.

TRACY, Phineas Lyman (brother of Albert Haller Tracy) (W N.Y.) Dec. 25, 1786-Dec. 22, 1876; House Nov. 5, 1827-33.

TRACY, Uri (D N.Y.) Feb. 8, 1764-July 21, 1838; House 1805-07, 1809-13.

TRACY, Uriah (F Conn.) Feb. 2, 1755-July 19, 1807; House 1793-Oct. 13, 1796; Senate Oct. 13, 1796-July 19, 1807; Pres. pro tempore 1800.

TRAEGER, William Isham (R Calif.) Feb. 26, 1880-Jan 20, 1935; House 1933-35.

TRAFICANT, James A. Jr. (D Ohio) May 8, 1941-—; House 1985-—.

TRAFTON, Mark (AP Mass.) Aug. 1, 1810-March 8 1901; House 1855-57.

TRAIN, Charles Russell (R Mass.) Oct. 18, 1817-July 28 1885; House 1859-63.

TRAMMELL, Park (D Fla.) April 9, 1876-May 8, 1936 Senate 1917-May 8, 1936; Gov. 1913-17.

TRANSUE, Andrew Jackson (D Mich.) Jan. 12, 1903-— House 1937-39.

TRAXLER, Jerome Bob (D Mich.) July 21, 1931-— House April 16, 1974-—.

TRAYNOR, Philip Andrew (D Del.) May 31, 1874-Dec 5, 1962; House 1941-43, 1945-47.

TREADWAY, Allen Towner (R Mass.) Sept. 16, 1867 Feb. 16, 1947; House 1913-45.

TREADWAY, William Marshall (D Va.) Aug. 24, 1807 May 1, 1891; House 1845-47.

TREDWELL, Thomas (grandfather of Thoma Treadwell Davis) (— N.Y.) Feb. 6, 1743-Dec. 30 1831; House May 1791-95.

TREEN, David Conner (R La.) July 16, 1928-—; Hous 1973-March 10, 1980; Gov. 1980-84.

TRELOAR, William Mitchellson (R Mo.) Sept. 21 1850-July 3, 1935; House 1895-97.

TREMAIN, Lyman (R N.Y.) June 14, 1819-Nov. 30 1878; House 1873-75.

TREZVANT, James (— Va.) ?-Sept. 2, 1841; Hous 1825-31.

TRIBBLE, Samuel Joelah (D Ga.) Nov. 15, 1869-Dec. 8 1916; House 1911-Dec. 8, 1916.

TRIBLE, Paul Seward Jr. (R Va.) Dec. 29, 1946-— House 1977-83; Senate 1983-—.

TRIGG, Abram (brother of John Johns Trigg) (— Va. 1750-?; House 1797-1809.

TRIGG, Connally Findlay (D Va.) Sept. 18, 1847-Apr 23, 1907; House 1885-87.

TRIGG, John Johns (brother of Abram Trigg) (— Va 1748-May 17, 1804; House 1797-May 17, 1804.

TRIMBLE, Carey Allen (R Ohio) Sept. 13, 1813-May 4 1887; House 1859-63.

TRIMBLE, David (D Ky.) June 1782-Oct. 20, 1842; House 1817-27.

TRIMBLE, James William (D Ark.) Feb. 3, 1894-March 10, 1972; House 1945-67.

TRIMBLE, John (R Tenn.) Feb. 7, 1812-Feb. 23, 1884; House 1867-69.

TRIMBLE, Lawrence Strother (D Ky.) Aug. 26, 1825-Aug. 9, 1904; House 1865-71.

TRIMBLE, South (D Ky.) April 13, 1864-Nov. 23, 1946; House 1901-07.

TRIMBLE, William Allen (— Ohio) April 4, 1786-Dec. 13, 1821; Senate 1819-Dec. 13, 1821.

TRIPLETT, Philip (W Ky.) Dec. 24, 1799-March 30, 1852; House 1839-43.

TRIPPE, Robert Pleasant (W Ga.) Dec. 21, 1819-July 22, 1900; House 1855-59.

TROTTER, James Fisher (D Miss.) Nov. 5, 1802-March 9, 1866; Senate Jan. 22-July 10, 1838.

TROTTI, Samuel Wilds (— S.C.) July 18, 1810-June 24, 1856; House Dec. 17, 1842-43.

TROUP, George Michael (SRD Ga.) Sept. 8, 1780-April 26, 1856; House 1807-15 (Democrat); Senate Nov. 13, 1816-Sept. 23, 1818, 1829-Nov. 8, 1833; Gov. 1823-27 (Democratic Republican).

TROUT, Michael Carver (D Pa.) Sept. 30, 1810-June 25, 1873; House 1853-55.

TROUTMAN, William Irvin (R Pa.) Jan. 13, 1905-Jan. 27, 1971; House 1943-Jan. 2, 1945.

TROWBRIDGE, Rowland Ebenezer (R Mich.) June 18, 1821-April 20, 1881; House 1861-63, 1865-69.

TRUAX, Charles Vilas (D Ohio) Feb. 1, 1887-Aug. 9, 1935; House 1933-Aug. 9, 1935.

TRUMAN, Harry S (D Mo.) May 8, 1884-Dec. 26, 1972; Senate 1935-Jan. 17, 1945; Vice President Jan. 20-April 12, 1945; President April 12, 1945-53.

TRUMBO, Andrew (W Ky.) Sept. 15, 1797-Aug. 21, 1871; House 1845-47.

TRUMBULL, Jonathan (uncle of Joseph Trumbull) (F Conn.) March 26, 1740-Aug. 7, 1809; House 1789-95; Speaker 1791-93; Senate 1795-June 10, 1796; Gov. 1797-1809.

TRUMBULL, Joseph (nephew of Jonathan Trumbull) (W Conn.) Dec. 7, 1782-Aug. 4, 1861; House Dec. 1, 1834-35, 1839-43; Gov. 1849-50.

TRUMBULL, Lyman (R Ill.) Oct. 12, 1813-June 25, 1896; Senate 1855-73.

TSONGAS, Paul Efthemios (D Mass.) Feb. 14, 1941-—; House 1975-79; Senate 1979-85.

TUCK, Amos (I N.H.) Aug. 2, 1810-Dec. 11, 1879; House 1847-53.

TUCK, William Munford (D Va.) Sept. 28, 1896-June 9, 1983; House April 14, 1953-69; Gov. 1946-50.

TUCKER, Ebenezer (— N.J.) Nov. 15, 1758-Sept. 5, 1845; House 1825-29.

TUCKER, George (cousin of Henry St. George Tucker) (D Va.) Aug. 20, 1775-April 10, 1861; House 1819-25.

TUCKER, Henry St. George (father of John Randolph Tucker, grandfather of Henry St. George Tucker, below, cousin of George Tucker, nephew of Thomas Tudor Tucker) (— Va.) Dec. 29, 1780-Aug. 28, 1848; House 1815-19.

TUCKER, Henry St. George (son of John Randolph Tucker, grandson of Henry St. George Tucker, above) (D Va.) April 5, 1853-July 23, 1932; House 1889-97, March 21, 1922-July 23, 1932.

TUCKER, James Guy (D Ark.) June 13, 1943-—; House 1977-79.

TUCKER, John Randolph (son of Henry St. George Tucker born in 1780, father of Henry St. George Tucker born in 1853) (D Va.) Dec. 24, 1823-Feb. 13, 1897; House 1875-87.

TUCKER, Starling (— S.C.) 1770-Jan. 3, 1834; House 1817-31.

TUCKER, Thomas Tudor (uncle of Henry St. George Tucker born in 1780) (F S.C.) June 25, 1745-May 2, 1828; House 1789-93; Cont. Cong. 1787-88.

TUCKER, Tilghman Mayfield (D Miss.) Feb. 5, 1802-April 3, 1859; House 1843-45; Gov. 1842-43.

TUFTS, John Quincy (R Iowa) July 12, 1840-Aug. 10, 1908; House 1875-77.

TULLY, Pleasant Britton (D Calif.) March 21, 1829-March 24, 1897; House 1883-85.

TUMULTY, Thomas James (D N.J.) March 2, 1913-Nov. 23, 1981; House 1955-57.

TUNNELL, James Miller (D Del.) Aug. 2, 1879-Nov. 14, 1957; Senate 1941-47.

TUNNEY, John Varick (D Calif.) June 26, 1934-—; House 1965-Jan. 2, 1971; Senate Jan. 2, 1971-Jan. 1, 1977.

TUPPER, Stanley Roger (R Maine) Jan. 25, 1921-—; House 1961-67.

TURLEY, Thomas Battle (D Tenn.) April 5, 1845-July 1, 1910; Senate July 20, 1897-1901.

TURNBULL, Robert (D Va.) Jan. 11, 1850-Jan. 22, 1920; House March 8, 1910-13.

TURNER, Benjamin Sterling (R Ala.) March 17, 1825-March 21, 1894; House 1871-73.

TURNER, Charles Henry (D N.Y.) May 26, 1861-Aug. 31, 1913; House Dec. 9, 1889-91.

TURNER, Charles Jr. (WD Mass.) June 20, 1760-May 16, 1839; House June 28, 1809-13.

TURNER, Clarence Wyly (D Tenn.) Oct. 22, 1866-March 23, 1939; House Nov. 7, 1922-23, 1933-March 23, 1939.

TURNER, Daniel (son of James Turner of N.C.) (D N.C.) Sept. 21, 1796-July 21, 1860; House 1827-29.

TURNER, Erastus Johnson (R Kan.) Dec. 26, 1846-Feb. 10, 1933; House 1887-91.

TURNER, George (Fus. Wash.) Feb. 25, 1850-Jan. 26, 1932; Senate 1897-1903.

TURNER, Henry Gray (D Ga.) March 20, 1839-June 9, 1904; House 1881-97.

TURNER, James (father of Daniel Turner) (D N.C.) Dec. 20, 1766-Jan. 15, 1824; Senate 1805-Nov. 21, 1816; Gov. 1802-05.

TURNER, James (D Md.) Nov. 7, 1783-March 28, 1861; House 1833-37.

TURNER, Oscar (father of Oscar Turner, below) (ID Ky.) Feb. 3, 1825-Jan. 22, 1896; House 1879-85.

TURNER, Oscar (son of Oscar Turner, above) (D Ky.) Oct. 19, 1867-July 17, 1902; House 1899-1901.

TURNER, Smith Spangler (D Va.) Nov. 21, 1842-April 8, 1898; House Jan. 30, 1894-97.

TURNER, Thomas (D Ky.) Sept. 10, 1821-Sept. 11, 1900; House 1877-81.

TURNER, Thomas Johnston (D Ill.) April 5, 1815-April 4, 1874; House 1847-49.

TURNEY, Hopkins Lacy (D Tenn.) Oct. 3, 1797-Aug. 1 1857; House 1837-43; Senate 1845-51.

TURNEY, Jacob (D Pa.) Feb. 18, 1825-Oct. 4, 1891; House 1875-79.

TURPIE, David (D Ind.) July 8, 1828-April 21, 1909; Senate Jan. 14-March 3 1863, 1887-99.

TURPIN, Charles Murray (R Pa.) March 4, 1878-June 4, 1946; House June 4, 1929-37.

TURPIN, Louis Washington (D Ala.) Feb. 22, 1849-Feb. 3, 1903; House 1889-June 4, 1890, 1891-95.

TURRILL, Joel (JD N.Y.) Feb. 22, 1794-Dec. 28, 1859 House 1833-37.

TUTEN, James Russell (D Ga.) July 23, 1911-Aug. 16 1968; House 1963-67.

TUTHILL, Joseph Hasbrouck (nephew of Selah Tuthill) (D N.Y.) Feb. 25, 1811-July 27, 1877; House 1871-73.

TUTHILL, Selah (uncle of Joseph Hasbrouck Tuthill (− N.Y.) Oct. 26, 1771-Sept. 7, 1821; House March 4-Sept. 7, 1821.

TUTTLE, William Edgar Jr. (D N.J.) Dec. 10, 1870-Feb. 11, 1923; House 1911-15.

TWEED, William Marcy (D N.Y.) April 3, 1823-April 12, 1878; House 1853-55.

TWEEDY, John Hubbard (W Wis.) Nov. 9, 1814-Nov. 12, 1891; House (Terr. Del.) 1847-May 29, 1848.

TWEEDY, Samuel (W Conn.) March 8, 1776-July 1 1868; House 1833-35.

TWICHELL, Ginery (R Mass.) Aug. 26, 1811-July 23 1883; House 1867-73.

TWYMAN, Robert Joseph (R Ill.) June 18, 1897-June 28, 1976; House 1947-49.

TYDINGS, Joseph Davies (son of Millard Evelyn Tydings) (D Md.) May 4, 1928- − ; Senate 1965-71

TYDINGS, Millard Evelyn (father of Joseph Davie Tydings) (D Md.) April 6, 1890-Feb. 9, 1961; House 1923-27; Senate 1927-51.

TYLER, Asher (W N.Y.) May 10, 1798-Aug. 1, 1875 House 1843-45.

TYLER, David Gardiner (son of John Tyler, grandson o Gov. John Tyler of Va.) (D Va.) July 12, 1846-Sept 5, 1927; House 1893-97.

TYLER, James Manning (R Vt.) April 27, 1835-Oct. 13 1926; House 1879-83.

TYLER, John (father of David Gardiner Tyler, son o Gov. John Tyler of Va.) (DR Va.) March 29, 1790-Jan. 18, 1862; House Dec. 16, 1817-21; Senate 1827-Feb. 29, 1836; Pres. pro tempore 1835-36; Gov. 1825-27; Vice President March 4-April 4, 1841 (Whig) President April 6, 1841-45 (Whig).

TYNDALL, William Thomas (R Mo.) Jan. 16, 1862-Nov. 26, 1928; House 1905-07.

TYNER, James Noble (R Ind.) Jan. 17, 1826-Dec. 5 1904; House 1869-75; Postmaster Gen. 1876-77.

TYSON, Jacob (− N.Y.) Oct. 8, 1773-July 16, 1848 House 1823-25.

TYSON, Joe Roberts (W Pa.) Feb. 8, 1803-June 27, 1858; House 1855-57.

TYSON, John Russell (D Ala.) Nov. 28, 1856-March 27, 1923; House 1921-March 27, 1923.

TYSON, Lawrence Davis (D Tenn.) July 4, 1861-Aug. 24, 1929; Senate 1925-Aug. 24, 1929.

UDALL, Morris King (brother of Stewart Lee Udall) (D Ariz.) June 15, 1922- —; House May 2, 1961- —.

UDALL, Stewart Lee (brother of Morris King Udall) (D Ariz.) Jan. 31, 1920- —; House 1955-Jan. 18, 1961; Secy. of the Interior 1961-69.

UDREE, Daniel (D Pa.) Aug. 5, 1751-July 15, 1828; House Oct. 12, 1813-15, Dec. 26, 1820-21, Dec. 10, 1822-25.

ULLMAN, Albert Conrad (D Ore.) March 9, 1914-Oct. 11, 1986; House 1957-81.

UMSTEAD, William Bradley (D N.C.) May 13, 1895-Nov. 7, 1954; House 1933-39; Senate Dec. 18, 1946-Dec. 30, 1948; Gov. 1953-54.

UNDERHILL, Charles Lee (R Mass.) July 20, 1867-Jan. 28, 1946; House 1921-33.

UNDERHILL, Edwin Stewart (D N.Y.) Oct. 7, 1861-Feb. 7, 1929; House 1911-15.

UNDERHILL, John Quincy (D N.Y.) Feb. 19, 1848-May 21, 1907; House 1899-1901.

UNDERHILL, Walter (W N.Y.) Sept. 12, 1795-Aug. 17, 1866; House 1849-51.

UNDERWOOD, John William Henderson (D Ga.) Nov. 20, 1816-July 18, 1888; House 1859-Jan. 23, 1861.

UNDERWOOD, Joseph Rogers (brother of Warner Lewis Underwood, grandfather of Oscar Wilder Underwood) (W Ky.) Oct. 24, 1791-Aug. 23, 1876; House 1835-43; Senate 1847-53.

UNDERWOOD, Mell Gilbert (D Ohio) Jan. 30, 1892-March 8, 1972; House 1923-April 10, 1936.

UNDERWOOD, Oscar Wilder (grandson of Joseph Rogers Underwood, grandnephew of Warner Lewis Underwood) (D Ala.) May 6, 1862-Jan. 25, 1929; House 1895-June 9, 1896, 1897-1915; House majority leader 1911-15; Senate 1915-27.

UNDERWOOD, Thomas Rust (D Ky.) March 3, 1898-June 29, 1956; House 1949-March 17, 1951; Senate March 19, 1951-Nov. 4, 1952.

UNDERWOOD, Warner Lewis (brother of Joseph Rogers Underwood, granduncle of Oscar Wilder Underwood) (AP Ky.) Aug. 7, 1808-March 12, 1872; House 1855-59.

UPDEGRAFF, Jonathan Taylor (R Ohio) May 13, 1822-Nov. 30, 1882; House 1879-Nov. 30, 1882.

UPDEGRAFF, Thomas (R Iowa) April 3, 1834-Oct. 4, 1910; House 1879-83, 1893-99.

UPDIKE, Ralph Eugene (R Ind.) May 27, 1894-Sept. 16, 1953; House 1925-29.

UPHAM, Charles Wentworth (cousin of George Baxter Upham and Jabez Upham) (W Mass.) May 4, 1802-June 15, 1875; House 1853-55.

UPHAM, George Baxter (brother of Jabez Upham, cousin of Charles Wentworth Upham) (— N.H.) Dec. 27 1768-Feb. 10, 1848; House 1801-03.

UPHAM, Jabez (brother of George Baxter Upham, cousin of Charles Wentworth Upham) (— Mass.) Aug. 23, 1764-Nov. 8, 1811; House 1807-10.

UPHAM, Nathaniel (D N.H.) June 9, 1774-July 10, 1829; House 1817-23.

UPHAM, William (W Vt.) Aug. 5, 1792-Jan. 14, 1853; Senate 1843-Jan. 14, 1853.

UPSHAW, William David (D Ga.) Oct. 15, 1866-Nov. 21, 1952; House 1919-27.

UPSON, Charles (R Mich.) March 19, 1821-Sept. 5, 1885; House 1863-69.

UPSON, Christopher Columbus (D Texas) Oct. 17, 1829-Feb. 8, 1902; House April 15, 1879-83.

UPSON, William Hanford (R Ohio) Jan. 11, 1823-April 13, 1910; House 1869-73.

UPTON, Charles Horace (R Va.) Aug. 23, 1812-June 17, 1877; House May 23, 1861-Feb. 27, 1862.

UPTON, Frederick Stephen (R Mich.) April 23, 1953- —; House 1987- —.

UPTON, Robert William (R N.H.) Feb. 3, 1884-April 28, 1972; Senate Aug. 14, 1953-Nov. 7, 1954.

URNER, Milton George (uncle of James Samuel Simmons) (R Md.) July 29, 1839-Feb. 9, 1926; House 1879-83.

UTT, James Boyd (R Calif.) March 11, 1899-March 1, 1970; House 1953-March 1, 1970.

UTTER, George Herbert (R R.I.) July 24, 1854-Nov. 3, 1912; House 1911-Nov. 3, 1912; Gov. 1905-07.

UTTERBACK, Hubert (cousin of John Gregg Utterback) (D Iowa) June 28, 1880-May 12, 1942; House 1935-37.

UTTERBACK, John Gregg (cousin of Hubert Utterback) (D Maine) July 12, 1872-July 11, 1955; House 1933-35.

VAIL, George (D N.J.) July 21, 1809-May 23, 1875; House 1853-57.

VAIL, Henry (D N.Y.) 1782-June 25, 1853; House 1837-39.

VAIL, Richard Bernard (R Ill.) Aug. 31, 1895-July 29, 1955; House 1947-49, 1951-53.

VAILE, William Newell (R Colo.) June 22, 1876-July 2, 1927; House 1919-July 2, 1927.

VALENTINE, Edward Kimble (R Neb.) June 1, 1843-April 11, 1916; House 1879-85.

VALENTINE, Tim (D N.C.) March 15, 1926- —; House 1983- —.

VALK, William Weightman (AP N.Y.) Oct. 12, 1806-Sept. 20, 1879; House 1855-57.

VALLANDIGHAM, Clement Laird (uncle of John A. McMahon) (D Ohio) July 29, 1820-June 17, 1871; House May 25, 1858-63.

VAN AERNAM, Henry (R N.Y.) March 11, 1819-June 1, 1894; House 1865-69, 1879-83.

VAN ALEN, James Isaac (half brother of Martin Van Buren) (F N.Y.) 1776-Dec. 23, 1870; House 1807-09.

VAN ALEN, John Evert (— N.Y.) 1749-March 1807; House 1793-99.

VAN ALSTYNE, Thomas Jefferson (D N.Y.) July 25, 1827-Oct. 26, 1903; House 1883-85.

VAN AUKEN, Daniel Myers (D Pa.) Jan. 15, 1826-Nov. 7, 1908; House 1867-71.

VAN BUREN, John (D N.Y.) May 13, 1799-Jan. 16, 1855; House 1841-43.

VAN BUREN, Martin (half brother of James Isaac Van Alen) (D N.Y.) Dec. 5, 1782-July 24, 1862; Senate 1821-Dec. 20, 1828; Gov. 1829; Secy. of State 1829-31; Vice President 1833-37; President 1837-41.

VANCE, John Luther (D Ohio) July 19, 1839-June 10, 1921; House 1875-77.

VANCE, Joseph (W Ohio) March 21, 1786-Aug. 24, 1852; House 1821-35 (Democrat), 1843-47; Gov. 1836-38.

VANCE, Robert Brank (uncle of Zebulon Baird Vance and Robert Brank Vance, below) (D N.C.) 1793-1827; House 1823-25.

VANCE, Robert Brank (nephew of Robert Brank Vance, above, brother of Zebulon Baird Vance) (D N.C.) April 24, 1828-Nov. 28, 1899; House 1873-85.

VANCE, Robert Johnstone (D Conn.) March 15, 1854-June 15, 1902; House 1887-89.

VANCE, Zebulon Baird (brother of Robert Brank Vance born in 1828, nephew of Robert Brank Vance born in 1793) (D N.C.) May 13, 1830-April 14, 1894; House Dec. 7, 1858-61; Senate 1879-April 14, 1894; Gov. 1862-65, 1877-79.

VAN CORTLANDT, Philip (brother of Pierre Van Cortlandt Jr.) (D N.Y.) Aug. 21, 1749-Nov. 1, 1831; House 1793-1809.

VAN CORTLANDT, Pierre Jr. (brother of Philip Van Cortlandt) (D N.Y.) Aug. 29, 1762-July 13, 1848; House 1811-13.

VAN DEERLIN, Lionel (D Calif.) July 25, 1914- —; House 1963-81.

VANDENBERG, Arthur Hendrick (R Mich.) March 22, 1884-April 18, 1951; Senate March 31, 1928-April 18, 1951; Pres. pro tempore 1947-49.

VANDERGRIFF, Tom (D Texas) Jan. 29, 1926- —; House 1983-85.

VANDER JAGT, Guy Adrian (R Mich.) Aug. 26, 1931- —; House Nov. 8, 1966- —.

VANDERPOEL, Aaron (D N.Y.) Feb. 5, 1799-July 18, 1870; House 1833-37, 1839-41.

VANDER VEEN, Richard Franklin (D Mich.) Nov. 26, 1922- —; House Feb. 18, 1974-77.

VANDERVEER, Abraham (D N.Y.) 1781-July 21, 1839; House 1837-39.

VANDEVER, William (R Calif.) March 31, 1817-Jul 23, 1893; House 1859-Sept. 24, 1861 (Iowa), 1887-91.

VANDIVER, Willard Duncan (D Mo.) March 30, 1854-May 30, 1932; House 1897-1905.

VAN DUZER, Clarence Dunn (D Nev.) May 4, 1866-Sept. 28, 1947; House 1903-07.

VAN DYKE, Carl Chester (D Minn.) Feb. 18, 1881-May 20, 1919; House 1915-May 20, 1919.

VAN DYKE, John (W N.J.) April 3, 1807-Dec. 24, 1878; House 1847-51.

VAN DYKE, Nicholas (F Del.) Dec. 20, 1769-May 21, 1826; House Oct. 6, 1807-11; Senate 1817-May 21, 1826.

VAN EATON, Henry Smith (D Miss.) Sept. 14, 1826-May 30, 1898; House 1883-87.

VAN GAASBECK, Peter (AF N.Y.) Sept. 27, 1754-1797; House 1793-95.

VAN HORN, Burt (R N.Y.) Oct. 28, 1823-April 1, 1896; House 1861-63, 1865-69.

AN HORN, George (D N.Y.) Feb. 5, 1850-May 3, 1904; House 1891-93.

AN HORN, Robert Thompson (R Mo.) May 19, 1824-Jan. 3, 1916; House 1865-71, 1881-83, Feb. 27, 1896-97.

AN HORNE, Archibald (− Md.) ?-1817; House 1807-11.

AN HORNE, Espy (D Pa.) 1795-Aug. 25, 1829; House 1825-29.

AN HORNE, Isaac (D Pa.) Jan. 13, 1754-Feb. 2, 1834; House 1801-05.

AN HOUTEN, Isaac B. (D N.Y.) June 4, 1776-Aug. 16, 1850; House 1833-35.

ANIK, Charles Albert (D Ohio) April 7, 1913-−; House 1955-81.

ANMETER, John Inskeep (W Ohio) Feb. 1798-Aug. 3, 1875; House 1843-45.

AN NESS, John Peter (D N.Y.) 1770-March 7, 1846; House Oct. 6, 1801-Jan. 17, 1803.

AN NUYS, Frederick (D Ind.) April 16, 1874-Jan. 25, 1944; Senate 1933-Jan. 25, 1944.

AN PELT, William Kaiser (R Wis.) March 10, 1905-−; House 1951-65.

AN RENSSELAER, Henry Bell (son of Stephen Van Rensselaer) (W N.Y.) May 14, 1810-March 23, 1864; House 1841-43.

AN RENSSELAER, Jeremiah (father of Solomon Van Vechten Van Rensselaer, cousin of Killian Killian Van Rensselaer) (− N.Y.) Aug. 27, 1738-Feb. 19, 1810; House 1789-91.

AN RENSSELAER, Killian Killian (cousin of Jeremiah Van Rensselaer, uncle of Solomon Van Vechten Van Renssealer) (D N.Y.) June 9, 1763-June 18, 1845; House 1801-11.

AN RENSSELAER, Solomon Van Vechten (son of Jeremiah Van Rensselaer, nephew of Killian Killian Van Rensselaer) (F N.Y.) Aug. 6, 1774-April 23, 1852; House 1819-Jan. 14, 1822.

AN RENSSELAER, Stephen (father of Henry Bell Van Rensselaer) (− N.Y.) Nov. 1, 1764-Jan. 26, 1839; House Feb. 27, 1822-29.

AN SANT, Joshua (D Md.) Dec. 31, 1803-April 8, 1884; House 1853-55.

AN SCHAICK, Isaac Whitbeck (uncle of Aaron Van Schaick Cochrane) (R Wis.) Dec. 7, 1817-Aug. 22, 1901; House 1885-87, 1889-91.

VAN SWEARINGEN, Thomas (− Va.) May 5, 1784-Aug. 19, 1822; House 1819-Aug. 19, 1822.

VAN TRUMP, Philadelph (D Ohio) Nov. 15, 1810-July 31, 1874; House 1867-73.

VAN VALKENBURGH, Robert Bruce (R N.Y.) Sept. 4, 1821-Aug. 1, 1888; House 1861-65.

VAN VOORHIS, Henry Clay (R Ohio) May 11, 1852-Dec. 12, 1927; House 1893-1905.

VAN VOORHIS, John (R N.Y.) Oct. 22, 1826-Oct. 20, 1905; House 1879-83, 1893-95.

VAN VORHES, Nelson Holmes (R Ohio) Jan. 23, 1822-Dec. 4, 1882; House 1875-79.

VAN WINKLE, Marshall (grandnephew of Peter Godwin Van Winkle) (R N.J.) Sept. 28, 1869-May 10, 1957; House 1905-07.

VAN WINKLE, Peter Godwin (granduncle of Marshall Van Winkle) (U W.Va.) Sept. 7, 1808-April 15, 1872; Senate Aug. 4, 1863-69.

VAN WYCK, Charles Henry (R Neb.) May 10, 1824-Oct. 24, 1895; House 1859-63, 1867-69, Feb. 17, 1870-71 (N.Y.); Senate 1881-87.

VAN WYCK, William William (D N.Y.) Aug. 9, 1777-Aug. 27, 1840; House 1821-25.

VAN ZANDT, James Edward (R Pa.) Dec. 18, 1898-Jan. 6, 1986; House 1939-Sept. 24, 1943, 1947-63.

VARDAMAN, James Kimble (D Miss.) July 26, 1861-June 25, 1930; Senate 1913-19; Gov. 1904-08.

VARE, William Scott (R Pa.) Dec. 24, 1867-Aug. 7, 1934; House April 24, 1912-Jan. 2, 1923, March 4, 1923-27; Senate (elected 1926 but never served).

VARNUM, John (F Mass.) June 25, 1778-July 23, 1836; House 1825-31.

VARNUM, Joseph Bradley (− Mass.) Jan. 29, 1750-Sept. 21, 1821; House 1795-June 29, 1811; Speaker 1807-11; Senate June 29, 1811-17; Pres. pro tempore 1813-14.

VAUGHAN, Horace Worth (D Texas) Dec. 2, 1867-Nov. 10, 1922; House 1913-15.

VAUGHAN, William Wirt (D Tenn.) July 2, 1831-Aug. 19, 1878; House 1871-73.

VAUGHN, Albert Clinton Sr. (R Pa.) Oct. 9, 1894-Sept. 1, 1951; House Jan. 3-Sept. 1, 1951.

VAUX, Richard (D Pa.) Dec. 19, 1816-March 22, 1895; House May 20, 1890-91.

VEEDER, William Davis (D N.Y.) May 19, 1835-Dec. 2, 1910; House 1877-79.

VEHSLAGE, John Herman George (D N.Y.) Dec. 20, 1842-July 21, 1904; House 1897-99.

VELDE, Harold Himmel (R Ill.) April 1, 1910-Sept. 1, 1985; House 1949-57.

VENABLE, Abraham Bedford (uncle of Abraham Watkins Venable) (− Va.) Nov. 20, 1758-Dec. 26, 1811; House 1791-99; Senate Dec. 7, 1803-June 7, 1804.

VENABLE, Abraham Watkins (nephew of Abraham Bedford Venable) (D N.C.) Oct. 17, 1799-Feb. 24, 1876; House 1847-53.

VENABLE, Edward Carrington (D Va.) Jan. 31, 1853-Dec. 8, 1908; House 1889-Sept. 23, 1890.

VENABLE, William Webb (D Miss.) Sept. 25, 1880-Aug. 2, 1948; House Jan. 4, 1916-21.

VENTO, Bruce Frank (D Minn.) Oct. 7, 1940-−; House 1977-−.

VERPLANCK, Daniel Crommelin (father of Gulian Crommelin Verplanck) (F N.Y.) March 19, 1762-March 29, 1834; House Oct. 17, 1803-09.

VERPLANCK, Gulian Crommelin (son of Daniel Crommelin Verplanck) (D N.Y.) Aug. 6, 1786-March 18, 1870; House 1825-33.

VERREE, John Paul (R Pa.) March 9, 1817-June 27, 1889; House 1859-63.

VEST, George Graham (D Mo.) Dec. 6, 1830-Aug. 9, 1904; Senate 1879-1903.

VESTAL, Albert Henry (R Ind.) Jan. 18, 1875-April 1, 1932; House 1917-April 1, 1932.

VEYSEY, Victor V. (R Calif.) April 14, 1915-−; House 1971-75.

VIBBARD, Chauncey (D N.Y.) Nov. 11, 1811-June 5, 1891; House 1861-63.

VICKERS, George (D Md.) Nov. 19, 1801-Oct. 8, 1879; Senate March 7, 1868-73.

VIDAL, Michel (R La.) Oct. 1, 1824-?; House July 18, 1868-69.

VIELE, Egbert Ludoricus (D N.Y.) June 17, 1825-April 22, 1902; House 1885-87.

VIGORITO, Joseph Phillip (D Pa.) Nov. 10, 1918-−; House 1965-77.

VILAS, William Freeman (D Wis.) July 9, 1840-Aug. 28, 1908; Senate 1891-97; Postmaster Gen. 1885-88; Secy. of the Interior 1888-89.

VINCENT, Beverly Mills (D Ky.) March 28, 1890-−; House 1937-45.

VINCENT, Bird J. (R Mich.) March 6, 1880-July 18 1931; House 1923-July 18, 1931.

VINCENT, Earl W. (R Iowa) March 27, 1886-May 22 1953; House June 4, 1928-29.

VINCENT, William Davis (P Kan.) Oct. 11, 1852-Feb. 28, 1922; House 1897-99.

VINING, John (− Del.) Dec. 23, 1758-Feb. 1802; House 1789-93; Senate 1793-Jan. 19, 1798; Cont. Cong 1784-86.

VINSON, Carl (D Ga.) Nov. 18, 1883-June 1, 1981 House Nov. 3, 1914-65.

VINSON, Frederick Moore (D Ky.) Jan. 22, 1890-Sept 8, 1953; House Jan. 12, 1924-29, 1931-May 12, 1938 Secy. of the Treasury 1945-46; Chief Justice United States 1946-53.

VINTON, Samuel Finley (W Ohio) Sept. 25, 1792-May 11, 1862; House 1823-37, 1843-51.

VISCLOSKY, Peter John (D Ind.) Aug. 13, 1949-− House 1985-−.

VIVIAN, Weston Edward (D Mich.) Oct. 25, 1924-− House 1965-67.

VOIGT, Edward (R Wis.) Dec. 1, 1873-Aug. 26, 1934 House 1917-27.

VOLK, Lester David (R N.Y.) Sept. 17, 1884-April 30 1962; House Nov. 2, 1920-23.

VOLKMER, Harold Lee (D Mo.) April 4, 1931-− House 1977-−.

VOLLMER, Henry (D Iowa) July 28, 1867-Aug. 24 1930; House Feb. 10, 1914-15.

VOLSTEAD, Andrew John (R Minn.) Oct. 31, 1860-Jan 20, 1947; House 1903-23.

VOORHEES, Charles Stewart (son of Daniel Wolsey Voorhees) (D Wash.) June 4, 1853-Dec. 26, 190 House (Terr. Del.) 1885-89.

VOORHEES, Daniel Wolsey (father of Charles Stewart Voorhees) (D Ind.) Sept. 26, 1827-April 9, 189 House 1861-Feb. 23, 1866, 1869-73; Senate Nov. 1877-97.

VOORHIS, Charles Henry (R N.J.) March 13, 183 April 15, 1896; House 1879-81.

VOORHIS, Horace Jerry (D Calif.) April 6, 1901-Sep 11, 1984; House 1937-47.

VORYS, John Martin (R Ohio) June 16, 1896-Aug. 2 1968; House 1939-59.

VOSE, Roger (F N.H.) Feb. 24, 1763-Oct. 26, 184 House 1813-17.

VREELAND, Albert Lincoln (R N.J.) July 2, 1901-May 3, 1975; House 1939-43.

VREELAND, Edward Butterfield (R N.Y.) Dec. 7, 1856-May 8, 1936; House Nov. 7, 1899-1913.

VROOM, Peter Dumont (D N.J.) Dec. 12, 1791-Nov. 18, 1873; House 1839-41; Gov. 1829-32, 1833-36.

VUCANOVICH, Barbara Farrell (R Nev.) June 22, 1921- —; House 1983- —.

VURSELL, Charles Wesley (R Ill.) Feb. 8, 1881-Sept. 21, 1974; House 1943-59.

WACHTER, Frank Charles (R Md.) Sept. 16, 1861-July 1, 1910; House 1899-1907.

WADDELL, Alfred Moore (D N.C.) Sept. 16, 1834-March 17, 1912; House 1871-79.

WADDILL, Edmund Jr. (R Va.) May 22, 1855-April 9, 1931; House April 12, 1890-91.

WADDILL, James Richard (D Mo.) Nov. 22, 1842-June 14, 1917; House 1879-81.

WADE, Benjamin Franklin (brother of Edward Wade) (R Ohio) Oct. 27, 1800-March 2, 1878; Senate March 15, 1851-69 (1851-57 Whig); Pres. pro tempore 1867-69.

WADE, Edward (brother of Benjamin Franklin Wade) (R Ohio) Nov. 22, 1802-Aug. 13, 1866; House 1853-61 (1853-55 Free-Soiler).

WADE, Martin Joseph (D Iowa) Oct. 20, 1861-April 16, 1931; House 1903-05.

WADE, William Henry (R Mo.) Nov. 3, 1835-Jan. 13, 1911; House 1885-91.

WADLEIGH, Bainbridge (R N.H.) Jan. 4, 1831-Jan. 24, 1891; Senate 1873-79.

WADSWORTH, James Wolcott (father of James Wolcott Wadsworth Jr., great-grandfather of James Wadsworth Symington) (R N.Y.) Oct. 12, 1846-Dec. 24, 1926; House Nov. 8, 1881-85, 1891-1907.

WADSWORTH, James Wolcott Jr. (son of James Wolcott Wadsworth, grandfather of James Wadsworth Symington, father-in-law of William Stuart Symington) (R N.Y.) Aug. 12, 1877-June 21, 1952; Senate 1915-27; House 1933-51.

WADSWORTH, Jeremiah (F Conn.) July 12, 1743-April 30, 1804; House 1789-95; Cont. Cong. 1787-88.

WADSWORTH, Peleg (— Mass.) May 6, 1748-Nov. 12, 1829; House 1793-1807.

WADSWORTH, William Henry (R Ky.) July 4, 1821-April 2, 1893; House 1861-65 (Unionist), 1885-87.

WAGENER, David Douglas (D Pa.) Oct. 11, 1792-Oct. 1, 1860; House 1833-41.

WAGGAMAN, George Augustus (NR La.) 1790-March 22, 1843; Senate Nov. 15, 1831-35.

WAGGONNER, Joseph David Jr. (D La.) Sept. 7, 1918- —; House Dec. 19, 1961-79.

WAGNER, Earl Thomas (D Ohio) April 27, 1908- —; House 1949-51.

WAGNER, Peter Joseph (W N.Y.) Aug. 14, 1795-Sept. 13, 1884; House 1839-41.

WAGNER, Robert Ferdinand (D N.Y.) June 8, 1877-May 4, 1953; Senate 1927-June 28, 1949.

WAGONER, George Chester Robinson (R Mo.) Sept. 3, 1863-April 27, 1946; House Feb. 26-March 3, 1903.

WAINWRIGHT, Jonathan Mayhew (R N.Y.) Dec. 10, 1864-June 3, 1945; House 1923-31.

WAINWRIGHT, Stuyvesant II (R N.Y.) March 16, 1921- —; House 1953-61.

WAIT, John Turner (R Conn.) Aug. 27, 1811-April 21, 1899; House April 12, 1876-87.

WAKEFIELD, James Beach (R Minn.) March 21, 1825-Aug. 25, 1910; House 1883-87.

WAKEMAN, Abram (W N.Y.) May 31, 1824-June 29, 1889; House 1855-57.

WAKEMAN, Seth (R N.Y.) Jan. 15, 1811-Jan. 4, 1880; House 1871-73.

WALBRIDGE, David Safford (R Mich.) July 30, 1802-June 15, 1868; House 1855-59.

WALBRIDGE, Henry Sanford (cousin of Hiram Walbridge) (W N.Y.) April 8, 1801-Jan. 27, 1869; House 1851-53.

WALBRIDGE, Hiram (cousin of Henry Sanford Walbridge) (D N.Y.) Feb. 2, 1821-Dec. 6, 1870; House 1853-55.

WALCOTT, Frederic Collin (R Conn.) Feb. 19, 1869-April 27, 1949; Senate 1929-35.

WALDEN, Hiram (D N.Y.) Aug. 21, 1800-July 21, 1880; House 1849-51.

WALDEN, Madison Miner (R Iowa) Oct. 6, 1836-July 24, 1891; House 1871-73.

WALDIE, Jerome Russell (D Calif.) Feb. 15, 1925- —; House June 7, 1966-75.

WALDO, George Ernest (R N.Y.) Jan. 11, 1851-June 16, 1942; House 1905-09.

WALDO, Loren Pinckney (D Conn.) Feb. 2, 1802-Sept. 8, 1881; House 1849-51.

WALDON, Alton R. Jr. (D N.Y.) Dec. 21, 1936- —; House July 29, 1986-87.

WALDOW, William Frederick (R N.Y.) Aug. 26, 1882-April 16, 1930; House 1917-19.

WALDRON, Alfred Marpole (R Pa.) Sept. 21, 1865-June 28, 1952; House 1933-35.

WALDRON, Henry (R Mich.) Oct. 11, 1819-Sept. 13, 1880; House 1855-61, 1871-77.

WALES, George Edward (— Vt.) May 13, 1792-Jan. 8, 1860; House 1825-29.

WALES, John (— Del.) July 31, 1783-Dec. 3, 1863; Senate Feb. 3, 1849-51.

WALGREN, Douglas (D Pa.) Dec. 28, 1940- —; House 1977- —.

WALKER, Amasa (R Mass.) May 4, 1799-Oct. 29, 1875; House Dec. 1, 1862-63.

WALKER, Benjamin (D N.Y.) 1753-Jan. 13, 1818; House 1801-03.

WALKER, Charles Christopher Brainerd (D N.Y.) June 27, 1824-Jan. 26, 1888; House 1875-77.

WALKER, David (brother of George Walker, grandfather of James David Walker) (— Ky.) ?-March 1, 1820; House 1817-March 1, 1820.

WALKER, E. S. Johnny (D N.M.) June 18, 1911- —; House 1965-69.

WALKER, Felix (D N.C.) July 19, 1753-1828; House 1817-23.

WALKER, Francis (brother of John Walker) (— Va.) June 22, 1764-March 1806; House 1793-95.

WALKER, Freeman (D Ga.) Oct. 25, 1780-Sept. 23, 1827; Senate Nov. 6, 1819-Aug. 6, 1821.

WALKER, George (brother of David Walker) (— Ky.) 1763-1819; Senate Aug. 30-Dec. 16, 1814.

WALKER, Gilbert Carlton (D Va.) Aug. 1, 1833-May 11, 1885; House 1875-79; Gov. 1869-74 (1870-77 Conservative).

WALKER, Isaac Pigeon (D Wis.) Nov. 2, 1815-March 29, 1872; Senate June 8, 1848-55.

WALKER, James Alexander (R Va.) Aug. 27, 1832-Oct. 21, 1901; House 1895-99.

WALKER, James David (grandson of David Walker, nephew of Finis Ewing McLean and John McLean of Ill., cousin of Wilkinson Call) (D Ark.) Dec. 13, 1830-Oct. 17, 1906; Senate 1879-85.

WALKER, James Peter (D Mo.) March 14, 1851-July 19, 1890; House 1887-July 19, 1890.

WALKER, John (brother of Francis Walker) (— Va.) Feb. 13, 1744-Dec. 2, 1809; Senate March 31-Nov. 9, 1790; Cont. Cong. 1780.

WALKER, John Randall (D Ga.) Feb. 23, 1874-?; House 1913-19.

WALKER, John Williams (father of Percy Walker) (D Ala.) Aug. 12, 1783-April 23, 1823; Senate Dec. 14, 1819-Dec. 12, 1822.

WALKER, Joseph Henry (R Mass.) Dec. 21, 1829-April 3, 1907; House 1889-99.

WALKER, Lewis Leavell (R Ky.) Feb. 15, 1873-June 30, 1944; House 1929-31.

WALKER, Percy (son of John Williams Walker) (AP Ala.) Dec. 1812-Dec. 31, 1880; House 1855-57.

WALKER, Prentiss Lafayette (R Miss.) Aug. 23, 1917- —; House 1965-67.

WALKER, Robert James (D Miss.) July 23, 1801-Nov. 11, 1869; Senate 1835-March 5, 1845; Secy. of the Treasury 1845-49; Gov. (Kan. Terr.) 1857.

WALKER, Robert Jarvis Cochran (R Pa.) Oct. 20, 1838-Dec. 19, 1903; House 1881-83.

WALKER, Robert Smith (R Pa.) Dec. 23, 1942- —; House 1977- —.

WALKER, Walter (D Colo.) April 3, 1883-Oct. 8, 1956; Senate Sept. 26-Dec. 6, 1932.

WALKER, William Adams (D N.Y.) June 5, 1805-Dec. 18, 1861; House 1853-55.

WALL, Garret Dorset (father of James Walter Wall) (D N.J.) March 10, 1783-Nov. 22, 1850; Senate 1835-41.

WALL, James Walter (son of Garret Dorset Wall) (D N.J.) May 26, 1820-June 9, 1872; Senate Jan. 14-March 3, 1863.

WALL, William (R N.Y.) March 20, 1800-April 20, 1872; House 1861-63.

WALLACE, Alexander Stuart (R S.C.) Dec. 30, 1810-June 27, 1893; House May 27, 1870-77.

WALLACE, Daniel (W S.C.) May 9, 1801-May 13, 1859; House June 12, 1848-53.

WALLACE, David (W Ind.) April 4, 1799-Sept. 4, 1859; House 1841-43; Gov. 1837-40.

WALLACE, James M. (— Pa.) 1750-Dec. 17, 1823; House Oct. 10, 1815-21.

WALLACE, John Winfield (R Pa.) Dec. 20, 1818-June 24, 1889; House 1861-63, 1875-77.

WALLACE, Jonathan Hasson (D Ohio) Oct. 31, 1824-Oct. 28, 1892; House May 27, 1884-85.

WALLACE, Nathaniel Dick (D La.) Oct. 27, 1845-July 16, 1894; House Dec. 9, 1886-87.

WALLACE, Robert Minor (D Ark.) Aug. 6, 1856-Nov. 9, 1942; House 1903-11.

WALLACE, Rodney (R Mass.) Dec. 21, 1823-Feb. 27, 1903; House 1889-91.

WALLACE, William Andrew (D Pa.) Nov. 28, 1827-May 22, 1896; Senate 1875-81.

WALLACE, William Copeland (R N.Y.) May 21, 1856-Sept. 4, 1901; House 1889-91.

WALLACE, William Henson (R Idaho) July 19, 1811-Feb. 7, 1879; House (Terr. Del. Wash.) 1861-63, Feb. 1, 1864-65; Gov. (Idaho Terr.) 1863.

WALLEY, Samuel Hurd (W Mass.) Aug. 31, 1805-Aug. 27, 1877; House 1853-55.

WALLGREN, Monrad Charles (D Wash.) April 17, 1891-Sept. 18, 1961; House 1933-Dec. 19, 1940; Senate Dec. 19, 1940-Jan. 9, 1945; Gov. 1945-49.

WALLHAUSER, George Marvin (R N.J.) Feb. 10, 1900-—; House 1959-65.

WALLIN, Samuel (R N.Y.) July 31, 1856-Dec. 1, 1917; House 1913-15.

WALLING, Ansel Tracy (D Ohio) Jan. 10, 1824-June 22, 1896; House 1875-77.

WALLOP, Malcolm (R Wyo.) Feb. 27, 1933-—; Senate 1977-—.

WALLS, Josiah Thomas (R Fla.) Dec. 30, 1842-May 5, 1905; House 1871-Jan. 29, 1873, 1873-April 19, 1876.

WALN, Robert (F Pa.) Feb. 22, 1765-Jan. 24, 1836; House Dec. 3, 1798-1801.

WALSH, Allan Bartholomew (D N.J.) Aug. 29, 1874-Aug. 5, 1953; House 1913-15.

WALSH, Arthur (D N.J.) Feb. 26, 1896-Dec. 13, 1947; Senate Nov. 26, 1943-Dec. 7, 1944.

WALSH, David Ignatius (D Mass.) Nov. 11, 1872-June 11, 1947; Senate 1919-25, Dec. 6, 1926-47; Gov. 1914-16.

WALSH, James Joseph (D N.Y.) May 22, 1858-May 8, 1909; House 1895-June 2, 1896.

WALSH, John Richard (D Ind.) May 22, 1913-—; House 1949-51.

WALSH, Joseph (R Mass.) Dec. 16, 1875-Jan. 13, 1946; House 1915-Aug. 2, 1922.

WALSH, Michael (D N.Y.) March 8, 1810-March 18, 1859; House 1853-55.

WALSH, Patrick (D Ga.) Jan. 1, 1840-March 19, 1899; Senate April 2, 1894-95.

WALSH, Thomas James (D Mont.) June 12, 1859-March 2, 1933; Senate 1913-March 2, 1933.

WALSH, Thomas Yates (W Md.) 1809-Jan. 20, 1865; House 1851-53.

WALSH, William (D Md.) May 11, 1828-May 17, 1892; House 1875-79.

WALSH, William Francis (R N.Y.) July 11, 1912-—; House 1973-79.

WALTER, Francis Eugene (D Pa.) May 26, 1894-May 31, 1963; House 1933-May 31, 1963.

WALTERS, Anderson Howell (R Pa.) May 18, 1862-Dec. 7, 1927; House 1913-15, 1919-23, 1925-27.

WALTERS, Herbert Sanford (D Tenn.) Nov. 17, 1891-Aug. 17, 1973; Senate Aug. 20, 1963-Nov. 3, 1964.

WALTHALL, Edward Cary (D Miss.) April 4, 1831-April 21, 1898; Senate March 9, 1885-Jan. 24, 1894, 1895-April 21, 1898.

WALTON, Charles Wesley (R Maine) Dec. 9, 1819-Jan. 24, 1900; House 1861-May 26, 1862.

WALTON, Eliakim Persons (R Vt.) Feb. 17, 1812-Dec. 19, 1890; House 1857-63.

WALTON, George (cousin of Matthew Walton) (— Ga.) 1749-Feb. 2, 1804; Senate Nov. 16, 1795-Feb. 20, 1796; Cont. Cong. 1776-78, 1780-81, 1787-88; Gov. 1789 (Democratic Republican).

WALTON, Matthew (cousin of George Walton) (D Ky.) ?-Jan. 18, 1819; House 1803-07.

WALTON, William Bell (D N.M.) Jan. 23, 1871-April 14, 1939; House 1917-19.

WALWORTH, Reuben Hyde (D N.Y.) Oct. 26, 1788-Nov. 27, 1867; House 1821-23.

WAMPLER, Fred (D Ind.) Oct. 15, 1909-—; House 1959-61.

WAMPLER, William Creed (R Va.) April 21, 1926-—; House 1953-55, 1967-83.

WANGER, Irving Price (R Pa.) March 5, 1852-Jan. 14, 1940; House 1893-1911.

WARBURTON, Herbert Birchby (R Del.) Sept. 21, 1916-July 30, 1983; House 1953-55.

WARBURTON, Stanton (R Wash.) April 13, 1865-Dec. 24, 1926; House 1911-13.

WARD, Aaron (uncle of Elijah Ward) (D N.Y.) July 5, 1790-March 2, 1867; House 1825-29, 1831-37, 1841-43.

WARD, Andrew Harrison (D Ky.) Jan. 3, 1815-April 16, 1904; House Dec. 3, 1866-67.

WARD, Artemas (father of Artemas Ward Jr.) (F Mass.) Nov. 26, 1727-Oct. 28, 1800; House 1791-95; Cont. Cong. 1780-82.

WARD, Artemas Jr. (son of Artemas Ward) (F Mass.) Jan. 9, 1762-Oct. 7, 1847; House 1813-17.

WARD, Charles Bonnell (R N.Y.) April 27, 1879-May 27, 1946; House 1915-25.

WARD, David Jenkins (D Md.) Sept. 17, 1871-Feb. 18, 1961; House June 6, 1939-45.

WARD, Elijah (nephew of Aaron Ward) (D N.Y.) Sept. 16, 1816-Feb. 7, 1882; House 1857-59, 1861-65, 1875-77.

WARD, Hallett Sydney (D N.C.) Aug. 31, 1870-March 31, 1956; House 1921-25.

WARD, Hamilton (R N.Y.) July 3, 1829-Dec. 28, 1898; House 1865-71.

WARD, James Hugh (D Ill.) Nov. 30, 1853-Aug. 15, 1916; House 1885-87.

WARD, Jasper Delos (R Ill.) Feb. 1, 1829-Aug. 6, 1902; House 1873-75.

WARD, Jonathan (D N.Y.) Sept. 21, 1768-Sept. 28, 1842; House 1815-17.

WARD, Marcus Lawrence (R N.J.) Nov. 9, 1812-April 25, 1884; House 1873-75; Gov. 1866-69; Chrmn. Rep. Nat. Comm. 1866-68.

WARD, Matthias (D Texas) Oct. 13, 1805-Oct. 5, 1861; Senate Sept. 27, 1858-Dec. 5, 1859.

WARD, Thomas (D N.J.) about 1759-March 4, 1842; House 1813-17.

WARD, Thomas Bayless (D Ind.) April 27, 1835-Jan. 1, 1892; House 1883-87.

WARD, William (R Pa.) Jan. 1, 1837-Feb. 27, 1895; House 1877-83.

WARD, Wiliam Lukens (R N.Y.) Sept. 2, 1856-July 16, 1933; House 1897-99.

WARD, William Thomas (W Ky.) Aug. 9, 1808-Oct. 12, 1878; House 1851-53.

WARDWELL, Daniel (R N.Y.) May 28, 1791-March 27, 1878; House 1831-37.

WARE, John Haines III (R Pa.) Aug. 29, 1908- —; House Nov. 3, 1970-1975.

WARE, Nicholas (— Ga.) 1769-Sept. 7, 1824; Senate Nov. 10, 1821-Sept. 7, 1824.

WARE, Orie Solomon (D Ky.) May 11, 1882-Dec. 16, 1974; House 1927-29.

WARFIELD, Henry Ridgely (F Md.) Sept. 14, 1774-March 18, 1839; House 1819-25.

WARNER, Adoniram Judson (D Ohio) Jan. 13, 1834-Aug. 12, 1910; House 1879-81, 1883-87.

WARNER, Hiram (D Ga.) Oct. 29, 1802-June 30, 1881; House 1855-57.

WARNER, John De Witt (D N.Y.) Oct. 30, 1851-May 27, 1925; House 1891-95.

WARNER, John William (R Va.) Feb. 18, 1927- —; Senate Jan. 2, 1979- —.

WARNER, Levi (brother of Samuel Larkin Warner) (D Conn.) Oct. 10, 1831-April 12, 1911; House Dec. 4, 1876-79.

WARNER, Richard (D Tenn.) Sept. 19, 1835-March 4, 1915; House 1881-85.

WARNER, Samuel Larkin (brother of Levi Warner) (R Conn.) June 14, 1828-Feb. 6, 1893; House 1865-67.

WARNER, Vespasian (R Ill.) April 23, 1842-March 31, 1925; House 1895-1905.

WARNER, Willard (R Ala.) Sept. 4, 1826-Nov. 23, 1906; Senate July 13, 1868-71.

WARNER, William (R Mo.) June 11, 1840-Oct. 4, 1916; House 1885-89; Senate March 18, 1905-11.

WARNOCK, William Robert (R Ohio) Aug. 29, 1838-July 30, 1918; House 1901-05.

WARREN, Cornelius (W N.Y.) March 15, 1790-July 28, 1849; House 1847-49.

WARREN, Edward Allen (D Ark.) May 2, 1818-July 2, 1875; House 1853-55, 1857-59.

WARREN, Francis Emroy (R Wyo.) June 20, 1844-Nov. 24, 1929; Senate Nov. 18, 1890-93, 1895-Nov. 24, 1929; Gov. 1885-86, 1889-90 (Wyo. Terr.), Sept. 11-Nov. 24, 1890.

WARREN, Joseph Mabbett (D N.Y.) Jan. 28, 1813-Sept. 9, 1896; House 1871-73.

WARREN, Lindsay Carter (D N.C.) Dec. 16, 1889-Dec. 28, 1976; House 1925-Oct. 31, 1940.

WARREN, Lott (W Ga.) Oct. 30, 1797-June 17, 1861; House 1839-43.

WARREN, William Wirt (D Mass.) Feb. 27, 1834-May 2, 1880; House 1875-77.

WARWICK, John George (D Ohio) Dec. 23, 1830-Aug. 14, 1892; House 1891-Aug. 14, 1892.

WASHBURN, Cadwallader Colden (brother of Israel Washburn Jr., Elihu Benjamin Washburne and William Drew Washburn) (R Wis.) April 22, 1818-May 15, 1882; House 1855-61, 1867-71; Gov. 1872-74.

WASHBURN, Charles Grenfill (R Mass.) Jan. 28, 1857-May 25, 1928; House Dec. 18, 1906-11.

WASHBURN, Henry Dana (R Ind.) March 28, 1832-Jan. 26, 1871; House Feb. 23, 1866-69.

WASHBURN, Israel Jr. (brother of Elihu Benjamin Washburne, Cadwallader Colden Washburn and William Drew Washburn) (R Maine) June 6, 1813-May 12, 1883; House 1851-Jan. 1, 1861 (1851-55 Whig); Gov. 1861-63.

WASHBURN, William Barrett (R Mass.) Jan. 31, 1820-Oct. 5, 1887; House 1863-Dec. 5, 1871; Senate April 17, 1874-75; Gov. 1872-74.

WASHBURN, William Drew (brother of Israel Washburn Jr., Elihu Benjamin Washburne and Cadwallader Colden Washburn) (R Minn.) Jan. 14, 1831-July 29, 1912; House 1879-85; Senate 1889-95.

WASHBURNE, Elihu Benjamin (brother of Israel Washburn Jr., Cadwallader Colden Washburn and William Drew Washburn) (W Ill.) Sept. 23, 1816-Oct. 22, 1887; House 1853-March 6, 1869; Secy. of State 1869.

WASHINGTON, George Corbin (grandnephew of Pres. George Washington) (— Md.) Aug. 20, 1789-July 17, 1854; House 1827-33, 1835-37.

WASHINGTON, Harold (D Ill.) April 15, 1922-—; House 1981-April 30, 1983.

WASHINGTON, Joseph Edwin (D Tenn.) Nov. 10, 1851-Aug. 28, 1915; House 1887-97.

WASHINGTON, William Henry (W N.C.) Feb. 7, 1813-Aug. 12, 1860; House 1841-43.

WASIELEWSKI, Thaddeus Francis Boleslaw (D Wis.) Dec. 2, 1904-April 25, 1976; House 1941-47.

WASKEY, Frank Hinman (D Alaska) April 20, 1875-Jan. 18, 1964; House (Terr. Del.) Aug. 14, 1906-07.

WASON, Edward Hills (R N.H.) Sept. 2, 1865-Feb. 6, 1941; House 1915-33.

WATERMAN, Charles Winfield (R Colo.) Nov. 2, 1861-Aug. 27, 1932; Senate 1927-Aug. 27, 1932.

WATERS, Russell Judson (R Calif.) June 6, 1843-Sept. 25, 1911; House 1899-1901.

WATKINS, Albert Galiton (D Tenn.) May 5, 1818-Nov. 9, 1895; House 1849-53 (Whig), 1855-59.

WATKINS, Arthur Vivian (R Utah) Dec. 18, 1886-Sept. 1, 1973; Senate 1947-59.

WATKINS, Elton (D Ore.) July 6, 1881-June 24, 1956; House 1923-25.

WATKINS, George Robert (R Pa.) May 21, 1902-Aug. 7, 1970; House 1965-Aug. 7, 1970.

WATKINS, John Thomas (D La.) Jan. 15, 1854-April 25, 1925; House 1905-21.

WATKINS, Wesley Wade (D Okla.) Dec. 15, 1938-—; House 1977-—.

WATMOUGH, John Goddard (— Pa.) Dec. 6, 1793-Nov. 27, 1861; House 1831-35.

WATRES, Laurence Hawley (R Pa.) July 18, 1882-Feb. 6, 1964; House 1923-31.

WATSON, Albert William (R S.C.) Aug. 30, 1922-—; House 1963-Feb. 1, 1965 (Democrat), June 15, 1965-71.

WATSON, Clarence Wayland (D W.Va.) May 8, 1864-May 24, 1940; Senate Feb. 1, 1911-13.

WATSON, Cooper Kinderdine (FS Ohio) June 18, 1810-May 20, 1880; House 1855-57.

WATSON, David Kemper (R Ohio) June 8, 1849-Sept. 28, 1918; House 1895-97.

WATSON, Henry Winfield (R Pa.) June 24, 1856-Aug. 27, 1933; House 1915-Aug. 27, 1933.

WATSON, James (D N.Y.) April 6, 1750-May 15, 1806; Senate Aug. 17, 1798-March 19, 1800.

WATSON, James Eli (R Ind.) Nov. 2, 1863-July 29, 1948; House 1895-97, 1899-1909; Senate Nov. 8, 1916-33; Senate majority leader 1929-33.

WATSON, Lewis Findlay (R Pa.) April 14, 1819-Aug. 25, 1890; House 1877-79, 1881-83, 1889-Aug. 25, 1890.

WATSON, Thomas Edward (D Ga.) Sept. 5, 1856-Sept. 26, 1922; House 1891-93 (Populist); Senate 1921-Sept. 26, 1922.

WATSON, Walter Allen (D Va.) Nov. 25, 1867-Dec. 24, 1919; House 1913-Dec. 24, 1919.

WATTERSON, Harvey Magee (father of Henry Watterson) (D Tenn.) Nov. 23, 1811-Oct. 11, 1891; House 1839-43.

WATTERSON, Henry (son of Harvey Magee Watterson, nephew of Stanley Matthews) (D Ky.) Feb. 16, 1840-Dec. 22, 1921; House Aug. 12, 1876-77.

WATTS, John (− N.Y.) Aug. 27, 1749-Sept. 3, 1836; House 1793-95.

WATTS, John Clarence (D Ky.) July 9, 1902-Sept. 24, 1971; House April 14, 1951-Sept. 24, 1971.

WATTS, John Sebrie (R N.M.) Jan. 19, 1816-June 11, 1876; House (Terr. Del.) 1861-63.

WAUGH, Daniel Webster (R Ind.) March 7, 1842-March 14, 1921; House 1891-95.

WAXMAN, Henry Arnold (D Calif.) Sept. 12, 1939-−; House 1975-−.

WAYNE, Anthony (father of Isaac Wayne) (− Ga.) Jan. 1, 1745-Dec. 15, 1796; House 1791-March 21, 1792.

WAYNE, Isaac (son of Anthony Wayne) (F Pa.) 1772-Oct. 25, 1852; House 1823-25.

WAYNE, James Moore (JD Ga.) 1790-July 5, 1867; House 1829-Jan. 13, 1835; Assoc. Justice Supreme Court 1835-67.

WEADOCK, Thomas Addis Emmet (D Mich.) Jan. 1, 1850-Nov. 18, 1938; House 1891-95.

WEAKLEY, Robert (N Tenn.) July 20, 1764-Feb. 4, 1845; House 1809-11.

WEARIN, Otha Donner (D Iowa) Jan. 10, 1903-−; House 1933-39.

WEATHERFORD, Zadoc Lorenzo (D Ala.) Feb. 4, 1888-−; House Nov. 5, 1940-41.

WEAVER, Archibald Jerard (grandfather of Phillip Hart Weaver) (R Neb.) April 15, 1844-April 18, 1887; House 1883-87.

WEAVER, Claude (D Okla.) March 19, 1867-May 19, 1954; House 1913-15.

WEAVER, James Baird (D/G-Lab. Iowa) June 12, 1833-Feb. 6, 1912; House 1879-81 (Greenbacker), 1885-89 (1885-87 Greenbacker).

WEAVER, James Dorman (R Pa.) Sept. 27, 1920-−; House 1963-65.

WEAVER, James Howard (D Ore.) Aug. 8, 1927-−; House 1975-87.

WEAVER, Phillip Hart (grandson of Archibald Jerard Weaver) (R Neb.) April 9, 1919-−; House 1955-63.

WEAVER, Walter Lowrie (R Ohio) April 1, 1851-May 26, 1909; House 1897-1901.

WEAVER, Zebulon (D N.C.) May 12, 1872-Oct. 29, 1948; House 1917-March 1, 1919, March 4, 1919-29, 1931-47.

WEBB, Edwin Yates (D N.C.) May 23, 1872-Feb. 7, 1955; House 1903-Nov. 10, 1919.

WEBB, William Robert (grandson of Richard Stanford) (D Tenn.) Nov. 11, 1842-Dec. 19, 1926; Senate Jan. 24-March 3, 1913.

WEBBER, Amos Richard (R Ohio) Jan. 21, 1852-Feb. 25, 1948; House Nov. 8, 1904-07.

WEBBER, George Washington (R Mich.) Nov. 25, 1825-Jan. 15, 1900; House 1881-83.

WEBER, Ed (R Ohio) July 26, 1931-−; House 1981-83.

WEBER, John Baptiste (R N.Y.) Sept. 21, 1842-Dec. 18, 1926; House 1885-89.

WEBER, Vin (R Minn.) July 24, 1952-−; House 1981-−.

WEBSTER, Daniel (W Mass.) Jan. 18, 1782-Oct. 24, 1852; House 1813-17 (Federalist N.H.), 1823-May 30, 1827 (Federalist); Senate May 30, 1827-Feb. 22, 1841 (Federalist), 1845-July 22, 1850; Secy. of State 1841-43, 1850-52.

WEBSTER, Edwin Hanson (R Md.) March 31, 1829-April 24, 1893; House 1859-July 1865.

WEBSTER, John Stanley (R Wash.) Feb. 22, 1877-Dec. 24, 1962; House 1919-May 8, 1923.

WEBSTER, Taylor (JD Ohio) Oct. 1, 1800-April 27, 1876; House 1833-39.

WEDEMEYER, William Walter (R Mich.) March 22, 1873-Jan. 2, 1913; House 1911-Jan. 2, 1913.

WEEKS, Edgar (cousin of John Wingate Weeks of Mass.) (R Mich.) Aug. 3, 1839-Dec. 17, 1904; House 1899-1903.

WEEKS, John Eliakim (R Vt.) June 14, 1853-Sept. 10, 1949; House 1931-33; Gov. 1927-31.

WEEKS, John Wingate (granduncle of John Wingate Weeks, below) (− N.H.) March 31, 1781-April 3, 1853; House 1829-33.

WEEKS, John Wingate (father of Sinclair Weeks, cousin of Edgar Weeks, grandnephew of John Wingate Weeks, above) (R Mass.) April 11, 1860-July 12, 1926; House 1905-March 4, 1913; Senate March 4, 1913-19; Secy. of War 1921-25.

WEEKS, Joseph (grandfather of Joseph Weeks Babcock) (D N.H.) Feb. 13, 1773-Aug. 4, 1845; House 1835-39.

WEEKS, Sinclair (son of John Wingate Weeks of Mass.) (R Mass.) June 15, 1893-Feb. 7, 1972; Senate Feb. 8-Dec. 19, 1944; Secy. of Commerce 1953-58.

WEEMS, Capell Lane (R Ohio) July 7, 1860-Jan. 5, 1913; House Nov. 3, 1903-09.

WEEMS, John Crompton (D Md.) 1778-Jan. 20, 1862; House Feb. 1, 1826-29.

WEFALD, Knud (FL Minn.) Nov. 3, 1869-Oct. 25, 1936; House 1923-27.

WEICHEL, Alvin F. (R Ohio) Sept. 11, 1891-Nov. 27, 1956; House 1943-55.

WEICKER, Lowell Palmer Jr. (R Conn.) May 16, 1931- –; House 1969-71; Senate 1971- –.

WEIDEMAN, Carl May (D Mich.) March 5, 1898-March 5, 1972; House 1933-35.

WEIGHTMAN, Richard Hanson (D N.M.) Dec. 28, 1816-Aug. 10, 1861; House (Terr. Del.) 1851-53.

WEIS, Jessica McCullough (R N.Y.) July 8, 1901-May 1, 1963; House 1959-63.

WEISS, Samuel Arthur (D Pa.) April 15, 1902-Feb. 1, 1977; House 1941-Jan. 7, 1946.

WEISS, Theodore S. (D N.Y.) Sept. 17, 1927- –; House 1977- –.

WEISSE, Charles Herman (D Wis.) Oct. 24, 1866-Oct. 8, 1919; House 1903-11.

WELBORN, John (R Mo.) Nov. 20, 1857-Oct. 27, 1907; House 1905-07.

WELCH, Adonijah Strong (R Fla.) April 12, 1821-March 14, 1889; Senate June 25, 1868-69.

WELCH, Frank (R Neb.) Feb. 10, 1835-Sept. 4, 1878; House 1877-Sept. 4, 1878.

WELCH, John (W Ohio) Oct. 28, 1805-Aug. 5, 1891; House 1851-53.

WELCH, Philip James (D Mo.) April 4, 1895-April 26, 1963; House 1949-53.

WELCH, Richard Joseph (R Calif.) Feb. 13, 1869-Sept. 10, 1949; House Aug. 31, 1926-Sept. 10, 1949.

WELCH, William Wickham (AP Conn.) Dec. 10, 1818-July 30, 1892; House 1855-57.

WELDON, W. Curtis (R Pa.) July 22, 1947- –; House 1987- –.

WELKER, Herman (R Idaho) Dec. 11, 1906-Oct. 30, 1957; Senate 1951-57.

WELKER, Martin (R Ohio) April 25, 1819-March 15, 1902; House 1865-71.

WELLBORN, Marshall Johnson (D Ga.) May 29, 1808-Oct. 16, 1874; House 1849-51.

WELLBORN, Olin (D Texas) June 18, 1843-Dec. 6, 1921; House 1879-87.

WELLER, John B. (UD Calif.) Feb. 22, 1812-Aug. 17, 1875; House 1839-45 (Democrat Ohio); Senate Jan. 30, 1852-57; Gov. 1858-60 (Democrat).

WELLER, Luman Hamlin (Nat.G/D Iowa) Aug. 24, 1833-March 2, 1914; House 1883-85.

WELLER, Ovington Eugene (R Md.) Jan. 23, 1862-Jan. 5, 1947; Senate 1921-27.

WELLER, Royal Hurlburt (D N.Y.) July 2, 1881-March 1, 1929; House 1923-March 1, 1929.

WELLING, Milton Holmes (D Utah) Jan. 25, 1876-May 28, 1947; House 1917-21.

WELLINGTON, George Louis (R Md.) Jan. 28, 1852-March 20, 1927; House 1895-97; Senate 1897-1903.

WELLS, Alfred (R N.Y.) May 27, 1814-July 18, 1867; House 1859-61.

WELLS, Daniel Jr. (D Wis.) July 16, 1808-March 18, 1902; House 1853-57.

WELLS, Erastus (D Mo.) Dec. 2, 1823-Oct. 2, 1893; House 1869-77, 1879-81.

WELLS, Guilford Wiley (R Miss.) Feb. 14, 1840-March 21, 1909; House 1875-77.

WELLS, John (W N.Y.) July 1, 1817-May 30, 1877; House 1851-53.

WELLS, John Sullivan (– N.H.) Oct. 18, 1803-Aug. 1, 1860; Senate Jan. 16-March 3, 1855.

WELLS, Owen Augustine (D Wis.) Feb. 4, 1844-Jan. 29, 1935; House 1893-95.

WELLS, William Hill (– Del.) Jan. 7, 1769-March 11, 1829; Senate Jan. 17, 1799-Nov. 6, 1804, May 28, 1813-17.

WELSH, George Austin (R Pa.) Aug. 9, 1878-Oct. 22, 1970; House 1923-May 31, 1932.

WELTNER, Charles Longstreet (D Ga.) Dec. 17, 1927- –; House 1963-67.

WELTY, Benjamin Franklin (D Ohio) Aug. 9, 1870-Oct. 23, 1962; House 1917-21.

WEMPLE, Edward (D N.Y.) Oct. 23, 1843-Dec. 18, 1920; House 1883-85.

WENDOVER, Peter Hercules (D N.Y.) Aug. 1, 1768-Sept. 24, 1834; House 1815-21.

WENE, Elmer H. (D N.J.) May 1, 1892-Jan. 25, 1957; House 1937-39, 1941-45.

WENTWORTH, John (R Ill.) March 5, 1815-Oct. 16, 1888; House 1843-51 (Democrat), 1853-55 (Democrat), 1865-67.

WENTWORTH, Tappan (W Mass.) Feb. 24, 1802-June 12, 1875; House 1853-55.

WERDEL, Thomas Harold (R Calif.) Sept. 13, 1905-Sept. 30, 1966; House 1949-53.

WERNER, Theodore B. (D S.D.) June 2, 1892- –; House 1933-37.

WERTZ, George M. (R Pa.) July 19, 1856-Nov. 19, 1928; House 1923-25.

WEST, Charles Franklin (D Ohio) Jan. 12, 1895-Dec. 27, 1955; House 1931-35.

WEST, George (R N.Y.) Feb. 17, 1823-Sept. 20, 1901; House 1881-83, 1885-89.

WEST, Joseph Rodman (R La.) Sept. 19, 1822-Oct. 31, 1898; Senate 1871-77.

WEST, Milton Horace (D Texas) June 30, 1888-Oct. 28, 1948; House April 22, 1933-Oct. 28, 1948.

WEST, William Stanley (D Ga.) Aug. 23, 1849-Dec. 22, 1914; Senate March 2-Nov. 3, 1914.

WESTBROOK, John (D Pa.) Jan. 9, 1789-Oct. 8, 1852; House 1841-43.

WESTBROOK, Theodoric Romeyn (D N.Y.) Nov. 20, 1821-Oct. 6, 1885; House 1853-55.

WESTCOTT, James Diament Jr. (D Fla.) May 10, 1802-Jan. 19, 1880; Senate July 1, 1845-49.

WESTERLO, Rensselaer (F N.Y.) April 29, 1776-April 18, 1851; House 1817-19.

WESTLAND, Aldred John "Jack" (R Wash.) Dec. 14, 1904-Nov. 3, 1982; House 1953-65.

WETHERED, John (D Md.) May 8, 1809-Feb. 15, 1888; House 1843-45.

WETMORE, George Peabody (R R.I.) Aug. 2, 1846-Sept. 11, 1921; Senate 1895-1907, Jan. 22, 1908-13; Gov. 1885-87.

WEVER, John Madison (R N.Y.) Feb. 24, 1847-Sept. 27, 1914; House 1891-95.

WEYMOUTH, George Warren (R Mass.) Aug. 25, 1850 Sept. 7, 1910; House 1897-1901.

WHALEN, Charles William Jr. (R Ohio) July 31, 1920 –; House 1967-79.

WHALEY, Kellian Van Rensalear (R W.Va.) May 6 1821-May 20, 1876; House 1861-63 (Va.), Dec. 7 1863-67.

WHALEY, Richard Smith (D S.C.) July 15, 1874-Nov. 8 1951; House April 29, 1913-21.

WHALLEY, John Irving (R Pa.) Sept. 14, 1902-March 8, 1980; House Nov. 8, 1960-73.

WHALLON, Reuben (JD N.Y.) Dec. 7, 1776-April 15 1843; House 1833-35.

WHARTON, Charles Stuart (R Ill.) April 22, 1875-Sep 4, 1939; House 1905-07.

WHARTON, James Ernest (R N.Y.) Oct. 4, 1899- – House 1951-65.

WHARTON, Jesse (grandfather of Wharton Jackson Green) (– Tenn.) July 29, 1782-July 22, 1833; House 1807-09; Senate March 17, 1814-Oct. 10, 1815.

WHEAT, Alan D. (D Mo.) Oct. 16, 1951- –; House 1983 –.

WHEAT, William Howard (R Ill.) Feb. 19, 1879-Jan. 16 1944; House 1939-Jan. 16, 1944.

WHEATON, Horace (D N.Y.) Feb. 24, 1803-June 23 1882; House 1843-47.

WHEATON, Laban (F Mass.) March 13, 1754-March 23, 1846; House 1809-17.

WHEELER, Burton Kendall (D Mont.) Feb. 27, 1882 Jan. 6, 1975; Senate 1923-47.

WHEELER, Charles Kennedy (D Ky.) April 18, 1863 June 15, 1933; House 1897-1903.

WHEELER, Ezra (D Wis.) Dec. 23, 1820-Sept. 19, 1871 House 1863-65.

WHEELER, Frank Willis (R Mich.) March 2, 1853-Aug 9, 1921; House 1889-91.

WHEELER, Grattan Henry (– N.Y.) Aug. 25, 1783 March 11, 1852; House 1831-33.

WHEELER, Hamilton Kinkaid (R Ill.) Aug. 5, 1848-Jul 19, 1918; House 1893-95.

WHEELER, Harrison H. (D Mich.) March 22, 1839-July 28, 1896; House 1891-93.

WHEELER, John (D N.Y.) Feb. 11, 1823-April 1, 1906 House 1853-57.

WHEELER, Joseph (D Ala.) Sept. 10, 1836-Jan. 25, 1906; House 1881-June 3, 1882, Jan. 15-March 3, 1883, 1885-April 20, 1900.

WHEELER, Loren Edgar (R Ill.) Oct. 7, 1862-Jan. 8, 1932; House 1915-23, 1925-27.

WHEELER, Nelson Platt (R Pa.) Nov. 4, 1841-March 3, 1920; House 1907-11.

WHEELER, William Almon (R N.Y.) June 30, 1819-June 4, 1887; House 1861-63, 1869-77; Vice President 1877-81.

WHEELER, William McDonald (D Ga.) July 11, 1915--; House 1947-55.

WHELCHEL, Benjamin Frank (D Ga.) Dec. 16, 1895-May 11, 1954; House 1935-45.

WHERRY, Kenneth Spicer (R Neb.) Feb. 28, 1892-Nov. 29, 1951; Senate 1943-Nov. 29, 1951.

WHIPPLE, Thomas Jr. (– N.H.) 1787-Jan. 23, 1835; House 1821-29.

WHITACRE, John Jefferson (D Ohio) Dec. 28, 1860-Dec. 2, 1938; House 1911-15.

WHITAKER, John Albert (grandson of Addison Davis James) (D Ky.) Oct. 31, 1901-Dec. 15, 1951; House April 17, 1948-Dec. 15, 1951.

WHITCOMB, James (D Ind.) Dec. 1, 1795-Oct. 4, 1852; Senate 1849-Oct. 4, 1852; Gov. 1843-49.

WHITE, Addison (cousin of John White) (W Ky.) May 1, 1824-Feb. 4, 1909; House 1851-53.

WHITE, Albert Smith (R Ind.) Oct. 24, 1803-Sept. 24, 1864; House 1837-39 (Whig), 1861-63; Senate 1839-45 (Whig).

WHITE, Alexander (F Va.) 1738-Sept. 19, 1804; House 1789-93.

WHITE, Alexander (R Ala.) Oct. 16, 1816-Dec. 13, 1893; House 1851-53 (Union Whig), 1873-75.

WHITE, Alexander Colwell (R Pa.) Dec. 12, 1833-June 11, 1906; House 1885-87.

WHITE, Allison (D Pa.) Dec. 21, 1816-April 5, 1886; House 1857-59.

WHITE, Bartow (– N.Y.) Nov. 7, 1776-Dec. 12, 1862; House 1825-27.

WHITE, Benjamin (D Maine) May 13, 1790-June 7, 1860; House 1843-45.

WHITE, Campbell Patrick (JD N.Y.) Nov. 30, 1787-Feb. 12, 1859; House 1829-35.

WHITE, Cecil Fielding (D Calif.) Dec. 12, 1900--; House 1949-51.

WHITE, Chilton Allen (D Ohio) Feb. 6, 1826-Dec. 7, 1900; House 1861-65.

WHITE, Compton Ignatius (father of Compton Ignatius White Jr.) (D Idaho) July 31, 1877-March 31, 1956; House 1933-47, 1949-51.

WHITE, Compton Ignatius Jr. (son of Compton Ignatius White) (D Idaho) Dec. 19, 1920--; House 1963-67.

WHITE, David (– Ky.) 1785-Oct. 19, 1834; House 1823-25.

WHITE, Dudley Allen (R Ohio) Jan. 3, 1901-Oct. 14, 1957; House 1937-41.

WHITE, Edward Douglas Sr. (son of James White, father of Edward Douglass White) (W La.) March 1795-April 18, 1847; House 1829-Nov. 15, 1834, 1839-43; Gov. 1835-39.

WHITE, Edward Douglass (grandson of James White, son of Edward Douglas White Sr.) (D La.) Nov. 3, 1845-May 19, 1921; Senate 1891-March 12, 1894; Assoc. Justice Supreme Court 1894-1910; Chief Justice United States 1910-21.

WHITE, Francis (– Va.) ?-Nov. 1826; House 1813-15.

WHITE, Francis Shelley "Frank" (D Ala.) March 13, 1847-Aug. 1, 1922; Senate May 11, 1914-15.

WHITE, Frederick Edward (D Iowa) Jan. 19, 1844-Jan. 14, 1920; House 1891-93.

WHITE, George (D Ohio) Aug. 21, 1872-Dec. 15, 1953; House 1911-15, 1917-19; Chrmn. Dem. Nat. Comm. 1920-21; Gov. 1931-35.

WHITE, George Elon (R Ill.) March 7, 1848-May 17, 1935; House 1895-99.

WHITE, George Henry (R N.C.) Dec. 18, 1852-Dec. 28, 1918; House 1897-1901.

WHITE, Harry (R Pa.) Jan. 12, 1834-June 23, 1920; House 1877-81.

WHITE, Hays Baxter (R Kan.) Sept. 21, 1855-Sept. 29, 1930; House 1919-29.

WHITE, Hugh (R N.Y.) Dec. 25, 1798-Oct. 6, 1870; House 1845-51.

WHITE, Hugh Lawson (– Tenn.) Oct. 30, 1773-April 10, 1840; Senate Oct. 28, 1825-Jan. 13, 1840; Pres. pro tempore 1832-33.

WHITE, James (father of Edward Douglas White Sr., grandfather of Edward Douglass White) (– Tenn.) June 16, 1749-Oct. 1809; House (Terr. Del.) Sept. 3, 1794-June 1, 1796; Cont. Cong. 1786-88 (N.C.).

WHITE, James Bain (R Ind.) June 26, 1835-Oct. 9, 1897; House 1887-89.

WHITE, James Bamford (D Ky.) June 6, 1842-March 25, 1931; House 1901-03.

WHITE, John (cousin of Addison White, uncle of John Daugherty White) (W Ky.) Feb. 14, 1802-Sept. 22, 1845; House 1835-45; Speaker 1841-43.

WHITE, John Daugherty (nephew of John White) (R Ky.) Jan. 16, 1849-Jan. 5, 1920; House 1875-77, 1881-85.

WHITE, Joseph Livingston (W Ind.) ?-Jan. 12, 1861; House 1841-43.

WHITE, Joseph M. (D Fla.) May 10, 1781-Oct. 19, 1839; House (Terr. Del.) 1825-37.

WHITE, Joseph Worthington (D Ohio) Oct. 2, 1822-Aug. 6, 1892; House 1863-65.

WHITE, Leonard (D Mass.) May 3, 1767-Oct. 10, 1849; House 1811-13.

WHITE, Michael Doherty (R Ind.) Sept. 8, 1827-Feb. 6, 1917; House 1877-79.

WHITE, Milo (R Minn.) Aug. 17, 1830-May 18, 1913; House 1883-87.

WHITE, Phineas (D Vt.) Oct. 30, 1770-July 6, 1847; House 1821-23.

WHITE, Richard Crawford (D Texas) April 29, 1923- —; House 1965-83.

WHITE, Samuel (F Del.) 1770-Nov. 4, 1809; Senate Feb. 28, 1801-Nov. 4, 1809.

WHITE, Sebastian Harrison (D Colo.) Dec. 24, 1864-Dec. 21, 1945; House Nov. 15, 1927-29.

WHITE, Stephen Mallory (D Calif.) Jan. 19, 1853-Feb. 21, 1901; Senate 1893-99.

WHITE, Stephen Van Culen (R N.Y.) Aug. 1, 1831-Jan. 18, 1913; House 1887-89.

WHITE, Wallace Humphrey Jr. (grandson of William Pierce Frye) (R Maine) Aug. 6, 1877-March 31, 1952; House 1917-31; Senate 1931-49; Senate majority leader 1947-49.

WHITE, Wilbur McKee (R Ohio) Feb. 22, 1890-Dec. 31, 1973; House 1931-33.

WHITE, William John (R Ohio) Oct. 7, 1850-Feb. 16, 1923; House 1893-95.

WHITEAKER, John (D Ore.) May 4, 1820-Oct. 2, 1902; House 1879-81; Gov. 1859-62.

WHITEHEAD, Joseph (D Va.) Oct. 31, 1867-July 8 1938; House 1925-31.

WHITEHEAD, Thomas (C Va.) Dec. 27, 1825-July 1 1901; House 1873-75.

WHITEHILL, James (son of John Whitehill, nephew o Robert Whitehill) (— Pa.) Jan. 31, 1762-Feb. 26 1822; House 1813-Sept. 1, 1814.

WHITEHILL, John (father of James Whitehill, brother of Robert Whitehill) (— Pa.) Dec. 11, 1729-Sept. 16 1815; House 1803-07.

WHITEHILL, Robert (brother of John Whitehill, uncle of James Whitehill, great-great-grandfather of John Crain Kunkel) (— Pa.) July 21, 1738-April 8, 1813 House Nov. 7, 1805-April 8, 1813.

WHITEHOUSE, John Osborne (LD N.Y.) July 19 1817-Aug. 24, 1881; House 1873-77.

WHITEHURST, George William (R Va.) March 12 1925- —; House 1969-87.

WHITELAW, Robert Henry (D Mo.) Jan. 30, 1854-July 27, 1937; House Nov. 4, 1890-91.

WHITELEY, Richard Henry (R Ga.) Dec. 22, 1830 Sept. 26, 1890; House Dec. 22, 1870-75.

WHITELEY, William Gustavus (D Del.) Aug. 7, 1819 April 23, 1886; House 1857-61.

WHITENER, Basil Lee (D N.C.) May 14, 1915- — House 1957-69.

WHITESIDE, Jenkin (— Tenn.) 1772-Sept. 25, 1822 Senate April 11, 1809-Oct. 8, 1811.

WHITESIDE, John (D Pa.) 1773-July 28, 1830; House 1815-19.

WHITFIELD, John Wilkins (D Kan.) March 11, 1818 Oct. 27, 1879; House (Terr. Del.) Dec. 20, 1854-Aug 1, 1856; Dec. 9, 1856-57.

WHITING, Justin Rice (D/G Mich.) Feb. 18, 1847-Jan 31, 1903; House 1887-95.

WHITING, Richard Henry (uncle of Ira Clifton Copley (R Ill.) Jan. 17, 1826-May 24, 1888; House 1875-77

WHITING, William (R Mass.) March 3, 1813-June 29 1873; House March 4-June 29, 1873.

WHITING, William (R Mass.) May 24, 1841-Jan. 1911; House 1883-89.

WHITLEY, Charles Orville (D N.C.) Jan. 3, 1927- — House 1977-87.

WHITLEY, James Lucius (R N.Y.) May 24, 1872-Ma 17, 1959; House 1929-35.

WHITMAN, Ezekiel (F Maine) March 9, 1776-Aug. 1, 1866; House 1809-11 (Mass.), 1817-21 (Mass.), 1821-June 1, 1822.

WHITMAN, Lemuel (D Conn.) June 8, 1780-Nov. 13, 1841; House 1823-25.

WHITMORE, Elias (D N.Y.) March 2, 1772-Dec. 26, 1853; House 1825-27.

WHITMORE, George Washington (R Texas) Aug. 26, 1824-Oct. 14, 1876; House March 30, 1870-71.

WHITNEY, Thomas Richard (AP N.Y.) May 2, 1807-April 12, 1858; House 1855-57.

WHITTAKER, Robert (R Kan.) Sept. 18, 1939- —; House 1979- —.

WHITTEMORE, Benjamin Franklin (R S.C.) May 18, 1824-Jan. 25, 1894; House July 18, 1868-Feb. 24, 1870.

WHITTEN, Jamie Lloyd (D Miss.) April 18, 1910- —; House Nov. 4, 1941- —.

WHITTHORNE, Washington Curran (D Tenn.) April 19, 1825-Sept. 21, 1891; House 1871-83, 1887-91; Senate April 16, 1886-87.

WHITTINGTON, William Madison (D Miss.) May 4, 1878-Aug. 20, 1962; House 1925-51.

WHITTLESEY, Elisha (uncle of William Augustus Whittlesey, cousin of Frederick Whittlesey and Thomas Tucker Whittlesey) (— Ohio) Oct. 19, 1783-Jan. 7, 1863; House 1823-July 9, 1838.

WHITTLESEY, Frederick (cousin of Elisha Whittlesey and Thomas Tucker Whittlesey) (W N.Y.) June 12, 1799-Sept. 19, 1851; House 1831-35.

WHITTLESEY, Thomas Tucker (cousin of Elisha Whittlesey and Frederick Whittlesey) (VBD Conn.) Dec. 8, 1798-Aug. 20, 1868; House April 29, 1836-39.

WHITTLESEY, William Augustus (nephew of Elisha Whittlesey) (D Ohio) July 14, 1796-Nov. 6, 1866; House 1849-51.

WHYTE, William Pinkney (D Md.) Aug. 9, 1824-March 17, 1908; Senate July 13, 1868-69, 1875-81, June 8, 1906-March 17, 1908; Gov. 1872-74.

WICK, William Watson (D Ind.) Feb. 23, 1796-May 19, 1868; House 1839-41, 1845-49.

WICKERSHAM, James (R Alaska) Aug. 24, 1857-Oct. 24, 1939; House (Terr. Del.) 1909-17, Jan. 7-March 3, 1919, March 1-3, 1921, 1931-33.

WICKERSHAM, Victor Eugene (D Okla.) Feb. 9, 1906- —; House April 1, 1941-47, 1949-57, 1961-65.

WICKES, Eliphalet (— N.Y.) April 1, 1769-June 7, 1850; House 1805-07.

WICKHAM, Charles Preston (R Ohio) Sept. 15, 1836-March 18, 1925; House 1887-91.

WICKLIFFE, Charles Anderson (grandfather of Robert Charles Wickliffe and John Crepps Wickliffe Beckham) (UW Ky.) June 8, 1788-Oct. 31, 1869; House 1823-33 (Democrat), 1861-63; Gov. 1839-40 (Whig); Postmaster Gen. 1841-45.

WICKLIFFE, Robert Charles (grandson of Charles Anderson Wickliffe, cousin of John Crepps Wickliffe Beckham) (D La.) May 1, 1874-June 11, 1912; House 1909-June 11, 1912.

WIDGERY, William (D Mass.) about 1753-July 31, 1822; House 1811-13.

WIDNALL, William Beck (R N.J.) March 17, 1906-Dec. 28, 1983; House Feb. 6, 1950-Dec. 31, 1974.

WIER, Roy William (D Minn.) Feb. 25, 1888-June 27, 1963; House 1949-61.

WIGFALL, Louis Tresvant (D Texas) April 21, 1816-Feb. 18, 1874; Senate Dec. 5, 1859-March 23, 1861.

WIGGINS, Charles Edward (R Calif.) Dec. 3, 1927- —; House 1967-79.

WIGGINTON, Peter Dinwiddie (D Calif.) Sept. 6, 1839-July 7, 1890; House 1875-77, Feb. 7, 1878-79.

WIGGLESWORTH, Richard Bowditch (R Mass.) April 25, 1891-Oct. 22, 1960; House Nov. 6, 1928-Nov. 13, 1958.

WIKE, Scott (D Ill.) April 6, 1834-Jan. 15, 1901; House 1875-77, 1889-93.

WILBER, David (father of David Forrest Wilber) (R N.Y.) Oct. 5, 1820-April 1, 1890; House 1873-75, 1879-81, 1887-April 1, 1890.

WILBER, David Forrest (son of David Wilber) (R N.Y.) Dec. 7, 1859-Aug. 14, 1928; House 1895-99.

WILBOUR, Isaac (F R.I.) April 25, 1763-Oct. 4, 1837; House 1807-09; Gov. 1806-07 (Democratic Republican).

WILCOX, James Mark (D Fla.) May 21, 1890-Feb. 3, 1956; House 1933-39.

WILCOX, Jeduthun (father of Leonard Wilcox) (F N.H.) Nov. 18, 1768-July 18, 1838; House 1813-17.

WILCOX, John A. (UW Miss.) April 18, 1819-Feb. 7, 1864; House 1851-53.

WILCOX, Leonard (son of Jeduthun Wilcox) (D N.H.) Jan. 29, 1799-June 18, 1850; Senate March 1, 1842-43.

WILCOX, Robert William (− Hawaii) Feb. 15, 1855-Oct. 23, 1903; House (Terr. Del.) Nov. 6, 1900-03.

WILDE, Richard Henry (D Ga.) Sept. 24, 1789-Sept. 10, 1847; House 1815-17, Feb. 7-March 3, 1825, Nov. 17, 1827-35.

WILDER, Abel Carter (R Kan.) March 18, 1828-Dec. 22, 1875; House 1863-65.

WILDER, William Henry (R Mass.) May 14, 1855-Sept. 11, 1913; House 1911-Sept. 11, 1913.

WILDMAN, Zalmon (D Conn.) Feb. 16, 1775-Dec. 10, 1835; House March 4-Dec. 10, 1835.

WILDRICK, Isaac (D N.J.) March 3, 1803-March 22, 1892; House 1849-53.

WILEY, Alexander (R Wis.) May 26, 1884-May 26, 1967; Senate 1939-63.

WILEY, Ariosto Appling (brother of Oliver Cicero Wiley) (D Ala.) Nov. 6, 1848-June 17, 1908; House 1901-June 17, 1908.

WILEY, James Sullivan (D Maine) Jan. 22, 1808-Dec. 21, 1891; House 1847-49.

WILEY, John McClure (D N.Y.) Aug. 11, 1846-Aug. 13, 1912; House 1889-91.

WILEY, Oliver Cicero (brother of Ariosto Appling Wiley) (D Ala.) Jan. 30, 1851-Oct. 18, 1917; House Nov. 3, 1908-09.

WILEY, William Halsted (R N.J.) July 10, 1842-May 2, 1925; House 1903-07, 1909-11.

WILFLEY, Xenophon Pierce (D Mo.) March 18, 1871-May 4, 1931; Senate April 30-Nov. 5, 1918.

WILKIN, James Whitney (father of Samuel Jones Wilkin) (D N.Y.) 1762-Feb. 23, 1845; House June 7, 1815-19.

WILKIN, Samuel Jones (son of James Whitney Wilkin) (D N.Y.) Dec. 17, 1793-March 11, 1866; House 1831-33.

WILKINS, Beriah (D Ohio) July 10, 1846-June 7, 1905; House 1883-89.

WILKINS, William (D Pa.) Dec. 20, 1779-June 23, 1865; Senate 1831-June 30, 1834 (Democratic/Anti Mason); House 1843-Feb. 14, 1844; Secy. of War 1844-45.

WILKINSON, Morton Smith (R Minn.) Jan. 22, 1819-Feb. 4, 1894; Senate 1859-65; House 1869-71.

WILKINSON, Theodore Stark (D La.) Dec. 18, 1847-Feb. 1, 1921; House 1887-91.

WILLARD, Charles Wesley (R Vt.) June 18, 1827-Jun 8, 1880; House 1869-75.

WILLARD, George (R Mich.) March 20, 1824-March 2 1901; House 1873-77.

WILLCOX, Washington Frederick (D Conn.) Aug. 2: 1834-March 8, 1909; House 1889-93.

WILLETT, William Forte Jr. (D N.Y.) Nov. 27, 186? Feb. 12, 1938; House 1907-11.

WILLEY, Calvin (D Conn.) Sept. 15, 1776-Aug. 2: 1858; Senate May 4, 1825-31.

WILLEY, Earle Dukes (R Del.) July 21, 1889-March 1? 1950; House 1943-45.

WILLEY, Waitman Thomas (R W.Va.) Oct. 18, 1811 May 2, 1900; Senate July 9, 1861-63 (Va.), Aug. 4 1863-71.

WILLFORD, Albert Clinton (D Iowa) Sept. 21, 187? March 10, 1937; House 1933-35.

WILLIAMS, Abram Pease (R Calif.) Feb. 3, 1832-Oc 17, 1911; Senate Aug. 4, 1886-87.

WILLIAMS, Alpheus Starkey (D Mich.) Sept. 20, 181? Dec. 20, 1878; House 1875-Dec. 20, 1878.

WILLIAMS, Andrew (R N.Y.) Aug. 27, 1828-Oct. ? 1907; House 1875-79.

WILLIAMS, Archibald Hunter Arrington (nephew ? Archibald Hunter Arrington) (D N.C.) Oct. 22, 184: Sept. 5, 1895; House 1891-93.

WILLIAMS, Arthur Bruce (R Mich.) Jan. 27, 1872-Ma 1, 1925; House June 19, 1923-May 1, 1925.

WILLIAMS, Benjamin (− N.C.) Jan. 1, 1751-July 2? 1814; House 1793-95; Gov. 1799-1802, 1807-08 (Den ocratic Republican).

WILLIAMS, Charles Grandison (R Wis.) Oct. 18, 182? March 30, 1892; House 1873-83.

WILLIAMS, Christopher Harris (grandfather of Joh Sharp Williams) (W Tenn.) Dec. 18, 1798-Nov. 2 1857; House 1837-43, 1849-53.

WILLIAMS, Clyde (D Mo.) Oct. 13, 1873-Nov. 12, 195 House 1927-29, 1931-43.

WILLIAMS, David Rogerson (D S.C.) March 8, 177? Nov. 17, 1830; House 1805-09, 1811-13; Gov. 1814-1 (Democrat Republican).

WILLIAMS, Elihu Stephen (R Ohio) Jan. 24, 1835-De 1, 1903; House 1887-91.

WILLIAMS, George Fred (D Mass.) July 10, 1852-Ju 11, 1932; House 1891-93.

WILLIAMS, George Henry (UR Ore.) March 23, 1823-April 4, 1910; Senate 1865-71; Atty. Gen. 1872-75.

WILLIAMS, George Howard (R Mo.) Dec. 1, 1871-Nov. 25, 1963; Senate May 25, 1925-Dec. 5, 1926.

WILLIAMS, George Short (R Del.) Oct. 21, 1877-Nov. 22, 1961; House 1939-41.

WILLIAMS, Guinn (D Texas) April 22, 1871-Jan. 9, 1948; House May 13, 1922-33.

WILLIAMS, Harrison Arlington Jr. (D N.J.) Dec. 10, 1919-—; House Nov. 3, 1953-57; Senate 1959-March 11, 1982.

WILLIAMS, Henry (D Mass.) Nov. 30, 1805-May 8, 1887; House 1839-41, 1843-45.

WILLIAMS, Hezekiah (D Maine) July 28, 1798-Oct. 23, 1856; House 1845-49.

WILLIAMS, Isaac Jr. (D N.Y.) April 5, 1777-Nov. 9, 1860; House Dec. 20, 1813-15, 1817-19, 1823-25.

WILLIAMS, James (D Del.) Aug. 4, 1825-April 12, 1899; House 1875-79.

WILLIAMS, James Douglas (D Ind.) Jan. 16, 1808-Nov. 20, 1880; House 1875-Dec. 1, 1876; Gov. 1877-80.

WILLIAMS, James Robert (D Ill.) Dec. 27, 1850-Nov. 8, 1923; House Dec. 2, 1889-95, 1899-1905.

WILLIAMS, James Wray (D Md.) Oct. 8, 1792-Dec. 2, 1842; House 1841-Dec. 2, 1842.

WILLIAMS, Jared (JD Va.) March 4, 1766-Jan. 2, 1831; House 1819-25.

WILLIAMS, Jared Warner (D N.H.) Dec. 22, 1796-Sept. 29, 1864; House 1837-41; Senate Nov. 29, 1853-July 15, 1854; Gov. 1847-49.

WILLIAMS, Jeremiah Norman (D Ala.) May 29, 1829-May 8, 1915; House 1875-79.

WILLIAMS, John (— N.Y.) Sept. 1752-July 22, 1806; House 1795-99.

WILLIAMS, John (brother of Lewis Williams and Robert Williams, father of Joseph Lanier Williams, cousin of Marmaduke Williams) (— Tenn.) Jan. 29, 1778-Aug. 10, 1837; Senate Oct. 10, 1815-23.

WILLIAMS, John (D N.Y.) Jan. 7, 1807-March 26, 1875; House 1855-57.

WILLIAMS, John Bell (D Miss.) Dec. 4, 1918-March 25, 1983; House 1947-Jan. 16, 1968; Gov. 1968-72.

WILLIAMS, John James (R Del.) May 17, 1904-—; Senate 1947-Dec. 31, 1970.

WILLIAMS, John McKeown Snow (R Mass.) Aug. 13, 1818-March 19, 1886; House 1873-75.

WILLIAMS, John Sharp (grandson of Christopher Harris Williams) (D Miss.) July 30, 1854-Sept. 27, 1932; House 1893-1909; Senate 1911-23.

WILLIAMS, John Stuart (D Ky.) July 10, 1818-July 17, 1898; Senate 1879-85.

WILLIAMS, Jonathan (— Pa.) May 20, 1750-May 16, 1815; House March 4-May 16, 1815.

WILLIAMS, Joseph Lanier (son of John Williams of Tenn., nephew of Lewis Williams and Robert Williams) (W Tenn.) Oct. 23, 1810-Dec. 14, 1865; House 1837-43.

WILLIAMS, Lawrence Gordon (R Pa.) Sept. 15, 1913-July 13, 1975; House 1967-75.

WILLIAMS, Lemuel (— Mass.) June 18, 1747-Nov. 8, 1828; House 1799-1805.

WILLIAMS, Lewis (brother of John Williams of Tenn. and Robert Williams, cousin of Marmaduke Williams, uncle of Joseph Lanier Williams) (— N.C.) Feb. 1, 1782-Feb. 23, 1842; House 1815-Feb. 23, 1842.

WILLIAMS, Lyle (R Ohio) Aug. 23, 1942-—; House 1979-85.

WILLIAMS, Marmaduke (cousin of John Williams of Tenn., Lewis Williams and Robert Williams) (D N.C.) April 6, 1774-Oct. 29, 1850; House 1803-09.

WILLIAMS, Morgan B. (R Pa.) Sept. 17, 1831-Oct. 13, 1903; House 1897-99.

WILLIAMS, Nathan (D N.Y.) Dec. 19, 1773-Sept. 25, 1835; House 1805-07

WILLIAMS, Pat (D Mont.) Oct. 30, 1937-—; House 1979-—.

WILLIAMS, Reuel (D Maine) June 2, 1783-July 25, 1862; Senate 1837-Feb. 15, 1843.

WILLIAMS, Richard (R Ore.) Nov. 15, 1836-June 19, 1914; House 1877-79.

WILLIAMS, Robert (brother of John Williams of Tenn. and Lewis Williams, cousin of Marmaduke Williams, uncle of Joseph Lanier Williams) (— N.C.) July 12, 1773-Jan. 25, 1836; House 1797-1803; Gov. (Miss. Terr.) 1805-09.

WILLIAMS, Seward Henry (R Ohio) Nov. 7, 1870-Sept. 2, 1922; House 1915-17.

WILLIAMS, Sherrod (W Ky.) 1804-?; House 1835-41.

WILLIAMS, Thomas (R Pa.) Aug. 28, 1806-June 16, 1872; House 1863-69.

WILLIAMS, Thomas (D Ala.) Aug. 11, 1825-April 13, 1903; House 1879-85.

WILLIAMS, Thomas Hickman (D Miss.) Jan. 20, 1801-May 3, 1851; Senate Nov. 12, 1838-39.

WILLIAMS, Thomas Hill (D Miss.) 1780-1840; Senate Dec. 10, 1817-29.

WILLIAMS, Thomas Scott (− Conn.) June 26, 1777-Dec. 22, 1861; House 1817-19.

WILLIAMS, Thomas Sutler (R Ill.) Feb. 14, 1872-April 5, 1940; House 1915-Nov. 11, 1929.

WILLIAMS, Thomas Wheeler (W Conn.) Sept. 28, 1789-Dec. 31, 1874; House 1839-43.

WILLIAMS, William (D N.Y.) Sept. 6, 1815-Sept. 10, 1876; House 1871-73.

WILLIAMS, William (R Ind.) May 11, 1821-April 22, 1896; House 1867-75.

WILLIAMS, William Brewster (R Mich.) July 28, 1826-March 4, 1905; House Dec. 1, 1873-77.

WILLIAMS, William Elza (D Ill.) May 5, 1857-Sept. 13, 1921; House 1899-1901, 1913-17.

WILLIAMS, William Robert (R N.Y.) Aug. 11, 1884-May 9, 1972; House 1951-59.

WILLIAMSON, Ben Mitchell (D Ky.) Oct. 16, 1864-June 23, 1941; Senate Dec. 1, 1930-31.

WILLIAMSON, Hugh (F N.C.) Dec. 5, 1735-May 22, 1819; House 1789-93; Cont. Cong. 1782-85, 1787-88.

WILLIAMSON, John Newton (R Ore.) Nov. 8, 1855-Aug. 29, 1943; House 1903-07.

WILLIAMSON, William (R S.D.) Oct. 7, 1875-July 15, 1972; House 1921-33.

WILLIAMSON, William Durkee (DR Maine) July 31, 1779-May 27, 1846; House 1821-23; Gov. 1821.

WILLIE, Asa Hoxie (D Texas) Oct. 11, 1829-March 16, 1899; House 1873-75.

WILLIS, Albert Shelby (D Ky.) Jan. 22, 1843-Jan. 6, 1897; House 1877-87.

WILLIS, Benjamin Albertson (D N.Y.) March 24, 1840-Oct. 14, 1886; House 1875-79.

WILLIS, Edwin Edward (D La.) Oct. 2, 1904-Oct. 24, 1972; House 1949-69.

WILLIS, Francis (− Ga.) Jan. 5, 1745-Jan. 25, 1829; House 1791-93.

WILLIS, Frank Bartlett (R Ohio) Dec. 28, 1871-March 30, 1928; House 1911-Jan. 9, 1915; Senate Jan. 14 1921-March 30, 1928; Gov. 1915-17.

WILLIS, Jonathan Spencer (R Del.) April 5, 1830-Nov 24, 1903; House 1895-97.

WILLIS, Raymond Eugene (R Ind.) Aug. 11, 1875 March 21, 1956; Senate 1941-47.

WILLITS, Edwin (R Mich.) April 24, 1830-Oct. 22 1896; House 1877-83.

WILLOUGHBY, Westel Jr. (D N.Y.) Nov. 20, 1769-Oct 3, 1844; House Dec. 13, 1815-17.

WILMOT, David (R Pa.) Jan. 20, 1814-March 16, 1868 House 1845-51 (Democrat); Senate March 14, 1861 63.

WILSHIRE, William Wallace (C Ark.) Sept. 8, 1830 Aug. 19, 1888; House 1873-June 16, 1874 (Republi can), 1875-77.

WILSON, Alexander (− Va.) ?-?; House Dec. 4, 1804 09.

WILSON, Benjamin (D W.Va.) April 30, 1825-April 26 1901; House 1875-83.

WILSON, Charles (D Texas) June 1, 1933-−; Hous 1973-−.

WILSON, Charles Herbert (D Calif.) Feb. 15, 1917-Jul 21, 1984; House 1963-81.

WILSON, Earl (R Ind.) April 18, 1906-−; House 194 59, 1961-65.

WILSON, Edgar (Sil.R/D Idaho) Feb. 25, 1861-Jan. 1915; House 1895-97 (Republican), 1899-1901.

WILSON, Edgar Campbell (son of Thomas Wilson (Va., father of Eugene McLanahan Wilson) (W Va Oct. 18, 1800-April 24, 1860; House 1833-35.

WILSON, Emmett (grandson of Augustus Emme Maxwell) (D Fla.) Sept. 17, 1882-May 29, 191 House 1913-17.

WILSON, Ephraim King (father of Ephraim King Wi son, below) (D Md.) Sept. 15, 1771-Jan. 2, 183 House 1827-31.

WILSON, Ephraim King (son of Ephraim King Wilso above) (D Md.) Dec. 22, 1821-Feb. 24, 1891; Hous 1873-75; Senate 1885-Feb. 24, 1891.

WILSON, Eugene McLanahan (son of Edgar Campbe Wilson, grandson of Thomas Wilson of Va., grea grandson of Isaac Griffin) (D Minn.) Dec. 25, 183 April 10, 1890; House 1869-71.

WILSON, Francis Henry (R N.Y.) Feb. 11, 1844-Sep 25, 1910; House 1895-Sept. 30, 1897.

WILSON, Frank Eugene (D N.Y.) Dec. 22, 1857-July 12, 1935; House 1899-1905, 1911-15.

WILSON, George Allison (R Iowa) April 1, 1884-Sept. 8, 1953; Senate Jan. 14, 1943-49; Gov. 1939-43.

WILSON, George Howard (D Okla.) Aug. 21, 1905-July 16, 1985; House 1949-51.

WILSON, George Washington (R Ohio) Feb. 22, 1840-Nov. 27, 1909; House 1893-97.

WILSON, Henry (D Pa.) 1778-Aug. 14, 1826; House 1823-Aug. 14, 1826.

WILSON, Henry (R Mass.) Feb. 16, 1812-Nov. 22, 1875; Senate Jan. 31, 1855-73; Vice President 1873-75.

WILSON, Isaac (— N.Y.) June 25, 1780-Oct. 25, 1848; House 1823-Jan. 7, 1824.

WILSON, James (father of James Wilson, below) (F N.H.) Aug. 16, 1766-Jan. 4, 1839; House 1809-11.

WILSON, James (son of James Wilson, above) (W N.H.) March 18, 1797-May 29, 1881; House 1847-Sept. 9, 1850.

WILSON, James (D Pa.) April 28, 1779-July 19, 1868; House 1823-39.

WILSON, James (father of John Lockwood Wilson) (R Ind.) April 9, 1825-Aug. 8, 1867; House 1857-61.

WILSON, James (R Iowa) Aug. 16, 1835-Aug. 26, 1920; House 1873-77, 1883-85; Secy. of Agriculture 1897-1913.

WILSON, James Clifton (D Texas) June 21, 1874-Aug. 3, 1951; House 1917-19.

WILSON, James Falconer (R Iowa) Oct. 19, 1828-April 22, 1895; House Oct. 8, 1861-69; Senate 1883-95.

WILSON, James Jefferson (D N.J.) 1775-July 28, 1834; Senate 1815-Jan. 8, 1821.

WILSON, Jeremiah Morrow (R Ind.) Nov. 25, 1828-Sept. 24, 1901; House 1871-75.

WILSON, John (— S.C.) Aug. 11, 1773-Aug. 13, 1828; House 1821-27.

WILSON, John (F Mass.) Jan. 10, 1777-Aug. 9, 1848; House 1813-15, 1817-19.

WILSON, John Frank (D Ariz.) May 7, 1846-April 7, 1911; House (Terr. Del.) 1899-1901, 1903-05.

WILSON, John Haden (D Pa.) Aug. 20, 1867-Jan. 28, 1946; House 1919-21.

WILSON, John Henry (R Ky.) Jan. 30, 1846-Jan. 14, 1923; House 1889-93.

WILSON, John Lockwood (son of James Wilson of Ind.) (R Wash.) Aug. 7, 1850-Nov. 6, 1912; House Nov. 20, 1889-Feb. 18, 1895; Senate Feb. 19, 1895-99.

WILSON, John Thomas (R Ohio) April 16, 1811-Oct. 6, 1891; House 1867-73.

WILSON, Joseph Franklin (D Texas) March 18, 1901-Oct. 13, 1968; House 1947-55.

WILSON, Joseph Gardner (cousin of James Willis Nesmith) (R Ore.) Dec. 13, 1826-July 2, 1873; House March 4-July 2, 1873.

WILSON, Nathan (D N.Y.) Dec. 23, 1758-July 25, 1834; House June 3, 1808-09.

WILSON, Pete (R Calif.) Aug. 23, 1933- —; Senate 1983- —.

WILSON, Riley Joseph (D La.) Nov. 12, 1871-Feb. 23, 1946; House 1915-37.

WILSON, Robert (U Mo.) Nov. 1803-May 10, 1870; Senate Jan. 17, 1862-Nov. 13, 1863.

WILSON, Robert Carlton (R Calif.) April 5, 1916- —; House 1953-81.

WILSON, Robert Patterson Clark (D Mo.) Aug. 8, 1834-Dec. 21, 1916; House Dec. 2, 1889-93.

WILSON, Stanyarne (D S.C.) Jan. 10, 1860-Feb. 14, 1928; House 1895-1901.

WILSON, Stephen Fowler (R Pa.) Sept. 4, 1821-March 30, 1897; House 1865-69.

WILSON, Thomas (father of Edgar Campbell Wilson, grandfather of Eugene McLanahan Wilson) (F Va.) Sept. 11, 1765-Jan. 24, 1826; House 1811-13.

WILSON, Thomas (D Pa.) 1772-Oct. 4, 1824; House May 4, 1813-17.

WILSON, Thomas (D Minn.) May 16, 1827-April 3, 1910; House 1887-89.

WILSON, Thomas Webber (D Miss.) Jan. 24, 1893-Jan. 31, 1948; House 1923-29.

WILSON, William (— Pa.) ?-?; House 1815-19.

WILSON, William (— Ohio) March 19, 1773-June 6, 1827; House 1823-June 6, 1827.

WILSON, William Bauchop (D Pa.) April 2, 1862-May 25, 1934; House 1907-13; Secy. of Labor 1913-21.

WILSON, William Edward (D Ind.) March 9, 1870-Sept. 29, 1948; House 1923-25.

WILSON, William Henry (R Pa.) Dec. 6, 1877-Aug. 11, 1937; House 1935-37.

WILSON, William Lyne (D W.Va.) May 3, 1843-Oct. 17, 1900; House 1883-95; Postmaster Gen. 1895-97.

WILSON, William Warfield (R Ill.) March 2, 1868-July 22, 1942; House 1903-13, 1915-21.

WINANS, Edwin Baruch (D Mich.) May 16, 1826-July 4, 1894; House 1883-87; Gov. 1891-93.

WINANS, James January (R Ohio) June 7, 1818-April 28, 1879; House 1869-71.

WINANS, John (ID Wis.) Sept. 27, 1831-Jan. 17, 1907; House 1883-85.

WINCHESTER, Boyd (D Ky.) Sept. 23, 1836-May 18, 1923; House 1869-73.

WINDOM, William (R Minn.) May 10, 1827-Jan. 29, 1891; House 1859-69; Senate July 15, 1870-Jan. 22, 1871, March 4, 1871-March 7, 1881, Nov. 15, 1881-83; Secy. of the Treasury 1881, 1889-91.

WINFIELD, Charles Henry (D N.Y.) April 22, 1822-June 10, 1888; House 1863-67.

WING, Austin Eli (W Mich.) Feb. 3, 1792-Aug. 27, 1849; House (Terr. Del.) 1825-29, 1831-33.

WINGATE, Joseph Ferdinand (D Maine) June 29, 1786-?; House 1827-31.

WINGATE, Paine (F N.H.) May 14, 1739-March 7, 1838; Senate 1789-93; House 1793-95; Cont. Cong. 1787-88.

WINGO, Effiegene Locke (widow of Otis Theodore Wingo, great-great-great-granddaughter of Matthew Locke) (D Ark.) April 13, 1883-Sept. 19, 1962; House Nov. 4, 1930-33.

WINGO, Otis Theodore (husband of Effiegene Locke Wingo) (D Ark.) June 18, 1877-Oct. 21, 1930; House 1913-Oct. 21, 1930.

WINN, Larry Jr. (R Kan.) Aug. 22, 1919- —; House 1967-85.

WINN, Richard (D S.C.) 1750-Dec. 19, 1818; House 1793-97, Jan. 24, 1803-13.

WINN, Thomas Elisha (Alliance D Ga.) May 2, 1839-June 5, 1925; House 1891-93.

WINSLOW, Samuel Ellsworth (R Mass.) April 11, 1862-July 11, 1940; House 1913-25.

WINSLOW, Warren (D N.C.) Jan. 1, 1810-Aug. 16, 1862; House 1855-61; Gov. 1854-55.

WINSTEAD, William Arthur (D Mass.) Jan. 6, 1904- —; House 1943-65.

WINSTON, Joseph (D N.C.) June 17, 1746-April 21, 1815; House 1793-95, 1803-07.

WINTER, Charles Edwin (R Wyo.) Sept. 13, 1870-April 22, 1948; House 1923-29.

WINTER, Elisha I. (F N.Y.) July 15, 1781-June 30, 1849; House 1813-15.

WINTER, Thomas Daniel (R Kan.) July 7, 1896-Nov. 7, 1951; House 1939-47.

WINTHROP, Robert Charles (W Mass.) May 12, 1809-Nov. 16, 1894; House Nov. 9, 1840-May 25, 1842, Nov. 29, 1842-July 30, 1850; Senate July 30, 1850-Feb. 1, 1851; Speaker 1847-49.

WIRTH, Timothy Endicott (D Colo.) Sept. 22, 1939- —; House 1975-87; Senate 1987- —.

WISE, George Douglas (cousin of John Sergeant Wise and Richard Alsop Wise, nephew of Henry Alexander Wise) (D Va.) June 4, 1831-Feb. 4, 1898; House 1881-April 10, 1890, 1891-95.

WISE, Henry Alexander (father of John Sergeant Wise and Richard Alsop Wise, uncle of George Douglas Wise, son-in-law of John Sergeant) (Tyler D Va.) Dec. 3, 1806-Sept. 12, 1876; House 1833-Feb. 12, 1844 (1833-37 Jackson Democrat, 1837-43 Whig); Gov. 1856-59 (Democrat).

WISE, James Walter (D Ga.) March 3, 1868-Sept. 8, 1925; House 1915-25.

WISE, John Sergeant (son of Henry Alexander Wise, grandson of John Sergeant, brother of Richard Alsop Wise, cousin of George Douglas Wise) (Read. Va.) Dec. 27, 1846-May 12, 1913; House 1883-85.

WISE, Morgan Ringland (D Pa.) June 7, 1825-April 13, 1903; House 1879-83.

WISE, Richard Alsop (son of Henry Alexander Wise, grandson of John Sergeant, brother of John Sergeant Wise, cousin of George Douglas Wise) (R Va.) Sep. 2, 1843-Dec. 21, 1900; House April 26, 1898-99, March 12-Dec. 21, 1900.

WISE, Robert Ellsworth Jr. (D W.Va.) Jan. 6, 1948- —; House 1983- —.

WITCHER, John Seashoal (R W.Va.) July 15, 1839-July 8, 1906; House 1869-71.

WITHERELL, James (D Vt.) June 16, 1759-Jan. 9, 1838; House 1807-May 1, 1808.

WITHERS, Garrett Lee (D Ky.) June 21, 1884-April 30, 1953; Senate Jan. 20, 1949-Nov. 26, 1950; House Aug. 2, 1952-April 30, 1953.

WITHERS, Robert Enoch (cousin of Thomas Withers Chinn) (C Va.) Sept. 18, 1821-Sept. 21, 1907; Senate 1875-81.

WITHERSPOON, Robert (great-great-grandfather of Robert Witherspoon Hemphill) (D S.C.) Jan. 29, 1767-Oct. 11, 1837; House 1809-11.

WITHERSPOON, Samuel Andrew (D Miss.) May 4, 1855-Nov. 24, 1915; House 1911-Nov. 24, 1915.

WITHROW, Gardner Robert (R Wis.) Oct. 5, 1892-Sept. 23, 1964; House 1931-39 (1835-39 Progressive), 1949-61.

WITTE, William Henry (D Pa.) Oct. 4, 1817-Nov. 24, 1876; House 1853-55.

WOFFORD, Thomas Albert (D S.C.) Sept. 27, 1908-Feb. 25, 1978; Senate April 5-Nov. 6, 1956.

WOLCOTT, Edward Oliver (R Colo.) March 26, 1848-March 1, 1905; Senate 1889-1901.

WOLCOTT, Jesse Paine (R Mich.) March 3, 1893-Jan. 28, 1969; House 1931-57.

WOLCOTT, Josiah Oliver (D Del.) Oct. 31, 1877-Nov. 11, 1938; Senate 1917-July 2, 1921.

WOLD, John Schiller (R Wyo.) Aug. 31, 1916- —; House 1969-71.

WOLF, Frank R. (R Va.) Jan. 30, 1939- —; House 1981- —.

WOLF, George (D Pa.) Aug. 12, 1777-March 11, 1840; House Dec. 9, 1824-29; Gov. 1829-35 (Jackson Democrat).

WOLF, Harry Benjamin (D Md.) June 16, 1880-Feb. 17, 1944; House 1907-09.

WOLF, Leonard George (D Iowa) Oct. 29, 1925-March 28, 1970; House 1959-61.

WOLF, William Penn (R Iowa) Dec. 1, 1833-Sept. 19, 1896; House Dec. 6, 1870-71.

WOLFE, Simeon Kalfius (D Ind.) Feb. 14, 1824-Nov. 18, 1888; House 1873-75.

WOLFENDEN, James (R Pa.) July 25, 1889-April 8, 1949; House Nov. 6, 1928-47.

WOLFF, Joseph Scott (D Mo.) June 14, 1878-Feb. 27, 1958; House 1923-25.

WOLFF, Lester Lionel (D N.Y.) Jan. 4, 1919- —; House 1965-81.

WOLFORD, Frank Lane (D Ky.) Sept. 2, 1817-Aug. 2, 1895; House 1883-87.

WOLPE, Howard Eliot (D Mich.) Nov. 2, 1939- —; House 1979- —.

WOLVERTON, Charles Anderson (R N.J.) Oct. 24, 1880-May 16, 1969; House 1927-59.

WOLVERTON, John Marshall (R W.Va.) Jan. 31, 1872-Aug. 19, 1944; House 1925-27, 1929-31.

WOLVERTON, Simon Peter (D Pa.) Jan. 28, 1837-Oct. 25, 1910; House 1891-95.

WON PAT, Antonio Borja (D Guam) Dec. 10, 1908- —; House 1973-85.

WOOD, Abiel (F Mass.) July 22, 1772-Oct. 26, 1834; House 1813-15.

WOOD, Alan Jr. (nephew of John Wood) (R Pa.) July 6, 1834-Oct. 31, 1902; House 1875-77.

WOOD, Amos Eastman (D Ohio) Jan. 2, 1810-Nov. 19, 1850; House Dec. 3, 1849-Nov. 19, 1850.

WOOD, Benjamin (brother of Fernando Wood) (D N.Y.) Oct. 13, 1820-Feb. 21, 1900; House 1861-65, 1881-83.

WOOD, Benson (R Ill.) March 31, 1839-Aug. 27, 1915; House 1895-97.

WOOD, Bradford Ripley (D N.Y.) Sept. 3, 1800-Sept. 26, 1889; House 1845-47.

WOOD, Ernest Edward (D Mo.) Aug. 24, 1875-Jan. 10, 1952; House 1905-June 23, 1906.

WOOD, Fernando (brother of Benjamin Wood) (D N.Y.) June 14, 1812-Feb. 13, 1881; House 1841-43 (Tammany Democrat), 1863-65, 1867-Feb. 13, 1881.

WOOD, Ira Wells (R N.J.) June 19, 1856-Oct. 5, 1931; House Nov. 8, 1904-13.

WOOD, John (uncle of Alan Wood Jr.) (R Pa.) Sept. 6, 1816-May 28, 1898; House 1859-61.

WOOD, John Jacob (JD N.Y.) Feb. 16, 1784-May 20, 1874; House 1827-29.

WOOD, John M. (R Maine) Nov. 17, 1813-Dec. 24, 1864; House 1855-59.

WOOD, John Stephens (D Ga.) Feb. 8, 1885-Sept. 12, 1968; House 1931-35, 1945-53.

WOOD, John Travers (R Idaho) Nov. 25, 1878-Nov. 2, 1954; House 1951-53.

WOOD, Reuben Terrell (D Mo.) Aug. 7, 1884-July 16, 1955; House 1933-41.

WOOD, Silas (D N.Y.) Sept. 14, 1769-March 2, 1847; House 1819-29.

WOOD, Thomas Jefferson (D Ind.) Sept. 30, 1844-Oct. 13, 1908; House 1883-85.

WOOD, Walter Abbott (R N.Y.) Oct. 23, 1815-Jan. 15, 1892; House 1879-83.

WOOD, William Robert (R Ind.) Jan. 5, 1861-March 7, 1933; House 1915-33.

WOODARD, Frederick Augustus (D N.C.) Feb. 12, 1854-May 8, 1915; House 1893-97.

WOODBRIDGE, Frederick Enoch (R Vt.) Aug. 29, 1818-April 25, 1888; House 1863-69.

WOODBRIDGE, William W. (W/D Mich.) Aug. 20, 1780-Oct. 20, 1861; House (Terr. Del.) 1819-Aug. 9, 1820; Senate 1841-47; Gov. 1840-41.

WOODBURN, William (R Nev.) April 14, 1838-Jan. 15, 1915; House 1875-77, 1885-89.

WOODBURY, Levi (D N.H.) Dec. 22, 1789-Sept. 4, 1851; Senate March 16, 1825-31, 1841-Nov. 20, 1845; Gov. 1823-24; Secy. of the Navy 1831-34; Secy. of the Treasury 1834-41; Assoc. Justice Supreme Court 1845-51.

WOODCOCK, David (D N.Y.) 1785-Sept. 18, 1835; House 1821-23, 1827-29.

WOODFORD, Stewart Lyndon (R N.Y.) Sept. 3, 1835-Feb. 14, 1913; House 1873-July 1, 1874.

WOODHOUSE, Chase Going (D Conn.) 1890-Dec. 12, 1984; House 1945-47, 1949-51.

WOODMAN, Charles Walhart (R Ill.) March 11, 1844-March 18, 1898; House 1895-97.

WOODRUFF, George Catlin (D Conn.) Dec. 1, 1805-Nov. 21, 1885; House 1861-63.

WOODRUFF, John (AP Conn.) Feb. 12, 1826-May 20, 1868; House 1855-57, 1859-61.

WOODRUFF, Roy Orchard (R Mich.) March 14, 1876-Feb. 12, 1953; House 1913-15 (Progressive Republican), 1921-53.

WOODRUFF, Thomas M. (D N.Y.) May 3, 1804-March 28, 1855; House 1845-47.

WOODRUM, Clifton Alexander (D Va.) April 27, 1887-Oct. 6, 1950; House 1923-Dec. 31, 1945.

WOODS, Frank Plowman (R Iowa) Dec. 11, 1868-April 25, 1944; House 1909-19.

WOODS, Henry (brother of John Woods of Pa.) (− Pa.) 1764-1826; House 1799-1803.

WOODS, James Pleasant (D Va.) Feb. 4, 1868-July 7, 1948; House Feb. 25, 1919-23.

WOODS, John (brother of Henry Woods) (F Pa.) 1761-Dec. 16, 1816; House (elected 1814 but never served).

WOODS, John (W Ohio) Oct. 18, 1794-July 30, 1855; House 1825-29.

WOODS, Samuel Davis (R Calif.) Sept. 19, 1845-Dec. 2 1915; House Dec. 3, 1900-03.

WOODS, William (D N.Y.) 1790-Aug. 7, 1837; Hou Nov. 3, 1823-25.

WOODSON, Samuel Hughes (father of Samuel Hugh Woodson, below) (− Ky.) Sept. 15, 1777-July 2 1827; House 1821-23.

WOODSON, Samuel Hughes (son of Samuel Hugh Woodson, above) (AP Mo.) Oct. 24, 1815-June 2 1881; House 1857-61.

WOODWARD, George Washington (D Pa.) March 2 1809-May 10, 1875; House Nov. 21, 1867-71.

WOODWARD, Gilbert Motier (D Wis.) Dec. 25, 183 March 13, 1913; House 1883-85.

WOODWARD, Joseph Addison (D S.C.) April 11, 180 Aug. 3, 1885; House 1843-53.

WOODWARD, William (− S.C.) ?-?; House 1815-17

WOODWORTH, James Hutchinson (R Ill.) Dec. 1804-March 26, 1869; House 1855-57.

WOODWORTH, Laurin Dewey (R Ohio) Sept. 10, 183 March 13, 1897; House 1873-77.

WOODWORTH, William W. (D N.Y.) March 16, 180 Feb. 13, 1873; House 1845-47.

WOODYARD, Harry Chapman (R W.Va.) Nov. 1 1867-June 21, 1929; House 1903-11, Nov. 7, 1916-2 1925-27.

WOOMER, Ephraim Milton (R Pa.) Jan. 14, 1844-Nc 29, 1897; House 1893-97.

WOOTEN, Dudley Goodall (D Texas) June 19, 186 Feb. 7, 1929; House July 13, 1901-03.

WORCESTER, Samuel Thomas (R Ohio) Aug. 30, 18(Dec. 6, 1882; House July 4, 1861-63.

WORD, Thomas Jefferson (W Miss.) ?-?; House May : 1838-39.

WORKS, John Downey (R Calif.) March 29, 1847-Ju 6, 1928; Senate 1911-17.

WORLEY, Francis Eugene (D Texas) Oct. 10, 1908-De 17, 1974; House 1941-April 3, 1950.

WORMAN, Ludwig (F Pa.) 1761-Oct. 17, 1822; Hou 1821-Oct. 17, 1822.

WORTENDYKE, Jacob Reynier (D N.J.) Nov. : 1818-Nov. 7, 1868; House 1857-59.

WORTHINGTON, Henry Gaither (R Nev.) Feb. 1828-July 29, 1909; House Oct. 31, 1864-65.

ORTHINGTON, John Tolley Hood (D Md.) Nov. 1, 1788-April 27, 1849; House 1831-33, 1837-41.

ORTHINGTON, Nicholas Ellsworth (D Ill.) March 30, 1836-March 4, 1916; House 1883-87.

ORTHINGTON, Thomas (D Ohio) July 16, 1773-June 20, 1827; Senate April 1, 1803-07, Dec. 15, 1810-Dec. 1, 1814; Gov. 1814-18 (Democratic Republican).

ORTHINGTON, Thomas Contee (grandnephew of Benjamin Contee) (D Md.) Nov. 25, 1782-April 12, 1847; House 1825-27.

ORTLEY, George C. (R N.Y.) Dec. 8, 1928- —; House 1981- —.

REN, Thomas (R Nev.) Jan. 2, 1826-Feb. 5, 1904; House 1877-79.

RIGHT, Ashley Bascom (R Mass.) May 25, 1841-Aug. 14, 1897; House 1893-Aug. 14, 1897.

RIGHT, Augustus Romaldus (D Ga.) June 16, 1813-March 31, 1891; House 1857-59.

RIGHT, Charles Frederick (brother of Myron Benjamin Wright) (R Pa.) May 3, 1856-Nov. 10, 1925; House 1899-1905.

RIGHT, Daniel Boone (D Miss.) Feb. 17, 1812-Dec. 27, 1887; House 1853-57.

RIGHT, Edwin Ruthvin Vincent (D N.J.) Jan. 2, 1812-Jan. 21, 1871; House 1865-67.

RIGHT, George Grover (brother of Joseph Albert Wright) (R Iowa) March 24, 1820-Jan. 11, 1896; Senate 1871-77.

RIGHT, George Washington (I Calif.) June 4, 1816-April 7, 1885; House Sept. 11, 1850-51.

RIGHT, Hendrick Bradley (D Pa.) April 24, 1808-Sept. 2, 1881; House 1853-55, July 4, 1861-63, 1877-81.

RIGHT, James Assion (D Pa.) Aug. 11, 1902-Nov. 7, 1963; House 1941-45.

RIGHT, James Claude Jr. (D Texas) Dec. 22, 1922- —; House 1955- —; House majority leader 1977-87; Speaker 1987- —.

RIGHT, John Crafts (Ad.D Ohio) Aug. 17, 1783-Feb. 13, 1861; House 1823-29.

RIGHT, John Vines (D Tenn.) June 28, 1828-June 11, 1908; House 1855-61.

RIGHT, Joseph Albert (brother of George Grover Wright) (D Ind.) April 17, 1810-May 11, 1867; House 1843-45; Senate Feb. 24, 1862-Jan. 14, 1863; Gov. 1849-57.

WRIGHT, Myron Benjamin (brother of Charles Frederick Wright) (R Pa.) June 12, 1847-Nov. 13, 1894; House 1889-Nov. 13, 1894.

WRIGHT, Robert (D Md.) Nov. 20, 1752-Sept. 7, 1826; Senate Nov. 19, 1801-Nov. 12, 1806; House Nov. 29, 1810-17, 1821-23; Gov. 1806-09 (Democratic Republican).

WRIGHT, Samuel Gardiner (W N.J.) Nov. 18, 1781-July 30, 1845; House March 4-July 30, 1845.

WRIGHT, Silas Jr. (D N.Y.) May 24, 1795-Aug. 27, 1847; House 1827-Feb. 16, 1829; Senate Jan. 4, 1833-Nov. 26, 1844; Gov. 1845-47.

WRIGHT, William (D N.J.) Nov. 13, 1790-Nov. 1, 1866; House 1843-47 (Clay Whig); Senate 1853-59, 1863-Nov. 1, 1866.

WRIGHT, William Carter (D Ga.) Jan. 6, 1866-June 11, 1933; House Jan. 24, 1918-33.

WURTS, John (NR Pa.) Aug. 13, 1792-April 23, 1861; House 1825-27.

WURZBACH, Harry McLeary (uncle of Robert Christian Eckhardt) (R Texas) May 19, 1874-Nov. 6, 1931; House 1921-29, Feb. 10, 1930-Nov. 6, 1931.

WYANT, Adam Martin (R Pa.) Sept. 15, 1869-Jan. 5, 1935; House 1921-33.

WYATT, Joseph Peyton Jr. (D Texas) Oct. 12, 1941- —; House 1979-81.

WYATT, Wendell (R Ore.) June 15, 1917- —; House Nov. 3, 1964-75.

WYDEN, Ron (D Ore.) May 3, 1949- —; House 1981- —.

WYDLER, John Waldemar (R N.Y.) June 9, 1924- —; House 1963-81.

WYLIE, Chalmers Pangburn (R Ohio) Nov. 23, 1920- —; House 1967- —.

WYMAN, Louis Crosby (R N.H.) March 16, 1917- —; House 1963-65, 1967-Dec. 31, 1974; Senate Dec. 31, 1974-75.

WYNKOOP, Henry (- Pa.) March 2, 1737-March 25, 1816; House 1789-91; Cont. Cong. 1779-83.

WYNN, William Joseph (UL/D Calif.) June 12, 1860-Jan. 4, 1935; House 1903-05.

WYNNS, Thomas (F N.C.) 1764-June 3, 1825; House Dec. 7, 1802-07.

YANCEY, Bartlett (cousin of John Kerr) (- N.C.) Feb. 19, 1785-Aug. 30, 1828; House 1813-17.

YANCEY, Joel (D Ky.) Oct. 21, 1773-April 1838; House 1827-31.

YANCEY, William Lowndes (uncle of Joseph Haynsworth Earle) (D Ala.) Aug. 10, 1814-July 28, 1863; House Dec. 2, 1844-Sept. 1, 1846.

YANGCO, Teodoro Rafael (Nat. P.I.) Nov. 9, 1861-April 20, 1939; House (Res. Comm.) 1917-20.

YAPLE, George Lewis (U Mich.) Feb. 20, 1851-Dec. 16, 1939; House 1883-85.

YARBOROUGH, Ralph Webster (D Texas) June 8, 1903- —; Senate April 29, 1957-71.

YARDLEY, Robert Morris (R Pa.) Oct. 9, 1850-Dec. 8, 1902; House 1887-91.

YATES, John Barentse (D N.Y.) Feb. 1, 1784-July 10, 1836; House 1815-17.

YATES, Richard Sr. (father of Richard Yates Jr.) (R Ill.) Jan. 18, 1818-Nov. 27, 1873; House 1851-55 (Whig); Senate 1865-71; Gov. 1861-65.

YATES, Richard Jr. (son of Richard Yates Sr.) (R Ill.) Dec. 12, 1860-April 11, 1936; House 1919-33; Gov. 1901-05.

YATES, Sidney Richard (D Ill.) Aug. 27, 1909- —; House 1949-63, 1965- —.

YATRON, Gus (D Pa.) Oct. 16, 1927- —; House 1969- —.

YEAMAN, George Helm (U Ky.) Nov. 1, 1829-Feb. 23, 1908; House Dec. 1, 1862-65.

YEATES, Jesse Johnson (D N.C.) May 29, 1829-Sept. 5, 1892; House 1875-79; Jan. 29-March 3, 1881.

YELL, Archibald (VBD Ark.) 1797-Feb. 22, 1847; House Aug. 1, 1836-39, 1845-July 1, 1846; Gov. 1840-44 (Democrat).

YOAKUM, Charles Henderson (D Texas) July 10, 1849-Jan. 1, 1909; House 1895-97.

YOCUM, Seth Hartman (R Pa.) Aug. 2, 1834-April 19, 1895; House 1879-81.

YODER, Samuel S. (D Ohio) Aug. 16, 1841-May 11, 1921; House 1887-91.

YON, Thomas Alva (D Fla.) March 14, 1882-Feb. 16, 1971; House 1927-33.

YORK, Tyre (LD N.C.) May 4, 1836-Jan. 28, 1916; House 1883-85.

YORKE, Thomas Jones (W N.J.) March 25, 1801-April 4, 1882; House 1837-39, 1841-43.

YORTY, Samuel William (D Calif.) Oct. 1, 1909- —; House 1951-55.

YOST, Jacob (R Va.) April 1, 1853-Jan. 25, 1933; Hou 1887-89, 1897-99.

YOST, Jacob Senewell (D Pa.) July 29, 1801-March 1872; House 1843-47.

YOUMANS, Henry Melville (D Mich.) May 15, 183 July 8, 1920; House 1891-93.

YOUNG, Andrew Jackson (D Ga.) March 12, 1932- House 1973-77.

YOUNG, Augustus (W Vt.) March 20, 1784-June 1857; House 1841-43.

YOUNG, Bryan Rust (brother of William Singlet Young, uncle of John Young Brown born in 1835) Ky.) Jan. 14, 1800-May 14, 1882; House 1845-47.

YOUNG, Charles William "Bill" (R Fla.) Dec. 16, 193 —; House 1971- —.

YOUNG, Clarence Clifton (R Nev.) Nov. 7, 1922- House 1953-57.

YOUNG, Donald Edwin (R Alaska) June 9, 1933- House March 6, 1973- —.

YOUNG, Ebenezer (F Conn.) Dec. 25, 1783-Aug. 1851; House 1829-35.

YOUNG, Edward Lunn (R S.C.) Sept. 7, 1920- —; Hou 1973-75.

YOUNG, George Morley (R N.D.) Dec. 11, 1870-May 1932; House 1913-Sept. 2, 1924.

YOUNG, Hiram Casey (D Tenn.) Dec. 14, 1828-Aug. 1899; House 1875-81, 1883-85.

YOUNG, Horace Olin (R Mich.) Aug. 4, 1850-Aug. 1917; House March 4, 1903-May 16, 1913.

YOUNG, Isaac Daniel (R Kan.) March 29, 1849-Dec. 1927; House 1911-13.

YOUNG, James (D Texas) July 18, 1866-April 29, 19 House 1911-21.

YOUNG, James Rankin (R Pa.) March 10, 1847-Dec. 1924; House 1897-1903.

YOUNG, John (W N.Y.) June 12, 1802-April 23, 18 House Nov. 9, 1836-37, 1841-43; Gov. 1847-49.

YOUNG, John Andrew (D Texas) Nov. 10, 1916- House 1957-79.

YOUNG, John Duncan (D Ky.) Sept. 22, 1823-Dec. 1910; House 1873-75.

YOUNG, John Smith (D La.) Nov. 4, 1834-Oct. 11, 19 House Nov. 5, 1878-79.

‎OUNG, Lafayette (R Iowa) May 10, 1848-Nov. 15, 1926; Senate Nov. 12, 1910-April 11, 1911.

‎OUNG, Milton Ruben (R N.D.) Dec. 6, 1897-May 31, 1983; Senate March 12, 1945-81.

‎OUNG, Pierce Manning Butler (D Ga.) Nov. 15, 1836-July 6, 1896; House July 25, 1868-69, Dec. 22, 1870-75.

‎OUNG, Richard (R N.Y.) Aug. 6, 1846-June 9, 1935; House 1909-11.

‎OUNG, Richard Montgomery (D Ill.) Feb. 20, 1798-Nov. 28, 1861; Senate 1837-43.

‎OUNG, Robert A. (D Mo.) Nov. 27, 1923- —; House 1977-87.

‎OUNG, Samuel Hollingsworth (R Ill.) Dec. 26, 1922- —; House 1973-75.

‎OUNG, Stephen Marvin (D Ohio) May 4, 1889-Dec. 1, 1984; House 1933-37, 1941-43, 1949-51; Senate 1959-71.

‎OUNG, Thomas Lowry (R Ohio) Dec. 14, 1832-July 20, 1888; House 1879-83; Gov. 1877-78.

‎OUNG, Timothy Roberts (D Ill.) Nov. 19, 1811-May 12, 1898; House 1849-51.

‎OUNG, William Albin (D Va.) May 17, 1860-March 12, 1928; House 1897-April 26, 1898, 1899-March 12, 1900.

‎OUNG, William Singleton (brother of Bryan Rust Young, uncle of John Young Brown born in 1835) (D Ky.) April 10, 1790-Sept. 20, 1827; House 1825-Sept. 20, 1827.

‎OUNGBLOOD, Harold Francis (R Mich.) Aug. 7, 1907- —; House 1947-49.

‎OUNGDAHL, Oscar Ferdinand (R Minn.) Oct. 13, 1893-Feb. 3, 1946; House 1939-43.

YOUNGER, Jesse Arthur (R Calif.) April 11, 1893-June 20, 1967; House 1953-June 20, 1967.

YULEE, David Levy (formerly David Levy) (WD Fla.) June 12, 1810-Oct. 10, 1886; House (Terr. Del.) 1841-45; Senate July 1, 1845-51, 1855-Jan. 21, 1861.

ZABLOCKI, Clement John (D Wis.) Nov. 18, 1912-Dec. 3, 1983; House 1949-Dec. 3, 1983.

ZEFERETTI, Leo C. (D N.Y.) July 15, 1927- —; House 1975-83.

ZELENKO, Herbert (D N.Y.) March 16, 1906-Feb. 23, 1979; House 1955-63.

ZENOR, William Tayor (D Ind.) April 30, 1846-June 2, 1916; House 1897-1907.

ZIEGLER, Edward Danner (D Pa.) March 3, 1844-Dec. 21, 1931; House 1899-1901.

ZIHLMAN, Frederick Nicholas (R Md.) Oct. 2, 1879-April 22, 1935; House 1917-31.

ZIMMERMAN, Orville (D Mo.) Dec. 31, 1880-April 7, 1948; House 1935-April 7, 1948.

ZION, Roger Herschel (R Ind.) Sept. 17, 1921- —; House 1967-75.

ZIONCHECK, Marion Anthony (D Wash.) Dec. 5, 1901-Aug. 7, 1936; House 1933-Aug. 7, 1936.

ZOLLICOFFER, Felix Kirk (SRW Tenn.) May 19, 1812-Jan. 19, 1862; House 1853-59.

ZORINSKY, Edward (D Neb.) Nov. 11, 1928-March 6, 1987; Senate Dec. 28, 1976-March 6, 1987.

ZSCHAU, Ed (R Calif.) Jan. 6, 1940- —; House 1983-87.

ZWACH, John Matthew (R Minn.) Feb. 8, 1907- —; House 1967-75.

Governors

Governors were not popular during the period of the American Revolution. During the colonial era, the British-appointed governors were the symbols of the mother country's control and, the revolutionaries argued, of tyranny.

During the years before the Revolutionary War, colonial assemblies were able to assert their control over appropriations and thus became the champions of colonial rights against the governors. Thus, when forming their own state constitutions, the newly freed Americans tended to look with suspicion on the office of governor and gave most of the power to the legislative bodies.

For these reasons, early American governors found themselves hemmed in by restrictions. Among such restrictions were both the length of the term of office and the method of election.

Length of Terms

As of 1789 the four New England states — Connecticut, Massachusetts, New Hampshire, and Rhode Island — held gubernatorial elections every year. Some of the Middle Atlantic states favored somewhat longer terms; New York and Pennsylvania had three-year terms for their governors, although New Jersey instituted a one-year term. The Border and Southern states had a mix: Maryland and North Carolina governors served a one-year term; South Carolina had a two-year term; and Delaware, Virginia, and Georgia had three-year terms. No state had a four-year term.

Over the years states have changed the length of gubernatorial terms. With some occasional back and forth movement, the general trend has been toward lengthening

terms. New York, for example, has changed the term of office of its governor four times. Beginning in 1777 with a three-year term, the state switched to a two-year term in 1820, back to a three-year term in 1876, back to a two-year term in 1894, and to a four-year term beginning in 1938.

Maryland provides another example of a state that has changed its gubernatorial term several times. Beginning with one year in 1776, the state extended the term to three years in 1838, then to four years in 1851. Regular gubernatorial elections were held every second odd year from then through 1923, when the state had one three-year term so that future elections would be held in even-numbered years, beginning in 1926. Thus, the state held gubernatorial elections in 1919, 1923, and 1926 and then every four years after that.

The trend toward longer gubernatorial terms shows up clearly by comparing the length of terms in 1900 and 1986. Of the 45 states in the Union in 1900, 22, almost half, had two-year terms. One (New Jersey) had a three-year term, while Rhode Island and Massachusetts were the only states left with one-year terms. The remaining 20 states had four-year gubernatorial terms. *(Length of Governor Terms, box, p. 345)*

By January 1986, 42 of those same states had four-year terms, and the five states admitted to the Union after 1900 — Oklahoma (1907), Arizona and New Mexico (1912), Alaska and Hawaii (1959) — had four-year gubernatorial terms. This left only three states with two-year terms: New Hampshire, Rhode Island, and Vermont.

During the November 1984 elections, voters in New Hampshire were asked to de-

343

Party Lineup of Governors

The figures below show the number of governorships held by the two parties after each election since 1950. D stands for Democrat; R, Republican; and I, Independent.

Year	D	R	I
1950	23	25	0
1952	18	30	0
1954	27	21	0
1956	29	19	0
1958	35	14	0
1960	34	16	0
1962	34	16	0
1964	33	17	0
1966	25	25	0
1968	19	31	0
1970	29	21	0
1972	31	19	0
1974	36	13	1
1976	37	12	1
1978	32	18	0
1980	26	24	0
1982	34	16	0
1984	34	16	0
1986	26	24	0

SOURCE: Republican National Committee

cide whether the governor should serve four years instead of two. In a fairly close ballot New Hampshire rejected the change, which would have required a two-thirds vote to pass. In November 1986, Rhode Island voters also rejected a constitutional amendment that would have lengthened the gubernatorial term to four years.

Elections in Nonpresidential Years

Along with the change to longer terms for governors came another trend — away from holding gubernatorial elections in presidential election years. Except for North Dakota, every state in the twentieth century that switched to four-year gubernatorial terms scheduled its elections in nonpresidential years. Moreover, Florida, which held its quadrennial gubernatorial elections in presidential years, changed to nonpresidential years in 1966. To make the switch, the state shortened to two years the term of the governor elected in 1964, then resumed the four-year term in 1966. Thus, Florida held gubernatorial elections in 1960, 1964, 1966, 1970, and every four years since then.

Illinois made a similar switch in 1976-78, leaving only nine states — Delaware, Indiana, Missouri, Montana, North Carolina, North Dakota, Utah, Washington, and West Virginia — holding quadrennial gubernatorial elections at the same time as the presidential election. (Louisiana holds its gubernatorial election in presidential years but not in November; New Hampshire, Rhode Island, and Vermont still had two-year terms, so every other gubernatorial election in these three states occurred in a presidential year. Arkansas, which switched from a two-year to a four-year term in 1984, chose to select its governors in nonpresidential election years beginning in 1986.)

Methods of Election

Yet another way in which Americans of the early federal period restricted their governors was by the method of election. In 1789, only in New York and the four New England states did the people directly choose their governors by popular vote. In the remaining eight states, governors were chosen by the state legislatures, thus enhancing the power of the legislatures in their dealing with the governors. But several factors — including the democratic trend to elect public officials directly, the increasing trust in the office of governor, and the need for a stronger and more independent chief executive — led to the gradual introduction of popular votes in all the states.

By the 1860s the remaining eight original states all had switched to popular ballots. Pennsylvania was first, in 1790, and was followed by Delaware in 1792, Georgia in 1824, North Carolina in 1835, Maryland in 1838, New Jersey in 1844, Virginia in 1851, and South Carolina in 1865, after the Civil War.

Length of Governor Terms

State	1900	1986	Year of change	State	1900	1986	Year of change
Alabama	2	4	1901	Montana	4	4	—
Alaska*	—	4	—	Nebraska	2	4	1966
Arizona*	—	4	1970	Nevada	4	4	—
Arkansas	2	4	1986	New Hampshire	2	2	—
California	4	4	—	New Jersey	3	4	1949
Colorado	2	4	1958	New Mexico*	—	4	1970
Connecticut	2	4	1950	New York	2	4	1938
Delaware	4	4	—	North Carolina	4	4	—
Florida	4	4	—	North Dakota	2	4	1964
Georgia	2	4	1942	Ohio	2	4	1958
Hawaii*	—	4	—	Oklahoma*	—	4	—
Idaho	2	4	1946	Oregon	4	4	—
Illinois	4	4	—	Pennsylvania	4	4	—
Indiana	4	4	—	Rhode Island	1	2	1912
Iowa	2	4	1974	South Carolina	2	4	1926
Kansas	2	4	1974	South Dakota	2	4	1974
Kentucky	4	4	—	Tennessee	2	4	1954
Louisiana	4	4	—	Texas	2	4	1974
Maine	2	4	1958	Utah	4	4	—
Maryland	4	4	—	Vermont	2	2	—
Massachusetts	1	4	1920, 1966†	Virginia	4	4	—
				Washington	4	4	—
Michigan	2	4	1966	West Virginia	4	4	—
Minnesota	2	4	1962	Wisconsin	2	4	1970
Mississippi	4	4	—	Wyoming	4	4	—
Missouri	4	4	—				

* Oklahoma was admitted to the Union in 1907, Arizona and New Mexico in 1912, and Alaska and Hawaii in 1959. Oklahoma, Alaska, and Hawaii have always had four-year gubernatorial terms; Arizona began with a two-year term and switched to four years in 1970. New Mexico (1912) began with a four-year term, changed to two years in 1916, and back to four years in 1970.
† Massachusetts switched from a one- to a two-year term in 1920 and to a four-year term in 1966.

SOURCE: State secretaries of state; *The Book of the States, 1986-1987*, vol. 26. Lexington, Ky.: The Council of State Governments, 1986.

All the states admitted to the Union after the original 13, with one exception, made provision from the very beginning for popular election of their governors. The exception was Louisiana, which from its admission in 1812 until a change in the state constitution in 1845 had a unique system of gubernatorial elections. The people partici-pated by voting in a first-step popular election. In a second step, the Legislature was to select the governor from the two candidates receiving the highest popular vote.

Number of Terms

Another limitation placed on governors is a restriction on the number of terms they are allowed to serve. In the early years at least three states had such limitations: governors of Maryland were eligible to serve three consecutive one-year terms and then were required to retire for at least one year; Pennsylvania allowed its governors three consecutive three-year terms and then forced retirement for at least one term; and in New Jersey, according to the constitution of 1844, a governor could serve only one three-year term before retiring for at least one term.

In 1986 just over half the states — 29 — placed some sort of limitation on the number of consecutive terms their governors could serve. Of these 29, 4 prohibited their governors from serving more than one term in a row, permitting the governors to serve again after an interim of at least one term. The remaining 25 states allowed their governors to seek reelection once but required that they step down after two terms for an interim of at least one term. Three exceptions to that general rule — Delaware, Missouri, and North Carolina — imposed an absolute two-term limit. That is, a governor could serve only two terms, however spaced, in his lifetime. The remaining 21 states imposed no limits on the number of consecutive terms a governor could serve. *(Limitations on Governor Terms, box, p. 347)*

Majority Vote Requirement

A peculiarity of gubernatorial voting that has almost disappeared from the American political scene is the requirement that the winning gubernatorial candidate receive a majority of the popular vote. Otherwise, the choice devolves upon the state legislature or, in one case, a runoff between the two highest candidates is required. Centered in New England, this practice was used mainly in the nineteenth century. All six present-day New England states and Georgia had such a provision in their state constitutions at one time. New Hampshire, Vermont, Massachusetts, and Connecticut already had the provision when they entered the Union between 1789 and 1791.

Rhode Island required a majority election but did not adopt a provision for legislative election until 1842; Maine adopted a

majority provision when it split off from Massachusetts to form a separate state in 1820; and Georgia put the majority provision in its constitution when it switched from legislative to popular election of governors in 1825.

The purpose of the majority provision appears to have been to safeguard against a candidate's winning with a small fraction of the popular vote in a multiple field. In most of New England, the provision was part of the early state constitutions, formed largely in the 1780s, before the development of the two-party system.

The prospect of multiple-candidate fields diminished with the coming of the two-party system. Nevertheless, each of these states had occasion to use the provision at least once. Sometimes, in an extremely close election, minor party candidates received enough of a vote to keep the winner from getting a majority of the total vote. And at other times strong third-party movements or disintegration of the old party structure resulted in the election's being thrown into the state legislature.

Vermont retains the majority vote provision and its Legislature chose the governor in January 1987, the first time it did so since 1912. Georgia maintains the requirement for a majority vote for governor but, instead of legislative election, provides for a runoff between the top two contenders three weeks after the general election. Mississippi has a majority vote provision under the 1890 state constitution, but the provision has not been used because the Democratic party nominee always has received a majority.

Following are the states that had the majority vote provision for governor (except Mississippi), the years in which the choice devolved on the legislature because of it, and the year, if any, in which the requirement was repealed or changed:

Connecticut. No gubernatorial candidate received a majority of the popular vote, thus throwing the election into the Legislature, in the following years subsequent to 1824: 1833, 1834, 1842, 1844, 1846, 1849, 1850, 1851, 1854, 1855, 1856, 1878, 1884, 1886, 1888, and 1890. Following the election of 1890, the Legislature was unable to

Limitations on Governor Terms
(As of 1986)

State	Maximum number of consecutive terms	State	Maximum number of consecutive terms
Alabama	2	Montana	No limit
Alaska	2	Nebraska	2
Arizona	No limit	Nevada	2
Arkansas	2	New Hampshire	No limit
California	No limit	New Jersey	2
Colorado	No limit	New Mexico	0
Connecticut	No limit	New York	No limit
Delaware	2*	North Carolina	2*
Florida	2	North Dakota	No limit
Georgia	2	Ohio	2
Hawaii	2	Oklahoma	2
Idaho	No limit	Oregon	2
Illinois	No limit	Pennsylvania	2
Indiana	2	Rhode Island	No limit
Iowa	No limit	South Carolina	2
Kansas	2	South Dakota	2
Kentucky	0	Tennessee	2
Louisiana	2	Texas	No limit
Maine	2	Utah	No limit
Maryland	2	Vermont	No limit
Massachusetts	No limit	Virginia	0
Michigan	No limit	Washington	No limit
Minnesota	No limit	West Virginia	2
Mississippi	0	Wisconsin	No limit
Missouri	2*	Wyoming	No limit

* Indicates an absolute two-term limit. That is, no person may serve more than two gubernatorial terms in his lifetime. In other states with limitations, a governor may serve as many terms as he may be elected to, provided he retires after one, or two, terms, depending on the constitutional provisions of his state, and stays out of office at least one term before running again.

0 Indicates the governor must retire at the end of his first term. After a one-term interim, he may serve again.

2 Indicates the governor must retire after two consecutive terms. After a one-term interim, he may serve again.

SOURCE: *The Book of the States, 1986-1987*, vol. 26. Lexington, Ky.: The Council of State Governments, 1986.

choose a new governor, so the outgoing governor, Morgan G. Bulkeley, R, continued to serve through the entire new term (1891-93). The provision was repealed in 1901. The years prior to 1824 in which the provision was used, if any, were unavailable from the Connecticut secretary of state's office.

Georgia. Although the majority vote requirement was contained in the constitution as early as 1825, it was not used until the twentieth century. In 1966, with an emerging Republican party, a controversial

Democratic nominee, and an Independent Democrat all affecting the gubernatorial race, no candidate received a majority. The Legislature chose Democrat Lester Maddox. It was the controversy surrounding this experience that led to the change from legislative choice to a runoff between the top two contenders. Earlier, in 1946, the Georgia Legislature also attempted to choose the governor, under unusual circumstances not covered by the majority vote requirement. The governor-elect, Eugene Talmadge, D, died before taking office. When it met, the Legislature chose Talmadge's son, Herman E. Talmadge, as the new governor. Herman Talmadge was eligible for consideration on the basis that he received enough write-in votes in the general election to make him the second-place candidate. But the state Supreme Court voided the Legislature's choice and declared that the lieutenant governor-elect, Melvin E. Thompson, D, should be governor.

Maine. Maine entered statehood in 1820 with a majority vote provision for governor but repealed it in 1880. During this 60-year span, the Legislature was called on to choose the governor nine times, in 1840, 1846, 1848, 1852, 1853, 1854, 1855, 1878, and 1879.

Massachusetts. Like the other New England states, Massachusetts originally had a requirement for majority voting in gubernatorial elections. However, after the Legislature was forced to choose the governor for six straight elections from 1848 to 1853, Massachusetts repealed the provision in 1855. The years in which it was used were 1785, 1833, 1842, 1843, 1845, 1848, 1849, 1850, 1851, 1852, and 1853.

New Hampshire. New Hampshire's mandated majority vote for governor was in force from 1784 through 1912, when it was repealed. The outcome of the following gubernatorial elections was determined by the Legislature: 1785, 1787, 1789, 1790, 1812, 1824, 1846, 1851, 1856, 1863, 1871, 1874, 1875, 1886, 1888, 1890, 1906, and 1912.

Rhode Island. Under the constitution of 1842, Rhode Island required a majority to win the gubernatorial election. Under this mandate, the Legislature chose the governor in the years 1846, 1875, 1876, 1880, 1889, 1890, and 1891. Because of a disagreement between the two houses of the state Legislature, the ballots for governor were not counted in 1893, and Gov. D. Russell Brown, R, continued in office for another term of one year. The provision for majority voting then was repealed.

Before 1842 there also was a requirement for a popular majority, but the Legislature was not allowed to choose a new governor if no candidate achieved a majority. Three times — in 1806, 1832, and 1839 — there was a lack of a majority in a gubernatorial election, with a different outcome each time. In 1806 the lieutenant governor-elect served as acting governor for the term. In 1832 the Legislature mandated a new election, but still no majority choice was reached; three more elections were held, all without a majority being achieved, so the same state officers were continued until the next regular election. And in 1839, when neither the gubernatorial nor lieutenant governor's race yielded a winner by majority, the senior state senator acted as governor for the term.

Vermont. Vermont's provision for majority gubernatorial election resulted in the Legislature's picking the governor 20 times: 1789, 1797, 1813, 1814, 1830, 1831, 1832, 1834, 1841, 1843, 1845, 1846, 1847, 1848, 1849, 1852, 1853, 1902, 1912, and 1987. On a 21st occasion, 1835, the Legislature failed to choose a new governor because of a deadlock and the lieutenant governor-elect served as governor for the term. The Vermont provision remains in force.

Governors: Biographies

This biographical summary lists, by state in chronological order of service, all governors of the United States since 1789. For each governor, the material is organized as follows: name; relationship to other governors, presidents, or vice presidents; political affiliation; date of birth; date of death (if applicable); dates of service as governor; congressional service, service as president, vice president, Supreme Court justice, member of the Cabinet, delegate to the Continental Congress, House or Senate majority leader, Speaker of the House, president pro tempore of the Senate, or chairman of the Democratic or Republican National Committee. *(Party abbreviations, box, p. x)*

An index of the governors in alphabetical order begins on page 411.

The major sources of information for this list were *The Book of the States, 1986-1987,* vol. 26 (Lexington, Ky.: Council of State Governments, 1986); Congressional Quarterly's *Guide to U.S. Elections,* 2d ed.; *Governors of the American States, Commonwealths, and Territories* (Washington, D.C.: National Governors' Association, 1983); Joseph E. Kallenbach and Jessamine S. Kallenbach, *American State Governors, 1776-1976,* 3 vols. (Dobbs Ferry, N.Y.: Oceana Publishing, 1977); and individual state offices and historical societies. *(State Sources for Governors, box, p. 410)*

Alabama

(Became a state Dec. 14, 1819)

BIBB, William Wyatt (brother of Thomas Bibb, cousin of David Bibb Graves) (DR) Oct. 2, 1781-July 10, 1820; Nov. 9, 1819-July 10, 1820; House 1807-13 (Ga.); Senate 1813-16 (Ga.).

BIBB, Thomas (brother of William Wyatt Bibb, cousin of David Bibb Graves) (DR) 1783-Sept. 20, 1839; July 15, 1820-Nov. 9, 1821.

PICKENS, Israel (DR) Jan. 30, 1780-April 24, 1827; Nov. 9, 1821-Nov. 25, 1825; House 1811-17 (N.C.); Senate 1826.

MURPHY, John (D) 1785-Sept. 21, 1841; Nov. 25, 1825-Nov. 25, 1829; House 1833-35.

MOORE, Gabriel (brother of Samuel B. Moore, below) (JD) 1785-June 9, 1845; Nov. 25, 1829-March 3, 1831; House 1821-29; Senate 1831-37.

MOORE, Samuel B. (brother of Gabriel Moore, above) (D) 1789-Nov. 7, 1846; March 3-Nov. 26, 1831.

GAYLE, John (W) Sept. 11, 1792-July 21, 1859; Nov. 26, 1831-Nov. 21, 1835 (Democrat); House 1847-49.

CLAY, Clement Comer (JD) Dec. 17, 1789-Sept. 7, 1866; Nov. 21, 1835-July 17, 1837; House 1829-35; Senate 1837-41.

McVAY, Hugh (D) 1788-May 9, 1851; July 17-Nov. 21, 1837.

BAGBY, Arthur Pendleton (D) 1794-Sept. 21, 1858; Nov. 21, 1837-Nov. 22, 1841; Senate 1841-48.

FITZPATRICK, Benjamin (D) June 30, 1802-Nov. 21, 1869; Nov. 22, 1841-Dec. 10, 1845; Senate 1848-49, 1853-61; Pres. pro tempore 1857-60.

MARTIN, Joshua Lanier (D) Dec. 5, 1799-Nov. 2, 1856; Dec. 10, 1845-Dec. 16, 1847; House 1835-39.

CHAPMAN, Reuben (D) July 15, 1799-May 16, 1882; Dec. 16, 1847-Dec. 17, 1849; House 1835-47.

COLLIER, Henry Watkins (D) Jan. 17, 1801-Aug. 28, 1855; Dec. 17, 1849-Dec. 20, 1853.

WINSTON, John Anthony (brother-in-law of Robert Burns Lindsay, below) (D) Sept. 4, 1812-Dec. 21, 1871; Dec. 20, 1853-Dec. 1, 1857.

MOORE, Andrew Barry (W) March 7, 1807-April 5, 1873; Dec. 1, 1857-Dec. 2, 1861.

SHORTER, John Gill (D) April 23, 1818-May 29, 1872; Dec. 2, 1861-Dec. 1, 1863.

WATTS, Thomas Hill (W) Jan. 3, 1819-Sept. 16, 1892; Dec. 1, 1863-April 12, 1865.

PARSONS, Lewis Eliphalet (W) April 28, 1817-June 8, 1895; (Provisional) June 21-Dec. 20, 1865.

PATTON, Robert Miller (W) July 10, 1809-Feb. 28, 1885; Dec. 20, 1865-July 14, 1868.

SMITH, William Hugh (D) April 26, 1826-Jan. 1, 1899; July 14, 1868-Nov. 26, 1870.

LINDSAY, Robert Burns (brother-in-law of John Anthony Winston, above) (D) July 4, 1824-Feb. 13, 1902; Nov. 26, 1870-Nov. 17, 1872.

LEWIS, David Peter (R) 1820-July 3, 1884; Nov. 25, 1872-Nov. 24, 1874.

HOUSTON, George Smith (D) Jan. 17, 1809-Dec. 31, 1879; Nov. 24, 1874-Nov. 28, 1878; House 1841-49, 1851-61 (Union Democrat); Senate 1879.

COBB, Rufus Wills (D) Feb. 25, 1829-Nov. 26, 1913; Nov. 28, 1878-Dec. 1, 1882.

O'NEAL, Edward Asbury (father of Emmet O'Neal, below) (D) Sept. 20, 1818-Nov. 7, 1890; Dec. 1, 1882-Dec. 1, 1886.

SEAY, Thomas (D) Nov. 20, 1846-March 30, 1896; Dec. 1, 1886-Dec. 1, 1890.

JONES, Thomas Goode (D) Nov. 26, 1844-April 28, 1914; Dec. 1, 1890-Dec. 1, 1894.

OATES, William Calvin (D) Dec. 1, 1835-Sept. 9, 1910; Dec. 1, 1894-Dec. 1, 1896; House 1881-94.

JOHNSTON, Joseph Forney (D) March 23, 1843-Aug. 8, 1913; Dec. 1, 1896-Dec. 1, 1900; Senate 1907-13.

JELKS, William Dorsey (D) Nov. 7, 1855-Dec. 13, 1931; Dec. 1-26, 1900, June 11, 1901-April 25, 1904, March 5, 1905-Jan. 14, 1907.

SAMFORD, William James (D) Sept. 16, 1844-June 11, 1901; Dec. 26, 1900-June 11, 1901; House 1879-81.

JELKS, William Dorsey (D) June 11, 1901-April 25, 1904 (for previous term see above).

CUNNINGHAM, Russell McWhortor (D) Aug. 25, 1855-June 6, 1921; April 25, 1904-March 5, 1905.

JELKS, William Dorsey (D) March 5, 1905-Jan. 14, 1907 (for previous terms see above).

COMER, Braxton Bragg (D) Nov. 7, 1848-Aug. 15, 1927; Jan. 14, 1907-Jan. 17, 1911; Senate 1920.

O'NEAL, Emmet (son of Edward Asbury O'Neal, above) (D) Sept. 23, 1853-Sept. 7, 1922; Jan. 17, 1911-Jan. 18, 1915.

HENDERSON, Charles (D) April 26, 1860-Jan. 7, 1937; Jan. 18, 1915-Jan. 20, 1919.

KILBY, Thomas Erby (D) July 9, 1865-Oct. 22, 1943; Jan. 20, 1919-Jan. 15, 1923.

BRANDON, William Woodward (D) June 5, 1868-Dec. 7, 1934; Jan. 15, 1923-Jan. 17, 1927.

McDOWELL, Charles Samuel (D) Oct. 17, 1871-May 22, 1943; July 10-11, 1924 (acting).

GRAVES, David Bibb (cousin of William Wyatt Bibb and Thomas Bibb, above) (D) April 1, 1873-March 14, 1942; Jan. 17, 1927-Jan. 19, 1931, Jan. 14, 1935-Jan. 17, 1939.

MILLER, Benjamin Meek (D) March 13, 1864-Feb. 6 1944; Jan. 19, 1931-Jan. 14, 1935.

GRAVES, David Bibb (D) Jan. 14, 1935-Jan. 17, 193* (for previous term see above).

DIXON, Frank Murray (D) July 25, 1892-Oct. 11, 1965 Jan. 17, 1939-Jan. 19, 1943.

SPARKS, George Chauncey (D) Oct. 8, 1884-Nov. 6 1968; Jan. 19, 1943-Jan. 20, 1947.

FOLSOM, James Elisha (D) Oct. 9, 1908- —; Jan. 20 1947-Jan. 15, 1951, Jan. 17, 1955-Jan. 19, 1959.

PERSONS, Seth Gordon (D) Feb. 5, 1902-May 29, 1965 Jan. 15, 1951-Jan. 17, 1955.

FOLSOM, James Elisha (D) Jan. 17, 1955-Jan. 19, 195* (for previous term see above).

PATTERSON, John Malcolm (D) Sept. 27, 1921- — Jan. 19, 1959-Jan. 14, 1963.

WALLACE, George Corley (husband of Lurleen Burn Wallace, below) (D) Aug. 25, 1919- —; Jan. 14, 1963 Jan. 16, 1967, Jan. 18, 1971-June 5, 1972, July 7 1972-Jan. 15, 1979, Jan. 17, 1983-Jan. 19, 1987.

WALLACE, Lurleen Burns (wife of George Corley Wal lace, above) (D) Sept. 19, 1926-May 7, 1968; Jan. 16 1967-May 7, 1968.

BREWER, Albert Preston (D) Oct. 26, 1928- —; May 7 1968-Jan. 18, 1971.

WALLACE, George Corley (D) Jan. 18, 1971-June 5 1972 (for previous term see above).

BEASLEY, Jere Locke (D) Dec. 12, 1935- —; June 5 July 7, 1972.

WALLACE, George Corley (D) July 7, 1972-Jan. 15 1979 (for previous terms see above).

JAMES, Forrest Hood "Fob" Jr. (D) Sept. 15, 1934- — Jan. 15, 1979-Jan. 17, 1983.

WALLACE, George Corley (D) Jan. 17, 1983-Jan. 19 1987 (for previous terms see above).

HUNT, Harold Guy (R) June 17, 1933- —; Jan. 19, 1987 —.

Alaska

(Became a state Jan. 3, 1959)

EGAN, William Allen (D) Oct. 8, 1914-May 6, 1984; Jan 3, 1959-Dec. 5, 1966, Dec. 5, 1970-Dec. 2, 1974.

HICKEL, Walter Joseph (D) Aug. 18, 1919- —; Dec. 5 1966-Jan. 29, 1969; Secy. of the Interior 1969-70.

MILLER, Keith Harvey (R) March 1, 1925- —; Jan. 29, 1969-Dec. 5, 1970.

EGAN, William Allen (D) Dec. 5, 1970-Dec. 2, 1974 (for previous term see above).

HAMMOND, Jay Sterner (R) July 21, 1922- —; Dec. 2, 1974-Dec. 6, 1982.

SHEFFIELD, William Jennings (D) June 26, 1928- —; Dec. 6, 1982-Dec. 1, 1986.

COWPER, Steve Camberling (D) Aug. 21, 1938- —; Dec. 1, 1986- —.

Arizona

Became a state Feb. 14, 1912)

HUNT, George Wylie Paul (D) Nov. 1, 1859-Dec. 24, 1934; Feb. 14, 1912-Jan. 1, 1917, Dec. 25, 1917-Jan. 6, 1919, Jan. 1, 1923-Jan. 7, 1929, Jan. 5, 1931-Jan. 2, 1933.

CAMPBELL, Thomas Edward (R) Jan. 18, 1878-March 1, 1944; Jan. 1, 1917-Dec. 25, 1917, Jan. 6, 1919-Jan. 1, 1923.

HUNT, George Wylie Paul (D) Dec. 25, 1917-Jan. 6, 1919 (for previous term see above).

CAMPBELL, Thomas Edward (R) Jan. 6, 1919-Jan. 1, 1923 (for previous term see above).

HUNT, George Wylie Paul (D) Jan. 1, 1923-Jan. 7, 1929 (for previous terms see above).

PHILLIPS, John C. (R) Nov. 13, 1870-June 25, 1943; Jan. 7, 1929-Jan. 5, 1931.

HUNT, George Wylie Paul (D) Jan. 5, 1931-Jan. 2, 1933 (for previous terms see above).

MOEUR, Benjamin Baker (D) Dec. 22, 1869-March 16, 1937; Jan. 2, 1933-Jan. 4, 1937.

STANFORD, Rawghlie Clement (D) Aug. 2, 1879-Dec. 15, 1963; Jan. 4, 1937-Jan. 2, 1939.

JONES, Robert Taylor (D) Feb. 8, 1884-June 11, 1958; Jan. 2, 1939-Jan. 6, 1941.

OSBORN, Sidney Preston (D) May 17, 1884-May 25, 1948; Jan. 6, 1941-May 25, 1948.

GARVEY, Daniel E. (D) June 19, 1886-Feb. 5, 1974; May 25, 1948-Jan. 1, 1951.

PYLE, John Howard (R) March 25, 1906- —; Jan. 1, 1951-Jan. 3, 1955.

McFARLAND, Ernest William (D) Oct. 9, 1894-June 8, 1984; Jan. 3, 1955-Jan. 5, 1959; Senate 1941-53; Senate majority leader 1951-53.

FANNIN, Paul Jones (R) Jan. 29, 1907- —; Jan. 5, 1959-Jan. 4, 1965; Senate 1965-76.

GODDARD, Samuel Pearson Jr. (D) Aug. 8, 1919- —; Jan. 4, 1965-Jan. 2, 1967.

WILLIAMS, John Richard (R) Oct. 29, 1909- —; Jan. 2, 1967-Jan. 6, 1975.

CASTRO, Raul Hector (D) June 12, 1916- —; Jan. 6, 1975-Oct. 20, 1977.

BOLIN, Wesley H. (D) July 1, 1908-March 4, 1978; Oct. 20, 1977-March 4, 1978.

BABBITT, Bruce Edward (D) June 27, 1938- —; March 4, 1978-Jan. 5, 1987.

MECHAM, Evan (R) May 12, 1924- —; Jan. 5, 1987- —.

Arkansas

(Became a state June 15, 1836)

CONWAY, James Sevier (brother of Elias Nelson Conway, below) (D) Dec. 9, 1798-March 3, 1855; Sept. 13, 1836-Nov. 4, 1840.

YELL, Archibald (VBD) Aug. 1799-Feb. 22, 1847; Nov. 4, 1840-April 29, 1844 (Democrat); House 1836-39, 1845-46.

ADAMS, Samuel (D) June 5, 1805-Feb. 27, 1850; April 29-Nov. 5, 1844.

DREW, Thomas Stevenson (D) Aug. 25, 1802-1879; Nov. 5, 1844-Jan. 10, 1849.

BYRD, Richard C. (D) 1805-June 1, 1854; Jan. 11-April 19, 1849.

ROANE, John Selden (D) Jan. 8, 1817-April 17, 1867; April 19, 1849-Nov. 15, 1852.

CONWAY, Elias Nelson (brother of James Sevier Conway, above) (D) May 17, 1812-Feb. 28, 1892; Nov. 15, 1852-Nov. 16, 1860.

RECTOR, Henry Massey (ID) May 1, 1816-Aug. 12, 1899; Nov. 16, 1860-Nov. 4, 1862.

FLETCHER, Thomas (D) April 8, 1819-Feb. 21, 1900; Nov. 4-15, 1862.

FLANAGIN, Harris (D) Nov. 3, 1817-Sept. 23, 1874; Nov. 15, 1862-April 18, 1864.

MURPHY, Isaac (U) Oct. 16, 1802-Sept. 8, 1882; April 18, 1864-July 2, 1868.

CLAYTON, Powell (R) Aug. 7, 1833-Aug. 25, 1914; July 2, 1868-March 17, 1871; Senate 1871-77.

HADLEY, Ozra A. (R) June 30, 1826-July 18, 1915; March 17, 1871-Jan. 6, 1873.

BAXTER, Elisha (R) Sept. 1, 1827-May 31, 1899; Jan. 6, 1873-Nov. 12, 1874.

GARLAND, Augustus Hill (D) June 11, 1832-Jan. 26, 1899; Nov. 12, 1874-Jan. 11, 1877; Senate 1877-85; Atty. Gen. 1885-89.

MILLER, William Read (D) Nov. 23, 1823-Nov. 29, 1887; Jan. 11, 1877-Jan. 13, 1881.

CHURCHILL, Thomas James (D) March 10, 1824-March 10, 1905; Jan. 13, 1881-Jan. 13, 1883.

BERRY, James Henderson (D) May 15, 1841-Jan. 30, 1913; Jan. 13, 1883-Jan. 17, 1885; Senate 1885-1907.

HUGHES, Simon P. (D) April 14, 1830-June 29, 1906; Jan. 17, 1885-Jan. 17, 1889.

EAGLE, James Philip (D) Aug. 10, 1837-Dec. 20, 1904; Jan. 17, 1889-Jan. 10, 1893.

FISHBACK, William Meade (D) Nov. 5, 1831-Feb. 9, 1903; Jan. 10, 1893-Jan. 18, 1895.

CLARKE, James Paul (D) Aug. 18, 1854-Oct. 1, 1916; Jan. 18, 1895-Jan. 12, 1897; Senate 1903-16; Pres. pro tempore 1913-16.

JONES, Daniel Webster (D) Dec. 15, 1839-Dec. 25, 1918; Jan. 12, 1897-Jan. 8, 1901.

DAVIS, Jeff (D) May 6, 1862-Jan. 3, 1913; Jan. 8, 1901-Jan. 8, 1907; Senate 1907-13.

LITTLE, John Sebastian (D) March 15, 1851-Oct. 29, 1916; Jan. 8-Feb. 11, 1907; House 1894-1907.

MOORE, John I. (D) Feb. 7, 1856-March 18, 1937; Feb. 11-May 11, 1907.

PINDALL, Xenophon Overton (D) Aug. 21, 1873-Jan. 2, 1935; May 15, 1907-Jan. 11, 1909.

MARTIN, Jesse M. (D) March 1, 1877-Jan. 22, 1915; Jan. 11-14, 1909.

DONAGHEY, George W. (D) July 1, 1856-Dec. 15, 1937; Jan. 14, 1909-Jan. 15, 1913.

ROBINSON, Joseph Taylor (D) Aug. 26, 1872-July 14, 1937; Jan. 15-March 10, 1913; House 1903-13; Senate 1913-37; Senate majority leader 1933-37.

OLDHAM, William Kavanaugh (D) May 29, 1865-May 6, 1938; March 10-13, 1913.

FUTRELL, Junius Marion (D) Aug. 14, 1870-June 20 1955; March 13-July 23, 1913, Jan. 10, 1933-Jan. 12 1937.

HAYS, George Washington (D) Sept. 23, 1863-Sept. 15 1927; July 23, 1913-Jan. 9, 1917.

BROUGH, Charles Hillman (D) July 9, 1876-Dec. 26 1935; Jan. 9, 1917-Jan. 11, 1921.

McRAE, Thomas Chipman (D) Dec. 21, 1851-June 2, 1929; Jan. 11, 1921-Jan. 13, 1925; House 1885-1903.

TERRAL, Thomas Jefferson (D) Dec. 21, 1882-March 9 1946; Jan. 13, 1925-Jan. 11, 1927.

MARTINEAU, John Ellis (D) Dec. 2, 1873-March 6 1937; Jan. 11, 1927-March 4, 1928.

PARNELL, Harvey (D) Feb. 28, 1880-Jan. 16, 1936 March 14, 1928-Jan. 10, 1933.

FUTRELL, Junius Marion (D) Jan. 10, 1933-Jan. 12 1937 (for previous term see above).

BAILEY, Carl Edward (D) Oct. 8, 1894-Oct. 23, 1948 Jan. 12, 1937-Jan. 14, 1941.

ADKINS, Homer Martin (D) Oct. 15, 1890-Feb. 26 1964; Jan. 14, 1941-Jan. 9, 1945.

LANEY, Benjamin Travis (D) Nov. 25, 1896-Jan. 21 1977; Jan. 9, 1945-Jan. 11, 1949.

McMATH, Sidney Sanders (D) June 14, 1912- —; Jan 11, 1949-Jan. 13, 1953.

CHERRY, Francis Adams (D) Sept. 5, 1908-July 15 1965; Jan. 13, 1953-Jan. 11, 1955.

FAUBUS, Orval Eugene (D) Jan. 7, 1910- —; Jan. 11 1955-Jan. 10, 1967.

ROCKEFELLER, Winthrop (brother of Vice Presiden Nelson Aldrich Rockefeller, uncle of John Daviso "Jay" Rockefeller IV of W.Va., grandson of Se Nelson Wilmarth Aldrich of R.I., nephew of Re Richard Steere Aldrich of R.I.) (R) May 1, 1912-Fe 22, 1973; Jan. 10, 1967-Jan. 12, 1971.

BUMPERS, Dale Leon (D) Aug. 12, 1925- —; Jan. 1 1971-Jan. 2, 1975; Senate 1975- —.

RILEY, Robert Cowley (D) Sept. 18, 1924- —; Jan. 2-1 1975.

PRYOR, David Hampton (D) Aug. 29, 1934- —; Jan. 1 1975-Jan. 3, 1979; House 1966-73; Senate 1979- —.

PURCELL, Joe (D) July 29, 1923- —; Jan. 3-9, 1979.

CLINTON, Bill (D) Aug. 19, 1946- —; Jan. 9, 1979-Jar 19, 1981, Jan. 11, 1983- —.

WHITE, Frank D. (R) June 4, 1933- —; Jan. 19, 1981-Jan. 11, 1983.

CLINTON, Bill (D) Jan. 11, 1983- — (for previous term see above).

California

(Became a state Sept. 9, 1850)

BURNETT, Peter Hardeman (ID) Nov. 15, 1807-May 17, 1895; Dec. 20, 1849-Jan. 9, 1851.

McDOUGAL, John (ID) 1818-March 30, 1866; Jan. 9, 1851-Jan. 8, 1852.

BIGLER, John (brother of William Bigler of Pa.) (D) Jan. 8, 1805-Nov. 29, 1871; Jan. 8, 1852-Jan. 9, 1856.

JOHNSON James Neely (ASP) Aug. 2, 1825-Aug. 31, 1872; Jan. 9, 1856-Jan. 8, 1858.

WELLER, John B. (D) Feb. 22, 1812-Aug. 17, 1875; Jan. 8, 1858-Jan. 9, 1860; House 1839-45 (Ohio); Senate 1852-57 (Union Democrat).

LATHAM, Milton Slocum (D) May 23, 1827-March 4, 1882; Jan. 9-14, 1860; House 1853-55; Senate 1860-63.

DOWNEY, John Gately (D) June 24, 1827-March 1, 1894; Jan. 14, 1860-Jan. 10, 1862.

STANFORD, Amasa Leland (R) March 9, 1824-June 21, 1893; Jan. 10, 1862-Dec. 10, 1863; Senate 1885-93.

LOW, Frederick Ferdinand (U) June 30, 1828-July 21, 1894; Dec. 10, 1863-Dec. 5, 1867; House 1862-63 (Republican).

HAIGHT, Henry Huntly (D) May 20, 1825-Sept. 2, 1878; Dec. 5, 1867-Dec. 8, 1871.

BOOTH, Newton (AM) Dec. 30, 1825-July 14, 1892; Dec. 8, 1871-Feb. 27, 1875 (Republican); Senate 1875-81.

PACHECO, Romualdo (R) Oct. 31, 1831-Jan. 23, 1899; Feb. 27-Dec. 9, 1875; House 1877-78, 1879-83.

IRWIN, William (D) 1827-March 15, 1886; Dec. 9, 1875-Jan. 8, 1880.

PERKINS, George Clement (R) Aug. 23, 1839-Feb. 26, 1923; Jan. 8, 1880-Jan. 10, 1883; Senate 1893-1915.

STONEMAN, George (D) Aug. 8, 1822-Sept. 5, 1894; Jan. 10, 1883-Jan. 8, 1887.

BARTLETT, Washington (D) Feb. 29, 1824-Sept. 12, 1887; Jan. 8-Sept. 12, 1887.

WATERMAN, Robert Whitney (R) Dec. 15, 1826-April 12, 1891; Sept. 13, 1887-Jan. 8, 1891.

MARKHAM, Henry Harrison (R) Nov. 16, 1840-Oct. 9, 1923; Jan. 8, 1891-Jan. 11, 1895; House 1885-87.

BUDD, James Herbert (D) May 18, 1851-July 30, 1908; Jan. 11, 1895-Jan. 3, 1899; House 1883-85.

GAGE, Henry Tifft (R) Dec. 25, 1852-Aug. 28, 1924; Jan. 3, 1899-Jan. 6, 1903.

PARDEE, George Cooper (R) July 25, 1857-Sept. 1, 1941; Jan. 6, 1903-Jan. 8, 1907.

GILLETT, James Norris (R) Sept. 20, 1860-April 20, 1937; Jan. 8, 1907-Jan. 3, 1911; House 1903-06.

JOHNSON, Hiram Warren (R, Prog.) Sept. 2, 1866-Aug. 6, 1945; Jan. 3, 1911-March 15, 1917; Senate 1917-45.

STEPHENS, William Dennison (R) Dec. 26, 1859-April 24, 1944; March 15, 1917-Jan. 9, 1923; House 1911-16.

RICHARDSON, Friend William (R) Dec. 1865-Sept. 6, 1943; Jan. 9, 1923-Jan. 4, 1927.

YOUNG, Clement Calhoun (R) April 28, 1869-Dec. 24, 1947; Jan. 4, 1927-Jan. 6, 1931.

ROLPH, James Jr. (R) Aug. 23, 1869-June 2, 1934; Jan. 6, 1931-June 2, 1934.

MERRIAM, Frank Finley (R) Dec. 22, 1865-April 25, 1955; June 2, 1934-Jan. 2, 1939.

OLSON, Culbert Levy (D) Nov. 7, 1876-April 13, 1962; Jan. 2, 1939-Jan. 4, 1943.

WARREN, Earl (R) March 19, 1891-July 9, 1974; Jan. 4, 1943-Oct. 5, 1953; Chief Justice United States 1954-69.

KNIGHT, Goodwin Jess (R) Dec. 9, 1896-May 22, 1970; Oct. 5, 1953-Jan. 5, 1959.

BROWN, Edmund Gerald "Pat" Sr. (father of Edmund Gerald Brown Jr., below) (D) April 21, 1905- —; Jan. 5, 1959-Jan. 2, 1967.

REAGAN, Ronald Wilson (R) Feb. 6, 1911- —; Jan. 5, 1967-Jan. 6, 1975; President 1981- —.

BROWN, Edmund Gerald "Jerry" Jr. (son of Edmund Gerald "Pat" Brown Sr., above) (D) April 7, 1928- —; Jan. 6, 1975-Jan. 3, 1983.

DEUKMEJIAN, George (R) June 6, 1928- —; Jan. 3, 1983- —.

Colorado

(Became a state Aug. 1, 1876)

ROUTT, John Long (R) April 25, 1826-Aug. 13, 1907; Nov. 3, 1876-Jan. 14, 1879, Jan. 13, 1891-Jan. 10, 1893.

PITKIN, Frederick Walker (R) Aug. 31, 1837-Dec. 18, 1886; Jan. 14, 1879-Jan. 9, 1883.

GRANT, James Benton (D) Jan. 2, 1848-Nov. 1, 1911; Jan. 9, 1883-Jan. 13, 1885.

EATON, Benjamin Harrison (R) Dec. 15, 1833-Oct. 29, 1904; Jan. 13, 1885-Jan. 11, 1887.

ADAMS, Alva (brother of William Herbert Adams, below) (D) May 14, 1850-Nov. 1, 1922; Jan. 11, 1887-Jan. 10, 1889, Jan. 12, 1897-Jan. 10, 1899, Jan. 10-March 17, 1905.

COOPER, Job Adams (R) Nov. 6, 1843-Jan. 20, 1899; Jan. 10, 1889-Jan. 13, 1891.

ROUTT, John Long (R) Jan. 13, 1891-Jan. 10, 1893 (for previous term see above).

WAITE, Davis Hanson (P) April 9, 1825-Nov. 27, 1901; Jan. 10, 1893-Jan. 8, 1895.

McINTIRE, Albert Wills (R) Jan. 15, 1853-Jan. 30, 1935; Jan. 8, 1895-Jan. 12, 1897.

ADAMS, Alva (D) Jan. 12, 1897-Jan. 10, 1899 (for previous term see above).

THOMAS, Charles Spalding (D) Dec. 6, 1849-June 24, 1934; Jan. 10, 1899-Jan. 8, 1901; Senate 1913-21.

ORMAN, James B. (D) Nov. 4, 1849-July 21, 1919; Jan. 8, 1901-Jan. 13, 1903.

PEABODY, James Hamilton (R) Aug. 21, 1852-Nov. 23, 1917; Jan. 13, 1903-Jan. 10, 1905, March 17, 1905.

ADAMS, Alva (D) Jan. 10-March 17, 1905 (for previous terms see above).

PEABODY, James Hamilton (R) March 17, 1905 (for previous term see above).

McDONALD, Jesse Fuller (R) June 30, 1858-Feb. 25, 1942; March 17, 1905-Jan. 8, 1907.

BUCHTEL, Henry Augustus (R) Sept. 30, 1847-Oct. 22, 1924; Jan. 8, 1907-Jan. 12, 1909.

SHAFROTH, John Franklin (D) June 9, 1854-Feb. 20, 1922; Jan. 12, 1909-Jan. 14, 1913; House 1895-97 (1895-97 Silver Republican, 1897-1903 Silver Republican/Democrat); Senate 1913-19.

AMMONS, Elias Milton (father of Teller Ammons, below) (D) July 28, 1860-May 20, 1925; Jan. 14, 1913-Jan. 12, 1915.

CARLSON, George Alfred (R) Oct. 23, 1876-Dec. 6, 1926; Jan. 12, 1915-Jan. 9, 1917.

GUNTER, Julius Caldeen (D) Oct. 31, 1858-Oct. 26, 1940; Jan. 9, 1917-Jan. 14, 1919.

SHOUP, Oliver Henry Nelson (R) Dec. 13, 1869-Sept. 30, 1940; Jan. 14, 1919-Jan. 9, 1923.

SWEET, William Ellery (D) Jan. 27, 1869-May 9, 1942; Jan. 9, 1923-Jan. 13, 1925.

MORLEY, Clarence J. (R) Feb. 9, 1869-Nov. 15, 1948; Jan. 13, 1925-Jan. 11, 1927.

ADAMS, William Herbert (brother of Alva Adams, above) (D) Feb. 15, 1861-Feb. 4, 1954; Jan. 11, 1927-Jan. 10, 1933.

JOHNSON, Edwin Carl (D) Jan. 1, 1884-May 30, 1970; Jan. 10, 1933-Jan. 2, 1937, Jan. 11, 1955-Jan. 8, 1957; Senate 1937-55.

TALBOT, Ray H. (D) Aug. 19, 1896-Jan. 31, 1955; Jan. 3-12, 1937.

AMMONS, Teller (son of Elias Milton Ammons, above) (D) Dec. 3, 1895-Jan. 16, 1972; Jan. 12, 1937-Jan. 10, 1939.

CARR, Ralph L. (R) Dec. 11, 1887-Sept. 22, 1950; Jan. 10, 1939-Jan. 12, 1943.

VIVIAN, John Charles (R) June 30, 1887-Feb. 10, 1964; Jan. 12, 1943-Jan. 14, 1947.

KNOUS, William Lee (D) Feb. 2, 1889-Dec. 13, 1959; Jan. 14, 1947-April 15, 1950.

JOHNSON, Walter Walfred (D) April 16, 1904--; April 15, 1950-Jan. 9, 1951.

THORNTON, Daniel Isaac J. (R) Jan. 31, 1911--; Jan. 9, 1951-Jan. 11, 1955.

JOHNSON, Edwin Carl (D) Jan. 11, 1955-Jan. 8, 1957 (for previous term see above).

McNICHOLS, Stephen L. R. (D) March 17, 1914--; Jan. 8, 1957-Jan. 8, 1963.

LOVE, John A. (R) Nov. 29, 1916--; Jan. 8, 1963-July 16, 1973.

VANDERHOOF, John David (R) May 27, 1922--; July 16, 1973-Jan. 14, 1975.

LAMM, Richard David (D) Aug. 3, 1935--; Jan. 14, 1975-Jan. 13, 1987.

ROMER, Roy (D) Oct. 31, 1928--; Jan. 13, 1987--.

Connecticut

(Ratified the Constitution Jan. 9, 1788)

HUNTINGTON, Samuel (uncle of Samuel H. Huntington of Ohio) (F) July 3, 1731-Jan. 5, 1796; May 11, 1786-Jan. 5, 1796; Cont. Cong. 1775-81 (President 1779-81).

WOLCOTT, Oliver Sr. (father of Oliver Wolcott Jr., uncle of Roger Griswold) (F) Dec. 20, 1726-Dec. 1, 1797; Jan. 5, 1796-Dec. 1, 1797; Cont. Cong. 1775-78, 1780-84.

TRUMBULL, Jonathan (uncle of Joseph Trumbull, below) (F) March 26, 1740-Aug. 7, 1809; Dec. 1, 1797-Aug. 7, 1809; House 1789-95; Speaker 1791-93; Senate 1795-96.

TREADWELL, John (F) Nov. 23, 1745-Aug. 18, 1823; Aug. 7, 1809-May 9, 1811; Cont. Cong. 1785-86.

GRISWOLD, Roger (nephew of Oliver Wolcott Sr., cousin of Oliver Wolcott Jr.) (F) May 21, 1762-Oct. 25, 1812; May 9, 1811-Oct. 25, 1812; House 1795-1805.

SMITH, John Cotton (F) Feb. 12, 1765-Dec. 7, 1845; Oct. 25, 1812-May 8, 1817; House 1800-06.

WOLCOTT, Oliver Jr. (son of Oliver Wolcott Sr., cousin of Roger Griswold) (DR) Jan. 11, 1760-June 1, 1833; May 8, 1817-May 2, 1827; Secy. of the Treasury 1795-1800.

TOMLINSON, Gideon (D) Dec. 31, 1780-Oct. 8, 1854; May 2, 1827-March 2, 1831 (Democratic Republican); House 1819-27 (Democratic Republican); Senate 1831-37.

PETERS, John Samuel (NR) Sept. 21, 1772-March 30, 1858; March 2, 1831-May 4, 1833.

EDWARDS, Henry Waggaman (D) Oct. 1779-July 22, 1847; May 4, 1833-May 7, 1834, May 6, 1835-May 2, 1838; House 1819-23; Senate 1823-27.

FOOTE, Samuel Augustus (W) Nov. 8, 1780-Sept. 15, 1846; May 7, 1834-May 6, 1835; House 1819-21, 1823-25, 1833-34; Senate 1827-33.

EDWARDS, Henry Waggaman (D) May 6, 1835-May 2, 1838 (for previous term see above).

ELLSWORTH, William Wolcott (W) Nov. 10, 1791-Jan. 15, 1868; May 2, 1838-May 4, 1842; House 1829-34.

CLEVELAND, Chauncey Fitch (D) Feb. 16, 1799-June 6, 1887; May 4, 1842-May 1844; House 1849-53.

BALDWIN, Roger Sherman (father of Simeon Eben Baldwin, below) (W) Jan. 4, 1793-Feb. 19, 1863; May 1844-May 6, 1846; Senate 1847-51.

TOUCEY, Isaac (D) Nov. 5, 1796-July 30, 1869; May 6, 1846-May 5, 1847; House 1835-39; Senate 1852-57; Atty. Gen. 1848-49; Secy. of the Navy 1857-61.

BISSELL, Clark (W) Sept. 7, 1782-Sept. 15, 1857; May 5, 1847-May 2, 1849.

TRUMBULL, Joseph (nephew of Jonathan Trumbull, above) (W) Dec. 7, 1782-Aug. 4, 1861; May 2, 1849-May 4, 1850; House 1834-35, 1839-43.

SEYMOUR, Thomas Hart (D) Sept. 29, 1807-Sept. 3, 1868; May 4, 1850-Oct. 13, 1853; House 1843-45.

POND, Charles Hobby (D) April 26, 1781-April 28, 1861; Oct. 13, 1853-May 1854.

DUTTON, Henry (W) Feb. 12, 1796-April 26, 1869; May 1854-May 1855.

MINOR, William Thomas (ASP) Oct. 3, 1815-Oct. 13, 1889; May 3, 1855-May 6, 1857.

HOLLEY, Alexander Hamilton (R) Aug. 12, 1804-Oct. 2, 1887; May 6, 1857-May 5, 1858.

BUCKINGHAM, William Alfred (R) May 28, 1804-Feb. 5, 1875; May 5, 1858-May 2, 1866; Senate 1869-75.

HAWLEY, Joseph Roswell (R) Oct. 31, 1826-March 17, 1905; May 2, 1866-May 1, 1867; House 1872-75, 1879-81; Senate 1881-1905.

ENGLISH, James Edward (D) March 13, 1812-March 2, 1890; May 1, 1867-May 5, 1869, May 4, 1870-May 16, 1871; House 1861-65; Senate 1875-76.

JEWELL, Marshall (R) Oct. 20, 1825-Feb. 10, 1883; May 5, 1869-May 4, 1870, May 16, 1871-May 7, 1873; Postmaster Gen. 1874-76; Chrmn. Rep. Nat. Comm. 1880-83.

ENGLISH, James Edward (D) May 4, 1870-May 16, 1871 (for previous term see above).

JEWELL, Marshall (R) May 16, 1871-May 7, 1873 (for previous term see above).

INGERSOLL, Charles Roberts (D) Sept. 16, 1821-Jan. 25, 1903; May 7, 1873-Jan. 3, 1877.

HUBBARD, Richard Dudley (D) Sept. 7, 1818-Feb. 28, 1884; Jan. 3, 1877-Jan. 9, 1879; House 1867-69.

ANDREWS, Charles Bartlett (R) Nov. 4, 1836-Sept. 12, 1902; Jan. 9, 1879-Jan. 5, 1881.

BIGELOW, Hobart B. (R) May 16, 1834-Oct. 12, 1891; Jan. 5, 1881-Jan. 3, 1883.

WALLER, Thomas MacDonald (D) 1839-Jan. 24, 1924; Jan. 3, 1883-Jan. 8, 1885.

HARRISON, Henry Baldwin (R) Sept. 11, 1821-Oct. 29, 1901; Jan. 8, 1885-Jan. 7, 1887.

LOUNSBURY, Phineas Chapman (brother of George Edward Lounsbury, below) (R) Jan. 10, 1841-June 22, 1925; Jan. 7, 1887-Jan. 10, 1889.

BULKELEY, Morgan Gardner (cousin of Edwin Dennison Morgan of N.Y.) (R) Dec. 26, 1837-Nov. 6, 1922; Jan. 10, 1889-Jan. 4, 1893; Senate 1905-11.

MORRIS, Luzon Burritt (D) April 16, 1827-Aug. 22, 1895; Jan. 4, 1893-Jan. 9, 1895.

COFFIN, Owen Vincent (R) June 20, 1836-Jan. 3, 1921; Jan. 9, 1895-Jan. 6, 1897.

COOKE, Lorrin Alamson (R) April 6, 1831-Aug. 12, 1902; Jan. 6, 1897-Jan. 4, 1899.

LOUNSBURY George Edward (brother of Phineas Chapman Lounsbury, above) (R) May 7, 1838-Aug. 16, 1904; Jan. 4, 1899-Jan. 9, 1901.

McLEAN, George Payne (R) Oct. 7, 1857-June 6, 1932; Jan. 9, 1901-Jan. 7, 1903; Senate 1911-29.

CHAMBERLAIN, Abiram (R) Dec. 7, 1837-May 15, 1911; Jan. 7, 1903-Jan. 4, 1905.

ROBERTS, Henry (R) Jan. 22, 1853-May 1, 1929; Jan. 4, 1905-Jan. 9, 1907.

WOODRUFF, Rollin Simmons (R) July 14, 1854-June 30, 1925; Jan. 9, 1907-Jan. 6, 1909.

LILLEY, George Leavens (R) Aug. 3, 1859-April 21, 1909; Jan. 6-April 21, 1909; House 1903-09.

WEEKS, Frank Bentley (R) Jan. 20, 1854-Oct. 2, 1935; April 21, 1909-Jan. 4, 1911.

BALDWIN, Simeon Eben (son of Roger Sherman Baldwin, above) (D) Feb. 5, 1840-Jan. 30, 1927; Jan. 4, 1911-Jan. 6, 1915.

HOLCOMB, Marcus Hensey (R) Nov. 28, 1884-March 5, 1932; Jan. 6, 1915-Jan. 5, 1921.

LAKE, Everett John (R) Feb. 8, 1871-Sept. 16, 1948; Jan. 5, 1921-Jan. 3, 1923.

TEMPLETON, Charles Augustus (R) March 3, 1871-Aug. 15, 1955; Jan. 3, 1923-Jan. 7, 1925.

BINGHAM, Hiram (R) Nov. 19, 1875-June 6, 1956; Jan. 7-8, 1925; Senate 1924-33.

TRUMBULL, John Harper (R) March 4, 1873-May 21, 1961; Jan. 8, 1925-Jan. 7, 1931.

CROSS, Wilbur Lucius (D) April 10, 1862-Oct. 5, 1948; Jan. 7, 1931-Jan. 4, 1939.

BALDWIN, Raymond Earl (R) Aug. 31, 1893-Oct. 4, 1986; Jan. 4, 1939-Jan. 8, 1941, Jan. 6, 1943-Dec. 27, 1946; Senate 1946-49.

HURLEY, Robert Augustine (D) Aug. 25, 1895-May 3, 1968; Jan. 8, 1941-Jan. 6, 1943.

BALDWIN, Raymond Earl (R) Jan. 6, 1943-Dec. 27, 1946 (for previous term see above).

SNOW, Charles Wilbert (D) April 6, 1884-Sept. 28, 1977; Dec. 27, 1946-Jan. 8, 1947.

McCONAUGHY, James Lukens (R) Oct. 21, 1887-March 7, 1948; Jan. 8, 1947-March 7, 1948.

SHANNON, James Coughlin (R) July 21, 1896- —; March 7, 1948-Jan. 5, 1949.

BOWLES, Chester Bliss (D) April 5, 1901-May 25, 1986; Jan. 5, 1949-Jan. 3, 1951; House 1959-61.

LODGE, John Davis (R) Oct. 20, 1903-Oct. 29, 1985; Jan. 3, 1951-Jan. 5, 1955; House 1947-51.

RIBICOFF, Abraham Alexander (D) April 9, 1910- —; Jan. 5, 1955-Jan. 21, 1961; House 1949-53; Senate 1963-81; Secy. of Health, Education and Welfare 1961-62.

DEMPSEY, John Noel (D) Jan. 3, 1915- —; Jan. 21, 1961-Jan. 6, 1971.

MESKILL, Thomas Joseph (R) Jan. 30, 1928- —; Jan. 6, 1971-Jan. 8, 1975; House 1967-71.

GRASSO, Ella Tambussi (D) May 10, 1919-Feb. 5, 1981; Jan. 8, 1975-Dec. 31, 1980; House 1971-75.

O'NEILL, William A. (D) Aug. 11, 1930- —; Dec. 31, 1980- —.

Delaware

(Ratified the Constitution Dec. 7, 1787)

CLAYTON, Joshua (son-in-law of Richard Bassett, below) (F) July 20, 1744-Aug. 11, 1798; June 2, 1789-Jan. 13, 1796; Senate 1798.

BEDFORD, Gunning Sr. (F) April 7, 1742-Sept. 28, 1797; Jan. 13, 1796-Sept. 28, 1797.

ROGERS, Daniel (F) Jan. 3, 1754-Feb. 2, 1806; Sept. 28, 1797-Jan. 9, 1799.

BASSETT, Richard (father-in-law of Joshua Clayton, above) (F) April 2, 1745-Aug. 15, 1815; Jan. 9, 1799-March 3, 1801; Senate 1789-93.

SYKES, James (F) March 27, 1761-Oct. 18, 1822; March 3, 1801-Jan. 19, 1802.

HALL, David (DR) Jan. 4, 1752-Sept. 18, 1817; Jan. 19, 1802-Jan. 15, 1805.

MITCHELL, Nathaniel (F) 1753-Feb. 21, 1814; Jan. 15, 1805-Jan. 19, 1808; Cont. Cong. 1786-88.

TRUITT, George (F) 1756-Oct. 8, 1818; Jan. 19, 1808-Jan. 15, 1811.

HASLET, Joseph (DR) 1769-June 20, 1823; Jan. 15, 1811-Jan. 18, 1814, Jan. 21-June 20, 1823.

RODNEY, Daniel (brother of Caleb Rodney, below) (F) Sept. 10, 1764-Sept. 2, 1846; Jan. 18, 1814-Jan. 21, 1817; House 1822-23; Senate 1826-27.

CLARK, John (F) Feb. 1, 1761-Aug. 14, 1821; Jan. 21, 1817-Jan. 15, 1820.

STOUT, Jacob (F) 1764-Nov. 1855; Jan. 15, 1820-Jan. 16, 1821.

COLLINS, John (DR) 1775-April 15, 1822; Jan. 16, 1821-April 15, 1822.

RODNEY, Caleb (brother of Daniel Rodney, above) (DR) April 29, 1767-April 29, 1840; April 15, 1822-Jan. 21, 1823.

HASLET, Joseph (DR) Jan. 21-June 20, 1823 (for previous term see above).

THOMAS, Charles (DR) June 23, 1790-Feb. 8, 1848; June 20, 1823-Jan. 20, 1824.

PAYNTER, Samuel (F) 1768-Oct. 2, 1845; Jan. 20, 1824-Jan. 16, 1827.

POLK, Charles (F) Nov. 15, 1788-Oct. 27, 1857; Jan. 16, 1827-Jan. 19, 1830, May 9, 1836-Jan. 17, 1837.

HAZZARD, David (D) May 18, 1781-July 8, 1864; Jan. 19, 1830-Jan. 15, 1833.

BENNETT, Caleb Prew (D) Nov. 11, 1758-May 9, 1836; Jan. 15, 1833-May 9, 1836.

POLK, Charles (F) May 9, 1836-Jan. 17, 1837 (for previous term see above).

COMEGYS, Cornelius Parsons (W) Jan. 15, 1780-Jan. 27, 1851; Jan. 17, 1837-Jan. 19, 1841.

COOPER, William B. (W) Dec. 16, 1771-April 27, 1849; Jan. 19, 1841-Jan. 21, 1845.

STOCKTON, Thomas (W) April 1, 1781-March 2, 1846; Jan. 21, 1845-March 2, 1846.

MAULL, Joseph (W) Sept 6, 1781-May 1, 1846; March 2-May 1, 1846.

TEMPLE, William (W) Feb. 28, 1814-May 28, 1863; May 1, 1846-Jan. 19, 1847.

THARP, William (grandfather of William T. Watson, below) (D) Nov. 27, 1803-Jan. 1, 1865; Jan. 19, 1847-Jan. 21, 1851.

ROSS, William Henry Harrison (D) June 2, 1814-June 29, 1887; Jan. 21, 1851-Jan. 16, 1855.

CAUSEY, Peter Foster (uncle of Trusten Polk of Mo.) (AW) Jan. 11, 1801-Feb. 15, 1871; Jan. 16, 1855-Jan. 18, 1859.

BURTON, William (D) Oct. 16, 1789-Aug. 5, 1866; Jan. 18, 1859-Jan. 20, 1863.

CANNON, William (U) March 15, 1809-March 1, 1865; Jan. 20, 1863-March 1, 1865.

SAULSBURY, Gove (D) May 29, 1815-July 31, 1881; March 1, 1865-Jan. 17, 1871.

PONDER, James (D) Oct. 31, 1819-Nov. 5, 1897; Jan. 17, 1871-Jan. 19, 1875.

COCHRAN, John P. (D) Feb. 7, 1809-Dec. 27, 1898; Jan. 19, 1875-Jan. 21, 1879.

HALL, John Wood (D) Jan. 1, 1817-Jan. 23, 1892; Jan. 21, 1879-Jan. 16, 1883.

STOCKLEY, Charles Clark (D) Nov. 6, 1819-April 20, 1901; Jan. 16, 1883-Jan. 18, 1887.

BIGGS, Benjamin Thomas (D) Oct. 1, 1821-Dec. 25, 1893; Jan. 18, 1887-Jan. 20, 1891; House 1869-73.

REYNOLDS, Robert John (D) March 17, 1838-June 10, 1909; Jan. 20, 1891-Jan. 15, 1895.

MARVIEL, Joshua Hopkins (R) Sept. 3, 1825-April 8, 1895; Jan. 15-April 8, 1895.

WATSON, William T. (grandson of William Tharp, above) (D) June 6, 1849-April 14, 1917; April 8, 1895-Jan. 19, 1897.

TUNNELL, Ebe Walter (D) Dec. 31, 1844-Dec. 13, 1917; Jan. 19, 1897-Jan. 15, 1901.

HUNN, John (R) June 23, 1849-Sept. 1, 1926; Jan. 15, 1901-Jan. 17, 1905.

LEA, Preston (R) Nov. 12, 1841-Dec. 4, 1916; Jan. 17, 1905-Jan. 19, 1909.

PENNEWILL, Simeon Selby (R) July 23, 1867-Sept. 9, 1935; Jan. 19, 1909-Jan. 21, 1913.

MILLER, Charles R. (R) Sept. 30, 1857-Sept. 18, 1927; Jan. 21, 1913-Jan. 17, 1917.

TOWNSEND, John Gillis Jr. (R) May 31, 1871-April 10, 1964; Jan. 17, 1917-Jan. 18, 1921; Senate 1929-41.

DENNEY, William Du Hamel (R) March 31, 1873-Nov. 22, 1953; Jan. 18, 1921-Jan. 20, 1925.

ROBINSON, Robert P. (R) March 28, 1869-March 4, 1939; Jan. 20, 1925-Jan. 15, 1929.

BUCK, Clayton Douglass (R) March 21, 1890-Jan. 27, 1965; Jan. 15, 1929-Jan. 19, 1937; Senate 1943-49.

McMULLEN, Richard Cann (D) Jan. 2, 1868-Feb. 18, 1944; Jan. 19, 1937-Jan. 21, 1941.

BACON, Walter W. (R) Jan. 20, 1879-March 18, 1962; Jan. 21, 1941-Jan. 18, 1949.

CARVEL, Elbert Nostrand (D) Feb. 9, 1910- —; Jan. 18, 1949-Jan. 20, 1953, Jan. 17, 1961-Jan. 19, 1965.

BOGGS, James Caleb (R) May 15, 1909- —; Jan. 20, 1953-Dec. 30, 1960; House 1947-53; Senate 1961-73.

BUCKSON, David Penrose (R) July 25, 1920- —; Dec. 30, 1960-Jan. 17, 1961.

CARVEL, Elbert Nostrand (D) Jan. 17, 1961-Jan. 19, 1965 (for previous term see above).

TERRY, Charles Laymen Jr. (D) Sept. 17, 1900-Feb. 6, 1970; Jan. 19, 1965-Jan. 21, 1969.

PETERSON, Russell Wilbur (R) Oct. 3, 1916- —; Jan. 21, 1969-Jan. 16, 1973.

TRIBBITT, Sherman Willard (D) Nov. 9, 1922- —; Jan. 16, 1973-Jan. 18, 1977.

du PONT, Pierre Samuel "Pete" IV (R) Jan. 22, 1935- —; Jan. 18, 1977-Jan. 15, 1985; House 1971-77.

CASTLE, Michael N. (R) July 2, 1939- —; Jan. 15, 1985- —.

Florida

(Became a state March 3, 1845)

MOSELEY, William Dunn (D) Feb. 1, 1795-Jan. 4, 1863; June 25, 1845-Oct. 1, 1849.

BROWN, Thomas (W) Oct. 24, 1785-August 24, 1867; Oct. 1, 1849-Oct. 3, 1853.

BROOME, James E. (D) Dec. 15, 1808-Nov. 23, 1883; Oct. 3, 1853-Oct. 5, 1857.

PERRY, Madison Stark (D) 1814-March 1865; Oct. 5, 1857-Oct. 7, 1861.

MILTON, John (D) April 20, 1807-April 1, 1865; Oct. 7, 1861-April 1, 1865.

MARVIN, William (D) April 14, 1808-July 9, 1902; July 13-Dec. 20, 1865.

WALKER, David Shelby (C) May 2, 1815-July 20, 1891; Dec. 20, 1865-July 9, 1868.

REED, Harrison (R) Aug. 26, 1813-March 25, 1899; July 9, 1868-Jan. 7, 1873.

HART, Ossian Bingley (R) Jan. 17, 1821-March 18, 187? Jan. 7, 1873-March 18, 1874.

STEARNS, Marcellus Lovejoy (R) April 29, 1839-Dec. ? 1891; March 18, 1874-Jan. 2, 1877.

DREW, George Franklin (D) Aug. 6, 1827-Sept. 26, 190? Jan. 2, 1877-Jan. 4, 1881.

BLOXHAM, William Dunnington (D) July 9, 183? March 15, 1911; Jan. 4, 1881-Jan. 6, 1885, Jan. ? 1897-Jan. 8, 1901.

PERRY, Edward Alysworth (D) March 15, 1831-Oct. 1? 1889; Jan. 6, 1885-Jan. 8, 1889.

FLEMING, Francis Philip (D) Sept. 28, 1841-Dec. 2? 1908; Jan. 8, 1889-Jan. 3, 1893.

MITCHELL, Henry Laurens (D) Sept. 3, 1831-Oct. 1? 1903; Jan. 3, 1893-Jan. 5, 1897.

BLOXHAM, William Dunnington (D) Jan. 5, 1897-Jan? 8, 1901 (for previous term see above).

JENNINGS, William Sherman (D) March 24, 1863-Feb? 28, 1920; Jan. 8, 1901-Jan. 3, 1905.

BROWARD, Napoleon Bonaparte (D) April 19, 1857? Oct. 1, 1910; Jan. 3, 1905-Jan. 5, 1909.

GILCHRIST, Albert Waller (D) Jan. 15, 1858-May 1? 1926; Jan. 5, 1909-Jan. 7, 1913.

TRAMMELL, Park (D) April 9, 1876-May 8, 1936; Jan? 7, 1913-Jan. 2, 1917; Senate 1917-36.

CATTS, Sidney Johnston (Prohib.) July 31, 1863-March 9, 1936; Jan. 2, 1917-Jan. 4, 1921.

HARDEE, Cary Augustus (D) Nov. 13, 1876-Nov. 2? 1957; Jan. 4, 1921-Jan. 6, 1925.

MARTIN, John Wellborn (D) June 21, 1884-Feb. 2? 1958; Jan. 6, 1925-Jan. 8, 1929.

CARLTON, Doyle Elam (D) July 6, 1887-Oct. 25, 197? Jan. 8, 1929-Jan. 3, 1933.

SHOLTZ, David (D) Oct. 6, 1891-March 21, 1953; Jan. ? 1933-Jan. 5, 1937.

CONE, Frederick Preston (D) Sept. 28, 1871-July 2? 1948; Jan. 5, 1937-Jan. 7, 1941.

HOLLAND, Spessard Lindsey (D) July 10, 1892-Nov. ? 1971; Jan. 7, 1941-Jan. 2, 1945; Senate 1946-71.

CALDWELL, Millard Fillmore (D) Feb. 6, 1897-Oct. 2? 1984; Jan. 2, 1945-Jan. 4, 1949; House 1933-41.

WARREN, Fuller (D) Oct. 3, 1905-Sept. 23, 1973; Jan. ? 1949-Jan. 6, 1953.

McCARTY, Daniel Thomas (D) Jan. 18, 1912-Sept. 28, 1953; Jan. 6-Sept. 28, 1953.

JOHNS, Charley Eugene (D) Feb. 27, 1905- —; Sept. 28, 1953-Jan. 4, 1955.

COLLINS, Thomas LeRoy (D) March 19, 1909- —; Jan. 4, 1955-Jan. 3, 1961.

BRYANT, Cecil Farris (D) July 26, 1914- —; Jan. 3, 1961-Jan. 5, 1965.

BURNS, William Haydon (D) March 17, 1912- —; Jan. 5, 1965-Jan. 3, 1967.

KIRK, Claude Roy Jr. (R) Jan. 7, 1926- —; Jan. 3, 1967- Jan. 5, 1971.

ASKEW, Reubin O'Donovan (D) Sept. 11, 1928- —; Jan. 5, 1971-Jan. 2, 1979.

GRAHAM, Daniel Robert "Bob" (D) Nov. 9, 1936- —; Jan. 2, 1979-Jan. 3, 1987; Senate 1987- —.

MIXON, John Wayne (D) June 16, 1922- —; Jan. 3-6, 1987.

MARTINEZ, Robert (R) Dec. 25, 1934- —; Jan. 6, 1987- —.

Georgia

(Ratified the Constitution Jan. 2, 1788)

HANDLEY, George (DR) Feb. 9, 1752-Sept. 17, 1793; Jan. 26, 1788-Jan. 7, 1789.

WALTON, George (DR) 1749-Feb. 2, 1804; Jan. 7-Nov. 9, 1789; Cont. Cong. 1776-78, 1780-81, 1787-88; Senate 1795-96.

TELFAIR, Edward (DR) 1735-Sept. 17, 1807; Nov. 9, 1789-Nov. 7, 1793; Cont. Cong. 1778-82, 1784, 1788-89.

MATHEWS, George (DR) Aug. 30, 1739-Aug. 30, 1812; Nov. 7, 1793-Jan. 15, 1796; House 1789-91.

IRWIN, Jared (DR) 1750-March 1, 1818; Jan. 15, 1796-Jan. 12, 1798, Sept. 23, 1806-Nov. 10, 1809.

JACKSON, James (DR) Sept. 21, 1757-March 19, 1806; Jan. 12, 1798-March 3, 1801; House 1789-91; Senate 1793-95, 1801-06.

EMANUEL, David (DR) 1744-Feb. 19, 1808; March 31-Nov. 7, 1801.

TATTNALL, Josiah Jr. (DR) 1764-June 6, 1803; Nov. 7, 1801-Nov. 4, 1802; Senate 1796-99.

MILLEDGE, John (DR) 1757-Feb. 9, 1818; Nov. 4, 1802-Sept. 23, 1806; House 1792-93, 1795-99, 1801-1802; Senate 1806-09; Pres. pro tempore 1809.

IRWIN, Jared (DR) Sept. 23, 1806-Nov. 10, 1809 (for previous term see above).

MITCHELL, David Brydie (DR) Oct. 22, 1766-April 22, 1837; Nov. 10, 1809-Nov. 5, 1813, Nov. 10, 1815-March 4, 1817.

EARLY, Peter (DR) June 20, 1773-Aug. 15, 1817; Nov. 5, 1813-Nov. 10, 1815; House 1803-07.

MITCHELL, David Brydie (DR) Nov. 10, 1815-March 4, 1817 (for previous term see above).

RABUN, William (DR) April 8, 1771-Oct. 25, 1819; March 4, 1817-Oct. 24, 1819.

TALBOT, Matthew (DR) 1767-Sept.17, 1827; Oct. 24-Nov. 5, 1819.

CLARK, John (father of Edward Clark of Texas) (DR) Feb. 28, 1766-Oct. 2, 1832; Nov. 5, 1819-Nov. 7, 1823.

TROUP, George Michael (SRD) Sept. 8, 1780-April 26, 1856; Nov. 7, 1823-Nov. 7, 1827 (Democratic Republican); House 1807-15 (Democrat); Senate 1816-18, 1829-33.

FORSYTH, John (DR) Oct. 22, 1780-Oct. 21, 1841; Nov. 7, 1827-Nov. 4, 1829; House 1813-18, 1823-27; Senate 1818-19, 1829-34; Secy. of State 1834-41.

GILMER, George Rockingham (W) April 11, 1790-Nov. 16, 1859; Nov. 4, 1829-Nov. 9, 1831 (Democrat), Nov. 8, 1837-Nov. 6, 1839; House 1821-23 (Democrat), 1827-29 (Democrat), 1833-35 (Democrat).

LUMPKIN, Wilson (UD) Jan. 14, 1783-Dec. 28, 1870; Nov. 9, 1831-Nov. 4, 1835; House 1815-17, 1827-31; Senate 1837-41.

SCHLEY, William (UD) Dec. 10, 1786-Nov. 20, 1858; Nov. 4, 1835-Nov. 8, 1837; House 1833-35.

GILMER, George Rockingham (W) Nov. 8, 1837-Nov. 6, 1839 (for previous term see above).

McDONALD, Charles James (D) July 9, 1793-Dec. 16, 1860; Nov. 6, 1839-Nov. 8, 1843.

CRAWFORD, George Walker (W) Dec. 22, 1798-July 27, 1872; Nov. 8, 1843-Nov. 3, 1847; House 1843; Secy. of War 1849-50.

TOWNS, George Washington Bonaparte (D) May 4, 1801-July 15, 1854; Nov. 3, 1847-Nov. 5, 1851; House 1835-36, 1837-39, 1846-47 (1835-39 Union Democrat).

COBB, Howell (D) Sept. 7, 1815-Oct. 9, 1868; Nov. 5, 1851-Nov. 9, 1853 (Union Democrat); House 1843-51, 1855-57; Speaker 1849-51; Secy. of the Treasury 1857-60.

JOHNSON, Herschel Vespasian (D) Sept. 18, 1812-Aug. 16, 1880; Nov. 9, 1853-Nov. 6, 1857; Senate 1848-49.

BROWN, Joseph Emerson (father of Joseph Mackey Brown, below) (D) April 15, 1821-Nov. 30, 1894; Nov. 6, 1857-June 17, 1865; Senate 1880-91.

JOHNSON, James (D) Feb. 12, 1811-Nov. 20, 1891; (Provisional) June 17-Dec. 14, 1865; House 1851-53 (Unionist).

JENKINS, Charles Jones (D) Jan. 6, 1805-June 14, 1883; Dec. 14, 1865-Jan. 13, 1868.

RUGER, Thomas Howard; April 2, 1833-June 3, 1907; (Military) Jan. 13-July 4, 1868.

BULLOCK, Rufus Brown (R) March 28, 1834-April 27, 1907; July 4, 1868-Oct. 23, 1871.

CONLEY, Benjamin (R) March 1, 1815-Jan. 10, 1886; Oct. 30, 1871-Jan. 12, 1872.

SMITH, James Milton (D) Oct. 24, 1823-Nov. 25, 1890; Jan. 12, 1872-Jan. 12, 1877.

COLQUITT, Alfred Holt (D) April 20, 1824-March 26, 1894; Jan. 12, 1877-Nov. 4, 1882; House 1853-55; Senate 1883-94.

STEPHENS, Alexander Hamilton (D) Feb. 11, 1812-March 4, 1883; Nov. 4, 1882-March 4, 1883; House 1843-59, 1873-82.

BOYNTON, James Stoddard (D) May 7, 1833-Dec. 22, 1902; March 5-May 10, 1883.

McDANIEL, Henry Dickerson (D) Sept. 4, 1836-July 25, 1926; May 10, 1883-Nov. 9, 1886.

GORDON, John Brown (D) Feb. 6, 1832-Jan. 9, 1904; Nov. 9, 1886-Nov. 8, 1890; Senate 1873-80, 1891-97.

NORTHEN, William Jonathan (D) July 9, 1835-March 25, 1913; Nov. 8, 1890-Oct. 27, 1894.

ATKINSON, William Yates (D) Nov. 11, 1854-Aug. 8, 1899; Oct. 27, 1894-Oct. 29, 1898.

CANDLER, Allen Daniel (D) Nov. 4, 1834-Oct. 26, 1910; Oct. 29, 1898-Oct. 25, 1902; House 1883-91.

TERRELL, Joseph Meriwether (D) June 6, 1861-Nov. 17, 1912; Oct. 25, 1902-June 29, 1907; Senate 1910-11.

SMITH, Hoke (D) Sept. 2, 1855-Nov. 27, 1931; June 29, 1907-June 26, 1909, July 1-Nov. 16, 1911; Senate 1911-21; Secy. of the Interior 1893-96.

BROWN, Joseph Mackey (son of Joseph Emerson Brown, above) (D) Dec. 28, 1851-March 3, 1932; June 26, 1909-July 1, 1911, Jan. 25, 1912-June 28, 1913.

SMITH, Hoke (D) July 1-Nov. 16, 1911 (for previous term see above).

SLATON, John Marshall (D) Dec. 25, 1866-Jan. 11 1955; Nov. 16, 1911-Jan. 25, 1912, June 28, 1913-June 26, 1915.

BROWN, Joseph Mackey (D) Jan. 25, 1912-June 28 1913 (for previous term see above).

SLATON, John Marshall (D) June 28, 1913-June 26 1915 (for previous term see above).

HARRIS, Nathaniel Edwin (D) Jan. 21, 1846-Sept. 21 1929; June 26, 1915-June 30, 1917.

DORSEY, Hugh Manson (D) July 10, 1871-June 11 1948; June 30, 1917-June 25, 1921.

HARDWICK, Thomas William (D) Dec. 9, 1872-Jan. 31 1944; June 25, 1921-June 30, 1923; House 1903-14 Senate 1914-19.

WALKER, Clifford Mitchell (D) July 4, 1877-Nov. 9 1954; June 30, 1923-June 25, 1927.

HARDMAN, Lamartine Griffin (D) April 14, 1856-Feb 18, 1937; June 25, 1927-June 27, 1931.

RUSSELL, Richard Brevard Jr. (D) Nov. 2, 1897-Jan 21, 1971; June 27, 1931-Jan. 10, 1933; Senate 1933-71; Pres. pro tempore 1969-71.

TALMADGE, Eugene (father of Herman Eugene Talmadge, below) (D) Sept. 23, 1884-Dec. 21, 1946; Jan 10, 1933-Jan. 12, 1937, Jan. 14, 1941-Jan. 12, 1943

RIVERS, Eurith Dickinson (D) Dec. 1, 1895-June 11 1967; Jan. 12, 1937-Jan. 14, 1941.

TALMADGE, Eugene (D) Jan. 14, 1941-Jan. 12, 1943 (for previous term see above).

ARNALL, Ellis Gibbs (D) March 20, 1907- —; Jan. 12 1943-Jan. 14, 1947.

TALMADGE, Herman Eugene (son of Eugene Talmadge, above) (D) Aug. 9, 1913- —; Jan. 14-March 18, 1947, Nov. 17, 1948-Jan. 11, 1955; Senate 1957-81.

THOMPSON, Melvin Ernest (D) May 1, 1903-Oct. ? 1980; March 18, 1947-Nov. 17, 1948.

TALMADGE, Herman Eugene (D) Nov. 17, 1948-Jan 11, 1955 (for previous term see above).

GRIFFIN, Samuel Marvin (D) Sept. 4, 1907-June 13 1982; Jan. 11, 1955-Jan. 13, 1959.

NDIVER, Samuel Ernest Jr. (D) July 3, 1918- —; Jan. 13, 1959-Jan. 15, 1963.

NDERS, Carl Edward (D) July 15, 1925- —; Jan. 15, 1963-Jan. 10, 1967.

DDOX, Lester Garfield (D) Sept. 30, 1915- —; Jan. 11, 1967-Jan. 12, 1971.

RTER, James Earl "Jimmy" Jr. (D) Oct. 1, 1924- —; Jan. 12, 1971-Jan. 14, 1975; President 1977-81.

SBEE, George Dekle (D) Aug. 7, 1927- —; Jan. 14, 1975-Jan. 11, 1983.

RRIS, Joe Frank (D) Feb. 26, 1936- —; Jan. 11, 1983- —.

awaii

ecame a state Aug. 21, 1959)

INN, William Francis (R) July 31, 1919- —; Aug. 21, 1959-Dec. 3, 1962.

RNS, John Anthony (D) Nov. 30, 1909-April 5, 1975; Dec. 3, 1962-Dec. 2, 1974.

IYOSHI, George Ryoichi (D) March 12, 1926- —; Dec. 2, 1974-Dec. 1, 1986.

IHEE, John III (D) May 19, 1946- —; Dec. 1, 1986- —.

aho

ecame a state July 3, 1890)

OUP, George Laird (R) June 15, 1836-Dec. 21, 1904; July 3-Dec. 18, 1890; Senate 1890-1901.

LLEY, Norman Bushnell (R) March 25, 1838-Oct. 20, 1921; Dec. 19, 1890-Jan. 1, 1893.

CONNELL, William John (R) Sept. 18, 1839-March 30, 1925; Jan. 2, 1893-Jan. 4, 1897; Senate 1890-91.

EUNENBERG, Frank (D) Aug. 8, 1861-Dec. 30, 1905; Jan. 4, 1897-Jan. 7, 1901.

NT, Frank Williams (D) Dec. 16, 1871-Nov. 25, 1906; Jan. 7, 1901-Jan. 5, 1903.

RRISON, John Tracy (R) Dec. 25, 1860-Dec. 20, 1915; Jan. 5, 1903-Jan. 2, 1905.

ODING, Frank Robert (R) Sept. 16, 1859-June 24, 1928; Jan. 2, 1905-Jan. 4, 1909; Senate 1920-28.

ADY, James Henry (R) June 12, 1862-Jan. 13, 1918; Jan. 4, 1909-Jan. 2, 1911; Senate 1913-18.

HAWLEY, James Henry (D) Jan. 17, 1847-Aug. 3, 1929; Jan. 2, 1911-Jan. 6, 1913.

HAINES, John Michiner (R) Jan. 1, 1863-June 4, 1917; Jan. 6, 1913-Jan. 4, 1915.

ALEXANDER, Moses (D) Nov. 15, 1853-Jan. 4, 1932; Jan. 4, 1915-Jan. 6, 1919.

DAVIS, David William (R) April 23, 1873-Aug. 5, 1959; Jan. 6, 1919-Jan. 1, 1923.

MOORE, Charles Calvin (R) Feb. 26, 1866-March 19, 1958; Jan. 1, 1923-Jan. 3, 1927.

BALDRIGE, H. Clarence (R) Nov. 24, 1868-June 8, 1947; Jan. 3, 1927-Jan. 5, 1931.

ROSS, C. Ben (D) Dec. 27, 1876-March 31, 1946; Jan. 5, 1931-Jan. 4, 1937.

CLARK, Barzilla Worth (brother of Chase Addison Clark, below) (D) Dec. 22, 1880-Sept. 21, 1943; Jan. 4, 1937-Jan. 2, 1939.

BOTTOLFSEN, Clarence Alfred (R) Oct. 10, 1891-July 19, 1964; Jan. 2, 1939-Jan. 6, 1941, Jan. 4, 1943-Jan. 1, 1945.

CLARK, Chase Addison (brother of Barzilla Worth Clark, above) (D) Aug. 20, 1883-Dec. 29, 1966; Jan. 6, 1941-Jan. 4, 1943.

BOTTOLFSEN, Clarence Alfred (R) Jan. 4, 1943-Jan. 1, 1945 (for previous term see above).

GOSSETT, Charles Clinton (D) Sept. 2, 1888-Sept. 20, 1974; Jan. 1-Nov. 17, 1945; Senate 1945-47.

WILLIAMS, Arnold (D) May 21, 1898-May 25, 1970; Nov. 17, 1945-Jan. 6, 1947; Secy. of State 1959-66.

ROBINS, Charles Armington (R) Dec. 8, 1884-Sept. 20, 1970; Jan. 6, 1947-Jan. 1, 1951.

JORDAN, Leonard Beck (R) May 15, 1899-June 30, 1983; Jan. 1, 1951-Jan. 3, 1955; Senate 1962-73.

SMYLIE, Robert Eben (R) Oct. 31, 1914- —; Jan. 3, 1955-Jan. 2, 1967.

SAMUELSON, Don William (R) July 27, 1913- —; Jan. 2, 1967-Jan. 4, 1971.

ANDRUS, Cecil Dale (D) Aug. 25, 1931- —; Jan. 4, 1971-Jan. 24, 1977, Jan. 5, 1987- —; Secy. of the Interior 1977-81.

EVANS, John Victor (D) Jan. 18, 1925- —; Jan. 24, 1977-Jan. 5, 1987.

ANDRUS, Cecil Dale (D) Jan. 5, 1987- — (for previous term see above).

Illinois

(Became a state Dec. 3, 1818)

BOND, Shadrack (DR) Nov. 24, 1773-April 12, 1832; Oct. 6, 1818-Dec. 5, 1822; House (Terr. Del.) 1812-13 (Democrat).

COLES, Edward (brother-in-law of John Rutherford of Va.) (DR) Dec. 15, 1786-July 7, 1868; Dec. 5, 1822-Dec. 6, 1826.

EDWARDS, Ninian (NR) March 17, 1775-July 20, 1833; Dec. 6, 1826-Dec. 6, 1830; Senate 1818-24 (Democrat).

REYNOLDS, John (brother of Thomas Reynolds of Mo.) (D) Feb. 26, 1789-May 8, 1865; Dec. 6, 1830-Nov. 17, 1834 (National Republican); House 1834-37, 1839-43.

EWING, William Lee Davidson (JD) Aug. 31, 1795-March 25, 1846; Nov. 17-Dec. 3, 1834; Senate 1835-37.

DUNCAN, Joseph (W) Feb. 22, 1794-Jan. 15, 1844; Dec. 3, 1834-Dec. 7, 1838; House 1827-34 (Jackson Democrat).

CARLIN, Thomas (D) July 18, 1789-Feb. 14, 1852; Dec. 7, 1838-Dec. 8, 1842.

FORD, Thomas (D) Dec. 5, 1800-Nov. 3, 1850; Dec. 8, 1842-Dec. 9, 1846.

FRENCH, Augustus C. (D) Aug. 2, 1808-Sept. 4, 1864; Dec. 9, 1846-Jan. 10, 1853.

MATTESON, Joel Aldrich (D) Aug. 2, 1808-Jan. 31, 1873; Jan. 10, 1853-Jan. 12, 1857.

BISSELL, William Harrison (R) April 25, 1811-March 18, 1860; Jan. 12, 1857-March 18, 1860; House 1849-55 (Democrat).

WOOD, John (R) Dec. 20, 1798-June 11, 1880; March 21, 1860-Jan. 14, 1861.

YATES, Richard Sr. (father of Richard Yates Jr., below) (UR) Jan. 18, 1818-Nov. 27, 1873; Jan. 14, 1861-Jan. 16, 1865 (Republican); House 1851-55 (Whig); Senate 1865-71.

OGLESBY, Richard James (R) July 25, 1824-April 24, 1899; Jan. 16, 1865-Jan. 11, 1869, Jan. 13-23, 1873, Jan. 30, 1885-Jan. 14, 1889; Senate 1873-79.

PALMER, John McAuley (D) Sept. 13, 1817-Sept. 25, 1900; Jan. 11, 1869-Jan. 13, 1873 (Republican); Senate 1891-97.

OGLESBY, Richard James (R) Jan. 13-23, 1873 (for previous term see above).

BEVERIDGE, John Lourie (R) July 6, 1824-May 1910; Jan. 23, 1873-Jan. 8, 1877; House 1871-73.

CULLOM, Shelby Moore (R) Nov. 22, 1829-Jan. 1914; Jan. 8, 1877-Feb. 8, 1883; House 1865-71; S ate 1883-1913; Senate majority leader 1911-13.

HAMILTON, John Marshall (R) May 28, 1847-Sept. 1905; Feb. 16, 1883-Jan. 30, 1885.

OGLESBY, Richard James (R) Jan. 30, 1885-Jan. 1889 (for previous terms see above).

FIFER, Joseph Wilson (R) Oct. 28, 1840-Aug. 6, 19 Jan. 14, 1889-Jan. 10, 1893.

ALTGELD, John Peter (D) Dec. 30, 1847-March 1902; Jan. 10, 1893-Jan. 11, 1897.

TANNER, John Riley (R) April 4, 1844-May 23, 19 Jan. 11, 1897-Jan. 14, 1901.

YATES, Richard Jr. (son of Richard Yates Sr., abc (R) Dec. 12, 1860-April 11, 1936; Jan. 14, 1901-J 9, 1905; House 1919-33.

DENEEN, Charles Samuel (R) May 4, 1863-Feb. 1940; Jan. 9, 1905-Feb. 3, 1913; Senate 1925-31.

DUNNE, Edward Fitzsimmons (D) Oct. 12, 1853-N 14, 1937; Feb. 3, 1913-Jan. 8, 1917.

LOWDEN, Frank Orren (R) Jan. 26, 1861-March 1943; Jan. 8, 1917-Jan. 10, 1921; House 1906-11.

SMALL, Lennington (R) June 16, 1862-May 17, 19 Jan. 10, 1921-Jan. 14, 1929.

EMMERSON, Louis Lincoln (R) Dec. 27, 1883-Feb 1941; Jan. 14, 1929-Jan. 9, 1933.

HORNER, Henry (D) Nov. 30, 1879-Oct. 6, 1940; Jan 1933-Oct. 6, 1940.

STELLE, John Henry (D) Aug. 10, 1891-July 5, 19 Oct. 6, 1940-Jan. 13, 1941.

GREEN, Dwight Herbert (R) Jan. 9, 1897-Feb. 20, 19 Jan. 13, 1941-Jan. 10, 1949.

STEVENSON, Adlai Ewing II (grandson of Vice Pr dent Adlai Ewing Stevenson, father of Sen. Ac Ewing Stevenson III) (D) Feb. 5, 1900-July 14, 19 Jan. 10, 1949-Jan. 12, 1953.

STRATTON, William Grant (R) Feb. 26, 1914- ; J 12, 1953-Jan. 9, 1961; House 1941-43, 1947-49.

KERNER, Otto (D) Aug. 15, 1908-May 8, 1976; Jan 1961-May 22, 1968.

SHAPIRO, Samuel Harvey (D) April 25, 1907- ; N 22, 1968-Jan. 13, 1969.

GILVIE, Richard Buell (R) Feb. 2, 1923- —; Jan. 13, 1969-Jan. 8, 1973.

ALKER, Daniel (D) Aug. 6, 1922- —; Jan. 8, 1973-Jan. 10, 1977.

HOMPSON, James Robert (R) May 8, 1936- —; Jan. 10, 1977- —.

ndiana

3ecame a state Dec. 11, 1816)

NNINGS, Jonathan (D) 1784-July 26, 1834; Nov. 7, 1816-Sept. 12, 1822 (Democratic Republican); House 1822-31.

ON, Ratliff (JD) Jan. 18, 1781-Nov. 20, 1844; Sept. 12-Dec. 4, 1822; House 1825-27, 1829-39.

NDRICKS, William (uncle of Thomas Andrews Hendricks, below) (D) Nov. 12, 1782-May 16, 1850; Dec. 5, 1822-Feb. 12, 1825 (Democratic Republican); House 1816-22; Senate 1825-37.

Y, James Brown (AJD, I) Feb. 19, 1794-Aug. 4, 1848; Feb. 12, 1825-Dec. 7, 1831 (1828-31 Independent).

BLE, Noah (NR, W) Jan. 14, 1794-Feb. 8, 1844; Dec. 7, 1831-Dec. 6, 1837.

ALLACE, David (W) April 4, 1799-Sept. 4, 1859; Dec. 6, 1837-Dec. 9, 1840; House 1841-43.

GGER, Samuel (W) March 20, 1802-Sept. 9, 1846; Dec. 9, 1840-Dec. 6, 1843.

HITCOMB, James (father-in-law of Claude Matthews, below) (D) Dec. 1, 1795-Oct. 4, 1852; Dec. 6, 1843-Dec. 27, 1848; Senate 1849-52.

NNING, Paris Chipman (D) March 15, 1806-May 9, 1884; Dec. 27, 1848-Dec. 5, 1849.

RIGHT, Joseph Albert (D) April 17, 1810-May 11, 1867; Dec. 5, 1849-Jan. 12, 1857; House 1843-45; Senate 1862-63.

LLARD, Ashbel Parsons (D) Oct. 31, 1820-Oct. 4, 1860; Jan. 12, 1857-Oct. 4, 1860.

MMOND, Abram Adams (D) March 21, 1814-Aug. 27, 1874; Oct. 4, 1860-Jan. 14, 1861.

NE, Henry Smith (R) Feb. 24, 1811-June 18, 1881; Jan. 14-16, 1861; House 1840-43 (Whig); Senate 1861-67.

RTON, Oliver Hazard Perry Throck (UR) Aug. 4, 1823-Nov. 1, 1877; Jan. 16, 1861-Jan. 23, 1867 (Republican); Senate 1867-77.

KER, Conrad (R) Feb. 12, 1817-April 28, 1885; Jan. 24, 1867-Jan. 13, 1873.

HENDRICKS, Thomas Andrews (nephew of William Hendricks, above) (D) Sept. 7, 1819-Nov. 25, 1885; Jan. 13, 1873-Jan. 8, 1877; House 1851-55; Senate 1863-69; Vice President 1885.

WILLIAMS, James Douglas (D) Jan. 16, 1808-Nov. 20, 1880; Jan. 8, 1877-Nov. 20, 1880; House 1875-76.

GRAY, Isaac Pusey (D) Oct. 18, 1828-Feb. 14, 1895; Nov. 20, 1880-Jan. 10, 1881, Jan. 12, 1885-Jan. 14, 1889.

PORTER, Albert Gallatin (R) April 20, 1824-May 3, 1897; Jan. 10, 1881-Jan. 12, 1885; House 1859-63.

GRAY, Isaac Pusey (D) Jan. 12, 1885-Jan. 14, 1889 (for previous term see above).

HOVEY, Alvin Peterson (R) Sept. 6, 1821-Nov. 23, 1891; Jan. 14, 1889-Nov. 21, 1891; House 1887-89.

CHASE, Ira Joy (R) Dec. 7, 1834-May 11, 1895; Nov. 21, 1891-Jan. 9, 1893.

MATTHEWS, Claude (son-in-law of James Whitcomb, above) (D) Dec. 14, 1845-April 28, 1898; Jan. 9, 1893-Jan. 11, 1897.

MOUNT, James Atwell (R) March 24, 1843-Jan. 16, 1901; Jan. 11, 1897-Jan. 14, 1901.

DURBIN, Winfield Taylor (R) May 4, 1847-Dec. 18, 1928; Jan. 14, 1901-Jan. 9, 1905.

HANLY, James Franklin (R) April 4, 1863-Aug. 1, 1920; Jan. 9, 1905-Jan. 11, 1909; House 1895-97.

MARSHALL, Thomas Riley (D) March 14, 1854-June 1, 1925; Jan. 11, 1909-Jan. 13, 1913; Vice President 1913-21.

RALSTON, Samuel Moffett (D) Dec. 1, 1857-Oct. 14, 1925; Jan. 13, 1913-Jan. 8, 1917; Senate 1923-25.

GOODRICH, James Putnam (R) Feb. 18, 1864-Aug. 15, 1940; Jan. 8, 1917-Jan. 10, 1921.

McCRAY, Warren Terry (R) Feb. 4, 1865-Dec. 19, 1938; Jan. 10, 1921-April 30, 1924.

BRANCH, Emmett Forest (R) May 16, 1874-Feb. 23, 1932; April 30, 1924-Jan. 12, 1925.

JACKSON, Edward L. (R) Dec. 27, 1873-Nov. 18, 1954; Jan. 12, 1925-Jan. 14, 1929.

LESLIE, Harry Guyer (R) Aug. 6, 1878-Dec. 10, 1937; Jan. 14, 1929-Jan. 9, 1933.

McNUTT, Paul Vories (D) July 19, 1891-March 24, 1955; Jan. 9, 1933-Jan. 11, 1937.

TOWNSEND, Maurice Clifford (D) Aug. 11, 1884-Nov. 11, 1954; Jan. 11, 1937-Jan. 13, 1941.

SCHRICKER, Henry Frederick (D) Aug. 30, 1883-Dec. 28, 1966; Jan. 13, 1941-Jan. 8, 1945, Jan. 10, 1949-Jan. 12, 1953.

GATES, Ralph Fesler (R) Feb. 24, 1893-July 28, 1978; Jan. 8, 1945-Jan. 10, 1949.

SCHRICKER, Henry Frederick (D) Jan. 10, 1949-Jan. 12, 1953 (for previous term see above).

CRAIG, George North (R) Aug. 6, 1909- —; Jan. 12, 1953-Jan. 14, 1957.

HANDLEY, Harold Willis (R) Nov. 27, 1909-Aug. 30, 1972; Jan. 14, 1957-Jan. 9, 1961.

WELSH, Matthew Empson (D) Sept. 15, 1912- —; Jan. 9, 1961-Jan. 11, 1965.

BRANIGIN, Roger Douglas (D) July 26, 1902-Nov. 19, 1975; Jan. 11, 1965-Jan. 13, 1969.

WHITCOMB, Edgar Doud (R) Nov. 6, 1917- —; Jan. 13, 1969-Jan. 8, 1973.

BOWEN, Otis Ray (R) Feb. 26, 1918- —; Jan. 8, 1973-Jan. 12, 1981; Secy. of Health and Human Services 1985- —.

ORR, Robert Dunkerson (R) Nov. 17, 1917- —; Jan. 12, 1981- —.

Iowa

(Became a state Dec. 28, 1846)

BRIGGS, Ansel (D) Feb. 3, 1806-May 5, 1881; Dec. 3, 1846-Dec. 4, 1850.

HEMPSTEAD, Stephen P. (D) Oct. 1, 1812-Feb. 16, 1883; Dec. 4, 1850-Dec. 9, 1854.

GRIMES, James Wilson (R) Oct. 20, 1816-Feb. 7, 1872; Dec. 9, 1854-Jan. 13, 1858 (Whig); Senate 1859-69.

LOWE, Ralph Phillips (R) Nov. 27, 1805-Dec. 22, 1883; Jan. 13, 1858-Jan. 11, 1860.

KIRKWOOD, Samuel Jordan (R) Dec. 20, 1813-Sept. 1, 1894; Jan. 11, 1860-Jan. 14, 1864, Jan. 13, 1876-Feb. 1, 1877; Senate 1866-67, 1877-81; Secy. of the Interior 1881-82.

STONE, William Milo (R) Oct. 14, 1827-July 8, 1893; Jan. 14, 1864-Jan. 16, 1868.

MERRILL, Samuel (R) Aug. 7, 1822-Aug. 31, 1899; Jan. 16, 1868-Jan. 11, 1872.

CARPENTER, Cyrus Clay (R) Nov. 24, 1829-May 29, 1898; Jan. 11, 1872-Jan. 13, 1876; House 1879-83.

KIRKWOOD, Samuel Jordan (R) Jan. 13, 1876-Feb. 1877 (for previous term see above).

NEWBOLD, Joshua G. (R) May 12, 1830-June 10, 190 Feb. 1, 1877-Jan. 17, 1878.

GEAR, John Henry (R) April 7, 1825-July 14, 1900; Ja 17, 1878-Jan. 12, 1882; House 1887-91, 1893-95; Se ate 1895-1900.

SHERMAN, Buren Robinson (R) May 28, 1836-Nov. 1904; Jan. 12, 1882-Jan. 14, 1886.

LARRABEE, William (R) Jan. 20, 1832-Nov. 16, 191 Jan. 14, 1886-Feb. 26, 1890.

BOIES, Horace (D) Dec. 7, 1827-April 4, 1923; Feb. 2 1890-Jan. 11, 1894.

JACKSON, Frank Darr (R) Jan. 26, 1854-Nov. 16, 193 Jan. 11, 1894-Jan. 16, 1896.

DRAKE, Francis Marion (R) Dec. 30, 1830-Nov. 2 1903; Jan. 16, 1896-Jan. 13, 1898.

SHAW, Leslie Mortier (R) Nov. 2, 1848-March 28, 193 Jan. 13, 1898-Jan. 16, 1902; Secy. of the Treasu 1902-07.

CUMMINS, Albert Baird (R) Feb. 15, 1850-July 3 1926; Jan. 16, 1902-Nov. 24, 1908; Senate 1908-192 Pres. pro tempore 1919-25.

GARST, Warren (R) Dec. 4, 1850-Oct. 5, 1924; Nov. 2 1908-Jan. 14, 1909.

CARROLL, Beryl Franklin (R) March 15, 1860-Dec. 1 1939; Jan. 14, 1909-Jan. 16, 1913.

CLARKE, George W. (R) Oct. 24, 1852-Nov. 28, 193 Jan. 16, 1913-Jan. 11, 1917.

HARDING, William Lloyd (R) Oct. 3, 1877-Dec. 1 1934; Jan. 11, 1917-Jan. 13, 1921.

KENDALL, Nathan Edward (R) March 17, 1868-Nc 5, 1936; Jan. 13, 1921-Jan. 15, 1925; House 1909-1

HAMMILL, John (R) Oct. 14, 1875-April 6, 1936; Ja 15, 1925-Jan. 15, 1931.

TURNER, Daniel Webster (R) March 17, 1877-April 1 1969; Jan. 15, 1931-Jan. 12, 1933.

HERRING, Clyde LaVerne (D) May 3, 1879-Sept. 1 1945; Jan. 12, 1933-Jan. 14, 1937; Senate 1937-43

KRASCHEL, Nelson George (D) Oct. 27, 1889-Mar 15, 1957; Jan. 14, 1937-Jan. 12, 1939.

WILSON, George Allison (R) April 1, 1884-Sept. 8, 19 Jan. 12, 1939-Jan. 14, 1943; Senate 1943-49.

ICKENLOOPER, Bourke Blakemore (R) July 21, 1896-Sept. 4, 1971; Jan. 14, 1943-Jan. 11, 1945; Senate 1945-69.

LUE, Robert Donald (R) Sept. 24, 1898- —; Jan. 11, 1945-Jan. 13, 1949.

EARDSLEY, William S. (R) May 17, 1901-Nov. 21, 1954; Jan. 13, 1949-Nov. 21, 1954.

LTHON, Leo (R) June 9, 1898-April 16, 1967; Nov. 22, 1954-Jan. 13, 1955.

OEGH, Leo Arthur (R) March 30, 1908- —; Jan. 13, 1955-Jan. 17, 1957.

OVELESS, Herschel Celiel (D) May 5, 1911- —; Jan. 17, 1957-Jan. 12, 1961.

RBE, Norman Arthur (R) Oct. 25, 1919- —; Jan. 12, 1961-Jan. 17, 1963.

UGHES, Harold Everett (D) Feb. 10, 1922- —; Jan. 17, 1963-Jan. 1, 1969; Senate 1969-75.

ULTON, Robert David (D) May 13, 1929- —; Jan. 1-16, 1969.

AY, Robert D. (R) Sept. 26, 1928- —; Jan. 16, 1969-Jan. 14, 1983.

RANSTAD, Terry E. (R) Sept. 17, 1946- —; Jan. 14, 1983- —.

Kansas

Became a state Jan. 29, 1861)

OBINSON, Charles Lawrence (R) July 21, 1818-Aug. 17, 1894; Feb. 9, 1861-Jan. 12, 1863.

ARNEY, Thomas (R) Aug. 20, 1824-July 28, 1888; Jan. 12, 1863-Jan. 9, 1865.

RAWFORD, Samuel Johnson (father-in-law of Arthur Capper, below) (R) April 10, 1835-Oct. 21, 1913; Jan. 9, 1865-Nov. 4, 1868.

REEN, Nehemiah (R) March 8, 1837-Jan. 12, 1890; Nov. 4, 1868-Jan. 11, 1869.

ARVEY, James Madison (R) Sept. 21, 1833-April 15, 1894; Jan. 11, 1869-Jan. 13, 1873; Senate 1874-77.

SBORN, Thomas Andrew (R) Oct. 26, 1836-Feb. 4, 1898; Jan. 13, 1873-Jan. 18, 1877.

NTHONY, George Tobey (R) June 9, 1824-Aug. 5, 1896; Jan. 18, 1877-Jan. 13, 1879.

T. JOHN, John Pierce (R) Feb. 25, 1833-Aug. 31, 1916; Jan. 13, 1879-Jan. 8, 1883.

GLICK, George Washington (D) July 4, 1827-April 13, 1911; Jan. 8, 1883-Jan. 13, 1885.

MARTIN, John Alexander (R) March 10, 1839-Oct. 2, 1889; Jan. 13, 1885-Jan. 14, 1889.

HUMPHREY, Lyman Underwood (R) July 25, 1844-Sept. 12, 1915; Jan. 14, 1889-Jan. 9, 1893.

LEWELLING, Lorenzo Dow (P) Dec. 21, 1846-Sept. 3, 1900; Jan. 9, 1893-Jan. 14, 1895.

MORRILL, Edmund Needham (R) Feb. 12, 1834-March 14, 1909; Jan. 14, 1895-Jan. 11, 1897; House 1883-91.

LEEDY, John Whitnah (P) March 4, 1849-March 24, 1935; Jan. 11, 1897-Jan. 9, 1899.

STANLEY, William Eugene (R) Dec. 28, 1844-Oct. 13, 1910; Jan. 9, 1899-Jan. 12, 1903.

BAILEY, Willis Joshua (R) Oct. 12, 1854-May 19, 1932; Jan. 12, 1903-Jan. 9, 1905; House 1899-1901.

HOCH, Edward Wallis (R) March 17, 1849-June 1, 1925; Jan. 9, 1905-Jan. 11, 1909.

STUBBS, Walter Roscoe (R) Nov. 7, 1858-March 25, 1929; Jan. 11, 1909-Jan. 13, 1913.

HODGES, George Hartshorn (D) Feb. 6, 1866-Oct. 7, 1947; Jan. 13, 1913-Jan. 11, 1915.

CAPPER, Arthur (son-in-law of Samuel Johnson Crawford, above) (R) July 14, 1865-Dec. 19, 1951; Jan. 11, 1915-Jan. 13, 1919; Senate 1919-49.

ALLEN, Henry Justin (R) Sept. 11, 1868-Jan. 17, 1950; Jan. 13, 1919-Jan. 8, 1923; Senate 1929-30.

DAVIS, Jonathan McMillan (D) April 27, 1871-June 27, 1943; Jan. 8, 1923-Jan. 12, 1925.

PAULEN, Benjamin Sanford (R) July 14, 1869-July 11, 1961; Jan. 12, 1925-Jan. 14, 1929.

REED, Clyde Martin (R) Oct. 9, 1871-Nov. 8, 1949; Jan. 14, 1929-Jan. 12, 1931; Senate 1939-49.

WOODRING, Harry Hines (D) May 31, 1887-Sept. 9, 1967; Jan. 12, 1931-Jan. 9, 1933; Secy. of War 1936-40.

LANDON, Alfred Mossman (R) Sept. 9, 1887- —; Jan. 9, 1933-Jan. 11, 1937.

HUXMAN, Walter Augustus (D) Feb. 16, 1887-June 26, 1972; Jan. 11, 1937-Jan. 9, 1939.

RATNER, Payne Harry (R) Oct. 3, 1896-Dec. 27, 1974; Jan. 9, 1939-Jan. 11, 1943.

SCHOEPPEL, Andrew Frank (R) Nov. 23, 1894-Jan. 21, 1962; Jan. 11, 1943-Jan. 13, 1947; Senate 1949-62.

CARLSON, Frank (R) Jan. 23, 1893--; Jan. 13, 1947-Nov. 28, 1950; House 1935-47; Senate 1950-69.

HAGAMAN, Frank Leslie (R) June 1, 1894-June 23, 1966; Nov. 28, 1950-Jan. 8, 1951.

ARN, Edward Ferdinand (R) May 19, 1906--; Jan. 8, 1951-Jan. 10, 1955.

HALL, Frederick Lee (R) July 24, 1916-March 18, 1970; Jan. 10, 1955-Jan. 3, 1957.

McCUISH, John Berridge (R) June 22, 1906-March 12, 1962; Jan. 3-14, 1957.

DOCKING, George (father of Robert Blackwell Docking, below) (D) Feb. 23, 1904-Jan. 20, 1964; Jan. 14, 1957-Jan. 9, 1961.

ANDERSON, John Jr. (R) May 8, 1917--; Jan. 9, 1961-Jan. 11, 1965.

AVERY, William Henry (R) Aug. 11, 1911--; Jan. 11, 1965-Jan. 9, 1967; House 1955-65.

DOCKING, Robert Blackwell (son of George Docking, above) (D) Oct. 9, 1925-Oct. 8, 1983; Jan. 9, 1967-Jan. 13, 1975.

BENNETT, Robert Frederick (R) May 23, 1927--; Jan. 13, 1975-Jan. 8, 1979.

CARLIN, John (D) Aug. 3, 1940--; Jan. 8, 1979-Jan. 12, 1987.

HAYDEN, John Michael "Mike" (R) March 16, 1944--; Jan. 12, 1987--.

Kentucky

(Became a state June 1, 1792)

SHELBY, Isaac (DR) Dec. 11, 1750-July 18, 1826; June 4, 1792-June 7, 1796, June 1, 1812-June 1, 1816.

GARRARD, James (DR) Jan. 14, 1749-Jan. 19, 1822; June 7, 1796-June 1, 1804.

GREENUP, Christopher (DR) 1749-April 27, 1818; June 1, 1804-June 1, 1808.

SCOTT, Charles (DR) 1739-Oct. 22, 1813; June 1, 1808-June 1, 1812.

SHELBY, Isaac (DR) June 1, 1812-June 1, 1816 (for previous term see above).

MADISON, George (DR) 1763-Oct. 14, 1816; June 1-Oct. 14, 1816.

SLAUGHTER, Gabriel (DR) Dec. 12, 1767-Sept. 19, 1830; Oct. 21, 1816-June 1, 1820.

ADAIR, John (D) Jan. 9, 1757-May 19, 1840; June 1820-June 1, 1824; Senate 1805-06; House 1831-33

DESHA, Joseph (DR) Dec. 9, 1768-Oct. 12, 1842; June 1824-June 1, 1828; House 1807-19 (Democrat).

METCALFE, Thomas (D) March 20, 1780-Aug. 18 1855; June 1, 1828-June 1, 1832 (National Republican); House 1819-28; Senate 1848-49.

BREATHITT, John (D) Sept. 9, 1786-Feb. 21, 1834 June 1, 1832-Feb. 21, 1834.

MOREHEAD, James Turner (cousin of John Motley Morehead of N.C.) (W) May 24, 1797-Dec. 28, 185 Feb. 22, 1834-June 1, 1836 (Democrat); Senate 1841 47.

CLARK, James (W) Jan. 16, 1779-Oct. 5, 1839; June 1836-Oct. 5, 1839; House 1813-16 (Clay Democrat 1825-31 (Clay Democrat).

WICKLIFFE, Charles Anderson (father of Rober Charles Wickliffe of La., grandfather of John Crip Wickliffe Beckham) (UW) June 8, 1788-Oct. 3 1869; Oct. 5, 1839-June 1, 1840 (Whig); House 182 33 (Democrat), 1861-63; Postmaster Gen. 1841-45

LETCHER, Robert Perkins (W) Feb. 10, 1788-Jan. 2 1861; June 1, 1840-June 1, 1844; House 1823-: (1823-27 Clay Democrat), 1834-35.

OWSLEY, William (W) March 24, 1782-Dec. 9, 186 June 1, 1844-June 1, 1848.

CRITTENDEN, John Jordan (uncle of Thomas Theodore Crittenden of Mo.) (U) Sept. 10, 1787-July 2 1863; June 1, 1848-July 31, 1850 (Whig); Senat 1817-19 (Whig), 1835-41 (Whig), 1842-48 (Whig 1855-61 (Whig); House 1861-63; Atty. Gen. 184 1850-53.

HELM, John Larue (W) July 4, 1802-Sept. 8, 1867; Ju 31, 1850-Sept. 2, 1851, Sept. 3-8, 1867.

POWELL, Lazarus Whitehead (D) Oct. 6, 1812-July 1867; Sept. 2, 1851-Sept. 1, 1855; Senate 1859-65.

MOREHEAD, Charles Slaughter (ASP) July 7, 180 Dec. 21, 1868; Sept. 1, 1855-Aug. 30, 1859; Hou 1847-51 (Whig).

MAGOFFIN, Beriah (D) April 18, 1815-Feb. 28, 188 Aug. 30, 1859-Aug. 16, 1862.

ROBINSON, James Fisher (D) Oct. 4, 1800-Oct. 3 1882; Aug. 18, 1862-Sept. 1, 1863.

BRAMLETTE, Thomas E. (UD) Jan. 3, 1817-Jan. 1 1875; Sept. 1, 1863-Sept. 3, 1867.

HELM, John Larue (D) Sept. 3-8, 1867 (for previou term see above).

TEVENSON, John White (D) May 4, 1812-Aug. 10, 1886; Sept. 8, 1867-Feb. 13, 1871; House 1857-61; Senate 1871-77.

ESLIE, Preston Hopkins (D) March 8, 1819-Feb. 7, 1907; Feb. 13, 1871-Aug. 31, 1875.

IcCREARY, James Bennett (D) July 8, 1838-Oct. 8, 1918; Aug. 31, 1875-Aug. 31, 1879, Dec. 12, 1911-Dec. 7, 1915; House 1885-97; Senate 1903-09.

LACKBURN, Luke Pryor (D) June 16, 1816-Sept. 14, 1887; Sept. 2, 1879-Sept. 4, 1883.

NOTT, James Procter (D) Aug. 29, 1830-June 18, 1911; Sept. 4, 1883-Aug. 30, 1887; House 1867-71, 1875-83.

UCKNER, Simon Bolivar (D) April 1, 1823-Jan. 8, 1914; Aug. 30, 1887-Sept. 1, 1891.

ROWN, John Young (D) June 28, 1835-Jan. 11, 1904; Sept. 1, 1891-Dec. 10, 1895; House 1859-61, 1873-77.

RADLEY, William O'Connell (uncle of Edwin Porch Morrow, below) (R) March 18, 1847-May 23, 1914; Dec. 10, 1895-Dec. 12, 1899; Senate 1909-14.

AYLOR, William Sylvester (R) Oct. 10, 1853-Aug. 2, 1928; Dec. 12, 1899-Jan. 31, 1900.

OEBEL, William (D) Jan. 4, 1856-Feb. 3, 1900; Jan. 31-Feb. 3, 1900.

ECKHAM, John Crepps Wickliffe (grandson of Charles Anderson Wickliffe, nephew of Robert Charles Wickliffe of La.) (D) Aug. 5, 1869-Jan. 9, 1940; Feb. 3, 1900-Dec. 10, 1907; Senate 1915-21.

ILLSON, Augustus Everett (R) Oct. 13, 1846-Aug. 24, 1931; Dec. 10, 1907-Dec. 12, 1911.

IcCREARY, James Bennett (D) Dec. 12, 1911-Dec. 7, 1915 (for previous term see above).

TANLEY, Augustus Owsley (D) May 21, 1867-Aug. 13, 1958; Dec. 7, 1915-May 19, 1919; House 1903-15; Senate 1919-25.

LACK, James Dixon (D) Sept. 24, 1849-Aug. 4, 1938; May 19-Dec. 9, 1919.

ORROW, Edwin Porch (nephew of William O'Connell Bradley, above) (R) Nov. 28, 1877-June 15, 1935; Dec. 9, 1919-Dec. 11, 1923.

IELDS, William Jason (D) Dec. 29, 1874-Oct. 21, 1954; Dec. 11, 1923-Dec. 13, 1927; House 1911-23.

AMPSON, Flemon Davis (R) Jan. 25, 1875-May 25, 1967; Dec. 13, 1927-Dec. 8, 1931.

AFOON, Ruby (D) Jan. 15, 1869-March 1, 1941; Dec. 8, 1931-Dec. 10, 1935.

CHANDLER, Albert Benjamin "Happy" (D) July 14, 1898- —; Dec. 10, 1935-Oct. 9, 1939, Dec. 13, 1955-Dec. 9, 1959; Senate 1939-45.

JOHNSON, Keen (D) Jan. 12, 1896-Feb. 7, 1970; Oct. 9, 1939-Dec. 7, 1943.

WILLIS, Simeon Slavens (R) Dec. 1, 1879-April 2, 1965; Dec. 7, 1943-Dec. 9, 1947.

CLEMENTS, Earle Chester (D) Oct. 22, 1896-March 12, 1985; Dec. 9, 1947-Nov. 27, 1950; House 1945-47; Senate 1950-57.

WETHERBY, Lawrence Winchester (D) Jan. 2, 1908- —; Nov. 27, 1950-Dec. 13, 1955.

CHANDLER, Albert Benjamin "Happy" (D) Dec. 13, 1955-Dec. 8, 1959 (for previous term see above).

COMBS, Bertram Thomas (D) Aug. 13, 1911- —; Dec. 8, 1959-Dec. 10, 1963.

BREATHITT, Edward Thompson (D) Nov. 26, 1926- —; Dec. 10, 1963-Dec. 12, 1967.

NUNN, Louis Broady (R) March 8, 1924- —; Dec. 12, 1967-Dec. 7, 1971.

FORD, Wendell Hampton (D) Sept. 8, 1924- —; Dec. 7, 1971-Dec. 28, 1974; Senate 1974- —.

CARROLL, Julian Morton (D) April 16, 1931- —; Dec. 28, 1974-Dec. 11, 1979.

BROWN, John Young Jr. (D) Dec. 28, 1933- —; Dec. 11, 1979-Dec. 13, 1983.

COLLINS, Martha Layne (D) Dec. 7, 1936- —; Dec. 13, 1983- —.

Louisiana

(Became a state April 30, 1812)

CLAIBORNE, William Charles Cole (D) 1775-Nov. 23, 1817; July 30, 1812-Dec. 16, 1816 (Democratic Republican), House 1797-1801 (Jefferson Democrat, Tenn.); Gov. 1801-03 (Democratic Republican, Miss. Terr.), 1804-12 (Democratic Republican, Orleans Terr.); Senate 1817.

VILLERE, Jacques Philippe (DR) April 28, 1760-March 7, 1830; Dec. 17, 1816-Dec. 18, 1820.

ROBERTSON, Thomas Bolling (brother of Wyndham Robertson of Va.) (DR) Feb. 27, 1779-Oct. 5, 1828; Dec. 18, 1820-Nov. 15, 1824; House 1812-1818.

THIBODEAUX, Henry Schuyler (DR) 1769-Oct. 24, 1827; Nov. 15-Dec. 13, 1824.

JOHNSON, Henry S. (W) Sept. 14, 1783-Sept. 4, 1864; Dec. 13, 1824-Dec. 15, 1828 (Democratic Republican); Senate 1818-24, 1844-49; House 1834-39.

DERBIGNY, Pierre Auguste Charles Bourguignon (NR) 1767-Oct. 6, 1829; Dec. 15, 1828-Oct. 6, 1829.

BEAUVAIS, Armand (NR) Sept. 6, 1783-Nov. 18, 1843; Oct. 6, 1829-Jan. 14, 1830.

DUPRE, Jacques (NR) Feb. 12, 1773-Sept. 14, 1846; Jan. 14, 1830-Jan. 31, 1831.

ROMAN, Andre Bienvenu (W) March 5, 1795-Jan. 26, 1866; Jan. 31, 1831-Feb. 4, 1835 (National Republican), Feb. 4, 1839-Jan. 30, 1843.

WHITE Edward Douglas Sr. (W) March 1795-April 18, 1847; Feb. 2, 1835-Feb. 4, 1839; House 1829-34, 1839-43.

ROMAN, Andre Bienvenu (W) Feb. 4, 1839-Jan. 30, 1843 (for previous term see above).

MOUTON, Alexandre (D) Nov. 19, 1804-Feb. 12, 1885; Jan. 30, 1843-Feb. 12, 1846; Senate 1837-42.

JOHNSON, Isaac (D) Nov. 1, 1803-March 15, 1853; Feb. 12, 1846-Jan. 27, 1850.

WALKER, Joseph Marshall (D) July 1, 1784-Jan. 21, 1856; Jan. 28, 1850-Jan. 17, 1853.

HEBERT, Paul Octave (D) Dec. 12, 1818-Aug. 29, 1880; Jan. 18, 1853-Jan. 28, 1856.

WICKLIFFE, Robert Charles (son of Charles Anderson Wickliffe of Ky., uncle of John Crepps Wickliffe Beckham of Ky.) (D) Jan. 6, 1819-April 18, 1895; Jan. 28, 1856-Jan. 22, 1860.

MOORE, Thomas Overton (D) April 10, 1804-June 25, 1876; Jan. 23, 1860-Jan. 25, 1864.

SHEPLEY, George Foster; Jan. 1, 1819-July 20, 1878; (Military) June 10, 1862-March 4, 1864.

ALLEN, Henry Watkins (D) April 29, 1820-April 22, 1866; Jan. 25, 1864-June 2, 1865.

HAHN, Michael (R) Nov. 24, 1830-March 15, 1886; March 4, 1864-March 3, 1865 (State Rights Free Trader); House 1862-63 (Unionist), 1885-86.

WELLS, James Madison (ND) Jan. 8, 1808-Feb. 28, 1899; March 4, 1865-June 3, 1867.

FLANDERS, Benjamin Franklin; Jan. 26, 1816-March 13, 1896; (Military) June 6, 1867-Jan. 8, 1868; House 1862-63 (Unionist).

BAKER, Joshua; March 23, 1799-April 16, 1885; (Military) Jan. 2-June 27, 1868.

WARMOTH, Henry Clay (R) May 9, 1842-Sept. 30 1931; June 29, 1868-Dec. 9, 1872.

PINCHBACK, Pinckney Benton Stewart (R) May 10 1837-Dec. 21, 1921; Dec. 9, 1872-Jan. 13, 1873.

KELLOGG, William Pitt (R) Dec. 8, 1830-Aug. 10, 191. Jan. 13, 1873-Jan. 8, 1877; Senate 1868-72, 1877-8 House 1883-85.

NICHOLLS, Francis Redding Tillou (D) Aug. 20, 183 Jan. 4, 1912; Jan. 8, 1877-Jan. 13, 1880, May 2 1888-May 10, 1892.

WILTZ, Louis Alfred (D) Jan. 21, 1843-Oct. 16, 188 Jan. 14, 1880-Oct. 16, 1881.

McENERY, Samuel Douglas (D) May 28, 1837-June 2 1910; Oct. 16, 1881-May 20, 1888; Senate 1897-191

NICHOLLS, Francis Redding Tillou (D) May 21, 188 May 10, 1892 (for previous term see above).

FOSTER, Murphy James (cousin of Jared Young San ers, below) (D) Jan. 12, 1849-June 12, 1921; May 1 1892-May 21, 1900 (Anti Lottery Democrat); Sena 1901-13.

HEARD, William Wright (D) April 28, 1853-June 1926; May 21, 1900-May 10, 1904.

BLANCHARD, Newton Crain (D) Jan. 29, 1849-Ju 22, 1922; May 10, 1904-May 18, 1908; House 1881-9 Senate 1894-97.

SANDERS, Jared Young (cousin of Murphy James Fo ter, above) (D) Jan. 29, 1867-March 23, 1944; Ma 18, 1908-May 14, 1912; House 1917-21.

HALL, Luther Egbert (D) Aug. 30, 1869-Nov. 6, 192 May 20, 1912-May 15, 1916.

PLEASANT, Ruffin Golson (D) June 2, 1871-Sept. 1 1937; May 15, 1916-May 17, 1920.

PARKER, John Milliken (D) March 16, 1863-May 2 1939; May 17, 1920-May 19, 1924.

FUQUA, Henry Luce (D) Nov. 8, 1865-Oct. 11, 192 May 19, 1924-Oct. 11, 1926.

SIMPSON, Oramel Hinckley (D) March 20, 1870-No 17, 1932; Oct. 11, 1926-May 21, 1928.

LONG, Huey Pierce "the Kingfish" (father of Sen. Ru sell B. Long, brother of Earl Kemp Long, below) (I Aug. 30, 1893-Sept. 10, 1935; May 21, 1928-Jan. 2 1932; Senate 1932-35.

KING, Alvin Olin (D) June 21, 1890-Feb. 21, 1958; Ja 25-May 16, 1932.

ALLEN, Oscar Kelly (D) Aug. 8, 1882-Jan. 28, 193 May 16, 1932-Jan. 28, 1936.

)E, James Albert (D) Dec. 21, 1893-April 2, 1976; Jan. 28-May 12, 1936.

:CHE, Richard Webster (D) May 17, 1898-Feb. 22, 1965; May 12, 1936-June 26, 1939.

)NG, Earl Kemp (brother of Huey Pierce "the Kingfish" Long, above, uncle of Sen. Russell B. Long) (D) Aug. 26, 1895-Sept. 5, 1960; June 26, 1939-May 14, 1940, May 11, 1948-May 13, 1952, May 15, 1956-May 10, 1960.

)NES, Sam Houston (D) July 15, 1897-Feb. 8, 1978; May 14, 1940-May 9, 1944.

AVIS, James Houston (D) Sept. 11, 1902- –; May 9, 1944-May 11, 1948, May 10, 1960-May 12, 1964.

)NG, Earl Kemp (D) May 11, 1948-May 13, 1952 (for previous term see above).

ENNON, Robert Floyd (D) Aug. 21, 1902- –; May 13, 1952-May 8, 1956.

)NG, Earl Kemp (D) May 15, 1956-May 10, 1960 (for previous terms see above).

AVIS, James Houston (D) May 10, 1960-May 12, 1964 (for previous term see above).

cKEITHEN, John Julian (D) May 28, 1918- –; May 12, 1964-May 9, 1972.

)WARDS, Edwin Washington (D) Aug. 7, 1927- –; May 9, 1972-March 10, 1980, March 12, 1984- –; House 1965-72.

REEN, David Conner (R) July 16, 1928- –; March 10, 1980-March 12, 1984; House 1973-80.

)WARDS, Edwin Washington (D) March 12, 1984- – (for previous term see above).

Iaine

ecame a state March 15, 1820)

NG, William (DR) Feb. 9, 1768-June 17, 1852; May 31, 1820-May 28, 1821.

ILLIAMSON, William Durkee (D) July 31, 1779-May 27, 1846; May 29-Dec. 25, 1821 (Democratic Republican); House 1821-23.

MES, Benjamin (DR) Oct. 30, 1778-Sept. 28, 1835; Dec. 25, 1821-Jan. 2, 1822.

)SE, Daniel (DR) 1771-Oct. 25, 1833; Jan. 2-5, 1822.

RRIS, Albion Keith (DR) Jan. 19, 1788-Feb. 22, 1857; Jan. 5, 1822-Jan. 3, 1827; House 1815-18 (Democrat, Mass.); Senate 1827-28.

LINCOLN, Enoch (son of Levi Lincoln of Mass., brother of Levi Lincoln Jr. of Mass., granduncle of Frederick Robie) (DR) Dec. 28, 1788-Oct. 8, 1829; Jan. 3, 1827-Oct. 8, 1829; House 1818-21 (Mass.), 1821-26.

CUTLER, Nathan (D) May 29, 1775-June 8, 1861; Oct. 12, 1829-Feb. 5, 1830.

HALL, Joshua (D) Oct. 22, 1768-Dec. 25, 1862; Feb. 5-10, 1830.

HUNTON, Jonathan Glidden (NR) March 14, 1781-Oct. 12, 1851; Feb. 10, 1830-Jan. 5, 1831.

SMITH, Samuel Emerson (JD) March 12, 1788-March 3, 1860; Jan. 5, 1831-Jan. 1, 1834.

DUNLAP, Robert Pinckney (D) Aug. 17, 1794-Oct. 20, 1859; Jan. 1, 1834-Jan. 3, 1838; House 1843-47.

KENT, Edward (W) Jan. 8, 1802-May 19, 1877; Jan. 3, 1838-Jan. 2, 1839, Jan. 13, 1841-Jan. 5, 1842.

FAIRFIELD, John (D) Jan 30, 1797-Dec. 24, 1847; Jan. 2, 1839-Jan. 6, 1841, Jan. 5, 1842-March 7, 1843; House 1835-38; Senate 1843-47.

VOSE, Richard H. (–) Nov. 8, 1803-?; Jan. 12-13, 1841.

KENT, Edward (W) Jan. 13, 1841-Jan. 5, 1842 (for previous term see above).

FAIRFIELD, John (D) Jan. 5, 1842-March 7, 1843 (for previous term see above).

KAVANAGH, Edward (D) April 27, 1795-Jan. 20, 1844; March 7, 1843-Jan. 1, 1844; House 1831-35.

DUNN, David (D) Jan. 17, 1811-Feb. 17, 1894; Jan. 1-3, 1844.

DANA, John Winchester (D) June 21, 1808-Dec. 22, 1867; Jan. 3-5, 1844, May 13, 1847-May 8, 1850.

ANDERSON, Hugh Johnston (D) May 10, 1801-May 31, 1881; Jan. 5, 1844-May 12, 1847; House 1837-41.

DANA, John Winchester (D) May 13, 1847-May 8, 1850 (for previous term see above).

HUBBARD, John (D) March 22, 1794-Feb. 6, 1869; May 8, 1850-Jan. 5, 1853.

CROSBY, William George (W) Sept. 10, 1805-March 21, 1881; Jan. 5, 1853-Jan. 3, 1855.

MORRILL, Anson Peaslee (brother of Lot Myrick Morrill, below) (R) June 10, 1803-July 4, 1887; Jan. 3, 1855-Jan. 2, 1856; House 1861-63.

WELLS, Samuel (D) Aug. 15, 1801-July 15, 1868; Jan. 2, 1856-Jan. 8, 1857.

HAMLIN, Hannibal (R) Aug. 27, 1809-July 4, 1891; Jan. 8-Feb. 25, 1857; House 1843-47 (Democrat); Senate 1848-57 (Democrat), 1857-61, 1869-81; Vice President 1861-65.

WILLIAMS, Joseph Hartwell (R) June 2, 1814-July 19, 1896; Feb. 26, 1857-Jan. 8, 1858.

MORRILL, Lot Myrick (brother of Anson Peaslee Morrill, above) (R) May 3, 1813-Jan. 10, 1883; Jan. 8, 1858-Jan. 2, 1861; Senate 1861-69, Sept. 1869-76; Secy. of the Treasury 1876-77.

WASHBURN, Israel Jr. (brother of Cadwallader Colden Washburn of Wis.) (R) June 6, 1813-May 12, 1883; Jan. 2, 1861-Jan. 7, 1863; House 1851-61 (1851-55 Whig).

COBURN, Abner (R) March 22, 1803-Jan. 4, 1885; Jan. 7, 1863-Jan. 6, 1864.

CONY, Samuel (R) Feb. 27, 1811-Oct. 5, 1870; Jan. 6, 1864-Jan. 2, 1867

CHAMBERLAIN, Joshua Lawrence (R) Sept. 8, 1828-March 2, 1908; Jan. 2, 1867-Jan. 4, 1871.

PERHAM, Sidney (R) March 27, 1819-April 10, 1907; Jan. 4, 1871-Jan. 7, 1874; House 1863-69.

DINGLEY, Nelson Jr. (R) Feb. 15, 1832-Jan. 13, 1899; Jan. 7, 1874-Jan. 5, 1876; House 1881-99.

CONNOR, Seldon (R) Jan. 25, 1839-July 9, 1917; Jan. 5, 1876-Jan. 8, 1879.

GARCELON, Alonzo (D) May 6, 1813-Dec. 8, 1906; Jan. 8, 1879-Jan. 17, 1880.

DAVIS, Daniel Franklin (R) Sept. 12, 1843-Jan. 9, 1897; Jan. 17, 1880-Jan. 13, 1881.

PLAISTED, Harris Merrill (father of Frederick William Plaisted, below) (D) Nov. 2, 1828-Jan. 31, 1898; Jan. 13, 1881-Jan. 3, 1883; House 1875-77 (Republican).

ROBIE, Frederick (great-grandnephew of Levi Lincoln of Mass., grandnephew of Levi Lincoln Jr. of Mass. and Enoch Lincoln) (R) Aug. 12, 1822-Feb. 3, 1912; Jan. 3, 1883-Jan. 5, 1887.

BODWELL, Joseph Robinson (R) June 18, 1818-Dec. 15, 1887; Jan. 5-Dec. 15, 1887.

MARBLE, Sebastian Streeter (R) March 1, 1817-May 10, 1902; Dec. 16, 1887-Jan. 2, 1889.

BURLEIGH, Edwin Chick (R) Nov. 27, 1843-June 16, 1916; Jan. 2, 1889-Jan. 4, 1893; House 1897-1911; Senate 1913-16.

CLEAVES, Henry B. (R) Feb. 6, 1840-June 22, 1912; Jan. 4, 1893-Jan. 6, 1897.

POWERS, Llewellyn (R) Oct. 14, 1836-July 28, 19▪ Jan. 6, 1897-Jan. 2, 1901; House 1877-79, 1901-0

HILL, John Fremont (R) Oct. 29, 1855-March 16, 19 Jan. 2, 1901-Jan. 4, 1905.

COBB, William Titcomb (R) July 23, 1857-July 24, 19 Jan. 4, 1905-Jan. 6, 1909.

FERNALD, Bert Manfred (R) April 3, 1859-Aug. 1926; Jan. 6, 1909-Jan. 4, 1911; Senate 1916-26.

PLAISTED, Frederick William (son of Harris Mer Plaisted, above) (D) July 26, 1865-March 4, 19 Jan. 4, 1911-Jan. 1, 1913.

HAINES, William Thomas (R) Aug. 7, 1854-June 1919; Jan. 1, 1913-Jan. 6, 1915.

CURTIS, Oakley Chester (D) March 29, 1865-Feb. 1924; Jan. 6, 1915-Jan. 3, 1917.

MILLIKEN, Carl Elias (R) July 13, 1877-May 1, 19▪ Jan. 3, 1917-Jan. 5, 1921.

PARKHURST, Frederick Hale (R) Nov. 5, 1864-J▪ 31, 1921; Jan. 5-31, 1921.

BAXTER, Percival Proctor (R) Nov. 22, 1876-June 1969; Jan. 31, 1921-Jan. 8, 1925.

BREWSTER, Ralph Owen (R) Feb. 22, 1888-Dec. 1961; Jan. 8, 1925-Jan. 2, 1929; House 1935-41; S▪ ate 1941-52.

GARDINER, William Tudor (R) June 12, 1892-Aug 1953; Jan. 2, 1929-Jan. 4, 1933.

BRANN, Louis Jefferson (D) July 6, 1876-Feb. 3, 19▪ Jan. 4, 1933-Jan. 6, 1937.

BARROWS, Lewis Orin (R) June 7, 1893-Jan. 30, 19 Jan. 6, 1937-Jan. 1, 1941.

SEWALL, Sumner (R) June 17, 1897-Jan. 25, 1965; J 1, 1941-Jan. 3, 1945.

HILDRETH, Horace Augustus (R) Dec. 2, 1901-—; J 3, 1945-Jan. 5, 1949.

PAYNE, Frederick George (R) July 24, 1904-June 1978; Jan. 5, 1949-Dec. 25, 1952; Senate 1953-59▪

CROSS, Burton Melvin (R) Nov. 15, 1902-—; Dec. 1952-Jan. 5, 1955.

MUSKIE, Edmund Sixtus (D) March 28, 1914-—; J 5, 1955-Jan. 3, 1959; Senate 1959-80; Secy. of St 1980-81.

HASKELL, Robert Nelson (R) Aug. 24, 1903-—; Jan 8, 1959.

CLAUSON, Clinton Amos (D) March 24, 1898-Dec. 1959; Jan. 8-Dec. 30, 1959.

ED, John Hathaway (R) Jan. 5, 1921-—; Dec. 30, 1959-Jan. 5, 1967.

RTIS, Kenneth M. (D) Feb. 8, 1931-—; Jan. 5, 1967-Jan. 1, 1975; Chrmn. Dem. Nat. Comm. 1977-78.

NGLEY, James Bernard (I) April 22, 1924-Aug. 16, 1980; Jan. 2, 1975-Jan. 3, 1979.

ENNAN, Joseph E. (D) Nov. 2, 1934-—; Jan. 3, 1979-Jan. 7, 1987; House 1987-—.

KERNAN, John R. Jr. (R) May 20, 1948-—; Jan. 7, 1987-—; House 1983-87.

aryland

ntified the Constitution April 28, 1788)

WARD, John Eager (father of George Howard, below) (F) June 4, 1752-Oct. 12, 1827; Nov. 24, 1788-Nov. 14, 1791; Cont. Cong. 1784-88; Senate 1796-1803; Pres. pro tempore 1801.

ATER, George (F) Nov. 8, 1735-Feb. 10, 1792; Nov. 14, 1791-Feb. 10, 1792; Cont. Cong. 1778-81.

ICE, James (F) Aug. 26, 1746-July 11, 1801; Feb. 13-April 5, 1792.

E, Thomas Sim (great-great-grandfather of John Lee Carroll, below) (F) Oct. 29, 1745-Nov. 9, 1819; April 5, 1792-Nov. 14, 1794.

NE, John Hoskins (F) 1745-Oct. 5, 1804; Nov. 14, 1794-Nov. 17, 1797.

NRY, John (great-grandfather of Henry Lloyd, below) (F) Nov. 1750-Dec. 16, 1798; Nov. 17, 1797-Nov. 14, 1798; Cont. Cong 1778-81, 1784-87; Senate 1789-97.

LE, Benjamin (F) Jan. 27, 1749-July 6, 1809; Nov. 14, 1798-Nov. 10, 1801.

RCER, John Francis (DR) May 17, 1759-Aug. 30, 1821; Nov. 10, 1801-Nov. 15, 1803; Cont. Cong. (Va.) 1782-85; House 1792-94 (Democrat).

WIE, Robert (DR) March 1750-Jan. 8, 1818; Nov. 15, 1803-Nov. 10, 1806, Nov. 16, 1811-Nov. 25, 1812.

IGHT, Robert (father-in-law of Philip Francis Thomas, below) (D) Nov. 20, 1752-Sept. 7, 1826; Nov. 12, 1806-May 6, 1809 (Democratic Republican); Senate 1801-06; House 1810-17 (Democratic Republican), 1821-23.

TCHER, James (DR) ?-Jan. 12, 1824; May 6-June 9, 1809.

LLOYD, Edward (grandfather of Henry Lloyd, granduncle of Lloyd Lowndes Jr.) (D) July 22, 1779-June 2, 1834; June 9, 1809-Nov. 16, 1811 (Democratic Republican); House 1806-09; Senate 1819-26.

BOWIE, Robert (DR) Nov. 16, 1811-Nov. 25, 1812 (for previous term see above).

WINDER, Levin (F) Sept. 4, 1757-July 1, 1819; Nov. 25, 1812-Jan. 2, 1816.

RIDGELY, Charles Carnan (father-in-law of George Howard, below) (F) Dec. 6, 1762-July 17, 1829; Jan. 2, 1816-Jan. 8, 1819.

GOLDSBOROUGH, Charles (F) July 15, 1765-Dec. 13, 1834; Jan. 8-Dec. 20, 1819; House 1805-17.

SPRIGG, Samuel (DR) 1783-April 21, 1855; Dec. 20, 1819-Dec. 16, 1822.

STEVENS, Samuel Jr. (DR) July 13, 1778-Feb. 7, 1860; Dec. 16, 1822-Jan. 9, 1826.

KENT, Joseph (NR) Jan. 14, 1779-Nov. 24, 1837; Jan. 9, 1826-Jan. 15, 1829 (Democratic Republican); House 1811-15 (Federalist), 1819-26 (Republican); Senate 1833-37.

MARTIN, Daniel (AJD) 1780-July 11, 1831; Jan. 15, 1829-Jan. 15, 1830, Jan. 13-July 11, 1831.

CARROLL, Thomas King (JD) April 29, 1793-Oct. 3, 1873; Jan. 15, 1830-Jan. 13, 1831.

MARTIN, Daniel (AJD) Jan. 13-July 11, 1831 (for previous term see above).

HOWARD, George (son of John Eager Howard, son-in-law of Charles Carnan Ridgely) (AJD) Nov. 21, 1789-Aug. 2, 1846; July 22, 1831-Jan. 17, 1833.

THOMAS, James (AJD) March 11, 1785-Dec. 25, 1845; Jan. 17, 1833-Jan. 14, 1836.

VEAZEY, Thomas Ward (W) Jan. 31, 1774-July 1, 1842; Jan. 14, 1836-Jan. 7, 1839.

GRASON, William (D) March 11, 1788-July 2, 1868; Jan. 7, 1839-Jan. 3, 1842.

THOMAS, Francis (son-in-law of James McDowell of Va.) (UR) Feb. 3, 1799-Jan. 22, 1876; Jan. 3, 1842-Jan. 6, 1845 (Democrat); House 1831-41 (Jackson Democrat), 1861-69.

PRATT, Thomas George (W) Feb. 18, 1804-Nov. 9, 1869; Jan. 6, 1845-Jan. 3, 1848; Senate 1850-57 (1856-57 Conservative Democrat).

THOMAS, Philip Francis (son-in-law of Robert Wright, above) (D) Sept. 12, 1810-Oct. 2, 1890; Jan. 3, 1848-Jan. 6, 1851; House 1839-41, 1875-77; Secy. of the Treasury 1860-61.

LOWE, Enoch Louis (D) Aug. 10, 1820-Aug. 23, 1892; Jan. 6, 1851-Jan. 11, 1854.

LIGON, Thomas Watkins (D) May 10, 1810-Jan. 12, 1881; Jan. 11, 1854-Jan. 13, 1858; House 1845-49.

HICKS, Thomas Holliday (UR) Sept. 2, 1798-Feb. 14, 1865; Jan. 13, 1858-Jan. 8, 1862 (American Party); Senate 1862-65.

BRADFORD, Augustus Williamson (UR) Jan. 9, 1806-March 1, 1881; Jan. 8, 1862-Jan. 10, 1866.

SWANN, Thomas (D) Feb. 3, 1809-July 24, 1883; Jan. 10, 1866-Jan. 13, 1869 (Union Democrat); House 1869-79.

BOWIE, Oden (D) Nov. 10, 1826-Dec. 4, 1894; Jan. 13, 1869-Jan. 10, 1872.

WHYTE, William Pinkney (D) Aug. 9, 1824-March 17, 1908; Jan. 10, 1872-March 4, 1874; Senate 1868-69, 1875-81, 1906-08.

GROOME, James Black (D) April 4, 1838-Oct. 5, 1893; March 4, 1874-Jan. 12, 1876; Senate 1879-85.

CARROLL, John Lee (great-great-grandson of Thomas Sim Lee, above) (D) Sept. 30, 1830-Feb. 27, 1911; Jan. 12, 1876-Jan. 14, 1880.

HAMILTON, William Thomas (D) Sept. 8, 1820-Oct. 26, 1888; Jan. 14, 1880-Jan. 9, 1884; House 1849-55; Senate 1869-75.

McLANE, Robert Milligan (D) June 23, 1815-April 16, 1898; Jan. 9, 1884-March 27, 1885; House 1847-51, 1879-83.

LLOYD, Henry (grandson of Edward Lloyd, great-grandson of John Henry) (D) Feb. 21, 1852-Dec. 30, 1920; March 27, 1885-Jan. 11, 1888.

JACKSON, Elihu Emory (D) Nov. 3, 1836-Dec. 27, 1907; Jan. 11, 1888-Jan. 13, 1892.

BROWN, Frank (D) Aug. 8, 1846-Feb. 3, 1920; Jan. 13, 1892-Jan. 8, 1896.

LOWNDES, Lloyd Jr. (grandnephew of Edward Lloyd, above) (R) Feb. 21, 1845-Jan. 8, 1905; Jan. 8, 1896-Jan. 10, 1900; House 1873-75.

SMITH, John Walter (D) Feb. 5, 1845-April 19, 1925; Jan. 10, 1900-Jan. 13, 1904; House 1899-1900; Senate 1908-21.

WARFIELD, Edwin (D) May 7, 1848-March 31, 1920; Jan. 13, 1904-Jan. 8, 1908.

CROTHERS, Austin Lane (D) May 17, 1860-May 25, 1912; Jan. 8, 1908-Jan. 10, 1912.

GOLDSBOROUGH, Phillips Lee (R) Aug. 6, 1865-Oct. 22, 1946; Jan. 10, 1912-Jan. 12, 1916; Senate 1929-35.

HARRINGTON, Emerson Columbus (D) March 1864-Dec. 15, 1945; Jan. 12, 1916-Jan. 14, 1920.

RITCHIE, Albert Cabell (D) Aug. 29, 1876-Feb. 1936; Jan. 14, 1920-Jan. 9, 1935.

NICE, Harry Whinna (R) Dec. 5, 1877-Feb. 25, 19 Jan. 9, 1935-Jan. 11, 1939.

O'CONOR, Herbert Romulus (D) Nov. 17, 1896-Ma 4, 1960; Jan. 11, 1939-Jan. 3, 1947; Senate 1947

LANE, William Preston Jr. (D) May 12, 1892-Feb 1967; Jan. 3, 1947-Jan. 10, 1951.

McKELDIN, Theodore Roosevelt (R) Nov. 20, 19 Aug. 10, 1974; Jan. 10, 1951-Jan. 14, 1959.

TAWES, John Millard (D) April 8, 1894-June 25, 19 Jan. 14, 1959-Jan. 25, 1967.

AGNEW, Spiro Theodore (R) Nov. 9, 1918- —; Jan. 1967-Jan. 7, 1969; Vice President 1969-73.

MANDEL, Marvin (D) April 19, 1920- —; Jan. 7, 19 June 1977.

LEE, Blair III (D) May 19, 1916-Oct. 25, 1985; J 1977-Jan. 15, 1979.

HUGHES, Harry R. (D) Nov. 13, 1926- —; Jan. 17, 19 Jan. 20, 1987.

SCHAEFER, William Donald (D) Nov. 2, 1921- —; 21, 1987- —.

Massachusetts

(Ratified the Constitution Feb. 6, 1788)

HANCOCK, John (—) Jan. 23, 1737-Oct. 8, 1793; 30, 1787-Oct. 8, 1793; Cont. Cong. 1775-77 (Pr dent), 1785-86.

ADAMS, Samuel (DR) Sept. 27, 1722-Oct. 2, 1803; 8, 1793-June 2, 1797; Cont. Cong. 1774-82.

SUMNER, Increase (F) Nov. 27, 1746-June 7, 19 June 2, 1797-June 7, 1799.

GILL, Moses (F) Jan. 18, 1734-May 20, 1800; Jun 1799-May 20, 1800.

STRONG, Caleb (F) Jan. 9, 1745-Nov. 7, 1819; May 1800-May 29, 1807, June 5, 1812-May 30, 1816; S ate 1789-96.

SULLIVAN, James (brother of John Sullivan of N (DR) April 22, 1744-Dec. 10, 1808; May 29, 18 Dec. 10, 1808; Cont. Cong. 1782, 1784-85.

LINCOLN, Levi (father of Levi Lincoln Jr. and Enoch Lincoln of Maine, great-granduncle of Frederick Robie of Maine) (DR) May 15, 1749-April 14, 1820; Dec. 10, 1808-May 1, 1809; House 1800-01 (Democrat); Atty. Gen. 1801-05.

GORE, Christopher (F) Sept. 21, 1758-March 1, 1827; May 1, 1809-June 2, 1810; Senate 1813-16.

GERRY, Elbridge (DR) July 17, 1744-Nov. 23, 1814; June 2, 1810-June 5, 1812; Cont. Cong. 1776-81, 1782-85; House 1789-93 (Anti Federalist); Vice President 1813-14.

STRONG, Caleb (F) June 5, 1812-May 30, 1816 (for previous term see above).

BROOKS, John (F) May 4, 1752-March 1, 1825; May 30, 1816-May 31, 1823.

EUSTIS, William (DR) June 10, 1753-Feb. 6, 1825; May 31, 1823-Feb. 6, 1825; House 1801-05, 1820-23; Secy. of War 1809-13.

MORTON, Marcus (D) Dec. 19, 1784-Feb. 6, 1864; Feb. 6-May 26, 1825 (Democratic Republican), Jan. 18, 1840-Jan. 7, 1841, Jan. 17, 1843-Jan. 3, 1844; House 1817-21.

LINCOLN, Levi Jr. (son of Levi Lincoln, brother of Enoch Lincoln of Maine, granduncle of Frederick Robie of Maine) (W) Oct. 25, 1782-May 29, 1868; May 26, 1825-Jan. 9, 1834 (1825-29 Anti Democrat, 1829-34 National Republican); House 1834-41.

DAVIS, John (W) Jan. 13, 1787-April 19, 1854; Jan. 9, 1834-March 1, 1835, Jan. 7, 1841-Jan. 17, 1843; House 1825-34 (National Republican); Senate 1835-40, 1845-53.

ARMSTRONG, Samuel Turell (IW) April 29, 1784-March 26, 1850; March 1, 1835-Jan. 13, 1836.

EVERETT, Edward (W) April 11, 1794-Jan. 15, 1865; Jan. 13, 1836-Jan. 18, 1840; House 1825-35; Senate 1853-54; Secy. of State 1852-53.

MORTON, Marcus (D) Jan. 18, 1840-Jan. 7, 1841 (for previous term see above).

DAVIS, John (W) Jan. 7, 1841-Jan. 17, 1843 (for previous term see above).

MORTON, Marcus (D) Jan. 17, 1843-Jan. 3, 1844 (for previous terms see above).

BRIGGS, George Nixon (W) April 12, 1796-Sept. 11, 1861; Jan. 3, 1844-Jan. 11, 1851; House 1831-43.

BRIGGS, George Nixon (W) April 12, 1796-Sept. 11, 1861; Jan. 3, 1844-Jan. 11, 1851; House 1831-43.

BOUTWELL, George Sewall (R) Jan. 28, 1818-Feb. 27, 1905; Jan. 11, 1851-Jan. 14, 1853 (Democrat); House 1863-69; Senate 1873-77; Secy. of the Treasury 1869-73.

CLIFFORD, John Henry (W) Jan. 16, 1809-Jan. 2, 1876; Jan. 14, 1853-Jan. 4, 1854.

WASHBURN, Emory (W) Feb. 14, 1800-March 18, 1877; Jan. 12, 1854-Jan. 4, 1855.

GARDNER, Henry Joseph (ASP) June 14, 1819-July 21, 1892; Jan. 4, 1855-Jan. 6, 1858.

BANKS, Nathaniel Prentice (R) Jan. 30, 1816-Sept. 1, 1894; Jan. 6, 1858-Jan. 2, 1861; House 1853-57, 1865-73, 1875-79, 1889-91; Speaker 1855-59 (1853-55 Coalition Democrat, 1855-57 American Party, 1865-67 Union Republican, 1875-79 Liberal Republican).

ANDREW, John Albion (R) May 31, 1818-Oct. 30, 1867; Jan. 2, 1861-Jan. 4, 1866.

BULLOCK, Alexander Hamilton (R) March 2, 1816-Jan. 17, 1882; Jan. 4, 1866-Jan. 7, 1869.

CLAFLIN, William (R) March 6, 1818-Jan. 5, 1905; Jan. 7, 1869-Jan. 4, 1872; House 1877-81; Chrmn. Rep. Nat. Comm. 1868-72.

WASHBURN, William Barrett (R) Jan. 31, 1820-Oct. 5, 1887; Jan. 3, 1872-April 29, 1874; House 1863-71; Senate 1874-75.

TALBOT, Thomas (R) Sept. 7, 1818-Oct. 6, 1886; April 29, 1874-Jan. 6, 1875, Jan. 1, 1879-Jan. 7, 1880.

GASTON, William (D) Oct. 3, 1820-Jan. 19, 1894; Jan. 6, 1875-Jan. 5, 1876.

RICE, Alexander Hamilton (R) Aug. 30, 1818-July 22, 1895; Jan. 5, 1876-Jan. 1, 1879; House 1859-67.

TALBOT, Thomas (R) Jan. 1, 1879-Jan. 7, 1880 (for previous term see above).

LONG, John Davis (R) Oct. 27, 1838-Aug. 28, 1915; Jan. 8, 1880-Jan. 4, 1883; House 1883-89; Secy. of the Navy 1897-1902.

BUTLER, Benjamin Franklin (father-in-law of Adelbert Ames of Miss.) (D/G) Nov. 5, 1818-Jan. 11, 1893; Jan. 4, 1883-Jan. 3, 1884; House 1867-75 (Republican), 1877-79 (Greenbacker).

ROBINSON, George Dexter (R) Jan. 20, 1834-Feb. 22, 1896; Jan. 3, 1884-Jan. 5, 1887; House 1877-84.

AMES, Oliver (R) Feb. 4, 1831-Oct. 22, 1895; Jan. 5, 1887-Jan. 1, 1890.

BRACKETT, John Quincy Adams (R) June 8, 1842-April 6, 1918; Jan. 1, 1890-Jan. 7, 1891.

RUSSELL, William Eustis (D) Jan. 6, 1857-July 14, 1896; Jan. 7, 1891-Jan. 3, 1894.

GREENHALGE, Frederic Thomas (R) July 19, 1842-March 5, 1896; Jan. 3, 1894-March 5, 1896; House 1889-91.

WOLCOTT, Roger (R) July 13, 1847-Dec. 21, 1900; March 5, 1896-Jan. 4, 1900.

CRANE, Winthrop Murray (R) April 23, 1853-Oct. 2, 1920; Jan. 4, 1900-Jan. 8, 1903; Senate 1904-13.

BATES, John Lewis (R) Sept. 18, 1859-June 8, 1946; Jan. 8, 1903-Jan. 5, 1905.

DOUGLAS, William Lewis (D) Aug. 22, 1845-Sept. 17, 1924; Jan. 5, 1905-Jan. 4, 1906.

GUILD, Curtis Jr. (R) Feb. 2, 1860-April 6, 1915; Jan. 4, 1906-Jan. 7, 1909.

DRAPER, Eben Sumner (R) June 17, 1858-April 9, 1914; Jan. 7, 1909-Jan. 5, 1911.

FOSS, Eugene Noble (D) Sept. 24, 1858-Sept. 13, 1939; Jan. 5, 1911-Jan. 8, 1914; House 1910-11.

WALSH, David Ignatius (D) Nov. 11, 1872-June 11, 1947; Jan. 8, 1914-Jan. 6, 1916; Senate 1919-25, 1926-47.

McCALL, Samuel Walker (R) Feb. 28, 1851-Nov. 4, 1923; Jan. 6, 1916-Jan. 2, 1919; House 1893-1913.

COOLIDGE, John Calvin (cousin of William Wallace Stickney of Vt.) (R) July 4, 1872-Jan. 5, 1933; Jan. 2, 1919-Jan. 6, 1921; Vice President 1921-23; President 1923-29.

COX, Channing Harris (R) Oct. 28, 1879-Aug. 20, 1968; Jan. 6, 1921-Jan. 8, 1925.

FULLER, Alvan Tufts (R) Feb. 27, 1878-April 30, 1958; Jan. 8, 1925-Jan. 3, 1929; House 1917-21.

ALLEN, Frank G. (R) Oct. 6, 1874-Oct. 9, 1950; Jan. 3, 1929-Jan. 8, 1931.

ELY, Joseph Buell (D) Feb. 22, 1881-June 13, 1956; Jan. 8, 1931-Jan. 3, 1935.

CURLEY, James Michael (D) Nov. 20, 1874-Nov. 12, 1958; Jan. 3, 1935-Jan. 7, 1937; House 1911-14, 1943-45.

HURLEY, Charles Francis (D) Nov. 24, 1893-March 24, 1946; Jan. 7, 1937-Jan. 5, 1939.

SALTONSTALL, Leverett (R) Sept. 1, 1892-June 17, 1979; Jan. 5, 1939-Jan. 3, 1945; Senate 1945-67.

TOBIN, Maurice Joseph (D) May 22, 1901-July 19, 1953; Jan. 3, 1945-Jan. 2, 1947; Secy. of Labor 1948-53.

BRADFORD, Robert Fiske (R) Dec. 15, 1902-March 18, 1983; Jan. 2, 1947-Jan. 6, 1949.

DEVER, Paul Andrew (D) Jan. 15, 1903-April 11, 1958; Jan. 6, 1949-Jan. 8, 1953.

HERTER, Christian Archibald (R) March 28, 1895-Dec. 30, 1966; Jan. 8, 1953-Jan. 3, 1957; House 1943-53; Secy. of State 1959-61.

FURCOLO, Foster John (D) July 29, 1911- —; Jan. 3, 1957-Jan. 5, 1961; House 1949-52.

VOLPE, John Anthony (R) Dec. 8, 1908- —; Jan. 5, 1961, Jan. 3, 1963, Jan. 7, 1965-Jan. 22, 1969; Secy. of Transportation 1969-73.

PEABODY, Endicott "Chub" (D) Feb. 15, 1920- —; Jan. 3, 1963-Jan. 7, 1965.

VOLPE, John Anthony (R) Jan. 7, 1965-Jan. 22, 1969 (for previous term see above).

SARGENT, Francis Williams (R) July 29, 1915- —; Jan. 22, 1969-Jan. 2, 1975.

DUKAKIS, Michael Stanley (D) Nov. 3, 1933- —; Jan. 2, 1975-Jan. 4, 1979, Jan. 6, 1983- —.

KING, Edward J. (D) May 11, 1925- —; Jan. 4, 1979-Jan. 6, 1983.

DUKAKIS, Michael Stanley (D) Jan. 6, 1983- — (for previous term see above).

Michigan

(Became a state Jan. 26, 1837)

WOODBRIDGE, William (W) Aug. 20, 1780-Oct. 20, 1861; Jan. 7, 1840-Feb. 23, 1841; Senate 1841-47.

GORDON, James Wright (W) 1809-Dec. 1853; Feb. 23, 1841-Jan. 3, 1842.

BARRY, John Stewart (D) Jan. 29, 1802-Jan. 14, 1870; Jan. 3, 1842-Jan. 5, 1846, Jan. 7, 1850-Jan. 1, 1851.

FELCH, Alpheus (D) Sept. 28, 1804-June 13, 1896; Jan. 5, 1846-March 3, 1847; Senate 1847-53.

GREENLY, William L. (D) Sept. 18, 1813-Nov. 29, 1883; March 3, 1847-Jan. 3, 1848.

RANSOM, Epaphroditus (D) Feb. 1787-Nov. 9, 1859; Jan. 3, 1848-Jan. 7, 1850.

BARRY, John Stewart (D) Jan. 7, 1850-Jan. 1, 1851 (for previous term see above).

McCLELLAND, Robert (D) Aug. 1, 1807-Aug. 30, 1880; Jan. 1, 1851-March 7, 1853; House 1843-49; Secy. of the Interior 1853-57.

PARSONS, Andrew (D) July 22, 1817-June 6, 1855; March 7, 1853-Jan. 3, 1855.

INGHAM, Kinsley Scott (R) Dec. 16, 1808-Oct. 5, 1861; Jan. 3, 1855-Jan. 5, 1859; House 1847-51 (Democrat); Senate 1859-61.

ISNER, Moses (R) June 3, 1815-Jan. 5, 1863; Jan. 5, 1859-Jan. 2, 1861.

LAIR, Austin (R) Feb. 8, 1818-Aug. 6, 1894; Jan. 2, 1861-Jan. 4, 1865; House 1867-73.

RAPO, Henry Howland (R) May 22, 1804-July 22, 1869; Jan. 4, 1865-Jan. 6, 1869.

ALDWIN, Henry Porter (R) Feb. 22, 1814-Dec. 31, 1892; Jan. 6, 1869-Jan. 1, 1873; Senate 1879-81.

AGLEY, John Judson (R) July 24, 1832-Dec. 27, 1881; Jan. 1, 1873-Jan. 3, 1877.

ROSWELL, Charles Miller (R) Oct. 31, 1825-Dec. 13, 1886; Jan. 3, 1877-Jan. 1, 1881.

EROME, David Howell (R) Nov. 17, 1869-April 23, 1896; Jan. 1, 1881-Jan. 1, 1883.

EGOLE, Josiah William (D) Jan. 20, 1815-June 6, 1896; Jan. 1, 1883-Jan. 1, 1885; House 1873-75.

LGER, Russell Alexander (R) Feb. 27, 1836-Jan. 24, 1907; Jan. 1, 1885-Jan. 1, 1887; Senate 1902-07; Secy. of War 1897-99.

UCE, Cyrus Gray (R) July 2, 1824-March 18, 1905; Jan. 1, 1887-Jan. 1, 1891.

INANS, Edwin Baruch (D) May 16, 1826-July 4, 1894; Jan. 1, 1891-Jan. 1, 1893; House 1883-87.

ICH, John Treadway (R) April 23, 1841-March 28, 1926; Jan. 1, 1893-Jan. 1, 1897.

INGREE, Hazen Stuart (R) Aug. 30, 1840-June 18, 1901; Jan. 1, 1897-Jan. 1, 1901.

LISS, Aaron Thomas (R) May 22, 1837-Sept. 16, 1906; Jan. 1, 1901-Jan. 1, 1905; House 1889-91.

ARNER, Fred Maltby (R) July 21, 1865-April 17, 1823; Jan. 1, 1905-Jan. 1, 1911.

SBORN, Chase Salmon (R) June 22, 1860-April 11, 1949; Jan. 1, 1911-Jan. 1, 1913.

ERRIS, Woodbridge Nathan (D) Jan. 6, 1853-March 23, 1928; Jan. 1, 1913-Jan. 1, 1917; Senate 1923-28.

LEEPER, Albert Edson (R) Dec. 31, 1862-May 13, 1934; Jan. 1, 1917-Jan. 1, 1921.

ROESBECK, Alexander Joseph (R) Nov. 7, 1873-March 10, 1953; Jan. 1, 1921-Jan. 1, 1927.

REEN, Fred Warren (R) Oct. 20, 1871-Nov. 30, 1936; Jan. 1, 1927-Jan. 1, 1931.

BRUCKER, Wilber Marion (R) June 23, 1894-Oct. 28, 1968; Jan. 1, 1931-Jan. 1, 1933; Secy. of the Army 1955-61.

COMSTOCK, William Alfred (D) July 2, 1877-June 16, 1949; Jan. 1, 1933-Jan. 1, 1935.

FITZGERALD, Frank Dwight (R) Jan. 27, 1885-March 16, 1939; Jan. 1, 1935-Jan. 1, 1937, Jan. 2-March 16, 1939.

MURPHY, Francis William (D) April 13, 1890-July 19, 1949; Jan. 1, 1937-Jan. 1, 1939; Atty. Gen. 1939; Assoc. Justice Supreme Court 1940-49.

FITZGERALD, Frank Dwight (R) Jan. 2-March 16, 1939 (for previous term see above).

DICKENSON, Luren Dudley (R) April 15, 1859-April 22, 1943; March 16, 1939-Jan. 1, 1941.

VAN WAGONER, Murray Delos (D) March 18, 1898-June 12, 1986; Jan. 1, 1941-Jan. 1, 1943.

KELLY, Harry Francis (R) April 19, 1895-Feb. 8, 1971; Jan. 1, 1943-Jan. 1, 1947.

SIGLER, Kim (R) May 2, 1894-Nov. 30, 1953; Jan. 1, 1947-Jan. 1, 1949.

WILLIAMS, Gerhard Mennen (D) Feb. 23, 1911-—; Jan. 1, 1949-Jan. 2, 1961.

SWAINSON, John Burley (D) July 30, 1925-—; Jan. 2, 1961-Jan. 1, 1963.

ROMNEY, George Wilcken (R) July 8, 1907-—; Jan. 1, 1963-Jan. 22, 1969; Secy. of Housing and Urban Development 1969-72.

MILLIKEN, William Grawn (R) March 26, 1922-—; Jan. 22, 1969-Jan. 1, 1983.

BLANCHARD, James Johnston (D) Aug. 8, 1942-—; Jan. 1, 1983-—; House 1975-83.

Minnesota

(Became a state May 11, 1858)

SIBLEY, Henry Hastings (D) Feb. 20, 1811-Feb. 18, 1891; May 24, 1858-Jan. 2, 1860.

RAMSEY, Alexander (R) Sept. 8, 1815-April 22, 1903; Jan. 2, 1860-July 10, 1863; House 1843-47 (Whig, Pa.); Senate 1863-75; Secy. of War 1879-81.

SWIFT, Henry Adoniram (R) March 23, 1823-Feb. 25, 1869; July 10, 1863-Jan. 11, 1864.

MILLER, Stephen (R) Jan. 17, 1816-Aug. 18, 1881; Jan. 11, 1864-Jan. 8, 1866.

MARSHALL, William Rogerson (R) Oct. 17, 1825-Jan. 8, 1896; Jan. 8, 1866-Jan. 9, 1870.

AUSTIN, Horace (R) Oct. 15, 1831-Nov. 2, 1905; Jan. 9, 1870-Jan. 7, 1874.

DAVIS, Cushman Kellogg (R) June 16, 1838-Nov. 27, 1900; Jan. 7, 1874-Jan. 7, 1876; Senate 1887-1900.

PILLSBURY, John Sargent (R) July 29, 1828-Oct. 10, 1901; Jan. 7, 1876-Jan. 10, 1882.

HUBBARD, Lucius Frederick (R) Jan. 26, 1836-Feb. 5, 1913; Jan. 10, 1882-Jan. 5, 1887.

McGILL, Andrew Ryan (R) Feb. 19, 1840-Oct. 31, 1905; Jan. 5, 1887-Jan. 9, 1889.

MERRIAM, William Rush (R) July 26, 1849-Feb. 18, 1931; Jan. 9, 1889-Jan. 4, 1893.

NELSON, Knute (R) Feb. 2, 1843-April 28, 1923; Jan. 4, 1893-Jan. 31, 1895; House 1883-89; Senate 1895-1923.

CLOUGH, David Marston (father-in-law of Roland Hill Hartley of Wash.) (R) Dec. 27, 1846-Aug. 28, 1924; Jan. 31, 1895-Jan. 2, 1899.

LIND, John (D) March 25, 1854-Sept. 18, 1930; Jan. 2, 1899-Jan. 7, 1901; House 1887-93 (Republican), 1903-05.

VAN SANT, Samuel Rinnah (R) May 11, 1844-Oct. 3, 1936; Jan. 7, 1901-Jan. 4, 1905.

JOHNSON, John Albert (D) July 28, 1861-Sept. 21, 1909; Jan. 4, 1905-Sept. 21, 1909.

EBERHART, Adolph Olson (R) June 23, 1870-Dec. 6, 1944; Sept. 21, 1909-Jan. 5, 1915.

HAMMOND, Winfield Scott (D) Nov. 17, 1863-Dec. 30, 1915; Jan. 5-Dec. 30, 1915; House 1907-15.

BURNQUIST, Joseph Alfred Arner (R) July 21, 1879-Jan. 12, 1961; Dec. 30, 1915-Jan. 5, 1921.

PREUS, Jacob Aall Ottesen (R) Aug. 28, 1883-May 24, 1961; Jan. 5, 1921-Jan. 6, 1925.

CHRISTIANSON, Theodore (R) Sept. 12, 1885-Dec. 9, 1948; Jan. 6, 1925-Jan. 6, 1931; House 1933-37.

OLSON, Floyd Bjornstjerne (FL) Nov. 13, 1891-Aug. 22, 1936; Jan. 6, 1931-Aug. 22, 1936.

PETERSEN, Hjalmar (FL) Jan. 2, 1890-March 29, 1968; Aug. 22, 1936-Jan. 4, 1937.

BENSON, Elmer Austin (FL) Sept. 22, 1895-March 13, 1985; Jan. 4, 1937-Jan. 2, 1939.

STASSEN, Harold Edward (R) April 13, 1907- —; Jan. 2, 1939-April 27, 1943.

THYE, Edward John (R) April 26, 1896-Aug. 28, 196 April 27, 1943-Jan. 8, 1947; Senate 1947-59.

YOUNGDAHL, Luther Wallace (R) May 29, 1896-Jur 21, 1978; Jan. 8, 1947-Sept. 27, 1951.

ANDERSON, Clyde Elmer (R) March 16, 1912- —; Sep 27, 1951-Jan. 5, 1955.

FREEMAN, Orville Lothrop (DFL) May 9, 1918- - Jan. 5, 1955-Jan. 2, 1961; Secy. of Agriculture 196 69.

ANDERSEN, Elmer Lee (R) June 17, 1909- —; Jan. 1961-March 25, 1963.

ROLVAAG, Karl Fritjof (DFL) July 18, 1913- —; Mar 25, 1963-Jan. 2, 1967.

LEVANDER, Harold (R) Oct. 10, 1910- —; Jan. 2, 196 Jan. 4, 1971.

ANDERSON, Wendell Richard (DFL) Feb. 1, 1933- - Jan. 4, 1971-Dec. 29, 1976; Senate 1976-78.

PERPICH, Rudolph George "Rudy" (DFL) June 2 1928- —; Dec. 29, 1976-Jan. 1, 1979, Jan. 3, 1983- -

QUIE, Albert Harold (IR) Sept. 18, 1923- —; Jan. 1979-Jan. 3, 1983; House 1958-79.

PERPICH, Rudolph George "Rudy" (DFL) Jan. 1983- — (for previous term see above).

Mississippi

(Became a state Dec. 10, 1817)

HOLMES, David (DR) March 10, 1769-Aug. 20, 183 Dec. 10, 1817-Jan. 5, 1820, Jan. 7-July 25, 182 House 1797-1809 (Va.); Senate 1820-25.

POINDEXTER, George (D) 1779-Sept. 5, 1855; Jan. 1820-Jan. 7, 1822 (Democratic Republican); Hou (Terr. Del.) 1807-13 (Democratic Republicar (Rep.) 1817-19 (Democratic Republican); Sena 1830-35; Pres. pro tempore 1834.

LEAKE, Walter (DR) May 25, 1762-Nov. 17, 1825; Ja 7, 1822-Nov. 17, 1825; Senate 1817-20.

BRANDON, Gerard Chittoque (JD) Sept. 15, 178 March 28, 1850; Nov. 17, 1825-Jan. 7, 1826 (Dem cratic Republican), July 25, 1826-Jan. 9, 1832.

HOLMES, David (DR) Jan. 7-July 25, 1826 (for prev ous term see above).

BRANDON, Gerard Chittoque (JD) July 25, 1826-Ja 9, 1832 (for previous term see above).

SCOTT, Abram Marshall (NR) 1785-July 12, 1833; Ja 9, 1832-June 12, 1833.

LYNCH, Charles (W) 1783-Feb. 9, 1853; June 12-Nov. 20, 1833, Jan. 7, 1836-Jan. 8, 1838.

RUNNELS, Hiram George (uncle of Hardin R. Runnels of Texas) (JD) Dec. 15, 1796-Dec. 15, 1857; Nov. 20, 1833-Nov. 20, 1835.

QUITMAN, John Anthony (D) Sept. 1, 1799-July 17, 1858; Dec. 3, 1835-Jan. 7, 1836, Jan. 10, 1850-Feb. 3, 1851; House 1855-58.

LYNCH, Charles (W) Jan. 7, 1836-Jan. 8, 1838 (for previous term see above).

McNUTT, Alexander Gallatin (D) Jan. 3, 1802-Oct. 22, 1848; Jan. 8, 1838-Jan. 10, 1842.

TUCKER, Tilghman Mayfield (D) Feb. 5, 1802-April 3, 1859; Jan. 10, 1842-Jan. 10, 1844; House 1843-45.

BROWN, Albert Gallatin (D) May 31, 1813-June 12, 1880; Jan. 10, 1844-Jan. 10, 1848; House 1839-41, 1847-53; Senate 1854-61.

MATTHEWS, Joseph W. (D) 1812-Aug. 27, 1862; Jan. 10, 1848-Jan. 10, 1850.

QUITMAN, John Anthony (D) Jan. 10, 1850-Feb. 3, 1851 (for previous term see above).

GUION, John Isaac (D) Nov. 18, 1802-June 26, 1855; Feb. 3-Nov. 4, 1851.

WHITFIELD, James (D) Dec. 15, 1791-June 25, 1875; Nov. 24, 1851-Jan. 10, 1852.

FOOTE, Henry Stuart (U) Feb. 28, 1804-May 19, 1880; Jan. 10, 1852-Jan. 5, 1854; Senate 1847-52.

PETTUS, John Jones (D) Oct. 9, 1813-Jan. 28, 1867; Jan. 5-10, 1854, Nov. 21, 1859-Nov. 16, 1863.

McRAE, John Jones (SRD) Jan. 10, 1815-May 30, 1868; Jan. 10, 1854-Nov. 16, 1857 (Democrat); Senate 1851-52 (Democrat); House 1858-61.

McWILLIE, William (D) Nov. 17, 1795-March 3, 1869; Nov. 16, 1857-Nov. 21, 1859; House 1849-51.

PETTUS, John Jones (D) Nov. 21, 1859-Nov. 16, 1863 (for previous term see above).

CLARK, Charles (D) Feb. 19, 1810-Dec. 18, 1877; Nov. 16, 1863-May 22, 1865.

SHARKEY, William Lewis; July 12, 1798-April 29, 1873; (Provisional) June 13-Oct. 16, 1865.

HUMPHREYS, Benjamin Grubb (D) Aug. 26, 1808-Dec. 20, 1822; Oct. 16, 1865-June 15, 1868.

AMES, Adelbert (son-in-law of Benjamin Franklin Butler of Mass.) Oct. 31, 1835-April 12, 1933; (Military) June 15, 1868-March 10, 1870, Jan. 4, 1874-March 20, 1876 (Republican); Senate 1870-74 (Republican).

ALCORN, James Lusk (R) Nov. 4, 1816-Dec. 19, 1894; March 10, 1870-Nov. 30, 1871; Senate 1871-77.

POWERS, Ridgely Ceylon (R) Dec. 24, 1836-Nov. 11, 1912; Nov. 30, 1871-Jan. 4, 1874.

AMES, Adelbert (R) Jan. 4, 1874-March 20, 1876 (for previous term see above).

STONE, John Marshall (D) April 30, 1830-March 2, 1900; March 29, 1876-Jan. 29, 1882, Jan. 13, 1890-Jan. 20, 1896.

LOWRY, Robert (D) March 10, 1831-Jan. 18, 1910; Jan. 29, 1882-Jan. 13, 1890.

STONE, John Marshall (D) Jan. 13, 1890-Jan. 20, 1896 (for previous term see above).

McLAURIN, Anselm Joseph (D) March 26, 1848-Dec. 22, 1909; Jan. 20, 1896-Jan. 16, 1900; Senate 1894-95, 1900-09.

LONGINO, Andrew Houston (D) May 16, 1855-Feb. 24, 1942; Jan. 16, 1900-Jan. 19, 1904.

VARDAMAN, James Kimble (D) July 26, 1861-June 25, 1930; Jan. 19, 1904-Jan. 21, 1908; Senate 1913-19.

NOEL, Edmond Favor (D) March 4, 1856-July 30, 1927; Jan. 21, 1908-Jan. 16, 1912.

BREWER, Earl LeRoy (D) Aug. 11, 1869-March 10, 1942; Jan. 16, 1912-Jan. 18, 1916.

BILBO, Theodore Gilmore (D) Oct. 13, 1877-Aug. 21, 1947; Jan. 18, 1916-Jan. 20, 1920, Jan. 17, 1928-Jan. 19, 1932; Senate 1935-47.

RUSSELL, Lee Maurice (D) Nov. 16, 1875-May 16, 1943; Jan. 20, 1920-Jan. 22, 1924.

WHITFIELD, Henry Lewis (D) June 20, 1868-March 18, 1927; Jan. 22, 1924-March 18, 1927.

MURPHREE, Herron Dennis (D) Jan. 6, 1886-Feb. 9, 1949; March 18, 1927-Jan. 17, 1928, Dec. 26, 1943-Jan. 18, 1944.

BILBO, Theodore Gilmore (D) Jan. 17, 1928-Jan. 19, 1932 (for previous term see above).

CONNER, Martin Sennett "Mike" (D) Aug. 31, 1891-Sept. 16, 1950; Jan. 19, 1932-Jan. 21, 1936.

WHITE, Hugh Lawson (D) Aug. 19, 1881-Sept. 20, 1965; Jan. 21, 1936-Jan. 16, 1940, Jan. 22, 1952-Jan. 17, 1956.

JOHNSON, Paul Burney (father of Paul Burney Johnson Jr., below) (D) March 23, 1880-Dec. 26, 1943; Jan. 16, 1940-Dec. 26, 1943; House 1919-23.

MURPHREE, Herron Dennis (D) Dec. 26, 1943-Jan. 18, 1944 (for previous term see above).

BAILEY, Thomas Lowry (D) Jan. 6, 1888-Nov. 2, 1946; Jan. 18, 1944-Nov. 2, 1946.

WRIGHT, Fielding Lewis (D) May 16, 1895-May 4, 1956; Nov. 2, 1946-Jan. 22, 1952.

WHITE, Hugh Lawson (D) Jan. 22, 1952-Jan. 17, 1956 (for previous term see above).

COLEMAN, James Plemon (D) Jan. 9, 1914- −; Jan. 17, 1956-Jan. 19, 1960.

BARNETT, Ross Robert (D) Jan. 22, 1898- −; Jan. 19, 1960-Jan. 21, 1964.

JOHNSON, Paul Burney Jr. (son of Paul Burney Johnson, above) (D) Jan. 23, 1916- −; Jan. 21, 1964-Jan. 16, 1968.

WILLIAMS, John Bell (D) Dec. 4, 1918-March 25, 1983; Jan. 16, 1968-Jan. 18, 1972; House 1947-68.

WALLER, William Lowe (D) Oct. 21, 1926- −; Jan. 18, 1972-Jan. 20, 1976.

FINCH, Charles Clifton (D) April 4, 1927- −; Jan. 20, 1976-Jan. 22, 1980.

WINTER, William Forrest (D) Feb. 21, 1923- −; Jan. 22, 1980-Jan. 10, 1984.

ALLAIN, William A. (D) Feb. 14, 1928- −; Jan. 10, 1984- −.

Missouri

(Became a state Aug. 10, 1821)

McNAIR, Alexander (DR) May 5, 1775-March 18, 1826; Aug. 10, 1821-Nov. 15, 1824.

BATES, Frederick (AR) June 23, 1777-Aug. 4, 1825; Nov. 15, 1824-Aug. 4, 1825.

WILLIAMS, Abraham J. (DR) Feb. 26, 1781-Dec. 30, 1839; Aug. 4, 1825-Jan. 20, 1826.

MILLER, John (VBD) Nov. 25, 1781-March 18, 1846; Jan. 20, 1826-Nov. 14, 1832 (Jackson Democrat); House 1837-43.

DUNKLIN, Daniel (D) Jan. 14, 1790-July 25, 1844; Nov. 14, 1832-Sept. 13, 1836.

BOGGS, Lilburn W. (D) Dec. 14, 1792-March 14, 1860; Sept. 13, 1836-Nov. 16, 1840.

REYNOLDS, Thomas (brother of John Reynolds of Ill.) (D) March 12, 1796-Feb. 9, 1844; Nov. 16, 1840-Feb. 9, 1844.

MARMADUKE, Meredith Miles (father of John Sappington Marmaduke, brother-in-law of Claiborne Fox Jackson) (D) Aug. 25, 1791-March 26, 1864; Feb. 9-Nov. 20, 1844.

EDWARDS, John Cummins (D) June 24, 1804-Sept. 17, 1888; Nov. 20, 1844-Nov. 27, 1848; House 1841-43.

KING, Austin Augustus (UD) Sept. 21, 1802-April 22, 1870; Nov. 27, 1848-Jan. 3, 1853 (Democrat); House 1863-65.

PRICE, Sterling (D) Sept. 20, 1809-Sept. 29, 1867; Jan. 3, 1853-Jan. 5, 1857; House 1845-46.

POLK, Trusten (nephew of Peter Foster Causey of Del.) (D) May 29, 1811-April 16, 1876; Jan. 5-Feb. 27, 1857; Senate 1857-62.

JACKSON, Hancock Lee (D) May 12, 1796-March 19, 1876; Feb. 27-Oct. 22, 1857.

STEWART, Robert Marcellus (D) March 12, 1815-Sept. 21, 1871; Oct. 22, 1857-Jan. 3, 1861.

JACKSON, Claiborne Fox (brother-in-law of Meredith Miles Marmaduke, above) (D) April 4, 1806-Dec. 6, 1862; Jan. 3-July 30, 1861.

GAMBLE, Hamilton Rowan (U) Nov. 29, 1798-Jan. 31, 1864; July 31, 1861-Jan. 31, 1864.

HALL, Willard Preble (U) May 9, 1820-Nov. 2, 1882; Jan. 31, 1864-Jan. 2, 1865; House 1847-53 (Democrat).

FLETCHER, Thomas Clement (UR) Jan. 21, 1827-March 25, 1899; Jan. 2, 1865-Jan. 12, 1869.

McCLURG, Joseph Washington (R) Feb. 22, 1818-Dec. 2, 1900; Jan. 12, 1869-Jan. 9, 1871; House 1863-68 (1863-65 Emancipationist, 1865-68 Radical).

BROWN, Benjamin Gratz (LR) May 28, 1826-Dec. 13, 1885; Jan. 9, 1871-Jan. 8, 1873; Senate 1863-67 (Democrat).

WOODSON, Silas (D) May 18, 1819-Oct. 9, 1896; Jan. 8, 1873-Jan. 12, 1875.

HARDIN, Charles Henry (D) July 15, 1820-July 29, 1892; Jan. 12, 1875-Jan. 8, 1877.

PHELPS, John Smith (D) Dec. 22, 1814-Nov. 20, 1886; Jan. 8, 1877-Jan. 10, 1881; House 1845-63.

CRITTENDEN, Thomas Theodore (nephew of John Jordan Crittenden of Ky.) (D) Jan. 1, 1832-May 29, 1909; Jan. 10, 1881-Jan. 12, 1885; House 1873-75, 1877-79.

MARMADUKE, John Sappington (son of Meredith Miles Marmaduke, great-grandson of John Breathitt of Ky.) (D) March 14, 1833-Dec. 28, 1887; Jan. 12, 1885-Dec. 28, 1887.

MOREHOUSE, Albert Pickett (D) July 11, 1835-Sept. 30, 1891; Dec. 28, 1887-Jan. 14, 1889.

FRANCIS, David Rowland (D) Oct. 1, 1850-Jan. 15, 1927; Jan. 14, 1889-Jan. 9, 1893; Secy. of the Interior 1896-97.

STONE, William Joel (D) May 7, 1848-April 14, 1918; Jan. 9, 1893-Jan. 11, 1897; House 1885-91; Senate 1903-18.

STEPHENS, Lawrence Vest "Lon" (D) Dec. 21, 1858-Jan. 10, 1923; Jan. 11, 1897-Jan. 14, 1901.

DOCKERY, Alexander Monroe (D) Feb. 11, 1845-Dec. 26, 1926; Jan. 14, 1901-Jan. 9, 1905; House 1883-99.

FOLK, Joseph Wingate (D) Oct. 28, 1869-May 28, 1923; Jan. 9, 1905-Jan. 11, 1909.

HADLEY, Herbert Spencer (R) Feb. 20, 1872-Dec. 1, 1927; Jan. 11, 1909-Jan. 13, 1913.

MAJOR, Elliot Woolfolk (D) Oct. 20, 1864-July 9, 1949; Jan. 13, 1913-Jan. 8, 1917.

GARDNER, Frederick D. (D) Nov. 6, 1869-Dec. 18, 1933; Jan. 8, 1917-Jan. 10, 1921.

HYDE, Arthur Mastick (R) July 12, 1877-Oct. 17, 1947; Jan. 10, 1921-Jan. 12, 1925; Secy. of Agriculture 1929-33.

BAKER, Samuel Aaron (R) Nov. 7, 1874-Sept. 16, 1933; Jan. 12, 1925-Jan. 14, 1929.

CAULFIELD, Henry Stewart (R) Dec. 9, 1873-May 11, 1966; Jan. 14, 1929-Jan. 9, 1933; House 1907-09.

PARK, Guy Brasfield (D) June 10, 1872-Oct. 1, 1946; Jan. 9, 1933-Jan. 11, 1937.

STARK, Lloyd Crow (D) Nov. 23, 1886-Sept. 17, 1972; Jan. 11, 1937-Jan. 13, 1941.

DONNELL, Forrest C. (R) Aug. 20, 1884-March 3, 1980; Jan. 13, 1941-Jan. 8, 1945; Senate 1945-51.

DONNELLY, Philip Matthew (D) March 6, 1891-Sept. 12, 1961; Jan. 8, 1945-Jan. 10, 1949, Jan. 12, 1953-Jan. 14, 1957.

SMITH, Forrest (D) Feb. 14, 1886-March 8, 1962; Jan. 10, 1949-Jan. 12, 1953.

DONNELLY, Philip Matthew (D) Jan. 12, 1953-Jan. 14, 1957 (for previous term see above).

BLAIR, James Thomas Jr. (D) March 15, 1902-July 12, 1962; Jan. 14, 1957-Jan. 9, 1961.

DALTON, John Montgomery (D) Nov. 9, 1900-July 7, 1972; Jan. 9, 1961-Jan. 11, 1965.

HEARNES, Warren E. (D) July 24, 1923- −; Jan. 11, 1965-Jan. 8, 1973.

BOND, Christopher S. "Kit" (R) March 6, 1939- −; Jan. 8, 1973-Jan. 10, 1977, Jan. 12, 1981-Jan. 14, 1985; Senate 1987- −.

TEASDALE, Joseph P. (D) March 29, 1936- −; Jan. 10, 1977-Jan. 12, 1981.

BOND, Christopher S. "Kit" (R) Jan. 12, 1981-Jan. 14, 1985 (for previous term see above).

ASHCROFT, John (R) May 9, 1942- −; Jan. 14, 1985- −.

Montana

(Became a state Nov. 8, 1889)

TOOLE, Joseph Kemp (D) May 12, 1851-March 11, 1929; Nov. 8, 1889-Jan. 2, 1893, Jan. 7, 1901-April 1, 1908.

RICKARDS, John Ezra (R) July 23, 1848-Dec. 26, 1927; Jan. 2, 1893-Jan. 4, 1897.

SMITH, Robert Burns (P, D) Dec. 29, 1854-Nov. 16, 1908; Jan. 4, 1897-Jan. 7, 1901.

TOOLE, Joseph Kemp (D) Jan. 7, 1901-April 1, 1908 (for previous term see above).

NORRIS, Edwin Lee (D) Aug. 16, 1865-April 25, 1924; April 1, 1908-Jan. 5, 1913.

STEWART, Samuel Vernon (D) Aug. 2, 1872-Sept. 15, 1939; Jan. 6, 1913-Jan. 2, 1921.

DIXON, Joseph Moore (R) July 31, 1867-May 22, 1934; Jan. 3, 1921-Jan. 4, 1925; House 1903-07; Senate 1907-13.

ERICKSON, John Edward (D) March 14, 1863-May 25, 1946; Jan. 5, 1925-March 13, 1933; Senate 1933-34.

COONEY, Frank Henry (D) Dec. 31, 1872-Dec. 15, 1935; March 13, 1933-Dec. 15, 1935.

HOLT, William Elmer (D) Oct. 14, 1884-March 1, 1945; Dec. 16, 1935-Jan. 4, 1937.

AYERS, Roy Elmer (D) Nov. 9, 1882-May 23, 1955; Jan. 4, 1937-Jan. 6, 1941; House 1933-37.

FORD, Samuel Clarence (R) Nov. 7, 1882-Nov. 25, 1961; Jan. 6, 1941-Jan. 3, 1949.

BONNER, John Woodrow (D) July 16, 1902-March 28, 1970; Jan. 3, 1949-Jan. 5, 1953.

ARONSON, John Hugo (R) Sept. 1, 1891-Feb. 25, 1978; Jan. 5, 1953-Jan. 4, 1961.

NUTTER, Donald Grant (R) Nov. 28, 1915-Jan. 25, 1962; Jan. 4, 1961-Jan. 25, 1962.

BABCOCK, Tim M. (R) Oct. 27, 1919- —; Jan. 26, 1962-Jan. 6, 1969.

ANDERSON, Forrest Howard (D) Jan. 30, 1913- —; Jan. 6, 1969-Jan. 1, 1973.

JUDGE, Thomas Lee (D) Oct. 12, 1934- —; Jan. 1, 1973-Jan. 5, 1981.

SCHWINDEN, Ted (D) Aug. 31, 1925- —; Jan. 5, 1981- —.

Nebraska

(Became a state March 1, 1867)

BUTLER, David C. (R) Dec. 15, 1829-May 25, 1891; March 27, 1867-June 2, 1871.

JAMES, William Hartford (R) Oct. 16, 1831-Feb. 1, 1920; June 2, 1871-Jan. 13, 1873.

FURNAS, Robert Wilkinson (R) May 5, 1824-June 1, 1905; Jan. 13, 1873-Jan. 12, 1875.

GARBER, Silas (R) Sept. 21, 1833-Jan. 12, 1905; Jan. 12, 1875-Jan. 9, 1879.

NANCE, Albinus (R) March 30, 1848-Dec. 7, 1911; Jan. 9, 1879-Jan. 4, 1883.

DAWES, James William (R) Jan. 8, 1844-Oct. 8, 1918; Jan. 4, 1883-Jan. 6, 1887.

THAYER, John Milton (R) Jan. 24, 1820-March 19, 1906; Jan. 6, 1887-Jan. 15, 1891, May 5, 1891-Feb. 8, 1892; Senate 1867-71.

BOYD, James E. (D) Sept. 9, 1834-April 30, 1906; Jan. 15-May 5, 1891, Feb. 8, 1892-Jan. 13, 1893.

THAYER, John Milton (R) May 5, 1891-Feb. 8, 1892 (for previous term see above).

BOYD, James E. (D) Feb. 8, 1892-Jan. 13, 1893 (for previous term see above).

CROUNSE, Lorenzo (R) Jan. 26, 1834-May 13, 1909; Jan. 13, 1893-Jan. 3, 1895; House 1873-77.

HOLCOMB, Silas Alexander (P) Aug. 25, 1858-April 25, 1920; Jan. 3, 1895-Jan. 5, 1899.

POYNTER, William Amos (Fus) May 29, 1848-April 5, 1909; Jan. 5, 1899-Jan. 3, 1901.

DIETRICH, Charles Henry (R) Nov. 26, 1853-April 10, 1924; Jan. 3-May 1, 1901; Senate 1901-05.

SAVAGE, Ezra Perin (R) April 3, 1842-Jan. 8, 1920; May 1, 1901-Jan. 8, 1903.

MICKEY, John Hopwood (R) Sept. 30, 1845-June 2, 1910; Jan. 8, 1903-Jan. 3, 1907.

SHELDON, George Lawson (R) May 31, 1870-April 4, 1960; Jan. 3, 1907-Jan. 7, 1909.

SHALLENBERGER, Ashton Cockayne (D) Dec. 23, 1862-Feb. 22, 1938; Jan. 7, 1909-Jan. 5, 1911; House 1901-03, 1915-19, 1923-29, 1931-35.

ALDRICH, Chester Hardy (R) Nov. 10, 1862-March 10, 1924; Jan. 5, 1911-Jan. 9, 1913.

MOREHEAD, John Henry (D) Dec. 3, 1861-May 30, 1942; Jan. 9, 1913-Jan. 4, 1917; House 1923-35.

NEVILLE, M. Keith (D) Feb. 25, 1884-Dec. 4, 1959; Jan. 4, 1917-Jan. 9, 1919.

McKELVIE, Samuel Roy (R) April 15, 1881-Jan. 6, 1956; Jan. 9, 1919-Jan. 3, 1923.

BRYAN, Charles Wayland (D) Feb. 10, 1867-March 4, 1945; Jan. 4, 1923-Jan. 8, 1925, Jan. 8, 1931-Jan. 3, 1935.

McMULLEN, Adam (R) June 12, 1872-March 2, 1959; Jan. 8, 1925-Jan. 3, 1929.

WEAVER, Arthur J. (R) Nov. 18, 1873-Oct. 17, 1945; Jan. 3, 1929-Jan. 8, 1931.

BRYAN, Charles Wayland (D) Jan. 8, 1931-Jan. 3, 1935 (for previous term see above).

COCHRAN, Robert LeRoy (D) Jan. 28, 1886-Feb. 23, 1963; Jan. 3, 1935-Jan. 9, 1941.

GRISWOLD, Dwight Palmer (R) Nov. 27, 1893-April 12, 1954; Jan. 9, 1941-Jan. 9, 1947; Senate 1952-54.

PETERSON, Val Frederick Demar Erastus (R) July 18, 1903-Oct. 17, 1983; Jan. 9, 1947-Jan. 8, 1953.

CROSBY, Robert Berkey (R) March 26, 1911- —; Jan. 8, 1953-Jan. 6, 1955.

ANDERSON, Victor Emanuel (R) March 30, 1902-Aug. 15, 1962; Jan. 6, 1955-Jan. 8, 1959.

BROOKS, Ralph Gilmour (D) July 6, 1898-Sept. 9, 1960; Jan. 8, 1959-Sept. 9, 1960.

BURNEY, Dwight Willard (R) Jan. 7, 1892- —; Sept. 9, 1960-Jan. 5, 1961.

MORRISON, Frank Brenner (D) May 20, 1905- —; Jan. 5, 1961-Jan. 5, 1967.

TIEMANN, Norbert Theodore (R) July 18, 1924- — Jan. 5, 1967-Jan. 7, 1971.

EXON, John James (D) Aug. 9, 1921- —; Jan. 7, 1971-Jan. 3, 1979; Senate 1979- —.

THONE, Charles (R) Jan. 4, 1924- —; Jan. 4, 1979-Jan. 6, 1983; House 1971-79.

KERREY, Robert (D) Aug. 27, 1943- —; Jan. 6, 1983-Jan. 9, 1987.

ORR, Kay A. (R) Jan. 2, 1939- —; Jan. 9, 1987- —.

Nevada

(Became a state Oct. 31, 1864)

BLASDEL, Henry Goode (R) Jan. 20, 1825-July 26, 1900; Dec. 5, 1864-Jan. 2, 1871.

BRADLEY, Lewis Rice (D) Feb. 18, 1805-March 21, 1879; Jan. 3, 1871-Jan. 6, 1879.

KINKEAD, John Henry (R) Dec. 10, 1826-Aug. 15, 1924; Jan. 7, 1879-Jan. 1, 1883.

ADAMS, Jewett William (D) Aug. 6, 1835-June 18, 1920; Jan. 2, 1883-Jan. 3, 1887.

STEVENSON, Charles Clark (R) Feb. 20, 1826-Sept. 21, 1890; Jan. 4, 1887-Sept. 2, 1890.

BELL, Francis Jardine (R) Jan. 28, 1840-Feb. 13, 1927; Sept. 21, 1890-Jan. 5, 1891.

COLCORD, Roswell Keyes (R) April 25, 1839-Oct. 30, 1939; Jan. 6, 1891-Jan. 7, 1895.

JONES, John Edward (Sil.D) Dec. 5, 1840-April 10, 1896; Jan. 8, 1895-April 10, 1896.

SADLER, Reinhold (Sil.R) Jan. 10, 1948-Jan. 30, 1906; April 10, 1896-Jan. 1, 1903.

SPARKS, John (Sil.D) Aug. 30, 1843-May 22, 1908; Jan. 1, 1903-May 22, 1908.

DICKERSON, Denver Sylvester (Sil.D) Jan. 24, 1872-Nov. 28, 1925; May 22, 1908-Jan. 2, 1911.

ODDIE, Tasker Lowndes (R) Oct. 24, 1870-Feb. 18, 1950; Jan. 2, 1911-Jan. 4, 1915; Senate 1921-33.

BOYLE, Emmet Derby (D) July 26, 1879-Jan. 3, 1926; Jan. 4, 1915-Jan. 1, 1923.

SCRUGHAM, James Graves (D) Jan. 19, 1880-June 2, 1945; Jan. 1, 1923-Jan. 3, 1927; House 1933-42; Senate 1942-45.

BALZAR, Frederick Bennett (R) June 15, 1880-March 21, 1934; Jan. 3, 1927-March 21, 1934.

GRISWOLD, Morley Isaac (R) Oct. 10, 1890-Oct. 3, 1951; March 21, 1934-Jan. 7, 1935.

KIRMAN, Richard Sr. (D) Jan. 14, 1877-Jan. 19, 1959; Jan. 7, 1935-Jan. 2, 1939.

CARVILLE, Edward Peter (D) May 14, 1885-June 27, 1956; Jan. 2, 1939-July 24, 1945; Senate 1945-47.

PITTMAN, Vail Montgomery (D) Sept. 17, 1883-Jan. 29, 1964; July 24, 1945-Jan. 1, 1951.

RUSSELL, Charles Hinton (R) Dec. 27, 1903- —; Jan. 1, 1951-Jan. 5, 1959; House 1947-49.

SAWYER, Grant "Frank" (D) Dec. 14, 1918- —; Jan. 5, 1959-Jan. 2, 1967.

LAXALT, Paul Dominique (R) Aug. 2, 1922- —; Jan. 2, 1967-Jan. 4, 1971; Senate 1974-87.

O'CALLAGHAN, Donald Neil "Mike" (D) Sept. 10, 1929- —; Jan. 4, 1971-Jan. 1, 1979.

LIST, Robert Frank (R) Sept, 1, 1936- —; Jan. 1, 1979-Jan. 3, 1983.

BRYAN, Richard H. (D) July 16, 1936- —; Jan. 3, 1983- —.

New Hampshire

(Ratified the Constitution June 21, 1788)

SULLIVAN, John (brother of James Sullivan of Mass.) (F) Feb. 17, 1740-Jan. 23, 1795; June 6, 1789-June 5, 1790; Cont. Cong. 1774-75, 1780-81.

BARTLETT, Josiah (DR) Nov. 21, 1729-May 19, 1795; June 5, 1790-June 5, 1794.

GILMAN, John Taylor (F) Dec. 19, 1753-Sept. 1, 1828; June 5, 1794-June 6, 1805, June 13, 1813-June 6, 1816; Cont. Cong. 1782-86.

LANGDON, John (DR) June 26, 1741-Sept. 18, 1819; June 6, 1805-June 8, 1809, June 7, 1810-June 5, 1812; Senate 1789-1801; Pres. pro tempore 1789, 1792-94; Cont. Cong. 1775-76, 1783.

SMITH, Jeremiah (F) Nov. 29, 1759-Sept. 21, 1842; June 8, 1809-June 7, 1810; House 1791-97.

LANGDON, John (DR) June 7, 1810-June 5, 1812 (for previous term see above).

PLUMER, William (DR) June 25, 1759-Dec. 22, 1850; June 5, 1812-June 3, 1813, June 6, 1816-June 3, 1819; Senate 1802-07 (F).

GILMAN, John Taylor (F) June 13, 1813-June 6, 1816 (for previous term see above).

PLUMER, William (DR) June 6, 1816-June 3, 1819 (for previous term see above).

BELL, Samuel (brother of John Bell, uncle of Charles Henry Bell) (DR) Feb. 9, 1770-Dec. 23, 1850; June 3, 1819-June 5, 1823; Senate 1823-35.

WOODBURY, Levi (DR) Dec. 22, 1789-Sept. 4, 1851; June 5, 1823-June 2, 1824; Senate 1825-31, 1841-45; Secy. of the Navy 1831-34; Secy. of the Treasury 1834-41; Assoc. Justice Supreme Court 1845-51.

MORRILL, David Lawrence (DR) June 10, 1772-Jan. 28, 1849; June 3, 1824-June 7, 1827; Senate 1817-23.

PIERCE, Benjamin (JD) (father of President Franklin Pierce) Dec. 25, 1757-April 1, 1839; June 7, 1827-June 5, 1828 (Democratic Republican), June 4, 1829-June 3, 1830.

BELL, John (brother of Samuel Bell, father of Charles Henry Bell) (NR) July 20, 1765-March 22, 1836; June 5, 1828-June 4, 1829.

PIERCE, Benjamin (JD) June 4, 1829-June 3, 1830 (for previous term see above).

HARVEY, Matthew (JD) June 21, 1781-April 7, 1866; June 3, 1830-Feb. 28, 1831; House 1821-25 (Democrat).

HARPER, Joseph Morrill (D) June 21, 1787-Jan. 15, 1865; Feb. 28-June 2, 1831; House 1831-35.

DINSMOOR, Samuel (father of Samuel Dinsmoor Jr., below) (JD) July 1, 1766-March 15, 1835; June 2, 1831-June 5, 1834; House 1811-13 (War Democrat).

BADGER, William (D) Jan. 13, 1779-Sept. 21, 1852; June 5, 1834-June 2, 1836.

HILL, Isaac (D) April 6, 1788-March 22, 1851; June 2, 1836-June 5, 1839; Senate 1831-36.

PAGE, John (D) May 21, 1787-Sept. 8, 1865; June 5, 1839-June 2, 1842; Senate 1836-37.

HUBBARD, Henry (D) May 3, 1784-June 5, 1857; June 2, 1842-June 6, 1844; House 1829-35; Senate 1835-41.

STEELE, John Hardy (D) Jan. 4, 1789-July 3, 1865; June 6, 1844-June 4, 1846.

COLBY, Anthony (W) Nov. 13, 1795-July 13, 1873; June 4, 1846-June 3, 1847.

WILLIAMS, Jared Warner (D) Dec. 22, 1796-Sept. 29, 1864; June 3, 1847-June 7, 1849; House 1837-41; Senate 1853-54.

DINSMOOR, Samuel Jr. (son of Samuel Dinsmoor, above) (D) May 8, 1799-Feb. 24, 1869; June 7, 1849-June 3, 1852.

MARTIN, Noah (D) July 26, 1801-May 28, 1863; June 3, 1852-June 8, 1854.

BAKER, Nathaniel Bradley (D) Sept. 29, 1818-Sept. 11 1876; June 8, 1854-June 7, 1855.

METCALF, Ralph (ASP) Nov. 21, 1798-Aug. 26, 1858 June 7, 1855-June 4, 1857.

HAILE, William (R) May 1807-July 22, 1876; June 4 1857-June 2, 1859.

GOODWIN, Ichabod (R) Oct. 10, 1796-July 4, 1882 June 2, 1859-June 6, 1861.

BERRY, Nathaniel Springer (R) Sept. 1, 1796-April 27, 1894; June 6, 1861-June 3, 1863.

GILMORE, Joseph Albree (R) June 10, 1811-April 7 1867; June 3, 1863-June 8, 1865.

SMYTH, Frederick (U) March 9, 1819-April 22, 1899 June 8, 1865-June 6, 1867.

HARRIMAN, Walter (R) April 8, 1817-July 25, 1884; June 6, 1867-June 2, 1869.

STEARNS, Onslow (R) Aug. 30, 1810-Dec. 29, 1878; June 3, 1869-June 8, 1871.

WESTON, James Adams (D) Aug. 27, 1827-May 8, 1895; June 14, 1871-June 6, 1872, June 3, 1874-June 10, 1875.

STRAW, Ezekiel Albert (R) Dec. 30, 1819-Oct. 23, 1882; June 6, 1872-June 3, 1874.

WESTON, James Adams (D) June 3, 1874-June 10, 1875 (for previous term see above).

CHENEY, Person Colby (R) Feb. 25, 1828-June 19, 1901; June 10, 1875-June 6, 1877; Senate 1886-87.

PRESCOTT, Benjamin Franklin (R) Feb. 26, 1833-Feb. 21, 1895; June 7, 1877-June 5, 1879.

HEAD, Nathaniel (R) May 20, 1828-Nov. 12, 1883; June 5, 1879-June 2, 1881.

BELL, Charles Henry (son of John Bell, nephew of Samuel Bell) (R)'Nov. 18, 1823-Nov. 11, 1893; June 2, 1881-June 7, 1883; Senate 1879.

HALE, Samuel Whitney (R) April 2, 1823-Oct. 16, 1891; June 7, 1883-June 4, 1885.

CURRIER, Moody (R) April 22, 1806-Aug. 23, 1898; June 4, 1885-June 2, 1887.

SAWYER, Charles Henry (R) March 30, 1840-Jan. 18, 1908; June 2, 1887-June 6, 1889.

GOODELL, David Harvey (R) May 6, 1834-Jan. 22, 1915; June 6, 1889-Jan. 8, 1891.

TUTTLE, Hiram Americus (R) Oct. 16, 1837-Feb. 10, 1911; Jan. 8, 1891-Jan. 5, 1893.

SMITH, John Butler (R) April 12, 1838-Aug. 10, 1914; Jan. 5, 1893-Jan. 3, 1895.

BUSIEL, Charles Albert (R) Nov. 24, 1842-Aug. 29, 1901; Jan. 3, 1895-Jan. 7, 1897.

RAMSDELL, George Allen (R) March 11, 1834-Nov. 16, 1900; Jan. 7, 1897-Jan. 5, 1899.

ROLLINS, Frank West (R) Feb. 24, 1860-Oct. 27, 1915; Jan. 5, 1899-Jan. 3, 1901.

JORDAN, Chester Bradley (R) Oct. 15, 1839-Aug. 24, 1914; Jan. 3, 1901-Jan. 1, 1903.

BATCHELDER, Nahum Josiah (R) Sept. 3, 1859-April 22, 1934; Jan. 1, 1903-Jan. 5, 1905.

McLANE, John (R) Feb. 27, 1852-April 13, 1911; Jan. 5, 1905-Jan. 3, 1907.

FLOYD, Charles Miller (R) June 5, 1861-Feb. 3, 1923; Jan. 3, 1907-Jan. 7, 1909.

QUINBY, Henry Brewer (R) June 10, 1846-Feb. 8, 1924; Jan. 7, 1909-Jan. 5, 1911.

BASS, Robert Perkins (R) Sept. 11, 1873-July 29, 1960; Jan. 5, 1911-Jan. 2, 1913.

FELKER, Samuel Demeritt (D) April 16, 1859-Nov. 14, 1932; Jan. 2, 1913-Jan. 7, 1915.

SPAULDING, Rolland Harty (brother of Huntley Nowel Spaulding, below) (R) March 15, 1873-March 14, 1942; Jan. 7, 1915-Jan. 3, 1917.

KEYES, Henry Wilder (R) May 23, 1863-June 19, 1938; Jan. 3, 1917-Jan. 2, 1919; Senate 1919-37.

BARTLETT, John Henry (R) March 15, 1869-March 19, 1952; Jan. 2, 1919-Jan. 6, 1921.

BROWN, Albert Oscar (R) July 18, 1853-March 28, 1937; Jan. 6, 1921-Jan. 4, 1923.

BROWN, Fred Herbert (D) April 12, 1879-Feb. 3, 1955; Jan. 4, 1923-Jan. 1, 1925; Senate 1933-39.

WINANT, John Gilbert (R) Feb. 23, 1889-Nov. 3, 1947; Jan. 1, 1925-Jan. 6, 1927, Jan. 1, 1931-Jan. 3, 1935.

SPAULDING, Huntley Nowel (brother of Rolland Harty Spaulding, above) (R) Oct. 20, 1869-Nov. 14, 1955; Jan. 6, 1927-Jan. 3, 1929.

TOBEY, Charles William (R) July 22, 1880-July 24, 1953; Jan. 3, 1929-Jan. 1, 1931; House 1933-39; Senate 1939-53.

WINANT, John Gilbert (R) Jan. 1, 1931-Jan. 3, 1935 (for previous term see above).

BRIDGES, Henry Styles (R) Sept. 9, 1898-Nov. 26, 1961; Jan. 3, 1935-Jan. 7, 1937; Senate 1937-61; Pres. pro tempore 1953-55.

MURPHY, Francis Parnell (R) Aug. 16, 1877-Dec. 19, 1958; Jan. 7, 1937-Jan. 2, 1941.

BLOOD, Robert Oscar (R) Nov. 10, 1887-Aug. 3, 1975; Jan. 2, 1941-Jan. 4, 1945.

DALE, Charles Milby (R) March 8, 1893-Sept. 28, 1978; Jan. 4, 1945-Jan. 6, 1949.

ADAMS, Sherman (R) Jan. 8, 1899-Oct. 27, 1986; Jan. 6, 1949-Jan. 1, 1953; House 1945-47.

GREGG, Hugh (R) Nov. 22, 1917- —; Jan. 1, 1953-Jan. 6, 1955.

DWINELL, Lane (R) Nov. 14, 1906- —; Jan. 6, 1955-Jan. 1, 1959.

POWELL, Wesley (R) Oct. 13, 1915-Jan. 6, 1981; Jan. 1, 1959-Jan. 3, 1963.

KING, John William (D) Oct. 10, 1918- —; Jan. 3, 1963-Jan. 2, 1969.

PETERSON, Walter Rutherford (R) Sept. 19, 1922- —; Jan. 2, 1969-Jan. 4, 1973.

THOMSON, Meldrim Jr. (R) March 8, 1912- —; Jan. 4, 1973-Jan. 4, 1979.

GALLEN, Hugh J. (D) July 30, 1924-Dec. 29, 1982; Jan. 4, 1979-Nov. 11, 1982.

MONIER, Robert B. (D) March 5, 1922- —; Nov. 11-30, 1982.

GARDNER, William Michael (D) Oct. 26, 1948- —; Nov. 30-Dec. 1, 1982.

ROY, Vesta M. (R) March 26, 1925- —; Dec. 1, 1982-Jan. 6, 1983.

SUNUNU, John Henry (R) July 2, 1939- —; Jan. 6, 1983- —.

New Jersey

(Ratified the Constitution Dec. 18, 1787)

LIVINGSTON, William (father-in-law of John Jay of N.Y.) (F) Nov. 30, 1723-July 25, 1790; Aug. 27, 1776-July 25, 1790; Cont. Cong. 1774-76.

LAWRENCE, Elisha (F) 1746-July 23, 1799; July 25-Oct. 30, 1790.

PATERSON, William (F) Dec. 24, 1745-Sept. 9, 1806; Oct. 30, 1790-March 4, 1793; Cont. Cong. 1780-81, 1787; Senate 1789-90; Assoc. Justice Supreme Court 1793-1806.

HENDERSON, Thomas (F) Aug. 15, 1743-Dec. 15, 1824; March 30-June 3, 1793; House 1795-97.

HOWELL, Richard (F) Oct. 25, 1754-April 28, 1802; June 3, 1793-Oct. 31, 1801.

BLOOMFIELD, Joseph (DR) Oct. 5, 1753-Oct. 3, 1823; Oct. 31, 1801-Oct. 28, 1802, Oct. 29, 1803-Oct. 29, 1812; House 1817-21.

LAMBERT, John (DR) Feb. 24, 1746-Feb. 4, 1823; Nov. 15, 1802-Oct. 29, 1803; House 1805-09; Senate 1809-15.

BLOOMFIELD, Joseph (DR) Oct. 29, 1803-Oct. 29, 1812 (for previous term see above).

OGDEN, Aaron (granduncle of Daniel Haines, below) (F) Dec. 3, 1756-April 19, 1839; Oct. 29, 1812-Oct. 29, 1813; Senate 1801-03.

PENNINGTON, William Sandford (father of William Pennington Jr., below) (DR) 1757-Sept. 18, 1826; Oct. 29, 1813-June 19, 1815.

KENNEDY, William (DR) ?-Jan. 1, 1826; June 19-Oct. 25, 1815.

DICKERSON, Mahlon (brother of Philemon Dickerson, below) (DR) April 17, 1770-Oct. 5, 1853; Oct. 26, 1815-Feb. 1, 1817; Senate 1817-29; Secy. of the Navy 1834-38 (Democrat).

WILLIAMSON, Isaac Halstead (F) Sept. 27, 1767-July 10, 1844; Feb. 6, 1817-Oct. 30, 1829.

VROOM, Peter Dumont (D) Dec. 12, 1791-Nov. 18, 1873; Nov. 6, 1829-Oct. 26, 1832, Oct. 25, 1833-Oct. 28, 1836; House 1839-41.

SOUTHARD, Samuel Lewis (W) June 9, 1787-June 26, 1842; Oct. 26, 1832-Feb. 27, 1833 (Republican); Senate 1821-23 (Democratic Republican), 1833-42; Pres. pro tempore 1841-42; Secy. of the Navy 1823-29.

SEELEY, Elias P. (W) Nov. 10, 1791-Aug. 23, 1846; Feb. 27-Oct. 23, 1833.

VROOM, Peter Dumont (D) Oct. 25, 1833-Oct. 28, 1836 (for previous term see above).

DICKERSON, Philemon (brother of Mahlon Dickerson, above) (JD) Jan. 11, 1788-Dec. 10, 1862; Nov. 3, 1836-Oct. 27, 1837 (Democrat); House 1833-36 (Democrat), 1839-41.

PENNINGTON, William Jr. (son of William Sandford Pennington, above) (R) May 4, 1796-Feb. 16, 1862; Oct. 27, 1837-Oct. 27, 1843 (Democratic Republican); House 1859-61; Speaker 1859-61.

HAINES, Daniel (grandnephew of Aaron Ogden, above) (D) Jan. 6, 1801-Jan. 26, 1877; Oct. 27, 1843-Jan. 21, 1845, Jan. 18, 1848-Jan. 20, 1851.

STRATTON, Charles Creighton (W) March 6, 1796-March 30, 1859; Jan. 21, 1845-Jan. 18, 1848; House 1837-39, 1841-43.

HAINES, Daniel (D) Jan. 18, 1848-Jan. 20, 1851 (for previous term see above).

FORT, George Franklin (uncle of John Franklin Fort below) (D) March 1809-April 22, 1872; Jan. 21, 1851-Jan. 17, 1854.

PRICE, Rodman McCamley (D) May 5, 1816-June 7 1894; Jan. 17, 1854-Jan. 20, 1857; House 1851-53.

NEWELL, William Augustus (R) Sept. 5, 1817-Aug. 8 1901; Jan. 20, 1857-Jan. 17, 1860; House 1845-51 (Whig), 1865-67.

OLDEN, Charles Smith (R) Nov. 19, 1799-April 7, 1876 Jan. 17, 1860-Jan. 20, 1863.

PARKER, Joel (D) Nov. 24, 1816-Jan. 2, 1888; Jan. 20 1863-Jan. 16, 1866, Jan. 16, 1872-Jan. 19, 1875.

WARD, Marcus Lawrence (R) Nov. 9, 1812-April 25 1884; Jan. 16, 1866-Jan. 19, 1869; House 1873-75 Chrmn. Rep. Nat. Comm. 1866-68.

RANDOLPH, Theodore Fitz (D) June 24, 1826-Nov. 7, 1883; Jan. 19, 1869-Jan. 16, 1872; Senate 1875-81.

PARKER, Joel (D) Jan. 16, 1872-Jan. 19, 1875 (for previous term see above).

BEDLE, Joseph Dorsett (D) Jan. 5, 1821-Oct. 21, 1894 Jan. 19, 1875-Jan. 15, 1878.

McCLELLAN, George Brinton (D) Dec. 3, 1826-Oct. 29, 1885; Jan. 15, 1878-Jan. 18, 1881.

LUDLOW, George Craig (D) April 6, 1830-Dec. 18, 1900; Jan. 18, 1881-Jan. 15, 1884.

ABBETT, Leon (D) Oct. 8, 1836-Dec. 4, 1894; Jan. 15 1884-Jan. 18, 1887, Jan. 21, 1890-Jan. 17, 1893.

GREEN, Robert Stockton (D) March 25, 1831-May 7 1895; Jan. 18, 1887-Jan. 21, 1890; House 1885-87.

ABBETT, Leon (D) Jan. 21, 1890-Jan. 17, 1893 (for previous term see above).

WERTS, George Theodore (D) March 24, 1846-Jan. 17 1910; Jan. 17, 1893-Jan. 21, 1896.

GRIGGS, John William (R) July 10, 1849-Nov. 28, 1927 Jan. 21, 1896-Jan. 31, 1898; Atty. Gen. 1898-1901.

VOORHEES, Foster MacGowan (R) Nov. 5, 1856-June 14, 1927; Feb. 1-Oct. 18, 1898, Jan. 17, 1899-Jan. 21 1902.

WATKINS, David Ogden (R) June 8, 1862-June 20, 1938; Oct. 18, 1898-Jan. 16, 1899.

VOORHEES, Foster MacGowan (R) Jan. 17, 1899-Jan. 21, 1902 (for previous term see above).

MURPHY, Franklin (R) Jan. 3, 1846-Feb. 24, 1920; Jan. 21, 1902-Jan. 17, 1905.

STOKES, Edward Casper (R) Dec. 22, 1860-Nov. 4, 1942; Jan. 17, 1905-Jan. 21, 1908.

FORT, John Franklin (nephew of George Franklin Fort, above) (R) March 20, 1852-Nov. 17, 1920; Jan. 21, 1908-Jan. 17, 1911.

WILSON, Thomas Woodrow (D) Dec. 28, 1856-Feb. 3, 1924; Jan. 17, 1911-March 1, 1913; President 1913-21.

FIELDER, James Fairman (D) Feb. 26, 1867-Dec. 2, 1954; March 1-Oct. 28, 1913, Jan. 20, 1914-Jan. 15, 1917.

TAYLOR, Leon R. (D) Oct. 26, 1883-April 1, 1924; Oct. 28, 1913-Jan. 20, 1914.

FIELDER, James Fairman (D) Jan. 20, 1914-Jan. 15, 1917 (for previous term see above).

EDGE, Walter Evans (R) Nov. 20, 1873-Oct. 29, 1956; Jan. 15, 1917-May 16, 1919, Jan. 18, 1944-Jan. 21, 1947; Senate 1919-29.

RUNYON, William Nelson (R) March 5, 1871-Nov. 9, 1931; May 16, 1919-Jan. 13, 1920.

CASE, Clarence Edwards (R) Sept. 24, 1877-Sept. 3, 1961; Jan. 13-20, 1920.

EDWARDS, Edward Irving (D) Dec. 1, 1863-Jan. 26, 1931; Jan. 20, 1920-Jan. 15, 1923; Senate 1923-29.

SILZER, George Sebastian (D) April 14, 1870-Oct. 16, 1940; Jan. 15, 1923-Jan. 19, 1926.

MOORE, Arthur Harry (D) July 3, 1879-Nov. 18, 1952; Jan. 19, 1926-Jan. 15, 1929, Jan. 19, 1932-Jan. 3, 1935, Jan. 18, 1938-Jan. 21, 1941; Senate 1935-38.

LARSON, Morgan Foster (R) June 15, 1882-March 21, 1961; Jan. 15, 1929-Jan. 19, 1932.

MOORE, Arthur Harry (D) Jan. 19, 1932-Jan. 3, 1935 (for previous term see above).

POWELL, Clifford R. (R) July 26, 1893-March 28, 1973; Jan. 3-8, 1935.

PRALL, Horace Griggs (R) March 6, 1881-April 23, 1951; Jan. 8-15, 1935.

HOFFMAN, Harold Giles (R) Feb. 7, 1896-June 4, 1954; Jan. 15, 1935-Jan. 18, 1938; House 1927-31.

MOORE, Arthur Harry (D) Jan. 18, 1938-Jan. 21, 1941 (for previous terms see above).

EDISON, Charles (D) Aug. 3, 1890-July 31, 1969; Jan. 21, 1941-Jan. 18, 1944; Secy. of the Navy 1939-40.

EDGE, Walter Evans (R) Jan. 18, 1944-Jan. 21, 1947 (for previous term see above).

DRISCOLL, Alfred Eastlack (R) Oct. 25, 1902-March 9, 1975; Jan. 21, 1947-Jan. 19, 1954.

MEYNER, Robert Baumle (D) July 3, 1908- —; Jan. 19, 1954-Jan. 16, 1962.

HUGHES, Harold Joseph (D) Aug. 10, 1909- —; Jan. 16, 1962-Jan. 20, 1970.

CAHILL, William Thomas (R) June 25, 1912- —; Jan. 20, 1970-Jan. 15, 1974; House 1959-70.

BYRNE, Brendan Thomas (D) April 1, 1924- —; Jan. 15, 1974-Jan. 19, 1982.

KEAN, Thomas H. (R) April 21, 1935- —; Jan. 19, 1982- —.

New Mexico

(Became a state Jan. 6, 1912)

McDONALD, William C. (D) July 25, 1858-April 11, 1918; Jan. 6, 1912-Jan. 1, 1917.

DE BACA, Ezequiel Cabeza (D) Nov. 1, 1864-Feb. 18, 1917; Jan. 1-Feb. 18, 1917.

LINDSEY, Washington Ellsworth (R) Dec. 20, 1862-April 5, 1926; Feb. 19, 1917-Jan. 1, 1919.

LARRAZOLO, Octaviano Amrosio (R) Dec. 7, 1859-April 7, 1930; Jan. 1, 1919-Jan. 1, 1921; Senate 1928-29.

MECHEM, Merrit Cramer (uncle of Edwin Leard Mechem, below) (R) Oct. 10, 1870-May 24, 1946; Jan. 1, 1921-Jan. 1, 1923.

HINKLE, James Fielding (D) Oct. 20, 1862-March 26, 1951; Jan. 1, 1923-Jan. 1, 1925.

HANNETT, Arthur Thomas (D) Feb. 17, 1884-March 18, 1966; Jan. 1, 1925-Jan. 1, 1927.

DILLON, Richard Charles (R) June 24, 1877-Jan. 4, 1966; Jan. 1, 1927-Jan. 1, 1931.

SELIGMAN, Arthur (D) June 14, 1871-Sept. 25, 1933; Jan. 1, 1931-Sept. 25, 1933.

HOCKENHULL, Andrew W. (D) Jan. 16, 1877-June 20, 1974; Sept. 25, 1933-Jan. 1, 1935.

TINGLEY, Clyde (D) Jan. 5, 1883-Dec. 24, 1960; Jan. 1, 1935-Jan. 1, 1939.

MILES, John Esten (D) July 28, 1884-Oct. 7, 1971; Jan. 1, 1939-Jan. 1, 1943; House 1949-51.

DEMPSEY, John Joseph (D) June 22, 1879-March 11, 1958; Jan. 1, 1943-Jan. 1, 1947; House 1935-41, 1951-58.

MABRY, Thomas Jewett (D) Oct. 17, 1884-Dec. 23, 1962; Jan. 1, 1947-Jan. 1, 1951.

MECHEM, Edwin Leard (nephew of Merrit Cramer Mechem, above) (R) July 2, 1912- —; Jan. 1, 1951-Jan. 1, 1955, Jan. 1, 1957-Jan. 1, 1959, Jan. 1, 1961-Nov. 30, 1962; Senate 1962-64.

SIMMS, John Field Jr. (D) Dec. 18, 1916-April 11, 1975; Jan. 1, 1955-Jan. 1, 1957.

MECHEM, Edwin Leard (R) Jan. 1, 1957-Jan. 1, 1959 (for previous term see above).

BURROUGHS, John (D) April 7, 1907-May 21, 1978; Jan. 1, 1959-Jan. 1, 1961.

MECHEM, Edwin Leard (R) Jan. 1, 1961-Nov. 30, 1962 (for previous terms see above).

BOLACK, Thomas Felix (R) May 18, 1918- —; Nov. 30, 1962-Jan. 1, 1963.

CAMPBELL, John M. "Jack" (D) Sept. 10, 1916- —; Jan. 1, 1963-Jan. 1, 1967.

CARGO, David Francis (R) Jan. 13, 1929- —; Jan. 1, 1967-Jan. 1, 1971.

KING, Bruce (D) April 6, 1924- —; Jan. 1, 1971-Jan. 1, 1975, Jan. 1, 1979-Jan. 1, 1983.

APODACA, Raymond S. "Jerry" (D) Oct. 3, 1934- —; Jan. 1, 1975-Jan. 1, 1979.

KING, Bruce (D) Jan. 1, 1979-Jan. 1, 1983 (for previous term see above).

ANAYA, Toney (D) April 29, 1941- —; Jan. 1, 1983-Jan. 1, 1987.

CARRUTHERS, Garrey E. (R) Aug. 29, 1939- —; Jan. 1, 1987- —.

New York

(Ratified the Constitution July 26, 1788)

CLINTON, George (father of Rep. George Clinton, uncle of Rep. James Graham Clinton and De Witt Clinton, below) (DR) July 26, 1739-April 20, 1812; July 30, 1777-June 30, 1795, July 1, 1801-July 1, 1804; Cont. Cong. 1775-76; Vice President 1805-12.

JAY, John (son-in-law of William Livingston of N.J.) (F) Dec. 12, 1745-May 17, 1829; July 1, 1795-June 30 1801; Cont. Cong. 1774-75, 1777, 1778-79 (president); Secy. of Foreign Affairs 1784-89; Chief Justice United States 1789-95.

CLINTON, George (DR) July 1, 1801-July 1, 1804 (for previous term see above).

LEWIS, Morgan (F) Oct. 16, 1754-April 7, 1844; July 1 1804-July 1, 1807.

TOMPKINS, Daniel D. (DR) June 21, 1774-June 11 1825; July 1, 1807-Feb. 24, 1817; Vice President 1817-25.

TAYLER, John (DR) July 4, 1742-April 19, 1829; Feb 24-July 1, 1817.

CLINTON, De Witt (nephew of George Clinton, hal brother of James Graham Clinton, cousin of Rep George Clinton) (Clinton R) March 2, 1769-Feb. 11 1828; July 1, 1817-Jan. 1, 1823 (Democratic Republi can), Jan. 1, 1825-Feb. 11, 1828; Senate 1802-03 (Democratic Republican).

YATES, Joseph Christopher (DR) Nov. 9, 1768-March 19, 1837; Jan. 1, 1823-Dec. 31, 1824.

CLINTON, De Witt (Clinton R) Jan. 1, 1825-Feb. 11 1828 (for previous term see above).

PITCHER, Nathaniel (D) Nov. 30, 1777-May 25, 1836 Feb. 11-Dec. 31, 1828 (Democratic Republican) House 1819-23, 1831-33.

VAN BUREN, Martin (half brother of Rep. James Isaac Van Alen) (D) Dec. 5, 1782-July 24, 1862; Jan. 1 March 12, 1829; Senate 1821-28; Secy. of State 1829 31; Vice President 1833-37; President 1837-41.

THROOP, Enos Thompson (JD) Aug. 21, 1784-Nov. 1 1874; March 12, 1829-Jan. 1, 1833; House 1815-16 (Democrat).

MARCY, William Learned (JD) Dec. 12, 1786-July 4 1857; Jan. 1, 1833-Jan. 1, 1839; Senate 1831-33; Secy of War 1845-49; Secy. of State 1853-57.

SEWARD, William Henry (W) May 16, 1801-Oct. 10 1872; Jan. 1, 1839-Jan. 1, 1843; Senate 1849-61 (1855-61 Republican); Secy. of State 1861-69.

BOUCK, William C. (D) Jan. 7, 1786-April 19, 1859; Jan 1, 1843-Jan. 1, 1845.

WRIGHT, Silas Jr. (D) May 24, 1795-Aug. 27, 1847; Jan 1, 1845-Jan. 1, 1847; House 1827-29; Senate 1833-44

YOUNG, John (W) June 12, 1802-April 23, 1852; Jan. 1 1847-Jan. 1, 1849; House 1836-37, 1841-43.

FISH, Hamilton (W) Aug. 3, 1808-Sept. 7, 1893; Jan. 1 1849-Jan. 1, 1851; House 1843-45; Senate 1851-57 Secy. of State 1869-77.

HUNT, Washington (W) Aug. 5, 1811-Feb. 2, 1867; Jan. 1, 1851-Jan. 1, 1853; House 1843-49.

SEYMOUR, Horatio (D) May 31, 1810-Feb. 12, 1886; Jan. 1, 1853-Jan. 1, 1855, Jan. 1, 1863-Jan. 1, 1865.

CLARK, Myron Holley (W/FS) Oct. 23, 1806-Aug. 23, 1892; Jan. 1, 1855-Jan. 1, 1857.

KING, John Alsop (R) Jan. 3, 1788-July 7, 1867; Jan. 1, 1857-Jan. 1, 1859; House 1849-51 (W).

MORGAN, Edwin Dennison (cousin of Morgan Gardner Bulkeley of Conn.) (R) Feb. 8, 1811-Feb. 14, 1883; Jan. 1, 1859-Jan. 1, 1863; Senate 1863-69; Chrmn. Rep. Nat. Comm. 1856-64, 1872-76.

SEYMOUR, Horatio (D) Jan. 1, 1863-Jan. 1, 1865 (for previous term see above).

FENTON, Reuben Eaton (R) July 4, 1819-Aug. 25, 1885; Jan. 1, 1865-Jan. 1, 1869; House 1853-55, 1857-64; Senate 1869-75.

HOFFMAN, John Thompson (D) Jan. 10, 1828-March 24, 1888; Jan. 1, 1869-Jan. 1, 1873.

DIX, John Adams (R) July 24, 1798-April 21, 1879; Jan. 1, 1873-Jan. 1, 1875; Senate 1845-49 (Democrat), Secy. of the Treasury 1861.

TILDEN, Samuel Jones (D) Feb. 9, 1814-Aug. 4, 1886; Jan. 1, 1875-Jan. 1, 1877.

ROBINSON, Lucius (D) Nov. 4, 1810-March 23, 1891; Jan. 1, 1877-Jan. 1, 1880.

CORNELL, Alonzo B. (R) Jan. 22, 1832-Oct. 15, 1904; Jan. 1, 1880-Jan. 1, 1883.

CLEVELAND, Stephen Grover (D) March 18, 1837-June 24, 1908; Jan. 1, 1883-Jan. 6, 1885; President 1885-89, 1893-97.

HILL, David Bennett (D) Aug. 29, 1843-Oct. 20, 1910; Jan. 6, 1885-Jan. 1, 1892; Senate 1892-97.

FLOWER, Roswell Pettibone (D) Aug. 7, 1835-May 12, 1899; Jan. 1, 1892-Jan. 1, 1895; House 1881-83, 1889-91.

MORTON, Levi Parsons (R) May 16, 1824-May 16, 1920; Jan. 1, 1895-Jan. 1, 1897; House 1879-81; Vice President 1889-93.

BLACK, Frank Swett (R) March 8, 1853-March 22, 1913; Jan. 1, 1897-Jan. 1, 1899; House 1895-97.

ROOSEVELT, Theodore (R) Oct. 27, 1858-Jan. 6, 1919; Jan. 1, 1899-Jan. 1, 1901; Vice President 1901; President 1901-09.

ODELL, Benjamin Baker Jr. (R) Jan. 14, 1854-May 9, 1826; Jan. 1, 1901-Jan. 1, 1905; House 1895-99.

HIGGINS, Frank Wayland (R) Aug. 18, 1856-Feb. 12, 1907; Jan. 1, 1905-Jan. 1, 1907.

HUGHES, Charles Evans (R) April 11, 1862-Aug. 27, 1948; Jan. 1, 1907-Oct. 6, 1910; Assoc. Justice Supreme Court 1910-16; Secy. of State 1921-25; Chief Justice United States 1930-41.

WHITE, Horace (R) Oct. 7, 1865-Nov. 26, 1943; Oct. 6, 1910-Jan. 1, 1911.

DIX, John Alden (D) Dec. 25, 1860-April 9, 1928; Jan. 1, 1911-Jan. 1, 1913.

SULZER, William (D) March 18, 1863-Nov. 6, 1941; Jan. 1-Oct. 17, 1913; House 1895-1912.

GLYNN, Martin Henry (D) Sept. 27, 1871-Dec. 14, 1924; Oct. 17, 1913-Jan. 1, 1915; House 1899-1901.

WHITMAN, Charles Seymour (R) Aug. 28, 1868-March 29, 1947; Jan. 1, 1915-Jan. 1, 1919.

SMITH, Alfred Emanuel (D) Dec. 30, 1873-Oct. 4, 1944; Jan. 1, 1919-Jan. 1, 1921, Jan. 1, 1923-Jan. 1, 1929.

MILLER, Nathan Lewis (R) Oct. 10, 1868-June 26, 1953; Jan. 1, 1921-Jan. 1, 1923.

SMITH, Alfred Emanuel (D) Jan. 1, 1923-Jan. 1, 1929 (for previous term see above).

ROOSEVELT, Franklin Delano (D) Jan. 30, 1882-April 12, 1945; Jan. 1, 1929-Jan. 1, 1933; President 1933-45.

LEHMAN, Herbert Henry (D) March 28, 1878-Dec. 5, 1963; Jan. 1, 1933-Dec. 3, 1942; Senate 1949-57.

POLETTI, Charles (D) July 2, 1903- -; Dec. 3, 1942-Jan. 1, 1943.

DEWEY, Thomas Edmund (R) March 24, 1902-March 16, 1971; Jan. 1, 1943-Jan. 1, 1955.

HARRIMAN, William Averell (D) Nov. 15, 1891-July 7, 1986; Jan. 1, 1955-Jan. 1, 1959.

ROCKEFELLER, Nelson Aldrich (brother of Winthrop Rockefeller of Ark., uncle of Sen. John Davison "Jay" Rockefeller IV, nephew of Rep. Richard Steere Aldrich, grandson of Sen. Nelson Wilmarth Aldrich) (R) July 8, 1908-Jan. 26, 1979; Jan. 1, 1959-Dec. 18, 1973; Vice President 1974-77.

WILSON, Malcolm (R) Feb. 26, 1914- -; Dec. 18, 1973-Jan. 1, 1975.

CAREY, Hugh Leonard (D) April 11, 1919- -; Jan. 1, 1975-Jan. 1, 1983; House 1961-74.

CUOMO, Mario Matthew (D) June 15, 1932- -; Jan. 1, 1983- -.

North Carolina

(Ratified the Constitution Nov. 21, 1789)

JOHNSTON, Samuel (F) Dec. 15, 1733-Aug. 17, 1816; Dec. 20, 1787-Dec. 17, 1789; Cont. Cong. 1780-82; Senate 1789-93.

MARTIN, Alexander (F) 1740-Nov. 10, 1807; Dec. 17, 1789-Dec. 14, 1792; Senate 1793-99.

SPAIGHT, Richard Dobbs Sr. (father of Richard Dobbs Spaight Jr., below) (D) March 25, 1758-Sept. 6, 1802; Dec. 14, 1792-Nov. 19, 1795 (Anti Federalist); Cont. Cong. 1782-85; House 1798-1801.

ASHE, Samuel (AF) 1725-Feb. 3, 1813; Nov. 19, 1795-Dec. 7, 1798.

DAVIE, William Richardson (F) June 20, 1756-Nov. 18, 1820; Dec. 7, 1798-Nov. 23, 1799.

WILLIAMS, Benjamin (DR) Jan. 1, 1751-July 20, 1814; Nov. 23, 1799-Dec. 6, 1802, Dec. 1, 1807-Dec. 12, 1808; House 1793-95.

TURNER, James (DR) Dec. 20, 1766-Jan. 15, 1824; Dec. 6, 1802-Dec. 10, 1805; Senate 1805-16 (Democrat).

ALEXANDER, Nathaniel (DR) March 5, 1756-March 8, 1808; Dec. 10, 1805-Dec. 1, 1807; House 1803-05.

WILLIAMS, Benjamin (DR) Dec. 1, 1807-Dec. 12, 1808 (for previous term see above).

STONE, David (D) Feb. 17, 1770-Oct. 7, 1818; Dec. 12, 1808-Dec. 5, 1810 (Democratic Republican); House 1799-1801; Senate 1801-07, 1813-14.

SMITH, Benjamin (DR) Jan. 10, 1756-Jan. 27, 1826; Dec. 5, 1810-Dec. 9, 1811.

HAWKINS, William (DR) Oct. 10, 1777-May 17, 1819; Dec. 9, 1811-Dec. 7, 1814.

MILLER, William (DR) 1770-1825; Dec. 7, 1814-Dec. 3, 1817.

BRANCH, John (D) Nov. 4, 1782-Jan. 4, 1863; Dec. 6, 1817-Dec. 7, 1820 (Democratic Republican); Senate 1823-29; House 1831-33; Secy. of the Navy 1829-31.

FRANKLIN, Jesse (DR) March 24, 1760-Aug. 31, 1823; Dec. 7, 1820-Dec. 7, 1821; House 1795-97 (Democrat); Senate 1799-1805 (Democrat), 1806-13 (Democrat); Pres. pro tempore 1804-05.

HOLMES, Gabriel (DR) 1769-Sept. 26, 1829; Dec. 7, 1821-Dec. 7, 1824; House 1825-29.

BURTON, Hutchins Gordon (F) 1774-April 21, 1836; Dec. 7, 1824-Dec. 8, 1827; House 1819-24 (Anti Democrat).

IREDELL, James Jr. (D) Nov. 2, 1788-April 13, 1853; Dec. 8, 1827-Dec. 12, 1828 (Democratic Republican); Senate 1828-31.

OWEN, John (DR) Aug. 1787-Oct. 9, 1841; Dec. 12, 1828-Dec. 18, 1830.

STOKES, Montfort (D) March 12, 1762-Nov. 4, 1842; Dec. 18, 1830-Dec. 6, 1832; Senate 1816-23.

SWAIN, David Lowry (W) Jan. 4, 1801-Aug. 27, 1868; Dec. 6, 1832-Dec. 10, 1835.

SPAIGHT, Richard Dobbs Jr. (son of Richard Dobbs Spaight Sr., above) (D) 1796-Nov. 2, 1850; Dec. 10, 1835-Dec. 31, 1836; House 1823-25.

DUDLEY, Edward Bishop (W) Dec. 15, 1789-Oct. 30, 1855; Dec. 31, 1836-Jan. 1, 1841; House 1829-31 (National Republican).

MOREHEAD, John Motley (cousin of James Turner Morehead of Ky.) (W) July 4, 1796-Aug. 27, 1866; Jan. 1, 1841-Jan. 1, 1845.

GRAHAM, William Alexander (W) Sept. 5, 1804-Aug. 11, 1875; Jan. 1, 1845-Jan. 1, 1849; Senate 1840-43; Secy. of the Navy 1850-52.

MANLY, Charles (W) May 13, 1795-May 1, 1871; Jan. 1, 1849-Jan. 1, 1851.

REID, David Settle (D) April 19, 1813-June 19, 1891; Jan. 1, 1851-Dec. 6, 1854; House 1843-47; Senate 1854-59.

WINSLOW, Warren (D) Jan. 1, 1810-Aug. 16, 1862; Dec. 6, 1854-Jan. 1, 1855; House 1855-61.

BRAGG, Thomas (D) Nov. 9, 1810-Jan. 21, 1872; Jan. 1, 1855-Jan. 1, 1859; Senate 1859-61.

ELLIS, John Willis (D) Nov. 23, 1820-July 7, 1861; Jan. 1, 1859-July 7, 1861.

CLARK, Henry Toole (D) Feb. 7, 1808-April 14, 1874; July 7, 1861-Sept. 8, 1862.

VANCE, Zebulon Baird (D) May 13, 1830-April 14, 1894; Sept. 8, 1862-May 29, 1865, Jan. 1, 1877-Feb. 5, 1879; House 1858-61; Senate 1879-94.

HOLDEN, William Woods (R) Nov. 24, 1818-March 1, 1892; May 29, 1865-Dec. 15, 1865, July 1, 1868-Dec. 15, 1870.

WORTH, Jonathan (D) Nov. 18, 1802-Sept. 5, 1869; Dec. 15, 1865-July 1, 1868.

HOLDEN, William Woods (R) July 1, 1868-Dec. 15, 1870 (for previous term see above).

CALDWELL, Tod Robinson (R) Feb. 19, 1818-July 11, 1874; Dec. 15, 1870-July 11, 1874.

BROGDEN, Curtis Hooks (R) Nov. 6, 1816-Jan. 5, 1901; July 11, 1874-Jan. 1, 1877; House 1877-79.

VANCE, Zebulon Baird (D) Jan. 1, 1877-Feb. 5, 1879 (for previous term see above).

JARVIS, Thomas Jordan (D) Jan. 18, 1836-June 17, 1915; Feb. 5, 1879-Jan. 21, 1885; Senate 1894-95.

SCALES, Alfred Moore (D) Nov. 26, 1827-Feb. 9, 1892; Jan. 21, 1885-Jan. 17, 1889; House 1857-59, 1875-84.

FOWLE, Daniel Gould (D) March 3, 1831-April 7, 1891; Jan. 17, 1889-April 7, 1891.

HOLT, Thomas Michael (D) July 15, 1831-April 11, 1896; April 8, 1891-Jan. 18, 1893.

CARR, Elias (D) Feb. 25, 1839-July 22, 1900; Jan. 18, 1893-Jan. 12, 1897.

RUSSELL, Daniel Lindsay (R) Aug. 7, 1845-May 14, 1908; Jan. 12, 1897-Jan. 15, 1901; House 1879-81.

AYCOCK, Charles Brantley (D) Nov. 1, 1859-April 4, 1912; Jan. 15, 1901-Jan. 11, 1905.

GLENN, Robert Brodnax (D) Aug. 11, 1854-May 16, 1920; Jan. 11, 1905-Jan. 12, 1909.

KITCHIN, William Walton (D) Oct. 9, 1866-Nov. 9, 1924; Jan. 12, 1909-Jan. 15, 1913; House 1897-1909.

CRAIG, Locke (D) Aug. 16, 1860-June 9, 1924; Jan. 15, 1913-Jan. 11, 1917.

BICKETT, Thomas Walter (D) Feb. 28, 1869-Dec. 28, 1921; Jan. 11, 1917-Jan. 12, 1921.

MORRISON, Cameron (D) Oct. 5, 1869-Aug. 20, 1953; Jan. 12, 1921-Jan. 14, 1925; Senate 1930-32; House 1943-45.

McLEAN, Angus Wilton (D) April 20, 1870-June 21, 1935; Jan. 14, 1925-Jan. 11, 1929.

GARDNER, Oliver Max (brother-in-law of Clyde Roark Hoey, below) (D) March 22, 1882-Feb. 6, 1947; Jan. 11, 1929-Jan. 5, 1933.

EHRINGHAUS, John Christoph Blucher (D) Feb. 5, 1882-July 31, 1949; Jan. 5, 1933-Jan. 7, 1937.

HOEY, Clyde Roark (brother-in-law of Oliver Max Gardner, above) (D) Dec. 11, 1877-May 12, 1954; Jan. 7, 1937-Jan. 9, 1941; House 1919-21; Senate 1945-54.

BROUGHTON, Joseph Melville (D) Nov. 17, 1888-March 6, 1949; Jan. 9, 1941-Jan. 4, 1945; Senate 1948-49.

CHERRY, Robert Gregg (D) Oct. 17, 1891-June 25, 1957; Jan. 4, 1945-Jan. 6, 1949.

SCOTT, William Kerr (father of Robert Walter Scott, below) (D) April 17, 1896-April 16, 1958; Jan. 6, 1949-Jan. 8, 1953; Senate 1954-58.

UMSTEAD, William Bradley (D) May 13, 1895-Nov. 7, 1954; Jan. 8, 1953-Nov. 7, 1954; House 1933-39; Senate 1946-48.

HODGES, Luther Hartwell (D) March 9, 1898-Oct. 6, 1974; Nov. 7, 1954-Jan. 5, 1961; Secy. of Commerce 1961-65.

SANFORD, Terry (D) Aug. 20, 1917- – ; Jan. 5, 1961-Jan. 8, 1965; Senate 1987- – .

MOORE, Daniel Killian (D) April 2, 1906-Sept. 7, 1986; Jan. 8, 1965-Jan. 3, 1969.

SCOTT, Robert Walter (son of William Kerr Scott, above) (D) June 13, 1929- – ; Jan. 3, 1969-Jan. 5, 1973.

HOLSHOUSER, James Eubert Jr. (R) Oct. 8, 1934- – ; Jan. 5, 1973-Jan. 8, 1977.

HUNT, James Baxter Jr. (D) May 16, 1937- – ; Jan. 8, 1977-Jan. 5, 1985.

MARTIN, James Grubbs (R) Dec. 11, 1935- – ; Jan. 5, 1985- – ; House 1973-85.

North Dakota

(Became a state Nov. 2, 1889)

MILLER, John (R) Oct. 6, 1843-Oct. 26, 1908; Nov. 4, 1889-Jan. 6, 1891.

BURKE, Andrew Horace (R) May 15, 1850-Nov. 17, 1918; Jan. 7, 1891-Jan. 3, 1893.

SHORTRIDGE, Eli C. D. (I) March 29, 1830-Feb. 4, 1908; Jan. 4, 1893-Jan. 7, 1895.

ALLIN, Roger (R) Dec. 18, 1848-Jan. 1, 1936; Jan. 7, 1895-Jan. 5, 1897.

BRIGGS, Frank Arlington (R) Sept. 16, 1858-Aug. 9, 1898; Jan. 5, 1897-Aug. 9, 1898.

DEVINE, Joseph McMurray (R) March 15, 1861-Aug. 31, 1938; Aug. 9, 1898-Jan. 3, 1899.

FANCHER, Frederick Bartlett (R) April 2, 1852-Jan. 10, 1944; Jan. 3, 1899-Jan. 10, 1901.

WHITE, Frank (R) Dec. 12, 1856-March 23, 1940; Jan. 10, 1901-Jan. 4, 1905.

SARLES, Elmore Yocum (R) Jan. 15, 1859-Feb. 14, 1929; Jan. 5, 1905-Jan. 9, 1907.

BURKE, John (D) Feb. 25, 1859-May 14, 1937; Jan. 9, 1907-Jan. 8, 1913.

HANNA, Louis Benjamin (R) Aug. 9, 1861-April 23, 1948; Jan. 8, 1913-Jan. 3, 1917; House 1909-13.

FRAZIER, Lynn Joseph (R) Dec. 21, 1874-Jan. 11, 1947; Jan. 3, 1917-Nov. 23, 1921; Senate 1923-41.

NESTOS, Ragnvald Anderson (R) April 12, 1877-July 15, 1942; Nov. 23, 1921-Jan. 7, 1925.

SORLIE, Arthur Gustav (R) April 26, 1874-Aug. 28, 1928; Jan. 7, 1925-Aug. 28, 1928.

MADDOCK, Walter Jeremiah (R) Sept. 13, 1880-Jan. 25, 1951; Aug. 28, 1928-Jan. 9, 1929.

SHAFER, George F. (R) Nov. 23, 1888-Aug. 13, 1948; Jan. 9, 1929-Dec. 31, 1932.

LANGER, William (R) Sept. 30, 1886-Nov. 8, 1959; Dec. 31, 1932-July 17, 1934, Jan. 6, 1937-Jan. 5, 1939 (Independent); Senate 1941-59.

OLSON, Ole H. (R) Sept. 19, 1872-Jan. 29, 1954; July 17, 1934-Jan. 7, 1935.

MOODIE, Thomas Hilliard (D) May 26, 1878-March 3, 1948; Jan. 7-Feb. 2, 1935.

WELFORD, Walter (R) May 21, 1868-June 28, 1952; Feb. 2, 1935-Jan. 6, 1937.

LANGER, William (R) Jan. 6, 1937-Jan. 5, 1939 (Independent) (for previous term see above).

MOSES, John (D) June 12, 1885-March 3, 1945; Jan. 5, 1939-Jan. 4, 1945; Senate 1945.

AANDAHL, Fred George (R) April 9, 1897-April 7, 1966; Jan. 4, 1945-Jan. 3, 1951; House 1951-53.

BRUNSDALE, Clarence Norman (R) July 9, 1891-Jan. 27, 1978; Jan. 3, 1951-Jan. 9, 1957; Senate 1959-60.

DAVIS, John Edward (R) April 18, 1913-—; Jan. 9, 1957-Jan. 4, 1961.

GUY, William Lewis (D) Sept. 30, 1919-—; Jan. 4, 1961-Jan. 2, 1973.

LINK, Arthur Albert (D) May 24, 1914-—; Jan. 2, 1973-Jan. 7, 1981; House 1971-73.

OLSON, Allen Ingvar (R) Nov. 5, 1938-—; Jan. 7, 1981-Jan. 8, 1985.

SINNER, George (D) May 29, 1928-—; Jan. 8, 1985-—.

Ohio

(Became a state March 1, 1803)

TIFFIN, Edward (brother-in-law of Thomas Worthington, below) (DR) June 19, 1766-Aug. 9, 1829; March 3, 1803-March 4, 1807; Senate 1807-09.

KIRKER, Thomas (DR) 1760-Feb. 20, 1837; March 4 1807-Dec. 12, 1808.

HUNTINGTON, Samuel H. (nephew of Samuel Huntington of Conn.) (DR) Oct. 4, 1765-June 8, 1817 Dec. 12, 1808-Dec. 8, 1810.

MEIGS, Return Jonathan Jr. (DR) Nov. 17, 1765-March 29, 1825; Dec. 8, 1810-March 24, 1814; Senate 1808-10; Postmaster Gen. 1814-23.

LOOKER, Othneil (DR) Oct. 4, 1757-July 23, 1845, March 24-Dec. 8, 1814.

WORTHINGTON, Thomas (brother-in-law of Edward Tiffin, above) (DR) July 16, 1773-June 20, 1827 Dec. 8, 1814-Dec. 14, 1818; Senate 1803-07, 1810-14.

BROWN, Ethan Allen (DR) July 4, 1776-Feb. 24, 1852, Dec. 14, 1818-Jan. 4, 1822; Senate 1822-25.

TRIMBLE, Allen (NR) Nov. 24, 1783-Feb. 3, 1870; Jan 4-Dec. 28, 1822 (Federalist), Dec. 19, 1826-Dec. 18, 1830.

MORROW, Jeremiah (JD) Oct. 6, 1771-March 22, 1852, Dec. 28, 1822-Dec. 19, 1826; House 1803-13 (Democrat), 1840-43 (Whig); Senate 1813-19 (Democrat).

TRIMBLE, Allen (NR) Dec. 19, 1826-Dec. 18, 1830 (for previous term see above).

McARTHUR, Duncan (NR) January 14, 1772-April 29, 1839; Dec. 18, 1830-Dec. 7, 1832; House 1813, 1823-25 (1813-25 Democrat).

LUCAS, Robert (JD) April 1, 1781-Feb. 7, 1853; Dec. 7, 1832-Dec. 12, 1836.

VANCE, Joseph (W) March 21, 1786-Aug. 24, 1852; Dec. 12, 1836-Dec. 13, 1838; House 1821-35 (Democrat), 1843-47.

SHANNON, Wilson (D) Feb. 24, 1802-Aug. 30, 1877; Dec. 13, 1838-Dec. 16, 1840, Dec. 14, 1842-April 15, 1844; House 1853-55.

CORWIN, Thomas (R) July 29, 1794-Dec. 18, 1865; Dec. 16, 1840-Dec. 14, 1842 (Whig); House 1831-40 (Whig), 1858-61; Senate 1845-50 (Whig); Secy. of the Treasury 1850-53.

SHANNON, Wilson (D) Dec. 14, 1842-April 15, 1844 (for previous term see above).

BARTLEY, Thomas Welles (son of Mordecai Bartley, below) (D) Feb. 11, 1812-June 20, 1885; April 15-Dec. 3, 1844.

BARTLEY, Mordecai (father of Thomas Welles Bartley, above) (W) Dec. 16, 1783-Oct. 10, 1870; Dec. 3, 1844-Dec. 12, 1846; House 1823-31.

BEBB, William (W) Dec. 2, 1801-Oct. 23, 1873; Dec. 12, 1846-Jan. 22, 1849.

FORD, Seabury (W) Oct. 15, 1801-May 8, 1855; Jan. 22, 1849-Dec. 12, 1850.

WOOD, Reuben (D) 1792-Oct. 1, 1864; Dec. 12, 1850-July 13, 1853.

MEDILL, William (D) Feb. 1802-Sept. 2, 1865; July 13, 1853-Jan. 14, 1856; House 1839-43.

CHASE, Salmon Portland (father-in-law of William Sprague of R.I.) (FSD, R) Jan. 13, 1808-May 7, 1873; Jan. 14, 1856-Jan. 9, 1860; Senate 1849-55, 1861; (1849-57 Free Soil Democrat, 1857-61 Republican); Secy. of the Treasury 1861-64; Chief Justice United States 1864-73.

DENNISON, William Jr. (R) Nov. 23, 1815-June 15, 1882; Jan. 9, 1860-Jan. 13, 1862; Postmaster Gen. 1864-66.

TOD, David (U) Feb. 21, 1805-Nov. 13, 1868; Jan. 13, 1862-Jan. 11, 1864.

BROUGH, John (U) Sept. 17, 1811-Aug. 29, 1865; Jan. 11, 1864-Aug. 29, 1865.

ANDERSON, Charles (U) June 1, 1814-Sept. 2, 1895; Aug. 29, 1865-Jan. 8, 1866.

COX, Jacob Dolson (R) Oct. 27, 1828-Aug. 4, 1900; Jan. 8, 1866-Jan. 13, 1868; Secy. of the Interior 1869-70; House 1877-79.

HAYES, Rutherford Birchard (R) Oct. 4, 1822-Jan. 17, 1893; Jan. 13, 1868-Jan. 8, 1872, Jan. 10, 1876-March 2, 1877; House 1865-67; President 1877-81.

NOYES, Edward Follansbee (R) Oct. 3, 1832-Sept. 4, 1890; Jan. 8, 1872-Jan. 12, 1874.

ALLEN, William (D) Dec. 27, 1803-July 11, 1879; Jan. 12, 1874-Jan. 10, 1876; House 1833-35; Senate 1837-49.

HAYES, Rutherford Birchard (R) Jan. 10, 1876-March 2, 1877 (for previous term see above).

YOUNG, Thomas Lowry (R) Dec. 14, 1832-July 20, 1888; March 2, 1877-Jan. 14, 1878; House 1879-83.

BISHOP, Richard Moore (D) Nov. 4, 1812-March 2, 1893; Jan. 14, 1878-Jan. 12, 1880.

FOSTER, Charles (R) April 12, 1828-Jan. 9, 1904; Jan. 12, 1880-Jan. 14, 1884; House 1871-79; Secy. of the Treasury 1891-93.

HOADLY, George (D) July 31, 1826-Aug. 26, 1902; Jan. 14, 1884-Jan. 11, 1886.

FORAKER, Joseph Benson (R) July 5, 1846-May 10, 1917; Jan. 11, 1886-Jan. 13, 1890; Senate 1897-1909.

CAMPBELL, James Edwin (D) July 7, 1843-Dec. 18, 1924; Jan. 13, 1890-Jan. 11, 1892; House 1884-89.

McKINLEY, William Jr. (R) Jan. 29, 1843-Sept. 14, 1901; Jan. 11, 1892-Jan. 13, 1896; House 1877-84, 1885-91; President 1897-1901.

BUSHNELL, Asa Smith (R) Sept. 16, 1834-Jan. 15, 1904; Jan. 13, 1896-Jan. 8, 1900.

NASH, George Kilborn (R) Aug. 14, 1842-Oct. 28, 1904; Jan. 8, 1900-Jan. 11, 1904.

HERRICK, Myron Timothy (R) Oct. 9, 1854-March 31, 1929; Jan. 11, 1904-Jan. 8, 1906.

PATTISON, John M. (D) June 13, 1847-June 18, 1906; Jan. 8-June 18, 1906; House 1891-93.

HARRIS, Andrew Lintner (R) Nov. 17, 1835-Sept. 13, 1915; June 18, 1906-Jan. 11, 1909.

HARMON, Judson (D) Feb. 3, 1846-Feb. 22, 1927; Jan. 11, 1909-Jan. 13, 1913.

COX, James Middleton (D) March 31, 1870-July 15, 1957; Jan. 13, 1913-Jan. 11, 1915, Jan. 8, 1917-Jan. 10, 1921; House 1909-13.

WILLIS, Frank Bartlett (R) Dec. 28, 1871-March 30, 1928; Jan. 11, 1915-Jan. 8, 1917; House 1911-15; Senate 1921-28.

COX, James Middleton (D) Jan. 8, 1917-Jan. 10, 1921 (for previous term see above).

DAVIS, Harry Lyman (R) Jan. 25, 1878-May 21, 1950; Jan. 10, 1921-Jan. 8, 1923.

DONAHEY, Alvin Victor (D) July 7, 1873-April 8, 1946; Jan. 8, 1923-Jan. 14, 1929; Senate 1935-41.

COOPER, Myers Young (R) Nov. 25, 1873-Dec. 7, 1958; Jan. 14, 1929-Jan. 12, 1931.

WHITE, George (D) Aug. 21, 1872-Dec. 15, 1953; Jan. 12, 1931-Jan. 14, 1935; House 1911-15, 1917-19; Chrmn. Dem. Nat. Comm. 1920-21.

DAVEY, Martin Luther (D) July 25, 1884-March 31, 1946; Jan. 14, 1935-Jan. 9, 1939; House 1918-21, 1923-29.

BRICKER, John William (R) Sept. 6, 1893-March 22, 1986; Jan. 9, 1939-Jan. 8, 1945; Senate 1947-59.

LAUSCHE, Frank John (D) Nov. 14, 1895- —; Jan. 8, 1945-Jan. 13, 1947, Jan. 10, 1949-Jan. 3, 1957; Senate 1957-69.

HERBERT, Thomas James (R) Oct. 28, 1894-Oct. 26, 1974; Jan. 13, 1947-Jan. 10, 1949.

LAUSCHE, Frank John (D) Jan. 10, 1949-Jan. 3, 1957 (for previous term see above).

BROWN, John William (R) Dec. 28, 1913- —; Jan. 3-14, 1957.

O'NEILL, C. William (R) Feb. 14, 1916-Aug. 20, 1978; Jan. 14, 1957-Jan. 12, 1959.

DI SALLE, Michael Vincent (D) Jan. 6, 1908-Sept. 16, 1981; Jan. 12, 1959-Jan. 14, 1963.

RHODES, James Allen (R) Sept. 13, 1909- —; Jan. 14, 1963-Jan. 11, 1971, Jan. 13, 1975-Jan. 10, 1983.

GILLIGAN, John Joyce (D) March 22, 1921- —; Jan. 11, 1971-Jan. 13, 1975; House 1965-67.

RHODES, James Allen (R) Jan. 13, 1975-Jan. 10, 1983 (for previous term see above).

CELESTE, Richard F. (D) Nov. 11, 1937- —; Jan. 10, 1983- —.

Oklahoma

(Became a state Nov. 16, 1907)

HASKELL, Charles Nathaniel (D) March 13, 1860-July 5, 1933; Nov. 16, 1907-Jan. 9, 1911.

CRUCE, Lee (D) July 8, 1863-Jan. 16, 1933; Jan. 9, 1911-Jan. 11, 1915.

WILLIAMS, Robert Lee (D) Dec. 20, 1868-April 10, 1948; Jan. 11, 1915-Jan. 13, 1919.

ROBERTSON, James Brooks Ayers (D) March 15, 1871-March 7, 1938; Jan. 13, 1919-Jan. 8, 1923.

WALTON, John Calloway "Jack" (D) March 6, 1881-Nov. 25, 1949; Jan. 8-Nov. 19, 1923.

TRAPP, Martin Edwin (D) April 19, 1877-July 27, 1951; Nov. 19, 1923-Jan. 10, 1927.

JOHNSTON, Henry Simpson (D) Dec. 30, 1870-Jan. 7, 1965; Jan. 10, 1927-March 20, 1929.

HOLLOWAY, William Judson (D) Dec. 15, 1888-Jan. 28, 1970; March 20, 1929-Jan. 12, 1931.

MURRAY, William Henry (father of Johnston Murray, below) (D) Nov. 21, 1869-Oct. 15, 1956; Jan. 12, 1931-Jan. 14, 1935; House 1913-17.

MARLAND, Ernest Whitworth (D) May 8, 1874-Oct. 3 1941; Jan. 14, 1935-Jan. 9, 1939; House 1933-35.

PHILLIPS, Leon Chase (D) Dec. 9, 1890-March 27 1958; Jan. 9, 1939-Jan. 11, 1943.

KERR, Robert Samuel (D) Sept. 11, 1896-Jan. 1, 1963 Jan. 11, 1943-Jan. 13, 1947; Senate 1949-63.

TURNER, Roy Joseph (D) Nov. 6, 1894-June 11, 1973 Jan. 13, 1947-Jan. 8, 1951.

MURRAY, Johnston (son of William Henry Murray, above) (D) July 21, 1902-April 16, 1974; Jan. 8, 1951-Jan. 10, 1955.

GARY, Raymond Dancel (D) Jan. 21, 1908- —; Jan. 10, 1955-Jan. 19, 1959.

EDMONDSON, James Howard (D) Sept. 27, 1925-Nov 17, 1971; Jan. 12, 1959-Jan. 6, 1963; Senate 1963-64.

NIGH, George Patterson (D) June 9, 1927- —; Jan. 6-14, 1963, Jan. 3, 1979-Jan. 12, 1987.

BELLMON, Henry Louis (R) Sept. 3, 1921- —; Jan. 14, 1963-Jan. 9, 1967, Jan. 12, 1987- —; Senate 1969-81.

BARTLETT, Dewey Follett (R) March 28, 1919-March 1, 1979; Jan. 9, 1967-Jan. 11, 1971; Senate 1973-79.

HALL, David (D) Oct. 20, 1930- —; Jan. 11, 1971-Jan. 13, 1975.

BOREN, David Lyle (D) April 21, 1941- —; Jan. 13, 1975-Jan. 3, 1979; Senate 1979- —.

NIGH, George (D) Jan. 3, 1979-Jan. 12, 1987 (for previous term see above).

BELLMON, Henry Louis (R) Jan. 12, 1987- — (for previous term see above).

Oregon

(Became a state Feb. 14, 1859)

WHITEAKER, John (D) May 4, 1820-Oct. 2, 1902; March 3, 1859-Sept. 10, 1862; House 1879-81.

GIBBS, Addison Crandall (UR) July 9, 1825-Dec. 29, 1886; Sept. 10, 1862-Sept. 12, 1866.

WOODS, George Lemuel (R) July 30, 1832-Jan. 7, 1890; Sept. 12, 1866-Sept. 14, 1870.

GROVER, La Fayette (D) Nov. 29, 1823-May 10, 1911; Sept. 14, 1870-Feb. 1, 1877; House 1859; Senate 1877-83.

CHADWICK, Stephen Fowler (D) Dec. 25, 1825-Jan. 15, 1895; Feb. 1, 1877-Sept. 11, 1878.

HAYER, William Wallace (D) July 15, 1827-Oct. 15, 1899; Sept. 11, 1878-Sept. 13, 1882.

OODY, Zenas Ferry (R) May 27, 1832-March 14, 1917; Sept. 13, 1882-Jan. 12, 1887.

ENNOYER, Sylvester (PD) July 6, 1831-May 30, 1902; Jan. 12, 1887-Jan. 14, 1895.

ORD, William Paine (R) July 1, 1839-Feb. 17, 1911; Jan. 14, 1895-Jan. 9, 1899.

EER, Theodore Thurston (R) March 12, 1851-Feb. 21, 1924; Jan. 9, 1899-Jan. 14, 1903.

HAMBERLAIN, George Earle (D) Jan. 1, 1854-July 9, 1928; Jan. 14, 1903-Feb. 28, 1909; Senate 1909-21.

ENSON, Frank Williamson (R) March 20, 1858-April 14, 1911; March 1, 1909-June 17, 1910.

OWERMAN, Jay (R) Aug. 15, 1876-Oct. 25, 1957; June 17, 1910-Jan. 8, 1911.

/EST, Oswald (D) May 20, 1873-Aug. 22, 1960; Jan. 10, 1911-Jan. 12, 1915.

'ITHYCOMBE, James (R) March 21, 1854-March 3, 1919; Jan. 12, 1915-March 3, 1919.

LCOTT, Ben Wilson (R) Oct. 15, 1872-July 21, 1952; March 3, 1919-Jan. 8, 1923.

IERCE, Walter Marcus (D) May 30, 1861-March 27, 1954; Jan. 8, 1923-Jan. 10, 1927; House 1933-43.

ATTERSON, Isaac Lee (R) Sept. 17, 1859-Dec. 21, 1929; Jan. 10, 1927-Dec. 21, 1929.

ORBLAD, Albin Walter (R) March 19, 1881-April 17, 1960; Dec. 22, 1929-Jan. 12, 1931.

IEIER, Julius L. (I) Dec. 31, 1874-July 14, 1937; Jan. 12, 1931-Jan. 14, 1935.

IARTIN, Charles Henry (D) Oct. 1, 1863-Sept. 22, 1946; Jan. 14, 1935-Jan. 9, 1939; House 1931-35.

PRAGUE, Charles Arthur (R) Nov. 12, 1887-March 13, 1969; Jan. 9, 1939-Jan. 11, 1943.

NELL, Earl Wilcox (R) July 11, 1895-Oct. 28, 1947; Jan. 11, 1943-Oct. 28, 1947.

IALL, John Hubert (R) Feb. 7, 1899-Nov. 14, 1970; Oct. 30, 1947-Jan. 10, 1949.

IcKAY, Douglas (R) June 24, 1893-July 22, 1959; Jan. 10, 1949-Dec. 27, 1952; Secy. of the Interior 1953-56.

ATTERSON, Paul Linton (R) July 18, 1900-Jan. 31, 1956; Dec. 27, 1952-Jan. 31, 1956.

MITH, Elmo Everett (R) Nov. 19, 1909-July 15, 1968; Feb. 1, 1956-Jan. 14, 1957.

HOLMES, Robert Denison (D) May 11, 1909-June 6, 1976; Jan. 14, 1957-Jan. 12, 1959.

HATFIELD, Mark Odom (R) July 12, 1922- —; Jan. 12, 1959-Jan. 9, 1967; Senate 1967- —.

McCALL, Thomas Lawson (R) March 22, 1913-Jan. 8, 1983; Jan. 9, 1967-Jan. 13, 1975.

STRAUB, Robert William (D) May 6, 1920- —; Jan. 13, 1975-Jan. 8, 1979.

ATIYEH, Victor G. (R) Feb. 20, 1923- —; Jan. 8, 1979-Jan. 12, 1987.

GOLDSCHMIDT, Neil (D) June 16, 1940- —; Jan. 12, 1987- —; Secy. of Transportation 1979-80.

Pennsylvania

(Ratified the Constitution Dec. 12, 1787)

MIFFLIN, Thomas (DR) Jan. 10, 1744-Jan. 20, 1800; Dec. 21, 1790-Dec. 17, 1799.

McKEAN, Thomas (DR) March 19, 1734-June 24, 1817; Dec. 17, 1799-Dec. 20, 1808.

SNYDER, Simon (DR) Nov. 5, 1789-Nov. 9, 1819; Dec. 20, 1808-Dec. 16, 1817.

FINDLAY, William (father-in-law of Francis Rawn Shunk, below) (D) June 20, 1768-Nov. 12, 1846; Dec. 16, 1817-Dec. 19, 1820 (Democratic Republican); Senate 1821-27.

HIESTER, Joseph (DR) Nov. 18, 1752-June 10, 1832; Dec. 19, 1820-Dec. 16, 1823; House 1799-1805 (Federalist), 1815-20.

SHULZE, John Andrew (JD) July 19, 1775-Nov. 18, 1852; Dec. 16, 1823-Dec. 15, 1829.

WOLF, George (JD) Aug. 12, 1777-March 11, 1840; Dec. 15, 1829-Dec. 15, 1835; House 1824-29 (Democrat).

RITNER, Joseph (AMas.) March 25, 1780-Oct. 16, 1869; Dec. 15, 1835-Jan. 15, 1839.

PORTER, David Rittenhouse (D) Oct. 31, 1788-Aug. 6, 1867; Jan. 15, 1839-Jan. 21, 1845.

SHUNK, Francis Rawn (son-in-law of William Findlay, above) (D) Aug. 7, 1788-July 20, 1848; Jan. 21, 1845-July 9, 1848.

JOHNSTON, William Freame (W) Nov. 29, 1808-Oct. 25, 1872; July 26, 1848-Jan. 20, 1852.

BIGLER, William (brother of John Bigler of Calif.) (D) Jan. 11, 1814-Aug. 9, 1880; Jan. 20, 1852-Jan. 16, 1855; Senate 1856-61.

POLLOCK, James (W) Sept. 11, 1810-April 19, 1890; Jan. 16, 1855-Jan. 19, 1858; House 1844-49.

PACKER, William Fisher (D) April 2, 1807-Sept. 27, 1870; Jan. 19, 1858-Jan. 15, 1861.

CURTIN, Andrew Gregg (R) April 22, 1815-Oct. 7, 1894; Jan. 15, 1861-Jan. 15, 1867; House 1881-87 (Democrat).

GEARY, John White (R) Dec. 30, 1819-Feb. 8, 1873; Jan. 15, 1867-Jan. 21, 1873.

HARTRANFT, John Frederick (R) Dec. 16, 1830-Oct. 17, 1889; Jan. 21, 1873-Jan. 18, 1879.

HOYT, Henry Martyn (R) June 8, 1830-Dec. 1, 1892; Jan. 21, 1879-Jan. 16, 1883.

PATTISON, Robert Emory (D) Dec. 8, 1850-Aug. 1, 1904; Jan. 16, 1883-Jan. 18, 1887, Jan. 20, 1891-Jan. 15, 1895.

BEAVER, James Addams (R) Oct. 21, 1837-Jan. 31, 1914; Jan. 18, 1887-Jan. 20, 1891.

PATTISON, Robert Emory (D) Jan. 20, 1891-Jan. 15, 1895 (for previous term see above).

HASTINGS, Daniel Hartman (R) Feb. 26, 1849-Jan. 9, 1903; Jan. 15, 1895-Jan. 17, 1899.

STONE, William Alexis (R) April 18, 1846-March 1, 1920; Jan. 17, 1899-Jan. 20, 1903; House 1891-98.

PENNYPACKER, Samuel Whitaker (R) April 9, 1843-Sept. 2, 1916; Jan. 20, 1903-Jan. 15, 1907.

STUART, Edwin Sydney (R) Dec. 28, 1853-March 21, 1937; Jan. 15, 1907-Jan. 17, 1911.

TENER, John Kinley (R) July 25, 1863-May 19, 1946; Jan. 17, 1911-Jan. 19, 1915.

BRUMBAUGH, Martin Grove (R) April 14, 1862-March 14, 1930; Jan. 19, 1915-Jan. 21, 1919.

SPROUL, William Cameron (R) Sept. 16, 1870-March 21, 1928; Jan. 21, 1919-Jan. 16, 1923.

PINCHOT, Gifford (R) Aug. 11, 1865-Oct. 4, 1946; Jan. 16, 1923-Jan. 18, 1927, Jan. 20, 1931-Jan. 15, 1935.

FISHER, John Stuchell (R) May 25, 1867-June 25, 1940; Jan. 18, 1927-Jan. 20, 1931.

PINCHOT, Gifford (R) Jan. 20, 1931-Jan. 15, 1935 (for previous term see above).

EARLE, George Howard III (D) Dec. 5, 1890-Dec. 30, 1974; Jan. 15, 1935-Jan. 17, 1939.

JAMES, Arthur Horace (R) July 14, 1883-April 27, 1973; Jan. 17, 1939-Jan. 19, 1943.

MARTIN, Edward (R) Sept. 18, 1879-March 19, 196 Jan. 19, 1943-Jan. 2, 1947; Senate 1947-59.

BELL, John Cromwell Jr. (R) Oct. 25, 1892-March 1 1974; Jan. 2-21, 1947.

DUFF, James Henderson (R) Jan. 21, 1883-Dec. 2 1969; Jan. 21, 1947-Jan. 16, 1951; Senate 1951-57

FINE, John Sydney (R) April 10, 1893-May 21, 197 Jan. 16, 1951-Jan. 18, 1955.

LEADER, George Michael (D) Jan. 17, 1918- —; Jan. 1 1955-Jan. 20, 1959.

LAWRENCE, David Leo (D) June 18, 1889-Nov. 2 1966; Jan. 20, 1959-Jan. 15, 1963.

SCRANTON, William Warren (R) July 19, 1917- —; Ja 15, 1963-Jan. 17, 1967; House 1961-63.

SHAFER, Raymond Philip (R) March 5, 1917- —; Ja 17, 1967-Jan. 19, 1971.

SHAPP, Milton Jerrold (D) June 25, 1912- —; Jan. 1 1971-Jan. 16, 1979.

THORNBURGH, Richard L. (R) July 16, 1932- —; Ja 16, 1979-Jan. 20, 1987.

CASEY, Robert Patrick (D) Jan. 9, 1932- —; Jan. 2 1987- —.

Rhode Island

(Ratified the Constitution May 29, 1790)

FENNER, Arthur (father of James Fenner, below) (AF Dec. 10, 1745-Oct. 15, 1805; May 5, 1790-Oct. 1 1805.

SMITH, Henry (DR) Feb. 10, 1766-June 28, 1818; Oc 15, 1805-May 7, 1806.

WILBOUR, Isaac (F) April 25, 1763-Oct. 4, 1837; May 1806-May 6, 1807 (Democratic Republican); Hous 1807-09.

FENNER, James (son of Arthur Fenner, above (L&OW) Jan. 22, 1771-April 17, 1846; May 6, 1807 May 1, 1811 (Democratic Republican), May 5, 1824 May 4, 1831 (Democratic Republican), May 2, 184 May 6, 1845; Senate 1805-07 (Democrati Republican).

JONES, William (F) Oct. 8, 1753-April 9, 1822; May 1811-May 7, 1817.

KNIGHT, Nehemiah Rice (D) Dec. 31, 1780-April 1 1854; May 7, 1817-Jan. 9, 1821 (Democratic Republi can); Senate 1821-41 (1821-35 Anti Federalist).

WILCOX, Edward (DR) July 5, 1783-Sept. 7, 1838; Jan. 9-May 2, 1821.

GIBBS, William Channing (DR) Feb. 10, 1789-Feb. 24, 1871; May 2, 1821-May 5, 1824.

FENNER, James (L&OW) May 5, 1824-May 4, 1831 (Democratic Republican) (for previous term see above).

ARNOLD, Lemuel Hastings (great-granduncle of Theodore Francis Green, below) (LW) Jan. 29, 1792-June 27, 1852; May 4, 1831-May 1, 1833 (Democratic Republican); House 1845-47.

FRANCIS, John Brown (L&OW) May 31, 1791-Aug. 9, 1864; May 1, 1833-May 2, 1838 (Democrat); Senate 1844-45.

SPRAGUE, William (uncle of William Sprague, below) (W) Nov. 3, 1799-Oct. 19, 1856; May 2, 1838-May 1, 1839; House 1835-37; Senate 1842-44.

KING, Samuel Ward (W) May 22, 1786-Jan. 20, 1851; May 2, 1839-May 2, 1843.

FENNER, James (L&OW) May 2, 1843-May 6, 1845 (for previous terms see above).

JACKSON, Charles (LW) March 3, 1797-Jan. 21, 1876; May 6, 1845-May 6, 1846.

DIMAN, Byron (L&OW) Aug. 5, 1795-Aug. 1, 1865; May 6, 1846-May 4, 1847.

HARRIS, Elisha (father-in-law of Henry Howard, below) (W) 1791-Feb. 1, 1861; May 4, 1847-May 1, 1849.

ANTHONY, Henry Bowen (R) April 1, 1815-Sept. 2, 1884; May 1, 1849-May 6, 1851 (Whig); Senate 1859-84; Pres. pro tempore 1869-73.

ALLEN, Philip (TD) Sept. 1, 1785-Dec. 16, 1865; May 6, 1851-July 20, 1853; Senate 1853-59.

DIMOND, Francis M. (D) 1796-April 23, 1859; July 20, 1853-May 2, 1854.

HOPPIN, William Warner (AW) Sept. 1, 1807-April 19, 1890; May 2, 1854-May 26, 1857.

DYER, Elisha II (father of Elisha Dyer III, below) (R) July 20, 1811-May 17, 1890; May 26, 1857-May 31, 1859.

TURNER, Thomas Goodwin (R) Oct. 24, 1810-Jan. 3, 1875; May 31, 1859-May 29, 1860.

SPRAGUE, William (nephew of William Sprague, son-in-law of Salmon Portland Chase of Ohio) (R) Sept. 12, 1830-Sept. 11, 1915; May 29, 1860-March 3, 1863 (Unionist); Senate 1863-75.

COZZENS, William Cole (Fus) Aug. 26, 1811-Dec. 17, 1876; March 3-May 26, 1863.

SMITH, James Youngs (UR) Sept. 15, 1809-March 26, 1876; May 26, 1863-May 29, 1866.

BURNSIDE, Ambrose Everett (R) May 23, 1824-Sept. 13, 1881; May 29, 1866-May 25, 1869; Senate 1875-81.

PADELFORD, Seth (R) Oct. 3, 1807-Aug. 26, 1878; May 25, 1869-May 27, 1873.

HOWARD, Henry (son-in-law of Elisha Harris, above) (R) April 2, 1826-Sept. 22, 1905; May 27, 1873-May 25, 1875.

LIPPITT, Henry (father of Charles Warren Lippitt, below) (R) Oct. 9, 1818-June 5, 1891; May 25, 1875-May 29, 1877.

VAN ZANDT, Charles Collins (R/Prohib.) Aug. 10, 1830-June 4, 1894; May 29, 1877-May 25, 1880.

LITTLEFIELD, Alfred Henry (R) April 2, 1829-Dec. 21, 1893; May 25, 1880-May 29, 1883.

BOURN, Augustus Osborn (R) Oct. 1, 1834-Jan. 28, 1925; May 29, 1883-May 26, 1885.

WETMORE, George Peabody (R) Aug. 2, 1846-Sept. 11, 1921; May 26, 1885-May 31, 1887; Senate 1895-1907, 1908-13.

DAVIS, John William (D) March 7, 1826-Jan. 26, 1907; May 31, 1887-May 29, 1888, May 27, 1890-May 26, 1891.

TAFT, Royal Chapin (R) Feb. 14, 1823-June 4, 1912; May 29, 1888-May 28, 1889.

LADD, Herbert Warren (R) Oct. 15, 1843-Nov. 29, 1913; May 28, 1889-May 27, 1890, May 26, 1891-May 31, 1892.

DAVIS, John William (D) May 27, 1890-May 26, 1891 (for previous term see above).

LADD, Herbert Warren (R) May 26, 1891-May 31, 1892 (for previous term see above).

BROWN, Daniel Russell (R) March 28, 1848-Feb. 28, 1919; May 31, 1892-May 29, 1895.

LIPPITT, Charles Warren (son of Henry Lippitt, above) (R) Oct. 8, 1846-April 4, 1924; May 29, 1895-May 25, 1897.

DYER, Elisha III (son of Elisha Dyer II, above) (R) Nov. 29, 1839-Nov. 29, 1906; May 25, 1897-May 29, 1900.

GREGORY, William (R) Aug. 3, 1849-Dec. 16, 1901; May 29, 1900-Dec. 16, 1901.

KIMBALL, Charles Dean (R) Sept. 13, 1859-Dec. 8, 1930; Dec. 16, 1901-Jan. 6, 1903.

GARVIN, Lucius Fayette Clark (D) Nov. 13, 1841-Oct. 22, 1922; Jan. 6, 1903-Jan. 3, 1905.

UTTER, George Herbert (R) July 24, 1854-Nov. 3, 1912; Jan. 3, 1905-Jan. 1, 1907; House 1911-12.

HIGGINS, James Henry (D) Jan. 22, 1876-Sept. 16, 1927; Jan. 1, 1907-Jan. 5, 1909.

POTHIER, Aram J. (R) July 26, 1854-Feb. 3, 1928; Jan. 5, 1909-Jan. 5, 1915, Jan. 6, 1925-Feb. 4, 1928.

BEECKMAN, Robert Livingston (R) April 15, 1866-Jan. 21, 1935; Jan. 5, 1915-Jan. 4, 1921.

SAN SOUCI, Emery John (R) July 24, 1857-Aug. 10, 1936; Jan. 4, 1921-Jan. 2, 1923.

FLYNN, William Smith (D) Aug. 14, 1885-April 6, 1966; Jan. 2, 1923-Jan. 6, 1925.

POTHIER, Aram J. (R) Jan. 6, 1925-Feb. 4, 1928 (for previous term see above).

CASE, Norman Stanley (R) Oct. 11, 1888-Oct. 9, 1967; Feb. 4, 1928-Jan. 3, 1933.

GREEN, Theodore Francis (great-grandnephew of Lemuel Hastings Arnold, above) (D) Oct. 2, 1867-May 19, 1966; Jan. 3, 1933-Jan. 5, 1937; Senate 1937-61.

QUINN, Robert Emmet (D) April 2, 1894-May 20, 1975; Jan. 5, 1937-Jan. 3, 1939.

VANDERBILT, William Henry (R) Nov. 24, 1901-April 14, 1981; Jan. 3, 1939-Jan. 7, 1941.

McGRATH, James Howard (D) Nov. 28, 1903-Sept. 2, 1966; Jan. 7, 1941-Oct. 6, 1945; Senate 1947-49; Chrmn. Dem. Nat. Comm. 1947-49; Atty. Gen. 1949-52.

PASTORE, John Orlando (D) March 17, 1907- —; Oct. 6, 1945-Dec. 19, 1950; Senate 1950-76.

McKIERNAN, John Sammon (D) Oct. 15, 1911- —; Dec. 19, 1950-Jan. 2, 1951.

ROBERTS, Dennis Joseph (D) April 8, 1903- —; Jan. 2, 1951-Jan. 6, 1959.

DEL SESTO, Christopher (R) March 10, 1907-Dec. 23, 1973; Jan. 6, 1959-Jan. 3, 1961.

NOTTE, John Anthony Jr. (D) May 3, 1909-March 7, 1983; Jan. 3, 1961-Jan. 1, 1963.

CHAFEE, John Hubbard (R) Oct. 22, 1922- —; Jan. 1, 1963-Jan. 7, 1969; Secy. of the Navy 1969-72; Senate 1976- —.

LICHT, Frank (D) March 13, 1916- —; Jan. 7, 1969-Jan. 2, 1973.

NOEL, Philip William (D) June 6, 1931- —; Jan. 2, 1973-Jan. 4, 1977.

GARRAHY, John Joseph (D) Nov. 26, 1930- —; Jan. 4 1977-Jan. 1, 1985.

DiPRETE, Edward Daniel (R) July 8, 1934- —; Jan. 1 1985- —.

South Carolina

(Ratified the Constitution May 23, 1788)

PINCKNEY, Charles (father-in-law of Robert Youn‚ Hayne, below) (DR) Oct. 26, 1757-Oct. 29, 1824; Jan 26, 1789-Dec. 5, 1792, Dec. 8, 1796-Dec. 6, 1798, Dec 9, 1806-Dec. 10, 1808; Cont. Cong. 1784-87; Senat 1798-1801; House 1819-21.

MOULTRIE, William (F) Nov. 23, 1730-Sept. 27, 1805 Dec. 5, 1792-Dec. 17, 1794.

VAN der HORST Arnoldus (F) March 21, 1748-Jan. 29 1815; Dec. 17, 1794-Dec. 8, 1796.

PINCKNEY, Charles (DR) Dec. 8, 1796-Dec. 6, 179₄ (for previous term see above).

RUTLEDGE, Edward (brother-in-law of Henry Middle ton, below) (F) Nov. 23, 1749-Jan. 23, 1800; Dec. 18 1798-Jan. 23, 1800; Cont. Cong. 1774-77.

DRAYTON, John (DR) June 22, 1767-Nov. 27, 1822 Jan. 23, 1800-Dec. 8, 1802, Dec. 10, 1808-Dec. 8 1810.

RICHARDSON, James Burchill (uncle of John Peter Richardson II and Richard Irvine Manning I, grand uncle of John Peter Richardson III and Joh Laurence Manning, great-granduncle of Richard Irvine Manning III) (DR) Oct. 28, 1770-April 28 1836; Dec. 8, 1802-Dec. 7, 1804.

HAMILTON, Paul (DR) Oct. 16, 1762-June 30, 1816 Dec. 7, 1804-Dec. 9, 1806.

PINCKNEY, Charles (DR) Dec. 9, 1806-Dec. 10, 180 (for previous terms see above).

DRAYTON, John (DR) Dec. 10, 1808-Dec. 8, 1810 (fc previous term see above).

MIDDLETON, Henry (brother-in-law of Edward Rut ledge, above) (DR) Sept. 28, 1770-June 14, 184 Dec. 10, 1810-Dec. 10, 1812; House 1815-19 (Dem crat).

ALSTON, Joseph (son-in-law of Vice President Aaro Burr, brother-in-law of John Lyde Wilson) (DR 1779-Sept. 10, 1816; Dec. 10, 1812-Dec. 10, 1814.

WILLIAMS, David Rogerson (DR) March 8, 1776-No 17, 1830; Dec. 10, 1814-Dec. 5, 1816; House 1805-0 1811-13 (1805-13 Democrat).

ICKENS, Andrew (father of Francis Wilkinson Pickens, below) (DR) Nov. 13, 1779-July 1, 1838; Dec. 5, 1816-Dec. 8, 1818.

EDDES, John (DR) Dec. 25, 1777-March 4, 1828; Dec. 8, 1818-Dec. 7, 1820.

ENNETT, Thomas (DR) Aug. 14, 1781-Jan. 30, 1865; Dec. 20, 1820-Dec. 7, 1822.

ILSON, John Lyde (brother-in-law of Joseph Alston, above) (DR) May 24, 1784-Feb. 12, 1849; Dec. 7, 1822-Dec. 3, 1824.

ANNING, Richard Irvine I (father of John Laurence Manning, grandfather of Richard Irvine Manning III, nephew of James Burchill Richardson, cousin of John Peter Richardson II, second cousin of John Peter Richardson III) (D) May 1, 1789-May 1, 1836; Dec. 3, 1824-Dec. 9, 1826 (Democratic Republican); House 1834-36.

AYLOR, John (DR) May 4, 1770-April 16, 1832; Dec. 9, 1826-Dec. 10, 1828.

ILLER, Stephen Decatur (D) May 8, 1787-March 8, 1838; Dec. 10, 1828-Dec. 9, 1830; House 1817-19; Senate 1831-33 (Nullifier).

AMILTON, James Jr. (SRD) May 8, 1786-Nov. 15, 1857; Dec. 9, 1830-Dec. 13, 1832; House 1822-29 (States Rights Free Trader).

AYNE, Robert Young (son-in-law of Charles Pinckney, above) (SRD) Nov. 10, 1791-Sept. 24, 1839; Dec. 13, 1832-Dec. 11, 1834; Senate 1823-32 (Tariff Democrat).

cDUFFIE, George (father-in-law of Wade Hampton, below) (D) Aug. 10, 1790-March 11, 1851; Dec. 11, 1834-Dec. 10, 1836 (States Rights Democrat); House 1821-34); Senate 1842-46.

UTLER, Pierce Mason (SRD) April 11, 1798-Aug. 20, 1847; Dec. 10, 1836-Dec. 10, 1838.

OBLE, Patrick (SRD) 1787-April 7, 1840; Dec. 10, 1838-April 7, 1840.

ENAGAN, Barnabas Kelet (D) June 7, 1798-Jan. 10, 1855; April 7-Dec. 10, 1840.

ICHARDSON, John Peter II (father of John Peter Richardson III, nephew of James Burchill Richardson, cousin of Richard Irvine Manning I, second cousin of John Laurence Manning) (SRD) April 14, 1801-Jan. 24, 1864; Dec. 10, 1840-Dec. 8, 1842; House 1836-39.

AMMOND, James Henry (SRD) Nov. 15, 1807-Nov. 13, 1864; Dec. 8, 1842-Dec. 7, 1844 (Democrat); House 1835-36 (States Rights Free Trader); Senate 1857-60.

AIKEN, William (D) Aug. 4, 1806-Sept. 7, 1887; Dec. 7, 1844-Dec. 8, 1846; House 1851-57.

JOHNSON, David (D) Oct. 3, 1782-Jan. 7, 1855; Dec. 8, 1846-Dec. 12, 1848.

SEABROOK, Whitemarsh Benjamin (D) June 30, 1792-April 16, 1855; Dec. 12, 1848-Dec. 13, 1850.

MEANS, John Hugh (SRD) Aug. 18, 1812-Aug. 29, 1862; Dec. 13, 1850-Dec. 9, 1852.

MANNING, John Laurence (son of Richard Irvine Manning I, grandnephew of James Burchill Richardson, uncle of Richard Irvine Manning III, second cousin of John Peter Richardson II) (SRD) Jan. 29, 1816-Oct. 29, 1889; Dec. 9, 1852-Dec. 11, 1854.

ADAMS, James Hopkins (SRD) March 15, 1812-July 13, 1861; Dec. 11, 1854-Dec. 9, 1856.

ALLSTON, Robert Francis Withers (D) April 21, 1801-April 7, 1864; Dec. 9, 1856-Dec. 10, 1858.

GIST, William Henry (SRD) Aug. 20, 1809-Sept. 30, 1874; Dec. 10, 1858-Dec. 17, 1860.

PICKENS, Francis Wilkinson (son of Andrew Pickens, above) (SRD) April 7, 1805-Jan. 25, 1869; Dec. 14, 1860-Dec. 17, 1862; House 1834-43 (Nullifier Democrat).

BONHAM, Milledge Luke (Confed.D) Dec. 25, 1813-Aug. 27, 1890; Dec. 17, 1862-Dec. 20, 1864; House 1857-60 (States Rights Democrat).

McGRATH, Andrew Gordon (Confed.D) Feb. 8, 1813-April 9, 1893; Dec. 20, 1864-May 25, 1865.

PERRY, Benjamin Franklin (UD) Nov. 20, 1805-Dec. 3, 1886; (Provisional) June 30, 1865-Nov. 29, 1865.

ORR, James Lawrence (R) May 12, 1822-May 5, 1873; Nov. 29, 1865-July 6, 1868; House 1849-59 (Democrat); Speaker 1857-59.

SCOTT, Robert Kingston (R) July 3, 1826-Aug. 13, 1900; July 9, 1868-Dec. 7, 1872.

MOSES, Franklin J. Jr. (R) 1838-Dec. 11, 1906; Dec. 7, 1872-Dec. 1, 1874.

CHAMBERLAIN, Daniel Henry (R) June 23, 1835-April 14, 1907; Dec. 1, 1874-April 10, 1877.

HAMPTON, Wade (son-in-law of George McDuffie, above) (D) March 28, 1818-April 11, 1902; Dec. 14, 1876-Feb. 26, 1879; Senate 1879-91.

SIMPSON, William Dunlap (D) Oct. 27, 1823-Dec. 26, 1890; Feb. 26, 1879-Sept. 1, 1880.

JETER, Thomas Bothwell (D) Oct. 13, 1827-May 20, 1883; Sept. 1-Nov. 30, 1880.

HAGOOD, Johnson (D) Feb. 21, 1829-Jan. 4, 1898; Nov. 30, 1880-Dec. 5, 1882.

THOMPSON, Hugh Smith (D) Jan. 24, 1836-Nov. 20, 1904; Dec. 5, 1882-July 10, 1886.

SHEPPARD, John Calhoun (D) July 5, 1850-Oct. 17, 1931; July 10-Nov. 30, 1886.

RICHARDSON, John Peter III (son of John Peter Richardson II, grandnephew of James Burchill Richardson, second cousin of Richard Irvine Manning I) (D) Sept. 25, 1831-July 6, 1899; Nov. 30, 1886-Dec. 4, 1890.

TILLMAN, Benjamin Ryan (D) Aug. 11, 1847-July 3, 1918; Dec. 4, 1890-Dec. 4, 1894; Senate 1895-1918.

EVANS, John Gary (D) Oct. 15, 1863-June 27, 1942; Dec. 4, 1894-Jan. 18, 1897.

ELLERBE, William Haselden (D) April 7, 1862-June 2, 1899; Jan. 18, 1897-June 2, 1899.

McSWEENEY, Miles Benjamin (D) April 18, 1855-Sept. 29, 1909; June 2, 1899-Jan. 20, 1903.

HEYWARD, Duncan Clinch (D) June 24, 1864-Jan. 23, 1943; Jan. 20, 1903-Jan. 15, 1907.

ANSEL, Martin Frederick (D) Dec. 12, 1850-Aug. 24, 1945; Jan. 15, 1907-Jan. 17, 1911.

BLEASE, Coleman Livingston (D) Oct. 8, 1868-Jan. 19, 1942; Jan. 17, 1911-Jan. 14, 1915; Senate 1925-31.

SMITH, Charles Aurelius (D) Jan. 22, 1861-April 1, 1916; Jan. 14-19, 1915.

MANNING, Richard Irvine III (grandson of Richard Irvine Manning I, nephew of John Laurence Manning, great-grandnephew of James Burchill Richardson) (D) Aug. 15, 1859-Sept. 11, 1931; Jan. 19, 1915-Jan. 21, 1919.

COOPER, Robert Archer (D) June 12, 1874-Aug. 7, 1953; Jan. 21, 1919-May 20, 1922.

HARVEY, Wilson Godfrey (D) Sept. 8, 1866-Oct. 7, 1932; May 20, 1922-Jan. 16, 1923.

McLEOD, Thomas Gordon (D) Dec. 17, 1868-Dec. 11, 1932; Jan. 16, 1923-Jan. 18, 1927.

RICHARDS, John Gardiner (D) Sept. 11, 1864-Oct. 9, 1941; Jan. 18, 1927-Jan. 20, 1931.

BLACKWOOD, Ibra Charles (D) Nov. 21, 1878-Feb. 12, 1936; Jan. 20, 1931-Jan. 15, 1935.

JOHNSTON, Olin Dewitt Talmadge (D) Nov. 18, 1896-April 18, 1965; Jan. 15, 1935-Jan. 17, 1939, Jan. 19, 1943-Jan. 2, 1945; Senate 1945-65.

MAYBANK, Burnet Rhett (D) March 7, 1899-Sept. 1954; Jan. 17, 1939-Nov. 4, 1941; Senate 1941-54.

HARLEY, Joseph Emile (D) Sept. 14, 1880-Feb. 27 1942; Nov. 4, 1941-Feb. 27, 1942.

JEFFRIES, Richard Manning (D) Feb. 27, 1889-Apr 20, 1964; March 2, 1942-Jan. 19, 1943.

JOHNSTON, Olin Dewitt Talmadge (D) Jan. 19, 1943 Jan. 2, 1945 (for previous term see above).

WILLIAMS, Ransome Judson (D) Jan. 4, 1892-Jan. 1970; Jan. 2, 1945-Jan. 21, 1947.

THURMOND, James Strom (D) Dec. 5, 1902- -; Jan 21, 1947-Jan. 16, 1951; Senate 1954- - (1964- - Republican); Pres. pro tempore 1981-87.

BYRNES, James Francis (D) May 2, 1879-April 9, 197; Jan. 16, 1951-Jan. 18, 1955; House 1911-25; Senat 1931-41; Assoc. Justice Supreme Court 1941-4; Secy. of State 1945-47.

TIMMERMAN, George Bell Jr. (D) Aug. 11, 1912- - Jan. 18, 1955-Jan. 20, 1959.

HOLLINGS, Ernest Frederick "Fritz" (D) Jan. 1, 1922 - -; Jan. 20, 1959-Jan. 15, 1963; Senate 1966- -.

RUSSELL, Donald Stuart (D) Feb. 22, 1906- -; Jan. 1 1963-April 22, 1965; Senate 1965-67.

McNAIR, Robert Evander (D) Dec. 14, 1923- -; Apr 22, 1965-Jan. 19, 1971.

WEST, John Carl (D) Aug. 27, 1922- -; Jan. 19, 1971 Jan. 21, 1975.

EDWARDS, James Burrows (R) June 24, 1927- -; Jar 21, 1975-Jan. 10, 1979.

RILEY, Richard Wilson (D) Jan. 2, 1933- -; Jan. 1(1979-Jan. 14, 1987.

CAMPBELL, Carroll Ashmore Jr. (R) July 24, 1940- - Jan. 14, 1987- -; House 1979-87.

South Dakota

(Became a state Nov. 2, 1889)

MELETTE, Arthur Calvin (R) June 23, 1842-May 2; 1896; Nov. 2, 1889-Jan. 3, 1893.

SHELDON, Charles Henry (R) Sept. 12, 1840-Oct. 2(1898; Jan. 3, 1893-Jan. 5, 1897.

LEE, Andrew Erickson (uncle of Carl Gunderson, below (P) March 18, 1847-March 19, 1934; Jan. 5, 1897 Jan. 8, 1901.

ERREID, Charles Nelson (R) Oct. 20, 1857-July 6, 1928; Jan. 8, 1901-Jan. 3, 1905.

LROD, Samuel Harrison (R) May 1, 1856-July 13, 1935; Jan. 3, 1905-Jan. 8, 1907.

RAWFORD, Coe Isaac (R) Jan. 14, 1858-April 25, 1944; Jan. 8, 1907-Jan. 5, 1909; Senate 1909-15.

ESSEY, Robert Scadden (R) May 16, 1858-Oct. 18, 1929; Jan. 5, 1909-Jan. 7, 1913.

YRNE, Frank Michael (R) Oct. 23, 1858-Dec. 24, 1927; Jan. 7, 1913-Jan. 2, 1917.

ORBECK, Peter (R) Aug. 27, 1870-Dec. 20, 1936; Jan. 2, 1917-Jan. 4, 1921; Senate 1921-36.

cMASTER, William Henry (R) May 10, 1877-Sept. 14, 1968; Jan. 4, 1921-Jan. 6, 1925; Senate 1925-31.

UNDERSON, Carl (nephew of Andrew Erickson Lee, above) (R) June 20, 1864-Feb. 26, 1933; Jan. 6, 1925-Jan. 4, 1927.

ULOW, William John (D) Jan. 13, 1869-Feb. 26, 1960; Jan. 4, 1927-Jan. 6, 1931; Senate 1931-43.

REEN, Warren Everett (R) March 10, 1870-April 27, 1945; Jan. 6, 1931-Jan. 3, 1933.

ERRY, Thomas Matthew (D) April 23, 1879-Oct. 30, 1951; Jan. 3, 1933-Jan. 5, 1937.

NSEN, Leslie (R) Sept. 15, 1892-Dec. 14, 1964; Jan. 5, 1937-Jan. 3, 1939.

USHFIELD, Harlan John (R) Aug. 6, 1882-Sept. 27, 1948; Jan. 3, 1939-Jan. 5, 1943; Senate 1943-48.

HARPE, Merrell Quentin (R) Jan. 11, 1888-Jan. 22, 1962; Jan. 5, 1943-Jan. 7, 1947.

ICKELSON, George Theodore (father of George Speaker Mickelson, below) (R) July 23, 1903-Feb. 28, 1965; Jan. 7, 1947-Jan. 2, 1951.

NDERSON, Sigurd (R) Jan. 22, 1904-—; Jan. 2, 1951-Jan. 4, 1955.

SS, Joseph Jacob (R) April 17, 1915-—; Jan. 4, 1955-Jan. 6, 1959.

ERSETH, Ralph E. (D) July 2, 1909-Jan. 24, 1969; Jan. 6, 1959-Jan. 3, 1961.

UBBRUD, Archie M. (R) Dec. 31, 1910-—; Jan. 3, 1961-Jan. 5, 1965.

OE, Nils Andreas (R) Sept. 10, 1913-—; Jan. 5, 1965-Jan. 7, 1969.

ARRAR, Frank Leroy (R) April 2, 1929-—; Jan. 7, 1969-Jan. 5, 1971.

KNEIP, Richard Francis (D) Jan. 7, 1933-March 9, 1987; Jan. 5, 1971-July 24, 1978.

WOLLMAN, Harvey L. (D) May 14, 1935-—; July 24, 1978-Jan. 1, 1979.

JANKLOW, William John (R) Sept. 13, 1939-—; Jan. 1, 1979-Jan. 6, 1987.

MICKELSON, George Speaker (son of George Theodore Mickelson, above) (R) Jan. 31, 1941-—; Jan. 6, 1987-—.

Tennessee

(Became a state June 1, 1796)

SEVIER, John (DR) Sept. 23, 1745-Sept. 24, 1815; March 30, 1796-Sept. 23, 1801, Sept. 23, 1803-Sept. 19, 1809; House 1789-91 (Democrat N.C.), 1811-15 (Democrat Tenn.).

ROANE, Archibald (DR) 1760-Jan. 18, 1819; Sept. 23, 1801-Sept. 23, 1803.

SEVIER, John (DR) Sept. 23, 1803-Sept. 19, 1809 (for previous term see above).

BLOUNT, William (great-great-grandfather of Harry Hill McAlister, below) (DR) April 18, 1768-Sept. 10, 1835; Sept. 20, 1809-Sept. 27, 1815.

McMINN, Joseph (DR) June 27, 1758-Nov. 17, 1824; Sept. 27, 1815-Oct. 1, 1821.

CARROLL, William (D) March 3, 1788-March 22, 1844; Oct. 1, 1821-Oct. 1, 1827 (Democratic Republican), Oct. 1, 1829-Oct. 12, 1835.

HOUSTON, Samuel (father of Rep. Andrew Jackson Houston, cousin of Rep. David Hubbard) (D) March 2, 1793-July 26, 1863; Oct. 1, 1827-April 16, 1829, Dec. 21, 1859-March 16, 1861 (Texas); House 1823-27; Senate 1846-59 (Texas).

HALL, William (D) Feb. 11, 1775-Oct. 7, 1856; April 16-Oct. 1, 1829 (Democratic Republican); House 1831-33.

CARROLL, William (D) Oct. 1, 1829-Oct. 12, 1835 (for previous term see above).

CANNON, Newton (W) May 22, 1781-Sept. 16, 1841; Oct. 12, 1835-Oct. 14, 1839; House 1814-17 (Democrat), 1819-23 (Democrat).

POLK, James Knox (brother of Rep. William Hawkins Polk) (D) Nov. 2, 1795-June 15, 1849; Oct. 14, 1839-Oct. 15, 1841; House 1825-39; Speaker 1835-39; President 1845-49.

JONES, James Chamberlain (W) June 7, 1809-Oct. 29, 1859; Oct. 15, 1841-Oct. 14, 1845; Senate 1851-57.

BROWN, Aaron Venable (D) Aug. 15, 1795-March 8, 1859; Oct. 14, 1845-Oct. 16, 1847; House 1839-45; Postmaster Gen. 1857-59.

BROWN, Neill Smith (brother of John Calvin Brown, below) (W) April 18, 1810-Jan. 30, 1886; Oct. 17, 1847-Oct. 16, 1849.

TROUSDALE, William (D) Sept. 23, 1790-March 27, 1872; Oct. 16, 1849-Oct. 16, 1851.

CAMPBELL, William Bowen (D) Feb. 1, 1807-Aug. 19, 1867; Oct. 16, 1851-Oct. 16, 1853 (Whig); House 1837-43 (Whig), 1866-67.

JOHNSON, Andrew (father-in-law of Sen. David Trotter Patterson) (R) Dec. 29, 1808-July 31, 1875; Oct. 17, 1853-Nov. 3, 1857 (Democrat), (Military) March 12, 1862-March 4, 1865; House 1843-53 (Democrat); Senate 1857-62 (Democrat), 1875; Vice President 1865; President 1865-69.

HARRIS, Isham Green (D) Feb. 10, 1818-July 8, 1897; Nov. 3, 1857-March 12, 1862; House 1849-53; Senate 1877-97; Pres. pro tempore 1893-95.

JOHNSON, Andrew (R) (Military) March 12, 1862-March 4, 1865 (for previous term see above).

EAST, Edward Hazzard (Prohib.) Oct. 1, 1830-Nov. 12, 1904; March 4-April 5, 1865.

BROWNLOW, William Gannaway (W, R) Aug. 29, 1805-April 28, 1877; April 5, 1865-Feb. 25, 1869; Senate 1869-75 (Republican).

SENTER, DeWitt Clinton (CR) March 26, 1830-June 14, 1898; Feb. 25, 1869-Oct. 10, 1871.

BROWN, John Calvin (brother of Neill Smith Brown, father-in-law of Benton McMillin) (D, LR) Jan. 6, 1827-Aug. 17, 1889; Oct. 10, 1871-Jan. 18, 1875.

PORTER, James Davis Jr. (D) Dec. 7, 1828-May 18, 1912; Jan. 18, 1875-Feb. 16, 1879.

MARKS, Albert Smith (D) Oct. 16, 1836-Nov. 4, 1891; Feb. 16, 1879-Jan. 17, 1881.

HAWKINS, Alvin (R) Dec. 2, 1821-April 27, 1905; Jan. 17, 1881-Jan. 15, 1883.

BATE, William Brimage (D) Oct. 7, 1826-March 9, 1905; Jan. 15, 1883-Jan. 17, 1887; Senate 1887-1905.

TAYLOR, Robert Love (brother of Alfred Alexander Taylor, below) (D) July 31, 1850-March 31, 1912; Jan. 17, 1887-Jan. 19, 1891, Jan. 21, 1897-Jan. 16, 1899; House 1879-81; Senate 1907-12.

BUCHANAN, John Price (D) Oct. 24, 1837-May 14, 1930; Jan. 19, 1891-Jan. 16, 1893.

TURNEY, Peter (D) Sept. 27, 1827-Oct. 28, 1903; Jan. 16, 1893-Jan. 21, 1897.

TAYLOR, Robert Love (D) Jan. 21, 1897-Jan. 16, 189? (for previous term see above).

McMILLIN, Benton (son-in-law of John Calvin Brown, above) (D) Sept. 11, 1845-Jan. 8, 1933; Jan. 16, 189? Jan. 19, 1903; House 1879-99.

FRAZIER, James Beriah (D) Oct. 18, 1856-March 2? 1937; Jan. 19, 1903-March 21, 1905; Senate 1905-1?

COX, John Isaac (D) Nov. 23, 1855-Sept. 5, 1946; Marc? 21, 1905-Jan. 17, 1907.

PATTERSON, Malcolm Rice (D) June 7, 1861-March ? 1935; Jan. 17, 1907-Jan. 26, 1911; House 1901-06.

HOOPER, Ben Walker (R) Oct. 13, 1870-April 18, 195? Jan. 26, 1911-Jan. 17, 1915.

RYE, Thomas Clarke (D) June 2, 1863-Sept. 12, 195? Jan. 17, 1915-Jan. 15, 1919.

ROBERTS, Albert Houston (D) July 4, 1868-June 2? 1946; Jan. 15, 1919-Jan. 15, 1921.

TAYLOR, Alfred Alexander (brother of Robert Lo? Taylor, above) (R) Aug. 6, 1848-Nov. 25, 1931; Ja? 15, 1921-Jan. 16, 1923; House 1889-95.

PEAY, Austin III (D) June 1, 1876-Oct. 2, 1927; Jan. ? 1923-Oct. 2, 1927.

HORTON, Henry Hollis (D) Feb. 17, 1866-July 2, 193? Oct. 3, 1927-Jan. 17, 1933.

McALISTER, Harry Hill (great-great-grandson of W? liam Blount, above) (D) July 15, 1875-Oct. 30, 195? Jan. 17, 1933-Jan. 15, 1937.

BROWNING, Gordon (D) Nov. 22, 1889-May 23, 197? Jan. 15, 1937-Jan. 16, 1939, Jan. 17, 1949-Jan. 1? 1953; House 1923-35.

COOPER, William Prentice (D) Sept. 28, 1895-May ? 1969; Jan. 16, 1939-Jan. 16, 1945.

McCORD, James Nance (D) March 17, 1879-Sept. ? 1968; Jan. 16, 1945-Jan. 17, 1949; House 1943-45.

BROWNING, Gordon (D) Jan. 17, 1949-Jan. 15, 19? (for previous term see above).

CLEMENT, Frank Goad (D) June 2, 1920-Nov. 4, 196? Jan. 15, 1953-Jan. 16, 1959, Jan. 15, 1963-Jan. ? 1967.

ELLINGTON, Earl Buford (D) June 27, 1907-April ? 1972; Jan. 19, 1959-Jan. 15, 1963, Jan. 16, 1967-Ja? 16, 1971.

CLEMENT, Frank Goad (D) Jan. 15, 1963-Jan. 16, 19? (for previous term see above).

ELLINGTON, Earl Buford (D) Jan. 16, 1967-Jan. ? 1971 (for previous term see above).

UNN, Bryant Winfield Culberson (R) July 1, 1927--; Jan. 16, 1971-Jan. 18, 1975.

LANTON, Leonard Ray (D) April 10, 1930--; Jan. 18, 1975-Jan. 17, 1979; House 1967-73.

LEXANDER, Lamar (R) July 3, 1940--; Jan. 17, 1979-Jan. 17, 1987.

lcWHERTER, Ned Ray (D) Oct. 15, 1930--; Jan. 17, 1987--.

Texas

Became a state Dec. 29, 1845)

ENDERSON, James Pinckney (SRD) March 31, 1808-June 4, 1858; Feb. 19, 1846-Dec. 21, 1847; Senate 1857-58.

OOD, George Thomas (D) March 12, 1795-Sept. 3, 1858; Dec. 21, 1847-Dec. 21, 1849.

ELL, Peter Hansborough (D) March 11, 1810-March 8, 1898; Dec. 21, 1849-Nov. 23, 1853; House 1853-57.

ENDERSON, James Wilson (D) Aug. 15, 1817-Aug. 30, 1880; Nov. 23-Dec. 21, 1853.

EASE, Elisha Marshall (D) Jan. 3, 1812-Aug. 26, 1883; Dec. 21, 1853-Dec. 21, 1857, Aug. 8, 1867-Sept. 30, 1869.

UNNELS, Hardin Richard (nephew of Hiram George Runnels of Miss.) (D) Aug. 30, 1820-Dec. 25, 1873; Dec. 21, 1857-Dec. 21, 1859.

OUSTON, Samuel (father of Rep. Andrew Jackson Houston, cousin of Rep. David Hubbard) (I, D) March 2, 1793-July 26, 1863; Dec. 21, 1859-March 16, 1861, Oct. 1, 1827-April 16, 1829 (Tenn.); House 1823-27 (Tenn.); Senate 1846-59.

LARK, Edward (son of John Clark of Ga.) (D) April 1, 1815-May 4, 1880; March 16-Nov. 7, 1861.

UBBOCK, Francis Richard (D) Oct. 16, 1815-June 22, 1905; Nov. 7, 1861-Nov. 5, 1863.

URRAH, Pendleton (D) 1824-Aug. 4, 1865; Nov. 5, 1863-June 11, 1865.

TOCKDALE, Fletcher S. (D) 1823-1902; June 11-16, 1865.

AMILTON, Andrew Jackson (ID) Jan. 28, 1815-April 11, 1875; June 17, 1865-Aug. 9, 1866; House 1859-61.

HROCKMORTON, James Webb (C) Feb. 1, 1825-April 21, 1894; Aug. 9, 1866-Aug. 8, 1867; House 1875-79, 1883-87.

PEASE, Elisha Marshall (D) Aug. 8, 1867-Sept. 30, 1869 (for previous term see above).

DAVIS, Edmund Jackson (R) Oct. 2, 1827-Feb. 7, 1883; Jan. 8, 1870-Jan. 15, 1874.

COKE, Richard (D) March 13, 1829-May 14, 1897; Jan. 15, 1874-Dec. 1, 1876; Senate 1877-95.

HUBBARD, Richard Bennett (D) Nov. 1, 1832-July 12, 1901; Dec. 1, 1876-Jan. 21, 1879.

ROBERTS, Oran Milo (D) July 9, 1815-May 19, 1898; Jan. 21, 1879-Jan. 16, 1883.

IRELAND, John (D) Jan. 21, 1827-March 5, 1896; Jan. 16, 1883-Jan. 18, 1887.

ROSS, Lawrence Sullivan "Sul" (D) Sept. 27, 1838-Jan. 3, 1898; Jan. 18, 1887-Jan. 20, 1891.

HOGG, James Stephen (D) March 24, 1851-March 3, 1906; Jan. 20, 1891-Jan. 15, 1895.

CULBERSON, Charles Allen (D) June 19, 1855-March 19, 1925; Jan. 15, 1895-Jan. 17, 1899; Senate 1899-1923.

SAYERS, Joseph Draper (D) Sept. 23, 1841-May 15, 1929; Jan. 17, 1899-Jan. 20, 1903; House 1885-89.

LANHAM, Samuel Willis Tucker (D) July 4, 1846-July 29, 1908; Jan. 20, 1903-Jan. 15, 1907; House 1883-93, 1897-1903.

CAMPBELL, Thomas Mitchell (D) April 22, 1856-April 1, 1923; Jan. 15, 1907-Jan. 17, 1911.

COLQUITT, Oscar Branch (D) Dec. 16, 1861-March 8, 1940; Jan. 17, 1911-Jan. 19, 1915.

FERGUSON, James Edward "Pa" (husband of Miriam Amanda "Ma" Ferguson, below) (D) Aug. 31, 1871-Sept. 21, 1944; Jan. 19, 1915-Aug. 25, 1917.

HOBBY, William Pettus (D) March 26, 1878-June 7, 1964; Aug. 25, 1917-Jan. 18, 1921.

NEFF, Patrick Morris (D) Nov. 26, 1871-Jan. 20, 1952; Jan. 18, 1921-Jan. 20, 1925.

FERGUSON, Miriam Amanda "Ma" (wife of James Edward "Pa" Ferguson, above) (D) June 13, 1875-June 25, 1961; Jan. 20, 1925-Jan. 18, 1927, Jan. 17, 1933-Jan. 15, 1935.

MOODY, Daniel J. (D) June 1, 1893-May 22, 1966; Jan. 18, 1927-Jan. 20, 1931.

STERLING, Ross Shaw (D) Feb. 11, 1875-March 25, 1949; Jan. 20, 1931-Jan. 17, 1933.

FERGUSON, Miriam Amanda "Ma" (D) Jan. 17, 1933-Jan. 15, 1935 (for previous term see above).

ALLRED, James V. (D) March 29, 1889-Sept. 24, 1959; Jan. 15, 1935-Jan. 17, 1939.

O'DANIEL, Wilbert Lee "Pappy" (D) March 11, 1890-May 11, 1969; Jan. 17, 1939-Aug. 4, 1941; Senate 1941-49.

STEVENSON, Coke Robert (D) March 20, 1888-June 28, 1975; Aug. 4, 1941-Jan. 21, 1947.

JESTER, Beauford Halbert (D) Jan. 12, 1893-July 11, 1949; Jan. 21, 1947-July 11, 1949.

SHIVERS, Allan (D) Oct. 5, 1907-Jan. 14, 1985; July 11, 1949-Jan. 15, 1957.

DANIEL, Price Marion (D) Oct. 10, 1910- —; Jan. 15, 1957-Jan. 15, 1963; Senate 1953-57.

CONNALLY, John Bowden (D) Feb. 27, 1917- —; Jan. 15, 1963-Jan. 21, 1969; Secy. of the Navy 1961; Secy. of the Treasury 1971-72.

SMITH, Preston Earnest (D) March 8, 1912- —; Jan. 21, 1969-Jan. 16, 1973.

BRISCOE, Dolph Jr. (D) April 23, 1923- —; Jan. 16, 1973-Jan. 16, 1979.

CLEMENTS, William P. Jr. (R) April 13, 1917- —; Jan. 16, 1979-Jan. 18, 1983, Jan. 20, 1987- —.

WHITE, Mark (D) March 17, 1940- —; Jan. 18, 1983-Jan. 20, 1987.

CLEMENTS, William P. Jr. (R) Jan. 20, 1987- — (for previous term see above).

Utah

(Became a state Jan. 4, 1896)

WELLS, Heber Manning (R) Aug. 11, 1859-March 12, 1938; Jan. 6, 1896-Jan. 2, 1905.

CUTLER, John Christopher (R) Feb. 5, 1846-July 30, 1928; Jan. 2, 1905-Jan. 4, 1909.

SPRY, William (R) Jan. 11, 1864-April 21, 1929; Jan. 4, 1909-Jan. 1, 1917.

BAMBERGER, Simon (D) Feb. 27, 1846-Oct. 6, 1926; Jan. 1, 1917-Jan. 3, 1921.

MABEY, Charles Rendell (R) Oct. 4, 1877-April 26, 1959; Jan. 3, 1921-Jan. 5, 1925.

DERN, George Henry (D) Sept. 8, 1872-Aug. 27, 1936; Jan. 5, 1925-Jan. 2, 1933.

BLOOD, Henry Hooper (D) Oct. 1, 1872-June 19, 1942; Jan. 2, 1933-Jan. 6, 1941.

MAW, Herbert Brown (D) March 11, 1893- —; Jan. 1941-Jan. 3, 1949.

LEE, Joseph Bracken (R) Jan. 7, 1899- —; Jan. 3, 1949 Jan. 7, 1957.

CLYDE, George Dewey (R) July 21, 1898-April 2, 197 Jan. 7, 1957-Jan. 4, 1965.

RAMPTON, Calvin Lewellyn (D) Nov. 6, 1913- —; Ja 4, 1965-Jan. 3, 1977.

MATHESON, Scott Milne (D) Jan. 8, 1929- —; Jan. 1977-Jan. 7, 1985.

BANGERTER, Norman H. (R) Jan. 4, 1933- —; Jan. 1985- —.

Vermont

(Became a state March 4, 1791)

CHITTENDEN, Thomas (father of Martin Chittende father-in-law of Jonas Galusha) Jan. 6, 1730-Aug. 2 1797; March 4, 1791-Aug. 25, 1797.

BRIGHAM, Paul (DR) Jan. 6, 1746-June 15, 1824; Au 25, 1797-Oct. 16, 1797.

TICHENOR, Isaac (F) Feb. 8, 1754-Dec. 11, 1838; Oc 16, 1797-Oct. 9, 1807, Oct. 17, 1808-Oct. 14, 180 Senate 1796-97, 1815-21.

SMITH, Israel (DR) April 4, 1759-Dec. 2, 1810; Oct. 1807-Oct. 14, 1808; House 1791-97, 1801-03; Senat 1803-07.

TICHENOR, Isaac (F) Oct. 17, 1808-Oct. 14, 1809 (f previous term see above).

GALUSHA, Jonas (son-in-law of Thomas Chittende brother-in-law of Martin Chittenden) (DR) Feb. 1 1753-Sept. 24, 1834; Oct. 14, 1809-Oct. 23, 1813, Oc 14, 1815-Oct. 13, 1820.

CHITTENDEN, Martin (son of Thomas Chittende brother-in-law of Jonas Galusha) (F) March 1 1769-Sept. 5, 1840; Oct. 23, 1813-Oct. 14, 181 House 1803-13.

GALUSHA, Jonas (DR) Oct. 14, 1815-Oct. 13, 1820 (f previous term see above).

SKINNER, Richard (DR) May 30, 1778-May 23, 183 Oct. 13, 1820-Oct. 10, 1823; House 1813-15.

VAN NESS, Cornelius P. (DR) Jan. 26, 1782-Dec. 1 1852; Oct. 10, 1823-Oct. 13, 1826.

BUTLER, Ezra (DR) Sept. 24, 1763-July 12, 1838; Oc 13, 1826-Oct. 10, 1828; House 1813-15.

RAFTS, Samuel Chandler (NR) Oct. 6, 1768-Nov. 19, 1853; Oct. 10, 1828-Oct. 18, 1831; House 1817-25; Senate 1842-43.

ALMER, William Adams (AMas.D) Sept. 12, 1781-Dec. 3, 1860; Oct. 18, 1831-Nov. 2, 1835; Senate 1818-25.

ENISON, Silas Hemenway (W) May 17, 1791-Sept. 30, 1849; Nov. 2, 1835-Oct. 15, 1841.

AINE, Charles (W) April 15, 1799-July 6, 1853; Oct. 15, 1841-Oct. 13, 1843.

ATTOCKS, John (W) March 4, 1777-Aug. 14, 1847; Oct. 13, 1843-Oct. 11, 1844; House 1821-23, 1825-27, 1841-43.

LADE, William (W) May 9, 1786-Jan. 18, 1859; Oct. 11, 1844-Oct. 9, 1846; House 1831-43.

ATON, Horace (W) June 22, 1804-July 4, 1855; Oct. 9, 1846-Oct. 1848.

OOLIDGE, Carlos (W) June 25, 1792-Aug. 15, 1866; Oct. 1848-Oct. 11, 1850.

ILLIAMS, Charles Kilborn (W) Jan. 24, 1782-March 9, 1853; Oct. 11, 1850-Oct. 18, 1852.

AIRBANKS, Erastus (father of Horace Fairbanks, below) (W) Oct. 28, 1792-Nov. 20, 1864; Oct. 18, 1852-Nov. 2, 1853, Oct. 12, 1860-Oct. 11, 1861.

OBINSON, John Staniford (D) Nov. 10, 1804-April 25, 1860; Nov. 2, 1853-Oct. 13, 1854.

OYCE, Stephen (W, R) Aug. 12, 1787-Nov. 11, 1868; Oct. 13, 1854-Oct. 10, 1856.

LETCHER, Ryland (R) Feb. 18, 1799-Dec. 19, 1885; Oct. 10, 1856-Oct. 10, 1858.

ALL, Hiland (R) July 20, 1795-Dec. 18, 1885; Oct. 10, 1858-Oct. 12, 1860; House 1833-43 (Whig).

AIRBANKS, Erastus (R) Oct. 12, 1860-Oct. 11, 1861 (for previous term see above).

OLBROOK, Frederick (R) Feb. 15, 1813-April 28, 1909; Oct. 11, 1861-Oct. 9, 1863.

MITH, John Gregory (father of Edward Curtis Smith, below) (R) July 22, 1818-Nov. 6, 1891; Oct. 9, 1863-Oct. 13, 1865.

LLINGHAM, Paul Jr. (father of William Paul Dillingham, below) (R) Aug. 10, 1799-July 16, 1891; Oct. 13, 1865-Oct. 13, 1867; House 1843-47 (Democrat).

AGE, John Boardman (R) Feb. 25, 1826-Oct. 24, 1885; Oct. 13, 1867-Oct. 15, 1869.

WASHBURN, Peter Thacher (R) Sept. 7, 1814-Feb. 7, 1870; Oct. 15, 1869-Feb. 7, 1870.

HENDEE, George Whitman (R) Nov. 30, 1832-Dec. 6, 1906; Feb. 7, 1870-Oct. 6, 1870; House 1873-79.

STEWART, John Wolcott (R) Nov. 24, 1825-Oct. 29, 1915; Oct. 6, 1870-Oct. 3, 1872; House 1883-91; Senate 1908.

CONVERSE, Julius (R) Dec. 17, 1798-Aug. 16, 1885; Oct. 3, 1872-Oct. 8, 1874.

PECK, Asahel (R) Feb. 6, 1803-May 18, 1879; Oct. 8, 1874-Oct. 5, 1876.

FAIRBANKS, Horace (son of Erastus Fairbanks, above) (R) March 21, 1820-March 17, 1888; Oct. 5, 1876-Oct. 3, 1878.

PROCTOR, Redfield Sr. (father of Fletcher Dutton Proctor and Redfield Proctor Jr., grandfather of Mortimer Robinson Proctor) (R) June 1, 1831-March 4, 1908; Oct. 3, 1878-Oct. 7, 1880; Senate 1891-1908; Secy. of War 1889-91.

FARNHAM, Roswell (R) July 23, 1827-Jan. 5, 1903; Oct. 7, 1880-Oct. 5, 1882.

BARSTOW, John Lester (R) Feb. 21, 1832-June 28, 1913; Oct. 5, 1882-Oct. 2, 1884.

PINGREE, Samuel Everett (R) Aug. 2, 1832-June 1, 1922; Oct. 2, 1884-Oct. 7, 1886.

ORMSBEE, Ebenezer Jolls (R) June 8, 1834-April 3, 1924; Oct. 7, 1886-Oct. 4, 1888.

DILLINGHAM, William Paul (son of Paul Dillingham Jr., above) (R) Dec. 12, 1843-July 12, 1923; Oct. 4, 1888-Oct. 2, 1890; Senate 1900-23.

PAGE, Carroll Smalley (R) Jan. 10, 1843-Dec. 3, 1925; Oct. 2, 1890-Oct. 6, 1892; Senate 1908-23.

FULLER, Levi Knight (R) Feb. 24, 1841-Oct. 10, 1896; Oct. 6, 1892-Oct. 4, 1894.

WOODBURY, Urban Andrain (R) July 11, 1838-April 15, 1915; Oct. 4, 1894-Oct. 8, 1896.

GROUT, Josiah (brother of William Wallace Grout, below) (R) May 28, 1841-July 19, 1925; Oct. 8, 1896-Oct. 6, 1898.

SMITH, Edward Curtis (son of John Gregory Smith, above) (R) Jan. 5, 1854-April 6, 1925; Oct. 6, 1898-Oct. 4, 1900.

STICKNEY, William Wallace (cousin of President John Calvin Coolidge) (R) March 21, 1853-Dec. 15, 1932; Oct. 4, 1900-Oct. 3, 1902.

McCULLOUGH, John Griffith (R) Sept. 16, 1835-May 29, 1915; Oct. 3, 1902-Oct. 6, 1904.

BELL, Charles James (R) March 10, 1845-Sept. 25, 1909; Oct. 6, 1904-Oct. 4, 1906.

PROCTOR, Fletcher Dutton (father of Mortimer Robinson Proctor, son of Redfield Proctor Sr., brother of Redfield Proctor Jr.) (R) Nov. 7, 1860-Sept. 27, 1911; Oct. 4, 1906-Oct. 8, 1908.

PROUTY, George Herbert (R) March 4, 1862-Aug. 19, 1918; Oct. 8, 1908-Oct. 5, 1910.

MEAD, John Abner (R) April 20, 1841-Jan. 12, 1920; Oct. 5, 1910-Oct. 3, 1912.

FLETCHER, Allen Miller (R) Sept. 25, 1853-May 11, 1922; Oct. 3, 1912-Jan. 7, 1915.

GATES, Charles Winslow (R) Jan. 12, 1856-July 1, 1927; Jan. 7, 1915-Jan. 4, 1917.

GRAHAM, Horace French (R) Feb. 7, 1862-Nov. 23, 1941; Jan. 4, 1917-Jan. 9, 1919.

CLEMENT, Percival Wood (R) July 7, 1846-Jan. 9, 1927; Jan. 9, 1919-Jan. 6, 1921.

HARTNESS, James (R) Sept. 3, 1861-Feb. 2, 1934; Jan. 6, 1921-Jan. 4, 1923.

PROCTOR, Redfield Jr. (son of Redfield Proctor Sr., brother of Fletcher Dutton Proctor, uncle of Mortimer Robinson Proctor) (R) April 13, 1879-Feb. 5, 1957; Jan. 4, 1923-Jan. 8, 1925.

BILLINGS, Franklin Swift (R) May 11, 1862-Jan. 16, 1935; Jan. 8, 1925-Jan. 6, 1927.

WEEKS, John Eliakim (R) June 14, 1853-Sept. 10, 1949; Jan. 6, 1927-Jan. 8, 1931; House 1931-33.

WILSON, Stanley Calef (R) Sept. 10, 1879-Oct. 5, 1967; Jan. 8, 1931-Jan. 10, 1935.

SMITH, Charles Manley (R) Aug. 3, 1868-Aug. 12, 1937; Jan. 10, 1935-Jan. 7, 1937.

AIKEN, George David (R) Aug. 20, 1892-Nov. 19, 1984; Jan. 7, 1937-Jan. 9, 1941; Senate 1941-75.

WILLS, William Henry (R) Oct. 26, 1882-March 6, 1946; Jan. 9, 1941-Jan. 4, 1945.

PROCTOR, Mortimer Robinson (son of Fletcher Dutton Proctor, grandson of Redfield Proctor Sr., nephew of Redfield Proctor Jr.) (R) May 30, 1889-April 28, 1968; Jan. 4, 1945-Jan. 9, 1947.

GIBSON, Ernest William (R) March 6, 1901-Nov. 4, 1969; Jan. 9, 1947-Jan. 16, 1950; Senate 1940-41.

ARTHUR, Harold John (R) Feb. 9, 1904-July 19, 1971; Jan. 16, 1950-Jan. 4, 1951.

EMERSON, Lee Earl (R) Dec. 19, 1898-May 21, 1976; Jan. 4, 1951-Jan. 6, 1955.

JOHNSON, Joseph Blaine (R) Aug. 29, 1893-Oct. ? 1986; Jan. 6, 1955-Jan. 8, 1959.

STAFFORD, Robert Theodore (R) Aug. 8, 1913-—; Ja 8, 1959-Jan. 5, 1961; House 1961-71; Senate 1971-·

KEYSER, Frank Ray Jr. (R) Aug. 17, 1927-—; Jan. 1961-Jan. 10, 1963.

HOFF, Philip Henderson (D) June 29, 1924-—; Jan. ▮ 1963-Jan. 9, 1969.

DAVIS, Deane Chandler (R) Nov. 7, 1900-—; Jan. 1969-Jan. 4, 1973.

SALMON, Thomas Paul (D) Aug. 19, 1932-—; Jan. 1973-Jan. 6, 1977.

SNELLING, Richard Arkwright (R) Feb. 18, 1927-Jan. 3, 1977-Jan. 10, 1985.

KUNIN, Madeleine May (D) Sept. 28, 1933-—; Jan. 1985-—.

Virginia

(Ratified the Constitution June 25, 1788

RANDOLPH, Beverley (−) 1754-Feb. 1797; Dec. 1788-Dec. 1, 1791.

LEE, Henry (F) Jan. 29, 1756-March 25, 1818; Dec. 1791-Dec. 1, 1794; Cont. Cong. 1785-88; House 179 1801.

BROOKE, Robert (DR) 1751-Feb. 27, 1799; Dec. 1794-Dec. 1, 1796.

WOOD, James (F) 1747-June 16, 1813; Dec. 1, 1796-D▮ 1, 1799.

MONROE, James (uncle of Rep. James Monroe) (D▮ April 28, 1758-July 4, 1831; Dec. 1, 1799-Dec. 1802, Jan. 16-April 3, 1811; Cont. Cong. 1783-▮ Senate 1790-94; Secy. of State 1811-17; Preside 1817-25.

PAGE, John (DR) April 17, 1744-Oct. 11, 1808; Dec. 1802-Dec. 1, 1805; House 1789-97.

CABELL, William Henry (DR) Dec. 16, 1772-Jan. ▮ 1853; Dec. 7, 1805-Dec. 1, 1808.

TYLER, John (father of President John Tyler, grand▮ ther of Rep. David Gardiner Tyler) (DR) Feb. ▮ 1747-Jan. 6, 1813; Dec. 1, 1808-Jan. 15, 1811.

MONROE, James (DR) Jan. 16-April 3, 1811 (for pre▮ ous term see above).

SMITH, George William (DR) 1762-Dec. 26, 1811; Ap▮ 6-Dec. 26, 1811.

RANDOLPH, Peyton (DR) 1779-Dec. 26, 1828; Dec. 27, 1811-Jan. 3, 1812.

BARBOUR, James (AD/SR) June 10, 1775-June 7, 1842; Jan. 3, 1812-Dec. 1, 1814; Senate 1815-25; Pres. pro tempore 1819; Secy. of War 1825-28.

NICHOLAS, Wilson Cary (DR) Jan. 31, 1761-Oct. 10, 1820; Dec. 1, 1814-Dec. 1, 1816; Senate 1799-1804; House 1807-09.

PRESTON, James Patton (brother-in-law of John Floyd, uncle of James McDowell and John Buchanan Floyd) (DR) June 21, 1774-May 4, 1853; Dec. 1, 1816-Dec. 1, 1819.

RANDOLPH, Thomas Mann (son-in-law of President Thomas Jefferson) (DR) Oct. 1, 1768-June 20, 1828; Dec. 1, 1819-Dec. 1, 1822; House 1803-07.

PLEASANTS, James Jr. (DR) Oct. 24, 1769-Nov. 9, 1836; Dec. 1, 1822-Dec. 10, 1825; House 1811-19; Senate 1819-22.

TYLER, John (son of John Tyler, father of Rep. David Gardiner Tyler) (W) March 29, 1790-Jan. 18, 1862; Dec. 10, 1825-March 4, 1827 (Democratic Republican); House 1817-21 (Democratic Republican); Senate 1827-36 (Democratic Republican); Pres. pro tempore 1835-36; Vice President 1841; President 1841-45.

GILES, William Branch (D) Aug. 12, 1762-Dec. 4, 1830; March 4, 1827-March 4, 1830; House 1790-98 (Anti Federalist), 1801-03; Senate 1804-15.

FLOYD, John (father of John Buchanan Floyd, uncle of James McDowell, brother-in-law of James Patton Preston) (D) April 24, 1783-Aug. 17, 1837; March 4, 1830-March 31, 1834; House 1817-29.

TAZEWELL, Littleton Waller (D) Dec. 17, 1774-May 6, 1860; March 31, 1834-April 30, 1836; House 1800-01; Senate 1824-32; Pres. pro tempore 1832.

ROBERTSON, Wyndham (brother of Thomas Bolling Robertson of La.) (SRD) Jan. 26, 1803-Feb. 11, 1888; April 30, 1836-March 31, 1837.

CAMPBELL, David (W) Aug. 2, 1779-March 19, 1859; March 31, 1837-March 31, 1840.

GILMER, Thomas Walker (D) April 6, 1802-Feb. 28, 1844; March 31, 1840-March 1, 1841 (Whig); House 1841-43 (Whig), 1843-44; Secy. of the Navy 1844.

PATTON, John Mercer (SRW) Aug. 10, 1797-Oct. 29, 1858; March 18-31, 1841; House 1830-38 (Democrat).

RUTHERFORD, John (brother-in-law of Edward Coles of Ill.) (SRW) Dec. 6, 1792-Aug. 3, 1866; March 31, 1841-March 31, 1842.

GREGORY, John Munford (SRW) July 8, 1804-April 9, 1884; March 31, 1842-Jan. 1, 1843.

McDOWELL, James (nephew of James Patton Preston and John Floyd, cousin of John Buchanan Floyd, father-in-law of Francis Thomas of Md.) (D) Oct. 13, 1796-Aug. 24, 1851; Jan. 1, 1843-Jan. 1, 1846; House 1846-51.

SMITH, William (Confed.D) Sept. 6, 1797-May 18, 1887; Jan. 1, 1846-Jan. 1, 1849 (Democrat), Jan. 1, 1864-April 1865; House 1841-43 (Democrat), 1853-61 (Democrat).

FLOYD, John Buchanan (son of John Floyd, nephew of James Patton Preston, cousin of James McDowell) (D) June 1, 1806-Aug. 26, 1863; Jan. 1, 1849-Jan. 16, 1852; Secy. of War 1857-60.

JOHNSON, Joseph (D) Dec. 19, 1785-Feb. 27, 1877; Jan. 16, 1852-Dec. 31, 1855; House 1823-27, 1833, 1835-41, 1845-47.

WISE, Henry Alexander (D) Dec. 3, 1806-Sept. 12, 1876; Jan. 1, 1856-Dec. 31, 1859; House 1833-44 (1833-37 Jackson Democrat, 1837-43 Whig, 1843-44 Tyler Democrat).

LETCHER, John (D) March 29, 1813-Jan. 26, 1884; Jan. 1, 1860-Dec. 31, 1863; House 1851-59.

SMITH, William (Confed.D) Jan. 1, 1864-April 1865 (for previous term see above).

PIERPOINT, Francis Harrison (U) Jan. 25, 1814-March 24, 1899; June 20, 1861-April 4, 1868 (1865-68 Provisional).

WELLS, Henry Horatio; Sept. 17, 1823-Feb. 13, 1890; (Provisional) April 4, 1868-Sept. 21, 1869.

WALKER, Gilbert Carlton (D) Aug. 1, 1833-May 11, 1885; (Provisional) Sept. 21, 1869-Jan. 1, 1870, Jan. 1, 1870-Jan. 1, 1874 (Conservative); House 1875-79 (1875-77 Conservative).

KEMPER, James Lawson (D) June 11, 1823-April 7,

HOLLIDAY, Frederick William Mackey (D) Feb. 22, 1828-May 29, 1899; Jan. 1, 1878-Jan. 1, 1882.

CAMERON, William Ewan (Read) Nov. 29, 1842-Jan. 26, 1927; Jan. 1, 1882-Jan. 1, 1886.

LEE, Fitzhugh (D) Nov. 19, 1835-April 28, 1905; Jan. 1, 1886-Jan. 1, 1890.

McKINNEY, Philip Watkins (D) May 1, 1832-March 1, 1899; Jan. 1, 1890-Jan. 1, 1894.

O'FERRALL, Charles Triplett (D) Oct. 21, 1840-Sept. 22, 1905; Jan. 1, 1894-Jan. 1, 1898; House 1884-93.

TYLER, James Hoge (D) Aug. 11, 1846-Jan. 3, 1925; Jan. 1, 1898-Jan. 1, 1902.

MONTAGUE, Andrew Jackson (D) Oct. 3, 1862-Jan. 24, 1937; Jan. 1, 1902-Feb. 1, 1906; House 1913-37.

SWANSON, Claude Augustus (D) March 31, 1862-July 7, 1939; Feb. 1, 1906-Feb. 1, 1910; House 1893-1906; Senate 1910-33; Secy. of the Navy 1933-39.

MANN, William Hodges (D) July 30, 1843-Dec. 12, 1927; Feb. 1, 1910-Feb. 1, 1914.

STUART, Henry Carter (D) Jan. 18, 1855-July 24, 1933; Feb. 1, 1914-Feb. 1, 1918.

DAVIS, Westmoreland (D) Aug. 21, 1859-Sept 7, 1942; Feb. 1, 1918-Feb. 1, 1922.

TRINKLE, Elbert Lee (D) March 12, 1876-Nov. 25, 1939; Feb. 1, 1922-Feb. 1, 1926.

BYRD, Harry Flood (D) June 10, 1887-Oct. 20, 1966; Feb. 1, 1926-Jan. 15, 1930; Senate 1933-65.

POLLARD, John Garland (D) Aug. 9, 1871-April 28, 1937; Jan. 15, 1930-Jan. 17, 1934.

PEERY, George Campbell (D) Oct. 28, 1873-Oct. 14, 1952; Jan. 17, 1934-Jan. 19, 1938; House 1923-29.

PRICE, James Hubert (D) Sept. 7, 1878-Nov. 22, 1943; Jan. 19, 1938-Jan. 21, 1942.

DARDEN, Colgate Whitehead Jr. (D) Feb. 11, 1897-June 9, 1981; Jan. 21, 1942-Jan. 16, 1946; House 1933-37, 1939-41.

TUCK, William Munford (D) Sept. 28, 1896-June 9, 1983; Jan. 16, 1946-Jan. 18, 1950; House 1953-69.

BATTLE, John Stewart (D) July 11, 1890-April 9, 1972; Jan. 18, 1950-Jan. 20, 1954.

STANLEY, Thomas Bahnson (D) July 16, 1890-July 10, 1970; Jan. 20, 1954-Jan. 11, 1958; House 1946-53.

ALMOND, James Lindsay Jr. (D) June 15, 1898- —; Jan. 11, 1958-Jan. 13, 1962; House 1946-48.

HARRISON, Albertis Sydney Jr. (D) Jan. 11, 1907- —; Jan. 13, 1962-Jan. 15, 1966.

GODWIN, Mills Edwin Jr. (R) Nov. 19, 1914- —; Jan. 16, 1966-Jan. 17, 1970 (Democrat), Jan. 12, 1974-Jan. 14, 1978.

HOLTON, Abner Linwood Jr. (R) Sept. 21, 1923- —; Jan. 17, 1970-Jan. 12, 1974.

GODWIN, Mills Edwin Jr. (R) Jan. 12, 1974-Jan. 14, 1978 (for previous term see above).

DALTON, John Nichols (R) July 11, 1931-July 30, 1986; Jan. 14, 1978-Jan. 16, 1982.

ROBB, Charles Spittal (D) June 26, 1939- —; Jan. 16, 1982-Jan. 18, 1986.

BALILES, Gerald L. (D) July 8, 1940- —; Jan. 18, 1986- —.

Washington

(Became a state Nov. 11, 1889)

FERRY, Elisha Peyre (R) Aug. 9, 1825-Oct. 14, 1895 Nov. 11, 1889-Jan. 9, 1893.

McGRAW, John Harte (R) Oct. 4, 1850-June 23, 1910 Jan. 9, 1893-Jan. 11, 1897.

ROGERS, John Rankin (PD) Sept. 4, 1838-Dec. 26 1901; Jan. 11, 1897-Dec. 26, 1901.

McBRIDE, Henry (R) Feb. 7, 1856-Oct. 6, 1937; Dec. 26 1901-Jan. 9, 1905.

MEAD, Albert Edward (R) Dec. 14, 1861-March 19 1913; Jan. 9, 1905-Jan. 27, 1909.

COSGROVE, Samuel Goodlove (R) April 10, 1847 March 28, 1909; Jan. 27-March 28, 1909.

HAY, Marion E. (R) Dec. 9, 1865-Nov. 21, 1933; March 29, 1909-Jan. 11, 1913.

LISTER, Ernest (D) June 15, 1870-June 14, 1919; Jan 11, 1913-June 14, 1919.

HART, Louis Folwell (R) Jan. 4, 1862-Dec. 5, 1929; Jun 14, 1919-Jan. 12, 1925.

HARTLEY, Roland Hill (son-in-law of David Martson Clough of Minn.) (R) June 26, 1864-Sept. 21, 1952 Jan. 12, 1925-Jan. 9, 1933.

MARTIN, Clarence Daniel (D) June 29, 1887-Aug. 11 1955; Jan. 9, 1933-Jan. 13, 1941.

LANGLIE, Arthur Bernard (R) July 25, 1900-July 24 1966; Jan. 13, 1941-Jan. 8, 1945, Jan. 10, 1949-Jan 14, 1957.

WALLGREN, Monrad Charles (D) April 17, 1891-Sept 18, 1961; Jan. 8, 1945-Jan. 10, 1949; House 1933-40 Senate 1940-45.

LANGLIE, Arthur Bernard (R) Jan. 10, 1949-Jan. 14 1957 (for previous term see above).

ROSELLINI, Albert Dean (D) Jan. 21, 1910- —; Jan. 14 1957-Jan. 11, 1965.

EVANS, Daniel Jackson (R) Oct. 16, 1925- —; Jan. 11 1965-Jan. 12, 1977; Senate 1983- —.

RAY, Dixy Lee (D) Sept. 3, 1914- —; Jan. 12, 1977-Jan 14, 1981.

SPELLMAN, John D. (R) Dec. 29, 1926- —; Jan. 14 1981-Jan. 16, 1985.

GARDNER, Booth (D) Aug. 21, 1936- —; Jan. 16, 1985 —.

West Virginia

Became a state June 19, 1863)

BOREMAN, Arthur Inghram (R) July 24, 1823-April 19, 1896; June 20, 1863-Feb. 26, 1869; Senate 1869-75.

FARNSWORTH, Daniel Duane Tompkins (R) Dec. 28, 1819-Dec. 5, 1892; Feb. 27-March 4, 1869.

STEVENSON, William Erskine (R) March 18, 1820-Nov. 29, 1883; March 4, 1869-March 4, 1871.

JACOB, John Jeremiah (D/I) Dec. 9, 1829-Nov. 24, 1893; March 4, 1871-March 4, 1877.

MATHEWS, Henry Mason (D) March 29, 1834-April 28, 1884; March 4, 1877-March 4, 1881.

JACKSON, Jacob Beeson (D) April 6, 1829-Dec. 11, 1893; March 4, 1881-March 4, 1885.

WILSON, Emanuel Willis (D) Aug. 11, 1844-May 28, 1909; March 4, 1885-Feb. 5, 1890.

FLEMING, Aretas Brooks (D) Oct. 15, 1839-Oct. 13, 1923; Feb. 5, 1890-March 4, 1893.

MacCORKLE, William Alexander (D) May 7, 1857-Sept. 24, 1930; March 4, 1893-March 4, 1897.

ATKINSON, George Wesley (R) June 29, 1845-April 4, 1925; March 4, 1897-March 4, 1901; House 1890-91.

WHITE, Albert Blakeslee (R) Sept. 22, 1856-July 3, 1941; March 4, 1901-March 4, 1905.

DAWSON, William Mercer Owens (R) May 21, 1853-March 12, 1916; March 4, 1905-March 4, 1909.

GLASSOCK, William Ellsworth (R) Dec. 13, 1862-April 12, 1925; March 4, 1909-March 4, 1913.

HATFIELD, Henry Drury (R) Sept. 15, 1875-Oct. 23, 1962; March 4, 1913-March 4, 1917; Senate 1929-35.

CORNWELL, John Jacob (D) July 11, 1867-Sept. 8, 1953; March 4, 1917-March 4, 1921.

MORGAN, Ephraim Franklin (R) Jan. 16, 1869-Jan. 15, 1950; March 4, 1921-March 4, 1925.

GORE, Howard Mason (R) Oct. 12, 1877-June 20, 1947; March 4, 1925-March 4, 1929; Secy. of Agriculture 1924-25.

CONLEY, William Gustavus (R) Jan. 8, 1866-Oct. 21, 1940; March 4, 1929-March 4, 1933.

KUMP, Herman Guy (D) Oct. 31, 1877-Feb. 14, 1962; March 4, 1933-Jan. 18, 1937.

HOLT, Homer Adams (D) March 1, 1898-Jan. 16, 1975; Jan. 18, 1937-Jan. 12, 1941.

NEELY, Matthew Mansfield (D) Nov. 9, 1874-Jan. 18, 1958; Jan. 13, 1941-Jan. 15, 1945; House 1913-21, 1945-47; Senate 1923-29, 1931-41, 1949-58.

MEADOWS, Clarence Watson (D) Feb. 11, 1904-Sept. 12, 1961; Jan. 15, 1945-Jan. 17, 1949.

PATTESON, Okey Leonidas (D) Sept. 14, 1898- —; Jan. 17, 1949-Jan. 19, 1953.

MARLAND, William Casey (D) March 26, 1918-Nov. 26, 1965; Jan. 19, 1953-Jan. 13, 1957.

UNDERWOOD, Cecil Harland (R) Nov. 5, 1922- —; Jan. 13, 1957-Jan. 16, 1961.

BARRON, William Wallace (D) Dec. 8, 1911- —; Jan. 16, 1961-Jan. 18, 1965.

SMITH, Hulett Carlson (D) Oct. 12, 1918- —; Jan. 18, 1965-Jan. 13, 1969.

MOORE, Arch Alfred Jr. (R) April 16, 1923- —; Jan. 13, 1969-Jan. 17, 1977, Jan. 14, 1985- —; House 1957-69.

ROCKEFELLER, John Davidson "Jay" IV (nephew of Vice President Nelson Aldrich Rockefeller and Winthrop Rockefeller of Ark., great-grandson of Sen. Nelson Wilmarth Aldrich, granduncle of Rep. Richard Steere Aldrich) (D) June 18, 1937- —; Jan. 17, 1977-Jan. 14, 1985; Senate 1985- —.

MOORE, Arch Alfred Jr. (R) Jan. 14, 1985- — (for previous term see above).

Wisconsin

(Became a state May 29, 1848)

DEWEY, Nelson (D) Dec. 19, 1813-July 21, 1889; June 7, 1848-Jan. 5, 1852.

FARWELL, Leonard James (W) Jan. 5, 1819-April 11, 1889; Jan. 5, 1852-Jan. 2, 1854.

BARSTOW, William Augustus (D) Sept. 13, 1813-Dec. 13, 1865; Jan. 2, 1854-March 21, 1856.

MacARTHUR, Arthur (D) Jan. 26, 1815-Aug. 26, 1896; March 21-25, 1856.

BASHFORD, Coles (R) Jan. 24, 1816-April 25, 1878; March 25, 1856-Jan. 4, 1858.

RANDALL, Alexander Williams (R) Oct. 31, 1819-July 26, 1872; Jan. 4, 1858-Jan. 6, 1862.

HARVEY, Louis Powell (R) July 22, 1820-April 19, 1862; Jan. 6-April 19, 1862.

SALOMON, Edward P. (R) Aug. 11, 1828-April 21, 1909; April 19, 1862-Jan. 4, 1864.

LEWIS, James Taylor (R) Oct. 30, 1819-Aug. 4, 1904; Jan. 4, 1864-Jan. 1, 1866.

FAIRCHILD, Lucius (R) Dec. 27, 1831-May 23, 1896; Jan. 1, 1866-Jan. 1, 1872.

WASHBURN, Cadwallader Colden (brother of Israel Washburn Jr. of Maine) (R) April 22, 1818-May 14, 1882; Jan. 1, 1872-Jan. 5, 1874; House 1867-71.

TAYLOR, William Robert (D) July 10, 1820-March 17, 1909; Jan. 5, 1874-Jan. 3, 1876.

LUDINGTON, Harrison (R) July 30, 1812-June 17, 1891; Jan. 3, 1876-Jan. 7, 1878.

SMITH, William E. (R) June 18, 1824-Feb. 13, 1883; Jan. 7, 1878-Jan. 2, 1882.

RUSK, Jeremiah McLain (R) June 17, 1830-Nov. 21, 1893; Jan. 2, 1882-Jan. 7, 1889; House 1871-77; Secy. of Agriculture 1889-93.

HOARD, William Dempster (R) Oct. 10, 1836-Nov. 22, 1918; Jan. 7, 1889-Jan. 5, 1891.

PECK, George Wilbur (D) Sept. 28, 1840-April 16, 1916; Jan. 5, 1891-Jan. 7, 1895.

UPHAM, William Henry (R) May 3, 1841-July 2, 1924; Jan. 7, 1895-Jan. 4, 1897.

SCOFIELD, Edward (R) March 28, 1842-Feb. 3, 1925; Jan. 4, 1897-Jan. 7, 1901.

LA FOLLETTE, Robert Marion (father of Philip Fox La Follette, below) (R) June 14, 1855-June 18, 1925; Jan. 7, 1901-Jan. 1, 1906; House 1885-91; Senate 1906-25.

DAVIDSON, James Ole (R) Feb. 10, 1854-Dec. 16, 1922; Jan. 1, 1906-Jan. 2, 1911.

McGOVERN, Francis Edward (R) Jan. 21, 1866-May 16, 1946; Jan. 2, 1911-Jan. 4, 1915.

PHILIPP, Emanuel Lorenz (R) March 25, 1861-June 15, 1925; Jan. 4, 1915-Jan. 3, 1921.

BLAINE, John James (R) May 4, 1875-April 16, 1934; Jan. 3, 1921-Jan. 3, 1927; Senate 1927-33.

ZIMMERMAN, Fred R. (R) Nov. 20, 1880-Dec. 14, 1954; Jan. 3, 1927-Jan. 7, 1929.

KOHLER, Walter Jodok Sr. (father of Walter Jodok Kohler Jr., below) (R) March 3, 1875-April 21, 1940; Jan. 7, 1929-Jan. 5, 1931.

LA FOLLETTE, Philip Fox (son of Robert Marion La Follette, above) (Prog.) May 8, 1897-Aug. 18, 1965; Jan. 5, 1931-Jan. 2, 1933 (Republican), Jan. 7, 1935-Jan. 2, 1939.

SCHMEDEMAN, Albert George (D) Nov. 25, 1864; Nov. 26, 1946; Jan. 2, 1933-Jan. 7, 1935.

LA FOLLETTE, Philip Fox (Prog.) Jan. 7, 1935-Jan. 1939 (for previous term see above).

HEIL, Julius Peter (R) July 24, 1876-Nov. 30, 1949; Jan. 2, 1939-Jan. 4, 1943.

GOODLAND, Walter Samuel (R) Dec. 22, 1862-March 12, 1947; Jan. 4, 1943-March 12, 1947.

RENNEBOHM, Oscar (R) May 25, 1889-Oct. 15, 196; March 12, 1947-Jan. 1, 1951.

KOHLER, Walter Jodok Jr. (son of Walter Jodok Kohler Sr., above) (R) April 4, 1904-March 21, 1976; Jan. 1, 1951-Jan. 7, 1957.

THOMSON, Vernon Wallace (R) Nov. 5, 1905- —; Jan. 7, 1957-Jan. 5, 1959; House 1961-74.

NELSON, Gaylord Anton (D) June 4, 1916- —; Jan. 1959-Jan. 7, 1963; Senate 1963-81.

REYNOLDS, John Whitcome (D) April 4, 1921- —; Jan. 7, 1963-Jan. 4, 1965.

KNOWLES, Warren Perley (R) Aug. 19, 1908- —; Jan. 1965-Jan. 4, 1971.

LUCEY, Patrick Joseph (D) March 21, 1918- —; Jan. 1971-July 7, 1977.

SCHREIBER, Martin James (D) April 8, 1939- —; July 7, 1977-Jan. 1, 1979.

DREYFUS, Lee Sherman (R) June 20, 1926- —; Jan. 1979-Jan. 3, 1983.

EARL, Anthony Scully (D) April 12, 1936- —; Jan. 1983-Jan. 5, 1987.

THOMPSON, Tommy George (R) Nov. 19, 1941- — Jan. 5, 1987- —.

Wyoming

(Became a state July 10, 1890)

WARREN, Francis Emroy (R) June 20, 1884-Nov. 2 1929; Sept. 11-Nov. 24, 1890; Senate 1890-93, 189 1929.

BARBER, Amos Walker (R) July 25, 1861-May 1 1915; Nov. 24, 1890-Jan. 2, 1893.

OSBORNE, John Eugene (D) June 19, 1858-April 2 1953; Jan. 2, 1893-Jan. 7, 1895; House 1897-99.

RICHARDS, William Alford (R) March 9, 1849-July 2 1912; Jan. 7, 1895-Jan. 2, 1899.

RICHARDS, DeForest (R) Aug. 6, 1846-April 28, 1903; Jan. 2, 1899-April 28, 1903.

CHATTERTON, Fenimore (R) July 21, 1860-May 9, 1958; April 28, 1903-Jan. 2, 1905.

BROOKS, Bryant Butler (R) Feb. 5, 1861-Dec. 7, 1944; Jan. 2, 1905-Jan. 2, 1911.

CAREY, Joseph Maull (father of Robert Davis Carey, below) (R) Jan. 19, 1845-Feb. 5, 1924; Jan. 2, 1911-Jan. 4, 1915; Senate 1890.

KENDRICK, John Benjamin (D) Sept. 6, 1857-Nov. 3, 1933; Jan. 4, 1915-Feb. 26, 1917; Senate 1917-33.

HOUX, Frank L. (D) Dec. 12, 1860-April 3, 1941; Feb. 26, 1917-Jan. 6, 1919.

CAREY, Robert Davis (son of Joseph Maull Carey, above) (R) Aug. 12, 1878-Jan. 17, 1937; Jan. 6, 1919-Jan. 1, 1923; Senate 1930-37.

ROSS, William Bradford (husband of Nellie Tayloe Ross, below) (D) Dec. 4, 1873-Oct. 2, 1924; Jan. 1, 1923-Oct. 2, 1924.

LUCAS, Franklin Earl (R) Aug. 4, 1876-Nov. 26, 1948; Oct. 2, 1924-Jan. 5, 1925.

ROSS, Nellie Tayloe (wife of William Bradford Ross, above) (D) Nov. 29, 1876-Dec. 19, 1977; Jan. 5, 1925-Jan. 3, 1927; Co-Chrmn. Dem. Nat. Comm. 1932.

EMERSON, Frank Collins (R) May 26, 1882-Feb. 18, 1931; Jan. 3, 1927-Feb. 18, 1931.

CLARK, Alonzo Monroe (R) Aug. 13, 1868-Oct. 12, 1952; Feb. 18, 1931-Jan. 2, 1933.

MILLER, Leslie Andrew (D) Jan. 29, 1886-Sept. 29, 1970; Jan. 2, 1933-Jan. 2, 1939.

SMITH, Nels Hanson (R) Aug. 27, 1884-July 5, 1976; Jan. 2, 1939-Jan. 4, 1943.

HUNT, Lester Calloway (D) July 8, 1892-June 19, 1954; Jan. 4, 1943-Jan. 3, 1949; Senate 1949-54.

CRANE, Arthur Griswold (R) Sept. 1, 1877-Aug. 12, 1955; Jan. 3, 1949-Jan. 1, 1951.

BARRETT, Frank Aloysius (R) Nov. 10, 1892-May 30, 1962; Jan. 1, 1951-Jan. 3, 1953; House 1942-50; Senate 1953-59.

ROGERS, Clifford Joy "Doc" (R) Dec. 20, 1897-May 18, 1962; Jan. 3, 1953-Jan. 3, 1955.

SIMPSON, Milward Lee (R) Nov. 12, 1897- −; Jan. 3, 1955-Jan. 5, 1959.

HICKEY, John Joseph (D) Aug. 22, 1911-Sept. 22, 1970; Jan. 5, 1959-Jan. 2, 1961; Senate 1961-62.

GAGE, Jack Robert (D) Jan. 13, 1899-March 14, 1970; Jan. 2, 1961-Jan. 6, 1963.

HANSEN, Clifford Peter (R) Oct. 16, 1912- −; Jan. 6, 1963-Jan. 2, 1967; Senate 1967-78.

HATHAWAY, Stanley Knapp (R) July 19, 1924- −; Jan. 2, 1967-Jan. 6, 1975; Secy. of the Interior 1975.

HERSCHLER, Edgar J. (D) Oct. 27, 1918- −; Jan. 6, 1975-Jan. 5, 1987.

SULLIVAN, Michael John (D) Sept. 22, 1939- −; Jan. 5, 1987- −.

State Sources for Governors

The following individual state archives, historical societies, libraries, and secretary of state offices provided information used to compile the governors' biographies. *(Other sources, p. 349)*

Ala.: State of Alabama, Department of Archives and History; **Alaska:** State Archives of Alaska; **Ariz.:** State of Arizona, Department of Library, Archives, and Public Records; **Ark.:** Arkansas State Library, Office of State Library Services; **Calif.:** California State Library; **Colo.:** State of Colorado, Division of Archives and Public Records; Colorado Historical Society; **Del.:** State of Delaware, Bureau of Archives and Records Management; **Fla.:** Historic Tallahassee Preservation Board, Florida; **Ga.:** State of Georgia, Department of Archives and History; **Hawaii:** Office of Janice C. Lipsen, Washington representative, State of Hawaii; **Idaho:** Idaho State Historical Society; **Ind.:** Indiana Historical Bureau; **Iowa:** Iowa State Historical Department, Division of Historical Museums and Archives; **Kan.:** Kansas State Historical Society; **Ky.:** Kentucky Historical Society; **La.:** Louisiana State Library; **Maine:** Maine State Archives; **Md.:** Maryland State Law Library; Maryland State Archives; **Mass.:** Commonwealth of Massachusetts State Library, George Fingold Library; **Mich.:** Library of Michigan; **Minn.:** Minnesota Historical Society; **Mo.:** State of Missouri, Office of the Secretary of State; **Mont.:** Montana Historical Society Library; **Neb.:** Nebraska Historical Society; **Nev.:** Nevada State Library and Archives, Division of Archives and Records; **N.J.:** State of New Jersey, Division of Archives and Records Management; **N.M.:** State of New Mexico, State Records Center and Archives; **N.Y.:** New York State Library; **N.C.:** North Carolina Department of Cultural Resources; **N.D.:** State Historical Society of North Dakota; **Ohio:** Ohio Historical Society; **Okla.:** Oklahoma Historical Society, Library Resources Division; **Ore.:** Oregon Historical Society; **Pa.:** Commonwealth of Pennsylvania Historical and Museum Commission; **R.I.:** Office of the Secretary of State, Rhode Island State Archives; **S.D.:** South Dakota Historical Society; **Tenn.:** Tennessee State Library and Archives; **Texas:** Texas Historical Commission; **Utah:** Utah State Historical Society; **Vt.:** State of Vermont, Office of the Secretary of State; **Va.:** Commonwealth of Virginia State Library; **W.Va.:** West Virginia Department of Culture and History; **Wis.:** The State Historical Society of Wisconsin; **Wyo.:** Wyoming State Archives, Museums, and Historical Department.

Index to Governors

411

BAXTER, Percival Proctor (Maine) - 370
BEARDSLEY, William S. (Iowa) - 365
BEASLEY, Jere Locke (Ala.) - 350
BEAUVAIS, Armand (La.) - 368
BEAVER, James Addams (Pa.) - 394
BEBB, William (Ohio) - 391
BECKHAM, John Crepps Wickliffe (Ky.) - 367
BEDFORD, Gunning Sr. (Del.) - 356
BEDLE, Joseph Dorsett (N.J.) - 384
BEECKMAN, Robert Livingston (R.I.) - 396
BEGOLE, Josiah William (Mich.) - 375
BELL, Charles Henry (N.H.) - 382
BELL, Charles James (Vt.) - 404
BELL, Francis Jardine (Nev.) - 381
BELL, John (N.H.) - 382
BELL, John Cromwell Jr. (Pa.) - 394
BELL, Peter Hansborough (Texas) - 401
BELL, Samuel (N.H.) - 382
BELLMON, Henry Louis (Okla.) - 392
BENNETT, Caleb Prew (Del.) - 357
BENNETT, Robert Frederick (Kan.) - 366
BENNETT, Thomas (S.C.) - 397
BENSON, Elmer Austin (Minn.) - 375
BENSON, Frank Williamson (Ore.) - 393
BERRY, James Henderson (Ark.) - 352
BERRY, Nathaniel Springer (N.H.) - 382
BERRY, Thomas Matthew (S.D.) - 399
BEVERIDGE, John Lourie (Ill.) - 362
BIBB, Thomas (Ala.) - 349
BIBB, William Wyatt (Ala.) - 349
BICKETT, Thomas Walter (N.C.) - 389
BIGELOW, Hobart B. (Conn.) - 355
BIGGER, Samuel (Ind.) - 363
BIGGS, Benjamin Thomas (Del.) - 357
BIGLER, John (Calif.) - 353
BIGLER, William (Pa.) - 393
BILBO, Theodore Gilmore (Miss.) - 377
BILLINGS, Franklin Swift (Vt.) - 403
BINGHAM, Hiram (Conn.) - 356
BINGHAM, Kinsley Scott (Mich.) - 375
BISHOP, Richard Moore (Ohio) - 391
BISSELL, Clark (Conn.) - 355
BISSELL, William Harrison (Ill.) - 362
BLACK, Frank Swett (N.Y.) - 387
BLACK, James Dixon (Ky.) - 367
BLACKBURN, Luke Pryor (Ky.) - 367
BLACKWOOD, Ibra Charles (S.C.) - 398
BLAINE, John James (Wis.) - 408
BLAIR, Austin (Mich.) - 375
BLAIR, James Thomas Jr. (Mo.) - 379
BLANCHARD, James Johnston (Mich.) - 375
BLANCHARD, Newton Crain (La.) - 368
BLANTON, Leonard Ray (Tenn.) - 401
BLASDEL, Henry Goode (Nev.) - 380
BLEASE, Coleman Livingston (S.C.) - 398
BLISS, Aaron Thomas (Mich.) - 375
BLOOD, Henry Hooper (Utah) - 402
BLOOD, Robert Oscar (N.H.) - 383
BLOOMFIELD, Joseph (N.J.) - 384
BLOUNT, William (Tenn.) - 399
BLOXHAM, William Dunnington (Fla.) - 358
BLUE, Robert Donald (Iowa) - 365
BODWELL, Joseph Robinson (Maine) - 370
BOE, Nils Andreas (S.D.) - 399
BOGGS, James Caleb (Del.) - 358

BOGGS, Lilburn W. (Mo.) - 378
BOIES, Horace (Iowa) - 364
BOLACK, Thomas Felix (N.M.) - 386
BOLIN, Wesley H. (Ariz.) - 351
BOND, Christopher S. "Kit" (Mo.) - 379
BOND, Shadrack (Ill.) - 362
BONHAM, Milledge Luke (S.C.) - 397
BONNER, John Woodrow (Mont.) - 379
BOON, Ratliff (Ind.) - 363
BOOTH, Newton (Calif.) - 353
BOREMAN, Arthur Inghram (W.Va.) - 407
BOREN, David Lyle (Okla.) - 392
BOTTOLFSEN, Clarence Alfred (Idaho) - 361
BOUCK, William C. (N.Y.) - 386
BOURN, Augustus Osborn (R.I.) - 395
BOUTWELL, George Sewall (Mass.) - 373
BOWEN, Otis Ray (Ind.) - 364
BOWERMAN, Jay (Ore.) - 393
BOWIE, Oden (Md.) - 372
BOWIE, Robert (Md.) - 371
BOWLES, Chester Bliss (Conn.) - 356
BOYD, James E. (Neb.) - 380
BOYLE, Emmet Derby (Nev.) - 381
BOYNTON, James Stoddard (Ga.) - 360
BRACKETT, John Quincy Adams (Mass.) - 373
BRADFORD, Augustus Williamson (Md.) - 372
BRADFORD, Robert Fiske (Mass.) - 374
BRADLEY, Lewis Rice (Nev.) - 381
BRADLEY, William O'Connell (Ky.) - 367
BRADY, James Henry (Idaho) - 361
BRAGG, Thomas (N.C.) - 388
BRAMLETTE, Thomas E. (Ky.) - 366
BRANCH, Emmett Forest (Ind.) - 363
BRANCH, John (N.C.) - 388
BRANDON, Gerard Chittoque (Miss.) - 376
BRANDON, William Woodward (Ala.) - 350
BRANIGIN, Roger Douglas (Ind.) - 364
BRANN, Louis Jefferson (Maine) - 370
BRANSTAD, Terry E. (Iowa) - 365
BREATHITT, Edward Thompson (Ky.) - 367
BREATHITT, John (Ky.) - 366
BRENNAN, Joseph E. (Maine) - 371
BREWER, Albert Preston (Ala.) - 350
BREWER, Earl LeRoy (Miss.) - 377
BREWSTER, Ralph Owen (Maine) - 370
BRICE, James (Md.) - 371
BRICKER, John William (Ohio) - 391
BRIDGES, Henry Styles (N.H.) - 383
BRIGGS, Ansel (Iowa) - 364
BRIGGS, Frank Arlington (N.D.) - 389
BRIGGS, George Nixon (Mass.) - 373
BRIGHAM, Paul (Vt.) - 402
BRISCOE, Dolph Jr. (Texas) - 401
BROGDEN, Curtis Hooks (N.C.) - 389
BROOKE, Robert (Va.) - 404
BROOKS, Bryant Butler (Wyo.) - 409
BROOKS, John (Mass.) - 373
BROOKS, Ralph Gilmour (Neb.) - 380
BROOME, James E. (Fla.) - 358
BROUGH, Charles Hillman (Ark.) - 352
BROUGH, John (Ohio) - 391
BROUGHTON, Joseph Melville (N.C.) - 389
BROWARD, Napoleon Bonaparte (Fla.) - 358
BROWN, Aaron Venable (Tenn.) - 400
BROWN, Albert Gallatin (Miss.) - 377

FENNER, Arthur (R.I.) - 394
FENNER, James (R.I.) - 394, 395
FENTON, Reuben Eaton (N.Y.) - 387
FERGUSON, James Edward "Pa" (Texas) - 401
FERGUSON, Miriam Amanda "Ma" (Texas) - 401
FERNALD, Bert Manfred (Maine) - 370
FERRIS, Woodbridge Nathan (Mich.) - 375
FERRY, Elisha Peyre (Wash.) - 406
FIELDER, James Fairman (N.J.) - 385
FIELDS, William Jason (Ky.) - 367
FIFER, Joseph Wilson (Ill.) - 362
FINCH, Charles Clifton (Miss.) - 378
FINDLAY, William (Pa.) - 393
FINE, John Sydney (Pa.) - 394
FISH, Hamilton (N.Y.) - 386
FISHBACK, William Meade (Ark.) - 352
FISHER, John Stuchell (Pa.) - 394
FITZGERALD, Frank Dwight (Mich.) - 375
FITZPATRICK, Benjamin (Ala.) - 349
FLANAGIN, Harris (Ark.) - 351
FLANDERS, Benjamin Franklin (La.) - 368
FLEMING, Aretas Brooks (W.Va.) - 407
FLEMING, Francis Philip (Fla.) - 358
FLETCHER, Allen Miller (Vt.) - 404
FLETCHER, Ryland (Vt.) - 403
FLETCHER, Thomas (Ark.) - 351
FLETCHER, Thomas Clement (Mo.) - 378
FLOWER, Roswell Pettibone (N.Y.) - 387
FLOYD, Charles Miller (N.H.) - 383
FLOYD, John (Va.) - 405
FLOYD, John Buchanan (Va.) - 405
FLYNN, William Smith (R.I.) - 396
FOLK, Joseph Wingate (Mo.) - 379
FOLSOM, James Elisha (Ala.) - 350
FOOTE, Henry Stuart (Miss.) - 377
FOOTE, Samuel Augustus (Conn.) - 355
FORAKER, Joseph Benson (Ohio) - 391
FORD, Samuel Clarence (Mont.) - 379
FORD, Seabury (Ohio) - 391
FORD, Thomas (Ill.) - 362
FORD, Wendell Hampton (Ky.) - 367
FORSYTH, John (Ga.) - 359
FORT, George Franklin (N.J.) - 384
FORT, John Franklin (N.J.) - 385
FOSS, Eugene Noble (Mass.) - 374
FOSS, Joseph Jacob (S.D.) - 399
FOSTER, Charles (Ohio) - 391
FOSTER, Murphy James (La.) - 368
FOWLE, Daniel Gould (N.C.) - 389
FRANCIS, David Rowland (Mo.) - 379
FRANCIS, John Brown (R.I.) - 395
FRANKLIN, Jesse (N.C.) - 388
FRAZIER, James Beriah (Tenn.) - 400
FRAZIER, Lynn Joseph (N.D.) - 390
FREEMAN, Orville Lothrop (Minn.) - 376
FRENCH, Augustus C. (Ill.) - 362
FULLER, Alvan Tufts (Mass.) - 374
FULLER, Levi Knight (Vt.) - 403
FULTON, Robert David (Iowa) - 365
FUQUA, Henry Luce (La.) - 368
FURCOLO, Foster John (Mass.) - 374
FURNAS, Robert Wilkinson (Neb.) - 380
FUTRELL, Junius Marion (Ark.) - 352

GAGE, Henry Tifft (Calif.) - 353

GAGE, Jack Robert (Wyo.) - 409
GALLEN, Hugh J. (N.H.) - 383
GALUSHA, Jonas (Vt.) - 402
GAMBLE, Hamilton Rowan (Mo.) - 378
GARBER, Silas (Neb.) - 380
GARCELON, Alonzo (Maine) - 370
GARDINER, William Tudor (Maine) - 370
GARDNER, Booth (Wash.) - 406
GARDNER, Frederick D. (Mo.) - 379
GARDNER, Henry Joseph (Mass.) - 373
GARDNER, Oliver Max (N.C.) - 389
GARDNER, William Michael (N.H.) - 383
GARLAND, Augustus Hill (Ark.) - 352
GARRAHY, John Joseph (R.I.) - 396
GARRARD, James (Ky.) - 366
GARST, Warren (Iowa) - 364
GARVEY, Daniel E. (Ariz.) - 351
GARVIN, Lucius Fayette Clark (R.I.) - 395
GARY, Raymond Dancel (Okla.) - 392
GASTON, William (Mass.) - 373
GATES, Charles Winslow (Vt.) - 404
GATES, Ralph Fesler (Ind.) - 364
GAYLE, John (Ala.) - 349
GEAR, John Henry (Iowa) - 364
GEARY, John White (Pa.) - 394
GEDDES, John (S.C.) - 397
GEER, Theodore Thurston (Ore.) - 393
GERRY, Elbridge (Mass.) - 373
GIBBS, Addison Crandall (Ore.) - 392
GIBBS, William Channing (R.I.) - 395
GIBSON, Ernest William (Vt.) - 404
GILCHRIST, Albert Waller (Fla.) - 358
GILES, William Branch (Va.) - 405
GILL, Moses (Mass.) - 372
GILLETT, James Norris (Calif.) - 353
GILLIGAN, John Joyce (Ohio) - 392
GILMAN, John Taylor (N.H.) - 381
GILMER, George Rockingham (Ga.) - 359
GILMER, Thomas Walker (Va.) - 405
GILMORE, Joseph Albree (N.H.) - 382
GIST, William Henry (S.C.) - 397
GLASSOCK, William Ellsworth (W.Va.) - 407
GLENN, Robert Brodnax (N.C.) - 389
GLICK, George Washington (Kan.) - 365
GLYNN, Martin Henry (N.Y.) - 387
GODDARD, Samuel Pearson Jr. (Ariz.) - 351
GODWIN, Mills Edwin Jr. (Va.) - 406
GOEBEL, William (Ky.) - 367
GOLDSBOROUGH, Charles (Md.) - 371
GOLDSBOROUGH, Phillips Lee (Md.) - 372
GOLDSCHMIDT, Neil (Ore.) - 393
GOODELL, David Harvey (N.H.) - 382
GOODING, Frank Robert (Idaho) - 361
GOODLAND, Walter Samuel (Wis.) - 408
GOODRICH, James Putnam (Ind.) - 363
GOODWIN, Ichabod (N.H.) - 382
GORDON, James Wright (Mich.) - 374
GORDON, John Brown (Ga.) - 360
GORE, Christopher (Mass.) - 373
GORE, Howard Mason (W.Va.) - 407
GOSSETT, Charles Clinton (Idaho) - 361
GRAHAM, Daniel Robert "Bob" (Fla.) - 359
GRAHAM, Horace French (Vt.) - 404
GRAHAM, William Alexander (N.C.) - 388
GRANT, James Benton (Colo.) - 354

HENDRICKS, Thomas Andrews (Ind.) - 363
HENDRICKS, William (Ind.) - 363
HENRY, John (Md.) - 371
HERBERT, Thomas James (Ohio) - 392
HERREID, Charles Nelson (S.D.) - 399
HERRICK, Myron Timothy (Ohio) - 391
HERRING, Clyde LaVerne (Iowa) - 364
HERSCHLER, Edgar J. (Wyo.) - 409
HERSETH, Ralph E. (S.D.) - 399
HERTER, Christian Archibald (Mass.) - 374
HEYWARD, Duncan Clinch (S.C.) - 398
HICKEL, Walter Joseph (Alaska) - 350
HICKENLOOPER, Bourke Blakemore (Iowa) - 365
HICKEY, John Joseph (Wyo.) - 409
HICKS, Thomas Holliday (Md.) - 373
HIESTER, Joseph (Pa.) - 393
HIGGINS, Frank Wayland (N.Y.) - 387
HIGGINS, James Henry (R.I.) - 396
HILDRETH, Horace Augustus (Maine) - 370
HILL, David Bennett (N.Y.) - 387
HILL, Isaac (N.H.) - 382
HILL, John Fremont (Maine) - 370
HINKLE, James Fielding (N.M.) - 385
HOADLY, George (Ohio) - 391
HOARD, William Dempster (Wis.) - 408
HOBBY, William Pettus (Texas) - 401
HOCH, Edward Wallis (Kan.) - 365
HOCKENHULL, Andrew W. (N.M.) - 385
HODGES, George Hartshorn (Kan.) - 365
HODGES, Luther Hartwell (N.C.) - 389
HOEGH, Leo Arthur (Iowa) - 365
HOEY, Clyde Roark (N.C.) - 389
HOFF, Philip Henderson (Vt.) - 404
HOFFMAN, Harold Giles (N.J.) - 385
HOFFMAN, John Thompson (N.Y.) - 387
HOGG, James Stephen (Texas) - 401
HOLBROOK, Frederick (Vt.) - 403
HOLCOMB, Marcus Hensey (Conn.) - 356
HOLCOMB, Silas Alexander (Neb.) - 380
HOLDEN, William Woods (N.C.) - 388
HOLLAND, Spessard Lindsey (Fla.) - 358
HOLLEY, Alexander Hamilton (Conn.) - 355
HOLLIDAY, Frederick William Mackey (Va.) - 405
HOLLINGS, Ernest Frederick "Fritz" (S.C.) - 398
HOLLOWAY, William Judson (Okla.) - 392
HOLMES, David (Miss.) - 376
HOLMES, Gabriel (N.C.) - 388
HOLMES, Robert Denison (Ore.) - 393
HOLSHOUSER, James Eubert Jr. (N.C.) - 389
HOLT, Homer Adams (W.Va.) - 407
HOLT, Thomas Michael (N.C.) - 389
HOLT, William Elmer (Mont.) - 379
HOLTON, Abner Linwood Jr. (Va.) - 406
HOOPER, Ben Walker (Tenn.) - 400
HOPPIN, William Warner (R.I.) - 395
HORNER, Henry (Ill.) - 362
HORTON, Henry Hollis (Tenn.) - 400
HOUSTON, George Smith (Ala.) - 350
HOUSTON, Samuel (Tenn.) - 399
HOUSTON, Samuel (Texas) - 401
HOUX, Frank L. (Wyo.) - 409
HOVEY, Alvin Peterson (Ind.) - 363
HOWARD, George (Md.) - 371
HOWARD, Henry (R.I.) - 395
HOWARD, John Eager (Md.) - 371

HOWELL, Richard (N.J.) - 384
HOYT, Henry Martyn (Pa.) - 394
HUBBARD, Henry (N.H.) - 382
HUBBARD, John (Maine) - 369
HUBBARD, Lucius Frederick (Minn.) - 376
HUBBARD, Richard Bennett (Texas) - 401
HUBBARD, Richard Dudley (Conn.) - 355
HUGHES, Charles Evans (N.Y.) - 387
HUGHES, Harold Everett (Iowa) - 365
HUGHES, Harold Joseph (N.J.) - 385
HUGHES, Harry R. (Md.) - 372
HUGHES, Simon P. (Ark.) - 352
HUMPHREY, Lyman Underwood (Kan.) - 365
HUMPHREYS, Benjamin Grubb (Miss.) - 377
HUNN, John (Del.) - 357
HUNT, Frank Williams (Idaho) - 361
HUNT, George Wylie Paul (Ariz.) - 351
HUNT, Harold Guy (Ala.) - 350
HUNT, James Baxter Jr. (N.C.) - 389
HUNT, Lester Calloway (Wyo.) - 409
HUNT, Washington (N.Y.) - 387
HUNTINGTON, Samuel (Conn.) - 355
HUNTINGTON, Samuel H. (Ohio) - 390
HUNTON, Jonathan Glidden (Maine) - 369
HURLEY, Charles Francis (Mass.) - 374
HURLEY, Robert Augustine (Conn.) - 356
HUXMAN, Walter Augustus (Kan.) - 365
HYDE, Arthur Mastick (Mo.) - 379

INGERSOLL, Charles Roberts (Conn.) - 355
IREDELL, James Jr. (N.C.) - 388
IRELAND, John (Texas) - 401
IRWIN, Jared (Ga.) - 359
IRWIN, William (Calif.) - 353

JACKSON, Charles (R.I.) - 395
JACKSON, Claiborne Fox (Mo.) - 378
JACKSON, Edward L. (Ind.) - 363
JACKSON, Elihu Emory (Md.) - 372
JACKSON, Frank Darr (Iowa) - 364
JACKSON, Hancock (Mo.) - 378
JACKSON, Jacob Beeson (W.Va.) - 407
JACKSON, James (Ga.) - 359
JACOB, John Jeremiah (W.Va.) - 407
JAMES, Arthur Horace (Pa.) - 394
JAMES, Forrest Hood "Fob" Jr. (Ala.) - 350
JAMES, William Hartford (Neb.) - 380
JANKLOW, William John (S.D.) - 399
JARVIS, Thomas Jordan (N.C.) - 389
JAY, John (N.Y.) - 386
JEFFRIES, Richard Manning (S.C.) - 398
JELKS, William Dorsey (Ala.) - 350
JENISON, Silas Hemenway (Vt.) - 403
JENKINS, Charles Jones (Ga.) - 360
JENNINGS, Jonathan (Ind.) - 363
JENNINGS, William Sherman (Fla.) - 358
JENSEN, Leslie (S.D.) - 399
JEROME, David Howell (Mich.) - 375
JESTER, Beauford Halbert (Texas) - 402
JETER, Thomas Bothwell (S.C.) - 397
JEWELL, Marshall (Conn.) - 355
JOHNS, Charley Eugene (Fla.) - 359
JOHNSON James Neely (Calif.) - 353
JOHNSON, Andrew (Tenn.) - 400
JOHNSON, David (S.C.) - 397

Appendix

Presidents and Vice Presidents of the United States

President and Political Party	Born	Died	Age at inguration	Native of—	Elected from—	Term of Service	Vice President
George Washington (F)	1732	1799	57	Va.	Va.	April 30, 1789-March 4, 1793	John Adams
George Washington (F)			61			March 4, 1793-March 4, 1797	John Adams
John Adams (F)	1735	1826	61	Mass.	Mass.	March 4, 1797-March 4, 1801	Thomas Jefferson
Thomas Jefferson (DR)	1743	1826	57	Va.	Va.	March 4, 1801-March 4, 1805	Aaron Burr
Thomas Jefferson (DR)			61			March 4, 1805-March 4, 1809	George Clinton
James Madison (DR)	1751	1836	57	Va.	Va.	March 4, 1809-March 4, 1813	George Clinton
James Madison (DR)			61			March 4, 1813-March 4, 1817	Elbridge Gerry
James Monroe (DR)	1758	1831	58	Va.	Va.	March 4, 1817-March 4, 1821	Daniel D. Tompkins
James Monroe (DR)			62			March 4, 1821-March 4, 1825	Daniel D. Tompkins
John Q. Adams (DR)	1767	1848	57	Mass.	Mass.	March 4, 1825-March 4, 1829	John C. Calhoun
Andrew Jackson (D)	1767	1845	61	S.C.	Tenn.	March 4, 1829-March 4, 1833	John C. Calhoun
Andrew Jackson (D)			65			March 4, 1833-March 4, 1837	Martin Van Buren
Martin Van Buren (D)	1782	1862	54	N.Y.	N.Y.	March 4, 1837-March 4, 1841	Richard M. Johnson
W. H. Harrison (W)	1773	1841	68	Va.	Ohio	March 4, 1841-April 4, 1841	John Tyler
John Tyler (W)	1790	1862	51	Va.	Va.	April 6, 1841-March 4, 1845	
James K. Polk (D)	1795	1849	49	N.C.	Tenn.	March 4, 1845-March 4, 1849	George M. Dallas
Zachary Taylor (W)	1784	1850	64	Va.	La.	March 4, 1849-July 9, 1850	Millard Fillmore
Millard Fillmore (W)	1800	1874	50	N.Y.	N.Y.	July 10, 1850-March 4, 1853	
Franklin Pierce (D)	1804	1869	48	N.H.	N.H.	March 4, 1853-March 4, 1857	William R. King
James Buchanan (D)	1791	1868	65	Pa.	Pa.	March 4, 1857-March 4, 1861	John C. Breckinridge
Abraham Lincoln (R)	1809	1865	52	Ky.	Ill.	March 4, 1861-March 4, 1865	Hannibal Hamlin
Abraham Lincoln (R)			56			March 4, 1865-April 15, 1865	Andrew Johnson
Andrew Johnson (R)	1808	1875	56	N.C.	Tenn.	April 15, 1865-March 4, 1869	
Ulysses S. Grant (R)	1822	1885	46	Ohio	Ill.	March 4, 1869-March 4, 1873	Schuyler Colfax
Ulysses S. Grant (R)			50			March 4, 1873-March 4, 1877	Henry Wilson
Rutherford B. Hayes (R)	1822	1893	54	Ohio	Ohio	March 4, 1877-March 4, 1881	William A. Wheeler
James A. Garfield (R)	1831	1881	49	Ohio	Ohio	March 4, 1881-Sept. 19, 1881	Chester A. Arthur
Chester A. Arthur (R)	1830	1886	50	Vt.	N.Y.	Sept. 20, 1881-March 4, 1885	

President	Born	Died	Age	Birthplace	Home State	Term	Vice President
Grover Cleveland (D)	1837	1908	47	N.J.	N.Y.	March 4, 1885-March 4, 1889	Thomas A. Hendricks
Benjamin Harrison (R)	1833	1901	55	Ohio	Ind.	March 4, 1889-March 4, 1893	Levi P. Morton
Grover Cleveland (D)			55			March 4, 1893-March 4, 1897	Adlai E. Stevenson
William McKinley (R)	1843	1901	54	Ohio	Ohio	March 4, 1897-March 4, 1901	Garret A. Hobart
William McKinley (R)			58		Ohio	March 4, 1901-Sept. 14, 1901	Theodore Roosevelt
Theodore Roosevelt (R)	1858	1919	42	N.Y.	N.Y.	Sept. 14, 1901-March 4, 1905	
Theodore Roosevelt (R)			46			March 4, 1905-March 4, 1909	Charles W. Fairbanks
William H. Taft (R)	1857	1930	51	Ohio	Ohio	March 4, 1909-March 4, 1913	James S. Sherman
Woodrow Wilson (D)	1856	1924	56	Va.	N.J.	March 4, 1913-March 4, 1917	Thomas R. Marshall
Woodrow Wilson (D)			60			March 4, 1917-March 4, 1921	Thomas R. Marshall
Warren G. Harding (R)	1865	1923	55	Ohio	Ohio	March 4, 1921-Aug. 2, 1923	Calvin Coolidge
Calvin Coolidge (R)	1872	1933	51	Vt.	Mass.	Aug. 3, 1923-March 4, 1925	
Calvin Coolidge (R)			52			March 4, 1925-March 4, 1929	Charles G. Dawes
Herbert Hoover (R)	1874	1964	54	Iowa	Calif.	March 4, 1929-March 4, 1933	Charles Curtis
Franklin D. Roosevelt (D)	1882	1945	51	N.Y.	N.Y.	March 4, 1933-Jan. 20, 1937	John N. Garner
Franklin D. Roosevelt (D)			55			Jan. 20, 1937-Jan. 20, 1941	John N. Garner
Franklin D. Roosevelt (D)			59			Jan. 20, 1941-Jan. 20, 1945	Henry A. Wallace
Franklin D. Roosevelt (D)			63			Jan. 20, 1945-April 12, 1945	Harry S Truman
Harry S Truman (D)	1884	1972	60	Mo.	Mo.	April 12, 1945-Jan. 20, 1949	
Harry S Truman (D)			64			Jan. 20, 1949-Jan. 20, 1953	Alben W. Barkley
Dwight D. Eisenhower (R)	1890	1969	62	Texas	N.Y.	Jan. 20, 1953-Jan. 20, 1957	Richard Nixon
Dwight D. Eisenhower (R)			66		Pa.	Jan. 20, 1957-Jan. 20, 1961	Richard Nixon
John F. Kennedy (D)	1917	1963	43	Mass.	Mass.	Jan. 20, 1961-Nov. 22, 1963	Lyndon B. Johnson
Lyndon B. Johnson (D)	1908	1973	55	Texas	Texas	Nov. 22, 1963-Jan. 20, 1965	
Lyndon B. Johnson (D)			56			Jan. 20, 1965-Jan. 20, 1969	Hubert H. Humphrey
Richard Nixon (R)	1913		56	Calif.	N.Y.	Jan. 20, 1969-Jan. 20, 1973	Spiro T. Agnew
Richard Nixon (R)			60		Calif.	Jan. 20, 1973-Aug. 9, 1974	Spiro T. Agnew / Gerald R. Ford
Gerald R. Ford (R)	1913		61	Neb.	Mich.	Aug. 9, 1974-Jan. 20, 1977	Nelson A. Rockefeller
Jimmy Carter (D)	1924		52	Ga.	Ga.	Jan. 20, 1977-Jan. 20, 1981	Walter F. Mondale
Ronald Reagan (R)	1911		69	Ill.	Calif.	Jan. 20, 1981-Jan. 20, 1985	George Bush
Ronald Reagan (R)			73			Jan. 20, 1985-	George Bush

Abbreviations: (D) Democrat, (DR) Democratic Republican, (F) Federalist, (R) Republican, (W) Whig

Political Party Affiliations in Congress and the Presidency

Year	Congress	HOUSE Majority party	HOUSE Principal minority party	HOUSE Other (except vacancies)	SENATE Majority party	SENATE Principal minority party	SENATE Other (except vacancies)	President
1987-1989	100th	D-258	R-177	-	D-55	R-45	-	R (Reagan)
1985-1987	99th	D-252	R-182	-	R-53	D-47	-	R (Reagan)
1983-1985	98th	D-268	R-166	-	R-55	D-45	-	R (Reagan)
1981-1983	97th	D-243	R-192	-	R-53	D-46	1	R (Reagan)
1979-1981	96th	D-276	R-157	-	D-58	R-41	1	D (Carter)
1977-1979	95th	D-292	R-143	-	D-61	R-38	1	D (Carter)
1975-1977	94th	D-291	R-144	-	D-60	R-37	2	R (Ford)
1973-1975	93d	D-239	R-192	1	D-56	R-42	2	R (Nixon-Ford)
1971-1973	92d	D-254	R-180	-	D-54	R-44	2	R (Nixon)
1969-1971	91st	D-243	R-192	-	D-57	R-43	-	R (Nixon)
1967-1969	90th	D-247	R-187	-	D-64	R-36	-	D (L. Johnson)
1965-1967	89th	D-295	R-140	-	D-68	R-32	-	D (L. Johnson)
1963-1965	88th	D-258	R-177	-	D-67	R-33	-	D (L. Johnson)
								D (Kennedy)
1961-1963	87th	D-263	R-174	-	D-65	R-35	-	D (Kennedy)
1959-1961	86th	D-283	R-153	-	D-64	R-34	-	R (Eisenhower)
1957-1959	85th	D-233	R-200	-	D-49	R-47	-	R (Eisenhower)
1955-1957	84th	D-232	R-203	-	D-48	R-47	1	R (Eisenhower)
1953-1955	83d	R-221	D-211	1	R-48	D-47	1	R (Eisenhower)
1951-1953	82d	D-234	R-199	1	D-49	R-47	-	D (Truman)
1949-1951	81st	D-263	R-171	1	D-54	R-42	-	D (Truman)
1947-1949	80th	R-245	D-188	1	R-51	D-45	-	D (Truman)
1945-1947	79th	D-242	R-190	2	D-56	R-38	1	D (Truman)
1943-1945	78th	D-218	R-208	4	D-58	R-37	1	D (F. Roosevelt)
1941-1943	77th	D-268	R-162	5	D-66	R-33		D (F. R...)

Years	Congress	House majority	House minority	House other	Senate majority	Senate minority	Senate other	President
1939-1941	76th	D-261	R-164	4	D-69	R-23	4	D (F. Roosevelt)
1937-1939	75th	D-331	R-89	13	D-76	R-16	4	D (F. Roosevelt)
1935-1937	74th	D-319	R-103	10	D-69	R-25	2	D (F. Roosevelt)
1933-1935	73d	D-310	R-117	5	D-60	R-35	1	D (F. Roosevelt)
1931-1933	72d	D-220	R-214	1	R-48	D-47	1	R (Hoover)
1929-1931	71st	R-267	D-167	1	R-56	D-39	1	R (Hoover)
1927-1929	70th	R-237	D-195	3	R-49	D-46	1	R (Coolidge)
1925-1927	69th	R-247	D-183	4	R-56	D-39	1	R (Coolidge)
1923-1925	68th	R-225	D-205	5	R-51	D-43	2	R (Coolidge)
1921-1923	67th	R-301	D-131	1	R-59	D-37	-	R (Harding)
1919-1921	66th	R-240	D-190	3	R-49	D-47	-	D (Wilson)
1917-1919	65th	D-216	R-210	6	D-53	R-42	-	D (Wilson)
1915-1917	64th	D-230	R-196	9	D-56	R-40	-	D (Wilson)
1913-1915	63d	D-291	R-127	17	D-51	R-44	1	D (Wilson)
1911-1913	62d	D-228	R-161	1	R-51	D-41	1	R (Taft)
1909-1911	61st	R-219	D-172	-	R-61	D-32	-	R (Taft)
1907-1909	60th	R-222	D-164	-	R-61	D-31	-	R (T. Roosevelt)
1905-1907	59th	R-250	D-136	-	R-57	D-33	-	R (T. Roosevelt)
1903-1905	58th	R-208	D-178	-	R-57	D-33	-	R (T. Roosevelt)
1901-1903	57th	R-197	D-151	9	R-55	D-31	4	R (T. Roosevelt)
1899-1901	56th	R-185	D-163	9	R-53	D-26	8	R (McKinley)
1897-1899	55th	R-204	D-113	40	R-47	D-34	7	R (McKinley)
1895-1897	54th	R-244	D-105	7	R-43	D-39	6	R (McKinley)
1893-1895	53d	D-218	R-127	11	D-44	R-38	3	D (Cleveland)
1891-1893	52d	D-235	R-88	9	R-47	D-39	2	D (Cleveland)
1889-1891	51st	R-166	D-159	-	R-39	D-37	-	R (B. Harrison)
1887-1889	50th	D-169	R-152	4	R-39	D-37	-	R (B. Harrison)
1885-1887	49th	D-183	R-140	2	R-43	D-34	-	D (Cleveland)
1883-1885	48th	D-197	R-118	10	R-38	D-36	2	R (Arthur)

Year	Congress	HOUSE Majority party	Principal minority party	Other (except vacancies)	SENATE Majority party	Principal minority party	Other (except vacancies)	President
1881–1883	47th	R-147	D-135	11	R-37	D-37	1	R (Arthur) / R (Garfield)
1879–1881	46th	D-149	R-130	14	D-42	R-33	1	R (Hayes)
1877–1879	45th	D-153	R-140	-	R-39	D-36	1	R (Hayes)
1875–1877	44th	D-169	R-109	14	R-45	D-29	2	R (Grant)
1873–1875	43d	R-194	D-92	14	R-49	D-19	5	R (Grant)
1871–1873	42d	R-134	D-104	5	R-52	D-17	5	R (Grant)
1869–1871	41st	R-149	D-63	-	R-56	D-11	-	R (Grant)
1867–1869	40th	R-143	D-49	-	R-42	D-11	-	R (A. Johnson)
1865–1867	39th	U-149	D-42	-	U-42	D-10	-	R (A. Johnson) / R (Lincoln)
1863–1865	38th	R-102	D-75	9	R-36	D-9	5	R (Lincoln)
1861–1863	37th	R-105	D-43	30	R-31	D-10	8	R (Lincoln)
1859–1861	36th	R-114	D-92	31	D-36	R-26	4	D (Buchanan)
1857–1859	35th	D-118	R-92	26	D-36	R-20	8	D (Buchanan)
1855–1857	34th	R-108	D-83	43	D-40	R-15	5	D (Pierce)
1853–1855	33d	D-159	W-71	4	D-38	W-22	2	D (Pierce)
1851–1853	32d	D-140	W-88	5	D-35	W-24	3	W (Fillmore)
1849–1851	31st	D-112	W-109	9	D-35	W-25	2	W (Fillmore) / W (Taylor)
1847–1849	30th	W-115	D-108	4	D-36	W-21	1	D (Polk)
1845–1847	29th	D-143	W-77	6	D-31	W-25	-	D (Polk)
1843–1845	28th	D-142	W-79	1	W-28	D-25	1	W (Tyler)
1841–1843	27th	W-133	D-102	6	W-28	D-22	2	W (Tyler) / W (W. Harrison)
1839–1841	26th	D-124	W-118	-	D-28	W-22	-	D (Van Buren)

1837-1839	25th	D-108	W-107	24	D-30	W-18	4	D (Van Buren)
1835-1837	24th	D-145	W-98	-	D-27	W-25	-	D (Jackson)
1833-1835	23d	D-147	AM-53	60	D-20	NR-20	8	D (Jackson)
1831-1833	22d	D-141	NR-58	14	D-25	NR-21	2	D (Jackson)
1829-1831	21st	D-139	NR-74	-	D-26	NR-22	-	D (Jackson)
1827-1829	20th	J-119	Ad-94	-	J-28	Ad-20	-	DR (John Q. Adams)
1825-1827	19th	Ad-105	J-97	-	Ad-26	J-20	-	DR (John Q. Adams)
1823-1825	18th	DR-187	F-26	-	DR-44	F-4	-	DR (Monroe)
1821-1823	17th	DR-158	F-25	-	DR-44	F-4	-	DR (Monroe)
1819-1821	16th	DR-156	F-27	-	DR-35	F-7	-	DR (Monroe)
1817-1819	15th	DR-141	F-42	-	DR-34	F-10	-	DR (Monroe)
1815-1817	14th	DR-117	F-65	-	DR-25	F-11	-	DR (Madison)
1813-1815	13th	DR-112	F-68	-	DR-27	F-9	-	DR (Madison)
1811-1813	12th	DR-108	F-36	-	DR-30	F-6	-	DR (Madison)
1809-1811	11th	DR-94	F-48	-	DR-28	F-6	-	DR (Madison)
1807-1809	10th	DR-118	F-24	-	DR-28	F-6	-	DR (Jefferson)
1805-1807	9th	DR-116	F-25	-	DR-27	F-7	-	DR (Jefferson)
1803-1805	8th	DR-102	F-39	-	DR-25	F-9	-	DR (Jefferson)
1801-1803	7th	DR-69	F-36	-	DR-18	F-13	-	DR (Jefferson)
1799-1801	6th	F-64	DR-42	-	F-19	DR-13	-	F (John Adams)
1797-1799	5th	F-58	DR-48	-	F-20	DR-12	-	F (John Adams)
1795-1797	4th	F-54	DR-52	-	F-19	DR-13	-	F (Washington)
1793-1795	3d	DR-57	F-48	-	F-17	DR-13	-	F (Washington)
1791-1793	2d	F-37	DR-33	-	F-16	DR-13	-	F (Washington)
1789-1791	1st	Ad-38	Op-26	-	Ad-17	Op-9	-	F (Washington)

NOTE: Figures are for the first session of each Congress.

Abbreviations: Ad—Administration; AM—Anti Masonic; D—Democratic; DR—Democratic Republican; F—Federalist; J—Jeffersonian; NR—National Republican; Op—Opposition; R—Republican; U—Unionist; W—Whig.

SOURCES: Congressional Quarterly Weekly Report; U.S. Bureau of the Census. Historical Statistics of the United States, Colonial Times to 1970. Washington, D.C.: Government Printing Office, 1975; U.S. Bureau of the Census. Statistical Abstract of the United States, 1985. Washington, D.C.: Government Printing Office, 1984; U.S. Congress. Joint Committee on Printing. Official Congressional Directory. Washington, D.C.: Government Printing Office, 1967– .

Sessions of the U.S. Congress, 1789-1987

Congress	Session	Date of beginning[1]	Date of adjournment[2]	Length in days	President pro tempore of the Senate[3]	Speaker of the House of Representatives
1st	1	Mar. 4, 1789	Sept. 29, 1789	210	John Langdon of New Hampshire[4]	Frederick A. C. Muhlenberg of Pennsylvania
	2	Jan. 4, 1790	Aug. 12, 1790	221		
	3	Dec. 6, 1790	Mar. 3, 1791	88		
2d	1	Oct. 24, 1791	May 8, 1792	197	Richard Henry Lee of Virginia	Jonathan Trumbull of Connecticut
	2	Nov. 5, 1792	Mar. 2, 1793	119	John Langdon of New Hampshire	
3d	1	Dec. 2, 1793	June 9, 1794	190	Langdon Ralph Izard of South Carolina	Frederick A. C. Muhlenberg of Pennsylvania
	2	Nov. 3, 1794	Mar. 3, 1795	121	Henry Tazewell of Virginia	
4th	1	Dec. 7, 1795	June 1, 1796	177	Tazewell Samuel Livermore of New Hampshire	Jonathan Dayton of New Jersey
	2	Dec. 5, 1796	Mar. 3, 1797	89	William Bingham of Pennsylvania	
5th	1	May 15, 1797	July 10, 1797	57	William Bradford of Rhode Island	Dayton
	2	Nov. 13, 1797	July 16, 1798	246	Jacob Read of South Carolina Theodore Sedgwick of Massachusetts	George Dent of Maryland[5]
	3	Dec. 3, 1798	Mar. 3, 1799	91	John Laurence of New York James Ross of Pennsylvania	
6th	1	Dec. 2, 1799	May 14, 1800	164	Samuel Livermore of New Hampshire Uriah Tracy of Connecticut	Theodore Sedgwick of Massachusetts

Congress	Session	Date convened	Date adjourned	Days	President pro tempore of the Senate	Speaker of the House
	2	Nov. 17, 1800	Mar. 3, 1801	107	John E. Howard of Maryland; James Hillhouse of Connecticut	
7th	1	Dec. 7, 1801	May 3, 1802	148	Abraham Baldwin of Georgia	Nathaniel Macon of North Carolina
	2	Dec. 6, 1802	Mar. 3, 1803	88	Stephen R. Bradley of Vermont	
8th	1	Oct. 17, 1803	Mar. 27, 1804	163	John Brown of Kentucky; Jesse Franklin of North Carolina; Joseph Anderson of Tennessee	Macon
	2	Nov. 5, 1804	Mar. 3, 1805	119		
9th	1	Dec. 2, 1805	Apr. 21, 1806	141	Samuel Smith of Maryland	Macon
	2	Dec. 1, 1806	Mar. 3, 1807	93		
10th	1	Oct. 26, 1807	Apr. 25, 1808	182	Smith	Joseph B. Varnum of Massachusetts
	2	Nov. 7, 1808	Mar. 3, 1809	117	Stephen R. Bradley of Vermont; John Milledge of Georgia	
11th	1	May 22, 1809	June 28, 1809	38	Andrew Gregg of Pennsylvania	Varnum
	2	Nov. 27, 1809	May 1, 1810	156	John Gaillard of South Carolina	
	3	Dec. 3, 1810	Mar. 3, 1811	91	John Pope of Kentucky	
12th	1	Nov. 4, 1811	July 6, 1812	245	William H. Crawford of Georgia	Henry Clay of Kentucky
	2	Nov. 2, 1812	Mar. 3, 1813	122	Crawford	
13th	1	May 24, 1813	Aug. 2, 1813	71	Joseph B. Varnum of Massachusetts	Clay
	2	Dec. 6, 1813	Apr. 18, 1814	134	John Gaillard of South Carolina	
	3	Sept. 19, 1814	Mar. 3, 1815	166		
14th	1	Dec. 4, 1815	Apr. 30, 1816	148	Gaillard	Langdon Cheves of South Carolina[6]; Henry Clay of Kentucky
	2	Dec. 2, 1816	Mar. 3, 1817	92	Gaillard	
15th	1	Dec. 1, 1817	Apr. 20, 1818	141	Gaillard	Clay
	2	Nov. 16, 1818	Mar. 3, 1819	108	James Barbour of Virginia	

Congress	Session	Date of beginning	Date of adjournment	Length in days	President pro tempore of the Senate	Speaker of the House of Representatives
16th	1	Dec. 6, 1819	May 15, 1820	162	John Gaillard of South Carolina	Clay
	2	Nov. 13, 1820	Mar. 3, 1821	111	Gaillard	John W. Taylor of New York[7]
17th	1	Dec. 3, 1821	May 8, 1822	157	Gaillard	Philip P. Barbour of Virginia
18th	2	Dec. 2, 1822	Mar. 3, 1823	92	Gaillard	
	1	Dec. 1, 1823	May 27, 1824	178	Gaillard	Henry Clay of Kentucky
	2	Dec. 6, 1824	Mar. 3, 1825	88	Gaillard	
19th	1	Dec. 5, 1825	May 22, 1826	169	Nathaniel Macon of North Carolina	John W. Taylor of New York
20th	2	Dec. 4, 1826	Mar. 3, 1827	90	Macon	
	1	Dec. 3, 1827	May 26, 1828	175	Samuel Smith of Maryland	Andrew Stevenson of Virginia
21st	2	Dec. 1, 1828	Mar. 3, 1829	93	Smith	
	1	Dec. 7, 1829	May 31, 1830	176	Smith	Stevenson
	2	Dec. 6, 1830	Mar. 3, 1831	88	Littleton Waller Tazewell of Virginia	
22d	1	Dec. 5, 1831	July 16, 1832	225	Tazewell	Stevenson
	2	Dec. 3, 1832	Mar. 2, 1833	91	Hugh Lawson White of Tennessee	
23d	1	Dec. 2, 1833	June 30, 1834	211	George Poindexter of Mississippi	Stevenson
	2	Dec. 1, 1834	Mar. 3, 1835	93	John Tyler of Virginia	John Bell of Tennessee[8]
24th	1	Dec. 7, 1835	July 4, 1836	211	William R. King of Alabama	James K. Polk of Tennessee
	2	Dec. 5, 1836	Mar. 3, 1837	89	King	
25th	1	Sept. 4, 1837	Oct. 16, 1837	43	King	Polk
	2	Dec. 4, 1837	July 9, 1838	218	King	
	3	Dec. 3, 1838	Mar. 3, 1839	91	King	
26th	1	Dec. 2, 1839	July 21, 1840	233	King	Robert M. T. Hunter of Virginia
	2	Dec. 7, 1840	Mar. 3, 1841	87		Polk
27th	1	May 31, 1841	Sept. 13, 1841	106	Samuel L. Southard of New Jersey	John White of Kentucky

Congress	Session	Convened	Adjourned	Page	President pro tempore of the Senate	Speaker of the House
	2	Dec. 6, 1841	Aug. 31, 1842	269	Willie P. Mangum of North Carolina	
28th	3	Dec. 5, 1842	Mar. 3, 1843	89	Mangum	John W. Jones of Virginia
	1	Dec. 4, 1843	June 17, 1844	196	Mangum	
29th	2	Dec. 2, 1844	Mar. 3, 1845	92	Mangum	
	1	Dec. 1, 1845	Aug. 10, 1846	253	David R. Atchison of Missouri	John W. Davis of Indiana
30th	2	Dec. 7, 1846	Mar. 3, 1847	87	Atchison	
	1	Dec. 6, 1847	Aug. 14, 1848	254	Atchison	Robert C. Winthrop of Massachusetts
31st	2	Dec. 4, 1848	Mar. 3, 1849	90	Atchison	
	1	Dec. 3, 1849	Sept. 30, 1850	302	William R. King of Alabama	Howell Cobb of Georgia
32d	2	Dec. 2, 1850	Mar. 3, 1851	92	King	
	1	Dec. 1, 1851	Aug. 31, 1852	275	King	Linn Boyd of Kentucky
33d	2	Dec. 6, 1852	Mar. 3, 1853	88	David R. Atchison of Missouri	
	1	Dec. 5, 1853	Aug. 7, 1854	246	Atchison	Boyd
34th	2	Dec. 4, 1854	Mar. 3, 1855	90	Jesse D. Bright of Indiana; Lewis Cass of Michigan	
	1	Dec. 3, 1855	Aug. 18, 1856	260	Jesse D. Bright of Indiana	Nathaniel P. Banks of Massachusetts
	2	Aug. 21, 1856	Aug. 30, 1856	10	Bright	
35th	3	Dec. 1, 1856	Mar. 3, 1857	93	James M. Mason of Virginia; Thomas J. Rusk of Texas	
	1	Dec. 7, 1857	June 14, 1858	189	Benjamin Fitzpatrick of Alabama	James L. Orr of South Carolina
36th	2	Dec. 6, 1858	Mar. 3, 1859	88	Fitzpatrick	
	1	Dec. 5, 1859	June 25, 1860	202	Fitzpatrick	William Pennington of New Jersey
37th	2	Dec. 3, 1860	Mar. 3, 1861	93	Jesse D. Bright of Indiana	
	1	July 4, 1861	Aug. 6, 1861	34	Solomon Foot of Vermont	Galusha A. Grow of Pennsylvania
	2	Dec. 2, 1861	July 17, 1862	228	Foot	
	3	Dec. 1, 1862	Mar. 3, 1863	93	Foot	

Congress	Session	Date of beginning	Date of adjournment	Length in days	President pro tempore of the Senate	Speaker of the House of Representatives
38th	1	Dec. 7, 1863	July 4, 1864	209	Foot	Schuyler Colfax of Indiana
	2	Dec. 5, 1864	Mar. 3, 1865	89	Daniel Clark of New Hampshire / Clark	
39th	1	Dec. 4, 1865	July 28, 1866	237	Lafayette S. Foster of Connecticut	Colfax
	2	Dec. 3, 1866	Mar. 3, 1867	91	Benjamin F. Wade of Ohio	
40th	1	Mar. 4, 1867[9]	Dec. 2, 1867	274	Wade	Colfax
	2	Dec. 2, 1867[10]	Nov. 10, 1868	345	Wade	
	3	Dec. 7, 1868	Mar. 3, 1869	87	Wade	Theodore M. Pomeroy of New York[11]
41st	1	Mar. 4, 1869	Apr. 10, 1869	38	Henry B. Anthony of Rhode Island	James G. Blaine of Maine
	2	Dec. 6, 1869	July 15, 1870	222	Anthony	
	3	Dec. 5, 1870	Mar. 3, 1871	89	Anthony	
42d	1	Mar. 4, 1871	Apr. 20, 1871	48	Anthony	Blaine
	2	Dec. 4, 1871	June 10, 1872	190	Anthony	
	3	Dec. 2, 1872	Mar. 3, 1873	92	Anthony	
43d	1	Dec. 1, 1873	June 23, 1874	204	Matthew H. Carpenter of Wisconsin / Carpenter	Blaine
	2	Dec. 7, 1874	Mar. 3, 1875	87	Henry B. Anthony of Rhode Island	
44th	1	Dec. 6, 1875	Aug. 15, 1876	254	Thomas W. Ferry of Michigan	Michael C. Kerr of Indiana[12] / Samuel S. Cox of New York, pro tempore[13] / Milton Sayler of Ohio, pro tempore[14] / Samuel J. Randall of Pennsylvania
	2	Dec. 4, 1876	Mar. 3, 1877	90	Ferry	Randall
45th	1	Oct. 15, 1877	Dec. 3, 1877	50	Ferry	
	2	Dec. 3, 1877	June 20, 1878	200	Ferry	
	3	Dec. 2, 1878	Mar. 3, 1879	92	Ferry	
46th	1	Mar. 18, 1879	July 1, 1879	106	Allen G. Thurman of	Randall

	Session	Convened	Adjourned		President pro tempore of the Senate	Speaker
	2	Dec. 1, 1879	June 16, 1880	199	Thurman	
	3	Dec. 6, 1880	Mar. 3, 1881	88	Thurman	
47th	1	Dec. 5, 1881	Aug. 8, 1882	247	Thomas F. Bayard of Delaware; David Davis of Illinois; George F. Edmunds of Vermont	J. Warren Keifer of Ohio
	2	Dec. 4, 1882	Mar. 3, 1883	90	Edmunds	
48th	1	Dec. 3, 1883	July 7, 1884	218	Edmunds	John G. Carlisle of Kentucky
	2	Dec. 1, 1884	Mar. 3, 1885	93		
49th	1	Dec. 7, 1885	Aug. 5, 1886	242	John Sherman of Ohio	Carlisle
	2	Dec. 6, 1886	Mar. 3, 1887	88	John J. Ingalls of Kansas	
50th	1	Dec. 5, 1887	Oct. 20, 1888	321	Ingalls	Carlisle
	2	Dec. 3, 1888	Mar. 3, 1889	91	Ingalls	
51st	1	Dec. 2, 1889	Oct. 1, 1890	304	Ingalls	Thomas B. Reed of Maine
	2	Dec. 1, 1890	Mar. 3, 1891	93	Charles F. Manderson of Nebraska	
52d	1	Dec. 7, 1891	Aug. 5, 1892	251	Manderson	Charles F. Crisp of Georgia
	2	Dec. 5, 1892	Mar. 3, 1893	89	Isham G. Harris of Tennessee	
53d	1	Aug. 7, 1893	Nov. 3, 1893	89	Harris	Crisp
	2	Dec. 4, 1893	Aug. 28, 1894	268	Harris	
	3	Dec. 3, 1894	Mar. 3, 1895	97	Matt W. Ransom of North Carolina; Isham G. Harris of Tennessee	
54th	1	Dec. 2, 1895	June 11, 1896	193	William P. Frye of Maine	Thomas B. Reed of Maine
	2	Dec. 7, 1896	Mar. 3, 1897	87		
55th	1	Mar. 15, 1897	July 24, 1897	131	Frye	Reed
	2	Dec. 6, 1897	July 8, 1898	215	Frye	
	3	Dec. 5, 1898	Mar. 3, 1899	89	Frye	
56th	1	Dec. 4, 1899	June 7, 1900	186	Frye	David B. Henderson of Iowa
	2	Dec. 3, 1900	Mar. 3, 1901	91	Frye	
57th	1	Dec. 2, 1901	July 1, 1902	212	Frye	Henderson
	2	Dec. 1, 1902	Mar. 3, 1903	93	Frye	

Congress	Session	Date of beginning	Date of adjournment	Length in days	President pro tempore of the Senate	Speaker of the House of Representatives
58th	1	Nov. 9, 1903	Dec. 7, 1903	29	Frye	Joseph G. Cannon of Illinois
	2	Dec. 7, 1903	Apr. 28, 1904	144	Frye	
	3	Dec. 5, 1904	Mar. 3, 1905	89	Frye	
59th	1	Dec. 4, 1905	June 30, 1906	209	Frye	Cannon
	2	Dec. 3, 1906	Mar. 3, 1907	91	Frye	
60th	1	Dec. 2, 1907	May 30, 1908	181	Frye	Cannon
	2	Dec. 7, 1908	Mar. 3, 1909	87	Frye	
61st	1	Mar. 15, 1909	Aug. 5, 1909	144	Frye	Cannon
	2	Dec. 6, 1909	June 25, 1910	202	Frye	
	3	Dec. 5, 1910	Mar. 3, 1911	89	Frye	
62d	1	Apr. 4, 1911	Aug. 22, 1911	141	Frye[15]	Champ Clark of Missouri
	2	Dec. 4, 1911	Aug. 26, 1912	267	Augustus O. Bacon of Georgia[16], Frank B. Brandegee of Connecticut[17]; Charles Curtis of Kansas[18]; Jacob H. Gallinger of New Hampshire[19], Henry Cabot Lodge of Mass.[20]	
	3	Dec. 2, 1912	Mar. 3, 1913	92	Bacon[21]; Gallinger[22]	
63d	1	Apr. 7, 1913	Dec. 1, 1913	239	James P. Clarke of Arkansas	Clark
	2	Dec. 1, 1913	Oct. 24, 1914	328	Clarke	
	3	Dec. 7, 1914	Mar. 3, 1915	87	Clarke	
64th	1	Dec. 6, 1915	Sept. 8, 1916	278	Clarke[23]	Clark
	2	Dec. 4, 1916	Mar. 3, 1917	90	Willard Saulsbury of Delaware	
65th	1	Apr. 2, 1917	Oct. 6, 1917	188	Saulsbury	Clark
	2	Dec. 3, 1917	Nov. 21, 1918	354	Saulsbury	
	3	Dec. 2, 1918	Mar. 3, 1919	92	Saulsbury	
66th	1	May 19, 1919	Nov. 19, 1919	185	Albert B. Cummins of	Frederick H. Gillett

Congress	Session	Convened	Adjourned	Days	President pro tempore of the Senate	Speaker of the House
	2	Dec. 1, 1919	June 5, 1920	188	Cummins	Gillett
	3	Dec. 6, 1920	Mar. 3, 1921	88	Cummins	
67th	1	Apr. 11, 1921	Nov. 23, 1921	227	Cummins	
	2	Dec. 5, 1921	Sept. 22, 1922	292	Cummins	
	3	Nov. 20, 1922	Dec. 4, 1922	15	Cummins	
	4	Dec. 4, 1922	Mar. 3, 1923	90	Cummins	
68th	1	Dec. 3, 1923	June 7, 1924	188	Cummins	Gillett
	2	Dec. 1, 1924	Mar. 3, 1925	93	Cummins	
69th	1	Dec. 7, 1925	July 3, 1926	209	George H. Moses of New Hampshire	Nicholas Longworth of Ohio
	2	Dec. 6, 1926	Mar. 3, 1927	88	Moses	
70th	1	Dec. 5, 1927	May 29, 1928	177	Moses	Longworth
	2	Dec. 3, 1928	Mar. 3, 1929	91	Moses	
71st	1	Apr. 15, 1929	Nov. 22, 1929	222	Moses	Longworth
	2	Dec. 2, 1929	July 3, 1930	214	Moses	
	3	Dec. 1, 1930	Mar. 3, 1931	93	Moses	
72d	1	Dec. 7, 1931	July 16, 1932	223	Moses	John N. Garner of Texas
	2	Dec. 5, 1932	Mar. 3, 1933	89	Moses	
73d	1	Mar. 9, 1933	June 15, 1933	99	Key Pittman of Nevada	Henry T. Rainey of Illinois[24]
	2	Jan. 3, 1934	June 18, 1934	167	Pittman	
74th	1	Jan. 3, 1935	Aug. 26, 1935	236	Pittman	Joseph W. Byrns of Tennessee[25]
	2	Jan. 3, 1936	June 20, 1936	170	Pittman	William B. Bankhead of Alabama[26]
75th	1	Jan. 5, 1937	Aug. 21, 1937	229	Pittman	Bankhead
	2	Nov. 15, 1937	Dec. 21, 1937	37	Pittman	
	3	Jan. 3, 1938	June 16, 1938	165	Pittman	
76th	1	Jan. 3, 1939	Aug. 5, 1939	215	Pittman	Bankhead[27]
	2	Sept. 21, 1939	Nov. 3, 1939	44	Pittman	
	3	Jan. 3, 1940	Jan. 3, 1941	366	Pittman[28]; William H. King of Utah[30]	Sam Rayburn of Texas[29]
77th	1	Jan. 3, 1941	Jan. 2, 1942	365	Pat Harrison of Mississippi[31]; Carter Glass of Virginia[32]	Rayburn
	2	Jan. 5, 1942	Dec. 16, 1942	346	Carter Glass of Virginia	
78th	1	Jan. 6, 1943[33]	Dec. 21, 1943	350	Glass	Rayburn

Congress	Session	Date of beginning	Date of adjournment	Length in days	President pro tempore of the Senate	Speaker of the House of Representatives
79th	2	Jan. 10, 1944[34]	Dec. 19, 1944	345	Glass	Rayburn
	1	Jan. 3, 1945[35]	Dec. 21, 1945	353	Kenneth McKellar of Tennessee	
80th	2	Jan. 14, 1946[36]	Aug. 2, 1946	201	McKellar	Joseph W. Martin Jr. of Massachusetts
	1	Jan. 3, 1947[37]	Dec. 19, 1947	351	Arthur H. Vandenberg of Michigan	
81st	2	Jan. 6, 1948[38]	Dec. 31, 1948	361	Vandenberg	Sam Rayburn of Texas
	1	Jan. 3, 1949	Oct. 19, 1949	290	Kenneth McKellar of Tennessee	
82d	2	Jan. 3, 1950[39]	Jan. 2, 1951	365	McKellar	Rayburn
	1	Jan. 3, 1951[40]	Oct. 20, 1951	291	McKellar	
	2	Jan. 8, 1952[41]	July 7, 1952	182	McKellar	
83d	1	Jan. 3, 1953[42]	Aug. 3, 1953	213	Styles Bridges of New Hampshire	Joseph W. Martin Jr. of Massachusetts
	2	Jan. 6, 1954[43]	Dec. 2, 1954	331	Bridges	
84th	1	Jan. 5, 1955[44]	Aug. 2, 1955	210	Walter F. George of Georgia	Sam Rayburn of Texas
	2	Jan. 3, 1956[45]	July 27, 1956	207	George	Rayburn
85th	1	Jan. 3, 1957[46]	Aug. 30, 1957	239	Carl Hayden of Arizona	
	2	Jan. 7, 1958[47]	Aug. 24, 1958	230	Hayden	
86th	1	Jan. 7, 1959[48]	Sept. 15, 1959	252	Hayden	Rayburn
	2	Jan. 6, 1960[49]	Sept. 1, 1960	240	Hayden	
87th	1	Jan. 3, 1961[50]	Sept. 27, 1961	268	Hayden	Rayburn[51]
	2	Jan. 10, 1962[52]	Oct. 13, 1962	277	Hayden	John W. McCormack of Massachusetts[53]
88th	1	Jan. 9, 1963[54]	Dec. 30, 1963	356	Hayden	McCormack
	2	Jan. 7, 1964[55]	Oct. 3, 1964	270	Hayden	
89th	1	Jan. 4, 1965	Oct. 23, 1965	293	Hayden	McCormack
	2	Jan. 10, 1966[56]	Oct. 22, 1966	286	Hayden	
90th	1	Jan. 10, 1967[57]	Dec. 15, 1967	340	Hayden	McCormack
	2	Jan. 15, 1968[58]	Oct. 14, 1968	274	Hayden	
91st	1	Jan. 3, 1969[59]	Dec. 23, 1969	355	Richard B. Russell of Georgia	McCormack
	2	Jan. 19, 1970[60]	Jan. 2, 1971	349	Russell	

92d	1	Jan. 21, 1971[61]	Dec. 17, 1971	331	Russell[62], Allen J. Ellender of Louisiana[63]	Carl Albert of Oklahoma
	2	Jan. 18, 1972[64]	Oct. 18, 1972	275	Ellender[65], James O. Eastland of Mississippi[66]	
93d	1	Jan. 3, 1973[67]	Dec. 22, 1973	354	Eastland	Albert
	2	Jan. 21, 1974[68]	Dec. 20, 1974	334	Eastland	
94th	1	Jan. 14, 1975[69]	Dec. 19, 1975	340	Eastland	Albert
	2	Jan. 19, 1976[70]	Oct. 2, 1976	258	Eastland	
95th	1	Jan. 4, 1977[71]	Dec. 15, 1977	346	Eastland	Thomas P. O'Neill Jr. of Massachusetts
	2	Jan. 19, 1978[72]	Oct. 15, 1978	270	Eastland	
96th	1	Jan. 15, 1979[73]	Jan. 3, 1980	354	Warren G. Magnuson of Washington	O'Neill
	2	Jan. 3, 1980[74]	Dec. 16, 1980	349	Magnuson	
97th	1	Jan. 5, 1981[75]	Dec. 16, 1981	347	Strom Thurmond of South Carolina	O'Neill
	2	Jan. 25, 1982[76]	Dec. 23, 1982	333	Thurmond	
98th	1	Jan. 3, 1983[77]	Nov. 18, 1983	320	Thurmond	O'Neill
	2	Jan. 23, 1984[78]	Oct. 12, 1984	264	Thurmond	
99th	1	Jan. 3, 1985[79]	Dec. 20, 1985	352	Thurmond	O'Neill
	2	Jan. 21, 1986[80]	Oct. 18, 1986	271	Thurmond	
100th	1	Jan. 6, 1987			John D. Stennis of Mississippi	Jim Wright of Texas

1. The Constitution (art. I, sec. 4) provided that "The Congress shall assemble at least once in every year ... on the first Monday in December, unless they shall by law appoint a different day." Pursuant to a resolution of the Continental Congress, the first session of the First Congress convened March 4, 1789. Up to and including May 20, 1820, 18 acts were passed providing for the meeting of Congress on other days in the year. After 1820 Congress met regularly on the first Monday in December until 1934, when the Twentieth Amendment to the Constitution became effective changing the meeting date to Jan. 3. [Until then, brief special sessions of the Senate only were held at the beginning of each presidential term to confirm Cabinet and other nominations—and occasionally at other times for other purposes. The Senate last met in special session from March 4 to March 6, 1933.]

   The first and second sessions of the First Congress were held in New York City. Subsequently, including the first session of the Sixth Congress, Philadelphia was the meeting place; since then, Congress has convened in Washington.

2. Until adoption of the Twentieth Amendment, the deadline for adjournment of Congress in odd-numbered years was March 3. However, the expiring Congress often extended the "legislative day" of March 3 up to noon of March 4, when the new Congress came officially into being. After ratification of the Twentieth Amendment, the deadline for adjournment of Congress in odd-numbered years was noon on Jan. 3.

3. Until recent years the appointment or election of a president pro tempore was considered by the Senate to be for the occasion only, so that more than one appears in several sessions and in others none was chosen. Since March 12, 1890, they have served until "the Senate otherwise ordered."

4. Elected to count the vote for president and vice president, which was done April 6, 1789, because there was a quorum of the Senate for the first time. John Adams, vice president, appeared April 21, 1789, and took his seat as president of the Senate.

5. Elected Speaker pro tempore for April 20, 1798, and again for May 28, 1798.

6. Elected Speaker Jan. 19, 1814, to succeed Henry Clay, who resigned Jan. 19, 1814.

7. Elected Speaker Nov. 15, 1820, to succeed Henry Clay, who resigned Oct. 28, 1820.

8. Elected Speaker June 2, 1834, to succeed Andrew Stevenson of Virginia, who resigned.

9. There were recesses in this session from Saturday, Mar. 30, to Wednesday, July 1, and from Saturday, July 20, to Thursday, Nov. 21.

10. There were recesses in this session from Monday, July 27, to Monday, Sept. 21, to Friday, Oct. 16, and to Tuesday, Nov. 10. No business was transacted subsequent to July 27.

11. Elected Speaker Mar. 3, 1869, and served one day.

12. Died Aug. 19, 1876.

13. Appointed Speaker pro tempore Feb. 17, May 12, June 19.

14. Appointed Speaker pro tempore June 4.

15. Resigned as president pro tempore Apr. 27, 1911.

16. Elected to serve Jan. 11-17, Mar. 11-12, Apr. 8, May 10, May 30 to June 1 and 3, June 13 to July 5, Aug. 1-10, and Aug. 27 to Dec. 15, 1912.

17. Elected to serve May 25, 1912.

18. Elected to serve Dec. 4-12, 1911.

19. Elected to serve Feb. 12-14, Apr. 26-27, May 7, July 6-31, Aug. 12-26, 1912.

20. Elected to serve Mar. 25-26, 1912.

21. Elected to serve Aug. 27 to Dec. 15, 1912, Jan. 5-18, and Feb. 2-15, 1913.

22. Elected to serve Dec. 16, 1912, to Jan. 4, 1913, Jan. 19 to Feb. 1, and Feb. 16 to Mar. 3, 1913.

23. Died Oct. 1, 1916.

24. Died Aug. 19, 1934.

25. Died June 4, 1936.

26. Elected June 4, 1936.

27. Died Sept. 15, 1940.

28. Died Nov. 10, 1940.

29. Elected Sept. 16, 1940.

30. Elected Nov. 19, 1940.

31. Elected Jan. 6, 1941; died June 22, 1941.

32. Elected July 10, 1941.

33. There was a recess in this session from Thursday, July 8, to Tuesday, Sept. 14.

34. There were recesses in this session from Saturday, Apr. 1, to Wednesday, Apr. 12; from Friday, June 23, to Tuesday, Aug. 1; and from Thursday, Sept. 21, to Tuesday, Nov. 14.

35. The House was in recess in this session from Saturday, July 21, 1945, to Wednesday, Sept. 5, 1945, and the Senate from Wednesday, Aug. 1, 1945, to Wednesday, Sept. 5, 1945.

36. The House was in recess in this session from Thursday, Apr. 18, 1946, to Tuesday, Apr. 30, 1946.

37. There was a recess in this session from Sunday, July 27, 1947, to Monday, Nov. 17, 1947.

38. There were recesses in this session from Sunday, June 20, 1948, to Monday, July 26, 1948, and from Saturday, Aug. 7, 1948, to Friday, Dec. 31, 1948.

39. The House was in recess in this session from Thursday, Apr. 6, 1950, to Tuesday, Apr. 18, 1950, and both the Senate and the House were in recess from Saturday, Sept. 23, 1950, to Monday, Nov. 27, 1950.

40. The House was in recess in this session from Thursday, Mar. 22, 1951, to Monday, Apr. 2, 1951, and from Thursday, Aug. 23, 1951, to Wednesday, Sept. 12, 1951.

41. The House was in recess in this session from Thursday, Apr. 10, 1952, to Tuesday, Apr. 22, 1952.

42. The House was in recess in this session from Thursday, Apr. 2, 1953, to Monday, Apr. 13, 1953.

43. The House was in recess in this session from Thursday, Apr. 15, 1954, to Monday, Apr. 26, 1954, and adjourned sine die Aug. 20, 1954. The Senate was in recess in this session from Friday, Aug. 20, 1954, to Monday, Nov. 8, 1954; from Thursday, Nov. 18, 1954, to Monday, Nov. 29, 1954, and adjourned sine die Dec. 2, 1954.

44. There was a recess in this session from Monday, Apr. 4, 1955, to Wednesday, Apr. 13, 1955.

45. There was a recess in this session from Thursday, Mar. 29, 1956, to Monday, Apr. 9, 1956.

46. There was a recess in this session from Thursday, Apr. 18, 1957, to Monday, Apr. 29, 1957.

47. There was a recess in this session from Thursday, Apr. 3, 1958, to Monday, Apr. 14, 1958.

48. There was a recess in this session from Thursday, Mar. 26, 1959, to Tuesday, Apr. 7, 1959.

49. The Senate was in recess in this session from Thursday, Apr. 14, 1960, to Monday, Apr. 18, 1960; from Friday, May 27, 1960, to Tuesday, May 31, 1960, and from Sunday, July 3, 1960, to Monday, Aug. 8, 1960. The House was in recess in this session from Thursday, Apr. 14, 1960, to Monday, Apr. 18, 1960; from Friday, May 27, 1960, to Tuesday, May 31, 1960, and from Sunday, July 3, 1960, to Monday, Aug. 15, 1960.

50. The House was in recess in this session from Thursday, Mar. 30, 1961, to Monday, Apr. 10, 1961.

51. Died Nov. 16, 1961.

52. The House was in recess in this session from Thursday, Apr. 19, 1962, to Monday, Apr. 30, 1962.

53. Elected Jan. 10, 1962.

54. The House was in recess in this session from Thursday, Apr. 11, 1963, to Monday, Apr. 22, 1963.

55. The House was in recess in this session from Thursday, Mar. 26, 1964, to Monday, Apr. 6, 1964; from Thursday, July 2, 1964, to Monday, July 20, 1964; from Friday, Aug. 21, 1964, to Monday, Aug. 31, 1964. The Senate was in recess in this session from Friday, July 10, 1964, to Monday, July 20, 1964; from Friday, Aug. 21, 1964, to Monday, Aug. 31, 1964.

56. The House was in recess in this session from Thursday, Apr. 7, 1966, to Monday, Apr. 18, 1966; from Thursday, June 30, 1966, to Monday, July 11, 1966. The Senate was in recess in this session from Thursday, Apr. 7, 1966, to Wednesday, Apr. 13, 1966; from Thursday, June 30, 1966, to Monday, July 11, 1966.

57. There was a recess in this session from Thursday, Mar. 23, 1967, to Monday, Apr. 3, 1967; from Thursday, June 29, 1967, to Monday, July 10, 1967; from

Thursday, Aug. 31, 1967, to Monday, Sept. 11, 1967; and from Wednesday, Nov. 22, 1967, to Monday, Nov. 27, 1967.

58. The House was in recess this session from Thursday, Apr. 11, 1968, to Monday, Apr. 22, 1968; from Wednesday, May 29, 1968, to Monday, June 3, 1968; from Wednesday, July 3, 1968, to Monday, July 8, 1968; from Friday, Aug. 2, 1968, to Wednesday, Sept. 4, 1968. The Senate was in recess this session from Thursday, Apr. 11, 1968, to Wednesday, Apr. 17, 1968; from Wednesday, May 29, 1968, to Monday, June 3, 1968; from Wednesday, July 3, 1968, to Monday, July 8, 1968; from Friday, Aug. 2, 1968, to Wednesday, Sept. 4, 1968.

59. The House was in recess this session from Friday, Feb. 7, 1969, to Monday, Feb. 17, 1969; from Thursday, Apr. 3, 1969, to Monday, Apr. 14, 1969; from Wednesday, May 28, 1969, to Monday, June 2, 1969; from Wednesday, July 2, 1969, to Monday, July 7, 1969; from Wednesday, Aug. 13, 1969, to Wednesday, Sept. 3, 1969; from Thursday, Nov. 6, 1969, to Wednesday, Nov. 12, 1969; from Wednesday, Nov. 26, 1969, to Monday, Dec. 1, 1969. The Senate was in recess this session from Friday, Feb. 7, 1969, to Monday, Feb. 17, 1969; from Thursday, Apr. 3, 1969, to Monday, Apr. 14, 1969; from Wednesday, July 2, 1969, to Monday, July 7, 1969; from Wednesday, Aug. 13, 1969, to Wednesday, Sept. 3, 1969; from Wednesday, Nov. 26, 1969, to Monday, Dec. 1, 1969.

60. The House was in recess this session from Tuesday, Feb. 10, 1970, to Monday, Feb. 16, 1970; from Thursday, Mar. 26, 1970, to Tuesday, Mar. 31, 1970; from Wednesday, May 27, 1970, to Monday, June 1, 1970; from Wednesday, July 1, 1970, to Monday, July 6, 1970; from Friday, Aug. 14, 1970, to Wednesday, Sept. 9, 1970; from Wednesday, Oct. 14, 1970, to Monday, Nov. 16, 1970; from Wednesday, Nov. 25, 1970, to Monday, Nov. 30, 1970; from Tuesday, Dec. 22, 1970, to Tuesday, Dec. 29, 1970. The Senate was in recess this session from Tuesday, Feb. 10, 1970, to Monday, Feb. 16, 1970; from Thursday, Mar. 26, 1970, to Tuesday, Mar. 31, 1970; from Wednesday, Sept. 2, 1970, to Tuesday, Sept. 8, 1970; from Wednesday, Oct. 14, 1970, to Monday, Nov. 16, 1970; from Wednesday, Nov. 25, 1970, to Monday, Nov. 30, 1970; from Tuesday, Dec. 22, 1970, to Monday, Dec. 28, 1970.

61. The House was in recess this session from Wednesday, Feb. 10, 1971, to Wednesday, Feb. 17, 1971; from Wednesday, Apr. 7, 1971, to Monday, Apr. 19, 1971; from Thursday, May 27, 1971, to Tuesday, June 1, 1971; from Thursday, July 1, 1971, to Tuesday, July 6, 1971; from Friday, Aug. 6, 1971, to Wednesday, Sept. 8, 1971; from Thursday, Oct. 7, 1971, to Tuesday, Oct. 12, 1971; from Thursday, Oct. 21, 1971, to Tuesday, Oct. 26, 1971; from Friday, Nov. 19, 1971, to Monday, Nov. 29, 1971. The Senate was in recess this session from Thursday, Feb. 11, 1971, to Wednesday, Feb. 17, 1971; from Wednesday, Apr. 7, 1971, to Wednesday, Apr. 14, 1971; from Wednesday, May 26, 1971, to Tuesday, June 1, 1971; from Wednesday, June 30, 1971, to Tuesday, July 6, 1971; from Friday, Aug. 6, 1971, to Wednesday, Sept. 8, 1971; from Thursday, Oct. 21, 1971, to Tuesday, Oct. 26, 1971; from Wednesday, Nov. 24, 1971, to Monday, Nov. 29, 1971.

62. Died Jan. 21, 1971.

63. Elected Jan. 22, 1971.

64. The House was in recess this session from Wednesday, Feb. 9, 1972, to Wednesday, Feb. 16, 1972; from Wednesday, Mar. 29, 1972, to Monday, Apr. 10, 1972; from Wednesday, May 24, 1972, to Tuesday, May 30, 1972; from Friday, June 30, 1972, to Monday, July 17, 1972; from Friday, Aug. 18, 1972, to Tuesday, Sept. 5, 1972. The Senate was in recess this session from Wednesday, Feb. 9, 1972, to Monday, Feb. 14, 1972; from Thursday, Mar. 30, 1972, to Tuesday, Apr. 4, 1972; from Thursday, May 25, 1972, to Tuesday, May 30, 1972; from Friday, June 30, 1972, to Monday, July 17, 1972; from Friday, Aug. 18, 1972, to Tuesday, Sept. 5, 1972.

65. Died July 27, 1972.

66. Elected July 28, 1972.

67. The House was in recess this session from Thursday, Feb. 8, 1973, to Monday, Feb. 19, 1973; from Thursday, Apr. 19, 1973, to Monday, Apr. 30, 1973; from Thursday, May 24, 1973, to Tuesday, May 29, 1973; from Saturday, June 30, 1973, to Tuesday, July 10, 1973; from Friday, Aug. 3, 1973, to Wednesday, Sept. 5, 1973; from Thursday, Oct. 4, 1973, to Tuesday, Oct. 9, 1973; from Thursday, Oct. 18, 1973, to Tuesday, Oct. 23, 1973; from Thursday, Nov. 15, 1973 to Monday, Nov. 26, 1973. The Senate was in recess this session from Thursday, Feb. 8, 1973, to Thursday, Feb. 15, 1973; from Wednesday, Apr. 18, 1973, to Monday, Apr. 30, 1973; from Wednesday, May 23, 1973, to Tuesday, May 29, 1973; from Saturday, June 30, 1973, to Monday, July 9, 1973; from Friday, Aug. 3, 1973, to Wednesday, Sept. 5, 1973; from Thursday, Oct. 18, 1973, to Tuesday, Oct. 23, 1973; from Wednesday, Nov. 21, 1973, to Monday, Nov. 26, 1973.

68. The House was in recess this session from Thursday, Feb. 7, 1974, to Wednesday, Feb. 13, 1974; from Thursday, Apr. 11, 1974, to Monday, Apr. 22, 1974; from Thursday, May 23, 1974, to Tuesday, May 28, 1974; from Thursday, Aug. 22, 1974, to Wednesday, Sept. 11, 1974; from Thursday, Oct. 17, 1974, to Monday, Nov. 18, 1974; from Tuesday, Nov. 26, 1974, to Tuesday, Dec. 3, 1974. The Senate was in recess this session from Friday, Feb. 8, 1974, to Monday, Feb. 18, 1974; from Wednesday, Mar. 13, 1974, to Tuesday, Mar. 19, 1974; from Thursday, Apr. 11, 1974, to Monday, Apr. 22, 1974; from Wednesday, May 23, 1974, to Tuesday, May 28, 1974; from Thursday, Aug. 22, 1974, to Wednesday, Sept. 4, 1974; from Thursday, Oct. 17, 1974, to Monday, Nov. 18, 1974; from Tuesday, Nov. 26, 1974, to Monday, Dec. 2, 1974.

69. The House was in recess this session from Wednesday, Mar. 26, 1975, to Monday, Apr. 7, 1975; from Thursday, May 22, 1975, to Monday, June 2, 1975; from Thursday, June 26, 1975, to Tuesday, July 8, 1975; from Friday, Aug. 1, 1975, to Wednesday, Sept. 3, 1975; from Thursday, Oct. 9, 1975, to Monday, Oct. 20, 1975; from Thursday, Oct. 23, 1975, to Tuesday, Oct. 28, 1975; from Thursday, Nov. 20, 1975, to Monday, Dec. 1, 1975. The Senate was in recess this session from Wednesday, Mar. 26, 1975, to Monday, Apr. 7, 1975; from Thursday, May 22, 1975, to Monday, June 2, 1975; from Friday, June 27, 1975, to Monday, July 7, 1975; from Friday, Aug. 1, 1975, to Wednesday, Sept. 3, 1975; from Thursday, Oct. 9, 1975, to Monday, Oct. 20, 1975; from Thursday, Oct. 23, 1975, to Tuesday, Oct. 28, 1975; from

Thursday, Nov. 20, 1975, to Monday, Dec. 1, 1975.

70. The House was in recess this session from Wednesday, Feb. 11, 1976, to Monday, Feb. 16, 1976; from Wednesday, Apr. 14, 1976, to Monday, Apr. 26, 1976; from Thursday, May 27, 1976, to Tuesday, June 1, 1976; from Friday, July 2, 1976, to Monday, July 19, 1976; from Tuesday, Aug. 10, 1976, to Monday, Aug. 23, 1976; from Thursday, Sept. 2, 1976, to Wednesday, Sept. 8, 1976. The Senate was in recess this session from Friday, Feb. 6, 1976, to Monday, Feb. 16, 1976; from Wednesday, Apr. 14, 1976, to Monday, Apr. 26, 1976; from Friday, May 28, 1976, to Wednesday, June 2, 1976; from Friday, July 2, 1976, to Monday, July 19, 1976; from Tuesday, Aug. 10, 1976, to Monday, Aug. 23, 1976; from Wednesday, Sept. 1, 1976, to Tuesday, Sept. 7, 1976.

71. The House was in recess this session from Wednesday, Feb. 9, 1977, to Wednesday, Feb. 16, 1977; from Wednesday, Apr. 6, 1977, to Monday, Apr. 18, 1977; from Thursday, May 26, 1977, to Wednesday, June 1, 1977; from Thursday, June 30, 1977, to Monday, July 11, 1977; from Friday, Aug. 5, 1977, to Wednesday, Sept. 7, 1977; from Thursday, Oct. 6, 1977, to Tuesday, Oct. 11, 1977. The Senate was in recess this session from Friday, Feb. 11, 1977, to Monday, Feb. 21, 1977; from Thursday, Apr. 7, 1977, to Monday, Apr. 18, 1977; from Friday, May 27, 1977, to Monday, June 6, 1977; from Thursday, June 30, 1977, to Monday, July 11, 1977; from Saturday, Aug. 6, 1977, to Wednesday, Sept. 7, 1977.

72. The House was in recess this session from Thursday, Feb. 9, 1978, to Tuesday, Feb. 14, 1978; from Wednesday, Mar. 22, 1978, to Monday, Apr. 3, 1978; from Thursday, May 25, 1978, to Wednesday, May 31, 1978; from Thursday, June 29, 1978, to Monday, July 10, 1978; from Thursday, Aug. 17, 1978, to Wednesday, Sept. 6, 1978. The Senate was in recess this session from Friday, Feb. 10, 1978, to Monday, Feb. 20, 1978; from Thursday, Mar. 23, 1978, to Monday, Apr. 3, 1978; from Friday, May 26, 1978, to Monday, June 5, 1978; from Thursday, June 29, 1978, to Monday, July 10, 1978; from Friday, Aug. 25, 1978, to Wednesday, Sept. 6, 1978.

73. The House was in recess this session from Thursday, Feb. 8, 1979, to Tuesday, Feb. 13, 1979; from Tuesday, Apr. 10, 1979, to Monday, Apr. 23, 1979; from Thursday, May 24, 1979, to Wednesday, May 30, 1979; from Friday, June 29, 1979, to Monday, July 9, 1979; from Thursday, Aug. 2, 1979, to Wednesday, Sept. 5, 1979; from Tuesday, Nov. 20, 1979, to Monday, Nov. 26, 1979. The Senate was in recess this session from Friday, Feb. 9, 1979, to Monday, Feb. 19, 1979; from Tuesday, Apr. 10, 1979, to Monday, Apr. 23, 1979; from Friday, May 25, 1979, to Monday, June 4, 1979; from Friday, Aug. 3, 1979, to Wednesday, Sept. 5, 1979; from Tuesday, Nov. 20, 1979, to Monday, Nov. 26, 1979.

74. The House was in recess this session from Wednesday, Feb. 13, 1980, to Tuesday, Feb. 19, 1980; from Wednesday, Apr. 2, 1980, to Tuesday, Apr. 15, 1980; from Thursday, May 22, 1980, to Wednesday, May 28, 1980; from Wednesday, July 2, 1980, to Monday, July 21, 1980; from Friday, Aug. 1, 1980, to Monday, Aug. 18, 1980; from Thursday, Aug. 28, 1980, to Wednesday, Sept. 3, 1980; from Thursday, Oct. 2, 1980, to Monday, Nov. 12, 1980. The Senate was in recess this session from Monday, Feb. 11, 1980, to Thursday, Feb. 14, 1980; from Thursday, Apr. 3, 1980, to

Tuesday, Apr. 15, 1980; from Thursday, May 22, 1980, to Wednesday, May 28, 1980; from Wednesday, July 2, 1980, to Monday, July 21, 1980; from Wednesday, Aug. 6, 1980, to Monday, Aug. 18, 1980; from Wednesday, Aug. 27, 1980, to Wednesday, Sept. 3, 1980; from Wednesday, Oct. 1, 1980, to Wednesday, Nov. 12, 1980; from Monday, Nov. 24, 1980, to Monday, Dec. 1, 1980.

75. The House was in recess this session from Friday, Feb. 6, 1981, to Tuesday, Feb. 17, 1981; from Friday, Apr. 10, 1981, to Monday, Apr. 27, 1981; from Friday, June 26, 1981, to Wednesday, July 8, 1981; from Tuesday, Aug. 4, 1981, to Wednesday, Sept. 9, 1981; from Wednesday, Oct. 7, 1981, to Tuesday, Oct. 13, 1981; from Monday, Nov. 23, 1981, to Monday, Nov. 30, 1981. The Senate was in recess this session from Friday, Feb. 6, 1981, to Monday, Feb. 16, 1981; from Friday, Apr. 10, 1981, to Monday, Apr. 27, 1981; from Thursday, June 25, 1981, to Wednesday, July 8, 1981; from Monday, Aug. 3, 1981, to Wednesday, Sept. 9, 1981; from Wednesday, Oct. 7, 1981, to Wednesday, Oct. 14, 1981; from Tuesday, Nov. 24, 1981, to Monday, Nov. 30, 1981.

76. The House was in recess this session from Wednesday, Feb. 10, 1982, to Monday, Feb. 22, 1982; from Tuesday, Apr. 6, 1982, to Tuesday, Apr. 20, 1982; from Thursday, May 27, 1982, to Wednesday, June 2, 1982; from Thursday, July 1, 1982, to Monday, July 12, 1982; from Friday, Aug. 20, 1982, to Wednesday, Sept. 8, 1982; from Friday, Oct. 1, 1982, to Monday, Nov. 29, 1982. The Senate was in recess this session Thursday, Feb. 11, 1982, to Monday, Feb. 22, 1982; from Thursday, Apr. 1, 1982, to Tuesday, Apr. 13, 1982; from Thursday, May 27, 1982, to Tuesday, June 8, 1982; from Thursday, July 1, 1982, to Monday, July 12, 1982; from Friday, Aug. 20, 1982, to Wednesday, Sept. 8, 1982; from Friday, Oct. 1, 1982, to Monday, Nov. 29, 1982.

77. The House adjourned for recess this session Friday, Jan. 7, 1983, to Tuesday, Jan. 25, 1983; Thursday, Feb. 17, 1983, to Tuesday, Feb. 22, 1983; Thursday, March 24, 1983, to Tuesday, Apr. 5, 1983; Thursday, May 26, 1983, to Wednesday, June 1, 1983; Thursday, June 30, 1983, to Monday, July 11, 1983; Friday, Aug. 5, 1983, to Wednesday, Sept. 12, 1983; Friday, Oct. 7, 1983, to Tuesday, Oct. 17, 1983. The Senate adjourned for recess this session Monday, Jan. 3, 1983, to Tuesday, Jan. 25, 1983; Friday, Feb. 4, 1983, to Monday, Feb. 14, 1983; Friday, March 25, 1983, to Tuesday, Apr. 5, 1983; Friday, May 27, 1983, to Monday, June 6, 1983; Friday, July 1, 1983, to Monday, July 11, 1983; Friday, Aug. 5, 1983, to Monday, Sept. 12, 1983; Monday Oct. 10, 1983, to Monday, Oct. 17, 1983.

78. The House adjourned for recess this session Thursday, Feb. 9, 1984, to Tuesday, Feb. 21, 1984; Thursday, Apr. 13, 1984, to Tuesday, Apr. 24, 1984; Friday, May 25, 1984, to Wednesday, May 30, 1984; Friday, June 29, 1984, to Monday, July 23, 1984; Friday, Aug. 10, 1984, to Wednesday, Sept. 5, 1984. The Senate adjourned for recess this session Friday, Feb. 10, 1984, to Monday, Feb. 20, 1984; Friday, Apr. 13, 1984, to Tuesday, Apr. 24, 1984; from Friday, June 29, 1984, to Monday, July 23, 1984; Friday, Aug. 10, 1984, to Wednesday, Sept. 5, 1984.

79. The House adjourned for recess this session Monday, Jan. 7, 1985, to Monday, Jan. 21, 1985; Thursday, Feb. 7, 1985, to Tuesday, Feb. 19, 1985; Thursday, March 7, 1985, to Tuesday, March 19, 1985; Thursday, April 4, 1985, to Monday, April 15, 1985; Thursday, May 23, 1985, to Monday, June 3, 1985; Thursday, June 27, 1985, to Monday, July 8, 1985; Thursday, Aug. 1, 1985, to Wednesday, Sept. 4, 1985; Thursday, Nov. 21, 1985, to Monday, Dec. 2, 1985. The Senate adjourned for recess this session Monday, Jan. 7, 1985, to Monday, Jan. 21, 1985; Thursday, Feb. 7, 1985, to Monday, Feb. 18, 1985; Tuesday, March 12, 1985, to Thursday, March 14, 1985; Thursday, April 4, 1985, to Monday, April 15, 1985; Friday, May 24, 1985, to Monday, June 3, 1985; Thursday, June 27, 1985, to Monday, July 8, 1985; Thursday, Aug. 1, 1985, to Monday, Sept. 9, 1985; Saturday, Nov. 23, 1985, to Monday, Dec. 2, 1985.

80. The House adjourned for recess this session Tuesday, Jan. 7, 1986, to Tuesday, Jan. 21, 1986; Friday, Feb. 7, 1986, to Tuesday, Feb. 18, 1986; Tuesday, March 25, 1986, to Tuesday, April 8, 1986; Thursday, May 22, 1986, to Tuesday, June 3, 1986; Thursday, June 26, 1986, to Monday, July 14, 1986; Friday, Aug. 15, 1986, to Monday, Sept. 8, 1986. The Senate adjourned for recess this session Tuesday, Jan. 7, 1986, to Tuesday, Jan. 21, 1986; Friday, Feb. 7, 1986, to Monday, Feb. 17, 1986; Thursday, March 27, 1986, to Tuesday, April 8, 1986; Wednesday, May 21, 1986, to Monday, June 2, 1986; Thursday, June 26, 1986, to Monday, July 14, 1986; Friday, Aug. 15, 1986, to Monday, Sept. 8, 1986.

SOURCE: *Official Congressional Directory*.

Leaders of the House since 1899

Congress	House Floor Leaders		House Whips	
	Majority	Minority	Majority	Minority
56th (1899-1901)	Sereno E. Payne (R N.Y.)	James D. Richardson (D Tenn.)	James A. Tawney (R Minn.)	Oscar W. Underwood (D Ala.)[6]
57th (1901-1903)	Payne	Richardson	Tawney	James T. Lloyd (D Mo.)
58th (1903-1905)	Payne	John Sharp Williams (D Miss.)	Tawney	Lloyd
59th (1905-1907)	Payne	Williams	James E. Watson (R Ind.)	Lloyd
60th (1907-1909)	Payne	Williams/Champ Clark (D Mo.)[1]	Watson	Lloyd[7]
61st (1909-1911)	Payne	Clark	John W. Dwight (R N.Y.)	None
62d (1911-1913)	Oscar W. Underwood (D Ala.)	James R. Mann (R Ill.)	None	John W. Dwight (R N.Y.)
63d (1913-1915)	Underwood	Mann	Thomas M. Bell (D Ga.)	Charles H. Burke (R S.D.)
64th (1915-1917)	Claude Kitchin (D N.C.)	Mann	None	Charles M. Hamilton (R N.Y.)
65th (1917-1919)	Kitchin	Mann	None	Hamilton
66th (1919-1921)	Franklin W. Mondell (R Wyo.)	Clark	Harold Knutson (R Minn.)	None
67th (1921-1923)	Mondell	Claude Kitchin (D N.C.)	Knutson	William A. Oldfield (D Ark.)
68th (1923-1925)	Nicholas Longworth (R Ohio)	Finis J. Garrett (D Tenn.)	Albert H. Vetal (R Ind.)	Oldfield
69th (1925-1927)	John Q. Tilson (R Conn.)	Garrett	Vestal	Oldfield
70th (1927-1929)	Tilson	Garrett	Vestal	Oldfield/John McDuffie (D Ala.)[8]
71st (1929-1931)	Tilson	John N. Garner (D Texas)	Vestal	McDuffie
72d (1931-1933)	Henry T. Rainey (D Ill.)	Bertrand H. Snell (R N.Y.)	John McDuffie (D Ala.)	Carl G. Bachmann (R W.Va.)
73d (1933-1935)	Joseph W. Byrns (D Tenn.)	Snell	Arthur H. Greenwood (D Ind.)	Hary L. Englebright (R Calif.)
74th (1935-1937)	William B. Bankhead (D Ala.)[2]	Snell	Patrick J. Boland (D Pa.)	Englebright
75th (1937-1939)	Sam Rayburn (D Texas)	Snell	Boland	Englebright
76th (1939-1941)	Rayburn/John W. McCormack (D Mass.)[3]	Joseph W. Martin Jr. (R Mass.)	Boland	Englebright
77th (1941-1943)	McCormack	Martin	Boland/Robert Ramspeck (D Ga.)[9]	Englebright
78th (1943-1945)	McCormack	Martin	Ramspeck	Leslie C. Arends (R Ill.)
79th (1945-1947)	McCormack	Martin	Ramspeck/John J. Sparkman (D Ala.)[10]	Arends
80th (1947-1949)	Charles A. Halleck (R Ind.)	Sam Rayburn (D Texas)	Leslie C. Arends (R Ill.)	John W. McCormack (D Mass.)
81st (1949-1951)	McCormack	Martin	J. Percy Priest (D Tenn.)	Arends
82d (1951-1953)	McCormack	Martin	Priest	Arends

Congress	Speaker	Majority Leader	Minority Leader	Majority Whip	Minority Whip
83d (1953–1955)			Rayburn	Arends	McCormack
84th (1955–1957)	Rayburn	McCormack	Martin	Carl Albert (D Okla.)	Arends
85th (1957–1959)	Rayburn	McCormack	Martin	Albert	Arends
86th (1959–1961)	Rayburn	McCormack	Charles A. Halleck (R Ind.)	Albert	Arends
87th (1961–1963)	Rayburn/McCormack	McCormack/Carl Albert (D Okla.)[4]	Halleck	Albert/Hale Boggs (D La.)[11]	Arends
88th (1963–1965)	McCormack	Albert	Halleck	Boggs	Arends
89th (1965–1967)	McCormack	Albert	Gerald R. Ford (R Mich.)	Boggs	Arends
90th (1967–1969)	McCormack	Albert	Ford	Boggs	Arends
91st (1969–1971)	McCormack	Albert	Ford	Boggs	Arends
92d (1971–1973)	Carl Albert (D Okla.)	Hale Boggs (D La.)	Ford	Thomas P. O'Neill Jr. (D Mass.)	Arends
93d (1973–1975)	Albert	Thomas P. O'Neill Jr. (D Mass.)	Ford/John J. Rhodes (R Ariz.)[5]	John J. McFall (D Calif.)	Arends
94th (1975–1977)	Albert	O'Neill	Rhodes	McFall	Robert H. Michel (R Ill.)
95th (1977–1979)	Thomas P. O'Neill Jr. (D Mass.)	Jim Wright (D Texas)	Rhodes	John Brademas (D Ind.)	Michel
96th (1979–1981)	O'Neill	Wright	Rhodes	Brademas	Michel
97th (1981–1983)	O'Neill	Wright	Robert H. Michel (R Ill.)	Thomas S. Foley (D Wash.)	Trent Lott (R Miss.)
98th (1983–1985)	O'Neill	Wright	Michel	Foley	Lott
99th (1985–1987)	O'Neill	Wright	Michel	Foley	Lott
100th (1987–1989)	Jim Wright (D Texas)	Thomas S. Foley (D Wash.)	Michel	Tony Coelho (D Calif.)	Lott

1. Clark became minority leader in 1908.
2. Bankhead became Speaker of the House on June 4, 1936. The post of majority leader remained vacant until the next Congress.
3. McCormack became majority leader on Sept. 26, 1940, filling the vacancy caused by the elevation of Rayburn to the post of Speaker of the House on Sept. 16, 1940.
4. Albert became majority leader on Jan. 10, 1962, filling the vacancy caused by the elevation of McCormack to the post of Speaker of the House on Jan. 10, 1962.
5. Rhodes became minority leader on Dec. 7, 1973, filling the vacancy caused by the resignation of Ford on Dec. 6, 1973, to become vice president.
6. Underwood did not become minority whip until 1901.
7. Lloyd resigned to become chairman of the Democratic Congressional Campaign Committee in 1908. The post of minority whip remained vacant until the beginning of the 62nd Congress.
8. John McDuffie became minority whip after the death of William Oldfield on Nov. 19, 1928.
9. Ramspeck became majority whip on June 8, 1942, filling the vacancy caused by the death of Boland on May 18, 1942.
10. Sparkman became majority whip on Jan. 14, 1946, filling the vacancy caused by the resignation of Ramspeck on Dec. 31, 1945.
11. Boggs became majority whip on Jan. 10, 1962, filling the vacancy caused by the elevation of Albert to the post of majority leader on Jan. 10, 1962.

SOURCES: Ripley, Randall B. Party Leaders in the House of Representatives. Washington, D.C.: Brookings Institution, 1967; U.S. Congress. Joint Committee on Printing. Official Congressional Directory. Washington, D.C.: Government Printing Office, 1967– –; U.S. Congress. Senate. Biographical Directory of the American Congress, 1774–1971. Compiled by Lawrence F. Kennedy. 92d Cong, 1st sess., 1971. S Doc. 8.

Leaders of the Senate since 1911

	Senate Floor Leaders		Senate Whips	
Congress	**Majority**	**Minority**	**Majority**	**Minority**
62d (1911-1913)	Shelby M. Cullom (R Ill.)	Thomas S. Martin (D Va.)	None	None
63d (1913-1915)	John W. Kern (D Ind.)	Jacob H. Gallinger (R N.H.)	J. Hamilton Lewis (D Ill.)	None
64th (1915-1917)	Kern	Gallinger	Lewis	James W. Wadsworth Jr. (R N.Y.) Charles Curtis (R Kan.)[a]
65th (1917-1919)	Thomas S. Martin (D Va.)	Gallinger/Henry Cabot Lodge (R Mass.)[1]	Lewis	Curtis
66th (1919-1921)	Henry Cabot Lodge (R Mass.)	Martin/Oscar W. Underwood (D Ala.)[2]	Charles Curtis (R Kan.)	Peter G. Gerry (D R.I.)
67th (1921-1923)	Lodge	Underwood	Curtis	Gerry
68th (1923-1925)	Lodge/Charles Curtis (R Kan.)[3]	Joseph T. Robinson (D Ark.)	Curtis/Wesley L. Jones (R Wash.)[9]	Gerry
69th (1925-1927)	Curtis	Robinson	Jones	Gerry
70th (1927-1929)	Curtis	Robinson	Jones	Gerry
71st (1929-1931)	James E. Watson (R Ind.)	Robinson	Simeon D. Fess (R Ohio)	Morris Sheppard (D Texas)
72d (1931-1933)	Watson	Robinson	Fess	Sheppard
73d (1933-1935)	Joseph T. Robinson (D Ark.)	Charles L. McNary (R Ore.)	Lewis	Felix Hebert (R R.I.)
74th (1935-1937)	Robinson	McNary	Lewis	None
75th (1937-1939)	Robinson/Alben W. Barkley (D Ky.)[4]	McNary	Lewis	None
76th (1939-1941)	Barkley	McNary	Sherman Minton (D Ind.)	None
77th (1941-1943)	Barkley	McNary	Lister Hill (D Ala.)	None
78th (1943-1945)	Barkley	McNary	Hill	Kenneth Wherry (R Neb.)
79th (1945-1947)	Barkley	Wallace H. White Jr. (R Maine)	Hill	Wherry
80th (1947-1949)	Wallace H. White Jr. (R Maine)	Alben W. Barkley (D Ky.)	Kenneth Wherry (R Neb.)	Scott Lucas (D Ill.)
81st (1949-1951)	Scott W. Lucas (D Ill.)	Kenneth S. Wherry (R Neb.)	Francis Myers (D Pa.)	Leverett Saltonstall (R Mass.)
82d (1951-1953)	Ernest W. McFarland (D Ariz.)	Wherry/Styles Bridges (R N.H.)[5]	Lyndon B. Johnson (D Texas)	Saltonstall
83d (1953-1955)	Robert A. Taft (R Ohio)/William F. Knowland (R Calif.)[6]	Lyndon B. Johnson (D Texas)	Leverett Saltonstall (R Mass.)	Earle Clements (D Ky.)
84th (1955-1957)	Lyndon B. Johnson (D Texas)	William F. Knowland (R Calif.)	Earle Clements (D Ky.)	Saltonstall

(86th 1959–1961)	Johnson	Everett McKinley Dirksen (R Ill.)	Mansfield	Thomas H. Kuchel (R Calif.)
87th (1961-1963)	Mike Mansfield (D Mont.)	Dirksen	Hubert H. Humphrey (D Minn.)	Kuchel
88th (1963-1965)	Mansfield	Dirksen	Humphrey	Kuchel
89th (1965-1967)	Mansfield	Dirksen	Russell Long (D La.)	Kuchel
90th (1967-1969)	Mansfield	Dirksen	Long	Kuchel
91st (1969-1971)	Mansfield	Dirksen/Hugh Scott (R Pa.)[7]	Edward M. Kennedy (D Mass.)	Hugh Scott (R Pa.)/ Robert P. Griffin (R Mich.)[10]
92d (1971-1973)	Mansfield	Scott	Robert C. Byrd (D W.Va.)	Griffin
93d (1973-1975)	Mansfield	Scott	Byrd	Griffin
94th (1975-1977)	Mansfield	Scott	Byrd	Griffin
95th (1977-1979)	Robert C. Byrd (D W.Va.)	Howard H. Baker Jr. (R Tenn.)	Alan Cranston (D Calif.)	Ted Stevens (R Alaska)
96th (1979-1981)	Byrd	Baker	Cranston	Stevens
97th (1981-1983)	Howard H. Baker Jr. (R Tenn.)	Robert C. Byrd (D W.Va.)	Ted Stevens (R Alaska)	Alan Cranston (D Calif.)
98th (1983-1985)	Baker	Byrd	Stevens	Cranston
99th (1985-1987)	Robert J. Dole (R Kan.)	Byrd	Alan K. Simpson (R Wyo.)	Cranston
100th (1987-1989)	Robert C. Byrd (D W.Va.)	Robert J. Dole (R Kan.)	Alan Cranston (D Calif.)	Alan K. Simpson (R Wyo.)

1. Lodge became minority leader on Aug. 24, 1918, filling the vacancy caused by the death of Gallinger on Aug. 17, 1918.
2. Underwood became minority leader on April 27, 1920, filling the vacancy caused by the death of Martin on Nov. 12, 1919. Gilbert M. Hitchcock (D Neb.) served as acting minority leader in the interim.
3. Curtis became majority leader on Nov. 28, 1924, filling the vacancy caused by the death of Lodge on Nov. 9, 1924.
4. Barkley became majority leader on July 22, 1937, filling the vacancy caused by the death of Robinson on July 14, 1937.
5. Bridges became minority leader on Jan. 8, 1952, filling the vacancy caused by the death of Wherry on Nov. 29, 1951.
6. Knowland became majority leader on Aug. 4, 1953, filling the vacancy caused by the death of Taft on July 31, 1953. Taft's vacant seat was filled by a Democrat, Thomas Burke, on Nov. 10, 1953. The division of the Senate changed to 48 Democrats, 47 Republicans, and 1 Independent, thus giving control of the Senate to the Democrats. However, Knowland remained as majority leader until the end of the 83rd Congress.
7. Scott became minority leader on Sept. 24, 1969, filling the vacancy caused by the death of Dirksen on Sept. 7, 1969.
8. Wadsworth served as minority whip for only one week, from Dec. 6 to Dec. 13, 1915.
9. Jones became majority whip filling the vacancy caused by the elevation of Curtis to the post of majority leader. (Footnote 3)
10. Griffin became minority whip on Sept. 24, 1969, filling the vacancy caused by the elevation of Scott to the post of minority leader. (Footnote 7)

SOURCES: Oleszek, Walter J. "Party Whips in the United States Senate." *Journal of Politics* 33 (November 1971): 955-979; U.S. Congress. Joint Committee on Printing. *Official Congressional Directory.* Washington, D.C.: Government Printing Office, 1967--; U.S. Congress. Senate. *Biographical Directory of the American Congress, 1774-1971.* Compiled by Lawrence F. Kennedy. 92d Cong, 1st sess., 1971. S Doc. 8; U.S. Congress. Senate. *Majority and Minority Leaders of the Senate.* Compiled by Floyd M. Riddick. 94th Cong, 1st sess., 1975. S Doc. 66.